The Broad Canvas

The Broad Canvas

portraits of women by women

by Linda Rogers
with photographs by Barbara Pedrick

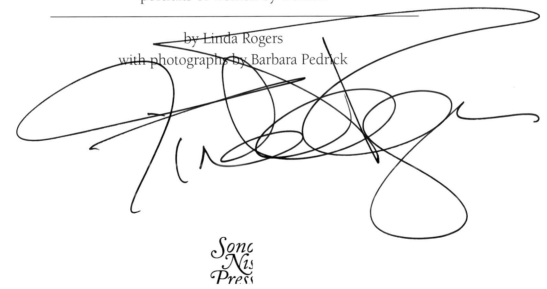

Sono
Nis
Press

Victoria   British Columbia   Canada

Canadian Cataloguing in Publication Data

Main entry under title:

The broad canvas

ISBN 1-55039-097-X

   1. Women authors, Canadian (English)—20th century—Interviews.*
2. Women artists—Canada—Interviews. 3. Women authors, Canadian
(English)—20th century—Portraits.* 4. Women artists—Canada—
Portraits. I. Rogers, Linda, 1944– II. Pedrick, Barbara.
NX513.Z8B76 1999   700'.92'271   C99-910383-0

Sono Nis Press gratefully acknowledges the support of the Canada Council for the Arts and its publishing program. We acknowledge the assistance of the Province of British Columbia, through the British Columbia Arts Council.

Cover design by Jim Brennan
Page design and composition by Annie Weeks

Published by
SONO NIS PRESS
P.O. Box 5550, Stn. B
Victoria, British Columbia
Canada   V8R 6S4
http://www.islandnet.com/sononis/
sono.nis@islandnet.com

Printed and bound in Canada by Friesens

THE CANADA COUNCIL | LE CONSEIL DES ARTS
FOR THE ARTS | DU CANADA
SINCE 1957 | DEPUIS 1957

This book is for the women in my family.

With thanks to every woman who shared her life in art, to Barb who photographed them with so much loving care, to Diane, Heather, and Dawn, geniuses of Sono Nis Press, and to Patricia, my silent friend.

My husband Rick has been so much help, as always.

Barbara Colebrook Peace has the eye of an eagle, the ear of a dog, and the patience of Jobette. Her editorial advice is much appreciated.

Contents

Dear Max, From now on it's our world.

ANNE SEXTON TO MAXINE KUMIN

Introduction

"WHAT WOULD HAPPEN," the poet Muriel Rukeyser wrote, "if one woman told the truth about her life?" This was a question that began to haunt me as women I knew billowed into maturity, some of them lighter than air, going on to the last freedom. I thought others would be interested in the lives of mature women and began to take dictation. *The Broad Canvas* has been a collaborative process between myself, Barbara Pedrick, and the subjects themselves, drawn from the broad canvas of Canadian life.

I know there is a pun in the title *Broad Canvas*, but then puns have traditionally been male territory and feminists have been accused of lacking humour. So here it is, an empowering cartoon for our mural depicting the renaissance lives of women I have known. All the subjects live in or around the art world. Connected by friendship in the family of Canadian artists, we have been redefining each other in our process.

We have learned so much from interviews, many of them lunches, *nous avons du poids*, that took us well beyond the surface of art and casual friendship to the gestalt that is the DNA of every creative woman.

In her book *The Obstacle Race,* Germaine Greer analyzed the reasons why women in history were typically relegated to the domestic arts. These reasons no longer apply. Now that we have the freedom of our minds and bodies, we have the broadest possible canvas to paint on because we enjoy the full range of human experience.

I grew up during the fifties, when women with ideas were frequently tranquillized to keep them passive. My own mother, whose organizational skills are legendary, was described as "ambitious," which was, next to "common" or "slatternly," one of the most pejorative adjectives used to describe a woman. My mother was ambitious for a better society, something all the women in this book have in common. Now in her seventies and working for people living with AIDS, she looks back on a life of accomplishment which includes blueprints for the arts and social welfare sectors.

When I was a child, my mother complimented me when I did things "like a boy." She was proud of my fearlessness and my intelligence. However, when adolescence put an end to some of those freedoms, even she, worrying that I might not withstand the criticism she had endured, began to impose the social sanctions that were typical of the time. It wasn't what we did but what we were seen to do that invoked judgement. We were all trapped in that as surely as our bodies were imprisoned in the girdles that held up our stockings. If we didn't become young ladies we were doomed to be Something Else, that grey area where Women of Spirit were sent by the conventional wisdom.

Mothers are the keepers of custom, even when those rituals are physical and emotional trusses that confine our freedom of expression. The mother-daughter relationship was the most volatile area of conversation with the women in this book. Mothers visit their fear on their children. Adele Wiseman, an exemplary feminist whose principles were frustrated in her marriage, said that to give birth to a daughter is to be born to fear. This is a terrible legacy with which we wrestle in every poem or painting, every song. We are the breakthrough generation and our work is not only artistically but historically significant.

As I was growing up, I heard stories about the men of accomplishment in my family. The novelist Anthony Trollope was one, Gerard Manley Hopkins another. Peter Skene Ogden, the explorer, gave my mother her middle name. A several-greats grandfather gave (bad) spiritual advice to mad King George III. An uncle was a distinguished Canadian diplomat. Another was the official historian for Scotland.

I rarely heard about the women who dissembled in various shades of competence, rebellion, and martyrdom. All had artistic gifts that were god-given so that they might decorate themselves and their houses and places of worship appropriately. My grandmothers sang and danced, embroidered and painted watercolours. My great-grandmother was a brilliant horticulturalist. In this family, one side genteel, the other aristocratic, my mother was a mutation. She became known by her first name, coming out from the cover of marriage.

If I didn't want to be just like her, because I could see her struggle within the female social context, I wanted at the least to be an honorary boy. I played with boys and I played hard. However, when the prospect of marriage loomed as the only way to have children, and children are my passion, I caved in. I let a boy give the valedictory speech after I had been appointed. I gave up medicine as a choice after coming first in the province in biology. I declined admission to Oxford University when male advisors opined it would be a waste of money to send a girl to be educated in England.

I had contempt for women and the womanly arts even though I made sure my own glass house was a *maison lumière*.

That was then.

Things have changed since the days of gloves and girdles, and many of the mothers of girls I never played with have moved on. When people I knew and cared about started dying, I began to wonder about their experience of being female and, in particular, seeing a creative function beyond their biological destiny. I became determined to ask the questions that led to this collection of stories.

At the same time, Barbara Pedrick, who had grown up in the constrained atmosphere of the Midwestern Bible belt, was leaving her marriage and her past and embarking on a new life. Because she was facing her own ghosts in the marriage crisis, she was intrigued by women as photographic portrait subjects.

We found the beautiful in everyone. There isn't a single subject who sat for us who doesn't have typically feminine insecurities about some aspect of her appearance or work. So much goes back to the relationship with the mothers who, frequently, visited their own lack of confidence on their daughters. One of the most pleasant aspects of our quest to meet the inner women was to discover the appreciation they have for one another. This is what we have been learning to do. It is the first step to liking ourselves.

Some stunning metaphors have surfaced in the discussions and photo sessions that made doing this book such an amazing experience. When Phyllis Serota told me she painted with her whole being, every chakra at once, I realized we were all making body prints in our work. This is what makes women's art so compelling.

When dramatist Lina de Guevara described the evolution of her *Puente* (bridge) project for immigrant women in terms of the mutating folding chairs they used for sets, we could hear them opening and shutting, scraping across the floor as they defined the limited physical world of the actors. Articulate props, the chairs became beds for seduction and *accouchement* and barricades in domestic wars. Stacked on one another, precariously balanced, they evolved a metaphor for struggle as the actors climbed toward resolution.

I was reminded of my childhood, when my hearing-impaired aunt, who lives in a silent world, sat me down on a worn rug and transformed it into a magic carpet of storytelling that took us to the fertile country of her imagination.

"I like a difficulty," de Guevara said, describing her exile from Chile after the *coup d'etat* of the colonels. She could have been speaking for Comfort Adesuwa or Jody Paterson or Lynda Raino.

Every woman in this book has experienced the difficulties of a woman's life. We have overcome conditioning, prejudice, civil war, and physical and emotional pain to create. We all say the same thing about our work. We do it because we must.

Do women whose bodies and minds are dedicated to transformation of the ordinary into the extraordinary easily embrace the rapture at the end of the day? Is death only one more miracle in the miracle of life? Is it the willingness to take risks that makes art resonate?

For some the risk has been physical. Comfort Adesuwa gambled with her own position of privilege when she spoke out against tyranny in her Nigerian homeland. Myfanwy Pavelić paints past the pain of arthritis. For others, like poet Inge Israel, one of the few in her extended family to escape the Holocaust, poetry is a necessary component of healing.

Many stories are told for the first time in this book. Even an artist, used to revelation, needs courage to dance through the final veil, her personal history. We have trusted one another to make this mural, which, we hope, will also reflect the lives and struggles of those who read it.

There is a particular vitality in the passionately engaged. These women, constantly transformed and rejuvenated by their creative lives, move to the light wearing the expression of eager discovery that is a bridge from the reality of the flesh to that of the spirit. Barbara has caught this joy in her photographs of our friends.

Gathered from the luminous web of world community, we are every colour in the broad canvas of life: daughters, wives, mothers, grandmothers, aunts. In music, writing, theatre, visual art, and dance, we tell what it is to be a woman in the segue to the twenty-first century. What we are is female, but what we make is not gender specific. It is for everyone, so that we might know one another better.

The Broad Canvas

ELISABETH MARGARET HOPKINS

PAINTER (1894, ISLAND OF JERSEY–1991, SALT SPRING ISLAND)

Hopy painted her relationship with God, who was faithful and tolerant of her slightly buck-toothed Anglican plainness.

HOPY, WHO DID ANYTHING but go gentle into her good night, saw the God in everything and almost always put God first, except possibly the time she made the magenta-robed bishop holding his box of holy smoke communion baubles wait on a hard chair outside her hospital room equipped with a ladies' bar, one bottle of sherry and one of gin, while she entreated my husband me to sing a song we had written about nose picking for the enjoyment of the ladies sharing bed and board at the Lady Minto Hospital on Salt Spring Island.

The ladies laughed about boogers, but the Bishop did not. He did, however, return for her funeral where we sang a lusty "New Jerusalem" as she lay in the nave, a bride at last, after ninety-seven years, in an embroidered nightie she had saved for the occasion.

Elisabeth, nurse to the Empire, retired at the age of sixty to the Gulf Islands of British Columbia. She came hot on the trail of interesting antecedents: Peter Skene Ogden, the explorer; Frances Trollope, the widely travelled mother of the novelist Anthony; and step-grandmother Francis Hopkins, Canadian wilderness painter. Settling at last on Galiano Island, she began to grow a wild garden in the best English tradition.

Elisabeth had been, by her own admission, a naughty, outspoken child, her rebellion held down by God just as her cousin Gerard Manley suppressed the wild bump in his cassock and the impulse to write down many of the poems in his sin-filled Anglo-Catholic brain. She grew into a kind but querulous spinster who only gave in to the urge to paint, which was her wildness, when the garden became too much for her. Hopy painted her relationship with

God, who was faithful and tolerant of her slightly buck-toothed Anglican plainness, in watercolours that shout the joy of Paradise found when the lion lies down with the lamb. In dozens of what are now, in the folk revival, called "naif paintings," she celebrated the lives of animals with human foibles in a post-feminist jungle of exuberant colour.

Commentators, who have mistaken the simple joy of a learned ironist for primitivism and called the Island of Jersey's most volatile export since milk "Canada's Grandma Moses," must be feeling the force of rancid curds from heaven, from whose pearly gate Elisabeth Margaret Hopkins, former *enfant terrible,* is now delivering her judgement. She hated that, wasn't "Canada's Anybody" except herself.

Her paintings, pen and ink filled in with Pelikan, always Pelikan, watercolours are evidence of a better world, a jungle, where lust is the hunger of larger for smaller creatures and carnivores are forgiven their cannibal crimes.

She celebrated the lives of

animals with human foibles.

Jane Rule wrote of Elisabeth's painting: "Only domestic animals, in particular cats, are often allowed their fallen nature, shown in arched-back, fur-risen fury, with torn ears and lost eyes, cruising back alleys. At their picnics, though they are allowed rows of carefully arranged dead mice and fish, no birds are ever served."

In her eighth and ninth decades, Hopy enjoyed a Naissance, her Coming Out into glory, as twice a year for years her paintings bantered strange animal and English dialects on the walls of the Bau-Xi Galleries in Vancouver and Toronto and in one book, *The Painted Cougar*, a children's classic.

The stories of her alleged crabbiness are as legendary as those of her kindness. Allergic children disallowed candies were sent bulging anonymous packages in the mail. Questioning parents were dismissed with the imperious contempt of a geriatric child who was stamping her foot and getting her own way at last.

Was she ruined by fame and moderate royalties? Yes. Elisabeth became the centre of an epicurean assemblage known as the Picnics Parties and Balls Society. The PPBS made the giggling rounds of Haute Canada: openings, readings, hors d'oeuvres, gin, canapes, and birthday cakes cut with the hell-raising sword

of the archangel Michael on wild beaches and mountain meadows, with Elisabeth as the spoiled adorable Perennial Surprise in her Chinese slippers and quilted satin jackets in evangelical colours.

Every year she started the rumour that This Birthday was going to be her last. That self-generated premature obituary would start an avalanche of invitations and plans that made the month of April so much less cruel for the members of her inner circle who were able to renounce those private moments of mortification on the bathroom scale.

The days of praise and celebration took themselves at last to Salt Spring Island and the Lady Minto Hospital, where Our Irrepressible Patient with the Impeccable Pitch of a Crow usurped the privileges of doctors and nurses, driving her wheelchair in at the most critical moments, waving her arms, waving her oxygen away, directing God's most critical choir with her defrocked midwife's "Push!"

With life came death, which she planned like a wedding. Her only. Elisabeth hung out with the gay literati. The bishop was one of the few straight boys who visited her, and he was more mentor than suitor. One of our favourite parlour games was speculation. Was she on the bowling team, a friend of Dorothy's?

She hated being called Canada's Grandma Moses, wasn't "Canada's Anybody" but herself.

Every birthday she started the rumour that it was going to be her last.

Were the Nurse stories true? Or had she loved a soldier in one of England's green and pleasant colonial armies? Was she only in love with her personal saviour? One ambiguous clue. She adored the soaps on television and only grudgingly forgave those (including myself and my mother, who were, after all, cousins) who divorced or broke up, ruining her picture of true romance.

Once we saw The Nightie, we thought we knew. She was saving herself for the big honeymoon in the sky.

On her last birthday, there was going to be a party in the hospital. Fresh bottles of gin and sherry were procured in the usual ways and smuggled in. The nurses baked a painterly cake with polychromatic icing.

Hopy was a scholar and a lady, one of the first to become a famous painter for reasons known only to the wife of the Sphinx, still sweeping sand in the desert. If John Milton and other notorious and famous men could be born and die on their birthdays, so could she. This was her determination, in spite of an unspoken understanding that she really ought to wait at least until she had earned a centenary telegram from Brenda Windsor in London. The almost Birthday Girl made her announcement on the penultimate day, as if she were an excited child with white envelopes to deliver: "I am going to die on my birthday!" And she did, give an hour or two.

They say the last thing you give up is your hearing. When my son played "Happy Birthday" on his trumpet one last time, the sleeping lady smiled. And she kept on smiling as they washed her body and put on her beautiful nightgown.

My allergic children, who had been sent so much contraband in the mail, were her pallbearers, and after they carried her body into the little Anglican church at Ganges on Salt Spring, so far from the Island of Jersey where she was born, they sat down beside her and unwrapped her favourite Zero bars as the congregation sang her favourite hymns. The boys were going to send the chocolate with her into the furnace, but decided the saviour waiting on the other side was all the pleasure she would require in Paradise.

Elisabeth Margaret Hopkins' last birthday candles were blown out by the youngest child at her wake. It took a while as he was asthmatic, wheezing in such close proximity to sugar. Gin and sherry were served with the cake, of course.

MAGGIE JACK

SALISH BASKET WEAVER (?, SQUIRREL COVE, CORTES ISLAND, BRITISH COLUMBIA–1977, CHEMAINUS, BRITISH COLUMBIA)

It was good for her to be in charge and good for me to learn that book-learning city girls don't know everything after all.

AGE WAS AN ISSUE for my friend Maggie Jack. On the one hand, she wanted to be younger than she was because she had a young husband, Vernon, more recently known to residents and tourists in Victoria as Sassy (short for Sasquatch), the forest spirit with the button collection who plays harmonica for change on the corner of Victoria's Government and Yates and recently waded through rush hour traffic to shake my hand at a stop light. On the other, she was trying to make the stretch to compete with a family record. Her father, a Cortes Islander whose coming of age predated the most devastating effects of contact, had lived to be one hundred and four.

I met Maggie at the Penelekut Reserve in 1972. She was giving a class in Salish basket weaving and was having trouble beating the bushes for First Nations women willing to risk their manicured nails in the brutal task of preparing the cedar roots. There were two honkies in the class and even though we were teased, me for my left-handed ass-backwards problem solving and Annette MacDonald for her chronic lateness, we both managed to complete with face.

Maggie's face was a work of art. She had red kewpie lips and great dark circumflexes drawn on her forehead. She dyed and curled her hair, which surprised me because most of the Native People I knew took great pride in their long straight hair, washed in the cold water of the Chemainus river and dried in the sun. Some of the women (never the men, who also wore their hair long) sold it for large sums of money to carvers for ceremonial masks that required beautiful hair. As fish provided much of the local diet, my family used to say more of the pog (welfare money) went downriver in shampoo than up (the direction of the grocery store) for food.

Maggie was dolling herself up for her child groom.

Whenever Vernon's lustful eye strayed beyond the front porch of their cabin in the direction of a lovelier, younger kloochma, Maggie would pick up a handy piece of kindling and beat him across the shoulders. This seemed to be some sort of good-humoured married people game, but I saw how serious she was when I met the real Maggie underneath the painted smiles and Miss Clairol as she lay in the hospital enduring her final illness. By then, her face was her own and her hair was silver and braided. She was a beautiful old woman. Herself. Even then, she was reluctant to relinquish control over her young husband, and she made me promise to keep an eye on Vernon after she went to spirit; an impossible task, although I solemnly swore.

The stories of Vernon's waywardness and her discipline were always good-naturedly recounted. Indian humour was a new genre to me and Maggie broke it wide open. Almost every non-Indian behaviour was a non sequitur. Why grow grass, for example, if you're not going to eat it?

Maggie had three natural sons and a host of boys who adopted her because she was a comfort woman. There was always something to eat and a bed at her shack, even though the price was something like staying at the Sally Ann Mission: you had to promise to be good, and take the consequences when you weren't.

Maggie made cedar root baskets and Cowichan sweaters to supplement her government money. This she had to pin to her bra because it would be stolen at night while she was sleeping, either by her boyish husband or one of those loving brats who stayed up late watching the wrestling on TV.

The First Nations kids who lived on the res called the boys "Sam and them" because they were too many to name, a ragged progress of aboriginal men that made its way to town and the jungle, a cedar clearing not too far from the liquor store, where they drank in peace so long as the whisky was shared. When it wasn't, there was war. Once I was chased down the highway by a posse of Indian cars when I gave a lift to a brother who had ripped his fellow boys off for a mickey, the volatile prize hidden under his jacket.

She was happy to pass this knowledge on, even to a white person, because she loved her culture.

Vernon wasn't all truant. He helped with the carding and spinning of wool and preparation of the baskets. The search for suitable roots was a spring sacrament, not unlike the hunt for Easter eggs. A good root grew long and straight and the ones by the river were best.

When I went with Maggie and Vernon on the expeditions, I tolerated the honky humour, their amusement over my left-handedness and general foreignness in woods they knew intimately. They were the stars, and I, the daughter of opportunity, just a sword carrier in the theatre of the bush. It was good for them to be in charge and good for me to learn that book-learning city girls don't know everything after all. They led me past my awkwardness with patience and good humour and I learned how to make a tolerable basket, sacrificing my fingernails to become part of a sacred task passed down from mother to daughter in her nation.

In my culture, everything had been learned verbally or from books. Maggie showed me the Indian way: how to dig the roots and strip them, how to keep them supple in water, then weave and decorate them with the darker cherry bark. She was happy to pass this knowledge on, even to a white person, because she loved her culture and was dismayed to see the traditional ways dying out.

Maggie and Vernon were photographed by Ulli Steltzer, whom Maggie called "that German woman," for a book recording Indian artists at work. There are photos of Vernon on his porch and at the river demonstrating his canoe

bailer, made from tree bark at the expense of the tree. My ex-husband used to say Vernon was harder on trees than rabbits. Maggie appears in full paint, stripping a root with her teeth.

By then she was dying. She must have known. She was so angry that she had been teased with an invitation to the book launch in Vancouver, but had no way to get there. Maggie had no money for travel. She could barely afford an occasional taxi to town to pick up her groceries and lost boys in the jungle. The book launch would have been her last glory trip on earth. Maggie liked her fun and her treats. Sometimes I would swing by and pick her up for a raiding party on the Overwaitea store in Chemainus, which stocked a greater variety of sweets than the grocery store at the Crofton Corner.

When recurring stomach cancer was too painful to paint over, she made her last trip to town in an ambulance to the little hospital where she spent several months refusing to die. This was the time her cultures collided. Raised a Catholic, she also had faith in the old ways. I was sent to find a shaman who made medicine. She said the tonic was derived from a certain tree. Maggie had been cured before. But the shaman, who had been living by the

butter church (so named because a farmer priest exchanged butter for rocks delivered to the top of the hill at Tzouhalem where his monument to God was being built stone by stone), had gone to the United States. Now, of course, we realize the tree, recently proven efficacious in white man's medicine, was yew. Meanwhile, the Catholic priest was visiting her and preparing her for a Catholic death.

On Mother's Day, I ignored the new "Natives Only" sign on the bridge to the Penelakut Reserve and drove to her cabin to offer the boys a ride to the hospital for a visit. It was going to be the last time. No one wanted to say goodbye. I had never experienced adult Indian death first-hand before, only the frequent deaths by accident of children, who were sailed to heaven on waves of grief. The boys were not about to relinquish their mother. They were going to crawl into a bottle and I was supposed to show them the money so they could call the bootlegger who drove the taxi in town. As it happened, I only had a few dollars and I wasn't about to pay up for booze. I went by myself to visit Maggie and found Vernon already there, washing her face and braiding her long silver hair.

On the way back from the hospital, I stopped at the store and bought cheese and

My ex-husband used to say Vernon was harder on trees than rabbits.

bread and milk, dropping it off at the cabin, which was quiet. Too quiet. I could hear a slight breeze pushing the plastic covering the broken windows and the mice at work under the floor.

The next morning, Leonard Peter, the Cowichan elder who drove my kids' school bus, told me "Sam and them" had all poisoned themselves that afternoon. They had broken into the Kuper Island residential school, where most of them had been brutally abused as children, and stolen Gestetner fluid, which they drank in Maggie's kitchen. The next two months were pure hell. Maggie was in agony. As a Catholic, she knew she had a balcony ticket, but she wasn't going to budge until she got to see her only remaining son and all the adult children whose Indian welfare cheques had been made out to her. She pleaded for them to come and no one would tell her they were dead. The priest had ordered it.

I don't know why I was intimidated by Father Green. He wasn't my priest. I realized Maggie needed her children to release her, but I also knew first-hand the unspeakable agony of having your children die before you. It became harder and harder to visit and to make up excuses for "Sam and them," who had long been buried in the Indian cemetery, where too many graves were decorated with children's toys.

I was relieved when Maggie forgot the English language and reverted to the dialect aboriginal children had been beaten for speaking at residential schools. I only understood a few words. She would have to forgive my silence. I held her hand and tried not to look into her eyes. Sooner or later, she would have to give up.

Finally, she died and went, I hope, to the heavenly riverbank where "Sam and them" and her other children had already scouted the best roots and where her father was fishing peacefully with a pipe in his mouth.

Maggie would have loved her funeral, held in the same church that had dispatched "Sam and them." I decided to be her daughter, since none of her children survived her to grieve, gathering all the baskets Maggie had given us and others we knew. It was July and there were many beautiful wildflowers growing in the fields and ditches. I picked them all: dog roses, lupin, wild snapdragon, sweetpea, and daisy, filling her baskets. The church was glorious with flowers and praise and summer light coming through the stained glass windows.

Brother Abel, a tiny man whose feet barely made it to the pedals, played "Amazing Grace"

There was chaos in the church that wanted her for Jesus.

on the organ. The women carried on like kids at the dentist, howling and caterwauling in contrast to my restrained Anglican experiences of death. Annette, who was always late, was late, and everyone stopped their wailing to laugh when the Tussie Road chapel door slammed behind her. Men stood on the porch collecting money for the coffin and the priest. You could hear trucks peeling in and out of the gravel parking lot. There were quite a few who wouldn't come into the church. For those, the sight of a man in ecclesiastical vestments was the equivalent of being served a dead rat on a plate during the Plague.

The best part of Maggie's funeral was saved for the last. There was a fight. Right in the middle of the service, a woman chief from up north arrived in a pick-up to take the body home to Cortes Island, where she said it belonged. The locals wanted to keep her too. After an extremity of sound-enhanced disputation, a storm of adversarial kin swamped the nave, taking opposite ends of the open coffin where Maggie lay smiling in a new pantsuit Vernon bought at the Woodward's mall, taking a taxi both ways to Nanaimo. She must have liked the adversarial kin rocking her back and forth, a motion she remembered from her childhood on the water.

There was chaos in the church that wanted her for Jesus. In the end, the North Family won and they took her home to Cortes, leaving her worldly goods for the Tussie Road people to burn, which is the custom. The smoke followed her to her new life.

Her baskets, of course, went home with people who treasured them. Mine are part of our daily life. We use the last tray from the wonderful tree we found together, woven partly by her and partly by Vernon after her death, for tea in the garden. Her last basket holds my sewing things. Each of my children has a basket to remember her. Once a year, we immerse them in water to keep them from drying out. Even though all things belong to the earth and return to the earth, we want to keep Maggie's work alive as long as we can.

LISTENING

for Maggie

I kept listening for her everywhere,
a voice in the woods at night,
her breath in the leaves,
one raven laughing louder than the rest.

And then, one day, under a pear tree,
I met one who seemed to be waiting there,
who seemed to know me;
a rabbit white as her hospital hair.

There had been injuries in the orchard.
"Trees bleed," my husband said,
his jacket stained with the blood of animals.
"Rabbits eat bark."
Oh no, she was always gentle, always said thanks
to the tree for her baskets.

My husband raised his axe.
It was the end of our marriage.
When the rabbit screamed,
her voice was just like a woman's.

LINDA ROGERS, 1978

HILDA HALE

WRITER AND PAINTER (1907, YORKSHIRE, ENGLAND–)

What a miracle to be living on her own, trimming her own stems and arranging them in a crystal vase, with a steady hand, at age ninety.

HILDA HALE IS A NEW FRIEND. Barb Pedrick had intrigued me with a full frontal photograph of the silk-clad dowager standing in front of a carved Chinese chest and her own painting, in the Chinese style, of a blackbird on a mulberry branch. I had to meet her.

I had heard Hilda described as indomitable and formidable, so I armed myself with an armful of voluptuous tulips before knocking on the door of her Oak Bay house in Victoria. Built in the colonial manner, with a fine verandah and cool sprawling rooms, it fits her perfectly. What a miracle to be living on her own, trimming her own stems and arranging them in a crystal vase, with a steady hand, at age ninety.

I was soon to learn that the list of Hilda's skills is more detailed than the Christmas catalogue from Simpsons Sears. Not only is she confident with the matrimonial crystal but

also with her sable paint brushes and a pen from Buckingham Palace. When I told Hilda the Duchess of York stole stationery from the Royal households before her wedding to the Duke, she laughed and assured me hers was a gift bought by a friend in support of the restoration of Windsor Castle after the fire.

She took me through the darkened rooms, softly lit to rest her eyes, introducing various paintings, carpets, embroideries, and pieces of magnificent furniture as if they were old friends. I felt myself falling back to a time in my childhood when there were many elderly ladies of her ilk who spoke Mandarin with houseboys left over from colonial days, and who spoke *sotto voce* of children conceived by "accommodating" brothers in China while they smoked opium in their lonely quarters at night.

Hilda was born in England but, in the tradition of the British Empire, has lived on five continents—Europe, Asia, Africa, North America, and India. Her father, a pioneer in aeronautics, gave his family a geographical education it is almost impossible to imagine today, when, due in part to his efforts, the global village is a smaller place, but neither as rich nor diverse as it was.

The first born in her family, with the first child's adventurous spirit, it is clear she was indomitable from the start, living out the prediction of a gypsy that she was lucky and would travel far and see much. Her life is a scrapbook of exotic impressions, beginning with an early childhood recollection of a washerwoman from the South African kraal who slung her pendulous breast over her shoulder to feed the infant on her back.

One image follows another as the traveller recounts nine decades of passionate journey.

Hilda herself is something to look at. She is theatrical in her presentation, a blend of the artistic English girl with the oriental stamp of the impressionable colonial wife. She is now receiving a special pension for war survivors. This, she says, pays for the hairdo that is as essential now as it was in China before the war. One must keep up appearances.

As a child, Hilda mastered piano and mandolin and became an expert English

country dancer. Later on, these skills made her invaluable to the British community in China where her husband was posted with Thomas Cook and Sons. They must have saved her sanity when, in a Japanese internment camp during the Second World War, she taught the children the things she loved to do, keeping pride and awareness of their own culture alive for them during hard times.

Already familiar with the exotic from childhood travel with her parents, Hilda accepted an engagement ring made of diamonds from the ring of a Chinese concubine and married her husband in Japan before moving with him to Beijing, where her two daughters were born.

Her happy marriage was silk embroidered, like the present from a Mandarin princess that miraculously followed her through adversity and still hangs in her house today. In pre-war China, the Hales had servants, a car, and a social life, and Hilda was busy teaching her artistic and musical skills to the women and children in the expatriate community. As the wife of an executive in the travel business, she met and befriended fascinating people, including Edwina, the sexually adventurous Lady Mountbatten, who gave her a beautiful jade sculpture of Ho Hsien Ku, the only female Chinese immortal.

The shadow on this charmed life, as a colonial wife with an "evolved" husband who encouraged her independence, was the war. Hilda's physician in China, Dr. von Wolff, was later reported to have become the personal physician to Hitler. This could be an apocryphal story, the sort of urban myth to start in expatriate communities, where all foreigners are bonded in co-dependence whatever their national differences. These brushes with past danger are relished in the telling.

The Hale family were under house arrest and finally interned in the Weihsien Internment Camp in Shantung province, northern China, for more than two years. This is the time the real Hilda emerged in her glory. Through sheer will and what they used to call pluck, she pulled her daughters through disease and deprivation, creating with her devoted husband a real family life in the dreadful conditions while they were imprisoned. Rather than giving in to depression, the Beijing social butterfly drew on her Yorkshire heritage and made English pudding out of virtual stones. I sense the Hale daughters did well in this enforced intimacy.

The list of Hilda's skills is more detailed than the Christmas catalogue from Simpsons Sears.

Despite physical deprivation, they had wonderful emotional nourishment from both parents. Hilda, who had no adult social distractions, taught them to read and sew in addition to the fine arts she was teaching other camp children.

One daughter did not live to be old, perhaps the effect of childhood trauma. Both girls were nursed by their mother through whooping cough and paratyphoid while in the internment camp.

The camp liberator believed he had discovered a village of the dead when the gates were opened. Several became seriously ill when they wolfed down provisions brought by the American soldiers, a common footnote to starvation. Hilda, the ever-resourceful Yorkshirewoman, had augmented her family's camp rations with black market deals that happened at night over the wall around the camp. During one inspection for contraband, she painted her children with measles to discourage the inquisitive Japanese from looking under their blanket of fur coats from better days.

Weihsien was more than a train journey away from the privilege of Beijing, where Hilda had her underwear embroidered in an orphanage run by nuns. Now, of course, we know as she does that those children did and still do go blind from the work, the alternative to death by exposure, a common fate for unwanted girls in China. China is full of such paradoxes, she says, having experienced both sides of privilege.

Hilda's physician in China was later reported to have become the personal physician to Hitler.

Hilda clearly enjoyed the glamour of English colonial life, especially such perks as taking the decadent Lady Mountbatten to choose her furs, but the sensible Yorkshirewoman rose and took charge whenever the going got tough. You see it in her portrait now, the straight lady in front of her delicate painting. It is the contradictions that make her so interesting. She is a survivor, just as surely as the fields of her home country come up green every spring.

After the war, colonial life as they knew it was history. The Hales spent some time in India and then moved to Victoria, where Hilda has been President of the Asian Arts Society, an affiliate of the Art Gallery of Victoria, and a member of the Monarchist League.

When I went to the Art Gallery to buy her

autobiography, *Indomitably Yours*, she was decked out in one of those Chinese furs and flourishing the Palace pen. Hilda, with her defiant mid-Pacific accent, is a legend in her own time.

You get the sense that she is determined to savour every day of her life. She is still painting on silk and rice paper in spite of a cataract operation two years ago, and she still teaches mah-jong to the dowagers of Oak Bay who must ante up for the Asian Arts Society in return for her precious time. Her book, based on a lifetime supply of memorabilia pack-ratted from one continent to another, well-written and as rich in detail as her beloved embroideries, was self-published because, at her age, she wasn't going to wait around for the right publisher.

There is nothing like the sound of mah-jong tiles clicking together on polished wood. The importance of China is recalled in sensory impressions like this that reprise a happy marriage. I have a feeling Hilda will enjoy passing over to that other side she first experienced after a difficult childbirth in a Chinese hospital.

What is death but another birth for the adventurous, especially if her husband is waiting for her as he did in those other times of separation and adversity? No doubt Hilda will cross over in a beautiful dress and immaculate coiffure, wearing the concubine's diamonds and clutching the Chinese guest book, her favourite wedding present. When I signed it, I could see it was almost filled.

Hilda accepted an engagement ring made of diamonds from the ring of a Chinese concubine.

DOROTHY LIVESAY

POET AND ACTIVIST (1909, WINNIPEG, MANITOBA–1996, VICTORIA, BRITISH COLUMBIA)

Dorothy Livesay, warrior, was born in a storm and when she died in a storm no one was surprised.

DOROTHY LIVESAY, WARRIOR, was born in a storm and when she died in a storm no one was surprised.

Some people came to her memorial service at the Victoria Art Gallery, a suitable compromise between her pagan and Christian selves, to honour a life spent fighting dragons and other apposite beings. She *was* a dragon and the mourners had business to finish at a time when the fires in her fighting mouth were banked. Even though she wrote the script for her own funeral service, Dee left room, in her surprisingly fair-minded way, for rebuttals to the hymns and testimonials to her life as pugilist.

Dorothy was born to a pair of non-conforming journalists who paid indulgent inattention to daughters born in the autumn of their lives. Dee and Sophie, whose dresses were good but not always cleaned and mended, grew up in a chaos of words and music and domestic dispute. Mother was an untidy Christian with unruly hair and father a sometimes responsible hedonist who may have put his tongue in his daughters' mouths when he'd been drinking. Dee wasn't sure she remembered exactly. Nor was she certain whether his death on the evening of a significant birthday was natural or not.

The poet child of this neurotic household was strong willed and highly sexed, unlike her mother, who suffered the attentions of her passionate husband. She was a girl who was comfortable in weather, whether it was family conflict or a wild ride on her swing. From the beginning, her life was motivated by passion and intuition.

When she married Duncan McNair, possibly to extend the child in her to another generation, she warned him that she was a bride of the wind. Eventually, that nomadic determination took her to Africa and into the arms of other men and women, some of whom suffered as her amanuenses.

A sea wind brought her back to the west coast where she settled for a time in the unquiet island community that included Audrey Thomas, Elisabeth Hopkins, Jane Rule, and Helen Sonthoff, all artists. The word "secretary" took on new meaning as women with buns and sensible skirts took the ferry to and from Galiano Island, where Dee spent the youthful part of her old age drinking up a storm and womanizing like there was no tomorrow. It was hard not to giggle on being introduced to these two-dimensional women (Olive Oyl and Agnes Gooch come to mind) who usually walked a few paces behind the Great Lady, wearing the expressions of academic wives, carrying her papers and her scarves.

The real poems are being written in outports
on backwoods farms
in passageways where pantries still exist
or where geraniums
nail light to the window
while out of the window boy in the flying field
is pulled to heaven on the keel of a kite.

All Dee's finding of causes and people to raise up and love was documented in poetry that was, until the end—when the cutting edge of poetry exceeded even her liberal parameters by slipping into what she considered to be vulgar street rhetoric and post-feminist babble—at least a step ahead of its time. ("One step forward? Two steps back.") There was just a hint of possession in her and her poetry, those "voices singing under ice" she acknowledged in her poem "The Uninvited." This tendency became more marked when she was slowly gathered up in the final storm of a passionate dementia.

When I entered the unorthodox contract that was friendship with Dee, she was starting to lose the grip on her teeth and her mind, and it made her furious. Her grey-blue eyes raged out of that shrinking face with the pain a wild girl feels when she finally recognizes the crone passing the shop window as herself. As always, Livesay was candid about the mutual betrayal of her body and her brain. Even though her mind was rusty, her arthritic hands still couldn't keep up with her need to bang out her fury at time's cruel joke. The tyranny of a failing bladder kept her at home. She refused drinks when out, fighting for control. It made her bitchy.

On one occasion, when she had mistakenly waited in the lane for a ride to a lunch party, she berated me for parking around the front of the Oxford Street rest home, the first of many stops at levels of increasing care. It was Dorothy who taught me tough love works as well for the hormone-challenged elder as it does for the adolescent. I told her to behave or she would henceforth be taking a taxi to the literary events she enjoyed so much.

Dorothy loved children, possibly because she never left her childhood, her impulsiveness, her enthusiasm, her self-centredness behind. It was a naive idealism that led her into the barricades as a young woman to fight hunger, racism, and tyranny, with just a hint of noblesse oblige, taking now-legislated positions long before they were fashionable. The country honoured Dorothy with medals and she loved to wear them, a whole pride on her chest, on every public occasion. Like the feathers of an aboriginal freedom fighter, her medals gave her credibility in the ongoing battle for human rights.

There were representatives of First Nations and Japanese Canadian communities, Quakers, feminists, family, poets, and children at Dee's memorial service, making a potpourri of remembrance for a garden with no fences.

From the beginning, her life was motivated by passion and intuition.

She was one of the first women in Canada to advocate for difference. Not conventionally beautiful, she relished her sexuality. Not male in a time of masculine domination of politics and poetry, she defiantly celebrated her gender. In return, she was adored in the way public people often are, from a distance.

Those who knew her well were often at odds with this odd character who, although politically correct, was not comfortable with the social graces.

At a reading, "The Unquiet Bed," held by the League of Canadian Poets, everyone rose to the pitch of P.K. Page's helium-filled poem, "But We Rhyme in Heaven," which was about the difficulty of rhyming on earth with Dorothy Livesay, *femme terrible*.

> *It is so irrational.*
> *What is the bloody bone*
> *we struggle and fight for?*
> *Not my bone. Not hers.*
> *An astrological quirk?*

Elizabeth Brewster confided about sharing a lover with Dee; Patrick Lane recounted a horrible insult: Dorothy had told him the wrong brother died when Pat's brother Red passed away. Someone else resurrected the rumour that Dee had had an affair (actually it was all reported to have happened in one limousine ride to the Kremlin) with the tyrant Stalin, anticipating the movie about Stalin's love affair with a political idealist in which Australian actress Judy Davis played the Dee part—right up to her famous brown lips.

I remember an often cranky old lady who loved flowers and music and babies, smiling in recognition when I took my grandchild Sophie to visit (partly because the name was an echo of her own childhood and her sister Sophie). Each morning she phoned with a list of ways I was supposed to change the world that day, my number and a few others written in large print on a chalkboard near her bed, lest she forget. She hoped we would drop everything and run to the barricades as she had, never mind that some of us had husbands and children to consider. Would I just fly off to the latest flood and give inoculations for typhus?

Dorothy wanted to become a wise woman. She did not plan to lose her mind. She raged against the body that leaked and hurt and forgot, but she still loved the world and believed she could fix it, and if she couldn't she'd get someone else to.

Each morning she phoned with a list of ways I was supposed to change the world that day.

And so the whole that I possess
Is still much less—
They move triumphant through my head:
I am the one
Uncomforted.

She valued the legacy of poetry in its highest function, the world made perfect with beautiful and meaningful language, making every attempt to encourage and inspire. There is still debate about her own work. Some venerate her poetry and some condescend, calling her most banal poetry propaganda, ignoring the sublime in her best work. In *Archive for Our Times*, a collection and analysis of Dorothy's poetry, editor Dean Irvine (a former student I saved from poetry, he says, by suggesting he become an editor instead) has shown that there is much value in the "singing under ice," even those poems written when she was raging against the dying of the light. She was as hard on herself as others were, ruthlessly cutting the poems that lacked a cutting edge.

Dorothy used to complain to me about unintelligible poetry, sometimes picking on poets who had been chosen to receive the prize named after her. She wanted poetry to be clear and effective, so everyone could understand and share it, and hers was always that.

When her father made his last journey, with Montaigne's essays on his bedside table, an ivory paper cutter between the pages, Dorothy read, "The greatest thing in the world is to belong to ourselves." When her own journey with her selves ended in a last battle with the snow angel of dementia, no one would argue that she hadn't. Dorothy Livesay had written her own book right up to the time when words failed her and you could only remember the words that could be her epitaph:

Speak through me, mountains
Till the other voices be silent
Till the sirens cease and the guns muffle their thunder
Till the monstrous voice of man is sheltered by quiet—
Speak through me, speak till I remember
Movement in the womb and green renewal
Sundrenched maples in September
And the sweep of time as a gull's wing slanting.

WHITE ELEPHANTS
for Dee

Now the old lady is white in her bed,
white as the sheets she hemmed
to make love in, long ago.

Now she is pale as the drowned boy
she saw run out of the water,
his naked body a chandelier,
who brought her pale
anemones from his garden
and danced with her on the beach
leaving the scent of tides
in the folds of her organdy dress,
while her father's portable radio played
"God Bless the Child" by a blues singer
with holes in her arms,
her ship going down,
the gardenia in her hair
dying in the finite space of a song.

Now the old lady smiles
like a boat full of children
sailing through storms,
her lips a fugue, the baby
teeth of elephants stolen at night,
banging the shores of Africa,
where she saw plant-eating matriarchs
herd their families back to the ocean.

This is the wind she's been waiting for.
At last, she hears ivory singing,
white elephants circling her hospital bed,
white trunks raised, smelling of Emerald
Cities beneath the sea,
lifting her white nightgown,
filling her cotton sail.

Linda Rogers, 1996

P. K. PAGE

POET AND PAINTER (1916, SWANAGE-BY-THE-SEA, ENGLAND–)

I am a tin whistle
Blow through me
Blow through me
And make my tin
Gold

IF EVER A SWAN WAS BORN in Swanage, it must be Patricia Kathleen, eldest and only daughter of Lionel and Rose, sister to the mythically beautiful Michael, who in his infant photographs could be the future Siegfried, so perfect is the strength and beauty of his face. The family mouth and curls, the stature, must have set brother and sister apart from other children the moment they both sailed out in their pram.

The public P.K. is a woman described in the words of fairy tale. She is handsome, a goddess, commanding, majestic, the Aurora for her time, dressed in swansdown or, more likely, something sculptured from a store that sells wearable art. Her jewelry could be borrowed from the border of a medieval illumination.

My husband calls P.K. "the Jeweller." Her beautifully crafted poems are, from every angle, the literary equivalent of the Imperial eggs the artist Faberge created for the Royal Family of Russia, precious jewels articulating the surface of a holy idea. Dazzled by the dramatic readings that have made Page the Dowager Queen of Canadian poetry, we have become familiar with one aspect of a complex intelligence. She is bright. Her poetry is brilliant. The brilliance, which finds its resonance in all the references to light, precious metal, and reflection in her poetry, is insight. For some, even her granddaughter, Christine, who uses the word in her loving essay "My Grandmother's Luggage," it is "intimidating."

P.K., who has made a study of philosophy and Sufism, may be willing the sea to lie down as she would iron the wrinkles on the surface of the earth in one of her most beautiful poems. There is underpainting she would calm with her meditations and "holy surfaces." In medieval painting, a ground of red bole gives the gold leaf its vibrancy. Only the blood surging beneath the stories of snow disturbs the serenity of Page's art.

Images, P.K. believes, are out there in the phenomenal world, like pears on a tree, for artists to select. In spite of the evident craftsmanship of her work, she says that, unlike writers who stick to schedules, she is undisciplined in the regularity of her devotions; that the lines summon her to the writing desk. The discipline came in the beginning when, as a teenager, she made herself write a sonnet a day, all of them, she says, bad. It was practice and much reading that made the ink flow smoothly.

The daughter of an army officer, P.K. inherited the stature of that fine horseman who joined the cavalry because it provided the opportunity to ride for a living. Not "the very model of a modern Major-General," he taught her that joy is the fundamental premise of work. Her father also possessed a sense of humour, the playfulness that marks his daughter's obsession with line and language.

Her social composure aside, there is turbulence in the inside air of the poems that resonates on the surface, giving them a dynamic that pulls the reader in. P.K. says she

was always an outsider, the *étranger* who watches and listens. She has an eye for detail and a good ear. A tall girl with a funny accent who did not attend Sunday School, she felt "different" from the beginning. This may have been the impetus for the antithetical moments in her personal journey, which sometimes led to conflict.

There are a number of poems about conflict and resolution, which have, even in this time of unbridled revelation, an astonishing candour. What child hasn't craved "forgiveness for thy just rebukes as I still crave thy praise"? Startled by the "thys" of this poem, I once asked P.K. if the Bible had been her primer. Despite the fact P.K. did time in an Anglican school, her parents were religious nonconformists, which partially explains her attraction to Eastern philosophy.

In the gravity-defying, air-filled skirt of the whirling Sufi is found her personal archetype, the circle (or eye, "I") that dominates both her writing and the painting that came later in life when the voice detoured in colour and silence, the visual poetry of her middle age. Painting, which surprised P.K., as C.S. Lewis was surprised by Joy, is the gift of her mother, Rose, daughter of an artistic family, who illustrated the poems P.K.'s father sent home from the

Her beautifully crafted poems are, from every angle, the literary equivalent of the Imperial eggs the artist Faberge created for the Royal Family of Russia.

front for their infant daughter. She is perhaps the gypsy P.K. sometimes allows us to glimpse in herself. It is the gypsy who calls her work "play," which all art might be and all artists, in the vernacular of the New Age, still their "inner children."

Play perhaps. Not as opposed to work. But spontaneous involvement which is its own reward: done for the sheer joy of doing it; for the discovery, invention, sensuous pleasure. "Taking a line for a walk," manipulating sounds, rhythms.

There are stories of P.K. as a young woman at the time Canadian poetry was in its adolescence, when poets became a tribe. P.K. danced on tables, I have heard. She threw back her head and laughed. But there were factions, even then. Her initiation to the politics of poetry came with the Preview Poets, writers like Patrick Anderson and F.R. Scott, themselves scholarly and intimidating, who took the young poet into their cell. In grand opposition stood that baroque individualist Irving Layton, who suggested a literary purgative for the likes of those he saw as the embodiment of Wasp repression.

The outspoken and sometimes careless Dorothy Livesay was another angel to wrestle. How interesting that Page follows Livesay in

this book, and that Page has the final say. The last word is graceful. They had disagreed about poetry, about style, but P.K. wrote her now-famous poem around a promise Dee had made about "rhyming in heaven," and the poem says Amen to that. She says, "magnets pull us together and we go for each other." It is an interesting and revealing line about someone preoccupied with the properties of metal. Freud said conflict is the mother of creativity. When you read through the canon of P.K. Page and search the paintings for clues to the character of the eye that has seen and recorded so many human events, you begin to know the daughter of sun and moon in terms of alchemy, gold and silver.

She refers to her fictitious gypsy and real progenitors as if they were armies inside a walled garden, one in the house and one camping in caravans. They are the figurative seat of the negative attraction. P.K. Page may well be the Queen of Canadian poetry, but the gypsy lurks. You catch the flash of her silver jewelry, the flirtatious locus of her moving skirts.

P.K. kept the English love of garden and language and an accent that stops at about the place the Titanic sank. Perhaps her desire to embroider comes from an obsessive reaction

to dust and endless horizons. She is still English, in the enclosed garden where poets like Edith Sitwell and fellow émigré Anne Szumigalski flourish.

When P.K. married the widowed Commissioner of the National Film Board in Ottawa, where she had been working, she assumed the life of a corporate wife. Arthur Irwin, a recent centenarian, was a management bureaucrat and diplomat, who worked with my uncle, Dana Wilgress, Canadian Ambassador to London, Moscow, and NATO, in External Affairs, another cross-stitch in this family fabric. Diplomatic missions in Brazil, Australia, and Mexico with her new husband awakened the painter and shushed the poet, who found her pen looping and cross-hatching, hungering to put down the shapes of her new landscapes, and, eventually, when courage filled her diplomatic elbow-length gloves with paint, the colours as well.

P.K. does tell one story about letting the gypsy out in her diplomatic life. She was having lunch at Government House in Victoria with the Queen Mother and her various aides. P.K., who probably knew you never ask the Queen Mum (who, at home, apparently refers to herself as an "old Queen" in her household of elderly male servants) a personal question, did ask a personal question. The Queen Mother, astonishingly, talked about fatigue making one vulnerable, whereupon P.K. asked if she had ever been invulnerable. It sounds perfectly logical, but the Queen Mum waved her sceptre and P.K. was levitated and left on the cold side of the room. She had accomplished invisibility.

In the Major key, Page has written fine public poetry like the beautiful glosa "Planet Earth":

It has to be made bright, the skin of this planet
till it shines in the sun like gold leaf.

Archangels then will attend to its metals
and polish the rods of its rain.

These are the words she would like us to remember.

The gypsy has sometimes shown her face boldly in poems and paintings about private life. These are the domestic sketches which have their literary equivalent in poems like "Deaf Mute in the Pear Tree," where his "locked throat finds a little door / and through it feathered joy / flies screaming like a jay."

P.K. was always a painter, even before she knew it. Poets are required to capture truth in snapshots, or in the case of such a colourful writer, in paint and precious metal, so that the eye becomes the "I" of the poem and we see with her clarity.

We know from her writing that the moon has a dark side. Like all of us, she has had her disappointments. There has never been a child of her own making to crown with the glory of gold sunlight in her tempera paintings. The angel she wrestles now is very real. It lives in her, in the bones that ache and torment her.

As one grief piles on another, an exhausted world, the death of friends, the act of God that brought down a favourite Douglas-fir tree, she continues to be, in accordance with Mother Teresa's direction to all of us, "a pencil in the hand of God." This is the confidence instilled by parents who also taught her a responsibility to her gifts, and the will of a woman determined to iron the wrinkles and gild the ceremonial moments.

One night when she was small, P.K.'s mother took her outside. Indicating the night sky, she asked, "How can we believe in only one way when heaven is so various?" These are the landscapes behind the eye which accommodate every possible variation. The sky may have been the permanent home to an army child who moved so often her mother

These are the landscapes behind the eye which accommodate every possible variation.

refused to make jam because she would have to pack it around.

She could still be watching for those messengers she writes about who bring truths from places more evolved than Planet Earth. P.K. says if she were a dictator she would command that everyone read Doris Lessing's "inner-space fiction," *Shikasta,* which puts forward the premise that there is intelligence greater than our own and made Page believe she was "hearing the truth for the first time." There are voices out there. They dictate the poems which she "sometimes understands later."

Between the poet and the voices there are arras curtains of her own making, on which she transcribes her worlds and ours.

ARRAS

Consider a new habit—classical,
and trees espaliered on the wall like candelabra.
How still upon that lawn our sandalled feet.

But a peacock rattling his rattan tail and screaming
has found a point of entry. Through whose eye
did it insinuate in furled disguise
to shake its jewels and silks upon that grass?

The peaches hang like lanterns. No one joins
those figures on the arras.
                                    Who am I
or who am I become that walking here
I am observer, other, Gemini,
starred for a green garden of cinema?

I ask, what did they deal me in this pack?
The cards, all suits, are royal when I look.
My fingers slipping on a monarch's face
twitch and grow slack.
I want a hand to clutch, a heart to crack.

No one is moving now, the stillness is
infinite. If I should make a break . . .
take to my springy heels . . . ? But nothing moves.
The spinning world is stuck upon its poles,
the stillness points a bone at me. I fear
the future on this arras.

                I confess:

It was my eye.
Voluptuous it came.
Its head the ferrule and its lovely tail
folded so sweetly; it was strangely slim
to fit the retina. And then it shook
and was a peacock—living patina,
eye-bright—maculate!
Does no one care?

I thought their hands might hold me if I spoke.
I dreamed the bite of fingers in my flesh,
their poke smashed by an image, but they stand
as if within a treacle, motionless,
folding slow eyes on nothing. While they stare
another line has trolled the encircling air,
another bird assumes its furled disguise.

P.K. PAGE

MYFANWY PAVELIĆ

PAINTER (1916, VICTORIA, BRITISH COLUMBIA–)

Every time painter Myfanwy Pavelić looks out her living room window, she sees her life on a green, arbutus-interrupted lawn that leads to the sea.

EVERY TIME PAINTER MYFANWY PAVELIĆ looks out her living room window, she sees her life on a green, arbutus-interrupted lawn that leads to the sea. This is the beach she toddled toward with her earliest steps, the place where later she sketched Pierre Trudeau and painted her friend Katherine Hepburn in a red scarf. The sea is changing colour and light, every note of a vast concerto playing itself the same and differently every day. What luxury to wake up each morning and hear the same picture in its infinite variety and ultimate simplicity.

Older cultures than our own afford this sense of continuity as generation after generation live in the same houses, farm the same land, and worship in the same churches. The sense of family and village is the first imprint. It is more complicated for us. Born to wanderers, we continue to search for ourselves.

Myfanwy, an animated eighty-two, is still a character in search of family. Her arms move like a dancer's, in spite of her reluctant bones, as she introduces a lifetime's collection of friends hanging on her walls. An only child in a tribe of cousins, she has spent her life selecting the friendships and portraits that surround her in her parents' summer house.

When she parted with the large portion of her work that entered the permanent collection of the University of Victoria, her first reaction was relief, the way mothers feel the first day all their children go to school. Now she had space and breathing room. She could rest. Before long, maternal anxiety set in. She missed her favourites, the ongoing non-verbal conversations that occur between painter and subject.

Born into a successful mercantile family, Myfanwy Spencer might have turned out like

The piano stands in her studio, tuned and ready like a fresh canvas.

most of her contemporaries, content with growing up in privilege, "coming out" (which used to mean being introduced in Society), marrying, and playing bridge. This was not to be the chosen road for one of the best-known figurative painters of our time. Myfanwy was as different as her melodious Welsh name and Eggs Myf, a breakfast concoction at the Algonquin, New York's famous literary hotel, where Dorothy Parker presided at the round table and Myf must have found favour with the cook as her own particular version of Heloise.

Like many artists, Myfanwy had a solitary childhood, in her case as an invalid "only." The sick child and the only child have the luxury of contemplation. Hours spent alone with books and paints as playmates set the pattern for lateral thinking. Myfanwy was different, fragile and alone, but strong in character. Born a Taurus, she resisted the mould of her time and place, determining early that she would be an artist. Only ill health stood in the way of her determination to have a career in music. Demonstrating her flexible floppy thumbs, she allows you into the full circle of her grief.

The piano stands in her studio, tuned and ready like a fresh canvas. All her life she has had a passion for music and musicians, a

passion that is reflected in her fine portraits of friends like Yehudi Menuhin, whose first concert at Carnegie Hall she attended, and pianist Jan Cherniavsky, my children's uncle.

She tells a wonderful story about Jan. Visiting New York during the war, when financial restrictions were in effect, she was dreaming of attending his performance in the famous concert hall. She was allowed in the country with barely enough money to rent herself a bed, let alone a fine meal or a ticket to a concert. While Myfanwy was pondering her dilemma in Grand Central Station, she looked up to see a poster: her beautiful drawing of the pianist in lyric pencil lines. That was her concert, his portrait and the sound of rushing feet.

Hanging over the piano in her studio, a high-ceilinged room with generous windows and the comfortable intimacy of books and worn rugs, is Myfanwy's portrait of her formidable mother, the portrait's length accentuating the elegant legs crossed in the foreground. Mother is having the last word as you interrupt the dialogue between painter and subject, the inevitable bicker pastel, softened by good manners and the intervening years. Mother is everything the painter is not. She is coiffure, tea gown, and silk stockings, a figure aware of her femininity, but properly. She knows her legs are perfect, but her knees are just covered. Looking up, the daughter, her curls in a defiant ponytail, her slender figure dressed in androgynous shirt and slacks, is her own person.

There are self-portraits too. In my favourite, the artist is turning away, her back and the pose of her arm telling everything about her impatience with her own body and physical appearance.

As a talented only child, Myfanwy was allowed to explore her gifts, never pushed or exploited, but not entirely appreciated for herself. Sometimes the apparent indifference of the significant parent triggers a need to please. Myfanwy, like many other women artists, wanted her mother to love what she made. For many mothers this was complicated because their own creativity had been stifled by social demands. It was far safer for a daughter to be pretty and marry well than to risk being an artist or a person with opinions.

Myfanwy is a beautiful woman, but, like most of Barbara's subjects, she was nervous about her appearance. This astonishing phenomenon led us to the realization that many mothers are competitive in their definition of feminine beauty. Somehow they

give their daughters the message that they leave something to be desired. The most rewarding aspect of this project for me has been the privilege of seeing our subjects through Barbara's eyes. All have been pleased and surprised by what they saw.

What is immediately recognizable in her work is the compassionate line. You realize that they are all about relationship, something that cannot be generalized.

When it came time for Myfanwy to be photographed in her studio and in front of her portrait of Hepburn, the self-consciousness vanished and she had the professional composure of the portrait-painter who knows exactly what to do with the head and the hands. Her attention to such details accounts for the outstanding character of her portraits. When I asked Myfanwy what she wanted to capture, she insisted that every painting was isolated in the experience of that moment. She never thinks ahead to its public life. What is immediately recognizable in her work is the compassionate line. You realize that they are all about relationship, something that cannot be generalized.

Individually and in total her paintings are, one by one, about community. They are her small world and her friendships released to embrace the strangers who experience their intimacy. If they make a statement beyond their artistic value, then it is about the character and values of her subjects, all of whom share a common humanity.

Although I met Myfanwy relatively recently, my life has been populated by these portraits. In the houses of friends and relatives, they have been a warm reminder of relationship. I understand how she felt when she sent some of her favourites away to the university gallery.

Even though she has birthed many paintings, Pavelić has only one child, Tessa, who lives with her at Spencerwood, her house by the sea. After a first marriage that pleased her mother and ended in divorce, as many marriages of that sort are bound to do, she found a soulmate in Nicki Pavelić, a Yugoslav lawyer who emigrated after the war. Nicki recently died in his nineties, leaving the two women and Tessa's kind but slowed-down sheepdog alone in a house that is coloured by family history.

Myfanwy's big concern has been to leave Tessa in a circle of familial friends. This she has seen to as she has taken care of every detail of her daughter's life. A woman who has been honoured in every way, from painting a Prime Minister and some of the most beloved artists of our time, to public decoration, she will tell you that the greatest moment of her life was Tessa's graduation from a school for differently gifted children in New York. Tessa, challenged from birth, has realized her maximum potential because of the strength and conviction of her mother, who does not give in to physical or mental limitations of any kind.

Tessa works with young children and is considered an angel by her co-workers. She plays the piano and Myfanwy twinkles when she tells you about the musical conversations between her daughter and Menuhin, the former gifted child. Music, the language of angels, is level ground for two people united by obsession.

Myfanwy Pavelić is not a quitter. In her eighty-first year, when many would be satisfied with expending the effort to blow out that number of candles, she celebrated by organizing a magnificent concert in honour of Menuhin, with the proceeds donated to his school for performing artists.

When it looked as if her enemies, osteoporosis and arthritis, were attempting to beat down her muse, Pavelić had a harness designed that would allow maximum movement around her large canvases. Every morning, religiously, she works out in a warm pool doing the "squishies," hand and leg exercises that ensure maximum flexibility.

In spite of the artist's need for solitude, it is Myf's inherited sociability that continues to be the impetus for her life in art. Myfanwy concedes that although her elegant mother was not an artist, her life was art, every detail of her household perfect in its execution. Her own life is also well ordered in spite of the ragged goodbyes that tear the symmetry of her household.

Recently, her brush has turned from the beloved faces, all of them filled with character and light, to the landscape around the familiar house which has grown to fit her own life, always keeping the simple profile of the original rooms with their graceful inclusion of the outdoors. In the exhibition that accompanied the Menuhin concert, there was an extraordinary series of paintings excluding the human figure. The perspective was intense as the painter took us through rows of spent trees toward the light. These are portraits of her world the way she sees it when she wakes up alone.

When a famous photographer explained to me that the best moment for capturing the vulnerable human face was when they were brought out of darkness, as from a movie theatre into a bright afternoon, sitting her subjects in the dark and lighting them the moment before the shutter blinked, I thought of the impossibility of that phenomenon in any other medium. That was before I saw the recent landscapes of Myfanwy Pavelić. She has captured nature blinking in that primal illumination.

I thought perhaps this series was a valedictory statement. This is what it is like to move into the light. However, looking back, I see that this perception has always been her gift, and what she has chosen to select in that first light is the most noble aspect of her subjects. Whether the intelligence of the thoughtful child, revealed in her eyes or hands, or the gentle profile of Pierre Trudeau, philosopher king, or a portrait of her aging husband, triumphant after his promenade around the driveway, always it is grace that turns to her light.

Glenn Gould—Hands
1982
Pencil on paper

EURITHE PURDY

MUSE (1924, McARTHUR'S MILLS, ONTARIO–)

Eurithe knows she is one of those rare women who have been immortalized.

AL CLAIMS EURITHE LIED about her age when they eloped in 1941. She says not, that she was legal—nearly seventeen, a mature girl from a big family. He likes to think of himself as a cradle robber; it goes with the rogue poet persona. He and Eurithe are a couple of gypsies riding the rails, writing and rewriting the love song that has been their complicated life in poetry. If Eurithe did fib to nail the love of her life, it might be her one and only conscious deception. It is her pragmatic, no-nonsense, non-fiction approach that has kept the two of them on track for over fifty years. It is Eurithe who has balanced the books and steered through some pretty rough terrain, not excluding those irritating and time-consuming poetry wannabes who sometimes tie themselves to the fast track of the famous.

Eurithe Purdy came from a large, agrarian, Ontario family. The stories about how she got together with the greatest narrative poet in Canada vary according to the storyteller. Al does most of the talking. However, it is Eurithe who, with the ironies of her strategic feminine intelligence, undercuts all the fictitious meandering with minimalist linguistic missiles. He listens to her.

Her unusual name and unorthodox life are matched by a face in a million. Eurithe has the inscrutable beauty of a woman who has lived for a thousand years, most of them spent in the humid environment of talking men. Her face is the model of discretion. Only the eyes and editorial smile betray her lurking intelligence. She is that interesting anomaly, the artist's wife, simultaneously muse and servant to the muse. Al would not be Al as we know him without her. She is the one who has taken the small earnings and made them into a comfortable life. She is the one at the centre of many great poems. If she is not the direct inspiration, then she is the listener, his best. When the "F" word, fame, is spoken, she knows it is theirs, a mutual achievement. "We" is the matrix in which language is transformed into beauty.

There are many ink wells in which a pen can be dipped. A poet's wife sleeps with one eye open. Still, home is where the heart is. When asked what has kept them together for fifty-seven years, he is quick to exclaim "Love!" while she looks somewhat skeptical. I have heard stories of Al Purdy bereft in London and the Arctic without his compass, the woman who points him home.

> *And you you*
> > *bitch no irritating*
> *questions re love and permanence only*
> > *an unrolling lifetime here*
> *between your rocking thighs*
>
> > *and the semblance of motion*

While her husband wrote and sometimes held down a job, Eurithe steadily toiled as teacher and secretary. She took the grant and prize money and invested it in real estate. Al, the school dropout who rode the rails during the depression and once worked in a mattress factory, is now something of a poetry plutocrat. Al and Eurithe have property in Ontario, where he also has agrarian roots, and in British Columbia, where her heart sings in the proximity to the Pacific Ocean.

We were so pleased when Eurithe agreed to have her picture taken on the creek beside their Sidney, British Columbia, house. The creek leads to the sea where she beachcombs for their fireplace. Eurithe likes to be warm. As the second eldest in an Ontario family of eleven children, all of whom are hard workers and achievers, she has earned her comfort. It is hard for the working poet to admit to privilege, but, apart from the aches and pains of aging, Al and Eurithe have managed to transform the rocks on the bumpy trail to Olympus into silk cushions, a comfy lifestyle.

I met this lanky pair in the sixties but it wasn't until the mid-eighties that we became family. By this time, the Purdys, who have suffered their share of beans, were eating in middle-class restaurants. We had roast beef the first time we ate together, and Al still complains that Mexico has gone to the Mexican dogs, who have eaten all the available steaks. The Mexican beer is still OK but now he is forbidden his favoured brown maiden because of blood

A poet's wife sleeps with one eye open.

pressure problems. All that is left of his former vices is the piece of the true cross held between his lips, his ubiquitous toothpick. Eurithe has been drinking tea forever. Someone had to remember what happened and where they were going to sleep that night.

Eurithe makes a great pie and is still struggling to create the perfect loaf of bread. The first time I tried to show her, at Roblin Lake in the A-frame they built and where Al has written many beautiful poems, she put the rising bread into the oven in the plastic bowl I was using for mixing, while I was having my morning swim in the lake. The result was great sculpture but inedible. The second time, when I gave her a lesson with the poet Lorna Crozier, we left out the salt and the fat in deference to Eurithe's tired heart and the poet complained, excoriating me for undermining the bread for female territorial reasons!

Eurithe has either learned or knew intuitively that throwing her lot in with the great ego of a great voice was a lot like making bread. It has to do with hot air rising.

I could see at once that she loved me
tho it was cleverly concealed—
For the next few weeks I had to distribute
the meals she prepared among neighbouring
dogs because of the rat poison and
addressed her as Missus Borgia—

One baby in many, she made the decision many offspring from large families make and had only one herself. Eurithe says that most

of her maternal energy has been consumed by the poet and the poetry she has fed in the literal and figurative sense. It is as if she has given herself to history.

There was a time when Eurithe wanted to be a doctor, but the life in poetry made no room for that. Now she says she is happy to have lived on the road, each turn a surprise. She loves antiquity, be it old buildings or broken pottery.

When Eurithe abandons her silence, it is usually when her son is the issue or the rights of women, both subjects she takes very seriously.

I asked her once, when she had commented on the claustrophobic life of a woman her age whose world was defined by Kraft marshmallow recipes, someone I perceived to have a lot more personal freedom than Eurithe, if she found it paradoxical that she was so strong on the rights of women and so willing to lie down for poetry, leaving her own dreams in a drawer. She responded that she and Al are both devoted to the same god and her autonomy rests in that.

Eurithe is not a conventional woman of her age. She is a sexual being in her eighth decade. The sparks fly between them. You have the sense the irritable romance will proceed as long as both of them breathe.

Al says he acts and she reacts, showing the white mark on her wrist when he circles it with his hand. It may be the other way round. Great poems certainly prove that. So many of them move from her ironic glance to the epiphanies in the lyrics. Whatever the dynamics, they are a team. At yard sales, he lurks rare books while she sniffs out china, especially her favourite with the green edge. Together they have shopped the global village, admiring its antiquities.

I once spent a happy morning with them while they stalked the wild asparagus around Belleville, Ontario. Bonnie and Clyde, the omnivores, they hunted the ditches, Eurithe at the wheel, gunning her engine, while Al loped off, whooping, to purloin the precious greens we ate with the drunken jubilation of pirates, chins the greasy hue of stolen gold.

There is an awareness that, for Al and Eurithe, freedom is guarded contraband. Pulses are taken. Fat is cut. Poems run through the hourglass. They do not exchange presents on birthdays and at Christmas. The holy events on calendars have nothing to do with poetry. The days that are marked are those in which language articulated in the full voice of the

Someone had to remember what happened and where they were going to sleep that night.

Canadian landscape comes as the only gift that is truly valued.

The evening in 1987 when Al was presented with the Order of Ontario, along with Ben Johnson, Celia Franca, and Gene Kinisky, in a pair of short shoes he bought second-hand because he was too inured to poverty to go retail even in a year of large cash prizes, Eurithe almost cracked her mask laughing over the phone in their deluxe bathroom in the King Edward Hotel, a long way from the flashing neon of former domiciles. Should we phone Atwood?

Death is respected as the moment the symbiotic relationship that produces poetry will pass into history. Eurithe knows she is one of those rare women who have been immortalized. As long as our language is read and understood she will be known. There may be no grandchildren who carry her face, but it is in the poems, in every recorded glance and word. She does not react when the poet announces to a crowded audience, there in part because every reading might be his last, that he and his bride no longer buy green bananas or play long-playing records. It is only theatre and she has had a lifetime of that. Theatre is fugitive. Poetry is forever.

These are my children
these are my grandchildren
they have green hair
their bones grow from my bones
when rain comes they drink the sky
I am their mother and grandmother
I am their past
their memory is my thousand years
of growing and waiting for them

AL PURDY

RONA MURRAY

WRITER (1924, LONDON, ENGLAND–)

Perhaps it was taught in those times when children were seen and not heard, but Rona has the ability to listen.

"JOURNEY" IS A WORD THAT appears twice in the titles of writer Rona Murray's books. It is the life motif of this daughter of the Raj who has spent forever between two worlds, where East meets West.

Born in London to English parents who were themselves children of India, Rona now lives with her husband, respected potter Walter Dexter, at the western edge of Canada where the next perspective is the Orient. When Rona walks through her lovely English garden, so much in character with gardens she remembers from her childhood, she can look out over the sea and imagine the outline of the Himalayas beyond the Pacific, which makes comforting sounds on the beach below their house.

Perhaps it was taught in those times when children were seen and not heard, but Rona has the ability to listen. This is what has made her such an entertaining storyteller. In poems and plays and her astonishingly vivid account of her return to India, *Journey Back to Peshawar,* there is always the voice of the narrator who has taken note of every aural and visual detail.

Her house and garden, full of virtual memories, are the projection of an imagination that came to life in an exotic place of loud colour and sound and pungent odours. There Rona was an in-between, neither Indian nor English but somehow suspended between two worlds. She says she still feels like an extraterrestrial, a Canadian with an English accent.

It wasn't an altogether happy childhood. Like most middle- and upper-class English children of that era, Rona and her sister were subjected to the tyranny of the nanny. Rona recounts many small cruelties, many of them having to do with natural body functions. This behaviour made children stick pins in dolls and make wishes. Rona's nanny took the hint and left in a spectacular way. She retired herself after an earthquake, proving she had one by dying of a heart attack.

The journey back to Peshawar ends in the graveyard where Rona cannot even remember the nanny's name. As much as she is a child of the Raj, she is the daughter of a nameless surrogate mother. This is the circle of her life. Along the way, she has named everything in stories and poems that bring alive the various landscapes that conform and contrast to what she remembers from her early years, roots that were pulled up when her family emigrated to Canada. "Finished" on the west coast of Canada, she still bears the signature of an English family carrying its identity in the family luggage.

What she learned from India, in addition to the smells of spices and flowers, especially the lantana which changes colour like a chameleon through its long season, was the Indian ability to live in the moment instead of rushing to the next. There was a sweeper, an Untouchable, on her family property, who sat on his haunches and really listened to the small child. He was the only one. Parents had a social agenda. Nanny had her potty training to attend

to. The sweeper may have been the father of her imagination, which observes and renders fantastic the ordinary details of life.

The Indians I knew lived in the moment, and the moment always gave them time to be wholly where they were, even if that was merely sitting on a verandah, brush in hand, listening to a small child, or showing a little girl how a lizard was still "alive" when its amputated sections moved off in different directions.

In her biographical writing and poetry, Rona, though raised in the polite English tradition, never flinches from the grim or the ugly. I once commented that reading *Journey Back to Peshawar* made me wish I had the Kaopectate (anti-diarrhetic) monopoly for India. Between Rona's bemused observation of Indian custom ("no problem" the necessary third world mantra) and description of the country's magnificent culture, is the ongoing comedy of a middle-aged couple force-marching their bodies through culture shock. Walter is the good-natured schlemeil who sometimes loses patience. These are all the elements of good storytelling, where the beautiful and the ugly compete as the forces of good and evil.

I have been into the halls of the dead;
the old man said I wore white,
and white makes the woman invulnerable,
he said.

White is the colour worn by secluded widows in India, those women who live in the interzone between usefulness and death. Married to a potter, a low caste in India, where the potter's work is used and smashed, returned to the earth, Rona has the Oriental awareness of life's transience. She is the river Sutra, music taking the shape of the day and returning to its natural element, water. She lives by the ocean. It reminds her daily that everything changes and stays the same.

In *Adam and Eve in Middle Age,* a collaboration with painter Phyllis Serota, she wrote:

Out there a heron
writes on water,
four swans fly
down the sky, a man
paddles an over-freighted
coffin
across the bay.

Fantastic as this may sound, something from a surreal imagination from the subcontinent, Rona and Walter live near a medium security prison known as "Club Fed." Inmates have attempted escape by water in improvised boats, in one case a prop coffin from a prison play. In Rona's writing the conscious and subconscious are woven with the same craft as the lovely cashmere shawl she passed through her wedding ring, according to custom, before purchasing it in India.

Living near prisoners in what would appear to be Paradise is another reminder of India, where the view from a luxurious hotel includes a child sifting through garbage looking for something to eat. We are all prisoners of one kind or another. It is the small mercies, a perfect bowl from the potter's wheel, the ecstatic sound of a gull, or the smell of a flowering bush, that are the miracles she records.

Rona and Walter, by their combined effort, have a comfortable life. They are both respected for their work in art. Rona was recently awarded the Hawthorne Society's Ivy Mickelson Award for her service to the arts community. Still, in Canada, the poet is only an adjunct to the national identity. She was as surprised in India, as I was recently in Cuba, to be reminded that poetry is the conscience of a nation.

In her poems, Rona reflects on community, which begins with people listening to one another. Her poems are about intimacy that begins with two. It is her ease with conversation, learned from an Untouchable, that gives her writing the vitality of real life.

She blows smoke in mirrors, but the imaginary is always informed by the ordinary, things learned by the practical child who survived childhood tyrannies.

Mothers used to abandon their children to ayahs and nannies so they could carry on with their social lives. Abandonment is an issue that haunts her. Rona describes turning points in her life, all of which involve loss. The first was loss of her ayah when Nana was hired. The second was losing India when the family settled on Vancouver Island. The third epiphany occurred when she had a mastoid operation as a young teenager. The recuperation time gave her the pause that often becomes a moment of dedication for an artist. This did happen. The bookish girl, who was also an athlete and future head girl of her boarding school, determined that writing was her life. She also came to the inevitable realization, when her mother squeezed a hospital visit in her lunch hour, that she was not anywhere near the centre of the maternal universe, as children have a right to expect.

I told Rona I ended a marriage after a similar experience, but you don't divorce mothers. Because Rona presents as the colonial Englishwoman, raised with horses and silent domestics, I asked what taboos informed her

The sweeper may have been the father of her imagination, which observes and renders fantastic the ordinary details of life.

*Rona has the
Oriental awareness of
life's transience.*

writing. She says the answers will come "in time." There is at least one book that will not be published while the mother who did not see abuse is alive.

Like many writers, Murray, who did not read until she was eight due to the indifference of the British colonials to the formal education of their daughters, believes herself to be right-brained and not a wizard at the mechanics of writing. Still, she knew her vocation at a young age, and on the strength of a scholarship to Mills College, where she won a prize for writing, began to work to that end.

She first married at twenty and went to England to be with her "charming" RAF pilot husband. After three children and nineteen years of marriage, Rona found herself a single mother working toward a Ph.D. in English literature. The marriage had died of boredom and "financial discrepancies" as many do. Her husband had gone to work for her parents when the couple came to Canada, and that involvement with the family business was suffocating. She remembers her father taking her aside and explaining that, while it was lovely that she was interested in writing, she should remember that the focus of her energy and ambition should be on her husband's

career. It is hard to imagine a father getting away with that now.

By the time she reached early middle age, Rona was writing plays, poetry, and short stories that were winning recognition. In her controversial biography of poet Earl Birney, Elspeth Cameron describes Birney as a major influence on Rona. Rona, however, says he thanked her for the pleasure of her friendship by blocking her Ph.D. application. His excuse was that the academic life would impoverish her creativity. Perhaps that should have been Rona's decision, not his. That is how uppity women were treated by male academics in the sixties. She later won a scholarship to complete her Ph.D. in England.

When her book *The Enchanted Adder* went too far for the sensibilities of an upper-middle-class colonial family, who looked the other way when their children reported abuses and always had a good address even when they couldn't afford it, Rona was excoriated. She was intimidated but not stopped by this reaction to her honesty. In spite of her proper demeanour (silver hair, cushy voice, and straight posture), Rona lives the credo she preaches to creative writing students: "Be prepared to be honest. Go naked." Writers are only as valuable as their candour, sometimes making the wretched beautiful by giving it grace.

When asked what goals she has as a writer in her seventh decade, she says, "To explain the past"; perhaps to understand it herself as well as enlighten readers who benefit from her wide experience of the world as it was and is. She wonders if her accent, sounding of the Raj, makes her an anachronism, but that does not stop the flow.

That stopped only briefly. A few years ago, Rona was in an automobile accident. This was the final turning point. She says it left her "calm." The writing slowed down. She continued with the lively theatre reviews that appeared in Victoria's *Monday Magazine* and with literary criticism, which brought in small but necessary income, but the major literary projects were not happening. This is slowly changing. She is buying new dresses again. A collection of short fiction is turning into memoirs which have her gripped. After a late morning start, she faces the sea at the south-facing end of their bedroom and writes about the past that surfaces in so many enchanting variations.

Rona and Walter, who have been together for two decades, live carefully but comfortably in Metchosin on Vancouver Island, where both can see the ocean from their places of work. They could be Adam and Eve, as one of her titles suggests. However, when we left Paradise, Barb and I noticed that some callow neighbour was letting loose with a ghetto blaster in the probable absence of parental units. Rona, who was in the house, would say it was like India; those sounds far away, but loud.

EMILY HEARN

WRITER AND PRODUCER (1925, MARKHAM, ONTARIO–)

EMILY HEARN IS A YEAR YOUNGER than my mother. Those years of Egyptian Revival, the renaissance of classical beauty in design, were a vintage time. Its most memorable daughters are indefatigable. Like little birds, they dance in the air, fringes blowing in the wind. Perhaps it was the frantic music of the twenties, the ragtime, that set the pace for their lives.

At seventy-two, Emily is still vivacious, loquacious, and flirtatious. She has the energy of a hyperactive four-year-old who has inhaled helium, floating on a tough bubble of enthusiasms. It had to be tough. Emily has been through some rough weather, but she is still the perky optimist raised by a strong and loving mother who was widowed young. Emily's father was gassed in the trenches, contracted rheumatic fever, and never regained his strength. An enthusiastic presence in the household, he went to spirit when Emily was five, leaving a legacy of optimism.

A war pension allowed Emily's mother to stay at home and raise Emily and her brother. When Emily was old enough, she supplemented the family income by teaching piano and playing music wherever and whenever she was wanted. Because everyone pitched in, Emily's mother was able to keep her home through the Great Depression and raise children with strong egos. This is nothing short of amazing in Emily's case because, even as a woman in a time when women had their wings clipped, she grew up believing she could do anything she set her mind to. And she did. Her pioneering work in the media of radio and television is especially remarkable; she was a woman ahead of her time.

The key to Emily's personality is self-esteem. She remembers her mother teaching

She has the energy of a hyperactive four-year-old who has inhaled helium.

without teaching, allowing her children to grow in confidence. This "passive teaching" left the children directing their own passions. When Emily reacted positively to some Strauss waltzes, her mother made sure the music was on the piano the next time her daughter sat down to play. Such quiet coincidences resulted in self-motivated learning. This is the credo of Emily's professional and family life. Children learn with their enthusiasms. Because these enthusiasms can be fragile, the teacher is more supporter than pedagogue.

It has served Emily well. She has raised two handfuls of her own and spousal children, all of whom are remarkable, and has guided several generations of Canadian readers, radio listeners, and television viewers who learn by doing. Much of what is admirable in Canadian television is due to this soft approach. Her stories and textbooks broke ground in mirroring the Canadian land and mindscape for young readers.

I used to compare Canadian to American television when my children were small. The Canadian programs were visits which left the children inspired to draw or play music or dress up. The American counterparts left them overwhelmed with sensory bombardment.

Our media taught children to create rather than consume.

Emily divides her life b.c. and a.c., before and after children. Because she was and is perpetual motion, the advent of motherhood in her twenties was a change in tempo for the gifted girl who had danced all night and

Like her mother, who died around this time of Emily's loneliness, she became stronger and more self-reliant in adversity.

worked all day. Her husband, whom she had met when they were both working for the National Film Board, disappeared into a project in Tibet and there was no communication because the Tibetans were pirating radio equipment to make jewelry. Like her mother, who died around this time of Emily's loneliness, she became stronger and more self-reliant in adversity.

There was more to come. After two more children, it became clear that Emily was really a beard for her husband, whose heart was not in the marriage, and she moved on to marry an actor and have his baby. This marriage of strong personalities lasted into the psychedelic sixties. Emily, with her first handful born over a spread of twenty years and a radio show, *Playroom,* under her belt, moved into her third and final marriage to widower Doug, with his four daughters, and into the era of television. She wrote songs and scripts for the ground-breaking *Polka Dot Door,* which kept kids humming through the next two decades and beyond. Emily understood the importance of kinesthetic activities in linking the body and the mind. Children in her audiences were always active participants.

Collaboration with artist Mike Thurman saw them talking and drawing their way

through one hundred fifty episodes of "Mighty Mites" for *Owl Magazine* and several of the popular Franny Books, one of which is in progress. There is no stopping her. She is a kid herself with the energy of a gerbil on a candy diet.

You would not call Emily retired. She has passed her philosophy on to the next generation of television and created a canon of living texts for Canadian schoolchildren, and is still restless and ambitious for our shared babies. I met her online a few years ago when we both went to work for "Writers in Electronic Residence," the cyberspace for young Canadian writers. Once again, Emily is in the front line, pushing the frontiers of communication. She applies the same energy to this demanding program as she gave to her previous undertakings. The gentle but uncompromising encouragement she was given by her own mother is now offered to the thousands of young writers she encounters on the Internet. The cyber-generation have the advantage of a direct relationship with Emily as she nudges them to self-expression in conversations online. Their mothers and fathers met her directly and indirectly in the work she did as acquisitions editor for Nelson, the textbook publisher.

When Emily got her wings and travelled, she says, every inch of this country gathering stories and poems for new Canadian readers, she opened a window on a whole new writing genre. As she experienced the country, elementary schoolchildren learned it was something to write about.

Emily says she will die with her wings on. A human hummingbird, she travels light and ready to go anywhere, anytime. Every bit of her energy is for the journey, wherever it takes her. She laughs at silence. Rings on her fingers, bells on her toes. There is music wherever she goes.

Her strength carried her through the death of her son Tim several years ago. Tim, who followed his father into filmmaking, was enjoying a good career and a good family life when a seizure led to the diagnosis of brain cancer. Only mothers who have buried their children know the pain of it. Emily does not dismiss this agony, but she is able to celebrate Tim's life. Recently, the family planted a sugar maple for Tim. Its sweetness will survive the hard winters her ancestors braved when they came to the cold Promised Land.

Death has already done its worst to Emily and she is not afraid. Perhaps because she survived grief in childhood, when her father was taken from her, she has not been stopped by the cruelty of Tim's premature death, but focuses her love for him on his children. Friendship with Emily involves a thousand considerations around the celebration of life. Those who are absent or gone still have a place at her table.

Doug, the ultimate husband and clearly a major Hearn fan, recently had lunch with us at il Terrone in Toronto. He spoke enthusiastically of a writing program he is initiating in Toronto schools, a project that includes a high school publication for young writers. This volunteer job is a new direction for a committed teacher. Obviously in love, the two have a common dedication to young people, passing on what they have been given. By encouraging the creativity of young people, they believe they are nourishing the essence of community. An understanding of the ephemeral nature of life and the importance of teaching the values that make a civilization is their gift. You don't see their names flashed on every newsbreak in the country, but people like Doug and Emily are the architects of our culture.

Emily is one of the lucky ones. She is still beautiful and she knows it, describing herself as a "pretty nerd!", one of those unusual bright/

She is a kid herself with the energy of a gerbil on a candy diet.

*Death has already
done its worst to
Emily and she is
not afraid.*

pretty girls whose obsessions extend past what they see in the mirror to the world around them. This is the confidence instilled by her mother, who built character on love and encouragement rather than criticism. Emily has always felt accepted for her grace and for her intelligence at a time when young women were encouraged to bury their gifts and ambitions in order to fit gender stereotypes. Because she has been able to balance her life as a woman with her intellectual curiosity, she has had it all: scholarship, motherhood, pleasure in music and the written word.

In interviewing women, I have noticed how critical it is for a human being to feel strong in her sense of physical and intellectual beauty. It is a pity that so many are not given this birthright to confidence. This is the pillar of Emily's wisdom. We and our children are lucky that she cares enough to tell us in so many ways. If every mother had her grace, then ours would be a golden civilization, every child fulfilling his or her potential.

In every life there is pain. Some are blessed with the ability to transform that information into beauty. It takes a great energy. This is the not-so-quiet Emily behind the scenes in the life we have heard and watched as our country has grown into the third millennium. She is creating a legacy of advocacy for children.

SPOONFUL OF SUGAR

for Emily

Meshugge, they say when someone goes crazy
in the language made by people
who hid their children in the woods.
Shug, a name in fiction for sugar.
It makes you think of a funeral parade,
umbrellas with tinsel,
a dusty black car with a child
lying white and still in a box
made of the cheap wood you might use
for cigars or a funky guitar,
and trumpets and trombones, tubas,
those fast tunes slowed down as traffic
slows down when the crazy lady
steals another baby at night
when everyone else is looking the other way
to the place where midwives circle the fire
in skirts with flashing threads
making the low sound women know
for girls who lie down in white dresses
waiting for the earth to move.

This is the so-called heaven on earth,
where marble children play
behind wrought-iron fences,
where we plant our afterbirth
and red tulips grow by themselves.
These are the tulips the crazy lady sees
when she lights a cigar
and blows the smoke in mirrors.
This is where she comes once a year
with scissors to cut the tulips
and make red tea with a spoonful of sugar
that puts her stolen children to sleep.

What the crazy lady doesn't know,
because it's a recipe written in the sweet
milk of mothers who never forget
the right way into the woods
where the real children live,
is that she has the wrong children
and the right children are living in trees
with sweet blood in their veins
that sings every year in winter
when the tulips and the wrong children
are fast asleep in the ground.

LINDA ROGERS, 1996

PHYLLIS WEBB

WRITER AND PAINTER (1927, VICTORIA, BRITISH COLUMBIA–)

The poet in his tree of hell
will see life steadily and see it well.

IT WAS LATE DECEMBER and Phyllis, Barbara, and I were having lunch in Phyllis's kitchen on Salt Spring Island. "Are you vegetarian?" Phyllis asked, her fork poised over our plate of leftover ham. "Yes!" we answered in unison, our forks diving in. Waste not, want not was our reciprocal anthem. Disgusted, Phyllis's cats, for whom ham is a desecration of the beatific pink trotter, fled for the outdoors.

"It's the noise, actually," she apologized. Our arrival in the temple of their familiar with cameras and Christmas leftovers must have felt like a home invasion. Surrounded by trees and ocean, Phyllis's cats are accustomed to the harmony of wind and wave, the poet's *sotto voce,* and the pleasant daily rotation of her can opener.

Phyllis is the mutable goddess of Canadian poetry. The oracle spoke, posed the question, then laughed. You may have been taken in by a luminous intelligence, her mysterious fog, droplets of air, each one the crystal breath of a dragon hanging from her vision tree, the holy place where philosopher fools hang out, hang in, hang fire, but she has vanished in smoke— again.

Webb, who has abandoned her covenant with nicotine, has also stopped writing, disappeared into thick air, leaving the questions behind. Only the tree remains, its shape, its remarkable decorations. They could be imagined or real. You are never sure. We looked out her kitchen window and thought we saw a heron standing on the highest branch of the cedar by her gate. "The branch isn't moving," she said, a hint, without telling us what we were all going to think. Someone

Phyllis is the
mutable goddess of
Canadian poetry.

might have conjured the fisher-bird. It might have been her.

Magic is the essence of transformation, the medium for spirit religion and the poems hanging on Phyllis's metaphorical tree. Just as she temporarily inhabited the body of one of her cats for a graceful feline photo shoot, her hands as eloquent as the "long beautiful hands" she describes in her poem about her father, so do her poems move in and out of different realities. Most writers aspire to move from the particular to the universal through the selection of metaphors from the phenomenal world. Webb does that easily, but like a skater who adds a loop to an impossible figure, she lands another visual pun. Her timing is perfect. This is the gift of the comedian.

Everyone knows great comedians are uncomfortable people. They make us laugh because they draw attention to our shared discomfort. This intense sensitivity is what has given us Webb's great poetry and profound commentary. In her tenure as executive producer of the CBC public affairs program *Ideas*, Phyllis threw herself into informing the ethic of a generation of Canadians. When I asked her about the child who preceded this extraordinary woman, she said that was another mystery.

For the woman who asks so many questions, the question is painful. "My life has been based on questions and not being able to answer them."

What are you sad about?

*that all my desire goes
out to the impossibly
beautiful*

Her timing is perfect.
This is the gift of the
comedian.

Phyllis was born in an impossibly philistine Victoria, when the city at the end of things was the living end of the British Empire, and where working mothers and divorcees were as welcome as the plague in polite society. She was the youngest of three. Her father worked in a bank, a humble but genteel profession, and was unable to provide for the family when her parents divorced. Her mother was left with the task of raising Phyllis and her brothers, which she did by driving a taxi and working in the Boeing plant on Yates Street during the war.

Phyllis's mother, a strong character who passed her hundredth birthday, made sure her children had cultural enrichment. One son became a painter. Her bright daughter went to a good school and on to university. It was at St. Margaret's, where she was a free scholar, that Phyllis met the teacher she calls Ms. Godson. Ms. Godson taught mathematics and English. Phyllis, a typically disnumeric lefty, bombed in the former and soared in the latter. Because Ms. Godson was a behaviourist, she punished and rewarded. Phyllis experienced the true ambivalence of fairy tale: Your fairy godmother who reads wonderful stories is easily transformed into the wicked witch. This is conditional love, a lesson painfully absorbed by the shy, sensitive child who longed to please.

Webb, through her own effort and help from her mother, studied English and philosophy at UBC. While working for the CCF party, she met F.R. Scott, fell in love with him, and moved to Montreal, where she became part of a poetry milieu that included Louis Dudek, Miriam Waddington, Eli Mandel, Irving Layton, and Leonard Cohen.

Sensitivity and exposure to pain, the recollection of abandonment and betrayal, a pattern she learned to control by seeking impossible romantic relationships with men and women almost as sensitive and troubled as she was, has rendered Phyllis vulnerable. She has been called the priestess of pain, but that is to overlook the survivor. She is, after all, her mother's daughter. Humour is the hallmark of intelligence. Her ability to transcend almost any situation with levity has saved her from the very bottom of the pond of despair that has called some of her closest friends. She has seen that muddy place, but somehow found the resilience to surface and breathe and tell us what it is like in poems of wit and clarity.

Rose-coloured glasses, a shift in the mood, or indigo, odd
angles, surfaces like mica, cosmos and microcosmos,
glazed and changing.

That same energy has transformed the poet into a painter in her seventh decade. We all joke about the cells that die in middle age. The hair falls out, the hearing and vision fade. We can't remember the name of a certain flower or the bird that visits the same flowering bush every spring. Naming is everything to poets. When Phyllis noticed she was stumbling over boulders she could not identify, she decided it was time to switch media and save her creativity. "Another part of my brain has been waiting to be used."

Phyllis was amazed by the easy transition she made from writing to visual art. In the beginning, she used scissors and glue, choosing her images carefully from photographs and paintings. I found these collages interesting, cerebral, and was unprepared for the easel she stacked for our visit. So loaded with canvases it almost toppled over, the easel displayed, in one painting after another, a palette I could only describe as going to the light. There was no evidence of the dark energy of depression. The paintings are a glorious exploration of the human potential for joy.

There are florid trips to the vortex, a descent into the feminine centre of the universe, where "the light is mauve" and her "eye's iris blooms into the nightmare of riderless horse." In these paintings, she takes risks with her earlier vision, the more careful collages. She gets on that horse and rides. "I love her palette," Barb and I said in unison. It is the colours of the garden—not the garden of the sea, where death by drowning is the end possibility, but Paradise, where women flourish and cant is overpowered by light.

Her mother and father lived into their tenth and eleventh decades respectively. Phyllis, the moth, may be "morphing" again. She told us she abruptly stopped painting, just as she stopped smoking, in the fall of this year. Perhaps she was frightened by the freedom of her palette, the openness of her paintings. Maybe they want to fly. Now she sits on her striped sofa, her wings stretched out, looking at her most recent work as the winter solstice passes and the world takes another direction.

"My life has been based on questions and not being able to answer them."

*She has changed
shape so many times,
living in the moment,
making it bearable by
making it beautiful.*

Maybe the paintings should be taken out into the world, like a child who has been taught to shake hands and say hello. She is considering her options.

"Did you ever think of marriage or a permanent relationship or children?" I asked the exotic moth on her sofa. Phyllis almost repeated verbatim what novelist Adele Wiseman said about giving birth to fear. Phyllis's covenant is with the voices that compel her life in art. She needs a lot of room and privacy for that vocation and for the resolution of her private agonies. The world is too much with her. And so after a while were we. When we left, she made us take the rest of the ham, the urban zucchini, zucchini being a Gulf Island joke with surplus squash turning up like foundling babies on people's doorsteps.

On the way to the ferry, I told Barb I first heard the words "Phyllis Webb," recited like a canticle by one of my poem-infected friends, in 1962, the year I started undergraduate studies at UBC. My friend was lucky enough to have Phyllis as her first-year English literature instructor and she had been stopped in her tracks, stunned by the ironic intelligence and powerful dramatic presence of one of Canada's outstanding poets and critical commentators.

I experienced that epiphany when Phyllis read at a women's festival. She was an exotic, low notes and diaphanous veils (the moth again), her poetry a fusion of church and Wicca, or so I believed when I was fresh out of my first communion veil. I was in awe of this amazing presence, especially when she had the generosity to notice and encourage a younger poet. Phyllis comes from a time when poetry was less a career and more a vocation, when Canada was looking for an identity and poetry was more than a postmodernist abnormality in the age of information. "In the early days," she said, "poets were a mutually supportive community" (and, she might have added, "supported by the community").

Thirty years have passed between then and now. There are hundreds of poets where there used to be a few. We have seen each other in and out of years. Some of our mutual friends, Elisabeth Hopkins and Dorothy Livesay among them, have gone to spirit. I asked Phyllis, who has said on many occasions that death was her friend, how she was affected by aging. She has changed shape so many times, living in the moment, making it bearable by making it beautiful.

Listen. If I have known beauty
let's say I came to it
asking.

The questions beg answers. Phyllis says she hates being asked questions. Still, she wrote in response to a request from her editor:

THERE ARE THE POEMS

An editor asks me to put it all down: the
reasons I write. And I thought 'it' was a gift.
Homo ludens at play among the killing fields
of dry grasses. Playful woman making a space
to breathe. 'There are the poems,' Sharon says,
she means, between the critical flash. There
are the poems, like fists wearing birthstones
and bracelets, her 'roses & bliss'. Or they're
like legs running, bounding over the fields of
force, momentum, for a quick roll in Darwin's
tangled bank. And there are the poets doing
what? And why, the editor asks. What does he
want? Contributions to knowledge? Civil-
isation and its discontents? Chaos among the
order—or, oh yes, french doors opening onto
a deck and a small pool where we can watch
our weird reflections shimmering and
insubstantial? The proper response to a poem
is another poem. We burrow into the paper to
court in secret the life of plants, the shifty
moon's space-walks, the bliss, the roses, the
glamorous national debt. Someone to talk to,
for God's sake, something to love that will
never hit back.

INGE ISRAEL

POET (1927, FRANKFURT, GERMANY–)

Inge is a nomad for whom nowhere is truly home.

I WAS HAVING LUNCH with poet Inge Israel at the Oak Bay Marina in Victoria. We both had views of the sea, seals swimming up to beg and crows and seagulls fighting over the remains of lunch served on the terrace. When I told her my great-grandmother had lived just down the road in a large stone house and this was the landscape of my childhood, I realized how comfortable it felt to be rooted in this place. Like her biblical predecessors, who wandered the desert until they found the Promised Land and then lost it and wandered again in the Great Diaspora, Inge is a nomad for whom nowhere is truly home. As we ate our rich dessert, we talked about the deprivation of her childhood and the journey that has brought her from then to now.

Inge likes restaurants. Food is a sacrament that brings her together with people, a luxury she never quite gets used to. Her husband, a theoretical physicist obsessed with black holes, is an ascetic in this department. This has made her independent. She has worked her way through the cafés and restaurants of several continents, celebrating life and making friends and observations that inform her poetry and short fiction.

Her story began in Frankfurt in 1927, where she was the second daughter born into a Polish Jewish family. Her father, who had served in the German army and was taken prisoner on the first day he went to war against the Russians, met her mother in Siberia, where her Orthodox family had recently taken refuge. Inge's mother's new in-laws condescended to the Russian bride of twenty and even burned her trousseau, for fear it had been contaminated with whatever grows in the skirts of Siberian girls. They gave the small-framed woman a large set of keys, which she found intolerably heavy. This became a metaphor for life in a justifiably frightened German-Jewish community.

While the sound of keys drove Inge's mother mad, her father took note of the ominous sound of boots in the street. By the early thirties, it became obvious to him that Frankfurt, the birthplace of Heidi, for several generations a symbol of childhood innocence, was an unsafe place to raise his daughters. The family wrenched itself from the comfortable bosom of the German bourgeoisie and began the odyssey that, for Inge, has never ended. Almost all of those who stayed behind in Germany died in Auschwitz. She remembers only one who survived.

Inge was taken first to Belgium and then France, where her mother and sister were granted visas. Her father, who was not, emigrated to Ireland. He was not, at first, allowed to bring the family because he had no means of support.

This is the moment when Inge's fork stops in midair and her blue Russian eyes cloud over. Her mother was down and out in Paris with no marketable skills. The children were taken to a children's home in a Paris suburb, a home that was sponsored by the Rothschild family but definitely not up to the level of comfort of the Rothschild residences. The food was inadequate and the children were treated with cruelty. Inge will not say why her sister was removed soon after, but it is clearly a painful

subject. She rarely heard from her mother who, as a Jewish émigré in an anti-Semitic Catholic country, had neither the confidence nor the train fare to visit her child.

Inge remembers a boy who was afraid of heights being hoisted to the tallest branch of the tallest tree as punishment for a small misdemeanour. She says she was not often punished. She was good, she says with much pain in her eyes, something I once saw in the eyes of a nun who also told me she was good, as if good was a terrible burden, like the dead bird a chicken-killing dog is forced to wear around his neck.

This is not a time she likes to remember. It is the ravine between then and now, the time without a mother that ended when her mother was emotionally and financially able to plan the next move.

Inge was the shy daughter of a woman who was humiliated by history. She says her mother was faced with so much adversity it made her daughter strong. Inge mothered the sister born in Dublin after the family was reunited, and she taught herself to tell the story of her life in stories and poems.

The way Inge presents herself is elegant. She has the exquisite appearance and manners of Europeans born into a certain class at a certain time. I suspect she is an iron butterfly with the necessary strength of a survivor. I haven't asked Inge Israel how her appearance has affected her life. She is so comfortable with herself, so beautiful at the end of her sixth decade that I don't have to. In an adolescent photo, she looks like a young Ingrid Bergman. Her beauty may have saved her life at a time when she looked like the Aryan ideal, light boned and fair. Certainly she was a favourite at the children's home, where much of her pain was experienced vicariously in witnessing the torment of other, less beautiful children. Beauty is at once a burden and a privilege.

Her mother eventually learned the art of millinery in Paris and she and the children were reunited. Interestingly, her father, taking a parallel path in ladies' accessories, had begun to make purses in Dublin, replicating the success of his family in business in Frankfurt. Inge describes her parents' life in Ireland as volatile but durable. Neither parent socialized and the family stayed apart from both the Catholic and Jewish communities, even though the latter had helped the mother and daughters emigrate just before World War II broke out in Europe.

When asked what it was like to grow up in a Catholic country after experiencing racism elsewhere, Inge says she was fascinated by the exotic orientalism of the Catholic faith. We agreed that most Jewish conversos we knew had chosen Catholicism over the more ascetic Protestant alternative.

The Judaism of her ancestors and her observant sister is now a secular humanism first articulated by her mother, a socialist who always had a lineup of supplicants at her Dublin door. Inge lives in the moment with an awareness of everything around her. My mother categorizes people as animals, all falling in the general categories of horse, dog, etc. Inge is definitely a bird person. Married to a scientist exploring the holes in space, she travels light.

The Israels currently perch in an apartment near the ocean in Oak Bay, Victoria. Unlike other Europeans of their generation, there is very little in their home that tells where they came from, no ancestral portraits or samovars, no jewels smuggled in skirts. There is a consciousness of ephemerality that speaks in the empty spaces. They could unfold themselves and fly away at any moment.

She has a bird's-eye view, an ironic understanding that comes from lofty observation points. When I commented on an Italian poet we both know, she told me about a bag of chestnuts she once bought in Switzerland. On the bag, the chestnuts were described in three languages—French, Italian, and German. The French said chestnuts were delicious, the German that they were good for you, the Italian that they were Italian! This was the observation of a woman who understands the subtleties of translation and transformation.

Inge says she doesn't ever expect to find home, even though she looks for pieces of the torn family photograph wherever she goes. On a recent trip to Japan, she said she felt as comfortable as she has anywhere. She just blended in. This may be the acquired skill of a little girl who avoided detection and punishment in alien places. Her younger sister has found religion and a home in Israel. This is a mystery to Inge, for whom there are no easy answers, just fascinating questions.

She has a granddaughter now. When I asked her what she wanted the child to know of her story, she said she was too busy relearning the business of childhood herself. Inge never got to be a child in the way every child has the right to be. The child invites her in. This, for her, is the moment of absolute equilibrium.

Inge lives in the moment with an awareness of everything around her.

UNMARKED DOORS

My father did his best,
covered his heartbeat
with a pocket watch,
checked it by every clock, at night
kept it near to rewind
should it stop,
though he had no illusions.

Stateless, he moved
through unmarked doors—
childhood, his only homeland—
a stranger trying to fit in,
the watch, a link, a rudder
steering him into accepted channels,
now, in this Dublin graveyard,
a stranger still.
I place reluctant pebbles on his grave.

Sunday morning bells fill
the soft Irish air, not for him,
under this angular stone slab
in rows of fearful symmetry.
No weathered curves. No flower
whose roots might split genealogies.

He remains a paradox of conformity
here where history is an epic
of rebellion yet days no more free-float
than beards, his one wish always
to have my mother at his side.
But she lies half-way across the world
in another symmetry.

He was a silent man,
his brief moments of happiness
before my time.

When I knew him
he stepped through happiness
as through a minefield, did not sing
like his brother who skipped
me along Sèvres streets
when I was four, teaching me a song,
    "On va bien s'amuser
    On va bien rigoler
    Avec les pom-pom
    Avec les pom-pom
    Aaah-vec les pompiers!"
My fun-loving uncle
who perished in Auschwitz.

I see my father
walking along Sandymount Strand
touching his hat to neighbours
barely glancing at them
for fear of intruding,
brooding if they looked
too hard at him. I want to slip
my arm through his and say:
It's alright. Really!

I want to stroke his smooth cheek
and ask: What colour
would the stubble be
if just once you didn't shave?

If I had the 78-record
of canned laughter he once bought
I would drop the needle on it
and cry. It was the only thing
that made him laugh.

INGE ISRAEL

PAT MARTIN BATES

PRINTMAKER (1927, SAINT JOHN, NEW BRUNSWICK–)

Her prints and drawings reveal a feminine attention to detail articulated by small hands.

PAT MARTIN BATES HAS CAPTURED the light in an exquisite canon of work that only could have been produced by a woman artist. Never decorative, her prints and drawings reveal a feminine attention to detail articulated by small hands. You want to tear her work off the walls and wear the fine and witty lace made of paper and other serendipitous things. Their curves and chiaroscuro are the body print of a complex woman whose sense of humour is the frill around an architecture of darkness.

When you first meet Pat, you are disarmed by her adorable presence. She has the voice of a matinee princess and is liable to break into song and dance in the middle of even the most serious conversations. A child of the airwaves, brought up in the musical Maritimes in the golden age of Marconi, she must know the words to every song and will admit to a secret adolescent ambition to be the Quaker Oats Girl in radio advertisements. The voice comes out of a beautifully appointed mouth, the scarlet punctuation in her creamy Celtic complexion. Black hair, green eyes, and that amazing skin tell the story of her Welsh and Irish heritage.

Martin Bates has taken the extremes of those island cultures and defined them in the print media that have made her a celebrated international artist. In her "light boxes," drawings, lithos, and serigraphs there is always a fascinating struggle between light and darkness. You see it in her face and on her walls. Her house, a virtual gallery, is an arts and crafts masterpiece with beautiful windows and dark panelling that echo the chiaroscuro in her work and in a personality forged in love and loss.

When I commented to Martin Bates that she leaves my husband, an obsessive collector, in the dust, she explained her overflowing rooms with a touching recollection of grief. When she was eight years old, her father died suddenly. He was his widowed mother's only child. Two weeks after his death, Martin Bates's grandmother took a walk around the garden,

then lay down on her bed and folded her hands on her chest. Some of us choose our death. Pat and her younger brother were taken to live with relatives. Her pregnant mother caved in to grief and then gave birth to a second daughter who was cared for by another relative. Pat never saw her first home again, or her toys, or any of the birthday gifts she had recently been given. A hand came down from the unintelligible sky and erased her childhood. No wonder the heavens fascinate her.

"These days," I said, "you get to keep your toys," and she smiled. Everything in her overflowing life transcends, by nature of its sentimental or artistic value. The walls are covered with her own work and that of her friends, particularly the Limners, a group whose members include herself, Myfanwy Pavelić, and Carole Sabiston.

One of the best known of the Limners, Martin Bates had already made a major reputation before she moved to Victoria, where she taught in the University of Victoria Fine Arts Department and earned an Excellence in Teaching Award. Still on the west coast, she continues refining her love affair with ink, paper, and light.

The child of grief has a compulsion to manage.

*A hand came
down from the
unintelligible sky and
erased her childhood.*

A feminist, Martin Bates presents a beguiling femininity. She is definitely deco, her design dictated by Egyptian Queens and the stars of silent movies. Her beautifully crafted face and dress are the artistic expression of a very beautiful inner woman. She likes to get everything right, from the appropriate texture of paper for a print to the proper descent of a curl. The child of grief has a compulsion to manage. She has taken control of her life, even though she does like to extend that velvet glove for what appears to be a soft handshake and says she is just a passenger in a speeding car.

What is out of control is the passage of time. Beloved friends are going to spirit. There is so much work to do and the body begins to ache and complain. When Martin Bates, who has mastered every aspect of printmaking, is asked what she has left out and yearns to include, she says sculpture.

I told her about jeweller Martha Sturdy, who studied sculpture at art school but was arrested by a family of three and financial impecunity. She resorted to a cottage jewelry business, which has expanded to become a corporation with many employees executing her designs. Now that her children have grown apace with her bank account, it seems it would

be hard for her to return to the monumental work of her early imagining, that risk taking.

But jewelry *is* sculpture, Martin Bates asserted, correctly. She is descended on her father's side from jewellers. You see it in her work, the gem-studded collages and pin pricks of light perforating her prints and drawings, the light boxes designed by her and assembled by her husband, a retired army officer, who proudly showed us his Christmas Castle made of small marshmallows for visiting children.

Pat and Al have been married for half a century. That is on record, something to celebrate. Some dates are chased away as irrelevant. She is here and the light dances around her. That is enough. She says she never knows or cares how old anyone is because she looks at their eyes. They are what matter.

The first time she laid her eyes on Al, they were both playing in a youth orchestra in Moncton, New Brunswick. She says she played bad second fiddle, but he was divine on the cello. As an added bonus, he was as handsome as the father she wanted to remember and naturally idealized. The cellist disappeared in the aftermath of war and came out a warrior. A career in the military was not Pat's idea of a romantic vocation, but married they were and they now have two children to prove it. Pat says they have separated a few times over the years, but there is much history between them and so much real affection they are beginning to sound like one another. He is making marshmallow castles. That is a long way from raising the red ensign.

This raises the question of the married artist. Pat has worked throughout her marriage and has had the freedom to travel to every part of the world, winning awards and representing Canada at major exhibitions. It is a tribute to the strength of their respect for one another and her self-respect that she has persevered where other women have faltered.

Perhaps what toughened her was the terrible double grief of losing her mother and father, one after the other. Even though mother and daughter found each other again, there is a deep chasm between then and now, a darkness the artist leaps over in every quest to experience the sky by leaping over every sidewalk crack. Pat's mother was not prepared for the catastrophe of losing her mate and provider. Pat herself knows how to provide. She has never lost sight of herself or the conviction that she has an important statement to make. A Gemini, Martin Bates is articulate as she navigates the dual aspects, water and air, of her personality. You feel it flow in her conversation and in the art which has won her international recognition.

In this country, the biggest reputations are reserved for artists who work in the "durable" media: stone, canvas, and paint. Because paper is ephemeral, printmakers and photographers have been relegated to a passive second level of recognition. This is not true in Europe and the Orient, where more respect is given to artists who work with paper and print techniques. Martin Bates, who takes such delight in the phenomenal world, her gathering of friends and amulets from friends, seems unconcerned by fame, which distracts lesser artists from their vision. She is happy to play, evidence of a true vocation.

We talked about numbers and the corresponding chakras. Martin Bates likes the number five, which may have something to do with the five-pointed star, a favourite archetype in her work. I told her I liked the number nine. She said yes, the neighbour to bliss, but not quite. She likes nine too. I remembered what Lina de Guevara said about needing a difficulty. It is always good to fall a little short of your expectations, to have to reach.

Pat Martin Bates has had a lifetime struggle with the loneliness of her childhood. She was

She says she never knows or cares how old anyone is because she looks at their eyes.

She is happy to

play, evidence of a

true vocation.

afraid of the dark that took her parents to death and despair. That feeling pervades everything she creates and resonates in the viewer along with relief when the light perseveres. When that happens, you are transported to sparkling heavens or to the soft place where precious stones dance into the collarbone of a beautiful woman.

The artist may never get around to that monumental sculpture, the three-hundred-sixty-degree celestial light box imprinted on her mind when she closes her eyes at night. Or perhaps she has, graphing sections of heaven in every two-dimensional piece that reflects pieces of sky. This is what she sees when she lies on her back saying hello to her mother and father, together again.

There was a back injury once when she fell through a coal chute. Martin Bates was long on her back and, after her convalescence, continued to be fascinated by black holes and stars that implode. Her favourite childhood quotation from her son, Philip, was his observation that the moon was broken. For her, this is a perfect metaphor for broken light, the motif of her life and her art.

At the moment, Pat is working on a series called "The Angel of Blue Skies Cries Parallax Tears," which is dedicated to the orphans of

Yugoslavia. It is not hard to imagine why her energy is devoted to such a cause or why she was a legendary teacher of young artists. She is a bubbling hot spring of renewal, feeding on her naive curiosity and delight in the phenomenal world.

When I told a friend I had been talking to Pat, she said, "Oh, P.M.B., she is an angel." Like the heavenly messengers, she is a precursor of storms that light up the sky.

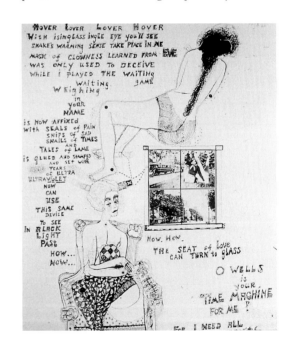

Flying Women Series #4
1969
Drawing with watercolour
22.5 in x 30.5 in

WHERE GRIEF TOOK YOU
for Pat

For millennia, we've been lying on our backs,
sometimes sneaking a look at our watches,
making grocery lists, or retrieving
the words to popular songs.

That would be you, wouldn't it,
remembering the radio lady
singing hits from your childhood,
your aunt's treble church voice
and the pipe organ in the parlour.

The angel on top, your husband
wearing gold braid and medals,
plays beautiful cello.
Sounds like her, you say to yourself,
the silent game of charades and your mother,
someone you look for at night, in heaven,
where grief took you both that time
you remember perfectly, every glad
detail in every print you make.

Your son said the moon was broken,
its dark pieces falling to the earth.
There is a spell for mending
children fragmented by shadows.
Mot-her, you say, searching the galaxy,
pricks in a canvas lit from behind.
Her word is the language
you are compelled to reinvent
because it lets in the light.

You lie on your back, assuming
the position for sex and art,
making prints with your perforated
body the world understands
better than painted ceilings,
those old cathedrals our ancestors
built for worshipping saints,
because, sooner or later, everyone
and everything you have ever known,
man, woman, child, song,
passes through you for us.

LINDA ROGERS, 1998

ADELE WISEMAN

NOVELIST (1928, WINNIPEG, MANITOBA–1992, TORONTO, ONTARIO)

A lifelong concern for the well-being of others was founded in her belief in mitzvah (good work) and storytelling.

A YEAR AFTER THE DEATH of novelist Adele Wiseman, my husband and I walked through Cabbagetown in Toronto, making a pilgrimage to the Kensington Market. There I had spent many entertaining and sometimes hysterical hours with the novelist, who had died of cancer. We were retracing the steps so my husband could get the feel of the early part of a friendship that was eventually shared by us both.

It was a summer afternoon and we had just performed at the Stephen Leacock poetry festival in Orillia, Ontario. I had money to burn, in the denominations that poets squander, and having noticed a house that advertised second-hand books, I pulled my husband in.

The place was painted entirely white and could have been an anteroom to heaven. There was no furniture, only bookshelves, and only one book, its black-and-white cover beckoning. The book was a paperback copy of Adele's *Crackpot,* the story of Hoda, the daughter of a hunchback and a blind basketmaker, who finds redemption through sex. It is perhaps one of the finest novels written in the English language.

We bought this orphan copy, of course, even though I had a drawerful at home that I had been dispensing to the uninitiated. I felt it was an amulet. In those white rooms, ready to receive the books Adele loved to read and write, she was properly enshrined.

The first time I met Adele, in the art- and kitsch-filled house she shared with her daughter Tamara and husband Dmitri, she looked so much like Picasso's paintings of Gertrude Stein it took my breath away. "Soul come back," the Balinese say when air is exhaled involuntarily. Adele had enough soul for a full-figured gospel choir.

Adele, who died in Toronto in 1992, was born in Winnipeg to Pesach (meaning Passover, the time of renewal) and Chaika, both tailors. Behind the shop, she and her three siblings had a traditional Jewish family life.

By the time Adele reached adolescence, the shape of the adult was recognizable. She won creative writing prizes at school and worked with children in her free time. A lifelong concern for the well-being of others was founded in her belief in *mitzvah* (good work) and storytelling. "I knew that I was meant to be a writer, that my writing was going to bring truth and understanding and love to the world and make everything and everybody happy and perfect." Her effort to will that equilibrium in her family and social environment was a life struggle that she has passed on to her only child.

At the age of nineteen, Adele began the most significant friendship of her lifetime, with novelist Margaret Laurence. A beginning in the Promised Land of the Canadian Prairie gave a biblical gestalt to the fiction of both women, who rewrote the Old Testament in the language of their different cultures. Both Wiseman and Laurence found grace in the articulation of the

sacred and the profane, the chiaroscuro of pre-Christian biblical writing. They supported one another through the controversies that particularly marked the life and premature death of Laurence, a spirit wrestler if there ever was one. Remarkably, Wiseman, as earthy, as honest in her description of the human condition, moved more easily through the politics of literary criticism. However, like the children of Holocaust survivors who learn to internalize conflict, her demons would also eat her insides.

Adele studied English and psychology at the University of Manitoba and wrote her Governor General's Award-winning first novel, *The Sacrifice,* under the tutelage of professor Malcolm Ross, an inspired mentor. Her precocity augured well for a brilliant career in writing. The new novelist worked and travelled, filling in the gaps in her knowledge and experience. She was extremely observant, her beautiful dark eyes taking in everything, silently commenting with the most subtle change in expression.

Early on, Adele, who had the Jewish love of conversation and an ear for dialogue, experimented with playwriting. Both *The Lovebound* and the later *Testimonial Dinner* were privately printed. My mother, who was in one

Both Wiseman and Laurence found grace in the articulation of the sacred and the profane.

of her incarnations a theatrical producer, advised Adele there were too many characters in her later play. This may have been prophetic. It was Adele's generosity in relationships with everyone from family to students that undermined the precious time she needed to write.

Her second novel, *Crackpot,* introduced the stubborn theme of incest. It was already almost a wrap by the time her daughter, Tamara, was born. Tamara was the centre of the universe. There was never a more doting mother than this woman, previously delivered of a tumour, who gave birth to a live child, a miracle, in her forty-second year, paralleling the experience of her character Hoda, who expected a tumour like the one that took her hunchback mother but surprised herself with a baby.

In the years of her marriage, Adele wrote *Old Woman at Play,* the story of her dollmaking mother; children's stories; and the disturbingly titled *Memoirs of a Book Molesting Childhood.* The next novel, which required the selfishness of isolation to write, did not come.

When marriage became a nightmare in spite of Adele's heroic efforts, she turned to the cryptic language of poetry to express the unspeakable. There are some who would argue with my judgement, but Adele's poetry, except for some pithy phrases, was not good. The poems, although full of the anger of a woman and mother betrayed, do not have the epiphanies of her translucent fiction. She was a woman who needed the larger canvas to paint on.

Adele began presenting her doll show (a dramatic narrative based on her mother's trunk full of homemade scrap treasures) and seeking positions as writer-in-residence, often receiving the invisible treatment sometimes accorded women writers of a certain age. When I suggested to the (now mercifully retired) head of a Creative Writing Department that Adele would be an ideal university teacher, I was told the department did not need dinosaurs. I did not take this remark kindly and reported it to Carol Shields, who told me of identical experiences in her own teaching career. Her betrayal found its fictional home in her award-winning novel *The Stone Diaries*. We are vindicated.

Fortunately, Rachel Wyatt, who later translated *Crackpot* into the language of the theatre, made sure of Adele's tenure at the Banff School of Writing, where she was a nurturing and effective head until the year of her death.

The penultimate time I saw my little friend Hatele ("Little Hat," my name for her because she wore her many hats so well) was at Banff. I had been for a week's visit and when I left, Adele put her head through the front door of my departing bus for one last look. I shivered, feeling the angel of death hovering in the clear mountain air, and began to mourn the most astonishing and intelligent eyes I had ever seen.

The week in that narcotic mountain air was somewhat surreal. Tamara had also been visiting, and had begun work in the centre of Adele's tiny apartment on a large lump of clay taking the shape of a man with exaggerated genitals. Adele stepped around her daughter's astonishing sculpture, keeping up a non-stop mission statement about her intention to maintain a celibate peace in the mountains, where the monks and nuns of poetry and prose could focus on their literary work.

She asked me to watch out for lechery at parties where students and faculty mixed. Male writers known for their appreciation of women were not invited to teach in her department. Anyone who breached etiquette, including one faculty member who was fired for dating a student who later became his wife, was severely reprimanded by the tiny Mussolinette I called Hatele.

It was Adele's generosity in relationships with everyone from family to students that undermined the precious time she needed to write.

She was a woman who needed the larger canvas to paint on.

I remembered back to the Mother's Day Tamara's father had cooked steaks on the barbecue. Tamara's gift was a nude portrait of her mother in several poses. Mother and daughter were more like sisters, both comfortable with this intimate rendering of the chubby but shapely little body in which Adele was at home. I suggested the addition of a hat. It would have made a fine cover for her book of essays, *Memoirs of a Book Molesting Childhood.*

Adele was very close to her mother, the Russian-Jewish immigrant dressmaker who sewed dolls for pleasure. In *Old Woman at Play,* she lovingly described the scraps her mother transformed into art, much the same way she herself made stories by slowly stitching the rags that made a character. "She kept us on the long leash of an endless rope of language, looping and knotting us as firmly to her as ever she stitched edge to edge in a seam." When her mother became ill, Adele created a hospice in her house, making something beautiful out of the process of dying. Her mother died surrounded by love.

It wasn't quite the same for Adele, who had delivered herself, for several years running, of more benign tumours. First it was the brain. Her sense of smell and taste had been wacky for some time. We teased her about her lack of taste and she laughed and nodded off. The nodding and her legendary snore were a clue to the monster growing in her head. That was duly removed, and she recovered quickly, telling everyone, with a novelist's clarity, how her brain had been separated from her body. We could imagine the fiction that would slowly evolve from this true "out of body" experience.

Adele wrote slowly. She was the perfector of her craft and of many friendships, which she savoured like sips of Russian tea, served in a glass. There would be time when Tamara grew up, evolving into the great visual artist she was expected to become, for the magnificent novel of her mother's maturity. It was hard to imagine another character as brilliantly conceived as Hoda, the humanist hooker of *Crackpot,* but we all expected it.

The next tumour was in her kidney and she proudly reported it was about the size of a human infant. Again she went back to writing, while running the school at Banff and dissolving her marriage and often inappropriately suspecting sexual misconduct in her colleagues and misogyny and racism in their work.

On her last visit to us, we took her to Cowichan Bay to attend the Picture Dance for deceased members of a First Nations family I had known for twenty years. She was fascinated by the story of a young man whose life had so many parallels to that of Hoda. But this boy did not live out the full cycle of his dysfunctional family, as did Hoda (in one memorable tragicomic scene, her sexual services are hired by her own adolescent son). Instead, our young friend committed suicide, an epidemic among those children of the First Nations whose legacy is incest and despair.

Adele's own time of dying was a sad counterpoint to that of her mother. Her public battles became private ones. If she did not heal the family that had been the focus of her public and private life, she might die unshriven. Adele, the purveyor of truth in fiction, would not name her psychic wound, except obliquely in the raging poems that charted her conflicted final years: "Every mother is delivered into fear." By this time, we were not having our famous late-night marathon conversations on the phone any longer, and Adele had stopped writing. I sent her regular notes, with a continent between myself and her imperfect farewell.

I heard this careful practitioner of language died with the most loaded word on her lips. Seeking refuge in the safe place from which she had come, she reached out her arms and called for her mother.

Tamara, her mother's doll, who came to sit Shiva in a house with covered mirrors in the Jewish tradition, is Adele's literary executrix. I wonder if she grieves for that last book that might have explained her young life to her.

A good part of the art of self-defence
is to survive what you are learning.

I have talked to Tamara once since her mother died. We ran into one another at Word on the Street in Toronto in the fall of 1997. I thought I was seeing a ghost, so much is she like her mother as a young woman. Her compassionate memoir, a feminist manifesto in which the word "father" does not appear, is part of *We Who Can Fly*, a collection of poems, essays, and memories in honour of Adele, edited by Elizabeth Greene. Tamara is putting on the armour belonging to the warrior who gave birth to her: "My mother died from fighting. My mother died fighting."

ANGELA GODSELL ADDISON

EDITOR (1930, TORONTO, ONTARIO–)

I have watched her fall in love with the genius in many men.

THE FIRST TIME I MET Angela Addison, she was selling beautiful things at the flea market. She knew, though I did not, that she was soon to be my editor, but that is another story. The more important thing I did not know was that letting go, transcending the physical, was the key to her character.

A few years later, Angela moved out of her too-expensive, oak-panelled, turn-of-the-century apartment over Wellburn's Grocery at the corner of Cook and Pandora in Victoria. She had the queen of all moving sales, serving sherry and cheese biscuits to buyers who were stripping the place down to the walls. Paintings of and by beloved friends, including Glenn Gould and Myfanwy Pavelić, were, with her desk, favourite books and photos, and a few essentials, all that she kept.

The gathering that matters to Angela, who was born an Anglo-Scots-Irish Upper Canada blend in Toronto and schooled at the Toronto Conservatory of Music, is as ephemeral as music. Performance shy, she chose, instead of a career in music, the romance of friendship, an abstraction she has raised to an art form, which finds its many voices in music, poetry, and paintings inspired by her. Like Eurithe Purdy, she made the choice to become one of those women who enable artists, as editor and sometimes muse.

There is a line in a song my husband sings about Voodoo Queen Marie, Marie Leveau, the legendary Creole witch of New Orleans: "Other women walk on the earth / This one sails through the air." Angela, now in her sixties, actually does. In spite of the arthritis that plagues her, she floats.

The daughter of a controlling mother, Addison would have been an amusing child to observe as she acted out her determination to remain at all times several inches off the ground. It was her father who began the great romance with men that has had many permutations over the years. I have watched her fall in love with the genius in many men, from poets she has edited to one of my sons, who has something of the same artistic gifts and transcendent spirit. Some of these romantic impulses were acted upon in the real world. Her son once told me his earliest childhood recollections were of his mother following some free spirit, the male incarnation of the muse of poetry or music, and being returned to the family by his grandfather in one of the classic cars of the time. I can picture her sitting in the back seat, the picture of Isadora Duncan, arms crossed, wearing sunglasses, a big hat, and the moue of a denied debutante.

Her father, albeit responsible to the family, did initiate the picaresque that is Angela's life story. He gave her the love of romance, adventures of the mind and the feet. He travelled in his work and sometimes took his young daughter with him, giving her a taste for a moving landscape. She tells of a silver Buick touring car with red leather upholstery that might have been a powerful horse in the mythology of less-unusual adolescent girls.

Together, they absorbed the stately pleasures of the eastern seaboard, staying in boarding houses in old, elm-shaded American towns, sometimes in elegant hotels like the Peabody

in Memphis, giving her a silver spoon asceticism, her non-acquisitive appreciation for comfort and beauty.

Like many women of her generation, Angela made an effort at conformity. She

Like many women of her generation, Angela made an effort at conformity.

married, she says, to get away from her domineering and critical mother, and to have children, because Angela is one of those rare adults who really delights in childhood. Her view of the world is innocent in spite of her learning and experience. Even though she left when they were still young, Angela is affectionately engaged with her children and grandchildren, who mostly appreciate her eccentricities, recognizing the child in her, while she respects the adult in them. Many of her favourite books are children's stories. She loves to play games and, as you would expect from someone raised in the Anglo Upper-Canadian manner, attaches little importance to winning or losing but much to how the game is played.

Her rules, in life and art, are somewhat personal and she enforces them fiercely. Freedom and beauty emerge as the important criteria. Since these concepts are abstract, they fit her like a pair of transparent stockings. Her first marriage, to a businessman chosen by her mother, was imperfect. Therefore, escaping was an act of purification. This last rebellion happened while she was in England after the death of her father in an accident in one of his beautiful cars. This time there was no one to bring her back to an ill-fitting marriage.

While living in London, Angela looked up her godson and cousin, an airplane pilot. Love took off and so did Angela, who left her husband and three young children for this man fifteen years her junior (she had seen him naked before, she told me, having changed his diapers). They moved to Sidney on Vancouver Island.

Looking over her old photographs, she smiled and said she would do it all again. I wondered at her calm, had no idea that, like many women of her generation, there was a time she put a little extra something in her tea to help her though the long afternoons. We used to call that splash "mother's little helper," its presence a clue that mother is not quite as serene as she is expected to be.

When I was a child, divorce still made a ripple. I can imagine the waves crashing in teacups in Toronto when Angela made her bid for freedom. Leaving your marriage for someone who promised new beginnings was then the prerogative of men.

Perhaps because he longed for the part of his life he had skipped, her second husband left her after nearly two decades Angela describes as "art." The French talk about *éclat de vieux*, that moment when age comes over your face like a veil. Angela says she grieved

Elisabeth Hopkins

The Birthday Party
1977
Watercolour 14.6 cm x 22 cm
Permission of Patricia Hall

Maggie Jack

Coast Salish Basket
Barbara Pedrick photo

P.K. Page

Stone Fruit
1959
Oil pastel

The Broad Canvas

Myfanwy Pavelić

Katherine Hepburn
1982
acrylic on canvas

The Broad Canvas

Myfanwy Pavelić

Yehudi Menuhin
1998
charcoal and conté drawing

Myfanwy Pavelić

First Limner Painting
1973
acrylic on canvas

T h e   B r o a d   C a n v a s

Phyllis Webb

The Sea of Galilee
1995
Photo collage

Pat Martin Bates

Parallax Tears
1998
Perforated configuration:
papers, inks, threads, grommets,
black Rives

Pat Martin Bates

Let the Star of 8 Sing a Song of
Cutting the Moon into Star Pieces
1977
B.F.K. Rives, painting on paper

The Broad Canvas

Claire Weissman Wilks

Totem
Bronze
42 in x 26 in

Phyllis Serota

Contrasts
1998
Mixed media on canvas
44 in x 60 in

The Broad Canvas

Phyllis Serota

Order and Chaos
1998
Mixed media on canvas
60 in x 132 in

The Broad Canvas

Phyllis Serota

Near The Sea Of Galilee
(At The Baths)
1999
Acrylic on canvas
52 in x 60 in

Carole Sabiston

*Take Off: Point of
Departure and Mode of
Travel*
1988
Textile assemblage
240 in x 144 in x 144 in

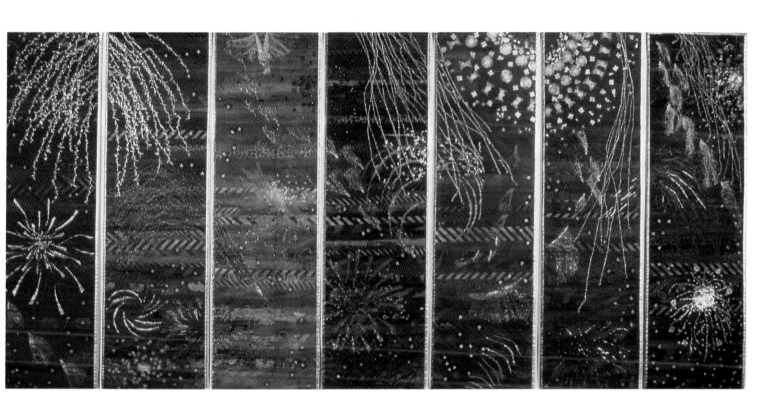

Carole Sabiston

Sky Alive
1988-90
Textile assemblage
84 in x 180 in

Susan Musgrave

*Susan Musgrave and her
daughter Sophie Musgrave Reid
in their art car*
Barbara Pedrick photo

in her friend Myfanwy's studio for several days and came out changed. She no longer regarded herself as beautiful. Still, she claims she has never been attached to her body or appearance, which is unusual in a woman, especially one who grew up when women (whose appearance was their currency) lost cachet in the aging process.

In any case, it was not long before another young lover, a musician who rode a bicycle, presented himself and burned in her tolerant presence until he died of alcoholic anorexia a few years later.

The way Angela presents as a woman in her sixties is serene. Her slow movements are graceful. Her silver hair matches her faultless understated surround, rooms that glow. She decorates herself simply and beautifully, the way you would expect an elegant ghost to dress. I would not be surprised to see Angela walk through a wall. She recently read to me a passage from Aldous Huxley in which he described the transparency she aspires to as sun breathing so fiercely (into shadow) it is like walking through the ghost of a zebra. Her old friend, poet D.G. Jones, described it perfectly in a poem written for Angela several decades ago: "And I confess / what I protect is your capacity for loss, your freedom to be no

one / look so naked from that window / you are lost in light."

When she talks about hitting walls, it is not death or the end of her impermanence that bothers her. She looks forward to the release from anxiety and to the incandescent mind she sees at the door where she leaves her body behind. What Angela fears is the physical claustrophobia of increasingly smaller rooms and a body that might deny her the movement her mind requires.

At this time, she is living in a green room at the top of an old house in an old neighbourhood. While my husband and I sleep in the graceful sleigh bed with curved wooden ends she bought with her great love, she rests on a couch covered with embroidered cushions and looks out her window at the moon and blooming trees. In her daytimes, she reads letters of unrequited love from friends and walks and visits the gardens at Government House, where she most admires the white flowers.

She loves to be given white flowers and poems for which the anarchist beauty of her white stems and mind are the inspiration. Angela recognizes Being in the exquisite absence of colour. It is fragile music, the white notes, that she most admires. There is room

Leaving your marriage for someone who promised new beginnings was then the prerogative of men.

She decorates herself
simply and
beautifully, the way
you would expect an
elegant ghost to dress.

in these fugitive intervals for a woman of spirit.

In spite of her otherworldliness, Angela has her little vanities. When a designer friend irecently commented on the shapeliness of her legs, she was over the top. She told me photos taken of her for stocking advertisements in *Vogue* magazine were among her favourites.

Although she eschews excess, she says it is the Romantic composers Brahms and Schumann she identifies with. In the subtext of this spiritual *ménage à trois* lurks Clara Schumann, a brilliant musician in her own right, who sacrificed worldly success for love, as women did and still do, as Angela has. In spite of her nineteenth-century identification with an intense romantic triangle, one woman and two men, she says she also yearns for Scarlatti, the clarity of passion articulated by genius. These are the contradictions in Angela and in music itself, both of which have an architecture of learning and a point where everything known is abandoned to intuition.

As a poetry editor, Angela is beautifully non-present, her judgements subtle, her understanding of the music in language completely assimilated. The words play on her. There are no obvious interventions, just reaction. Her approach to the practical side of publishing is superseded by her devotion to

aesthetics. Art as business is anathema to her. A poem should never be tarnished by ambition or commerce. This idealism appealed to me and our friendship has transcended the business of publishing.

When I have tea with Angela, I feel the philosopher's cave has been transformed into the book- and picture-filled office of an inspired headmistress, where anything that glows is loved and appreciated. She takes me around the room and introduces me to all the small luminosities. As she pours tea and the steam escapes, I realize she is presiding at a vanishing. This is the light that has attracted her throughout her life and which she describes as the end, a phenomenon articulated in the recent paintings of her friend Myfanwy Pavelić. The mundane really does not interest her. I would be surprised to hear Angela changed her own lightbulbs. I cannot imagine it. Her light comes from a different source.

She is an enthusiast who plays the old recordings and reads the old books over and over. The biography of Glenn Gould she went to London to research years ago remains unfinished. Too many have desecrated his memory, she says. Hers are her own, as fragile as the web in the tree outside her window. The unspoken has a beautiful clarity. It is air, her element.

In any case, Angela desires no monument beyond the poems written in friendship to her. Her creative canon glows in acts of passion. There are books started and not finished, baroque concerti abandoned in the middle of a phrase, but Angela is not concerned with her material canon. She has been muse and bemused, the partner in many creative dances with men she has loved. Like those women of antiquity mentioned in poems and songs and painted by the Great Masters, she rests content. She looks back on a life of roads taken and would do it all again, she says, follow her informed heart wherever it took her. Even the pain has been beautiful. It all flies in the wind, like music abandoned and books unwritten. The Angela ashes will no doubt take a spirit already evident on a magnificent journey.

JANE RULE

NOVELIST AND ESSAYIST (1931, PLAINFIELD, NEW JERSEY–)

Jane has become the spokesperson of reason for a generation whose greatest wish is its own political obsolescence.

JANE RULE HAS A FACE LIKE A PUPPY DOG, her big brown eyes full of the ironic intelligence that ensures puppies get fed like clockwork. You might even call Jane charming if that word had not been pre-empted by egregious males. Perhaps acute social intuition would be the appropriate phrase for someone who has walked through minefields with perfect posture all her life.

Rule, whom Barb and I visited at the beautifully situated log house on Galiano Island she shares with Helen Sonthoff, her partner of over forty years, is part of that endangered species I call the *comme il faut* people, her good manners perfected over a lifetime of adaptation. She knows exactly what to say and how to behave in every virtual and "fictional" situation, the hard-to-control dimple the only giveaway that her sense of humour is operating parallel to perfect social behaviour.

This is what has made her a writer of note and articulate advocate for humanitarian issues, all the once-dangerous but now politically correct "isms" of the postmodernist period. At once a social observer and social commentator, Jane has become the spokesperson of reason for a generation whose greatest wish is its own political obsolescence. If everyone were like her, responsible anarchy would rule. Jane Austen, her own ironies wrinkling the silk surface of eighteenth-century reason, is her literary foremother.

Born to gentle people, a mother whose only distraction from her children was giving piano lessons to others and a U.S. naval officer father who taught his tall brood to stand tall, military style, Rule is one exception to the rule that writers come from dysfunctional families. She and her brother Art and sister Libby were raised in confidence. A critical grandmother had taught her mother the wisdom of positive reinforcement for children. Years later, when Jane, who belongs to two minority groups, dyslexics and lesbians, emerged into responsible adulthood, she did so from a base of self-esteem nurtured by extraordinary parents.

While Jane is an exception to the pattern of dysfunction in the childhoods of many writers, music is what connects her to the privileged daughters of musical mothers. Even though she found her childhood violin "awfully heavy" and admits the chief allure in her clarinet was the woody taste of the reed, music has always given her pleasure and may have tuned her ear to dialogue, one of her strengths as a writer.

The constant challenge of adapting to new geographic and social environments as her family moved from the east coast to the west and several places between, made Jane an observer of behaviour. She played the chameleon, adapting her speech patterns and dress code for every new milieu. In her words, she "learned to roll her socks the right way" to fit in everywhere. Even after her father retired from the military and became a builder, the family moved often. Jane recalls entering school mid-year more times than she can count, despite the fact that she is proficient at math, an aberration in lefties, the disnumeric subculture.

Rule is one exception to the rule that writers come from dysfunctional families.

While adapting, a certain cynicism arose as the future novelist noticed that "correct" was as variable as the weather. "Ma'am," proper in the South, was an insult in San Francisco, where full names were required from a polite child. Her response was a satiric pragmatism. Rules are made to be broken, by everyone but the writer who bends with the wind. Observation made Jane into a politician who could speak across class differences, and a novelist whose observation of mores gave distinction to her characters and credibility to her social commentary. "You are the stranger—make others comfortable" was the ultimate rule of her strategic mother, advice we might all remember. It is the omniscient voice of her constant narrator and the underlying premise of her fiction and her public life.

The novelist's childhood picaresque with sympathetic parents was regularized by summer visits to family in the redwood forest of California. In Rule's life and work there is a devotion to community that was patterned by ecstatic summers with a tribe of cousins. Wherever they have gone, she and Helen have recreated this community. Now isolated from old friends by death and geography, Jane and Helen are surrounded in their perfect country house by the chatting paintings of friends John Koerner, Tak Tanabe, Gordon Smith, Molly Bobak, and my cousin Elisabeth Hopkins, who lived down the road and enjoyed their solicitous friendship in the last years of her life.

"Chatting" is the operative word. Jane inherited a love of humour and conversation from her gregarious mother, whose needlepoint is the centrepiece of Jane's sartorial splendour, a wardrobe of colourful vests. Dextrous conversation is the locus of her stories, which weave complex relationships in a tapestry that finally depicts enlightened community: men, women, and children living together in civilized microcosms. Jane is the "hot-eyed moderate" who can speak every dialect. She uses social homily to reconcile the irreconcilable, even to the inclusion of men in her compassionate aura.

In *A Hot-Eyed Moderate*, a collection of her essays, Rule says, "It is not only women but men who must stand up and say, 'No, that is not who we are.' Women, in stating our own case against our misrepresentation in the fantasy life of the world and therefore our lack of representation in the real world, sometimes don't want to hear that men are as, if differently, victimized."

In a family of Janes, Rule became "Jinx," perhaps a weaver of spells, but definitely not "bad luck." Her charmed life is the result of hard work and a willing flexibility in everything except the routine that has her, these days, swimming in the morning, lunching promptly at noon, and, at one p.m., watching her beloved soaps, which she refers to as "the school of orthodox heterosexuality," a subject she clearly finds amusing and exotic.

You know that underneath the floating humour this Aries person is stubborn because she has struggled to overcome prejudice against homosexuals, lefties, and dyslexics. Jane was always bright in school, but a slow reader. Her spelling was and is creative. It wasn't until grade eight, when she attended private school, that a perceptive teacher noticed her eyes and brain were not working at the same speed. Rule, the aural learner, daughter of a musician, had also been confused by the number of dialects she had assimilated in the family picaresque.

The judgements involved in early assessment of her fluctuating intellectual skills (she was a performing student with a less-than-flashy IQ) only reinforced the civilized disobedience of her late adolescence, which resulted in her eventual expulsion from school.

You don't get the impression that this termination with prejudice was ever regarded as a tragedy by Jane, for whom it surfaces like a brownie badge. She later wrote, "Questioning conventional morality can be the beginning of a moral education from which we can learn to make choices based on understanding rather than blind faith or great fear."

Told she had deliberately failed testing to shame her school, Rule was turfed out with only negative recommendations forthcoming, which made college entrance a bit of a challenge. This challenge, however, the ever-flexible Jane was finally able to meet and overcome when she met a trustee of Mills College, her intellectual haven, and "rolled her socks the right way," convincing the educator that she was worth educating. Already Jane was learning compensatory strategies. The marvel is that she had been given the confidence to challenge prejudice against differently enabled scholars by a nurturing family.

Patterns emerge. Mills College was also a haven for Rona Murray. Murray, Page, and Rule are all daughters of army officers.

Jane had already learned many survival skills. She wrote in spite of difficulties with language, practising to perfection. She stood

In her words, she "learned to roll her socks the right way" to fit in everywhere.

You know that underneath the floating humour this Aries person is stubborn because she has struggled to overcome prejudice against homosexuals, lefties, and dyslexics.

tall and made a room her own when she entered it. She used her humour to dismantle discomfort, even prejudice, in a world disposed to despise and fear difference. She even learned not to speak in public toilets, where her deep voice convinced a fellow sitter that a man had invaded that sacrosanct place.

Giving up the idea of studying medicine when she found out it was more about science than about people, she focused on the reach which might have seemed to exceed her grasp. The slow reader and creative speller with the basement IQ was determined to become a writer. Her professors told the Phi Beta Kappa with her own spelling rules that they would meet her halfway, if only she would learn to spell "metaphor" and "simile" the way scholars do. This she did, earning her wings.

A garret year in London, where she says "American" was an eight-letter obscenity, as an occasional student at the University of London (which allowed "drop in" students at selected lectures), produced chilblains, semi-starvation, and the first of two "drawer novels." The jejeune fiction, she says with the conviction of a child with caged crickets, is very happy in the drawer.

Graduate school at Stanford University, which she viewed as a cultural meat market whose chief attraction was that it had formerly refused her, had one shining moment, a lecture on point of view by the English novelist Joyce Carey. Rule's distaste for competition was the black border on her graduate degree.

Recently, she was awarded the Order of British Columbia. I took the opportunity to discuss competition in the arts with someone who is not without honour in her own adopted country. This is where Rule draws the line between art, her vocation, and politics, her calling. Whatever helps focus on human rights issues she accommodates in spite of her conviction that all saints have feet of clay, a variation on "the Queen uses the toilet too" motif that is the underlying principle of an egalitarian education. She accepts the honours on behalf of her constituency even though she is not overly impressed with gold braid.

A slight edge of cynicism enters the conversation when we talk about the "Public Jane." It is as if the creative personality is reluctantly taking a back seat to the public crusader. Perhaps Jane suspects her reputation rests on a number of firsts that only describe the "outside person," usually on her best behaviour. The inside is harder to know. Jane smokes; in fact, she was expelled from school for smoking and other minor challenges to the status quo. She has come a long way, baby, but not because of the clandestine cigarettes. Public life has a price she, above all, is aware of. For one thing, fame made demands on private time she needed to write, particularly as her process of writing was slow and careful.

Nobody messes with Jane Rule's integrity or her time. The "Women Working" sign she and Helen posted outside their house with its alluring swimming pool, the jewel in their crown, has a serious purpose. Writing was a craft she approached with dedication, specified hours for work, and no room for exploitation.

She wrote, "Writing is, more than is often acknowledged, a craft that has to be practised, like tennis or the flute. Just as an athlete or a musician works long hours in solitary repetition of the hardest techniques of the craft before performing them in game or concert, so a writer needs to concentrate, particularly at first, on what is most difficult."

Because Rule, like Livesay, has become something of a holy icon in the women's movement, particularly in the area of gay rights, she has had to be her own temple pekingese barking at the well-intentioned intrusions that make the *funktionslust* impossible. This has meant the abandonment of the "difficult to maintain" friendships that are the burden of many women artists. There is an aspect of Jane that is ruthless. Compartmentalizing her lives is a balancing act that separates the politician from the writer. That process is exhausting, particularly for someone who suffers from an affliction that makes movement from mode to mode, moment to moment, painful. Rule has suffered from arthritis for the last two decades. This, and a belief that her case rests, made the decision to retire easier for her than for many others who do work they like.

One of the perks of artistic self-employment, which lacks the overt benefits of pension and dental and medical plans, is the freedom to work to your own timetable. Night people get to work at night. Old people can choose to share their considerable resources of wisdom and experience longer than their contemporaries in the ordinary work force. Having weighed these freedoms against the prison sentence of living in an arthritic body, Rule is content to enjoy her trees and her four-decade relationship with Helen, who says, "Being old takes a lot of time." The two of them have been partners in a great adventure which began over forty years ago, at Concord Academy where they were teaching, and which

She wrote, "Writing is, more than is often acknowledged, a craft that has to be practised, like tennis or the flute."

Rule is content to enjoy her trees and her four-decade relationship with Helen, who says, "Being old takes a lot of time."

brought them to the west coast of Canada almost by accident.

Jane knew she was home when she experienced the physical charms of Vancouver in the sixties. Helen followed and began her own legendary teaching career at UBC (where she was on my M.A. thesis committee), which also employed Jane until she realized that tenure would mean the comfortable suffocation of her creativity.

When *The Desert of the Heart*, a virtual and metaphorical "coming out" novel, was a hit, she knew she could call herself a writer. In book after book, advocating the civilized integration of human beings with different DNA and different profiles, she has proven it. The peripheral fun of Jane Rule T-shirts for National Book Week and Jane Rule iconization by feminists has been icing on the cake, which is the joy of writing.

Creating her utopian village in sympathetic communities fashioned on her own experience, Rule has participated in the life cycle. She has earned her elevation to the position of wise elder or grandmother, her offspring at her feet in a garden of fuchsias and begonias, flowers that last all summer because she hates goodbyes, possibly because her world and her fiction are built on an interdependent network of fragile relationships. Stoic about her own ephemerality, Rule says being born is like "winning the lottery." Immortality is a deal with the devil. She just wishes her friends and loved ones would have the decency to die after her.

Life is the focus of her novel *Memory Board*, in which one of the characters is living with AIDS:

we die in any case, sex the mortal bomb, used, abused, neglected, it didn't matter, set at our conception to tick away until it triggered the spewing of seed on barren or fertile ground, it didn't matter, set finally to fail in any case, that crucial failure in the complex and intricate design of a system meant to self-destruct.

The graceful father who made Jane comfortable with her own body has gone to spirit, but the laughing, singing mother who made her childhood a delight is still perking along at ninety. Jane likes that. Hers is an ordered world, based on an ethical system which is flexible only so long as its variations are based on compassion and tolerance, and the soaps are on at one.

My husband says being a good musician means not playing the wrong notes. Still the naughty anarchist, the daughter of a loving teacher repeats her mother's words—"all you need is bad examples"—and lights a cigarette while I cast the most recent stone, a lame allergic cough, and Barb poises to take the forbidden photograph.

A hand goes up. The interview is over.

LINA DE GUEVARA

DRAMATIST (1933, SANTIAGO, CHILE–)

The major emotional transition of her life has been emigration.

LINA SAID THE MOST AMAZING THING in the middle of a conversation about life and politics and art: "I like to live with a difficulty." No wonder Lina has the face of a female Buddha. She has climbed quite a few mountains (and folding chairs).

I met Lina de Guevara, actor/director/writer/producer, in the mid-eighties, when she directed a theatrical performance of poetry gathered by P.K. Page. The actors were the writers and there were a couple of dancers for those moments when words failed us. Somehow she wrestled the unruly actors—Leon Rooke, Susan Musgrave, and myself—into a transcendent theatre piece called *Angels*.

This began an explosion of performance poetry, the place where the printed word meets the stage and becomes accessible to larger audiences. We were all grateful to Lina for that. Aware that she was a political refugee from

Chile, I have noted her work over the years and met her in passing, always wondering about her story, especially as she began to re-work it in public forums.

When I have asked women about major transitions in their lives, those periods of adjustment usually determined by biological factors, their answers have been similar. Childbearing is an abrupt banishment from the self-absorption of childhood. Divorce and menopause are the markers that either end youth or initiate a feminist renaissance. Death is another end and beginning, but for Lina, a political daughter of Chile, the major emotional transition of her life has been emigration. This is the theme she has brought to her understanding and dramatic interpretation of problems of identity and racism. As an immigrant, she has stood outside the mainstream of Canadian artists and held a two-sided mirror up for us to see both ourselves and the newcomers who have pulled up their roots to participate in our culture.

Lina was born in Santiago, Chile, the daughter of romance. Her father was a Chilean painter and professor and her mother a Dane. They met in Paris. He was studying art and she the French language. He sketched her at the *Closerie des lilas*, the Bohemian restaurant where Hemingway wrote, and the rest is family history. Even though her mother was a nurturer, cooking, canning, and sewing their clothes, Lina and her brother grew up in an artistic milieu which did not discriminate between girls and boys. She always knew she was an entitled worker.

The child loved to dance and studied drama as a means to improve her interpretation of the music. Even now, suffering from "frozen shoulder," a painful mid-life curse of many women, Lina's arms are graceful in telling the story of exile and fulfilment.

Practicality dictated a teaching degree in history and geography. During her university years in Chile, she met Celso, and the passionate bond that is their successful marriage began in physical attraction and an intense commitment to the politics of the left.

Lina soon realized that the chairs were a metaphor for the transformation of human lives.

The political aspect of their relationship is manifested in intuitive understanding, community commitment, and mutual care. Unlike the stereotypical Hispanic husband, Celso, an engineer, always assumed Lina's work was important. They shared the raising of two children, Cristian and Valentina, who grew up with a practical understanding of gender balance.

The night Lina celebrated her nomination for a Woman of Distinction Award with the women friends who had nominated her and her daughter and granddaughter, Celso absented himself from the intense kitchen feast. He went to Valentina's house, where he spent the evening polishing her pots. We were impressed. That doesn't happen in Chile!

That summer party was typical of Lina, who was aware that the cost of the awards dinner exceeded the budget of her artist friends. We admired the outfit she had chosen for the following evening, ate beautiful food, and talked about our gardens. There is a large photo in her house of the wisteria-covered house in Santiago where she was born. "Wisteria is my roots," she said, wistfully. "I planted one here and it has never bloomed." The room went silent for a moment and then the actress's face transformed again as she

saved the upbeat tone of the evening: "But Chile is crazy."

Work took her young family away from Chile during the turbulent sixties. They were in Cuba during the Missile Crisis, Celso working for the government and Lina with Teatro Estudio, where she taught, acted, and directed from a repertoire that included American and Spanish political plays. Because theatre is the most political of the written arts, dealing directly with issues and relationships, her politics and art were an easy symbiosis.

When Celso did his M.A. at the University of Toronto, the family had their first taste of life in Canada, one that made their eventual emigration easier than it was for many of the refugees fleeing the totalitarian dictatorship of Pinochet and his colonels after the assassination of Chilean President Salvador Allende in 1973. The coup made life in Chile impossible for political activists of the left and centre. Lina and her family were lucky to escape and seek asylum in Canada.

When she felt obliged to leave Chile, Lina looked forward to her new life in Canada, a country she had found inviting during their previous visit. Looking for ways to make her art meaningful in the new community, Lina began to look beyond the standard repertoire, considering the problems of immigration in a country largely populated by first and second generation immigrants. Even though she had broken into the Canadian theatre community, she still felt apart. Surely that apartness could be the matrix for her own homecoming.

In 1987, Lina went home to Chile and had her tarot cards read by her former sister-in-law, a sculptor. The cards showed Lina and her world as separate in spite of auspicious chemistry between them. This was a challenge that had its resolution in the *Puente* (bridge) project that saw the creation of a revolutionary theatrical genre in this country.

Using Manpower grants for the employment of immigrant women, Lina hired five women from the new Hispanic community and made them into actors by challenging them to tell their own stories and interview others. Improvisation led to scriptwriting and before long there was a play, *I Wasn't Born Here*. Therapeutic for new Canadians, the play educated the community at large about the problems of emigration, assimilation, and racism. In rehearsal, the group used folding chairs as fluent settings, arranging them into various configurations to complement the action. Lina soon realized that the chairs were

a metaphor for the transformation of human lives.

Working with women led to a curiosity about men. Having grown up in a classless household, Lina says she learned for the first time about gender difference when she moved her project into the world of men. Wanting to expand public awareness about the effects of emigration on husbands and fathers and sons of the women she had been working with, she invited them to her next project and was surprised by their openness. The Latinos in *Crossing Borders*, the male equivalent to *I Wasn't Born Here*, were more tribal than the women she had directed in the earlier project. Apart from their mothers, the women in their lives were not mentioned in improvisation and life stories. Unlike the women, who defined themselves as mothers and daughters, the male self-definition came through their work and bonding with other men.

Lina says the men were easier to work with because group cooperation was intuitively understood. Her comments made me think about Naomi Wolfe's advocacy of "Difference Feminism" based on tolerance, abandoning the judgement and sexual rivalry which have undermined the feminist movement. They also reinforced the pattern of mother-daughter competition that was emerging in our interviews. Lina agrees that women's political effectiveness has been neutralized by more than just their relationships with men. We have checked one another inside and outside the family.

Both projects were embraced by the public. Lina, of course, moved on. Starting with dance, her life has been about movement. For her final project in the "bridge" trilogy, she employed professional actors to illustrate the problems of social and private adjustment. The play *Canadian Tango*, which dealt with the ways in which emigration affects a relationship, articulated the problem in a schematic diagram of an intensely sexual dance.

Again, Lina de Guevara did not stand still. The only constant for her is family, and this is perhaps what sustains her in change. Today she is working with the problem of racism among adolescents. Her *Forum* project takes multicultural actors into the schools, where they perform racist incidents from scripts. The audience may intervene to change the outcome, but only by taking the role of the oppressed or a bystander. In an incident involving prejudice, it is the victim who is motivated to change the dynamic of the situation.

In Victoria, where a young girl of East Indian descent was recently tormented, tortured, thrown in the Gorge waterway, and left to drown by her adolescent schoolmates, this service is essential. If only there were more Linas to fill the need. When I asked if she was willing to be cloned, she laughed and said it would be nice to do all the things you dream of. There will be more change and growth in spite of the cranky muscles that make her shoulder hurt. So long as there are chairs to arrange and permutations of chairs, Lina will be moving them.

Lina agrees that women's political effectiveness has been neutralized by more than just their relationships with men.

CLAIRE WEISSMAN WILKS

SCULPTOR (1933, TORONTO, ONTARIO–)

Claire was the

paradigm of power.

WHEN I MET CLAIRE WEISSMAN WILKS, she was the Queen of Toronto. She had the presence of Boadicea or Esther, the biblical queen who saved the Jews. Claire was handsome, with a sculptor's powerful hands. In photographs from that time, ten years ago, her sculptural jewelry might have been armour as she readied herself to do battle with the philistines who were about to take political control.

She and her partner, poet/painter/ journalist/musician/horse player/editor/ teacher/bon vivant Barry Callaghan, had Toronto, boomtown of Canadian Culture, sewn up in gold thread. While holding down a demanding job as visual researcher for *The Fifth Estate* at the CBC, she was drawing and sculpting, collaborating on books with poets like D.M. Thomas and John Montague, mounting international exhibitions of her work, and hosting a salon in her house where

the front line of the new Canadian culture had great food and great conversation by her grace. What more could a woman want? Claire was the paradigm of power. Little did I know that this protean woman was as vulnerable as any and that her struggle had been as monumental as her grand but very human life studies.

Claire is the daughter of assimilated Jews, one of two children of lower-middle-class parents who were highly cultured—part of a larger family that included musicians, professors, dancers. Music was the matrix of family pleasure. Her mother, after separating from her father, struggled to support her two daughters by playing piano at the silent movies. Uncle Harold was second violinist for the Toronto Symphony; Aunt Esther was pianist for the National Ballet. Her sister, Wilma Pinkus, became a well-known watercolourist. Claire studied piano and violin, too. Her first pleasurable recollections of drawing include sitting at a table working and listening to the Texaco Opera Broadcasts on Saturdays.

One of her cousins, who lives in Jerusalem, is a violist with the Jerusalem Symphony, and another studied with Bartok. Another is David Cronenberg, one of our finest filmmakers. These children had parents who made family life and education a priority. Music was not Claire's first passion but it informs her work with a legato that is visually apparent. From the beginning, she loved to draw dancers, the movement of trees. The focus of everything she has done is the light of the roots, the sound of light moving up into the branches, feeding the leaves that bind one human figure to another with the promise of redemption from the dark.

When Claire was old enough, she was chosen to be one of the privileged Saturday morning students at the Art Gallery of Ontario. George Hees killed this program when he was elected, and Claire's mother never forgave the Conservatives for this travesty, of the sort that has become a tradition with Ontario Conservative governments.

Claire remembers the joy of her Saturday lessons, the smells of lino and clay and the treats afterward on the way home, smoked salmon from the downtown delis.

Like many creative people who found a pause somewhere between childhood and artistic maturity, Claire had a period of invalidism in the midst of adolescence. Somehow, perhaps from a tubercular tenant in her house "who liked to spit in the bathtub," or from her father, who served in France with my grandfather in World War I and was gassed by the Germans at Ypres, she contracted tuberculosis, which was, thanks to the only humane corollary of World War II, treatable for the first time with antibiotics. She spent two and a half years in a sanatorium, and finally had surgery on one lung. For many, like writer Robert Louis Stevenson, this is dream time and feeds the imagination. In view of Claire's leaps into sculpture, the no woman's land of art, it could be assumed that brushes with death gave her a vivid appreciation of life and a willingness to take risks in its interpretation and enjoyment.

If anything marks her work, it is vigour, a hungry sensuality that ensures the continuation of the human race. It is interesting that her evolution as an artist parallels the miracle of post-war Jewish children born to those who might have been wasted, as European Jewry, caught in another diaspora, determinedly replaced itself against the odds.

While she was in hospital, Claire, whose family had celebrated Christmas and, she believes, introduced the term "Chanukah bush" to the vernacular, met her husband, who was from an observant Jewish family. They called her their "little goyim," so ignorant was she of Jewish ritual practices. Like Phyllis Serota, who was born around the same time, Claire married and went suburban, playing The Wife and producing four children, two sons and two daughters. She was happy with motherhood, but determined at the same time to continue her study of art. Her husband felt threatened by her assertion of this aspect of her creativity. As it does in those marriages where men feel shut out by their spouses' intellectual pursuits, her divided focus created marital tension that led to the breakdown of the relationship and her family.

Somewhere on the road to creative licence, Claire took bad legal advice and gave up custody of her children. The agony of this has been visited on them and is apparent in her hundreds of drawings of mothers and children, the ambivalence of mothering as an energy source and energy drain. In many of the

This is the energy apparent in Claire's work, continuous circles linking the body and spirit the way roots and branches co-operate in the life of a tree.

drawings, the mother lies with the serene repose of the Madonna in what could be a litter of human puppies. The infants proliferate in her hair like lice. In some drawings they are adored and in others the mother, in the midst of birthing, straddles the child with the indifference of pigs who roll over on the newly born.

This is the drawing and redrawing of loss as a mother agonizes over her function as Creator. At this point, Barry Callaghan, who has returned from an afternoon spent watching the horses and writing at the race track, his Office, with an offertory bowl of won ton soup, breaks in to suggest that Claire is what T.S. Eliot had in mind when he conjured his Hyacinth Woman, the giver of life.

After her divorce, Claire, who had her children on weekends, found a job as a receptionist at the CBC. Because of her superb organizational skills, the job quickly became a career in visual research, and she eventually won two Emmy Awards, an Oscar, an Annik Award, and an ACTRA Award. She was becoming the toast of the town. One fine day her male equivalent walked into the CBC and they began a collaboration which became a life in art. Barry Callaghan, son of Morley, one of the finest fiction writers and moralists of

his age, was a man with talent and energy to match hers.

While managing her job, freelance work, and a man with enormous appetite for life, Claire moved beyond drawing into sculpture, the three-dimensional realization of her vision, a dance with shapes. My husband, who describes her drawing style as free and exhilarating, reminded me of a classical drawing exercise in which a pencil is held in both hands at once and the drawing rendered in big arm movements. This is the energy apparent in Claire's work, continuous circles linking the body and spirit the way roots and branches co-operate in the life of a tree.

It would seem the page is not big enough for her. Indeed, Claire, who talked to me on the eve of her sixty-fifth birthday, has as her long-range goal commissions for large outdoor sculpture, figures interacting with the elements in the way a tree experiences life's transitions, renewing itself with every season.

A Lipschitz show at the Art Gallery of Ontario opened a window in her three-dimensional landscape. Her enthusiasm for his work verges on worship:

I saw a man of never-ending energy and imaginative inventiveness, an artist who always took enormous risks. My multifigural compositions break out into the same primal shape that Lipschitz's sculptures take, becoming, I hope, the source of light, a symbol of hope and continuation of a people. But I have to say I happen to be a Canadian who happens to be a Jew. The proliferation of the race looks after itself. This is the wonder of life implied in Lipschitz's Tree of Life—the roots feed in the darkness, the tree leafs in the light. In Lipschitz's sculpture, I saw the living shape that I also find seductive in a menorah. That is where the totem sculptures take off.

There is a story about an epiphany during a holiday in Cuba. She was sitting on the beach watching a Cuban family bury one of their children in sand. The women were laughing as they spooned sand on the infant, who was not enjoying it. In fact, Claire's attention was commanded by the child's protests. She remembered an incident in high school, in which a young German refugee recalled the earth crying when children were buried alive in the camp where he had been interned. At that point, Claire realized her function. "It was to bring them back to life."

Another clear influence was Claire's discovery in the early eighties of the photo-graphy of Hannah Maynard, whose work was lost in the archives of the BC Provincial Museum. Her book on Maynard, *The Magic Box*, describes the surreal imagination of a fellow risk taker and documents the influence of Maynard's astonishing photography on her own sculpture. In Maynard's "Gem Collages" of babies, we see the human multiplicity that also distinguishes Claire's drawings of mothers and children and her totem sculptures, bodies on bodies, all symbiotic. Like Maynard, Claire is an exception, a woman in what has been male territory, taking the phenomenal world in both hands and wrestling with it. Many visual artists I have interviewed reveal a longing for sculpture, the three-dimensional form, but few have had the confidence to embrace a form that challenges the technical limitations of art.

Claire's life is an extension of her art, a house full of books and beautiful things made by friends who decorate the lyrical line of her domestic tableau. No wonder everybody came. Unfortunately, there have been intruders, thieves and an arsonist who laid waste to their home on Sullivan Street. When Barry's father died, they grieved him and the old place, moving to Morley's large house in Rosedale. This is Barry's sentimental home, but Claire is

This is the drawing and redrawing of loss as a mother agonizes over her function as Creator.

From
Hillmother
by
Claire Weissman Wilks
Exile Editions 1983

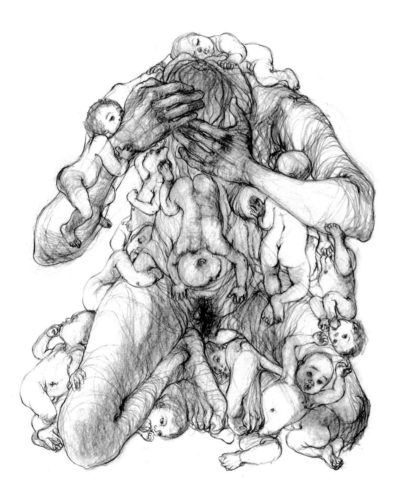

still struggling to make it hers. These violations added to the new climate of philistinism in Canadian and world politics, which elevates information over wisdom and conformity over thought. It has taken its toll on the couple, as it has on the general well-being of our culture. The values present in Claire's childhood home, elevating music and art over the marketplace, are no longer prevalent in our popular culture.

Claire has felt the inertia of depression as she has watched public evaluation of the artist plummet. This is a fight she and Barry are fighting, but, when power is money and there is not enough to take care of the physical needs of our population, art is suffering. When you watch the powerful sculptor's hands moving in the afternoon sunlight, when you understand what she has already overcome in public and personal grief, you believe she will triumph as do the figures climbing to the light in the sculpture in her upstairs hall. So long as there is wind in her branches, Claire will never stop moving.

FINOLA FOGARTY

ARCHITECT (1934, COUNTY LIMERICK, IRELAND–)

She says it has something to do with the Irish weather, which permanently mutates fog into the body chemistry.

FINOLA WON MY HEART THE EVENING I met her by telling me right off the top she was enjoying my eejit banter, having been born in a loony bin in County Limerick. This was her offhand Irish way of saying her Da was a live-in shrink and her first playmates were inmates. Of course, she was right about me, and true to her heritage, she has more recently confided that only the mad are worth knowing.

Finola's dad, a spoiled, adored mind worker, was as crazy as his patients, falling occasionally into the Irish despond as do his children and grandchildren. She says it has something to do with the Irish weather, which permanently mutates fog into the body chemistry. Her mother was a good Catholic wife, whose husband was the god of the household. The children came next. I told Finola all the women I had been talking to fit the pattern of good or bad relationships with their mothers. There are no neutrals. Finola says she is definitely in the latter category, but did fall in love with her mother's memory as soon as she died. It is not easy being married to a mood-swinging god. Mother Fogarty had an enormous vegetable garden and many slaves to do her bidding. The loonies, as they were called, were drafted into what her mother "euphemized" as occupational therapy, activities that kept the family primed.

Raised a Catholic, Finola has little good to say about the church and definitely will not be buried on consecrated ground, even though she did send two of her sons to Jesuit schools. At least, she muses, the Jesuits were worldly enough to ignore the hypocrisy of celibacy and its corollary, interference with little scholars, and, besides, it was the best school in Ireland, the alma mater of James Joyce and generations of men in Finola's family.

Born on a storm-tossed island, she never stops kicking her feet in turbulent waters.

You have to get up very early in the morning to keep up with Finola, who keeps her mind sharp reading books and swimming every day. Born on a storm-tossed island, she never stops kicking her feet in turbulent waters. In fact, she chose her profession just because she admired a local architect who looked magnificent in his bathing suit. No one objected to her vocational choice. In holy Ireland, amazingly, there was less prejudice against her as a professional woman than she later found in Canada, however foolish the reason for the decision which led her to become one of four female architecture students in a class of one hundred.

Now, she says, the problem is ageism. Many offend her with their surprise that a woman in her sixties would want to continue doing work she loves.

Irish to her marrow, Finola is a woman who is impressed easily by poetry in all its forms. She lost herself to the lyrically shaped architect and later to a young veterinary surgeon. The latter had achieved a certain notoriety by boldly divesting the Tate Gallery in London of a well-known Irish painting, presenting it to his own embassy where it apparently hangs to this day. She wrote him a letter and he responded. The rest was a wild picaresque ending in divorce.

This was a man she could have babies with, and she did, five of them. When that wasn't enough, she was impressed by the romance of people who adopted minority children, so she did that too, raising her First Nations daughter with the Irish tribe she had brought to Canada.

But I am romping ahead. Finola's husband was a passionate creature who enjoyed the national pastime. Finola says the Irish drink because Catholicism has taught them a state of grace can only be entered through the portal in the face. Transformation by whisky is the gospel of renovated heathens.

In the beginning, the recklessness was attractive, and it did keep the family on the move. Her husband was congenitally unfaithful. In racist South Africa, there were black women, not *comme il faut*, and the man known as the "Elephant Doctor" got himself stabbed in the face by a stalwart defender of apartheid.

Through most of these times, apart from the half-dozen years when she was "always pregnant," Finola worked at home with the help of babysitters and nannies. Having a studio in the house, with children around, may have introduced her habit of working at night, during the quiet hours. In Canada, the Fogartys finally split and Finola's husband, Billy, returned to Ireland. There he now lives in a house owned by their son Angus, who received a settlement because he is suffering the effect of thalidomide.

Finola loves little children. That is clear. She is kind to my grandchildren and dotes on her own. I had to ask how she came to take drugs while pregnant. Why would pregnancy have meant depression and lack of sleep to someone who embraced the idea of childbearing? The thalidomide, prescribed by her mother-in-law, was for nausea and insomnia brought on by the frequent absences of her husband.

I asked if hers was a typical Irish marriage. In Ireland, Finola says, it was more acceptable to be unfaithful than to use birth control. The whole country was inside out and upside down. She longed for a new start and, in the beginning, Canada was a fresh sheet of paper to draw on. Now she finds Canadians complacent and stares at her maps with longing. Marriage and childrearing behind her, Finola describes herself as a non-sexual adventurer. She is more interested in new milieus than new men. Perhaps this has something to do with experience and

something to do with the antidepressants she needs to dispel her greys.

We talked about mental illness and chemical dependencies. Finola worries about her children: a doctor, a lawyer, an environmental strategist, a biologist, a logger, and a First Nations band council worker. Will they quit on their marriages as she and her husband did? Will the Irish Fog inevitably complicate their lives?

This is a heavy load for a woman living alone in a house she constantly apologizes for, because "it is never finished," but nevertheless has character, as does she. Houses tell a lot about their owners. Finola's house on Victoria's historic South Turner Street, known for its cherry blossoms, has great profile and refinement. She burns driftwood from the nearby ocean in her fireplaces and sleeps in a bed surrounded by a magnificent plum- and moss-coloured arras curtain. When I said "Arras?" she replied only "Polonius" and didn't add "Stupid!", tactful for once.

Addicted to coffee, Finola burns the midnight oil in a glassed-in verandah where she keeps her drafting table. She works better at night even though she suffers from darkness. All Ireland is darkness, as are parts of her house, which she forsakes for this porch where neighbours watch her fantasies take shape in bright artificial light.

We had lunch one rainy afternoon. The rain, she said, was good, dramatic. It is the grey that ought to be feared. Wind and rain transport the stalled spirit. Even though she says there is prejudice against women architects in this country, Finola continues to do the work she loves. Why should she retire? She is good at her work and it satisfies her.

The balance she struggles to achieve is a combination of liveable and aesthetically pleasing. She has gained a reputation for designs of family-friendly buildings. Her blueprint for the Lasqueti Island school revolutionized the concept of education in that rural community by opening the rather traditional schoolhouse to the possibilities of performance and group activity. She has brought special understanding to her designs for transition houses for battered women. When there was no place else to go, she had to take her tribe to a motel to escape the negative attention of an Irish drunk. Her designs for women's shelters take into account the physical and emotional needs of families in trauma. They are as much like home as possible. Community is the bottom line in her architectural aesthetic. *People* live in buildings.

Hers is a female approach to design. The grand statement does not always make for the fine living spaces that are her desiderata. Thinking of all the bipolar artists whose moments of euphoria lead to works of genius, I asked Finola if her top notes ever result in professional risk-taking. She replied, "That is for geniuses." I had to remind her of Jean

Irish to her marrow, Finola is a woman who is impressed easily by poetry in all its forms.

Genet's definition: "Genius is not a gift but the way one invents in difficult situations." This is the sort of challenge Finola prefers to meet with a female pragmatism. Form follows function.

Her "greys" have made her aware of the human need for light and comfort. One award-winning design for a shelter has as its precept physical and emotional encirclement. The building feels safe, with every child visible in the central playground from every kitchen window. Each unit is different in format to reflect the individuality of its occupants. This is not a prison for families but a place to grow in confidence.

It is this sensitivity that marks her designs and her face, which is at once kind and intelligent. It is typical of Finola's self-deprecating wit that she described Barbara as a genius when the proofs from her photo shoot were delivered. It is possibly true that she is unaware of her great beauty. Barbara says this is a face made for a crown or the face of a coin.

Finola describes her desideratum as transcendence of the physical body that is beginning to humiliate her with its aches and pains. She echoes the theme of invisibility that I have heard from other women of a certain age. With the sacrifice of the sexual woman comes a clarity that allows women to present as human beings as opposed to sexual beings. This is the crown of old age and one she will grasp and put on herself. "It is marvellous coming out of myself and leaving the female behind."

Six decades into her adventurous life, Finola Fogarty is beautiful, witty, and strong, well designed and well made like her buildings. She has to be.

PHYLLIS SEROTA

PAINTER (1938, CHICAGO, ILLINOIS–)

Painting is the ultimate form of prayer for Serota.

PAINTER SEROTA IS A STAINED GLASS window of mysteries and transparencies. One of the most direct people I have ever met, she is also a contemplative, someone for whom the Jungian journey and the mystic pragmatism of Judaism are compatible.

We talked in her studio on a sunny late afternoon in early September. Phyllis kept moving her chair to enjoy various relationships with the light. She was curious that I stayed where I was. Perhaps there is some significance. Serota (her Russian-Jewish surname means "orphan") is a Piscean. Like a fish, she moves as she describes the various transformations in her life.

Born to a second-generation Jewish émigré family in Chicago, she grew up in the intensity of a displaced *shtetl* household. Her father was a man of complex intensity. Because her older sister dissembled and conformed as first daughters often do, Phyllis was the one who stood up to his will. Early practice in family warfare made her strong and determined, which is just as well in a competitive field like visual art, where tenacity is essential.

Phyllis's mother wanted her second child to be a son. The six-year interval before a son appeared was enough to imprint a strong sense of bewilderment. Phyllis was sometimes jokingly called *Mieskeit*, the ugly one. Looking back at photographs, she knows she was just as attractive as her older sister, but it was a well-kept secret. When I told Phyllis that there appeared to be a strain of maternal disapproval in the history of women artists, she agreed that the desire to render herself less invisible, less ugly, was paramount in her struggle for acceptance.

As a child, she liked to make sculpture out of papier mâché and clay. Indeed, there is still a strong sculptural aspect to her painting. Her earliest memory of artistic rejection is of standing in the kitchen showing a drawing while her mother washed the dishes with her back to her. She would not look. When I ask Phyllis now about her greatest ambition, she admits it would be for her mother to see her work and comment positively about it.

Serota, who maintains that art and politics are separate, describes the epiphanies in her life as largely political. At her high school, there was a teacher who was persecuted for her liberal politics. To a young Jew, with the sound of Cossack horses in her blood, the ostracism of a mentor may have raised the spectre of the religious persecution from which her family had fled.

When the McCarthy witch hunts began, many Jews went underground, rejecting their names and their culture. Others went to jail for leftist politics or aligned themselves with the fledgling civil rights movement. In her early adult life, Serota, who was from an Orthodox family, sublimated her natural inclination to rebellion, choosing middle-class behaviour over politics. She married her childhood sweetheart at nineteen, went to the 'burbs, and had a baby when she was twenty.

She says she slept through her twenties, bearing three children in her sleep and ignoring her husband's infidelities. The most telling anecdote of that period is the paint-by-number set she bought and completed, a bizarre artistic initiation and metaphor for her life. From then on, her most awake time was spent at art classes, even though she kept her painting clothes clean and stayed in the safe realm of the still life.

She woke up in 1968 to the revelation of her spouse's inappropriate behaviour and the shocking events of the Democratic Convention

The most telling anecdote of that period is the paint-by-number set she bought and completed, a bizarre artistic initiation and metaphor for her life.

in Chicago, where a young activist was beaten on the hood of the car in which she was travelling. She realized then that her middle-class life was ugly and America was ugly.

The next year, she and her family drove to Vancouver Island because they had heard it was warm. Settling in Maple Bay, the family became involved in encounter groups and the religion of self-discovery. She remembers this as a good period even though the risks of sexual freedom and experimental drugs led to family breakdown and spousal abuse. When the dust had cleared, Phyllis, who remembers a school crush on a girl as her earliest awakening, discovered that she was indeed a lesbian.

She has been with her partner, graphic and lighting designer Annie Weeks, for twenty-five years. The relationship is strong. Her only regrets are the changes her children underwent with her. Not everyone is resilient. Though painting had always been part of her life, she became serious inside the time with Annie. Both women returned to school. Phyllis felt untouched by the largely academic experience, but she found the courage to call herself an artist. Sometime in the late seventies, Judy Chicago gave a workshop for women in Vancouver and, in order to be accepted, Phyllis

had to declare her vocation, the final turning point.

Study of Jungian psychology and analysis, Judaism, and feminism are probably the most obvious social influences on Serota's paintings which, several years ago, I would have described as secular Chagall. Serota acknowledges the influence of the Russian painter, celebrating his joy and the fluidity of line and colour that describe his relationship with light. There is much in common; their cultural background, an awareness of suffering, and the need to transcend pain. But there is a point where they diverge. Serota says painting like the dark poetry of Montreal's Betty Goodwin is a stronger influence on her present work. The dark side of Phyllis Serota is reflected in a new series of Holocaust paintings and in her controversial crucified woman, which takes the primary Christian metaphor into post-feminist mythology. She has just finished a Holocaust triptych which fills a whole wall of her studio, contrasting the dark images of despair with the relief of lace.

In the centre panel there is a pyramid of bodies in a pit. It reverberates an image from the play about the bigot Zundel, in which a camp commandant sentimentally recalls skiing in the Alps, comparing the experience of the camp to skiing down a mountain of eyeglasses. It is the exquisite, a piece of lace in the left panel, that brings it all home with such force, the exodus of gentle people into the horror of horrors. The focus of the centre panel is a Christ-like figure. His body, the body of a mind worker, a scholar, or a musician, reminds me of my husband. It is a totally vulnerable man.

When I asked Phyllis if she felt a social obligation to paint such images, she responded that painting was now a compulsion, a life function, echoing what so many women artists have said to me: "I do it because I have to." Even though her pivotal moments have been around social issues like bigotry, political persecution, and feminism, she says the art is for art's sake.

Judaism infuses her painting with joy and a sense of family and social connection. If she experiences religious ecstasy, it is a visceral reaction to light and music and familiar things from her culture. Painting is the ultimate form of prayer for Serota. It is this love and serenity that she sees as her real legacy to her children and grandchildren.

Like many women, Phyllis, whose painted figures are solid, what my stepdaughter describes as "pudgy but shapely," has always considered herself the *mieskeit* of her childhood. Looking at old photographs, we discovered that she was not fat at all, but lovely, her face doll-like. I told her many of the women I talked to have had the same experience. We wondered if living with criticism, unrealistic social expectations, made women struggle harder for approval.

Phyllis wishes she always had the confidence she has now. On the other hand, experiencing the outside has sharpened her compassion and provided the impetus that took her out of the grey invisibility of her former life. Now Serota is a woman in her prime, with beautiful thick hair and vibrant skin. She paints with the force and energy of her formidable intellect. Is she afraid of the future possibility, the diminishing of those powers? Of course, she says; the spectre of her family was a grandmother with dementia.

Her mother may never notice, but by now joy in her work has overtaken the desire to please her parent, which is the impetus for so much art. Phyllis has the approval of Annie and the critics and all those people who hang her paintings in their homes and places of business and worship. The shadows of the past inform the light she is moving into. That is a good place to be going.

Phyllis's mother wanted her second child to be a son.

CAROLE SABISTON

TEXTILE ARTIST (1939, BUSHY HEATH, LONDON–)

The musicality that is fundamental to dancing has transposed itself to art.

BARBARA HAS A WAY OF DISARMING her subjects, making the most self-conscious follow in the jetstream of her conversation. The day she photographed textile artist Carole Sabiston, Barbara had been up all night following the dislanded on the Internet in her quest for information about the Zapatistas. Her passion was contagious and she soon had her reactive subject wired.

Since she was born in Bushy Heath, a village in the great village of London, Carole revealed a whim to present as "Bushy Heathen," the total woman with electric hair. After taking a portrait of the artist with her Tutankhamen piece, we carried the photo gear up to her room and stood her in front of the beautiful lace curtains that once belonged to her husband's Oakville grandmother. Carole began to move like a woman possessed, taking her hair in her hands, letting it go wherever it

wanted. You could almost hear the castanets. There was so much uninhibited grace in her, I was not surprised when she later revealed her first ambition had been to dance.

The daughter of English immigrants, Carole grew up in West Vancouver and Victoria, the outposts of empire, where snobbery was having its final flourish among the nouveau riche of the last earthly frontier. Her father was a butcher and her mother worked in the shop. When Carole went round to deliver meat to the kitchens of her well-heeled schoolmates, the daughter of parents who left a country where social position was written in stone felt awkward and self-conscious.

Carole exudes confidence in herself as a dressed-up, fragile, beautiful woman and as an artist, but she does not like to be patronized. We are the children of our childhoods. An only child, Carole was not spoiled, but appreciated. She had no idea until her mid-twenties that her parents had wished for a son. It is perhaps unthinkable to young women nowadays, in our part of the world, that a girl would have to struggle for recognition, that girls would not be valuable, but we remember that being told we did something "like a boy" was the highest form of compliment. It came as a shock when Carole's parents finally told her in her young adulthood that they were proud of her, that "for a girl" she was something special.

"Something special" meant that every fibre of her energetic being was a blotter for sensual impressions. A talented dancer, she was also distinguishing herself as a visual artist. The decision not to dance was in the end a choice against an ascetic lifestyle that ran counter to her need for spontaneous expression.

The musicality that is fundamental to dancing has transposed itself to art. In the magnificent pieces that make up her canon, from large wall hangings to intimate pieces to operatic sets, there is a flow of light and colour that could be musical notation, a modern baroque.

A favourite image is sails, the air-filled canvas transporting her work from the real to the surreal, where sound and shape are the

The glittering strands that are picked from her environment the way a crow chooses shiny objects are more about the transient light than nesting.

witty metaphors for truth. "I've always lived on islands, and my work is a lot about changes in atmosphere, where the only thing constant is change; you always know that the horizon is there, but what goes on with the colours, back and forth, the dark and white, is always in flux." The titles of her work are most often about motion; "Flying," "Sailing," and "Restless Legacies" are as much about her life as her art, both of which are characterized by kinetic energy. This is the evolution of a girl with red shoes.

The glittering strands that are picked from her environment the way a crow chooses shiny objects are more about the transient light than nesting. Because her work is so labour intensive, its practical origins in craft, I asked Carole if she saw her wall hangings and sewn and bejewelled theatrical scrims as an extension of traditional women's work. Did she intend to take the traditional medium for female creativity and translate it for the postmodernist marketplace? Her reasons, she says, are not political. A whiz in home economics and a wearer of theatrical clothing she made herself, she liked to sew and sewing was the most practical way for a young mother to express herself in a limited space. She could fold a tapestry and put it away when it was

time to make dinner. Paint with its smells and expansive presence was not so obliging, so the choice was obvious.

Carole had been to college and married Brian Sabiston. Her work as a craftswoman helped put him through graduate school in eastern Canada. During the sixties, she joined the craft renaissance of our generation, elevating home art to marketable media in order to survive the impecunious student life. The marriage did not survive those exciting times. Sabiston returned to Victoria and made her living as an artist and teacher. She eventually met and married Jim Munro, the owner of one of Canada's most elegant bookstores, with its extraordinary hangings by one of Canada's finest artists (surprise!), Carole Sabiston. She now has the room to make major pieces that sing in majestic architectural spaces.

Jim and Carole live on Rockland Avenue in an old house that could be an extension of the Victoria Art Gallery. Somehow this Victorian near-mansion has evolved from "dignified" to "exquisite." Grandmother's lace curtains hang in the bedroom and her beaded flapper dresses slumber in the closet. The brilliantly hued walls are covered with sentimental pieces. There is light everywhere, and, where there isn't, there are candles to compensate.

The ghost of Alice Munro, Jim's first wife, the mother of his three grown daughters, and one of Canada's most respected prose writers, has been relegated to a closet, where some of her papers were left behind. I asked Carole if she ever felt she was the second Mrs. Munro, and she threw back her head and laughed. Needless to say, they are both formidable. What Jim tactfully leaves out of conversation about his famous wives might be written in cryptic script in his ubiquitous notebook.

Carole has a son by her first marriage. Andrew is one of the whiz kids from St. Michael's University School who parlayed a school theatre project into the megamusical *Napoleon*. Is Carole proud? Of course, but we agreed over lunch that a mother's proudest wish is to see her children happy as opposed to rich or famous. Andrew is recently married, and Carole might wish for a granddaughter who could slip into all the beautiful costumes she has sewn and collected.

Carole has been one of those women who dress theatrically, as if she were putting on a costume or stepping into a painting. "Isn't this fun?" she might be asking as she hooks up the four hundredth button. A natural mannequin with a dancer's grace, she sailed through three decades in a blaze of gauzy skirts, emerging a confident, mature woman.

How does a beautiful woman with a strong sculptural awareness in her choice of shoes and dresses and jewelry feel about getting older? She has always been the presence inside the dress. Now, she says, she is settling down into neutral colours. She doesn't want to be the woman at the centre of attention. Her role models are women who have aged gracefully and are centred in their lives. Her wisdom radiates on the outside. She moves beautifully. She dresses beautifully. She speaks beautifully, with the balance of a Libran who has found her articulate colours in a woman's place.

Nowadays, no one condescends to the woman translated from the eight-year-old girl who lost her cockney accent as fast as she could after moving to Canada. However, she says with a sparkle, she could still do Eliza Doolittle to a T. This is the irony that shades her work. Her awareness that gold shines in relation to the darker tones of poverty and ignorance raises her work above the merely decorative. Like Mozart, she wilfully undermines her own high seriousness, lest we take the jewelled surfaces too seriously. It is the tension between surface and substance that layers her work

I asked Carole if she ever felt she was the second Mrs. Munro, and she threw back her head and laughed.

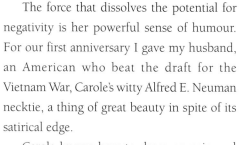

with meaning, just as her lurking dimple hints at hidden ironies.

Having raised "women's work" to the level of art, Carole has been honoured by her country and by public and private patrons, from corporations to theatre and opera companies, who commission her major works. She has been awarded an honorary doctorate, a Confederation Medal from the Governor General, and the Order of British Columbia. She also has a well-adjusted son and a husband who is a pillar of his community. Nevertheless, she has not forgotten her origins in a country where some people always use the back door. Moral judgement, the prerogative of the outsider, surfaces as integrity in her life and art, both of which are a celebration of light, the way you see it coming through her fine flax-coloured hair.

Like the proverbial crow foraging for treasure to line its nest, Carole has spent her life seeking out the gold threads and working them into her oeuvre. However, the preoccupation with beauty doesn't mean she tolerates bigotry or condones suffering. She is far too sensitive to be unaware of inequity.

The force that dissolves the potential for negativity is her powerful sense of humour. For our first anniversary I gave my husband, an American who beat the draft for the Vietnam War, Carole's witty Alfred E. Neuman necktie, a thing of great beauty in spite of its satirical edge.

Carole knows how to dress up pain and poverty and take it out for dinner. This has been the leitmotif of her life, a theme rarely learned in the nurseries of the privileged. An insider now, she is in a position to enlighten those who have not had her broad range of experience.

There is no colour for cruelty in Sabiston's palette. Like Sarastro, the wizard in Mozart's *Magic Flute*, for which she has provided elegant sets and costumes, she banishes darkness. She simply obliterates the shadows she has experienced first-hand, choosing instead the hues for community and hope, the hands that reach out of her amazing tapestries to remind us we are connected to each other and to the light.

*Moving Through a
Fragmented London Life*
1986
120 in x 120 in
Textile assemblage

The Broad Canvas

Sister Eileen Curteis, SSA

Poet and Reiki Master (1942, Victoria, British Columbia–)

Her journey has been spiritual, physical, and psychological, a classic case of mind over body.

ROCK AND ROLL! Sister Eileen reminds me of the nuns I once knew who played baseball wearing T-shirts that read "Tiny but Tough" under their habits. After we sat and chatted for a while in the gazebo at Queenswood, a beautifully landscaped retreat centre a short prayer away from the Pacific Ocean, I realized it would be unkind to mention this. Sister Eileen was one of those girls who never got picked, except by the one secular love she alludes to, but the appeal of marriage and children of her own was not as strong as the desire to be consumed by God's love. Her calling led her to enter religious life at the age of nineteen.

A painful social life with only God as a true friend led Eileen Curteis (the spelling is an anglicization of the French Courtois, a family that crossed the English Channel with William the Conqueror) to a vocation where she could work with children, giving her a chance to rediscover her own childhood in the enthusiasm of children she taught. A shy wee person, she called herself "Small" in a voice that faith took past self-pity into action.

Small
is a little girl
who lived sometime
after the war was over
but for Small
the war was never over.

It is interesting that another Victorian, Emily Carr, also called herself "Small," a name that comes easily to girls with a shrunken confidence. Elspeth Rogers Cherniavsky, my children's great-aunt, wrote to me that Miss Carr "smelt" when she taught at Crofton House School. Eileen has the rose-coloured odour of

sanctity, the garden she brings into her convent room.

A religious experience shortly after she graduated from St. Anne's Academy in Victoria determined the path that has taken many strange turns, as a minute voiceless child transformed herself into a channel for the Holy Spirit, a poet, and a reiki master.

The daughter of a school principal, Eileen was small for her age and tongue-tied. Her mother spoke for her at home, and at school the children silenced her with cruelty. Although she was bright, she was scared paralytic and unable to perform in class. By the time Eileen was in her mid-twenties, she was in constant pain. The tension in her body and the effort to make herself appear taller than her tiny four feet ten had a crippling effect on her spine, with severe scoliosis as the result.

Her journey has been spiritual, physical, and psychological, a classic case of mind over body. The high expectations of a Catholic childhood and a secular school system inflexible to her needs had a profound effect on her body and her spirit. Since her apprehensive mind had destroyed her health, she would use it to bring herself back by exploring her own faith and the teachings of ancient practitioners.

An emotional and physical breakdown at the age of thirty-nine she now sees as her moment of enlightenment. I am reminded of Lina de Guevara's "needing a difficulty," the inhumanity that made her an exile from Chile and Comfort Adesuwa an exile from Nigeria. Sister Eileen exiled herself from the body that made her less herself than she needed to be to do her work.

Today Eileen is a fighter, relentlessly cheerful. A feminist in a patriarchal church, she is smiling her way through pain and suffering to glory, the vibrant realization that everyone is equal in the eyes of God.

Eileen says that, although she is celibate, she has experienced her sensuality, first in her work channelling God's love in her teaching and then in her healing ministries. Although she has not experienced motherhood in the conventional sense, she has mothered thousands. Because as a child she only felt safe at home and in the arms of God, as an adult she was determined to make the school experience positive for her charges. Every child who passed through her classrooms in twenty-seven years of teaching would feel empowered by her caring. That is quite a compelling mission, but she had to leave it behind when she felt called to a "hands-on" healing ministry

at the beginning of her personal search for balance and health.

As her body heals, she says, she feels a harmony that brings her into physical relationship with the cosmos—animal, vegetable, and mineral. She is a small hummingbird feeding on the mysteries of nature.

When asked how she could reconcile controversy around the church, particularly with respect to children, with her own benevolent humanism, she answered that she could only serve by example. Being exemplary is difficult, when there is evidence of betrayal all around you. The modern world is so problematic there is no dogma that serves to provide the answers. Diplomacy is essential to women living in community. Sister Eileen was not comfortable with the difficult questions I asked about the treatment of children in residential schools. It was as if the question hurt her, as it does all of us, because, as Jesus said, "We are only as strong as the weakest among us."

In some of her drawings, Sister Eileen describes a woman with a stone on her shoulder. The shoulder is where women classically carry their rage. This is one explanation for frozen shoulder, which affects

A feminist in a patriarchal church, she is smiling her way through pain and suffering to glory.

so many women during menopause. Among the subjects of this book, Eurithe Purdy, Angela Addison, and Lina de Guevara have all experienced this mid-life curse. Eileen's whole body has been frozen. The miracle is her thaw.

I first met Sister Eileen Curteis at a reading in Fernwood, Victoria. She was launching her second book, *Moving On*, poems and sketches from the inner world. In simple line drawings, a woman is created and recreated. Sometimes her internal organs are shown, heart and womb, as she reaches for her own truth and descends the chakras to find the being she left behind.

In every drawing, the eyes are black, like Little Orphan Annie's. I asked Eileen if they were blank and she said no, the lenses were open to the light. I believe her. If she weren't advancing toward the radiance she feels reflected in herself, I doubt she would have made it this far.

The poems are candid. She says they are the children of her journey toward the light. Depression, a woman's anger, is a new word in her vocabulary. She has had to invent a liturgy for survival through transcendence of her former self. Eileen is not angry with anyone, but with the absence of love that leads children, born innocent, to callousness. This

She is a small hummingbird feeding on the mysteries of nature.

is her incantation that came to her in a dream: "I hate you almost, but I love you more." Passion is where the energy for transformation is found.

Eileen now combines her ministry with hands-on healing. Wasn't that an act of arrogance, I asked, assuming that she had the power to heal in herself? But I misunderstood. She believes she is a channel, that the love of God passes through her hands into the body and mind of those who suffer as she has.

In my church
there'll be no more rules
no more dogma
just God
putting a kite
on my splintered tongue
letting me fly
thorn free.

On a second visit to Queenswood, we walked through the quiet halls past a drawing of hands by Myfanwy Pavelić. Myfanwy has also suffered from crippling disease. The synchronicities are everywhere. Upstairs, overlooking the garden, Eileen has transformed a convent room in order to practise her healing art. There are perfumed candles and paintings of flowers. The beds are covered with homey crocheted shawls. The teachers Jesus and Buddha, represented in icons, are comfy together in this peaceful place, and Barbara, the fallen Baptist, has been forgiven for starting her cafeteria dinner without waiting for grace, even though Eileen did remind her with a sharp tap of her fork on her water glass and I unsuccessfully tried to hide my giggle behind a paper napkin. We were the naughty children Jesus beckoned.

I asked Eileen, who has spent so much time with children, about original sin. She questions the church's traditional teachings because she cannot look at a newborn face and believe it is anything but the vessel of love. Birth is original blessing.

She views herself not as a doctrinaire pedant, but as a wounded healer who feels called to empower and facilitate others to find their own healing energies with dignity. "This last ache has made you real. Go now to the others."

When I asked her about the impact of Vatican II on church and religious life, particularly that of women like herself, she said it lifted some of the burden but that for her the only true healing came years later when she moved into the holistic Eastern art of Reiki.

She had an abbreviated response when I commented on the recent appointment of yet another conservative cardinal by the aging pope John Paul; just widened her eyes significantly.

Ridiculous!
And, yet, here I am
a brittle bird
still trapped
in the warped wood
of my anatomy
removing the last of these nails.

This is August, her holiday month. She is finishing up a third book, *Wind Daughter*, which includes a suite of autobiographical poems and photography. Is publishing not vanity, I wanted to know, remembering the torment of my great-grandfather's cousin Gerard Manley Hopkins, a priest who was too ashamed to have pride in his beautiful poetry. How was her book regarded within the religious community? Her answer was the same as the one about Reiki, the Buddhist healing technique. Times have changed. Tolerance is the touchstone of the new gospel. Even though she has been writing since the sixties, she is only now "going public."

Her catch phrase is "the gospel of reality." When I asked her what that meant, she said it taught her not to bury her light under a bushel. Most of us go through a bushel of matches. But we are not nuns.

We talked about the near-death experience phenomenon, going into the light, which so many people describe. Although she has had serious illnesses and many ecstatic experiences, she has never seen the brilliant face of heaven. I was not afraid to ask Sister Eileen how she felt about "moving into the mystery," and she says she is excited about the journey. When I mentioned the "pearly gates" of gospel songs, she gave me the schoolteacher's lecture about cliché. I told her I had a theory that the entrance to heaven was decorated with teeth purchased from children by the tooth fairy, but she remained unimpressed by that charming metaphor. Every metaphor falls short of a spiritual realm beyond human imagining.

Passion is where the energy for transformation is found.

CAROLYN SADOWSKA

ACTOR AND PAINTER (1944, QUEBEC CITY, QUEBEC–)

There is a private side to this very public performer.

AFTER SHE TOLD ME SHE HAD BEEN STONED as a child in a francophone village outside of Quebec City, I did not have to ask Carolyn Sadowska, whom most people know as "Her Majesty the Queen Impersonator," why she kept the surname of the husband she divorced, as opposed to her maiden name or the name of her deceased second husband. For Carolyn, whose Anglo pedigree and Anglican religion were a neighbourhood crime, the Polish surname has the same comfort and exotic allure as childhood fantasies that saved her from despair.

We were having lunch in the garden at the Water Club in Victoria. It was Carolyn's birthday, she said her fifty-fourth. When I asked her what year she had been born, she told me 1944. That would make you fifty-three, I told her. How could an intelligent woman born in a legitimate union not know her age?

She explained it was like setting your clock ahead when you are afraid you will oversleep. If she lost a year somewhere, sleeping in or undergoing a transformation, something the invisible child learns to do, she would come out balanced.

You don't contradict the Queen. While she sipped her strawberry mango soup from a silver spoon, I asked if the Queen business was suffering in the perennial recession. "What recession?" she asked in the same imperial tone Brenda (as the real Queen is known in her own neighbourhood) might use to dismiss the frayed edges of her royal tapestry.

Carolyn has been intimate with the Queen all her life. Because the local priest told children they would go to hell if they played with her, she made friends with her dolls, all royal princesses. Later, when she was old enough to go on the bus by herself, she escaped her expected milieu, taking serendipitous journeys, hanging out in juke joints in the historic lower town, where she drew obsessively while the music played, selling her drawings on the streets of Old Quebec City.

There is a private side to this very public performer. Her restored Edwardian house (on the same street in Victoria where Barbara Pedrick and Finola live) is cool and serenely furnished. Its high ceilings are perfect for portraits of the Royal Family. The Queen hangs over the four-poster bed Carolyn shares with her partner John Dewhirst and a three-legged white cat my husband calls "the trivet." Apart from her own paintings on the walls, the house could be a museum, occupied by enigmatic figures. There is little clutter to reveal their inner life. They too are cats, burying their treasure.

Carolyn's paintings are beautiful. The colour schemes that are her dress code, something between the purples and oranges of Maxfield Parrish and the blues, golds, and greens of the pre-Raphaelites and -Bloomsburys, soften the neo-expressionist paintings of blurred figures in static

landscapes. She studied art hoping to become a full-time painter, but when her first marriage to a scientist ended, she made the decision to go back to school, with the intention of studying theology and becoming an Anglican minister.

Her moment of disillusionment crystallized around the revelation from someone she knew that religious experience can be reproduced by stimulating a certain area of the brain. This was my chance to ask Carolyn the question about aging. She is not a woman obsessed with her appearance, in spite of a brief period of anorexia after her husband died which had as much to do with grief as body image. Here is a woman apparently comfortable with her retro-deco physical presentation, even though she says she is sure she could be slimmer. They say women invent themselves. Gloria Steinem says we are all female impersonators! Carolyn very definitely looks like someone who paints her own portrait, and the private woman is in contrast with the frumpy Queen we see dressed up for her gig.

Instead of asking her how she felt about not eating here any more, I asked how she thought her life would be affected by the death of the incumbent. She fixed those steady blue eyes on me, a trick she learned from Diana, whom she met in the early days of Diana's marriage to Charles, and said, "The Queen is not about to die." As I stuck my fork in the voluptuous three-berry flan that followed the soup and wilted spinach salad, I thought it might be true. Those who know Brenda say she never eats dessert.

Carolyn has already survived the death of a partner and she knows the ways in which life is ephemeral. After her second husband, a pilot, died in a plane crash in the north where she had been teaching school, she took control of her life, learning martial arts, working out excessively at the gym, and deciding to transform herself once again.

If religion was not to be her salvation, then humour was. She is one of those quiet people who wait to say something interesting or funny. She might sit quietly and watch a hundred hats go by at a garden party before commenting, "Never wear a hat more interesting than you are." The only exception to intermittent wit is the intense tête-à-tête that is sometimes the trademark of a shy person.

Carolyn enchanted John, who says they will marry Thanksgiving weekend, 2004, their twentieth anniversary. They moved to Victoria and she became the Queen of special events

and television movies, which she loves because of the unreality of limousines and flowers in extravagant hotel rooms, things to giggle about with John, who calls her Binky.

I recently met them "on a mission" in the garden section at Capitol Iron. They were reluctant to reveal what the mission was, and I assumed it was to buy something toxic for their weeds. With much scuffing of her toes, Carolyn explained they were shopping for earthquake provisions. I felt I could be watching a rehearsed comedy sketch. Carolyn and John are like that. You always have the feeling they do a lot of laughing under the covers, just as the real Queen might giggle over her subjects in private.

There have been times when Carolyn and John, an archaeologist, have eaten beans. Now that they are entering an economic comfort zone, she looks amused when she tells you how she gets paid for the play-acting she has done for nothing since she was little and lonely. Security is important to her for obvious reasons. She has had the rug pulled out from under her.

Once it was purple. Doing a Queen gig during a Royal visit to Victoria, she made a gloved wave close to the face just as Prince Philip passed in the background and a photographer snapped. Somehow, the photo came out looking as though she was thumbing her nose at the Royal Stud. The town bullies went ballistic, making Carolyn, who thought Victoria was the last place on earth she would be shunned, believe that not only was no place like home, but home was no place. This has changed, but it took her wind when she realized how willingly the insecurities of childhood surface.

Carolyn has no children apart from the three-legged cat. She says it is difficult for the childless woman to measure life's transitions. There is no sudden absence of voices in her house, no grandchild to announce she is on the threshold of winter. To her this is strange and amorphous. When I asked her if she thought the aging process was easier on workers such as painters and musicians, who maintain an identity, as opposed to those who retire or grow out of parenting, she admitted her dream was to paint full-time again.

Carolyn's "park" in James Bay, the old part of Victoria, is as far away and as close as you can get in Canada from and to the grave of the husband who died in the other, northern James Bay. It is an English garden, with daisies, phlox, poppies, and Himalayan impatiens, the tall, thick-stalked perennial that attacks you with seed at the end of summer. There is a cottage at the back, her studio, a replica of the well-appointed house, where the painter will be born again. For now, its enigmatic walls are as blank as Carolyn's celestial blue irises.

For her party the evening of her birthday, the garden was decorated with lanterns and parasols and wicker furniture. Carolyn's hairdresser, Frederick, the author of her signature mahogany deco shingle, who has a reputation for transforming the lives of worshipful customers, presided over the triple fudge cake. Celtic musicians, a surprise from John, played under an ancient umbrella-shaped cherry tree. Carolyn, who keeps her sense of humour even on her birthday, handed Death by Chocolate on a plate adorned with the image of Queen Elizabeth to a singer from County Limerick in Ireland. "What Irish problem?" she responded when asked. Her timing is perfect.

In spite of the humiliating incident with Philip, with whom she was only trying to have fun, Carolyn has great affection for the royals. It is just that everything she likes has a funny side. This is how Carolyn has survived sadness.

When the sun went down on her July birthday, poet bill bissett shivered and Carolyn gave him the cosy sweater she wore mountain

climbing in Nepal. The sweater has magic, she said. She had been suffering from altitude sickness and somehow made it to the top, something she says she must always do, once she has set her mind on it. You have the feeling her house is at the top of the world.

As we filed out past her perennial border, Carolyn gave us a poem she had written. Beneath the last line—"It appears there are no choices when anticipation sizzles under the breastbone"—is a photo of the writer, fallen on her knees, ready for dubbing, or love, or a mountain.

DAISY DeBOLT

SINGER/SONGWRITER (1945, WINNIPEG [FORT ROUGE], MANITOBA–)

Daisy noticed she liked the adrenalin kick when she sang.

GODDESS IS THE WORD. Daisy DeBolt, five-oh, has gone AWOL from the Milton Acorn Festival with a handful of poets and our babysitter, Ojibwa artist Irv Marshall, who heard the beat of a different drum and took us to paradise PEI, a red beach, angel-blue sky, musical shells, and nipple-tightening sea. Les girls, Daisy, Sky Dancer, Paulette Dube, the omniscient first person present, and our muse, Newfie poet Al Pittman, smoke in one hand and a beer in the other, putting in good time before his quadruple bypass, have come down the road singing lyrics by Daisy at the tops of our metaphor-inflated lungs, shaking the proper windows in the proper white houses in Charlottetown, where the festival organizers are watching their watches and making out detention slips.

Daisy always shows up, but she gets there on her own terms. Herding kittens comes to mind. In my photo, she stands triumphant on the red beach wrapped in pink and yellow cotton and the jewelry of an Afghani queen, the sun behind her revealing the Rubensian shape of her legs. Daisy is holding a staff wrapped in seaweed. We call her Neptuna. She is the Boss Chick.

Daisy, Canada's pre-eminent blues diva, took charge the moment she emerged red-faced and bawling on a warm day in July, 1945. She already had a brother but this girl was what her mother wanted, a friend in music, a doll to dress. Daisy was one of those curls-and-tap-shoes kids with the homemade velvet outfits. She might have been a Shirley Temple clone. Her mum loved her to bits and taught her to play piano, accordion, guitar, your heartstrings, whatever came to mind.

Mum, who is now in her eighties and still playing music for "old people" in rest homes, was first chair violin in the Winnipeg Symphony and piano teacher to many a scrubbed and unwilling prodigy. It was lucky she worked so hard because Daisy's dad was a dreamer, and everyone knows your dreams don't all come true.

The eldest of twelve legitimate siblings and a baker's dozen sprinkled around western Canada, Daisy's dad left school in grade four to help support his younger brothers and sisters when his father allowed himself to be led north and west by the brainless voyageur between his legs. When it came time to parent himself, Daisy's old man had no time. He had full parental responsibility at the age of nine. All he knew was work and his dream of Eldorado, a dream life for the wife he adored, which ended when a car fell on him and severed his spinal cord.

He wasn't the only wounded in the house. The sun rose and set on Daisy. Her mother ran up matching mother and daughter outfits and doted on her golden girl, who was belting solos in local churches and tapping her feet to the popular recordings played at home. Her dad liked country and her mother big band. No one even saw her brother, until he made sure they noticed him by setting the house on fire. The DeBolts, descended from firebrand French Protestants, are a passionate lot!

Her father survived the terrible car accident, living on for twenty years as a paraplegic, but the accident did sever Daisy's dream of going to France and studying at the Sorbonne. Even though music was everyone's first love, Daisy wanted to design buildings because of primal experiences with her dad's carpentry, one thing he actually settled into at home. As her father resigned himself to the fact he would never walk again, Daisy gave up her dream of architecture, then art, and left home, where his depression had made life intolerable. She was only fifteen.

At this point, ambition pulled on two separate leashes. A retail job in Ladies' Wear at Eaton's led to an interest in dress design. Hanging around clubs gave her the impetus to become a diva. Daisy noticed she liked the adrenalin kick when she sang. She could and still can shake the foundation of any building with her big voice. Almost a Leo, she relishes her place in the sun. That time led to one of those fortuitous friendships with Lennie Breau, junkie and genius guitar player, who taught her the unique voicings and guitar changes that are her trademark, before he died in tragic and mysterious circumstances in Los Angeles.

She is the Boss Chick.

One year led to another, and Daisy found herself in the musical and emotional relationship that made her a hippie household name. As Fraser and DeBolt, she and Allan Fraser charmed the OshKosh overalls off the gumboot activists of the seventies. Their mutual passion and musicianship, Daisy's poetic and socially relevant lyrics, and her death-defying vocal range made them flavour of the decade until the decade and their relationship went sour.

She hit the sound barrier in what had become a deafening collaboration. Daisy recalls being onstage with Fraser one night and hearing a powerful silence, no music, nothing, the audience opening and closing their mouths like goldfish. When she heard the white sound of her own terror, she walked off the stage and out of that life.

Her feminist buttons were now attached to her trademark accordion. The next band was called "Don't Push Me Against the Fridge," and you can imagine the notes for that. The seventies were a great time for great names right from the primal source.

Meanwhile, the stunt vocalist who calls herself a white soul singer studied opera to improve her range and technique and continued her patterning after the great musical sculptors of black American music—Mahalia Jackson, Ella Fitzgerald, and Sarah Vaughan, among others. These were all powerful role models, mothers of invention.

Soon Daisy was a mother too. The man she now prefers to call "the sperm donor," an abusive academic, already had two sons. Daisy retreated to raise them and her own Jacob, born in July 1977. This accounts for a decade or two—mothering, gardening, cooking, some theatre work, and enough songs for an album, *Soul Stalking*, which came out at the end of the marriage.

I met Daisy when she was touring to promote the next album, a mantra, *I Can*, in 1994. She was back on the road. At that time, Daisy was playing ping-pong on the Internet, experimenting in collaborative songwriting with poets. She has written songs with Michael Ondaatje, Patrick Lane, and, of course, les girls.

Jake is a big boy now. When we were rising in a jetstream over PEI, sans Daisy who was getting back her own way, les girls placed their first airplane-to-ground phone call admonishing Jake to clean up before mommy got home. He did. Daisy threatens to take him on tour when his feet stop smelling. That could be any day now, and she says he has the family talent for music plus a technical edge.

Solidly into her fifties, Daisy still smokes. She has the energy to climb mountains and paddle rivers. She hopes, before she dies, to get rich enough not to worry and to find the one man who can get his teeth into a slice of sirloin diva.

Even though she grew up singing in churches, DeBolt is not attracted to the gospel lifestyle she could sing the pants off. Hers is a New Age approach to spirituality. She believes in the healing power of music and her large personality, which fills a room. She grows her vegetables in a neighbourhood garden and bikes in Toronto. This keeps her mind and body on the sixteen tracks she composes as she goes. She dreams about her own place in the country, where she would grow vegetables and feed a multitude of friends.

I'm just a country girl
Like it raw and steady
Like it early in the morning
Like it in the afternoon
When the sun comes down
I like it when all my friends are around

This is one of my granddaughter's favourite dancing songs. When Daisy hits the soaring

As Fraser and DeBolt, she and Allan Fraser charmed the OshKosh overalls off the gumboot activists of the seventies.

notes for "Paradise," Sophie's feet leave the ground.

When I asked Daisy about getting old, she said she wouldn't mind doing what her mother does, one day and one note at a time. She would, however, like to die in somebody's arms. That somebody is different every time we meet her. There is always a maybe man down the road, a possibility. She writes a heartbreaking grief song for every one of those travelling men.

Like many of the sixties women who traded their mothers' gloves and girdles for magic sandals and gypsy dresses, Daisy is paying the price of freedom. There is no pension waiting around the next corner and the old guys with guitars are rarely sugar daddies. The counterpoint to this is the amazing courage that has seen Daisy bury her lives and resurrect several times, thanks to the confidence she was given as a child by her adoring mother.

Daisy radiates the confidence of someone who has been properly loved at least once. She is comfortable in her body and in her music, which tells the story of adventurers who climb mountains just for the view. It is all about going up and coming down. Both sides make the other worthwhile and, for her, "The river always sings in E."

She said she wouldn't mind doing what her mother does, one day and one note at a time.

BARBARA PEDRICK

PHOTOGRAPHER (1947, KALAMAZOO, MICHIGAN–)

The Baptist girl from Kalamazoo packed up her stuff and went to find the idealism she had lost.

IF ELVIS IS DEAD, HOW COME we hear him every time we think back? In his album *Flaming Pie,* Paul McCartney explains why music and poetry refuse to lie down: "It always comes back to the songs we were singing at any particular time."

Barbara Pedrick, born in Kalamazoo, Michigan, a small town made famous by Orville Gibson, the stringed instrument manufacturer, has written the script for her life around music. The daughter of a hairdresser and a Baptist school superintendent, some of the notes were transposed by the tension of her parents' marriage.

There wasn't much to do in Kalamazoo between church and choir practice. When Barb and her sister and her girl cousins were old enough to drive, they took the car to choir practice, tooling around afterward, singing at the tops of their lungs. Barb's mother, who washed and set her daughters' hair, saved up and bought the girls a convertible, the closest their father let them get to dancing. Getting there is half the fun.

What he gave his daughters was the discipline that persists and gets them through crises, and a spirituality that extends beyond church to the music of the cosmos. When he laid down a life plan that included marriage and children, but excluded an education, and when Lyndon Johnson extended Kennedy's war in Vietnam, the Baptist girl from Kalamazoo packed up her stuff and went to find the idealism she had lost.

The generation that grew up in America in the fifties left it in the sixties. They tuned out and turned on. How could Jesus, who said, "Suffer the little children to come unto me," be on the side of people who bombed children with yellow skin and slanty eyes? Like thousands of young Americans during the psychedelic era, Barb turned against an idealism based on bigotry.

She says she has never been so angry as when Robert MacNamara, a Catholic on a heaven track, apologized in his autobiography for the arrogance and stupidity that sent a generation of kids either to war or damnation. The two names that still raise her blood pressure are Robert MacNamara and Billy Graham. She says she can't hear the evangelist's voice without having her stomach clench. Barb, her sisters, and her cousins all went to church on Sunday morning, but Sunday afternoon was for family fun at the lake, with the kids swimming and picnicking together. Baptists, however, can't have too much fun. On the drive back to town Sunday evening, Billy Graham was on the radio. She can remember looking out the window and crying. "What did hellfire have to do with being a good person?" she still asks.

Her life has been her response to that question as she wrestles with issues of morality and hypocrisy. Essentially ethical, she abhors dogma. It is a hard walk; in Barbara's case, a dance, forbidden to Baptists.

Years later, Barb, who left home after seeing Fonteyn and Nureyev on television, believing dance might be magic, blamed the red shoes that danced her into the culture of drugs and free love for the tragedy that tested her in the eighties and nineties. Everyone was reacting then, looking for new places to put love and trust when God and the country turned out to have feet of clay.

She is still dancing. A passion for flamenco, everything Spanish, the antithesis of her fundamentalist background, kept her second marriage, to a guitar player, going long past the death of infants and respect. Now Barbara is reaching that age when we see our parents every time we look in the mirror. When I met her, the music she conjured was operatic, perhaps Wagnerian. She wore her hair braided around her head. She could have been the twin of Amanda, her tall, blonde, adolescent daughter standing with her on the stairs at the opera. The opera should have been *Die Valkyrie,* but it was *La Cenerentola,* by Rossini, the story of Cinderella.

I originally thought there was something horsey, very stirrup cup, about Barbara. Later, I learned she and her polo-playing, former-hippie second husband, the guitar player, owned a company that gave carriage tours past the house of Emily Carr in James Bay, the Victoria old town. They also ran a bed and breakfast in their Victorian house. I was wrong. What I took for "good breeding," meaning family of pedigree and means, in Barbara Pedrick, née Blied, was the pioneer strength of Middle America, the backbone that comes from generations of trial and triumph over adversity and the weaknesses of the flesh. Even though Barbara has tested her weaknesses, the spirit persists.

A true daughter of rock and roll, one of the many transformed by American politics and music in the sixties, she could be the love child of Billy Graham and Carmen Miranda, so many are the contradictions in her background and nature. This could be the contest of her parents' marriage, "by the book" father versus spontaneous mother, which is also reflected in her photography, at its best when technical competence gives way to the serendipitous moment.

The name of everybody who was anybody in Greenwich Village or Haight Ashbury in the sixties drops off her tongue like honey from Moroccan bees. Taking pictures in New York or working in THE radio station in San Francisco, she met absolutely everyone passing through their fifteen minutes of fame.

The photographer says the first time she made love, she was listening to "Four Strong

Winds" by Ian Tyson. The title, based in the religion of our indigenous people, is also an anthem for a generation of spiritual nomads who have been searching for the certainty that was given as their birthright and taken when they collectively lost their innocence.

Barb's exodus from "America and My Right" had taken her and her suitcase and camera to the baths and bazaars of Morocco, where she met her first husband, a Dutchman, then to Holland, and finally to Salt Spring Island in Canada, where Dan Pedrick, the polo player, was playing in a string band Barb happened upon. She must have danced well, because their daughter was born eighteen months after his daughter, Heron, whose mother later died in a house fire. Barb says she loved Dan's guitar playing and he made her laugh. Her Baptist father did not attend that wedding either.

Now her daughter Amanda is grown and attending art school, and Barbara is facing fallout from the sixties, a liver biopsy, which is causing her to confront death; hard when you are facing a new beginning after divorce. It is not a new tune in her life. Shortly before I met her, she lost twin daughters at birth, cords wrapped around their tiny necks. When the twins were born, they were shown to

Barbara and twelve-year-old Amanda, and then photographed together, the way they went to paradise. Barb has never looked at that picture, but she says she takes comfort in knowing someone cared to record the tiny girls before they were buried. She sees them in the children she photographs.

It is the pictures of children that stand out: my granddaughter, naked, peeking around her father's sculpture of a serpent; or my friend Ann West's daughter, Jaima Yates, lifting her skirt and laughing outside the old wooden church in Saanich where she was recently married. The serpent is in all of them.

Shortly after her children died, Barb discovered she had breast cancer. She kept her breast and underwent therapy. Until that time she had been an insomniac. The marijuana tea that was prescribed to combat the nausea of chemotherapy gave her the gift of sleep. She says she relinquished control at that point to whatever higher power was her destiny. She remembers a great serenity in that decision, giving herself up to rest, even if it meant eternal sleep.

When she was offered the option of removing the radiation scar on her neck, she refused. She decided it was better to confront her demons and wear them as trophies than

Her mother is dead now, and Barbara is honouring the woman who brought out feminine beauty her own way.

back down or pretend to ignore them as women did in the fifties, when she was growing up.

Barbara recently felt her angel fly over twice in one week. The first was a bittersweet encounter on the Internet with Leonard Cohen, who e-mailed a poem from his Buddhist retreat at Mount Baldy, California. The second was the sad announcement of the death of Linda McCartney in Santa Cruz, California. McCartney, who died surrounded by her family, had taken her candid photographs to the stratosphere of fame and had found a happy family life. She had made living with cancer inspirational, her chemo haircut an emblem of faith.

Barbara's radiation burns are beautiful, as are her photographs of women, all of them proud of the scars, visible and invisible, that inform their art. In the process of researching this book, we have discovered so much to admire in and behind the faces illuminated by her flash. We were so excited when each subject in turn admired the portraits of her predecessors. We hoped each would see what we found beautiful in her. As Barbara worked, I saw her look for the compassionate angle, the one in which the subject could comfortably be herself.

Like most of the women she photographed, Barbara's relationship with her mother is central to her life and work. Barbara's mother, living in that particular box which was post-war America, repressed the wild side that became her daughter, working at hairdressing, an acceptable job for an artistic woman, and secretly imbibing when her Baptist husband turned his back.

Her mother is dead now, and Barbara is honouring the woman who brought out feminine beauty her own way, with brushes and curlers. She is taking pictures and cherishing her friendships, particularly with her sister Leslie, daughter Amanda, and stepdaughter Heron, anchors in the winds of change.

COMFORT ADESUWA

POET AND ACTIVIST (1947, UDO, NIGERIA–)

Comfort is a traditional mother, struggling to maintain the old values in her new home.

"COMFORT" IS *oyibo*, white man's name. Adesuwa, a Nigerian political refugee, comes from a family revolutionized by Christianity. In her heart, where she is the daughter of Africa and an Edo chief, she is Adesuwa, her home name.

In Canada, where she is living, she hopes temporarily, Comfort is most often Comfort, her identity permutating as she adjusts to a new climate and new political and social realities under the sponsorship of the Anglican Church. Still, in her head and her Cridge Centre, Victoria, apartment home, she is her father's daughter, thinking in her mother tongue, one of the many dialects she understands.

Emigration is only one more adaptation in a life constantly challenged by a changing Africa. Comfort wrote:

The new African child is born
unto a crossroad of confusion.
His all frail and laboured being
is geared to just one need
Bread!

Comfort was one of nine children in the family of a hereditary leader and a mother who converted to Catholicism after marriage. While her father maintained paternalistic tribal traditions, her mother asserted a revolutionary attitude, the freedom of women to choose their own form of worship. Comfort went to an Anglican school in her village and later to Catholic school and university in the neighbouring city of Benin. Her origin in the autocratic ruling class of her culture was moderated by the Christian influence. In the hymns of her childhood were sewn the seeds of humanitarianism, her coming of age. There is no sign of arrogance in this woman born to entitlement, only a sense of responsibility to others.

At university, where she studied French with the intention of teaching, she met her husband, a research scientist specializing in agriculture. They have six children.

I first met Comfort at a poetry reading at Glenlyon Norfolk School. She introduced herself as a poet hungry for contact with other writers and meaningful work, which she has since found in Lina de Guevara's acting company, a collection of émigrés anxious to identify themselves in the new society they have abruptly entered.

At home, Comfort was a member of the National Conscience of Nigeria, an organization persecuted by the military dictatorship because of its advocacy of free speech. The president, Ken Saro Wiwa, was executed by the state.

I thought of my friend Susan Musgrave, Chair of the Writers' Union of Canada, and myself, President of the League of Canadian Poets, and the potential consequences of free expression in a totalitarian country, where advocacy, which is our job description, could be perceived as treason punishable by death. This is the atmosphere in which Comfort was

Homesickness is a debilitating affliction for émigrés who must work vigorously to establish themselves in a new environment.

raising her bright and responsible young family of six.

In her stories about life in Africa, Comfort wrote about children scrounging for food in nuisance grounds, the refuse dumps where vultures are the natural predators and poor families leave their dead children wrapped like Christmas parcels to protect them from desecration. She says there are no benefits for the Nigerian poor and hospitalization is only effective for those who can provide their own medical supplies. Those without have only the compassion of overworked staff to rely on at times of illness and injury.

There is no coherent social plan in post-colonial Nigeria, an oil-exporting country where the rich get richer as the poor get poorer. Comfort's response to these inequities is poetry, and poetry that questions the status quo in Nigeria is silenced by the most severe forms of censorship, banishment and death.

Comfort is in Canada, ostensibly, to educate her children. The second-eldest attended Lester B. Pearson College, where lucky students, potential leaders of their countries, are translated from all corners of the Commonwealth of Nations to the woods of British Columbia and given an opportunity to learn in a privileged microcosm of the Global Village. The real reason is that her family is at risk in a volatile political situation.

I had one of her younger children in a creative writing class one recent summer. I.K., as she is known because her peers in Canada have trouble pronouncing her melodious given name, Ikponmwosa, was experiencing culture shock. At the age of fifteen, she was bearing the added weight of making life's most difficult transition from adolescence to adulthood in a new culture, one which pays little respect to the wisdom of elders, which is the foundation of Edo society.

Comfort is a traditional mother, struggling to maintain the old values in her new home. When she writes of her own mother, she describes her ideal self.

Scolding she does
with love undertones.
Her kingdom is every part of the home.
With joy she sings and dances,
as each little one is rocked to sleep
to a sweet and gentle lullaby
on her soft and sweaty back.
She is a queen, my mother.

One wet afternoon, Comfort assured Barb and me that as soon as the totalitarian regime is brought down, she will return to her homeland, where the joyous colours of her descriptive writing are as fresh as rare summer mornings in our rainforest.

The rooster rushes in ahead
of its coo-coo chicks hurrying to the homestead.
The wingless sun is aglow,
sinking in the quicksand of time, steady and slow.
It throws its glowing orange and gold tongues
in slow pale thrusts
kissing warmly the earthbrown rafters
that crown the village huts with laughter.

Homesickness is a debilitating affliction for émigrés who must work vigorously to establish themselves in a new environment. It saps the energy. Comfort struggles with the inevitable depression that comes from events as basic as the weather. To someone used to sunlight, the lack of it is a serious deprivation. In order to keep her family functional, she wills herself to transcend sorrow. Writing and acting are her tools. In explaining her African homeland, she keeps it alive in herself and alerts the world to its exploitation.

This determination is given impetus by the ongoing tragedy of her homeland, an oil-rich country with criminal poverty. The suspicious death of political prisoner Moshood Abiola and subsequent riots underline the importance of her advocacy for humanitarian reform. There is no doubt in Comfort's mind about her mandate as a writer. When I asked if she had written love poems and would like to be part of a Valentine's Day reading, her expression became ironic. Who had time for erotic poetry in a country where children were starving and civil war was normal? My question hung in the air like a piece of frivolous lace around a box of chocolates.

In Edo culture, the ritual language and practices are fixed. Her permission to write political poetry comes from her Christian self, the Christian-Judaic tradition of theological debate. She is her mother's daughter as much as her father's, believing the two are ultimately compatible because both are based in high principles.

This is the year Comfort turned fifty, and there is so much work to be done she has hardly given any thought to the personal implications. She lives for her children and for the future of Africa, where her descendants will have a better life in community if her voice is heard and acted upon. Wrinkles and waistlines take up about as much space in her inventive mind as love poems. She loves her

She lives for her children and for the future of Africa.

country. Her children are part of its tradition and its future. Evolution is her mission.

Finding African food, the plantains and yams that populate her stories and poems about hunger, is a problem in Canada. When Comfort took a break from rehearsing with Lina de Guevara's acting company to have lunch in a deli with Barbara and me, her longing for the African market was palpable as she made her slow choice from an unfamiliar menu. The grey sky of west coast winter weighs heavy upon her. Like a nursing mother separated from her infant, her voice has the flat edge of desperation. Africa is her mother and she in turn is compelled to mother her. That is the dialectic her heart knows.

When we returned from lunch, the troupe began to familiarize themselves with papier mâché masks they had made from their own faces the day before. There was music. As she danced into the mask, the transformation of Comfort to Adesuwa was amazing. A young black woman with sensitive body language stayed close, as if to protect her. Another actor approached and picked at her sweater the way our primate ancestors groomed one another in recognition of family bonds.

This is the beginning of storytelling, Susan Musgrave recently told me. We begin by picking fleas and evolve to gossip, refined social behaviour. Our curiosity about one another is the precursor to community.

As her body slowly released itself from the self-conscious social posture of the *étranger*, she became a graceful dancer, a woman at home in herself. There is one reason why the Nigerian poet is living and working among us, spreading the message of tolerance in our schools with de Guevara's troupe. "Who will bell the cat?" is the question that ends a political story by Comfort Adesuwa. You know perfectly well she does.

Africa is her mother and she in turn is compelled to mother her.

LYNDA RAINO

DANCER (1948, VANCOUVER, BRITISH COLUMBIA–)

Lynda developed an early sense of community.

DANCER LYNDA RAINO has been surprising people from day one. During the months she shared a womb with her twin sister, Sandy, they were to be the large, wanted boy who came after two girls. Because there was only one noticeable heartbeat, the twins' premiere appearance was a sensation that was only upstaged, at last, by the birth of a mid-life baby brother.

One of seven at dinner and one of the gang in a working-class neighbourhood, Lynda developed an early sense of community, something that has dictated her grassroots approach to art. She is still involved in the ongoing familial dialogue.

Her father was a jazz musician who died of a heart attack while making love to his wife when Lynda was seventeen. In her kinesthetic mind, she sees his translation from one ecstasy to another, the music of conjugal pleasure linking this world to the next. This is the gestalt of her own gestures that link the life cycle to other realities, animal and spiritual. Her mother, a Scots midwife, gave practical mothering to her half-Italian brood through the sixties; they came out the other end rooted in family and committed to ideals that many flower children have long since forsaken. It is the family that has centred Linda and been her focus no matter what it cost in terms of professional opportunity. Her dance, however, is informed by this groundedness which is the only springboard to abstract ideas.

Music was the matrix of the Raino family and the kids, raised Christian and taught music by their father, sang in churches through their childhood. Lynda always had an urge to move to the music, but, in a struggling family with five children to feed and clothe, there was no extra money for lessons. Instead, she expended her supernatural energy in free recreation, every sport imaginable.

Being members of a pair did not mean the girls ever did anything by halves. Lynda was the whole body, her sister the whole brain. If Lynda was moving through air, Sandy was navigating. Lynda says being a twin and a mother are the raw materials of her being. The twin part has meant an extraordinary relationship with another human being, but it has had its downside. Lynda expected the world to reveal itself through intuition, the way she and her sister communicate. This naïveté is beautiful, but it has led to disappointment and, sometimes, to the failure of relationships in which she expected nothing less than the mutual understanding that defines the twin-sisterly friendship.

In high school, Lynda dressed up and crossed the tracks to meet the politically aware in coffee houses of West Vancouver, her Valhalla. Revolution is the privilege of the middle class. Most of the neighbourhood kids were working too hard to notice the world was undergoing a violent change in its attitudes toward human rights. Lynda listened to the folk singers of the sixties and determined she too would effect change, but she wasn't yet sure exactly how.

After her father's death, she and Sandy were able to go to university, thanks to bursaries from the Department of Veterans' Affairs. Lynda chose recreation as a major and lasted until she was faced with a choice between dance and university. The decision made itself. She had begun dance classes with Paula Ross and was immediately recognized as a soloist. School soon became an irritating interruption in her new routine of rehearsal and performance. In dance, she could articulate the stories that had always been pre-empted by her more verbal twin. Sandy was the mouth, she says. But the body had a voice of its own.

She has not stopped speaking. A "literal dancer," Lynda tells the stories everyone knows. Through her movement, audiences are connected to their own feelings. The reaction is always emotional. This is what she wants. Any artist who only speaks to the mind is telling half the story. For Lynda, every movement is literal. What she learned to intuit, sister to sister, now has a broader base in her understanding of human behaviour and its reflection in body language.

In 1968, she moved to Montreal, then the culture capital of Canada. She did her first work as a choreographer for Les Ballets Modernes du Quebec, whereupon she was

Lynda was the whole body, her sister the whole brain.

fired for the impact of her work, which upstaged that of the current director. How often do we encounter that scenario? From Lynda Raino to Carol Shields, I hear the same story. To transpose the Victorian shibboleth about children: "Women are better seen than heard." Lynda is a half-full glass person, and so she took from that experience the lesson of her success rather than indulging in bitterness over the unfairness of artistic politics or male domination of dance.

She took her optimism to Shango Dance Circus, where she had artistic freedom, enjoying the days of subsidy when one new work after another was supported by Local Initiatives Program grants. Those were the times when Canadians were eager to support the quest for a Canadian artistic identity.

Lynda stopped riding her notorious motorcycle long enough to meet the father of her children, a Chinese-American architect. She says she determined early on to have mixed-race children because she thought that was the only way to end intolerance. It may take more than that gesture, but it is true that Paolo and Sorell, the children of grace, represent the best of both worlds. In any case, Lynda, with her Scots-Italian parents, is the

balanced result of intercultural breeding herself.

Lynda has always had an issue with size. She is not a tall person, but neither is she a bird, the ideal shape for ballet. All the lessons in the world have not changed the fact that she has flat feet, bowed legs, and a full woman's body, whereas the contemporary archetype for a dancer is something on the other side of starvation. She has been through the low self-esteem and starvation visited upon dancers, but she had the wisdom to realize early that many dancers burn out physically because they do not nourish the body or the spirit. Neurosis about body type has destroyed many dancers and many human beings. It is a plague among adolescent women in our culture, and Lynda is doing her best to dispel those notions that ruin a woman's self-worth.

At Lynda Raino Dance, students are encouraged to celebrate their bodies, whatever age or shape. At a time when anorexia is rampant among dancers and gymnasts, it is a valuable model. Recently she has had a big-boned dancer with a "shrinking" body language as a student. "Be Big!" Lynda has been telling her. "You are the spokesperson for the undiminished." Pride is the essence of her message to her students and her audience. "Like yourself and the world will like you."

When Lynda was pregnant with Paolo, she made the decision that she would have a life *and* art as opposed to a life in art. Lynda says she never regretted her choice. She says that was the Turning Point and reminded me of the movie. She had the Shirley MacLaine part. Her professional sisterhood with Margie Gillis, who made the other decision, is a valuable reference point as she experiences life's transitions. As both women transform from the procreative to creative plateaus, Lynda realizes she has "had it all," and that her art is enriched by the ongoing experience of motherhood.

Although Lynda is well known in this country and in dance circles internationally, she does not have the immediate recognition of artists who choose fame over family. In the end, when the world looks away, a lucky woman has her children with her.

Her relationship with the architect ended during her second pregnancy, and she opted to live in Victoria because her family had moved to the Garden City. Her first professional appearance here was a performance, seven months pregnant, of *Mother Moon,* an event no one who saw it has

But the body had a voice of its own.

forgotten. She is known as an artist who takes the ordinary and makes it extraordinary. Such mundane occurrences as folding diapers and sleeping beside a snoring husband become metaphors for absolutes in the life cycle. We are trapped in our bodies and our lives. Music is the medium for transcendence and dance the expression of desire. Lynda has taken her universal interpretation of the human condition as far abroad as Japan and Brazil, where she performed at the Theatre of the Oppressed Festival.

While there, she was able to translate "politically correct" into the international language of humour. A natural satirist with a gift for timing and sensitivity to the physical business at the root of humour, she finds her greatest satisfaction in the funny pieces. Humour is the matrix of change as the impossible is translated into the possible. Lynda has often been asked if she studied with Charlie Chaplin. This is the highest compliment, given that Chaplin had a genius for understanding human behaviour and the social awareness to bring it to our attention. Her Chaplinesque *Cruelty of Ballet,* performed in a cross-Canada tour, exposed all the rigid conventions of that art form to ridicule. She did the fat dancer, the sexual dancer, and the non-stereotypical female dancer, hoisting her tutu-ed male partner to the delight of audiences.

There have been many collaborations, in particular with her friend Constantine Darling. Constantine is the cerebral dancer and she the intuitive. The partnership, which ended in 1983, was greater than the sum of its parts, satisfying to both of them.

Lynda says the summits of her professional and personal lives have been appearances with her sons. She joined Paolo, who has been studying jazz at Malaspina College (which produced Diana Krall, among others), in *The Wall,* a gymnastic piece in which she collaborated with choreographer Debbie Brown. She also appeared with both Sorell and his brother in a performance of *Romeo and Juliet.* This was the circle of completion that meant more to her than curtain calls in the theatre of ambition.

Pushing herself beyond what can reasonably be expected on a forty-something physical apparatus, Lynda damaged her back and is now in chronic pain, with nerve damage to her legs and feet. While that has done nothing to slow down her teaching and choreography, it does limit her motion. My sense of her recent work is that it is similar to

Pride is the essence of her message to her students and her audience.

the unfinished sculpture of Michelangelo, all the more eloquent for its limitations. We struggle with what we have.

The same aesthetic motivates her teaching. She takes what her students have and brings it out in appropriate movement. Her Big Dance class, a group of soft-built women, who are not above self-parody, a judgement on the world for judging them, has changed the conventional wisdom about what constitutes a dancer. The group has been invited to perform in Europe and this is a great source of satisfaction to Lynda, who believes dance is for everyone, every shape and size and age.

As she deals with aging, particularly with the physical limitations that puts upon her, she is determined to express the meaning of life in movement that tells her story. She has experienced menopause and injury. Her children are leaving home. There are many dances in the life cycle.

Mid-life sexuality is a reason to celebrate. Raino remembers her father and his beautiful death. Her mother has just died, the way an Italian widow is supposed to pass on, dressed for a reconciliation with the husband who died in her arms. Lynda herself has been given the gift of a new love, Paul, a significant name,

Her recent work is similar to the unfinished sculpture of Michelangelo, all the more eloquent for its limitations.

whom she met in the hospital during her recovery.

In her nomination letter for Lynda's Women of Distinction Award, director Glynis Leyshon described her "work embraced as dance an act of joy, much like the brilliant paintings of Matisse, a joy unfettered by strict classical shapes and vocabularies" and gave the highest praise to her teaching. "Her task is not just to impart a physical vocabulary but to free the creative soul in each of her students, allowing them to grow not just as dancers but as men and women."

Leyshon had collaborated with Raino and author Rachel Wyatt on *A Leg to Stand On,* the theatre piece that celebrated Lynda's return from the hell of physical infirmity. That piece and *Saying Goodbye to My Brother,* a duet she choreographed for herself and Shawn Costello, who was soon to die of AIDS, was one of many memorable moments in the theatre that Lynda has created to raise public awareness of suffering. Her career is highlighted by such moments, when the most powerful muscle in the human body is the true soloist.

SUSAN MUSGRAVE

POET (1951, SANTA CRUZ, CALIFORNIA TO CANADIAN PARENTS, FOURTH-GENERATION VANCOUVER ISLANDERS–)

"You are not mad,"

the wise man told her.

"You are a poet."

THE VERY MOMENT Mother Teresa breathed her last and the hearse carrying the Princess of Wales drove through the gates of Kensington Palace in London, poet Susan Musgrave talked to me about what these things meant to her as we parked her art car for a photographer in downtown Victoria. Susan's car, covered in the icons that decorate shrines in other parts of the world, makes people smile as she drives by. It is an idiosyncratic representation of the risks she takes to prove to herself and others that she is alive.

Mother Teresa said we must all do something beautiful for God. There is nothing more beautiful in our age of unreason than a car covered with the faces of dolls and the reactions of people on the street. Reaction is Susan's oeuvre.

we scream the vowels
of freedom,
the wheel tracks freshen
as hell falls through—

When Wiccan poet Robin Skelton died, Susan reminded the world that he had visited her in hospital when everyone else had decided she was a mad adolescent. "You are not mad," the wise man told her. "You are a poet." Robin did many good deeds, not the least of which was including Susan in his own family and encouraging her gift. Good deeds are the stock-in-trade of those who believe in reincarnation, for, whatever else Susan Musgrave may be, she is someone who fixes her karma in incantations that wash and sting and sometimes heal a wounded planet.

Let's not invent any more weapons.
Let's grope in the fog
wearing coarse underwear instead.
Let's be kind to one another
and let's not write any more hate poetry.

Let's pretend we're in love with one another.
You go first.

In fearless poetry that uses humour or horror, whatever it takes, to unmask herself and the reader, Susan digs for the bare truth, even in her own family relationships.

But when you told me you loved me less
I didn't know how to cure it.
The bed became smaller than cruelty
with just enough room for the two of us
and the night came over me
like a backhand over the mouth
like my father with steak blood
in the corner of his mouth
holding up a photograph of his
shy, wild daughter.

Characteristically, she does not wear makeup, but she does cover her television with a Connemara widow's shawl. Because her integrity is legendary—"we just sit around telling the truth about everything"—we assume this has to do with aesthetics as opposed to dissembling intellectual snobbery. Now, my husband and I NEVER watch television. Our set, so large it would require the death shroud of Mama Cass to cover it, is for movies only. However, we did recently happen upon a Knowledge Network documentary on the last days of the Raj. There, in living colour, was a mad and beautiful maharanee living in her empty palace with only a starving dog for company. That could be Susan, we said in unison. There is something of the fallen aristocrat about Musgrave. No matter how tarty her leathers, her zippers, and outrageous silver jewelry, Susan could still be the déclassé mistress of some austere castle on the moors.

I once said to her husband, novelist and retired "gentleman of spirit" Stephen Reid, "Susan would be using linen napkins in a mud hut." Double damask tablecloths and candles in silver sticks. Susan, whose personality and genius contest for public attention, is a ritualist. Wicca, the healing art taught by the older poet who visited her when she was in the hospital, is part of her country heritage and complementary to Susan's life in the great rainforests of British Columbia. Friendship with Skelton led to a job babysitting Robin and Sylvia's children and her first love, poet Seán Virgo, who took her to the Queen Charlottes to live.

If Susan has become a personality, it is because she is a woman of her time, a grace note to the period in history that preceded the Whitecomers. She is the wild white woman of the woods, a mask that speaks poetry. It is interesting that her husband is part Ojibwa, connected by birth to her adopted aboriginal mythology, which resonates with the English pagan in her DNA.

The antlered ghosts of my ancestors were
vanishing; I envied them their shifty universe.

One of four children, Musgrave grew up in a colonial family at the end of Empire. Her father, who read to her as a child, willing her first delight in language, was also a yachtsman who relished the captain's authoritarian prerogatives and gave her a lasting distaste for boats, surprising in someone so identified with the wilful landscape of her homeland.

Susan's own wildness is part inherent, part crafted. Although she presents herself as an intuitive personality, her decision making is a neurotic process. She is a very good cook who occasionally takes direction and follows recipes ("mostly while baking—the rest flows from my fridge") and a poet who researches every allusion, every detail of pleasure.

Currant bread, simnel cake and
coloured eggs were eaten on the
picnic. Oh, it was a good
picnic, an elegant one.

We spread the ground with food
for the beautiful women.

Even the humorous anecdotes that make her a popular public personality are crafted with care. When I recently taught her creative writing class, I was amazed at her detailed instructions and copious teaching notes. Musgrave's poems, bursting with surreal energy, are architectural wonders. Even her e-mails are works of art. A recent one described the heart as a "lonely muscle" as she recounted her dream of a bicycle ride with her husband in watery English meadows. "We liked being lost," she wrote, echoing her aesthetic credo that art is about loss.

There are some who believe more time is spent on the persona of the sea witch than on the craft of writing. The reality is that Susan has worked to help support herself and her children, Charlotte and Sophie, since she was hardly more than a child herself. In a world that does not reward poets, this is unusual. It takes a lot of the proverbial lame gigs, time-sucking jobs with negligible pay, to retire a mortgage, as Susan and Stephen did in the beach ceremony that also saw his parole warrant go up in smoke in the summer of 1996.

Stephen lost his lucky amethyst bracelet, a gift from Susan, when he was thrown into the water by writer friends celebrating his successful evolution from con man to family man. That evening Susan, a keeper of amulets, fretted at the shoreline with a flashlight until the tide returned it.

Susan has two daughters. Charlotte is a ringer for supermodel Kate Moss, and Sophie, like her mother, has the gift of tongues. One hot day, she told me she needed a drink RIGHT NOW because her throat was dry and her blood felt like sand sifting through her veins. She once saw crows flying out of her eyes. This is how poets talk at age eight. Robin Skelton must have heard this when he found her unhappy parent crouched over a typewriter in the hospital, where sensitivity sent her.

Perhaps the approval seeking that is an ingredient in the personality of most artists comes from the ongoing dynamic of the perennial adolescent. Susan says her search for identity has less to do with approval seeking than disapproval seeking. In everything she does, she looks for the strong reaction. That reaction is evidence of the moral order for which she must have empirical proof. For all her audacity—the nude photograph and damaging article that are the subjects of an ongoing legal conflict, the surprising elopements and marriages to two outlaws and one criminal lawyer, the outspoken

There is something of the fallen aristocrat about Musgrave.

frankness—Musgrave is a vulnerable person who, when not performing, is uncomfortable in a crowd, wearing a mask of crusty humour to deflect hurt.

It is hard to believe that there is an agonized private face to the relaxed and witty public performer glowing in the flashbulbs, a face she so frankly reveals in the poems. A writer's writer, Susan is, in spite of her stunning theatrical presentation, uncomfortable with ambition. She is known among writers as an enthusiastic supporter and was elected president of the Writers' Union of Canada based on that confidence. In a country where few artists are rewarded for their work and literary rivalry is legendary, this is not the norm.

Susan reduces almost every aspect of human behaviour to humour, self-parody not excluded. When the idea of the art car germinated in the wake of Lorna Crozier's purchase of a shiny new Miata convertible, I got a phone call. Would I come over, preferably with my glue gun, preferably with my granddaughter and her toys? Susan wanted to decorate her, oh, let's be charitable, near-beater with toys and glitter. Susan's car, beautifully appointed, is characteristically attracting a lot of attention. Some might say Susan has a genius for publicity. And they would be right. Susan would say her car is a poem in progress. She would be right too.

Even though Musgrave's ancestors are from the other side of the Irish Sea, it is Ireland that has called her from those early moments in childhood when she knew she was different and began to cultivate the difference. Long before Celtic mythology began to be marketed in pop culture, she was attracted to the greening ruins of that ancient culture where there are spells for everything, and every word uttered is poetry, whether it is expressed in blasphemy or prayer.

Recently, several of Susan's friends and fellow poets have gone to spirit, creating the need for a new genre in the Musgrave canon. For Charles Lillard, Robin Skelton, and bibliophile Bill Hoffar there are the grace notes of jewelled obituaries, every facet shone by the poet who takes care with everything from her legendary scones to her footnotes.

I have reached an age where even a spring rain falling on spring ground can make me less of what I am. So I told her then what I've tried to believe in my life, that we don't have to die, ever. Victorious she turned to me, like the flowers of this world, the brilliance sliding from her.

"We liked being lost," she wrote, echoing her aesthetic credo that art is about loss.

Her own famous last words are always on her mind. She stays out of the sun and keeps her medical dictionary beside her cookbook. Mordant and morbid have their roots in food and death; humour is the leaven of a morbid imagination. Susan has probably filed her obituary in the recipe file under M. In the meantime, she promises to take that black Irish shawl off her TV set and wear it to celebrate the moment she steps into cronehood. We will keep our eyes on it as she sits behind the wheel of her art car, fringes in the wind, going wherever it takes her.

Hot damn says Jane.
We hoof it.

YOU COULD UNDERSTAND THIS

I'm reading your book, the part
where your mother's life being too much
for him, your father takes a gun
from the trunk of the car and empties it
in her head, and she dies slowly, then he
shoots himself and that's only the beginning
of the first chapter

when suddenly I hear crying
at the front door and I look up
and it's my own parents standing there,
pleading with me to let them come in.

For thirty-five years I've been unable
to let them in. Come in
I say to my father, who loved the sea.
Come in I say to my mother
who looks like me.

And then—after all those years—
I don't know what else to say to them.
You could understand this.
So I look at my mother and say, "How's
it been?" And my mother replies only,
"He's going to leave me, finally."

I look at my father. "She says she wants me
to go," he whispers.
                    After all those years
your mother wants her life back

and suddenly you understand
your father. Forgive him. And then the world
stops, with tears on its young face.
The world comes to an end.
Or it just keeps on.

SUSAN MUSGRAVE

SHEILA RYAN

SINGER AND SONGWRITER (1953, COUNTY LIMERICK, IRELAND–)

"You had to be

there to

understand."

YOU'D THINK SHE WAS QUEEN of the Land, sipping tea on the grand front porch of her stone mansion right across the street from Government House, Victoria, where the Lieutenant-Governor of British Columbia entertains the Royal Family and waves to Sheila when he drives by in his big fancy car.

The fact is Sheila Ryan, folk singer and songwriter from County Limerick, Ireland, rents out every bedroom from basement to attic, including the one she shares with her husband, when the bed and breakfast trade is brisk. There is a rumour that Sheila will sleep under the majestic dining room table when necessary.

Necessity is the mother of invention, and Sheila has invented a life that would seem a fairy tale to the girl she used to be, back home. "You had to be there to understand," an Irish friend once told me when I asked her what

made Sheila—who runs before breakfast, cooks the full Anglo-Irish, swims around the island in the middle of Thetis Lake with her friend Finola Fogarty, makes beds, writes a song, and then puts on one of her green lacy gowns and does a concert in a typical day—tick, which is the way Sheila pronounces "thick."

Ryan, who will tell you cream rises to the middle, was born lower middle, number eight of a dozen in a dairy-farming family in County Limerick. One of many, she learned early about hard work and sharing, responsibilities that only come to many of us with the prerogatives of adulthood.

Sheila's father, older than her mother, a dairymaid from the farm next door who bore his first child when she was hardly more than a child herself, was a hard-working, typical Irishman. He gave his children the rough love that has to be shared twelve ways, along with the bread and the shoes and the Saturday bath. Sheila's slice came in the barn, where he taught her the songs she still sings while they milked the cows together.

Singing was their bond. Her father sang in church and in the pub where he played cards several nights a week. Years later, when he died, the nuns prevented her from singing a song at his funeral, a song she had written especially for him. This last cruelty of nuns who made her childhood miserable will be on the list at their day of judgement, when Sheila just might be the one who decides who is in and who out of the holy choir. No doubt the finger of expulsion will also be pointed at old Master Daily, the teacher/cleric who cleaned his ears and nails in class and beat his scholars with a bamboo stick when they forgot their catechism.

There was no money for music lessons. Sheila taught herself to play guitar and harp later on, to accompany herself in Canada. The word "conservatory" never passed her lips, but she did mention a *maison lumière* to her father, a vision she had of a big house where music was played and performed all day long. The farmer shrugged and kept milking.

There was no money for music lessons.

Her mother, who stayed home like other Irish women while their husbands socialized in the pub, whistled. Sheila remembers the dairymaid who left school at eleven was a good whistler. When I suggested it might have been the frustrated release of tuneful air, something I remember my mother doing when she was upset, Sheila said she hadn't thought of it. She missed her mother's whistling, comforting as a tea kettle, when she was gone.

They say you lose a tooth for every child. Sheila's mother had none of hers. Teeth were for church only. Every Sunday, her mother put in her dentures and painted a red circle around her mouth. She endured the annual ritual of babies and Catholic misogyny beyond the palliative effect of whistling until she called a taxi and left, leaving the children's morning porridge lumping up on the stove.

The townspeople speculated about what Mrs. MacDonald might be doing. The truth was she was over the water, in London, taking care of rich people and rich people's houses, being paid for her drudgery and feeling validated for the first time in her life. At school, the nuns silently taught the other students to isolate Sheila, who now had total responsibility for caring for the younger children. Excluded by grief and stigmatization, and missing her mother, Sheila cried herself to sleep every night until the day she married, when she was nineteen.

There were moments of relief in a life of hard work and social ostracism. Sheila was an athlete, good at sports like grass hockey, and on St. Stephen's Day, when according to custom, Irish children carrying branches festooned with ribbons canvas the citizens for treats, she was the stellar one. "Sing us a song, Sheila" was the most frequent request and the small freckled daughter of sorrow broke their hearts with her pure tone, earning herself the extra pennies. It must have been hard singing for the very parents who taught their children to shun the daughter of iniquity, an Irish mother who left.

Never one to sit still and read, it is understandable that books remind Sheila of school and the frequent humiliation of children who share a bed and rationed food. "I move, therefore I am" might be her reason for being and the only exit from the grey, low-ceilinged rooms of her childhood.

When Sheila and her husband Frank met and fell in love, his family warned him about her pedigree, to which he properly replied, "It is the daughter I am marrying." After a short period of domesticity in Limerick, where they learned charity and religion are not necessarily synonymous in Irish culture, the new family of three emigrated to Canada, where many of our ancestors arrived with good reason for leaving home. Frank and Sheila were determined to transcend their parochial childhoods. For them, Canada was the Promised Land.

As landed immigrants, they blarneyed their way into bank loans and began to build a life, first in Fort St. John, where he developed real estate until a brief recession in the early eighties wiped them out. As if that weren't enough, Sheila and her children were in a car accident that has left her still struggling with her body. For a year, she could not open her mouth to sing.

When they came to Victoria and established their first bed and breakfast, she and Frank struck a deal. The idea was that the business would allow the Ryans and their two small children to enjoy a comfortable life in shared surroundings they might not otherwise afford, and Sheila would be able to write songs and sing in the free time that life afforded her.

Anyone who has been in the bed and breakfast business knows there is no such thing as privacy. You are on your best behaviour always, can't raise your voice, can't cook smelly fish. The house has to look ready to be photographed for a magazine, with all the beds turned down and all the linen crisp. You make scones every day until you are sick of them and you set your face in the pose for sympathetic listening even when you are totally exhausted or dying to get back to your harp and practise, practise, practise.

Sheila is a self-taught musician, except for what her father showed her while they were hanging out with the cows. She carries songs in her head the way folk musicians always have and plays harp and guitar, lamenting even as she plays that there aren't enough hours in her day.

The freckled children, Jeanette and Shane, grew up, and the Ryans decided to lease the fanciful *belle époque* mansion they own on Superior Street. My husband and I thought perhaps the days of hard work would be put behind them and Sheila would concentrate on the singing, especially since everything Irish has been in vogue during the recent Celtic renaissance. "You had to be there," the woman said as we stood on the sidewalk in front of the new house and the new neighbour swished by with the Prince of Wales in his back seat.

Now the Ryans are at it again, renovating yet another house, taking off the overalls

Frank and Sheila were determined to transcend their parochial childhoods.

minutes before the curtain goes up. Conflicted by her dream of wider acceptance as a musician and her hunger for economic security, which only those who have been there can understand, Sheila continues to prioritize.

Perhaps this is the insecurity of the child who sang for an audience that treated her with contempt when she wasn't in the singer persona. I am reminded of the sapper in Michael Ondaatje's novel, *The English Patient,* who, as a person of colour in racist England, knew himself to be invisible except when he was performing the dangerous and necessary task of disabling bombs. Sheila knows the double-edged sword of contempt and acceptance.

Nevertheless, her recordings outsell any other on the BC Ferries, where they play constantly. She charms all her bed and breakfast customers into buying boxes of "product," the tapes and CDs made with her band, Sarsfield. These days it is difficult to market an independent label internationally but Sheila sells briskly, even in Japan, where her lyrics are simply sound. She is delighted that an article extolling her singing appeared in *Hibernia Magazine* alongside one of actress Meg Ryan. "Not bad," she says.

Sheila has lived the stories in the ballads she is singing.

Sheila has the charming voice of a child singing through adversity. It has a vulnerability, which is also the story of the Irish people. Hers is the true, idiosyncratic sound of Ireland, where hearth and history are stained with blood and suffering.

Like many a modern musician, Sheila records and promotes her own work. Because of the accessibility of recording studios and recording equipment, there is a lot of product competing for attention. That Sheila is heard often is a tribute to the authenticity of her sound and to the loyalty of her fans, many of them Irish.

Sheila enjoys sitting on her big front porch having a cuppa, her baby finger artfully raised, being seen by the plutocrats in her neighbourhood. Her comfort zone is the security she wouldn't have dared dream of in the barn back home. No one is going to talk her out of her big house, even if she does share it with the world. "We are used to the big rooms now." None of them has a dirt floor.

Her mother comes from London to visit. So do her brothers and sisters, who a few years ago actually put their father's coffin down on the road and wrestled one another over whether the mother who left them should walk with them to the graveyard. "You had to be there." When Sheila recollects, there is always the smile that tells you this is an Irish fairy tale, especially when the prince in overalls is Frank Ryan. "Just fooling," she says, whether you have just been ruthlessly teased or treated to a bit of family history.

Sheila has lived the stories in the ballads she is singing. In her life, she has known death and betrayal. She and Frank have built a life that will allow their children to make choices not open to their parents. Frank is a well-read man who had to leave school at twelve to help support his family. In the folk tradition, Sheila's only teachers are the lessons of experience. For the Ryans, the dream was giving their children the opportunity to choose. Now that Jeanette and Shane are grown, Sheila can make more time to do what she loves best.

It doesn't matter who is in the audience and whether or not she is getting paid. This is what she must do. More and more, she is singing at benefits because helping people is more rewarding than competing with hungry artists for a limited entertainment dollar. What Sheila is seizing when she stands in front of an audience is the moment when her light burns brightly. The nuns told her to do something beautiful for God. She remembers that and tries to forget the rest. When she sings with her eyes closed, she is alone with the songs her father taught her.

JODY PATERSON

JOURNALIST (1956, SASKATOON, SASKATCHEWAN–)

Jody was given the mandate to excel and the heavy burden of expectation which falls on any first-born or only.

IT IS FITTING that the last collector of stories in this collection of women's stories, a late boomer, will be under fifty and still breaking the sound barrier, women's silence, in the year 2000. Jody Paterson, newspaperwoman, happened to the Canadian Prairie in the fifties. This was the time when returning soldiers were getting acclimatized to life as usual, while many of their wives pulled on white gloves and rushed out to fill prescriptions for the mind-altering drugs they needed to stay at home after the expedient wartime emancipation of women in the workplace.

Jody's mother was a nurse and her father served in the Royal Canadian Air Force, a prescription for the average, hohum, Dick and Jane life of the fifties. What made the Patersons unusual was the diverse gene pool that gave their daughter zero tolerance for hot air, bagpipes excepted. Her father was of Scottish descent, a solid Canadian pedigree. The railroad that joined Canada east to west was a vision largely realized by Scottish ingenuity and Chinese labour. The Chinese workers, who came believing the New World Gold Mountain would ensure a dignified future for their families, found prejudice instead. This is the legacy of Jody's mother, a volatile Chinese-Romanian cocktail.

Recently, Jody wrote a piece for the *Victoria Times Colonist,* where she oversees the editorial page, that described her mother's experiences with racism in a country united by a railway system built by coolie labourers, many of whom gave their lives to fulfill the national dream of mercantile Scots. Her mother was refused admission to a "whites only" prairie dance, bigotry echoing the racism of west coast restaurants with names like "The White Lunch" and "The White Spot" that advertised no Chinese cooks touched the food served there.

Right away, as her mother's only daughter, Jody was given the mandate to excel and the heavy burden of expectation which falls on any first-born or only, especially those whose parents have experienced humiliation in an alien culture. All this sat on a frail child with multiple allergies and no fixed address, the plight of military children.

The family settled in Comox, British Columbia, where her father eventually left the military to give his family the stability of a permanent home. Jody was a pleaser, one of the natural excellers who are good students with multiple gifts. Out of school, she studied piano, and in class, her teachers nourished her obvious gift for writing. By the time Jody was an adolescent, she was dreaming about her first Pulitzer prize; not a typical projection for a small-town girl. Jody, who had already busted a few shibboleths, would eventually light her own virtual cigar in the exclusive men's club of journalism.

Like many writers, Jody, who suffers from asthma and other allergic responses, had the dream time of an invalid childhood. A traumatic illness at age seven changed her appearance, making her alternately the object

of ridicule and sympathy. This affected her profoundly and may have sharpened a natural sympathy for those who suffer. Her strong editorials advocating for the meek are modern homilies that sometimes pit Jody against the status quo. You never doubt she is writing with her head and her heart.

The segue from adolescence to the post-feminist world of journalism, where Jody now rules, was about as genteel as a walk through a minefield. Jody rebelled with all the pent up energy of pediatric homework slaves and, by the time she was seventeen, was married with a son, now in his mid-twenties and an environmental guerrilla. Daniel was followed by a sister, Regan. Paterson got her teaching certificate from the Toronto Conservatory and earned what our mothers called "pin money" (as opposed to "mad money" you pinned to your underwear in case you had to make a hasty exit from a car during a date). It was her first independent income. Anyone who has taught piano to inattentive children with pushy mothers knows that is not often satisfying work. Jody's persistent daytime fantasy during her years of housewifery was to become a deejay, but, when she found out riding records was high pressure with minimal intellectual input, she refocused on journalism.

After earning a certificate in Communications, her first formal post-secondary education, she started freelancing for the *Kamloops Daily Sentinel* and worked her way into a reporting job for the *Kamloops Daily News*. This was the start of a ride which may be taking her somewhere else. She is a person who likes a journey.

Jody has the fidgeting personality profile of the allergic. Her first marriage, which she describes as traditional, ended in divorce, as did her second, which was blessed with daughter Rachelle. When Jody says the word marriage, it lassoes your auditory heart with barbed wire. She does, however, maintain friendly co-parenting with her ex-husbands.

Jody, who came to the *Victoria Times Colonist* in 1989 as a reporter, drew attention to herself with good writing and, let's face it, it was time to hire women for management positions, so she skated into the jobs of City Editor, then Managing Editor, and now Chief Editorial Writer, a job that suits her hands-on humanistic approach to newspaper writing. She has achieved what her foremothers in the newspaper industry could not, translating her natural ability into power jobs within the system, with the agenda of changing the apparatus that exploits those outside.

I have just made a note to tell her that my mother, who has had a distinguished career in the public sector, was given a job on the Women's Page when she was a cub reporter at the *Vancouver Province*. This pink ghetto was the only niche for intelligent newspaper-women in those days.

Now that Jody, who took Women's Studies at the University of Victoria, has transcended the rage that made her a reporter and arrived at a place of wisdom, she envisions a life of travel and reflection, making sense of the global village.

When I asked if she had the common newsperson's fantasy of chucking the day job and plunging into the crocodile-infested waters of creative writing, she admitted a longing to write creative nonfiction, a genre that has produced some brilliant books for our time.

Jody, who is colourful, a strong personality with attractive vulnerabilities, uses the word "grey" a lot in conversation. I thought of the men in grey flannel suits who dominated the decade of her birth and have risen again in the new bureaucracies of the age of technocracy—Voltaire's bastards, more than adequately described by John Ralston Saul, whose feet I have kissed and apparently Jody would do likewise.

Though she is from the rising grey, conformist generation that amazingly passed through the sixties untouched by its idealism and put information ahead of wisdom in the compromise of the century, Jody is one of the dissenters. Perhaps this is the legacy of a mother who wanted to lose herself in a racist society and couldn't. Or it could be the primal protest of a different child who, rather than conform, would prefer to change an imperfect social environment.

Having already accomplished most of her vocational goals, Jody is setting her sight on the world, which she plans to visit with her various children and perhaps the one man she feels has manifested a willingness to accommodate himself to her flexible life plan and her unwillingness to cook on demand.

Although I had been reading Jody's intelligent and articulate commentaries in the paper, I didn't meet her in the context of her work. She turned up with a handful of extra-vocational poetry at a Valentine's Day writing contest I was co-judging. I liked her cinnamon hearts wrapped up in typewriter ribbon. They had the bite and sweetness of a woman in balance.

When her children grow up, she will live in a cabin with only the man and her

When Jody says the word marriage, it lassoes your auditory heart with barbed wire.

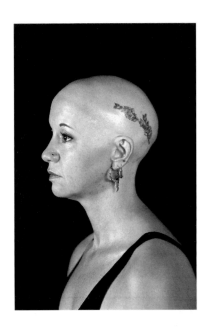

typewriter for companions. Then she will create folklore from the stories she has been gathering. This is the prerogative of the wise woman and a first step in correcting a civilization that has not been listening.

Recently, Victoria hosted an international summit for sexually exploited youth. Jody was there, tactfully interfacing the delegates and an underinformed public with the disgraceful reality of the enslavement of children in the sex trade. The participants, who came from all over North and South America to tell their stories, gradually revealed a pattern of abuse that implicates all of us when we refuse to recognize the problem and advocate for reform. Those who participated came to understand what Jody calls "the grey area of overlapping experience." In her case, it was a common physical vulnerability.

Most of the young prostitutes expressed a resentment that they were not seen as human beings, that their covers told the whole story as far as most of the public was concerned. This is also the frustration for public women who are most frequently described in physical as opposed to functional terms.

There was a recent letter to the editor attacking Jody's former hairstyle, which was short and funky and covered her eyes, a good device, I thought, for someone who watches. I winced when I read about it but I had no idea how cruel and devastating an effect the criticism had on her.

Women are still subject to judgement based on appearance. One young woman, in the writing workshop I was giving with Patricia Young to help the abused young people find a voice, told me there was no way she would take up my invitation to swim in the hotel pool. Her method of distancing herself from men who had sexually abused her was an eating disorder and she no longer wore a bathing suit. Others did take their imperfections and painful childhood memories to the primal waters, as did the newswoman they had to trust because she was their link to public awareness of their situation.

Jody, the success paradigm of her generation, smart, articulate, and elegant, mother about to become grandmother, took off her business suit and her watch and, last of all, her wig, revealing a perfectly smooth skull, her secret, decorated with a rose tattoo.

That put the *N* back in nonfiction.

BARBARA LIVINGSTON

SOPRANO (1958, COMOX, BRITISH COLUMBIA–)

In the buzz of fanning programs and the rattling of diamonds, no one mentioned the soprano.

THE ORCHESTRA WAS TUNING UP. Jody Paterson settled into her seat in the gods, near ours. Victoria was plastered with pictures of the hometown boy with the voice from heaven. Everyone came to Pacific Opera's summer production of Verdi's *Un Ballo in Maschera* to hear Richard Margison sing the part of Riccardo, Count of Warwick, the incorrect lover in love with Amelia, his best friend's wife.

In the buzz of fanning programs and the rattling of diamonds, no one mentioned the soprano. Her name didn't even appear on the six-foot posters of Richard's masked face in every bus stop in town. It was Cinderella's appearance at the ball. No one was expecting her.

The soprano, as the whole world will undoubtedly know sooner than later, was Barbara Livingston, halfway down the cast list in print so small I couldn't read it without my glasses, way smaller than the presence producing a flow of sound like spun sugar in the second scene. Barbara Livingston, who hardly knew opera from the juke box in the local family restaurant, was making her debut opposite the fastest-rising tenor in North America, and he was singing his pants off to keep up with the huge voice coating the dome in the Royal Theatre.

Jaws dropped and the audience exhaled in unison at the end of the first act. Someone had just driven down the gravel road from Campbell River, where people cut trees and fish, and made a fast turn into the fast lane and fame. What was that? It didn't seem real. Jody, who is a musician when she isn't relentlessly pursuing social justice on the editorial page of the local paper, remembered a tall girl who sang back home, up-island as they say. Her name was Barbara something.

"Barbara something" was the daughter of just plain folks. Her father had a job with the municipality and her mother stayed home. Perhaps they wanted more. Her mother was someone Barbara always felt she ought to take care of. She remembers standing in the kitchen in a spilled pile of powdered milk trying to make formula for her baby sister when she was not quite three years old. Like many oldest children, she took responsibility for family harmony without even being aware of it.

She is an intuitive singer. Harmony is her gift and her goal. Just as she has transcended family dysfunction, she has risen, it would appear, without effort, like cream to the top of the bottle. While other divas grow long fingernails and scratch their way to recognition ("Sopranos are a dime a dozen"), Barbara just opens her mouth and sings.

Music was the salvation of her household. Her mother sang popular songs while she vacuumed and washed the dishes. Barbara grew up loving show tunes, musical comedy, and she studied flute and piano when her family finally got their hands on one. Her high school music teachers couldn't help but notice a huge natural instrument and singled her out for solos, even though they had to ask her to pipe down for the sake of the school windows.

She remembers Jody from music festivals at this time. Thinking she would never be as good on the piano as the awesome older girl, she also knew Jody was paying a price for her music prizes.

Right from the start, Barbara was a tall girl with a big voice and she was comfortable, she says, with both. "I could look over the heads of other kids," something she has found she also likes doing in a large theatre. "A tall person is automatically the centre of attention on stage." This is true, and it has been proven that tall politicians benefit from the advantage of loftiness. I wondered if that was why the director of her first opera chose to have her stand so still, the music pouring out of her, some Valkyrie down from Valhalla, the fairy-tale castle of the goddesses of singing.

Unlike many tall women, the singer has beautiful posture. Maybe this is the backbone of the eldest child of some adversity. Her younger sister, who is taller than she is, has not been able to stand so straight, and this is a source of pain to Barbara, who is by birth order a fixer. Mother, father, and big sister walked on eggs to avoid conflict with the *enfant terrible* and this may be the key to Barbara's history of avoiding risks. The troubles of her dark sibling can be heard in the dark side of the singer's voice, where pain comes through and takes the listener to a place beyond words or music.

Like many sensitive children of houses where angels are wrestled, their silences loud, Barbara became a reader. Her appreciation of story colours her singing, which is rich with nuance. After high school, the practical child of a working-class family planned to become a music teacher and earn a sensible living. She enrolled in the music program at the University of Victoria. Sometimes university music programs are a better preparation for teachers than performers. Feeling the impulse of her true vocation, Barbara soon found the experience frustrating and she never finished her degree, although she did teach music in the long segue to now.

Back home, just short of whatever her practical goal had been, she took a job as a receptionist and started going out with the man who would become her husband and to whom, in small-town style, she was already connected in her network of friendships. Unlike her turbulent first family, Cal is the port in the storm. Older than Barbara, he is the strong, silent logger who has given her a comfortable middle-class life and a son with red hair, a sign of good luck in any culture.

Her appreciation of story colours her singing.

Her son, Graeme, and God help you if you spell it the other way, is pure jock with the ears of a dog. I told Barbara that we once had a terrier who howled and hid when my children sang or played musical instruments. It is like that with Graeme who, it must be admitted, got himself born to a mother with a voice as big as Mount Washington where the locals ski, from the top of which you can see forever.

Barbara's huge brown eyes roll when she recalls that Graeme brought earplugs to her operatic debut. Earlier, when he was four, he had taped a sign written in the secret language of children to her piano. When asked for a translation, he told her it said NO LOUD SINGING. She wasn't much comforted when I told her my five-year-old granddaughter will not allow her father to play trumpet in the house, after the house had been bought at least in part so he could blow without harassment from neighbours or the police.

These dog-eared children must be the noise police. When Graeme went to school, he was anxious to master the first two Rs so he could write a perfectly intelligible sign: KNOW SINGEING ALOWD. She is not the first priestess to be so chastised. I told her about a sign at the hot springs near Nelson,

NO CHANTING OR MOANING, which severely curtails the ritual bathing of local Tibetan monks.

When Barbara went to Toronto to audition for the Canadian Opera Company, Graeme was impressed by her proximity to the Hockey Hall of Fame. She should be allowed to cheer loudly at his games.

Her sensational appearance at Pacific Opera has had aftershocks all over North America. Most recently, she has sung in San Francisco for Lotfi Mansouri, surely the pinnacle in the opera world, a planet so foreign to her she still hasn't caught her breath or had time to consider the implications. There are languages to learn and parts to memorize. Coming up is the role of Leonora in *Il Trovatore* for Regina Opera, and the understudy for Amelia with Richard again in San Francisco.

Barbara is going to be busy. Her husband Cal, seven years older than his wife, is at the age and the time in history when loggers think of retirement. When I asked Barbara what they will do when she is out of this world, flying in airplanes to places beyond her imagination, seeing the whole wide world at last, she says they will go to hockey games, noodle about together in the aluminum boat pulled up on the beach near their waterfront house, and eat without feminine intervention, which means with their fingers. It sounds like Paradise to them. The real high-wire act may not be the career in the centre ring that now appears inevitable, but the demands the career will make on her private life. She will need to draw on the strong character that has brought her this far to draw the line between them and us, a line that will keep her and her family in balance. There is only fear and little joy in working without a net.

Barbara, who has been singing at weddings all along, with the unspoken dream on the back burner, is not intimidated by the notion of a late career. Like Elisabeth Hopkins, who became famous at eighty, she will enjoy whatever fate hands her. After all, it already gave her a voice to die for. Perhaps the early death of her parents has introduced her to the belief that life and a gift are only rentals.

Because the part of Amelia came to her through the intervention of friends who had faith in her ability and not from her own hunger for recognition, she may not be tempted by the downside of fame and fortune, the insecure behaviour of ambitious artists. Barbara Livingston still has the fingernails of a woman who does her own housework.

Before any of this happened, an angel sent her an airline ticket to Toronto and an appointment with singer Louis Quilico. That time the city scared her paralytic, but now she says she is ready for the free travel and the chances to open up and sing away from the censorship of ten-year-olds.

When contralto Maureen Forrester was asked about the maturation of her magnificent voice, she said she never sang well until life gave it the patina that only comes from experience. She needed to be a mother, and a brave one at that because she was one of the few of her generation to keep a child born out of wedlock, in order to understand what she was singing. Barbara Livingston comes late to the professional stage, but she has, in addition to a marvellous natural ability, the genius of life experiences.

When Barbara stood and sang her heart out in the Royal Theatre, her mother, whom she had been nursing while learning the demanding part of Amelia, lay dying at home. For a long time, diabetes had been robbing her mother of her sight and her limbs, and Barbara had been absorbing the sound of grief, something we heard in the character of Amelia. Her mother, who had shared her joy in music and movement with her daughter, died the morning of the third performance of *Un Ballo*

The real high-wire act may not be the career in the centre ring that now appears inevitable, but the demands the career will make on her private life.

in Maschera, and Barbara sang through it. Amazing grace, those who knew were thinking, but Barbara says the singing kept her sane.

For Barbara Livingston, singing is not so much about technique as letting the story flow. It is astonishing that she has accomplished so much just moving with the current of desire. Perhaps that freshness is part of the appeal of her voice, which has not been damaged by bad teaching or disappointment.

I was not surprised to find out she has shared Richard Margison's teacher, as did my son, retired in his twenties from the brilliant operatic career of his mother's fantasies. Some are born to teach and when you have a student like Barbara, the feeling is as glorious as actually standing there yourself and feeling the notes pour over the footlights.

That sensation is only the icing to Barbara, who already knows her cake is the royal prerogative of home, with real-life princes who leave their laundry lying about and drink from the milk bottle when mother is working. She intends to stay grounded and, if she gets rich and famous, to take her girlfriends from Campbell River to one of the gay capitals of the world, where they will translate their modest annual shopping trip over the U.S.

border to the spree of a lifetime. I can see them in their underwear in the dressing rooms at some posh emporium like Liberty's in London, the diva dresses hanging on gilded hooks. Who wouldn't give their right arm to be the photographer there?

When I asked Barbara what parts she would like to sing, perhaps Lucia or Norma, the sky is the limit, she shrugged her shoulders. It doesn't matter. She likes Verdi, the unbelievably demanding gymnastic demands of his vocal line almost effortless to her. "I have been given so much already, I can't afford to ask." Her mother and father died young. Barbara is not going to roll the dice. The dice must come to her.

When Barbara says this, she smiles the inherited smile of her singing mother lying in her last bed, listening to her daughter's voice on the tape of the first operatic performance. The video was sent by courier to the hospital where she was holding off the angel of death because she wanted to hear Barbara's debut, a pleasure we shared.

"I have been given so much already, I can't afford to ask."

CLIMBING THE CHAIRS

The metal chairs make the moaning
sound of a woman in labour
when the actors drag them across the floor,
when they open and stack them,
one on top of the other, until we feel it
raising the hairs on our arms,
lifting our arms from our sides.

So much of this is involuntary,
and the balance, body on body, chair on chair,
has to be perfect every time.

When the actors stack the chairs,
balancing one on the other,
you have to believe they are stairs
to climb and there will always be
someplace to go at the top.

There is no word for when
the chairs tremble and the actors fall,
hitting the floor head first,
the way most of us drop from our mothers
until and if we ever tuck up and turn
beautiful somersaults in the air
and wind up landing on our feet.

This is the right time for applause.

There are so many stories,
so many combinations of chairs.
None of the actors
sound the same in the dark,
dragging their voices over the floor
and the metal chairs that are all the same
until they stack them, this way and that,
so the chairs become
a bed to make love or be born in,
a shallow grave, the actor's feet sticking out,
so bare and rude, the soles dirty,
no one ever thought a naked
foot could look so fragile
when the lights come on
and the story begins again.

LINDA ROGERS, 1998

Notes

ELISABETH MARGARET HOPKINS
p. 3 Jane Rule quote from the essay "Elisabeth Hopkins" in *A Hot-Eyed Moderate* (Tallahassee, FL: The Naiad Press, 1985).

DOROTHY LIVESAY
p. 18 Excerpt from Dorothy Livesay's poem "Without Benefit of Tape" in *Collected Poems: The Two Seasons* (Toronto: McGraw-Hill Ryerson, 1972).
p. 19 Reference to Dorothy Livesay's poem "The Uninvited" in *Collected Poems*.
p. 20 Excerpt from P.K. Page's poem "But We Rhyme in Heaven" in *The Hidden Room: Collected Poems in Two Volumes* (Erin, ON: The Porcupine's Quill, 1997).
p. 21 "And so the whole that I possess . . . " excerpted from Dorothy Livesay's poem "The Three Emily's" in *Collected Poems*.
p. 21 Final excerpt from Dorothy Livesay's poem "Speak through Me" in *Collected Poems*.

P.K. PAGE
p. 23 Opening poem ("I am a tin whistle . . . ") is titled "Request to the Alchemist," from Volume 2 of *The Hidden Room: Collected Poems in Two Volumes* by P.K. Page (Erin, ON: The Porcupine's Quill, 1997).
p. 23 Christine Irwin's essay, "My Grandmother's Luggage," appeared in a special issue of *The Malahat Review* (No. 117) devoted to P.K. Page.
p. 23 The reference to "one of her most beautiful poems" is to "Planet Earth," from Volume 2 of *The Hidden Room*.
p. 24 ". . . forgiveness for thy just rebukes . . ." is from P.K. Page's poem "Melanie's Nite-Book: Father" in Volume 1 of *The Hidden Room*.
p. 27 Excerpt from P.K. Page's poem "Planet Earth" in Volume 2 of *The Hidden Room*.
p. 27 Brief excerpt from P.K. Page's poem "Deaf Mute in the Pear Tree" in Volume 2 of *The Hidden Room*.
p. 29 Closing poem, "Arras," by P.K. Page, from Volume 1 of *The Hidden Room*.

EURITHE PURDY
p. 38 Excerpt from Al Purdy's poem "Song of the Impermanent Husband" in *Rooms for Rent in the Outer Planets: Selected Poems 1962–1996*, selected and edited by Al Purdy and Sam Solecki (Madeira Park, BC: Harbour Publishing, 1996).
p. 39 Excerpt from Al Purdy's poem "Home-Made Beer" in *Rooms for Rent in the Outer Planets*.
p. 41 Closing excerpt from Al Purdy's poem "The Nurselog" in *The Collected Poems of Al Purdy*, edited by Russell Brown (Toronto: McClelland & Stewart, 1986).

RONA MURRAY

p. 43 "The Indians I knew . . ." quote from *Journey Back to Peshawar* by Rona Murray (Victoria, BC: Sono Nis Press, 1993).

p. 44 Excerpt from Rona Murray's poem "I have been into the halls of the dead" in *Selected Poems* (Victoria, BC: Sono Nis Press, 1974).

p. 44 Excerpt from Rona Murray's poem "He returns:" in *Adam and Eve in Middle Age* (with paintings by Phyllis Serota) (Victoria, BC: Sono Nis Press, 1984).

PHYLLIS WEBB

p. 54 Opening excerpt from Phyllis Webb's poem "Two Versions: 2. In Situ" in *Selected Poems: The Vision Tree*, edited with an introduction by Sharon Thesen (Vancouver: Talonbooks, 1982).

p. 55 Excerpt from Phyllis Webb's poem "Some Final Questions" in *Selected Poems*.

p. 57 Excerpt from Phyllis Webb's poem "Anaximander" in *Hanging Fire* (Toronto: Coach House Books, 1990).

p. 57 "The light is mauve" and "eye's iris blooms. . ." are from Phyllis Webb's poem "Father" in *Selected Poems*.

p. 59 Excerpt from Phyllis Webb's poem "Some Final Questions" in *Selected Poems*.

p. 59 Closing poem, "There *Are* the Poems," by Phyllis Webb, from *Hanging Fire*.

INGE ISRAEL

p. 64 Closing poem, "Unmarked Doors," from the book *Unmarked Doors* by Inge Israel (Vancouver: Cacanadadada Press, 1992).

ADELE WISEMAN

p. 73 "I knew I was meant to be a writer . . ." quote from *Old Woman at Play,* by Adele Wiseman (Toronto: Clarke, Irwin & Co., 1978).

p. 77 "Every mother is delivered into fear" quote from "Selections from the Poetry—Adele Wiseman" in *We Who Can Fly: Poems, Essays and Memories in Honour of Adele Wiseman,* edited by Elizabeth Greene (Dunvegan, ON: Cormorant, 1997).

p. 77 "A good part of the art of self-defence . . ." quote from "Selections from the Poetry—Adele Wiseman" in *We Who Can Fly*.

ANGELA ADDISON

p. 78 The song "Voodoo Queen Marie" is written and performed by the Holy Modal Rounders on the album *Alleged in Their Own Time*, Rounder Records.

p. 81 Excerpt from D.G. Jones' poem "On a Picture of Your House" in *A Throw of Particles: The New and Selected Poems of D.G. Jones* (Toronto: General Publishing, 1983).

JANE RULE

p. 86 "It is not only women but men . . ." quote from the essay "Censorship" in *A Hot-Eyed Moderate*, by Jane Rule (Tallahassee, FL: The Naiad Press, 1985).

p. 87 "Questioning conventional morality . . ." quote from the essay "On a Moral Education" in *A Hot-Eyed Moderate*.

p. 89 "Writing is, more than is often acknowledged, a craft . . ." quote from the essay "The Practice of Writing" in *A Hot-Eyed Moderate*.

p. 90 Quote from the novel *Memory Board* by Jane Rule (Toronto: Macmillan, 1987).

CLAIRE WEISSMAN WILKS

p. 100 Quote regarding Lipschitz from personal communication with Claire.

CAROLE SABISTON

p. 114 "I've always lived on islands . . ." quote from personal communication with Carole.

SISTER EILEEN CURTEIS

p. 117 Excerpt from Eileen Curteis's poem "Small's World" in *Wind Daughter* (Victoria, BC: Ekstasis Editions, 1998).

p. 120 Excerpt from Eileen Curteis's poem "Kite That Sets You Free" in *Wind Daughter*.

p. 121 Excerpt from Eileen Curteis's poem "Kite That Sets You Free."

DAISY DEBOLT

p. 131 Excerpt from the song "Paradise" on Daisy DeBolt's self-produced album, *I Can*.

COMFORT ADESUWA

p. 138 Excerpt from unpublished poem "The New African Child" by Comfort Adesuwa.

p. 140 Excerpt from unpublished poem "My Queen, My Mother" by Comfort Adesuwa.

p. 141 Excerpt from unpublished poem "African Twilight" by Comfort Adesuwa.

SUSAN MUSGRAVE

p. 149 Excerpt from Susan Musgrave's poem "After the Rain" in *Songs of the Sea-Witch* (Victoria, BC: Sono Nis Press, 1970).

p. 150 "Let's not invent any more weapons . . . " excerpt from Susan Musgrave's poem "Canadian Roulette" in *Forcing the Narcissus* (Toronto: McClelland & Stewart, 1994).

p. 150 "But when you told me you loved me less . . . " excerpt from Susan Musgrave's poem "Here it Comes—Grief's Beautiful Blow-Job" in *Forcing the Narcissus*.

p. 151 "The antlered ghosts . . . " excerpt from Susan Musgrave's poem "The Judas Goat" in *A Man to Marry, A Man to Bury* (Toronto: McClelland & Stewart, 1979).

p. 152 "Currant bread, simnel cake . . . "excerpt from Susan Musgrave's poem "Elisa and Mary" in *A Man to Marry, A Man to Bury*.

p. 153 Excerpt from Susan Musgrave's poem "One Evening, the Wind Rising, It Began" in *Forcing the Narcissus*.

p. 154 Excerpt from Susan Musgrave's poem "Three Witches Go for Lunch in Elora" in *Cocktails at the Mausoleum* (Toronto: McClelland & Stewart, 1985).

p. 155 Closing poem, "You Could Understand This," by Susan Musgrave, from *Forcing the Narcissus*.

Alan Greenwood launched *Vintage Guitar* magazine in 1986 and in 1990 created *The Official Vintage Guitar Price Guide* (visit www.VintageGuitar.com to see everything *VG* now offers). His collection includes several vintage guitars, amps, effects, and ukuleles from the '20s to the '80s, as well as newer instruments. He lives in Bismarck, North Dakota.

Ram Tuli began collecting guitars as a teenager while he was in the U.S. Navy. He spent most of his professional life working as an engineer and production-plant manager. He has been keeping track of vintage instrument values for more than 40 years, and for the last 20 has been singing and playing lead guitar for the Phoenix-based blues band Psychedelic Mooj. Besides making music, Ram also loves writing detective stories and books about guitars and the Navy.

The Official Vintage Guitar® Price Guide 2025
By Alan Greenwood and Ram W. tuli
ISBN: 978-1-884883-01-9

Vintage Guitar, PO Box 7301, Bismarck, ND 58507, publishers of Vintage Guitar® magazine and Vintage Guitar® Online at www.VintageGuitar.com. Vintage Guitar is a registered trademark of Vintage Guitar, Inc.

Cover: 1959 Flying V, 1967 in Sparkling Burgundy, and a '71 Medallion: Jeff Lisec.
Back: 1969 Flying V in Walnut, 1981 in Holly Green, and a '67 sunburst: Jeff Lisec. Daniel Escauriza: Chicago Music Exchange. Jake Andrews courtesy of J. Andrews. Neal and Cathy Shelton: Neal's Music Store. Richard Tozzoli courtesy of R. Rozzoli. Laurence Wexer: Laurence Wexer, Ltd.

Cover Design: Doug Yellow Bird/Vintage Guitar, Inc.

Printed in the United States of America

In loving memory of Jack David Greenwood, 1990-2020

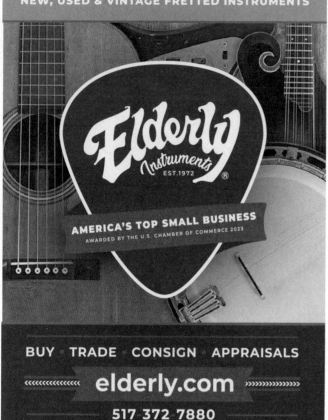

TABLE OF CONTENTS

Kay model 300 and 1949 Silvertone amp by Danelectro. Lynn Wheelwright.

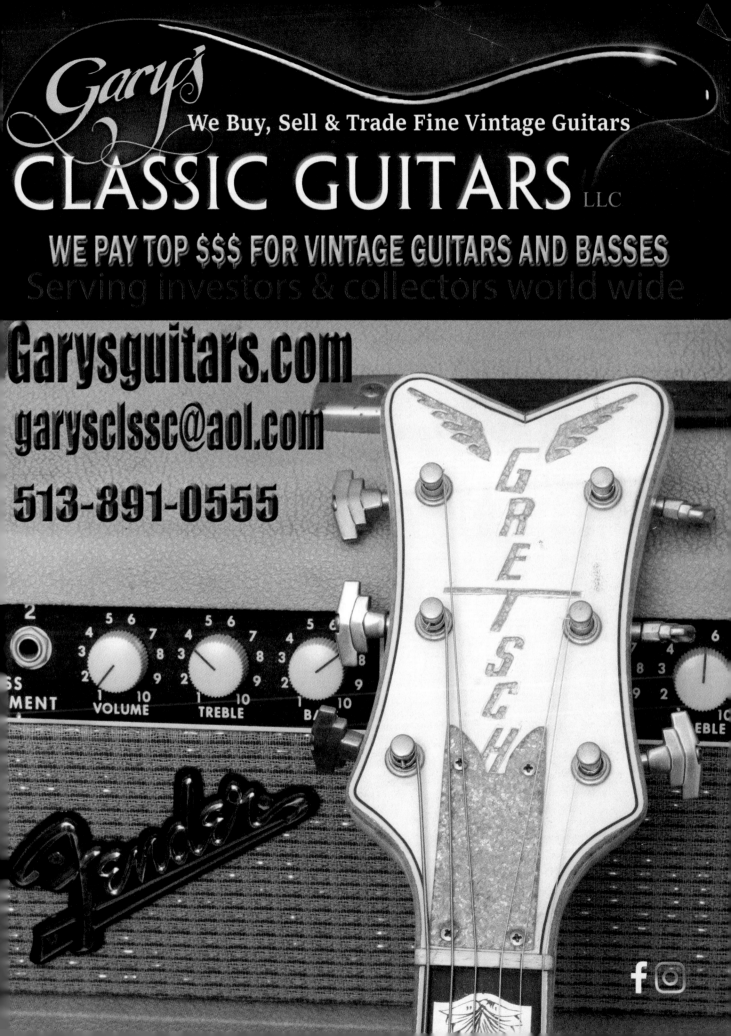

"Strato-Crazy"
Specialized Shop in Japan
Please Choose your best Vintage Stratocaster!!

USING THE GUIDE

UNDERSTANDING THE VALUES

Values presented in *The Official Vintage Guitar Price Guide* are for excellent-condition, all-original instruments. Our definition of excellent condition allows for some wear, but the instrument should be well-maintained, with no significant blemishes, wear, repairs, or damage. All-original means the instrument has the parts and finish it had when it left the factory. Replacement parts and refinishes can greatly affect value, as can the appropriate case (or cover) in excellent condition. In many instances, a "wrong" case will not greatly affect value, but with the top-dollar collectibles, it can.

The exception to this is the range on amplifiers, which operate in a high-voltage, high-temperate environment, being manhandled most of their life. Here, the low value is for ones showing wear and tear, but being regularly maintained. They will likely have grounded electrical plugs and non-original electrolytic capacitors. All other passive components in the electrical circuit should be original.

The second price shown is the premium paid for an all-original amp that functions perfectly and is in excellent cosmetic condition.

We use a range of excellent-condition values, as there is seldom agreement on a single price point for vintage and used instruments. A tighter range suggests there is a general consensus, while a wide range means the market isn't in strict agreement. A mint-condition instrument can be worth more than the values listed here.

Repairs affect value differently. Some repair is necessary to keep an instrument in playable condition. The primary concern is the level of expertise displayed in the work and an amateurish repair will lower the value

more than one that is obviously professional. A refinished guitar, regardless of the quality of the work, is generally worth 50% or less of the values shown in *The Guide*. A poorly executed neck repair or significant body repair can mean a 50% reduction in a guitar's value. A professional re-fret or minor, nearly invisible body repair will reduce a guitar's value by only 5%.

The values in *The Guide* are for unfaded finishes. Slight color fade reduces value by only 5%, but heavy fading can reduce value by 25% to 50%.

FINDING THE INFORMATION

The table of contents shows the major sections and each is organized in alphabetical order by brand, then by model. In a few instances, there are separate sections for a company's most popular models, especially when there is a large variety of similar instruments. Examples include Fender's Stratocasters, Telecasters, Precision and Jazz basses, and Gibson's Les Pauls. The outer top corner of each page includes a dictionary-type index that tells the models or brands on that page. This provides a quick way to navigate each section.

The Guide has excellent brand histories and in most cases the guitar section has the most detailed information for each brand. When possible, *The Guide* lists each model's years of availability and any design changes that affect values.

More information on many of the brands covered in *The Guide* is available in the pages of *Vintage Guitar* magazine and on the "Features" section of our website, www.Vintage-Guitar.com.

The authors of *The Guide* appreciate your help, so if you find any errors or have additional information on certain brands or models, please drop us a line at Ram@VintageGuitar.com.

NEW RETAIL PRICING INFORMATION

The Guide contains information on individual luthiers and smaller shops. It's difficult to develop values on used instruments produced by these builders because much of their output is custom work, production is low, and/or they haven't been producing for a period of time sufficient to see their instruments enter the used/resale market. To give you an idea about their instruments, we've developed five grades of retail values for new product. These convey only the prices charged by the builder, and are not indicative of the quality of construction.

The five retail-price grades are:
Budget - up to $500,
Intermediate - $501 to $1,500,
Professional - $1,501 to $3,000,
Premium - $3,001 to $10,000,
Presentation - more than $10,000.

The Guide uses the terms "production" and "custom" to differentiate between builders who do true custom work versus those who offer standard production models. "Production" means the company offers specific models, with no variations. "Custom" means they do only custom orders, and "production/custom" indicates they do both. Here's an example:

Bismarck Sound Guitars
2016-present. Premium grade, custom solidbody guitars built by luthier Alan Greenwood in Bismarck, North Dakota.

This tells who the builder is, the type of instruments they build, where they build them, how long they've been operating under that brand, that they do only custom work, and that they ask between $3,000 and $10,000 for their guitars (premium-grade).

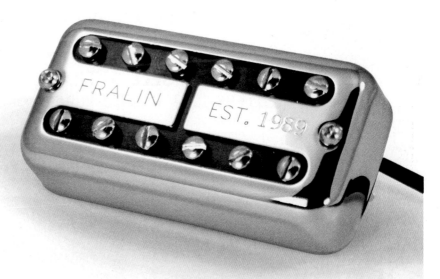

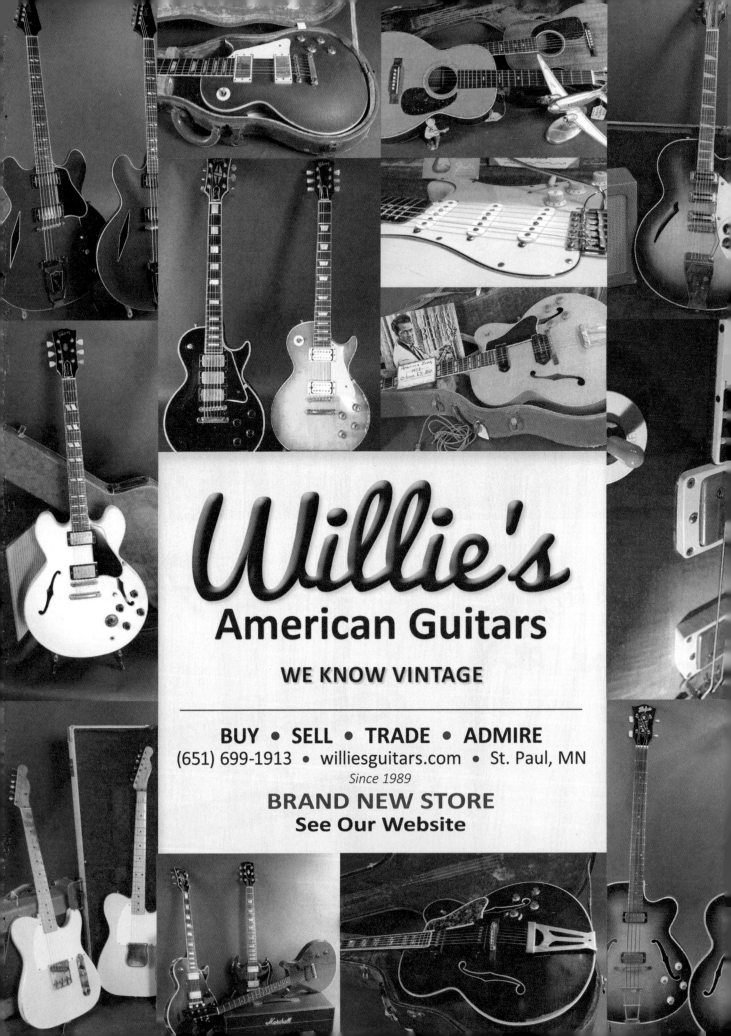

MAY 2-4 2025

DALLAS INTERNATIONAL GUITAR FESTIVAL

47th ANNUAL · 47th ANNUAL

DALLAS MARKET HALL

EST. 1978

WWW.GUITARSHOW.COM

INTRODUCTION

While the explosive pandemic-era growth in the collectible-guitar market has slowed, it is still experiencing impressive expansion. Since 1991, *Vintage Guitar*'s 42-Guitar Index has tracked the cumulative value of key models from the three largest companies of the "classic era" (see list at the end of this section). In 2024, that index rose 10%. Also, the overall market remains strong, as shown by our 3,000-Guitar Index, which tracks 34 brands. It rose 17%, repeating gains from 2023.

A comparison of the two indices shows that the blue-chip bubble of 2008 is now a distant memory. The 42-Guitar Index stabilized in 2013 and has since tracked much like the 3,000-Guitar Index. Both remained steady, with fluctuations of 2% to 3% until 2021. Figure 2 shows these indices after '21, when the current uptrend began.

For the first time, we've incorporated an index that compares how the S&P 500's growth during its "lost decade" (the period from 1999 to '09, one of the rare instances it had a negative return over a decade, at -0.9%) compared with the growth in the two guitar indices.

The longest bull run on stocks began March 9, 2009, and lasted until March 11, 2020, during which the S&P 500 grew by more than 300%. In that period, both guitar indices remained steady, reflecting minimal year-to-year fluctuations. Both rose significantly following the stock market decline of '22. Recent trends are similar to those from the mid '90s, when the stock market and guitar market tracked upward together. That ended when the dot-com bubble began in '95; the guitar market dropped by about 20% and didn't regain traction until 2000.

The 3,000-Guitar Index can be subdivided by brand. The traditional market is dominated by big five – Fender, Gibson, Gretsch, Martin, and Rickenbacker (as summarized on page 21). The Gretsch and Martin indices did well this year, rising 24% and 23%, receptively. The Gibson and Rickenbacker indices also did well, rising 16% and 14%, respectively. Fender rose 11%.

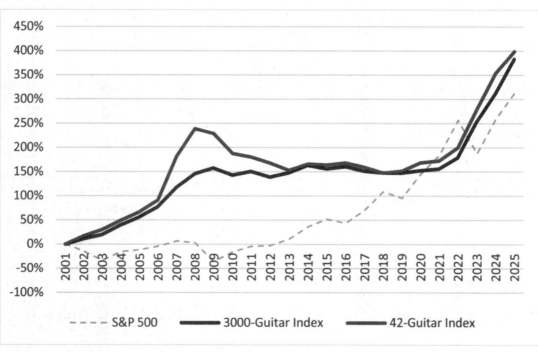

A Comparison of the 42-Guitar and 3000-Guitar Indices Since 2001

GRETSCH

The Gretsch index was dominated by the increase in value of early single-cut G-branded 6120s and White Falcons. Early-'60s double-cut Falcons jumped 92%, mid-'50s single-cut Falcons jumped 79%, and early G-branded 6120s rose 67%. Others rising (40% to 50%) include early-'60s Double Cut Silver Jets, mid-'60s Hi-Lo pickup Tennesseans, and late-'60s Country Clubs. Other Gretsches had negligible gains or experienced small decreases.

MARTIN

The Martin index did well because *all* flat-tops did well, especially pre-war models. Mahogany models did best, with many jumping 30% to 40%. Pre-war Brazilian rosewood Style 28, 42, and 45 appointments increased 20% to 30%. Shade-top pre-war D-18s and D-28s had their best year ever; a '34 D-18 shade-top now sells for twice what it did a few years ago.

GIBSON

The EDS-1275 had another amazing year, and the earliest special-order hollowbodies have quintupled in value since 2021. Over the last 10 years, they also have the highest annual return rate in The Guide, at 27%. That means they've doubled in value three times in that span. The most-desired models with SG bodies (a la Jimmy Page) now have an average return of around 11% per year. Models from the '70s rose 82% and have an annual return of about 9%. To put that in perspective, a '57 Strat has an annual

return of 7.5%.

It's no coincidence that the cover of the this year's *Guide* features the Flying V, as it and Explorer from all eras rose significantly in value, with Medallion and Heritage jumping at least 65%. The Cherry Red '66 stop-bar Flying V has quadrupled since '21. These highs carry over to similar models by Hamer, Jackson, and Dean.

All Les Paul models increased, with most gaining at least 10%. The mid-'50s goldtop with P-90s and Tune-O-Matic tailpieces did best, jumping 42%. The Les Paul Standard "'Burst" and PAF-equipped goldtop rose 15% to 18%, while Les Paul Customs from all eras saw the smallest gains, rising only 8%.

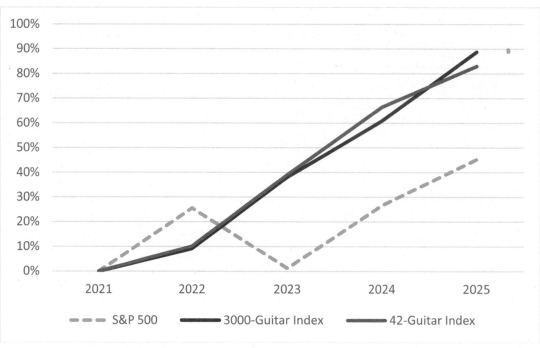

A Comparison of the 42-Guitar and 3000-Guitar Indices Since 2021

SURVEY ADVISORY BOARD

The information refined on these pages comes from several sources, including the input of many knowledgeable guitar dealers. Without the help of these individuals, it would be very hard for us to provide the information here and in each issue of *Vintage Guitar* magazine. We deeply appreciate the time and effort they provide.

Brian Goff
Bizarre Guitars

Garrett Tung
Boingosaurus Music

Dave Belzer
Burst Brothers

Kim Sherman
Carter Vintage

Daniel Escauriza
Chicago Music Exchange

John Majdalani
Cream City Music

Dave Rogers
Dave's Guitar Shop

David Davidson and Paige Davidson
Davidson's Well Strung Guitars

Drew Berlin
Drew Berlin's Vintage Guitars

Stan Werbin & S.J. "Frog" Forgey
Elderly Instruments

Dewey Bowen
Freedom Guitar

Rick Hogue
Garrett Park Guitars

Gary Dick
Gary's Classic Guitars

Eric Newell
Gruhn Guitars

Richard Johnston
Gryphon Strings

J.D. McDonald
Guitar Maverick

Kennard Machol & Leonard Coulson
Intermountain Guitar & Banjo

Jim Singleton
Jim's Guitars

Kevin Borden
Kebo's BassWorks

Dave Hinson
Killer Vintage

Timm Kummer
Kummer's Vintage Instruments

Buzzy Levine
Lark Street Music

Larry Wexer
Laurence Wexer, Ltd.

Artie Leider
McKenzie River Music

Neal Shelton
Neals Music (California)

Lowell Levinger
Players Vintage Instruments

Howie Statland
Rivington Guitars

Eliot Michael
Rumble Seat Music

Eric Schoenberg
Schoenberg Guitars

Richard Gellis
Union Grove Music

Fred Oster
Vintage Instruments

Richard Friedman
We Buy Guitars

Nate Westgor
Willie's American Guitars

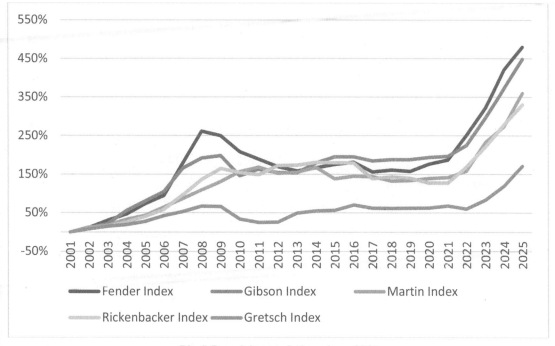

Big 5 Brand Appreciation since 2001

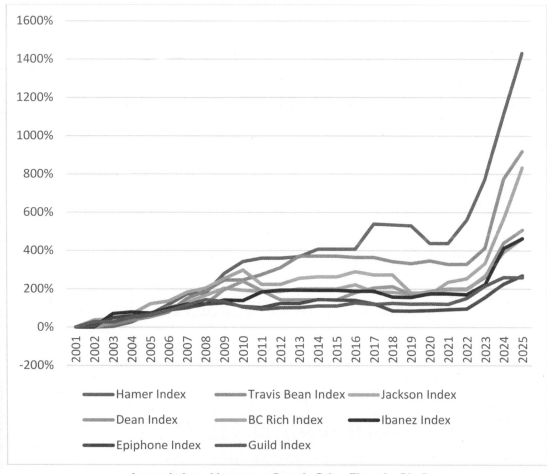

Appreciation of Important Brands Other Than the Big 5

L-5 rose 30%, while the '35 Super 400 was more typical, rising 10%. Electric archtops like the ES-175 and L-7CES realized their best gains in years, with PAF-equipped ES-175Ds jumping 30%. Many are no longer made and collectors are taking a closer look. Traditionally, electric and acoustic archtops have poor long-term returns, but this year was an anomaly. Gibson semi-hollow-bodies had negligible gains this year, with the exception of the '59 and '63 ES-335, which increased 23% and 15%, respectively.

RICKENBACKER

The Rickenbacker index was stagnant from 2009 to '16, then dipped and didn't gain momentum until '21. Now, it rivals Fender. Rose Morris models continue to dominate; the '64 Model 1993RM with flat tailpiece, and the later version with R tailpiece are up almost 500% since '21.

Almost every early Capri thick-body rose at least 30%, while mid-'60s models are also doing well, many doubling in value since '21.

FENDER

Pre-CBS Fenders have been hot for years, but this year saw a slight contrac-

Mid-century Gibson flat-tops did well, with the earliest Folk-singer and Hummingbird jumping 75% and 33%, respectively.

Gibson archtops had a good year. The '24 Loar-signed

tion, with Strats and Teles having smaller gains than the past three years. It makes sense that a slow-down would emerge with these models, since they dominated the market as it expanded; '71 Tele Thinlines, '85-'87 Made-in-Japan Strats, '50 Broadcasters, '65-'69 rare-color Jazzmasters, and '65-'69 rare-color Jaguars had the best returns this year, achieving 140%, 56%, 50%, 43%, and 41%, respectively.

THE EMERGING MARKET

The emerging market is dominated by the brands in the chart on page 21. Guitars made by these brands typically sell for under $5,000, and some at least doubled in value this year, including the '86 Kramer Liberty, Valenos made from '73-'76, any less-common '56-'69 Wandré, '83 B.C. Rich Wave, '86-'87 Hamer FB I/FB II, '95-'96 Hamer Korina Standard, '94-'95 Jackson Kelly Pro and Standard, '95-2012 Jackson Randy Rhoads Pro Series RR3 and RR5, '96-'99 Jackson Randy Rhoads Roswell, 2000-'02 Jackson Y2KV Dave Mustaine Signature, '75-'78 Ibanez Iceman 2663 (Flash I/II/III), and lawsuit era Ibanez Model 2387 Rocket Roll. The '91-'96 Music Man Eddie Van Halen also had a great year, rising 83%. ....

Almost 80% of the values shown in *The Guide* are for guitars that sell for less than $5,000, and nearly 60% of the guitars made after 1980 had negligible gains this year, likely because their segment has become saturated. This was predicted, given the

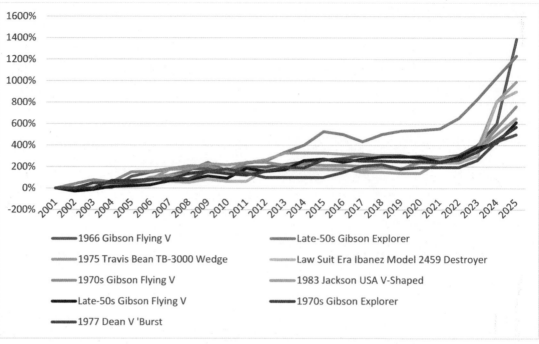

Appreciation of Selected Flying Vs and Explorers

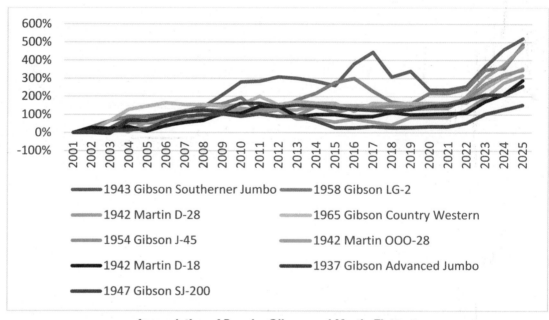

Appreciation of Popular Gibson and Martin Flattops

UPDATES AND CORRECTIONS

If you spot errors in the information about brands and models, have information on a brand you'd like to see included, or produce instruments for sale and would like to be included in the next edition of *The Guide*, email Wanda at Library@VintageGuitar.com.

If a model is missing from *The Guide*, or if you spot something that needs to be clarified, please drop a line to Ram@VintageGuitar.com.

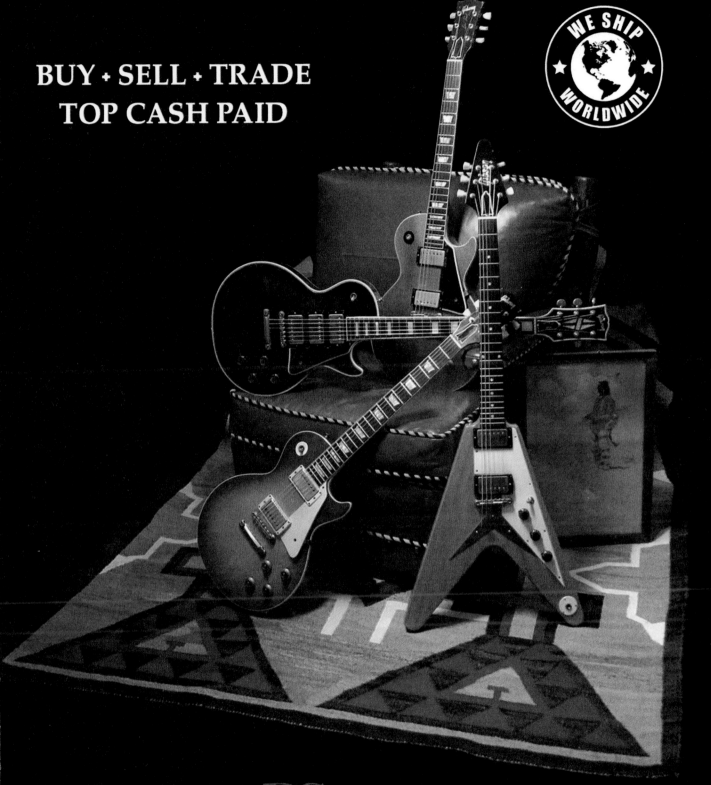

large number of guitars purchased during the pandemic, and many are being recirculated.

BASSES

The Precision Bass, Jazz Bass, and Rickenbacker 4001 continue to dominate the bass market. Basses mostly cooled this year, the exceptions being '60s Precisions (up 14% to 25%), '80s Rick 4001s (up 10%), and '60s Rickenbacker 4001s (up 4% to 7%). Other models that rose at least 10% were the '70s Travis Bean TB-2000, '75-'79 Hamer Standard, mid-'60s Burns Nu-Sonic, mid-'60s Baldwin Vibraslim, '77-'83 Dean ML, '70s Travis Bean TB-4000 Wedge, mid-'60s Ampeg AEB-1 and ASB-1 Devil, and '61 Höfner Model 500/1 lefty.

There were a few surprises among Gibsons; the '69 EB-0 and '70 EB doubled in price, while the '69-'73 EB-3L jumped 79% and the '80 silverburst Ripper rose 65%. Most other Gibsons lost value.

Many basses made after 1980 are rising in value, most notably, the Squire Bullet and certain post-2000 Hamer imports are both up 68%.

The Guide *authors Alan Greenwood and Ram W. Tuli.*

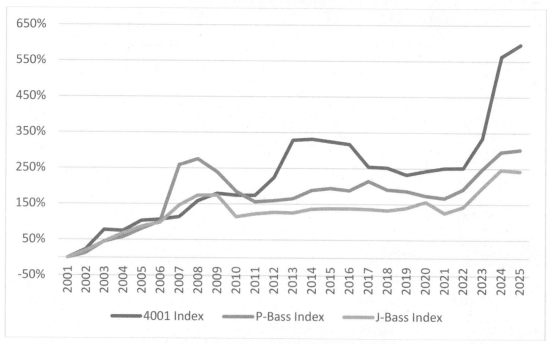

Appreciation of the Big 3 Vintage Basses

AMPS

Fender amps continued to climb, albeit at a slower pace. The best-performing index this year was Gibson, which rose 35%, primarily driven by the high values of Fender amps. The Fender and Mesa/Boogie indices both rose only 3%, while Marshalls rose 13% and Ampegs rose 12%. Vox is down 3%.

The best-performing Gibson is the '55-'57 two-tone/salt-maroon and '58-59 blue/blond GA-40 Les Paul, which are both up 67%, along with the '52-55 brown-grille GA-40 Les Paul (60%),

and the '50-54 GA-20 brown G-logo (40%). The Fender with best year-to-year jump was the '65-'67 black-face AA764 Champ (50%). The best Marshall increase was the JCM800, up 43%.

MORE INFORMATION

Much of the information in this book comes from *Vintage Guitar magazine*, which is offered in both print and digital formats; you can subscribe at www.VintageGuitar.com. VintageGuitar.com has a trove of feature interviews,

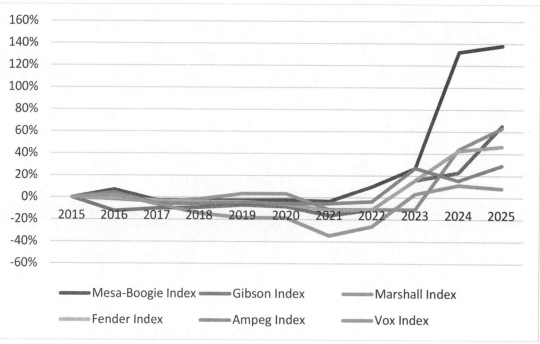

Vintage Amp Appreciation Since 2015

instrument histories and profiles, gear and music reviews, along with historical information on the brands and models covered in this book. You'll also find links to exclusive lessons, *VG* podcasts, our online archives of *VG* back issues, the *VG* YouTube channel, and our free e-mail *VG Overdrive* newsletter. Find us on Facebook, Twitter, YouTube, and Instagram, where we talk guitars and offer prizes. We'd love to have you join us.

ACKNOWLEDGEMENTS

Guitars beg for personal inspection to inspire a sale, and having a constituency of players nearby will influence the "localized" price. That is why *The Guide* uses dealers from all over the world, and we are especially grateful to the Survey Advisory Board for its help, as well as Rich Walter, Alex Kiedaisch, Larry Briggs, Joe Spann, Fred Stucky, Collin Whitley, Brett Coleman, Charlie Gelber, Peter Fung, John Dannert, Lee Jackson, James Pittman, Parker Lundgren, Michael Slubowski, Tucker Beirne, Kris Blakely, and Jeff Lisec.

Wanda Huether, as Editor of *The Guide*, keeps us all on deadline and makes all this possible. Doug Yellow Bird continues his fine work on the design and layout of the book. Larry Huether and Ward Meeker helped with editing and proofreading, James Jiskra, Johnny Zapp, and Mike Naughton handled the advertising and directory listings. We thank all of them for their usual fine work.

Thank you,
Alan Greenwood and Ram Tuli.

THE 42 GUITAR INDEX

FENDER MODELS
1952 blond Precision Bass
1952 blond Esquire
1953 blond Telecaster
1956 sunburst Stratocaster
1958 sunburst Jazzmaster
1958 blond Telecaster
1960 sunburst Stratocaster
1961 sunburst, stack knob, Jazz Bass
1962 sunburst, 3-knob, Jazz Bass

1963 sunburst Telecaster Custom
1963 sunburst Esquire Custom
1964 Lake Placid Blue Jaguar
1964 sunburst Precision Bass
1966 Candy Apple Red Stratocaster

GIBSON MODELS
1952 sunburst ES-5
1952 Les Paul Model
1954 Les Paul Jr.
1958 sunburst EB-2 Bass
1958 Les Paul Custom

1958 natural ES-335
1958 Super 400CES
1959 Les Paul Jr.
1959 J-160E
1961 ES-355
1961 Les Paul SG
1964 sunburst Thunderbird II Bass
1965 EB-3 Bass
1969 sunburst Citation

MARTIN
1931 OM-28

1936 00-28
1935 D-18
1944 scalloped-brace 000-28
1944 D-28
1950 D-28
1958 000-18
1959 D-18
1959 D-28E
1962 D-28
1967 GT-75
1968 000-18
1969 N-20
1969 D-45

THE 3,000-GUITAR INDEX

FENDER ELECTRICS
Duo-Sonic ('56 to '69)
Electric XII (All Colors, '65 to '69)
Esquire ('51 to '70)
Jaguar (All Colors, '62 to '75)
Jazzmaster (All Colors, '58 to '81)
Musicmaster ('56 to '81)
Mustang (All Colors, '64 to '81)
Stratocaster (All Colors, '54 to '81)
Telecaster (All Colors, '50 to '81)
Telecaster Custom ('59 to '72)
Telecaster Thinline ('68 to '78)

GIBSON ELECTRICS
Barney Kessel Regular ('61 to '73)
Barney Kessel Custom ('61 to '73)
Byrdland ('56 to '81)
EDS-1275 ('58 to '67; '77 to '81)
ES-120 T ('62 to '70)
ES-125 ('35 to '43; '47 to '70)
ES-125 C ('66 to '70)
ES-125 CD ('65 to '69)
ES-125 T ('56 to '68)
ES-125 TD ('57 to '63)
ES-125 TC ('60 to '70)
ES-125 TDC ('60 to '71)
ES-135 ('54 to '59)
ES-150 ('36 to '42; '46 to '56)
ES-175 ('49 to '71)
ES-175 N ('49 to '59)
ES-175 D ('52 to '81)
ES-175 DN ('52 to '66)
ES-225 T ('55 to '59)
ES-225 TN ('55 to '58)
ES-225 TD ('56 to '59)
ES-225 TDN ('56 to '59)
ES-250 ('39 to '40)
ES-250 N ('39 to '40)
ES-295 ('52 to '58)
ES-300 ('40 to '42; '45 to '53)
ES-300 N ('40 to '42; '45 to '53)
ES-330 T ('59 to '63)
ES-330 TN ('59 to '61)
ES-330 TD ('59 to '72)
ES-330 TDN ('59 to '61)
ES-335 TD ('58 to '81)
ES-335 TDN ('58 to '60)

ES-345 TD ('59 to '81)
ES-345 TDN ('59 to '60)
ES-350 ('47 to '56)
ES-350 N ('47 to '56)
ES-350 T ('56 to '63; '77 to '81)
ES-350 TN ('56 to '63; '77 to '81)
ES-355 TD ('58 to '70)
ES-355 TDSV ('58 to '81)
ES-5 ('49 to '62)
ES-5 N ('49 to '60)
Explorer ('58 to '59; '63 old parts; '75 to '81)
Firebird I ('63 to '69)
Firebird III ('63 to '69)
Firebird V ('63 to '69)
Firebird VII ('63 to '69)
Flying V ('58 to '59; '66 to '70; '75 to '81)
Johnny Smith ('61 to '81)
Johnny Smith D ('61 to '81)
L-4 CES ('58 and '69)
L-4 CESN ('58 and '69)
L-5 CES ('51 to '81)
L-5 CESN ('51 to '81)
L-7 E ('48 to '54)
L-7 CE ('48 to '54)
Les Paul Model ('52 to '57)
Les Paul Standard ('58 to '63; '68 to '69; '71 to '81)
Les Paul Custom ('54 to '63; '68 to '81)
Les Paul Deluxe ('69 to '81)
Les Paul Junior ('54 to '63)
Les Paul Special ('55 to '59)
Les Paul TV ('54 to '59)
Melody Maker ('59 to '70)
Melody Maker D ('60 to '70)
Melody Maker III ('67 to '71)
SG Custom ('63 to '80)
SG Deluxe ('71 to '73)
SG Junior ('63 to '71)
SG Special ('60 to '78)
SG Standard ('63 to '81)
SG TV ('59 to '61)
Super 400 CES ('51 to '81)
Super 400 CESN ('52 to '81)
Tal Fallow ('62 to '71)
Trini Lopez Standard ('64 to '70)
Trini Lopez Deluxe ('64 to '70)

GIBSON ACOUSTICS
Advanced Jumbo ('37)

Country Western ('65)
Everly Brothers ('62)
Hummingbird ('63)
J-45 ('54)
L-5 ('25 to '29)
LG-2 ('58)
SJ-200 ('47)
Southern Jumbo ('43)
Super 400 ('35)

GRETSCH ELECTRICS
Anniversary ('58 to '72)
Atkins Hollowbody 6120 ('54 to '80)
Atkins Solidbody 6121 ('55 to '63)
Astro Jet ('65 to '67)
Country Club ('54 to '81)
Country Gentleman ('57 to '81)
Duo-Jet ('53 to '71)
Jet Firebird ('55 to '71)
Monkees ('66 to '68)
Round Up ('54 to '60)
Silver Jet ('54 to '63)
Tennessean ('58 to '80)
White Falcon ('55 to '81)
White Penguin ('56 to '62)

GRETSCH ACOUSTICS
Rancher ('54)

MARTIN
O-18 (1898 to '81)
O-21 (1889 to '81)
O-28 (1874 to '31)
O-42 (1890 to '42)
O-45 ('04 to '39)
OO-18 (1898 to '81)
OO-21 (1898 to '81)
OO-28 (1898 to '41)
OO-42 (1898 to '43)
OO-45 ('04 to '29)
OOO-18 ('06 to '81)
OOO-28 ('02 to '81)
OOO-42 ('18 to '43)
OOO-45 ('06 to '42)
D-18 ('31 to '81)
D-21 ('55 to '69)
D-28 ('31 to '81)
D-28 E ('59 to '64)
D-45 ('36 to '42)
GT-75 ('65 to '67)
N-20 ('68 to '80)
OM-28 ('29 to '33)

OM-45 ('30 to '33)

RICKENBACKERS
A-22 ('32 to '36)
Combo 400 ('56 to '58)
Combo 420 ('65 to '81)
Combo 425 ('58 to '73)
Combo 450 ('57 to '66)
Combo 600 ('54 to '58)
Combo 650 ('57 to '59)
Combo 800 ('54 to '59)
Combo 850 ('57 to '59)
Combo 900 ('57 to '66)
Combo 950 ('57 to '80)
Electric Spanish ('46 to '49)
ES Ken Roberts ('35 to '39)
Model B Spanish ('35 to '43)
Model 310 ('58 to '70)
Model 315 ('58 to '74)
Model 320 ('58 to '81)
Model 325 ('58 to '75)
Model 330 ('58 to '81)
Model 330 12 ('64 to '81)
Model 331 Light Show ('70 to '75)
Model 335 ('58 to '77)
Model 340 ('58 to '81)
Model 345 ('58 to '74)
Model 360 ('58 to '81)
Model 360 12 ('64 to '81)
Model 365 ('58 to '74)
Model 370 ('58 to '81)
Model 370 12 ('66; '80 to '81)
Model 375 ('58 to '74)
Model 381 ('58 to '74)
Model 420 ('65 to '81)
Model 450 ('70 to '81)
Model 450 12 ('64 to '81)
Model 460 ('61 to '81)
Model 615 ('62 to '77)
Model 625 ('62 to '77)
Model 1000 ('56 to '70)
Model '93 RM ('64 to '67)
Model '96 RM ('64 to '67)
Model '97 RM ('64 to '67)
Model '98 RM ('64 to '67)
S-29 ('40 to '41)

SELECT OTHERS
Ampeg Dan Armstrong Lucite ('69 to '71)
B.C. Rich Bich-10 ('77)
B.C. Rich Bich Supreme ('78 to '79)

B.C. Rich Mockingbird ('76)
B.C. Rich Seagull II ('77)
B.C Rich Warlock ('86)
Bigsby ('48 to '56)
Bourgeois JOM Brazilian ('93)
Burns Bison ('61 to '62)
Burns Marvin ('64)
Charvel Pre-Pro ('80 to '81)
Charvel EVH Art Series (2004 to 2007)
Charvel Model 4 ('87)
Charvel San Dimas ('81 to '86)
Chapman Stick ('70 to '75)
Collings D-2H Brazilian ('94)
Collings SJ ('92)
Coral Sitar 3S19 ('67 to '69)
Danelectro Convertible ('65)
Danelectro Double Neck 3922 ('60)
Danelectro Guitarlin ('63)
Danelectro U2 ('58)
Danelectro Pro-1 ('63)
D'Angelico New Yorker ('38 to '41)
Dean Cadillac ('79)
Dean ML 'Burst ('77 to '86)
Dean V 'Burst ('77 to '81)
Dobro Model 27 Cyclops ('33)
EKO Rocket ('67 to '69)

Epiphone Casino ('61 to '70)
Epiphone Coronet ('60 to '69)
Epiphone Crestwood Custom ('61 to '69)
Epiphone FT-30 Caballero ('59)
Epiphone FT-45 Cortez ('59)
Epiphone FT-79 Texan ('59)
Epiphone Olympic Double ('60 to '63)
Epiphone Rivera ('63)
Epiphone Sheraton ('58)
Epiphone Wilshire ('62 to '66)
Gallagher Doc Watson ('74)
Grammer G-30 ('65)
Guild Aristocrat ('54 to '63)
Guild Bluegrass Special D-50 ('63)
Guild DE-500 ('62 to '65)
Guild Navarre F-50 ('57)
Guild Starfire III ('60 to '66)
Guild Troubadour F-20 ('57)
Hamer Chaparral ('86)
Hamer Standard ('74)
Hamer Standard ('85)
Hamer Sunburst ('77)
Harmony Buck Owens ('69)
Ibanez GB-20 ('81)
Ibanez PS-10 ('78)

Ibanez JEM 77 ('80 to '90)
Ibanez JEMY2KDNA (2000)
Ibanez JEM 10th Anniversary ('96)
Ibanez Joe Satriani 10th Anniversary ('98)
Ibanez 2459 Destroyer ('75 to '79)
Jackson Kelly Custom ('86)
Jackson Randy Rhoads U.S.A. Concorde ('83)
Jackson Soloist w/Floyd Rose ('84 to '86)
Kay K161 Jimmy Reed ('52 to '58)
Kramer Baretta ('84)
Kramer DMZ 3000 ('78)
Larrivee D-70 ('92)
Mosrite Combo Mark I ('66)
Mosrite Joe Maphis Mark XVIII ('64)
Mosrite Ventures ('63 to '68)
Mossman Winter Wheat ('76)
Music Man Edward Van Halen ('91 to '95)
Music Man Sabre II ('78)
Music Man Steve Morse ('87)
Music Man Stingray II ('76)
National Glenwood-99 ('62

to '65)
National Newport 88 ('64)
National Tri-Cone ('29)
National Style-O ('33)
Ovation Adamas 1587 ('80)
Ovation Breadwinner ('75)
PRS Custom 24 "Yellow" ('85)
PRS Custom 24 ('90)
PRS Dragon I ('92)
PRS McCarty Model ('94)
PRS Santana ('96)
Santa Cruz OM ('87)
Santa Cruz Tony Rice ('76)
Stella Flat Top 12 String ('30)
Steinberger GL ('79 to '84)
Taylor 410 ('93)
Taylor 810 ('75)
Travis Bean TB-500 Standard ('75)
Travis Bean TB-1000 Standard ('75)
Travis Bean TB-3000 Wedge ('75)
Tokai Les Paul Reborn ('76 to '82)
Tokai Springy Sound ('76 to '82)
Vox Phantom VI ('62)
Vox Mark VII ('64 to '67)

GUITARS

GUITARS

Airline Archtop
Tom Pfeifer

1960s Alamo Fiesta
Imaged by Heritage Auctions, HA.com

MODEL YEAR	FEATURES	EXC. COND. LOW	HIGH

17th Street Guitars

2004-2009. Founded by Dave Levine and Colin Liebich. Professional grade, production/custom, solidbody guitars built by luthier John Carruthers in Venice, California.

A Fuller Sound

Luthier Warren Fuller began building professional and premium grade, custom nylon and steel-string flat-tops in '98 in Oakland, California.

Abel

Custom aircraft-grade aluminum body, wood neck, guitars built by twins Jim and Jeff Abel in Evanston, Wyoming. They offered the Abel Axe from '94-'96 and 2000-'01, and still do custom orders. They also made the Rogue Aluminator in the late '90s.

Axe

1994-1996. Offset double-cut aluminum body with dozens of holes in the body, wood neck, various colors by anodizing the aluminum body. Abel Axe logo on the headstock.

1994-1996	Non-trem or trem	$900	$1,250

Abilene

Budget and intermediate grade, production, acoustic and electric guitars imported by Samick.

Abyss

See listing under Pederson Custom Guitars.

Acme

1960s. Imported inexpensive copy electric guitar models for the student market.

Acoustic

Ca. 1965-ca. 1987, 2001-2005, 2008-present. Mainly known for solidstate amps, the Acoustic Control Corp. of Los Angeles, California, did offer guitars and basses from around '69 to late '74. The brand has been revived with a new line of amps.

Black Widow

1969-1970, 1972-1974. Double-cut body, 2 pickups, and protective pad on back. The early version (AC500) had 22 frets, ebonite 'board and later one was 24 frets, rosewood 'board. Acoustic outsourced production, possibly to Japan, but final 200 or so guitars produced by Semie Moseley. The AC700 Black Widow 12-string was also available for '69-'70.

1969-1970		$1,875	$2,500
1972-1974		$1,625	$2,250

Agile

1985-present. Budget grade, production, acoustic and electric guitars imported by Rondo Music of Union, New Jersey. They also offer mandolins.

Aims

Ca. 1972-ca. 1976. Aims (American International Music Sales, Inc.) instruments, distributed by Randall Instruments in the mid-'70s, were copies of classic American guitar and bass models. They also offered a line of Aims amps during the same time.

MODEL YEAR	FEATURES	EXC. COND. LOW	HIGH

Airline

Ca. 1958-1968, 2004-present. Airline originally was a brand used by Montgomery Ward on acoustic, electric archtop and solidbody guitars and basses, amplifiers, steels, and possibly banjos and mandolins. Instruments manufactured by Kay, Harmony and Valco. In '04, the brand was revived by Eastwood guitars on a line of imported intermediate grade, production, reissue guitars and lap steels.

Acoustic Res-O-Glas Resonator

1964. Res-o-glas, coverplate with M-shaped holes, asymmetrical peghead.

1964		$1,125	$1,500

Amp-In-Case Model

1960s. Double-cut, single pickup, short scale guitar with amplifier built into the case, Airline on grille.

1960s		$750	$975

Archtop Acoustic

1950s-1960s. Various models.

1950s-60s	Higher-end	$350	$450
1950s-60s	Lower-end	$175	$225

Electric Hollowbody

1950s-1960s. Various models.

1950s	Kay B Kessel copy	$1,125	$1,500
1960s	ES-175 copy	$550	$650
1960s	Harmony H-54 copy	$550	$650
1960s	Harmony H-75 copy	$650	$825
1960s	Harmony H-76 copy	$925	$1,250
1960s	Kay B Kessel Swingmaster copy	$800	$1,000
1960s	Kay Swingmaster copy	$550	$750
1960s	Kay Tuxedo copy	$900	$1,250
1960s	National Town & Country copy	$1,125	$1,500

Electric Res-O-Glas

1960s. Res-o-glas is a form of fiberglass. The bodies and sometimes the necks were made of this material.

1960s	Jack White style	$2,375	$3,250
1960s	JB Hutto style	$2,375	$3,250
1960s	Other styles, 1 pu	$550	$750
1960s	Other styles, 2 pus	$1,125	$1,500
1960s	Other styles, 3 pus	$1,125	$1,500

Electric Res-O-Glas Resonator

1960s, 2010-present. Res-o-glas is a form of fiberglass. These models have resonator cones in the body.

1960s		$1,000	$1,375
2010-2023	Folkstar	$750	$975

Electric Solidbody (Standard)

1950s-1960s. Various models.

1950s-60s	Lower-end	$800	$1,000

Electric Solidbody (Deluxe)

1950s-1960s. Appointments may include multiple pickups, block inlays, additional logos, more binding.

1950s-60s	Higher-end	$1,125	$1,500

Flat-Top Acoustic

1950s-1960s. Various models.

1950s-60s	Higher-end, 14"-15"	$400	$525
1950s-60s	Lower-end, 13"	$225	$300

MODEL YEAR	FEATURES	EXC. COND. LOW	HIGH

Alamo

1947-1982. Founded by Charles Eilenberg, Milton Fink, and Southern Music, San Antonio, Texas, and distributed by Bruno & Sons. Alamo started out making radios, phonographs, and instrument cases. In '49 they added amplifiers and lap steels. From '60 to '70, the company produced beginner-grade solidbody and hollow-core body electric Spanish guitars. The amps were all-tube until the '70s. Except for a few Valco-made examples, all instruments were built in San Antonio.

Electric Hollowbody

1950s-70s	Higher-end	$1,125	$1,500
1950s-70s	Lower-end	$625	$800

Electric Solidbody

1950s-70s	Higher-end	$1,125	$1,500
1950s-70s	Lower-end	$625	$800

Alamo Guitars

1999-2008. The Alamo brand was revived for a line of handcrafted, professional grade, production/custom, guitars by Alamo Music Products, which also offered Robin and Metropolitan brand guitars and Rio Grande pickups.

Tonemonger

1999-2005. Ash or African Fakimba offset double cut solidbody, 3 single coils, tremolo.

1999-2005		$1,000	$1,375

Alan Carruth

1970-present. Professional and premium grade, production/custom, classical and archtop guitars built by luthier Alan Carruth in Newport, New Hampshire. He started building dulcimers and added guitars in '74. He also builds violins and harps.

Albanus

Ca. 1954-1977. Luthier Carl Albanus Johnson built around 75 high quality custom archtop guitars in Chicago, Illinois. He died in '77. He also built violins and at least two mandolins.

Alberico, Fabrizio

1998-present. Luthier Fabrizio Alberico builds his premium grade, custom, flat-top and classical guitars in Cheltenham, Ontario.

Alden

2005-present. Budget and intermediate grade, production, acoustic and electric guitars, and basses designed by Alan Entwhistle and imported from China.

Alden (Chicago)

1960s. Chicago's Alden was a department store and mail-order house offering instruments from Chicago builders such as Harmony.

H-45 Stratotone

1960s. Alden's version of the H45 Stratotone Mars model, single plain cover pickup.

1960s		$525	$675

Alembic

1969-present. Premium and presentation grade, production/custom, guitars, baritones, and 12-strings built in Santa Rosa, California. They also build basses. Established in San Francisco by Ron and Susan Wickersham, Alembic started out as a studio working with the Grateful Dead and other bands on a variety of sound gear. By '70 they were building custom basses, later adding guitars and cabinets. By '73, standardized models were being offered.

California Special

1988-2009. Double-cut neck-thru solidbody, six-on-a-side tuners, various colors.

1988-2009		$2,500	$3,500

Distillate

1979-1991. Various wood options.

1979-1991		$2,750	$4,000

Little Darling

2006-present. Exotic woods offered, heart inlay at 12th fret, brass bird tailpiece.

2006-2023		$6,000	$7,500

Orion

1990-present. Offset double-cut glued neck solidbody, various colors.

1990-2016		$2,500	$3,750

Series I

1972-present. Neck-thru, double-cut solidbody, book matched koa, black walnut core, 3 pickups, optional body styles available, natural.

1970s-2013	12-string	$7,500	$10,000
1970s-2023	6-string	$7,500	$10,000

Alfieri Guitars

1990-present. Luthier Don Alfieri builds his premium and presentation grade, custom/production, acoustic and classical guitars in Long Island, New York.

Alhambra

1930s. The Alhambra brand was most likely used by a music studio (or distributor) on instruments made by others, including Regal-built resonator instruments.

Allen Guitars

1982-present. Premium grade, production resonators, steel-string flat-tops, and mandolins built by Luthier Randy Allen, Colfax, California.

Alleva-Coppolo Basses and Guitars

1995-present. Professional and premium grade, custom/production, solidbody electric guitars and basses built by luthier Jimmy Coppolo in Dallas Texas for '95-97, in New York City for '98-2008, Upland, CA for "99-'21 and in Gadsden AL 2021-present.

Aloha

1935-1960s. Private branded by Aloha Publishing and Musical Instruments Company, Chicago, Illinois. Made by others. There was also the Aloha

1964 Alden Chicago
Tom Pfeifer

Alembic Little Darling

AlumiSonic Evo-Classic

1992 Alvarez Dana Scoop
Tom Pfeifer

MODEL		EXC. COND.	
YEAR	FEATURES	LOW	HIGH

Manufacturing Company of Honolulu which made musical instruments from around 1911 to the late '20s.

Alosa
1947-1958. Luthier Alois Sandner built these acoustic archtop guitars in Germany.

Alpha
1970s-1980s. One of the brand names of guitars built in the Egmond plant in Holland. Sold by Martin for a while in the 1980s.

Alray
1967. Electrics and acoustics built by the Holman-Woodell guitar factory in Neodesha, Kansas, who also marketed similar models under the Holman brand.

Alternative Guitar and Amplifier Company
Intermediate grade, custom/production, solid-body electric guitars and basses made in Piru, California, by luthiers Mal Stich and Sal Gonzales and imported from Korea, beginning in 2006, under the Alternative Guitar and Amplifier Company, and Mal n' Sal brands.

AlumiSonic
2006-present. Luthier Ray Matter builds his production/custom, professional grade, aluminum/wood hybrid electric guitars in Bohemia and West Islip, New York.

Alvarez
1965-present. Intermediate and professional grade, production, acoustic guitars imported by St. Louis Music. They also offer lap steels, banjos and mandolins. Initially high-quality handmade guitars Yairi made by K. (Kazuo) Yairi were exclusively distributed, followed by the lower-priced Alvarez line. In '90 the Westone brand used on electric guitars and basses was replaced with the Alvarez name; these Alvarez electrics were offered until '02. Many Alvarez electric models designed by luthier Dana Sutcliffe; several models designed by Dan Armstrong.

Alvarez Yairi
1966-present. Alvarez Yairi guitars are hand-crafted and imported by St. Louis Music.

Alvarez, Juan
1952-2019. Professional and premium grade, production/custom, classical and flamenco guitars made in Madrid, Spain, originally by luthier Juan Alvarez Gil (died in 2001), then by son Juan Miguel Alvarez.

American Acoustech
1993-2001. Production steel string flat-tops made by Tom Lockwood (former Guild plant manager)

and Dave Stutzman (of Stutzman's Guitar Center) as ESVL Inc. in Rochester, New York.

American Archtop Guitars
1995-present. Premium and presentation grade, custom 6- and 7-string archtops by luthier Dale Unger, in Stroudsburg, Pennsylvania.

American Conservatory (Lyon & Healy)
Late-1800s-early-1900s. Guitars, mandolins and harp guitars built by Chicago's Lyon & Healy and sold mainly through various catalog retailers. Mid-level instruments above the quality of Lyon & Healy's Lakeside brand, and generally under their Washburn brand. Generally of negligible value because repair costs often exceed their market value.

Acoustic

MODEL		EXC. COND.	
YEAR	FEATURES	LOW	HIGH
1920s	Spanish 6-string	$650	$850
1920s	Tenor 4-string	$650	$850

G2740 Monster Bass
Early-mid-1900s. Two 6-string neck (one fretless), acoustic flat-top harp guitar, spruce top, birch back and sides with rosewood stain, natural. Their catalog claimed it was "Indispensable to the up-to-date mandolin and guitar club."

1917		$3,500	$4,500

Style G Series Harp Guitar
Early-1900s. Two 6-string necks with standard tuners, 1 neck fretless, rosewood back and sides, spruce top, fancy rope colored wood inlay around soundhole, sides and down the back center seam.

1917	Natural	$3,250	$4,500

American Showster
1986-2004, 2010-2011. Established by Bill Meeker and David Haines, Bayville, New Jersey, building guitars shaped like classic car tailfins or motorcycle gas tanks. The Custom Series was made in the U.S.A., while the Standard Series (introduced in '97) was made in Czechoslovakia. They also made a bass. Bill Meeker started production again around 2010 until his death in late '11.

AS-57 Classic
1987-2004. American-made until 2000, body styled like a '57 Chevy tail fin, basswood body, bolt-on neck, 1 humbucker or 3 single-coils, various colors.

1987-1999	US-made	$4,250	$5,500
2000-2004	Import	$1,500	$2,000

The Biker/Tank
1987-1989. Alder body shaped like motorcycle gas tank, 3 single-coil or 2 humbucker pickups, maple neck, rosewood 'board.

1987-1989		$1,375	$1,750

Ampeg
1949-present. Founded in '49 by Everett Hull as the Ampeg Bassamp Company in New York and has built amplifiers throughout its history. In '62 the company added instruments with the introduction of their Baby Bass and from '63 to '65, they carried a

line of guitars and basses built by Burns of London and imported from England. In '66 the company introduced its own line of basses. In '67, Ampeg was acquired by Unimusic, Inc. From '69–'71 contracted with Dan Armstrong to produce lucite "see-through" guitars and basses with replaceable slide-in pickup design. In '71 the company merged with Magnavox. Beginning around '72 until '75, Ampeg imported the Stud Series copy guitars from Japan. Ampeg shut down production in the spring of '80. MTI bought the company and started importing amps. In '86 St. Louis Music purchased the company. In '97 Ampeg introduced new and reissue American-made guitar and bass models. They discontinued the guitar line in '01 but offered the Dan Armstrong plexi guitar again starting in '05, adding wood-bodied versions in '08. They also offered a bass. In '05 LOUD Technologies acquired SLM and the Ampeg brand. In '18, the brand was sold to Yamaha.

AMG1

1999-2001. Dan Amstrong guitar features, but with mahogany body with quilted maple top, 2 P-90-style or humbucker-style pickups.

1999-2001	Hums, gold hw	$650	$850
1999-2001	Kent Armstrong pickups	$475	$625
1999-2001	P-90s, standard hw	$475	$625

Dan Armstrong Lucite

1969-1971. Clear plexiglas solidbody, with interchangeable pickups, Dan Armstrong reports that around 9,000 guitars were produced, introduced in '69, but primary production was in '70-'71, reissued in '98.

1969-1971	Clear	$3,625	$4,750
1969-1971	Smoke	$4,375	$5,750

Dan Armstrong Plexi

1998-2001, 2006-2011. Reissue of Lucite guitar, produced by pickup designer Kent Armstrong (son of Dan Armstrong), offered in smoked (ADAG2) or clear (ADAG1). Latest version is Japanese-made ADA6.

1998-2011	Clear or Smoke	$850	$1,250

Heavy Stud (GE-150/GEH-150)

1973-1975. Import from Japan, single-cut body, weight added for sustain, single-coils or humbuckers (GEH).

1973-1975		$500	$650

Sonic Six (By Burns)

1964-1965. Solidbody, 2 pickups, tremolo, cherry finish, same as the Burns Nu-Sonic guitar.

1964-1965		$550	$725

Stud (GE-100/GET-100)

1973-1975. Import from Japan, double-cut, inexpensive materials, weight added for sustain, GET-100 included tremolo.

1973-1975		$500	$650

Super Stud (GE-500)

1973-1975. Double-cut, weight added for sustain, top-of-the-line in Stud Series.

1973-1975		$500	$650

Thinline (By Burns)

1963-1964. Semi-hollowbody, 2 f-holes, 2 pickups, double-cut, tremolo, import by Burns of London, same

as the Burns TR2 guitar.

1963-1964		$725	$950

Wild Dog (By Burns)

1963-1964. Solidbody, 3 pickups, shorter scale, tremolo, sunburst finish, import by Burns of London, same as the Burns Split Sound.

1963-1964		$775	$1,000

Wild Dog De Luxe (By Burns)

1963-1964. Solidbody, 3 pickups, bound neck, tremolo, sunburst finish, import by Burns of London, same as the Burns Split Sonic guitar.

1963-1964		$825	$1,125

Anderberg

2002-present. Professional and premium grade, production/custom, electric guitars and basses built by luthier Michael Anderberg in Jacksonville, Florida.

Andersen Stringed Instruments

Luthier Steve Andersen builds premium and presentation grade, production/custom flat-tops and archtops in Seattle, Washington, starting in 1978 and he also builds mandolins.

Andreas

1995-2004. Luthier Andreas Pichler built his aluminum-necked, solidbody guitars and basses in Dollach, Austria.

Andrew White Guitars

2000-present. Premium and presentation grade, custom, acoustic flat-top guitars built by luthier Andrew White in Morgantown, West Virginia. He also imports a production line of intermediate and professional grade, acoustic guitars from his factory in Korea.

Andy Powers Musical Instrument Co.

1996-2010. Luthier Andy Powers built his premium and presentation grade, custom, archtop, flat-top, and semi-hollow electric guitars in Oceanside, California. He also built ukes and mandolins.

Angelica

Ca. 1967-ca. 1990s. Entry-level guitars and basses imported from Japan.

Acoustic

1967-1972	Various models	$225	$500

Electric Solidbody

1967-1972	Various models	$300	$650

Angus

1976-present. Professional and premium grade, custom-made steel and nylon string flat-tops built by Mark Angus in Laguna Beach, California.

1976 Alvarez Yairi DY-74
Tom Pfeifer

Ampeg Super Stud GE-500
Imaged by Heritage Auctions, HA.com

1984 Aria Pro II ZZ Deluxe
Kris Fox

1979 Aria Pro II ES-800
Imaged by Heritage Auctions, HA.com

MODEL YEAR	FEATURES	EXC. COND. LOW	HIGH

Antares

1980s-1990s. Korean-made budget electric and acoustic guitars imported by Vega Music International of Brea, California.

Acoustic

1980s-90s	Various models	$135	$175

Double Neck 6/4

1990s. Cherry finish double-cut.

1990s		$650	$850

Solidbody

1980s-90s	Various models	$200	$300

Antique Acoustics

1970s-present. Luthier Rudolph Blazer builds production/custom flat-tops, 12 strings, and archtops in Tubingen, Germany.

Antonio Hermosa

Imported budget grade, production, acoustic and acoustic/electric classical guitars from The Music Link, starting in 2006.

Antonio Lorca

Intermediate and professional grade, production, classical guitars made in Valencia, Spain.

Apollo

Ca. 1967-1972. Entry-level guitars imported by St. Louis Music. They also offered basses and effects.

Electric

1967-1972 Japanese imports, various models

1967-1972		$1,500	$2,000

Applause

1976-present. Budget grade, production, acoustic and acoustic/electric guitars, basses, mandolins and ukes and previously solidbody electrics. Originally Kaman Music's entry-level Ovation-styled brand, it is now owned by Drum Workshop, Inc. The instruments were made in the U.S. until around '82 when production was moved to Korea. On the U.S.-made guitars, the back of the neck was molded Urelite, with a cast aluminum neck combining an I-beam neck reinforcement, fingerboard, and frets in one unit. The Korean models have traditional wood necks.

AA Models

1976-1990s. Acoustic, laminate top, plastic or composition body. Specs and features can vary on AA Models.

1976-1981	US-made	$175	$250
1980s-90s	Import	$100	$150

AE Models

1976-2000s. Acoustic/electric, laminate top, plastic or composition body. Specs and features can vary on AE Models.

1976-1981	US-made	$225	$300
1980-2000s	Import	$125	$175

Applegate

2001-present. Premium grade, production/custom, acoustic and classical guitars built by luthier Brian Applegate in Minneapolis, Minnesota.

APS Custom

2005-present. Luthier Andy Speake builds his production/custom, professional and premium grade, solidbody guitars in Victoria, British Columbia.

Arbor

1983-ca. 2013. Budget and intermediate grade, production, classical, acoustic, and solid and semi-hollow body electric guitars imported by Musicorp (MBT). They also offered basses.

Acoustic

1980s-2013	Various models	$100	$200

Electric

1980s-2013	Various models	$250	$400

Arch Kraft

1933-1934. Full-size acoustic archtop and flat-top guitars. Budget brand produced by the Kay Musical Instrument Company and sold through various distributors.

Aria Diamond

1960s. Brand name used by Aria in the '60s.

Electric

1960s. Various models and appointments in the '60s.

1960s		$550	$750

Aria/Aria Pro II

1956-present. Budget, intermediate, and professional grade, production, electric, acoustic, acoustic/electric, and classical guitars. They also make basses, mandolins, and banjos. Aria was established in Japan in '56 and started production of instruments in '60 using the Arai, Aria, Aria Diamond, and Diamond brands. The brand was renamed Aria Pro II in '75. Aria Pro II was used mainly on electric guitars, with Aria used on others. Over the years, they have produced acoustics, banjos, mandolins, electrics, basses, amplifiers, and effects. Around '87 production of cheaper models moved to Korea, reserving Japanese manufacturing for more expensive models. Around '95 some models were made in U.S., though most contemporary guitars sold in U.S. are Korean. In '01, the Pro II part of the name was dropped altogether.

Early Arias don't have serial numbers or pot codes. Serial numbers began to be used in the mid '70s. At least for Aria guitars made by Matsumoku, the serial number contains the year of manufacture in the first one or two digits (Y##### or YY####). Thus, a guitar from 1979 might begin with 79####. One from 1981 might begin with 1#####. The scheme becomes less sure after 1987. Some Korean-made guitars use a serial number with year and week indicated in the first four digits (YYWW####). Thus 9628#### would be from the 28th week of 1996. However, this is not the case on all guitars, and some have serial numbers which are not date coded.

Models have been consolidated by sector unless specifically noted.

Acoustic Solid Wood Top
1960s-present. Steel string models, various appointments, generally mid-level imports.

1960s-2023		$625	$850

Acoustic Veneer Wood Top
1960s-present. Steel string models, various appointments, generally entry-level imports.

1960s-2023		$275	$375

Classical Solid Wood Top
1960s-present. Various models, various appointments, generally mid-level imports.

1960s-2023		$325	$450

Classical Veneer Wood Top
1960s-present. Various models, various appointments, generally entry-level imports.

1960s-2023		$200	$250

Fullerton Series
1995-2000. Various models with different appointments and configurations based on the classic offset double-cut soldibody.

1995-2000		$550	$775

Herb Ellis (PE-175/FA-DLX)
1978-1987 (Model PE-175) and 1988-1993 (Model FA-DLX). Archtop hollowbody, ebony 'board, 2 humbuckers.

1978-1993		$850	$1,500

Solidbody
1960s-present. Various models, various appointments, generally mid-level imports.

1960s-2023		$675	$1,500

Titan Artist (TA) Series
1967-2012. Double cut, semi-hollow bodies, 2 pickups, various models.

1967-2012		$675	$1,500

Aristides
2010-present. Dutch engineer Aristides Poort developed the material (arium) used to build production/custom, premium grade, solidbody electric guitars in the Netherlands. They also build basses.

ARK - New Era Guitars
2006-present. Luthier A. R. Klassen builds his professional and premium grade, production/custom, reproductions of vintage Larson Brothers instruments in Chesterton, Indiana.

Armstrong, Rob
Custom steel- and nylon-string flat-tops, 12 strings, and parlor guitars made in Coventry, U.K. by luthier Rob Armstrong, starting in 1971. He also builds mandolins and basses.

Arpeggio Korina
1995-present. Professional, premium and presentation grade, production/custom, korina wood solidbody guitars built by luthier Ron Kayfield in Pennsylvania.

Art & Lutherie
Budget and intermediate grade, production, steel- and nylon-string acoustic and acoustic/electric guitars. Founded by luthier Robert Godin, who also has the Norman, Godin, Seagull, and Patrick & Simon brands of instruments.

Artesano
Intermediate and professional grade, production, classical guitars built in Valencia, Spain, and distributed by Juan Orozco. Orozco also made higher-end classical Orozco Models 8, 10 and 15.

Artinger Custom Guitars
1997-present. Luthier Matt Artinger builds his professional and premium grade, production/custom, hollow, semi-hollow, and chambered solidbody guitars and basses in Emmaus, Pennsylvania.

Artur Lang
1949-1975. German luthier Artur Lang is best known for his archtops but did build classicals early on. His was a small shop and much of his output was custom ordered. The instruments were mostly unbranded, but some had L.A. engraved on the headstock.

Asama
1970s-1980s. Some models of this Japanese line of solidbody guitars featured built-in effects. They also offered basses, effects, drum machines and other music products.

Ashborn
1848-1864. James Ashborn, of Wolcottville, Connecticut, operated one of the largest guitar making factories of the mid-1800s. Models were small parlor-sized instruments with ladder bracing and gut strings. Most of these guitars will need repair. Often of more interest as historical artifacts or museum pieces versus guitar collections.

Model 2
1848-1864. Flat-top, plain appointments, no position markers on the neck, identified by Model number.

1855	Fully repaired	$575	$750

Model 5
1848-1864. Flat-top, higher appointments.

1855	Fully repaired	$1,250	$1,625

Asher
1982-present. Luthier Bill Asher builds his professional grade, production/custom, solidbody electric guitars in Venice, California. He also builds lap steels.

Ashland
Intermediate grade, production, acoustic and acoustic/electric guitars made by Korea's Crafter Guitars.

Aristides 080s

Asher T Deluxe

Avalon Americana

B.C. Rich Assassin

Imaged by Heritage Auctions, HA.com

MODEL		EXC. COND.	
YEAR	FEATURES	LOW	HIGH

Astro
1963-1964. The Astro AS-51 was a 1 pickup kit guitar sold by Rickenbacker. German luthier Arthur Strohmer also built archtops bearing this name.

Asturias
Professional and premium grade, production, classical guitars built on Kyushu Island, in Japan.

Atkin Guitars
1995-present. Luthier Alister Atkin builds his production/custom steel and nylon string flat-tops in Canterbury, U.K. He also builds mandolins.

Atlas
Archtop guitars, and possibly other types, built in East Germany and by Zero Sette in Italy.

Atomic
2006-present. Production/custom, intermediate and professional grade, solidbody electric guitars and basses built by luthiers Tim Mulqueeny and Harry Howard in Peoria, Arizona.

Audiovox
Ca. 1935-ca. 1950. Paul Tutmarc's Audiovox Manufacturing, of Seattle, Washington, was a pioneer in electric lap steels, basses, guitars and amps. Tutmarc was a talented Hawaiian steel guitarist and ran a music school and is credited with inventing the electric bass guitar in '35, which his company started selling in the late '30s.

Austin
1999-present. Budget and intermediate grade, production, acoustic, acoustic/electric, resonator, and electric guitars, basses, amps, mandolins, ukes and banjos imported by St. Louis Music.

Acoustic Flat-Top

1999-2023	Various models	$125	$200

Solidbody Electric

1999-2023	Various models	$175	$300

Austin Hatchet
Mid-1970s-mid-1980s. Trademark of distributor Targ and Dinner, Chicago, Illinois.

Hatchet
1981. Travel guitar.

1981		$500	$650

Solidbody Electric
1970s-1980s. Various classic designs.

1970s-80s		$425	$550

Avalon
1920s. Instruments built by the Oscar Schmidt Co. and possibly others. Most likely a brand made for a distributor.

Avalon (Ireland)
2002-present. Luthiers Stevie Graham, Mark Lyttle, Ernie McMillan, Balazs Prohaszka and Robin

Thompson build premium and presentation grade, production/custom, steel-string and classical, acoustic and electro-acoustic guitars in Northern Ireland. In '04-'05 their Silver series was imported from South Korea, and '05 the Gold series from Czech Republic.

Avante
1997-2007. Intermediate grade, production, imported sharp cutaway acoustic baritone guitars designed by Joe Veillette and Michael Tobias and offered by MusicYo. Originally higher priced instruments offered by Alvarez, there was the baritone, a 6-string and a bass.

AV-2 Baritone
1997-2007. Baritone guitar tuned B to B, solid spruce cutaway top, mahogany sides and back.

1997-2007		$350	$450

Avanti
1964-late 1960s. Italian-made guitar brand imported by European Crafts, of Los Angeles. Earlier models were plastic covered; later ones had paint finishes.

Electric Solidbody
1960s. Solidbody, 3 single-coils, dot markers.

1960s		$275	$400

Avar
Late-1960s. Import copy models from Japan, not unlike Teisco, for the U.S. student market.

Solidbody Electric

1969		$275	$400

Aztec
1970s. Japanese-made copy guitars imported into Germany by Hopf.

B.C. Rich
Ca. 1966/67-present. Budget, intermediate, and premium grade, production/custom, import and U.S.-made, electric and acoustic guitars. They also offer basses. Founded by Bernardo Chavez Rico in Los Angeles, California. As a boy he worked for his guitar-maker father Bernardo Mason Rico (Valencian Guitar Shop, Casa Rico, Bernardo's Guitar Shop), building first koa ukes and later, guitars, steel guitars and Martin 12-string conversions. He started using the BC Rich name ca. '66-'67 and made about 300 acoustics until '68, when first solidbody electric made using a Fender neck.

Rich's early models were based on Gibson and Fender designs. The first production instruments were in '69 with 10 fancy Gibson EB-3 bass and 10 matching Les Paul copies, all carved out of single block of mahogany. Early guitars with Gibson humbuckers, then Guild humbuckers, and, from '74-'86, DiMarzio humbuckers. Around 150 BC Rich Eagles were imported from Japan in '76. Ca. '76 or '77 some boltneck guitars with parts made by Wayne Charvel were offered. Acoustic production ended in '82 (acoustics were again offered in '95).

MODEL YEAR	FEATURES	EXC. COND. LOW	HIGH

For '83-'86 the BC Rich N.J. Series (N.J. Nagoya, Japan) was built by Masan Tarada. U.S. Production Series (U.S.-assembled Korean kits) in '84. From '86 on, the N.J. Series was made by Cort in Korea. Korean Rave and Platinum series began around '86. In '87, Rich agreed to let Class Axe of New Jersey market the Korean Rave, Platinum and N.J. Series. Class Axe (with Neal Moser) introduces Virgin in '87 and in '88 Rave and Platinum names are licensed to Class Axe. In '89, Rico licensed the BC Rich name to Class Axe. Both imported and American-made BC Riches are offered during Class Axe management. In 2000, BC Rich became a division of Hanser Music Group.

During '90-'91, Rico begins making his upscale Mason Bernard guitars (approx. 225 made). In '94, Rico resumed making BC Rich guitars in California. He died in 1999.

First 340-360 U.S.-built guitars were numbered sequentially beginning in '72. In '74, serial numbers change to YYZZZ pattern (year plus consecutive production). As production increased in the late-'70s, the year number began getting ahead of itself. By '80 it was 2 years ahead; by '81 as much as 4 years ahead. No serial number codes on imports.

The American B.C. Rich company was first and foremost a custom shop, therefore surprising variants are possible for the models described below, especially in the early years of the company. Many of the first models were offered as either a Standard (also called Deluxe) model or as an upgrade called the Supreme model (technically speaking the Supreme model only applied to the Mockingbird, Eagle, Bich, and Wave).

The prime collector's market for B.C. Rich is the '72-'85 era. The Seagull, Eagle, Mockingbird, Bich, and Wave models are the true vintage models from that '72-'85 epoch. Pre-1985 BC Rich Standard Finishes were Natural, Gloss White, Black, Competition Red, Medium Blue, Metallic Red, and Cherry. Any other finish would be a Custom Color. Most custom colors started appearing in late 1978. Prior to '78, guitars had two tone transparent burst finishes, natural finishes and occasional one-color paint schemes. Custom Color finishes are worth 10% more than standard finish colors.

Assassin
1986-1998, 2000-2010. Double-cut body, 2 humbuckers, maple thru-neck dot markers, various colors.

1986-1989	1st Rico era	$850	$1,125
1989-1993	Class Axe era	$850	$1,125
1994-1998	2nd Rico era USA	$550	$750
2000-2010	Includes QX & PX	$300	$400

B-28 Acoustic
Ca.1967-1982. Acoustic flat-top, hand-built, herringbone trim, pearl R headstock logo.

1967-1982		$2,250	$3,000

B-30 Acoustic
Ca.1967-1982. Acoustic flat-top.

1967-1982		$2,250	$3,000

B-38 Acoustic
Ca.1967-1982. Acoustic flat-top, herringbone trim.

1967-1982		$2,250	$3,000

MODEL YEAR	FEATURES	EXC. COND. LOW	HIGH

B-41 Acoustic
1970s. Acoustic flat-top.

1970s		$2,375	$3,250

B-45 Acoustic
1970s. Hand-built, D-style acoustic flat-top.

1970s		$2,875	$3,750

Beast (U.S.A. Custom Shop)
1999-2015. Exaggerated four point cutaway body, flamed or quilted top.

1999-2015		$1,000	$1,375

Bich 6-String (U.S.A. Assembly)
1980-1998. Four-point sleek body, came in Standard top or Supreme with highly figured maple body and active EQ.

1980-1985	Standard/Deluxe	$4,000	$5,000
1986-1988	Standard/Deluxe	$2,000	$2,500
1988	Supreme	$3,500	$4,500
1989-1993	Class Axe era	$2,000	$2,500
1994-1998	2nd Rico era USA	$2,000	$2,500

Bich 10-String
1977-2015. U.S.-made, doubles on 4 low strings.

1977-1982	Koa	$8,500	$10,500
1977-1982	Opaque finish	$6,500	$8,500
1978-1982	Highly flamed	$7,500	$9,500
1985	Highly quilted	$7,000	$9,000
2005-2015	Highly quilted	$6,500	$8,500

Black Hole
1988. Bolt neck, rosewood 'board, integrated pickup design, Floyd Rose.

1988		$250	$350

Body Art Collection
2003-2006. Imports, 'Body Art Collection' headstock logo, different graphics/different models issued each month from January '03 to March '04, 25th Anniversary model available into '06.

2003-2006	Various models	$250	$350

Bronze Series
2001-2007. Made in China. Includes 2 models: Mockingbird and Warlock.

2001-2007		$75	$125

Doubleneck
1980-1988. Doublenecks were sporadically made, specs (and values) may vary.

1980-1988	Bich	$10,000	$12,500
1980-1988	Eagle	$12,500	$15,500
1980-1988	Iron Bird	$9,500	$11,500
1980-1988	Mockingbird	$12,500	$15,500
1980-1988	Seagull	$13,500	$16,500

Eagle
1975-1982, 2000-2004. Made in USA, often called the Eagle model, but also called Eagle Deluxe or Eagle Standard, features include diamond inlays, unbound rosewood fretboard, 3-on-a-side tuners, generally solid mahogany body, some rare examples with maple body or other woods, some with runners or stringers of alternate exotic wood. (See additional notes in the Eagle Supreme listing.)

1975-1982		$4,000	$6,000

Eagle Special (U.S.A.)
1977-1982. A variant of the Eagle with even more switches and electronic options, the extra options are

1982 B.C. Rich Bich
Erik Van Gansen

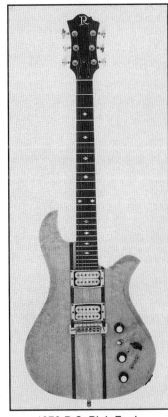

1978 B.C. Rich Eagle
Imaged by Heritage Auctions, HA.com

GUITARS

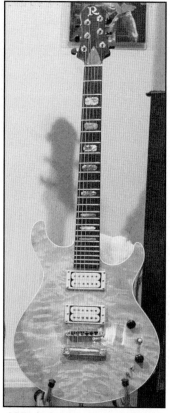

2001 B.C. Rich Exclusive EM I

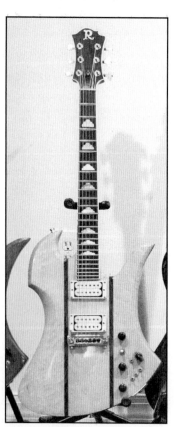

1979 B.C. Rich
Mockingbird Supreme

MODEL YEAR	FEATURES	EXC. COND. LOW	HIGH

not particularly considered an advantage in the BC Rich collector community, therefore an Eagle Special is worth less than the Standard or Eagle Supreme.

| 1977-1982 | | $4,500 | $5,750 |

Eagle Supreme

1975-1982, 2000-2004. Made in USA, Eagle body style with specific options including cloud inlays, fully bound ebony fretboard, 3-on-a-side headstock, various woods including solid koa, maple, highly-figured maple (birdseye, quilted, curly), other exotic woods offered, most with runners or stringers of alternating wood, also available as single solid wood, mid-'80s with original Kahler tremolo unit option, custom colors and sunburst finishes generally on a custom order basis, certain custom colors are worth more than the values shown, early models ca. '75-'82 had a Leo Quan Badass bridge option and those models are highly favored by collectors, early style control knobs with silver metal inserts, full electronics with Varitone and PreAmp and Grover Imperial bullseye tuners, the earliest models had red head mini-switches (later became silver-chrome switches).

| 1975-1982 | | $5,500 | $7,500 |
| 2000-2004 | | $4,000 | $5,000 |

Eagle Supreme Condor

1983-1987. Less than 50 made, simplified electronics system based on customer's requests, features can include cloud inlays, fully bound ebony fretboard neck, bound 3-on-a-side headstock, book matched figured maple top over solid mahogany body with slight arch, no runners or stringers, basic electronics with master volume, master tone, and pickup switch, also commonly called Condor Supreme.

| 1983-1987 | | $2,500 | $3,500 |

Elvira

2001. Elvira (the witch) photo on black Warlock body, came with Casecore coffin case.

| 2001 | | $500 | $650 |

Exclusive EM I

1996-2004. Platinum Series, offset double-cut, bound top, 2 humbuckers.

| 1996-2004 | | $165 | $250 |

Gunslinger

1987-1999. Inverted headstock, 1 (Gunslinger I) or 2 (Gunslinger II) humbuckers, recessed cutout behind Floyd Rose allows player to pull notes up 2 full steps.

1987-1989	Graphic designs	$800	$1,000
1987-1989	Standard finish	$750	$950
1989-1993	Class Axe era	$750	$950
1994-1999	2nd Rico era, bolt-on	$650	$800
1994-1999	2nd Rico era, neck-thru	$650	$800

Ironbird

1983-2004. Pointy body and headstock.

1983-1989		$1,500	$1,875
1989-1993	Class Axe era	$1,250	$1,500
1994-1998	2nd Rico era	$1,250	$1,500

Kerry King Wartribe 1 Warlock

2004-2015. Tribal Fire finish, 2 pickups.

| 2004-2015 | | $165 | $250 |

MODEL YEAR	FEATURES	EXC. COND. LOW	HIGH

Mockingbird

1976-present. Made in USA, also called the Mockingbird Standard or Mockingbird Deluxe, diamond inlays, unbound rosewood 'board, solid mahogany body, rare examples with maple body or other woods, some with runners or stringers of alternate exotic wood. In 2016 'Mk' was added to name (Mk1, Mk3, Mk5, Mk7, Mk9, Mk11). (See additional notes in the Mockingbird Supreme listing.)

1976		$4,500	$6,000
1977-1978	Short horn	$4,500	$6,000
1979-1983	Long horn	$4,500	$6,000
1984		$4,000	$5,000
1985		$4,000	$5,000
1986-1989	Last of 1st Rico era	$3,000	$3,750
1989-1993	Class Axe era	$3,000	$3,750
1994-1999	2nd Rico era, bolt-on	$2,500	$3,250
2000-2023	Custom Shop (COA)	$4,000	$5,000

Mockingbird Ice Acrylic

2004-2006. See-thru acrylic body.

| 2004-2006 | | $300 | $400 |

Mockingbird Legacy

2019-present. Mahogany body, koa or quilted maple top, 2 humbucker pickups, Floyd Rose or STQ hardtail, various colors.

| 2019-2023 | | $950 | $1,250 |

Mockingbird Supreme

1976-1989. Made in USA, Mockingbird body style with options including cloud inlays, fully bound ebony fretboard, 3-on-a-side headstock, various woods including solid koa, maple, highly-figured maple (birdseye, quilted, curly), other exotic woods offered, most with runners or stringers of alternating wood, also available as single solid wood, mid-'80s with original Kahler trem option, custom colors and sunburst finishes generally on a custom order basis, certain custom colors are worth more than the values shown, early models ca. '76-'82 had a Leo Quan Badass bridge option and those models are highly favored by collectors, early style control knobs with silver metal inserts, full electronics with Varitone and PreAmp and Grover Imperial bullseye tuners, the earliest models had red head mini-switches (later became silver-chrome switches).

1976-1978	Earlier short horn	$6,000	$7,500
1976-1978	Short horn	$6,000	$7,500
1979-1982	Later long horn	$6,000	$7,500
1983-1985		$4,500	$5,500
1986-1989		$4,250	$5,250
1989-1993	Class Axe era	$4,000	$5,000
1994-1999	2nd Rico era	$3,750	$4,750

Nighthawk

1978-ca.1982. Eagle-shaped body with bolt neck.

| 1978-1982 | | $800 | $1,125 |

NJ Series/NJC Series

1983-2006. Earlier models made in Japan. Made in Korea '86 forward. All NJ models fall within the same price range. Models include Assassin, Beast, Bich, Ironbird, Eagle, Mockingbird, Outlaw, ST III, Virgin, Warlock. C for Classic added in '06.

| 1983-1984 | Early NJ Japan | $600 | $750 |

MODEL YEAR	FEATURES	EXC. COND. LOW	HIGH
1985-1986	Later Japan	$500	$1,500
1987-2006	Made in Korea	$500	$1,250

Phoenix

1977-ca.1982. Mockingbird-shaped with bolt neck.

1977-1982		$1,000	$1,500

Platinum Series

1986-2006. Lower-priced import versions including Assassin, Beast, Bich, Ironbird, ST, Warlock.

1986-2006		$300	$400

Rave Series

1986-ca. 1990. Korean-made down-market versions of popular models.

1986-1990		$300	$400

Seagull

1972-1975. Single-cut solidbody, neck-thru, 2 humbuckers.

1972-1973	Earliest, 30 made	$3,500	$4,500
1973-1974		$3,500	$4,500
1975		$3,500	$4,500

Seagull II

1974-1977. Double-cut solidbody, neck-thru, 2 humbuckers. Transitional model in '75 between Seagull and Eagle, Seagull Jr. is used interchangable with Seagull II, the company made several variants during this period which some collectors consider to be Seagull Jr. while others consider to be Seagull II. The II/Jr. design was finally changed and called the Eagle.

1974	1st 50, Gibson pus	$3,500	$4,500
1974	Moser, 16 made	$3,500	$4,500
1974	Other from '74	$3,500	$4,500
1976-1977		$3,250	$4,000

Seagull II/Seagull Jr.

1975-1977. Another transitional model starting in '75, the model name Seagull Jr. is used interchangable with Seagull II, the company made several variants during this period which some collectors consider to be Seagull Jr. while others consider to be Seagull II. The design was finally changed and called the Eagle.

1975-1977	II and Jr	$2,500	$3,250

Stealth I Series

1983-1989. Includes Standard (maple body, diamond inlays) and Series II (mahogany body, dot inlays), 2 pickups.

1983-1989	Series II	$2,000	$2,500
1983-1989	Standard	$2,000	$2,500

ST-III (U.S.A.)

1987-1998. Double-cut solidbody, hum/single/single or 2 humbucker pickups, Kahler tremolo.

1987-1989	Bolt-on	$850	$1,125
1987-1989	Neck-thru	$875	$1,250
1989-1993	Class Axe era	$850	$1,250
1994-1998	New Rico era	$850	$1,250

The Mag

2000. U.S. Handcrafted Series Mockingbird Acoustic Supreme, solid spruce top, quilt maple back and sides, pickup with preamp and EQ optional, dark sunburst.

2000		$600	$800

Warlock

1981-present. Made in the USA, also called Warlock Standard, 4-point sleek body style with widow head-

stock. In 2016 'Mk' was added to name (Mk1, Mk3, Mk5, Mk7, Mk9, Mk11).

1981-1989	Standard	$2,500	$3,500
1990-1999	2nd Rico era, bolt-on	$1,500	$2,000
1990-1999	2nd Rico era, neck-thru	$1,500	$2,000

Warlock Extreme

2019-present. Mahogany body, spalted maple and quilted maple top, 2 humbucker pickups, Floyd Rose, various colors.

2019-2023		$1,125	$1,500

Warlock Ice Acrylic

2004-2006. See-thru acrylic body.

2004-2006		$300	$400

Wave

1983. U.S.-made, very limited production based upon the Wave bass.

1983		$8,000	$10,000

B.C. Rico

1978-1982. B.C. Rich's first Japan-made guitars were labeled B.C. Rico until they were sued for patent infringement on the Rico name. They made around 200 guitars and basses with the Rico headstock logo. After '82, B.C. Rich offered the NJ Series (Import) models.

Eagle

1978-1982. All mahogany, rosewood 'board, Dimarzio pickups, mother-of-pearl headstock logo.

1978-1982		$3,500	$4,500

Mockingbird

1978-1982. All mahogany, rosewood 'board, Dual DiMarzio humbuckers.

1978-1982		$3,500	$4,500

RW-2A

1978-1982. Acoustic D-style, Brazilian rosewood laminate body, spruce top, herringbone trim, natural finish.

1978-1982		$900	$1,250

RW-7

1978-1982. D-style, spruce top, Brazilian rosewood back and sides, abalone markers, natural finish.

1978-1982		$900	$1,250

b3 Guitars

2004-present. Premium grade, custom/production, solid, chambered and hollow-body guitars built by luthier Gene Baker in Arroyo Grande, California. He previously made Baker U.S.A. guitars.

Babicz

2004-present. Started by luthier Jeff Babicz and Jeff Carano, who worked together at Steinberger, the company offers intermediate, professional, and premium grade, production/custom, acoustic and acoustic/electric guitars made in Poughkeepsie, New York, and overseas.

b3 Phoenix

Babicz Identity Series
Dreadnought

**1968 Baldwin Model
525 Double Six**

Imaged by Heritage Auctions, HA.com

1967 Baldwin Model 706 V

Rivington Guitars

MODEL YEAR	FEATURES	EXC. COND. LOW	HIGH

Bacon & Day

Established in 1921 by David Day and Paul Bacon, primarily known for fine quality tenor and plectrum banjos in the '20s and '30s. Purchased by Gretsch ca. '40.

Belmont
1950s. Gretsch era, 2 DeArmond pickups, natural.

1950s		$1,500	$2,000

Flat-Top
1930s-1940s. Large B&D headstock logo, fancy or plain appointments.

1930s	Fancy	$3,000	$4,000
1930s	Plain	$2,250	$3,000
1940s	Fancy	$2,500	$3,250
1940s	Plain	$2,000	$2,500

Ramona Archtop
1938-1940. Sunburst.

1938-1940		$1,000	$1,500

Senorita Archtop
1940. Lower-end, sunburst, mahogany back and sides.

1940		$2,250	$3,000

Silver Bell Style 1 Guitar Banjo (Bacon)
1920s. F-hole flange.

1920s		$3,750	$5,000

Style B Guitar Banjo (Bacon)
1920s. Banjo-resonator body with 6-string guitar neck.

1920s		$1,250	$1,625

Sultana I
1930s. Large 18 1/4" acoustic archtop, Sultana engraved on tailpiece, block markers, bound top and back, sunburst.

1938		$4,250	$5,500

Baden

Founded in 2006, by T.J. Baden, a former vice president of sales and marketing at Taylor guitars, initial production based on six models built in Vietnam, intermediate retail-price grade.

Baker U.S.A.

1997-present. Professional and premium grade, production/custom, solidbody electric guitars. Established by master builder Gene Baker after working at the Custom Shops of Gibson and Fender, Baker produced solid- and hollowbody guitars in Santa Maria, California. They also built basses. Baker also produced the Mean Gene brand of guitars from '88-'90. In September '03, the company was liquidated and the Baker U.S.A. name was sold to Ed Roman. Gene Baker currently builds b3 Guitars.

Baldwin

1965-1970. Founded in 1862, in Cincinnati, when reed organ and violin teacher Dwight Hamilton Baldwin opened a music store that eventually became one of the largest piano retailers in the Midwest. By 1965, the Baldwin Piano and Organ company was ready to buy into the guitar market but was outbid by CBS for Fender. Baldwin did procure

Burns of London in September '65 and sold the guitars in the U.S. under the Baldwin name. Baldwin purchased Gretsch in '67. English production of Baldwin guitars ends in '70, after which Baldwin concentrates on the Gretsch brand.

Baby Bison (Model 560)
1965-1970. Double-cut solidbody, V headstock, 2 pickups, shorter scale, tremolo, black, red or white finishes.

1965-1966		$1,250	$1,750
1966-1970	Model 560	$1,000	$1,500

Bison (Model 511)
1965-1970. Double-cut solidbody, scroll headstock, 3 pickups, tremolo, black or white finishes.

1965-1966		$2,000	$2,500
1966-1970	Model 511	$1,500	$2,000

Double Six (Model 525)
1965-1970. Offset double-cut solidbody, 12 strings, 3 pickups, green or red sunburst.

1965-1966		$2,000	$2,500
1966-1970	Model 525	$2,000	$2,500

G.B. 65
1965-1966. Baldwin's first acoustic/electric, single-cut D-style flat-top, dual bar pickups.

1965-1966		$800	$1,000

G.B. 66 De Luxe
1965-1966. Same as Standard with added density control on treble horn, golden sunburst.

1965-1966		$1,125	$1,500

G.B. 66 Standard
1965-1966. Thinline Electric archtop, dual Ultra-Sonic pickups, offset cutaways, red sunburst.

1965-1966		$800	$1,000

Jazz Split Sound/Split Sound (Model 503)
1965-1970. Offset double-cut solidbody, scroll headstock, 3 pickups, tremolo, red sunburst or solid colors.

1965-1966		$1,250	$1,625
1966-1970	Model 503	$1,125	$1,500

Marvin (Model 524)
1965-1970. Offset double-cut solidbody, scroll headstock, 3 pickups, tremolo, white or brown finish.

1965-1966		$1,750	$2,250
1966-1970	Model 524	$1,750	$2,250

Model 706
1967-1970. Double-cut semi-hollowbody, scroll headstock, 2 pickups, 2 f-holes, no vibrato, red or golden sunburst.

1967-1970		$1,000	$1,500

Model 706V
1967-1970. Model 706 with vibrato.

1967-1970		$1,000	$1,500

Model 712R Electric XII
1967-1970. Double-cut semi-hollow body with regular neck, red or gold sunburst.

1967-1970		$750	$1,000

Model 712T Electric XII
1967-1970. Model 712 with thin neck, red or gold sunburst.

1967-1970		$750	$1,000

MODEL		EXC. COND.	
YEAR	FEATURES	LOW	HIGH

Model 801CP Electric Classical
1968-1970. Grand concert-sized classical with transducer based pickup system, natural pumpkin finish.

1968-1970		$750	$1,000

Nu-Sonic
1965-1966. Solidbody electric student model, 6-on-a-side tuners, black or cherry finish.

1965-1966		$750	$1,000

Vibraslim (Model 548)
1965-1970. Double-cut semi-hollowbody, 2 pickups, vibrato, 2 f-holes, red or golden sunburst. Notable spec changes with Model 548 in '66.

1965-1966		$1,250	$1,625
1966-1970	Model 548	$1,125	$1,500

Virginian (Model 550)
1965-1970. Single-cut flat-top, 2 pickups (1 on each side of soundhole), scroll headstock, tremolo, natural.

1965-1966		$1,000	$1,500
1966-1970	Model 550	$1,000	$1,500

Ballurio
Luthier Keith Ballurio builds his intermediate, professional, and premium grade, production/custom, solidbody and chambered guitars in Manassas, Virginia, starting in 2000.

Baltimore
2007-2008. Budget grade, production, solidbody electric guitars imported by The Music Link.

Bambu
1970s. Short-lived brand name on a line of guitars built by Japan's Chushin Gakki Co., which also built models for several other manufacturers.

Baranik Guitars
1995-present. Premium grade, production/custom steel-string flat-tops made in Tempe, Arizona by luthier Mike Baranik.

Barclay
1960s. Thinline acoustic/electric archtops, solidbody electric guitars and basses imported from Japan. Generally shorter scale beginner guitars.

Electric Solidbody
1960s. Various models and colors.

1960s		$275	$400

Barcus-Berry
Founded by John Berry and Les Barcus, in 1964, introducing the first piezo crystal transducer. Martin guitar/Barcus-Berry products were offered in the mid-'80s. They also offered a line of amps from around '76 to ca. '80.

Barrington
1988-1991. Imports offered by Barrington Guitar Werks, of Barrington, Illinois. Models included solidbody guitars and basses, archtop electrics, and acoustic flat-tops. Barrington Music Products is still in the music biz, offering LA saxophones and other products.

Acoustic/Electric
1988-1991. Acoustic/electric, flat-top single-cut with typical round soundhole, opaque white.

1988-1991		$250	$350

Solidbody
1988-ca 1991. Barrington's line of pointy headstock, double-cut solidbodies, black.

1988-1991		$250	$350

Bartell of California
1964-1969. Founded by Paul Barth (Magnatone) and Ted Peckles. Mosrite-inspired designs.

Double Neck

1967		$2,500	$3,250

Electric 12
1967. Mosrite-style body.

1967		$1,500	$2,000

Barth
1950s-1960s. Paul Barth was involved with many guitar companies including National, Rickenbacker, Magnatone and others. He also built instruments under his own brand in California, including guitars, lap steels and amps. Most will have either a Barth logo on plastic plate, or decal.

Mark VIII
1959. Double-cut solidbody, 2 pickups, dot markers, Barth headstock logo.

1959		$2,750	$3,500

Bartolini
1960s. European-made (likely Italian) guitars made for the Bartolini Accordion Company. Similar to Gemelli guitars, so most likely from the same manufacturer. Originally plastic covered, they switched to paint finishes by the mid '60s.

Solidbody

1960s		$600	$775

Bashkin Guitars
1998-present. Luthier Michael Bashkin builds his premium grade, custom, steel-string acoustics in Fort Collins, Colorado.

Basone Guitars
1999-present. Luthier Chris Basaraba builds his custom, professional grade, solid and hollowbody electric guitars and basses in Vancouver, British Columbia.

Bauer, George
1894-1911. Luthier George Bauer built guitars, mandolins, and banjos in Philadelphia, Pennsylvania. He also built instruments with Samuel S. Stewart (S.S. Stewart).

Baxendale
1974-present. Luthier Scott Baxendale builds his professional and premium grade, custom, steel-string acoustic and solidbody electric guitars in Athens, Georgia and previously in Colorado, Tennessee, and Texas.

Baranik

Bashkin The SJ

Bazzolo Guitarworks

Bedell Wildfire

MODEL YEAR	FEATURES	EXC. COND. LOW	HIGH

Bay State

Ca.1890-ca.1910. Bay State was a trademark for Boston's John C. Haynes & Co. and offered guitars and banjos.

Parlor

1890-1910. Small parlor size, mahogany body with salt & pepper binding.

1890-1910		$1,000	$1,500

Bazzolo Guitarworks

1983-2023. Luthier Thomas Bazzolo began building his premium grade, production/custom, classical and flat-top guitars in Lebanon, Connecticut and since 2008 in Sullivan, Maine. He retired in '23.

BC Kingston

1977-present. From 1977 to '96, luthier Brian Kingston built flat-top and semi-hollow acoustic guitars along with a few solidbodies. Presently he builds premium grade, production/custom, archtop jazz and semi-hollow guitars in Prince Edward Island, Canada.

Bear Creek Guitars

Luthier Bill Hardin worked for OMI Dobro and Santa Cruz Guitar before introducing his own line of professional and premium grade, custom-made Weissenborn-style guitars in 1995, made in Kula, Hawaii. He also builds ukes.

Beardsell Guitars

1996-present. Production/custom flat-tops, classical, and electric solidbody guitars built by luthier Allan Beardsell in Toronto, Ontario.

Beaulieu

2006-present. Luthier Hugues Beaulieu builds his production/custom, professional and premium grade, flat-top, flamenco and classical guitars in Pont-Rouge, Quebec.

Beauregard

1992-present. Luthier Mario Beauregard builds his premium and presentation grade, production/custom, flat-top, archtop and jazz guitars in Montreal, Quebec.

Bedell Guitars

1964-present. Intermediate and premium grade, production/custom, flat-top guitars built in Spirit Lake, Iowa and imported from China, designed by luthier Tom Bedell, Dan Mills and Sophia Yang. They also offer Great Divide Guitars and in 2010 acquired Breedlove.

Behringer

1989-present. The German professional audio products company added budget, production, solidbody guitars in '03, sold in amp/guitar packages. They also offer effects and amps.

MODEL YEAR	FEATURES	EXC. COND. LOW	HIGH

Beltona

1990-present. Production/custom metal body resonator guitars made in New Zealand by Steve Evans and Bill Johnson. Beltona was originally located in England. They also build mandolins and ukes.

Beltone

1920s-1930s. Acoustic and resonator guitars made by others for New York City distributor Perlberg & Halpin. Martin did make a small number of instruments for Beltone, but most were student-grade models, most likely made by one of the big Chicago builders. They also made mandolins.

Archtop

1920s-30s		$450	$575

Resonator Copy

1930s. Resonator copy but without a real resonator, rather just an aluminum plate on a wooden top, body mahogany plywood.

1938		$600	$775

Beltone (Import)

1950s-1960s. Japan's Teisco made a variety of brands for others, including the Beltone line of guitars, basses and amps. Carvin sold some of these models in the late 1960s. Italy's Welson guitars also marketed marble and glitter-finished guitars in the U.S. under this brand.

Electric Solidbody

1960s. Japan, 4 pickups.

1960s		$400	$550

Benedetto

1968-present. Premium and presentation grade, production/custom archtop and chambered solidbody guitars, built by luthier Robert Benedetto. He has also built a few violins and solidbodies. He was in East Stroudsburg, Pennsylvania, up to '99; in Riverview, Florida, for '00-'06; and in Savanah, Georgia, since '07. He is especially known for refining the 7-string guitar. From '99 to '06 he licensed the names of his standard models to Fender (see Benedetto FMIC); during that period, Benedetto only made special order instruments. In '06, Howard Paul joined Benedetto as President of the company to begin manufacturing a broader line of more affordable professional instruments.

Benedetto (FMIC)

1999-2006. Premium and presentation, production/custom, acoustic and electric archtops. From '99 to '06, Bob Benedetto had an agreement with Fender (FMIC) to build Benedetto guitars under his guidance and supervision. The guitars were originally built in the FMIC Guild Custom Shop in Nashville, and later in Fender's Corona, California, facility.

Benedict

1988-present. Founded by Roger Benedict. Professional and premium grade, production/custom,

MODEL		EXC. COND.	
YEAR	FEATURES	LOW	HIGH

solid and semi-hollow body guitars and basses built by luthier Bill Hager in Cedar, Minnesota.

Beneteau

1974-present. Custom, premium grade, classical, baritone and steel string acoustic guitars built first in Ottawa, Ontario, and since 1986 in St. Thomas, Ontario by luthier Marc Beneteau. He also builds ukuleles.

Bennett Music Labs

1998-present. Custom guitars built by luthier Bruce Bennett, who helped design the first Warrior line of instruments with J.D. Lewis. He also built amps and Brown Sound effects and guitars for J. Backlund Designs.

Bently

Ca.1985-1998. Student and intermediate grade copy style acoustic and electric guitars imported by St. Louis Music Supply. Includes the Series 10 electrics and the Songwriter acoustics (which have a double reversed B crown logo on the headstock). St. Louis Music replaced the Bently line with the Austin brand.

Berkowitz Guitars

1995-present. Luthier David D. Berkowitz builds his premium grade, custom/production, steel string and baritone guitars and basses in Washington, D.C.

Bernie Rico Jr. Guitars

Professional and premium grade, production/custom, solidbody electrics guitars and basses built by luther Bernie Rico, Jr., the son of B.C. Rich founder, in Hesperia, California.

Bertoncini Stringed Instruments

Luthier Dave Bertoncini began building in 1995, premium grade, custom, flat-top guitars in Olympia, Washington. He has also built solidbody electrics, archtops, mandolins, and ukuleles.

Beyond The Trees

1976-present. Luthier Fred Carlson offers a variety of innovative designs for his professional and presentation grade, production/custom 6- and 12-string flat-tops in Santa Cruz, California. He also produces the Sympitar (a 6-string with added sympathetic strings) and the Dreadnautilus (a unique shaped headless acoustic).

Big Lou Guitar

Mid-2010-present. Located in Perris, California, owner Louis Carroll imports his intermediate grade, production, electric guitars from China.

Big Tex Guitars

Production/custom, professional grade, vintage-style replica guitars, started in 2000, built for owner

Eric Danheim, by luthiers James Love, Mike Simon and Eddie Dale in Houston and Dripping Springs, Texas and Seattle, Washington.

Bigsby

1947-1965, 2002-present. Pedal steel guitars, hollow-chambered electric Spanish guitars, electric mandolins, doublenecks, replacement necks on acoustic guitars, hand vibratos, all handmade by Paul Arthur Bigsby, machinist and motorcycle enthusiast (designer of '30s Crocker motorcycles), in Downey, California. Initially built for special orders.

Bigsby was a pioneer in developing pedal steels. He designed a hand vibrato for Merle Travis. In '48, his neck-through hollow electrics (with Merle Travis) influenced Leo Fender, and Bigsby employed young Semie Moseley. In '56, he designed the Magnatone Mark series guitars and 1 Hawaiian lap steel. He built guitars up to '63.

He built less than 50 Spanish guitars, 6 mandolins, 70 to 150 pedal steels and 12 or so neck replacements. SN was stamped on the end of fingerboard: MMDDYY. In '65, the company was sold to Gibson president Ted McCarty who moved the tremolo/vibrato work to Kalamazoo. Bigsby died in '68. Fred Gretsch purchased the Bigsby company from Ted McCarty in '99 and sold it to Fender in 2019. A solidbody guitar and a pedal steel based upon the original Paul Bigsby designs were introduced in January 2002. These were modeled on the 1963 Bigsby catalog but look very similar to typical Bigsby solidbodys made in the early '50s. Early Bigsby guitars command high value on the collectible market and values here assume authentication by an industry expert.

Standard (Japan)

2007-2008. Various models made in Japan.

2007	Model BY-48N	$1,500	$2,000
2007	Model BY-50	$1,500	$2,000
2007	Model BYS-48	$1,500	$2,000

Standard Solidbody (Spanish)

Late-1940s-1950s, 2002. Standard Guitar, solidbody, natural. Reissue offered in '02.

1948		$250,000	$500,000
1949		$250,000	$500,000
1950-1956		$250,000	$500,000
2002	Reissue	$3,500	$5,000

Bil Mitchell Guitars

1979-present. Luthier Bil Mitchell builds his professional and premium grade, production/custom, flat-top and archtop guitars originally in Wall, New Jersey, and since '02 in Riegelsville, Pennsylvania.

Bill Foley Fine Instruments

2012-present. Luthiers Bill Foley, his son Sam, and Brad Lewis build professional and premium grade, custom electric guitars and basses in Columbus, Ohio.

Benedetto Bambino Elite

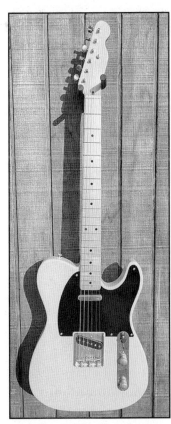

Bennett Music Labs

Bilt ESG

Bischoff 9-String

MODEL		EXC. COND.	
YEAR	FEATURES	LOW	HIGH

Bilt Guitars

2010-present. Professional grade, production/custom, solidbody and semi-hollowbody electric guitars built in Des Moines, Iowa by luthiers Bill Henss and Tim Thelen.

Birdsong Guitars

2001-present. Luthiers Scott Beckwith and Jamie Hornbuckle build their professional grade, production/custom, solidbody guitars and basses in Wimberley, Texas.

Bischoff Guitars

1975-present. Professional and premium-grade, custom-made flat-tops built by luthier Gordy Bischoff in Eau Claire, Wisconsin.

Bishline

1985-present. Luthier Robert Bishline, of Tulsa, Oklahoma, mainly builds banjos, but did build flat-tops and resonators in the past, and still does occasionally.

Black Jack

1960s. Violin-body hollowbody electric guitars and basses, possibly others. Imported from Japan by unidentified distributor. Manufacturers unknown, but some may be Arai.

Blackbird

2006-present. Luthier Joe Luttwak builds his professional grade, production/custom, carbon fiber acoustic guitars in San Francisco, California. He also offers a uke.

Blackshear, Tom

1958-2023. Premium and presentation grade, production, classical and flamenco guitars made by luthier Tom Blackshear in San Antonio, Texas, until his death in '23.

Blade

1987-present. Intermediate and professional grade, production, solidbody guitars and basses from luthier Gary Levinson and his Levinson Music Products Ltd. located in Switzerland.

California Custom
1994-2010. California Standard with maple top and high-end appointments.

1994-2010		$1,000	$1,375

California Deluxe/Deluxe
1994-1995. Standard with mahogany body and maple top.

1994-1995		$650	$850

California Hybrid
1998-1999. Standard with piezo bridge pickup.

1998-1999		$575	$750

California Standard
1994-2007. Offset double-cut, swamp ash body, bolt neck, 5-way switch.

1994-2007		$425	$550

R3
1988-1993. Offset double-cut maple solidbody, bolt maple neck, 3 single-coils or single/single/humbucker.

1988-1993		$625	$850

R4
1988-1993. R3 with ash body and see-thru color finishes.

1988-1992		$625	$850

Texas Series
2003-present. Includes Standard (3 single-coils) and Deluxe (gold hardware, single/single/hum pickups).

2003-2023	Deluxe	$500	$650
2003-2010	Special	$475	$625
2003-2023	Standard	$475	$625

Blanchard Guitars

1994-present. Luthier Mark Blanchard builds premium grade, custom steel-string, and classical guitars originally in Mammoth Lakes, California, and since May '03, in northwest Montana.

Blindworm Guitars

2008-present. Luthiers Andrew J. Scott and Steven Sells build premium and presentation grade, production/custom, acoustic, electric and electric-acoustic guitars, basses, mandolins, banjos and others in Colorado Springs, Colorado.

Blount

Professional and premium grade, production/custom, acoustic flat-top guitars built by luthier Kenneth H. Blount Jr. in Sebring, Florida. He started in 1985.

Blue Star

Luthier Bruce Herron began building production/custom guitars in 1984, in Fennville, Michigan. He also builds mandolins, lap steels, dulcimers and ukes.

Bluebird

1920s-1930s. Private brand with Bluebird painted on headstock, built by the Oscar Schmidt Co. and possibly others. Most likely made for distributor.

13" Flat-Top

1930s		$175	$250

Bluebird Guitars

2011-present. Luthiers Rob Bluebird and Gian Maria Camponeschi build premium grade, custom, archtop and solidbody guitars in Rome, Italy. They build production resonator guitars in Bali, Indonesia. They also offer basses and ukuleles.

Blueridge

Early 1980s-present. Intermediate and professional grade, production, solid-top acoustic guitars distributed by Saga. In '00, the product line was redesigned with the input of luthier Greg Rich (Rich and Taylor guitars).

MODEL YEAR	FEATURES	EXC. COND. LOW	HIGH

Bluesouth

1991-ca. 2006. Custom electric guitars built by luthier Ronnie Knight in Muscle Shoals, Alabama. He also built basses.

Boaz Elkayam Guitars

Presentation grade, custom steel, nylon, and flamenco guitars made by luthier Boaz Elkayam, starting in 1985, in Chatsworth, California.

Boedigheimer Instruments

2000-present. Luthier Brian Boedigheimer builds his professional and premium grade, production/custom, semi-hollowbody electric guitars in Red Wing, Minnesota.

Bohmann

1878-ca. 1926. Acoustic flat-top guitars, harp guitars, mandolins, banjos, violins made in Chicago Illinois, by Joseph Bohmann (born 1848, in Czechoslovakia). Bohmann's American Musical Industry founded 1878. Guitar body widths are 12", 13", 14", 15". He had 13 grades of guitars by 1900 (Standard, Concert, Grand Concert sizes). Early American use of plywood. Some painted wood finishes. Special amber-oil varnishes. Tuner bushings. Early ovalled fingerboards. Patented tuner plates and bridge design. Steel engraved label inside. Probably succeeded by son Joseph Frederick Bohmann.

Ca. 1896 12" body faux rosewood, 13", 14" and 15" body faux rosewood birch, 12", 13", 14" and 15" body sunburst maple, 12", 13", 14" and 15" body rosewood. By 1900 Styles 0, 1, 2 and 3 Standard, Concert and Grand Concert maple, Styles 1, 2, 3, 4, 5, 6, 7, 8, 9, 10, 11 and 12 in Standard, Concert, and Grand Concert rosewood.

14 3/4" Flat-Top

Solid spruce top, veneered Brazilian rosewood back and sides, wood marquetry around top and soundhole, natural. Each Bohmann should be valued on a case-by-case basis.

1896-1900	Brazilian	$1,250	$1,750
1896-1900	Other woods	$650	$850

Harp Guitar

1896-1899	All styles	$3,500	$4,500

Bolin

1978-present. Professional and premium grade, production/custom, solidbody guitars and basses built by luthier John Bolin in Boise, Idaho. Bolin is well-known for his custom work. His Cobra guitars are promoted and distributed by Sanderson Sales and Marketing as part of the Icons of America Series.

NS

1996-2011. Slot-headstock, bolt-on neck, single-cut solidbody, Seymour Duncan passive pickups or EMG active, from '96 to the fall of 2001 custom-built serial numbers to 0050 then from the fall of '01 to the present production model build starting with SN 0051.

1996-2001	Custom-built	$2,500	$3,250
2001-2011	Standard production	$950	$1,250

Bolt

1988-1991. Founded by luthier Wayne Bolt and Jim Dala Pallu in Schnecksville, Pennsylvania, Bolt's first work was CNC machined OEM necks and bodies made for Kramer and BC Rich. In '90, they started building solidbody Bolt guitars, many with airbrushed graphics. Only about 100 to 125 were built, around 40 with graphics.

Bond

1984-1985. Andrew Bond made around 1,400 Electraglide guitars in Scotland. Logo says 'Bond Guitars, London'.

ElectraGlide

1984-1985. Black carbon graphite 1-piece body and neck, double-cut, 3 single-coils (2 humbuckers were also supposedly available), digital LED controls that required a separate transformer.

1984-1985	With attachments	$1,500	$2,000

Borges Guitars

2000-present. Luthier Julius Borges builds his premium grade, production/custom, acoustic guitars in Groton, Massachusetts.

Boucher

2005-present. Professional and premium grade, acoustic guitars built by luthier Robin Boucher in Quebec.

Boulder Creek Guitars

2007-present. Intermediate and professional grade, production, imported dreadnought, classical, and 12-string guitars, basses and ukes distributed by Morgan Hill Music of Morgan Hill, California.

Bourgeois

1993-1999, 2000-present. Luthier Dana Bourgeois builds his professional and premium grade, production/custom, acoustic and archtop guitars in Lewiston, Maine. Bourgeois co-founded Schoenberg guitars and built Schoenberg models from '86-'90. Bourgeois' 20th Anniversary model was issued in '97. Bourgeois Guitars, per se, went out of business at the end of '99. Patrick Theimer created Pantheon Guitars, which included 7 luthiers (including Bourgeois) working in an old 1840s textile mill in Lewiston, Maine and Bourgeois models continue to be made as part of the Pantheon organization.

A-500

Top-of-the-line acoustic cutaway archtop, natural.

1997		$5,000	$6,500

Blues

1996. D-style, all koa.

1996		$3,000	$4,000

Country Boy

1998-present. Pre-war D-style designed for Ricky Skaggs, Sitka spruce top, mahogany back and sides, Ricky Skaggs label, natural.

1998-2023		$3,000	$4,000

Blade Texas Deluxe

Boulder Creek Grand Auditorium

GUITARS

GUITARS

1998 Bourgeois OM

Tom Pfeifer

Breedlove Oregon Concert CE

MODEL YEAR FEATURES	EXC. COND. LOW	HIGH

Country Boy Custom

1999-2016. Adirondack spruce top, figured mahogany back and sides.

| 1999-2016 | $3,000 | $4,000 |

Country Boy Deluxe

2003-2015. Country Boy with Adirondack spruce top, rosewood binding.

| 2003-2015 | $3,000 | $4,000 |

D - 20th Anniversary

1997. 20 made, bear claw spruce top, rosewood back and sides, mother-of-pearl 'board, ornate abalone floral pattern inlay, abalone rosette and border, natural.

| 1997 | $3,000 | $4,000 |

D-150/Style 150/"One-Fifty"

2002-present. Brazilian rosewood, premium Adirondack, abalone rosette. Called Style 150 in '20, then "One-Fifty" in '22.

| 2002-2023 | $5,750 | $7,500 |

DBJC

Jumbo cutaway, Indian rosewood back and sides, redwood top, gloss finish.

| 2007 | $3,500 | $4,500 |

Georgia Dreadnought

2003. Mahogany, Adirondack.

| 2003 | $2,500 | $3,000 |

JOM

1993-2015. Jumbo Orchestra Model flat-top, 15 5/8". Model includes one with cedar top, mahogany back and sides, and one with spruce top, Brazilian rosewood back and sides.

1993	Brazilian rosewood	$6,000	$7,500
1993	Mahogany	$3,000	$4,000
1993-2015	Indian rosewood	$3,000	$4,000

JOMC/OMC

1995-2015. Jumbo Orchestra cutaway, figured mahogany (OMC) and Indian rosewood (JOMC).

| 1995-2011 | OMC, mahogany | $4,000 | $5,500 |
| 1995-2015 | JOMC200, Indian rw | $3,500 | $4,500 |

JR-A

1990s. Artisan Series, 15 5/8", spruce top, rosewood back and sides.

| 1990s | $1,500 | $2,000 |

LC4 Archtop Limited Edition

2002. Limited edition of 12, signed and numbered, premium Sitka and carved curly maple.

| 2002 | $11,000 | $14,000 |

Martin Simpson

1997-2003. Grand auditorium with unusual cutaway that removes one-half of the upper treble bout, Englemann spruce top, Indian rosewood back and sides, natural.

| 1997-2003 | $2,500 | $3,250 |

OM

1993-1999. Standard size OM, spruce top, rosewood back and sides.

| 1993-1999 | $3,500 | $4,500 |

OM Deluxe Artisan

2002. Indian rosewood, Sitka.

| 2002 | $2,500 | $3,250 |

MODEL YEAR FEATURES	EXC. COND. LOW	HIGH

OM Soloist

1990s-present. Full-sized, soft cutaway flat-top, Adirondack spruce top, figured Brick Red Brazilian rosewood back and sides, natural. Named just Soloist in '22.

| 1990-2023 | $6,000 | $7,500 |

Ricky Skaggs Signature

1998. D-style, rosewood sides and back, spruce top.

| 1998 | $3,500 | $4,500 |

Slope D

1993-2021. D-size, 16", spruce top, mahogany back and sides.

| 1993-2021 | $4,000 | $5,250 |

Vintage D

2000-present. Adirondack spruce (Eastern red spruce) top, optional rosewood back and sides. D dropped from name in '22.

| 2000-2023 | Indian rosewood | $2,750 | $3,500 |
| 2000s | Brazilian rosewood | $6,000 | $7,500 |

Vintage OM

2005. Madagascar rosewood and Italian spruce top.

| 2005 | $3,750 | $5,000 |

Bown Guitars

Luthier Ralph Bown builds custom steel-string, nylon-string, baritone, and harp guitars, starting 1981, in Walmgate, U.K.

Bozo

1964-present. Bozo (pronounced Bo-zho) Podunavac learned instrument building in his Yugoslavian homeland and arrived in the United States in '59. In '64 he opened his own shop and built a variety of high-end, handmade, acoustic instruments, many being one-of-a-kind. He has built around 570 guitars over the years. There were several thousand Japanese-made (K. Yairi shop) Bell Western models bearing his name made from '79-'80; most of these were sold in Europe. He currently builds premium and presentation grade, custom guitars in Port Charlotte, Florida.

Acoustic

1970s-1980s. US-made, 6- and 12-string, appointments vary.

| 1970s-80s | Various models | $2,250 | $10,000 |

Bradford

Mid-1960s. Brand name used by the W.T. Grant Company, one of the old Five & Ten style retail stores similar to F.W. Woolworth and Kresge. Many of these guitars and basses were made in Japan by Guyatone.

Acoustic Flat-Top

| 1960s | | $225 | $300 |

Electric Solidbody

1960s	1 or 2 pickups	$225	$300
1960s	3 pickups	$325	$450
1960s	4 pickups	$375	$475

Bradley

1970s. Budget Japanese copy models imported by Veneman's Music Emporium.

MODEL YEAR FEATURES	EXC. COND. LOW	HIGH

Brawley Basses

Headquartered in Temecula, California, and designed by Keith Brawley, offering solidbody guitars and basses made in Korea.

Brazen

Starting in 2005, owner Steve Tsai, along with luthier Eddie Estrada, offered professional and premium grade, production, electric guitars. Steve also imports a line of intermediate grade guitars from China which are set up in the U.S.

Breedlove

1990-present. Founded by Larry Breedlove and Steve Henderson. Intermediate, professional, premium, and presentation grade, production/custom, steel, and nylon string flat-top built in Bend, Oregon and imported. They also build mandolins, basses, lapsteels and ukes. Several available custom options may add to the values listed here. They offered chambered electric guitars starting in 2008 but in January 2010, Breedlove discontinued all electric guitar production. Also, in '10, they became part of Two Old Hippies.

Brentwood

1970s. Student models built by Kay for store or jobber.

K-100

1970s. 13" student flat-top, K-100 label inside back, K logo on 'guard.

1970s	$55	$100

Brian May Guitar Company

2006-present. Guitarist Brian May teamed up with Barry Moorhouse and Pete Malandrone to offer versions of his Red Special Guitar. They also offered a bass.

Brian May Special

2006-present. Mahogany solidbody, 3 pickups, various colors.

2006-2023	$500	$650

Brian Moore

1992-present. Founded by Patrick Cummings, Brian Moore and Kevin Kalagher in Brewster, New York; they introduced their first guitars in '94. Initially expensive custom shop guitars with carbon-resin bodies with highly figured wood tops; later went to all wood bodies cut on CNC machines. The intermediate and professional grade, production, iGuitar/i2000series was introduced in 2000 and made in Korea but set up in the U.S. Currently the premium grade, production/custom, Custom Shop Series guitars are handcrafted in La Grange, New York. They also build basses and electric mandolins.

C/DC/MC Series

1994-2011. Various models.

1994-2011	$1,500	$2,000

iGuitar Series

2000-present. Various models.

2000-2023	$850	$1,250

MODEL YEAR FEATURES	EXC. COND. LOW	HIGH

Brian Stone Classical Guitars

Luthier Brian Stone builds his classical guitars in Corvallis, Oregon.

Briggs

1999-present. Luthier Jack Briggs builds his professional and premium grade, production/custom, chambered and solidbody guitars in Raleigh, North Carolina.

Broman

1930s. The Broman brand was most likely used by a music studio (or distributor) on instruments made by others, including Regal-built resonator instruments.

Bronson

Ca. 1934-early 1960s. George Bronson was a steel guitar instructor in the Detroit area and his instruments were made by other companies. They were mainly lap steels (usually sold with a matching amp), but some other types were also offered.

Honolulu Master Hawaiian

1938	$3,750	$4,750

Student Hawaiian (Acoustic)

1930s	13" flat-top	$250	$350

Brook Guitars

1993-present. Simon Smidmore and Andy Petherick build their production/custom Brook steel-string, nylon-strings, and archtops in Dartmoor, U.K.

Brown's Guitar Factory

1982-present. Luthier John Brown builds professional and premium grade, production/custom, solidbody guitars, basses and lap steels in Inver Grove Heights, Minnesota.

Bruné, R. E.

1966-present. Luthier Richard Bruné builds his premium and presentation grade, custom, classical and flamenco guitars in Evanston, Illinois. He also offers his professional and premium grade Model 20 and Model 30, which are handmade in a leading guitar workshop in Japan. Bruné's "Guitars with Guts" column appears quarterly in Vintage Guitar magazine.

Bruno and Sons

Distributor Bruno and Sons marketed a variety of brands, including their own. Later became part of Kaman Music.

Harp Guitar

1924	$2,500	$4,000

Hollowbody Electric

1960s-1970s. Various imported models.

1960s	$175	$300

1999 Brian Moore C90
Imaged by Heritage Auctions, HA.com

R. E. Bruné 30-S

Buddy Blaze

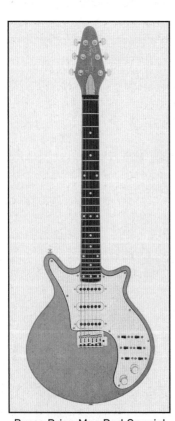

Burns Brian May Red Special

Imaged by Heritage Auctions, HA.com

MODEL YEAR	FEATURES	EXC. COND. LOW	HIGH
Parlor Guitar			
1880-1920. Various woods used on back and sides.			
1880-1920	Birch	$650	$850
1880-1920	Brazilian rosewood	$1,500	$2,000
1880-1920	Mahogany	$750	$975

Buddy Blaze

1985-present. Professional and premium grade, custom/production, solidbody electric guitars built by luthier Buddy Blaze from '85 to '87 in Arlington, Texas, and presently in Kailua Kona, Hawaii. He also designs intermediate grade models which are imported.

Bunker

1961-present. Founder Dave Bunker built custom guitars and basses while performing in Las Vegas in the '60s and developed a number of innovations. Around '92 Bunker began PBC Guitar Technology with John Pearse and Paul Chernay in Coopersburg, Pennsylvania, building instruments under the PBC brand and, from '94-'96, for Ibanez' USA Custom Series. PBC closed in '97 and Bunker moved back to Washington State to start Bunker Guitar Technology and resumed production of several Bunker models. In early 2002, Bunker Guitars became part of Maple Valley Tone Woods of Port Angeles, Washington. Currently Bunker offers intermediate, professional, and premium grade, production/custom, guitars, and basses built in Port Angeles. Most early Bunker guitars were pretty much custom-made in low quantities.

Burke

Ca. 1960-ca. 1966. 6- and 12- string electric guitars built by Glen Burke's Tuning Fork Guitar Company in Eugene and Grants Pass, Oregon and mostly sold in kit form. The guitars featured an aluminum neck-thru design with the body portion of the neck shaped being a rectangular box where the body wings are attached. Being kit guitars finishes, pickups, options and build quality will vary.

Burlesk Guitars

1994-present. Professional and premium grade, custom, solidbody electric guitars and basses, built by luthier James Burley in Alberta, Canada.

Burly Guitars

Luthier Jeff Ayers, starting in 2007, builds professional and premium grade, custom, solid and semi-hollowbody guitars, in Land O' Lakes, Wisconsin.

Burns

1960-1970, 1974-1983, 1992-present. Intermediate and professional grade, production, electric guitars built in the U.K. and Asia. They also build basses. Jim Burns began building guitars in the late-'50s and established Burns London Ltd in '60. Baldwin Organ (see Baldwin listing) purchased the company in '65 and offered the instruments until '70. The Burns name was revived in '91 by Barry Gibson as Burns London, with Jim Burns' involvement, offering reproductions of some of the classic Burns models of the '60s. Jim Burns passed away in August '98. In 2020, it was announced new instruments for '21.

MODEL YEAR	FEATURES	EXC. COND. LOW	HIGH
Baby Bison			
1965. Double-cut solidbody, scroll headstock, 2 pickups, shorter scale, tremolo.			
1965		$1,250	$1,625
Bison			
1964-1965, 2003-2020. Double-cut solidbody, 3 pickups, tremolo, black or white, scroll-headstock, replaced flat headstock Black Bison. Has been reissued with both types of headstocks.			
1961-1962	Black, 4 pus, flat hs	$3,500	$5,000
1962-1965	Black, 3 pus, scroll hs	$3,000	$4,000
1962-1965	White, 3 pus, scroll hs	$3,000	$4,000
2003-2020	Reissue	$550	$750
Brian May Signature - Red Special			
2001-2006. A replica of May's original 'Red Special' but with added whammy-bar, red finish. Korean-made.			
2001-2006		$850	$1,500
Cobra			
2004-2020. Double-cut solid, 2 pickups.			
2004-2020		$150	$200
Double Six			
1964-1965, 2003-2020. Solidbody 12-string, double-cut, 3 pickups, greenburst. Reissue made in Korea.			
1964-1965		$2,500	$3,000
2003-2020		$300	$400
Flyte			
1974-1977. Fighter jet-shaped solidbody, pointed headstock, 2 humbucking pickups, silver, has been reissued.			
1974-1977		$875	$1,250
GB66 Deluxe			
1965. Like 66 Standard, but with bar pickups and add Density control.			
1965		$1,125	$1,500
GB66 Deluxe Standard			
1965. Offset double-cut, f-holes, 2 Ultra-Sonic pickups.			
1965		$1,000	$1,375
Jazz			
1962-1965. Offset double-cut solid, shorter scale, 2 pickups.			
1962-1965		$1,375	$1,750
Jazz Split Sound			
1962-1965. Offset double-cut solid, 3 pickups, tremolo, red sunburst.			
1962-1965		$1,750	$2,250
Marquee			
2000-2020. Offset double-cut solid, 3 pickups, scroll headstock.			
2000-2020		$300	$400

MODEL YEAR FEATURES	EXC. COND. LOW	HIGH
Marvin		
1964-1965. Hank Marvin, offset double-cut solidbody, scroll headstock, 3 pickups, tremolo, white.		
1964-1965	$2,500	$3,500
Nu-Sonic		
1964-1965. Solidbody, 2 pickups, tremolo, white or cherry, has been reissued.		
1964-1965	$1,250	$1,625
Sonic		
1960-1964. Double shallow cut solid, 2 pickups, cherry.		
1960-1964	$925	$1,250
Split Sonic		
1962-1964. Solidbody, 3 pickups, bound neck, tremolo, red sunburst.		
1962-1964	$1,375	$1,750
Steer		
2000-2020. Semi-hollowbody, sound-hole, 2 pickups, non-cut and single-cut versions.		
2000-2020	$425	$550
TR-2		
1963-1964. Semi-hollow, 2 pickups, red sunburst.		
1963-1964	$1,375	$1,750
Vibra Artist		
1960-1962. Double-cut, mahogany, 3 pickups, 6 knobs.		
1960-1962	$1,375	$1,750
Vibraslim		
1964-1965. Double-cut, f-holes, 2 pickups, red sunburst.		
1964-1965	$1,375	$1,750
Virginian		
1964-1965. Burns of London model, later offered as Baldwin Virginian in '65.		
1964-1965	$1,375	$1,750
Vista Sonic		
1962-1964. Offset double-cut solid, 3 pickups, red sunburst.		
1962-1964	$1,375	$1,750

Burnside
1987-1988. Budget solidbody guitars imported by Guild.

Solidbody Electric/Blade
1987-1988. Solidbody, fat pointy headstock.

1987-1988	$200	$250

Burns-Weill
1959. Jim Burns and Henry Weill teamed up to produce three solidbody electric and three solidbody bass models under this English brand. Models included the lower end Fenton, a small single-cutaway, 2 pickups and an elongated headstock and the bizarrely styled RP2G. Henry Weill continued to produce a slightly different RP line under the re-named Fenton-Weill brand.

Burny
1980s-1990s. Solidbody electric guitars from Fernandes and built in Japan, Korea, or China.

Burrell
1984-2010. Luthier Leo Burrell built his professional grade, production/custom, acoustic, semi-hollow, and solidbody guitars and basses in Huntington, West Virginia. Leo retired in '10.

Burton Guitars
1980-present. Custom classical guitars built by luthier Cynthia Burton in Portland, Oregon.

Buscarino Guitars
1981-present. Luthier John Buscarino builds his premium and presentation grade, custom archtops and steel-string and nylon-string flat-tops in Franklin, North Carolina.

Byers, Gregory
1984-present. Premium grade, custom classical and Flamenco guitars built by luthier Gregory Byers in Willits, California.

Byrd
1998-present. Custom/production, professional and premium grade, V-shaped electric guitars, built by luthiers James Byrd and Joe Riggio, in Seattle and several other cities in the state of Washington.

C. Fox
1997-2002. Luthier Charles Fox built his premium grade, production/custom flat-tops in Healdsburg, California. In '02 he closed C. Fox Guitars and moved to Portland, Oregon to build Charles Fox Guitars.

C.F. Mountain
1970s-early 1980s. Japanese copy acoustics made by Hayashi Musical Instrument Ltd with headstock logo that looks very much like that of a certain classic American guitar company.

Acoustic

1970s-80s	$85	$150

CA (Composite Acoustics)
1999-2010, 2011-present. Professional grade, production, carbon fiber composite guitars that were built in Lafayette, Louisiana. The company ceased production in February, '10. At the end of '10 CA was acquired by Peavey, which launched the new Meridian, Mississippi-based line in January, '11.

Califone
1966. Six and 12-string guitars and basses made by Murphy Music Industries (maker of the Murph guitars) for Rheem Califone-Roberts which manufactured tape recorders and related gear. Very few made.

Callaham
1989-present. Professional, production/custom, solidbody electric guitars built by luthier Bill Callaham in Winchester, Virginia. They also make tube amp heads.

1965 Burns GB66 Deluxe
Peter Hvidegaard

Gregory Byers

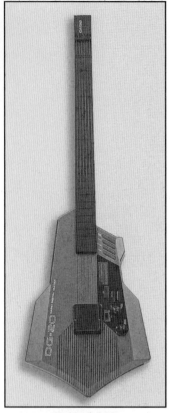

Casio DG20

Casper CGT-20 Classic

MODEL YEAR	FEATURES	EXC. COND. LOW	HIGH

Camelli
1960s. Line of solidbody electric guitars imported from Italy.
Solidbody Electric

1960s		$650	$850

Cameo
1960s-1970s. Japanese- and Korean-made electric and acoustic guitars. They also offered basses.
Electric

1960s-70s	Various models	$350	$450

Campbell American Guitars
2005-2015. Luthier Dean Campbell built his intermediate and professional grade, production/custom, solidbody guitars originally in Pawtucket, Rhode Island, then in Westwood, Massachusetts. From '02 to '05, he built guitars under the Greene & Campbell brand.

Campellone
1978-present. Luthier Mark Campellone builds his premium grade, custom archtops in Greenville, Rhode Island. He also made electrics and basses in the '70s and '80s, switching to archtops around '90.
Deluxe
1990-present. 16" to 18" archtop, middle of the company product line, blond or sunburst.

1990-2023		$5,000	$6,500

Special
1994-present. 16" to 18" archtop, top of the company product line, carved spruce top, carved flamed maple back, flamed maple sides, blond or sunburst.

1994-2023		$5,500	$7,250

Standard
2000-present. 16" to 18" archtop, lower of the 3 model lines offered.

2000-2023		$3,750	$5,000

Canvas
2004-2012. Budget and intermediate grade, production, acoustic and electric guitars, and basses imported from China by America Sejung Corp. until '11, then in South Korea.

Carbonaro
Luthier Robert Carbonaro began building in 1975, premium grade, production/custom, archtop and flat-top guitars in Santa Fe, New Mexico. Relocated his shop to Mexico in 2016, then Vietnam in '19.

Carl Fischer
1920s. Most likely a brand made for a distributor. Instruments built by the Oscar Schmidt Co. and possibly others.

Carlos
Ca.1976-late 1980s. Imported copies of classic American acoustics distributed by Coast Wholesale Music.

MODEL YEAR	FEATURES	EXC. COND. LOW	HIGH

Acoustic Flat-Top

1976-1980s	Various models	$200	$250

Carson Robison
1933-1938. Wards sold guitars endorsed by popular country artist Carson Robison. Built by Gibson, the guitars were the same as models sold under the Kalamazoo brand.
Model K
1933-1938. Flat top, ladder, K #926 same as Kalamazoo KG-11, K #1281/#1115 same as Kalamazoo K-14. Becomes the Recording King (Ward's main brand) Model K in '38.

1933-1935	K#926	$1,500	$2,000
1936-1938	K#1281/1115	$2,250	$3,000

Carvin
1946-present. Intermediate and professional grade, production/custom, acoustic and electric guitars, and basses built in San Diego, California. They also offer amps and mandolins. Founded in Los Angeles by Hawaiian guitarist and recording artist Lowell C. Kiesel as the L.C. Kiesel Co. making pickups for guitars. Bakelite Kiesel-brand electric Hawaiian lap steels are introduced in early-'47. Small tube amps introduced ca. '47. By late-'49, the Carvin brand is introduced, combining parts of names of sons Carson and Gavin. Carvin acoustic and electric Spanish archtops are introduced in '54. Instruments are sold by mail-order only. Kiesel brand name revived by Carvin in '15 for use on their guitars.

2,000-4,000 guitars made prior to '70 with no serial number. First serial number appeared in '70, stamped on end of fingerboard, beginning with #5000. All are consecutive. Later SN on neck plates.

Approximate SN ranges include:
1970: First serial number #5000 to 10019 ('79).
'80-'83: 10768 to 15919.
'84-'87: 13666 to 25332.
'88-'90: 22731 to 25683.
'91-'94: 25359 to 42547.
'95-'99: 45879 to 81427.
'00-present: 56162 upward.

Acoustic-Electric AC/AE Series

1990s-2020	Various models	$450	$1,750

Solidbody B/C/D Series (Mid-Level)

1990s-2020	Various models	$450	$1,750

Solidbody Carved-Top (Higher-End)

2000s-2020	Various models	$1,000	$2,000

Solidbody DN/DB/DS Series (Doubleneck)

1975-2020	Various models	$1,500	$3,500

Casa Montalvo
1987-present. Intermediate and professional grade, production/custom flamenco and classical guitars made in Mexico for George Katechis of Berkeley Musical Instrument Exchange.

MODEL YEAR	FEATURES	EXC. COND. LOW	HIGH

Casio

In 1987 Casio introduced a line of digital MIDI guitars imported from Japan, sporting plastic bodies and synthesizer features. They offered them for just a few years.

DG1
1980s. Squared plastic body.

1980s		$85	$150

DG10
1987-1989. Self-contained digital guitar.

1987-1989		$175	$250

DG20
1987-1989. Midi-capable digital guitar.

1987-1989		$250	$350

MG-500 Series MIDI Guitar
1987-1989. Cut-off teardrop (MG-500) or Strat-shaped (MG-510), basswood body, maple neck, rosewood 'board, 3 pickups.

1987-1989	500	$575	$750
1987-1989	510	$500	$650

PG-300
1988-1989. Similar to PG-380, but with less features.

1988-1989		$400	$550

PG-310
1988-1989. Similar to PG-380, but with less features.

1988-1989		$500	$650

PG-380
1988-1989. Guitar synth, double-cut, over 80 built-in sounds, midi controller capable.

1988-1989		$675	$875

Casper Guitar Technologies

Professional grade, production/custom, solid-body electric guitars and basses built by luthier Stephen Casper in Leisure City, Florida, starting in 2009.

Cat's Eyes

1980s. Made by Tokai, Cat's Eyes headstock logo, see Tokai guitar listings.

Champion

Ca. 1894-1897. Chicago's Robert Maurer built this brand of instruments before switching to the Maurer brand name around 1897.

Champlin Guitars

2006-present. Professional and premium grade, custom, flat-top and archtop guitars, and mandolinettos, built by Devin Champlin in Bellingham, Washington.

Chandler

Intermediate and professional grade, production/custom, solidbody electric guitars built by luthiers Paul and Adrian Chandler in Chico, California. They also build basses, lap steels and pickups. Chandler started making pickguards and accessories in the '70s, adding electric guitars, basses, and effects in '84.

555 Model
1992-2000s. Sharp double-cut, 3 mini-humbuckers, TV Yellow.

1992-2000s		$750	$975

Austin Special
1991-1999. Resembles futuristic Danelectro, lipstick pickups, available in 5-string version.

1991-1999		$650	$850

Austin Special Baritone
1994-1999. Nicknamed Elvis, gold metalflake finish, mother-of-toilet-seat binding, tremolo, baritone.

1994-1999		$650	$850

LectraSlide
2000s. Single-cut, Rezo 'guard, 2 pickups.

2000s		$675	$875

Metro
1995-2000. Double-cut slab body, P-90 in neck position and humbucker in the bridge position.

1995-2000		$650	$850

Telepathic
1994-2000. Classic single-cut style, 3 models; Basic, Standard, Deluxe.

1994-2000	Basic	$525	$675
1994-2000	Deluxe 1122 Model	$625	$850
1994-2000	Standard	$575	$750

Chantus

Premium grade, production/custom, classical and flamenco guitars built in Austin, Texas, by luthier William King starting in '84. He also builds ukes.

Chapin

Professional and premium grade, production/custom, semi-hollow, solidbody, and acoustic electric guitars built by luthiers Bill Chapin and Fred Campbell in San Jose, California.

Chapman

1970-present. Made by Emmett Chapman, the Stick features 10 strings and is played by tapping both hands. The Grand Stick features 12 strings.

Stick
1970-present. Touch-tap hybrid electric instrument, 10 or 12 strings.

1970-2023	10- or 12-string	$3,000	$5,000

Char

1985-present. Premium grade, custom, classical and steel string acoustic guitars built in Portland, Oregon by luthier Kerry Char. He also builds harp-guitars and ukuleles.

Charis Acoustic

1996-present. Premium grade, custom/production, steel-string guitars built by luthier Bill Wise in Bay City, Michigan.

Charles Fox Guitars

1968-present. Luthier Charles Fox builds his premium and presentation grade, custom, steel and nylon string guitars in Portland, Oregon. He

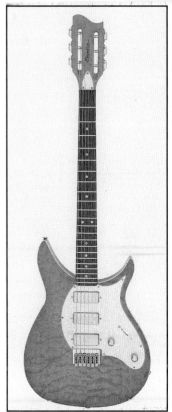

Chandler 555
Imaged by Heritage Auctions, HA.com

Charis Acoustic SJ

EVH Art Series (by Charvel)

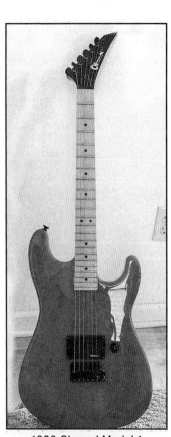

1986 Charvel Model 1
Tritium Guita Worx Randy

MODEL YEAR	FEATURES	EXC. COND. LOW	HIGH

also produced GRD acoustic and electric guitars for '78-'82 and C. Fox acoustic guitars for '97-'02. He also operates The American School of Lutherie in Portland.

Charles Shifflett Acoustic Guitars

Premium grade, custom, classical, flamenco, resonator, and harp guitars, basses and banjos built by luthier Charles Shifflett, starting 1990, in High River, Alberta.

Charvel

1976 (1980)-present. Intermediate and professional grade, production, solidbody electric guitars. They also build basses. Founded by Wayne Charvel as Charvel Manufacturing in '76, making guitar parts in Asuza, California. Moved to San Dimas in '78. Also, in '78 Grover Jackson bought out Charvel. In '79 or early '80 Charvel branded guitars are introduced. U.S.-made to '85, a combination of imports and U.S.-made post-'85. Charvel also manufactured the Jackson brand.

Charvel licensed its trademark to IMC (Hondo) in '85. IMC bought Charvel in '86 and moved the factory to Ontario, California. On October 25, 2002, Fender Musical Instruments Corp. (FMIC) took ownership of Jackson/Charvel Manufacturing Inc.

Pre-Pro (Pre-Production) Charvels began in November 1980 and ran until sometime in 1981. These are known as 'non-plated' indicating pre-production versus a production neck plate. Production serialized neck plates are considered to be San Dimas models which have a Charvel logo, serial number, and a PO Box San Dimas notation on the neck plate. These Serialized Plated Charvels came after Pre-Pros. Late '81 and '82 saw the early serialized guitars with 21-fret necks; these are more valuable. During '82 the 22-fret neck was introduced. The so-called Soft Strat-, Tele-, Flying V-, and Explorer-style headstocks are associated with the early San Dimas Charvel models. In late '82 the pointy headstock, called the Jackson style, was introduced. In '82 the Superstrat style with a neck plate was introduced. Superstrats with a Kahler tailpiece have a lower value than the Pre-Pro models (with Fender-style trem tailpiece).

Collectors of vintage Charvels look for the vintage Charvel 3-on-a-side logo. This is a defining feature and a cutoff point for valuations. Bogus builders are replicating early Charvels and attempting to sell them as originals so fakes can be a problem for Charvel collectors, so buyer beware.

Other electric guitar manufacturing info:
1986-1989 Japanese-made Models 1 through 8
1989-1991 Japanese-made 550 XL, 650 XL/ Custom, 750 XL (XL=neck-thru)
1989-1992 Japanese-made Models 275, 375, 475, 575
1990-1991 Korean-made Charvette models
1992-1994 Korean-made Models 325, 425

MODEL YEAR	FEATURES	EXC. COND. LOW	HIGH

Early Charvel serial numbers (provided by former Jackson/Charvel associate Tim Wilson):
The first 500 to 750 guitars had no serial number, just marked "Made In U.S.A." on their neckplates. Five digit serial numbers were then used until November '81 when 4-digit numbers were adopted, starting with #1001.
1981: 1001-1095
1982: 1096-1724
1983: 1725-2938
1984: 2939-4261
1985: 4262-5303
1986: 5304-5491

Pre-Pro
November 1980-1981. Pre-Pros came in different configurations of body styles, pickups, and finishes. There are five basic Pre-Pro formats: the Standard Body, the Bound Body, the Graphic Body, the Flamed Top, and the Matching Headstock. It is possible to have a combination, such as a Bound Body and Matching Headstock. Line items are based on body style and can feature any one of four neck/headstock-styles used: the so-called Tele-headstock, Strat-headstock, Flying V headstock, and Explorer headstock. Finishes included white, black, red, metallic Lake Placid Blue, and special graphics. All original parts adds considerable value and it is often difficult to determine what is original on these models, so expertise is required. An original Fender brass trem tailpiece, for example, adds considerable value. The Pre-Pro models were prone to modification such as added Kahler and Floyd Rose trems.

1980-1981	Various options	$9,000	$12,000

275 Deluxe Dinky
1989-1991. Made in Japan, offset double-cut solidbody, 1 single-coil and 1 humbucker in '89, 2 humbuckers after, tremolo.

1989-1991		$400	$550

325SL
1992-1994. Dot inlays.

1992-1994		$500	$650

325SLX
1992-1994. Surfcaster-like thinline acoustic/electric, dual cutaways, f-hole, on-board chorus, shark inlays, made in Korea.

1992-1994		$500	$650

375 Deluxe
1989-1991. Maple or rosewood 'board, dot inlays, single-single-humbucker.

1989-1991		$750	$1,000

475 Deluxe/475 Special
1989-1991. Introduced as Special, changed to Deluxe in '90, bound rosewood board, shark tooth inlays, 2 oval stacked humbuckers and 1 bridge humbucker. Was also offered as Deluxe Exotic with figured top and back.

1989-1991		$850	$1,250

525
1989-1994. Acoustic-electric, single-cut.

1989-1994		$400	$550

MODEL YEAR	FEATURES	EXC. COND. LOW	HIGH

550XL
1987-1989. Neck-thru (XL), dot markers, 1 single-coil and 1 bridge humbucker.

1987-1989		$750	$1,000

625-C12
1993-2000. Acoustic-electric cutaway 12-string, spruce top.

1993-2000		$400	$550

625F/625ACEL
1993-1995. Acoustic-electric cutaway, figured maple top.

1993-1995		$500	$650

650XL/Custom
1989-1990. Introduced as neck-thru XL and discontinued as Custom, shark fin markers, 2 stacked oval humbuckers and 1 bridge humbucker, custom version of 550XL.

1989-1990		$850	$1,250

750XL Soloist
1989-1990. Shark fin markers, cutaway body, 2 humbuckers, large Charvel logo.

1989-1990		$1,000	$1,500

Avenger
1990-1991. Randy Rhoads-style batwing-shaped solidbody, 1 humbucker, 1 single-coil, tremolo, made in Japan.

1990-1991		$500	$650

Charvette
1989-1991. Charvette Series made in Korea, superstrat-style, model number series 100 through 300.

1990-1991		$400	$550

CX Series
1991-1994. Imported solidbodies, body-mounted or pickguard mounted pickups, standard or deluxe tremolo.

1991-1994		$300	$400

EVH Art Series (by Charvel)
2004-2007. Offset double-cut solidbody, 1 humbucker, striped finish.

2004-2007	Black/white	$3,500	$4,500
2004-2007	Black/white on red	$3,500	$4,500
2004-2007	Black/yellow	$4,500	$5,500

Fusion Deluxe
1989-1991. Double-cut solidbody, tremolo, 1 humbucker and 1 single-coil, made in Japan.

1989-1991		$900	$1,250

Fusion Standard/AS FX 1
1993-1996. Double-cut solidbody, tremolo, 1 regular and 2 mini humbuckers, made in Japan, also named AS FX1.

1993-1996		$900	$1,250

Model 1/1A/1C
1986-1988. Offset double-cut solidbody, bolt-on maple neck, dot inlays, 1 humbucker, tremolo, made in Japan. Model 1A has 3 single-coils. Model 1C has 1 humbucker and 2 single-coils.

1986-1988		$900	$1,250

Model 2
1986-1988. As Model 1, but with rosewood 'board.

1986-1988		$900	$1,250

Model 3/3A/3DR/3L
1986-1989. As Model 2, but with 1 humbucker, 2 single coils. Model 3A has 2 humbuckers. Model 3DR has 1 humbucker and 1 single-coil.

1986-1989		$900	$1,250

Model 4/4A
1986-1988. As Model 2, but with 1 regular humbucker and 2 stacked humbuckers (no pickguard), active electronics, dots in '86, shark-fin inlays after. Model 4A has 2 regular humbuckers and dot markers.

1986-1988		$1,000	$1,500

Model 5/5A
1986-1988. As Model 4A, but neck-thru, with JE1000TG active electronics. Model 5A is single humbucker and single knob version, limited production, made in Japan.

1986-1988		$1,000	$1,500

Model 6
1986-1988. As HSS Model 4, but with shark's tooth inlays, standard or various custom finishes.

1986-1988		$1,000	$1,500

Model 7
1988-1989. Single-cut solidbody, bound top, reversed headstock, 2 single-coils, made in Japan.

1988-1989		$1,000	$1,500

Model 88 LTD
1988. Double-cut solidbody, 1 slanted humbucker, shark fin inlay, 1000 built, made in Japan.

1988		$1,000	$1,500

Predator
1989-1991. Offset double-cut, bridge humbucker, single-coil neck, bolt-on.

1989-1991		$650	$900

San Dimas Serialized Plated
1981-1986, 1995-1997. U.S.-made with San Dimas neck plate, bolt neck, rounded headstock early production, pointy headstock later, reissued in mid-'90s.

1981-1982	Soft headstock	$5,000	$8,500
1982-1986	Pointy headstock	$3,000	$5,000
1995-1997	Soft headstock	$1,500	$2,500

San Dimas LTD 25th Anniversary
2006. About 100 made, 25th Anniversary logo on neck plate with production number, highly figured top, high-end appointments.

2006		$1,750	$2,500

San Dimas Reissue (FMIC)
2004-present. USA Select series, alder body, bolt neck.

2004-2011	Custom Shop	$2,000	$2,500
2004-2023	Factory model	$1,000	$1,500

So-Cal Series
2008-2012. Offset double-cut solidbody.

2008-2012	Various options	$950	$1,250

ST Custom
1990-1991. Offset double-cut ash solidbody, 2 single-coils and 1 humbucker, rosewood 'board, tremolo, made in Japan.

1990-1991		$400	$550

ST Deluxe
1990-1991. Same as ST Custom but with maple 'board.

1990-1991		$400	$550

1986 Charvel Model 3
Imaged by Heritage Auctions, HA.com

Charvel San Dimas
Select Series

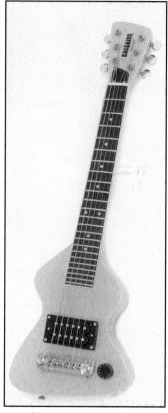

Chiquita Travel Guitar

Citron CF1

MODEL YEAR	FEATURES	EXC. COND. LOW	HIGH

Standard
2002-2003. Typical offset double-cut Charvel body, 2 Seymour Duncan humbucker pickups, various opaque colors.

2002-2003		$400	$550

Star
1980-1981. The Star is considered by early-Charvel collectors to be Charvel's only original design with its unique four-point body.

1980-1981		$2,500	$3,500

Surfcaster
1991-1996. Offset double-cut, f-hole, various pickup options, bound body, tremolo, made in Japan.

1991-1996	1 single, 1 hum	$1,500	$2,000
1991-1996	2 singles, hardtail	$1,500	$2,000
1991-1996	2 singles, vibrato	$1,500	$2,000

Surfcaster 12
1991-1996. Made in Japan, 12-string version of Surfcaster, no tremolo.

1991-1996		$1,500	$2,000

Surfcaster Doubleneck
1992. Very limited production, 6/12 double neck, Charvel logo on both necks, black.

1992		$2,250	$3,000

Surfcaster HT (Model SC1)
1996-2000. Made in Japan. Hard Tail (HT) non-tremolo version of Surfcaster, has single-coil and bridge humbucker.

1996-2000		$1,500	$2,000

Chiquita
1979-present. Intermediate grade, production guitars made by Erlewine Guitars in Austin, Texas (see that listing). There was also a mini amp available.

Travel Guitar
1979-present. Developed by Mark Erlewine and ZZ Top's Billy Gibbons, 27" overall length solidbody, 1 or 2 pickups, various colors.

1979-2023		$600	$800

Chris George
1966-present. Professional and premium grade, custom, archtop, acoustic, electric and resonator guitars built by luthier Chris George, in Tattershall Lincolnshire, U.K.

Christopher Carrington
1988-present. Production/custom, premium grade, classical and flamenco acoustic guitars built by luthier Chris Carrington in Rockwall, Texas.

Chrysalis Guitars
1998-2015. Luthier Tim White built his premium grade, production/custom Chrysalis Guitar System, which included interchangeable components that can be quickly assembled into a full-size electric/ acoustic guitar, in New Boston, New Hampshire. White introduced his new brand, Ridgewing in 2016.

Cimar/Cimar by Ibanez
Early-1980s. Private brand of Hoshino Musical Instruments, Nagoya, Japan, who also branded Ibanez. Headstock with script Cimar logo or Cimar by Ibanez, copy models and Ibanez near-original models such as the star body.

Cimar
1982	Classical	$100	$150
1982	Double-cut solidbody	$300	$400
1982	Star body style	$300	$400

Cimarron
1978-present. Luthiers John Walsh and Clayton Walsh build their professional grade, production/ custom, flat-top acoustic guitars in Ridgway, Colorado. Between '94 and '98 they also produced electric guitars.

Cipher
1960s. Solidbody electric guitars and basses imported from Japan by Inter-Mark. Generally strange-shaped bodies.

Electric Solidbody
1960s. For any student-grade import, a guitar with any missing part, such as a missing control knob or trem arm, is worth much less.

1960s		$250	$350

Citron
1995-present. Luthier Harvey Citron builds his professional and premium grade, production/custom solidbody guitars and basses in Woodstock, New York. He also builds basses. In '75, Citron and Joe Veillette founded Veillette-Citron, which was known for handcrafted, neck-thru guitars and basses. That company closed in '83.

Clark
1985-present. Custom, professional grade, solidbody electric guitars and basses, built by luthier Ed Clark, first in Amityville, New York ('85-'90), then Medford ('91-'99) and presently Lake Ronkonkoma.

Clifford
Clifford was a brand manufactured by Kansas City, Missouri instrument wholesalers J.W. Jenkins & Sons. First introduced in 1895, the brand also offered mandolins.

Clovis
Mid-1960s. Private brand guitars, most likely made by Kay.

Electric Solidbody
Mid-1960s. Kay slab solidbody, 2 pickups.

1965		$375	$500

CMG Guitars
2012-present. Owner Chris Mitchell imports intermediate grade, acoustic and acoustic-electric guitars from China. He also offers professional grade, production/custom, electric guitars built by

GUITARS

MODEL		EXC. COND.	
YEAR	FEATURES	LOW	HIGH

luthiers Russell Jones and James Horel in Statesboro, Georgia.

Cole

1890-1919. W.A. Cole, after leaving Fairbanks & Cole, started his own line in 1890. He died in 1909 but the company continued until 1919. He also made mandolins and banjos.

Parlor

1897. Small size, Brazilian rosewood sides and back, spruce top, ebony 'board, slotted headstock, dot markers.

1897		$925	$1,250

Coleman Guitars

1976-1983. Custom made presentation grade instruments made in Homosassa, Florida, by luthier Harry Coleman. No headstock logo, Coleman logo on inside center strip.

Collings

1986-present. Professional, premium, and presentation grade, production/custom, flat-top, archtop and electric guitars built in Austin, Texas. They also build mandolins and ukuleles. Bill Collings started guitar repair and began custom building guitars around '73. In '80, he relocated his shop from Houston to Austin and started Collings Guitars in '86. In '06 they moved to a new plant in southwest Austin.

01

2005-present. Mother-of-pearl inlays, Sitka spruce, mahogany neck, back & sides, ebony 'board and bridge, high gloss lacquer finish.

2005-2023		$3,500	$4,500

01A

2010-2017. As 01 with Adirondack spruce top.

2010-2017		$4,250	$5,500

01G

As 01 with German spruce top.

2009		$4,250	$5,500

01SB

Sitka spruce, mahogany.

2006-2015		$4,250	$5,500

02G

German spruce, sunburst.

1996		$4,500	$6,000

02H

Parlor, 12 frets.

2008		$3,500	$4,500

02SB

Parlor, 12 frets, 12-string.

2016		$4,500	$6,000

001G

German spruce.

2009		$4,250	$5,500

001MH

All mahogany body.

2010		$4,250	$5,500

002H

1999-present. Indian rosewood.

1999-2023		$3,500	$4,500

0041

2001. Premium Brazilian rosewood back and sides, Adirondack spruce top, abalone top purfling.

2001		$8,500	$11,000

0001 ICC

0001 with Indian rosewood back and sides.

2003-2013		$3,500	$4,500

0001 Series

1990s-present. 12-fret 000 size, Sitka spruce top (standard) or other top wood options, including mahogany, Adirondack, Honduran mahogany, etc.

1990s-2023	0001 Sitka	$3,500	$4,500
1990s-2023	0001A Adirondack	$4,500	$6,000
2006-2023	0001Mh Mahogany	$4,250	$5,500
2013-2023	0001 Cutaway	$3,500	$4,500

0002H

1994-present. 15" 000-size, 12-fret, Indian rosewood back and sides, spruce top, slotted headstock. AAA Koa back and sides in '96.

1994-1995	Indian rosewood	$3,500	$4,500
1996	AAA Koa	$4,500	$6,000
2007-2023	Indian rosewood	$3,500	$4,500

0002HAC

2009-present. With cutaway and herringbone trim.

2009-2023		$4,250	$5,500

00041

1999. Indian rosewood sides and back, Sitka spruce top, slotted headstock.

1999		$5,250	$7,000

290 Series

2004-present. Solid Honduran mahogany body, East Indian rosewood 'board, 2 P-90 style pickups, '50s style wiring, high gloss lacquer finish.

2004-2023	Custom/Deluxe	$2,500	$3,500

360 Baritone

2020-present. Solid ash body, doghair finish.

2020		$3,250	$4,250

360 LT

2015-present. Solidbody electric, level top (LT), mahogany, ash or alder body, rosewood 'board, high gloss nitro finish.

2015-2023		$3,250	$4,250

AT 16

2006-present. 16" archtop, limited numbers built, fully carved premium figured maple body and neck, carved solid spruce top, f-holes, high-end appointments, high gloss nitro finish.

2006-2023		$15,000	$20,000

AT 17

2008-present. 17" single-cut archtop, limited numbers built, S-holes, Adirondack or European spruce top, premium flamed maple back and sides, and premium appointments, sunburst or blonde. Options include scale length, pickup and bindings.

2008-2023		$15,000	$20,000

Baby Series

1997-present. Various 3/4 size models, Englemann (E) or German (G) spruce top, rosewood back and sides, Ivoroid with herringbone trim, tortoise 'guard, gloss nitro lacquer finish.

1997-2023	Various models	$3,000	$4,000

Collings 01

Collings 0001

To get the most from this book, be sure to read "Using *The Guide*" in the introduction.

Collings CL Deluxe

Collings DS2H

C10

1986-present. 000-size, mahogany back and sides, spruce top, sunburst or natural.

1986-2023		$3,500	$5,000

C10 Deluxe

1986-present. C10 with Indian rosewood back and sides (mahogany, flamed maple or koa optional), sunburst or natural.

1986-2023	Indian rosewood	$4,500	$6,000
1994-2000s	Flamed maple	$4,250	$5,500
1994-2000s	Koa option	$4,250	$5,500
1994-2000s	Varnish	$4,250	$5,500
1994-2023	Mahogany	$4,250	$5,500

C100

1986-1994, 2019-present. Quadruple 0-size, mahogany back and sides, spruce top, natural, replaced by CJ Jumbo. Reintroduced '19 with Honduran mahogany back, sides and neck.

1986-1994		$4,250	$5,500
2019-2023		$4,250	$5,500

C100 Deluxe

1986-1994, 2019-present. C-100 with rosewood back and sides. Reintroduced in '19 with East Indian rosewood and Honduran mahogany.

1986-1994		$4,250	$5,500

CJ

1995-present. Quadruple 0-size, Sitka spruce top (standard), Indian rosewood back and sides, natural. Various other wood options available.

1995-2023	Sitka, Indian	$4,000	$5,000

CJ A

2019. Adirondack spruce top, Indian rosewood back and sides.

2019		$4,250	$5,500

CJ Koa ASB

2007. Adirondack spruce top, scalloped bracing ASB, flamed koa sides and back.

2007		$4,500	$6,000

CJ Mh

2020-present. Sitka spruce top (standard), Honduran mahogany back, sides and neck, sunburst. Various other wood options available.

2020-2023	Sitka, mahogany	$4,000	$5,000

CJ-35

2014-present. Sitka spruce top (standard), Honduran mahogany back, sides and neck, tigerstripe 'guard. Various other wood options available.

2014-2023	Sitka, mahogany	$4,000	$5,000

CL Series (City Limits)

2004-present. City Limits Jazz series, fully carved flame maple top, solid Honduran mahogany body, East Indian rosewood 'board, high gloss lacquer finish.

2004-2023		$4,250	$5,500

Clarence White

1989-2000. Adirondack top, Brazilian rosewood back and sides (CW-28), or mahogany (CW-18), herringbone trim.

1989-2000	CW-28, Brazilian	$9,000	$12,000
1993-2000	CW-18, Mahogany	$4,500	$6,000

CW Indian A

2019-present. Collings Winfield (CW), named after the Walnut Valley Festival in Winfield, Kansas, modified version of standard dreadnought, Adirondack spruce top, East Indian rosewood back and sides, ivoroid binding with herringbone purfling.

2019-2023		$4,500	$6,000

D1 Gruhn

1989. Short run for Gruhn Guitars, Nashville, Gruhn script headstock logo, signed by Bill Collings, choice of Indian rosewood or curly maple back and sides, Engelman spruce top.

1989		$4,000	$5,000

D1 Series

1992-present. Dreadnought, Sitka spruce top (standard), mahogany back and sides. Various other wood options available.

1992-2018	D1A, Adirondack	$4,500	$6,000
1992-2018	D1H, Herringbone	$3,500	$4,500
1992-2023	D1, Mahogany	$3,500	$4,500
2010	D1VN, Vintage neck	$4,500	$6,000
2016-2023	D1AT, Adirondack, Torrefied	$5,500	$7,000

D2 Series

1986-present. Dreadnought, Sitka spruce top (standard), Indian rosewood back and sides. Various other wood options available.

1986-1995	D2, Sitka, Indian	$3,500	$5,000
1986-2023	D2H, Herringbone	$3,500	$5,000
1994	D2HV, Vintage neck	$3,500	$5,000
1994-2005	D2HB, Brazilian	$8,500	$11,000
2004-2010	D2HAV, Varnish	$4,750	$6,000
2004-2023	D2HA, Adirondack	$4,500	$5,750
2008	D2HGV, German spruce	$5,500	$7,500
2017-2023	D2HT, Traditional	$4,500	$6,000

D3 Series

1990-present. Dreadnought, Sitka spruce top (standard), Brazilian or Indian rosewood back and sides. Various other wood options available.

1990-1999	D3, Brazilian	$9,500	$12,500
2000-2023	D3, Indian	$4,000	$5,000
2004-2023	D3A, Adirondack	$5,000	$6,500

D42

2000s. Brazilian rosewood back and sides, fancy.

2000s		$9,500	$12,500

DS1/DS1A

2004-present. D-size, slope shoulders, 12 fret neck, slotted headstock, mahogany back and sides, A is Adirondack upgrade.

2004-2023		$4,500	$6,000

DS2H/DS2HA

1995-present. D-size, 12-fret, slotted headstock, Sitka spruce top, Indian rosewood back and sides, herringbone purfling. A is Adirondack upgrade.

1995-2023		$4,500	$6,000

DS41

1995-2007. Indian rosewood, fancy, abalone top trim, snowflake markers.

1995-2007		$5,000	$6,500

MODEL YEAR	FEATURES	EXC. COND. LOW	HIGH
I-30			

2017-present. Flamed maple top, f-holes, mahogany neck, 2 P-90 pickups.

MODEL YEAR	FEATURES	EXC. COND. LOW	HIGH
2017-2023		$4,500	$6,000
I-35 Deluxe			

2007-present. Premium flamed maple top (standard), mahogany body, gloss lacquer finish. Various other wood options available.

2007-2023	Various options	$5,250	$7,000
OM1 Series			

1994-present. Orchestra model, Sitka spruce top (standard), mahogany back and sides, natural. Various other wood options available.

1994-2023	OM1, Mahogany	$3,500	$4,500
1994-2023	OM1A, Adirondack	$4,250	$5,500
2000-2016	OM1, Koa	$3,500	$4,500
2000-2016	OM1MH, Mahogany	$3,500	$4,500
2007-2016	OM1A, Cutaway, Adirondack	$4,500	$6,000
2016-2023	OM1T, Traditional	$4,500	$6,000
2018-2023	OM1AT, Adirondack	$6,250	$8,500
2020-2023	OM1JL, Julian Lage	$5,000	$6,500
OM2 Series			

1990-present. Sitka spruce top (standard), Indian rosewood back and sides. Various other wood options available.

1990-2020	OM2, Sitka, Indian	$4,000	$6,000
1990-2023	OM2H, Herringbone	$4,250	$5,500
1998	OM2HAV, Varnish	$8,500	$11,000
2001	OM2H SSB, Brazilian	$8,500	$11,000
2003-2018	OM2HA, Adirondack	$4,500	$6,000
2008	OM2H GSS, German spruce	$4,500	$6,000
2018-2023	OM2HAT, Traditional, Adirondack	$5,500	$7,500
OM3 Series			

1986-present. Sitka spruce top (standard), first Brazilian later Indian rosewood back and sides. Various other wood options available.

1986-1996	OM3HC Cutaway, Indian	$4,500	$6,000
1986-1999	OM3B, Brazilian	$8,500	$11,000
1994-2007	OM3HBA, Adirondack, Brazilian	$8,500	$11,000
2000-2023	OM3, Indian	$4,000	$5,000
2003	OM3, Figured maple	$4,000	$5,000
2004-2023	OM3A, Adirondack	$4,500	$6,000
2008-2023	OM3, Mahogany	$4,000	$5,000
OM41BrzGCut			

2007. Brazilian rosewood sides and back, German spruce top, rounded cutaway.

2007		$9,500	$12,500
OM42B			

Brazilian rosewood back and sides, Adirondack spruce top, fancy rosette and binding.

2000		$10,000	$13,000
OM42G			

German spruce top, Indian rosewood back and sides.

1999		$5,500	$7,500
OMC2H			

Adirondack top, Brazilian rosewood back and sides, herringbone trim.

2008		$9,000	$12,000
SJ			

1986-present. Spruce top, quilted maple back and sides or Indian rosewood (earlier option), later mahogany.

1986-2023	Various options	$4,250	$5,500
SJ41			
1996		$4,250	$5,500
SoCo Deluxe			

2007-present. Premium figured maple top over semi-hollow mahogany body, rosewood 'board, f-holes, various finish options.

2007-2023		$4,250	$5,500
Winfield			

2004-2006. D-style, Adirondack spruce top, Brazilian or Indian rosewood back and sides, later mahogany.

2004	Indian	$4,250	$5,500
2005-2006	Brazilian	$4,250	$5,500
2006	Mahogany	$4,250	$5,500

Collings OM2H T

Columbia

Late 1800s-early 1900s. The Columbia brand name was used on acoustic guitars by New York's James H. Buckbee Co. until c.1987 and afterwards by Galveston's Thomas Goggan and Brothers.

Comins

1992-present. Premium and presentation grade, custom archtops built by luthier Bill Comins in Willow Grove, Pennsylvania. He also builds mandolins and offers a combo amp built in collaboration with George Alessandro.

Commander

Late 1950s-early 1960s. Archtop acoustic guitars made by Harmony for the Alden catalog company.

Concertone

Ca. 1914-1930s. Concertone was a brand made by Chicago's Slingerland and distributed by Montgomery Ward. The brand was also used on other instruments such as ukuleles.

Conklin

1984-present. Intermediate, professional and premium grade, production/custom, 6-, 7-, 8-, and 12-string solid and hollowbody electrics, by luthier Bill Conklin. He also builds basses. Originally located in Lebanon, Missouri, in '88 the company moved to Springfield, Missouri. Conklin instruments are made in the U.S. and overseas.

Comins 16 Vintage Burst Concert Model

GUITARS

Conrad Acoustical
Slimline 12-String

Imaged by Heritage Auctions, HA.com

Conrad Resonator Acoustic

Jack Welch

MODEL YEAR	FEATURES	EXC. COND. LOW	HIGH

Conn Guitars

Ca.1968-ca.1978. Student to mid-quality classical and acoustic guitars, some with bolt-on necks, also some electrics. Imported from Japan by band instrument manufacturer and distributor Conn/Continental Music Company, Elkhart, Indiana.

Acoustic

1968-1978	Various models	$200	$650

Classical

1968-1978	Student-level	$125	$200

Electric Solidbody

1968-1978	Various models	$250	$350

Connor, Stephan

1995-present. Luthier Stephan Connor builds his premium grade, custom nylon-string guitars in Waltham, Massachusetts.

Conrad Guitars

Ca. 1968-1978. Mid- to better-quality copies of glued-neck Martin and Gibson acoustics and bolt-neck Gibson and Fender solidbodies. They also offered basses, mandolins and banjos. Imported from Japan by David Wexler and Company, Chicago, Illinois.

Acoustic 12-String

1970s. Dreadnought size.

1970s		$175	$250

Acoustical Slimline (40080/40085)

1970s. Rosewood 'board, 2 or 3 DeArmond-style pickups, block markers, sunburst.

1970s		$450	$600

Acoustical Slimline 12-String (40100)

1970s. Rosewood 'board, 2 DeArmond-style pickups, dot markers, sunburst.

1970s		$450	$600

Bison (40035/40030/40065/40005)

1970s. 1 through 4 pickups available, rosewood 'board with dot markers, six-on-side headstock.

1970s		$450	$600

Bumper (40223)

1970s. Clear Lucite solidbody.

1970s		$575	$750

Classical Student (40150)

1970s		$135	$175

De Luxe Folk Guitar

1970s. Resonator acoustic, mahogany back, sides and neck, Japanese import.

1970s		$275	$350

Master Size (40178)

1972-1977. Electric archtop, 2 pickups.

1972-1977		$400	$550

Resonator Acoustic

1970s. Flat-top with wood, metal resonator and 8 ports, round neck.

1970s		$500	$650

Violin-Shaped 12-String Electric (40176)

1970s. Scroll headstock, 2 pickups, 500/1 control panel, bass side dot markers, sunburst.

1970s		$550	$725

MODEL YEAR	FEATURES	EXC. COND. LOW	HIGH

Violin-Shaped Electric (40175)

1970s. Scroll headstock, 2 pickups, 500/1 control panel, bass side dot markers, vibrato, sunburst.

1970s		$500	$650

White Styrene (1280)

1970s. Solid maple body covered with white styrene, 2 pickups, tremolo, bass side dot markers, white.

1970s		$450	$600

Contessa

1960s. Acoustic, semi-hollow archtop, solidbody and bass guitars made in Italy by Zero Sette and imported by Hohner. They also made banjos.

Acoustic

1960s	Various models	$110	$250

Electric Solidbody

1960s	Various models	$250	$425

Contreras

See listing for Manuel Contreras and Manuel Contreras II.

Coral

1967-1969. In '66 MCA bought Danelectro and in '67 introduced the Coral brand of guitars, basses and amps.

Bellzouki 7021

1967. 12-string electric, modified teardrop shape with body points on treble and bass bouts, 2 pickups.

1967		$1,375	$1,750

Combo/Vincent Bell Combo

1967-1969. Cutaway acoustic/electric, 1 or 2 pickups.

1967-1969	V1N6, 1 pu	$2,375	$3,250
1967-1969	V2N6, 2 pu	$2,875	$3,750

Firefly

1967-1969. Double-cut, f-holes, 2 pickups, vibrato available (2V) and 12-string (2N12), red or sunburst.

1967-1969	F2N, no vibrato	$975	$1,250
1967-1969	F2V, vibrato	$1,125	$1,500
1968-1969	F2N12, 12-string	$1,125	$1,500

Hornet (2 Pickups)

1967-1969. Solidbody, 2 pickups, vibrato available (2V or 3V), sunburst, black or red.

1967-1969	H2N, black or red	$1,125	$1,500
1967-1969	H2N, sunburst	$1,000	$1,375
1967-1969	H2V, black or red	$1,125	$1,500
1967-1969	H2V, sunburst	$1,000	$1,375

Hornet (3 Pickups)

1967-1969. As above with 3 pickups, with or without vibrato.

1967-1969	H3N, black or red	$1,375	$1,750
1967-1969	H3N, sunburst	$1,375	$1,750
1967-1969	H3V, black or red	$1,375	$1,750
1967-1969	H3V, sunburst	$1,375	$1,750

Long Horn

1967-1969. Deep double-cut hollowbody, 2 lipstick tube pickups, 6-string (2N6) or 12 (2N12), sunburst.

1967-1969	L2N12	$1,875	$2,500
1967-1969	L2N6	$1,875	$2,500

MODEL		EXC. COND.	
YEAR	FEATURES	LOW	HIGH

Scorpion
1967-1969. Offset double-cut solidbody, 12-string, 2 or 3 lipstick tube pickups, vibrato available (2V or 3V).

1967-1969	S2N12, black or red	$1,125	$1,500
1967-1969	S2N12, sunburst	$1,125	$1,500
1967-1969	S2V12, black or red	$1,125	$1,500
1967-1969	S2V12, sunburst	$1,125	$1,500
1967-1969	S3N12, black or red	$1,125	$1,500
1967-1969	S3N12, sunburst	$1,125	$1,500
1967-1969	S3V12, black or red	$1,375	$1,750
1967-1969	S3V12, sunburst	$1,125	$1,500

Sitar
1967-1969. Six-string guitar with drone strings and 3 pickups (2 under the 6 strings, 1 under the drones), kind of a USA-shaped body.

1967-1969	3S18, 18-string	$3,375	$4,250
1967-1969	3S19, 19-string	$3,500	$4,500
1967-1969	3S9, 9-string	$3,125	$4,000

Teardrop
1967-1969. Teardrop shaped hollowbody, 2 lipstick tube pickups.

1967-1969	T2N6	$1,375	$1,750

Córdoba
Line of classical guitars handmade in Portugal and imported by Guitar Salon International. By '13, U.S. production was added.

Classical

2000s	Higher-end	$1,750	$2,250
2000s	Mid-level	$450	$600
2000s	Student-level	$300	$375

Cordova
1960s. Classical nylon string guitars imported by David Wexler of Chicago.

Grand Concert Model WC-026
1960s. The highest model offered by Cordova, 1-piece rosewood back, laminated rosewood sides, spruce top, natural.

1960s		$300	$375

Corey James Custom Guitars
2005-present. Luthier Corey James Moilanen builds his professional and premium grade, production/custom solidbody guitars and basses in Howell, Michigan.

Coriani, Paolo
1984-present. Production/custom nylon-string guitars and hurdy-gurdys built by luthier Paolo Coriani in Modeila, Italy.

Cort
1973-present. North Brook, Illinois-based Cort offers budget, intermediate and professional grade, production/custom, acoustic and solidbody, semi-hollow, hollow body electric guitars and basses built in Korea.

Cort was the second significant Korean private label (Hondo brand was the first) to come out of Korea. Jack Westheimer entered into an agreement with Korea's Cort to do Cort-brand, private-label, and Epiphone-brand guitars.

CP Thornton Guitars
1985-present. Luthier Chuck Thornton builds professional and premium grade, production/custom, semi-hollow and solidbody electric guitars in Sumner, Maine. Up to '96 he also built basses.

Crafter
1986-present. Crafter offers budget and intermediate grade, production, classical, acoustic, acoustic/electric, and electric guitars, basses and mandolins made in Korea. They also offer the Cruzer and Ashland brands of instruments. From '72 to '86 they made Sungeum classical guitars.

Cranium
Introduced 1996, professional grade, production/custom, hollow, semi-hollow, and solidbody electrics built by luthier Wayne O'Connor in Peterborough, Ontario.

Crescent Moon
Professional grade, production/custom, solidbody guitars and basses built by luthier Craig Muller in Baltimore, Maryland, starting 1999.

Creston
2004-present. Professional grade, custom, solidbody electric guitars and basses built by luthier Creston Lea in Burlington, Vermont.

Crestwood
1970s. Copies of the popular classical guitars, flat-tops, electric solidbodies and basses of the era, imported by La Playa Distributing Company of Detroit.

Acoustic 12-String

1970s		$225	$300

Electric
1970s. Various models include near copies of the 335 (Crestwood model 2043, 2045 and 2047), Les Paul Custom (2020), Strat (2073), Jazzmaster (2078), Tele (2082), and the SG Custom (2084).

1970s		$300	$600

Crimson Guitars
2005-present. Luthiers Benjamin Crowe and Aki Atrill build professional and premium grade, custom, solidbody guitars and basses in Somerset, U.K.

Cromwell
1935-1939. Budget model brand built by Gibson and distributed by mail-order businesses like Grossman, Continental, Richter & Phillips, and Gretsch & Brenner.

1967 Coral Sitar
Izzy Miller

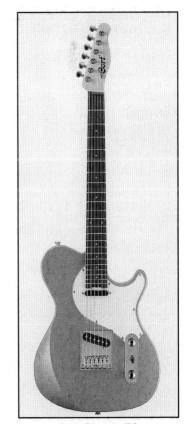

Cort Classic TC

CSR Serenata

1966 Custom Kraft Lexington
Rivington Guitars

MODEL		EXC. COND.	
YEAR	FEATURES	LOW	HIGH

Acoustic Archtop
1935-1939. Archtop acoustic, f-holes, pressed mahogany back and sides, carved and bound top, bound back, 'guard and 'board, no truss rod.

1935-1939	Various models	$1,125	$1,500
1935-1939	With '30s era pu	$1,500	$2,000

Acoustic Flat-Top
1935-1939	G-2 (L-00)	$2,000	$2,500

GT-2 Tenor
1935-1939	1474" flat-top	$1,000	$1,500

GT-4 Tenor
1935-1939	16" archtop	$1,000	$1,500

Cromwell (Guild)
1963-1964. Guild imported these 2- or 3-pickup offset double cut solidbodies from Hagstrom. These were basically part of Hagstrom's Kent line with laminated bodies and birch necks. About 500 were imported into the U.S.

Solidbody
1963-1964		$1,125	$1,500

Crook Custom Guitars
1997-present. Professional grade, custom, solidbody electric guitars and basses built in Moundsville, West Virginia by luthier Bill Crook.

Crossley
2005-present. Professional grade, production/custom, solidbody and chambered electric guitars built in Melbourne, Victoria, Australia by luthier Peter Crossley.

Crown
1960s. Violin-shaped hollowbody electrics, solidbody electric guitars and basses, possibly others. Imported from Japan.

Acoustic Flat-Top
1960s. 6-string and 12-string.
1960s		$150	$250

Electric Archtop
1960s. Double pointed cutaways, 2 humbucking pickups, laminated top, full-depth body.
1960s		$400	$600

Electric Solidbody/Semi-Hollow
1960s. Student-level Japanese import.
1960s	Copy models	$375	$500
1960s	Standard models	$225	$300
1960s	Violin-shaped body	$350	$450

Crucianelli
Early 1960s. Italian guitars imported into the U.S. by Bennett Brothers of New York and Chicago around '63 to '64. Accordion builder Crucianelli also made Imperial, Elite, PANaramic, and Elli-Sound brand guitars.

Cruzer
Intermediate grade, production, solidbody electric guitars, basses, amps, and effects made by Korea's Crafter Guitars.

CSR
1996-present. Father and daughter luthiers Roger and Courtney Kitchens build their premium grade, production/custom, archtop guitars and basses in Byron, Georgia.

Cumpiano
1974-present. Professional and premium grade, custom steel-string and nylon-string guitars, and acoustic basses built by luthier William Cumpiano in Northampton, Massachusetts.

Curbow String Instruments
1994-2007. Premium grade, production/custom, solidbody guitars and basses built by luthier Doug Somervell in Morganton, Georgia. Founded by Greg Curbow who passed away in '05.

Custom
1980s. Line of solidbody guitars and basses introduced in the early '80s by Charles Lawing and Chris Lovell, owners of Strings & Things in Memphis, Tennessee.

Custom Kraft
Late-1950s-1968. A house brand of St. Louis Music Supply, instruments built by Valco and Kay. They also offered basses and amps.

Electric Solidbody
1950s-1960s. U.S.-made or import, entry-level, 1or 2 pickups.
1950s-60s	Import	$225	$300
1950s-60s	USA, Kay, 2 pu	$600	$775

Sound Saturator
1960s	12-string	$500	$650

Super Zapp
1960s		$550	$750

Thin Twin Jimmy Reed (style)
Late-1950s-early-1960s. Single cut, 2 pickups, 4 knobs and toggle, dot markers.
1950s-60s	US-made	$850	$1,125

D.J. Hodson
1994-2007. Luthier David J. Hodson built his professional and premium grade, production/custom, acoustic guitars in Loughborough, Leicestershire, U.K. He also built ukes. He passed away in '07.

Daddy Mojo String Instruments Inc.
2005-present. Luthiers Lenny Piroth-Robert and Luca Tripaldi build their intermediate and professional grade, production/custom, solidbody electric, resonator and cigar box guitars in Montreal, Quebec.

Dagmar Custom Guitars
Luthier Pete Swanson builds custom, premium and presentation grade, acoustic and electric archtop guitars in Niagara, Ontario, starting in 2008.

MODEL		EXC. COND.	
YEAR	FEATURES	LOW	HIGH

D'Agostino

1976-early 1990s. Acoustic and electric solidbody guitars and basses imported by PMS Music, founded in New York City by former Maestro executive Pat D'Agostino, his brother Steven D'Agostino, and Mike Confortti. First dreadnought acoustic guitars imported from Japan in '76. First solidbodies manufactured by the EKO custom shop beginning in '77. In '82 solidbody production moved to Japan. Beginning in '84, D'Agostinos were made in Korea. Overall, about 60% of guitars were Japanese, 40% Korean. They also had basses.

Acoustic Flat-Top
1976-1990. Early production in Japan, by mid-'80s, most production in Korea.

1976-1990		$550	$725

Electric Semi-Hollowbody
1981-early 1990s. Early production in Japan, later versions from Korea.

1981-1990		$180	$775

Electric Solidbody
1977-early 1990s. Early models made in Italy, later versions from Japan and Korea.

1981-1990		$180	$775

Daily Guitars

1976-present. Luthier David Daily builds his premium grade, production/custom classical guitars in Sparks, Nevada.

Daion

1978-1984. Mid- to higher-quality copies imported from Japan. Original designs were introduced in the '80s. Only acoustics were offered at first; in '81 they added acoustic/electric and solid and semi-hollow electrics. They also had basses.

Acoustic
1978-1985. Various flat-top models.

1978-1985	Higher-end	$675	$1,500
1978-1985	Lower-end	$225	$600

Electric
1978-1985. Various solid and semi-hollow body guitars.

1978-1985	Higher-end	$675	$1,500
1978-1985	Lower-end	$225	$600

Daisy Rock

2001-present. Budget and intermediate grade, production, full-scale and 3/4 scale, solidbody, semi-hollow, acoustic, and acoustic/electric guitars and basses. Founded by Tish Ciravolo as a Division of Schecter Guitars, the Daisy line is focused on female customers.

D'Ambrosio

2001-present. Luthier Otto D'Ambrosio builds his premium grade, custom/production, acoustic and electric archtop guitars in Providence, Rhode Island.

MODEL		EXC. COND.	
YEAR	FEATURES	LOW	HIGH

Dan Armstrong

Dan Armstrong started playing jazz in Cleveland in the late-'50s. He moved to New York and started doing repairs, eventually opening his own store on 48th Street in '65. By the late-'60s he was designing his Lucite guitars for Ampeg (see Ampeg for those listings). He moved to England in '71, where he developed his line of colored stomp boxes. He returned to the States in '75. Armstrong died in '04.

Wood Body
1973-1975. Sliding pickup, wood body, brown.

1973-1975		$2,000	$2,500

Wood Body AMG 100 (reissue)
Various wood body options, BLD (blond, swamp ash), CH (cherry, mahogany) and BK (black, alder).

2008-2009	BK	$400	$550
2008-2009	BLD	$700	$950
2008-2009	CH	$500	$650

Dan Armstrong Guitars

Introduced 2015, professional grade, production/custom, acrylic solidbody electrics based on the original Dan Armstrong models, built in Everett, Washington.

Dan Kellaway

1976-present. Production/custom, premium grade, classical and steel string guitars built by luthier Dan Kellaway in Singleton NSW, Australia. He also builds mandolins and lutes.

Danelectro

1946-1969, 1996-present. Founded in Red Bank, New Jersey, by Nathan I. (Nate or Nat) Daniel, an electronics enthusiast with amplifier experience. In 1933, Daniel built amps for Thor's Bargain Basement in New York. In '34 he was recruited by Epiphone's Herb Sunshine to build the earliest Electar amps and pickup-making equipment. From '35 to '42, he operated Daniel Electric Laboratories in Manhattan, supplying Epiphone. He started Danelectro in '46 and made his first amps for Montgomery Ward in '47. Over the years, Danelectro made amplifiers, solidbody, semi-hollow and hollowbody electric guitars and basses, electric sitar, and the Bellzouki under the Danelectro, Silvertone, and Coral brands. In '48, began supplying Silvertone amps for Sears (various coverings), with his own brand (brown leatherette) distributed by Targ and Dinner as Danelectro and S.S. Maxwell. He developed an electronic vibrato in '48 on his Vibravox series amps. In '50 he developed a microphone with volume and tone controls and outboard Echo Box reverb unit. In the fall of '54, Danelectro replaced Harmony as provider of Silvertone solidbody guitars for Sears. Also, in '54, the first Danelectro brand guitars appeared with tweed covering, bell headstock, and pickups under the pickguard. The Coke bottle headstock debuts as Silvertone Lightning Bolt in '54 and was used on Danelectros from '56 to '66. The company moved to Red Bank, New Jersey in '57, and in '58 relocated to

2016 Dan Armstrong 50th Anniversary Custom
Imaged by Heritage Auctions, HA.com

1965 Danelectro Combo/ Vincent Bell

1967 Danelectro Dane B
Rivington Guitars

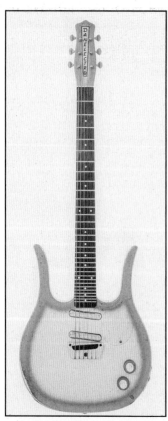

1960s Danelectro Guitaralin
Imaged by Heritage Auctions, HA.com

Neptune, New Jersey. In '59, Harmony and Kay guitars replaced all but 3 Danelectros in Sears catalog. In '66, MCA buys the company (Daniel remains with company), but by mid-'69, MCA halts production and closes the doors. Some leftover stock is sold to Dan Armstrong, who had a shop in New York at the time. Armstrong assembled several hundred Danelectro guitars as Dan Armstrong Modified with his own pickup design.

Rights to name acquired by Anthony Marc in late-'80s, who assembled several thinline hollow-body guitars, many with Longhorn shape, using Japanese-made bodies and original Danelectro necks and hardware. In '96, the Evets Corporation, of San Clemente, California, introduced a line of effects bearing the Danelectro brand. Amps and guitars, many of which were reissues of the earlier instruments, soon followed. In early 2003, Evets discontinued offering guitar and amps, but revived the guitar and bass line in '05.

MCA-Danelectro-made guitars were called the Dane Series with model numbers starting with an A, B, C, or a D, with A models being the least expensive going up to the D models. All Dane Series instruments came with 1, 2 or 3 pickups and with hand vibrato options. The Dane Series was made from '67 to '69. MCA did carry over the Convertible, Guitarlin 4123, Long Horn Bass-4 and Bass-6 and Doubleneck 3923. MCA also offered the Bellzouki Double Pickup 7021. Each Dane Series includes an electric 12-string. Danelectro also built Coral brand instruments (see Coral).

Prices for pre-MCA Danelectros include the period-correct case. A non-original case can drop the value of the guitar by 10%. In the mid- to late-'50s, these cases were referred to as "coffin cases" because of their unique shape.

Baritone 6-String Reissue
1999-2003, 2008-present. Danelectro has offered several models with 6-string baritone tuning, often with various reissue-year designations, single- or double-cut, 2 or 3 pickups.

1999-2023 Various models	$500	$600

Bellzouki
1963-1969. 12-string electric. Teardrop-shaped body, 1 pickup, sunburst (7010) for '63-'66. Vincent Bell model (7020) with modified teardrop shape with 2 body points on both treble and bass bouts and 2 pickups for '63-'66. Same body as Coral Electric Sitar for '67-'69.

1963-1969 1 pu, teardrop body	$1,000	$1,500
1963-1969 2 pu, pointy body	$1,250	$1,750
1967-1969 2 pu, sitar body	$1,875	$2,500

Companion
1959-1960. Hollowbody double-cut, 2 pickups, concentric TV knobs.

1959-1960	$1,500	$2,000

Convertible
1959-1969. Acoustic/electric, double-cut, guitar was sold with or without the removable single pickup.

1959-1969 Acoustic, no pu, natural	$600	$775

MODEL YEAR	FEATURES	EXC. COND. LOW	HIGH
1959-1969	Pickup installed, natural	$950	$1,250
1967-1969	Red, white, blue	$1,375	$1,750

Convertible Reissue
1999, 2000-2003. The Convertible Pro was offered '00-'03 with upgraded Gotoh tuners and metalflake and pearl finishes.

1999-2003	Blond or green	$300	$400

Dane A Series
1967-1969. 1or 2 pickups, with or without vibrato (V), solid wood slab body, hard lacquer finish with 4 color options, 12-string also offered.

1967-1969	1N12, 12-string	$1,375	$1,750
1967-1969	2N12, 12-string	$1,500	$2,000
1967-1969	N, 1 pickup	$1,000	$1,375
1967-1969	N, 2 pickpus	$1,250	$1,625
1967-1969	V, 1 pu, vibrato	$1,250	$1,625
1967-1969	V, 2 pu, vibrato	$1,375	$1,750

Dane B Series
1967-1969. 2 or 3 pickups, with or without vibrato (V), semi-solid Durabody, 6 or 12 strings.

1967-1969	12-string	$1,250	$1,625
1967-1969	6-string, 2 pu	$1,000	$1,375
1967-1969	6-string, 3 pu	$1,125	$1,500

Dane C Series
1967-1969. 2 or 3 pickups, with or without vibrato (V), semi-solid Durabody with 2-tone Gator finish, 6 or 12 strings.

1967-1969	12-string	$1,875	$2,500
1967-1969	6-string	$1,625	$2,125

Dane D Series
1967-1969. 2 or 3 pickups, with or without vibrato (V), solid wood sculptured thinline body, 'floating adjustable pickguard-fingerguide', master volume with 4 switches, 6 or 12 strings.

1967-1969	12-string	$1,500	$2,000
1967-1969	6-string, 2 pu	$1,125	$1,500
1967-1969	6-string, 3 pu	$1,375	$1,750

Danoblaster Series
2000-2003. Offset double-cuts, 3 pickups, built-in effects – distortion on the Hearsay, distortion, chorus, trem and echo on Innuendo. Also in 12-string and baritone.

2000-2003	$200	$275

DC-2 Model 3021
1959-1966. Jimmy Page model, shorthorn, double pickup.

1959-1966	$1,500	$2,000

DC-3/DDC-3
1999-2003. Shorthorn double-cut, 3 pickups, seal-shaped pickguard, Coke bottle headstock, solid and sparkle finishes.

1999-2003	$375	$500

DC-12/Electric XII
1999-2003. 12-string version of 59-DC.

1999-2003	$450	$600

59-DC/'59 Dano (Reissue)
1998-1999, 2007. Shorthorn double-cut, 2 pickups, seal-shaped pickguard, Coke bottle headstock, '07 version called '59 Dano.

1998-1999	$350	$500

MODEL YEAR	FEATURES	EXC. COND. LOW	HIGH
Deluxe Single Pickup			
1959-1966. Double-cut, Coke bottle headstock, 1 pickup, 2 knobs.			
1959-1960	Walnut or white	$1,375	$1,750
1961-1966	Walnut, white, honey	$1,250	$1,625
Deluxe Double Pickup			
1959-1966. As Single above, but with 2 pickups, and added master volume on later models.			
1959-1960	Walnut or white	$1,500	$2,000
1961-1966	Walnut, white, honey	$1,375	$1,750
Deluxe Triple Pickup			
1959-1966. As Single above, but with 3 pickups, 3 knobs, and added master volume on later models.			
1959-1960	Walnut or white	$1,500	$2,000
1961-1966	Walnut, white, honey	$1,375	$1,750
Doubleneck (3923)			
1958-1966. A shorthorn double-cut, bass and 6-string necks, 1 pickup on each neck, Coke bottle headstocks, white sunburst.			
1958-1966		$3,500	$4,500
Doubleneck Reissue			
1999-2003. Baritone 6-string and standard 6-string double neck, shorthorn body style, or the 6-12 model with a 6-string and 12-string neck. Price includes $75 for a guitar case, but many sales do not seem to include a guitar case because of unusual body size.			
1999-2003		$550	$800
Electric Sitar			
1968-1969. Traditional looking, oval-bodied sitar, no drone strings as on the Coral Sitar of the same period.			
1968-1969		$3,500	$4,500
Guitarlin (4123)			
1958-1966. The Longhorn guitar, 2 huge cutaways, 31-fret neck, 2 pickups.			
1958-1960		$3,500	$5,000
1961-1966		$3,000	$4,000
Hand Vibrato Single Pickup (4011)			
1958-1966. Short horn double-cut, 1 pickup, batwing headstock, simple design vibrato, black w/ white guard.			
1958-1966		$1,125	$1,500
Hand Vibrato Double Pickup (4021)			
1958-1966. Same as Single Pickup, but with 2 pickups and larger pickguard.			
1958-1966		$1,250	$1,625
Hawk			
1967-1969. Offered with 1 or 2 pickups, vibrato (V models) or non-vibrato (N models), 12-string model also offered.			
1967-1969	1N, 1 pickup	$1,125	$1,500
1967-1969	1N12, 12-string	$1,375	$1,750
1967-1969	1V, vibrato, 1 pu	$1,250	$1,625
1967-1969	2N, 2 pickups	$1,250	$1,625
1967-1969	2N12, 12-string	$1,625	$2,125
1967-1969	2V, vibrato, 2 pu	$1,625	$2,125
Hodad/Hodad 12-String			
1999-2003. Unique double-cut with sharp horns, 6 or 12 strings, sparkle finish.			
1999-2003		$375	$500

MODEL YEAR	FEATURES	EXC. COND. LOW	HIGH
Model C			
1955. Single-cut, 1 or 2 pickups, ginger colored vinyl cover.			
1955-1958		$750	$975
Pro 1			
1963-1964. Odd-shaped double-cut electric with squared off corners, 1 pickup.			
1963-1964		$1,000	$1,500
Pro Reissue			
2007. Based on '60s Pro 1, but with 2 pickups.			
2007		$300	$400
Slimline (SL) Series			
1967-1969. Offset waist double-cut, 2 or 3 pickups, with or without vibrato, 6 or 12 string.			
1967-1969	12-string	$1,375	$1,750
1967-1969	6-string, 2 pu	$1,000	$1,375
1967-1969	6-string, 3 pu	$1,250	$1,625
Standard Single Pickup			
1958-1966. Nicknamed the Shorthorn, double-cut, 1 pickup, 2 regular control knobs, kidney-shaped pickguard originally, seal-shaped 'guard by ca. 1960, Coke bottle headstock, in black or bronze.			
1958-1959	Kidney guard	$1,000	$1,500
1960-1966	Seal guard	$1,000	$1,500
Standard Double Pickup			
1958-1966. As Single Pickup above but with 2 pickups and 2 stacked, concentric volume/tone controls, in black, bronze and later blond. The black, seal-shaped pickguard version of this guitar is often referred to as the Jimmy Page model because he used one. Reissued in 1998 as 59-DC.			
1958-1959	Kidney guard, black	$1,250	$1,625
1960-1966	Bronze	$1,250	$1,625
1960-1966	Jimmy Page, black	$1,500	$2,000
1961-1966	Blond	$1,625	$2,125
Standard Triple Pickup			
1958. As Single Pickup above but with 3 pickups and 3 stacked, concentric pointer volume/tone controls, in white to bronze sunburst, very rare.			
1958		$1,500	$2,000
Tweed Model			
1954-1955. First production models, single-cut, bell-shape headstock, 1 or 2 pickups, tweed vinyl cover.			
1954-1955	1 pickup	$4,500	$5,500
1954-1955	2 pickups	$5,000	$6,000
U-1			
1955-1958. Single-cut, 1 pickup, 2 regular knobs, bell-shape headstock originally, switching to Coke bottle in late '55. The U Series featured Dano's new 'solid center' block construction.			
1955	Enamel, bell hdsk	$1,000	$1,500
1956-1957	Enamel, Coke hdsk	$1,000	$1,500
1956-1957	Ivory, Coke hdsk	$1,250	$1,750
1956-1957	Rare color	$3,000	$4,000
1958	Enamel, Coke hdsk	$1,000	$1,500
1958	Ivory, Coke hdsk	$1,250	$1,750
U-1 '56 Reissue			
1998-1999. Reissue of '56 U-1, various colors.			
1998-1999		$250	$350

Danelectro Standard
Single Pickup

Tom Pfeifer

1963 Danelectro Standard
Double Pickup

Trey Rabinek

GUITARS

1957 Danelectro U2
Rivington Guitars

Late-'30s D'Angelico Style B
Andy Nelson

MODEL YEAR	FEATURES	EXC. COND. LOW	HIGH
U-2			

1955-1958. As U-1, but with 2 pickups and 2 stacked concentric volume/tone controls.

MODEL YEAR	FEATURES	EXC. COND. LOW	HIGH
1955	Enamel, bell hdsk	$2,000	$2,500
1956-1957	Enamel, Coke hdsk	$2,000	$2,500
1956-1957	Ivory, Coke hdsk	$2,500	$3,000
1956-1957	Rare color	$5,500	$7,500
1958	Enamel, Coke hdsk	$2,000	$2,500
1958	Ivory, Coke hdsk	$2,500	$3,000

U-2 '56 Reissue

1998-2003. Reissue of '56 U-2, various colors.

1998-2003		$275	$400

U-3

1955-1958. As U-2, but with 3 pickups and 3 stacked concentric volume/tone controls.

1958	Enamel, Coke hdsk	$2,500	$3,000

U-3 '56 Reissue

1999-2003. Reissue of '56 U-3, various colors.

1999-2003		$250	$350

D'Angelico

John D'Angelico built his own line of archtop guitars, mandolins, and violins from 1932 until his death in 1964. His instruments are some of the most sought-after by collectors. The binding on some D'Angelico guitars can become deteriorated and requires replacing.

D'Angelico (L-5 Snakehead)

1932-1935. D'Angelico's L-5-style with snakehead headstock, his first model, sunburst.

1932-1935		$11,500	$14,500

Excel/Exel (Cutaway)

1947-1964. Cutaway, 17" width, 1- and 3-ply bound f-hole.

1947-1949	Natural, original binding	$30,000	$40,000
1947-1949	Sunburst, original binding	$30,000	$40,000
1950-1959	Natural, original binding	$30,000	$40,000
1950-1959	Sunburst, original binding	$30,000	$40,000
1960-1964	Natural	$30,000	$40,000
1960-1964	Sunburst	$30,000	$40,000

Excel/Exel (Non-Cutaway)

1936-1949. Non-cut, 17" width, 1- and 3-ply bound f-hole, natural finishes were typically not offered in the '30s, non-cut Excels were generally not offered after '49 in deference to the Excel cutaway.

1936-1939	Sunburst, straight f-hole	$16,000	$20,000
1938-1939	Sunburst, standard f-hole	$16,000	$20,000
1940-1949	Natural	$17,000	$22,000
1940-1949	Sunburst	$14,000	$18,000

New Yorker (Non-Cutaway)

1936-1949. Non-cut, 18" width, 5-ply-bound f-hole, New Yorker non-cut orders were overshadowed by the cut model orders starting in '47.

1936-1939	Sunburst	$20,000	$28,000
1940-1949	Natural	$22,000	$30,000
1940-1949	Sunburst	$20,000	$28,000

New Yorker Deluxe (Cutaway)

1947-1964. Cutaway, 18" width, 5-ply-bound f-hole, New Yorker non-cut orders were overshadowed by the cut model orders starting in '47.

1947-1949	Natural	$48,000	$62,000
1947-1949	Sunburst	$40,000	$52,000
1950-1959	Natural	$48,000	$62,000
1950-1959	Sunburst	$40,000	$52,000
1960-1964	Natural	$42,000	$55,000
1960-1964	Sunburst	$35,000	$45,000

New Yorker Special

1950-1964. Also called Excel New Yorker or Excel Cutaway New Yorker Cutaway, 17" width, New Yorker styling, not to be confused with D'Angelico Special (A and B style).

1950-1959	Natural	$30,000	$40,000
1950-1959	Sunburst	$27,000	$35,000
1960-1964	Natural	$27,000	$35,000
1960-1964	Sunburst	$24,000	$31,000

Special (Cutaway)

1950-1964. Generally, Style A and B-type instruments made for musicians on a budget, plain specs with little ornamentation, not to be confused with New Yorker Special.

1950-1959	Sunburst	$10,000	$13,000
1960-1964	Sunburst	$9,000	$12,000

Special (Non-Cutaway)

1950-1964. Non-cut Special, not to be confused with New Yorker Special.

1950-1959	Sunburst	$6,000	$7,750
1960-1964	Sunburst	$5,250	$6,750

Style A

1936-1945. Archtop, 17" width, unbound f-holes, block 'board inlays, multi-pointed headstock, nickel-plated metal parts.

1936-1939	Sunburst	$10,000	$13,000
1940-1945	Sunburst	$9,500	$12,000

Style A-1

1936-1945. Unbound f-holes, 17" width, arched headstock, nickel-plated metal parts.

1936-1939	Sunburst	$10,000	$13,000
1940-1945	Sunburst	$9,500	$12,000

Style B

1933-1948. Archtop 17" wide, unbound F-holes, block 'board inlays, gold-plated parts.

1936-1939	Sunburst	$11,000	$15,000
1940-1948	Sunburst	$10,000	$14,000

Style B Special

1933-1948. D'Angelico described variations from standard features with a 'Special' designation, Vintage dealers may also describe these instruments as 'Special'.

1936-1939	Sunburst	$12,000	$15,000
1940-1948	Sunburst	$11,000	$14,000

D'Angelico (D'Angelico Guitars of America)

1988-present. Intermediate and professional grade, production/custom, archtop, flat-top, and solidbody guitars made in South Korea and imported by D'Angelico Guitars of America, of Colts Neck,

MODEL		EXC. COND.	
YEAR	FEATURES	LOW	HIGH

New Jersey. From 1988 to '04, they were premium and presentation grade instruments built in Japan by luthier Hidesato Shino and Vestax. In '12, GTR announced they bought the brand name and are offering premium grade D'Angelicos built in the U.S.

D'Angelico (Lewis)

1994-2011. Luthier Michael Lewis built presentation grade, custom/production, D'Angelico replica guitars in Grass Valley, California, under an agreement with the GHS String Company, which owned the name in the U.S. He also builds guitars and mandolins under the Lewis name.

D'Angelico II

Mid-1990s. Archtops built in the U.S. and distributed by Archtop Enterprises of Merrick, New York. Mainly presentation grade copies of Excel and New Yorker models, but also made lower cost similar models.

Jazz Classic

1990s. Electric archtop, cutaway, carved spruce top, figured maple back and sides, single neck pickup, transparent cherry.

1990s		$2,500	$3,250

Daniel Friederich

1955-2015. Luthier Daniel Friederich built his custom/production, classical guitars in Paris, France.

D'Aquisto

1965-1995. James D'Aquisto apprenticed under D'Angelico until the latter's death, at age 59, in '64. He started making his own brand instruments in '65 and built archtop and flat-top acoustic guitars, solidbody and hollowbody electric guitars. He also designed guitars for Hagstrom and Fender. He died in '95, at age 59.

Avant Garde

1987-1994. 18" wide, non-traditional futuristic model, approximately 5 or 6 instruments were reportedly made, because of low production this pricing is for guidance only.

1990	Blond	$75,000	$95,000

Centura/Centura Deluxe

1993-1994. 17" wide, non-traditional art deco futuristic archtop, approximately 10 made, the last guitars made by this luthier, due to the low production this pricing is for guidance only.

1993-1994	Centura	$90,000	$115,000
1993-1994	Deluxe	$98,000	$127,000

Excel (Cutaway)

1965-1992. Archtop, 17" width, with modern thin-logo started in '81.

1965-1967	Blond	$32,000	$42,000
1965-1967	Sunburst	$30,000	$40,000
1968-1981	Blond	$32,000	$42,000
1968-1981	Sunburst	$30,000	$40,000
1982-1992	Blond	$34,000	$44,000
1982-1992	Sunburst	$33,000	$42,000

Excel (Flat-Top)

1970s-1980s. Flat-top, 16", flamed maple back and sides, Sitka spruce top, about 15 made, narrow Excel-style headstock, oval soundhole, D'Aquisto script logo on headstock.

1970s-80s		$17,000	$22,000

Hollow Electric

Early model with bar pickup, D'Aquisto headstock, '70s model with humbuckers.

1960s-80s		$14,000	$18,000

Jazz Special

1985	1st version	$15,000	$20,000
1988	2nd version	$21,500	$28,000

New Yorker Classic (Archtop)

1986. Single-cut acoustic archtop with new modern design features such as large S-shaped sound holes.

1986		$51,000	$65,000

New Yorker Classic (Solidbody)

1980s. Only 2 were reported to be made, therefore this pricing is for guidance only.

1980s		$16,000	$20,000

New Yorker Deluxe (Cutaway)

1965-1992. Most are 18" wide.

1965-1981	Blond	$42,000	$55,000
1965-1981	Sunburst	$35,000	$45,000
1982-1992	Blond	$42,000	$55,000
1982-1992	Sunburst	$38,000	$50,000

New Yorker Special (7-String)

1980s. Limited production 7-string, single-cut.

1980s		$30,000	$40,000

New Yorker Special (Cutaway)

1966-1992. Most are 17" wide.

1966-1992	Blond	$26,000	$35,000
1966-1992	Sunburst	$24,000	$30,000

Solo/Solo Deluxe

1992-1993. 18" wide, non-traditional non-cut art deco model, only 2 reported made, because of low production this pricing is for guidance only.

1992-1993		$95,000	$125,000

D'Aquisto (Aria)

May 2002-2013. Premium grade, production, D'Aquisto designs licensed to Aria of Japan by D'Aquisto Strings, Inc., Deer Park, New York.

Various Models

2002-2013		$2,500	$3,500

Dauphin

1970s-late 1990s. Classical and flamenco guitars imported from Spain and Japan by distributor George Dauphinais, located in Springfield, Illinois.

Dave King Acoustics

1980-present. Premium grade, custom/production, acoustic and resonator guitars built by luthier Dave King in Berkshire, U.K.

Dave Maize Acoustic Guitars

1991-present. Luthier Dave Maize builds his professional and premium grade, production/custom, flat-tops and basses in Cave Junction, Oregon.

1967 D'Aquisto New Yorker
Imaged by Heritage Auctions, HA.com

2002 D'Aquisto (Aria)
New Yorker
Mike Thompson

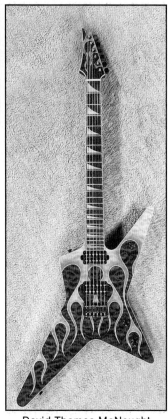

David Thomas McNaught

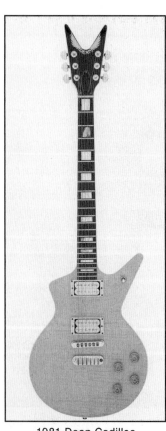

1981 Dean Cadillac

David Rubio

1960s-2000. Luthier David Spink built his guitars, lutes, violins, violas, cellos, and harpsichords first in New York, and after '67, in the U.K. While playing in Spain, he acquired the nickname Rubio, after his red beard. He died in '00.

David Thomas McNaught

1989-present. Professional, premium, and presentation grade, custom, solidbody guitars built by luthier David Thomas McNaught and finished by Dave Mansel in Locust, North Carolina. In '97, they added the production/custom DTM line of guitars.

Davis, J. Thomas

1975-present. Premium and presentation grade, custom, steel-string flat-tops, 12-strings, classicals, archtops, Irish citterns and flat-top Irish bouzoukis made by luthier J. Thomas Davis in Columbus, Ohio.

Davoli

See Wandre listing.

DBZ

2008-2012. Solidbody electric guitars from Dean B. Zelinsky, founder of Dean Guitars, and partners Jeff Diamant and Terry Martin. Dean left the partnership February, '12 and established Dean Zelinsky Private Label guitars.

de Jonge, Sergei

1972-present. Premium grade, production/custom classical and steel-string guitars built by luthier Sergei de Jonge originally in Oshawa, Ontario, and since '04 in Chelsea, Quebec.

De Paule Stringed Instruments

1969-1980, 1993-2008. Custom steel-string, nylon-string, archtop, resonator, and Hawaiian guitars built by luthier C. Andrew De Paule in Eugene, Oregon.

Dean

1976-present. Intermediate, professional and premium grade, production/custom, solidbody, hollowbody, acoustic, acoustic/electric, and resonator guitars made in the U.S., Korea, the Czech Republic and China. They also offer basses, banjos, mandolins, and amps. Founded in Evanston, Illinois, by Dean Zelinsky. Original models were upscale versions of Gibson designs with glued necks, fancy tops, DiMarzio pickups and distinctive winged headstocks (V, Z and ML), with production beginning in '77. In '80 the factory was relocated to Chicago. Dean's American manufacturing ends in '86 when all production shifts to Korea. In '91 Zelinsky sold the company to Tropical Music in Miami, Florida. For '93-'94 there was again limited U.S. (California) production of the E'Lite, Cadillac and

ML models under the supervision of Zelinsky and Cory Wadley. Korean versions were also produced. In '95, Elliott Rubinson's Armadillo Enterprises, of Clearwater, Florida, bought the Dean brand. In '97 and '98, Dean offered higher-end USA Custom Shop models. In '98, they reintroduced acoustics. From 2000 to '08, Zelinsky was once again involved in the company.

Dating American models: First 2 digits are year of manufacture. Imports have no date codes.

Baby ML

1982-1986, 2000-2014. Downsized version of ML model.

1982-1986	Import	$550	$750
1982-1986	US-made	$850	$1,125

Baby V

1982-1986, 2000-2014. Downsized version of the V model.

1982-1986	Import	$500	$650
1982-1986	US-made	$850	$1,125

Baby Z

1982-1986, 2000-2014. Downsized version of the Z model.

1982-1986	Import	$500	$650
1982-1986	US-made	$850	$1,125

Bel Aire

1983-1984. Solidbody, possibly the first production guitar with humbucker/single/single pickup layout, U.S.-made, an import model was introduced in '87.

1980s	Import	$450	$600
1983-1984	US-made	$650	$900

Budweiser Guitar

Ca.1987. Shaped like Bud logo.

1987	$375	$750

Cadillac (U.S.A.)

1979-1985. Single long treble horn on slab body.

1979-1985	$2,250	$3,000

Cadillac 1980

2006-2018. Block inlays, 2 humbuckers, gold hardware.

2006-2018	$500	$650

Cadillac Deluxe (U.S.A.)

1993-1994, 1996-1997. Made in U.S., single longhorn shape, various colors.

1993-1997	$1,750	$2,250

Cadillac Reissue (Import)

1992-1994. Single longhorn shape, 2 humbuckers, various colors.

1992-1994	$350	$450

Cadillac Select

2009-2017. Made in Korea, figured maple top, mahogany, pearl block inlays.

2009-2017	$500	$650

Cadillac Standard

1996-1997. Slab body version.

1996-1997	$1,750	$2,250

Del Sol

2008. Import, small double-cut thinline semi-hollow, ES-335 style body, rising sun fretboard markers.

2008	$400	$550

The Official Vintage Guitar magazine Price Guide 2025 **Dean** Dime O Flame (ML) — **Dean Zelinsky Private Label** **69**

GUITARS

MODEL YEAR	FEATURES	EXC. COND. LOW	HIGH

Dime O Flame (ML)
2005-2018. ML-body, Dimebuckers, burning flames finish, Dime logo on headstock.

2005-2018		$450	$575

Eighty-Eight (Import)
1987-1990. Offset double-cut solidbody, import.

1987-1990		$225	$300

E'Lite
1978-1985, 1994-1996. Single-horn shape.

1978-1985		$1,750	$2,250
1994-1996		$1,250	$1,650

E'Lite Deluxe
1980s. Single-horn shape.

1980s		$1,750	$2,250

EVO XM
2004-present. Single-cut slab body, 2 humbuckers.

2004-2023		$150	$200

Golden E'Lite
1980. Single pointy treble cutaway, fork headstock, gold hardware, ebony 'board, sunburst.

1980		$1,750	$2,250

Hollywood Z (Import)
1985-1986. Bolt-neck Japanese copy of Baby Z, Explorer shape.

1985-1986		$250	$325

Jammer (Import)
1987-1989. Offset double-cut body, bolt-on neck, dot markers, six-on-a-side tuners, various colors offered.

1987-1989		$250	$325

Leslie West Standard
2008-2017. Flame maple top, mahogany body, rosewood 'board.

2008-2017		$525	$675

Mach I (Import)
1985-1986. Limited run from Korea, Mach V with six-on-a-side tunes, various colors.

1985-1986		$250	$325

Mach V (Import)
1985-1986. Pointed solidbody, 2 humbucking pickups, maple neck, ebony 'board, locking trem, various colors, limited run from Korea.

1985-1986		$250	$325

Mach VII (U.S.A.)
1985-1986. Mach I styling, made in America, offered in unusual finishes.

1985-1986		$1,750	$2,250

ML (ML Standard/U.S.A.)
1977-1986. There is a flame model and a standard model.

1977-1986	Burst flamed top	$4,500	$5,500
1977-1986	Burst plain top	$4,000	$5,000
1977-1986	Common opaque	$3,500	$4,500

ML (Import)
1983-1990. Korean-made.

1983-1990		$600	$775

ML Dimebag Darrell Rust From Hell
2005. USA Custom Shop, limited run of 120, distressed airbrush finish.

2005		$5,000	$7,500

Soltero SL
2007-2010. Made in Japan, single-cut solidbody, 2 pickups, flame maple top.

2007-2010		$1,750	$2,250

USA Time Capsule Exotic V
2005-2014. Flying V style, solid mahogany body with exotic spalted and flamed maple top, Dean V neck profile (split V headstock).

2005-2014		$2,500	$3,250

USA Time Capsule Z
2000-2014. Explorer style body, figured maple top.

2000-2014		$2,500	$3,500

V Standard (U.S.A.)
1977-1986. V body, there is a standard and a flame model offered.

1977-1981	Burst flamed top	$4,500	$5,500
1977-1981	Burst plain top	$4,000	$4,500
1977-1981	Common opaque	$3,000	$4,000
1982-1986	Burst flamed top	$3,500	$4,500
1982-1986	Burst plain top	$3,000	$4,000
1982-1986	Common opaque	$2,500	$3,500

Z Standard (U.S.A.)
1977-1986. Long treble cutaway solidbody, 2 humbuckers.

1977-1983	Common finish	$3,000	$4,000
1977-1983	Rare finish	$3,500	$4,500

Z Autograph (Import)
1985-1987. The first Dean import from Korea, offset double-cut, bolt neck, dot markers, offered in several standard colors.

1985-1987		$350	$450

Z Coupe/Z Deluxe
1997-1998. US Custom Shop, mahogany body offered in several standard colors, Z Deluxe with Floyd Rose tremolo.

1997-1998		$1,250	$1,625

Z Korina
1997-1998. US Custom Shop, Z Coupe with korina body, various standard colors.

1997-1998		$1,375	$1,750

Z LTD
1997-1998. US Custom Shop, Z Coupe with bound neck and headstock, offered in several standard colors.

1997-1998		$1,375	$1,750

Dean Markley
The string and pickup manufacturer offered a limited line of guitars and basses for a time in the '80s. They were introduced in '84.

Dean Zelinsky Private Label
2012-present. Premium grade, production/custom, hollow, semi-hollow and solidbody electric guitars built in Chicago, Illinois by luthier Dean Zelinsky, founder of Dean Guitars. He also imports a line of intermediate grade guitars from South Korea and Indonesia.

1981 Dean ML

1979 Dean Z Standard

To get the most from this book, be sure to read "Using *The Guide*" in the introduction.

DeArmond M-70
Vic Hines

Delirium Bettie Red

MODEL		EXC. COND.	
YEAR	FEATURES	LOW	HIGH

DeArmond Guitars

1999-2004. Solid, semi-hollow and hollow body guitars based on Guild models and imported from Korea by Fender. They also offered basses. The DeArmond brand was originally used on pickups, effects and amps built by Rowe Industries.

Electric

1999-2004. Various import models, some with USA electronic components.

1999-2004 Various models	$300	$950

Dearstone

1993-2017. Luthier Ray Dearstone built his professional and premium grade, custom, archtop and acoustic/electric guitars in Blountville, Tennessee. He also built mandolin family instruments and violins.

Decar

1950s. A private brand sold by Decautur, Illinois music store, Decar headstock logo.

Stratotone H44

1956. Private branded Stratotone with maple neck and fretboard instead of the standard neck/fretboard, 1 pickup and other Harmony H44 Stratotone attributes, bolt-on neck.

1956	$675	$875

DeCava Guitars

1983-present. Professional and premium grade, production/custom, archtop and classical guitars built by luthier Jim DeCava first in Stratford, then Ansonia, Connecticut. He also builds ukes, banjos, and mandolins.

Decca

Mid-1960s. Acoustic, solid and hollow body guitars, basses and amps made in Japan by Teisco and imported by Decca Records, Decca headstock logo, student-level instruments.

Acoustic Flat-Top

1960s. Decca label on the inside back.

1960s	$200	$300

Electric Solidbody

1960s. Teisco-made in Japan, 3 pickups, sunburst.

1960s	$400	$550

Defil

Based out of Lubin, Poland, Defil made solid and semi-hollowbdy electric guitars at least from the 1970s to the '90s.

DeGennaro

2003-present. Premium grade, custom/production, acoustic, archtop, semi-hollow and solidbody guitars, basses and mandolins built by luthier William DeGennaro in Grand Rapids, Michigan.

Del Oro

1930s-1940s. Flat-top (including cowboy stencil models) and resonator guitars, built by Kay. At least the cowboy stencils were sold by Spiegel.

MODEL		EXC. COND.	
YEAR	FEATURES	LOW	HIGH

Small Acoustic

1930s	13" to 14" body	$250	$350

Del Pilar Guitars

1956-1986. Luthier William Del Pilar made his classical guitars in Brooklyn, New York.

Classical

1950s-1980s. Brazilian rosewood back and sides, cedar top, quilt rosette, 9-ply top binding.

1960-1969	$4,750	$6,250

Del Vecchio

1902-present. Casa Del Vecchio builds a variety of Spanish instruments including acoustic and resonator guitars in São Paulo, Brazil.

Delaney Guitars

2004-present. Luthier Mike Delaney builds his professional grade, production/custom, chambered, solidbody, and semi-hollowbody electric guitars and basses in Atlanta, Georgia. Prior to 2008 he built in Florence, Montana.

Delgado

1928-present. Delgado began in Torreon, Coahuila, Mexico, then moved to Juarez in the '30s with a second location in Tijuana. In '48 they moved to California and opened a shop in Los Angeles. Since 2005, Manuel A. Delgado, a third-generation luthier, builds his premium and presentation grade, production/custom, classical, flamenco and steel string acoustic guitars in Nashville, Tennessee. He also builds basses, mandolins, ukuleles, and banjos.

Delirium Custom Guitars

Luthiers Patrick and Vincent Paul-Victor along with Gael Canonne build their professional and premium grade, production/custom, solidbody electric guitars in Paris and Toulouse, France.

Dell'Arte

1997-present. Production/custom Maccaferri-style guitars from John Kinnard and Alain Cola. In '96, luthier John Kinnard opened a small shop called Finegold Guitars and Mandolins. In '98 he met Alain Cola, a long-time jazz guitarist who was selling Mexican-made copies of Selmer/Maccaferri guitars under the Dell'Arte brand. Cola wanted better workmanship for his guitars, and in October '98, Finegold and Dell'Arte merged. As of May '99, all production is in California.

Delta Guitars

2005-2010. Acoustic, acoustic/electric, and solidbody electric guitars from Musician's Wholesale America, Nashville, Tennessee.

Dennis Hill Guitars

Premium and presentation grade, production/custom, classical and flamenco guitars built by luthier Dennis Hill in Panama City, Florida. He has also built dulcimers, mandolins, and violins.

MODEL		EXC. COND.	
YEAR	FEATURES	LOW	HIGH

Desmond Guitars

1991-present. Luthier Robert B. Desmond builds his premium grade, production/custom classical guitars in Orlando, Florida.

DeTemple

1995-present. Premium grade, production/custom, solidbody electric guitars and basses built by luthier Michael DeTemple in Sherman Oaks, California.

DeVoe Guitars

1975-present. Luthier Lester DeVoe builds his premium grade, production/custom flamenco and classical guitars in Nipomo, California.

Diamond

Ca. 1963-1964. Line of sparkle finish solidbody guitars made in Italy for the Diamond Accordion company.

Ranger

Ca. 1963-1964. Rangers came with 1, 2, 3, or 4 pickups, sparkle finish.

1960s		$675	$900

Dick, Edward Victor

1975-present. Luthier Edward Dick currently builds his premium grade, custom, classical guitars in Denver, Colorado (he lived in Peterborough and Ottawa, Ontario until '95). He also operates the Colorado School of Lutherie.

Dickerson

1937-1947. Founded by the Dickerson brothers in '37, primarily for electric lap steels and small amps. Instruments were also private branded for Cleveland's Oahu company, and for the Gourley brand. By '47, the company changed ownership and was renamed Magna Electronics (Magnatone).

Dillion

1996-2021. Dillion, of Cary, North Carolina, offers intermediate grade, production, acoustic, acoustic/electric, hollow-body and solidbody guitars, basses and mandolins made in Korea and Vietnam. Stopped making instruments in '21.

Dillon

1975-2006. Professional and premium grade, custom, flat-tops and basses built by luthier John Dillon in Taos, New Mexico, and in Bloomsburg, Pennsylvania ('81-'01).

Dino's Guitars

Custom, professional grade, electric solidbody guitars built by a social co-op company founded by Alessio Casati and Andy Bagnasco, in Albisola, Italy. They also build effects.

DiPinto

1995-present. Intermediate and professional grade, production retro-vibe guitars and basses from luthier Chris DiPinto of Philadelphia, Pennsylvania. Until late '99, all instruments built in the U.S., since then all built in Korea.

Ditson

1835-1937. Started in Boston by music publisher Oliver Ditson, by the end of the 1800s the company was one of the East Coast's largest music businesses, operating in several cities and was also involved in distribution and manufacturing of a variety of instruments, including guitars and ukes. From 1916-1930 Ditson guitars were made by Martin. The majority of Martin production was from '16 to '22 with over 500 units sold in '21. Ditson also established Lyon and Healy in Chicago and the John Church Company in Cincinnati.

Values for Ditson Models 111 and 1-45 would be equivalent to those for Martin models from that era with similar specs.

Concert

1916-1922. Similar in size to Martin size 0. Models include Style 1, Style 2 and Style 3.

1916-1922	Style 1	$5,500	$7,000
1916-1922	Style 2	$6,500	$8,500
1916-1922	Style 3	$7,500	$9,500

Standard

1916-1922. Small body similar to Martin size 3, plain styling. Models include Style 1, Style 2 and Style 3.

1916-1922	Style 1	$4,000	$5,000
1916-1922	Style 2	$4,500	$5,500
1916-1922	Style 3	$6,000	$7,750

D'Leco Guitars

1991-2003. Guitarist Maurice Johnson and luthier James W. Dale built premium grade, production/custom archtops in Oklahoma City, Oklahoma.

DM Darling Guitars

Luthier Denis Merrill, began in 2006, builds professional and premium grade, custom, acoustic, classical, resonator and solidbody guitars in Tacoma, Washington. From 1978 to '06 he built under his own name and Merrill Custom Shop. He also builds mandolin family instruments.

Dobro

1929-1942, ca. 1954-2019. Currently, professional, and premium grade, production, wood and metal body resophonic guitars offered by Gibson.

Founded 1929 in Los Angeles by John Dopyera, Rudy Dopyera, Ed Dopyera and Vic Smith (Dobro stands for Dopyera Brothers). Made instruments sold under the Dobro, Regal, Norwood Chimes, Angelus, Rex, Broman, Montgomery Ward, Penetro, Bruno, Alhambra, More Harmony, Orpheum, and Magno-tone brands.

Dobro instruments have a single cone facing outward with a spider bridge structure and competed

DeTemple Spirit Series
Stellacasta

DiPinto Belvedere Deluxe

1976 Dobro Bicentennial
James Seldin

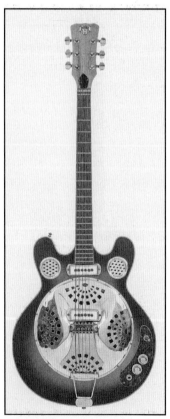

1968 Dobro D-100 Californian
Imaged by Heritage Auctions, HA.com

with National products. Generally, model names are numbers referring to list price and therefore materials and workmanship (e.g., a No. 65 cost $65). Because of this, the same model number may apply to different instruments. However, model numbers are never identified on instruments!

In '30, the company name was changed to Dobro Corporation, Ltd. In '32, Louis Dopyera buys Ted Kleinmeyer's share of National. Louis, Rudy and Ed now hold controlling interest in National, but in '32 John Dopyera left Dobro to pursue the idea of a metal resophonic violin. In December of '34 Ed Dopyera joins National's board of directors (he's also still on Dobro board), and by March of '35 Dobro and National have merged to become the National Dobro Corporation. Dobro moves into National's larger factory but continues to maintain separate production, sales and distribution until relocation to Chicago is complete. Beginning in early-'36 National Dobro starts relocating its offices to Chicago. L.A. production of Dobros continued until '37, after which some guitars continue to be assembled from parts until '39, when the L.A. operations were closed down.

All resonator production ended in '42. Victor Smith, Al Frost and Louis Dopyera bought the company and changed the name to the Valco Manufacturing Company. The Dobro name does not appear when production resumes after World War II.

In mid-'50s - some sources say as early as '54 - Rudy and Ed Dopyera began assembling wood-bodied Dobros from old parts using the name DB Original. In about '59, some 12-fret DB Originals were made for Standel, carrying both DB Original and Standel logos. In around '61, production was moved to Gardena, California, and Louis Dopyera and Valco transferred the Dobro name to Rudy and Ed, who produce the so-called Gardena Dobros. At this time, the modern Dobro logo appeared with a lyre that looks like 2 back-to-back '6s'. Dobro Original debuts ca. '62. In late-'64 the Dobro name was licensed to Ed's son Emil (Ed, Jr.) Dopyera. Ed, Jr. designs a more rounded Dobro (very similar to later Mosrites) and has a falling out with Rudy over it.

In '66 Semi Moseley acquires the rights to the Dobro brand, building some in Gardena, and later moving to Bakersfield, California. Moseley introduced Ed, Jr's design plus a thinline double-cutaway Dobro. He also made MoBros during this time. Moseley Dobros use either Dobro or National cones. In '67 Ed, Sr., Rudy and Gabriella Lazar started the Original Music Instrument Company (OMI) and produced Hound Dog brand Dobros. In '68 Moseley went bankrupt and in '70 OMI obtained the rights to the Dobro brand and begins production of OMI Dobros. In '75 Gabriella's son and daughter, Ron Lazar and Dee Garland, take over OMI. Rudy Dupyera makes and sells Safari brand resonator mandolins. Ed, Sr. dies in '77 and Rudy in '78. In '84 OMI was sold to Chester and Betty Lizak. Both wood and metal-bodied Dobros were produced in Huntington Beach, California. Chester Lizak died in '92. Gibson purchased Dobro in '93 and made Dobros in Nashville, Tennessee.

MODEL		EXC. COND.	
YEAR	FEATURES	LOW	HIGH

Dobros generally feature a serial number which, combined with historical information, provides a clue to dating. For prewar L.A. guitars, see approximation chart below adapted from "Gruhn's Guide to Vintage Guitars." No information exists on DB Originals.

Gardena Dobros had D prefix plus 3 digits beginning with 100 and going into the 500s (reportedly under 500 made). No information is available on Moseley Dobros.

OMI Dobros from '70-'79 have either D prefix for wood bodies or B prefix for metal bodies, plus 3 or 4 numbers for ranking, space, then a single digit for year (D XXXX Y or B XXX Y; e.g., D 172 8 would be wood body #172 from '78). For '80-'87 OMI Dobros, start with first number of year (decade) plus 3 or 4 ranking numbers, space, then year and either D for wood or B for metal bodies (8 XXXX YD or 8 XXX YB; e.g., 8 2006 5B would be metal body #2008 from '85). From '88-'92, at least, a letter and number indicate guitar style, plus 3 or 4 digits for ranking, letter for neck style, 2 digits for year, and letter for body style (AX XXXX NYYD or AX XXX NYYB).

L.A. Guitars (approx. number ranges, not actual production totals):

1929-30	900-2999
1930-31	3000-3999
1931-32	BXXX (Cyclops models only)
1932-33	5000-5599
1934-36	5700-7699
1937-42	8000-9999

Angelus
1933-1937. Wood body, round or square neck, 2-tone walnut finish, continues as Model 19 in Regal-made guitars.

1933-1937	Round neck	$1,500	$2,000
1933-1937	Square neck	$1,375	$1,750

Artist M-16
1934-1935. German silver alloy body, engraved.

1934-1935	H square neck	$4,000	$5,000
1934-1935	M round neck	$6,500	$8,000

Columbia D-12
1967-1968. Acoustic 12-string, typical Dobro resonator with spider style bridge, made during Dobro-Moseley era.

1967-1968		$900	$1,125

Cyclops 45
1932-1933. Bound walnut body, 1 screen hole.

1932-1933	Round neck	$2,875	$3,500
1932-1933	Square neck	$3,250	$4,000

D-40 Texarkana
1965-1967. Mosrite-era (identified by C or D prefix), traditional Dobro style cone and coverplate, dot inlays, Dobro logo on headstock, sunburst wood body. Red and blue finishes available.

1965-1967		$1,000	$1,375

D-40E Texarkana
1965-1967. D-40 electric with single pickup and 2 knobs.

1965-1967		$1,125	$1,500

MODEL YEAR	FEATURES	EXC. COND. LOW	HIGH
D-100 The Californian			
1965-1969. Dobro's version of Mosrite (thus nicknamed the "Mobro") thinline double-cut, resonator, 2 small metal ports, 2 pickups, 2 knobs, sunburst.			
1965-1969		$1,625	$2,125
DM-33 California Girl/DM-33H			
1996-2006. Chrome-plated bell brass body, biscuit bridge, spider resonator, rosewood 'board. Girl or Hawaiian-scene (H) engraving.			
1996-2006		$1,500	$2,000
Dobjo			
Dobro body, banjo neck, 5-string.			
1989		$1,125	$1,500
Dobro/Regal Model 19			
Ca.1934-1938. In the 1930s Dobro licensed Chicago's Regal Company to build Dobro-style guitars. The headstocks on these models can have a Dobro logo, Regal logo, or no logo at all. The 19 is a lower-end model, round holes in coverplate, square neck.			
1934-1938		$1,375	$1,750
Dobro/Regal Model 46/47			
1935-1942. Dobro/Regal 46, renamed 47 in '39, aluminum body, round neck, 14 frets, slotted headstock, silver finish. Degraded finish was a common problem with the Dobro/Regal 47.			
1935-1938	Model 46	$1,625	$2,000
1939-1942	Model 47	$2,250	$2,750
Dobro/Regal Model 62/65			
1935-1942. Renamed Model 65 in '39, nickel-plated brass body, Spanish dancer etching, round or square neck. Note: Dobro/Regal 65 should not be confused with Dobro Model 65 which was discontinued earlier.			
1935-1942	Model 62	$2,625	$3,250
1935-1942	Model 65	$2,625	$3,250
Dobro/Regal Tenor 27-1/2			
1930. Tenor version of Model 27.			
1930		$600	$800
Dobrolektric			
1996-2005. Resonator guitar with single-coil neck pickup, single-cut.			
1996-2005		$1,375	$1,750
DS-33/Steel 33			
1995-2000. Steel body with light amber sunburst finish, resonator with coverplate, biscuit bridge.			
1995-2000		$1,000	$1,375
DW-90C			
2001-2006. Single sharp cutaway, wood body, metal resonator, f-hole upper bass bout.			
2001-2006		$975	$1,250
E3 (C, M, W, B)			
Late 1970s-1986. Double-cut solidbodies with necks and bodies of laminated select hardwoods, Cinnamon (C), Maple (M), Walnut (W) or plain Black (B) finish, 2 pickups.			
1979-1986		$1,250	$1,625
F-60/F-60S			
1986-2005. Round neck (60, discontinued '00) or square neck (60S), f-holes, brown sunburst.			
1986-2005		$1,250	$1,625

MODEL YEAR	FEATURES	EXC. COND. LOW	HIGH
Gardena			
1968. Electric Dobro body, 2 knobs, single-coil soap bar pickup.			
1968		$850	$1,125
Hound Dog			
2002-2019. Laminated wood, 10 1/2" spider-bridge resonator.			
2002-2019		$425	$550
Hula Blues			
1987-1999. Dark brown wood body (earlier models have much lighter finish), painted Hawaiian scenes, round neck.			
1987-1999		$1,250	$1,625
Jerry Douglas			
1995-2005. Mahogany body, square neck, limited run of 200 with signature, but also sold without signature.			
1995-2005		$2,125	$2,750
Josh Graves			
1995-2005. The first 200 made were signed, single bound ample body, spider cone, nickel plated. Includes DW Josh Graves and Uncle Josh Limited models.			
1995	Signed	$1,750	$2,250
1996-2005	Unsigned	$1,500	$2,000
Leader 14M/14H			
1934-1935. Nickel plated brass body, segmented f-holes.			
1934-1935	H square neck	$2,375	$3,000
1934-1935	M round neck	$2,250	$2,750
Model 25			
1930-1935. Sunburst wood body, f-holes upper bout, large single metal cone, square neck.			
1930-1935		$1,625	$2,000
Model 27 (OMI)			
1976-1994. Wood body, square neck.			
1976-1994		$1,500	$2,000
Model 27 Cyclops			
1932-1933.			
1932-1933	Round neck	$1,875	$2,250
1932-1933	Square neck	$2,000	$2,500
Model 27 Deluxe			
1995-2005. 27 with figured maple top, nicer appointments.			
1996-2005		$1,750	$2,250
Model 27/27G			
1933-1937. Regal-made, wooden body.			
1933-1937	Round neck	$1,625	$2,000
1933-1937	Square neck	$1,875	$2,250
Model 32			
1939-1941. Regal-made, wooden body.			
1939-1941		$2,250	$2,750
Model 33 (Duolian)			
1972. Only made in '72, becomes Model 90 in '73.			
1972		$1,125	$1,500
Model 33 H			
1973-1997 (OMI & Gibson). Same as 33 D, but with etched Hawaiian scenes, available as round or square neck.			
1980s-90s	Round neck	$1,625	$2,000
1980s-90s	Square neck	$1,625	$2,000

2003 Dobro Hound Dog
Tom Pfeifer

1932 Dobro Model 27 Cyclops

1977 Dobro Model 60
Rivington Guitars

1973 Dobro Model 63
Imaged by Heritage Auctions, HA.com

MODEL YEAR	FEATURES	EXC. COND. LOW	HIGH

Model 35 (32)
1935-1942. Metal body, called Model 32 (not to be confused with wood body 32) for '35-'38.

1935-1942		$2,125	$2,750

Model 36
1932-1937. Wood body with resonator, round or square neck.

1932-1937	Round neck	$1,500	$2,000
1932-1937	Square neck	$1,875	$2,500

Model 36/36S
1970s-1997, 2002-2005. Chrome-plated brass body, round or square (S) neck, dot markers, engraved rose floral art.

1970s-2005		$1,625	$2,125

Model 37
1933-1937. Regal-made wood body, mahogany, bound body and 'board, round or square 12-fret neck.

1933-1937	Round neck	$1,625	$2,000
1933-1937	Square neck	$2,000	$2,500

Model 37 Tenor
1933-1937 (Regal). Tenor version of No. 37.

1933-1937		$1,000	$1,375

Model 45
1934-1939. Regal-made wood body, round or square neck.

1934-1939	Round neck	$2,000	$2,500
1934-1939	Square neck	$2,375	$3,000

Model 55/56 Standard
1929-1934. Model 55 Standard, renamed 56 Standard 1932-1934. Unbound wood body, metal resonator, bound neck, sunburst.

1929-1934	Round neck	$1,875	$2,250
1929-1934	Square neck	$2,125	$2,750

Model 60
1933-1936. Similar to Model 66/66B.

1933-1936	Round neck	$4,250	$5,500
1933-1936	Square neck	$5,000	$6,500

Model 60 Cyclops
1932-1933. Round neck, 12-fret model, black walnut finish.

1932-1933		$4,250	$5,500

Model 60/ 60D (OMI)/ 60DS
1970-1993. Wood body (laminated maple) with Dobro resonator cone, model 60 until '73 when renamed 60 D, and various 60 model features offered, post-'93 was Gibson-owned production.

1970-1993	Model 60 Series	$1,000	$1,500

Model 63
1973-1996. Wood body, 8-string, square neck.

1973-1996		$1,125	$1,500

Model 64
1980s-1995. Walnut body, tree-of-life inlay.

1982		$1,500	$2,000

Model 65/66/66B
1929-1933. Wood body with sandblasted ornamental design top and back, metal resonator, sunburst. Model 66 B has bound top.

1929-1931	Model 65	$2,375	$3,000
1932-1933	Model 66	$2,375	$3,000
1932-1933	Model 66B	$2,375	$3,000

Model 66/66 S
1972-1995. Wood body with sandblasted ornamental design top and back, metal resonator, sunburst, round or square (S) neck.

1972-1995		$925	$1,250

Model 75/Lily of the Valley
1972-1997, 2002-2005. Chrome plated bell brass body resonator, round neck, Lily of the Valley engraving.

1972-1997		$1,875	$2,500

Model 85/86
1929-1934. Wood body, triple-bound, round or square neck, renamed 86 in '32.

1929-1934		$2,625	$3,500

Model 90 (Duolian) (OMI)
1972-1995. Chrome-plated, f-holes, etched Hawaiian scene.

1972-1995	Various models	$1,250	$1,625

Model 90 (Woodbody)/WB90G/WB90S
1984-2005. Maple body with upper bout f-holes or sound holes, round neck, metal resonator with spider bridge, sunburst.

1984-2005		$1,125	$1,500

Model 125 De Luxe
1929-1934. Black walnut body, round or square neck, Dobro De Luxe engraved, triple-bound top, back and 'board, nickel-plated hardware, natural.

1929-1934	Round neck	$5,500	$7,000
1929-1934	Square neck	$10,000	$13,000

Professional 15M/15H
1934-1935. Engraved nickel body, round (M) or square (H) neck, solid peghead.

1934-1935	H square neck	$2,875	$3,750
1934-1935	M round neck	$2,625	$3,500

Dodge
1996-present. Luthier Rick Dodge builds his intermediate and professional grade, production, solidbody guitars with changeable electronic modules in Tallahassee, Florida. He also builds basses.

Doitsch
1930s. Acoustic guitars made by Harmony, most likely for a music store or studio.

Domino
Ca. 1967-1968. Solidbody and hollowbody electric guitars and basses imported from Japan by Maurice Lipsky Music Co. of New York, New York, previously responsible for marketing the Orpheum brand. Models are primarily near-copies of EKO, Vox, and Fender designs, plus some originals. Models were made by Arai or Kawai. Earlier models may have been imported, but this is not yet documented.

Electric
1967-1968. Various models including the Baron, Californian, Californian Rebel, Dawson, and Spartan.

1967-1968		$300	$900

MODEL		EXC. COND.	
YEAR	FEATURES	LOW	HIGH

Dommenget

1978-1985, 1988-present. Luthier Boris Dommenget (pronounced dommen-jay) builds his premium grade, custom/production, solidbody, flat-top, and archtop guitars in Balje, Germany. From '78 to '85 he was located in Wiesbaden, and from '88-'01 in Hamburg. He and wife Fiona also make pickups.

Don Musser Guitars

Luthier Don Musser, in 1976, began building custom, classical, and flat-top guitars in Silver City, New Mexico. He later moved his shop to Cotopaxi, Colorado.

Doolin Guitars

1997-present. Luthier Mike Doolin builds his premium grade, production/custom acoustics featuring his unique double-cut in Portland, Oregon.

Dorado

Ca. 1972-1973. Six- and 12-string acoustic guitars, solidbody electrics and basses. Brand used briefly by Baldwin/Gretsch on line of Japanese imports.

Acoustic Flat-Top/Acoustic Dobro

1972-1973. Includes folk D, jumbo Western, and grand concert styles (with laminated rosewood back and sides), and Dobro-style.

1972-1973	Higher-end	$350	$500
1972-1973	Lower-end	$200	$400
1972-1973	Mid-level	$250	$350

Solidbody Electric

1972-1973. Includes Model 5985, a double-cut with 2 P-90-style pickups.

1972-1973		$300	$500

Douglas Ching

Luthier Douglas J. Ching builds his premium grade, production/custom, classical, acoustic, and harp guitars currently in Chester, Virginia, and previously in Hawaii ('76-'89) and Michigan ('90-'93). He also builds ukes, lutes and violins.

D'Pergo Custom Guitars

2002-present. Professional, premium, and presentation grade, production/custom, solidbody guitars built in Windham, New Hampshire. Every component of the guitar is built by D'Pergo.

Dragge Guitars

1982-2010. Luthier Peter Dragge builds his custom, steel-string and nylon-string guitars in Ojai, California.

Dragonfly Guitars

1994-present. Professional grade, production/custom, sloped cutaway flat-tops, semi-hollow body electrics, basses and dulcitars built by luthier Dan Richter in Roberts Creek, British Columbia.

Drive

Ca. 2001-ca. 2011. Budget grade, production, import solidbody electric guitars and basses. They also offered solidstate amps.

DTM

See David Thomas McNaught listing.

Dudley Custom Guitars

2005-present. Luthier Peter Dudley builds his custom, premium grade, chambered solidbody electric guitars in Easton, Maryland.

Duelin Guitars

Professional grade, production/custom, 6 ½ string guitars designed by Don Scheib of Simi Valley and built by luthier Mike Lipe in Sun Valley, California.

Duesenberg

1995-present. Professional and premium grade, production/custom, solid and hollow body electric guitars and basses built by luthier Dieter Goelsdorf in Hannover, Germany. Rockinger had a Duesenberg guitar in the 1980s.

Dunwell Guitars

Professional and premium grade, custom, flat-tops built by luthier Alan Dunwell in Nederland, Colorado.

Dupont

Luthier Maurice Dupont builds his classical, archtop, Weissenborn-style and Selmer-style guitars in Cognac, France.

Dwight

See info under Epiphone Dwight guitar.

Dyer

1902-1939. The massive W. J. Dyer & Bro. store in St. Paul, Minnesota, sold a complete line of music related merchandise though they actually built nothing but a few organs. The Larson Brothers of Chicago were commissioned to build harp guitar and harp mandolin pieces for them somewhat following the harp guitar design of Chris Knutsen, until 1912 when the Knutsen patent expired. Although the body design somewhat copied the Knutsen patent the resulting instrument was in a class by itself in comparison. These harp guitars have become the standard by which all others are judged because of their ease of play and the tremendous, beautiful sound they produce. Many modern builders are using the body design and the same structural ideas evidenced in the Larson originals. They were built in Styles 4 (the plainest), 5, 6, 7 and 8. The ornamentation went from the no binding, dot inlay Style 4 to the full treatment, abalone trimmed, tree-of-life fingerboard of the Style 8. All had mahogany back and sides with ebony fingerboard and bridge. There are also a very few Style 3 models found of late that are smaller than the standard and have a lower bout body point. Other Dyer instruments were built by Knutsen. Dyer also carried Stetson brand instruments made by the Larson Brothers.

1965 Domino Californian
Rivington Guitars

Dragonfly Guitars

GUITARS

Eastwood Sidejack Pro DLX

Ehlers 15" SJC

Nort Graham

MODEL YEAR	FEATURES	EXC. COND. LOW	HIGH
Harp Guitar Style 3			
1902-1920s Small, short scale		$4,000	$5,500
Harp Guitar Style 4			
1902-1920s No binding		$4,000	$5,500
Harp Guitar Style 5			
1902-1920s Bound top		$5,000	$6,500
Harp Guitar Style 6			
1902-1920s Bound top/bottom		$5,500	$7,500
Harp Guitar Style 7			
1902-1920s Fancy inlays		$6,500	$8,500
Harp Guitar Style 8			
1902-1920s Tree-of-life		$9,000	$12,000

Dynacord

1950-present. Dynacord is a German company that makes audio and pro sound amps, as well as other electronic equipment. In 1966-'67 they offered solidbody guitars and basses from the Welson Company of Italy. They also had the Cora guitar and bass which is the center part of a guitar body with a tube frame in a guitar outline. They also offered tape echo machines.

Dynelectron

1960s-late 1970s. This Italian builder offered a variety of guitars and basses but is best known today for their almost exact copies of Danelectro Longhorns of the mid-'60s.

E L Welker

Luthier Eugene L. Welker began building in 1984, premium and presentation grade, production/custom, leather-wrapped archtop guitars in Claremont, New Hampshire.

E.L. Bashore Guitars

2011-present. Professional grade, custom, steel string and classical acoustic and solidbody electric guitars, basses and banjos built by luthier Eric L. Bashore in Danville, Pennsylvania.

Earthwood

1972-1985. Acoustic designs by Ernie Ball with input from George Fullerton and made in Newport Beach, California. One of the first to offer acoustic basses.

Eastman

1992-present. Intermediate and professional grade, production, archtop and flat-top guitars and basses, mainly built in China, with some from Germany and Romania. Beijing, China-based Eastman Strings started out building violins and cellos. They added guitars in '02 and mandolins in '04.

Eastwood

1997-present. Mike Robinson's company imports budget and intermediate grade, production, solid and semi-hollowbody guitars, many styled after 1960s models. They also offer basses and mandolins.

Eaton, William

1976-present. Luthier William Eaton builds custom specialty instruments such as vihuelas, harp guitars, and lyres in Phoenix, Arizona. He is also the Director of the Robetto-Venn School of Luthiery.

Echopark Guitars

2010-present. Premium and presentation grade, production/custom, solidbody electric guitars built by luthier Gabriel Currie in Detroit, Michigan, formerly in Los Angeles, California.

Ed Claxton Guitars

1972-present. Premium grade, custom flat-tops made by luthier Ed Claxton, first in Austin, Texas, and currently in Santa Cruz, California.

Eduardo Duran Ferrer

Luthier Eduardo Duran Ferrer, since 1987, builds premium grade, classical guitars in Granada, Spain.

Edward Klein

1998-present. Premium grade, custom, guitars built by luthier Edward Klein in Mississauga, Ontario.

EER Custom

2005-present. Professional and premium grade, custom, soldibody and semi-hollowbody electric guitars built by luthier Ernest E. Roesler in Forks, Washington.

Egmond

1935-1972. Founded by Ulke Egmond, building acoustic, archtop, semi-hollow and solidbody guitars originally in Eindhoven, later in Best Holland. They also made basses. Egmond also produced instruments under the Orpheum (imported into U.S.), Rosetti (England), Miller, Wilson and Lion brands.

Electric

1960-1972. Solid or semi-hollow bodies.

1960-1972		$500	$700

Ehlers

1968-2011. Luthier Rob Ehlers built his premium grade, production/custom, flat-top acoustic guitars, originally in Oregon and from '06 to '11, in Veracruz, Mexico. Rob died in November 2011.

15 CRC

Cutaway, Western red cedar top, Indian rosewood back and sides.

1996		$2,500	$3,250

15 SRC

Cutaway, European spruce top, Indian rosewood back and sides.

1998		$2,500	$3,250

16 BTM

European spruce top, mahogany back and sides, Troubadour peghead, black lacquer finish.

1998		$2,500	$3,250

16 C
16" lower bout, cutaway, flamed maple sides and back, European spruce top.

1990		$2,500	$3,250

16 SK Concert
16" lower bout, relatively small upper bout, small waist, European spruce top, flamed koa back and sides, diamond markers, natural.

1993		$2,250	$3,000

16 SM
European spruce top, mahogany back and sides.

1999		$2,000	$2,500

16 SSC
Cutaway, European spruce top, English sycamore back and sides.

1996		$2,000	$2,500

25 C
Limited Edition Anniversary Model, European spruce top, Indian rosewood back and sides, abalone top border.

2001		$3,000	$4,000

GJ (Gypsy Jazz)

2000s	D-style	$2,000	$2,500

Eichelbaum Guitars
2006-present. Luthier David Eichelbaum builds his premium grade, custom, flat-tops in Santa Barbara, California.

EKO
1959-present. Originally acoustic, acoustic/electric, electric thinline and full-size archtop hollowbody, solidbody electric guitars and basses built by Oliviero Pigini and Company in Recanati, Italy, and imported by LoDuca Brothers, Milwaukee, Radio and Television Equipment Company in Santa Ana, California, and others. First acoustic guitars followed by sparkle plastic-covered electrics by '62. Sparkle finishes are gone ca. '66. Pigini dies ca. '67. LoDuca Bros. is phased out in early-'70s. By '75 EKO offers some copy guitars and they purchased a custom shop to make other brands by '78. In '85 they ceased production in Italy, continuing the brand for a few years with Asian imports, and continued to distribute other brands. By 2004, the Eko line of guitar was revived with budget and intermediate grade, production, classical, acoustic, acoustic/electric, solidbody, solidbody, and hollowbody guitars made in Asia. They also make basses and amps.

Barracuda VI
1966-ca.1978. Double-cut semi-hollow, 2 pickups, 6-string.

1966-1978		$700	$950

Barracuda XII
1966-ca.1978. Double-cut semi-hollow, 2 pickups, 12-string.

1966-1978		$750	$975

Cobra I/II/III/XII
1966-1978. Double-cut solidbody, 2 knobs. Cobra I has 1 pickup, II 2 pickups and III 3 pickups. 12-string Cobra XII offered '67-'69, has 2 pickups.

1966-1978	Cobra I	$450	$600
1966-1978	Cobra II	$550	$700
1966-1978	Cobra III	$600	$800
1966-1978	Cobra XII	$600	$800

Commander
1965. Single-cut archtop electric, 1 pickup, 2 controls, EKO logo on upper bass bout, maple body in 'dura-glos' finish.

1965		$475	$625

Condor
1966-ca.1969. Double-cut solidbody with 3 or 4 pickups.

1966-1969		$600	$775

Dragon
1967-ca.1969. Single-cut archtop, 2 f-holes, 3 pickups, tremolo.

1967-1969		$1,125	$1,500

Flat-Top Acoustic
1960s. Various student-level flat-top acoustic models.

1960s		$325	$425

Florentine
1964-ca.1969. Double-cut archtop, 2 pickups.

1964-1969		$675	$875

Kadett/Kadett XII
1967-ca.1978. Double-cut solidbody with point on lower bass side of body, 3 pickups, tremolo. 12-string Kadett XII offered '68-'69.

1967-1978	Kadett	$625	$825
1968-1969	Kadett XII	$625	$825

Lancer Stereo
1967-1969. Lancer VI with stereo output (route output to 2 amplifiers requires EKO stereo cable for stereo application).

1967-1969		$525	$675

Lancer VI
1967-ca.1969. Double-cut solidbody, 2 pickups.

1967-1969		$425	$550

Lancer XII
1967-1969. Double-cut solidbody electric, 12-string.

1967-1969		$500	$650

Lark I/II
1970. Thin hollow cutaway, sunburst. Lark I has 1 pickup and Lark II 2.

1970	Lark I	$575	$750
1970	Lark II	$575	$750

Model 180
1960s. Cutaway acoustic archtop.

1960s		$400	$525

Model 285 Modello
1960s. Thinline single-cut, 1 pickup.

1962		$525	$675

Model 290/2V
1963-1965. Maple body and neck, ebony 'board, dot markers, 2 pickups, tremolo, renamed Barracuda in '66.

1963-1965		$625	$825

Model 300/375
1962. Copy of Hofner Club-style electric, single-cut, 2 pickups, set-neck.

1962		$900	$1,250

1966 EKO Model P12
Rivington Guitars

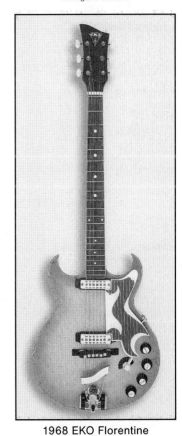

1968 EKO Florentine
Imaged by Heritage Auctions, HA.com

To get the most from this book, be sure to read "Using *The Guide*" in the introduction.

EKO Ranger 12
Seth Andrews

1977 Electra MPC
Rivington Guitars

MODEL YEAR	FEATURES	EXC. COND. LOW	HIGH

Model 400 Ekomaster
1960-1962. Jazzmaster-style, 1, 2 or 4 (2+2) pickups, sparkle finish.

| 1960-1962 | 4 pickups | $825 | $1,125 |

Model 500/1 and 500/1V
1961-1965. Plastic covered solidbody, 1 pickup. 500/1 no vibrato, 1V with vibrato.

| 1961-1965 | 500/1 | $700 | $925 |
| 1961-1965 | 500/1V | $775 | $1,000 |

Model 500/2 and 500/3V
1961-1964. Plastic covered solidbody, plastic sparkle finish. 500/2 no vibrato, 2 pickups. 3V with vibrato, 3 pickups.

| 1961-1965 | 500/2 | $775 | $1,000 |
| 1961-1965 | 500/3V | $825 | $1,125 |

Model 500/4 and 500/4V
1961-1964. Plastic covered solidbody, 4 pickups. 500/4 no vibrato, 4V with vibrato.

| 1961-1965 | 500/4 | $975 | $1,250 |
| 1961-1965 | 500/4V | $1,250 | $1,750 |

Model 540 (Classical)
1960s. Nylon-string classical guitar.

| 1960s | | $325 | $425 |

Model 700/3V
1961-1964. Map-shape/tulip-shape body, 3 pickups, vibrato, woodgrain plastic finish.

| 1961-1964 | | $1,375 | $1,750 |

Model 700/4V
1961-1967. Map-shape/tulip-shape body, 4 pickups, multiple switches, vibrato.

| 1961-1967 | Red, blue, silver sparkle | $1,625 | $2,125 |
| 1961-1967 | Standard finish | $1,375 | $1,750 |

Ranger 6/12
1967-ca.1982. D-size flat-top acoustic, large 3-point 'guard, dot inlays, EKO Ranger label. Ranger 12 is 12-string.

| 1967-1982 | Ranger 12 | $475 | $625 |
| 1967-1982 | Ranger 6 | $475 | $625 |

Ranger 6/12 Electra
1967. Ranger 6/12 with on-board pickup and 2 controls, 6-string with dot markers, 12-string with block markers.

| 1967 | 12 Electra | $525 | $700 |
| 1967 | 6 Electra | $525 | $700 |

Rocket VI/XII (Rokes)
1967-ca.1969. Rocket-shape design, solidbody, 6-string, says Rokes on the headstock, Rokes were a popular English band that endorsed EKO guitars, marketed as the Rocket VI in the U.S.; and as the Rokes in Europe, often called the Rok. Rocket XII is 12-string.

| 1967-1969 | Rocket VI | $1,375 | $1,750 |
| 1967-1969 | Rocket XII | $1,375 | $1,750 |

El Degas
Early 1970s-early '80s. Japanese-made copies of classic America electrics and acoustics, imported by Buegeleisen & Jacobson of New York, New York.

Solidbody
Copies of classic American models, including the Let's Play model.

| 1970s | | $375 | $550 |

El Maya
1970s-1980s. Also labeled Maya. Solidbody, archtop and semi-hollow guitars built by Japan's Chushin Gakki Co., which also built models for several other manufacturers.

Eleca
2004-present. Student/budget level, production, acoustic and electric guitars, imported by Eleca International. They also offer amps, effects and mandolins.

Electar
See Epiphone listing.

Electra
1970-1984, 2013-present. Imported from Japan by St. Louis Music. Most instruments made by Matsumoku in Japan. The Electra line replaced SLM's Japanese-made Apollo and U.S.-made Custom Kraft lines. The first guitar, simply called The Electra, was a copy of the Ampeg Dan Armstrong lucite guitar and issued in '70, followed quickly by a variety of bolt-neck copies of other brands. In '75 the Tree-of-Life guitars debut and the line is expanded. Open-book headstocks changed to wave or fan shape by '78. Some Korean production began in early-'80s. In the fall of '83, the Electra Brand became Electra Phoenix. By the beginning of '84, the brand became Electra-Westone and by the end of '84 just Westone. In 2013, the brand was revived with guitars built by luthiers Ben Chafin and Mick Donner in Tampa, Florida. Matsumoku-made guitars have serial numbers in which first 1 or 2 digits represent the year of manufacture. Thus, a guitar with a serial number beginning in 0 or 80 would be from 1980.

Concert Professional
Late 1970s. Howard Roberts style, single-cut electric flat-top with oval sound hole, single humbucking pickup, fancy markers.

| 1977 | | $900 | $1,250 |

Custom
1970s. Double-cut solidbody, 2 pickups, Custom logo on truss rod, cherry finish.

| 1970s | | $700 | $950 |

Elvin Bishop
1976-ca.1980. Double-cut semi-hollow body, tree-of-life inlay.

| 1976-1980 | | $800 | $1,125 |

Flying Wedge
1970s. V body, six-on-a-side tuners.

| 1970s | | $800 | $1,125 |

MPC Outlaw
1977-1980. Symmetric horn body, neck-thru, has separate modules (Modular Powered Circuits) that plug in for different effects. Includes X710 (peace sign burned into natural mahogany top), X720 (gray sunburst), X730 (tobacco sunburst) and X 740 (maple top).

| 1977-1980 | | $900 | $1,250 |
| 1977-1980 | MPC plug-in module | $150 | $200 |

MODEL YEAR FEATURES	EXC. COND. LOW	HIGH

MPC X310
1976-1980. MPC model, LP solidbody, 2 humbuckers (bridge w/ exposed zebra bobbins), 4 in-line control knobs plus 2 toggles, gold hardware, black finish.

1976-1980	$900	$1,250

MPC X320
1976-1980. Same as X310, but with transparent cherry red finish over mahogany top.

1976-1980	$900	$1,250

MPC X330
1976-1980. Same as X310, but with cherry sunburst finish on maple top.

1976-1980	$900	$1,250

MPC X340
1976-1980. Same as X310, but with Jacaranda rosewood top.

1976-1980	$900	$1,250

MPC X350
1977-1980. Same as X310, but with tobacco sunburst on a maple top.

1977-1980	$900	$1,250

Phoenix
1980-1984. Classic offset double-cut solidbody, Phoenix logo on headstock.

1980-1984	$400	$550

Rock
1971-1973. Single cut solidbody, becomes the Super Rock in '73.

1971-1973	$550	$725

Super Rock
1973-ca.1978. Renamed from Rock ('71-'73).

1973-1978	$600	$800

X135
1982. Offset double-cut solidbody, 2 humbucker pickups.

1982	$400	$550

X145 60th Anniversary
1982. Classic offset double-cut only made one year, Anniversary plate on back of headstock, single/single/hum pickups.

1982	$400	$550

X150
1975. Offset double-cut, 2 humbucker pickups.

1975	$550	$750

X220 Omega
1976-ca. 1980. Single-cut solidbody, block inlays, Omega logo on truss rod, black with rosewood neck, or natural with figured top and maple neck.

1976-1980	$550	$750

X280/X290 Working Man
1980-1984. Modified double-cut solidbody, 2 exposed-coil humbuckers, dot inlays, natural satin finish (X280) or jet black (X290).

1980-1984	$300	$400

X410
1975. Double-cut thinline acoustic archtop, 2 humbucker pickups, large split triangle markers, open-book style headstock shape.

1975	$900	$1,250

X420
1978. Double-cut thinline acoustic archtop, 2 humbucker pickups, dot markers, wave-shape style headstock.

1978	$600	$800

X935 Endorser
1983-1984. Double-cut solidbody, 2 humbucker pickups, tune-o-matic, dot markers.

1983-1984	$500	$650

X960 Ultima
1981. Hybrid single-cut with additional soft bass bout cutaway, slab solidbody, dot markers, 2 humbucker pickups, wave-shape style headstock.

1981	$550	$750

Electric Gypsy
See listing under Teye.

Electro
1964-1975. The Electro line was manufactured by Electro String Instruments and distributed by Radio-Tel. The Electro logo appeared on the headstock rather than Rickenbacker. Refer to the Rickenbacker section for models.

Electromuse
1940s-1950s. Mainly known for lap steels, Electromuse also offered acoustic and electric hollowbody guitars. They also had tube amps usually sold as a package with a lap steel.

Elferink
1993-present. Production/custom, premium grade, archtop guitars built in the Netherlands by luthier Frans Elferink.

Elijah Jewel
2009-present. Luthier Michael Kerry builds his professional grade, production/custom, acoustic guitars in Mineola, Texas. He also builds mandolins.

Elite
1960s. Guitars made in Italy by the Crucianelli accordion company, which made several other brands.

Elk
Late-1960s. Japanese-made by Elk Gakki Co., Ltd. Many were copies of American designs. They also offered amps and effects.

Elliott Guitars
1966-present. Premium and presentation grade, custom, nylon-string classical and steel-string guitars built by luthier Jeffrey Elliott in Portland, Oregon.

Ellis
2000-present. Luthier Andrew Ellis builds his production/custom, premium grade, steel string acoustic and resophonic guitars in Perth, Western Australia. In 2008 he also added lap steels.

Elijah Jewel

Elliott Raven

GUITARS

Epiphone AJ-500M Masterbilt
Rivington Guitars

Epiphone B.B. King Lucille

MODEL YEAR	FEATURES	EXC. COND. LOW	HIGH

Elli-Sound

1960s. Guitars made in Italy by the Crucianelli accordion company, which made several other brands.

Ellsberry Archtop Guitars

2003-2016. Premium and presentation grade, custom/production, acoustic and electric archtops built by luthier James Ellsberry first in Torrance and Harbor City, California, then in Huntington Beach.

Emperador

1966-1992. Guitars and basses imported from Japan by Westheimer Musical Instruments. Early models appear to be made by either Teisco or Kawai; later models were made by Cort.

Acoustic

1960s	Archtop or flat-top	$200	$300

Electric Solidbody

1960s		$250	$350

Empire

1997-present. Professional and premium grade, production/custom, solidbody guitars from Lee Garver's GMW Guitarworks of Glendora, California.

Encore

Mid-1960s-present. Budget grade, production, classical, acoustic, and electric guitars imported from China and Vietnam by John Hornby Skewes & Co. in the U.K. They also offer basses.

Engel Guitars

1990-present. Luthier Robert Engel builds his premium grade, production/custom, hollowbody and solidbody guitars in Stamford, Connecticut.

English Electronics

1960s. Lansing, Michigan, company named after owner, some private branded guitars and amps by Valco (Chicago), many models with large English Electronics vertical logo on headstock.

Tonemaster

1960s. National Val-Pro 84 with neck pickup and bridge mounted pickup, black.

1960s		$900	$1,250

Epcor

1967. Hollowbody electirc guitars and basses built by Joe Hall's Hallmark Guitars in Bakersfield, CA for manufacturer's rep Ed Preager (the EP in the name). Only about 35 were built.

Epi

1970s. Typical Japanese copy-import, Epi logo on headstock with capital letter split-E logo, inside label says "Norlin," probably for Japanese domestic market.

Acoustic Flat-Top

1970s. D-style, mahogany body.

1970s		$200	$300

Epiphone

Ca. 1873-present. Budget, intermediate, professional, and premium grade, production, solidbody, archtop, acoustic, acoustic/electric, resonator, and classical guitars made in the U.S. and overseas. They also offer basses, amps, mandolins, ukes and banjos. Founded in Smyrna, Turkey, by Anastasios Stathopoulos and early instruments had his label. He emigrated to the U.S. in 1903 and changed the name to Stathoupoulo. Anastasios died in '15 and his son, Epaminondas ("Epi") took over. The name changed to House of Stathopoulo in '17 and the company incorporated in '23. In '24 the line of Epiphone Recording banjos debuted and in '28 the company name was changed to the Epiphone Banjo Company. In '43 Epi Stathopoulo died and sons Orphie and Frixo took over. Labor trouble shut down the NYC factory in '51 and the company cut a deal with Conn/Continental and relocated to Philadelphia in '52. Frixo died in '57 and Gibson bought the company. Kalamazoo-made Gibson Epiphones debut in '58. In '69 American production ceased, and Japanese imports began. Some Taiwanese guitars were imported from '79-'81. Limited U.S. production resumed in '82 but sourcing shifted to Korea in '83. In '85 Norlin sold Gibson to Henry Juszkiewicz, Dave Barryman and Gary Zebrowski. In '92 Jim Rosenberg became president of the new Epiphone division.

AJ Masterbilt Series

2004-present. Sloped shoulder D size, solid spruce tops, solid rosewood or mahogany (M) back and sides.

2004-2023	Import	$650	$800

Alleykat

2000-2010. Single cut small body archtop, 1 humbucker and 1 mini-humbucker.

2000-2010		$300	$400

B.B. King Lucille

1997-2019. Laminated double-cut maple body, 2 humbuckers, Lucille on headstock.

1997-2019		$550	$700

Barcelona CE

1999-2000. Classical, solid spruce top, rosewood back and sides, EQ/preamp.

1999-2000		$325	$450

Barcelone (Classical)

1963-1968. Highest model of Epiphone '60s classical guitars, maple back and sides, gold hardware.

1963-1964		$800	$1,000
1965-1968		$700	$900

Bard 12-String

1962-1969. Flat-top, mahogany back and sides, natural or sunburst.

1962-1964		$1,625	$2,000
1965		$1,500	$1,875
1966-1969		$1,375	$1,750

Beverly

1931-1936. Flat-top, arched back, tenor or Hawaiian versions.

1931-1936	Hawaiian	$900	$1,250
1931-1936	Tenor	$575	$750

MODEL YEAR	FEATURES	EXC. COND. LOW	HIGH

Biscuit
1997-2000, 2002-2010. Wood body resonator, biscuit bridge, round neck.

1997-2010		$300	$400

Blackstone
1931-1950. Acoustic archtop, f-holes, sunburst.

1933-1934	Masterbilt	$1,500	$1,875
1935-1937		$1,250	$1,500
1938-1939		$1,125	$1,375
1940-1941		$1,000	$1,250
1948-1950		$850	$1,125

Blueshawk Deluxe
2015-2018. Single-cut semi-hollowbody, AAA flamed maple top, mahogany back and sides, 2 P-90s, Midnight Sapphire, Wine red or trans black.

2015-2018		$500	$650

Broadway (Acoustic)
1931-1958. Non-cut acoustic archtop.

1931-1938	Sunburst, walnut body	$4,000	$5,000
1939-1942	Sunburst, maple body	$4,000	$5,000
1946-1958	Natural	$3,500	$4,500
1946-1958	Sunburst	$3,000	$3,750

Broadway Regent (Acoustic Cutaway)
1950-1958. Single-cut acoustic archtop, sunburst.

1950-1958		$3,000	$3,750

Broadway (Electric)
1958-1969. Gibson-made electric archtop, single-cut, 2 New York pickups (mini-humbucking pickups by '61), Frequensator tailpiece, block inlays, sunburst or natural finish with cherry optional in '67 only.

1958-1959	Natural	$3,500	$4,500
1958-1959	Sunburst	$3,250	$4,000
1960-1964	Natural	$3,500	$4,500
1960-1964	Sunburst	$3,000	$3,750
1965	Natural	$3,000	$4,000
1965	Sunburst	$2,750	$3,500
1966-1967	Natural, cherry	$2,750	$3,500
1966-1967	Sunburst	$2,750	$3,500
1968-1969	Natural, cherry	$2,750	$3,500
1968-1969	Sunburst	$2,750	$3,500

Broadway Reissue
1997-2019. Full depth acoustic-electric single cut archtop, 2 humbuckers.

1997-2019		$500	$650

Broadway Tenor
1937-1953. Acoustic archtop, sunburst.

1937-1953		$1,375	$1,750

Byron
1949-ca.1955. Acoustic archtop, mahogany back and sides, sunburst.

1949-1955		$650	$825

C Series Classical (Import)
1995-2006. Nylon-string classical guitars, including C-25 (mahogany back & sides), C-40 (cedar top, mahogany), C-70-CE (rosewood).

1998-2005	C-40	$165	$225

Caiola Custom
1963-1970. Introduced as Caiola, renamed Caiola Custom in '66, electric thinbody archtop, 2 mini-humbuckers, multi-bound top and back, block inlays, walnut or sunburst finish (walnut only by '68).

1963-1964		$3,000	$3,750
1965		$2,875	$3,500
1966-1970		$2,500	$3,250

Caiola Standard
1966-1970. Electric thinbody archtop, 2 P-90s, single-bound top and back, dot inlays, sunburst or cherry.

1966-1967		$2,250	$2,875
1968-1970		$2,125	$2,625

Casino (1 Pickup)
1961-1969. Thinline hollowbody, double-cut, 1 P-90 pickup, various colors.

1961-1964		$7,250	$9,000
1965		$6,000	$7,500
1966-1969		$5,500	$6,875

Casino (2 Pickups)
1961-1970. Two pickup (P-90) version, various colors. '61-'63 known as Keith Richards model, '64-'65 known as Beatles model.

1961-1962		$10,500	$13,500
1963-1964		$9,000	$11,500
1965		$8,500	$10,500
1966-1970		$7,250	$9,000

Casino (Japan)
1982-1983. Epiphone built a few of its classic models, including the Casino, in Japan from mid-'82 to mid-'83.

1982-1983		$1,125	$1,500

Casino J.L. U.S.A. 1965
2003-2006. 1,965 made.

2003-2006		$2,500	$3,250

Casino Reissue
1995-2019. Import, sunburst.

1995-2019		$750	$975

Casino Revolution
1999-2005. Limited production 1965 reissue model, with certificate of authenticity, sanded natural.

1999-2005		$2,500	$3,250

50th Anniversary 1961 Casino
2011. Trapeze (TD) or TremTone vibrato (TDV), limited run of 1,961 built.

2011	TDV	$800	$1,125
2011	Trapeze	$800	$1,125

Century
1939-1970. Thinline archtop, non-cut, 1 pickup, trapeze tailpiece, walnut finish, sunburst finish available in '58, Royal Burgundy available '61 and only sunburst finish available by '68.

1939-1948	Oblong shape pu	$2,375	$3,000
1949-1958	NY pickup	$2,000	$2,500
1958-1962	P-90, plate logo	$2,375	$3,000
1963-1964	P-90, no plate logo	$2,375	$3,000
1965-1970	Sunburst, cherry	$2,000	$2,500

Classic (Classical)
1963-1970.

1963-1964		$525	$650
1965-1970		$475	$600

Collegiate
2004-2005. Les Paul-style body, 1 humbucker, various college graphic decals on body.

2004-2005		$200	$250

2014 Epiphone Casino Reissue
Paul Swanson

1953 Epiphone Century
Rivington Guitars

1964 Epiphone Coronet
Trey Rabinek

1998 Epiphone Del Ray
Rivington Guitars

MODEL YEAR	FEATURES	EXC. COND. LOW	HIGH

Coronet (Electric Archtop)
1939-1949. Electric archtop, laminated mahogany body, 1 pickup, trapeze tailpiece, sunburst, name continued as an electric solidbody in '58.

1939-1949		$1,375	$1,750

Coronet (Solidbody)
1958-1969. Solidbody electric, 1 New York pickup ('58-'59), 1 P-90 ('59-'69), cherry or black finish, Silver Fox finish available by '63, reintroduced as Coronet USA '90-'94, Korean-made '95-'98.

1958-1959	Cherry, NY pu	$6,000	$7,500
1959	Black (rare), NY pu	$9,500	$12,000
1960-1964	Various colors	$5,000	$6,500
1965	Standard color	$3,500	$4,500
1965-1966	Custom color	$6,750	$8,500
1966-1969	Standard color	$3,500	$4,500

Coronet U.S.A.
1990-1994. Made in Nashville, reverse banana headstock, typical Coronet styled body, single-coil and humbucker.

1990-1994		$900	$1,125

Coronet (Import)
1995-1998. Import version.

1995-1998		$400	$550

Crestwood Custom
1958-1970. Solidbody, 2 New York pickups ('58-'60), 2 mini-humbuckers ('61-'70), symmetrical body and 3+3 tuners ('58-'62), asymmetrical and 1x6 tuners ('63-'70), slab body with no Gibson equivalent model.

1958-1960	Cherry, NY pus	$5,500	$7,000
1959-1960	Sunburst, NY pus	$5,500	$7,000
1961-1962	Cherry, mini-hums	$5,000	$6,500
1961-1962	White, mini-hums	$5,500	$6,875
1963-1964	Cherry, mini-hums	$4,000	$5,000
1963-1964	Custom color	$6,500	$8,125
1965	Cherry	$3,375	$4,250
1965	Custom color	$6,500	$8,125
1966-1967	Cherry	$3,375	$4,250
1966-1967	Custom color	$4,250	$5,250
1968-1970	Cherry, white	$2,750	$3,500

Crestwood Deluxe
1963-1969. Solidbody with 3 mini-humbuckers, block inlay, cherry, white or Pacific Blue finish, 1x6 tuners.

1963-1964	Cherry, mini-hums	$4,000	$5,000
1963-1964	Custom color	$7,250	$9,000
1965	Cherry	$4,000	$5,000
1965	Custom color	$6,500	$8,125
1966-1967	Cherry	$3,375	$4,250
1966-1967	Custom color	$4,750	$6,000
1968-1969	Cherry, white	$3,375	$4,250

De Luxe
1931-1957. Non-cut acoustic archtop, maple back and sides, trapeze tailpiece ('31-'37), frequensator tailpiece ('37-'57), gold-plated hardware, sunburst or natural finish.

1931-1935	Sunburst, 1738"	$10,000	$12,500
1935-1944	Sunburst, 1638"	$8,000	$10,000
1939-1944	Natural	$8,000	$10,000
1945-1949	Natural	$7,000	$9,000
1945-1949	Sunburst	$6,500	$8,500

MODEL YEAR	FEATURES	EXC. COND. LOW	HIGH
1950-1957	Natural	$6,500	$8,500
1950-1957	Sunburst	$6,000	$7,500

De Luxe Regent (Acoustic Archtop)
1948-1952. Acoustic cutaway archtop, high-end appointments, rounded cutaway, natural finish, renamed De Luxe Cutaway in '53.

1948-1952	Natural	$10,500	$13,500
1948-1952	Sunburst	$8,500	$10,500

De Luxe Cutaway/Deluxe Cutaway
1953-1970. Renamed from De Luxe Regent, cataloged Deluxe Cutaway by Gibson in '58, special order by '64 with limited production because acoustic archtops were pretty much replaced by electric archtops. There is also a FT Deluxe Cutaway flat-top (see FT listings).

1953-1957	Natural	$10,000	$12,500
1953-1957	Sunburst	$8,500	$10,500
1958-1959		$9,500	$11,500
1960-1964	Gibson Kalamazoo	$7,500	$9,500
1965-1970	Special order only	$6,500	$8,500

De Luxe Electric (Archtop)
1954-1957. Single-cut electric archtop, 2 pickups, called the Zephyr De Luxe Regent from '48-'54. Produced with a variety of specs, maple or spruce tops, different inlays and pickup combinations.

1954-1957	Natural	$6,000	$7,500
1954-1957	Sunburst	$5,750	$7,250

Del Ray
1995-2000. Offset double-cut body, 2 blade humbuckers, tune-o-matic, flamed maple top.

1995-2000		$400	$550

Devon
1949-1957. Acoustic archtop, non-cut, mahogany back and sides, sunburst finish, optional natural finish by '54.

1950-1957	Sunburst	$1,875	$2,375
1954-1957	Natural	$1,875	$2,375

Don Everly (SQ-180)
1997-2004. Jumbo acoustic reissue, large double 'guard, black gloss finish.

1997-2004		$600	$775

Dot (ES-335 Dot)/Dot Archtop
2000-2020. Dot-neck ES-335.

2000-2020		$450	$600

Dot Studio
2004-2019. Simplified Dot, 2 control knobs, black hardware.

2004-2019		$350	$475

Dove Limited Edition
2008. Dove Limited Edition logo on label, Dove script logo on truss rod cover, classic dove logo art on 'guard and dove inlay on bridge, cherry or ebony.

2008		$300	$400

DR Series/Songmaker Series
2004-present. Dreadnought, spruce top, mahogany back and sides, various models including DR-100 (various colors), DR-200C (single-cut, natural or vintage sunburst), DR-212 (12-string, natural) and DR-500RNS (rosewood, natural satin).

2012-2023	Songmaker DR-212	$200	$275

MODEL YEAR	FEATURES	EXC. COND. LOW	HIGH

Dwight

1963, 1967. Coronet labeled as Dwight and made for Sonny Shields Music of St. Louis, 75 made in '63 and 36 in '67, cherry. National-Supro made Dwight brand lap steels in the '50s.

1963		$5,500	$7,000
1967		$4,000	$5,000

EA/ET/ES Series (Japan)

1970-1979. Production of the Epiphone brand was moved to Japan in '70. Models included the EA (electric thinline) and ET (electric solidbody).

1970-1975	EA-250 Riviera	$600	$750
1970-1975	ET-270	$650	$825
1970-1975	ET-275	$650	$825
1972	ES-255 Casino	$675	$850
1975-1979	ET-290 Crestwood	$650	$825

EJ-160E John Lennon

1997-2013. Based on John's Gibson acoustic/electric, sunburst, signature on body.

1997-2013		$400	$550

EJ-200 Series

1994-2020. Solid spruce top, laminate maple body.

1994-2020	Various models	$375	$500

EJ-300

2004-2006. Solid spruce top, laminate rosewood body.

2004-2006		$500	$650

El Diablo

1994-1995. Offset double-cut acoustic/electric, onboard piezo and 3-band EQ, composite back and sides, spruce top, cherry sunburst.

1994-1995		$450	$600

Electar Model M

1935-1939. Epiphone's initial entry into the new electric guitar market of the mid-'30s, 14 3/4" laminate maple archtop, horseshoe pickup, trap door on back for electronics, Electar logo on headstock, oblong pickup replaces horseshoe in late-'37.

1935-1936	2 control knobs	$1,375	$1,750
1937-1939	3 control knobs	$1,375	$1,750

Electar Model M Tenor

1937-1939. Electric tenor 4-string with Electar specs.

1937-1939	3 knobs, natural	$1,250	$1,625

Elitist Series

2003-2019. Made in Japan, higher-grade series, using finer woods and inlays and U.S.-made Gibson pickups.

2003-2004	J-200	$1,500	$2,000
2003-2004	L-00/VS	$1,250	$1,625
2003-2005	'61 SG Standard	$1,125	$1,500
2003-2005	'65 Texan	$1,500	$2,000
2003-2005	Riviera	$1,750	$2,250
2003-2008	'63 ES-335 Dot	$1,750	$2,250
2003-2008	Byrdland/L5	$2,250	$3,000
2003-2009	Broadway	$1,500	$2,000
2003-2009	LP Custom	$1,125	$1,500
2003-2009	LP Standard	$1,125	$1,500
2003-2009	LP Standard '57 Goldtop	$1,125	$1,500
2003-2009	LP Studio	$950	$1,250
2003-2009	Sheraton	$1,750	$2,250
2003-2019	Casino	$1,500	$2,000

MODEL YEAR	FEATURES	EXC. COND. LOW	HIGH
2004-2005	Jim Croce L-00	$1,125	$1,500
2005	Chet Atkins Country Gent	$1,500	$2,000
2007-2009	LP Plus	$1,125	$1,500
2012	D Yoakam Trash Casino	$1,500	$2,000

Emperor (Acoustic Archtop)

1935-1954. Acoustic archtop, non-cut, maple back and sides, multi-bound body, gold-plated hardware, sunburst, optional natural finish by '39.

1935-1939	Natural	$15,000	$20,000
1935-1939	Sunburst	$10,000	$12,500
1940-1949	Natural, Sunburst	$11,500	$14,500
1950-1954	Natural	$10,000	$12,500
1950-1954	Sunburst	$9,500	$11,500

Emperor Regent

1948-1953. Acoustic archtop with rounded cutaway, renamed Emperor Cutaway in '53.

1948-1953	Natural	$10,500	$13,500
1948-1953	Sunburst	$9,500	$12,000

Emperor Cutaway

1953-1957. Renamed from Emperor Regent, acoustic archtop, single-cut, maple back and sides, multi-bound body, gold-plated hardware, sunburst or natural.

1953-1957	Natural	$11,500	$14,500
1953-1957	Sunburst	$10,000	$12,500

Emperor Electric

1953-1957. Archtop, single-cut, 3 pickups, multibound body, sunburst, called the Zephyr Emperor Regent in '50-'53.

1953-1957		$5,500	$7,000

Emperor (Thinline Electric)

1958-1969. Single-cut, thinline archtop, 3 New York pickups in '58-'60, 3 mini-humbuckers '61 on, multibound, gold-plated hardware, sunburst or natural finish until '65 when only sunburst was made.

1958-1959	Natural, 3 NY pus	$13,500	$17,000
1958-1959	Sunburst, 3 NY pus	$10,500	$13,500
1960-1962	Natural	$12,500	$15,000
1960-1962	Sunburst	$10,000	$12,500
1963-1969	Special order	$8,500	$10,500

Emperor/Emperor II

1982-1994. Single-cut archtop jazz guitar, 2 humbuckers, blocks, gold hardware. II was added to name in '93, became Joe Pass Emperor II (see that listing) in '95, although his name was on the guitar as early as '91.

1982-1989	Matsumoku, Japan	$1,000	$1,375
1990-1994		$1,000	$1,375

Entrada (Classical)

1963-1968. Small classical, 13.25" bout, natural.

1963-1964		$550	$675
1965-1968		$500	$625

ES-175 Premium

2010-2019. Limited Edition, vintage "aged" lacquer finish, various colors.

2010-2019		$775	$1,000

ES-295

1997-2001, 2003-2016. Epiphone's version of classic Gibson goldtop.

1997-2016		$775	$1,000

Epiphone Songmaker DR-212

1967 Epiphone Emperor
RichardSarmento

GUITARS

1997 Epiphone Flying V

Johnny Zapp

1958 Epiphone FT45 Cortez

Jim Dikel

MODEL YEAR	FEATURES	EXC. COND. LOW	HIGH
ES-339 PRO/ES-339			
2012-present. Maple laminate body, 2 pickups. PRO dropped from name in 2020.			
2012-2023		$400	$550
Espana (Classical)			
1962-1968. Classical, U.S.-made, maple back and sides, natural, imported in '69 from Japan.			
1962-1964		$750	$975
1965-1968		$675	$900
Exellente			
1963-1969, 1994-1995. Flat-top, Brazilian rosewood back and sides (Indian rosewood '68-'69), cloud inlays. Name revived on Gibson Montana insturment in '90s.			
1963-1964	Brazilian	$10,000	$12,500
1965	Brazilian	$9,500	$12,000
1966-1967	Brazilian	$8,500	$10,500
1968-1969	Indian	$5,250	$6,500
1958 Korina Explorer			
1998-2011. Explorer with typical appointments, korina body. This guitar was produced with a variety of specs, ranging from maple tops to spruce tops, different inlay markers were also used, different pickup combinations have been seen, natural or sunburst finish.			
1998-2011		$550	$725
1958 Gothic Explorer/Flying V			
2002-2012. Flat black finish, V ends in 2010.			
2002-2012		$550	$725
Firebird			
1995-2000. Two mini-humbuckers, Firebird Red, dot markers.			
1995-2000		$550	$725
Firebird 300			
1986-1988. Korean import, Firebird Red.			
1986-1988		$550	$725
Firebird 500			
1986-1988. Korean import, Firebird Red.			
1986-1988		$550	$725
1963 Firebird VII/Firebird VII			
2000-2010. Reverse body, 3 mini-humbuckers, gold hardware, Maestro-style vibrato, block markers, Firebird Red. 1963 dropped from name in '03.			
2000-2010		$650	$850
Firebird I Joe Bonamassa			
2016. Artist Limited Edition, modeled after his Gibson '63 Firebird I (nicknamed "Treasure"), Tobacco Sunburst or Polymist Gold.			
2016		$1,375	$1,750
Firebird Studio			
2006-2011. Two humbuckers, with worn cherry finish.			
2006-2011		$550	$750
Flamekat			
1999-2005. Archtop, double dice position markers, 2 mini-humbuckers, Epiphone Bigsby, flame finish.			
1999-2005		$450	$600
Flying V/'67 Flying V			
1989-1998, 2003-2005. '67 or '58 specs, alder body, natural.			
1989-1998	'67 specs	$550	$725
2003-2005	'58 specs	$550	$725

MODEL YEAR	FEATURES	EXC. COND. LOW	HIGH
1958 Korina Flying V			
1998-2011, 2016. Typical Flying V configuration, korina body, veneer top. Limited Edition offered in '16 with solid korina, 2 humbucker pickups and gold hardware.			
1998-2011	Factory, veneer	$550	$725
2016	Limited Edition	$575	$750
1958 Korina Flying V Joe Bonamassa			
2017-2018. Limited Edition, modeled from his first '58 Korina Flying V (nicknamed "Amos"), '50s-style Flying V case, hand-signed COA.			
2017-2018		$950	$1,250
Flying V Prophecy			
2020-present. AAA figured maple top, Yellow Tiger or Black with aged gloss finish.			
2020-2023		$650	$850
FT 30			
1941-1949. Acoustic flat-top, brown stain, mahogany back and sides, reintroduced as Gibson-made FT 30 Caballero in '58.			
1941-1943		$1,625	$2,000
1944-1949		$1,375	$1,750
FT 30 Caballero			
1959-1970. Reintroduced from Epiphone-made FT 30, Gibson-made acoustic flat-top, natural, all mahogany body, dot inlay, tenor available '63-'68.			
1959-1961		$1,500	$1,875
1962-1964		$1,125	$1,500
1965		$950	$1,250
1966-1970		$825	$1,125
FT 45			
1941-1948. Acoustic flat-top, walnut back and sides, cherry neck, rosewood 'board, natural top, reintroduced as Gibson-made FT 45 Cortez in '58.			
1941-1943		$2,375	$3,000
1944-1948		$1,750	$2,250
FT 45 Cortez			
1958-1969. Reintroduced from Epiphone-made FT 45, Gibson-made acoustic flat-top, 16.5", mahogany back and sides, sunburst or natural top (sunburst only in '59-'62).			
1958-1959	Sunburst	$2,000	$2,500
1960-1964	Sunburst, natural	$2,000	$2,500
1965-1966	Sunburst, natural	$1,625	$2,000
1967-1969	Sunburst, natural	$1,250	$1,500
FT 79			
1941-1958. Acoustic 16" flat-top, square shoulder dreadnought, walnut back and sides until '49 and laminated maple back and sides '49 on, natural, renamed FT 79 Texan by Gibson in '58.			
1941-1943	Walnut	$3,250	$4,000
1944-1949	Walnut	$3,125	$4,000
1949-1958	Maple	$2,375	$3,000
FT 79 Texan			
1958-1970, 1993-1995. Renamed from Epiphone FT 79, Gibson-made acoustic flat-top, mahogany back and sides, sunburst or natural top, Gibson Montana made 170 in '93-'95.			
1958-1959		$4,250	$5,500
1960-1964		$3,875	$5,000
1965		$3,750	$4,750

The Official Vintage Guitar magazine Price Guide 2025 **Epiphone** P. McCartney 1964 Texan (U.S.A.) — Hollywood Masterbilt Tenor **85**

GUITARS

MODEL YEAR	FEATURES	EXC. COND. LOW	HIGH
1966-1967		$3,500	$4,500
1968-1969		$3,000	$3,750
1970		$2,625	$3,500

Paul McCartney 1964 Texan (U.S.A.)
2005-2006. Reproduction of McCartney's '64 Texan made in Gibson's Montana plant, two runs, one of 40 guitars ('05), second of 250 ('05-'06). The first 40 were hand-aged and came with Sir Paul's autograph, display case and certificate; the 250 run were not-hand aged, but have signed labels.

2005-2006		$3,750	$5,000

Paul McCartney 1964 Texan (Japan)
2006-2010. Limited run of 1,964 guitars.

2006-2010		$1,375	$1,750

1964 Texan (Inspired By Series)
2010-2019. Imported production model, acoustic/electric, non-adjustable bridge.

2010-2019		$300	$400

FT 85 Serenader 12-String
1963-1969. 12 strings, mahogany back and sides, dot inlay, natural.

1963-1964		$1,375	$1,750
1965		$1,125	$1,500
1966-1969		$1,125	$1,500

FT 90 El Dorado
1963-1970. Dreadnought flat-top acoustic, mahogany back and sides, multi-bound front and back, natural.

1963-1964		$3,125	$4,000
1965		$2,500	$3,250
1966-1967		$2,250	$3,000
1968-1970		$2,250	$3,000

FT 95 Folkster
1966-1969. 14" small body, mahogany back and sides, natural, double white 'guards.

1966-1969		$800	$1,125

FT 98 Troubadour
1963-1969. 16" square shouldered drednought, maple back and sides, gold-plated hardware, classical width 'board.

1963-1964		$2,750	$3,500
1965		$2,500	$3,250
1966-1969		$2,375	$3,000

FT 110
1941-1958. Acoustic flat-top, natural, renamed the FT 110 Frontier by Gibson in '58.

1941-1943	Square shoulder	$5,250	$6,500
1944-1949	Square shoulder	$4,875	$6,000
1949-1958	Round shoulder	$4,000	$5,000

FT 110 Frontier
1958-1970, 1994. Renamed from FT 110, acoustic flat-top, natural or sunburst, Gibson Montana made 30 in '94. Reintroduced '21, Antique Natural or Frontier Burst.

1958-1959		$7,000	$8,500
1960-1964		$6,500	$8,000
1965		$5,750	$7,250
1966-1970		$5,500	$7,000

FT Deluxe
1939-1941. Acoustic flat-top, 16.5".

1939-1941		$7,000	$9,500

FT Deluxe Cutaway (FT 210)
1954-1957. Acoustic flat-top, cutaway, 16.5". Some labeled FT 210.

1954-1957		$7,000	$9,500

FT Series (Flat-Tops Japan)
1970s. In '70 Epiphone moved production to Japan. Various 6- to 12-string models were made, nearly all with bolt necks and small rectangular blue labels on the inside back, ranging from the budget FT 120 to the top-of-the-line FT 570 Super Jumbo.

1970s	Various models	$550	$850

G 310
1989-2019. SG-style model with large 'guard and gig bag.

1989-2019		$250	$350

G 400
1989-2013. SG-style, 2 humbuckers, crown inlays.

1989-2013		$350	$475

G 400 Custom
1998-2000, 2003-2011. 3 humbucker version, gold hardware, block inlays.

1998-2011		$500	$650

G 400 Deluxe
1999-2007. Flame maple top version of 2 humbucker 400.

1999-2007		$525	$700

G 400 Limited Edition
2001-2002. 400 with Deluxe Maestro lyra vibrola, cherry red.

2001-2002		$525	$700

G 400 Tony Iommi
2003-2011. SG-style model with cross 'board inlay markers, black finish.

2003-2011		$525	$700

G 1275 Custom Double Neck
1996-2011. SG-style alder body, 6- & 12-string, maple top, mahogany neck, cherry red, set neck. Also offered as bolt-neck Standard for '96-'98.

1996-2011		$700	$950

Genesis
1979-1980. Double-cut solidbody, 2 humbuckers with coil-taps, carved top, red or black, available as Custom, Deluxe, and Standard models, Taiwan import.

1979-1980		$750	$975

Granada (Non-cutaway Thinbody)
1962-1969. Non-cut thinline archtop, 1 f-hole, 1 pickup, trapeze tailpiece, sunburst finish.

1962-1964		$2,250	$2,875
1965-1969		$2,000	$2,500

Granada (Cutaway)
1965-1970. Single-cut version.

1965-1970		$2,125	$2,625

Harry Volpe (E721/E722)
1955-1957. Hollow body, 1 pickup.

1955-1957	E721, Shaded	$1,500	$1,875
1955-1957	E722, Blonde	$1,500	$1,875

Hollywood Masterbilt Tenor
1931-1936. Tenor version of the Triumph, acoustic archtop 15.4", 19-fret Brazilian rosewood 'board, diagonal diamond markers.

1931-1936		$2,000	$2,500

1968 Epiphone FT-79 Texan
Rivington Guitars

1965 Epiphone FT 110 Frontier
Carter Vintage Guitars

To get the most from this book, be sure to read "Using *The Guide*" in the introduction.

1967 Epiphone Howard
Roberts Standard

Imaged by Heritage Auctions, HA.com

Epiphone Hummingbird Pro

MODEL YEAR	FEATURES	EXC. COND. LOW	HIGH

Howard Roberts Standard
1964-1970. Single-cut acoustic archtop, bound front and back, cherry or sunburst finish, listed in catalog as acoustic but built as electric.

| 1964-1970 | | $3,500 | $4,500 |

Howard Roberts Custom
1965-1970. Single-cut archtop, bound front and back, 1 pickup, walnut finish (natural offered '66 only).

| 1965-1970 | | $3,750 | $4,750 |

Howard Roberts III
1987-1991. Two pickups, various colors.

| 1987-1991 | | $725 | $950 |

Hummingbird/Pro/Studio
1994-present. Twin parallelogram inlays, hummingbird 'guard, replaced by Pro, with added electronics, in '13. Pro dropped from name in 2020, named Hummingbird Studio in 23.

| 1994-2023 | | $300 | $350 |

Inspiration Style A Tenor
1928-1929. Banjo resonator style body with round sound hole, A headstock logo, spruce top, walnut back, sides and neck.

| 1928-1929 | | $2,250 | $3,000 |

Joe Pass/Joe Pass Emperor II
1995-2019. Single-cut archtop jazz guitar, 2 humbuckers, blocks, gold hardware, natural or sunbusrt, renamed from Emperor II (see that listing). Limited Edition all-gold finish or Wine Red were available early on.

| 1995-2019 | | $575 | $750 |

Johnny A Signature Custom Outfit
2017-2018. Artist Signature series, Limited Edition, double-cut hollowbody, flamed maple top, 2 pickups, Bigsby tail, Sunset Glow gloss finish.

| 2017-2018 | | $950 | $1,250 |

Les Paul 100/LP-100
1993-2019. Affordable single-cut Les Paul, bolt-on neck.

| 1993-2019 | | $225 | $300 |

Les Paul '56 Goldtop
1998-2013. Made in China, based on '56 Goldtop specs with 2 P-90s. Black finish was offered starting in '09.

| 1998-2013 | Gold | $600 | $800 |
| 2009-2013 | Black | $600 | $800 |

Les Paul Ace Frehley
2001. Les Paul Custom 3-pickups, Ace's signature on 22nd fret, lightning bolt markers.

| 2001 | | $1,125 | $1,500 |

Les Paul Alabama Farewell Tour
2003. Limited production, 1 pickup single-cut Jr., American flag and Alabama logo graphics and band signatures on body, Certificate of Authenticity.

| 2003 | | $650 | $850 |

Les Paul Black Beauty
1997-2019. Classic styling with three gold plated pickups, black finish, block markers.

| 1997-2019 | | $650 | $850 |

Les Paul Classic
2003-2005. Classic Les Paul Standard specs, figured maple top, sunburst.

| 2003-2005 | | $650 | $850 |

MODEL YEAR	FEATURES	EXC. COND. LOW	HIGH

Les Paul Custom
1989-2011. Various colors.

| 1989-2011 | | $650 | $850 |

Les Paul Custom Plus (Flame Top)
1998-2010. Flamed maple top version of 2 pickup Custom, gold hardware, sunburst.

| 1998-2010 | | $650 | $850 |

Les Paul Custom Silverburst
2007-2008. 2 humbuckers, silverburst finish.

| 2007-2008 | | $650 | $850 |

Les Paul Dale Earnhardt
2003. Dale Earnhardt graphics, 1 humbucker.

| 2003 | | $650 | $850 |

Les Paul Deluxe
1998-2000. Typical mini-humbucker pickups.

| 1998-2000 | | $650 | $850 |

Les Paul ES Limited Edition
1999-2000. Les Paul semi-hollow body with f-holes, carved maple top, gold hardware, cherry sunburst and other color options.

| 1999-2000 | Custom | $675 | $875 |
| 1999-2000 | Standard | $675 | $875 |

Les Paul Gold Top
1994-1998. Goldtop, 2 humbuckers. Listed as Les Paul Standard Goldtop in '94.

| 1994-1998 | | $650 | $850 |

Les Paul Joe Perry Boneyard
2004-2006. Boneyard logo on headstock, figured Boneyard finish.

| 2004-2006 | | $650 | $850 |

Les Paul Jr. '57 Reissue
2006. '57 Reissue on truss rod cover, logo and script Les Paul Junior stencil on headstock, lower back headstock states 'Epiphone Limited Edition Custom Shop'.

| 2006 | | $300 | $400 |

Les Paul Music Rising
2006-2007. Music Rising (Katrina charity) graphics, LP Studio, 2 humbuckers.

| 2006-2007 | | $325 | $450 |

Les Paul Prophecy
2020-present. Modern Collection, mahogany body, AAA flame maple veneer top in Red Tiger or Olive Tiger aged gloss, or plain top in black aged gloss.

| 2020-2023 | | $650 | $850 |

Les Paul Sparkle L.E.
2001. Limited Edition LP Standard, silver, purple, red (and others) glitter finish, optional Bigsby.

| 2001 | | $650 | $850 |

Les Paul Special
1994-2000, 2020-present. Double-cut, bolt neck. Reintroduced in '20 with P-90 Pro pickups, CTS electronics, TV yellow finish.

| 1994-2000 | | $250 | $350 |

Les Paul Special II
1996-2019. Economical Les Paul, 2 pickups, single-cut, various colors.

| 1996-2016 | Guitar and amp | $125 | $175 |
| 1996-2019 | Guitar only | $100 | $130 |

The *Vintage Guitar Price Guide* shows values for all-original, excellent condition instruments and, where applicable, with original case.

MODEL YEAR	FEATURES	EXC. COND. LOW	HIGH
Les Paul Special/TV Special			
2006. Copy of single-cut late '50s Les Paul Special with TV finish.			
2006		$275	$350
Les Paul Standard			
1989-2019. Solid mahogany body, carved maple top, 2 humbuckers.			
1989-2019	Various colors	$375	$475
Les Paul Standard Baritone			
2004-2005. 27-3/4" long-scale baritone model.			
2004-2005		$650	$850
Les Paul Standard Plus FMT			
2003-2012. LP Standard figured curly maple sunburst top.			
2003-2012		$650	$850
Les Paul Standard Ultra/Ultra II			
2005-2012. LP Standard with chambered and contoured body, quilted maple top.			
2005-2012	Ultra	$650	$850
2005-2012	Ultra II	$650	$850
Les Paul Studio			
1995-present. Epiphone's version of Gibson LP Studio.			
1995-2023		$275	$400
Les Paul XII			
1998-2000. 12-string solidbody, trapeze tailpiece, flamed maple sunburst, standard configuration.			
1998-2000		$550	$725
Slash Les Paul			
1997-2000. Slash logo on body.			
1997-2000		$800	$1,125
Slash Les Paul Goldtop			
2008-2012. Limited Edition 2,000 made, goldtop finish, Seymour Duncan exposed humbuckers, Slash logo on truss rod cover, includes certificate of authenticity.			
2008-2012	With COA	$800	$1,125
Slash Les Paul Standard Plus Top			
2008-2012. Figured top, exposed humbuckers, includes certificate of authenticity.			
2008-2012	With COA	$900	$1,250
Zakk Wylde Les Paul Custom			
2002-2019. Bull's-eye graphic, block markers, split diamond headstock inlay.			
2002-2019		$550	$700
Madrid (Classical)			
1962-1969. Classical, natural.			
1962-1964		$450	$575
1965-1969		$325	$400
MD-30			
1993. D-size, round metal resonator, spruce top with dual screens.			
1993		$550	$750
Melody Tenor			
1931-1937. 23" scale, bound body.			
1931-1937	Masterbilt	$1,250	$1,625
Moderne			
2000. Copy of '58 Gibson Moderne design, dot markers, Moderne script logo on 'guard, black.			
2000		$675	$875

MODEL YEAR	FEATURES	EXC. COND. LOW	HIGH
Navarre			
1931-1940. Hawaiian flat-top, mahogany back and sides, bound top and back, dot inlay, brown finish.			
1931-1937	Masterbilt label	$3,000	$4,000
1938-1940	Standard label	$2,750	$3,500
Nighthawk Standard			
1995-2000. Epiphone's version of the Gibson Nighthawk, single-cut, bolt neck, figured top.			
1995-2000		$300	$400
Noel Gallagher Union Jack/Super Nova			
1997-2005. Limited edition, higher-end ES-335. Union Jack with British flag finish (introduced '99) or Supernova in solid blue.			
1997-2005		$1,000	$1,375
Olympic (Acoustic Archtop)			
1931-1949. Mahogany back and sides.			
1931-1936	Smaller body	$2,000	$3,000
1937-1939	Larger body	$1,500	$2,500
1940-1949		$1,500	$2,500
Olympic Tenor (Acoustic Archtop)			
1937-1949. 4-string version of the Olympic.			
1937-1949		$900	$1,250
Olympic Single (Solidbody)			
1960-1970. Slab body, the same as the mid-'60s Coronet, Wilshire and Crestwood Series, single-cut '60-'62, asymmetrical double-cut '63-'70, 2 Melody maker single-coil pickups, vibrato optional in '64 and standard by '65.			
1960-1962	Single-cut	$2,250	$2,875
1963-1964	Double-cut	$1,875	$2,375
1965-1970		$1,500	$1,875
Olympic Double (Solidbody)			
1960-1969. Slab body, the same as the mid-'60s Coronet, Wilshire and Crestwood Series, single-cut '60-'62, asymmetrical-cut '63-'70, 2 Melody Maker single-coils, vibrato optional in '64 and standard by '65.			
1960-1963	Single-cut	$3,375	$4,250
1963-1964	Double-cut	$3,000	$3,750
1965-1969	Cherry, sunburst	$2,500	$3,250
Olympic (3/4 Scale Solidbody)			
1960-1963. 22" scale, sunburst.			
1960-1963		$2,000	$2,500
Olympic Special (Solidbody)			
1962-1970. Short neck with neck body joint at the 16th fret (instead of the 22nd), single Melody Maker-style single-coil bridge pickup, small headstock, double-cut slab body, dot markers, Maestro or Epiphone vibrato optional '64-'65, slab body contour changes in '65 from symmetrical to asymmetrical with slightly longer bass horn, sunburst.			
1962-1964	Symmetrical	$1,125	$1,500
1965-1970	Asymmetrical	$1,000	$1,375
PR Series			
1980-2004. Budget acoustics, mainly D size but some smaller, cut and non-cut bodies.			
1980-2004	Various models	$300	$550
Pro 1			
1989-1996. Solidbody, double-cut, 1 single-coil and 1 humbucking pickup, bolt-on neck, various colors.			
1989-1996		$375	$500

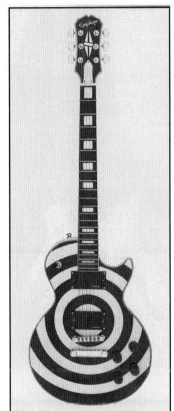

2004 Epiphone Zakk Wylde Les Paul Custom

1990 Epiphone PR-325

Dave Mullikin

1967 Epiphone Riviera 12 string
Dean Nissen

1961 Epiphone Triumph Regent
Carter Vintage Guitars

MODEL YEAR	FEATURES	EXC. COND. LOW	HIGH
Pro 2			
1995-1998. Higher-end Pro I with Steinberger DB bridge, set-neck, 2 humbuckers, various colors.			
1995-1998		$375	$500
Professional			
1962-1967. Double-cut, thinline archtop, 1 pickup, mahogany finish. Values include matching Professional amp.			
1962-1964	With matching amp	$3,000	$4,000
1965	With matching amp	$2,500	$3,250
1966-1967	With matching amp	$2,250	$3,000
Prophecy Extura			
2020-present. Modern Collection, mahogany body, AAA flame maple veneer top, 2 Fishman pickups, various colors with aged gloss finish.			
2020-2023		$600	$800
Recording A			
1928-1931. Asymmetrical body flat-top with exaggerated treble bout cutaway, celluloid headstock veneer, dot inlays. All Recording models were offered in concert or auditorium body sizes.			
1928-1931	Standard 6-string	$3,500	$4,500
1928-1931	Tenor 4-string	$2,000	$2,500
Recording B			
1928-1931. As Recording A but with arched back, bound fingerboard, fancier body binding and zigzagging double slotted-diamond inlays.			
1928-1931		$4,500	$5,500
Recording C			
1928-1931. As Recording B but with arched top.			
1928-1931		$4,500	$5,500
Recording D			
1928-1931. As Recording C, but with large cross-hatched block inlays.			
1928-1931		$5,500	$6,750
Recording E			
1928-1931. As Recording D, but with large floral engraved block inlays.			
1928-1931		$7,250	$9,500
Ritz			
1940-1949. 15.5" acoustic archtop, large cello f-holes, dot inlays, no headstock ornamentation other than script Epiphone inlay, blond finish.			
1940-1949		$1,250	$1,625
Riviera			
1962-1970. Double-cut thinline archtop, 2 mini-humbuckers, Royal Tan standard finish changing to sunburst in '65, cherry optional by '66-'70, additional 250 were made in Nashville in '93-'94, a Riviera import was available in '82 and for '94-'06.			
1962-1964	Tan or cherry	$6,500	$8,000
1964	Sunburst	$6,000	$7,500
1965	Sunburst, cherry	$5,500	$7,000
1966-1967	Sparkling Burgundy	$5,500	$7,000
1966-1970	Sunburst, cherry	$5,250	$6,500
1967-1968	Walnut	$5,250	$6,500
Riviera (U.S.A.)			
1993-1994. Made in U.S.A. on back of headstock.			
1993-1994		$1,375	$1,750

MODEL YEAR	FEATURES	EXC. COND. LOW	HIGH
Riviera Reissue (Korea)			
1994-2006. Korean-made contemporary reissue, natural.			
1994-2006		$550	$700
Riviera 12-String			
1965-1970. Double-cut, 12 strings, thinline archtop, 2 mini-humbuckers, sunburst or cherry.			
1965-1970		$3,500	$4,500
Riviera 12-String Reissue (Korea)			
1997-2000. Korean-made reissue, natural.			
1997	Humbuckers	$850	$1,125
1998-2000	Mini-hums	$550	$700
Royal			
1931-1935. 15 1/2" acoustic archtop, mahogany back and sides, dot markers, sunburst, bound top, back and neck, Masterbilt headstock logo.			
1931-1935		$2,000	$2,500
S-900			
1986-1989. Neck-thru-body, locking Bender tremolo system, 2 pickups with individual switching and a coil-tap control.			
1986-1989		$375	$500
SC350			
1976-1979. Mahogany solidbody, scroll bass horn, rosewood 'board, dot inlays, bolt neck, 2 humbuckers, made in Japan.			
1976-1979	Mahogany	$650	$850
SC450			
1976-1979. Like SC350, but with maple body, glued neck, and coil tap.			
1976-1979	Maple	$650	$850
SC550			
1976-1979. Like SC450, but with gold hardware, block inlays, neck and body binding, and ebony 'board.			
1976-1979	Maple, gold hdwr	$650	$850
Seville EC-100 (Classical)			
1938-1941, 1961-1969 (Gibson-made). Classical guitar, mahogany back and sides, natural, the '61-'63 version also available with a pickup.			
1961-1964		$550	$750
1965-1969		$475	$650
Prophecy SG			
2020-present. Modern Collection, mahogany body, AAA flame maple veneer top, 2 Fishman pickups, various colors with aged gloss finish.			
2020-2023		$650	$850
SG Special			
2000-present. SG body, dot markers, 2 open-coil humbuckers, later P-90s.			
2000-2016	Guitar and amp	$150	$200
2000-2023	Guitar only	$150	$200
Sheraton			
1958-1970. Double-cut thinline archtop, 2 New York pickups '58-'60, 2 mini-humbuckers '61 on, frequensator tailpiece, multi-bound, gold-plated hardware, sunburst or natural finish with cherry optional by '65. Reissued '93-'94.			
1958-1960	Natural, NY pus	$12,000	$15,000
1959-1964	Sunburst, mini-hums	$10,500	$13,500

MODEL YEAR	FEATURES	EXC. COND. LOW	HIGH
1961-1964	Natural, mini-hums	$12,000	$15,000
1962	Cherry, few made	$11,000	$14,000
1965	Cherry, natural	$8,000	$10,000
1965	Sunburst	$6,500	$8,500
1966-1967	Natural	$7,500	$9,500
1966-1970	Cherry, sunburst	$6,000	$7,500

Sheraton (Japan)

1982-1983. Early reissue, not to be confused with Sheraton II issued later, natural or sunburst.

1982-1983		$1,750	$2,250

Sheraton (Reissue U.S.A.)

1993-1994, 2005. An additional 250 American-made Sheratons were built from '93-'94.

1993-1994		$2,250	$3,000
2005		$2,250	$3,000

Sheraton II/Sheraton II PRO

1986-present. Contemporary archtop reissue, natural or sunburst.

1986-2023		$575	$750

Slasher

2001. Reverse offset double cut solidbody, bolt neck, six-on-a-side tuners, 2 pickups, dot markers.

2001		$375	$500

Sorrento (1 pickup)

1960-1970. Single-cut thinline archtop, 1 pickup in neck position, tune-o-matic bridge, nickel-plated hardware, sunburst, natural or Royal Olive finish, (cherry or sunburst by '68).

1960-1964		$2,500	$3,250
1965		$2,375	$3,000
1966-1970		$2,250	$2,875

Sorrento (2 pickups)

1960-1970. Single-cut thinline archtop, 2 pickups, tune-o-matic bridge, nickel-plated hardware, sunburst, natural or Royal Olive finish, (cherry or sunburst by '68).

1960-1964		$3,875	$4,875
1965		$3,250	$4,000
1966-1970		$3,000	$3,750

Sorrento (Reissue)

1994-2000. Reissue of 2 pickup model, import.

1994		$575	$750
1995-2000		$575	$750

Spartan

1934-1949. Acoustic archtop, 16 3/8", laminated maple body, multi-bound, trapeze tailpiece, sunburst or natural.

1934-1939	Sunburst	$1,500	$2,000
1940-1949	Sunburst	$1,250	$1,500
1941-1947	Natural	$1,250	$1,500

Special/SG Special (U.S.A.)

1979-1983. SG Special body style, dot markers, 2 exposed humbuckers, Special logo on truss rod cover.

1979-1983		$850	$1,125

Spider/The Spider

1997-2000. Wood body resonator, spider bridge, square neck.

1997-2000		$575	$750

Spirit I/Spirit II

1982. U.S.-made electric solidbody, double-cut, flat-top with 1 (I) or 2 (II) humbuckers, Epiphone U.S.A. script logo on headstock, Spirit logo on truss rod cover.

1982		$1,250	$1,625

SST

2007-2011. Acoustic/electric solidbody, either Classic (nylon) or Studio (steel). Chet Atkins model also available.

2007-2011		$300	$400

Tom Delonge Signature ES-333

2008-2019. One humbucker, dot inlays.

2008-2019		$600	$775

Trailer Park Troubadour Airscreamer

2003-2005. Airstream trailer-shaped body, identifying logo on headstock.

2003-2005		$550	$750

Triumph

1931-1957. 15 1/4" '31-'33, 16 3/8" '33-'36, 17 3/8" '36-'57, walnut back and sides until '33, laminated maple back and sides '33, solid maple back and sides '34, natural or sunburst.

1931-1932	Sunburst, laminated walnut	$2,750	$3,500
1933	Sunburst, laminated maple	$2,750	$3,500
1934-1935	Sunburst, solid maple	$3,000	$3,750
1936-1940	Sunburst 17 3/8" body	$3,000	$3,750
1941-1957	Natural	$3,000	$3,750
1941-1957	Sunburst	$3,000	$3,750

Triumph Regent (Cutaway)

1948-1969. Acoustic archtop, single-cut, F-holes, renamed Triumph Cutaway in '53, then Gibson listed this model as just the Triumph from '58-'69.

1948-1952	Regent, natural	$4,000	$5,000
1948-1952	Regent, sunburst	$4,000	$5,000
1953-1957	Cutaway, natural	$3,875	$4,875
1953-1957	Cutaway, sunburst	$3,500	$4,500
1958-1964	Sunburst	$3,875	$4,875
1965	Sunburst	$3,750	$4,625
1966-1969	Sunburst	$3,500	$4,375

USA Map Guitar

1982-1983. U.S.-made promotional model, solidbody electric, mahogany body shaped like U.S. map, 2 pickups, natural.

1982-1983		$3,500	$4,250

USA Map Guitar Limited Edition

2007	Import	$600	$800

Vee-Wee (Mini Flying V)

2003. Mini Flying V, single bridge pickup, gig bag.

2003		$125	$180

Wildkat

2001-2019. Thinline, single-cut, hollow-body, 2 P-90s, Bigsby tailpiece, various colors.

2001-2019		$400	$550

Wilshire

1959-1970. Double-cut solidbody, 2 pickups, tune-o-matic bridge, cherry.

1959	Symmetrical	$6,500	$8,500

1983 Epiphone USA Map Guitar

James Seldin

1964 Epiphone Wilshire

Imaged by Heritage Auctions, HA.com

1961 Epiphone Zephyr
Electric (Cutaway)

Jim Sliff

ESP Eclipse I

MODEL YEAR	FEATURES	EXC. COND. LOW	HIGH
1960-1962	Thinner-style, P-90s	$5,000	$6,500
1962-1963	Symmetrical, mini-hums	$5,000	$6,500
1963-1964	Asymmetrical, mini-hums	$4,500	$5,500
1965-1966	Custom color	$5,000	$6,500
1965-1966	Standard color	$4,000	$5,000
1967-1970		$3,500	$4,500

Wilshire 12-String
1966-1968. Solidbody, 2 pickups, cherry.

1966-1968		$3,125	$4,000

Wilshire II
1984-1985. Solidbody, maple body, neck and 'board, 2 humbuckers, 3-way switch, coil-tap, 1 tone and 1 volume control, various colors.

1984-1985		$550	$725

Windsor (1 Pickup)
1959-1962. Archtop, 1 or 2 pickups, single-cut thinline, sunburst or natural finish.

1959-1960	Natural, NY pu	$4,000	$5,000
1959-1960	Sunburst, NY pu	$3,750	$4,750
1961-1962	Natural, mini-hum	$3,000	$3,750
1961-1962	Sunburst, mini-hum	$2,750	$3,500

Windsor (2 Pickups)
1959-1962. Archtop, 1 or 2 pickups, single-cut thinline, sunburst or natural finish.

1959-1960	Natural, NY pu	$4,500	$5,500
1959-1960	Sunburst, NY pu	$4,000	$5,000
1961-1962	Natural, mini-hum	$3,500	$4,500
1961-1962	Sunburst, mini-hum	$3,000	$4,000

X-1000
1986-1989. Electric solidbody, Korean-made, various colors.

1986-1989		$350	$450

Zenith
1931-1969. Acoustic archtop, bound front and back, f-holes, sunburst.

1931-1933		$1,750	$2,125
1934-1935	14 3/4" body	$2,125	$2,625
1936-1949	16 3/8" body	$2,125	$2,625
1950-1957	Natural	$2,250	$2,875
1950-1957	Sunburst	$2,125	$2,625
1958-1969		$2,000	$2,500

Zephyr
1939-1957. Non-cut electric archtop, 1 pickup, bound front and back, blond or sunburst (first offered '53), called Zephyr Electric starting in '54.

1939-1940	Natural, metal handrest pu	$2,375	$3,000
1941-1943	Natural, no metal handrest	$2,375	$3,000
1944-1946	Natural, top mounted pu	$2,375	$3,000
1947-1948	17 3/8", metal covered pu	$2,375	$3,000
1949-1957	Natural, NY pu	$2,125	$2,625
1953-1957	Sunburst, NY pu	$2,000	$2,500

Zephyr Regent
1950-1953. Single-cut electric archtop, 1 pickup, natural or sunburst, called Zephyr Cutaway for '54-'57.

1950-1953	Natural	$3,750	$4,625
1950-1953	Sunburst	$3,000	$3,750

MODEL YEAR	FEATURES	EXC. COND. LOW	HIGH

Zephyr Cutaway
1954-1957. Cutaway version of Zephyr Electric, called Zephyr Regent for 1950-'53.

1954-1957	Natural	$3,750	$4,625
1954-1957	Sunburst	$3,375	$4,250

Zephyr Electric (Cutaway)
1958-1964. Gibson-made version, thinline archtop, single-cut, 2 pickups, natural or sunburst.

1958-1959	Natural	$4,375	$5,500
1958-1959	Sunburst	$3,750	$4,625
1960-1964	Natural	$3,750	$4,625
1960-1964	Sunburst	$3,375	$4,250

Zephyr De Luxe (Non-cutaway)
1941-1942, 1945-1954. Non-cut electric archtop, 1 or 2 pickups, multi-bound front and back, gold-plated hardware, natural or sunburst.

1941-1942	Natural	$3,375	$4,250
1945-1949	Natural, 1 pu	$3,750	$4,625
1945-1954	Natural, 2 pus	$4,000	$5,000
1950-1954	Sunburst, 2 pus	$3,750	$4,625

Zephyr De Luxe Regent (Cutaway)
1948-1954. Single-cut electric archtop, 1 or 2 pickups until '50, then only 2, gold-plated hardware, sunburst or natural finish. Renamed Deluxe Electric in '54.

1948-1949	Natural, 1 pu	$4,000	$5,000
1948-1949	Natural, 2 pus	$5,000	$6,250
1948-1949	Sunburst, 1 pu	$3,750	$4,625
1948-1949	Sunburst, 2 pus	$4,750	$6,000
1950-1954	Natural, 2 pus	$5,000	$6,250
1950-1954	Sunburst, 2 pus	$4,750	$6,000

Zephyr Emperor Regent
1950-1954. Archtop, single rounded cutaway, multi-bound body, 3 pickups, sunburst or natural finish, renamed Emperor Electric in '54.

1950-1954	Natural	$8,500	$10,500
1950-1954	Sunburst	$6,500	$8,500

Zephyr Tenor
1940-1950. Natural, figured top.

1940-1950		$1,500	$1,875

Zephyr Blues Deluxe
1999-2005. Based on early Gibson ES-5, 3 P-90 pickups.

1999-2005		$750	$950

Epoch

Economy level imports made by Gibson and sold through Target stores.

Equator Instruments

2006-present. Production/custom, professional and premium grade, solidbody, hollowbody, acoustic and classical guitars built in Chicago, Illinois by luthier David Coleman.

Erlewine

1979-present. Professional and premium grade, production/custom guitars built by luthier Mark Erlewine in Austin, Texas. Erlewine also produces the Chiquita brand travel guitar.

MODEL		EXC. COND.	
YEAR	FEATURES	LOW	HIGH

Esoterik Guitars

Professional grade, production/custom, electric guitars built in San Luis Obispo, California by luthier Ryan Cook. He began with guitars in 2010 and plans to add basses.

ESP

1983-present. Intermediate, professional, and premium grade, production/custom, Japanese-made solidbody guitars and basses. Hisatake Shibuya founded Electronic Sound Products (ESP), a chain of retail stores, in '75. They began to produce replacement parts for electric guitars in '83 and in '85 started to make custom-made guitars. In '87 a factory was opened in Tokyo. In '86 ESP opened a sales office in New York, selling custom guitars and production models. From around '98 to ca. '02 they operated their California-based USA custom shop. In '96, they introduced the Korean-made LTD brand and in '03 introduced the Xtone brand, which was folded into LTD in '10. Hisatake Shibuya also operated 48th Street Custom Guitars during the '90s but he closed that shop in 2003.

20th Anniversary
1995. Solidbody, double-cut, ESP95 inlaid at 12th fret, gold.

1995		$1,500	$2,000

25th Anniversary
2000. Slab body, single-cut.

2000		$3,500	$4,000

Eclipse Custom (U.S.A.)
1998-2002. U.S. Custom Shop-built, single-cut, mahogany body and maple top, various colors offered.

1998-2002		$1,000	$1,500

Eclipse Custom/Custom T (Import)
1986-1988, 2003-2010. Single-cut mahogany solidbody, earliest model with bolt dot marker neck, 2nd version with neck-thru and blocks, the Custom T adds locking trem. Current has quilt maple top.

1986-1987	Bolt-on, dots	$1,125	$1,500
1987-1988	Neck-thru, blocks	$1,125	$1,500
1987-1988	Neck-thru, Custom T	$1,125	$1,500

Eclipse Deluxe
1986-1988. Single-cut solidbody, 1 single-coil and 1 humbucker, vibrato, black.

1986-1988		$1,000	$1,500

Eclipse Series
1995-present. Recent Eclipse models.

1995-2000	Eclipse/Eclipse I	$750	$975
1996-2000	Eclipse Archtop	$750	$975

George Lynch M-1
2000s. Signature series, sunburst tiger finish.

1996-2023		$2,500	$3,250

Horizon (Import)
1986, 1996-2001. Double-cut neck-thru, bound ebony 'board, 1 single-coil and 1 humbucker, buffer preamp, various colors, reintroduced '96-'01 with bolt neck, curved rounded point headstock.

1986		$1,000	$1,375
1996-2001		$850	$1,125

Horizon Classic (U.S.A.)
1993-1995. U.S.-made, carved mahogany body, set-neck, dot markers, various colors, optional mahogany body with figured maple top also offered.

1993-1995		$2,000	$2,500

Horizon Custom (U.S.A.)
1998-2001. U.S. Custom Shop-made, mahogany body, figured maple top, bolt-on neck, mostly translucent finish in various colors.

1998-2001		$2,000	$2,500

Horizon Deluxe (Import)
1989-1992. Horizon Custom with bolt-on neck, various colors.

1989-1992		$1,250	$1,625

Hybrid I (Import)
1986 only. Offset double-cut body, bolt maple neck, dots, six-on-a-side tuners, vibrato, various colors.

1986		$600	$800

Hybrid II (Import)
1980s. Offset double-cut, rosewood 'board on maple bolt neck, lipstick neck pickup, humbucker at bridge, Hybrid II headstock logo.

1980s		$650	$850

James Hetfield Custom Explorer MX-250
1992. Limited production.

1992		$10,000	$12,000

Jeff Hanneman S & Key Inlay
2004. Only 12 made, camo or black.

2004		$25,000	$28,000

LTD EC-GTA Guitarsonist
2008. Flame graphic by Matt Touchard, 100 made.

2008		$1,500	$2,000

LTD EC-SIN Sin City
2008. Vegas graphic by Matt Touchard, 100 made.

2008		$1,500	$2,000

LTD Series
1998-present. Various Limited Edition models, range of prices due to wide range of specs.

1998-2023	Various models	$225	$1,500

Maverick/Maverick Deluxe
1989-1992. Offset double-cut, bolt maple or rosewood cap neck, dot markers, double locking vibrola, six-on-a-side tuners, various colors.

1989-1992		$700	$1,250

Metal I
1986 only. Offset double-cut, bolt maple neck, rosewood cap, dots, various colors.

1986		$650	$850

Metal II
1986 only. Single horn V body, bolt on maple neck with rosewood cap, dot markers, various colors.

1986		$650	$850

Metal III
1986 only. Reverse offset body, bolt maple neck with maple cap, dot markers, gold hardware, various colors.

1986		$650	$850

M-I Custom
1987-1994. Offset double-cut thru-neck body, offset block markers, various colors.

1987-1994		$950	$1,250

Esoterik DR1

ESP George Lynch M-1 Tiger

GUITARS

EVH Wolfgang Special

1968 Excelsior Dyno III
Rivington Guitars

MODEL YEAR	FEATURES	EXC. COND. LOW	HIGH

M-I Deluxe
1987-1989. Double-cut solidbody, rosewood 'board, 2 single-coils and 1 humbucker, various colors.

1987-1989		$950	$1,250

M-II
1989-1994, 1996-2000. Double-cut solidbody, reverse headstock, bolt-on maple or rosewood cap neck, dot markers, various colors.

1989-1994		$950	$1,250

M-II Custom
1990-1994. Double-cut solidbody, reverse headstock, neck-thru maple neck, rosewood cap, dot markers, various colors.

1990-1994		$950	$1,250

M-II Deluxe
1990-1994. Double-cut solidbody, reverse headstock, Custom with bolt-on neck, various colors.

1990-1994		$950	$1,250

Mirage Custom
1986-1990. Double-cut neck-thru solidbody, 2-octave ebony 'board, block markers, 1 humbucker and 2 single-coil pickups, locking trem, various colors.

1986-1990		$950	$1,250

Mirage Standard
1986 only. Single pickup version of Mirage Custom, various colors.

1986		$950	$1,250

Phoenix
1987 only. Offset, narrow waist solidbody, thru-neck mahogany body, black hardware, dots.

1987		$950	$1,250

Phoenix Contemporary
Late-1990s. 3 pickups vs. 2 on the earlier offering.

1998		$950	$1,250

S-454/S-456
1986-1987. Offset double-cut, bolt maple or rosewood cap neck, dot markers, various colors.

1986-1987		$800	$1,125

S-500
1991-1993. Double-cut figured ash body, bolt-on neck, six-on-a-side tuners, various colors.

1991-1993		$950	$1,250

SV-II
2009-2012. Part of Standard Series, made in Japan, neck-thru offset v-shaped solidbody, 2 pickups, dot inlays.

2009-2012		$2,000	$2,500

Traditional
1989-1990. Double-cut, 3 pickups, tremolo, various colors.

1989-1990		$950	$1,250

Vintage/Vintage Plus S
1995-1998. Offset double-cut, bolt maple or rosewood cap neck, dot markers, Floyd Rose or standard vibrato, various colors.

1995	20th Anniv Ed	$1,500	$2,000
1995-1998		$1,250	$1,625

Viper Series
2004-present. Offset double-cut SG style, 2 humbuckers, various models

2010	300M	$450	$600

Espana
1963-ca. 1973. Primarily acoustic guitars distributed by catalog wholesalers Bugeleisen & Jacobson. Built by Watkins in England.

Classical
1963-1973. Guitars with white spruce fan-braced tops with walnut, mahogany, or rosewood back and sides.

1963-1973		$275	$400

EL (Electric) Series
1963-1973. Various double-cut models, 2 or 3 pickups, tremolo, '63-ca. '68 with nitro finish, ca. '69-'73 poly finish.

1963-1973	EL-30, 2 pickups	$375	$500
1963-1973	EL-31, 3 pickups	$425	$550
1963-1973	EL-32, 12-string	$375	$500
1963-1973	EL-36, 2 pickups	$425	$550

Jumbo Folk
1969-1973. Natural.

1969-1973		$325	$450

Essex (SX)
1985-present. Budget grade, production, electric and acoustic guitars imported by Rondo Music of Union, New Jersey. They also offer basses.

Solidbody Electric
1980s-1990s. Copies of classic designs like the Les Paul and Telecaster.

1980s		$175	$250

Este
1909-1939. Luthier Felix Staerke's Este factory built classical and archtop guitars in Hamburg, Germany. They also built high-end banjos. The plant ceased instrument production in '39 and was destroyed in WW II.

Esteban
2002-present. Budget grade, production, acoustic and classical import guitars sold as packages with classical guitarist Esteban's (Stephen Paul) guitar lesson program, other miscellany and sometimes a small amp.

Steel and Nylon Acoustics

2002-2023	Various models	$45	$200

EtaVonni
2008-2010. Luthier Ben Williams built premium grade, production/custom, carbon fiber and aluminum electric guitars in Kentwood, Michigan.

Euphonon
1930-1944. A Larson brothers brand, most Euphonons date from 1934-'44. Body sizes range from 13 ½" to the 19" and 21" super jumbos. The larger body 14-fret neck sizes have body woods of Brazilian rosewood, mahogany, or maple. Ornamentation and features are as important to value as rosewood vs. mahogany. Production also included mandolins, and most models were A-style, with teardrop body and flat backs.

MODEL		EXC. COND.	
YEAR	FEATURES	LOW	HIGH

Everett Guitars

1977-present. Luthier Kent Everett builds his premium and presentation grade, production/custom, steel-string and classical guitars in Atlanta, Georgia. From '01 to '03, his Laurel Series guitars were built in conjunction with Terada in Japan and set up in Atlanta. He has also built archtops, semi-hollow and solidbody electrics, resonators, and mandolins.

Evergreen Mountain

1971-present. Professional grade, custom, flat-top and tenor guitars, basses and mandolins built by luthier Jerry Nolte in Cove, Oregon. He also built over 100 dulcimers in the '70s.

Everly Guitars

1982-2001. Luthier Robert Steinegger built these premium grade, production/custom flat-tops in Portland, Oregon (also see Steinegger Guitars).

EVH

2007-present. Eddie Van Halen worked with FMIC to create a line of professional and premium grade, production, solidbody guitars built in the U.S. and imported from other countries. Van Halen died October 2020, but the brand continues. They also build amps.

Wolfgang Special

2010-present. Made in Japan, offset double-cut solidbody, figured maple top over basswood body, birdseye maple 'board, 2 pickups, tremolo, opaque finish. Some more recent models made in Mexico.

2010-2023		$1,250	$2,000

Excelsior

The Excelsior Company started offering accordions in 1924 and had a large factory in Italy by the late '40s. They started building guitars around '62, which were originally plastic covered, switching to paint finishes in the mid '60s. They also offered classicals, acoustics, archtops and amps. By the early '70s they were out of the guitar business.

The Excelsior brand was also used ca.1885-ca.1890 on guitars and banjos by Boston's John C. Haynes & Co.

Dyno and Malibu

1960s. Offset, double cut, 2 or 3 pickups, vibrato.

1960s	Dyno I	$375	$500
1960s	Dyno II	$425	$600
1960s	Malibu I	$425	$600
1960s	Malibu II	$450	$650

Exlusive

2008-2013. Intermediate grade, production, electric guitars and basses, imported from Asia and finished in Italy by luthier Galeazzo Frudua.

Fairbuilt Guitar Co.

2000-present. Professional and premium grade, custom guitars and mandolins, built by luthier Martin Fair in Loudoun County, Virginia.

Falk

1989-present. Professional and premium grade, production/custom archtop guitars built by luthier Dave Falk, originally in Independence, Missouri, and currently in Amarillo, Texas. He also builds mandolins and dulcimers.

Fano

1995-present. Professional grade, production/custom, solidbody electric guitars and basses built by luthier Dennis Fano in Fleetwood, Pennsylvania.

Farnell

1989-present. Luthier Al Farnell builds his professional grade, production, solidbody guitars and basses in Ontario, California. He also offers his intermediate grade, production, C Series which is imported from China.

Fat Cat Custom Guitars

2004-present. Intermediate to premium grade, production/custom, solidbody and chambered electric guitars and basses built in Carpentersville, Illinois by luthier Scott Bond.

Favilla

1890-1973. Founded by the Favilla family in New York, the company began to import guitars in 1970, but folded in '73. American-made models have the Favilla family crest on the headstock. Import models used a script logo on the headstock.

Acoustic Classical

1960s-1973. Various nylon-string classical models.

1960s-1973		$165	$500

Acoustic Flat-Top

1960s-1973. Various flat-top models, 000 to D sizes, mahogany to spruce.

1960s-1973		$165	$500

Fell

One of the many guitar brands built by Japan's Matsumoku company.

Fender

1946 (1945)-present. Budget, intermediate, professional, and premium grade, production/custom, electric, acoustic, acoustic/electric, classical, and resonator guitars built in the U.S. and overseas. They also build amps, basses, mandolins, bouzoukis, banjos, lap steels, ukes, violins, and PA gear. Ca. 1939 Leo Fender opened a radio and record store called Fender Radio Service, where he met Clayton Orr 'Doc' Kauffman, and in '45 they started KF Company to build lap steels and amps. In '46 Kauffman left and Fender started the Fender Electric Instrument Company.

In January '65 CBS purchased the company and renamed it Fender Musical Instruments Corporation. The CBS takeover is synonymous with a perceived decline in quality among musicians and collectors, and Pre-CBS Fenders are more valuable. Fender

Farnell

Fat Cat Custom Guitars

1951 Fender Broadcaster

John Amaral

1969 Fender Bronco

Imaged by Heritage Auctions, HA.com

experienced some quality problems in the late-'60s. Small headstock is enlarged in '65 and the 4-bolt neck is replaced by the 3-bolt in '71. With high value and relative scarcity of Pre-CBS Fenders, even CBS-era instruments are now sought by collectors. Leo Fender was kept on as consultant until '70 and went on to design guitars for Music Man and G&L.

In '82 Fender Japan is established to produce licensed Fender copies for sale in Japan. Also, in '82, the Fender Squier brand debuts on Japanese-made instruments for the European market and by '83 they were imported into U.S. In March '85, the company was purchased by an investor group headed by Bill Schultz but the purchase does not include the Fullerton factory. While a new factory was being established at Corona, California, all Fender Contemporary Stratocasters and Telecasters were made either by Fender Japan or in Seoul, Korea. U.S. production resumes in late '85. The Fender Custom Shop, run by Michael Stevens and John Page, opens in '87. The Mexican Fender factory is established in '90. In '95, Fender purchased the Guild guitar company. On January 3, 2002, Fender Musical Instruments Corporation (FMIC) recapitalized a minority portion of common stock, with partners including Roland Corporation U.S. and Weston Presidio, a private equity firm in San Francisco. In 2003, Fred Gretsch Enterprises, Ltd granted Fender the exclusive rights to develop, produce, market, and distribute Gretsch guitars worldwide. Around the same time, Fender also acquired the Jackson/Charvel Guitar Company. In October, '04, Fender acquired Tacoma Guitars. On January 1, '08, Fender acquired Kaman Music Corporation and the Hamer, Ovation, and Genz Benz brands. The Groove Tubes brand was purchased by Fender in June, '08.

Dating older Fender guitars is an imprecise art form at best. While serial numbers were used, they were frequently not in sequence, although a lower number will frequently be older than a substantially higher number. Often necks were dated, but only with the date the neck was finished, not when the guitar was assembled. Generally, dating requires triangulating between serial numbers, neck dates, pot dates, construction details and model histories.

From '50 through roughly '65, guitars had more-or-less sequential numbers in either 4 or 5 digits, though some higher numbers may have an initial 0 or - prefix. These can range from 0001 to 99XXX.

From '63 into '65, some instruments had serial numbers beginning with an L prefix plus 5 digits (LXXXXX). Beginning in '65 with the CBS takeover into '76, 6-digit serial numbers were stamped on F neckplates roughly sequentially from 10XXXX to 71XXXX. In '76 the serial number was shifted to the headstock decal. From '76-'77, the serial number began with a bold-face 76 or S6 plus 5 digits (76XXXXX).

From '77 on, serial numbers consisted of a 2-place prefix plus 5 digits (sometimes 6 beginning in '91): '77 (S7, S8), '78 (S7, S8, S9), '79 (S9, E0), '80-'81 (S9, E0, E1), '82 (E1, E2, E3), '84-'85 (E4), '85-'86 (no U.S. production), '87 (E4), '88 (E4, E8), '89 (E8, E9), '90

(E9, N9, N0), '91 (N0), '92 (N2).

Serial numbers on guitars made by Fender Japan consist of either a 2-place prefix plus 5 digits or a single prefix letter plus 6 digits: '82-'84 (JV), '83-'84 (SQ), '85-'86+ (A, B, C), '86-'87 (F), '87-'88+ (G), '88-'89 (H), '89-'90 (I, J), '90-'91 (K), '91-'92 (L), '92-'93 (M).

Factors affecting Fender values: All Fender instruments shipped originally with a maple one-piece neck. A walnut "skunk stripe" plug was used on the back of the neck to cover the truss rod channel. The use of a rosewood fretboard beginning in 1959 changes the value of some models significantly. The sale to CBS in '65 is also a major point in Fender instrument values as CBS made many changes collectors feel affected quality. The '70s introduced the 3-bolt neck and other design changes that aren't as popular with guitarists. Custom color instruments, especially Strats from the '50s and early-'60s, can be valued much more than the standard sunburst finishes. In '75 Fender dropped the optional custom colors and started issuing the guitars in a variety of standard colors.

Custom colors are worth more than standard colors. For a Stratocaster, Telecaster Custom and Esquire Custom the standard color is sunburst, while the Telecaster and Esquire standard color is blond. The first Precision Bass standard color was blond but changed to sunburst in the late 1950s. The Jazz Bass standard color is sunburst. The Telecaster Thinline standard color is natural. All Fender guitars were available in a custom DuPont Duco or DuPont Lucite color. Some custom colors are rarer than others. Below is a list of the custom colors offered in 1960. They are sorted in ascending order with the most valuable color, Shell Pink, listed last. For example, Fiesta Red is typically worth 12% more than a Black or Blond, though all are in the Common Color category. In the Rare Color group, Foam Green is normally worth 8% more than Shoreline Gold. The two Very Rare colors are often worth 30% more than Shoreline Gold. In our pricing information we will list the standard color, then the relative value of a common custom color, and then the value of a rare custom color. Remember that the amount of fade also affects the price. These prices are for custom colors with slight or no fade, which implies a lighter color, but some examples can also be much darker in color due to the yellowing of the nitrocellulose clearcoat. Blue can fade to dark green. White can fade to deep yellow. The prices in the Guide are for factory original finishes only. It is important to understand that custom-colored Fenders are commonly forged. It is recommended to always buy from a reputable dealer when adding a custom-colored Pre-CBS Fender to your collection.

The various Telecaster and Stratocaster models are grouped under those general headings.

Common Color: Black, Blond, Candy Apple Red, Olympic White, Lake Placid Blue, Dakota Red, Daphne Blue, Fiesta Red

Rare Color: Shoreline Gold, Inca Silver, Burgundy Mist, Sherwood Green, Sonic Blue, Foam Green

MODEL YEAR	FEATURES	EXC. COND. LOW	HIGH

Rare (Very Rare) Pastel Color: Surf Green, Shell Pink

1960 - 1962: Black, Blond, Burgundy Mist, Dakota Red, Daphne Blue, Fiesta Red, Foam Green, Inca Silver, Lake Placid Blue, Olympic White, Shell Pink, Sherwood Green, Shoreline Gold, Sonic Blue, Sunburst, Surf Green

1963 - 1964: Black, Blond, Burgundy Mist, Candy Apple Red, Dakota Red, Daphne Blue, Fiesta Red, Foam Green, Inca Silver, Lake Placid Blue, Olympic White, Sherwood Green, Shoreline Gold, Sonic Blue, Sunburst, Surf Green

1965 - 1969: Black, Blond, Blue Ice, Candy Apple Red, Charcoal Frost, Dakota Red, Fiesta Red, Firemist Gold, Firemist Silver, Foam Green, Lake Placid Blue, Ocean Turquoise, Olympic White, Sonic Blue, Sunburst, Teal Green

1970 - 1971: Black, Blond, Candy Apple Red, Firemist Gold, Firemist Silver, Lake Placid Blue, Ocean Turquoise, Olympic White, Sonic Blue, Sunburst

1972: Black, Blond, Candy Apple Red, Lake Placid Blue, Olympic White, Sonic Blue, Sunburst

1973: Black, Blond, Candy Apple Red, Lake Placid Blue, Natural, Olympic White, Sunburst, Walnut

1974 - 1977: Black, Blond, Natural, Olympic White, Sunburst, Walnut

1978 - 1979: Antigua, Black, Blond, Natural, Olympic White, Sunburst, Walnut, Wine

Arrow
1969-1972. See listing for Musiclander.

Avalon
1985-1995. California Series, acoustic import, 6-on-a-side tuners, mahogany neck, back and sides (nato after '93), spruce top, various colors.

1985-1995		$225	$325

Balboa
1983-1987. California Series, acoustic import.

1983-1987		$375	$500

Brawler Baritone (Custom Shop)
2019-2020. Journeyman Relic, masterbuilt by Carlos Lopez.

2019-2020		$7,000	$9,000

Broadcaster
Mid-1950-early-1951. For a short time in early-'51, before being renamed the Telecaster, models had no Broadcaster decal; these are called No-casters by collectors.

1950	Blond	$150,000	$250,000
1951	Clipped decal, "No Caster"	$85,000	$125,000

Broadcaster Leo Fender Custom Shop
1999 only. Leo Fender script logo signature replaces Fender logo on headstock, Custom Shop certificate signed by Phyllis Fender, Fred Gretsch, and William Schultz, includes glass display case and poodle guitar case.

1999		$6,500	$8,500

'50s Relic/'51 NoCaster Custom Shop
1995-2014. Called the '50s Relic NoCaster for '96-'99, and '51 NoCaster in NOS, Relic, or Closet Classic versions 2000-'10, with the Relic Series being the highest offering. From June '95 to June '99 Relic work was done outside of Fender by Vince Cunetto and included a certificate noting model and year built, an instrument without the certificate is worth less than the value shown. Blonde or Honey Blonde finish. Also, in '09, the Limited '51 NoCaster Relic was offered with Twisted Tele neck pickup, 50 each in 2-tone sunburst or Dakota Red.

1995-1997	Cunetto built Relic	$3,500	$4,500
1997-1999	Cunetto era Closet Classic	$3,500	$4,500
1997-1999	Cunetto era NOS	$3,500	$4,500
1998-1999	Cunetto era Relic	$3,500	$4,500
2000-2009	Closet Classic	$3,000	$4,000
2000-2014	NOS	$3,000	$4,000
2000-2014	Relic	$3,000	$4,000

'51 NoCaster Limited Edition
2009. Custom Shop Limited Edition, as above but with Twisted Tele neck pickup, 50 each in 2-tone sunburst or Dakota Red.

2009	Relic	$3,000	$4,000

70th Anniversary Broadcaster Limited Edition
2020 only. Production model has ash body, black 'guard, '50s spaghetti logo, blonde lacquer finish. Custom Shop model available with aging Relic, Heavy Relic, NOS Time Capsule and Journeyman Relic.

2020	Custom Shop	$3,000	$4,000
2020	Production	$2,000	$2,500

Bronco
1967-1980. Slab solidbody, 1 pickup, tremolo, red.

1967-1968	Nitro	$1,500	$2,000
1969-1980	Poly	$1,500	$2,000

Buddy Miller Signature
2007-2009. Artist Design series, flat-top, Fishman Ellipse Aura, signature on headstock.

2007-2009		$800	$1,125

Bullet/Bullet Deluxe
1981-1983. Solidbody, came in 2- and 3-pickup versions (single-coil and humbucker), and single- and double-cut models, various colors. Becomes Squire Bullet in '85.

1981-1983	Various models	$825	$1,250

Catalina
1983-1995. California Series, acoustic dreadnought, import.

1983-1995		$250	$350

CC-60SCE Concert
2020-present. Single-cut, spruce top, mahogany back and sides, Fishman pickup, black or natural.

2020-2023		$250	$350

CD (Classic Design) Series
2006-present. Imported, intermediate grade, various models, acoustic or acoustic-electric, steel or nylon string.

2006-2023	Various models	$175	$350

1981 Fender Bullet
Rivington Guitars

Fender CC-60SCE Concert

GUITARS

1967 Fender Coronado II
Tom Pfeifer

1964 Fender Duo Sonic
Robbie Keene

MODEL YEAR	FEATURES	EXC. COND. LOW	HIGH

CG (Classical Guitar) Series
1995-2005. Imported, various nylon-string classical acoustic and acoustic/electric models, label on the inside back clearly indicates the model number, back and sides of rosewood, mahogany or other woods.

| 1995-2005 | Various models | $75 | $400 |

Concert
1963-1970. Acoustic flat-top slightly shorter than King/Kingman, spruce body, mahogany back and sides (optional Brazilian or Indian rosewood, zebrawood, or vermillion), natural, sunburst optional by '68.

| 1963-1970 | Natural or sunburst | $1,125 | $1,500 |

Concord
1986-1995. Dreadnought flat-top, 6-on-a-side headstock, natural.

| 1986-1995 | | $200 | $250 |

Coronado I
1966-1969. Thinline semi-hollowbody, double-cut, tremolo, 1 pickup, single-bound, dot inlay.

| 1966-1969 | Various colors | $1,750 | $2,250 |

Coronado II
1966-1969 (Antigua finish offered until '70). Thinline semi-hollowbody, double-cut, tremolo optional, 2 pickups, single-bound, block inlay, available in standard finishes but special issues offered in Antigua and 6 different Wildwood finishes (labeled on the pickguard as Wildwood I through Wildwood VI to designate different colors). Wildwood finishes were achieved by injecting dye into growing trees.

1966-1969	Various colors	$2,000	$2,500
1966-1969	Wildwood	$2,750	$3,500
1967-1970	Antigua	$2,000	$2,500

Coronado XII
1966-1969 (Antigua finish offered until '70). Thinline semi-hollowbody, double-cut, 12 strings, 2 pickups, block inlay, standard, Antigua and Wildwood finishes available.

1966-1969	Various colors	$2,250	$3,000
1966-1969	Wildwood	$2,750	$3,500
1967-1970	Antigua	$2,250	$3,000

Custom
1969-1971. Six-string solidbody that used up parts from discontinued Electric XII, asymmetrical-cut, long headstock, 2 split pickups, sunburst. Also marketed as the Maverick.

| 1969-1971 | | $6,500 | $8,500 |

Cyclone
1998-2006. Mexican import, solidbody, contoured offset waist, poplar body, various colors.

| 1998-2006 | Various options | $700 | $950 |

D'Aquisto Elite
1984, 1989-1994, 1994-2002. Part of Fender's Master Series, 16" laminated maple-side archtop, single-cut, glued neck, 1 pickup, gold hardware, made in Japan until '94, in '94 the Fender Custom Shop issued a version that retailed at $6,000, various colors.

| 1984-2002 | | $2,500 | $3,250 |

D'Aquisto Standard
1984 (Serial numbers could range from 1983-1985). Like D'Aquisto Elite, but with 2 pickups.

| 1984 | | $2,500 | $3,250 |

MODEL YEAR	FEATURES	EXC. COND. LOW	HIGH

D'Aquisto Ultra
1984, 1994-2000. USA Custom Shop, made under the supervision of James D'Aquisto, solid flamed maple back and sides, spruce top, ebony tailpiece, bridge and 'guard, all hand carved.

| 1994-2000 | | $4,000 | $5,000 |

DG (Dreadnought Guitar) Series
1995-1999, 2002-2014. Made in China, various lower-end acoustic and acoustic/electric models.

| 1995-2014 | Various models | $150 | $350 |

Duo-Sonic/Player Duo-Sonic
1956-1969, 2016-present. Solidbody, 3/4-size, 2 pickups, Desert Sand ('56-'61), sunburst ('61-'63), blue, red or white after, short- and long-scale necks, short-scale necks listed here (see Duo-Sonic II for long-scale), reissued Mexican-made in '94. In 2016 it becomes part of Player Series.

1956-1958	Desert Sand	$4,500	$5,500
1959	Maple neck	$4,500	$5,500
1960	Rosewood 'board	$3,500	$4,500
1961-1963	Desert Sand	$3,500	$4,500
1963	Sunburst (rare)	$3,000	$4,000
1964-1965	Blue, red, sunburst, white	$3,000	$4,000
1966-1969	Blue, red or white	$2,250	$3,000

Duo-Sonic II
1965-1969. Solidbody, 2 pickups, blue, red or white, long-scale neck, though the long-scale neck Duo-Sonic was not known as the Duo-Sonic II until '65, we have lumped all long-scales under the II for the purposes of this Guide.

| 1965-1969 | | $2,250 | $3,000 |

Duo-Sonic Reissue
1993-1997. Made in Mexico, black, red or white.

| 1993-1997 | | $325 | $450 |

Duo-Sonic HS/Player Duo-Sonic HS
2017-present. Player Series, humbucker and single-coil pickups.

| 2017-2023 | | $400 | $550 |

Electric XII
1965-1969. Solidbody, 12 strings, long headstock, 2 split pickups. Please refer to the Fender Guitar Intro Section for details on Fender color options.

1965-1969	Common color	$8,500	$12,000
1965-1969	Rare color	$11,000	$15,000
1965-1969	Sunburst	$6,000	$7,500

Electric XII Alternate Reality
2019. Modern updated reissue.

| 2019 | | $775 | $1,000 |

Ensenada Series
2005-2007. Made in Mexico acoustics, solid top, back and sides, A (grand auditorium), D (dreadnought), M (mini jumbo) and V (orchestra) sizes, E suffix denotes on-board electronics.

| 2005-2007 | Acoustic | $500 | $650 |
| 2005-2007 | Acoustic-electric | $550 | $750 |

Esprit Elite
1984. Master Series, made in Japan, double-cut, semi-hollow, carved maple top, 2 humbuckers, 4 controls, bound rosewood 'board, snowflake inlays.

| 1983-1985 | | $1,500 | $2,000 |

Esprit Standard

1984. Like Esprit Elite, but with dot inlays, 2 controls.

Model Year	Features	Low	High
1983-1985		$1,500	$2,000

Esprit Ultra

1984. Like Esprit Elite, but with bound ebony 'board, split-block inlays, gold hardware.

Model Year	Features	Low	High
1984		$1,500	$2,000

Esquire

1950-1970. Ash body, single-cut, 1 pickup, maple neck, black 'guard '50-'54, white 'guard '54 on. Please refer to the Fender Guitar Intro Section for details on Fender color options.

Model Year	Features	Low	High
1950-1951	Blond, black 'guard	$55,000	$70,000
1952-1953	Blond, black 'guard	$50,000	$65,000
1954	Blond, black 'guard	$45,000	$60,000
1954-1955	Blond, white 'guard	$35,000	$45,000
1956-1957	Blond	$35,000	$45,000
1958	Blond, backloader	$27,000	$38,000
1958	Blond, toploader	$25,000	$35,000
1959	Blond, maple 'board	$25,000	$35,000
1959	Blond, rosewood 'board	$25,000	$35,000
1960	Blond	$24,000	$32,000
1960	Sunburst	$25,000	$35,000
1961	Blond, slab 'board	$20,000	$25,000
1961	Custom color	$50,000	$65,000
1961	Sunburst, slab	$25,000	$35,000
1962	Blond, curved 'board	$18,000	$23,000
1962	Blond, slab	$20,000	$25,000
1962	Custom color	$45,000	$60,000
1962	Sunburst, curved	$25,000	$35,000
1962	Sunburst, slab	$25,000	$35,000
1963	Blond	$18,000	$23,000
1963	Common color	$30,000	$40,000
1963	Rare color	$40,000	$50,000
1963	Sunburst	$22,000	$30,000
1964	Blond	$17,000	$22,000
1964	Common color	$30,000	$40,000
1964	Rare color	$40,000	$50,000
1964	Sunburst	$22,000	$30,000
1965	Blond	$15,000	$20,000
1965	Common color	$25,000	$35,000
1965	Rare color	$35,000	$45,000
1965	Sunburst	$20,000	$25,000
1966	Blond	$13,000	$16,000
1966	Common color	$20,000	$25,000
1966	Rare color	$30,000	$40,000
1966	Sunburst	$15,000	$20,000
1967	Blond	$12,000	$15,500
1967	Blond, smuggler cavity	$12,500	$17,000
1967	Common color	$18,000	$23,500
1967	Rare color	$24,000	$31,500
1967	Sunburst	$13,000	$17,000
1968	Blond, nitro	$11,000	$15,000
1968	Common color, nitro	$18,000	$23,500
1968	Rare color, nitro	$24,000	$31,500
1968	Sunburst, nitro	$13,000	$17,000
1969	Blond, poly	$8,500	$11,000
1969	Common color, poly	$12,500	$16,500
1969	Rare color, poly	$17,000	$22,000
1969	Sunburst, poly	$12,000	$15,500
1970	Blond	$7,500	$9,750
1970	Common color	$11,500	$15,000
1970	Rare color	$15,000	$20,000
1970	Sunburst	$7,500	$9,750

Esquire (Japan)

1985-1994. Made in Japan, '54 specs.

Model Year	Features	Low	High
1985-1986		$1,125	$1,500
1987-1989	'50s Esquire	$1,125	$1,500
1990-1994	'50s Esquire	$1,125	$1,500

'50s Esquire (Mexico)

2005-2010. Maple neck, ash body.

Model Year	Features	Low	High
2005-2010		$600	$800

'52 Esquire

2012. Custom Shop, price includes Certificate of Authenticity.

Model Year	Features	Low	High
2012	NOS	$3,000	$4,000

'53 Esquire

2012. Custom Shop, price includes Certificate of Authenticity.

Model Year	Features	Low	High
2012	NOS	$3,000	$4,000

'59 Esquire

2003-2007, 2013-2016. Custom Shop, Relic version lasted to '07, then came back in '13 for limited run.

Model Year	Features	Low	High
2003-2013	Closet Classic	$3,000	$4,000
2003-2013	NOS	$3,000	$4,000
2003-2016	Relic	$3,000	$4,000

'60 Esquire

Custom Shop, NOS.

Model Year	Features	Low	High
2010		$3,000	$4,000

'70 Esquire

2008. Custom Shop, only 20 made.

Model Year	Features	Low	High
2008	Heavy Relic	$3,000	$4,000
2008	Relic	$3,000	$4,000

70th Anniversary Esquire

2020 only. Roasted pine body, 1-piece maple neck, 1 pickup, Anniversary neck plate, white blond.

Model Year	Features	Low	High
2020		$1,500	$2,000

Custom Esquire '95

1995. Custom Shop, limited run of 12 for Sam Ash Music, stealth pickup under 'guard, bird's-eye maple neck.

Model Year	Features	Low	High
1995		$2,750	$3,500

Esquire Custom

1959-1970. Same as Esquire, but with bound alder sunburst body and rosewood 'board.

Model Year	Features	Low	High
1959	Sunburst	$35,000	$50,000
1960	Custom color	$52,000	$75,000
1960	Sunburst	$35,000	$45,000
1961	Custom color	$45,000	$65,000
1961	Sunburst	$32,500	$44,000
1962	Custom color	$45,000	$60,000
1962	Sunburst, curve	$30,000	$40,000
1962	Sunburst, slab	$32,000	$45,000
1963	Custom color	$45,000	$60,000
1963	Sunburst	$30,000	$42,000

1965 Fender Electric XII
Thel Rountree

1986 Fender Esquire
Michael Alonzi

GUITARS

Fender Brad Paisley Esquire

1966 Fender Jaguar

Rob Zolezzi

MODEL YEAR	FEATURES	EXC. COND. LOW	HIGH
1964	Custom color	$37,000	$50,000
1964	Sunburst	$25,000	$35,000
1965	Custom color	$28,000	$40,000
1965	Sunburst	$22,000	$30,000
1966	Custom color	$25,000	$32,000
1966-1970	Sunburst	$15,500	$20,000

Esquire Custom (Import)

1983-1994. Made in Japan with all the classic bound Esquire features, sunburst.

1983-1987		$1,250	$1,625
1988-1994		$1,125	$1,500

Esquire Custom GT/Celtic/Scorpion

2003. Made in Korea, single-cut solidbody, 1 humbucker, 1 knob (volume), set-neck, solid colors.

2003		$600	$800

Esquire Z

2001. Custom Shop, black body and headstock, curly maple neck, ebony 'board, 25 made.

2001		$5,250	$6,750

Brad Paisley Esquire

2020-present. Spruce top and back, 2 single-coil pickups, black and silver paisley 'guard, road worn black sparkle finish.

2020-2023		$950	$1,250

Jeff Beck Tribute Esquire (Custom Shop)

2006. Also called Beck Artist Esquire or Tribute Series Jeff Beck Esquire, specs include an extremely lightweight 2-piece offset ash body with Beck's original contours, distressed for an appearance like Beck's original Esquire that was used on many Yardbird records.

2006		$10,000	$15,000

F (Flat-Top) Series

1969-1981. The F-Series were Japanese-made flat-top acoustics, included were Concert- and Dreadnought-size instruments with features running from plain to bound necks and headstocks and fancy inlays, there was also a line of F-Series classical, nylon-string guitars. A label on the inside indicates the model. FC-20 is a classical with Brazilian rosewood. There was also an Asian (probably Korean) import Standard Series for '82-'90 where the models start with a F.

1969-1981	Dreadnought, laminated	$85	$175
1969-1981	Dreadnought, solid top	$175	$400
1972-1981	Classical (FC)	$175	$400

FA (Fender Alternative) Series

2009-present. Entry-level acoustic series, various Concert, Dreadnought and Auditorium sized models.

2009-2023	FA-115, FA-125	$125	$175
2018-2023	FA-345CE	$300	$400

Flame Elite

1984. Master Series, made in Japan, neck-thru, offset double-cut, solidbody, 2 humbuckers, rosewood 'board, snowflake inlays.

1984-1988		$1,750	$2,250

Flame Standard

1984-1988. Like Flame Elite, but with dot inlays.

1984-1988		$1,750	$2,250

Flame Ultra

1984. Like Flame Elite, but with split block inlays (some with snowflakes), gold hardware.

1984-1988		$1,750	$2,250

FR-48 Resonator

2003-2009. Made in Korea, steel body.

2003-2009		$300	$400

FR-50 Resonator

2000-2015. Spruce top, mahogany back and sides, sunburst, optional square-neck.

2000-2015		$300	$400

FR-50CE Resonator

2000-2015. Same as FR-50 with cutaway and pickups.

2009-2015		$375	$500

FR-55 Hawaiian Resonator

2012-2013. Bell brass nickel-plated body etched with scenes of South Seas.

2012-2013		$400	$550

GA (Grand Auditorium) Series

2001-2009. Various grand auditorium models made in Korea, an oval label on the inside back clearly indicates the model number.

2001-2009		$175	$475

GC (Grand Concert) Series

1997-2009. Various grand concert models, an oval label on the inside back clearly indicates the model number.

1997-2009		$150	$200

GDO (Global Design Orchestra) Series

2004-2008. Various orchestra-sized acoustic models, an oval label on the inside back clearly indicates the model number.

2004-2008		$375	$550

Gemini Series

1983-1990. Korean-made flat-tops, label on inside indicates model. I is classical nylon-string, II, III and IV are dreadnought steel-strings, there is also a 12-string and an IIE acoustic/electric.

1984-1987	Gemini II	$100	$210
1984-1988	Gemini I	$90	$125
1987-1988	Gemini III	$150	$200
1987-1990	Gemini IIE	$150	$200
1987-1990	Gemini IV	$150	$200

GN (Grand Nylon) Series

2001-2007. Various grand nylon acoustic models, an oval label on the inside back clearly indicates the model number.

2001-2007		$350	$450

Harmony-Made Series

Late-1960s-1973. Various Harmony-made models, with white stencil Fender logo, mahogany, natural or sunburst.

1960s	D-style model	$300	$900
1970-1973	Stella model	$110	$200

Jag-Stang

1996-1999, 2003-2004. Made in Japan, designed by Curt Cobain, body similar to Jaguar, tremolo, 1 pickup, oversize Strat peghead, Fiesta Red or Sonic Blue. First year has 50th Anniversary label.

1996-2004		$900	$1,250

MODEL YEAR	FEATURES	EXC. COND. LOW	HIGH
Jaguar			
1962-1975. Reintroduced as Jaguar '62 in '95-'99. Please refer to the Fender Guitar Intro Section for details on Fender color options.			
1962-1964	Common color	$10,000	$15,000
1962-1964	Rare color	$15,000	$20,000
1962-1964	Sunburst	$6,000	$8,500
1965	Common color	$9,500	$12,500
1965	Rare color	$12,000	$16,000
1965	Sunburst	$5,000	$7,500
1966	Common color	$8,500	$12,000
1966	Rare color	$12,000	$16,000
1966	Sunburst	$5,000	$7,500
1967-1969	Common color	$8,000	$11,000
1967-1969	Rare color	$11,000	$15,000
1967-1969	Sunburst	$5,000	$7,500
1970	Common color	$7,000	$9,500
1970	Rare color	$9,000	$12,000
1970-1975	Sunburst	$4,500	$6,500
1971-1974	Custom color	$7,000	$9,500
1975	Custom color	$5,000	$7,000

Jaguar '62

1986-2012. Reintroduction of Jaguar, Japanese-made until '99, then U.S.-made American Vintage series, basswood body, rosewood 'board, various colors.

1986-1999	Import	$1,250	$1,625
1999-2012	USA	$1,500	$2,000

50th Anniversary Jaguar

2012. USA, modeled after '62, classic 24" scale, new one-degree neck-angle pocket, repositioned tremolo plate, redesigned hot Jaguar single-coils, lacquer finish in Lake Placid Blue, Candy Apple Red, or burgundy.

2012		$1,500	$2,000

American Vintage '62 Jaguar

2000. Export version, Lake Placid Blue, Candy Apple Red, Shell Pink, Burgundy Mist Metallic and Ice Blue Metallic with matching headstocks, a special run for Yamano, Japan. Limited to 50 in each color.

2000		$1,750	$2,250

Blacktop Jaguar HH

2010-2014. Stripped-down electronics with 2 humbuckers, 1 volume, 1 tone, single 3-way switch, maple neck, rosewood 'board, black 'guard, black or silver.

2010-2014		$625	$850

Jaguar Baritone Special HH

2005-2010. Japan, limited edition, Baritone Special logo on matching headstock, 2 humbuckers, no trem, black.

2005-2010		$750	$950

Jaguar Classic Player Special

2009-2019. Classic Player series, classic Jag look, tremolo, 2 single-coils

2009-2019		$700	$950

Jaguar Classic Player Special HH

2009-2019. Classic Player series. 2 humbucker version.

2009-2019		$700	$950

Jaguar FSR Classic '66 Reissue

2008-2010. Fender Special Run, '66 specs, block inlays, black logo, custom colors, limited edition.

2008-2010		$1,250	$1,625

MODEL YEAR	FEATURES	EXC. COND. LOW	HIGH
Jaguar FSR Thinline			
2012. Limited Edition, semi-hollowbody with f-hole, 2 vintage-style single-coil pickups.			
2012		$1,500	$2,000
Jaguar HH/Special Edition Jaguar HH			
2005-2014. Japan, 2 Dragster humbuckers, matching headstock, chrome knobs and pickup covers.			
2005-2014		$750	$1,000
Jaguar Limited Edition Classic Series			
2002-2003. Crafted in Japan.			
2002-2003	Various models	$1,125	$1,500
Johnny Marr Signature Jaguar			
2012-present. Artist series, based on Marr's '65 Jaguar, Olympic White or Metallic KO.			
2012-2023		$1,500	$2,000
Kurt Cobain Signature Jaguar			
2011-present. Artist Series, based on Cobain's '65 Jaguar, 3-color sunburst.			
2011-2023		$1,500	$2,000
Modern Player Jaguar			
2012-2014. Mahogany body, maple neck, rosewood 'board, 2-color chocolate burst, trans red or trans black.			
2012-2014		$350	$450
Pawn Shop Jaguarillo			
2012-2013. Alder body, maple neck, rosewood 'board, HSS pickups, various colors.			
2012-2013		$625	$850
Player Jaguar			
2018-present. Alder body, maple neck, 1 humbucker and 1 single-coil, various colors with gloss finish.			
2018-2023		$550	$750
Jazzmaster			
1958-1980. Contoured body, 2 pickups, rosewood 'board, clay dot inlay, reintroduced as Japanese-made Jazzmaster '62 in '94. Please refer to the Fender Guitar Intro Section for details on Fender color options.			
1958	Sunburst	$15,000	$20,000
1958	Sunburst, anodized guard	$22,000	$25,000
1958	Sunburst, maple 'board	$18,000	$23,000
1959	Custom color, includes rare	$28,000	$50,000
1959	Sunburst	$15,000	$20,000
1960-1961	Common color	$20,000	$25,000
1960-1961	Rare color	$25,000	$45,000
1960-1961	Sunburst	$12,000	$16,000
1962-1964	Common color	$20,000	$25,000
1962-1964	Rare color	$25,000	$45,000
1962-1964	Sunburst	$12,000	$16,000
1965	Common color	$12,000	$15,000
1965	Rare color	$20,000	$25,000
1965	Sunburst	$7,500	$10,000
1966-1969	Common color	$12,000	$15,000
1966-1969	Rare color	$20,000	$25,000
1966-1969	Sunburst	$7,500	$10,000
1970	Common color	$8,000	$10,000
1970	Rare color	$10,000	$13,000
1970-1980	Sunburst	$4,500	$6,000
1971-1974	Custom color	$7,000	$9,000

2010 Fender American
Vintage '62 Jaguar
Rivington Guitars

1962 Fender Jazzmaster
Kevin Rush

Fender American
Performer Jazzmaster

1963 Fender King
Rivington Guitars

MODEL YEAR	FEATURES	EXC. COND. LOW	HIGH
1975	Custom color	$6,000	$7,500
1976-1980	Custom color	$5,500	$7,000

Road Worn '60s Jazzmaster
2015-2019. '60s style with aged/worn alder body and maple neck, worn nitro-lacquer finish. Replaced by American Original '60s Jazzmaster.

2015-2019		$800	$1,125

Jazzmaster '62
1986-2012. Japanese-made reintroduction of Jazzmaster, basswood body, rosewood 'board, from '99 U.S.-made American Vintage series, various colors.

1986-1989	Import	$1,250	$1,625
1990-1998	Import	$1,250	$1,625
1999-2012	USA	$1,500	$2,000

Jazzmaster '65/American Vintage '65
2013-2018. Alder body, maple neck, mid-'60s neck profile, rosewood 'board. Part of American Vintage series in '16.

2013-2018		$1,625	$2,250

Jazzmaster '69
1986-1990s. Made in Japan.

1986-1989		$1,500	$2,000
1990-1999		$1,250	$1,625

American Performer Jazzmaster
Introduced Dec. 2018-present. Made in the US, new features include Yosemite single-coil pickups, Greasebucket tone system, various colors.

2018-2023		$800	$1,125

American Ultra Jazzmaster
2019-present. Alder or ash body, maple neck, rosewood 'board, 2 pickups.

2019-2023		$1,500	$2,000

Blacktop Jazzmaster HS
2010-2014. Stripped-down electronics with a single-coil and a humbucker, 1 volume, 1 tone, single 3-way switch, maple neck, rosewood 'board, black or sunburst.

2010-2014		$625	$850

Classic Player Jazzmaster Special
2008-2019. Alder body, maple neck, rosewood 'board, 2 single-coils, 3-color sunburst or black.

2008-2019		$700	$950

Elvis Costello Jazzmaster
2008-2010. Artist series, walnut stain, '70s neck, vintage style tremolo.

2008-2010		$1,500	$2,000

J Mascis Jazzmaster
2007-2009. Artist series, purple sparkle finish, matching headstock, Adjusto-Matic bridge, reinforced tremolo arm.

2007-2009		$1,500	$2,000

Noventa Jazzmaster
2021. Alder body, maple neck, 3 single-coil pickups, Fiesta Red, Surf Green, or Walnut.

2021		$800	$1,125

Pinup Girl Jazzmaster
1997. Custom Shop Limited Edition, pinup girl art on body, figured maple neck, 3 pickups, certificate of authenticity.

1997		$2,500	$3,250

Select Jazzmaster
2012-2013. Chambered alder body with a carved flame maple top, Fender Select headstock medallion, various finish options.

2012-2013		$2,000	$2,500

Sonic Youth Signature Jazzmaster
2009-2014. Lee Ranaldo and Thurston Moore Signature models based on their modified Jazzmasters which basically removed the standard control layout and replaced it with a 3-way switch.

2009-2014	Lee Ranaldo	$1,500	$2,000
2009-2014	Thurston Moore	$1,500	$2,000

The Ventures Limited Edition Jazzmaster
1996. Japanese-made, ash body, 2 pickups, block inlay, transparent purple/black.

1996		$1,500	$2,000

Troy Van Leeuwen Jazzmaster
2014-present. Alder body, maple neck, Oxblood finish, red tortoiseshell 'guard, matching headstock, various custom colors.

2014-2023		$900	$1,250

White Opal Jazzmaster HH
2016. Special Edition, made in Mexico, white opal body and headstock, pearloid 'guard, 2 humbuckers.

2016		$500	$650

JZM Deluxe
2007-2009. Electracoustic Series, acoustic/electric, Jazzmaster/Jaguar body styling, Fishman and Tele pickups, sunburst or trans amber.

2007-2009		$500	$650

Katana
1985-1986. Japanese-made wedge-shaped body, 2 humbuckers, set neck, triangle inlays, black.

1985-1986		$1,250	$2,000

King
1963-1965. Full-size 15 5/8" wide acoustic, natural. Renamed Kingman in '65.

1963-1965	Brazilian rosewood	$3,000	$4,000
1963-1965	Indian, Zebra, Vermillion	$1,750	$2,250

Kingman
1965-1971. Full-size 15 5/8" wide acoustic, slightly smaller by '70, offered in 3 Wildwood colors, referred to as the Wildwood acoustic which is a Kingman with dyed wood. Reissued as import in '06.

1965-1968		$1,750	$2,500
1969-1971		$1,500	$2,000

Kingman Antigua
1968-1971. Kingman in Antigua finish (silver to black sunburst).

1968-1971		$2,000	$2,500

Kingman ASCE
2008-2017. Cutaway acoustic-electric, mahogany back and sides.

2008-2017		$450	$600

Kingman SCE
2008-2017. Cutaway acoustic-electric, mahogany back and sides.

2008-2017		$450	$600

MODEL YEAR	FEATURES	EXC. COND. LOW	HIGH

Kingman USA Pro Custom
2013-2014. Custom Shop Pro series, limited run of 50, AA sitka spruce top, maple back/sides/neck, Firemist Gold.

2013-2014		$1,250	$1,625

Kingman USA Select
2012. All solid woods, rosewood 'board, Fishman electronics, 3-color sunburst.

2012		$1,250	$1,625

Kingman USA Select C
2012. Custom Shop limited edition of 150, Engelmann spruce top, mahogany back and sides, vintage C-shaped maple neck, rosewood 'board, Fiesta Red.

2012		$1,500	$2,000

Kingman/Elvis Kingman
2012-2013. Wildwood model as used by Elvis Presley in the '67 film 'Clambake', spruce top, mahogany back and sides, rosewood 'board, natural.

2012-2013		$400	$550

Lead I
1979-1982. Double-cut solidbody with 1 humbucker, maple or rosewood 'board, black or brown.

1979-1982		$800	$1,125

Lead II
1979-1982. Lead with 2 pickups, black or brown.

1979-1982		$900	$1,250

Lead III
1982. Lead with 2 split-coil humbuckers, 2 3-way switches, various colors.

1982		$900	$1,250

Player Lead II
2020-present. Reintroduced using late-70s and updated model features.

2020-2023		$450	$600

Player Lead III
2020-present. Reintroduced using late-70s and updated model features.

2020-2023		$450	$600

LTD
1969-1975. Archtop electric, single-cut, gold-plated hardware, carved top and back, 1 pickup, multi-bound, bolt-on neck, sunburst.

1969-1975		$8,000	$12,500

Malibu
1965-1971. Flat-top, spruce top, mahogany back and sides, black, mahogany or sunburst. Later version is import.

1965-1971		$850	$1,125

Malibu (California Series)
1983-1995. Made first in Japan, then Korea in '85.

1983-1995		$250	$350

Malibu SCE
2006-2013. Imported single-cut acoustic/electric, solid spruce top, laminated mahogany back and sides, block inlays.

2006-2013		$250	$350

Marauder
1965 only. The Marauder has 3 pickups, and some have slanted frets, only 8 were made, thus it is very rare. 1st generation has hidden pickups, 2nd has exposed.

1965	1st generation	$13,000	$16,500
1965	2nd generation	$10,000	$13,000

Marauder (Modern Player)
2011-2014. Jazzmaster-type body, 1 Jazzmaster pickup and 1 Triple Bucker, rosewood 'board.

2011-2014		$450	$600

Maverick Dorado (Parallel Universe)
2020. Parallel Universe Vol. II series, alder body, 22-fret maple neck, 2 pickups, Bigsby vibrato, Mystic Pine Green, Ultraburst and Firemist Gold.

2020		$1,750	$2,250

Meteora (Parallel Universe)
November 2018-2019. Parallel Universe Vol. II series, sleek offset body with both Jazzmaster and Telecaster features.

2018-2019		$650	$850

Mod Shop
2016-present. Models designed by customer by choosing options from a menu and built by Fender, 4 models offered – Jazz Bass, Precision Bass, Stratocaster and Telecaster. Values should be determined on case-by-case basis.

2016-2023		$2,250	$3,000

Montara (California Series)
1990-1995. Korean-made single-cut acoustic/electric flat-top, natural, sunburst or black. Maple with flamed sides starting '92.

1990-1995		$500	$650

Montego I/II
1968-1975 Electric archtop, single-cut, bolt-on neck, 1 pickup (I) or 2 pickups (II), chrome-plated hardware, sunburst

1968-1975	I	$7,500	$10,000
1968-1975	II	$7,750	$11,000

Musiclander
1969-1972. Also called Swinger and Arrow, solidbody, 1 pickup, arrow-shaped headstock, no model name on peghead, red, white, and blue. Fender used '66-'68 dated necks but final assembly did not begin until '69.

1969-1972		$4,500	$5,500

Musicmaster
1956-1980. Solidbody, 1 pickup, short-scale (3/4) neck, Desert Sand ('56-'61), sunburst ('61-'63), red, white, or blue after. Regular-scale necks were optional and are called Musicmaster II from '64 to '69, after '69 II is dropped and Musicmaster continues with regular-scale neck.

1956-1959	Blond	$3,500	$4,500
1960-1964	Blond	$2,000	$2,500
1964-1965	Nitro, red, white, blue	$2,000	$2,500
1966-1968	Nitro, red, white, blue	$1,750	$2,250
1969-1972	Poly, red, white, blue	$1,750	$2,250
1973-1980	Red, white, blue	$1,750	$2,250

Musicmaster II
1964-1969. Solidbody, 1 pickup, long regular-scale neck version of Musicmaster, red, white, or blue.

1964-1965		$2,000	$2,500
1966-1969		$1,750	$2,250

1980 Fender Lead II
Tom Pfeifer

1963 Fender Musicmaster
Cream City Music

GUITARS

Fender American
Performer Mustang

1969 Fender Palomino

MODEL YEAR	FEATURES	EXC. COND. LOW	HIGH

Mustang
1964-1982, 1997-1998, 2016-present. Solidbody, 2 pickups. Reissued as '69 Mustang in 1990s, name changed back to Mustang '97-'98. Dakota Red, Daphne Blue and Olympic White with Competition Red, Blue and Orange finishes with a racing stripe on the front of the body added '69-'73 (with matching headstock for '69-'70). Named Player Mustang in '16.

1964-1965	Red, white or blue	$3,250	$5,000
1966-1969	Red, white or blue	$2,750	$4,000
1969-1970	Competition blue or red	$3,000	$3,500
1969-1970	Competition orange	$5,500	$7,500
1970-1979	Contour body, poly	$2,000	$2,500
1978-1980	Antigua	$2,000	$2,500
1980-1982	Various colors	$1,500	$2,000

Vintera '60s Mustang
2019-present. Alder body, '60s C-neck, 2 single-coils, 3-color sunburst, Lake Placid Blue or Seafoam Green.

2019-2023		$650	$850

Mustang '65 Reissue
2006-2016. Made in Japan, Classic Series.

2006-2016		$850	$1,000

Mustang '69 Reissue
1986-1998, 2005. Japanese-made, blue or white.

1986-1998		$1,000	$1,375

Mustang 90/Player Mustang 90
2016-present. Made in Mexico, 2 MP-90 pickups. Named Player series in '20.

2016-2023		$450	$600

American Performer Mustang
Introduced Dec. 2018-present. Made in U.S.A., Yosemite single-coil pickups, Greasebucket tone system, various colors.

2018-2023		$850	$1,125

American Special Mustang
2017-2018. FSR model, 2 humbucking pickups, ash body with natural finish or alder Olympic White Pearl.

2017-2018		$850	$1,125

Ben Gibbard Mustang
2021-present. Artist series, chambered ash body, natural poly gloss finish.

2021-2023		$750	$1,000

Kurt Cobain Mustang
2012-2016. Artist Series, rosewood 'board, Fiesta Red finish.

2012-2016		$750	$1,000

Mustang Special
2011-2013. Pawn Shop series, 2 humbucker pickups. 3-color sunburst, Candy Apple Red or Lake Placid Blue.

2011-2013		$575	$750

Newporter
1965-1971. Acoustic flat-top, mahogany back and sides. Reissued as import.

1965-1968	Spruce top	$750	$1,000
1968-1971	Mahogany top	$700	$950

Newporter (California Series)
1983-1995. Made first in Japan, then Korea in '85.

1983-1995		$225	$300

MODEL YEAR	FEATURES	EXC. COND. LOW	HIGH

Newporter (Custom Shop USA)/ USA Select Newporter
2013-2014. Fishman electronics, 150 offered, certificate of authenticity.

2013-2014		$1,750	$2,250

Newporter Classic
2018-present. Spruce top, matching headstock, natural mahogany back and sides, pau ferro 'board.

2018-2023		$550	$750

Newporter Player
2018-present. California series, solid spruce top, mahogany back and sides, walnut 'board, various colors with gloss poly finish.

2018-2023		$300	$400

Palomino
1968-1971. Acoustic flat-top, spruce top, mahogany back and sides, triple-bound, black or mahogany.

1968-1971		$900	$1,250

Paramount Series
2016-2022. Various Standard and Deluxe acoustic models introduced at Jan. '16 NAMM.

2016-2022		$600	$800

Pawn Shop Series
2011-2014. All-new designs with diverse Fender components and the philosophy "guitars that never were but should have been".

2011-2014	Various models	$650	$850

Performer
1985-1986. Imported Swinger-like body design, 2 slanted humbuckers.

1985-1986		$1,750	$2,500

Prodigy
1991-1993. US-made, electric solidbody, double-cut, chrome-plated hardware, 2 single-coil and 1 humbucker pickups, blue or black.

1991-1993		$1,125	$1,500

Redondo
1969-1970. Mid-size flat-top, 14 3/8" wide, replaces Newport spruce top model.

1969-1970		$950	$1,250

Redondo (California Series)
1983-1995. Made first in Japan, then Korea in '85.

1983-1995		$225	$300

Redondo Player
2018-present. California series, solid Sitka spruce top, mahogany back and sides, walnut 'board, various colors with gloss poly finish.

2018-2023		$300	$400

Robben Ford Signature
1989-1994. Symmetrical double-cut, 2 pickups, glued-in neck, solidbody with tone chambers, multibound, gold-plated hardware, sunburst. After '94 made in Fender Custom Shop.

1989-1994		$1,875	$2,500
1995	Custom Shop	$3,000	$4,000

San Luis Rey (California Series)
1990-1995. Acoustic flat-top, solid spruce top, rosewood back and sides.

1990-1995		$300	$400

MODEL YEAR	FEATURES	EXC. COND. LOW	HIGH

San Miguel (California Series)
1990-1992. Acoustic cutaway flat-top, spruce top, mahogany back and sides.

1990-1992		$225	$300

Santa Maria (California Series)
1988-1992. Acoustic flat-top 12-string, spruce top, mahogany back and sides.

1988-1992		$225	$300

Santa Marino (California Series)
1990-1992. Acoustic flat-top, solid spruce top, mahogany back and sides.

1990-1992		$225	$300

Sergio Vallin Signature
2015-2017. New offset double-cut body shape, HSS pickups.

2015-2017		$550	$750

Shenandoah 12-String
1965-1971. Acoustic flat-top, spruce top, mahogany back and sides.

1965-1971	Antigua	$1,500	$2,000
1965-1971	Blond	$1,250	$1,625

Showmaster (Import)
2003-2007. Off-set double-cut solidbody, set neck, various models.

2003	Celtic, 1 bridge hum	$550	$750
2003-2007	HH, 2 hums	$550	$750
2004-2006	3 single coils	$550	$750

Showmaster FMT (Custom Shop)
2000-2007. Bound figured maple top (FMT), 2 single-coil pickups and a bridge position humbucker, maple neck, Custom Shop certificate.

2000-2007		$2,000	$2,500

Sonoran SCE (California Series)
2006-2018. Cutaway flat-top acoustic, 6-on-a-side tuners, spruce top, laminated mahogany back and sides, rosewood 'board, electronics options.

2006-2018		$225	$300

Squier Series
The following are all Squier Series instruments from Fender, listed alphabetically. Fender Japan was established in '82 with Squier production beginning that same year. Production was shifted to Korea in '87 and later allocated to China, India (Squier II '89-'90), Mexico and other countries.

Squier '51
2004-2006. Korean-made, Strat-style body with a Tele-style neck, various colors.

2004-2006		$130	$175

Squier Bullet
1983-1988, 1995-1996, 2000-2011. Strat style, early with Tele headstock, 1980s' models include H-2 ('83-'86, 2 humbuckers), S-3 ('83-'86, 3 single-coils), S-3T ('83-'88, 3 single-coils, vibrato). Name revived in 1995 (3 SC, vib.) and in 2000 on various models with 3 SC or 2 HB pickups.

1983-1984	S-3, T	$500	$650
1983-1986	H-2	$500	$650
1985-1988	S-3, T	$500	$650
2000-2011		$115	$150

Squier Bullet Stratocaster HT HSS
2017-present. Thin poplar body, maple neck, 1 humbucker and 2 single coil pickups, Shell Pink, Brown Sunburst or black.

2017-2023		$120	$160

Squier Duo-Sonic '50s (Classic Vibe Series)
2008-2010. Classic Vibe Series, made in China.

2008-2010		$225	$300

Squier Jaguar HH ST (Contemporary Series)
2021-present. Poplar body, roasted maple neck, Indian Laurel 'board, 2 humbucker pickups, stop tailpiece, Shorline Gold or Sky Burst Metallic.

2021-2023		$325	$425

Squier Jazzmaster (Classic Vibe Series)
2010-present. Includes both '60s ('10-present) and '70s ('10-'20) Jazzmaster, inspired by vintage-era models, various colors with gloss poly finish.

2010-2023	'60s or '70s	$275	$375

Squier Katana
1985-1987. Wedge-shaped body, 1 humbucker, bolt neck, dot inlays.

1985-1987		$775	$1,125

Squier Mini Stratocaster
2020-present. Poplar body, maple neck, 3 single-coil pickups, various colors. Dual humbucker pickups (HH) available.

2020-2023		$100	$150

Squier Showmaster Series
2002-2005. Made in China, various pickup configs.

2002-2005	Various models	$175	$225

Squier Stagemaster HH
1999-2002. 2 humbuckers, reverse headstock, 6- or 7-string.

1999-2002		$175	$225

Squier Standard Double Fat Strat
1999-2007. 2 humbucker pickups.

1999-2007		$125	$175

Squier Standard Fat Strat
1996-2006. Hum/single/single pickups. Replaced by the HSS.

1996-2006		$125	$175

Squier Standard Floyd Rose Strat
1992-1996. Floyd Rose tailpiece, black, white or foto flame finish, Fender and Squier headstock logos.

1992-1996		$425	$550

Squier Standard Stratocaster
1982-2019. Standard Series represent the classic designs.

1982-1984	1st logo, JV serial	$1,250	$1,625
1985-1989	2nd logo, SQ serial	$650	$850
1990-1999	Mexico	$400	$550
2000-2019	Indonesia	$180	$250

Squier II Stratocaster
1988-1992. Squier II models were targeted at a lower price point than regular Squier series. Mainly built in Korea but some early ones from India. Line was replaced by other models under regular Squier instruments.

1988-1992		$250	$350

Fender Redondo Player

2005 Fender Squier '51
Fred Schweng

Fender Squire Vintage
Modified Surf Stratocaster

Fender Squier Telecaster RH

MODEL YEAR	FEATURES	EXC. COND. LOW	HIGH

Squier Stratocaster (Affinity Series)
1997-present. Affinity Series, lower priced version, made in China.

1997-2023		$200	$250

Squier Stratocaster (Contemporary Series)
2020-present. Poplar body, roasted maple neck, 2 humbucker pickups, various colors with gloss poly finish. Floyd Rose tremolo available.

2020-2022	HH	$300	$400
2020-2023	HH FR, Floyd Rose	$350	$450

Squier Stratocaster '50s (Classic Vibe Series)
2008-present. China, alder body, maple 'board, white pickguard, 2-tone sunburst, Lake Placid Blue or Oly White.

2008-2023		$300	$400

Squier Stratocaster '60s (Classic Vibe Series)
2008-present. China, as '50s Classic Vibe but with rosewood 'board, tortoise pickguard, 3-tone sunburst or candy apple red.

2008-2023		$300	$400

Squier Stratocaster Pro-Tone
1996-1998. Korean-made, higher-end Squier series with solid ash bodies, one-piece maple necks, alnico single-coils.

1996-1998		$500	$650

Squier Stratocaster Special (Contemporary Series)
2021-present. Poplar body, roasted maple neck, 3 single-coil pickups, painted headstock with chrome logo, various colors with gloss poly finish. Hardtail bridge (HT) available.

2021-2023		$350	$450

Squier Tom Delonge Stratocaster
2002-2003. Hardtail, 1 humbucker.

2002-2003		$350	$450

Squier Standard Telecaster
1982-2019. Standard Series represent classic designs.

1982-1984	1st logo, JV serial	$1,250	$1,625
1985-1989	2nd logo, SQ serial	$650	$850
1990-1999	Mexico	$400	$550
2000-2019	Indonesia	$180	$250

Squier Standard Telecaster Special
2004-2007. Made in Indonesia, 1 humbucker, 1 single-coil.

2004-2007		$180	$250

Squier Telecaster (Affinity Series)
1998-present. Lower priced version, made in China.

1998-2023		$180	$250

Squier Telecaster HH/RH
2020-present. Contemporary series, poplar body, maple neck, 2 dual humbucking (HH) pickups, in '22 changed to RH (rail humbucker, hum), black metallic with pearl white 'guard or pearl white with black 'guard.

2020-2023		$350	$450

Squier Telecaster Custom/Custom II
2003-2012. 2 humbuckers, Custom II has 2 soapbar single-coils. Changed to Vintage Modified series in '12.

2003-2012		$180	$250

Squier J5 (John 5) Telecaster
2009-2020. Artist Series, black with chrome hardware or Frost Gold with gold hardware (introduced '14), matching headstock.

2014-2020		$350	$450

Squier Telecaster Thinline (Classic Vibe Series)
2014-2020. Semi-hollow mahogany body with f-hole.

2004-2020		$250	$350

Squier Venus
1997-1998. Offset double-cut solidbody, 2 pickups, co-designed by Courtney Love, also offered as 12-string.

1997-1998		$525	$725

Squier Vintage Modified Series
2012-2020. Imported, various models, large script Squier logo and small Fender logo on headstock.

2012-2016	Jazzmaster Special	$250	$350
2012-2016	Surf Stratocaster	$225	$300
2012-2016	Telecaster Special	$225	$300
2012-2020	'70s Stratocaster	$225	$300
2012-2020	Stratocaster HSS	$225	$300

Starcaster
1974-1980, 2014-2017. Offset double-cut, thinline semi-hollowbody, arched maple top and back, 2 humbuckers, 5 knobs (2 tone, 2 volume, 1 master volume), originally offered in tobacco sunburst, natural, walnut, black, white or custom blond finish. Model revived in Modern Player Series in '14 without master volume. Fender also used the Starcaster name as a brand on a line of budget guitars in the 2000s.

1974-1980	Various colors	$4,500	$6,000
2014-2017	Modern Player	$775	$1,000

Starcaster by Fender
2000s. Fender used the Starcaster brand on a line of budget versions of the Strat, Tele, and J- and P-Bass. They also offered small solid state amps and guitar packages with nylon- or steel-string acoustic or a Strat/amp combo. Sold in Costco and other discounters.

2000s	Acoustic	$150	$200
2000s	Electric guitar only	$150	$200
2000s	Guitar with amp & stand	$150	$200

Stratacoustic Series
2000-2019. Thinline acoustic/electric, single-cut, spruce top, fiberglass body, various colors. Stratacoustic discontinued '05, Deluxe begins '07 and Standard added in '09. Both Plus and Premier '14-'17.

2000-2019		$375	$500

Stratocaster
The following are all variations of the Stratocaster. The first six listings are for the main American-made line. All others are listed alphabetically after that in the following order:

Stratocaster
Standard Stratocaster

American Standard Stratocaster
American Series Stratocaster
American Professional Stratocaster
American Professional II Stratocaster
20th Century American Standard Stratocaster
21st Century American Standard Stratocaster
25th Anniversary Stratocaster
30th Anniversary Guitar Center Stratocaster
35th Anniversary Stratocaster
40th Anniversary 1954 Stratocaster Limited
    Edition
40th Anniversary American Standard Stratocaster
40th Anniversary Stratocaster Diamond Dealer
40th Anniversary Stratocaster ST62 (Japan)
'50s Stratocaster/Classic Series '50s Stratocaster
American Original '50s Stratocaster
Classic Player '50s Stratocaster
Classic Series '50s Stratocaster Lacquer
Road Worn '50s Stratocaster
50th Anniversary 1954 Stratocaster
50th Anniversary American Deluxe Stratocaster
50th Anniversary American Standard Stratocaster
50th Anniversary American Vintage 1957
    Stratocaster
50th Anniversary Stratocaster
50th Anniversary Stratocaster Relic
'54 Stratocaster (Custom Shop)
'54 Stratocaster FMT
'55 Stratocaster (Custom Shop)
'55 Dual-Mag Strat Journeyman Relic
'55 Historic 1955 NOS Stratocaster
'55 Rocking Dog Stratocaster
'55 Stratocaster Journeyman Relic
'56 Stratocaster (Custom Shop)
'56 Stratocaster Heavy Relic
'56 Stratocaster Journeyman Closet Classic
American Vintage '56 Stratocaster
American Vintage '56 Stratocaster Limited Edi-
    tion Roasted Ash
'57 Stratocaster (Custom Shop)
'57 Stratocaster (CS)
'57 Stratocaster (USA)
'57 Special Stratocaster
'57 Vintage Stratocaster (Japan)
American Vintage '57 Commemorative Strato-
    caster
Time Machine 1957 Stratocaster Relic
Vintage Custom 1957 Stratocaster NOS
Wildwood "10s" 1957 Limited Stratocaster Relic
'58 Stratocaster (Custom Shop)
'58 Stratocaster (Dakota Red)
'58 Limited Edition MIJ Stratocaster
'58 Stratocaster Journeyman Relic
Time Machine 1958 Stratocaster Heavy Relic
'59 Rocking Dog Stratocaster
'59 Stratocaster (Custom Shop)
1959 Stratocaster LTD Journeyman
American Vintage '59 Pine Stratocaster
American Vintage '59 Stratocaster
Time Machine 1959 Stratocaster
Wildwood "10s" 1959 Limited Stratocaster Relic
'60 Stratocaster (Custom Shop)
'60 Stratocaster FMT (Custom Shop)

Custom 1960 Stratocaster
'60s Stratocaster/Classic Series '60s Stratocaster
'60s Stratocaster/Time Machine 1960 Strato-
    caster
American Original '60s Stratocaster
Classic Player '60s Stratocaster
Classic Series '60s Stratocaster Lacquer
Limited Edition '60s Daybreak Stratocaster
Road Worn '60s Stratocaster
60th Anniversary '54 Stratocaster (Custom Shop)
60th Anniversary American Stratocaster
60th Anniversary American Vintage 1954
    Stratocaster
60th Anniversary Commemorative Stratocaster
60th Anniversary Presidential Stratocaster
'61 Stratocaster (Custom Shop)
Wildwood "10s" 1961 Limited Stratocaster
'62 Stratocaster (USA)
'62 Commemorative Stratocaster
'62 Heavy Relic Stratocaster
'62 Stratocaster ST62D/ST54 DEX2
'62 Stratocaster ST62US Reissue
'62 Vintage Stratocaster (Japan)
Dave's Guitar Shop American 1962 Stratocaster
Deluxe Vintage Player '62 Stratocaster
Vintage Custom 1962 Stratocaster
Willcutt Guitars True '62 Stratocaster
'63 Stratocaster (Custom Shop)
'63 Stratocaster Journeyman Relic
'64 Stratocaster (Custom Shop)
Time Machine 1964 Stratocaster Journeyman
    Relic
'65 Stratocaster (Custom Shop)
'65 Stratocaster Journeyman Closet Classic
American Vintage '65 Stratocaster
Time Machine 1965 Stratocaster Journeyman
    Relic
Total Tone '65 Stratocaster Relic
'66 Stratocaster (Custom Shop)
Time Machine 1967 Stratocaster Journeyman
    Relic Aged
Time Machine 1967 Stratocaster Journeyman
    Relic Custom Top
'68 Heavy Relic Stratocaster
'68 Reverse Strat Special (USA)
'68 Stratocaster (Japan)
'69 Stratocaster (Custom Shop)
Wildwood "10s" 1969 Limited Stratocaster
'70s Stratocaster/Classic Series '70s Stratocaster
American Vintage '70s Stratocaster
'72 Stratocaster (Japan)
'72 Stratocaster Limited Edition
75th Anniversary Commemorative Stratocaster
75th Anniversary Stratocaster
Acoustasonic Stratocaster
Aerodyne Classic Stratocaster
Aerodyne Stratocaster
Albert Hammond Jr. Signature Stratocaster
Aluminum Stratocaster (Custom Shop)
Aluminum Stratocaster American Standard
American Acoustasonic Stratocaster
American Classic Holoflake Stratocaster
American Classic Stratocaster

1976 Fender Starcaster
James Seldin

1954 Fender Stratocaster
Tony Sheedy

GUITARS

1954 Fender Stratocaster
Tony Sheedy

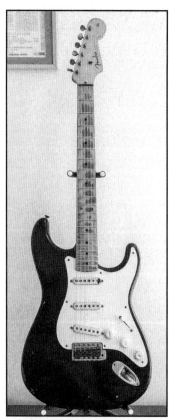

1956 Fender Stratocaster
David Stone

American Custom Stratocaster (Custom Shop)
American Deluxe Stratocaster
American Deluxe Stratocaster Dealer Event
American Deluxe Stratocaster Designer Series
American Deluxe Stratocaster FMT HSS
American Deluxe Stratocaster HSS Mahogany
American Elite Stratocaster
American Elite Stratocaster Limited Edition
American Longboard Stratocaster HSS
American Performer Stratocaster
American Special Stratocaster
American Standard Stratocaster Limited Edition
American Ultra Luxe Stratocaster
American Ultra Stratocaster
Ancho Poblano Stratocaster Journeyman Relic
Ancho Poblano Roasted Stratocaster Relic
Antigua Stratocaster
Artisan Series Stratocaster (Custom Shop)
Big Apple Stratocaster
Big Block Stratocaster
Big Head Stratocaster
Bill Carson Stratocaster
Billy Corgan Stratocaster
Blackie Stratocaster (Custom Shop)
Black Paisley Stratocaster
Blacktop Stratocaster
Mahogany Blacktop Stratocaster Limited Edition
Blue Flower Stratocaster
Bonnie Raitt Stratocaster
Bowling Ball/Marble Stratocaster
Buddy Guy Signature Stratocaster
Buddy Guy Standard Stratocaster
Buddy Holly Tribute Stratocaster
California Stratocaster/California Fat Strato-
  caster
Carroll Shelby Limited Edition Stratocaster
Carved Top Stratocaster HSS (Custom Shop)
Classic Player Stratocaster
Classic Player Stratocaster HH
Collector's Edition Stratocaster ('62 Reissue)
Contemporary Stratocaster (Custom Shop)
Contemporary Stratocaster (Import)
Crash Stratocaster
Custom Classic Stratocaster
Custom Deluxe Stratocaster
Custom Shop Limited Edition Stratocaster
Dave Murray Stratocaster
David Gilmour Signature Stratocaster
Deluxe Lone Star Stratocaster
Deluxe Players Special Edition Stratocaster
Deluxe Players Stratocaster
Deluxe Roadhouse Stratocaster
Deluxe Stratocaster
Deluxe Stratocaster HSS Plus Top With IOS
  Connectivity
Deluxe Stratocaster Plus
Dick Dale Stratocaster
Elite Stratocaster
EOB (Ed O'Brien) Sustainer Stratocaster
Eric Clapton Crossroads Stratocaster
Eric Clapton Gold Leaf Stratocaster
Eric Clapton Signature Journeyman Relic
  Stratocaster

Eric Clapton Signature Stratocaster (Custom
  Shop)
Eric Clapton Stratocaster
Eric Clapton Stratocaster (Custom Shop)
Eric Johnson 1954 "Virginia" Stratocaster
Eric Johnson Signature Stratocaster Thinline
Eric Johnson Stratocaster
Floyd Rose Classic Relic Stratocaster
Floyd Rose Classic Stratocaster (Strat HSS)
  (Strat HH)
Ford Shelby GT Stratocaster
Foto Flame Stratocaster
Freddy Tavares Aloha Stratocaster
FSR Stratocaster
George Fullerton 50th Anniversary '57 Strat
  Ltd. Ed. Set
George Harrison Rocky Stratocaster
Gold Stratocaster
Gold Elite Stratocaster
Gold Stratocaster (Custom Shop)
GT11 Stratocaster
H.E.R. Stratocaster
Hank Marvin Stratocaster
Hank Marvin 40th Anniversary Stratocaster
Harley-Davidson 90th Anniversary Stratocaster
Highway One Stratocaster/HSS
HM Strat (USA/Import)
HM Strat Limited Edition
Homer Haynes HLE Stratocaster
Hot Wheels Stratocaster
HRR Stratocaster/Floyd Rose HRR (Japan)
Ike Turner Tribute Stratocaster
Jeff Beck Signature Stratocaster (CS)
Jeff Beck Stratocaster
Jerry Donahue Hellecaster Stratocaster
Jim Root Stratocaster
Jimi Hendrix Limited Edition Stratocaster
  (Custom Shop)
Jimi Hendrix Monterey Pop Stratocaster
Jimi Hendrix Monterey Stratocaster
Jimi Hendrix Stratocaster
Jimi Hendrix Tribute Stratocaster
Jimi Hendrix Voodoo 29th Anniversary (Guitar
  Center) Stratocaster
Jimi Hendrix Voodoo Child Signature Strato-
  caster NOS
Jimi Hendrix Voodoo Child Stratocaster Jour-
  neyman Relic
Jimi Hendrix Voodoo Stratocaster
Jimmie Vaughan Tex-Mex Stratocaster
John Jorgenson Hellecaster Stratocaster
John Mayer Limited Edition Black1 Stratocaster
John Mayer Stratocaster
Kenny Wayne Shepherd Stratocaster
Koa Stratocaster
Kon Tiki Stratocaster
Lenny Stratocaster
Limited Roasted Tomatillo Stratocaster Relic
Lincoln Brewster Signature Stratocaster
Lite Ash Stratocaster Special Edition
Lone Star Stratocaster
Mark Kendrick Master Design '65 Stratocaster
Mark Knopfler Stratocaster

The *Vintage Guitar Price Guide* shows values for all-original, excellent condition instruments and, where applicable, with original case.

Masterbuilt Custom Shop Stratocaster
Matthias Jabs Signature Stratocaster
Michael Landau Signature Relic Stratocaster
   1963/1968
Milonga Deluxe Stratocaster
MLB Major League Baseball Stratocaster
Mod Shop Stratocaster
Modern Player Stratocaster HSH/HSS
Moto Limited Edition Stratocaster
Moto Set Stratocaster
Noventa Stratocaster
Orange Krush Limited Edition Stratocaster
Paisley Stratocaster
Parallel Universe Volume II Strat Jazz Deluxe
Parallel Universe Volume II Strat-Tele Hybrid
Playboy 40th Anniversary Stratocaster
Player Plus Stratocaster
Player Series Stratocaster
Post Modern Stratocaster (Custom Shop)
Post Modern Stratocaster Closet Classic (Custom Shop)
Post Modern Stratocaster Journeyman Relic (Custom Shop)
Post Modern Stratocaster NOS (Custom Shop)
Powerhouse/Powerhouse Deluxe Stratocaster
Proud Stratocaster
Rarities Stratocaster
Richie Sambora Stratocaster
Ritchie Blackmore Stratocaster
Ritchie Blackmore Tribute Stratocaster
Roadhouse Stratocaster
Robert Cray Signature Stratocaster
Robert Cray Stratocaster (Mexico)
Robin Trower Signature Stratocaster
Rory Gallagher Tribute Stratocaster
Sandblasted Stratocaster
Select Stratocaster
Set-Neck Stratocaster
Short-Scale (7/8) Stratocaster
So-Cal J.W. Black Stratocaster
So-Cal Speed Shop Stratocaster
Special Edition David Lozeau Art Stratocaster
Special Edition Stratocaster
Special Edition Stratocaster (Matching Headstock)
Special Edition White Opal Stratocaster
Splatter Stratocaster
Standard Roland Ready Stratocaster
Standard Stratocaster (Japan)
Standard Stratocaster (Mexico)
Standard Stratocaster Plus Top
Standard Stratocaster Satin Finish
Stevie Ray Vaughan Signature Stratocaster
Stevie Ray Vaughan Signature Stratocaster (Custom Shop)
Stevie Ray Vaughan Tribute #1 Stratocaster
Strat Plus
Stratocaster Junior
Stratocaster Pro Closet Classic (Custom Shop)
Stratocaster Pro NOS (Custom Shop)
Stratocaster Special
Stratocaster XII
Strat-o-Sonic
Sub Sonic Stratocaster

Super Stratocaster
Supreme Stratocaster
Tanqurey Tonic Stratocaster
Tash Sultana Stratocaster
Texas Special Stratocaster
The Edge Stratocaster
The Strat
Tie-Dye Stratocaster
Tom Delonge Stratocaster
Tom Morello "Soul Power" Stratocaster
Tree of Life Stratocaster
Turquoise Sparkle Stratocaster
U.S. Ultra/Ultra Plus Stratocaster
Ventures Limited Edition Stratocaster
VG Stratocaster
Vintage Hot Rod Stratocaster
Vintera Series Stratocaster
Walnut Elite Stratocaster
Walnut Stratocaster
Western Stratocaster
Whiteguard Stratocaster Limited Edition
Yngwie Malmsteen Signature Stratocaster (Custom Shop)
Yngwie Malmsteen Stratocaster

Stratocaster

1954-1981. Two-tone sunburst until '58, 3-tone after. Please refer to the Fender Guitar Intro Section for details on Fender color options.

Three-bolt neck '72-'81, otherwise 4-bolt. Unless noted, all Stratocasters listed have the Fender tremolo system. Non-tremolo models (aka hardtails) typically sell for less. Many guitarists feel the tremolo block helps produce a fuller range of sound. On average, many more tremolo models were made. One year, '58, seems to be a year where a greater percentage of non-tremolo models were made.

From '63-'70, Fender offered both the standard Brazilian rosewood fretboard and an optional maple fretboard. Prices listed here, for those years, are for the rosewood 'board models. Currently, the market considers the maple 'board (commonly referred to as a 'maple cap') to be a premium. The use of maple 'boards on Stratocasters was very rare and they can be worth up to 20% more than the values shown.

Renamed Standard Stratocaster for '82-'84 (see following listings), American Standard Stratocaster for '86-2000, the American Series Stratocaster for '00-'07, and the American Standard Stratocaster (again) for '08-'16. Currently called the American Professional Stratocaster.

MODEL YEAR	FEATURES	EXC. COND. LOW	EXC. COND. HIGH
1954	Very first '54, rare features	$200,000	$275,000
1954	Early-mid '54, typical features	$112,000	$210,000
1954	Sunburst, later production	$85,000	$120,000
1955	Late-'55, blond, nickel hw	$72,000	$150,000
1955	Sunburst, ash body	$62,000	$80,000
1956	Blond, nickel hw	$72,000	$150,000

1956 Fender Stratocaster (lefty)
HI Guitars

1959 Fender Stratocaster
Tracy Farmer

1962 Fender Statocaster

Tony Sheedy

1963 Fender Stratocaster

Scott Dailey

MODEL YEAR	FEATURES	EXC. COND. LOW	HIGH
1956	Mary Kaye, gold hw	$112,000	$165,000
1956	Sunburst, alder body	$56,000	$72,000
1956	Sunburst, ash body	$62,000	$80,000
1956	Sunburst, non-trem	$45,000	$55,000
1957	Blond, nickel hw	$65,000	$150,000
1957	Mary Kaye, gold hw	$110,000	$165,000
1957	Sunburst	$50,000	$60,000
1957	Sunburst, non-trem	$40,000	$50,000
1958	Blond, nickel hw	$60,000	$150,000
1958	Mary Kaye, gold hw	$90,000	$165,000
1958	Sunburst 2-tone, maple	$50,000	$60,000
1958	Sunburst 2-tone, non-trem	$40,000	$50,000
1958	Sunburst 3-tone, maple	$45,000	$55,000
1958	Sunburst 3-tone, non-trem	$38,000	$48,000
1959	Blond, nickel hw, maple 'board	$55,000	$150,000
1959	Blond, nickel hw, slab 'board	$50,000	$85,000
1959	Custom color	$85,000	$175,000
1959	Mary Kaye, gold hw, maple	$85,000	$165,000
1959	Mary Kaye, gold hw, slab	$85,000	$150,000
1959	Sunburst 3-tone, maple	$40,000	$50,000
1959	Sunburst, non-trem, slab	$30,000	$40,000
1959	Sunburst, slab, 1-ply 'guard	$35,000	$45,000
1959	Sunburst, slab, 3-ply 'guard	$35,000	$45,000
1960	Common color	$50,000	$75,000
1960	Rare color	$75,000	$175,000
1960	Sunburst	$36,000	$50,000
1961	Common color	$45,000	$75,000
1961	Rare color	$65,000	$175,000
1961	Sunburst	$36,000	$50,000
1962	Common color, early slab	$45,000	$75,000
1962	Common color, late curve	$40,000	$55,000
1962	Rare color, early slab	$65,000	$175,000
1962	Rare color, late curve	$55,000	$175,000
1962	Sunburst, early slab	$36,000	$50,000
1962	Sunburst, late curve	$32,000	$42,000
1963	Common color	$40,000	$55,000
1963	Rare color	$55,000	$175,000
1963	Sunburst	$32,000	$42,000

MODEL YEAR	FEATURES	EXC. COND. LOW	HIGH
1964	Common color	$40,000	$55,000
1964	Rare color	$55,000	$175,000
1964	Sunburst, spaghetti logo	$32,000	$42,000
1964	Sunburst, transition logo	$25,000	$33,000
1965	Common color	$35,000	$45,000
1965	Rare color	$50,000	$65,000
1965	Sunburst, early-'65 green 'guard	$25,000	$35,000
1965	Sunburst, late-'65 F-plate	$20,000	$25,000
1965	Sunburst, white 'guard	$23,000	$30,000
1966	Common color	$35,000	$45,000
1966	Common color, bound 'board (rare)	$36,000	$47,000
1966	Rare color	$45,000	$60,000
1966	Sunburst, block markers	$25,000	$33,000
1966	Sunburst, dot markers	$20,000	$25,000
1967	Common color	$30,000	$40,000
1967	Rare color	$45,000	$60,000
1967	Sunburst	$20,000	$25,000
1968	Common color, nitro	$30,000	$40,000
1968	Common color, poly	$28,000	$36,000
1968	Common color, poly body, nitro neck	$28,000	$36,000
1968	Rare color, nitro	$40,000	$50,000
1968	Rare color, poly	$36,000	$45,000
1968	Rare color, poly body, nitro neck	$36,000	$45,000
1968	Sunburst, nitro	$20,000	$25,000
1968	Sunburst, poly	$15,000	$20,000
1968	Sunburst, poly body, nitro neck	$16,000	$21,000
1969	Common color	$25,000	$30,000
1969	Rare color	$30,000	$40,000
1969	Sunburst	$15,000	$20,000
1970	Common color, 4-bolt	$18,000	$22,000
1970	Rare color, 4-bolt	$25,000	$30,000
1970	Sunburst, 4-bolt	$13,000	$17,000
1971	Common color, 4-bolt	$15,000	$20,000
1971	Early-mid '71, sunburst, 4-bolt	$12,000	$16,000
1971	Late '71, sunburst, 3-bolt	$5,500	$7,000
1971	Rare color, 4-bolt	$20,000	$25,000
1972	Common color, 3-bolt	$6,500	$8,500
1972	Rare color, 3-bolt	$10,000	$12,000
1972	Sunburst, 3-bolt	$5,500	$7,000
1973	Common color	$6,000	$8,000
1973	Natural	$4,500	$6,000
1973	Rare color	$8,000	$10,000

The *Vintage Guitar Price Guide* shows values for all-original, excellent condition instruments and, where applicable, with original case.

The Official Vintage Guitar magazine Price Guide 2025 **Fender** Standard Strat (includes "Smith Strat") — 40th Ann. 1954 Strat Ltd. Ed. **109**

GUITARS

MODEL YEAR	FEATURES	EXC. COND. LOW	HIGH
1973	Sunburst	$5,000	$6,500
1973	Walnut	$4,500	$6,000
1974	Black, blond, white (white parts)	$5,000	$6,500
1974	Natural (white parts)	$4,000	$5,500
1974	Sunburst (white parts)	$4,500	$6,000
1974	Walnut (white parts)	$4,500	$6,000
1975	Black, blond, white (black parts)	$4,500	$6,000
1975	Black, blond, white (white parts)	$5,000	$6,500
1975	Early-'75, sunburst (white parts)	$4,500	$6,000
1975	Late-'75, sunburst (black parts)	$4,000	$5,000
1975	Natural (black parts)	$3,500	$4,500
1975	Walnut (black parts)	$3,250	$4,250
1976-1977	Various colors	$3,500	$4,500
1978	Various colors	$3,000	$4,000
1979	Antiqua	$3,500	$4,500
1979	Various colors	$3,000	$4,000
1980	Various colors	$3,000	$4,000
1980-1981	International colors	$3,250	$4,250
1981	Various colors	$3,000	$4,000

Standard Stratocaster (includes "Smith Strat")

1981-1984. Replaces the Stratocaster. Renamed the American Standard Stratocaster for '86-'00 (see next listing). Renamed American Series Stratocaster in '00. From '81/'82 to mid-'83, 3 knobs same as regular Strat but with 4-bolt neck. In August '81, Dan Smith was hired by Bill Schultz and Fender produced an alder body, 4-bolt neck, 21-fret, small headstock Standard Stratocaster that has been nicknamed the Smith Strat (made from Dec. '81-'83). Mid-'83 to the end of '84 2 knobs and 'guard mounted input jack. Not to be confused with current Standard Stratocaster, which is made in Mexico.

1981-1983	Various colors	$2,500	$3,250
1983-1984	Sunburst, 2-knob	$1,375	$1,750
1983-1984	Various colors, 2-knob	$1,375	$1,750

American Standard Stratocaster

1986-1999, 2008-2016. Fender's new name for the American-made Strat when reintroducing it after CBS sold the company. The only American-made Strats made in 1985 were the '57 and '62 models. See Stratocaster and Standard Stratocaster for earlier models. Name used again for '08-'16, various pickup options including SSS, HH, HSH, HSS, Fat and HSS plus. Renamed American Series Stratocaster in 2000 and again renamed the American Professional Series Stratocaster in 2017.

1986-1999	Various colors & options	$1,000	$1,500
2008-2016	Various colors & options	$1,000	$1,375

American Series Stratocaster

2000-2007. Ash or alder body, rosewood or maple 'board, dot markers, various pickup options including HSS and HH, 5-way switch, hand polished fret edges. Renamed the American Standard Stratocaster again in '08.

2000-2007	Various colors & options	$1,000	$1,375
2004	50th Anniversary	$1,000	$1,375

American Professional Stratocaster

2017-2020. Model replaces American Standard Series Strat, redesign includes new V-Mod pickups, narrow-tall frets, new 'deep C' neck profile, genuine bone nut, various colors. Also available left-hand model. Renamed American Professional II in '20.

2017-2020	High-end features	$1,250	$1,625
2017-2020	Low-end features	$1,000	$1,375

American Professional II Stratocaster

2020-present. Various pickup options, woods and various colors.

2020-2023	HSS	$1,125	$1,500
2020-2023	Roasted Pine	$1,125	$1,500
2020-2023	Roasted Pine HSS	$1,125	$1,500
2020-2023	SSS	$1,125	$1,500

20th Century American Standard Stratocaster

1999. Limited Edition of the last 100 Strats off the line in 1999. COA signed by William Schultz. "20th Century American Standard" headstock stamp and neckplate.

1999		$1,250	$1,625

21st Century American Standard Stratocaster

2000. Limited Edition of the first 100 Strats off the line in 2000. COA signed by William Schultz. "21st Century American Standard" headstock stamp and neckplate.

2000		$1,250	$1,625

25th Anniversary Stratocaster

1979-1980. Limited Edition, 4-bolt neck plate, standard truss rod, has ANNIVERSARY on upper body horn, early-'79 has pearlescent finish which flaked, late-'79-'80 was changed to silver metallic.

1979	Early run, pearlescent	$2,250	$2,750
1979-1980	Silver	$2,500	$3,000

30th Anniversary Guitar Center Stratocaster

1994		$1,250	$1,625

35th Anniversary Stratocaster

1989-1991. Custom Shop, 500 made, figured maple top, Lace Sensor pickups, Eric Clapton preamp circuit.

1989-1991		$3,000	$4,000

40th Anniversary 1954 Stratocaster Limited Edition

1994. Standard production (not Custom Shop), 1,954 made, "40th Anniversary STRATOCASTER 1994" neck plate, serial number series xxxx of 1954, spaghetti logo, tremolo, Kluson tuners, solid maple neck, 2-tone sunburst semi-transparent finish on ash body.

1994		$2,500	$3,500

1983 Fender "Smith Strat"
Bill Beals

Fender American Professional II Stratocaster

**1996 Fender 50th
Anniversary Stratocaster**

Imaged by Heritage Auctions, HA.com

**2002 Fender '56 Stratocaster
NOS (Custom Shop)**

Cream City Music

MODEL YEAR	FEATURES	EXC. COND. LOW	HIGH

40th Anniversary American Standard Stratocaster
1994 only. US-made, American Standard model (not Custom Shop), plain top, appearance similar to a '54 maple-neck Strat, sunburst, 2 neck plates offered "40th Anniversary" and "40th Anniversary and still rockin'".

1994		$1,250	$1,625

40th Anniversary Stratocaster Diamond Dealer
1994 only. Custom Shop model, 150 made, 40th Anniversary headstock inlay, flamed maple top on ash body, '54-'94 inlay at 12th fret, gold etched 'guard, gold hardware, sunburst.

1994		$5,000	$7,000

40th Anniversary Stratocaster ST62 (Japan)
1994 only. Made in Japan, '62 reissue specs.

1994		$1,250	$1,625

'50s Stratocaster/Classic Series '50s Stratocaster
1985-2019. 'Made in Japan' logo until 'Crafted in Japan' logo mid-'97, basswood body, then mid-'99 made in Mexico with poplar or alder body. Foto-Flame finish offered '92-'94.

1985-1996	Made in Japan	$1,250	$1,625
1997-1999	Crafted in Japan	$800	$1,125
1999-2019	Mexico	$600	$800

American Original '50s Stratocaster
2018-2023. Vintage-style appointments, 3 pickups, alder or ash body (White Blonde only), 2-color sunburst or Aztec Gold.

2018-2023		$1,500	$2,000

Classic Player '50s Stratocaster
2006-2019. U.S.-made components but assembled in Mexico, alder body, maple neck and 'board, vintage-style pickups.

2006-2019		$600	$800
2014	50th Anniversary	$700	$950

Classic Series '50s Stratocaster Lacquer
2014-2019. Candy Apple Red nitro-lacquer finish.

2014-2019		$600	$800

Road Worn '50s Stratocaster
2009-2019. Made in Mexico, maple 'board, '50s specs, aged finish.

2009-2019		$800	$1,125

50th Anniversary 1954 Stratocaster
2004-2005. Custom Shop, celebrates 50 years of the Strat, 1954 specs and materials, replica form-fit case, certificate, Fender took orders for these up to December 31, 2004.

2004-2005		$3,500	$4,500

50th Anniversary American Deluxe Stratocaster
2004-2005. Deluxe series features, engraved neck plate, tweed case.

2004-2005		$1,500	$2,000

50th Anniversary American Standard Stratocaster
2004. Mexico, engraved neck plate, '54 replica pickups, tweed case.

2004		$800	$1,125

50th Anniversary American Vintage 1957 Stratocaster
1996. V serial number, 50th decal back of headstock.

1996		$1,625	$2,250

50th Anniversary Stratocaster
1995-1996. Custom Shop, 2500 made, flame maple top, 3 vintage-style pickups, gold hardware, gold 50th Anniversary (of Fender) coin on back of the headstock, sunburst.

1995-1996		$1,750	$2,500

50th Anniversary Stratocaster Relic
1995-1996. Custom Shop relic model, aged played-in feel, diamond headstock inlay, Shoreline Gold finish.

1995-1996		$3,500	$4,500

'54 Stratocaster (Custom Shop)
1992-1998. Classic reissue, ash body, Custom '50s pickups, gold-plated hardware.

1992-1998		$3,000	$4,000

'54 Stratocaster FMT
1992-1998. Custom Classic reissue, Flame Maple Top, also comes in gold hardware edition.

1992-1998		$3,000	$4,000

'55 Stratocaster (Custom Shop)
2006, 2013. 1st version is Limited Edition of 100 Relics with 2-tone sunburst; 2nd version is Closet Classic. Both include certificate of authenticity.

2006	Relic	$3,000	$4,000
2013	Closet Classic	$3,000	$4,000

'55 Dual-Mag Strat Journeyman Relic
2017-2019. Custom Shop Limited Edition, certificate of authenticity.

2017-2019		$3,000	$4,000

'55 Historic 1955 NOS Stratocaster
2018-2020. Custom Shop NOS, certificate of authenticity.

2018-2020		$3,000	$4,000

'55 Rocking Dog Stratocaster
2007. Custom Shop, commissioned by Garrett Park Guitars, various colors.

2007		$3,000	$4,000

'55 Stratocaster Journeyman Relic
2017. Custom Shop, vintage-correct appointments, certificate of authenticity.

2017		$3,000	$4,000

'56 Stratocaster (Custom Shop)
1996-2016. Most detailed replica (and most expensive to date) of '56 Strat, including electronics and pickups, offered with rosewood or maple 'board, gold hardware is +$100.

1996-1998	Cunetto built Relic	$3,500	$4,500
1997-1998	Cunetto era (staff built)	$3,000	$4,000
1999-2010	Closet Classic	$3,000	$4,000
1999-2010	NOS	$3,000	$4,000
1999-2014	Relic	$3,000	$4,000
2014-2016	Heavy relic	$3,000	$4,000

'56 Stratocaster Heavy Relic
2020. Custom Shop, certificate of authenticity.

2020		$3,000	$4,000

The *Vintage Guitar Price Guide* shows values for all-original, excellent condition instruments and, where applicable, with original case.

MODEL YEAR	FEATURES	EXC. COND. LOW	HIGH

'56 Stratocaster Journeyman Closet Classic

2020. Custom Shop, certificate of authenticity.

2020		$3,000	$4,000

American Vintage '56 Stratocaster

2013-2018. Vintage '56 style, maple 'board, black, Shell Pink or aged white blonde.

2013-2018		$1,500	$2,000

American Vintage '56 Stratocaster Limited Edition Roasted Ash

2017. Roasted ash body, roasted maple neck and 'board, nitro lacquer finish.

2017		$2,000	$2,500

'57 Stratocaster (Custom Shop)

1994-1996. Custom Shop models can be distinguished by the original certificate that comes with the guitar. Replaced by the more authentic, higher-detailed '56 Custom Shop Stratocaster by '99.

1994-1996	Various colors	$3,000	$4,000

'57 Stratocaster (CS)

2007, 2010-2016. Custom Shop models, Relic ('07), Closet Classic ('10-'13), Heavy Relic ('15-'16), NOS Dealer Select program ('13-'16) where models are built for specific dealers.

2007	Relic	$3,000	$4,000
2010-2013	Closet Classic	$3,000	$4,000
2013-2016	NOS	$3,000	$4,000
2015-2016	Heavy relic	$3,000	$4,000

'57 Stratocaster (USA)

1982-2012. U.S.-made at the Fullerton, California plant ('82-'85) and at the Corona, California plant ('85-'12), American Vintage series.

1982-1984	SN: V series	$3,500	$4,500
1986-1989	Common color	$2,000	$2,500
1986-1989	Rare color	$2,250	$3,000
1990-1999		$1,500	$2,000
1990-1999	Rare color	$2,000	$2,500
2000-2012	Various colors	$1,500	$2,000

'57 Special Stratocaster

1992-1993. Custom Shop, limited run of 60, flamed maple top, birdseye maple neck, sunburst.

1992-1993		$3,000	$4,000

'57 Vintage Stratocaster (Japan)

1982-1998. Made in Japan logo, JV serial numbers '82-'84, E serial '84-'87, Crafted in Japan logo by '98, various colors.

1982-1985	MIJ logo	$1,750	$2,250
1998	CIJ logo	$1,125	$1,500

American Vintage '57 Commemorative Stratocaster

2007. Limited production, 1957-2007 Commemorative logo neckplate.

2007-2012		$1,500	$2,000

Time Machine 1957 Stratocaster Relic

2020. Custom Shop Time Machine series, certificate of authenticity.

2020		$2,500	$3,250

Vintage Custom 1957 Stratocaster NOS

2019-present. Custom Shop, maple 'board, aged white blonde with gold hardware.

2019-2023		$3,000	$4,000

Wildwood "10s" 1957 Limited Stratocaster Relic

2014-2015. Custom Shop Dealer Select model for Wildwood Music, '57 specs with 3 single coil or HSS pickups, certificate of authenticity.

2014-2015		$3,000	$4,000

'58 Stratocaster (Custom Shop)

1996-1999. Ash body, Fat '50s pickups, chrome or gold hardware (gold is +$100.), Custom Shop models have certificate of authenticity.

1996-1999	Various colors	$3,000	$4,000

'58 Stratocaster (Dakota Red)

1996. Custom Shop, run of 30 made in Dakota Red with matching headstock, maple neck, Texas special pickups, gold hardware.

1996		$3,000	$4,000

'58 Limited Edition MIJ Stratocaster

2013. Made in Japan logo, 252 offered.

2013		$1,250	$1,625

'58 Stratocaster Journeyman Relic

2016. Custom Shop, vintage-correct appointments, certificate of authenticity.

2016		$3,000	$4,000

Time Machine 1958 Stratocaster Heavy Relic

2020. Custom Shop Time Machine series, certificate of authenticity.

2020		$3,000	$4,000

'59 Rocking Dog Stratocaster

2007. Custom Shop, commissioned by Garrett Park Guitars, based on '59 rosewood 'board Strat, various colors.

2007		$3,000	$4,000

'59 Stratocaster (Custom Shop)

2010-2013. Rosewood 'board, vintage appointments, COA, various colors with Relic or Heavy Relic finish.

2010-2013	Relic	$3,000	$4,000
2013	Heavy Relic	$3,000	$4,000

1959 Stratocaster LTD Journeyman

2019-2020. Custom Shop, limited edition, vintage and modern appointments, COA, various colors with Relic or Heavy Relic lacquer finish.

2019	Relic	$3,000	$4,000
2019-2020	Heavy Relic	$3,000	$4,000

American Vintage '59 Pine Stratocaster

2017. Limited Edition neck plate, pine body built from re-claimed 100-year-old wood, 3 vintage '59 single-coil pickups.

2017		$1,500	$2,000

American Vintage '59 Stratocaster

2013-2018. Maple or slab rosewood 'board.

2012-2018		$1,500	$2,000

Time Machine 1959 Stratocaster

2019-2021. Custom Shop Time Machine series, vintage and modern appointments, COA, various colors with Relic or Heavy Relic lacquer finish.

2019-2020	Relic	$3,000	$4,000
2020-2021	Heavy Relic	$3,000	$4,000

2003 Fender '57 Stratocaster
Rivington Guitars

Fender Vintage Custom 1957 Stratocaster NOS

Fender American Original
'60s Stratocaster

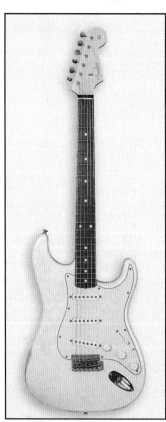

Fender Wildwood "10s"
1961 Limited Stratocaster

MODEL YEAR	FEATURES	EXC. COND. LOW	HIGH

Wildwood "10s" 1959 Limited Stratocaster Relic

2011-2017. Custom Shop, quartersawn maple neck, Brazilian rosewood 'board, 3 pickups, faded 3-color sunburst. Limited Edition neck plate decal, and certificate of authenticity.

2011	Maple 'board	$4,500	$5,500
2011-2017	Brazilian 'board	$7,500	$10,000

'60 Stratocaster (Custom Shop)

1992-1999. 3 Texas Special pickups, various colors, optional gold hardware is +$100, with certificate of authenticity. In 2000 the '60 Stratocaster name was applied to the Time Machine model (see following).

1992-1999		$3,000	$4,000

'60 Stratocaster FMT (Custom Shop)

1997-1999. Flame maple top (FMT).

1997-1999		$3,000	$4,000

Custom 1960 Stratocaster

1994. Short run of 20 custom ordered and specified instruments that have 1960 specs along with other specs such as a pearloid 'guard, matching headstock color, came with certificate of authenticity.

1994		$3,000	$4,000

'60s Stratocaster/Classic Series '60s Stratocaster

1985-2019. 'Made in Japan' logo until 'Crafted in Japan' logo mid-'97, basswood body, then mid-'99 made in Mexico with poplar or alder body. Foto-Flame finish offered '92-'94.

1985-1996	Made in Japan	$1,250	$1,625
1997-1999	Crafted in Japan	$800	$1,125
1999-2019	Mexico	$600	$800

'60s Stratocaster/Time Machine 1960 Stratocaster

1996-2020. Custom Shop Relic/Time Machine. For '96-'99 was called the '60s Stratocaster, in 2000 name was changed to Time Machine 1960 Stratocaster. Heavy Relic began late-'15. Optional gold hardware is +$100. Vince Cunetto and company did the aging of the guitars to mid-1999. The price includes the original Certificate of Authenticity, a guitar without the original COA is worth less than the values shown.

1996-1998	Cunetto built Relic	$3,500	$4,500
1997-1999	Cunetto era (staff built)	$3,000	$4,000
1999-2010	Closet Classic	$3,000	$4,000
1999-2010	NOS	$3,000	$4,000
1999-2015	Relic	$3,000	$4,000
2015-2020	Heavy relic	$3,000	$4,000

American Original '60s Stratocaster

2018-2023. Vintage-style appointments, 3 pickups, alder body, 3-color sunburst. Candy Apple Red or Olympic White.

2018-2023		$1,500	$2,000

Classic Player '60s Stratocaster

2006-2019. U.S.-made components but assembled in Mexico, alder body, maple neck, rosewood 'board, vintage-style pickups.

2006-2019		$600	$800

MODEL YEAR	FEATURES	EXC. COND. LOW	HIGH

Classic Series '60s Stratocaster Lacquer

2014-2019. Made in Mexico, 3-color sunburst nitro-lacquer finish.

2014-2019		$600	$800

Limited Edition '60s Daybreak Stratocaster

2019-2020. Traditional series, made in Japan, Olympic White with matching headstock, gold hardware.

2019-2020		$600	$800

Road Worn '60s Stratocaster

2009-2020. Rosewood 'board, '60s specs, aged finish. Renamed Vintera Road Worn '60s Strat in '20.

2009-2020		$600	$800

60th Anniversary '54 Stratocaster (Custom Shop)

2014. Heavy relic, certificate of authenticity, 60th guitar case.

2014		$3,000	$4,000

60th Anniversary American Stratocaster

2006-2007. Celebrates Fender's 60th, US-made, 'Sixty Years' decal logo on headstock, engraved 60th Anniversary neck plate, Z-series serial number, coin on back of headstock, sunburst only, paperwork.

2006-2007	American flag logo	$1,500	$2,000

60th Anniversary American Vintage 1954 Stratocaster

2014-2016. 1,954 built, came with reproduction 1954 paperwork and 1954 Anniversary Strat Certificate.

2014-2016		$1,500	$2,000

60th Anniversary Commemorative Stratocaster

2014. Celebrates the Strat's 60th, US-made, 60th Anniversary neckplate, 60th medallion on back of headstock, gold hardware, special case, commemorative book.

2014		$1,250	$1,625

60th Anniversary Presidential Stratocaster

2006. Custom Shop, Diamond (60th) anniversary, limited to 100, bookmatched maple top stained using grapes from Hill Family Winery (California), '1946-2006' logo on neck, 'Limited Edition 60th Anniv. Presidential' neck plate logo, certificate of authenticity.

2006		$6,500	$8,000

'61 Stratocaster (Custom Shop)

2001-2012. Relic, certificate of authenticity.

2001-2012		$3,000	$4,000

Wildwood "10s" 1961 Limited Stratocaster

2010-present. Custom Shop, NOS, relic or heavy relic, quartersawn maple and AA flame maple necks, 3 pickups, "faded" thin nitro finishes in multiple colors.

2010-2016	NOS	$3,000	$4,000
2010-2023	Relic	$3,000	$4,000

'62 Stratocaster (USA)

1982-1984, 1986-2012. Made at Fullerton plant ('82-'84) then at Corona plant ('86-2012), American Vintage series.

1982-1984	SN: V series	$3,500	$4,500
1986-1989	Common color	$2,000	$2,500
1986-1989	Rare color	$2,250	$3,000
1990-1999	Common color	$1,500	$2,000

MODEL YEAR	FEATURES	EXC. COND. LOW	HIGH
1990-1999	Rare color	$1,875	$2,500
2000-2012	Common color	$1,500	$2,000

'62 Commemorative Stratocaster

2007. Limited production, part of American Vintage Series, 1957-2007 Commemorative logo neckplate.

2007		$1,500	$2,000

'62 Heavy Relic Stratocaster

2007-2010. Custom Shop Dealer Select series, extreme Relic work.

2007-2010		$3,000	$4,000

'62 Stratocaster ST62D/ST54 DEX2

1996. Made in Japan, '54 maple neck, '62 body.

1996		$1,750	$2,250

'62 Stratocaster ST62US Reissue

2008-2012. Crafted in Japan, US-made 'vintage' pickups.

2008-2012		$700	$900

'62 Vintage Stratocaster (Japan)

1982-1984. Made in Japan, JV serial numbers, various colors.

1982-1984		$1,750	$2,250

Dave's Guitar Shop American 1962 Stratocaster

2019-2020. Limited Edition, various colors with nitro lacquer finish.

2019-2020		$1,500	$2,000

Deluxe Vintage Player '62 Stratocaster

2005-2006. Limited Edition, vintage and modern features based upon '62 specs, 3 Samarium Cobalt Noiseless pickups, Deluxe American Standard electronics, Olympic White or Ice Blue Metallic.

2005-2006		$1,500	$2,000

Vintage Custom 1962 Stratocaster

2019-present. Custom Shop Limited Edition, NOS finish, alder body, maple neck and 'board, 3-color sunburst.

2019-2023		$3,000	$4,000

Willcutt Guitars True '62 Stratocaster

2016-2020. Custom Shop, limited run for Bob Will-cutt Guitars, 4 models; 'V' neck, '59 'C' neck, '60s 'C' neck and large 'C' neck.

2016-2020		$3,000	$4,000

'63 Stratocaster (Custom Shop)

2015-2018. Time Machine series, Relic in '15-'17, Heavy Relic '18.

2015-2017	Relic	$3,000	$4,000
2018	Heavy Relic	$3,000	$4,000

'63 Stratocaster Journeyman Relic

2015. Custom Shop, vintage-correct appointments, alder body, bird's-eye maple neck, rosewood 'board, 3 single-coil pickups, certificate of authenticity.

2015		$3,000	$4,000

'64 Stratocaster (Custom Shop)

2009-2014. Relic or Closet Classic, certificate of authenticity.

2009-2012	Relic	$3,000	$4,000
2011-2014	Closet Classic	$3,000	$4,000

Time Machine 1964 Stratocaster Journeyman Relic

2018-2020. Custom Shop Time Machine series, vintage-correct appointments, certificate of authenticity.

2018-2020		$3,000	$4,000

'65 Stratocaster (Custom Shop)

1998-1999, 2003-2006, 2010 (no Closet Classic). Custom Shop model, '65 small-headstock specs, rosewood or maple cap 'board, transition logo, offered in NOS, Relic, or Closet Classic versions.

1998-1999	Cunetto era (staff built)	$3,000	$4,000
2003-2006	Closet Classic	$3,000	$4,000
2003-2010	NOS	$3,000	$4,000
2003-2010	Relic	$3,000	$4,000

'65 Stratocaster Journeyman Closet Classic

2019-2020. Custom Shop, vintage-correct appointments, certificate of authenticity.

2019-2020		$3,000	$4,000

American Vintage '65 Stratocaster

2013-2017. V serial number, flash coat finish, various colors, some with matching headstock.

2013-2017		$1,500	$2,000

Time Machine 1965 Stratocaster Journeyman Relic

2010. Custom Shop Time Machine series, vintage-correct appointments, certificate of authenticity.

2010		$3,000	$4,000

Total Tone '65 Stratocaster Relic

2013. Custom Shop Limited Edition, alder body, maple neck, reverse wound middle pickup for noise reduction, various colors with Relic nitro lacquer finish.

2013		$3,000	$4,000

'66 Stratocaster (Custom Shop)

2004-2008. Custom Shop model, offered in Closet Classic, NOS or Relic versions.

2004-2008	Closet Classic	$3,000	$4,000
2004-2008	NOS	$3,000	$4,000
2004-2008	Relic	$3,000	$4,000

Time Machine 1967 Stratocaster Journeyman Relic Aged

2020. Custom Shop Time Machine series, vintage-correct appointments.

2020		$3,000	$4,000

Time Machine 1967 Stratocaster Journeyman Relic Custom Top

2020. Custom Shop Time Machine series, vintage-correct appointments.

2020		$3,000	$4,000

'68 Heavy Relic Stratocaster

2007-2010. Custom Shop Dealer Select, extreme relic work.

2007-2010		$3,000	$4,000

'68 Reverse Strat Special (USA)

2001-2002. With special reverse left-hand neck, large headstock (post-CBS style).

2001-2002		$3,000	$4,000

'68 Stratocaster (Japan)

1996-1999, 2013. Part of Collectables Series, '68 specs including large headstock, sunburst, natural or Olympic White.

1996-1999		$1,250	$1,625
2013		$1,125	$1,400

2003 Fender '62 Stratocaster
Tom Pfeifer

1984 Fender '62 Vintage Stratocaster
Tom Pfeifer

GUITARS

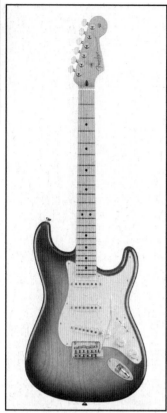

Fender 75th Anniversary
Commemorative Stratocaster

2010 Fender American
Deluxe Stratocaster
Cream City Music

MODEL YEAR	FEATURES	EXC. COND. LOW	HIGH

'69 Stratocaster (Custom Shop)
1997-2012, 2016. Large headstock, U-shaped maple neck with rosewood or maple cap options, '69-style finish, gold hardware is +$100, since 2000, offered in NOS, Relic, or Closet Classic (no CC after '08) versions. Heavy Relic in '16.

1997-1999	Cunetto era (staff built)	$3,000	$4,000
2000-2008	Closet Classic	$3,000	$4,000
2000-2009	NOS	$3,000	$4,000
2000-2012	Relic	$3,000	$4,000
2016	Heavy Relic	$3,000	$4,000

Wildwood "10s" 1969 Limited Stratocaster
2014. Custom Shop, Relic, Jimi Hendrix specs, certificate of authenticity.

2014		$3,000	$4,000

'70s Stratocaster/Classic Series '70s Stratocaster
1999-2019. Made in Mexico, large headstock, white pickups and knobs, rosewood 'board.

1999-2019		$600	$800

American Vintage '70s Stratocaster
2009-2012. Large '70s headstock, early '70s white pickups and knobs, 3-bolt neck. Hardtail version in '15.

2009-2012		$1,500	$2,000

'72 Stratocaster (Japan)
1985-1996. Basswood body, maple 'board, large headstock, various colors (does not include the Paisley '72).

1985-1996		$1,750	$2,250

'72 Stratocaster Limited Edition
2013. Made in Japan for US domestic sales, 144 made, large headstock, bullet truss rod, 3-bolt maple neck, 21 frets, 3 Alnico pickups.

2013		$750	$1,000

75th Anniversary Commemorative Stratocaster
2021-2023. US-made, limited edition, inlaid 75th Anniversary ingot back of headstock, gold hardware, 2-color Bourbon Burst gloss finish. Includes custom Inca Silver case with Lake Placid Blue interior.

2021-2023		$1,500	$2,000

75th Anniversary Stratocaster
2021-2023. Made in Mexico, 75th Anniversary neck plate, Diamond Anniversary satin finish with matching painted headstock.

2021-2023		$600	$800

Acoustasonic Stratocaster
2003-2009. Hollowed out alder Strat body with braceless graphite top, 3 in-bridge Fishman piezo pickups, acoustic sound hole.

2003-2009		$750	$975

Aerodyne Classic Stratocaster
2020. Limited run made in Japan, figured maple top, rosewood 'board, 3 pickups, various colors with gloss poly finish.

2020		$750	$950

Aerodyne Stratocaster
2004-2009. Import Strat with Aerodyne body profile, bound body, black.

2004-2009		$750	$975

Albert Hammond Jr. Signature Stratocaster
2018-present. Made in Mexico, styled after his 1985 reissue of a '72 Strat.

2018-2023		$600	$800

Aluminum Stratocaster (Custom Shop)
1994. Custom Shop aluminum bodies, chrome body with black 'guard, black body with chrome 'guard, or green with black lines and red swirls. There are also several Custom Shop one-offs with aluminum bodies.

1993-1994		$3,000	$4,000

Aluminum Stratocaster American Standard
1994-1995. Aluminum-bodied American Standard with anodized finish in blue marble, purple marble or red, silver and blue stars and stripes. Some with 40th Anniversary designation. There is also a Custom Shop version.

1994-1995	Various patterns & options	$2,000	$2,500

American Acoustasonic Stratocaster
2019-present. Solid A sitka spruce top, mahogany back and sides, ebony 'board, various colors. Also offered with cocobolo and ziricote top.

2019-2023		$1,500	$2,000
2020-2023	Cocobolo top	$2,250	$3,000

American Classic Holoflake Stratocaster
1992-1993. Custom Shop model, splatter/sparkle finish, pearloid 'guard.

1992-1993		$3,000	$4,000

American Classic Stratocaster
1992-1999. Custom Shop version of American Standard, 3 pickups, tremolo, rosewood 'board, nickel or gold-plated hardware, various colors.

1992-1999	Various options	$3,000	$4,000

American Custom Stratocaster (Custom Shop)
2020-present. Custom Shop American Custom series, various woods and colors.

2020-2023		$3,125	$4,000

American Deluxe Stratocaster
1998-2016. Premium alder or ash body, maple neck, various pickup options including SSS, HSS, HSH, HSS Plus, Fat and Shawbucker, various colors.

1998-2016	Various options	$1,375	$1,750

American Deluxe Stratocaster Dealer Event
2013. Sold at private dealer event at Fender Corona, various premium tonewoods, various colors and finishes.

2013		$1,500	$2,000

American Deluxe Stratocaster Designer Series
2004-2015. Limited production, various upgrades such as flamed maple top, mahogany, etc.

2004-2015		$1,500	$2,000

American Deluxe Stratocaster FMT HSS
2004-2009. Flame maple top version of the HSS.

2004-2009		$1,500	$2,000

The Official Vintage Guitar magazine Price Guide 2025 **Fender** American Deluxe Strat HSS — Mahogany Blacktop Strat Ltd. Ed. **115**

GUITARS

MODEL YEAR	FEATURES	EXC. COND. LOW	HIGH

American Deluxe Stratocaster HSS Mahogany

2015-2016. Limited Edition 10 for 15 series, 2-piece mahogany body.

| 2015-2016 | | $1,250 | $1,625 |

American Elite Stratocaster

2016-2019. Alder body, 3 single-coil pickups or HSS with Shawbucker.

| 2016-2019 | | $1,375 | $1,750 |

American Elite Stratocaster Limited Edition

2016. Various color options with matching head-stock.

| 2016 | | $1,500 | $2,000 |

American Longboard Stratocaster HSS

2015. Part of Fender's limited edition 10 for 15 series, vintage surfboard laminate top design.

| 2015 | | $1,000 | $1,375 |

American Performer Stratocaster

2018-present. Made in the US, new features include 3 Yosemite single-coil pickups, Greasebucket tone system, various colors.

| 2018-2023 | | $800 | $1,125 |

American Special Stratocaster

2010-2018. Limited Edition, '70s headstock with post-CBS black Stratocaster logo, Texas Special pickups (SSS or HSS), satin (early were gloss) finish.

| 2010-2018 | | $800 | $1,125 |

American Standard Stratocaster Limited Edition

1990s-2019. American Standard series, various limited-edition models.

1995-2000	Matching hdstk	$1,500	$2,000
2001	Standard hdstk	$1,500	$2,000
2009	Matching hdstk, Seafoam/Surf Green	$1,500	$2,000
2014-2017	Channel Bound	$1,000	$1,375
2015	Mystic Black	$1,000	$1,375
2015-2016	Mystic Aztec Gold	$1,000	$1,375
2015-2016	Oiled Ash	$1,000	$1,375
2015-2016	Vintage White	$1,000	$1,375
2017	Rosewood neck	$1,000	$1,375
2019	Pale Moon Quilt	$1,500	$2,000

American Ultra Luxe Stratocaster

2021-present. Pickups options and various colors.

| 2021-2023 | Floyd Rose HHS | $1,500 | $2,000 |
| 2021-2023 | SSS | $1,500 | $2,000 |

American Ultra Stratocaster

2019-present. Various options and colors.

| 2019-2023 | | $1,500 | $2,000 |

Ancho Poblano Stratocaster Journeyman Relic

2018-2019. Custom Shop Limited Edition series, alder body, 2-color sunburst or opaque white blonde, with Journeyman Relic nitro lacquer finish.

| 2018-2019 | | $2,750 | $3,500 |

Ancho Poblano Roasted Stratocaster Relic

2019-2020. Custom Shop Limited Edition series, roasted alder body with Relic lacquer finish, various colors.

| 2019-2020 | | $2,750 | $3,500 |

Antigua Stratocaster

2004. Made in Japan, limited-edition reissue, '70s features and antigua finish.

| 2004 | | $800 | $1,125 |

Artisan Series Stratocaster (Custom Shop)

2015-present. Features distinctively figured woods, gold hardware, hand-rubbed oil finishes, certificate of authenticity, various models: Okoume, Claro Walnut, Figured Rosewood, Spalted Maple, Tamo Ash, Thinline Koa.

2015	Okoume	$2,500	$3,000
2016-2019	Tamo Ash	$3,000	$4,000
2016-2022	Spalted Maple	$3,000	$4,000
2020-2023	Maple Burl	$3,000	$4,000

Big Apple Stratocaster

1997-2000. Two humbucking pickups, 5-way switch, rosewood 'board or maple neck, non-tremolo optional.

| 1997-2000 | Various colors | $1,250 | $1,500 |

Big Block Stratocaster

2005-2006. Pearloid block markers, black with matching headstock, 2 single coils (neck, middle) 1 humbucker (bridge), vintage style tremolo.

| 2005-2006 | | $700 | $950 |

Big Head Stratocaster

2020. Custom Shop Limited Edition series.

| 2020 | | $2,500 | $3,000 |

Bill Carson Stratocaster

1992. Based on the '57 Strat, birdseye maple neck, Cimarron Red finish, 1 left-handed and 100 right-handed produced, serial numbers MT000-MT100, made in Fender Custom Shop, and initiated by The Music Trader (MT) in Florida.

| 1992 | | $2,500 | $3,000 |

Billy Corgan Stratocaster

2008-2012. US-made, 3 DiMarzio pickups, string-thru hardtail bridge.

| 2008-2012 | | $1,250 | $1,625 |

Blackie Stratocaster (Custom Shop)

1987, 2006. Includes Certificate of Authenticity, 12 made in '87, in '06 185 made for U.S. market and 90 for export.

| 1987 | | $3,500 | $4,500 |
| 2006 | | $13,500 | $17,500 |

Black Paisley Stratocaster

2020. Made in Japan, Limited Edition, run of 300, silver and black paisley-print design on basswood body, rosewood 'board, 3 single-coil pickups.

| 2020 | | $700 | $950 |

Blacktop Stratocaster

2011-2015. Alder body, maple neck, rosewood or maple 'board, various pickup options including HH and HSH, various finish options. Floyd Rose version is also available.

| 2011-2015 | | $600 | $800 |

Mahogany Blacktop Stratocaster Limited Edition

2019. 2 or 3 Alnico humbuckers, mahogany body, black headstock, Oly White, black or crimson red, chrome or gold hardware.

| 2019 | | $600 | $800 |

Fender Artisan Series Spalted Maple Thinline Stratocaster

2005 Fender Big Block Stratocaster

Tom Pfeifer

Fender Dave Murray
Stratocaster

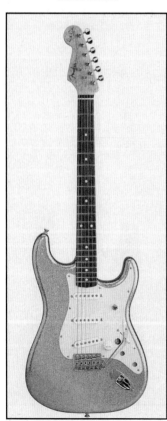

Fender Dick Dale Stratocaster

MODEL YEAR	FEATURES	EXC. COND. LOW	HIGH
Blue Flower Stratocaster			
1984-1997, 2002-2004. Made in Japan, '72 Strat reissue with a '68 Tele Blue Floral finish.			
1984-1987	1st issue	$1,750	$2,250
1988-1994	MIJ	$1,500	$2,000
1995-1997	CIJ	$1,125	$1,500
2002-2004	2nd issue	$850	$1,125
Bonnie Raitt Stratocaster			
1995-2001. Alder body, often in blueburst, Bonnie Raitt's signature on headstock.			
1995-2001		$2,250	$3,000
Bowling Ball/Marble Stratocaster			
1983-1984. Standard Strat with 1 tone and 1 volume control, jack on 'guard, called Bowling Ball due to the swirling color, blue, red or gold.			
1983-1984	Blue or red	$4,000	$5,000
1983-1984	Gold	$4,500	$9,500
Buddy Guy Signature Stratocaster			
1995-2009. Maple neck, 3 Gold Lace Sensor pickups, ash body, blond or sunburst.			
1995-2009		$1,250	$1,625
Buddy Guy Standard Stratocaster			
1996-present. Made in Mexico, maple neck, polkadot finish.			
1996-2023		$800	$950
Buddy Holly Tribute Stratocaster			
2014. Custom Shop, 50 made, '55 specs, with certificate of authenticity.			
2014		$7,250	$9,500
California Stratocaster/ California Fat Stratocaster			
1997-1999. Made in the U.S., painted in Mexico, 3 single coils, Fat has HSS, various colors.			
1997-1999	SSS or HSS	$850	$1,250
Carroll Shelby Limited Edition Stratocaster			
2009. Built for Ford Motor Co. as tribute to Shelby's life, graphic photo montage on front, engraved Shelby Automobiles logo on 'guard, only 100 produced.			
2009		$2,250	$3,000
Carved Top Stratocaster HSS (Custom Shop)			
1995-1998. Carved figured maple top, HSS (HH offered in '98), certificate of authenticity, various colors.			
1995-1998		$2,500	$3,000
Classic Player Stratocaster			
2000. Custom Shop, Standard Stratocaster with useful 'player-friendly features' such as noiseless stacked single-coil pickups and factory Sperzel locking tuners, black, gold anodized 'guard.			
2000		$1,750	$2,250
Classic Player Stratocaster HH			
2015-2016. Alder body, maple neck, bound rosewood 'board, 2 humbuckers, dark Mercedes Blue gloss finish with matching headstock.			
2015-2016		$600	$800
Collector's Edition Stratocaster ('62 Reissue)			
1997. Pearl inlaid '97 on 12th fret, rosewood 'board, alder body, gold hardware, tortoise 'guard, nitro finish, sunburst, 1997 made.			
1997		$1,500	$2,000

MODEL YEAR	FEATURES	EXC. COND. LOW	HIGH
Contemporary Stratocaster (Custom Shop)			
1989-1998. 7/8 scale body, hum/single/single pickups, various colors.			
1989-1998		$1,750	$2,250
Contemporary Stratocaster (Import)			
1985-1987. Import model used while the new Fender reorganized, black or natural headstock with silver-white logo, black or white 'guard, 2 humbucker pickups or single-coil and humbucker, 2 knobs and slider switch.			
1985-1987		$1,250	$1,625
Crash Stratocaster			
2005-2007. Master Built Custom Shop, hand painted by John Crash Matos, approximately 50, comes with a certificate, the prices shown include the original certificate.			
2005-2007		$5,500	$7,500
Custom Classic Stratocaster			
2000-2008. Custom Shop version of American Standard Strat.			
2000-2008		$2,500	$3,000
Custom Deluxe Stratocaster			
2009-2014. Custom Shop, birdseye maple neck, rosewood or maple 'board, certificate. Model also available with flame maple top.			
2009-2014		$3,500	$4,500
Custom Shop Limited Edition Stratocaster			
1992. Only 100 made, flame maple top, birdseye maple neck, rosewood 'board, gold hardware, trans red finish.			
1992		$3,000	$4,000
Dave Murray Stratocaster			
2009-present. Alder body, maple neck, rosewood 'board, 3 pickups, 2-color sunburst.			
2009-2023		$700	$950
David Gilmour Signature Stratocaster			
2008-2019. Custom Shop, NOS or Relic, based on Gilmour's '70 black Stratocaster, certificate of authenticity.			
2008-2019		$3,500	$4,500
Deluxe Lone Star Stratocaster			
2007-2016. Reissue of Lone Star Strat, made in Mexico, 1 humbucker and 2 single-coils, rosewood 'board.			
2007-2016		$400	$550
Deluxe Players Special Edition Stratocaster			
2007. Made in Mexico, Special Edition Fender oval sticker on back of headstock along with 60th Anniversary badge.			
2007		$450	$550
Deluxe Players Stratocaster			
2004-2016. Made in Mexico, 3 noiseless single-coils, push-button switching system.			
2004-2016		$500	$650
Deluxe Roadhouse Stratocaster			
2008-2021. Deluxe series reissue, Texas Special pickups.			
2008-2021		$600	$800

MODEL		EXC. COND.	
YEAR	FEATURES	LOW	HIGH

Deluxe Stratocaster
2016-2021. Mexico-made, double-cut, 3 vintage noiseless single-coils or 1 humbucker and 2 single-coils.

| 2016-2021 | SSS or HSS | $600 | $800 |

Deluxe Stratocaster HSS Plus Top With IOS Connectivity
2014-2016. Deluxe series, plugs into iOS devices.

| 2014-2016 | | $500 | $650 |

Deluxe Stratocaster Plus
1987-1998. Alder (poplar earlier) with ash veneer front and back, 3 Lace Sensor pickups, Floyd Rose, various colors. Becomes American Deluxe Strat Plus.

| 1987-1998 | | $1,375 | $1,750 |

Dick Dale Stratocaster
1994-present. Custom Shop signature model, alder body, reverse headstock, sparkle finish.

| 1994-2023 | | $3,000 | $4,000 |

Elite Stratocaster
1983-1984. The Elite Series features active electronics and noise-cancelling pickups, push buttons instead of 3-way switch, Elite script logo on 4-bolt neck plate, various colors. Also see Gold Elite Stratocaster and Walnut Elite Stratocaster.

| 1983-1984 | | $2,250 | $3,000 |

EOB (Ed O'Brien) Sustainer Stratocaster
2017-present. Alder body, maple neck and 'board, 3 pickups (Sustainer in neck position), custom "Flower of Life" neck plate, gloss poly white finish.

| 2017-2023 | | $800 | $1,125 |

Eric Clapton Crossroads Stratocaster
2007. Custom Shop Limited Edition of 100, Crossroads graphic, 50 sold with matching '57 Twin amp autographed by Clapton (and with other goodies) retailed at $30,000. The other 50 sold guitar alone (with less goodies) at $20,000.

2007	Guitar &		
	Twin Amp	$21,000	$28,000
2007	Guitar only	$18,000	$24,000

Eric Clapton Gold Leaf Stratocaster
2004. Custom Shop model, special build for Guitar Center, 50 made, 23k gold leaf finish/covering.

| 2004 | | $5,500 | $7,500 |

Eric Clapton Signature Journeyman Relic Stratocaster
2020-present. Custom Shop, Clapton's signature on the headstock, 2-color sunburst or aged white blonde.

| 2020 | | $4,000 | $5,000 |

Eric Clapton Signature Stratocaster (Custom Shop)
2019-present. Alder body, maple neck, three Vintage Noiseless pickups, Clapton's signature on headstock, black or Mercedes Blue.

| 2019-2023 | | $3,000 | $4,000 |

Eric Clapton Stratocaster
1988-present. U.S.-made, '57 reissue features, had Lace Sensor pickups until '01, when switched to Vintage Noiseless. Black versions have added "Blackie" decal on headstock.

1988-1999	Lace Sensors	$1,500	$2,000
2000	Lace Sensors	$1,375	$1,750
2001-2023	Noiseless	$1,375	$1,750

Eric Clapton Stratocaster (Custom Shop)
2004-2016. Custom Shop model, standard non-active single-coil pickups, black or blue finish.

| 2004-2016 | | $3,000 | $4,000 |

Eric Johnson 1954 "Virginia" Stratocaster
2020-present. Stories Collection, limited numbers offered from both Custom Shop (see Masterbuilt listing) and Corona production.

| 2020-2023 | Fender Corona | $2,000 | $2,500 |

Eric Johnson Signature Stratocaster Thinline
2018-2020. Alder body, maple neck and 'board, 3 single-coil pickups, 2-color sunburst or vintage white.

| 2017-2020 | | $1,250 | $1,625 |

Eric Johnson Stratocaster
2005-present. '57 spec body and 1-piece maple soft-v-neck, or, for '09 to '15, rosewood 'board, special design pickups, vintage tremolo with 4 springs, EJ initials and guitar-player figure engraved neck plate. Also listed as Eric Johnson Stratocaster Maple or Rosewood.

| 2005-2023 | Maple or rosewood | $1,500 | $2,000 |

Floyd Rose Classic Relic Stratocaster
1998. Custom Shop, late '60s large headstock, 1 humbucker and 1 Strat pickup.

| 1998 | | $3,000 | $4,000 |

Floyd Rose Classic Stratocaster (Strat HSS) (Strat HH)
1992-2002. Two single-coils, bridge humbucker, Floyd Rose tremolo, became Floyd Rose Classic Strat HSS or HH (2 humbuckers) in '98.

| 1992-2002 | | $1,375 | $1,625 |

Ford Shelby GT Stratocaster
2007. 200 made, black with silver Shelby GT racing stripe.

| 2007 | 200 made | $2,250 | $3,000 |

Foto Flame Stratocaster
1994-1996, 2000. Japanese-made Collectables model, alder and basswood body with Foto Flame (simulated woodgrain) finish on top cap and back of neck.

| 1994-2000 | | $775 | $1,000 |

Freddy Tavares Aloha Stratocaster
1993-1994. Custom Shop, hollow aluminum body with hand engraved Hawaiian scenes, custom inlay on neck, 153 made.

| 1993-1994 | | $7,500 | $9,500 |

FSR Stratocaster
2012-2019. Factory Special Run models might be 'dealer exclusive' or open to all dealers as limited run. FSR have a special set of appointments that are not standard to the core lineup.

2012	Antigua Strat	$600	$800
2013	Hot Rod Strat	$500	$650
2013-2017	Classic '60s Strat	$800	$1,125
2015-2016	Amer Std '54 Strat	$1,000	$1,375
2017-2019	Classic '50s Strat	$600	$800
2018-2019	Traditional '50s Strat	$600	$800

Fender Eric Clapton Signature Journeyman Relic Stratocaster
Tyler Willison

2017 Fender Eric Johnson Stratocaster

MODEL YEAR	FEATURES	EXC. COND. LOW	HIGH

Fender George Harrison
Rocky Stratocaster

George Fullerton 50th Anniversary '57 Strat Ltd. Ed. Set
2007. Limited Edition, 150 made, '57 Strat with matching relic Pro Junior tweed amp, 2 certificates of authenticity signed by Fullerton, commemorative neck plate.

2007		$4,000	$5,000

George Harrison Rocky Stratocaster
2020-present. Custom Shop Limited Edition, 2-piece alder body, 5A flame maple neck, 3 '60s Strat pickups, finish is designed from Harrison's psychedelic paint job including the "Grimwoods" decal, Sonic Blue with custom Rocky graphics top.

2020-2023		$16,500	$22,000

Gold Stratocaster
1981-1983. Gold metallic finish, gold-plated brass hardware, 4-bolt neck, maple 'board, skunk strip, trem.

1981-1983		$2,250	$3,000

Gold Elite Stratocaster
1983-1984. The Elite series features active electronics and noise-cancelling pickups, the Gold Elite has gold hardware and pearloid tuner buttons, also see Elite Stratocaster and Walnut Elite Stratocaster.

1983-1984		$2,250	$3,000

Gold Stratocaster (Custom Shop)
1989. Custom Shop, 500 made, gold finish with gold anodized and white 'guards included.

1989		$3,000	$4,000

GT11 Stratocaster
2019-2020. Custom Shop, exclusive models for Sweetwater, relic and heavy relic.

| 2019-2020 | Heavy Relic | $3,000 | $4,000 |
| 2019-2020 | Relic | $3,000 | $4,000 |

H.E.R. Stratocaster
2020-present. Made in Mexico, Artist Signature series, alder body with Chrome Glow finish, matching painted headstock.

2020-2023		$750	$975

Hank Marvin Stratocaster
1995-1996. Custom Shop, Feista Red.

1995-1996		$3,000	$4,000

Hank Marvin 40th Anniversary Stratocaster
1998. Custom Shop logo with '40 Years 1958-1998' marked on back of headstock, Fiesta Red, only 40 made, COA.

1998		$6,375	$8,500

Harley-Davidson 90th Anniversary Stratocaster
1993. Custom Shop, 109 total made, Harley-Davidson and Custom Shop V logo on headstock (Diamond Edition, 40 units), 9 units produced for the Harley-Davidson company without diamond logo, 60 units were not Diamond Edition, chrome-plated engraved metal body, engraved 'guard, COA necessary.

1993		$20,000	$35,000

Highway One Stratocaster/HSS
2002-2014. U.S.-made, alder body, satin lacquer finish, 3 single-coil pickups or HSS version has humbucker/single/single.

2002-2014		$700	$950

Fender H.E.R. Stratocaster

HM Strat (USA/Import)
1988-1992 ('88 Japanese-made, '89-'90 U.S.- and Japanese-made, '91-'92 U.S.-made). Heavy Metal Strat, Floyd Rose, regular or pointy headstock, black hardware, H, HH, SH, or SSH pickup options. Later models have a choice of SHH or SSH.

| 1988-1990 | Import | $1,000 | $1,375 |
| 1989-1992 | USA | $1,000 | $1,375 |

HM Strat Limited Edition
2020-2021. '88-'92 HM specs, available in era-correct Day-Glo colors, Frozen Yellow, Flash Pink, Ice Blue and Bright White.

2020-2021		$875	$1,125

Homer Haynes HLE Stratocaster
1988-1989. Custom Shop, limited edition of 500, '59 Strat basics with gold finish, gold anodized guard and gold hardware.

1988-1989		$3,000	$4,000

Hot Wheels Stratocaster
2003. Custom Shop model commissioned by Hot Wheels, 16 made, orange flames over blue background, large Hot Wheels logo.

2003		$2,500	$3,000

HRR Stratocaster/Floyd Rose HRR (Japan)
1990-1994. Made in Japan, hot-rodded vintage-style Strat, Floyd Rose tremolo system, H/S/S pickups, maple neck, sunburst or colors. Called the Floyd Rose HRR for '92-'94 (with optional Foto Flame finish).

1990-1994		$1,125	$1,400

Ike Turner Tribute Stratocaster
2005. Custom Shop model, 100 made, replica of Ike Turner's Sonic Blue Strat.

2005		$3,500	$4,500

Jeff Beck Signature Stratocaster (CS)
2004-present. Custom Shop, 3 Noiseless dual-coils, Olympic White or Surf Green.

| 2004-2019 | | $2,000 | $2,500 |
| 2020-2023 | | $3,500 | $4,500 |

Jeff Beck Stratocaster
1991-present. Alder body, originally 3 Lace Sensors (HSS) changing to 3 Noiseless dual-coils in '01, rosewood 'board, Olympic White and Surf Green (Midnight Purple until '02).

1991	1st issue, Lace Sensors	$2,250	$3,000
1992-1993	Lace Sensors	$2,000	$2,500
1994-2000	Lace Sensors	$1,500	$2,000
2001-2009	Noiseless	$1,500	$2,000
2010-2023	Artist Series	$1,500	$2,000

Jerry Donahue Hellecaster Stratocaster
1997. Made in the Fender Japan Custom Shop as one part of the 3-part Hellecasters Series, limited edition, Seymour Duncan pickups, maple, blue with blue sparkle guard.

1997		$1,000	$1,375

Jim Root Stratocaster
2010-present. Artist series, mahogany body, ebony or maple 'board, 2 active pickups, black hardware, black or white finish.

2010-2023		$1,125	$1,500

The Official Vintage Guitar magazine Price Guide 2025 **Fender** Jimi Hendrix Ltd. Ed. Strat (CS) — Mark Kendrick Master Design '65 Strat **119**

GUITARS

MODEL YEAR	FEATURES	EXC. COND. LOW	HIGH

Jimi Hendrix Limited Edition Stratocaster (Custom Shop)

2019-2021. Custom Artist series, designed from Hendrix's modified '68 Strat used at Woodstock ('69), aged Olympic White.

2019-2021		$5,500	$7,500

Jimi Hendrix Monterey Pop Stratocaster

1997-1998. Custom Shop, near replica of Monterey Pop Festival sacrifice guitar, red psychedelic-style finish.

1997-1998		$14,500	$19,000

Jimi Hendrix Monterey Stratocaster

2017-2018. Body art like Hendrix's hand-painted original that he destroyed at Monterey Pop Festival, custom neck plate, signature on headstock rear.

2017-2018		$600	$800

Jimi Hendrix Stratocaster

2015-present. Reverse headstock, silhouette and engraved 'Authentic Hendrix' on neckplate.

2015-2023		$600	$800

Jimi Hendrix Tribute Stratocaster

1997-2000. Left-handed guitar strung right-handed, maple cap neck, Olympic White. Fender headstock logo positioned upside down, made for right-handed player to look as if they are playing a left-handed guitar flipped over

1997-2000		$2,500	$3,000

Jimi Hendrix Voodoo 29th Anniversary (Guitar Center) Stratocaster

1993. Custom Shop made only 35 for Guitar Center, large 'Guitar Center 29th Anniversary' logo on neckplate, right-handed body with reverse left-handed headstock and reversed Fender headstock logo, purple sparkle finish.

1993		$3,000	$4,000

Jimi Hendrix Voodoo Child Signature Stratocaster NOS

2018-present. Custom Shop, Custom Artist series, 2-piece alder body, maple neck and 'board, 3 pickups, Olympic White or black, with NOS nitro lacquer finish.

2018-2023		$4,000	$5,000

Jimi Hendrix Voodoo Child Stratocaster Journeyman Relic

2020-present. Custom Shop, Olympic White or black with aged relic finish.

2020-2023		$4,000	$5,000

Jimi Hendrix Voodoo Stratocaster

1997-2002. Right-handed body with reverse headstock, maple neck, Olympic White, sunburst or black.

1997-2002		$2,500	$3,500

Jimmie Vaughan Tex-Mex Stratocaster

1997-present. Poplar body, maple 'board, signature on headstock, 3 Tex-Mex pickups, various colors.

1997-2023		$600	$800

John Jorgenson Hellecaster Stratocaster

1997. Fender Japan Custom Shop, part of the 3-part Hellecasters Series, limited edition, Seymour Duncan pickups, gold sparkle 'guard, gold hardware, split single-coils, rosewood 'board.

1997		$1,125	$1,500

John Mayer Limited Edition Black1 Stratocaster

2010. Custom Shop, 83 made, black finish NOS or extreme relic option, JC serial number, Custom Shop/ John Cruz logo on back of headstock includes personal letter from John Mayer.

2010	NOS	$3,000	$4,000

John Mayer Stratocaster

2005-2014. Alder body, special scooped mid-range pickups, vintage tremolo, special design gig bag with pocket for laptop computer.

2005-2014		$1,500	$2,000

Kenny Wayne Shepherd Stratocaster

2009-2016, 2020-present. Artist series, based on Shepherd's '61, rosewood 'board, jumbo frets, Artic White with cross, black with racing stripes or 3-color sunburst. Reintroduced '20, chambered ash body, 3 single-coil pickups, trans Faded Sonic Blue with matching painted headstock.

2009-2016	Import	$675	$900
2020-2023	US-made	$1,500	$2,000

Koa Stratocaster

2006-2008. Made in Korea, Special Edition series, sunburst over koa veneer top, plain script Fender logo, serial number on back of headstock with.

2006-2008		$500	$650

Kon Tiki Stratocaster

2003. Custom Shop, limited run of 25, Tiki Green including Tiki 3-color artwork on headstock.

2003		$3,000	$4,000

Lenny Stratocaster

Introduced Dec. 12, 2007 by Guitar Center stores, Custom Shop model, 185 guitars made, initial product offering price was 17K.

2007		$10,000	$13,000

Limited Roasted Tomatillo Stratocaster Relic

2019-2020. Custom Shop Limited Edition series, roasted alder body and 4A flame maple neck, various colors with Relic lacquer finish.

2019-2020		$3,125	$4,000

Lincoln Brewster Signature Stratocaster

2019-present. Ash body, 1-piece maple neck, 3 single-coil pickups, gold with lacquer finish.

2019-2023		$1,500	$2,000

Lite Ash Stratocaster Special Edition

2004-2007. Korea, light ash body, birds-eye maple neck.

2004-2007		$500	$650

Lone Star Stratocaster

1996-2001. Alder body, 1 humbucker and 2 single-coil pickups, rosewood 'board or maple neck, various colors.

1996	50th Anniv Badge	$925	$1,250
1997-2001		$925	$1,250

Mark Kendrick Master Design '65 Stratocaster

2004. Custom Shop Limited Edition, run of 65, alder body, maple neck, African rosewood 'board, Lake Placid Blue over Olympic White.

2004		$3,500	$4,500

Fender HM Strat Limited Edition

Fender Jimi Hendrix Voodoo Child Stratocaster Journeyman Relic

2006 Fender Masterbuilt Stratocaster
David Stone

Fender Noventa Stratocaster

MODEL YEAR	FEATURES	EXC. COND. LOW	HIGH

Mark Knopfler Stratocaster
2003-2013. '57 body with '62 maple neck.

2003-2013		$1,500	$2,000

Masterbuilt Custom Shop Stratocaster
2006-present. Builder Select series, various models and builders, specific identification to builder, must include certificate of authenticity.

2006-2023	Various models	$5,000	$20,000

Matthias Jabs Signature Stratocaster
1998. Made in Japan, 200 offered, Candy Apple Red.

1998		$1,125	$1,500

Michael Landau Signature Relic Stratocaster 1963/1968
2014-present. Custom Shop Artist series, Relic, alder body, rosewood 'board, '63 is worn Fiesta Red over 3-color sunburst, '68 is black or bleached 3-color sunburst.

2014-2023	1963 Relic	$3,000	$4,000
2014-2023	1968 Relic	$3,000	$4,000

Milonga Deluxe Stratocaster
2005. Special Edition made in Mexico, Vintage Noiseless pickups, rosewood 'board, Olympic White, gold hardware.

2005		$600	$800

MLB Major League Baseball Stratocaster
2014. Official team logos and imagery unique to each, licensed by Major League Baseball Properties.

2014	Various models	$600	$800

Mod Shop Stratocaster
2017-present. Mod Shop allows you to create your own factory-customized electric guitar or bass.

2017-2023		$1,625	$2,250

Modern Player Stratocaster HSH/HSS
2013-2015. Made in China, hum-single-hum or hum-single-single.

2013-2015		$600	$800

Moto Limited Edition Stratocaster
1995. Custom Shop model, pearloid cover in various colors, includes Certificate of Authenticity, not to be confused with white pearloid Moto Strat which is part of a guitar and amp set (as listed below).

1995		$3,000	$4,000

Moto Set Stratocaster
1995-1996. Custom Shop set including guitar, case, amp, and amp stand, white pearloid finish.

1995-1996	Red (few made)	$5,250	$6,750
1995-1996	White	$5,250	$6,750

Noventa Stratocaster
2021-present. Alder body, maple neck, Pau Ferro 'board, 2 single-coil pickups, Crimson Red Trans, Daphne Blue or Surf Green.

2021-2023		$750	$975

Orange Krush Limited Edition Stratocaster
1995. Custom Shop, 25 made, based on '57 Strat, orange finish with matching headstock, certificate of authenticity.

1995		$3,000	$4,000

Paisley Stratocaster
1984-1997, 2003-2004, 2008. Japanese-made '72 Strat reissue with a reissue '68 Tele Pink Paisley finish,

MODEL YEAR	FEATURES	EXC. COND. LOW	HIGH

large headstock until mid-'94, 'Made in Japan' logo used until early-'97, 'Crafted in Japan' after.

1984-1987	1st issue	$2,500	$3,000
1988-1994	MIJ	$1,500	$2,000
1995-1997	MIJ	$1,375	$1,750
2003-2004	CIJ	$800	$1,125
2008	2nd issue, 200 made	$800	$1,125

Parallel Universe Volume II Strat Jazz Deluxe
2019-2021. Limited Edition, alder body, 2 pickups, Mystic Surf Green with nitro lacquer finish.

2019-2021		$1,500	$2,000

Parallel Universe Volume II Strat-Tele Hybrid
2017-2018. Limited Edition, Tele body, Strat neck and headstock, 3 single-coil Strat pickups, 2-color sunburst with gloss nitro lacquer finish.

2017-2018		$1,500	$2,000

Playboy 40th Anniversary Stratocaster
1994. Custom Shop, 175 made, nude Marilyn Monroe graphic on body.

1994		$18,000	$22,000

Player Plus Stratocaster
2021-present. Alder body, maple neck, 3 Noiseless Stat pickups, various colors.

2021-2023		$600	$800

Player Series Stratocaster
2017-present. Various models include SSS, HSS, HSH, HSS Plus, Floyd Rose, SSS LH and SSS Plus, various colors and finishes.

2017-2019	SSS, HSS, HSH	$600	$700
2018-2023	Floyd Rose HSS	$600	$700
2018-2023	Plus Top SSS, HSS	$600	$700

Post Modern Stratocaster (Custom Shop)
2015-2019. Offered in Journeyman Relic, NOS, and lush Closet Classic finishes.

2015-2017	NOS	$2,750	$3,500
2016-2019	Journeyman Relic	$3,000	$4,000
2019	Closet Classic	$3,000	$4,000

Post Modern Stratocaster Closet Classic (Custom Shop)
2019-2020. Made exclusive for Sweetwater, certificate.

2019-2020	Aged natural	$3,000	$4,000

Post Modern Stratocaster Journeyman Relic (Custom Shop)
2019-2020. Made exclusively for Sweetwater, alder or ash, certificate.

2019-2020	Alder or ash	$3,000	$4,000

Post Modern Stratocaster NOS (Custom Shop)
2019-2020. Made exclusive for Sweetwater, certificate.

2019-2020	Aged natural	$3,000	$4,000

Powerhouse/Powerhouse Deluxe Stratocaster
1997-2010. Made in Mexico, Standard Strat configuration with pearloid 'guard, various colors.

1997-2010		$500	$650
2005	Powerbridge, TRS stereo	$500	$650

MODEL YEAR	FEATURES	EXC. COND. LOW	HIGH

Proud Stratocaster
2003. Custom Shop, 3 made to commemorate United Way and Rock & Roll Hall of Fame project, body painted in detail by Fender's artist.

2003		$6,000	$8,000

Rarities Stratocaster
2019-2020. Rarities Collection series, limited edition, models include Flame Maple Top, Flame KOA Top, Quilt Maple Top.

2019-2020	Various models	$1,750	$2,250

Richie Sambora Stratocaster
1993-2002. U.S. and Mexico models offered, alder body, Floyd Rose tremolo, maple neck, various colors.

1993-2002	USA	$3,000	$4,000
1994-2002	Mexico	$600	$800
1995-1997	Mexico, swirl color	$750	$1,000

Ritchie Blackmore Stratocaster
2009-present. Based on Blackmore's '70s large headstock model, scalloped rosewood 'board, Duncan Quarter Pound Flat pickups, Olympic White.

2009-2023		$800	$1,125

Ritchie Blackmore Tribute Stratocaster
2014. Custom Shop, '68 specs, maple neck.

2014		$4,500	$6,000

Roadhouse Stratocaster
1997-2000. U.S.-made, poplar body, tortoise shell 'guard, maple 'board, 3 Texas Special pickups, various colors.

1997-2000		$775	$1,000

Robert Cray Signature Stratocaster
1991-present. Custom Shop, rosewood 'board, chunky neck, lighter weight, non-trem, alder body, gold-plated hardware, various colors.

1991-2023		$3,000	$4,000

Robert Cray Stratocaster (Mexico)
1996-present. Artist series, chrome hardware.

1996-2023		$600	$800

Robin Trower Signature Stratocaster
2004-present. Custom Shop Custom Artist series, 100 made, large headstock (post '65-era), with '70s logo and 3-bolt neck, bullet truss rod, white.

2004-2023		$3,000	$4,000

Rory Gallagher Tribute Stratocaster
2004-present. Custom Shop, based on Gallagher's '61 model, heavily distressed, price includes the original certificate.

2004-2019		$3,500	$4,500
2020-2023		$4,000	$5,000

Sandblasted Stratocaster
2014-2015, 2019-2020. Limited Edition series, ash body, sandblasted finish. Limited run '19-'20 exclusive for Sweetwater USA.

2014-2015		$900	$1,250
2019-2020	Sweetwater	$900	$1,250

Select Stratocaster
2012-2015. Select Series, figured top, rear-headstock 'Fender Select' medallion, gloss-lacquer finish, various colors.

2012-2015		$2,000	$2,500

Set-Neck Stratocaster
1992-1999. Custom Shop model, mahogany body

and figured maple top, 4 pickups, glued-in neck, active electronics, by '96 ash body.

1992-1999		$3,000	$4,000

Short-Scale (7/8) Stratocaster
1989-1995. Similar to Standard Strat, but with 2 control knobs and switch, 24" scale vs. 25" scale, sometimes called a mini-Strat, Japanese import, various colors.

1989-1995		$650	$850

So-Cal J.W. Black Stratocaster
2000-2001. Custom Shop, So-Cal logo art on body, 20 offered.

2000-2001		$3,000	$4,000

So-Cal Speed Shop Stratocaster
2005-2006. Limited Edition for Musician's Friend, red, white, and black So-Cal paint job, basswood body, rosewood 'board, 1 humbucker, So-Cal Speed Shop decal.

2005-2006		$600	$800

Special Edition David Lozeau Art Stratocaster
2015-2016. Finishes include orange Tree of Life, blue Dragon, yellow Rose Tattoo and red Sacred Heart, etched David Lozeau neck plate.

2015-2016		$500	$650

Special Edition Stratocaster
2004-2009. Import model, Special Edition oval logo on back of headstock, various styles offered, '50s or '60s vintage copy specs, maple 'board, ash or koa body, see-thru or opaque finish.

2004-2009		$500	$650

Special Edition Stratocaster (Matching Headstock)
2016-2017. Made in Mexico, various colors with matching headstock.

2016-2017		$500	$650

Special Edition White Opal Stratocaster
2016. Made in Mexico, white opal body and headstock, pearloid 'guard, 3 humbuckers.

2016		$500	$650

Splatter Stratocaster
2003. Made in Mexico, splatter paint job, various color combinations, with gig bag.

2003		$650	$1,000

Standard Roland Ready Stratocaster
1998-2011. Made in Mexico, built-in Roland pickup system and 3 single-coils.

1998-2011		$450	$600

Standard Stratocaster (Japan)
1985-1989. Interim production in Japan while the new Fender reorganized, standard pickup configuration and tremolo system, 3 knobs with switch, traditional style input jack, traditional shaped headstock, offered in black, red or white.

1985-1989		$1,250	$1,625

Standard Stratocaster (Mexico)
1990-2018. Made in Mexico, renamed Player Series in '18. Not to be confused with the American-made Standard Stratocaster of '81-'84. Various models and colors, high-end range includes a hard guitar case, while low-end includes only a gig bag.

1990-2018	Various models	$400	$550

Fender Rory Gallagher
Tribute Stratocaster

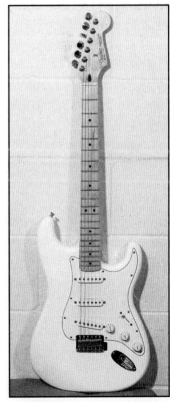

2005 Fender Standard
Stratocaster (Mexico)
Tom Pfeifer

1993 Fender U.S.
Ultra Stratocaster

Keith Myers

1952 Fender Telecaster

Trey Rabinek

MODEL YEAR	FEATURES	EXC. COND. LOW	HIGH

Standard Stratocaster Plus Top
2014-2018. Made in Mexico, alder body with flamed maple top. Renamed Player Series Plus Top in '18.

2014-2018		$450	$600

Standard Stratocaster Satin Finish
2003-2006. Basically Mexico-made Standard with satin finish.

2003-2006		$400	$550

Stevie Ray Vaughan Signature Stratocaster
1992-present. U.S.-made, alder body, sunburst, gold hardware, SRV 'guard, lefty tremolo, Brazilian rosewood 'board (pau ferro by '93).

1992	1st year, Brazilian	$4,000	$5,000
1992-2023	Pau Ferro	$1,500	$2,000

Stevie Ray Vaughan Signature Stratocaster (Custom Shop)
2019-present. Custom Artist series, 3-color sunburst with NOS or aged relic lacquer finish.

2019-2023	NOS	$3,500	$4,500
2019-2023	Relic	$3,500	$4,500

Stevie Ray Vaughan Tribute #1 Stratocaster
2004. Custom Shop Limited Edition, recreation of SRV's #1 made by Master Builder John Cruz in the Custom Shop, 100 made, $10,000 MSRP, includes flight case stenciled "SRV - Number One," and other goodies.

2004		$24,000	$30,000

Strat Plus
1987-1999. Three Lace Sensor pickups, alder (poplar available earlier) body, tremolo, rosewood 'board or maple neck, various colors. See Deluxe Strat Plus for ash veneer version.

1987-1999	Various colors	$1,250	$1,500

Stratocaster Junior
2004-2006. Import, short 22.7" scale, Alder body, non-trem hardtail bridge.

2004-2006		$400	$550

Stratocaster Pro Closet Classic (Custom Shop)
2006-2013. Ash body, early '60s neck, rosewood or maple board, solid or sunburst finish.

2006-2013		$3,000	$4,000

Stratocaster Pro NOS (Custom Shop)
2012-2016. Ash body, maple neck, rosewood 'board, solid or 3-tone sunburst.

2012-2016		$3,000	$4,000

Stratocaster Special
1993-1995. Made in Mexico, a humbucker and a single-coil pickup, 1 volume, 1 tone.

1993-1995		$400	$550

Stratocaster XII
1988-1997, 2003-2010. 1st version Japanese-made, alder body, 22-fret rosewood 'board. 2nd version is 21-fret Classic Series model for 2 years then Classic Series.

1988-1997	1st version	$1,250	$1,500
2003-2010	2nd version	$1,250	$1,500

Strat-o-Sonic
2003-2006. American Special Series, Stratocaster-style chambered body, includes Strat-o-Sonic Dove I (1 pickup, '03 only), Dove II/DV II (2 black P-90s, '03-'06) and HH (2 humbuckers, '05-'06).

2003	Dove I	$1,000	$1,375
2003-2006	Dove II/DV II	$1,000	$1,375
2003-2006	HH	$1,000	$1,375

Sub Sonic Stratocaster
2000-2001. Baritone model, offered in 2 production models - HH (2 humbuckers, 2000-'01), HSS (hum-single-single, '01) - and in a Custom Shop version of the HSS (2000-'01).

2000-2001		$1,000	$1,375
2000-2001	Custom Shop, COA	$2,500	$3,500

Super Stratocaster
1997-2003. Deluxe series, made in Mexico, 3 Super Fat single-coils, Super Switching gives 2 extra pickup options, gold tremolo.

1997-2003		$500	$650

Supreme Stratocaster
2017. Limited Edition, collaboration with Supreme (NY-based fashion brand), all white color with red Supreme logo on front.

2017		$6,500	$9,000

Tanqurey Tonic Stratocaster
1988. Made for a Tanqurey Tonic liquor ad campaign giveaway in '88, Tanqurey Tonic Green; many were given to winners around the country, ads said that they could also be purchased through Tanqurey, but that apparently didn't happen.

1988		$1,750	$2,250

Tash Sultana Stratocaster
2020-present. Artist series, all gold hardware, aged white pearl 'guard, trans cherry finish with matching painted headstock.

2020-2023		$800	$1,250

Texas Special Stratocaster
1991-1992. Custom Shop, 50 made, state of Texas map stamped on neck plate, Texas Special pickups, maple fretboard, sunburst.

1991-1992		$2,500	$3,500

The Edge Stratocaster
2016-2020. U2 guitarist The Edge signature on large '70s-style headstock, alder body, 1-piece quartersawn maple neck and 'board, 3 pickups, black.

2016-2020		$1,500	$2,000

The Strat
1980-1983. Alder body, 4-bolt neck, large STRAT on painted peghead, gold-plated brass hardware, various colors.

1980-1983		$1,500	$2,000

Tie-Dye Stratocaster
2004-2005. Single-coil neck and humbucker bridge pickups, Band of Gypsies or Hippie Blue tie-dye pattern, poly finish.

2004-2005		$600	$800

Tom Delonge Stratocaster
2001-2004. 1 humbucker, rosewood back and sides. Also in Squier version.

2001-2004		$800	$1,125

The *Vintage Guitar Price Guide* shows values for all-original, excellent condition instruments and, where applicable, with original case.

The Official Vintage Guitar magazine Price Guide 2025 | **Fender** Tom Morello "Soul Power" Stratocaster — Telecaster | **123**

GUITARS

MODEL YEAR	FEATURES	EXC. COND. LOW	HIGH

Tom Morello "Soul Power" Stratocaster
2020-present. Alder body, rosewood 'board, black with white 'guard. Shipped with "Soul Power" decal for face of guitar.

2020-2023		$900	$1,250

Tree of Life Stratocaster
1993. Custom Shop, 29 made, tree of life fretboard inlay, 1-piece quilted maple body.

1993		$5,500	$7,500

Turquoise Sparkle Stratocaster
2001. Custom Shop, limited run of 75 for Mars Music, turquoise sparkle finish.

2001		$1,750	$2,250

U.S. Ultra / Ultra Plus Stratocaster
1990-1997. Alder body with figured maple veneer on front and back, single Lace Sensor pickups in neck and middle, double Sensor at bridge, ebony 'board, sunburst.

1990-1997		$2,000	$2,500

Ventures Limited Edition Stratocaster
1996. Japanese-made tribute model, matches Jazzmaster equivalent, black.

1996		$1,375	$1,750

VG Stratocaster
2007-2009. American Series, modeling technology using Roland's VG circuitry, 5 guitar tone banks deliver 16 sounds.

2007-2009		$1,125	$1,500

Vintage Hot Rod Stratocaster
2007-2014. Vintage styling with modern features, '07-'13 named '57 Strat and '62 Strat, in '14 changed to '50s and '60s.

2007-2014	All models	$1,500	$2,000

Vintera Series Stratocaster
2019-present. Modified and non-modified '50s, '60s and '70s Strat models, various options and colors.

2019-2020	'70s	$700	$900
2019-2020	'70s modified	$700	$900
2019-2023	'50s	$700	$900
2019-2023	'50s modified	$700	$900
2019-2023	'60s	$700	$900
2019-2023	'60s modified	$700	$900

Walnut Elite Stratocaster
1983-1984. The Elite Series features active electronics and noise-cancelling pickups, Walnut Elite has a walnut body and neck, gold-plated hardware and pearloid tuner buttons. Also see Elite Stratocaster and Gold Elite Stratocaster.

1983-1984		$2,250	$3,000

Walnut Stratocaster
1981-1983. American black walnut body and 1-piece neck and 'board.

1981-1983		$2,000	$2,500

Western Stratocaster
1995. Custom Shop, only 5 made, featured in Fender Custom Shop book from the 1990s.

1995		$8,500	$11,000

Whiteguard Stratocaster Limited Edition
2018. Limited Edition neck plate, ash body, Tele hardware and white 'guard, 2 single-coil pickups, lacquer finish.

2018		$1,375	$1,750

MODEL YEAR	FEATURES	EXC. COND. LOW	HIGH

Yngwie Malmsteen Signature Stratocaster (Custom Shop)
2020-present. Custom Artist series, 2-piece select alder body, flat sawn maple neck, various colors with nitro lacquer finish.

2020-2023		$4,000	$5,000

Yngwie Malmsteen Stratocaster
1988-present. U.S.-made, maple neck, scalloped 'board, 3 single-coil pickups, Vintage White.

1988-2023		$1,250	$1,625

Swinger
1969-1972. See listing for Musiclander.

SX Series
1992-1995. Dreadnought and jumbo acoustics, ply or solid spruce tops with various wood options on back and sides, E models with electronics.

1992-1995	Various models	$200	$950

T-Bucket 300CE
2016-2018. Acoustic/electric, D-size, cutaway.

2016-2018		$225	$300

TC-90/TC-90 Thinline
2004-2007. Made in Korea, 2 single-coil P90s, double-cut, Vintage White or Black Cherry Burst.

2004-2007		$575	$750

Telecaster
The following are all variations of the Telecaster. Broadcaster and Nocaster models are under Broadcaster. The first five listings are for the main American-made line. All others are listed alphabetically after that in the following order:

Telecaster
Standard Telecaster
American Standard Telecaster
American Series Telecaster
American Professional/Professional II Telecaster
30th Anniversary Guitar Center Tree of Life Telecaster
40th Anniversary Telecaster
'50 Custom Telecaster
'50s Telecaster/Classic Series '50s Telecaster
Road Worn '50s Telecaster
50th Anniversary Spanish Guitar Set
50th Anniversary Telecaster
'52 Telecaster/American Vintage '52 Telecaster
American Vintage '52 Telecaster Korina (U.S.A.)
'52 Telecaster (Custom Shop)
'52 LTD Telecaster NOS
'52 Vintage Telecaster (Japan)
'54 Telecaster (Custom Shop)
'58 Telecaster (Custom Shop)
American Vintage '58 Telecaster (U.S.A.)
'60s Telecaster Custom
'60s Telecaster/Classic Series '60s Telecaster
American Original '60s Telecaster
American Original '60s Telecaster Thinline
'60 Telecaster Custom
60th Anniversary American Telecaster
60th Anniversary Telecaster (U.S.A.)
60th Anniversary Telecaster Limited Edition

1956 Fender Telecaster
Frank Manno

1961 Fender Telecaster
Gordon Kennedy

GUITARS

1963 Fender Telecaster
Kevin Rush

1966 Fender Telecaster
Rivington Guitars

'61 Telecaster Custom
'62 Telecaster Custom (Import)
'62 Telecaster Custom (U.S.A.)
'62 Mod Squad Custom Telecaster
'62 Telecaster Reissue (Japan)
Junkyard Dog 1962 Telecaster Relic
'63 Telecaster (Custom Shop)
'63 Telecaster Custom Relic LTD
'64 Telecaster Limited Relic
American Vintage '64 Telecaster
'67 Telecaster (Custom Shop)
'68 Telecaster Rosewood
'69 Tele/Telecaster Thinline (Import)
'69 Telecaster Thinline (Custom Shop)
'72 Telecaster Custom/Classic Series '72 Tele-
    caster Custom
'72 Telecaster Deluxe/Classic Series '72 Tele-
    caster Deluxe
'72 Telecaster Thinline American Vintage
'72 Telecaster Thinline/Classic Series Telecaster
    Thinline
1972 Telecaster Custom Closet Classic
75th Anniversary Commemorative Telecaster
75th Anniversary Telecaster
'90s Telecaster Deluxe
'90s Telecaster Thinline
1998 Collectors Edition Telecaster
Aerodyne Telecaster
Albert Collins Telecaster
Aluminum Telecaster
American Acoustasonic Telecaster
American Classic Holoflake Telecaster
American Classic Telecaster
American Deluxe HH Telecaster
American Deluxe Power Telecaster
American Deluxe Telecaster
American Deluxe/Elite Telecaster Thinline
American Elite Telecaster
American Nashville B-Bender Telecaster
American Performer Telecaster
American Professional II Telecaster Deluxe
American Professional Telecaster Deluxe
    Shawbucker
American Special Telecaster
American Standard Telecaster Limited Edition
American Standard Telecaster Special Edition
American Ultra Luxe Telecaster
American Ultra Telecaster
Andy Summers Masterbuilt Tribute Telecaster
Antigua Telecaster
Big Block Telecaster
Bigsby Telecaster
Blacktop Telecaster Series
Blue Flower Telecaster
Bowling Ball/Marble Telecaster
Britt Daniel Telecaster Thinline
Brown's Canyon Redwood Telecaster
Buck Owens Limited Edition Telecaster
Cabronita Telecaster (American Standard)
Cabronita Telecaster (Classic Player)
Cabronita Telecaster Thinline
California Fat Telecaster
California Telecaster

Chambered Mahogany Telecaster
Chrissie Hynde Telecaster
Clarence White Telecaster (Custom Shop)
Classic Player Baja Telecaster
Collector's Edition Telecaster
Contemporary Telecaster (Import)
Custom Carved Telecaster HH
Custom Classic Telecaster
Custom Deluxe Telecaster
Custom Telecaster
Danny Gatton Signature Telecaster
Deluxe Nashville Power Telecaster
Deluxe Nashville Telecaster (Mexico)
Deluxe Telecaster (U.S.A.)
Elite Nashville Telecaster
Elite Telecaster
Fat Telecaster
Foto Flame Telecaster
G.E. Smith Telecaster
Graham Coxon Special Run Telecaster
Highway One Telecaster/Texas Telecaster
HMT Telecaster (Import)
J5 Triple Telecaster Deluxe
James Burton Standard Telecaster
James Burton Telecaster
Jason Isbell Custom Telecaster
Jerry Donahue JD Telecaster
Jerry Donahue Telecaster
Jim Adkins JA-90 Telecaster Thinline
Jim Root Telecaster
Jimmy Bryant Tribute Telecaster
Jimmy Page Mirror Telecaster
Jimmy Page Telecaster
Joe Strummer Telecaster
John Jorgenson Telecaster
Jr. Telecaster
La Cabronita Especial Telecaster
Mahogany Offset Telecaster
Masterbuilt Custom Shop Telecaster
Matched Set Telecaster
Merle Haggard Signature Telecaster
Mod Shop Telecaster
Modern Player Telecaster Plus
Moto Limited Edition Telecaster
Muddy Waters Signature Telecaster Custom
Muddy Waters Tribute Telecaster
Nashville Telecaster
NHL Premier Edition Telecaster
Nokie Edwards Telecaster
Noventa Telecaster
Old Pine Telecaster
Paisley Telecaster
Palo Escrito Telecaster
Parallel Universe Jazz-Tele
Parallel Universe Troublemaker Telecaster
Parallel Universe Volume II Tele Mágico
Player Telecaster
Plus Telecaster
Rarities Telecaster
Richie Kotzen Telecaster
Rosewood Telecaster
Rosewood Telecaster (Japan)
Rosewood Telelcaster Limited Edition

MODEL YEAR	FEATURES	EXC. COND. LOW	HIGH
	Select Telecaster		
	Select Telecaster Thinline		
	Set-Neck Telecaster		
	Snakehead Telecaster		
	Sparkle Telecaster		
	Special Edition Custom Telecaster FMT HH		
	Special Edition Deluxe Ash Telecaster		
	Special Edition Koa Telecaster		
	Special Edition White Opal Telecaster		
	Special Telecaster/Telecaster Special		
	Standard Telecaster (Japan)		
	Standard Telecaster (Mexico)		
	Telecaster (Japanese Domestic)		
	Telecaster Custom		
	Telecaster Custom (Japan)		
	Telecaster Custom FMT HH (Korea)		
	Telecaster Stratocaster Hybrid		
	Telecaster Thinline		
	Tele-Sonic		
	Texas Special Telecaster		
	Twisted Telecaster Limited Edition		
	Two-Tone Telecaster Thinline		
	Vintage Hot Rod Telecaster		
	Waylon Jennings Tribute Telecaster		
	Will Ray Signature Jazz-A-Caster		
	Will Ray Signature Mojo Telecaster		

Telecaster

1951-1982. See Standard Telecaster (following listing) for '82-'85, American Standard Telecaster for '88-'00, the American Series Telecaster for '00-'07. and the American Standard Telecaster (again) for '08-'16. Currently called the American Professional Telecaster. Please refer to the Fender Guitar Intro Section for details on Fender color options.

In the late '60s and early '70s Fender began to increase their use of vibrato tailpieces. A vibrato tailpiece for this period is generally worth about 13% less than the values shown.

From '63-'70, Fender offered both the standard Brazilian rosewood fretboard and an optional maple fretboard. Prices listed here, for those years, are for the rosewood 'board models. Currently, the market considers the maple 'board to be a premium, so Telecasters with maple, for those years, are worth 10% to 15% more than the values shown.

MODEL YEAR	FEATURES	EXC. COND. LOW	HIGH
1951	Blond, black 'guard	$60,000	$80,000
1952	Blond, black 'guard	$55,000	$75,000
1953	Blond, black 'guard	$55,000	$75,000
1954	Blond, black 'guard	$55,000	$75,000
1954	Blond, white 'guard	$40,000	$52,000
1955	Blond, white 'guard	$40,000	$52,000
1956	Blond	$40,000	$52,000
1957	Blond, backloader	$35,000	$45,000
1958	Blond, backloader	$30,000	$40,000
1958	Blond, top loader	$28,000	$36,000
1958	Sunburst, backloader	$32,000	$42,000
1958	Sunburst, top loader	$30,000	$40,000
1959	Blond, maple	$27,000	$35,000

MODEL YEAR	FEATURES	EXC. COND. LOW	HIGH
1959	Blond, slab	$27,000	$35,000
1959	Custom color	$65,000	$85,000
1959	Sunburst, maple	$32,000	$42,000
1959	Sunburst, slab	$32,000	$42,000
1960	Blond, slab	$26,000	$34,000
1960	Common color	$42,000	$54,000
1960	Rare color	$53,000	$75,000
1960	Sunburst, slab	$30,000	$40,000
1961	Blond, slab	$24,000	$32,000
1961	Common color	$35,000	$45,000
1961	Rare color	$50,000	$65,000
1961	Sunburst, slab	$27,000	$34,000
1962	Blond, curve	$20,000	$26,000
1962	Blond, slab	$22,000	$28,000
1962	Common color	$32,000	$42,000
1962	Rare color	$42,000	$55,000
1962	Sunburst, curve	$22,000	$28,000
1962	Sunburst, slab	$25,000	$32,000
1963	Blond	$20,000	$26,000
1963	Common color	$32,000	$42,000
1963	Rare color	$42,000	$55,000
1963	Sunburst	$22,000	$28,000
1963-1964	Mahogany, see-thru cherry	$37,000	$48,000
1964	Blond	$17,000	$22,000
1964	Common color	$25,000	$32,000
1964	Rare color	$32,000	$45,000
1964	Sunburst	$20,000	$26,000
1965	Blond	$15,000	$20,000
1965	Common color	$22,000	$27,000
1965	Early '65, Sunburst	$18,000	$23,000
1965	Late '65, Sunburst	$17,000	$22,000
1965	Rare color	$30,000	$40,000
1966	Blond	$13,000	$17,000
1966	Common color	$18,000	$22,000
1966	Rare color	$23,000	$30,000
1966	Sunburst	$14,000	$18,000
1967	Blond	$12,000	$16,000
1967	Blond, smuggler	$15,000	$20,000
1967	Common color	$17,000	$22,000
1967	Rare color	$20,000	$26,000
1967	Sunburst	$14,000	$18,000
1968	Blond	$11,000	$15,000
1968	Blue Flora	$22,000	$30,000
1968	Common color	$15,000	$20,000
1968	Pink Paisley	$23,000	$32,000
1968	Rare color	$20,000	$26,000
1968	Sunburst	$13,000	$17,000
1969	Blond, poly	$9,000	$12,000
1969	Blue Flora	$18,500	$25,000
1969	Common color, poly	$12,500	$17,000
1969	Pink Paisley	$20,000	$25,000
1969	Rare color, poly	$20,000	$26,000
1969	Sunburst, poly	$10,000	$15,000
1970	Blond, poly	$8,000	$11,000
1970	Common color, poly	$11,000	$14,000
1970	Rare color, poly	$15,000	$20,000
1970	Sunburst, poly	$8,000	$11,000
1971	Blond	$7,000	$9,000

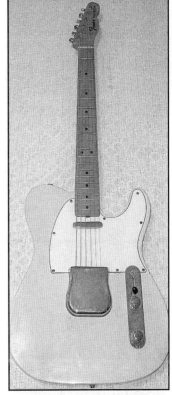

1967 Fender Telecaster
Lynn Rose

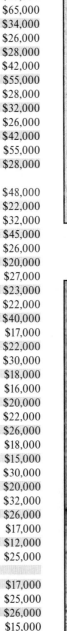

1970 Fender Telecaster
W. H. Stephens

1972 Fender Telecaster

John Hosford

Fender American Original
'60s Telecaster

MODEL YEAR	FEATURES	EXC. COND. LOW	HIGH
1971	Common color	$8,500	$11,000
1971	Rare color	$12,000	$15,000
1971	Sunburst	$7,000	$9,000
1972	Blond	$6,000	$8,000
1972	Common color	$8,500	$11,000
1972	Natural	$5,000	$6,500
1972	Rare color	$12,000	$15,000
1972	Sunburst	$6,000	$7,500
1973	Black, white	$4,500	$6,000
1973	Blond	$4,500	$6,000
1973	Natural	$4,000	$5,500
1973	Rare color	$8,500	$11,000
1973	Sunburst	$4,500	$6,000
1973	Walnut	$4,000	$5,500
1974	Blond, black, white	$4,250	$5,500
1974	Natural	$3,500	$4,500
1974	Sunburst	$4,500	$6,000
1974	Walnut	$3,500	$4,500
1975	Blond, black, white	$4,000	$5,000
1975	Natural	$3,500	$4,500
1975	Sunburst	$4,000	$5,500
1975	Walnut	$3,500	$4,500
1976	Blond, black, white	$3,500	$4,500
1976	Natural	$3,250	$4,250
1976	Sunburst	$3,500	$4,500
1976	Walnut	$3,250	$4,250
1977	Black, blond, white	$3,500	$4,500
1977	Natural	$3,250	$4,250
1977	Sunburst	$3,500	$4,500
1977	Walnut	$3,250	$4,250
1978-1979	All colors	$3,500	$4,500
1980-1981	All colors	$2,500	$3,250
1980-1981	International colors	$3,250	$4,250

Standard Telecaster
1982-1984. See Telecaster for '51-'82, and American Standard Telecaster (following listing) for '88-2000. Not to be confused with the current Standard Telecaster, which is made in Mexico.

1982	Blond, sunburst	$2,500	$3,250
1983-1984	Blond, sunburst	$1,500	$2,000

American Standard Telecaster
1988-2000, 2008-2016. Name used when Fender reissued the standard American-made Tele after CBS sold the company. The only American-made Tele available for '86 and '87 was the '52 Telecaster. See Telecaster for '51-'81, and Standard Telecaster for '82-'84. All '94 models have a metal 40th Anniversary pin on the headstock but should not be confused with the actual 40th Anniversary Telecaster model (see separate listing), all standard colors. Renamed the American Series Telecaster in 2000, then back to American Standard Series Telecaster in '08. Becomes American Professional in '17.

1988-2000		$1,000	$1,375
2008-2016		$1,000	$1,375

American Series Telecaster
2000-2007. See Telecaster for '51-'81, Standard Telecaster for '82-'84, and American Standard for '88-'99. Renamed American Standard again in '08.

2000-2007		$1,000	$1,375

American Professional/ Professional II Telecaster
2017-present. Model replaces American Standard Tele, redesign includes 2 V-Mod pickups, narrow-tall frets, new 'deep C' neck profile, various colors. Also available left-hand model. Renamed American Professional II in '20.

2017-2020	Pro	$1,000	$1,375
2020-2023	Pro II	$1,000	$1,375

30th Anniversary Guitar Center Tree of Life Telecaster
1994. Limited Edition, produced for 30th anniversary of Guitar Center, engraved neckplate with GC logo, tree-of-life 'board inlay.

1994		$5,500	$7,500

40th Anniversary Telecaster
1988, 1999. Custom Shop, limited edition run of 300, 2-piece flamed maple top, gold hardware ('88), flamed maple top over ash body, gold hardware ('99).

1988	1st run, high-end	$5,500	$7,000
1999	2nd run, plain top	$4,250	$5,500

'50 Custom Telecaster
1997. Custom Shop, limited run of 10, humbucker neck pickup, standard unbound body, highly figured maple neck, blackguard specs.

1997		$3,000	$4,000

'50s Telecaster/Classic Series '50s Telecaster
1990-2019. Made in Japan (basswood body) until mid '99, then in Mexico with ash body. Foto-Flame finish offered in '94 (see separate listing).

1990-1999	Japan	$1,000	$1,375
1999-2019	Mexico	$600	$800

Road Worn '50s Telecaster
2009-2019. Maple 'board, '50s specs, aged finish.

2009-2019		$800	$1,125

50th Anniversary Spanish Guitar Set
1996. Custom Shop, 50 sets made, Tele Prototype reproduction with similar era copy of woodie amp.

1996		$5,500	$7,000

50th Anniversary Telecaster
1995-1996. Custom Shop, flame maple top, 2 vintage-style pickups, gold hardware, sunburst, gold 50th Anniversary coin on back of the headstock, 1250 made.

1995-1996		$2,000	$2,500

'52 Telecaster/American Vintage '52 Telecaster
1982-1984, 1986-2017. Ash body, maple neck or rosewood 'board, blond. Replaced by the American Original '50s Telecaster.

1982-1984		$3,000	$4,000
1986-1999		$2,000	$2,500
1990-1999	Copper (limited)	$2,000	$2,500
2000-2009		$1,500	$2,000
2010-2017		$1,500	$2,000

American Vintage '52 Telecaster Korina (U.S.A.)
2015. Part of Fender's limited edition 10 for 15 series, Korina body, '52 specs.

2015		$2,000	$2,500

The Vintage Guitar Price Guide shows values for all-original, excellent condition instruments and, where applicable, with original case.

MODEL YEAR	FEATURES	EXC. COND. LOW	HIGH

'52 Telecaster (Custom Shop)
2004-2018. Custom Shop Dealer Select model, NOS, Relic and Closet Classic offered, changed to Heavy Relic in '15.

2004-2012	NOS	$3,000	$4,000
2004-2014	Relic	$3,000	$4,000
2010-2011	Closet Classic	$3,000	$4,000
2015-2018	Heavy Relic	$3,000	$4,000

'52 LTD Telecaster NOS
2020. Custom Shop, ash body, maple neck, faded blonde, lacquer finish.

2020		$2,500	$3,500

'52 Vintage Telecaster (Japan)
1982-1984. Made in Japan, JV serial numbers.

1982-1984		$1,750	$2,250

'54 Telecaster (Custom Shop)
1997-1998, 2013-2016. Relic, Closet Classic available with more recent model.

2013-2016	Relic	$3,000	$4,000

'58 Telecaster (Custom Shop)
2008. Custom Shop, relic and heavy relic.

2008	Heavy relic	$3,000	$4,000
2008	NOS	$3,000	$4,000
2008	Relic	$3,000	$4,000

American Vintage '58 Telecaster (U.S.A.)
2013-2018. Ash body, white 'guard, Aged White Blonde.

2013-2018		$1,500	$2,000

'60s Telecaster Custom
1997-1999. Custom Shop, bound alder body, sunburst, black or custom colors, nickel or gold hardware.

1997-1999		$3,000	$4,000

'60s Telecaster/Classic Series '60s Telecaster
1992-2019. Made in Japan (basswood body) until mid '99, then in Mexico with ash body. Foto-Flame finish offered in '94 (see separate listing). '06 version may have 60th Anniversary Badge on back of headstock.

1992-1996	Made in Japan	$1,000	$1,375
1997-1999	Crafted in Japan	$900	$1,250
1999-2019	Mexico	$600	$800

American Original '60s Telecaster
2018-2023. '60s specs, rosewood 'board, alder body.

2018-2023		$1,500	$2,000

American Original '60s Telecaster Thinline
2020-2023. '60s specs, ash body, maple neck, aged natural, 3-color sunburst or Surf Green.

2020-2023		$1,500	$2,000

'60 Telecaster Custom
2003-2004. Custom Shop Time Machine, bound alder body, offered in NOS, Closet Classic and Relic versions and in sunburst, CA Red and Sonic Blue.

2003-2004	Closet Classic	$3,000	$4,000
2003-2004	NOS	$3,000	$4,000
2003-2004	Relic	$3,000	$4,000

60th Anniversary American Telecaster
2006-2007. Special Edition commemorating Fender's 60th year, banner headstock 60th logo, neck plate reads Diamond Anniversary 1946-2006, made in U.S.A., rosewood 'board, sunburst.

2006-2007		$1,500	$2,000

60th Anniversary Telecaster (U.S.A.)
2011-2012. Celebrating 60 years of the Tele, commemorative chrome neck plate, ash body, blonde thin-skin finish.

2011-2012		$1,500	$2,000

60th Anniversary Telecaster Limited Edition
2006. Limited Edition of 1,000, 60 Diamond Anniversary 1946-2006 logo engraved in neck plate, American Flag logo on pickguard, '51 NoCaster pickup layout, 60 wood inlay on the face below bridge, clear nitro finish on natural ash body, silver guitar case with Fender 60 logo on inside lid.

2006		$2,000	$2,500

'61 Telecaster Custom
2010-2012. Custom Shop Dealer Select model, bound body Custom, NOS, Relic or Heavy Relic.

2010-2012	Closet Classic	$3,000	$4,000
2010-2012	NOS	$3,000	$4,000
2010-2012	Relic	$3,000	$4,000

'62 Telecaster Custom (Import)
1985-1999. Made in Japan, bound top and back, rosewood 'board, sunburst or red.

1985-1989		$1,250	$1,625
1990-1999		$1,250	$1,625

'62 Telecaster Custom (U.S.A.)
1999-2012. American Vintage Series, rosewood board.

1999-2012		$1,500	$2,000

'62 Mod Squad Custom Telecaster
2013. Custom Shop, Broadcaster bridge pickup and Duncan neck humbucker.

2013		$3,000	$4,000

'62 Telecaster Reissue (Japan)
1989-1990, 2005-2006. Made by Fender Japan.

1989-1990		$1,500	$2,000
2005-2006		$1,250	$1,625

Junkyard Dog 1962 Telecaster Relic
2014-2015. Custom Shop Dealer Select series, ash body, rosewood neck and 'board, white guard, Vintage Blonde.

2014-2015		$3,000	$4,000

'63 Telecaster (Custom Shop)
1999-2010, 2018-2019. Alder body (or blond on ash), original spec pickups, C-shaped neck, rosewood 'board. Relic offered in '07 and later heavy relic in '18.

1999-2010	Closet Classic	$3,000	$4,000
1999-2010	NOS	$3,000	$4,000
2007	Relic	$3,000	$4,000
2018-2019	Heavy relic	$3,000	$4,000

'63 Telecaster Custom Relic LTD
2006. Custom Shop, Limited Edition.

2006		$3,000	$4,000

'64 Telecaster Limited Relic
2009. Custom Shop, rosewood 'board, thin nitro finish, 50 each of black, aged white, and 3-tone chocolate sunburst.

2009		$3,000	$4,000

American Vintage '64 Telecaster
2013-2018. Ash body, mid-'60s 'C' neck profile, rounded rosewood 'board, 2 vintage single-coil pickups, White Blonde.

2013-2018		$1,500	$2,000

2012 Fender American Standard Telecaster
Steve Alvito

2006 Fender 60th Anniversary Telecaster Limited Edition
Imaged by Heritage Auctions, HA.com

GUITARS

Fender American
Ultra Telecaster

2001 Fender American
Deluxe Telecaster
Cream City Music

MODEL YEAR	FEATURES	EXC. COND. LOW	HIGH

'67 Telecaster (Custom Shop)
2005-2008, 2010-2011. Alder body, rosewood or maple 'board, Relic, NOS or Closet Classic, 2010 and later is rosewood 'board, Relic or NOS.

2005-2008	Closet Classic	$3,000	$4,000
2005-2011	NOS	$3,000	$4,000
2005-2011	Relic	$3,000	$4,000

'68 Telecaster Rosewood
Custom Shop, rosewood body.

2007	NOS	$3,000	$4,000

'69 Tele/Telecaster Thinline (Import)
1986-2015. Import, Classic Series, 2 Tele pickups.

1986-1996	Made in Japan	$1,250	$1,625
1997-1999	Crafted in Japan	$800	$1,125
2000-2015	Mexico	$675	$900

'69 Telecaster Thinline (Custom Shop)
2005-2006. Semi-hollow mahogany body, maple neck with maple 'board.

2005-2006		$3,000	$4,000

'72 Telecaster Custom/Classic Series '72 Telecaster Custom
1986-2019. Import, 1 humbucker and 1 single-coil, 2 humbuckers after '99.

1986-1989	Japan	$1,375	$1,750
1990-1999	Japan	$1,250	$1,625
2000-2019	Mexico	$600	$800

'72 Telecaster Deluxe/Classic Series '72 Telecaster Deluxe
2004-2019. Made in Mexico, alder body, large Deluxe 'guard, 2 humbuckers.

2004-2019		$600	$800

'72 Telecaster Thinline American Vintage
2012-2013. US-made, American Vintage FSR model, f-hole, 2 humbuckers.

2012-2013		$1,500	$2,000

'72 Telecaster Thinline/Classic Series Telecaster Thinline
1986-2019. Import, 2 humbuckers, f-hole.

1986-1999	Japan	$1,250	$1,625
2000-2019	Mexico	$600	$800

1972 Telecaster Custom Closet Classic
2013. Custom Shop, ash body, maple neck and 'board, 2 pickups, black finish.

2013		$3,000	$4,000

75th Anniversary Commemorative Telecaster
2021. US-made, limited edition, inlaid 75th Anniversary ingot back of headstock, gold hardware, 2-color Bourbon Burst gloss finish. Includes custom Inca Silver case with Lake Placid Blue interior.

2021		$1,750	$2,250

75th Anniversary Telecaster
2021. Made in Mexico, 75th Anniversary neck plate, Diamond Anniversary satin finish with matching painted headstock.

2021		$600	$800

'90s Telecaster Deluxe
1995-1998. Import, 1 Tele-style bridge pickup and 2 Strat-style pickups, rosewood 'board, Foto Flame '95-'97 and standard finishes '97-'98.

1995-1997	Foto-Flame	$800	$1,125
1997-1998	Standard finish	$800	$1,125

'90s Telecaster Thinline
1998-2001. Bound semi-hollow ash body, f-hole, white or brown shell 'guard, 2 single-coils, sunburst, black, natural, or transparent crimson.

1998-2001		$2,000	$2,500

1998 Collectors Edition Telecaster
1998. 1,998 made, 1998 logo inlay on 'board, maple, gold hardware.

1998		$1,500	$2,000

Aerodyne Telecaster
2004-2009. Imported Tele with Aerodyne body profile, bound body, black.

2004-2009		$700	$900

Albert Collins Telecaster
1990-2018. Custom Shop signature model, bound swamp ash body, humbucker pickup in neck position, natural or silver sparkle.

1990-2018		$3,000	$4,000

Aluminum Telecaster
1994-1995. Aluminum-bodied American Standard with anodized finish in blue marble, purple marble or red, silver and blue stars and stripes.

1994-1995	Flag option	$2,500	$3,000
1994-1995	Marble patterns	$2,500	$3,000

American Acoustasonic Telecaster
2019-present. Solid A Sitka spruce top, mahogany back, sides and neck, various colors.

2019-2023		$1,375	$1,750

American Classic Holoflake Telecaster
1996-1999. Custom Shop, splatter/sparkle finish, pearloid 'guard.

1996-1999		$3,000	$4,000

American Classic Telecaster
1996-1999. Custom Shop model, handcrafted version of American Standard, thin lacquer-finished ash body, maple or rosewood 'board, various options and colors, earlier versions had gold hardware and custom-color options.

1996-1999		$3,000	$4,000

American Deluxe HH Telecaster
2004-2006. Rosewood, maple top, 2 humbucker pickups.

2004-2006		$1,500	$2,000

American Deluxe Power Telecaster
1999-2001. Made in USA, with Fishman power bridge piezo pickups.

1999-2001		$1,500	$2,000

American Deluxe Telecaster
1998-2017. Premium ash or alder body with see-thru finishes.

1998-2017		$1,500	$2,000

American Deluxe/Elite Telecaster Thinline
2015-2019. Single-cut, alder body, f-hole, maple neck, 2 Noiseless pickups, various colors.

2015-2019		$1,750	$2,250

American Elite Telecaster
2016-2020. Single-cut, alder body, maple neck, rosewood 'board, 2 single-coil pickups, various colors.

2016-2020		$1,750	$2,250

The *Vintage Guitar Price Guide* shows values for all-original, excellent condition instruments and, where applicable, with original case.

MODEL YEAR	FEATURES	EXC. COND. LOW	HIGH

American Nashville B-Bender Telecaster
1998-2015. US-made, alder body, added Texas Special Strat pickup in middle position, white pearloid 'guard, Parsons-Fender B-string bender, 5-way switch.

| 1998-2015 | | $2,000 | $2,500 |

American Performer Telecaster
Introduced Dec. 2018-present. Made in the US, new features include Yosemite single-coil pickups, Greasebucket tone system, various colors.

| 2018-2023 | | $800 | $1,125 |

American Professional II Telecaster Deluxe
2020-present. Alder body, maple neck, 2 humbucking pickups, various colors with gloss finish.

| 2020-2023 | | $1,125 | $1,500 |

American Professional Telecaster Deluxe Shawbucker
2017-2018. With 2 ShawBucker humbucking pickups, various colors.

| 2017-2018 | | $1,250 | $1,625 |

American Special Telecaster
2010-2018. Alder body, gloss finish, Texas Special pickups.

| 2010-2018 | | $800 | $1,125 |

American Standard Telecaster Limited Edition
1990s-2019. American Standard series, various limited-edition models.

1995-1997	B-Bender	$2,000	$2,500
2009	Matching hdstk	$1,500	$2,000
2014-2015	Channel Bound	$1,250	$1,625
2015	Rosewood neck	$2,000	$2,500
2015-2016	HH	$1,250	$1,625

American Standard Telecaster Special Edition
2009. Surf Green, Fiesta Red or Daphne Blue with matching headstock.

| 2009 | | $1,500 | $2,000 |

American Ultra Luxe Telecaster
2021-present. 2 Noiseless single-coil or Floyd Rose with 2 humbucker, 2-color sunburst, trans Surf Green or black.

| 2021-2023 | Floyd Rose HH | $1,500 | $2,000 |
| 2021-2023 | SS | $1,500 | $2,000 |

American Ultra Telecaster
2019-present. Alder or ash body, upgrades include 2 Ultra Noiseless Vintage Tele single-coil pickups and 7 new colors with gloss poly finish.

| 2019-2023 | | $1,500 | $2,000 |

Andy Summers Masterbuilt Tribute Telecaster
2009. Custom shop, based on Summer's '61 Tele, heavy relic, 250 made, custom electronics rear-mounted overdrive unit controlled by a third knob, includes DVD, strap and Andy Summer's logo travel guitar case.

| 2009 | | $7,500 | $9,750 |

Antigua Telecaster
2004. Made in Japan, limited edition, 400 made, '70s features and antigua finish.

| 2004 | | $1,250 | $1,625 |

Big Block Telecaster
2005-2006. Pearloid block markers, black with matching headstock, 3 single-coils with center pickup reverse wound.

| 2005-2006 | | $700 | $950 |

Bigsby Telecaster
2003. Made in Mexico, standard Tele specs with original Fender-logo Bigsby tailpiece.

| 2003 | | $700 | $950 |

Blacktop Telecaster Series
2012-2015. Includes 2 humbucker HH and hum-single-single Baritone.

| 2012-2015 | Various models | $600 | $800 |

Blue Flower Telecaster
1985-1993, 2003-2004. Import, Blue Flower finish.

| 1985-1993 | 1st issue | $1,000 | $1,375 |
| 2003-2004 | 2nd issue | $800 | $1,125 |

Bowling Ball/Marble Telecaster
1983-1984. Standard Tele, called Bowling Ball Tele due to the swirling color, blue, red or gold.

| 1983-1984 | Blue or red | $4,000 | $5,000 |
| 1983-1984 | Gold | $4,500 | $9,500 |

Britt Daniel Telecaster Thinline
2019-present. Ash body, maple neck, 2 single-coil pickups, Amarillo Gold lacquer finish.

| 2019-2023 | | $1,500 | $2,000 |

Brown's Canyon Redwood Telecaster
2011. For Fender's 60th anniversary in 2011, they released 12 limited edition U.S.-made Tele-bration Telecasters, including this one with body made from 1890s California redwood.

| 2011 | | $1,750 | $2,250 |

Buck Owens Limited Edition Telecaster
1998-1999. Red, white and blue sparkle finish, 250 made, gold hardware, gold 'guard, rosewood 'board.

| 1998-1999 | | $2,000 | $2,500 |

Cabronita Telecaster (American Standard)
2011. For Fender's 60th anniversary in 2011, American Standard series, they released 12 limited edition U.S.-made Tele-bration Telecasters, including this one with 2 TV Jones Filter'Trons.

| 2011 | | $1,500 | $2,000 |

Cabronita Telecaster (Classic Player)
2014-2015. Mexico version, Classic Player series.

| 2014-2015 | | $500 | $650 |

Cabronita Telecaster Thinline
2012-2013. Made in Mexico, ash body, maple neck, 2 Fideli'Tron humbucking pickups, 2-Color Sunburst, Shoreline Gold or White Blonde.

| 2012-2013 | | $700 | $950 |

California Fat Telecaster
1997-1998. Alder body, maple fretboard, Tex-Mex humbucker and Tele pickup configuration.

| 1997-1998 | | $850 | $1,250 |

California Telecaster
1997-1998. Alder body, maple fretboard, sunburst, Tex-Mex Strat and Tele pickup configuration.

| 1997-1998 | | $850 | $1,250 |

Fender Antigua Telecaster

Fender Britt Daniel Telecaster Thinline

GUITARS

1974 Fender Custom Telecaster
Scott Casey

1977 Fender Deluxe Telecaster
Rivington Guitars

MODEL YEAR	FEATURES	EXC. COND. LOW	HIGH

Chambered Mahogany Telecaster
2006. U.S.-made, chambered mahogany body, Delta Tone System.

2006		$1,250	$1,625

Chrissie Hynde Telecaster
2021-present. Artist series, alder body with Faded Ice Blue Metallic Road Worn finish, chrome mirror 'guard.

2021-2023		$1,000	$1,375

Clarence White Telecaster (Custom Shop)
1994-2000. Parsons-White B-Bender and Scruggs-style tuners on both E strings, sunburst.

1994-2000		$9,000	$11,500

Classic Player Baja Telecaster
2007-2019. Made in Mexico, Custom Shop designed neck plate logo, thin gloss poly blond finish.

2007-2019		$700	$950

Collector's Edition Telecaster
1998. Mid-1955 specs including white 'guard, offered in sunburst with gold hardware (which was an option in '55), 1,998 made, Collector's Edition neck plate with serial number.

1998		$1,500	$2,000

Contemporary Telecaster (Import)
1985-1987. Japanese-made while the new Fender reorganized, 2 or 3 pickups, vibrato, black chrome hardware, rosewood 'board.

1985-1987		$750	$1,000

Custom Carved Telecaster HH
2013. Figured maple top, carved back, 2 humbucking pickups.

2013		$2,000	$2,500

Custom Classic Telecaster
2000-2008. Custom Shop, maple or rosewood 'board, certificate of authenticity.

2000-2008		$3,000	$4,000

Custom Deluxe Telecaster
2009-2014. Custom Shop model, ash body, AA birdseye maple neck, rosewood or maple 'board, abalone dot inlays, 2 pickups, certificate, black Bakelite 'guard, Aged White Blonde, Dakota Red or faded 2-color sunburst.

2009-2014		$3,500	$4,500

Custom Telecaster
1972-1981. One humbucking and 1 Tele pickup, standard colors, see Telecaster Custom for 2 Tele pickup/bound body version.

1972		$4,000	$5,500
1973-1974		$3,500	$4,500
1975-1977		$3,500	$4,500
1978-1979		$3,000	$4,000
1980-1981		$3,000	$4,000

Danny Gatton Signature Telecaster
1990-2018. Custom Shop, like '53 Telecaster, maple neck, 2 humbuckers.

1990-1999	Frost Gold	$4,000	$5,000
2000-2018	Various colors	$2,500	$3,000

Deluxe Nashville Power Telecaster
1999-2014. Like Deluxe Nashville, but with piezo transducer in each saddle.

1999-2014		$600	$800

Deluxe Nashville Telecaster (Mexico)
1997-2021. Tex-Mex Strat and Tele pickup configuration, various colors.

1997-2021		$600	$800

Deluxe Telecaster (U.S.A.)
1972-1981. Two humbuckers, various colors. Mexican-made version offered starting in 2004.

1972	Common color	$4,000	$5,500
1972	Less common color	$4,750	$6,500
1973-1974	Common color	$3,750	$5,000
1973-1974	Less common color	$4,750	$6,500
1975	Common color	$3,000	$4,000
1975	Less common color	$4,000	$5,500
1976-1977	Common color	$3,000	$4,000
1978-1979	Common color	$2,750	$3,500
1980-1981	Common color	$2,500	$3,250

Elite Nashville Telecaster
Custom Shop Limited Edition, ash body, 3 pickups, Antique Cherry Burst.

2016		$1,875	$2,500

Elite Telecaster
1983-1985. Two active humbucker pickups, 3-way switch, 2 volume knobs, 1 presence and filter controls, chrome hardware, various colors.

1983-1985		$2,250	$3,000

Fat Telecaster
1999-2001. Humbucker pickup in neck, Tele bridge pickup.

1999-2001		$750	$1,125

Foto Flame Telecaster
1994-1996. Import, sunburst or transparent.

1994-1996		$800	$1,125

G.E. Smith Telecaster
2007-2014. Swamp ash body, vintage style hardware, U-shaped neck, oval and diamond inlays.

2007-2014		$1,500	$2,000

Graham Coxon Special Run Telecaster
2011, 2013-2014. Blond, Tele bridge and humbucker neck pickup, rosewood 'board, limited run in 2011.

2011-2014		$1,250	$1,625

Highway One Telecaster/ Texas Telecaster
2003-2011. U.S.-made, alder body, satin lacquer finish, Texas version (introduced in '04) has ash body and Hot Vintage pickups.

2003-2011		$700	$950

HMT Telecaster (Import)
1990-1993. Japanese-made Heavy Metal Tele, available with or without Floyd Rose tremolo, 1 Fender Lace Sensor pickup and 1 DiMarzio bridge humbucker pickup, black.

1990-1993		$1,000	$1,375

J5 Triple Telecaster Deluxe
2007-2017. John 5 model, made in Mexico, 3 humbuckers, medium jumbo frets.

2007-2017		$800	$1,125

James Burton Standard Telecaster
1995-2016. Mexico, 2 Texas Special Tele pickups, standard colors (no paisley).

1995-2016		$650	$900

MODEL YEAR	FEATURES	EXC. COND. LOW	HIGH

James Burton Telecaster

1990-present. Ash body, 3 Fender Lace pickups, available in black with Gold Paisley, black with Candy Red Paisley, Pearl White, and Frost Red until '05. In '06 in black with red or blue flame-shaped paisley, or Pearl White.

1990-2005	Black & gold paisley, gold hw	$2,500	$3,250
1990-2005	Black & red paisley, black hw	$2,000	$2,500
1990-2010	Frost Red or Pearl White	$1,250	$1,625
1994	Blue Paisley, gold hw	$2,000	$2,500
2006-2023	Paisley flames	$1,250	$1,625

Jason Isbell Custom Telecaster

2021-present. Artist series, double-bound body, aged hardware, Road Worn Chocolate Sunburst with lacquer finish.

2021-2023		$1,250	$1,625

Jerry Donahue JD Telecaster

1993-1999. Made in Japan, Custom Strat neck pickup and Custom Tele bridge pickup, basswood body, special "V" shaped maple neck.

1993-1999		$1,250	$1,625

Jerry Donahue Telecaster

1992-2001. Custom Shop model designed by Donahue, Tele bridge pickup and Strat neck pickup, birdseye maple neck, top and back, gold hardware, passive circuitry, sunburst, transparent Crimson Red or Sapphire Blue. There was also a Japanese-made JD Telecaster.

1992-2001	Various colors	$2,500	$3,250

Jim Adkins JA-90 Telecaster Thinline

2008-present. Rosewood 'board, vintage-style P-90 soapbars.

2008-2023		$600	$800

Jim Root Telecaster

2007-present. Made in Mexico, black hardware, mahogany body.

2007-2023		$800	$1,125

Jimmy Bryant Tribute Telecaster

2004-2005. Custom Shop, hand-tooled leather 'guard overlay with JB initials.

2004-2005		$3,000	$4,000

Jimmy Page Mirror Telecaster

2019-present. Ash body with white blonde lacquer finish, rosewood 'board, 2 single-coil pickups, vintage-style tweed case, shipped with 8 round mirrors.

2019-2023		$2,000	$2,500

Jimmy Page Telecaster

2020-present. Ash body with gloss finish over Page's artwork, maple neck with Road Worn nitro finish, rosewood 'board.

2020-2023		$1,000	$1,375

Joe Strummer Telecaster

2007-2009. Limited edition, heavily relic'd based on Strummer's '66 Tele, Fender offered a limited-edition art customization kit as part of the package.

2007	Limited Edition	$1,000	$1,375
2007-2009	Standard run	$1,000	$1,375

John Jorgenson Telecaster

1998-2001. Custom Shop, korina body, double-coil stacked pickups, sparkle or black finish.

1998-2001	Sparkle	$3,000	$4,000

Jr. Telecaster

1994, 1997-2000. Custom Shop, transparent blond ash body, 2 P-90-style pickups, set neck, 11 tone chambers, 100 made in '94, reintroduced in '97.

1994		$3,000	$4,000
1997-2000		$3,000	$4,000

La Cabronita Especial Telecaster

2009-2010. Custom Shop relics, 1 or 2 TV Jones pickups. In '09, 10 each with 1 pickup in black or Shoreline Gold and 20 each with 2 pickups in black or Shoreline Gold. In '10, 10 each with 1 pickup in Candy Apple Red or Sonic Blue and 20 each with 2 pickups in Candy Apple Red or Sonic Blue.

2009-2010	Various colors	$3,750	$5,000

Mahogany Offset Telecaster

2020. Made in Japan series, mahogany body and neck, rosewood 'board, 2 pickups, natural finish.

2020		$750	$975

Masterbuilt Custom Shop Telecaster

2006-present. Various models and builders, specific identification to builder, must include certificate of authenticity.

2006-2023	Various models	$4,500	$8,500

Matched Set Telecaster

1994. Matching Tele and Strat Custom Shop models, model name on certificate is "Matched Set Telecaster", 3 sets were built, each set has serial number 1, 2, or 3.

1994		$5,000	$6,500

Merle Haggard Signature Telecaster

2009-2018. Custom Shop, figured maple body and neck, maple 'board, 2-color sunburst.

2009-2018		$3,500	$4,500

Mod Shop Telecaster

2017-present. Mod Shop allows you to create your own factory-customized electric guitar or bass.

2017-2023		$2,000	$2,500

Modern Player Telecaster Plus

2012-2018. Import, pine body, maple neck, HSS pickups, Honey Burst or Trans Charcoal.

2012-2018		$450	$600

Moto Limited Edition Telecaster

1990s. Custom Shop, pearloid cover in various colors. There were also Strat and Jag versions.

1990s		$3,000	$4,000

Muddy Waters Signature Telecaster Custom

2001-2009. Mexico, Fender amp control knobs, Telecaster Custom on headstock, Muddy Waters signature logo on neck plate, Candy Apple Red.

2001-2009		$800	$1,125

Muddy Waters Tribute Telecaster

2000. Custom Shop, 100 made, Fender amp control knobs, rosewood 'board, relic Candy Apple Red finish, certificate of authenticity.

2000		$3,500	$4,500

Fender Deluxe Nashville Telecaster (Mexico)

Fender Jason Isbell Custom Telecaster

GUITARS

1996 Fender Paisley Telecaster
Tom Pfeifer

Fender Richie Kotzen
Telecaster

MODEL YEAR FEATURES	EXC. COND. LOW	HIGH
Nashville Telecaster		
1995. Custom Shop model, 3 pickups.		
1995	$3,000	$4,000
NHL Premier Edition Telecaster		
1999-2000. Limited edition of 100 guitars with NHL hockey art logo on the top.		
1999-2000 All models	$1,000	$1,500
Nokie Edwards Telecaster		
1996. Made in Japan, limited edition, book matched flamed top, multi-lam neck, Seymour Duncan pickups, gold hardware, zero fret, tilted headstock.		
1996	$1,750	$2,250
Noventa Telecaster		
2021-present. Alder body, maple neck, maple or pau ferro 'board, single-coil pickup, 2-Color Sunburst, Fiesta Red or Vintage Blonde.		
2021-2023	$700	$950
Old Pine Telecaster		
2011. For Fender's 60th anniversary in 2011, they released 12 limited edition U.S.-made Tele-bration Telecasters, including this one with 100-year-old pine body, 300 made.		
2011	$1,500	$2,000
Paisley Telecaster		
1986-1998, 2003-2004, 2008. Import, 'Made in Japan' logo used until '98, 'Crafted in Japan' after, Pink Paisley finish.		
1986-1994	$1,250	$1,625
1995-1998	$1,125	$1,500
2003-2004	$800	$1,125
2008 600 made	$800	$1,125
Palo Escrito Telecaster		
2006-2007. Mexico, Classic series, palo escrito is tonewood from Mexico with unique grain patterns, natural finish.		
2006-2007	$800	$1,125
Parallel Universe Jazz-Tele		
June 2018. Parallel Universe series, limited edition, Tele body, 2 Jazzmaster single-coil pickups, 2-Color Sunburst or Surf Green.		
2018	$1,500	$2,000
Parallel Universe Troublemaker Telecaster		
July 2018. Parallel Universe series, limited edition, mahogany body, maple top, custom Cabronita 'guard, 2 ShawBucker (1T and 2T) humbucking pickups. Bigsby optional.		
2018	$1,500	$2,000
2018 with Bigsby	$1,500	$2,000
Parallel Universe Volume II Tele Mágico		
2020-2021. Parallel Universe Volume II series, limited edition, ash body, flame maple neck and 'board, Daphane Blue or Surf Green.		
2020-2021	$1,500	$2,000
Player Telecaster		
2018-present Alder body, maple neck, 2 SS or HH pickups, various colors with gloss finish		
2018-2023	$600	$700
Plus Telecaster		
1994-1997. Lace Sensor pickups, various colors.		
1994-1997	$2,000	$2,500

MODEL YEAR FEATURES	EXC. COND. LOW	HIGH
Rarities Telecaster		
2019-2020. Rarities Collection series, limited edition, models include Flame Maple Top, Quilt Maple Top, Red Mahogany Top.		
2019-2020	$2,000	$2,500
Richie Kotzen Telecaster		
2017-present. Ash body, bound flame maple top, 2 DiMarzio pickups, gold hardware, signature on headstock.		
2017-2023	$1,000	$1,375
Rosewood Telecaster		
1969-1972. Rosewood body and neck.		
1969-1972	$18,000	$23,000
Rosewood Telecaster (Japan)		
1986-1996. Japanese-made reissue, rosewood body and neck.		
1986-1996	$2,250	$3,000
Rosewood Telelcaster Limited Edition		
2014. Custom Shop, Limited Edition neck plate, based on George Harrison's rosewood Tele.		
2014	$4,500	$5,500
Select Telecaster		
2012-2013. Select Series, figured maple top, rear-headstock 'Fender Select' medallion, gloss-lacquer finish, chrome or gold hardware.		
2012-2013	$2,000	$2,500
Select Telecaster Thinline		
2012-2013. Select Series, rear-headstock 'Fender Select' medallion, chrome or gold hardware, various finish options.		
2012-2013	$2,000	$2,500
Set-Neck Telecaster		
1990-1996. Glued-in neck, Custom Shop, 2 humbucking pickups, Set-Neck CA (Country Artist) has 1 humbucker and 1 Tele pickup, various colors.		
1990-1996	$3,000	$4,000
Snakehead Telecaster		
Custom Shop Limited Edition, 45 offered.		
2010	$5,000	$6,500
Sparkle Telecaster		
1993-1995. Custom Shop model, poplar body, white 'guard, sparkle finish: champagne, gold, silver.		
1993-1995	$2,500	$3,000
Special Edition Custom Telecaster FMT HH		
2020-present. Mahogany body with carved flame maple top, 2 Seymour Duncan pickups, various colors with matching headstock.		
2020-2023	$500	$650
Special Edition Deluxe Ash Telecaster		
2009-2016. Mexico, butterscotch finish, ash body, 1-piece maple neck.		
2009-2016	$500	$650
Special Edition Koa Telecaster		
2006-2008. Made in Korea, standard Tele specs, koa veneer top over basswood body, pearloid 'guard, sunburst.		
2006-2008	$500	$650
Special Edition White Opal Telecaster		
2016. Made in Mexico, white opal body and headstock, pearloid 'guard.		
2016	$500	$650

The *Vintage Guitar Price Guide* shows values for all-original, excellent condition instruments and, where applicable, with original case.

MODEL YEAR	FEATURES	EXC. COND. LOW	HIGH

Special Telecaster/Telecaster Special
2004-2008. Made in Mexico, Special Edition logo with star logo sticker on back of headstock, special features like 6-way bridge and modern tuners.

2004-2008		$500	$650

Standard Telecaster (Japan)
1985-1989. In '85, the only Teles were interim production in Japan while the new Fender reorganized, no serial number, Japan headstock logo in '85, back of neck '86-'89.

1985-1989		$1,250	$1,625

Standard Telecaster (Mexico)
1990-2018. Guitar production at the Mexico facility started in '90. High end of range includes a hard guitar case, while the low end of the range includes only a gig bag, various colors. Replaced by Player Series.

1990-2018		$600	$800

Telecaster (Japanese Domestic)
1982-1997. Made in Japan for Japanese domestic market (not for export), suffix serial numbers JV5 ('82-'84) and A6 through V6 ('84-'97).

1982-1984	JV serial	$1,750	$2,250
1985-1989		$1,250	$1,625
1990-1997		$900	$1,250

Telecaster Custom
1959-1972. Body bound top and back, rosewood 'board, 2 Tele pickups, see Custom Telecaster for the 1 Tele/1 humbucker version. Please refer to the Fender Guitar Intro Section for details on Fender color options.

1959	Sunburst, maple	$36,000	$50,000
1960	Custom color	$52,000	$75,000
1960	Sunburst	$35,000	$45,000
1961	Custom color	$45,000	$65,000
1961	Sunburst	$34,000	$44,000
1962	Custom color	$45,000	$60,000
1962	Sunburst, curve	$32,000	$42,000
1962	Sunburst, slab	$35,000	$45,000
1963	Custom color	$45,000	$60,000
1963	Sunburst	$32,000	$42,000
1964	Custom color	$37,000	$50,000
1964	Sunburst	$27,000	$35,000
1965	Custom color	$30,000	$40,000
1965	Sunburst	$25,000	$30,000
1966	Custom color	$25,000	$32,000
1966	Sunburst	$16,000	$20,000
1967	Custom color	$25,000	$32,000
1967	Sunburst	$16,000	$20,000
1968	Custom color	$25,000	$32,000
1968	Sunburst	$16,000	$20,000
1969	Custom color	$25,000	$32,000
1969	Sunburst	$16,000	$20,000
1970	Custom color	$17,000	$22,000
1970	Sunburst	$14,000	$20,000
1971	Custom color, 4-bolt	$17,000	$22,000
1971	Sunburst, 3-bolt	$4,500	$6,000
1971	Sunburst, 4-bolt	$13,000	$18,000
1972	Custom color, 3-bolt	$9,000	$12,000
1972	Sunburst, 3-bolt	$4,500	$6,000

Telecaster Custom (Japan)
1985. Made in Japan during the period when Fender suspended all USA manufacturing in '85, Tele Custom specs including bound body.

1985		$1,250	$1,625

Telecaster Custom FMT HH (Korea)
2003-2019. Korean-made, flamed maple top, 2 humbuckers.

2003-2019		$800	$1,125

Telecaster Stratocaster Hybrid
2006. Tele body shape, Strat pickup system and wiring, Strat headstock shape, dot markers on rosewood board, reissue tremolo, includes Custom Shop COA that reads "Telecaster Stratocaster Hybrid".

2006		$3,000	$4,000

Telecaster Thinline
1968-1980. Semi-hollowbody, 1 f-hole, 2 Tele pickups, ash or mahogany body, in late-'71 the tilt neck was added and the 2 Tele pickups were switched to 2 humbuckers. Please refer to the Fender Guitar Intro Section for details on Fender color options.

1968	Common color	$17,000	$22,000
1968	Natural ash	$12,000	$16,000
1968	Natural mahogany	$12,000	$16,000
1968	Rare color	$22,000	$27,500
1968	Sunburst	$13,000	$18,000
1969	Common color	$16,000	$20,000
1969	Natural ash	$12,000	$16,000
1969	Natural mahogany	$12,000	$16,000
1969	Rare color	$20,000	$25,000
1969	Sunburst	$13,000	$18,000
1970	Common color	$16,000	$20,000
1970	Natural ash	$12,000	$16,000
1970	Natural mahogany	$12,000	$16,000
1970	Rare color	$20,000	$25,000
1970	Sunburst	$13,000	$18,000
1971	Color option, 3-bolt, hums	$10,000	$13,000
1971	Color option, 4-bolt, singles	$15,000	$18,000
1971	Natural ash, 3-bolt	$5,500	$7,500
1971	Natural ash, 3-bolt, hums	$5,500	$7,500
1971	Natural ash, 4-bolt, singles	$12,000	$15,000
1971	Natural mahogany, 3-bolt	$5,500	$7,500
1971	Natural mahogany, 3-bolt, hums	$5,500	$7,500
1971	Natural mahogany, 4-bolt, singles	$12,000	$15,000
1971	Sunburst, 3-bolt, hums	$5,500	$7,500
1971	Sunburst, 4-bolt, singles	$7,000	$9,500
1972	Color option	$9,000	$12,000
1972	Mahogany	$5,000	$6,500
1972	Natural ash	$5,000	$6,500
1972	Sunburst	$5,500	$7,000
1973	Color option	$6,500	$8,500
1973	Mahogany	$5,000	$6,500

1969 Fender Rosewood Telecaster

Keith Hardie

Fender Telecaster Custom

1972 Fender Telecaster Thinline

1968 Fender Villager 12-String
Imaged by Heritage Auctions, HA.com

MODEL YEAR	FEATURES	EXC. COND. LOW	HIGH
1973	Natural ash	$5,000	$6,500
1973	Sunburst	$5,500	$7,000
1974	Color option	$5,000	$6,500
1974	Mahogany	$4,000	$5,500
1974	Natural ash	$4,000	$5,500
1974	Sunburst	$4,500	$6,000
1975	Color option	$5,000	$6,500
1975	Natural ash	$4,000	$5,500
1975	Sunburst	$4,500	$6,000
1976	Color option	$3,500	$4,500
1976	Natural ash	$3,500	$4,500
1976	Sunburst	$3,500	$4,500
1977	Color option	$3,500	$4,500
1977	Natural ash	$3,500	$4,500
1977	Sunburst	$3,500	$4,500
1978	Color option	$3,250	$4,250
1978	Natural ash	$3,250	$4,250
1978	Sunburst	$3,250	$4,250

Tele-Sonic
1998-2000. U.S.A., chambered Telecaster body, 2 DeArmond pickups, dot markers, upper bass bout 3-way toggle switch.
1998-2000 $1,250 $1,625

Texas Special Telecaster
1991-1992. Custom Shop, 60 made, state of Texas outline on the 'guard, ash body with Texas Orange transparent finish, large profile maple neck, with certificate of authenticity.
1991-1992 $3,000 $4,000

Twisted Telecaster Limited Edition
2005. Custom Shop, 50 built by Master Builder Yuriy Shishkov, 100 built by the Custom Shop team, top loaded Bigsby.
2005 Shishkov built $5,000 $6,000
2005 Team built $3,000 $4,000

Two-Tone Telecaster Thinline
2019-2020. FSR Limited Edition, alder body, various top colors with matching headstock and white back and sides.
2019-2020 $1,500 $2,000

Vintage Hot Rod Telecaster
2007-2014. Vintage styling with modern features, '07-'13 named '52 Tele and '62 Tele, in '14 changed to '50s, and '60s.
2007-2014 All models $1,500 $2,000

Waylon Jennings Tribute Telecaster
1995-2003. Custom Shop, black with white leather rose body inlays.
1995-2003 $7,000 $9,000

Will Ray Signature Jazz-A-Caster
1997. Made in Fender Japan Custom Shop as one part of the three-part Hellecasters Series, limited edition, Strat neck on a Tele body with 2 soap-bar Seymour Duncan Jazzmaster-style pickups, gold leaf finish.
1997 $1,500 $2,000

Will Ray Signature Mojo Telecaster
1998-2001. Custom Shop, ash body, flamed maple Strat neck, locking tuners, rosewood 'board, skull inlays, double coil pickups, optional Hipshot B bender.
1998-2001 $3,000 $4,000

Telecoustic Series
2000-2016. Thinline acoustic/electric, single-cut, spruce top, fiberglass body, various colors. Telecoustic discontinued '05, Deluxe begins '07-'09 and Standard added in '09-'16. Both Plus and Premier '14-'16.
2000-2016 Various models $400 $550

Toronado/Deluxe/HH/Highway 1/GT HH
1998-2006. American Special series, various models and colors. Deluxe model made in Mexico.
1998-2006 $650 $850

Villager 12-String
1965-1969, 2011-present. Acoustic flat-top, spruce top, mahogany back and sides, 12 strings, natural. Reintroduced in '11 (California Series) with on-board Fishman System, made in China.
1965-1969 $975 $1,750
2011-2023 Reintroduced $350 $450

Violin - Electric
1958-1976, 2013. Violin-shape, solidbody, sunburst is the standard finish.
1958-1976 $2,500 $3,250
2013 $650 $850

Wildwood
1963-1971. Acoustic flat-top with Wildwood dyed top.
1966-1971 Various (unfaded) $2,250 $3,000

Fenix
Late 1980s-mid 1990s. Brand name of Korean manufacturer Young Chang, used on a line of original-design and copy acoustic, electric and bass guitars. They also built Squier brand guitars for Fender during that period.

Fenton-Weill
See info under Burns-Weill.

Fernandes
1969-present. Established in Tokyo. Early efforts were classical guitars, but they now offer a variety of intermediate grade, production, imported guitars and basses.

Fina
Production classical and steel-string guitars and acoustic basses built in Huiyang City, Guang Dong, China.

Finck, David
1986-present. Luthier David Finck builds custom, professional, and premium grade, acoustic guitars, presently in Valle Crucis, North Carolina. In the past, he has built in Pittsburg, Kansas and Reader, West Virginia.

Fine Resophonic
1988-present. Professional and premium grade, production/custom, wood and metal-bodied resophonic guitars (including reso-electrics) built by luthiers Mike Lewis and Pierre Avocat in Vitry Sur Seine, France. They also build ukes and mandolins.

MODEL		EXC. COND.	
YEAR	FEATURES	LOW	HIGH

Firefly

Independent brand, budget models produced in China.

Electric

Various copy models made in China.

2019-2023		$130	$250

First Act

1995-present. Budget and professional grade, production/custom, acoustic, solid and semi-hollow body guitars built in China and in their Custom Shop in Boston. They also make basses, violins, and other instruments.

Firth Pond & Company

1822-1867. An east coast retail distributor that sold Martin and Ashborn private brand instruments. The company operated as Firth and Hall from 1822-1841 (also known as Firth, Hall & Pond) in New York City and Litchfield, Connecticut. Most instruments were small parlor size (11" lower bout) guitars, as was the case for most builders of this era. Sometimes the inside back center seam will be branded Firth & Pond. Brazilian rosewood sides and back instruments fetch considerably more than most of the other tone woods and value can vary considerably based on condition. Guitars from the 1800s are sometimes valued more as antiques than working vintage guitars. In 1867 Firth & Sons sold out to Oliver Ditson Company.

Flammang Guitars

1990-present. Premium grade, custom/production, steel string guitars built by luthier David Flammang in Greene, Iowa and previously in East Hampton and Higganum, Connecticut.

Flaxwood

2004-present. Professional grade, production/custom, solid and semi-hollow body guitars built in Finland, with bodies of natural fiber composites.

Fleishman Instruments

Introduced in 1974, premium and presentation grade, custom flat-tops made by luthier Harry Fleishman in Sebastopol, California. He also offers basses and electric uprights. Fleishman is the director of Luthiers School International.

Fletcher Brock Stringed Instruments

1992-present. Custom flat-tops and archtops made by luthier Fletcher Brock originally in Ketchum, Idaho, and currently in Seattle, Washington. He also builds mandolin family instruments.

Flowers Guitars

1993-present. Premium grade, custom, archtop guitars built by luthier Gary Flowers in Baltimore, Maryland.

MODEL		EXC. COND.	
YEAR	FEATURES	LOW	HIGH

Floyd Rose

2004-2006. Floyd Rose, inventor of the Floyd Rose Locking Tremolo, produced a line of intermediate and professional grade, production, solidbody guitars from '04 to '06. They continue to offer bridges and other accessories.

Foggy Mountain

Intermediate grade, production, steel and nylon string acoustic and acoustic/electric guitars imported from China.

Fontanilla Guitars

1987-present. Luthier Allan Fontanilla builds his premium grade, production/custom, classical guitars in San Francisco, California.

Fouilleul

1978-present. Production/custom, classical guitars made by luthier Jean-Marie Fouilleul in Cuguen, France.

Fox Hollow Guitars

2004-present. Luthier Don Greenough builds his professional and premium grade, custom, acoustic and electric guitars in Eugene, Oregon. He also builds mandolins.

Fox or Rocking F

1983-present. Premium grade, custom, steel string acoustic guitars built in Seattle, Washington by luthier Cat Fox.

Foxxe

1990-1991. Short-lived brand of solidbodies offered by the same company that produced Barrington guitars, Korean-made.

Frame Works

1995-present. Professional grade, production/custom, steel- and nylon-string guitars built by luthier Frank Krocker in Burghausen, Germany. The instruments feature a neck mounted on a guitar-shaped frame. Krocker has also built traditional archtops, flat-tops, and classicals.

Framus

1946-1977, 1996-present. Professional and premium grade, production/custom, guitars made in Markneukirchen, Germany. They also build basses, amps, mandolins, and banjos. Frankische Musikindustrie (Framus) founded in Erlangen, Germany by Fred Wilfer, relocated to Bubenreuth in '54, and to Pretzfeld in '67. Begun as an acoustic instrument manufacturer, Framus added electrics in the mid-'50s. Earliest electrics were mostly acoustics with pickups attached. Electric designs began in the early-'60s. A unique feature was a laminated maple neck with many thin plies. By around '64-'65 upscale models featured the organtone, often called a spigot, a spring-loaded volume control that allowed you to

Flowers

Frame Works

1962 Framus Sorella
Model 5/59-50

Rivington Guitars

Fritz Brothers Roy
Buchanan Bluesmaster

MODEL YEAR	FEATURES	EXC. COND. LOW	HIGH

simulate a Leslie speaker effect. Better models often had mutes and lots of switches.

In the '60s, Framus instruments were imported into the U.S. by Philadelphia Music Company. Resurgence of interest in ca. '74 with the Jan Akkermann hollowbody followed by original mid-'70s design called the Nashville, the product of an alliance with some American financing.

The brand was revived in '96 by Hans Peter Wilfer, the president of Warwick, with production in Warwick's factory in Germany.

Amateur
Early-1960s to mid-1970s. Model 5/1, small flat-top, early without pickguard, plain, dot markers.

1960s-70s	Model 5/1	$250	$350

Atilla Zoller AZ-10
Early-1960s-early-1980s. Single-cut archtop, 2 pickups, neck glued-in until the '70s, bolt-on after, sunburst. Model 5/65 (rounded cutaway, made until late '60s) and Model 5/67 (sharp cutaway).

1960s	Model 5/65	$850	$1,125
1960s-70s	Model 5/67	$850	$1,125

Atlantic
Ca. 1965-ca. 1970. Model 5/110, single-cut thin body electric archtop, 2 pickups, tremolo optional.

1965-1970	Model 5/110	$750	$1,000

Atlantic Elec-12
Mid- to late-1960s. Model 5/011 and 5/013, double cut semi-hollow, 2 pickups, 12-string.

1960s	Model 5/011 & /013	$750	$1,000

Big 18 Doubleneck
Late-1960s. Model 5/200 is a solidbody and Model 5/220 is acoustic.

1960s	Model 5/200 & /220	$950	$1,250

Caravelle
Ca.1965-ca. 1975. Double-cut archtop, tremolo, model 5/117-52 has 2 pickups and 5/117-54 has 3.

1965-1975	Model 5/117	$850	$1,125

Gaucho
1967 to mid-1970s. Lower grade flat-top, concert size, spruce top, mahogany sides and back, rosewood bridge and 'board, sunburst or natural finish.

1967-70s	Model 5/194	$250	$350

Guitar-Banjo 6/76 Dixi, SL-76
Ca. 1957-early 1970s. Banjo body, guitar neck, silver hardware.

1957-1970s		$650	$850

Hollywood
1960s. Double-cut, 3 pickups, red sunburst.

1960s	Model 5/132	$1,000	$1,375

Jan Akkerman
1974-1977. Single-cut semi-hollowbody, 2 pickups, gold hardware.

1974-1977		$575	$750

Jumbo
1963 to late-1970s. Models earlier 5/97, later 5/197, jumbo flat-top, mahogany or maple sides and back.

1960s-70s		$600	$775

Jumbo 12-String
Late-1960s to mid-1970s. 12-string version.

1960s-70s	Model 5/297	$600	$775

Missouri (E Framus Missouri)
Ca.1955-ca. 1975. Originally non-cut acoustic archtop until early '60s when single-cut archtop with 1 or 2 pickups added.

1960s	Model 5/60	$650	$850

New Sound Series
1960s. Double-cut semi-hollowbody, model 5/116-52 has 2 pickups and 5/116-54 has 3.

1960s		$975	$1,250

Sorella Series
Ca.1955 to mid-1970s. Single-cut, Model 5/59 is acoustic archtop (with or without single pickup), 5/59-50 is 1-pickup electric archtop, 5/59-52 is electric 2-pickup.

1955-1975	Model 5/59	$850	$1,125
1965-1972	Model 5/59-50	$900	$1,250
1965-1972	Model 5/59-52	$900	$1,250

Sorento
Ca.1963-ca. 1970. Thinline archtop, single-cut, 2 pickups, organ effect, f-holes.

1963-1970	Model 5/112-53	$900	$1,125

Sorento 12
Ca.1963-ca. 1970. 12-string version.

1963-1970	Model 5/012	$950	$1,250

Sport
Early 1950s-mid-1970s. Small beginner flat-top, plain appointments, dot markers.

1950s-70s	Model 50/1	$225	$300

Strato de Luxe 12 String
Ca. 1963-ca. 1970. Model 5/067(metal pickguard) and 5/068 (wood grain pickguard and large gold cover plates), 2 pickups, tremolo.

1963-1970	Model 5/068	$925	$1,250

Strato de Luxe Series
Ca.1964-ca. 1970. Various models, 1 or 2 pickups (5/155, 5/167-52, 5/168-52), 3 pickups (5/167-54, 5/168-54), some models have gold hardware.

1964-1970	2 pickups	$800	$1,125
1964-1970	3 pickups	$850	$1,250

Strato Super
Early to late-1960s. Offset double-cut, 2 pickups.

1960s	Model 5/155-52	$825	$1,125

Studio Series
Late-1950s to mid-1970s. Model 5/51 (a.k.a. 030) is non-cut acoustic archtop (some with pickup - 5/51E), 5/108 is electric archtop, 1 pickup.

1960s-70s	Model 5/51	$250	$325
1960s-70s	Model 5/51E	$275	$350

Television Series
Early to late-1960s. Model 5/118-52 2 pickups and 5/118-54 3 pickups, offset double-cut thinline hollowbody.

1960s	Model 5/118-52	$750	$1,125
1960s	Model 5/118-54	$900	$1,250

Texan Series
Late-1960s to early-1980s. Model 5/196, 5/196E (with pickup) and 5/296 12-string flat-top, mahogany back and sides. 6-string ends in late '70s.

1960s-70s	6-string	$350	$450
1960s-80s	12-string	$350	$450

MODEL			EXC. COND.	
YEAR	FEATURES		LOW	HIGH

Western
1960s. Model 5/195, grand concert size, lower grade flat-top, spruce top, maple sides and back.

| 1960s | Model 5/195 | | $250 | $325 |

Franklin Guitar Company
1974-present. Premium and presentation grade, custom, flat-top steel string guitars built first in Franklin, Michigan and since 2003 in Rocheport, Missouri by luthier Nick Kukich. He also built in Idaho, Washington and Oregon.

Fraulini
2001-present. Luthier Todd Cambio builds his professional and premium grade, primarily custom, early 20th century style guitars, in Madison, Wisconsin.

FreeNote
Intermediate to professional grade, the innovative FreeNote 12-Tone Ultra Plus provides two frets for every traditional fret placement which provides an unlimited number of playable notes.

Fresher
1973-1985. The Japanese-made Fresher brand models were mainly copies of popular brands and limited numbers were imported into the U.S. They also made basses.

Solidbody Electric
1970s. Import from Japan, various models.

| 1970s | | | $225 | $500 |

Fret-King
2008-present. Luthier Trev Wilkinson builds professional and premium grade, production, solidbody and semi-hollow electric guitars and basses in Yorkshire, U.K., and offers a line imported from Korea.

Fritz Brothers
1988-present. Premium grade, production/custom, acoustic, semi-hollow, and solidbody guitars and basses built by luthier Roger Fritz, originally in Mobile, Alabama, then in Mendocino, California. In 2013 he again relocated to Mobile.

Froggy Bottom Guitars
1974-present. Luthier Michael Millard builds his premium and presentation grade, production/custom flat-tops in Newfane, Vermont (originally in Hinsdale, New York, and until '84 production was in Richmond, New Hampshire).

Frudua Guitar Works
1988-present. Luthier Galeazzo Frudua builds his intermediate to premium grade, production/custom, electric guitars, basses and amps in Imola, Italy.

Fukuoka Musical Instruments
1993-present. Custom steel- and nylon-string flat-tops and archtops built in Japan.

Furch
See listing for Stonebridge.

Furnace Mountain Guitar Works
1995-1999. Instruments built by luthier Martin Fair in New Mexico. He currently builds under the Fairbuilt Guitar Co. brand.

Fury
1962-2017. Founded by Glenn McDougall in Saskatoon, Saskatchewan, Fury offered production, hollow, semi-hollow and solidbody electric guitars and basses. McDougall died in early '17.

Futurama
1957-mid to late 1960s. Futurama was a brand name used by Selmer in the United Kingdom. Early instruments made by the Drevokov Cooperative in Czechoslovakia, models for '63-'64 made by Sweden's Hagstrom company. Some later '60s instruments may have been made in Japan. Beatles fans will recognize the brand name as Beatle George Harrison's first electric.

Futurama I/II/III
1957-1969. Offset double-cut, 2- or 3-pickup versions available, large Futurama logo on headstock with the reverse capital letter F. George Harrison purchased his Futurama in '59; maple neck, 3 pickups, 3 push button levels, 2 knobs, Futurama logo on 'guard. The price shown for the Harrison model assumes an all-original, excellent condition that exactly matches his '59 model.

| 1960-1969 | III, Harrison, maple | $2,000 | $5,000 |
| 1960-1969 | III, rosewood | $1,000 | $1,500 |

Fylde Guitars
1973-present. Luthier Roger Bucknall builds his professional and premium grade, production/custom acoustic guitars, basses, mandolins, mandolas, bouzoukis, and citterns in Penrith, Cumbria, UK.

G&L
1980-present. Intermediate and professional grade, production/custom, solidbody and semi-hollowbody electric guitars made in the U.S. and overseas. They also make basses. Founded by Leo Fender and George Fullerton following the severance of ties between Fender's CLF Research and Music Man. Company sold to John MacLaren and BBE Sound when Leo Fender died in '91. In '98 they added their Custom Creations Department. In '03 G&L introduced the Korean-made G&L Tribute Series. George Fullerton died in July, '09.

ASAT
1986-1998. Called the Broadcaster in '85. Two or 3 single-coil or 2 single-coil/1 humbucker pickup configurations until early-'90s, 2 single-coils after.

1986		$1,500	$1,875
1987	Leo sig on headstock	$1,500	$1,875
1988-1991	Leo sig on body	$1,500	$1,875
1992-1998	BBE era	$1,250	$1,625

Froggy Bottom Guitars

Futurama III

G&L ASAT Classic Bluesboy
Emmitt Omar

G&L ASAT Special

MODEL YEAR / FEATURES	EXC. COND. LOW	HIGH
ASAT 20th Anniversary		
2000. Limited Edition run of 50, ash body, tinted birdseye maple neck, 2-tone sunburst.		
2000	$1,500	$1,875
ASAT '50		
1999. Limited edition of 10.		
1999	$1,500	$1,875
ASAT Bluesboy Limited Edition		
1999. Limited edition of 20.		
1999	$1,375	$1,750
ASAT Bluesboy Semi-Hollow Limited Edition		
1999. Limited edition of 12, thin semi-hollow.		
1999	$1,375	$1,750
ASAT Classic		
1990-present. Two single-coil pickups, individually adjustable bridge saddles, neck-tilt adjustment and tapered string posts.		
1990-1991 Leo sig on body	$1,125	$1,500
1992-1997 3-bolt neck	$975	$1,250
1997-2023 4-bolt neck	$975	$1,250
ASAT Classic B-Bender		
1997. 12 made with factory-original B-Bender.		
1997	$1,250	$1,625
ASAT Classic Bluesboy		
2001-present. Humbucker neck pickup, single-coil at bridge.		
2001-2023	$1,125	$1,500
ASAT Classic Bluesboy Rustic		
2010-2015. Classic Bluesboy with Rustic aging and refinements.		
2010-2015	$1,375	$1,750
ASAT Classic Bluesboy Semi-Hollow		
1997-present. Chambered Classic with f-hole.		
1997-2023	$1,250	$1,625
ASAT Classic Commemorative/ Commemorative		
1991-1992. Leo Fender signature and birth/death dating, Australian lacewood (6 made) and Cherryburst or Sunburst (1,000 made).		
1991-1992 Australian	$7,000	$10,000
1991-1992 Cherryburst	$1,750	$2,250
1991-1992 Sunburst	$1,750	$2,250
ASAT Classic Custom		
1996-1997, 2002-2013. Large rectangular neck pickup, single-coil bridge pickup. 2nd version has 4-bolt neck.		
1996-1997 1st version	$1,250	$1,625
2002-2013 2nd version	$1,250	$1,625
ASAT Classic Custom Semi-Hollow		
2002-2013. Custom with f-hole.		
2002-2013	$1,125	$1,500
ASAT Classic S		
2007. Limited run of 50, certificate, swamp ash body, 3 single-coil pickups, Nashville pickup configuration.		
2007	$1,250	$1,625
ASAT Classic Semi-Hollow		
1997-2021. With f-hole.		
1997-2021	$1,250	$1,625

MODEL YEAR / FEATURES	EXC. COND. LOW	HIGH
ASAT Classic Signature		
1988-1991. Leo Fender signature on upper cutaway horn.		
1988-1991 Various colors	$1,875	$2,375
ASAT Classic Three		
1998. Limited Edition run of 100.		
1998	$1,375	$1,750
ASAT Custom		
1996. No pickguard, 25 to 30 made.		
1996	$1,125	$1,500
ASAT Deluxe		
1997-present. Flamed maple top, bound body, 2 humbuckers.		
1997 3-bolt neck	$1,375	$1,750
1997-2023 4-bolt neck	$1,375	$1,750
ASAT Deluxe Semi-Hollow		
1997-2018. Two humbuckers.		
1997-2018	$1,375	$1,750
ASAT III		
1988-1991, 1996-1998. Single-cut body, 3 single-coil pickups.		
1988-1991 Leo era, 150 made	$1,375	$1,750
1996-1998 Post Leo era	$1,250	$1,625
ASAT JD-5/Jerry Donahue JD-5		
2004-2007. Jerry Donahue model, single-cut, 2 single-coils, special wired 5-way switch.		
2004-2007	$1,375	$1,750
ASAT Junior		
1998-1999. Limited Edition run of 250, single-cut semi-hollowbody, 2 single-coils.		
1998-1999	$1,250	$1,625
ASAT S-3		
1998-2000. Three soap-bar single-coil pickups, limited production.		
1998-2000	$875	$1,125
ASAT Special		
1992-present. Like ASAT, but with 2 larger P-90-type pickups, chrome hardware, various colors.		
1992-1997 3-bolt neck	$1,125	$1,500
1997-2019 4-bolt neck	$1,125	$1,500
ASAT Special Semi-Hollow		
1997-2018. Semi-hollow version of ASAT Special.		
1997-2018	$875	$1,125
ASAT Special Deluxe		
2001-2015. No 'guard version of the Special with figured maple top.		
2001-2015	$1,250	$1,625
ASAT Special Detroit Muscle Series		
2015. Classic automobile colors include; Daytona Yellow, Hugger Orange, Cranberry Red and Marina Blue.		
2015	$1,125	$1,500
ASAT Z-2 Limited Edition		
1999. Limited run of 10, semi-hollow construction, natural ash, tortoise bound, engraved neckplate.		
1999	$1,250	$1,625
ASAT Z-3		
1998-2020. Three offset-style Z-3 high output pickups, sunburst.		
1998-2020	$1,125	$1,500

The *Vintage Guitar Price Guide* shows values for all-original, excellent condition instruments and, where applicable, with original case.

MODEL YEAR	FEATURES	EXC. COND. LOW	HIGH

ASAT Z-3 Semi-Hollow
1998-2020. F-hole version of Z-3.

1998-2020		$1,125	$1,500

Broadcaster
1985-1986. Solidbody, 2 single-coils with adjustable polepieces act in humbucking mode with selector switch in the center position, black parts and finish, name changed to ASAT in early-'86.

1985-1986	Kahler	$2,375	$3,000
1985-1986	Signed by Leo	$2,500	$3,125

Cavalier
1983-1986. Offset double-cut, 2 humbuckers, 700 made, sunburst.

1983-1986		$1,375	$1,750

Climax
1992-1996. Offset double-cut, bolt maple neck, six-on-a-side tuners, double locking vibrato, blue.

1992-1996		$1,000	$1,375

Climax Plus
1992-1996. Two humbuckers replace single-coils of the Climax, plus 1 single-coil.

1992-1996		$1,000	$1,375

Climax XL
1992-1996. Two humbuckers only.

1992-1996		$1,000	$1,375

Comanche V
1988-1991. Solidbody, 3 Z-shaped single-coil humbuckers, maple neck in choice of 3 radii, rosewood 'board, vibrato, fine tuners, Leo Fender's signature on the body, sunburst.

1988-1991		$1,625	$2,000

Comanche VI
1990-1991. Leo Fender's signature on the body, 6 mini-toggles.

1990-1991		$1,500	$2,000

Comanche (Reintroduced)
1998-present. Reissue with either swamp ash or alder body, bolt-on maple neck, 3 Z-coil pickups, standard or premium finish options.

1998-2023	Premium finish	$1,250	$1,625
1998-2023	Standard finish	$1,125	$1,500

Comanche Deluxe (Reintroduced)
2018-present. Fullerton Deluxe series, old style double-cut, 3 Z-coil pickups, alder or swamp ash top, various colors with vintage tint satin finish.

2018-2023		$1,125	$1,500

F-100 (Model I and II)
1980-1986. Offset double-cut solidbody, 2 humbuckers, natural. Came in an I and II model - only difference is the radius of the 'board.

1980-1986		$1,000	$1,375

F-100E (Model I and II)
1980-1982. Offset double-cut solidbody, 2 humbuckers, active electronics, pre-amp, natural. Came in an I and II model - only difference is the radius of the 'board.

1980-1982		$1,000	$1,375

Fallout
2013-present. SC-2 body style, P-90 and humbucker, swamp ash body on premier and alder on standard finishes, maple neck, maple or rosewood 'board.

2013-2023		$1,125	$1,500

Fullerton Deluxe Dohney
2018-present. Fullerton Deluxe series, old style, 2 pickups, alder or swamp ash top, various colors with vintage tint satin finish.

2018-2023		$1,125	$1,500

G-200/G-201
1981-1982. Mahogany solidbody, maple neck, ebony 'board, 2 humbucking pickups, coil-split switches, natural or sunburst, 209 made.

1981-1982	Front load	$2,250	$3,000
1981-1982	Rear load	$3,250	$4,250

GBL-LE (Guitars by Leo Limited Edition)
1999. Limited edition of 25, semi-hollowbody, 3 pickups.

1999		$1,250	$1,625

George Fullerton Signature
1995-2007. Double-cut solidbody, sunburst.

1995-1997	3-bolt neck	$1,375	$1,750
1997-2007	4-bolt neck	$1,375	$1,750

HG-1
1982-1983. Offset double-cut, 1 humbucker, dot inlays. Very rare as most were made into HG-2s.

1982-1983	5 made	$1,875	$2,500

HG-2
1982-1984. 2-humbucker HG, body changes to classic offset double-cut in '84.

1982-1983	Mustang-body	$1,500	$2,000
1984	Double-cut	$1,500	$2,000

Interceptor
1983-1991. To '86 an X-shaped solidbody, either 3 single-coils, 2 humbuckers, or 1 humbucker and 2 single-coils, '87-'91 was an offset double-cut solidbody.

1983-1985	1st X-body, 70 made	$2,875	$3,750
1985-1986	2nd X-body, 12 made	$2,875	$3,750
1987-1991	Double-cut	$1,500	$2,000

Invader
1984-1991, 1998-2018. Double-cut solidbody, 2 single-coil and 1 humbucker pickups.

1984-1991	1st version	$1,250	$1,625
1998-2018	2nd version	$1,250	$1,625

Invader Plus
1998-2018. Two humbuckers and single blade pickup in the middle position.

1998-2018		$1,125	$1,500

Invader XL
1998-2018. Fancy top, 2 humbuckers.

1998-2018		$1,250	$1,625

John Jorgenson Signature ASAT
1995. About 190 made, Silver Metalflake finish.

1995		$1,250	$1,625

Legacy
1992-present. Classic double-cut configuration, USA logo, 3-bolt neck until '97, 4-bolt after, various colors.

1992-1994	3-bolt, Duncans	$1,000	$1,375
1995-1997	3-bolt, Alnicos	$1,000	$1,375
1996-1997	Swirl finish	$1,125	$1,500
1998-2023	4-bolt, Alnicos	$1,000	$1,375

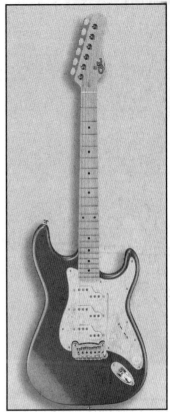

G&L Comanche

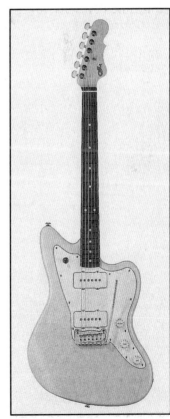

G&L Fullerton Deluxe Dohney

GUITARS

G&L S-500

G&L Tribute ASAT Classic

MODEL YEAR	FEATURES	EXC. COND. LOW	HIGH
Legacy Deluxe			
2001-2015. No 'guard, figured maple top.			
2001-2015		$1,000	$1,375
Legacy HH			
2001-2022. Two humbucker pickups.			
2001-2022		$1,000	$1,375
Legacy HSS			
2001-2023. One humbucker pickup at bridge position plus 2 single-coil pickups.			
2001-2023		$1,000	$1,375
Legacy Special			
1993-2023. Legacy with 3 humbuckers, various colors.			
1992-1997	3-bolt neck	$1,000	$1,375
1998-2023	4-bolt neck	$1,000	$1,375
Limited Edition 25th Anniversary			
2006. G&L Custom Creations, 250 made, combines appearance of '81 F-100 with contours and control layout of ASAT Super, single-cut mahogany body, 2 custom wound MFD humbuckers, custom blend 'root beer' finish.			
2006		$1,250	$1,625
Nighthawk			
1983. Offset double-cut solidbody, 269 made, 3 single-coil pickups, sunburst, name changed to Sky-hawk in '84.			
1983		$1,125	$1,500
Rampage			
1984-1991. Offset double-cut solidbody, hard rock maple neck, ebony 'board, 1 bridge-position humbucker pickup, sunburst. Currently available as Jerry Cantrell Signature Model.			
1984-1991	Common color	$1,250	$1,625
1984-1991	Rare color	$1,875	$2,500
Rampage (Reissue)			
2000. Limited Edition run of 70, supplied with gig bag and not hard case, ivory finish.			
2000		$750	$975
Rampage Jerry Cantrell Limited Edition			
2011. Limited Edition run of 50, blue dress decal.			
2011		$2,500	$5,000
S-500			
1982-present. Double-cut mahogany or ash solidbody, maple neck, ebony or maple 'board, 3 single-coil pickups, vibrato.			
1982-1987		$1,250	$1,625
1988-1991	Mini-toggle, Leo sig on body	$1,125	$1,500
1992-1997	3-bolt neck	$900	$1,125
1997-2023	4-bolt neck	$900	$1,125
S-500 Deluxe			
2001-2015. Deluxe Series features, including no 'guard and flamed maple top, natural.			
2001-2015		$1,125	$1,500
SC-1			
1982-1983. Offset double-cut solidbody, 1 single-coil pickup, tremolo, sunburst, 250 made.			
1981-1982		$1,125	$1,500
SC-2			
1982-1983, 2010-2018. Offset double-cut solidbody, shallow cutaways change to deeper pointed in '83, 2			

MODEL YEAR	FEATURES	EXC. COND. LOW	HIGH
MFD soapbar pickups, about 600 made in original run. Reissue maple or rosewood 'board.			
1982-1983		$1,500	$2,000
2010-2018	Reissue	$675	$875
SC-3			
1982-1991. Offset double-cut solidbody, shallow cutaway changes to deeper pointed in '84, 3 single-coil pickups, tremolo.			
1982-1987	No 'guard	$1,250	$1,625
1988-1991	With 'guard	$1,125	$1,500
Skyhawk			
1984-1991. Renamed from Nighthawk, offset double-cut, 3 single-coils, signature on headstock '84-'87, then on body '88-'91.			
1984-1987	Dual-Fulcrum or saddle lock	$1,000	$1,375
1984-1987	Kahler	$775	$1,000
1988-1991	Dual-Fulcrum or saddle lock	$850	$1,125
1988-1991	Kahler	$775	$1,000
Superhawk			
1984-1987. Offset double-cut, maple neck, ebony 'board, G&L or Kahler tremolos, 2 humbuckers, signature on headstock.			
1984-1987		$1,250	$1,500
Tribute Series			
2003-present. Imported versions of regular models.			
2003-2023	Various models	$250	$750
Trinity			
2006. Only 25 made, ASAT-style with 3 new style single-coils, designed by Tim Page of Buffalo Brothers, the last G&L to have COA signed by George Fullerton.			
2006		$1,750	$2,250
Will Ray Signature			
2002-2018. Will Ray signature on headstock, 3 Z-coil pickups, Hipshot B-Bender.			
2002-2018		$850	$1,125

G.L. Stiles

1960-1994. Built by Gilbert Lee Stiles primarily in the Miami, Florida area. First solidbody, including pickups and all hardware, built by hand in his garage. Stiles favored scrolls, fancy carving, and walnut fingerboards. His later instruments were considerably fancier and more refined. He moved to Hialeah, Florida by '63 and began making acoustic guitars and other instruments. Only his solidbodies had consecutive serial numbers. Stiles, who died in '94, made approximately 1000 solidbodies and 500 acoustics.

Gadotti Guitars

Luthier Jeanfranco Biava Gadotti, began in 1997, builds premium grade, custom/production, nylon- and steel-string, carved, chambered solidbodies in Orlando, Florida.

Gadow Guitars

2002-2019. Luthier Ryan Gadow built his professional and premium grade, custom/production, solid and semi-hollow body guitars and basses in Durham, North Carolina.

MODEL		EXC. COND.	
YEAR	FEATURES	LOW	HIGH

Gagnon

Luthier Bill Gagnon began building his premium and presentation grade, production/custom, archtop guitars in Beaverton, Oregon, starting in 1998.

Galanti

Ca.1962-ca.1967. Electric guitars offered by the longtime Italian accordion maker, some built by Zero Sette. They may have also offered acoustics.

Electric

1962-1967. Solidbody or hollowbody.

1962-1967	Fancy features	$650	$1,000
1962-1967	Plain features	$400	$700

Galiano

New Yorkers Antonio Cerrito and Raphael Ciani offered guitars under the Galiano brand during the early part of the last century. They used the brand both on guitars built by them and others, including The Oscar Schmidt Company. They also offered mandolins.

Gallagher

1965-present. Professional and premium grade, production/custom, flat-top guitars built in Wartrace, Tennessee. J. W. Gallagher started building Shelby brand guitars in the Slingerland Drum factory in Shelbyville, Tennessee in '63. In '65 he and his son Don made the first Gallagher guitar, the G-50. Doc Watson began using Gallagher guitars in '68. In '76, Don assumed operation of the business when J. W. semi-retired. J. W. died in '79.

71 Special

1970s-2015. Rosewood back and sides, spruce top, herringbone trim, bound ebony 'board, natural.

1970s-2015		$2,250	$3,250

72 Special

1977-2016. Rosewood back and sides, spruce top, abalone trim, bound ebony 'board, natural.

1977-2016		$3,750	$5,500

A-70 Ragtime Special

1978-2015. Smaller auditorium/00 size, spruce top, mahogany back and sides, G logo, natural.

1978-2015		$1,500	$2,500

Custom 12-String

Introduced in 1965-present. Mahogany, 12-fret neck, natural.

1965		$1,750	$2,500

Doc Watson

1968-present. Spruce top, mahogany back and sides, scalloped bracing, ebony 'board, herringbone trim, natural.

1968-2023		$2,750	$3,750

Doc Watson (Cutaway)

1975-2010. Spruce top, mahogany back and sides, scalloped bracing, ebony 'board, herringbone trim, natural.

1975-2010		$2,750	$3,750

Doc Watson 12-String

1995-2000. Natural.

1995-2000		$2,500	$3,500

MODEL		EXC. COND.	
YEAR	FEATURES	LOW	HIGH

Doc Watson Signature

2000-present. Signature inlay 12th fret.

2000-2023		$2,750	$3,750

G-45

1970-2008. Mahogany back and sides, spruce top, ebony 'board, natural.

1970-1979		$1,750	$2,500
1980-2008		$1,500	$2,250

G-50

1960s-2015. Mahogany back and sides, spruce top, ebony 'board, natural.

1960s		$2,500	$3,500
1970-2015		$2,000	$2,750

G-65

1980s-2015. Rosewood back and sides, spruce top, ebony 'board, natural.

1980s-2015		$2,000	$2,750

G-70

1978-present. Rosewood back and sides, herringbone purfling on top and sound hole, mother-of-pearl diamond 'board inlays, bound headstock, natural.

1978-2023		$2,000	$2,750

G-71

1970s. Indian rosewood, gold tuners.

1970s		$2,500	$3,250

Gallagher, Kevin

1996. Kevin Gallagher, luthier, changed name brand to Omega to avoid confusion with J.W. Gallagher. See Omega listing.

Gallotone

1950s-1960s. Low-end foreign brand similar to 1950s Stellas, the Gallotone Champion, a 3/4 size student flat-top, is associated with John Lennon as his early guitar.

Galloup Guitars

1994-present. Luthier Bryan Galloup builds his professional and premium grade, production/custom flat-tops in Big Rapids, Michigan. He also operates the Galloup School of Lutherie and The Guitar Hospital repair and restoration business.

Galveston

Budget and intermediate grade, production, imported acoustic, acoustic/electric, resonator and solidbody guitars. They also offer basses and mandolins.

Gamble & O'Toole

1978-present. Premium grade, custom classical and steel string guitars built by luthier Arnie Gamble in Sacramento, California, with design input and inlay work from his wife Erin O'Toole.

Ganz Guitars

1995-present. Luthier Steve Ganz builds his professional grade, production/custom classical guitars in Bellingham, Washington.

G&L Skyhawk
Imaged by Heritage Auctions, HA.com

Gallaher Doc Watson Signature

GUITARS

GUITARS

German DB6

1972 Giannini Craviola 12-String

Tom Pfeifer

MODEL YEAR	FEATURES	EXC. COND. LOW	HIGH

Garcia

Made by luthier Federico Garcia in Spain until late-1960s or very early-'70s when production moved to Japan.

Classical

1960s-1970s. Mid-level, '60s model is solid spruce top with solid mahogany, rosewood or walnut back and sides, '70s model is Spanish pine top with walnut back and sides.

1960s-70s	Various wood	$300	$400
1970s	Spanish pine/ Brazilian	$575	$750

Garrison

2000-2007. Intermediate and professional grade, production, acoustic and acoustic/electric guitars designed by luthier Chris Griffiths using his Active Bracing System (a single integrated glass-fiber bracing system inside a solid wood body). He started Griffiths Guitar Works in 1993 in St. John's, Newfoundland, and introduced Garrison guitars in 2000. In '07, the Garrison facility was acquired by Gibson.

Gary Kramer

2006-present. Intermediate and professional grade, production/custom, solidbody electric guitars built by luthier Gary Kramer in El Segundo, California, and imported. Kramer was one of the founders of the Kramer guitar company in the '70s.

Gauge Guitars

Luthier Aaron Solomon builds custom, professional and premium grade, solidbody and semi-solid electric guitars in New Jersey, starting in 2002.

Gemelli

Early 1960s-ca. 1966. European-made (likely Italian) guitars. Similar to Bartolini guitars, so most likely from the same manufacturer. Originally plastic covered, they switched to paint finishes by around '65.

Gemunder

1870s-1910s. New York shop that specialized in reproduction-aged violins, but also made parlor-sized guitars that were similar to Martin guitars of the era. An original label on the inside back identifies August Gemunder and Sons, New York.

Parlor

1870s-1910s. Style 28 appointments, rosewood body, spruce top.

1870-1910s		$1,250	$1,750

George

See listing under Chris George.

German Guitars

2001-present. Luthier Greg German builds his premium grade, custom/production, acoustic archtop guitars in Broomfield, Colorado.

MODEL YEAR	FEATURES	EXC. COND. LOW	HIGH

Giannini

1900-present. Classical, acoustic, and acoustic/electric guitars built in Salto, SP, Brazil near Sao Paolo. They also build violas, cavaquinhoes and mandolins. Founded by guitar-builder Tranquillo Giannini, an Italian who traveled to Brazil in 1890 and discovered the exotic woods of Brazil. The company was producing 30,000 instruments a year by '30. They began exporting their acoustic instruments to the U.S. in '63. They added electric guitars in '60, but these weren't imported as much, if at all. Gianninis from this era used much Brazilian Rosewood.

Classical

Early-1970s. Nylon string import, small body.

1970s	Brazilian rosewood	$525	$700
1970s	Pau ferro, mahogany	$225	$375

CraViola

1972-1974, 2004-present. Kidney bean-shaped rosewood body, acoustic, natural, line included a classical, a steel string, and a 12-string.

1972-1974		$650	$850

CraViola 12-String

1972-1974, 2004-present. Kidney bean-shaped body, 12 strings.

1972-1974		$650	$850

Gibson

1890s (1902)-present. Intermediate, professional, and premium grade, production/custom, acoustic and electric guitars made in the U.S. They also build basses, mandolins, amps, and banjos. Gibson also offers instruments under the Epiphone, Kramer, Steinberger, Dobro, Tobias, Valley Arts, Garrison, Slingerland (drums), Baldwin (pianos), Trace Elliot, Electar (amps), Maestro, Gibson Labs, Oberheim, and Echoplex brands.

Founded in Kalamazoo, Michigan by Orville Gibson, a musician and luthier who developed instruments with tops, sides and backs carved out of solid pieces of wood. Early instruments included mandolins, archtop guitars and harp guitars. By 1896 Gibson had opened a shop. In 1902 Gibson was bought out by a group of investors who incorporated the business as Gibson Mandolin-Guitar Manufacturing Company, Limited. The company was purchased by Chicago Musical Instrument Company (CMI) in '44. In '57 CMI also purchased the Epiphone guitar company, transferring production from Philadelphia to the Gibson plant in Kalamazoo. Gibson was purchased by Norlin in late-'69 and a new factory was opened in Nashville, Tennessee in '74. The Kalamazoo factory ceased production in '84. In '85, Gibson was sold to a group headed by Henry Juszkiewicz. Gibson purchased the Flatiron Company in '87 and built a new factory in '89, moving acoustic instrument production to Bozeman, Montana. In '18 Gibson went into Chapter 11 bankruptcy, emerging later in the year with KKR as new majority owner and James "JC" Curleigh as CEO.

The various models of Firebirds, Flying Vs, Les

MODEL		EXC. COND.	
YEAR	FEATURES	LOW	HIGH

Pauls, SGs, and Super 400s are grouped together under those general headings. Custom Shop and Historic instruments are listed with their respective main model (for example, the '39 Super 400 Historical Collection model is listed with the Super 400s).

Model specifications can cross model years. For example, it is possible that an early '60 Gibson guitar might have a specification, such as a wider-rounder neck, which is typically a '59 spec. In that case it is possible for the early '60 model to be valued more closely to the late '59 model than to a mid to late '60 model with a thinner-flatter neck profile.

Orville Gibson
1894-1902. Hand-made and carved by Orville Gibson, various models and sizes most with standard printed white rectangle label "O.H. Gibson" with photo of Orville Gibson and lyre-mandolin. Prices are for fully functional, original or refurbished examples. It is almost expected that a black Orville Gibson instrument has been refinished, and most of those were done by Gibson.

1894-1902	Very rare,		
	hand made	$65,000	$85,000

335 S Custom
1980-1981. Solidbody, 335-shaped, mahogany body, unbound rosewood 'board, 2 exposed Dirty Finger humbuckers, coil-tap, TP-6 tailpiece. Also available in natural finish, branded headstock Firebrand version.

1980-1981		$1,625	$2,250

335 S Deluxe
1980-1982. Same as 335 S Custom but with bound ebony 'board, brass nut.

1980-1982		$1,625	$2,250

335 S Limited Run
2011-2013. Maple body and neck, rosewood 'board, nitro-finish sunburst.

2011-2013		$1,375	$1,750

335 S Standard
1980-1981. Same as 335 S Custom except stop tailpiece, no coil-tap. Also available in natural finish, branded headstock Firebrand version.

1980-1981		$1,625	$2,250

Advanced Jumbo
1936-1940. Dreadnought, 16" wide, round shoulders, Brazilian rosewood back and sides, sunburst, reintroduced '90-'97.

1936-1940		$75,000	$85,000

Advanced Jumbo (Reissue)
1990-1999, 2002-2018. Issued as a standard production model, but soon available only as a special order for most of the '90s; currently offered as standard production. Renamed 1936 Advanced Jumbo for 1997-1998. There were also some limited-edition AJs offered during the '90s.

1990-1999	Reissue	$2,250	$3,000
2002-2018	Reintroduced	$2,500	$3,250

Advanced Jumbo 12
2015. 12-fret neck.

2015		$2,500	$3,250

Advanced Jumbo 75th Anniversary
2011-2012. 75th Anniversary label, 2nd edition 75 made with on-board electronics.

2011	1st edition	$2,500	$3,000
2012	2nd edition	$2,500	$3,000

1935 Advanced Jumbo
2013. Limited run of 35, Adirondack red spruce top, Indian rosewood back and sides, Vintage Sunburst.

2013		$4,500	$6,000

Advanced Jumbo Koa
2006. Custom Shop, koa back and sides, Adirondack top.

2006		$3,000	$4,000

Advanced Jumbo Luthier's Choice
2000-2008. Custom Shop, various wood options.

2000-2005	Brazilian	$7,000	$9,000
2008	Cocobolo	$3,375	$4,250

Advanced Jumbo Pro
2011-2013. Made for Guitar Center, Baggs pickup, Sitka top, solid rosewood back and sides.

2011-2013		$1,625	$2,125

Advanced Jumbo Red Spruce/ AJ Red Spruce
2013. Limited Edition, Adirondack red spruce top, rosewood back and sides.

2013		$2,500	$3,250

Advanced Jumbo Supreme
2007. Custom Shop, Madagascar rosewood back and sides, Adirondack spruce top.

2007		$3,000	$4,000

Iron Mountain Advanced Jumbo
2014. Custom Shop model, limited run of 65, Adirondack red spruce top, Birdseye maple back and sides, Honeyburst finish.

2014		$3,000	$4,000

Randy Scruggs Advanced Jumbo Limited Edition
2010-2018. Sitka spruce top, East Indian rosewood body, king's crown headstock logo on, crown markers, Fishman pickup, vintage sunburst.

2010-2018		$3,000	$4,000

All American I
1995-1997. Solidbody electric with vague double-cut Melody Maker body style, 1 pickup. Renamed the SG-X in '98.

1995-1997		$850	$1,125

All American II
1996-1997. As American I with 2 pickups.

1996-1997		$850	$1,125

B.B. King Custom
1980-1988. Lucille on peghead, 2 pickups, multi-bound, gold-plated parts, Vari-tone, cherry or ebony, renamed B.B. King Lucille in '88.

1980-1988		$3,000	$4,000

B.B. King Lucille
1988-2019. Introduced as B.B. King Custom, renamed B.B. King Lucille. Lucille on peghead, 2 pickups, multi-bound, gold-plated parts, Vari-tone, cherry or ebony. In '07 B.B. King logo and large king's crown on headstock with Lucille logo on truss rod cover.

1988-2019		$3,000	$4,000
2007-2009	King logo	$3,000	$4,000

1980 Gibson 335-S DeLuxe Professional
Ken MacSwan

1938 Gibson Advanced Jumbo
Imaged by Heritage Auctions, HA.com

2005 Gibson B.B. King
80th Birthday Lucille

Imaged by Heritage Auctions, HA.com

1963 Gibson Byrdland

Paul Lutzke

MODEL YEAR	FEATURES	EXC. COND. LOW	HIGH

B.B. King Standard
1980-1985. Like B.B. King Custom, but with stereo electronics and chrome-plated parts, cherry or ebony.

1980-1985		$2,875	$3,750

B.B. King 80th Birthday Lucille
2005. Custom Shop, limited run of 80, 'guard engraved with crown and signature, headstock engraved with artwork from King's birthday tribute album.

2005		$5,000	$6,500

B.B. King Super Lucille
2002-2004. Signed guard, abalone inlays, custom black sparkle finish.

2002-2004		$4,500	$5,750

B-15
1967-1971. Mahogany, spruce top, student model, natural finish.

1967-1971		$1,125	$1,500

B-20
1971-1972. 14.5" flat-top, mahogany back and sides, dot markers, decal logo, strip in-line tuners with small buttons.

1971-1972		$1,500	$1,875

B-25 3/4 / B-25N 3/4
1962-1968. Short-scale version, flat-top, mahogany body, cherry sunburst (natural finish is the B-25 3/4N).

1962	Wood bridge	$1,500	$1,875
1963-1964	Plastic bridge	$1,500	$1,875
1965		$1,250	$1,500
1966-1968		$1,125	$1,500

B-25/B-25N
1962-1977, 2008-2012. Flat-top, mahogany, bound body, upper belly on bridge (lower belly '68 on), cherry sunburst or black (natural finish is B-25N). Reissued in '08.

1962	Wood bridge	$2,875	$3,500
1963-1964	Plastic bridge	$2,875	$3,500
1965		$2,000	$2,500
1966-1968	Above belly bridge	$1,875	$2,375
1968	Black, white 'guard	$4,000	$5,000
1968	Red, white 'guard	$3,500	$4,500
1969	Below belly bridge	$1,500	$1,875
1970-1977		$1,500	$1,875
2008-2012	Reissue, black	$1,875	$2,375

B-25-12/B-25-12N
1962-1977. Flat-top 12-string version, mahogany, bound body, cherry sunburst (natural finish is the B-25-12N).

1962-1964	No tailpiece	$2,500	$3,500
1965	Trapeze tailpiece	$2,000	$2,500
1966-1968	Trapeze tailpiece	$1,875	$2,375
1969	Below belly bridge	$1,500	$1,875
1970-1977		$1,500	$1,875

B-45-12/B-45-12N
1960-1979. Flat-top 12-string, mahogany, round shoulders for '60-'61, square after, sunburst (natural finish is the B-45-12N).

1960	Early specs	$3,500	$4,500
1961-1962	Round shoulder	$3,000	$3,750
1962-1963	Square shoulder	$2,875	$3,500
1964	No tailpiece	$2,875	$3,500
1965	Trapeze tailpiece	$2,000	$2,500

1966-1968		$2,000	$2,500
1969	Below belly bridge	$1,625	$2,000
1970-1979		$1,500	$1,875

B-45-12 Limited Edition
1991-1992. Limited edition reissue with rosewood back and sides, natural.

1991-1992		$1,500	$1,875

Barney Kessel Custom
1961-1973. Double-cut archtop, 2 humbuckers, gold hardware, cherry sunburst.

1961	PAFs	$10,000	$12,500
1962	Pat #	$5,500	$6,875
1963-1964		$5,500	$6,875
1965		$5,000	$6,250
1966-1969		$4,750	$6,000
1970-1973		$3,625	$4,500

Barney Kessel Regular
1961-1974. Double-cut archtop, 2 humbuckers, nickel hardware, cherry sunburst.

1961	PAFs	$9,500	$12,000
1962	Pat #	$5,250	$6,500
1963-1964		$5,250	$6,500
1965		$4,750	$6,000
1966-1969		$4,500	$5,625
1970-1974		$3,500	$4,375

Blue Ridge
1968-1979, 1989-1990. Flat-top, dreadnought, laminated rosewood back and sides, natural finish, reintroduced for '89-'90.

1968-1969	Brazilian	$1,500	$1,875
1970-1979		$1,500	$1,875

Blue Ridge 12
1970-1978. Flat-top, 12 strings, laminated rosewood back and sides, natural finish.

1970-1978		$1,500	$1,875

Blues King
2012-2013. Acoustic/electric, non-cut, bubinga back and sides, dot inlays.

2012-2013		$1,875	$2,500

Blueshawk
1996-2006. Small single-cut, f-holes, 2 single-coil hum cancelling Blues 90 pickups, 6-way Varitone dial, gold hardware, Bigsby option starts '98.

1996-2006		$1,125	$1,500

B-SJ Blue Ridge
1989. Model name on the label is B-SJ, truss rod covers logo is Blue Ridge, SJ appointments but with narrow peghead shape.

1989		$1,500	$2,000

Byrdland
1955-1992. Thinline archtop, single-cut (rounded until late-'60, pointed '60-late-'69, rounded after '69, rounded or pointed '98-present), 2 pickups, now part of the Historic Collection.

1956-1957	Natural, Alnicos	$10,500	$13,500
1956-1957	Sunburst, Alnicos	$10,500	$13,500
1958-1959	Natural, PAFs	$17,500	$20,000
1958-1959	Sunburst, PAFs	$17,500	$20,000
1960-1962	Natural, PAFs	$15,000	$18,500
1960-1962	Sunburst, PAFs	$14,500	$18,000
1963-1964	Natural, pat #	$9,500	$15,000

MODEL YEAR	FEATURES	EXC. COND. LOW	HIGH
1963-1964	Sunburst, pat #	$9,500	$15,000
1965	Natural	$8,000	$10,000
1965	Sunburst	$8,000	$10,000
1966-1969	Natural	$6,500	$8,500
1966-1969	Sunburst	$6,500	$8,500
1970-1992	Various colors	$5,000	$6,500

Byrdland Historic Collection
1993-2018. Custom shop, various colors.

1993-2018		$5,500	$7,500

C-0 Classical
1962-1971. Spruce top, mahogany back and sides, bound top, natural.

1962-1964		$750	$975
1965		$650	$850
1966-1971		$575	$750

C-1 Classical
1957-1971. Spruce top, mahogany back and sides, bound body, natural.

1957-1959		$800	$1,000
1960-1964		$775	$1,000
1965		$700	$950
1966-1971		$625	$850

C-1 D Laredo
1963-1971. Natural spruce top, mahogany sides and back, upgrade to standard C-1.

1963-1965		$775	$1,000

C-1 E Classical Electric
1960-1967. C-1 with ceramic bridge pickup, catalog notes special matched amplifier that filters out fingering noises.

1960-1964		$775	$1,000
1965		$700	$950
1966-1967		$625	$850

C-1 S Petite Classical
1961-1966. Petite 13 1/4" body, natural spruce top, mahogany back and sides.

1961-1964		$775	$1,000
1965		$700	$950
1966-1967		$625	$850

C-2 Classical
1960-1971. Maple back and sides, bound body, natural.

1960-1964		$900	$1,125
1965		$775	$1,000
1966-1971		$775	$1,000

C-4 Classical
1962-1968. Maple back and sides, natural.

1962-1964		$900	$1,125
1965		$775	$1,000
1966-1968		$775	$1,000

C-6 Classical/Richard Pick
1958-1971. Rosewood back and sides, gold hardware, natural.

1958-1959	Brazilian	$1,875	$2,500
1960-1964	Brazilian	$1,750	$2,250
1965	Brazilian	$1,500	$2,000
1966-1969	Brazilian	$1,500	$2,000
1970-1971	Indian	$950	$1,250

C-8 Classical
1962-1969. Rosewood back and sides, natural.

1962-1964		$1,750	$2,250

MODEL YEAR	FEATURES	EXC. COND. LOW	HIGH
1965		$1,500	$2,000
1966-1969		$1,375	$1,750

C-100 Classical
1971-1972. Slotted peghead, spruce top, mahogany back and sides, ebony 'board, Gibson Master Model label, non-gloss finish.

1971-1972		$625	$850

C-200 Classical
1971-1972. C-100 with gloss finish.

1971-1972		$725	$950

C-300 Classical
1971-1972. Similar to C-100, but with rosewood 'board, wood binding, wider sound hole ring.

1971-1972		$725	$950

C-400 Classical
1971-1972. Rosewood sides and back, spruce top, high-end appointments, chrome hardware.

1971-1972		$775	$1,000

C-500 Classical
1971-1972. C-400 with gold hardware.

1971-1972		$850	$1,125

CF-100
1950-1958. Flat-top, pointed cutaway, mahogany back and sides, bound body, sunburst finish.

1950-1958		$5,500	$7,000

CF-100 E
1951-1959, 2009. CF-100 with a single-coil pickup. Also offered in '94 1950 CF-100 E limited edition and in '07 as a Custom Shop model.

1950-1959		$6,000	$7,750

CF-100 E Reissue
2007. Custom Shop, all maple body, ebony 'board, 24 made.

2007		$2,250	$3,000

Challenger I
1983-1985. Single-cut Les Paul-shaped solidbody, 1 humbucker, bolt-on maple neck, rosewood 'board, dot markers, silver finish standard.

1983-1985		$625	$850

Challenger II
1983-1985. 2 humbucker version.

1983-1985		$650	$875

Challenger III
1984. 3 single-coil version, never cataloged so could be very limited.

1984		$700	$950

Chet Atkins CE
1981-2005. CE stands for Classical Electric, single-cut, multi-bound body, rosewood 'board until '95, then ebony, standard width nut, gold hardware, various colors.

1981-2005		$1,750	$2,250

Chet Atkins CEC
1981-2005. Same as CE, but with ebony 'board and 2" classical width nut, black or natural.

1981-2005		$1,750	$2,250

Chet Atkins Country Gentleman
1986-2005. Thinline archtop, single rounded cutaway, 2 humbuckers, multi-bound, gold hardware, Bigsby. Part of Gibson's Custom line.

1986-2005		$2,875	$3,750

1967 Gibson C-O
Imaged by Heritage Auctions, HA.com

1982 Gibson Chet Atkins CE
Geoff Barker

To get the most from this book, be sure to read "Using *The Guide*" in the introduction.

GUITARS

1984 Gibson Corvus II
Imaged by Heritage Auctions, HA.com

Gibson Doves in Flight

MODEL		EXC. COND.	
YEAR	FEATURES	LOW	HIGH

Chet Atkins SST
1987-2006. Steel string acoustic/electric solidbody, single-cut, bridge transducer pickup, active bass and treble controls, gold hardware.

1987-1993	White	$2,250	$3,000
1987-2006	Black	$2,250	$3,000
1987-2006	Natural	$1,500	$2,000
1993	Red Wine or Antique	$2,250	$3,000
1994	Cherry Sunburst	$2,250	$3,000

Chet Atkins SST Celebrity
1991-1993. Gold hardware, 200 made, black body with unique white 'guard.

| 1991-1993 | | $2,250 | $3,000 |

Chet Atkins SST-12
1990-1994. 12-string model similar to 6-string, mahogany/spruce body, preamp circuit controls single transducer pickup, natural or ebony finish.

| 1990-1994 | | $1,500 | $2,000 |

Chet Atkins Super 4000
1997-2000. Custom Shop, figured curly maple back and sides, orange amber finish, 25 built, COA.

| 1997-2000 | | $20,000 | $25,000 |

Chet Atkins Tennessean
1990-2005. Single rounded cutaway archtop, 2 humbuckers, f-holes, bound body. Part of Gibson's Custom line.

| 1990-2005 | | $1,750 | $2,250 |

Chicago 35
1994-1995. Flat-top dreadnought, round shoulders, mahogany back and sides, prewar script logo.

| 1994-1995 | | $1,250 | $1,625 |

Citation
1969-1971. 17" full-depth body, single-cut archtop, 1 or 2 floating pickups, fancy inlay, natural or sunburst. Only 8 shipped for '69-'71, reissued the first time '79-'83 and as part of the Historic Collection in '93.

| 1969-1971 | | $20,000 | $25,000 |

Citation (1st Reissue)
1979-1983. Reissue of '69-'71 model, natural or sunburst. Reintroduced in '93 as part of Gibson's Historic Collection.

| 1979-1983 | | $20,000 | $25,000 |

Citation (2nd Reissue)
1993-2018. Limited production via Gibson's Historic Collection, natural or sunburst.

| 1994-2018 | | $15,000 | $20,000 |

Citation Vanderbilt Rose
2015. Custom Shop, very few made, Vanderbilt Rose lacquer finish with matching maple 'guard.

| 2015 | | $9,000 | $11,000 |

CJ-165/CJ-165 Modern Classic
2006-2008. Called J-165 in first year of production, classic small body non-cutaway flat-top, solid spruce top, maple or rosewood back and sides.

| 2006-2008 | | $2,000 | $2,500 |

CJ-165 EC Modern Classic
2007-2009. As above, but with single-cut, electronics, maple or rosewood back and sides.

| 2007-2009 | | $2,125 | $2,750 |

MODEL		EXC. COND.	
YEAR	FEATURES	LOW	HIGH

CL-10 Standard
1997-1998. Flat-top, solid spruce top, laminated mahogany back and sides.

| 1997-1998 | | $1,000 | $1,375 |

CL-20 Standard Plus
1997-1998. Flat-top, laminated back and sides, 4-ply binding with tortoiseshell appointments, abalone diamond inlays.

| 1997-1998 | | $1,125 | $1,500 |

CL-30 Deluxe
1997-1998. J-50 style dreadnought, solid spruce top, bubinga back and sides, factory electronics.

| 1997-1998 | | $1,250 | $1,625 |

CL-35 Deluxe
1998. Single cutaway CL-30.

| 1998 | | $1,375 | $1,750 |

CL-40 Artist
1997-1998. Flat-top, gold hardware, rosewood back and sides.

| 1997-1998 | | $1,875 | $2,500 |

CL-45 Artist
1997-1998. Single cutaway CL-40.

| 1997-1998 | | $2,000 | $2,500 |

CL-50
1997-1999. Custom Shop model, D-style body, higher-end appointments, offered with Brazilian rosewood.

| 1997-1999 | | $4,000 | $5,250 |

Corvus I
1982-1984. Odd-shaped solidbody with offset V-type cut, bolt maple neck, rosewood 'board, 1 humbucker, standard finish was silver gloss, but others available at an additional cost.

| 1982-1984 | | $1,125 | $1,500 |

Corvus II
1982-1984. Same as Corvus I, but with 2 humbuckers, 2 volume controls, 1 master tone control.

| 1982-1984 | | $1,250 | $1,625 |

Corvus III
1982-1984. Same as Corvus I, but with 3 single-coil pickups, master volume and tone control, 5-way switch.

| 1982-1984 | | $1,500 | $2,000 |

Crest Gold
1969-1971. Double-cut thinline archtop, Brazilian rosewood body, 2 pickups, bound top and headstock, bound f-holes, gold-plated parts. The Crest name was also used on a few (3-6) custom guitars based on the L-5CT built in 1959-'61.

| 1969-1971 | | $7,000 | $9,000 |

Crest Silver
1969-1972. Silver-plated parts version of Crest.

| 1969-1972 | | $6,500 | $8,500 |

CS Series
2002-2017. Custom Shop, scaled down ES-335 body style, plain top or F indicates figured top.

2002-2003	CS-356	$2,500	$3,250
2002-2012	CS-336F	$3,000	$4,000
2002-2014	CS-356F	$3,500	$4,500
2002-2017	CS-336	$2,750	$3,500

MODEL YEAR	FEATURES	EXC. COND. LOW	EXC. COND. HIGH

Dave Grohl DG-335
2007-2008. Custom Shop Inspired By series, Trini Lopez Standard specs, Certificate of Authenticity, Pelham Blue or black finish.

2007-2008		$8,000	$10,000

Dove
1962-1996, 1999-2013. Flat-top acoustic, maple back and sides, square shoulders, natural or sunburst.

1962-1964		$10,000	$15,000
1965	Early '65	$6,500	$8,250
1965	Late '65	$5,000	$6,250
1966-1969		$4,500	$5,750
1970-1979	Various colors	$3,000	$3,750
1980-1984	Double X	$2,750	$3,500
1985-1988	Single X	$2,750	$3,500
1989	New specs	$2,750	$3,500
1990-1996	Various colors	$2,750	$3,500
1999-2013	Reissue model	$2,750	$3,500

'60s Dove
1997-2004. Spruce top, maple back and sides, Dove appointments.

1997-2004		$2,750	$3,500

'60s Dove Limited Edition
2014. Sitka spruce top, flame maple back and sides, Indian rosewood 'board, Vintage Cherryburst finish.

2014	50 offered	$2,750	$3,500

Dove Artist
1999-2005. Sitka spruce, Indian rosewood.

1999-2005		$2,250	$3,000

Dove Commemorative
1994-1996. Commemorates Gibson's 100th anniversary, Heritage or Antique Cherry finish, 100 built.

1994-1996		$3,000	$4,000

Dove In Flight Limited Edition
1996-1997. Custom Shop, 250 made, figured maple sides and back, Adirondack top, Certificate of Authenticity, dove inlays on headstock.

1996-1997		$5,500	$7,500

Doves In Flight (Brazilian)
2003. Custom Shop, only 2 made.

2003		$12,000	$15,000

Doves In Flight (Production Model)
1996-present. Gibson Custom model, maple back and sides, doves in flight inlays.

1996-2023		$4,500	$6,500

Dove Elvis Presley Signature
2008-2010. Artist Series, Certificate of Authenticity, black.

2008-2010		$3,500	$4,500

Super Dove
2009-2012. Cutaway, on-board electronics, sold through certain retailers.

2009-2012		$3,250	$4,250

Duane Eddy Signature
2004-2009. Single rounded cut, flamed maple top and back, 2 single-coils and piezo, pearl 'moustache' markers, signature engraved on 'guard, Bigsby, Rockabilly Brown finish.

2004-2009		$5,000	$6,500

EAS Deluxe
1992-1994. Single-cut flat-top acoustic/electric, solid flamed maple top, bound rosewood 'board, trapezoid inlays, 3-band EQ, Vintage Cherry Sunburst.

1992-1994		$1,125	$1,500

EAS Standard/Classic
1992-1995. Like EAS Deluxe, but with spruce top, unbound top, dot inlays, called EAS Classic for '92.

1992-1995		$1,000	$1,375

EBS(F)-1250 Double Bass
1962-1968. Double-cut SG-type solidbody, double-neck with bass and 6-string, originally introduced as the EBSF-1250 because of a built-in fuzztone, which was later deleted, only 22 made.

1962-1964	Various colors	$40,000	$50,000
1965	Various colors	$20,000	$25,000
1966-1968	Various colors	$18,000	$22,500

EC-10 Standard
1997-1998. Jumbo single-cut, on-board electronics, solid spruce top, maple back and sides.

1997-1998		$1,125	$1,500

EC-20 Starburst
1997-1998. Jumbo single-cut, on-board electronics, solid spruce top, maple back and sides, renamed J-185 EC in '99.

1997-1998		$1,750	$2,250

EC-30 Blues King Electro (BKE)
1995-1998. Jumbo single-cut, on-board electronics, solid spruce top, maple back and sides, double parallelogram inlays, renamed J-185 EC in '99.

1995-1998		$2,000	$2,500

EDS-1275 Double 12
1958-1967, 1977-1990. Double-cut doubleneck with one 12- and one 6-string, thinline hollowbody until late-'62, SG-style solidbody '62 on.

1958-1961	Custom order	$150,000	$175,000
1962-1964	SG body	$40,000	$50,000
1965	SG body	$30,000	$40,000
1966-1967	SG body	$25,000	$30,000
1977-1979	Various colors	$10,000	$15,000
1977-1979	White	$10,000	$15,000
1980-1989	Various colors	$5,000	$6,500
1990	Various colors	$5,000	$6,500

EDS-1275 Double 12 (Historic Collection)
1991-2018. Custom Shop Historic Collection reissue.

1991-2018	Various colors	$5,000	$6,500

EDS-1275 Double 12 Centennial
1994. Guitar of the Month (May), gold medallion on back of headstock, cherry with gold hardware.

1994		$5,000	$6,500

EDS-1275 Double 12 Jimmy Page VOS Signature
2008. Custom Shop model with Certificate of Authenticity, 250 made.

2008		$20,000	$50,000

EDS-1275 Double Neck Alex Lifeson
2015-2016. Custom Shop model based on Lifeson's '70s Gibson, limited run of 100, first 25 signed and played by Alex, aged Arctic White.

2015-2016		$10,000	$20,000

Gibson Doves in Flight

1964 Gibson EDS-1275

John Wesley

1961 Gibson ES-125 TC

Jim King

1957 Gibson ES-140 3/4

Robbie Keene

MODEL YEAR	FEATURES	EXC. COND. LOW	HIGH
EDS-1275 Double Neck Don Felder 'Hotel California'			
2015-2016. Custom Shop limited edition, 50 aged/ signed, 100 aged/unsigned, 1 set of exposed pickups (VI), 1 set of covered pickups (XII), aged faded white nitro finish.			
2010	Signed	$30,000	$50,000
2010	Unsigned	$15,000	$20,000
EDS-1275 "Slash" 1966 Doubleneck			
2019. Custom Shop limited, 125 made and signed, authentic '66 replica, aged ebony.			
2019		$12,000	$15,000
EMS-1235 Double Mandolin			
1958-1963, 1965-1967. Double-cut, doubleneck with 1 regular 6-string and 1 short 6-string (the mandolin neck), thinline hollowbody until late-1962, SG-style solidbody '62-'68, black, sunburst or white, total of 61 shipped.			
1958-1961	Custom order	$40,000	$50,000
1962-1963	SG body	$30,000	$35,000
1965	SG body	$25,000	$32,500
1966-1967	SG body	$24,000	$30,000
ES-5/ES-5N			
1949-1955. Single-cut archtop, 3 P-90 pickups, sunburst or natural (5N). Renamed ES-5 Switchmaster in '55.			
1949-1955	Natural	$9,000	$12,000
1949-1955	Sunburst	$8,000	$10,000
ES-5 Switchmaster/ES-5N Switchmaster			
1956-1962. Renamed from ES-5, single-cut (rounded until late-'60, pointed after) archtop, 3 P-90s until end of '57, humbuckers after, switchmaster control.			
1956-1957	Natural, P-90s	$11,000	$14,000
1956-1957	Sunburst, P-90s	$10,000	$13,000
1957-1960	Natural, hums	$18,000	$22,000
1957-1960	Sunburst, hums	$16,000	$20,000
1960-1962	Pointed Florentine cutaway	$12,500	$16,000
ES-5/ES-5 Switchmaster Historic			
1995-2006. Custom Shop Historic Collection.			
1995-2002	ES-5, sunburst, P-90s	$4,000	$5,000
1995-2002	Switchmaster, Wine Red, hums	$4,000	$5,000
1995-2006	Switchmaster, natural, hums	$4,000	$5,000
1995-2006	Switchmaster, sunburst, hums	$4,000	$5,000
ES-100			
1938-1941. Archtop, 1 pickup, bound body, sunburst, renamed ES-125 in '41.			
1938-1941		$2,000	$2,500
ES-120 T			
1962-1970. Archtop, thinline, 1 f-hole, bound body, 1 pickup, sunburst.			
1962-1964		$1,625	$2,250
1965		$1,500	$2,000
1966-1970		$1,500	$2,000
ES-125			
1941-1943, 1946-1970. Archtop, non-cut, 1 pickup, sunburst, renamed from ES-100.			
1941-1943	Blade pickup	$2,625	$3,500

MODEL YEAR	FEATURES	EXC. COND. LOW	HIGH
1947-1949	1st non-adj, P-90s	$2,625	$3,500
1950	1st non-adj, P-90s	$2,500	$3,250
1951-1959	Adj P-90s with poles	$2,500	$3,250
1960-1964		$1,750	$2,250
1965		$1,625	$2,125
1966-1970		$1,500	$2,000
ES-125 C			
1966-1970. Wide body archtop, single pointed cutaway, 1 pickup, sunburst.			
1965		$1,875	$2,500
1966-1970		$1,750	$2,250
ES-125 CD			
1965-1970. Wide body archtop, single-cut, 2 pickups, sunburst.			
1965		$2,750	$3,500
1966-1970		$2,500	$3,250
ES-125 D			
1957. Limited production (not mentioned in catalog), 2 pickup version of thick body ES-125, sunburst.			
1957		$2,875	$3,750
ES-125 T			
1956-1968. Archtop thinline, non-cut, 1 pickup, bound body, sunburst.			
1956-1959		$2,500	$3,250
1960-1964		$2,250	$3,000
1965		$2,000	$2,750
1966-1968		$1,750	$2,250
ES-125 T 3/4			
1957-1968. Archtop thinline, short-scale, non-cut, 1 pickup, sunburst.			
1957-1960		$2,500	$3,250
1961-1964		$2,500	$3,250
1965		$2,500	$3,250
1966-1968		$2,500	$3,250
ES-125 TC			
1960-1970. Archtop thinline, single pointed cutaway, bound body, 1 P-90 pickup, sunburst.			
1960-1964		$2,500	$3,250
1965		$2,375	$3,125
1966-1970		$2,250	$3,000
ES-125 TD			
1957-1963. Archtop thinline, non-cut, 2 pickups, sunburst.			
1957-1963		$3,000	$4,000
ES-125 TDC or ES-125 TCD			
1960-1971. Archtop thinline, single pointed cutaway, 2 P-90 pickups, sunburst.			
1960-1964		$3,750	$5,000
1965	Early '65	$3,500	$4,500
1965	Late '65	$3,000	$4,000
1966-1971		$3,000	$4,000
ES-130			
1954-1956. Archtop, non-cut, 1 pickup, bound body, sunburst, renamed ES-135 in '56.			
1954-1959		$2,750	$3,500
ES-135			
1956-1958. Renamed from ES-130, non-cut archtop, 1 pickup, sunburst, name reused on a thin body in the '90s.			
1957-1959		$2,750	$3,500

MODEL YEAR	FEATURES	EXC. COND. LOW	HIGH

ES-135 (Thinline)

1991-2005. Single-cut archtop, laminated maple body, 2 humbuckers or 2 P-100s, stoptail or trapeze, chrome or gold hardware.

1991-2005		$1,625	$2,250

ES-137 Classic

2002-2015. Thin-body electric single cut, trapezoid inlays, 2 humbuckers, f-holes, gold hardware.

2002-2015		$1,625	$2,250

ES-137 Custom

2002-2011. Like Classic, but with split-diamond inlays and varitone.

2002-2011		$1,625	$2,250

ES-137 P (Premier)

2002-2005. Like Classic, but with exposed humbuckers, chrome hardware and very small trapezoid inlays.

2002-2005		$1,500	$2,000

ES-139

2013-2016. Semi-hollow Les Paul style body, 2 humbuckers, Guitar Center model.

2013-2016		$1,125	$1,500

ES-140 (3/4) or ES-140N (3/4)

1950-1956. Archtop, single-cut, 1 pickup, bound body, short-scale, sunburst or natural option (N).

1950-1956	Natural option	$3,500	$4,500
1950-1956	Sunburst	$3,000	$3,750

ES-140 (3/4) T or ES-140N (3/4) T

1957-1968. Archtop thinline, single-cut, bound body, 1 pickup, short-scale, sunburst or natural option (140N).

1957-1959	Natural option	$3,250	$4,000
1957-1959	Sunburst	$3,000	$3,750
1960-1964	Sunburst	$2,750	$3,500
1965	Sunburst	$2,625	$3,250
1966-1968	Sunburst	$2,375	$3,000

ES-150

1936-1942, 1946-1956. Historically important archtop, non-cut, bound body, Charlie Christian bar pickup from '36-'39, various metal covered pickups starting in '40, sunburst.

1936-1939	Charlie Christian pu	$7,500	$9,750
1940-1942	Metal covered pu	$7,000	$9,500
1946-1949	P-90 pickup	$3,500	$4,500
1950-1956	P-90 pickup	$3,000	$4,000

ES-150 DC

1969-1975. Archtop, double rounded cutaway, 2 humbuckers, multi-bound, cherry, natural or walnut.

1969-1975		$3,500	$4,500

ES-165 Herb Ellis

1991-2011. Single pointed cut hollowbody, 1 humbucker, gold hardware.

1991-2011		$2,500	$3,500

ES-175 or ES-175N

1949-1971. Archtop, single pointed cutaway, 1 pickup (P-90 from '49-early-'57, humbucker early-'57-'71), multi-bound, sunburst or natural option (175N).

1949-1956	Natural, P90	$6,500	$8,000
1949-1956	Sunburst, P-90	$6,500	$8,000
1957-1959	Natural, hum	$10,000	$12,500
1957-1963	Sunburst, PAF	$9,750	$12,250
1964	Sunburst, pat #	$7,500	$9,500
1965	Sunburst, hum	$4,750	$6,000
1966-1969	Sunburst, pat #	$4,000	$5,000
1967-1969	Black	$4,000	$5,000
1970-1971	Various colors	$3,500	$4,500

ES-175 CC

1978-1979. 1 Charlie Christian pickup, sunburst or walnut.

1978-1979		$3,250	$4,000

ES-175 D or ES-175N D

1952-2016. Archtop, single-cut, 2 pickups (P-90s from '53-early-'57, humbuckers early-'57 on), sunburst or natural option (175N D). Humbucker pickups were converted from PAF-stickers to Pat. No.-stickers in '62. Different models were converted at different times. An ES-175 model, made during the transitional time, with PAFs, will fetch more. In some of the electric-archtop models, the transition period may have been later than '62. Cataloged as the ES-175 Reissue in the '90s, currently as the ES-175 under Gibson Memphis.

1952-1956	Natural, P-90s	$7,000	$9,000
1952-1956	Sunburst, P-90s	$6,500	$8,000
1957-1963	Natural, PAFs	$16,500	$20,000
1957-1963	Sunburst, PAFs	$15,500	$19,500
1964	Natural, pat #	$8,000	$10,000
1964	Sunburst, pat #	$7,000	$8,750
1965	Natural, pat #	$7,000	$8,750
1965	Sunburst, hums	$6,250	$8,000
1966	Natural, pat #	$5,500	$7,000
1966	Sunburst, hums	$5,500	$7,000
1967-1969	Black	$5,500	$7,000
1967-1969	Various colors	$5,500	$7,000
1970-1979	Various colors	$4,250	$5,250
1980-2016	Various colors	$4,000	$5,000

ES-175 D Tenor

1966. Rare custom ordered tenor version, sunburst.

1966		$3,750	$5,000

ES-175 D-AN

1999-2000. Limited run, P-90s, Antique Natural finish.

1999-2000		$3,000	$4,000

ES-175 SP

2006. Single humbucker version, sunburst.

2006		$3,125	$4,000

ES-175 Steve Howe

2001-2007. Maple laminate body, multi-bound top, sunburst.

2001-2007		$3,500	$6,500

ES-175 T

1976-1980. Archtop thinline, single pointed cutaway, 2 humbuckers, various colors including international colors.

1976-1980		$3,250	$4,250

ES-225 T or ES-225N T

1955-1959. Thinline, single pointed cutaway, 1 P-90 pickup, bound body and neck, sunburst or natural option (225N T).

1955-1959	Natural	$5,500	$7,000
1955-1959	Sunburst	$4,000	$5,000

1952 Gibson ES-150

Frank Manno

1953 Gibson ES-175

Alex Clarke

1956 Gibson ES-225 T

1953 Gibson ES-295
Adam Turton

MODEL YEAR	FEATURES	EXC. COND. LOW	HIGH
ES-225 TD or ES-225N TD			
1956-1959. Thinline, single-cut, 2 P-90s, bound body and neck, sunburst or natural option (225N TD).			
1956-1959	Natural	$8,000	$10,000
1956-1959	Sunburst	$6,000	$7,500
1959 ES-225 Historic			
2014-2016. Single-cut TD reissue with 2 P-90s, sunburst.			
2014-2016		$2,750	$3,500
ES-235 Gloss			
2018-2020. Semi-hollow single-cut, maple neck, rosewood 'board, 2 pickups.			
2018-2020		$1,250	$1,625
ES-250 or ES-250N			
1939-1940. Archtop, carved top, special Christian pickup, multi-bound, high-end appointments, stairstep headstock '39 and standard in '40, sunburst or natural option (250N).			
1939	Natural, stairstep hs	$35,000	$45,000
1939	Sunburst, stairstep hs	$25,000	$30,000
1940	Natural, standard hs	$35,000	$45,000
1940	Sunburst, standard hs	$25,000	$30,000
ES-275			
2016-2019. Hollowbody archtop, single-cut, 2 humbucker pickups standard or optional P-90s, various colors and finishes, certificate of authenticity.			
2016	Gloss, opaque	$3,000	$4,000
2016-2019	Gloss, figured	$3,500	$4,500
2017	Gloss, P-90s	$3,500	$4,500
2018	Custom metallic	$3,500	$4,500
2019	Satin, opaque	$2,750	$3,500
ES-295			
1952-1958. Single pointed cutaway archtop, 2 pickups (P-90s from '52-late-'57, humbuckers after), gold finish, gold-plated hardware.			
1952-1957	P-90s	$11,500	$15,000
1957-1958	Humbuckers	$22,000	$28,000
ES-295 Historic Collection			
1990-2000. Custom Shop, 2 P-90 pickups, Bigsby, Antique Gold finish.			
1990-2000		$4,500	$6,000
ES-295 '52 Historic Collection			
2013-2015. Custom Shop. Limited VOS Vintage Cherry offered in '15.			
2013-2015		$4,000	$5,500
2015	Limited Cherry	$4,000	$5,500
ES-295 Scotty Moore Signature			
1999. Custom Shop, 15 produced, 12 with Scotty's actual signature on lower bout, Bullion Gold, trapeze tailpiece.			
1999		$8,000	$11,000
ES-300 or ES-300N			
1940-1942, 1945-1953. Archtop, non-cut, f-holes, had 4 pickup configurations during its run, sunburst or natural (300N).			
1940	Natural, oblong diagonal pu	$5,500	$7,000

MODEL YEAR	FEATURES	EXC. COND. LOW	HIGH
1940	Sunburst, oblong diagonal pu	$4,500	$5,750
1941-1942	Natural, 1 pu	$5,500	$7,000
1941-1942	Sunburst, 1 pu	$4,500	$5,750
1945	Black, 1 pu	$4,000	$5,000
1945-1949	Sunburst, 1 pu	$4,000	$5,000
1945-1953	Natural, 1 pu	$5,000	$6,500
1949-1953	Natural, 2 pus	$5,500	$7,000
1949-1953	Sunburst, 2 pus	$4,500	$5,500
ES-320 TD			
1971-1974. Thinline archtop, double-cut, 2 single-coil pickups, bound body, cherry, natural, or walnut.			
1971-1974		$2,000	$2,500
ES-325 TD			
1972-1978. Thinline archtop, double-cut, 2 mini-humbuckers, 1 f-hole, bound body, top mounted control panel, cherry or walnut.			
1972-1978		$2,500	$3,250
ES-330 L			
2009-2015. Custom Shop, classic 330 design, 2 dog-ear P-90 pickups, sunburst or black. 2015 model has humbuckers.			
2009-2015		$2,750	$3,500
ES-330 T or ES-330N T			
1959-1963. Double rounded cutaway, thinline, 1 pickup, bound body and neck, sunburst, cherry or natural option (330N T). In the '60s came with either an original semi-hard case (better than chip board) or a hardshell case. Prices quoted are for hardshell case; approximately $100 should be deducted for the semi-hard case.			
1959-1961	Natural	$10,500	$13,500
1959-1963	Cherry	$5,500	$7,250
1959-1963	Sunburst	$5,500	$7,250
ES-330 TD or ES-330N TD			
1959-1972. Double rounded cutaway, thinline, 2 pickups, bound body and neck, dot markers early then blocks, sunburst, cherry or natural option (330N TD). In the '60s came with either an original semi-hard case (better than chip board) or a hardshell case. Prices noted for the hardshell case; approximately $100 should be deducted for the semi-hard case.			
1959-1961	Natural	$14,500	$18,500
1959-1962	Cherry, dots	$9,000	$11,500
1959-1962	Sunburst, dots	$9,000	$11,500
1963-1964	Cherry, blocks	$7,750	$10,000
1963-1964	Sunburst, blocks	$7,750	$10,000
1965	Cherry, sunburst	$6,750	$8,500
1966-1968	Cherry, sunburst	$5,250	$6,500
1967-1968	Burgundy Metallic	$5,250	$6,500
1968	Walnut option	$5,250	$6,500
1969-1972	Various colors	$5,250	$6,500
ES-330 TDC			
1998-2000. Custom Shop model, block markers.			
1998-2000		$2,750	$3,500
1959 ES-330 Historic VOS			
2012-2019. Gibson Memphis, Historic series, P-90 pickups, trapeze tailpiece, certificate, VOS finish in sunburst, natural or cherry.			
2012-2019		$3,000	$4,000

1959 ES-330 Wildwood Spec

2015. Gibson Memphis, Limited Edition, figured top, natural, certificate.

MODEL YEAR	FEATURES	EXC. COND. LOW	HIGH
2015		$3,000	$4,000

1964 ES-330 Historic VOS

2015-2019. Historic series, vintage specs, P-90 pickups, trapeze tailpiece, certificate.

MODEL YEAR	FEATURES	EXC. COND. LOW	HIGH
2015-2019		$3,000	$4,000

ES-333

2002-2005. Economy ES-335, no 'guard, no headstock inlay, exposed coils, stencil logo, satin finish.

MODEL YEAR	FEATURES	EXC. COND. LOW	HIGH
2002-2005		$2,000	$2,500

ES-335 TD or ES-335N TD

1958-1981. The original design ES-335 has dot 'board inlays and a stop tailpiece, sunburst, cherry or natural option (335N). Block inlays replaced dots in mid-'62, in late-'64 the stop tailpiece was replaced with a trapeze tailpiece. Replaced by the ES-335 DOT in '81.

MODEL YEAR	FEATURES	EXC. COND. LOW	HIGH
1958	Natural, bound neck	$100,000	$120,000
1958	Natural, bound neck, Bigsby	$80,000	$100,000
1958	Natural, unbound neck	$95,000	$120,000
1958	Natural, unbound neck, Bigsby	$75,000	$90,000
1958	Sunburst, bound neck	$60,000	$75,000
1958	Sunburst, bound neck, Bigsby	$48,000	$62,000
1958	Sunburst, unbound neck	$55,000	$70,000
1958	Sunburst, unbound neck, Bigsby	$44,000	$55,000
1959	Cherry (early), stop tail	$120,000	$150,000
1959	Natural, bound neck	$150,000	$175,000
1959	Natural, bound neck, Bigsby	$120,000	$150,000
1959	Sunburst, bound neck	$80,000	$100,000
1959	Sunburst, bound neck, Bigsby	$65,000	$75,000
1960	Cherry, factory Bigsby	$40,000	$52,000
1960	Cherry, factory stop tail	$45,000	$55,000
1960	Natural, factory Bigsby	$78,000	$100,000
1960	Natural, factory stop tail	$95,000	$120,000
1960	Sunburst, factory Bigsby	$40,000	$52,000
1960	Sunburst, factory stop tail	$45,000	$55,000
1961	Cherry, factory Bigsby	$27,000	$35,000
1961	Cherry, factory stop tail	$35,000	$45,000
1961	Sunburst, factory Bigsby	$27,000	$35,000
1961	Sunburst, factory stop tail	$35,000	$45,000
1962	Cherry, blocks, PAFs	$25,000	$32,000
1962	Cherry, blocks, pat#	$20,000	$25,000
1962	Cherry, dots, PAFs	$32,000	$40,000
1962	Cherry, vibrola, pat#	$18,000	$22,000
1962	Sunburst, blocks, PAFs	$25,000	$32,000
1962	Sunburst, blocks, pat#	$20,000	$25,000
1962	Sunburst, dots, PAFs	$32,000	$40,000
1962	Sunburst, dots, pat#	$20,500	$25,500
1962	Sunburst, vibrola, pat#	$18,000	$22,000
1963-1964	Cherry, factory Bigsby	$20,000	$25,000
1963-1964	Cherry, factory Maestro	$20,000	$25,000
1963-1964	Cherry, factory stop tail	$25,000	$35,000
1963-1964	Sunburst, factory Bigsby	$20,000	$25,000
1963-1964	Sunburst, factory Maestro	$20,000	$25,000
1963-1964	Sunburst, factory stop tail	$23,000	$32,000
1965	Early '65, wide neck	$15,000	$20,000
1965	Mid '65, narrow neck	$8,500	$11,000
1966	Cherry, sunburst	$8,000	$10,000
1966	Pelham Blue	$17,000	$22,000
1966	Sparkling Burgundy	$10,000	$13,000
1967	Black	$12,500	$16,000
1967	Cherry, sunburst	$8,000	$10,000
1967	Pelham Blue	$17,000	$22,000
1967	Sparkling Burgundy	$10,000	$13,000
1968	Cherry, sunburst	$7,750	$10,000
1968	Pelham Blue	$17,000	$22,000
1968	Sparkling Burgundy	$10,000	$13,000
1969	Cherry, sunburst	$6,500	$8,500
1969	Walnut option	$5,500	$7,250
1970-1976	Cherry, sunburst	$4,000	$5,500
1970-1976	Walnut option	$3,750	$4,875
1977-1979	All colors	$3,500	$4,500
1980-1981	All colors	$3,000	$4,000

1959 Gibson ES-330 T
David Stone

1965 Gibson ES-335
K.C. Cormack

1979 Gibson ES-335 Pro

Michael Campbell

1990 Gibson ES-335 Studio

Kurt Davey

MODEL YEAR	FEATURES	EXC. COND. LOW	HIGH

ES-335 Dot
1981-1990. Reissue of '60 ES-335 and replaces ES-335 TD. Name changed to ES-335 Reissue. Various color options including highly figured wood.

1981	Black	$3,750	$5,000
1981-1984	Natural	$3,750	$5,000
1981-1990	Cherry, sunburst	$3,000	$4,000
1985-1990	Natural	$3,000	$4,000

ES-335 Dot CMT (Custom Shop)
1983-1985. Custom Shop ES-335 Dot with curly maple top and back, full-length center block, 2 PAF-labeled humbuckers, natural or sunburst.

| 1983-1985 | | $4,000 | $5,000 |

ES-335 Reissue/ES-335 '59 Dot Reissue/ES-335
1991-present. Replaced the ES-335 DOT, dot inlays, various color options including highly figured wood. Renamed the 1959 ES-335 Dot Reissue in '98 and currently just ES-335 followed by options - Dot, Block (added in '98), Fat Neck (added in '08), Figured (added in '06), Plain, Satin (added in '06).

1991-2020	Cherry, sunburst, walnut, black	$2,500	$3,250
1991-2023	Natural	$2,500	$3,250
2006-2017	Satin	$2,000	$2,500

ES-335 Dot P-90
2007. Custom Shop limited edition with black dog-ear P-90s, stop tailpiece.

| 2007 | | $2,750 | $3,500 |

ES-335-12
1965-1971. 12-string version of the 335.

| 1965-1968 | | $4,250 | $5,500 |

ES-335 '59 Dot Historic
1999-2000, 2002-2016. Custom Shop Historic Collection, based upon 1959 ES-335 dot neck, figured maple top on early series, plain on later, nickel hardware.

| 1999-2016 | Figured top | $4,000 | $5,000 |
| 2002-2016 | Plain top | $4,000 | $5,000 |

1959 ES-335 Dot Reissue Limited Edition
2009-2017. Custom Shop, plain laminated maple top/back/sides, rounded '59 neck profile, '57 Classic humbuckers, Certificate of Authenticity, 250 each to be made in Antique Vintage Sunburst or Antique Natural (standard gloss or V.O.S. treatments).

| 2009-2017 | | $4,000 | $5,250 |

1959 ES-335 Ultra Heavy Aged/Ultra Light Aged
2021-present. Custom Shop Murphy Lab Collection, ultra heavy aged (Vintage Natural) and ultra light (Ebony or Vintage Natural). Ultra light ends in '22.

| 2021-2023 | Ultra Heavy Aged | $6,500 | $8,500 |
| 2021-2023 | Ultra Light Aged | $4,000 | $5,250 |

ES-335 '60s Block Inlay
2004-2007. Made in Memphis facility, plain maple top, small block markers.

| 2004-2007 | | $2,500 | $3,250 |

50th Anniversary 1960 ES-335
2009-2010. Custom Shop, dot markers, natural.

| 2009-2010 | | $3,750 | $4,750 |

1961 ES-335 Heavy Aged/ Ultra Light Aged
2021-2022. Custom Shop Murphy Lab Collection, heavy or ultra light aged, Sixties Cherry finish. Ultra light ends in '22.

| 2021-2022 | Heavy Aged | $6,500 | $8,500 |
| 2021-2022 | Ultra Light Aged | $4,000 | $5,250 |

1961 ES-335 Reissue (Custom Shop)
2020-present. Historic series, 3-Ply maple/poplar/maple body, solid mahogany neck, Indian rosewood 'board, 2 Alnico pickups, Sixties Cherry or Vintage Burst.

| 2020-2023 | | $3,750 | $4,750 |

50th Anniversary 1963 Block ES-335TD/ES-335TDC
2010-2013. Memphis Custom Shop, block markers, double-ring vintage-style tuners, Antique Vintage Sunburst (TD), Antique Faded Cherry (TDC).

| 2010-2013 | TD, sunburst | $3,750 | $4,750 |
| 2010-2013 | TDC, cherry | $3,750 | $4,750 |

ES-335 '63 Block Historic
1998-2000, 2002-2018. Custom Shop Historic Collection, based upon 1963 ES-335 with small block markers, figured maple top on early series, plain on later, nickel hardware.

1998-2000	1st release, figured top	$4,000	$5,000
2002-2018	2nd release, figured top	$4,000	$5,000
2002-2018	Plain top	$3,750	$4,750

1964 ES-335 Ultra Light Aged
2021-2022. Custom Shop Murphy Lab Collection, Sixties Cherry finish.

| 2021-2022 | | $4,000 | $5,000 |

ES-335 Alvin Lee
2006-2007. Custom Division Nashville, 50 made, features reflect Alvin Lee's Big Red ES-335 complete with decal art, cherry red, includes certificate of authenticity (if missing value is reduced). There is also an unlimited version without a certificate.

| 2006-2007 | With certificate | $4,875 | $6,500 |

ES-335 Andy Summers
2002. Custom Shop, 50 made, script signature on 'guard, early dot neck specs, nitro cherry finish, certificate of authenticity.

| 2002 | | $3,750 | $4,750 |

ES-335 Artist
1981. Off-set dot markers, large headstock logo, metal truss rod plate, gold hardware, 3 control knobs with unusual toggles and input specification.

| 1981 | | $3,500 | $4,500 |

ES-335 Canadian Custom
2007. Custom Shop Canadian exclusive, run of 50, maple leaf 'Limited Edition' decal on back of headstock, 'Custom Made' engraved plate on guitar front, solid mahogany neck, pearloid block inlays, antique cherry finish with aged binding.

| 2007 | | $2,750 | $3,500 |

ES-335 Centennial
1994. Centennial edition, gold medallion in headstock, diamond inlay in tailpiece, cherry.

| 1994 | | $4,000 | $5,500 |

The *Vintage Guitar Price Guide* shows values for all-original, excellent condition instruments and, where applicable, with original case.

The Official Vintage Guitar magazine Price Guide 2025   **Gibson** ES-335 Chris Cornell — ES-345 TD or ES-345 TDSV   **153**

GUITARS

MODEL YEAR	FEATURES	EXC. COND. LOW	HIGH

ES-335 Chris Cornell
2012-2016. Olive Drab Green or black.

| 2012-2016 | | $3,500 | $4,500 |

ES-335 CRR/CRS
1979. Country Rock Regular with standard wiring and CRR logo. Country Rock Stereo with stereo wiring and CRS logo, 300 of each built, 2 pickups, coil-tap.

| 1979 | CRR | $3,250 | $4,250 |
| 1979 | CRS | $3,500 | $4,500 |

ES-335 Diamond Edition
2006. Trini Lopez style diamond f-holes, Bigsby tailpiece option, gold hardware, Pelham Blue, pearl white or black pearl.

| 2006 | | $2,750 | $3,500 |

ES-335 Eric Clapton Crossroads '64 Reissue
2005. Reissue of EC's, with certificate of authenticity.

| 2005 | | $11,000 | $14,500 |

ES-335 Goldtop
2013-2016. Gibson Memphis, limited edition, 2 Burstbucker humbuckers, gold finish.

| 2013-2016 | | $2,500 | $3,250 |

ES-335 Gothic
1998-1999. Gothic appointments including ebony 'board and black satin finish.

| 1998-1999 | | $1,500 | $2,000 |

ES-335 Government Series
2015-2016. Made from guitar bodies, necks and 'boards returned from Federal Government after '11 raid on Gibson, special run of 300 built, each with Certificate of Authenticity.

| 2015-2016 | | $2,500 | $3,000 |

ES-335 Jim Beam Limited Edition
1999. Promotional Custom Shop model, approximately 18 made, large Jim Beam notation on body, comes with certificate.

| 1999 | | $2,500 | $3,250 |

ES-335 Jimmy Wallace Reissue
Special order by Texas Gibson dealer Jimmy Wallace.

| 1980 | | $3,250 | $4,250 |

ES-335 Joe Bonamassa Signature
2012. Custom Shop, based on Joe's '61 335, VOS sunburst.

| 2012 | | $4,000 | $5,000 |

ES-335 King of the Blues
2006. Offered through Guitar Center, 150 made, based on B.B.'s Lucille, King of the Blues logo on 'guard.

| 2006 | | $3,000 | $4,000 |

ES-335 Larry Carlton
2002-2016. Mr. 335 logo on truss rod cover, block neck like Larry's guitar, vintage (faded) sunburst.

| 2002-2016 | | $3,750 | $4,750 |

ES-335 Lee Ritenour
2008. Custom Shop, COA, 50 signed and 100 unsigned, Antique Cherry finish.

| 2008 | | $3,750 | $4,750 |

ES-335 Limited Edition (P-90s)
2001. ES-335 style crown inlay on headstock, P-90 pickups.

| 2001 | | $2,625 | $3,500 |

ES-335 Nashville
1994. All serial numbers begin with 94, first year Custom Shop run (not the Centennial).

| 1994 | | $3,125 | $4,000 |

ES-335 Pro
1979-1981. Two humbucking pickups with exposed coils, bound 'board, cherry or sunburst.

| 1979-1981 | | $2,750 | $3,500 |

ES-335 Rich Robinson
2014-2016. Bigsby, small blocks, Cherry VOS finish.

| 2014-2016 | | $3,500 | $4,500 |

ES-335 Roy Orbison
2006. About 70 made, RO serial number, black finish.

| 2006 | | $4,000 | $5,000 |

ES-335 Rusty Anderson
2013. Figured maple, natural, dot neck specs.

| 2013 | | $4,000 | $5,000 |

ES-335 Showcase Edition
1988. Guitar of the Month series, limited production, black gothic-style hardware, EMG pickups, transparent white/beige finish.

| 1988 | | $2,750 | $3,500 |

ES-335 Studio
1986-1991, 2013-2020. Bound body, 2 Dirty Finger humbuckers, cherry or ebony. Reissued in '13 by Gibson Memphis using '58 specs but with Vintage Sunburst or ebony finish.

| 1986-1991 | | $2,000 | $2,500 |
| 2013-2020 | Memphis | $1,250 | $1,625 |

ES-335 Warren Haynes
2013-2015. Custom Shop model.

| 2013-2015 | 500 made | $3,500 | $4,500 |
| 2014 | 1961 Ltd Ed | $3,500 | $4,500 |

ESDT-335
2001-2009. Memphis Custom Shop, flame maple top and back, 2 humbucking pickups, various colors.

| 2001-2009 | | $3,000 | $4,000 |

ES-336
1996-1998. Custom Shop smaller sized ES-335 with smaller headstock, dot markers.

| 1996-1998 | All options | $2,500 | $3,250 |

ES-339
2007-present. Modern series, smaller-sized bound 335 body, 2 humbuckers, block inlays, various colors.

| 2007-2023 | All options | $2,250 | $3,000 |

ES-339 Studio
2013-2018. Stripped-down 339, no binding or pickguard, dot inlays.

| 2013-2018 | | $1,125 | $1,500 |

ES-339 Traditional Pro
2013. Figured or plain, cherry or vintage sunburst.

| 2013 | | $2,000 | $2,500 |

ES-340 TD
1968-1973. The 335 with a laminated maple neck, master volume and mixer controls, various colors.

| 1968-1973 | Natural, Walnut | $5,000 | $6,500 |

ES-345 TD or ES-345 TDSV
1959-1983. The 335 with Vari-tone, stereo, 2 humbuckers, gold hardware, double parallelogram inlays, stop tailpiece '59-'64 and '82-'83, trapeze tailpiece '65-'82. Cataloged as ES-345 TDSV by '80.

| 1959 | Cherry, Bigsby | $35,000 | $45,000 |

1967 Gibson ES-339

1959 Gibson ES-345 TD
Trey Rabinek

1967 Gibson ES-345
Scott Anderson

1962 Gibson ES-350 T
Landy Hardy

MODEL YEAR	FEATURES	EXC. COND. LOW	HIGH
1959	Cherry, stud tail	$40,000	$50,000
1959	Natural, Bigsby	$65,000	$85,000
1959	Natural, stud tail	$80,000	$110,000
1959	Sunburst, Bigsby	$32,000	$42,000
1959	Sunburst, stud tail	$40,000	$50,000
1960	Cherry, Bigsby	$30,000	$40,000
1960	Cherry, stud tail	$38,000	$48,000
1960	Natural, Bigsby	$60,000	$75,000
1960	Natural, stud tail	$75,000	$100,000
1960	Sunburst, Bigsby	$30,000	$40,000
1960	Sunburst, stud tail	$38,000	$50,000
1961	Cherry, Bigsby	$20,000	$25,000
1961	Cherry, stud tail	$25,000	$30,000
1961	Sunburst, Bigsby	$20,000	$25,000
1961	Sunburst, stud tail	$25,000	$30,000
1962	Bigsby, PAF	$18,000	$23,000
1962	Stud tail, PAF	$23,000	$30,000
1963-1964	Bigsby, pat #	$15,000	$20,000
1963-1964	Stud tail, pat #	$18,000	$23,000
1965	Early '65 wide neck	$9,500	$12,000
1965	Mid '65 narrow neck	$6,000	$7,750
1966-1969	Various colors	$5,000	$6,500
1970-1976	Various colors	$4,000	$5,500
1977-1979	Various colors	$3,500	$4,500
1980-1983	Various colors	$3,000	$4,000

ES-345 Historic

1998-1999. Custom Shop Historic Collection, stopbar, Bigsby or Maestro tailpiece, Viceroy Brown, Vintage Sunburst, Faded Cherry or natural.

1998-1999		$4,000	$5,000

ES-345 Reissue

2002-2010. 6-position Varitone selector, gold hardware, stop tailpiece, various colors.

2002-2010		$2,500	$3,250

1959 ES-345 TD

2014-2015. Period-correct '59 specs with VOS aged look, certificate of authenticity, Historic Burst or natural (TDN) finish.

2014	'59 reissue	$3,500	$4,500
2015	VOS	$4,000	$5,000

ES-346 Paul Jackson Jr.

1997-2006. Custom Shop, 335-like with figured or plain maple top, rosewood 'board, double-parallelogram inlays.

1997-2006		$4,000	$5,500

ES-347 TD or ES-347 S

1978-1985, 1987-1993. 335-style with gold hardware, tune-o-matic bridge, 2 Spotlight double-coil pickups, coil-tap, bound body and neck, S added to name in '87.

1978-1985	TD	$3,500	$5,500
1987-1993	S	$3,500	$5,500

ES-350 or ES-350N

1947-1956. Originally the ES-350 Premier, full body archtop, single-cut, 1 P-90 pickup until end of '48, 2 after, sunburst or natural (350N).

1947-1948	Natural, 1 pu	$9,000	$11,500
1947-1948	Sunburst, 1 pu	$8,500	$10,500
1949-1956	Natural, 2 pu	$9,500	$12,000
1949-1956	Sunburst, 2 pu	$9,000	$11,500

ES-350 Centennial

1994. Guitar of the Month, sunburst, gold hardware, gold medallion on back of headstock, diamond accents, 101 made with serial numbers from 1984-1994. Included a gold signet ring.

1994		$4,250	$5,500

ES-350 T or ES-350N T

1955-1963, 1977-1981, 1992-1993. Called the ES-350 TD in early-'60s, thinline archtop, single-cut (round '55-'60 and '77-'81, pointed '61-'63), 2 P-90 pickups '55-'56, humbuckers after, gold hardware. Limited runs were done in 1992-1993.

1956	Natural, P-90s	$9,000	$11,500
1956	Sunburst, P-90s	$8,500	$10,500
1957-1959	Natural, PAFs	$14,000	$17,500
1957-1959	Sunburst, PAFs	$14,000	$17,500
1960-1963	Natural, PAFs	$14,000	$17,500
1960-1963	Sunburst, PAFs	$14,000	$17,500
1977-1981	Natural, sunburst	$4,000	$5,000

ES-350 T Historic

1998-2000. Custom Shop Historic Collection reissue.

1998-2000		$4,000	$5,000

Chuck Berry 1955 ES-350 T

2019. Limited to 55, antique natural with VOS finish.

2019		$11,000	$14,000

ES-355 TD

1958-1970. 335-style with large block inlays, multibound body and headstock, 2 humbuckers, the 355 model was standard with a Bigsby, sideways or Maestro vibrato, non-vibrato models were an option. The prices shown assume a vibrato tailpiece, a factory stop tailpiece was considered an advantage and will fetch more. Early examples have factory Bigsby vibratos, early '60s have sideways vibratos, and late '60s have Maestro vibratos, cherry finish was the standard finish.

1958-1959	Cherry, PAFs, Bigsby, vibrato	$36,000	$45,000
1960-1962	Cherry, PAFs, Bigsby, vibrato	$25,000	$31,500
1962	Cherry, PAFs, side-pull, vibrato	$25,000	$31,500
1963-1964	Cherry, pat#, Bigsby, vibrato	$17,000	$21,500
1965	Early '65, wide neck	$12,000	$15,000
1965	Mid '65, narrow neck	$8,000	$10,000
1966-1968	Cherry or sunburst	$8,000	$10,000
1966-1968	Sparkling Burgundy	$12,000	$15,000
1969-1970	Cherry or sunburst	$6,500	$8,500

ES-355 TDSV

1959-1982. The stereo version of ES-355 with Varitone switch, a mono version was available, but few were made, the 355 model was standard with a Bigsby, sideways or Maestro vibrato, non-vibrato models were an option. The prices shown assume a vibrato tailpiece. A factory stop tailpiece was considered an advantage and will fetch more, early examples have factory Bigsby vibratos, early-'60s have sideways vibratos and late-'60s

MODEL YEAR	FEATURES	EXC. COND. LOW	HIGH

have Maestro vibratos, cherry finish was standard, walnut became available in '69.

1959	Bigsby	$26,000	$32,500
1959	Factory stop tail	$60,000	$75,000
1960	Bigsby	$22,000	$27,500
1961-1963	Sideways, late PAFs	$22,000	$27,500
1962	Maestro, late PAFs	$22,000	$27,500
1963-1964	Maestro, pat #	$15,000	$18,500
1965	Early '65 wide neck	$12,000	$15,000
1965	Mid '65 narrow neck	$7,500	$9,500
1966	Sparkling Burgundy	$12,000	$15,000
1966-1967	Cherry or sunburst, Maestro	$6,500	$8,500
1968	Various colors, Maestro	$6,500	$8,500
1969	Various colors, Bigsby	$6,000	$7,500
1970-1982	Various colors, Bigsby	$5,500	$7,000

ES-355/ES-355 TD (Custom Shop)
1994, 1997, 2006-2010. Mono, Bigsby or stop tail.

1994-2010		$4,000	$5,000

1959 ES-355 Light Aged/Ultra Light Aged
2021-present. Custom Shop Murphy Lab Collection, light aged (Watermelon Red) and ultra light (Ebony or Vintage Natural). Ultra light ends in '22.

2021-2023	Light Aged	$5,250	$6,750
2021-2022	Ultra Light Aged	$4,500	$6,000

ES-355 Alex Lifeson
2008-2010. Custom Shop Inspired By series, gold hardware, Alpine White finish.

2008-2010		$4,750	$6,250

ES-355 Centennial
1994. Guitar of the Month, sunburst, gold hardware, gold medallion on back of headstock, diamond accents, 101 made with serial numbers from 1984-1994. Included a gold signet ring.

1994		$4,000	$5,000

ES-355 Curly Maple Limited Edition
2010-2012. Figured flamed maple top, stop tailpiece, natural finish.

2010-2012		$4,500	$6,000

ES-355 Limited Edition (VOS)
2015-2018. Gibson Memphis, Bigsby, gold hardware, various colors with VOS finish.

2015-2018		$4,500	$6,000

ES-355 Summer Jam Series
2011. Custom Shop Summer Jam series, 25 made in Bourbon Burst.

2011		$4,000	$5,000

ES-359
2008-2016. Custom Shop, ES-335/ES-339 style with LP Custom style appointments, minor-figured top and back, sunburst.

2008-2016		$2,500	$3,250

MODEL YEAR	FEATURES	EXC. COND. LOW	HIGH

ES-369
1981-1982. A 335-style with 2 exposed humbucker pickups, coil-tap, sunburst.

1981-1982		$2,500	$3,250

ES-390
2014-2018. Memphis model, thinline hollow-body, rosewood 'board, 2 P-90s, Vintage Dark Burst finish.

2014-2018		$2,500	$3,250

ES-446
1999-2003. Single cut semi-hollow, 2 humbuckers, Bigsby, Custom Shop.

1999-2003	Various colors	$3,000	$4,000

ES-775
1990-1993. Single-cut hollowbody, 2 humbuckers, gold hardware, ebony, natural or sunburst.

1990-1993		$3,000	$4,000

ES-Artist
1979-1985. Double-cut thinline, semi-hollowbody, no f-holes, 2 humbuckers, active electronics, gold hardware, ebony, fireburst or sunburst. Moog electronics includes 3 mini-switches for compressor, expander, and bright boost.

1979-1985		$3,125	$4,000

EST-150
1937-1939. Tenor version of ES-150, Charlie Christian pickup, sunburst, renamed ETG-150 in '40.

1937-1939		$4,000	$5,000

ETG-150
1940-1942, 1947-1971. Renamed from EST-150, tenor version of ES-150, 1 metal-covered pickup '40-'42, P-90 after, sunburst.

1940-1942		$4,000	$5,000
1947-1959		$2,500	$3,250
1960-1971		$2,000	$2,500

Everly Brothers
1962-1972. Jumbo flat-top, huge double 'guard, star inlays, natural was optional in '63 and became the standard color in '68, reintroduced as the J-180 Everly Brothers in '86.

1962-1964	Black	$18,000	$22,500
1963	Natural option	$18,000	$22,500
1965	Early '65, black, large neck	$15,500	$20,000
1965	Late '65, black, small neck	$11,500	$14,500
1966-1967	Black	$10,000	$12,500
1968-1969	Natural	$7,500	$9,500
1970-1972	Natural	$6,500	$8,500

Explorer
1958-1959, 1963. Some '58s shipped in '63, korina body, 2 humbuckers. The Explorer market is a very specialized and very small market, with few genuine examples available and a limited number of high-end buyers. The slightest change to the original specifications can mean a significant drop in value. The narrow price ranges noted are for all original examples that have the original guitar case.

1958-1959		$1,000,000	$1,350,000
1963		$500,000	$750,000

1966 Gibson ES-355 TD
Ted Wulfers

1958 Gibson Explorer

GUITARS

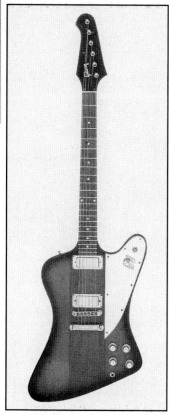

1996 Gibson Explorer '76
Rivington Guitars

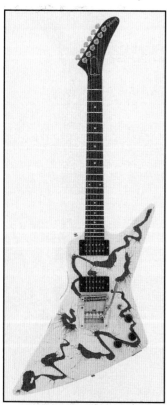

1984 Gibson Explorer
Designer Series
Imaged by Heritage Auctions, HA.com

MODEL YEAR	FEATURES	EXC. COND. LOW	HIGH

Explorer (Mahogany)
1975-1982. Mahogany body, 2 humbuckers, black, white or natural.

1975-1982	Black or white	$5,500	$7,000
1975-1982	Natural	$5,500	$7,000

Explorer I
1981-1982. Replaces Explorer (Mahogany), 2 Dirty Finger humbuckers, stoptail or Kahler vibrato, becomes Explorer 83 in '83.

1981-1982	$1,500	$1,875

Explorer 83 or Explorer (Alder)
1983-1989. Renamed Explorer 83 from Explorer I, changed to Explorer in '84, alder body, 2 humbuckers, maple neck, ebony 'board, dot inlays, triangle knob pattern.

1983-1984		$2,875	$3,500
1985-1989	Custom color, limited run	$2,500	$3,250
1985-1989	Standard finishes	$2,125	$2,625

Explorer II (E/2)
1978-1983. Five-piece maple and walnut laminate body sculptured like V II, ebony 'board with dot inlays, 2 humbuckers, gold-plated hardware, natural finish.

1978-1983	Figured top	$4,250	$5,500
1978-1983	Various colors	$4,000	$5,000

Explorer III
1984-1985. Alder body, 3 P-90 pickups, 2 control knobs, chrome or black hardware ('85 only), optional locking trem.

1984-1985	All options	$1,750	$2,500

Explorer '76/X-plorer/Explorer
1990-2014, 2019-present. Mahogany body and neck, rosewood 'board, dot inlays, 2 humbucking pickups, name changed to X-plorer in 2002 and to Explorer in '09. Reintroduced in '19.

1990-1999	Various colors	$1,500	$2,000
2002-2014	Various colors	$1,500	$2,000

Explorer 90 Double
1989-1990. Mahogany body and neck, 1 single-coil and 1 humbucker, strings-thru-body.

1989-1990	$2,125	$2,750

Explorer Baritone
2011-2013. 28"-scale, 2 exposed humbuckers.

2011-2013	$1,875	$2,500

Explorer Centennial
1994 only. Les Paul Gold finish, 100 year banner inlay at 12th fret, diamonds in headstock and gold-plated knobs, Gibson coin in rear of headstock, only 100 made.

1994	$7,500	$9,000

Explorer CMT/The Explorer
1981-1984. Flamed maple body, bound top, exposed-coil pickups, TP-6 tailpiece.

1981-1984	$4,000	$5,000

Explorer Custom Shop
2003-2012. Custom Shop model with Certificate of Authenticity, Korina body, gold hardware.

2003-2012	$6,500	$8,000

Explorer Designer Series
1983-1985. Custom paint finish.

1983-1985	$2,500	$3,250

Explorer Gothic
1998-2003. Gothic Series with black finish and hardware.

1998-2003	$1,500	$1,875

Explorer Government Series
2012-2016. Made from guitar bodies, necks and 'boards returned from Federal Government after '11 raid on Gibson, special run of 300 built, each with Certificate of Authenticity.

2013	$1,375	$1,750

Explorer Heritage
1983. Reissue of '58 Explorer, korina body, gold hardware, inked serial number, limited edition.

1983	Black, white, red	$6,500	$8,500
1983	Natural	$15,000	$20,000

Explorer Korina
1982-1984. Korina body and neck, 2 humbucking pickups, gold hardware, standard 8-digit serial (versus the inked serial number on the Heritage Explorer of the same era).

1982-1984	$6,000	$7,500

Explorer 1958 Korina/Split Headstock
1994. Split headstock, 50 made.

1994	$10,000	$12,500

Explorer 50th Anniversary '58 Korina
2007-2008. Custom Shop, natural korina, includes custom colors.

2007-2008	$10,000	$12,500

Explorer 50-Year Brimstone Commemorative
2008. Guitar of the month Oct. '08, solid mahogany body, AA figured maple top, higher-end appointments, 50th logo on truss rod cover, Brimstone Burst finish.

2008	$3,000	$4,000

Explorer 120
2014. 120th Anniversary inlay at 12th fret, mahogany body, cherry or black.

2014	$2,250	$3,000

Explorer Pro
2002-2005, 2007-2008. Explorer model updated with smaller, lighter weight mahogany body, 2 humbuckers, ebony or natural.

2002-2008	$1,625	$2,125

Allen Collins Tribute Explorer
2003. Custom Shop, limited production, korina body and neck, rosewood 'board, 2 humbucker pickups.

2003	$12,000	$15,000

Dethklok "Thunderhorse" Explorer
2011-2012. Limited Edition of 400, Thunderhorse logo on truss rod cover, silverburst finish.

2011-2012	$2,500	$3,250

Explorer Limited Edition (Korina)
1976. Limited edition korina body replaces standard mahogany body, natural.

1976	$7,500	$9,500

Explorer Limited Edition (Mahogany)
1999. Mahogany with natural finish.

1999	$2,500	$3,500

Explorer Robot
2008-2012. Announced Sept. '08, Robot Tuning System, trapezoid markers, 2 exposed humbuckers, red finish.

2008-2012	$1,625	$2,125

The *Vintage Guitar Price Guide* shows values for all-original, excellent condition instruments and, where applicable, with original case.

The Official Vintage Guitar magazine Price Guide 2025   **Gibson** Explorer Split Headstock Collection — Firebird III   **157**

GUITARS

MODEL YEAR	FEATURES	EXC. COND. LOW	HIGH
Explorer Split Headstock Collection			
2001. Custom Shop model, 25 made, Explorer body with V-split headstock.			
2001		$4,000	$5,500
Explorer T/Explorer 2016 T/2017 T			
2016-2018. Mahogany body, rosewood 'board, white 'guard, ebony or cherry finish.			
2016-2018		$1,625	$2,125
Explorer Voodoo			
2002-2004. Juju finish, red and black pickup coils.			
2002-2004		$1,875	$2,500
Explorer XPL Custom			
1985. Gibson Custom Shop logo on back of headstock, factory Gibson Kahler tremolo, extra cutaway on lower treble bout.			
1985		$1,500	$2,000
Holy Explorer			
2009-2011. Explorer body 7 routed holes, 1 knob, 2 exposed humbuckers, Limited Run Series certificate of authenticity, 350 made.			
2009-2011		$1,500	$2,000
Reverse Explorer			
2008. Guitar of the Month Sept. '08, 1,000 made, Antique Walnut finish, includes custom guitar case.			
2008		$2,000	$2,500
Sammy Hagar Signature Explorer			
2011-2013. Mahogany with Red Rocker finish, ghosted Chickenfoot logo on back.			
2011-2013		$2,500	$3,500
Shred X Explorer			
2008. Guitar of the Month June '08, 1,000 made, ebony finish, black hardware, 2 EMG 85 pickups, Kahler.			
2008		$2,000	$2,500
Tribal Explorer			
2009-2011. Black tribal graphics on white body. Limited run of 350.			
2009-2011		$1,500	$2,000
X-Plorer/X-Plorer V New Century			
2006-2007. Full-body mirror 'guard, mahogany body and neck, 2 humbuckers, mirror truss rod cover.			
2006-2007		$1,500	$2,000
Firebird I			
1963-1969. Reverse body and 1 humbucker '63-mid-'65, non-reversed body and 2 P-90s mid-'65-'69.			
1963	Sunburst, reverse, hardtail	$19,500	$24,500
1963	Sunburst, reverse, trem	$12,000	$15,000
1964	Cardinal Red, reverse	$25,000	$30,000
1964	Sunburst, reverse, hardtail	$18,500	$25,000
1964	Sunburst, reverse, trem	$10,500	$14,000
1965	Cardinal Red, reverse	$18,500	$25,000
1965	Custom color, non-reverse	$13,500	$16,500
1965	Sunburst, non-reverse, 2 P-90s	$5,500	$7,000

MODEL YEAR	FEATURES	EXC. COND. LOW	HIGH
1965	Sunburst, reverse	$8,500	$10,500
1966	Custom color, non-reverse	$10,000	$12,500
1966	Sunburst, non-reverse	$5,500	$7,000
1967	Custom color, non-reverse	$10,500	$12,500
1967	Sunburst, non-reverse	$5,500	$7,000
1968-1969	Sunburst, non-reverse	$5,500	$7,000
Firebird I (Custom Shop)			
1991-1992		$3,000	$4,000
Firebird I 1963 Reissue Historic			
2000-2006. Custom Shop Historic Collection, neck-thru, reverse body, Firebird logo on 'guard, various colors including sunburst and Frost Blue.			
2000-2006	Various colors	$3,000	$4,000
Eric Clapton 1964 Firebird I			
2019. Custom Shop, limited run of 100, mahogany body, mahogany/walnut neck, Indian rosewood 'board, signed backplate, 1 Alnico pickup, Vintage Sunburst, certificate.			
2019		$7,500	$9,750
Firebird 76			
1976-1978. Reverse body, gold hardware, 2 pickups.			
1976	Bicentennial	$6,500	$8,500
1976	Black	$6,000	$8,000
1976	Sunburst, red/white/blue 'guard logo	$6,500	$8,500
1977-1978	Sunburst	$6,000	$8,000
1977-1978	White	$6,000	$8,000
Firebird I/ Firebird 76			
1980-1982. Reintroduced Firebird 76 but renamed Firebird I.			
1980-1982		$4,000	$5,000
Firebird II/Firebird 2			
1981-1982. Maple body with figured maple top, 2 full size active humbuckers, TP-6 tailpiece.			
1981-1982		$5,000	$6,500
Firebird III			
1963-1969. Reverse body and 2 humbuckers '63-mid-'65, non-reversed body and 3 P-90s mid-'65-'69, various colors.			
1963	Cardinal Red	$25,000	$35,000
1963	Golden Mist	$25,000	$35,000
1963	Pastel Color	$65,000	$85,000
1963	Polaris White	$20,000	$25,000
1963	Sunburst	$13,500	$16,500
1964	Cardinal Red, reverse	$20,000	$25,000
1964	Golden Mist, reverse	$20,000	$25,000
1964	Pelham Blue	$20,000	$25,000
1964	Polaris White, reverse	$18,000	$22,500
1964	Sunburst, reverse	$13,500	$16,500
1965	Cherry, non-reverse, 3 P-90s	$7,500	$9,500
1965	Cherry, reverse	$13,500	$16,500

1965 Gibson Firebird I
Matt Carleson

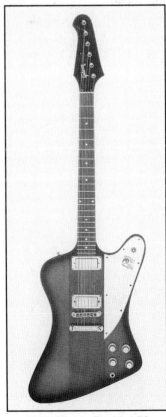

1976 Gibson Firebird 76
Imaged by Heritage Auctions, HA.com

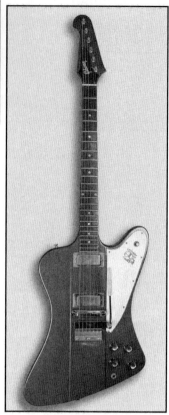

1964 Gibson Firebird III
Dave Rogers

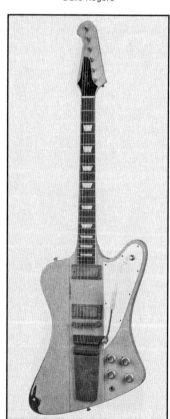

Gibson 1963 Firebird V
Murphy Lab Aged

MODEL YEAR	FEATURES	EXC. COND. LOW	HIGH
1965	Frost Blue, non-reverse	$13,500	$16,500
1965	Frost Blue, reverse	$16,500	$20,500
1965	Golden Mist, reverse	$16,500	$20,500
1965	Inverness Green, non-reverse	$13,500	$16,500
1965	Inverness Green, reverse	$16,500	$20,500
1965	Sunburst, non-reverse, 2 P-90s	$6,000	$7,500
1965	Sunburst, non-reverse, 3 P-90s	$6,500	$8,500
1965	Sunburst, reverse, 2 P-90s	$10,000	$12,500
1965	Sunburst, reverse, mini hums	$10,500	$13,500
1966	Frost Blue	$13,500	$16,500
1966	Pelham Blue	$13,500	$16,500
1966	Polaris White	$12,500	$15,500
1966-1969	Sunburst	$6,500	$8,500
1967	Cherry	$6,500	$8,500
1967	Frost Blue	$14,500	$18,500
1967-1969	Pelham Blue	$14,500	$18,500

Firebird III 1964 Reissue Historic
2000-2013. Custom Shop Historic Collection, Maestro, mini-humbuckers, sunburst or color option.

2000-2013		$3,500	$4,500

Firebird III 1965 Reissue Historic
2009. Custom Shop Historic Collection, reverse body, Maestro, 2 mini-humbuckers, sunburst.

2009		$3,000	$3,750

Firebird Non-Reverse
2002-2004. Non-reverse body, 2 humbuckers, standard finishes. There was also a limited edition in '02 with swirl finishes.

2002-2004		$1,750	$2,125

Firebird Studio Non-Reverse
2011-2012. Non-reverse body, 3 tapped P-90 pickups, 5-way pickup selector switch, dot markers, Vintage Sunburst or Pelham Blue nitro finish.

2011-2012		$1,500	$2,000

Firebird Studio Tribute/Studio T
2012-2017. Reverse mahogany body, '70s profile maple neck, 2 mini-humbuckers.

2012-2017		$1,500	$2,000

Firebird Studio/Firebird III Studio
2004-2010. Two humbuckers, dot markers, tune-o-matic and bar stoptail, reverse body, dark cherry finish.

2004-2010		$1,500	$2,000

Firebird V
1963-1969. Two humbuckers, reverse body '63-mid-'65, non-reversed body mid-'65-'69.

1963	Sunburst, reverse	$20,000	$25,000
1963-1964	Pelham Blue, reverse	$32,500	$40,000
1964	Cardinal Red, reverse	$25,000	$32,000
1964	Sunburst, reverse	$20,000	$25,000
1965	Cardinal Red, reverse	$25,000	$32,000

MODEL YEAR	FEATURES	EXC. COND. LOW	HIGH
1965	Sunburst, non-reverse	$9,500	$11,500
1965	Sunburst, reverse	$14,500	$18,500
1965	Pastel Color, reverse	$40,000	$50,000
1966-1967	Cardinal Red, non-reverse	$14,500	$18,500
1966-1969	Sunburst	$7,500	$9,500

Firebird V/Firebird V Reissue/ Firebird V 2010
1986-1987, 1990-2018. Based on Firebird V specs, reverse body, 2 pickups, tune-o-matic bridge, vintage sunburst, classic white or ebony with Cardinal Red optional in '91. Called Reissue for '90-'93, renamed V in '94, then V 2010 in '10.

1986-1987	Sunburst, white, black	$3,500	$4,500
1990	Sunburst, white, black	$3,500	$4,500
1991	Cardinal Red	$3,500	$4,500
1991-1999	Sunburst, white, black	$2,500	$3,500
2000-2018	Sunburst, white, black	$2,000	$2,500

Firebird V-12
1966-1967. Non-reverse Firebird V-style body with standard six-on-a-side headstock and split diamond headstock inlay (like ES-335-12 inlay), dot markers, special twin humbucking pickups (like mini-humbuckers).

1966-1967	Custom color	$13,500	$16,500
1966-1967	Sunburst	$6,000	$7,500

Firebird V 1963 Aged (Custom Shop)
2016. Reverse body, Vintage Sunburst, aged hardware.

2016		$4,000	$5,500

Firebird V 1963 Johnny Winter
2008. Johnny Winter script logo, certificate of authenticity.

2008		$8,500	$12,500

1963 Firebird V (Maestro Vibrola) Murphy Lab Aged
2021-present. Custom Shop Murphy Lab Collection, heavy aged (Antique Frost Blue), light aged (Cardinal Red) and ultra light (Ember Red or Pelham Blue).

2021-2023	Heavy aged	$5,750	$7,500
2021-2023	Light aged	$5,250	$6,750
2021-2022	Ultra Light aged	$5,000	$6,500

Firebird V 1964 Johnny Winter
2021-2023. Mahogany/walnut body, Indian rosewood 'board, 2 Alnico pickups, banjo tuners, Murphy Lab aged Polaris White finish.

2021-2023		$7,250	$9,500

Firebird V 1965 Reissue (Custom Shop)
2000-2013. Reverse body, 2 mini-humbuckers, Maestro tremolo, certificate, sunburst or colors.

2000-2013		$3,500	$4,500

Firebird V 50th Anniversary
2013. Gold hardware, '50th Anniversary 1963-2013' on 'guard, gold finish.

2013		$2,500	$3,000

*The **Vintage Guitar Price Guide** shows values for all-original, excellent condition instruments and, where applicable, with original case.*

MODEL		EXC. COND.	
YEAR	FEATURES	LOW	HIGH

Firebird V Celebrity Series
1990-1993. Reverse body, gold hardware, 2 humbuckers, various colors.

1990-1993		$3,500	$4,500

Firebird V Guitar Trader Reissue
1982. Guitar Trader commissioned Firebird reissue, only 15 made, sunburst or white.

1982		$4,500	$5,500

Firebird V Limited Edition Zebrawood
2007. Limited edition from Gibson USA, Guitar of the Week #12, 400 made, zebrawood reverse body.

2007		$2,500	$3,500

Firebird V Medallion
1972-1973. Reverse body, 2 humbuckers, Limited Edition medallion mounted on body.

1972-1973		$10,000	$12,500

Firebird VII
1963-1969. Three humbuckers, reverse body '63-mid-'65, non-reversed body mid-'65-'69, sunburst standard.

1963-1964	Sunburst, reverse	$30,000	$40,000
1964	Custom color, reverse	$50,000	$65,000
1965	Custom color, non-reverse	$30,000	$38,000
1965	Custom color, reverse	$45,000	$55,000
1965	Sunburst, non-reverse	$10,000	$12,500
1965	Sunburst, reverse	$18,500	$23,500
1966-1967	Custom color, non-reverse	$20,000	$25,000
1966-1969	Sunburst, non-reverse	$9,500	$11,500
1968	Custom color, non-reverse	$16,500	$20,500

Firebird VII (Reissue)
2002-2007. Designer collection, various production models, reverse and non-reverse, 3 pickups, block markers, vibrola, various color options with matching headstock.

2002-2007	All colors	$2,250	$2,750

Firebird VII 1965 Historic
1998-2013. Custom Shop Historic Collection, 3 mini-humbuckers, Vintage Sunburst or solid colors.

1998-2013		$3,375	$4,500

20th Anniversary 1965 Firebird VII
2014. Custom Shop, '65 specs, gold hardware, Golden Mist finish, certificate of authenticity.

2014		$5,500	$7,000

Firebird VII Centennial
1994 only. Headstock medallion, sunburst.

1994		$4,750	$6,000

Firebird X Limited Edition Robot
2011-2018. 1800 to be made, lightweight swamp ash body, 1-piece maple neck, curly maple 'board, 3 pickups, robot electronics, nitro lacquer finish in Redolution or Bluevolution.

2011-2018		$3,500	$4,500

Elliot Easton "Tikibird" Firebird
2013-2018. Reverse body, mahogany, rosewood 'board, 2 pickups, Tiki graphic on 'guard, signature on headstock back, Gold Mist Poly finish.

2013-2018		$3,000	$4,000

MODEL		EXC. COND.	
YEAR	FEATURES	LOW	HIGH

Firebird Custom Acoustic
2004-2018. Sitka spruce top, quilted maple back and sides, ebony 'board, mother-of-pearl headstock logo with MOP and abalone flames inlay, antique natural finish.

2004-2018		$3,500	$4,500

Firebird Zero
2016-2018. S Series, new body design, 2 pickups, poplar body, maple neck, rosewood 'board, various colors.

2016-2018		$650	$800

Flamenco 2
1963-1967. Natural spruce top, 14 3/4", cypress back and sides, slotted headstock, zero fret.

1963-1967		$1,500	$2,000

Flying V
1958-1959, 1962-1963. Only 81 shipped in '58 and 17 in '59, guitars made from leftover parts and sold in '62-'63, natural korina body, string-thru-body design. The original case with oxblood interior adds $2,500.

As with any ultra high-end instrument, each instrument should be evaluated on a case-by-case basis. The Flying V market is a very specialized market, with few untouched examples available, and a limited number of high-end buyers. The price ranges noted are for all-original, excellent condition guitars with the original Flying V case. The slightest change to the original specifications can mean a significant drop in value.

1958-1959		$500,000	$750,000

Flying V (Mahogany)
1966-1970, 1975-1981. Mahogany body, around 200 were shipped for '66-'70. Gibson greatly increased production of Flying Vs in '75. See separate listing for the '71 Medallion V version.

1966	Cherry, sunburst	$75,000	$85,000
1967-1970	Cherry, sunburst, sparkling burgundy, walnut	$65,000	$80,000
1975-1981	Various colors	$8,500	$12,000
1979	Silverburst	$8,500	$12,000
1980-1981	Silverburst	$8,500	$12,000

Flying V (Mahogany String-through-body)
1982. Mahogany body, string-thru-body design, only 100 made, most in white, some red or black possible.

1982	All colors	$4,250	$5,500

Flying V (Custom Shop)
2004-2008. A few made each year, figured maple top, options include standard point-headstock or split-headstock.

2004-2008	All options	$5,500	$6,750

Flying V Limited Registered Edition
1980. All gold.

1980		$10,000	$15,000

Flying V Heritage
1981-1982. Limited edition based on '58 specs, korina body, 4 colors available.

1981-1982	Natural	$6,500	$8,500
1981-1982	Various colors	$6,500	$8,500

Flying V I/V '83/Flying V (no pickguard)
1981-1988. Introduced as Flying V I, then renamed Flying V '83 in 1983, called Flying V from '84 on. Al-

1959 Gibson Flying V
Kris Blakely

1982 Gibson Flying V Heritage
Steve Evans

1998 Gibson Flying V '98

K.C. Cormack

1999 Gibson Historic
Korina Futura

Imaged by Heritage Auctions, HA.com

MODEL YEAR	FEATURES	EXC. COND. LOW	HIGH

der body, 2 exposed humbuckers, maple neck, ebony 'board, dot inlays, black rings, no 'guard, ebony or ivory finish, designed for lower-end market.

| 1981-1988 | | $3,000 | $4,000 |

Flying V Korina
1983. Name changed from Flying V Heritage, korina body, various colors.

| 1983 | | $6,500 | $8,500 |

Flying V Reissue/'67/Factor X/Flying V
1990-2014. Mahogany body, called Flying V Reissue first year, then '67 Flying V '91-'02, V Factor X '03-'08, Flying V '09-'14.

| 1990-2014 | Various colors | $1,500 | $2,000 |

Flying V II
1979-1982. Five-piece maple and walnut laminate sculptured body (1980 catalog states top is either walnut or maple), ebony 'board with dot inlays, 2 V-shaped pickups (2 Dirty Fingers humbuckers towards end of run), gold-plated hardware, natural.

| 1979-1982 | | $3,750 | $5,000 |
| 1982 | Silverburst | $3,750 | $5,000 |

Flying V 50th Anniversary
2008. Built as replica of '58 square shoulder V, 100 made, natural finish on korina body and neck, rosewood 'board, 8-series serial number, price includes original certificate.

| 2008 | | $8,000 | $10,000 |

Flying V '58 Historic
1991-2013. Custom Shop Historic Collection, based on '58 Flying V, gold hardware, natural korina.

| 1991-1999 | | $7,500 | $9,500 |
| 2000-2013 | | $6,500 | $8,500 |

Flying V 1958 Mahogany
2021-present. Custom Shop Designer series, mahogany with walnut finish.

| 2021-2023 | | $4,500 | $6,500 |

Flying V '59 (Custom Shop)

2001	Natural	$5,500	$7,000
2004	Cherry	$5,500	$7,000
2013	Natural	$4,500	$6,500
2014	Pelham Blue, 20 offered	$4,500	$6,500
2020	TV Black Gold	$4,000	$5,000

Flying V 1959 Mahogany
2014-2020. Custom Shop Designer series, mahogany with various colors.

| 2014-2020 | | $3,500 | $4,500 |

Flying V '67 Historic
1997-2004. Custom Shop Historic Collection, '67 Flying V specs, korina body, natural or opaque colors.

| 1997-2004 | | $3,500 | $4,500 |

Flying V '84 Silverburst
2007. Limited Edition Guitar of the Week.

| 2007 | | $1,875 | $2,500 |

Flying V '90 Double
1989-1990. Mahogany body, stud tailpiece, 1 single-coil and 1 double-coil humbucker, Floyd Rose tremolo, ebony, silver or white.

| 1989-1990 | | $2,500 | $3,000 |

Flying V '98
1998. Mahogany body, '58 style controls, gold or chrome hardware.

| 1998 | | $2,500 | $3,000 |

Flying V 120
2014. Mahogany body and neck, 120th Anniversary inlay at 12th fret, rosewood 'board, 2 BurstBucker pickups, ebony, classic white or Heritage Cherry.

| 2014 | | $2,000 | $2,500 |

Flying V 50-Year Commemorative
2008. Guitar of the Month March '08, 1,000 made, AA flamed maple top, higher-end appointments, 50th logo on truss rod cover, Brimstone Burst finish.

| 2008 | | $3,000 | $3,500 |

Flying V Brendon Small Snow Falcon
2013. Snow Falcon decal on headstock back, 2 Burstbucker pickups, chrome hardware, Snow Burst finish, limited run.

| 2013 | | $2,500 | $3,000 |

Flying V Centennial
1994 only. 100th Anniversary Series, all gold, gold medalion, other special appointments.

| 1994 | | $6,000 | $7,500 |

Flying V CMT/The V
1981-1985. Maple body with a curly maple top, 2 pickups, stud tailpiece, natural or sunburst.

| 1981-1985 | | $4,500 | $6,500 |

Flying V Custom
2002. Limited Edition, appointments similar to Les Paul Custom, including black finish, only 40 made.

| 2002 | | $6,500 | $8,500 |

Flying V Designer Series
1983-1984. Custom paint finish.

| 1983-1984 | | $3,000 | $4,000 |

Flying V Faded
2002-2012. Worn cherry finish.

| 2002-2012 | | $950 | $1,125 |

Flying V Gothic/'98 Gothic
1998-2003. Satin black finish, black hardware, moon and star markers.

| 1998-2003 | | $1,500 | $2,000 |

Flying V Government Series
2012-2016. Made from guitar bodies, necks and 'boards returned from Federal Government after '11 raid on Gibson, special run of 300 built, each with Certificate of Authenticity.

| 2013 | | $1,500 | $2,000 |

Flying V Hendrix Hall of Fame
Late-1991-1993. Limited Edition (400 made), numbered, black.

| 1991-1993 | | $4,250 | $5,500 |

Flying V Hendrix Psychedelic
2005-2006. Hand-painted 1967 Flying V replica, 300 made, includes certificate, instruments without the certificate are worth less than the amount shown.

| 2005-2006 | | $10,000 | $12,500 |

Flying V Kirk Hammett Signature
2012. Custom Shop, '76 specs, aged ebony.

| 2012 | | $6,000 | $7,500 |

The Vintage Guitar Price Guide shows values for all-original, excellent condition instruments and, where applicable, with original case.

MODEL YEAR FEATURES	EXC. COND. LOW	HIGH

Flying V Lenny Kravitz
2002. Custom Shop, 125 made.

| 2002 | $4,500 | $6,000 |

Flying V Lonnie Mack
1993-1995. Mahogany body with Lonnie Mack-style Bigsby vibrato, cherry.

| 1993-1995 | $6,000 | $7,500 |

Flying V LTD
2001. Limited Edition logo, certificate of authenticity.

| 2001 | $2,000 | $2,500 |

Flying V Medallion
1971, 1973-1974. Mahogany body, stud tailpiece, numbered Limited Edition medallion on bass side of V, 350 made in '71 (3 more were shipped in '73-'74).

| 1971-1974 | $25,000 | $30,000 |

Flying V New Century
2006-2007. Full-body mirror 'guard, mahogany body and neck, 2 humbuckers, Flying V style neck profile, mirror truss rod cover.

| 2006-2007 | $1,500 | $2,000 |

Flying V Pearl Block Marker
1979-1980. Pearl block inlays, various colors.

| 1979-1980 | $10,000 | $20,000 |

Flying V Primavera
1994. Primavera (light yellow/white mahogany) body, gold-plated hardware.

| 1994 | $3,000 | $4,000 |

Flying V Robot
2008-2011. Robot Tuning System.

| 2008-2011 | $1,750 | $2,125 |

Flying V T
2016-2017. Mahogany body, thicker 1-piece 'board.

| 2016-2017 | $1,750 | $2,125 |

Flying V The Holy V
2009. Guitar of the month for Jan. '09, large triangular cutouts in bouts, split diamond markers, 1 humbucker, 1 control knob.

| 2009 | $1,500 | $2,000 |

Flying V Voodoo
2002-2003. Black finish, red pickups.

| 2002-2003 | $2,500 | $3,500 |

Flying V XPL
1984-1986. Various colors with Purple 'Burst being rarest.

| 1984-1986 | $1,250 | $1,500 |

Limited Edition Flying V
2016. Dirty Fingers, faded amber finish, gig bag.

| 2016 | $750 | $950 |

Reverse Flying V
2006-2008. Introduced as part of Guitar of the Week program, reintroduced by popular demand in a '07 limited run, light colored solid mahogany body gives a natural Korina appearance or opaque white or black, V-shaped reverse body, traditional Flying V neck profile.

| 2006-2007 | | $2,125 | $2,500 |
| 2008 | Guitar of the Week | $1,875 | $2,375 |

Rudolf Schenker Flying V
1993. Only 103 made, black and white body and headstock, signature on 'guard.

| 1993 | $2,500 | $3,500 |

MODEL YEAR FEATURES	EXC. COND. LOW	HIGH

Rudolf Schenker Scorpions Flying V
1984. Custom Shop model, Kahler tremolo, mother-of-pearl inlays, black and white.

| 1984 | $4,000 | $5,000 |

Shred V
2008. Guitar of the Month, 1000 made, EMG humbuckers, Kahler, black.

| 2008 | $1,875 | $2,500 |

Tribal V
2009-2011. Black tribal graphics on white body. Limited run of 350.

| 2009-2011 | $1,500 | $1,875 |

Zakk Wylde Flying V
2007-2011. Custom Shop, with Floyd Rose and typical bullseye finish.

| 2007-2011 | $5,750 | $7,250 |

F-25 Folksinger
1963-1971. 14-1/2" flat-top, mahogany body, most have double white 'guard, natural.

1963-1964	$2,000	$2,500
1965	$1,750	$2,250
1966-1971	$1,750	$2,250

FJN Folk Singer
1963-1967. Jumbo flat-top, square shoulders, natural finish with deep red on back and sides.

1963-1964	$2,500	$3,250
1965	$2,375	$3,000
1966-1967	$2,250	$2,875

Futura
1982-1984. Deep cutout solidbody, 2 humbucker pickups, gold hardware, black, white or purple.

| 1982-1984 | $2,125 | $2,750 |

Historic Korina Futura
1998-1999. Custom Shop Historic Collection, Explorer body with V headstock.

| 1998-1999 | $8,000 | $10,500 |

G-00
2021-present. Generation Collection, parlor-sized, Sitka spruce top, walnut back and sides, natural finish.

| 2021-2023 | $725 | $950 |

G-45 (Standard/Studio)
2019-present. Slim body, Fishman pickup, solid Sitka spruce top, walnut back and sides, Antique Natural satin finish (standard) or gloss (studio).

| 2019-2021 | Gloss | $925 | $1,250 |
| 2019-2023 | Satin | $750 | $975 |

GB Series Guitar Banjos
See listings in Banjo section of the Price Guide.

GGC-700
1981-1982. Slab single-cut body, 2 exposed humbuckers, dots.

| 1981-1982 | $950 | $1,250 |

GK-55 Active
1979-1980. LP body style, 2 exposed Dirty Fingers humbuckers, bolt neck, dot markers.

| 1979-1980 | $1,000 | $1,375 |

Gospel
1973-1979. Flat-top, square shoulders, laminated maple back and sides, arched back, Dove of Peace headstock inlay, natural.

| 1973-1979 | $1,250 | $1,625 |

Gibson G-00

Gibson G-45 Standard

1937 Gibson HG-Century
Imaged by Heritage Auctions, HA.com

1963 Gibson Hummingbird
Craig Brody

MODEL YEAR	FEATURES	EXC. COND. LOW	HIGH

Gospel Reissue
1992-1997. Laminated mahogany back and sides, natural or sunburst (walnut added in '94, blue and red in '95), changes to old-style script logo and headstock ornamentation in '94.

| 1992-1993 | Reissue specs | $1,500 | $2,000 |
| 1994-1997 | Old-style specs | $1,500 | $2,000 |

GS-1 Classical
1950-1956. Mahogany back and sides.

| 1950-1956 | | $725 | $950 |

GS-2 Classical
1950-1956. Maple back and sides.

| 1950-1959 | | $800 | $1,000 |

GS-5 Custom Classic/C-5 Classical
1954-1960. Brazilian rosewood back and sides, renamed C-5 Classical in '57.

| 1954-1960 | | $1,750 | $2,250 |

GS-35 Classical/Gut String 35
1939-1942. Spruce top, mahogany back and sides, only 39 made.

| 1939-1942 | | $2,000 | $2,500 |

GS-85 Classical/Gut String 85
1939-1942. Brazilian rosewood back and sides.

| 1939-1942 | | $3,750 | $4,750 |

GY (Army-Navy)
1918-1921. Slightly arched top and back, low-end budget model, Sheraton Brown.

| 1918-1921 | | $850 | $1,125 |

Harley Davidson LTD
1994-1995. Limited Edition, 16" wide body, flat-top, Harley Davidson in script and logo, black, 1500 sold through Harley dealers to celebrate 100th Anniversary of Harley.

| 1994-1995 | | $3,000 | $4,000 |

Heritage
1965-1982. Flat-top dreadnought, square shoulders, rosewood back and sides (Brazilian until '67, Indian '68 on), bound top and back, natural finish.

| 1965-1967 | Brazilian | $4,500 | $5,500 |
| 1968-1982 | Indian | $2,250 | $3,000 |

Heritage-12
1968-1971. Flat-top dreadnought, 12 strings, Indian rosewood back and sides, bound top and back, natural finish.

| 1968-1971 | | $1,875 | $2,375 |

HG-00 (Hawaiian)
1932-1942. Hawaiian version of L-00, 14 3/4" flat-top, mahogany back and sides, bound top, natural.

| 1932-1947 | | $5,000 | $6,500 |

HG-20 (Hawaiian)
1929-1933. Hawaiian, 14 1/2" dreadnought-shaped, maple back and sides, round sound hole and 4 f-holes.

| 1929-1933 | | $5,000 | $6,500 |

HG-22 (Hawaiian)
1929-1932. Dreadnought, 14", Hawaiian, round sound hole and 4 f-holes, white paint logo, very small number produced.

| 1929-1932 | | $5,250 | $6,750 |

HG-24 (Hawaiian)
1929-1932. 16" Hawaiian, rosewood back and sides, round sound hole plus 4 f-holes, small number produced.

| 1929-1932 | | $7,250 | $9,500 |

HG-Century (Hawaiian)
1937-1938. Hawaiian, 14 3/4" L-C Century of Progress, pearloid 'board.

| 1937-1938 | | $5,000 | $6,500 |

Howard Roberts Artist
1976-1980. Full body single-cut archtop, sound hole, 1 humbucking pickup, gold hardware, ebony 'board, various colors.

| 1976-1980 | | $2,750 | $3,500 |

Howard Roberts Artist Double Pickup
1979-1980. Two pickup version of HR Artist.

| 1979-1980 | | $3,250 | $4,250 |

Howard Roberts Custom
1975-1981. Full body single-cut archtop, sound hole, 1 humbucking pickup, chrome hardware, rosewood 'board, various colors.

| 1975-1981 | | $3,000 | $4,000 |

Howard Roberts Fusion/ Fusion II/Fusion III
1979-2009. Single-cut, semi-hollowbody, 2 humbucking pickups, chrome hardware, ebony 'board (unbound until '78), TP-6 tailpiece, various colors, renamed Howard Roberts Fusion II in late-'88, and Howard Roberts Fusion III in '91.

| 1979-2009 | | $2,750 | $3,500 |

HP-415 W
2017-2018. High Performance series, slimmer round shoulder cutaway, Sitka spruce top, walnut back and sides.

| 2017-2018 | | $1,125 | $1,500 |

Hummingbird
1960-2020. Flat-top acoustic, square shoulders, mahogany back and sides, bound body and neck. Name changes to Hummingbird Standard in '20.

1960	Cherry Sunburst	$10,000	$15,000
1961-1964	Cherry Sunburst	$10,000	$15,000
1963-1965	Natural	$10,000	$15,000
1965	Cherry Sunburst	$6,500	$8,250
1966	Cherry Sunburst	$5,000	$6,500
1966	Natural	$5,000	$6,500
1967-1968	Natural, screwed 'guard	$5,000	$6,500
1967-1968	Sunburst, screwed 'guard	$4,500	$6,000
1969	Natural, screwed 'guard	$4,250	$5,500
1969	Sunburst, screwed 'guard	$4,250	$5,500
1970-1971	Natural, sunburst	$3,500	$4,500
1972-1979	Double X, block markers	$3,500	$4,500
1980-1985	Double X, block markers	$3,000	$4,000
1985-1988	Single X	$2,500	$3,500
1989	25 1/2" scale	$2,500	$3,500
1990-2020		$2,750	$3,500
1994	100 Years 1894-1994 label	$2,750	$3,500
2015-2020	Custom Shop, ebony	$2,750	$3,500

MODEL YEAR FEATURES	EXC. COND. LOW	HIGH

Hummingbird Standard
2020-present. Modern series, mahogany body with Sitka spruce top, Vintage Sunburst or ebony.

| 2020-2023 | $2,750 | $3,500 |

Hummingbird Historic
2005-2006. Custom Shop Historic Collection, Vintage Honeyburst.

| 2005-2006 | $2,500 | $3,250 |

50th Anniversary 1960 Hummingbird
2010-2012. Limited Edition, 200 made, 50th Anniversary logo on truss rod cover.

| 2010-2012 | $4,250 | $5,500 |

Hummingbird 12
2005-2011. Custom Shop, 12-string, Vintage Sunburst.

| 2005-2011 | $3,500 | $4,500 |

Hummingbird Artist
2007-2011. Plain (no Hummingbird) small 'guard, L.R. Baggs Element, sold through Guitar Center.

| 2007-2011 | $1,750 | $2,250 |

Hummingbird Custom Koa
2004, 2009-2018. Highly flamed koa back and sides, spruce top, gloss finish.

| 2004-2018 | $4,250 | $5,500 |

Hummingbird Limited Edition
1993-1994. Only 30 made, quilted maple top and back.

| 1993-1994 | $3,000 | $4,000 |

Hummingbird Madagascar Honeyburst
2009. Limited run of 20, figured Madagascar rosewood back and sides, factory electronics, certificate of authenticity.

| 2009 | $3,000 | $4,000 |

Hummingbird Modern Classic
2010-2012. Cherry sunburst or ebony finish, L.R. Baggs Element Active pickup system.

| 2010-2012 | $2,500 | $3,000 |

Hummingbird Pro
2010-2013. Non-cut, plain (no Hummingbird) small 'guard, L.R. Baggs Element, Guitar Center.

| 2010-2013 | $1,750 | $2,250 |

Hummingbird Pro EC
2010-2013. Cutaway version, Fishman Prefix Plus-T, Guitar Center.

| 2010-2013 | $1,750 | $2,250 |

Hummingbird Pro 12-String
2018. Custom Shop Limited Edition, Sitka spruce top, mahogany back and sides, Vintage Sunburst or Heritage Cherry Sunburst.

| 2018 | $1,750 | $2,250 |

Hummingbird Quilt Series

| 2007-2014 Custom Shop | $3,000 | $4,000 |

Hummingbird Silverburst
2007. Silverburst finish, 25 made.

| 2007 | $2,500 | $3,000 |

Hummingbird Studio
2019-2020. Slim body, on-board electronics, Antique Natural or Walnut Burst.

| 2019-2020 | $1,500 | $2,000 |

Hummingbird Studio Rosewood
2020-present. Sitka spruce top, rosewood back and sides, Antique Natural or Rosewood Burst.

| 2020-2023 | $2,000 | $2,500 |

Hummingbird Studio Walnut
2020-present. Sitka spruce top, walnut back and sides, Antique Natural or Walnut Burst.

| 2020-2023 | $1,500 | $2,000 |

Hummingbird True Vintage
2007-2013. Sitka spruce top, Madagascar rosewood bridge and 'board, special '60s Heritage Cherry or sunburst finish.

| 2007-2013 | $3,500 | $4,500 |

Invader
1983-1988. Single cutaway solid mahogany body, two humbucker pickups, four knobs with three-way selector switch, stop tailpiece, bolt-on maple neck.

| 1983-1988 All colors | $900 | $1,250 |

J-15/J-15 Standard
2014-2021. Acoustic-electric dreadnought, slope shoulder, walnut back and sides, Antique Natural.

| 2014-2021 | $1,375 | $1,750 |

J-25
1983-1985. Flat-top, laminated spruce top, synthetic semi-round back, ebony 'board, natural or sunburst.

| 1983-1985 | $575 | $750 |

J-29 Rosewood
2014-2016. Sitka spruce top, solid rosewood back and sides.

| 2014-2016 | $1,375 | $1,750 |

J-30
1985-1993. Dreadnought-size flat-top acoustic, mahogany back and sides, sunburst, Renamed J-30 Montana in '94.

| 1985-1993 | $1,750 | $2,250 |

J-30 Cutaway
1990-1995. Cutaway version of J-30, transducer pickup.

| 1990-1995 | $1,750 | $2,250 |

J-30 Montana
1994-1997. Renamed from J-30, dreadnought-size flat-top acoustic, mahogany back and sides, sunburst.

| 1994-1997 | $1,750 | $2,250 |

J-30 RCA Limited Edition
1991. Limited edition for RCA Nashville, RCA logo on headstock.

| 1991 | $1,750 | $2,250 |

J-35
1936-1942, 2012-2018. Sitka spruce top, mahogany back, sides and neck, rosewood 'board.

| 1936-1942 Original | $15,000 | $20,000 |
| 2012-2018 Reissue | $2,250 | $3,000 |

J-40
1971-1982. Dreadnought flat-top, mahogany back and sides, economy satin finish.

| 1971-1982 | $1,250 | $1,625 |

J-45
1942-1982, 1984-present. Dreadnought flat-top, mahogany back and sides, round shoulders until '68 and '84 on, square shoulders '69-'82, sunburst finish (see J-50 for natural version) then natural finish also available in '90s, renamed J-45 Western in '94, renamed Early J-45 in '97 then renamed J-45 Standard in '99. The prices noted are for all-original crack free instruments. A single professionally repaired minor crack that is nearly

Gibson Hummingbird
Studio Rosewood

2012 Gibson J-35
Bernunzio Uptown Music

1958 Gibson J-45

John Wesley

Gibson J-45 Studio Walnut

MODEL		EXC. COND.	
YEAR	FEATURES	LOW	HIGH

invisible will reduce the value only slightly. Two or more, or unsightly repaired cracks will devalue an otherwise excellent original acoustic instrument. Repaired cracks should be evaluated on a case-by-case basis.

1942-1945	Banner, Adirondack	$14,000	$18,500
1942-1945	Banner, mahogany	$13,500	$17,500
1945	Banner, Sitka	$11,000	$14,500
1946-1948	Script, Sitka	$11,000	$14,500
1949	Small 'guard	$9,500	$12,500
1950-1954		$8,500	$11,000
1955-1959	Big 'guard	$7,500	$10,000
1960-1964	Round shoulders	$5,500	$7,500
1965	Early '65, wide nut	$5,000	$6,500
1965	Late '65, slim nut	$4,000	$5,500
1966-1967	Round shoulders	$3,750	$5,000
1968	Black, Cherry	$6,000	$8,000
1968	Blue, Green	$7,750	$10,000
1968-1969	Sunburst, Gibson 'guard	$3,500	$4,500
1969	Square D-shape, late '69	$3,250	$4,250
1970	Square, sunburst	$2,500	$3,000
1971-1975	Deluxe, sunburst	$2,250	$3,000
1976-1979	Sunburst	$2,250	$3,000
1980-1982	Sunburst	$2,000	$2,500
1984-1993	Various Colors	$2,000	$2,500
1994-1997	Western	$2,000	$2,500
1997-1998	Early J-45	$2,000	$2,500
1999-2023	Standard	$2,000	$2,500

J-45 1942 Legend
2006-2014. Early J-45 specs, Adirondack red spruce body, mahogany back/sides/neck, rosewood 'board, Vintage Sunburst finish, certificate of authenticity.

2006-2014		$4,750	$6,250

J-45 1968 Reissue
2004-2007. Limited Edition, special run using '68 specs including Gibson logo 'guard, black or cherry finish.

2004-2007		$2,000	$2,500

J-45 Brad Paisley
2010-2016. Adirondack red spruce top, mahogany back and sides, cherry sunburst.

2010-2016		$3,250	$4,250

J-45 Buddy Holly
1995-1996. Limited Edition, 250 made.

1995-1996		$3,250	$4,250

J-45 Celebrity
1985. Acoustic introduced for Gibson's 90th anniversary, spruce top, rosewood back and sides, ebony 'board, binding on body and 'board, only 90 made.

1985		$2,000	$2,500

J-45 Custom
1999-2020. Custom logo on truss rod, maple, mahogany or rosewood body, abalone trim, fancy headstock inlay.

1999-2020	Various options	$2,000	$3,750

J-45 Custom Vine
1999-2010. Custom Shop, Indian rosewood back and sides, fancy pearl and abalone vine inlay in ebony 'board, pearl Gibson logo and crown, natural gloss finish.

1999-2010		$4,000	$5,000

J-45 Elite Mystic
2014. Figured back, limited edition, rosewood back and sides.

2014		$2,750	$3,500

J-45 Heart of Texas Rosewood
2004. Custom Shop, sound hole label signed by Master Luthier Ren Ferguson, Indian rosewood back and sides, abalone top trim.

2004		$4,000	$5,000

J-45 Historic
2005. Limited edition, 670 made, Historic Collection logo rear headstock, sunburst.

2005		$2,500	$3,000

J-45 John Hiatt
2010-2011. Signature on truss rod cover, 100 offered, Tri Burst top with Tobacco Brown back and sides.

2010-2011		$3,000	$4,000

J-45 Natural Anniversary
2009. Custom Shop Limited Edition, decal on headstock back, 20 made, spruce top, maple neck, zebrawood back and sides, natural finish.

2009		$3,000	$4,000

J-45 Red Spruce Edition
2007. Custom Shop limited edition, only 50 made.

2007		$3,250	$4,250

J-45 Rosewood
1999-2006. Indian rosewood body, spruce top.

1999-2006		$2,000	$2,500

J-45 Studio Rosewood
2020-present. Sitka spruce top, rosewood back and sides, Antique Natural or Rosewood Burst.

2020-2023		$1,500	$2,000

J-45 Studio Sustainable
2019-2020. Sitka spruce top, sustainably harvested North American walnut back and sides, hand-rubbed beeswax finish, Antique Natural.

2019-2020		$1,625	$2,125

J-45 Studio Walnut
2020-present. Sitka spruce top, walnut back and sides, Antique Natural or Walnut Burst.

2020-2023		$1,250	$1,625

J-45 True Vintage/J-45 Vintage
2007-2019. Part of Vintage Series, vintage sunburst finish. True dropped from name in '19.

2007-2019		$2,500	$3,000

J-45 Walnut Limited Edition
2015. Adirondack, flamed walnut.

2015		$3,250	$4,250

Working Man 45 (J-45)
1998-2005. Soft shoulder J-45 style, gloss finish spruce top, satin finish mahogany back and sides, dot markers, natural.

1998-2005		$1,250	$1,625

J-50
1942, 1945-1981, 1990-1995, 1998-2008 (present). Dreadnought flat-top, mahogany back and sides, round shoulders until '68, square shoulders after, natural finish (see J-45 for sunburst version). Though not labeled J-50, the J-45 Standard is now also available in natural finish.

1945	Banner logo	$13,500	$17,500

The Vintage Guitar Price Guide shows values for all-original, excellent condition instruments and, where applicable, with original case.

MODEL YEAR	FEATURES	EXC. COND. LOW	HIGH
1946-1948	Script logo	$11,500	$15,000
1949	Small 'guard	$10,500	$13,500
1950-1954	Small 'guard	$7,250	$9,500
1955	Big 'guard	$7,000	$9,000
1956-1959	Standard fixed bridge	$7,000	$9,000
1960-1964	Round shoulders	$5,500	$7,500
1965	Early '65, wide nut	$5,000	$6,500
1965	Late '65, slim nut	$4,000	$5,500
1966-1969	Round shoulders	$3,750	$5,000
1969	Late '69, square D-shape	$3,250	$4,500
1970-1979	Square shoulders	$2,500	$3,500
1980-2008		$2,500	$3,500

J-55
1935-1942. Mahogany.

1935-1942		$20,000	$25,000

J-55 (Jumbo 55) Limited Edition
1994 only. 16" flat-top, spruce top, mahogany back and sides, 100 made, sunburst.

1994		$2,000	$2,500

J-55 (Reintroduced)
1973-1982. Flat-top, laminated mahogany back and sides, arched back, square shoulders, sunburst. See Jumbo 55 listing for '39-'43 version.

1973-1982		$1,250	$1,625

J-60 Curly Maple
1993 and 1996. Curly maple back and sides, limited edition from Montana shop, natural.

1993,1996		$2,250	$2,750

J-60/J-60 Traditional
1992-1999. Solid spruce top dreadnought, square shoulders, Indian rosewood back and sides, ebony 'board, multiple bindings, natural or sunburst.

1992-1999		$1,625	$2,125

J-100/J-100 Custom
1970-1974, 1985-1997. Flat-top jumbo, multi-bound top and back, black 'guard, dot inlays, mahogany back and sides, '80s version has maple back and sides, dot inlays and tortoise shell 'guard, '90s model has maple back and sides, no 'guard, and J-200 style block inlays.

1970-1974	Mahogany	$1,500	$2,000
1985-1997	Maple	$1,500	$2,000

J-100 Xtra
1991-1997, 1999-2004. Jumbo flat-top, mahogany back and sides, moustache bridge, dot inlays, various colors, J-100 Xtra Cutaway also available, reintroduced in '99 with maple back and sides and single-bound body.

1991-2004		$1,750	$2,250

J-150/SJ-150 Maple
1999-2008. Super jumbo body, solid spruce top, figured maple back and sides (rosewood in '05), MOP crown inlays, moustache bridge with transducer. Renamed SJ-150 in 2006.

1999-2005	J-150	$2,500	$3,250
2006-2008	SJ-150	$2,500	$3,250

J-160E
1954-1979. Flat-top jumbo acoustic, 1 bridge P-90 pickup, tone and volume controls on front, sunburst finish, reintroduced as J-160 in '90.

1954-1964		$7,000	$9,500

MODEL YEAR	FEATURES	EXC. COND. LOW	HIGH
1965		$5,250	$7,000
1966-1969		$4,250	$5,500
1970-1979		$2,625	$3,500

J-160E Reissue/Standard/VS
1990-1997, 2003-2008. Reintroduced J-160E with solid spruce top, solid mahogany back and sides.

1990-2008		$2,250	$3,000

J-160E John Lennon Peace
2003-2013. J-160E with tortoise 'guard, natural, signature on truss rod cover.

2003-2013		$3,000	$4,000

J-160E John Lennon Peace Limited Edition
2009. Certificate of authenticity, 750 made.

2009		$3,250	$4,250

J-160E Montana Special
1995 only.

1995		$2,125	$2,750

J-160VS/John Lennon 70th
2010. Commemorative edition for John Lennon's 70th birthday, 500 made, vintage sunburst gloss finish.

2010		$2,750	$3,500

J-165 (Maple)
See CJ-165 listing.

J-180
2000s. Star logo on headstock, star position markers, black finish.

2000s		$3,000	$4,000

J-180 Billy Jo Armstrong
2011. Certificate of authenticity, 300 made.

2011		$3,000	$4,000

J-180/Everly Brothers/ The Everly Brothers
1986-2005. Everly Brothers flat-top model discontinued '72, but was reissued in '86 as the J-180. Star logo on headstock, star position markers, black finish. From '92-'93 was again called The Everly Brothers and in '94 name went back to J-180.

1986-2005		$2,750	$3,500

J-180 Special Edition
1993. Gibson Bozeman, only 36 made, Everly Brother specs, large double white pearloid 'guard.

1993		$3,000	$4,000

J-185/J-185N
1951-1959. Flat-top jumbo, figured maple back and sides, bound body and neck, sunburst (185) or natural (185N).

1951-1959	Natural, sunburst	$20,000	$25,000

J-185 Reissue
1990-1995, 1999-2018. Flat-top jumbo, figured maple back and sides, bound body and neck, natural or sunburst, limited run of 100 between '91-'92.

1990-2018		$3,000	$3,500

J-185-12
2001-2004. 12-string J-185, flamed maple sides and back.

2001-2004		$2,500	$3,000

1951 J-185 Limited Edition
1994-1995. Oct. '94 Centennial model, limited run of 100.

1994-1995		$4,000	$5,000

1994 Gibson J-100
Edward Sparks

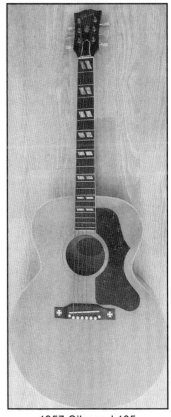

1957 Gibson J-185
Daniel Hess

2000 Gibson J-185 EC
Cream City Music

2002 Gibson J-200 Elvis
Presley Signature
Imaged by Heritage Auctions, HA.com

MODEL YEAR	FEATURES	EXC. COND. LOW	HIGH

J-185 Custom Vine
2004-2012. J-185 with abalone and mother-of-pearl vine 'board inlay.

2004-2012		$3,250	$4,250

J-185 EC
1999-2018. Acoustic/electric, rounded cutaway, flamed maple back and sides. Replaced EC-30 Blues King.

1999-2018		$2,000	$2,500

J-185 EC Custom
2005. Limited Edition, 200 made, spruce top, figured maple sides and back, pearl double parallelogram markers, Fishman Prefix Plus on-board electronics.

2005		$2,000	$2,500

J-185 EC Rosewood
2006-2018. Acoustic/electric, rounded cutaway, Indian rosewood back and sides.

2006-2018		$2,000	$2,500

J-185 EC Modern Rosewood
2020-2022. Slim body, Sitka spruce top, rosewood back and sides, Antique Natural or Rosewood Burst.

2020-2022		$2,000	$2,500

J-185 EC Modern Walnut
2020-2022. Slim body, Sitka spruce top, walnut back and sides, Antique Natural or Walnut Burst.

2020-2022		$1,750	$2,250

J-185 EC Quilt
2002. Quilted maple top, flamed maple body.

2002		$3,500	$4,500

J-190 EC Super Fusion
2001-2004. Jumbo single cut acoustic/electric, spruce top, curly maple back and sides, neck pickup and Fishman Piezo.

2001-2004		$2,750	$3,500

J-200/SJ-200/J-200N/SJ-200N
1946-present. Labeled SJ-200 until ca.'54. Super Jumbo flat-top, maple back and sides, see Super Jumbo 200 for '38-'42 rosewood back and sides model, called J-200 Artist for a time in the early-'70s, renamed '50s Super Jumbo 200 in '97 and again renamed SJ-200 Reissue in '99. Currently called the SJ-200 Original. 200N indicates natural option.

1946-1949	Natural, sunburst	$20,000	$25,000
1950-1959	Natural, sunburst	$16,500	$21,500
1960-1964	Natural, sunburst	$13,500	$17,500
1965	Natural, sunburst	$9,000	$11,500
1966-1969	Natural, sunburst	$6,500	$8,500
1970-1979	Natural, sunburst	$4,750	$6,250
1972	Artist (label)	$4,750	$6,250
1980-1989	Natural, sunburst	$4,250	$5,500
1990-1999	Natural, sunburst	$4,250	$5,500
2000-2009	Natural, sunburst	$4,250	$5,500
2010-2023	Natural, sunburst	$4,000	$5,250

J-200 Celebrity
1985-1987. Acoustic introduced for Gibson's 90th anniversary, spruce top, rosewood back, sides and 'board, binding on body and 'board, sunburst, only 90 made.

1985-1987		$4,000	$5,000

J-200 Custom/SJ-200 Custom
2009-2013. Additional abalone trim, gold hardware, sunburst or natural. Model name also used in 1993 on

J-200 with tree-of-life fingerboard inlay.

2009-2013		$4,000	$5,000

J-200 Deluxe Rosewood
1993-1996. Rosewood back and sides, abalone trim, gold hardware, sunburst or natural.

1993-1996		$5,000	$6,000

J-200 E
1986-1987. Built in Nashville, on-board volume control, sunburst.

1986-1987		$4,000	$5,250

J-200 Elvis Presley Signature
2002. 250 made, large block letter Elvis Presley name on 'board, figured maple sides and back, gloss natural spruce top, black and white custom designed 'guard after one of Presley's personal guitars.

2002		$5,000	$6,500

J-200 Jr.
1991-1996, 2002. Smaller 16" body, sunburst, natural, black or cherry.

1991-1996		$2,250	$2,750

J-200 Koa
1994-2013. Figured Hawaiian Koa back and sides, spruce top, natural.

1994-2013		$3,500	$4,500

J-200 M Trophy 75th Anniversary
2012-2013. Limited Edition, 75 made, quilt maple back and sides, rosewood 'board, abalone crown inlays, antique natural or vintage sunburst nitro finish.

2012-2013		$3,750	$4,750

J-200 Montana Gold Flame Maple
1998-2012. SJ-200 design, AAA Sitka spruce top with Eastern curly maple back and sides, ebony 'board, Custom Montana Gold banner peghead logo, antique natural.

1998-2012		$4,000	$5,000

J-200 Montana Western Classic Supreme
2016. Spruce top, rosewood back and sides, maple neck, Sunset Burst finish.

2016		$5,000	$6,500

J-200 Ron Wood/SJ-200 Ron Wood
1997. Based on a '57 SJ-200 with Wood's oversized double 'guard on either side of the sound hole, flame-pattern fretboard inlays, script signature inlay on headstock, natural.

1997		$5,500	$7,500

J-200 Rose
1994-1995. Centennial Series model, based on Emmylou Harris' guitar, black finish, rose 'guard, gold tuners, 100 built.

1994-1995		$5,500	$7,500

J-200 Rosewood
1991, 1994-1996. Made in Bozeman, rosewood back and sides.

1991-1996		$5,000	$6,000

J-200 Studio
2009-2018. Studio logo on truss rod cover, unbound 'board, plain 'guard.

2009-2018		$2,500	$3,250

J-200 Western Classic Pre-War
1999-2012. Indian rosewood.

1999-2012		$4,000	$5,000

MODEL YEAR	FEATURES	EXC. COND. LOW	HIGH

J-200 Western Classic Pre-War 200 Brazilian

2003. Custom Shop, limited run, based on Ray Whitley's '37 J-200, Brazilian rosewood back and sides.

2003		$10,000	$13,000

J-250 Monarch/SJ-250 Monarch

1995-2018. Rosewood back and sides, maple neck, ebony 'board, abalone trim, certificate of authenticity.

1995-2018		$15,000	$20,000

J-250 R

1972-1973, 1976-1978. A J-200 with rosewood back and sides, sunburst, only 20 shipped from Gibson.

1972-1978		$4,000	$5,500

J-1000/SJ-1000

1992-1994. Jumbo cutaway, spruce top, rosewood back and sides, on-board electronics, diamond-shape markers and headstock inlay.

1992-1994		$2,500	$3,250

J-1500

1992. Jumbo cutaway flat-top, higher-end appointments including Nick Lucas-style position markers, sunburst.

1992		$2,500	$3,250

J-2000/J-2000 Custom/J-2000R

1986, 1992-1999. Cutaway acoustic, rosewood back and sides (a few had Brazilian rosewood or maple bodies), ebony 'board and bridge, Sitka spruce top, multiple bindings, sunburst or natural. Name changed to J-2000 Custom in '93 when it became available only on a custom-order basis.

1986-1999	All models	$4,000	$5,500

Jackson Browne Signature

2011-2016. Based on '30s Jumbo style with increased body depth and upgraded tonewoods, Model 1 without pickup, Model A with pickups, Adirondack red spruce top, English walnut back and sides, nitro lacquer sunburst finish.

2011-2016	Model 1	$4,500	$5,750
2011-2016	Model A	$4,750	$6,250

JG-0

1970-1972. Economy, square shouldered jumbo, follows Jubilee model in '70.

1970-1972		$1,000	$1,500

JG-12

1970. Economy square shouldered jumbo 12-string, follows Jubilee-12 model in '70.

1970		$1,000	$1,500

Johnny A Signature Series

2004-2013. Thinline semi-hollow, sharp double-cut, flamed maple top, humbuckers, gold hardware, Bigsby, sunburst, includes certificate of authenticity.

2004-2013	Includes rare color option	$3,000	$4,000

Johnny Smith/Johnny Smith Double

1961-1989. Single-cut archtop, 1 or 2 humbucker pickups, gold hardware, multiple binding front and back, natural or sunburst. By '80 cataloged as JS and JSD models.

1961-1964		$14,000	$18,500
1965		$9,000	$11,500
1966-1969		$8,500	$11,000
1970-1989		$7,750	$10,000

Jubilee

1969-1970. Flat-top, laminated mahogany back and sides, single bound body, natural with black back and sides.

1969-1970		$1,125	$1,500

Jubilee Deluxe

1970-1971. Flat-top, laminated rosewood back and sides, multi-bound body, natural finish.

1970-1971		$1,125	$1,500

Jubilee-12

1969-1970. Flat-top, 12 strings, laminated mahogany back and sides, multi-bound, natural.

1969-1970		$1,125	$1,500

Jumbo

1934-1936. Gibson's first Jumbo flat-top, mahogany back and sides, round shoulders, bound top and back, sunburst, becomes the 16" Jumbo 35 in late-'36.

1934	Unbound	$31,000	$40,000
1935-1936	Bound	$23,500	$32,000

Jumbo 35/J-35

1936-1942. Jumbo flat-top, mahogany back and sides, silkscreen logo, sunburst, reintroduced as J-35, square-shouldered dreadnought, in '83.

1936-1938	Sunburst, 3 tone bars	$20,000	$25,000
1939	Natural, 3 tone bars	$20,000	$25,000
1940-1942	Sunburst, 2 tone bars	$15,000	$20,000

Jumbo 55/J-55

1939-1943. Flat-top dreadnought, round shoulders, mahogany back and sides, pearl inlaid logo, sunburst, reintroduced in '73 as J-55.

1939-1940	Stairstep	$20,000	$25,000
1941-1943	Non-stairstep	$20,000	$25,000

Jumbo Centennial Special

1994. Reissue of 1934 Jumbo, natural, 100 made.

1994		$3,250	$4,000

Junior Pro

1987-1989. Single-cut, mahogany body, KB-X tremolo system 1 humbucker pickup, black chrome hardware, various colors.

1987-1989		$650	$850

Kalamazoo Award Model

1978-1981. Single-cut archtop, bound f-holes, multi-bound top and back, 1 mini-humbucker, gold-plated hardware, woodgrain 'guard with bird and branch abalone inlay, highly figured natural or sunburst.

1978-1981	Natural	$15,000	$20,000
1978-1981	Sunburst	$15,000	$20,000

Keb' Mo' Royale

2016. Limited to 50, aged Adirondack red spruce top, vintage sunburst finish, label signed by artist, includes certificate of authenticity.

2016		$3,000	$4,000

Keb' Mo' Signature Bluesmaster

2010-2015. Limited run of 300, small-bodied flat-top acoustic, Baggs pickup, sound hole-mounted volume control, vintage sunburst or antique natural finish.

2010-2015		$2,500	$3,000

1964 Gibson J-200N
Smyth Jones

Gibson Johnny A Signature Series
Imaged by Heritage Auctions, HA.com

GUITARS

1942 Gibson L-0
David Stone

1935 Gibson L-00
David Stone

MODEL YEAR	FEATURES	EXC. COND. LOW	HIGH

Kiefer Sutherland KS-336
2007. Custom Shop Inspired By Artist series.

| 2007 | | $3,500 | $4,500 |

KZ II
1980-1981. Double-cut solidbody, 2 humbuckers, 4 knob and toggle controls, tune-o-matic, dot markers, stencil Gibson logo on headstock, KZ II logo on truss rod cover, walnut stain finish.

| 1980 | | $1,125 | $1,500 |

L-0
1926-1933, 1937-1942. Acoustic flat-top, maple back and sides '26-'27, mahogany after. Reissued '37 with spruce top.

1926-1928	13.5", maple	$6,000	$7,500
1928-1930	13.5", mahogany	$6,000	$7,500
1931-1933	14.75"	$6,500	$8,500
1937-1942	14.75", spruce	$6,500	$8,500

L-00
1932-1946. Acoustic flat-top, mahogany back and sides, bound top to '36 and bound top and back '37 on.

| 1932-1946 | | $6,500 | $8,000 |

L-00 1937 Legend
2006-2016. Part of the Vintage Series.

| 2006-2016 | | $3,375 | $4,500 |

L-00 Standard
2016-present. Small body, Sitka spruce top, mahogany back and sides, Vintage Sunburst nitro finish.

| 2016-2023 | | $2,000 | $2,500 |

L-00 Studio Walnut
2020-2023. Walnut back and sides, Fishman pickup, nitro finish, Antique Natural or Walnut Burst.

| 2020-2023 | | $1,125 | $1,500 |

L-00 Studio/Montana Studio
2019-2020. Sitka spruce top, walnut back and sides, Fishman pickup, aged nitro finish.

| 2019-2020 | | $1,125 | $1,500 |

L-00 Sustainable
2018-2021. Sitka spruce top, richlite 'board and bridge made from recycled trees pulp, Antique Natural.

| 2018-2021 | | $1,500 | $2,000 |

L-00/Blues King
1991-1997, 1999-2019. Reintroduced as L-00, called Blues King L-00 for '94-'97, back as L-00 for '99-'02, called Blues King '03-present.

| 1991-1997 | | $2,000 | $2,500 |
| 2003-2019 | | $2,000 | $2,500 |

L-1 (Archtop)
1902-1925. Acoustic archtop, single-bound top, back and sound hole, name continued on flat-top model in '26.

1902-1907	125"	$2,500	$3,500
1908-1919	135"	$2,500	$3,500
1920-1925	135", Loar era	$2,500	$3,500

L-1 (Flat-Top)
1926-1937. Acoustic flat-top, maple back and sides '26-'27, mahogany after.

1926-1929	135", 12-fret	$7,500	$9,500
1930-1931	1475", 13-fret	$8,000	$10,000
1932-1937	14-fret	$8,500	$10,500

MODEL YEAR	FEATURES	EXC. COND. LOW	HIGH

L-1 1928 Blues Tribute
2014-2018. Adirondack red spruce top, mahogany back and sides, rosewood 'board, faded Vintage Sunburst.

| 2014-2018 | | $2,500 | $3,500 |

L-1 CM Montana Special
1991-1993. Special Edition from Bozeman, Montana, limited run of 31, curly maple back and sides, Vintage Sunburst finish.

| 1991-1993 | | $3,000 | $4,000 |

L-1 Robert Johnson
2007-2016. 1926 specs, Robert Johnson inlay at end of 'board.

| 2007-2016 | | $2,000 | $2,500 |

L-1 Special
2016. Adirondack red spruce top, limited edition of 75.

| 2016 | | $2,500 | $3,000 |

L-2 (Archtop)
1902-1926. Round sound hole archtop, pearl inlay on peghead, 1902-'07 available in 3 body sizes: 12.5" to 16", '24-'26 13.5" body width.

| 1902-1907 | 125" | $2,500 | $3,500 |
| 1924-1926 | 135" | $2,500 | $3,500 |

L-2 (Flat-Top)
1929-1935. Acoustic flat-top, rosewood back and sides except for mahogany in '31, triple-bound top and back, limited edition model in '94.

| 1929-1933 | Brazilian | $22,500 | $30,000 |
| 1931-1932 | Mahogany | $18,500 | $25,000 |

L-2 1929 Reissue
1994 only. Spruce top, Indian rosewood back and sides, raised 'guard.

| 1994 | | $2,500 | $3,000 |

L-3 (Archtop)
1902-1933. Acoustic archtop, available in 3 sizes: 12.5", 13.5", 16".

1902-1907	125", round hole	$3,500	$4,500
1908-1919	135", round hole	$3,500	$4,500
1920		$3,500	$4,500
1921-1926	Loar era	$3,500	$4,500
1927-1928	135", oval hole	$3,500	$4,500
1929-1933	135", round hole	$3,500	$4,500

L-4
1912-1956. Acoustic archtop, 16" wide.

1912-1919	12-fret, oval hole	$3,500	$4,500
1920		$3,500	$4,500
1921-1924	Loar era	$3,500	$4,500
1925-1927	12-fret, oval hole	$3,500	$4,500
1928-1934	14-fret, round hole	$3,500	$4,500
1935-1946	Fleur-de-lis, f-holes	$4,500	$6,000
1947-1949	Crown, double-parallel	$4,500	$6,000
1950-1956		$4,000	$5,000

L-4 A or L-4 A EC
2003-2008. 15 3/4" lower bout, mid-size jumbo, rounded cutaway, factory electronics with preamp.

| 2003-2008 | | $1,875 | $2,500 |

L-4 C or L-4 CN
1949-1971. Single-cut acoustic archtop, sunburst or natural (CN).

| 1949-1959 | Natural | $6,500 | $8,500 |
| 1949-1959 | Sunburst | $6,000 | $7,500 |

MODEL YEAR	FEATURES	EXC. COND. LOW	HIGH
1960-1964	Natural	$6,000	$7,500
1960-1964	Sunburst	$4,750	$6,000
1965	Natural	$4,500	$5,500
1965	Sunburst	$4,000	$5,000
1966-1969	Natural, sunburst	$3,500	$4,500
1970-1971	Natural, sunburst	$3,000	$4,000

L-4 CES/L-4 CES Mahogany

1958, 1969, 1986-2018. Single pointed cutaway archtop, 2 humbuckers, gold parts, natural or sunburst, maple back and sides '58 and '69, mahogany laminate back and sides for '86-'93, became part of Gibson's Historic Collection (Custom Shop) with laminated maple back and sides for '94, renamed L-4 CES Mahogany with solid mahogany back and sides in '04.

1958	Natural, PAFs	$16,500	$22,000
1958	Sunburst, PAFs	$13,500	$17,500
1969	Natural, sunburst	$5,500	$7,500
1986-1993	Laminate mahogany	$4,000	$5,500
1994-2003	Laminate maple	$4,000	$5,500
2004-2018	Solid mahogany	$4,000	$5,500

L-4 Special Tenor/Plectrum

Late-1920s. Limited edition 4-string flat-top.

1929		$2,250	$3,000

L-5 '34 Non-Cutaway Historic

1994. 1934 specs including block pearl inlays, bound snakehead peghead, close grained solid spruce top, figured solid maple sides and back, replica Grover open back tuners, Cremona Brown Sunburst finish.

1994		$4,500	$5,750

L-5 Premier/L-5 P/L-5 PN

1939-1947. Introduced as L-5 Premier (L-5 P) and renamed L-5 C in '48, single rounded cutaway acoustic archtop, sunburst or natural option (PN).

1939-1947	Natural option	$25,000	$35,000
1939-1947	Sunburst	$20,000	$25,000

L-5/L-5N

1924-1958. Acoustic archtop, non-cut, multiple bindings, Lloyd Loar label in '24, 17" body by '35, Master Model label until '27, sunburst with natural option later.

1924	'24 ship date, Loar era	$65,000	$75,000
1925	Early '25, value per specs	$60,000	$70,000
1925	Late '25, value per specs	$35,000	$45,000
1926	'26 ship date, value per specs	$35,000	$45,000
1927	'27 ship date, value per specs	$35,000	$45,000
1928-1932	Value per specs	$30,000	$40,000
1933-1934	Value per specs	$15,000	$20,000
1935-1940	Value per specs	$10,000	$15,000
1939-1940	Natural option, value per specs	$13,000	$18,000
1946-1949	Natural option, value per specs	$12,000	$16,000
1946-1949	Sunburst, value per specs	$10,000	$15,000
1950-1958	Natural, value per specs	$10,000	$15,000

MODEL YEAR	FEATURES	EXC. COND. LOW	HIGH
1950-1958	Sunburst, value per specs	$7,500	$10,000

L-5 C/L-5 CN

1948-1982. Renamed from L-5 Premier (L-5 P), single rounded cutaway acoustic archtop, sunburst or natural option (CN)

1948-1949	Natural	$16,500	$22,000
1948-1949	Sunburst	$14,500	$20,000
1950-1959	Natural	$14,500	$20,000
1950-1959	Sunburst	$12,000	$15,000
1960-1964	Natural	$12,000	$15,000
1960-1964	Sunburst	$10,500	$13,000
1965	Natural	$9,000	$11,500
1965	Sunburst	$9,000	$11,500
1966-1969	Natural	$7,500	$9,500
1966-1969	Sunburst	$7,500	$9,500
1970-1982	Natural, sunburst	$5,500	$7,000

L-5 CES/L-5 CESN

1951-2018. Electric version of L-5 C, single round cutaway (pointed mid-'60-'69), archtop, 2 pickups (P-90s '51-'53, Alnico Vs '54-mid-'57, humbuckers after), sunburst or natural (CESN), now part of Gibson's Historic Collection.

1951-1957	Natural, single coils	$22,000	$27,500
1951-1957	Sunburst, single coils	$20,000	$25,000
1958-1959	Natural, PAFs	$25,000	$32,000
1958-1959	Sunburst, PAFs	$24,000	$30,000
1960-1962	Natural, PAFs	$24,000	$30,000
1960-1962	Sunburst, PAFs	$20,000	$25,000
1963-1964	Natural, pat #	$17,500	$22,000
1963-1964	Sunburst, pat #	$14,500	$18,500
1965	Natural, sunburst	$11,500	$14,500
1966-1969	Natural	$9,000	$12,000
1966-1969	Sunburst	$9,000	$12,000
1970-1979	Natural, sunburst	$7,500	$10,000
1980-1984	Kalamazoo made	$7,000	$9,500
1985-1992	Nashville made	$7,000	$9,500

L-5 CES Historic

1994-1997. Custom Shop Historic Collection series, sunburst or natural.

1994	100th Anniv, black	$5,750	$7,500
1994-1996	Natural, highly figured	$5,750	$7,500
1994-1996	Sunburst	$5,750	$7,500
1997	Wine Red	$5,750	$7,500

L-5 CT (George Gobel)

1959-1961. Single-cut, thinline archtop acoustic, some were built with pickups, cherry.

1959-1961		$21,000	$27,000

L-5 CT Reissue

1998-2007. Historic Collection, acoustic and electric versions, natural, sunburst, cherry.

1998-2007		$6,000	$8,000

L-5 S

1972-1985, 2004-2005. Single-cut solidbody, multi-bound body and neck, gold hardware, 2 pickups (low impedance '72-'74, humbuckers '75 on), offered in natural, cherry sunburst or vintage sunburst. 1 humbucker version issued in '04 from Gibson's Custom, Art & Historic division.

1972-2005	All options	$6,000	$7,500

1938 Gibson L-4
David Stone

1976 Gibson L-5 S
Frank Manno

1973 Gibson L-6 S
Tom Pfeifer

1967 Gibson L-7 CN
Imaged by Heritage Auctions, HA.com

MODEL YEAR	FEATURES	EXC. COND. LOW	HIGH

L-5 S Ron Wood
2015. Custom Shop, limited run of 250 with 1st 50 signed by Ron, certificate of authenticity, 2 Burstbucker pickups, ebony gloss finish.

2015		$5,000	$6,750

L-5 Signature
2001-2004. Carved spruce top, AAA maple back, tangerineburst or vintage sunburst.

2001-2004		$5,750	$7,500

L-5 Studio
1996-2000. Normal L-5 dual pickup features, marble-style 'guard, translucent finish, dot markers.

1996-2000		$2,750	$3,500

L-5 Wes Montgomery
1993-2018. Custom Shop, various colors.

1993-2018		$6,500	$10,000

L-6 S
1973-1975. Single-cut solidbody, 2 humbucking pickups, 6 position rotary switch, stop tailpiece, cherry or natural. Renamed L-6 S Custom in '75.

1973-1975	Cherry, natural	$1,750	$2,250

L-6 S Custom
1975-1980. Renamed from the L-6 S, 2 humbucking pickups, stop tailpiece, cherry or natural.

1975-1980		$1,750	$2,250
1978-1980	Silverburst option	$2,000	$2,500

L-6 S Deluxe
1975-1981. Single-cut solidbody, 2 humbucking pickups, no rotary switch, strings-thru-body design, cherry or natural.

1975-1981		$2,000	$2,500

L-6 S Reissue
2011-2012. With rotary switch, 2 humbuckers, natural or silverburst.

2011-2012		$1,000	$1,375

L-7/L-7N
1932-1956. Acoustic archtop, bound body and neck, fleur-de-lis peghead inlay, 16" body '32-'34, 17" body X-braced top late-'34, sunburst or natural (N).

1932-1934	16" body	$4,500	$6,000
1935-1939	17" body, X-braced	$4,500	$6,000
1940-1949	Natural	$4,250	$5,500
1940-1949	Sunburst	$4,000	$5,250
1950-1956	Natural	$4,000	$5,250
1950-1956	Sunburst	$3,750	$5,000

L-7 C/L-7 CN
1948-1972. Single-cut acoustic archtop, triple-bound top, sunburst or natural (CN). Gibson revived the L-7 C name for a new acoustic archtop in 2002.

1948-1949	Natural	$6,500	$8,500
1948-1949	Sunburst	$5,500	$7,500
1950-1959	Natural	$5,500	$7,500
1950-1959	Sunburst	$5,000	$6,500
1960-1964	Natural	$4,750	$6,250
1960-1964	Sunburst	$4,750	$6,250
1965	Natural	$4,500	$6,000
1965	Sunburst	$4,250	$5,500
1966-1972	Natural	$4,500	$6,000
1966-1972	Sunburst	$4,000	$5,500

L-7 Custom Electric
1936. L-7 with factory Christian-style pickup, limited production, often custom ordered.

1936		$10,000	$13,000

L-7 E/L-7 CE
1948-1954. L-7 and L-7 C with "McCarty" assembly of pickguard-mounted pickups (1 or 2), sunburst only.

1948-1954	L-7 CE, cutaway	$6,500	$8,500
1948-1954	L-7 E, non-cut	$5,000	$6,500

L-7 C (Custom Shop)
2002-2013. Custom Shop logo, Certificate of Authenticity.

2002-2013		$4,250	$5,500

L-10
1923-1939. Acoustic archtop, single-bound body and 'board, black or sunburst (added in '35).

1923-1934	16", F-holes	$6,500	$8,500
1935-1939	17", X-braced	$6,500	$8,500

L-12
1930-1955. Acoustic archtop, single-bound body, 'guard, neck and headstock, gold-plated hardware, sunburst.

1930-1934	16"	$7,000	$9,000
1935-1939	17", X-braced	$7,000	$9,000
1940-1941	Parallel top braced	$7,000	$9,000
1946-1949	Post-war	$4,500	$5,500
1950-1955		$4,000	$5,000

L-12 Premier/L-12 P
1947-1950. L-12 with rounded cutaway, sunburst.

1947-1950		$5,250	$6,500

L-20 20th Anniversary Limited Edition
2009. Custom Shop, 20 made, "20th Anniversary" logo on back of headstock and on label, Certificate of Authenticity.

2009		$3,250	$4,250

L-20 Special/L-20 K International Special
1993-1994. Rosewood or mahogany back and sides (Koa on the K), ebony 'board, block inlays, gold tuners, multi-bound.

1993-1994	L-20, mahogany	$2,250	$3,000
1993-1994	L-20, rosewood	$2,250	$3,000
1993-1994	L-20K, koa	$2,250	$3,000

L-30
1935-1943. Acoustic archtop, single-bound body, black or sunburst.

1935-1943		$1,875	$2,500

L-37
1937-1941. 14-3/4" acoustic archtop, flat back, single-bound body and 'guard, sunburst.

1937-1941		$1,875	$2,500

L-47
1940-1942. Acoustic archtop.

1940-1942		$2,500	$3,250

L-48
1946-1971. 16" acoustic archtop, single-bound body, mahogany sides, sunburst.

1946-1949		$2,250	$3,000
1950-1959		$2,250	$3,000
1960-1964		$2,000	$2,500
1965		$1,750	$2,000
1966-1969		$1,000	$1,250
1970-1971		$950	$1,125

MODEL YEAR	FEATURES	EXC. COND. LOW	HIGH

L-50

1932-1971. 14.75" acoustic archtop, flat or arched back, round sound hole or f-holes, pearl logo pre-war, decal logo post-war, maple sides, sunburst, 16" body late-'34.

1932-1934	1475" body	$3,125	$4,000
1934-1943	16" body	$3,125	$4,000
1946-1949	16", trapezoids	$3,000	$3,750
1950-1959		$2,375	$3,000
1960-1964		$2,125	$2,625
1965		$1,875	$2,375
1966-1969		$1,500	$1,875
1970-1971		$1,500	$1,875

L-75

1932-1939. 14.75" archtop with round sound hole and flat back, size increased to 16" with arched back in '35, small button tuners, dot markers, lower-end style trapeze tailpiece, pearl script logo, sunburst.

1932	1475", dot neck	$4,000	$5,000
1933-1934	1475", pearloid	$4,000	$5,000
1935-1939	16" body	$4,000	$5,000

L-130

1999-2005. 14 7/8" lower bout, small jumbo, solid spruce top, solid bubinga back and sides, rosewood 'board, factory electronics with preamp.

1999-2005	$1,250	$1,750

L-140

1999-2005. Like L-130 but with rosewood back and sides, ebony 'board.

1999-2005	$1,500	$2,000

L-200 Emmylou Harris

2001-2016. Smaller and thinner than standard 200, flamed maple sides and back, gold hardware, crest markers, natural or sunburst.

2001-2016	$2,500	$3,000

L-C Century

1933-1939. Curly maple back and sides, bound body, white pearloid 'board and peghead (all years) and headstock (until '38), sunburst.

1933-1938	Pearloid	$10,000	$12,500
1939		$9,500	$11,500

L-C Century Elvis Costello Limited

2016. Signed custom label, pearloid 'board, Adirondack red spruce top, AAA flamed maple back and sides, 300 made.

2016	$5,000	$6,500

L-C Century Reissue

1994. Pearloid headstock and 'board.

1994	$4,000	$5,000

L-Jr.

1918-1927. Archtop, solid carved spruce top, carved figured birch back, Sheraton Brown or natural finish.

1918-1927	$2,250	$2,750

LC-1 Cascade

2002-2006. LC-Series acoustic/electric, advanced L-00-style, solid quilted maple back and sides.

2002-2006	$2,000	$2,500

LC-2 Sonoma

2002-2006. Released November '02, LC-Series acoustic/electric, advanced L-00-style, solid walnut back and sides.

2002-2006	$2,500	$3,250

LC-3 Caldera

2003-2004. 14 3/4" flat-top, soft cutaway, solid cedar top, solid flamed Koa back and sides, fancy appointments.

2003-2004	$2,250	$3,000

Le Grande

1993-2010. Electric archtop, 17", formerly called Johnny Smith.

1993-2010	$9,000	$12,000

Les Paul

The following are models bearing the Les Paul name. In order to keep certain models grouped together, subheadings have been included for Classic, Custom, Deluxe, Goldtop, Junior, Special, Standard and Studio models. All others are then listed pretty much alphabetically as follows:

'60 Les Paul Corvette
Les Paul 25/50 Anniversary
Les Paul 40th Anniversary (from 1952)
Les Paul (All Maple)
Les Paul Artisan and Artisan/3
Les Paul Artist/L.P. Artist/Les Paul Active

Les Paul Classic

Following are Les Paul Classic models listed alphabetically.

Les Paul Classic
Les Paul Classic 1960 Mars Music
Les Paul Classic Antique Mahogany
Les Paul Classic Custom
Les Paul Classic H-90
Les Paul Classic Limited Edition
Les Paul Classic Mark III/MIII
Les Paul Classic Plus
Les Paul Classic Premium Plus
Les Paul Classic Premium Plus (Custom Shop)
Les Paul Classic Tom Morgan Limited Edition

Les Paul Custom

Following are Les Paul Custom models listed alphabetically.

Les Paul Custom
Les Paul Custom 25
Les Paul Custom '54
Les Paul Custom Historic '54
Les Paul Custom Historic '57 Black Beauty
1957 Les Paul Custom (2-Pickup) Ultra Light Aged
1957 Les Paul Custom (3-Pickup) Light Aged
Les Paul Custom Historic '68
1968 Les Paul Custom Reissue (Custom Shop)
1968 Les Paul Custom Ultra Light Aged
20th Anniversary Les Paul Custom
25th Anniversary (Guitar Center) Les Paul Custom
35th Anniversary Les Paul Custom
120th Anniversary Les Paul Custom
120th Anniversary Les Paul Custom Lite
Les Paul Custom Ace Frehley "Budokan"
Les Paul Custom Ace Frehley Signature

1935 Gibson L-30
Tyler Willison

1936 Gibson L-75
David Stone

1978 Gibson Les Paul Custom

Kevin Okanos

1969 Gibson Les Paul Deluxe

John Wesley

Les Paul Custom Adam Jones 1979
Les Paul Custom F (Custom Shop)
Les Paul Custom Jeff Beck 1954 Oxblood
Les Paul Custom Jimmy Page
Les Paul Custom John Sykes 1978
Les Paul Custom Lite
Les Paul Custom Lite (Show Case Edition)
Les Paul Custom Mick Ronson '68
Les Paul Custom Music Machine
Les Paul Custom Peter Frampton Signature
Les Paul Custom Plus
Les Paul Custom Showcase Edition
Les Paul Custom Silverburst
Les Paul Custom Steve Jones 1974
Les Paul Custom Zakk Wylde Signature

Les Paul Dale Earnhardt
Les Paul Dale Earnhardt Intimidator
Les Paul Dark Fire
Les Paul Dark Knight Quilt Top
Les Paul DC AA
Les Paul DC Classic
Les Paul DC Pro
Les Paul DC Standard (Plus)
Les Paul DC Studio

Les Paul Deluxe

Following are Les Paul Deluxe models listed alphabetically.
Les Paul Deluxe
Les Paul Deluxe 30th Anniversary
Les Paul Deluxe '69 Reissue
Les Paul Deluxe Hall of Fame
Les Paul Deluxe Limited Edition
Les Paul Deluxe Limited Edition AMS
Les Paul Deluxe Reissue
Les Paul Deluxe #1 Pete Townshend
Les Paul Deluxe #3 Pete Townshend
Les Paul Deluxe #9 Pete Townshend
Les Paul Pro Deluxe

Les Paul Dusk Tiger
Les Paul ES-Les Paul
Les Paul ES-Les Paul Custom
Les Paul ES-Les Paul Standard
Les Paul ES-Les Paul Studio
Les Paul Florentine Plus
Les Paul Supreme Florentine
Les Paul Futura
Les Paul Goddess

Les Paul Goldtop

Following are Les Paul Goldtop models listed alphabetically.
Les Paul Model
'52 Les Paul Goldtop
'52 Les Paul Tribute
'54 Les Paul Goldtop
'54 Les Paul Wildwood
1954 Les Paul Goldtop Heavy Aged
'55 Les Paul Goldtop Hot-Mod Wraptail
'56 Les Paul Goldtop
1956 Les Paul Goldtop "CME Spec"

1956 Les Paul Goldtop Reissue
1956 Les Paul Goldtop Ultra Light Aged
'57 Les Paul Goldtop
'57 Les Paul Goldtop (R-7 wrap-around)
1957 Les Paul Goldtop Darkback Light Aged
1957 Les Paul Goldtop Reissue
1957 Les Paul Goldtop Ultra Light/Ultra
    Heavy Aged
Les Paul 30th Anniversary
Les Paul 50th Anniversary 1956 Les Paul
    Standard Goldtop
Les Paul 50th Anniversary 1957 Les Paul
    Standard Goldtop
Les Paul Billy F. Gibbons Goldtop
Les Paul Centennial ('56 LP Standard Goldtop)
Les Paul Dickey Betts Goldtop
Les Paul Joe Bonamassa Aged Goldtop
Les Paul LP-295 Goldtop
Les Paul Pro Showcase Edition
Les Paul Reissue Goldtop
Les Paul Slash Signature Goldtop

Les Paul Government Series II
Les Paul GT
Les Paul HD.6-X Pro Digital
Les Paul Indian Motorcycle
Les Paul Jumbo

Les Paul Junior

Following are Les Paul Junior models listed alphabetically.
Les Paul Junior
Les Paul Junior 3/4
1957 Les Paul Junior (Single-Cut) Ultra Light
    Aged/Heavy Aged
1957 Les Paul Junior (Single-Cut) VOS
1958 Les Paul Junior (Double-Cut) VOS
'60 Les Paul Junior
1960 Les Paul Junior (Double-Cut) Ultra
    Heavy Aged
Les Paul J / LPJ
Les Paul Junior Billie Joe Armstrong Signature
Les Paul Junior DC Hall of Fame
Les Paul Junior Double Cutaway
Les Paul Junior Faded
Les Paul Junior John Lennon LTD
Les Paul Junior Lite
Les Paul Junior Special
Les Paul Junior Special Robot
Les Paul Junior Tenor/Plectrum
Les Paul TV
Les Paul TV 3/4
Les Paul TV Junior

Les Paul Limited Run 2016 Series
Les Paul Lou Pallo Signature
Les Paul Marc Bolan
Les Paul Menace
Les Paul Old Hickory
Les Paul Personal
Les Paul Professional
Les Paul Recording
Les Paul Richard Petty LTD

Les Paul Signature/L.P. Signature
Les Paul Silver Streak
Les Paul SM
Les Paul SmartWood Exotic
Les Paul SmartWood Standard
Les Paul SmartWood Studio

Les Paul Special

Following are Les Paul Special models listed alphabetically.

Les Paul Special
Les Paul 55
'60 Les Paul Special
Les Paul Special (Reissue)
Les Paul Special 100/100 Special
Les Paul Special 3/4
Les Paul Special Centennial
Les Paul Special Double Cutaway
Les Paul Special Faded
Les Paul Special New Century
Les Paul Special Robot
Les Paul Special Tenor
Les Paul Special Worn Cherry

Les Paul Standard

Following are Les Paul Standard models, beginning with the original model, then listed alphabetically.

Les Paul Standard (Sunburst)
Les Paul Standard (SG body)
Les Paul Standard (reintroduced)
'50s Les Paul Standard
'58 Les Paul Figured Top
'58 Les Paul Plaintop (VOS)
1958 Les Paul Standard "CME Spec"
1958 Les Paul Standard Light Aged/Heavy Aged
1958 Les Paul Standard Ultra Light Aged
'59 Les Paul Flametop/Reissue/Standard
'59 Les Paul Burst Brothers
'59 Les Paul Korina Reissue
'59 Les Paul Plaintop (VOS)
1959 Les Paul Standard "CME Spec"
1959 Les Paul Standard Heavy Aged
1959 Les Paul Standard Light Aged
1959 Les Paul Standard Reissue
1959 Les Paul Standard Ultra Heavy Aged
1959 Les Paul Standard Ultra Light Aged
True Historic 1959 Les Paul
'60s Les Paul Standard
'60 Les Paul Flametop/Standard '60s
'60 Les Paul Plaintop (VOS)
1960 Les Paul Standard Heavy Aged
1960 Les Paul Standard Light Aged
1960 Les Paul Standard Reissue
1960 Les Paul Standard Ultra Light Aged
True Historic 1960 Les Paul
'82 Les Paul Standard
Les Paul 10th Anniversary Chambered '58
    Reissue
Les Paul 40th Anniversary (from 1959)
Les Paul 50th Anniversary (Historic)
Les Paul 50th Anniversary 1956 Les Paul
    Standard

Les Paul 50th Anniversary 1959 Les Paul
    Standard
Les Paul 50th Anniversary 1960 Les Paul
    Standard
Les Paul 50th Anniversary DaPra
Les Paul 50th Anniversary Korina Tribute
Les Paul 50th Anniversary Les Paul Standard
    (Sweetwater)
Les Paul 60th Anniversary 1960 Les Paul
    Standard "CME Spec"
Les Paul 120th Anniversary
Les Paul Axcess Alex Lifeson
Les Paul Axcess Dave Amato
Les Paul Axcess Standard
Les Paul BFG
Les Paul Bird's-Eye Standard
Les Paul Carved Series
Les Paul Catalina
Les Paul Centennial ('59 LP Special)
Les Paul Class 5
Les Paul Cloud 9 Series
Les Paul Collector's Choice Series
Les Paul Dickey Betts Red Top
Les Paul Don Felder Hotel California 1959
Les Paul Duane Allman
Les Paul Duane Allman Hot 'Lanta
Les Paul Elegant
Les Paul Eric Clapton 1960
Les Paul Gary Moore BFG
Les Paul Gary Moore Signature
Les Paul Gary Rossington Signature
Les Paul Guitar Trader Reissue
Les Paul Heritage 80
Les Paul Heritage 80 Award
Les Paul Heritage 80 Elite
Les Paul Heritage 80/Standard 80
Les Paul Hot Rod Magazine '58 Standard
Les Paul Jim Beam (Custom Shop)
Les Paul Jimmy Page "Number Two"
Les Paul Jimmy Page (Custom Authentic)
Les Paul Jimmy Page Signature
Les Paul Jimmy Page Signature (Custom Shop)
Les Paul Jimmy Wallace Reissue
Les Paul Joe Bonamassa Bonabyrd
Les Paul Joe Bonamassa Skinnerburst 1959
Les Paul Joe Bonamassa 'Tomato Soup Burst'
    Limited Edition
Les Paul Joe Perry 1959
Les Paul Joe Perry Signature
Les Paul KM (Kalamazoo Model)
Les Paul Korina
Les Paul Leo's Reissue
Les Paul Limited Edition (3-tone)
Les Paul Modern
Les Paul Music Machine 25th Anniversary
Les Paul Music Machine Brazilian Stinger
Les Paul Music Rising Katrina
Les Paul Neal Schon Signature
Les Paul Peace
Les Paul Reissue Flametop
Les Paul SG '61 Reissue
Les Paul SG Standard Authentic
Les Paul SG Standard Reissue

1953 Gibson Les Paul Model

1959 Gibson Les Paul Special 3/4
Alex Sauceda

GUITARS

2019 Gibson Les
Paul Traditional

1977 Gibson Les Paul Artisan

Tony Jones

Les Paul Signature "T"
Les Paul Slash Appetite
Les Paul Slash Appetite For Destruction
Les Paul Slash Signature
Les Paul Slash Signature VOS
Les Paul Slash Snakepit
Les Paul Southern Rock Tribute 1959
Les Paul Spider-Man
Les Paul Spotlight Special
Les Paul Standard 100
Les Paul Standard 2008
Les Paul Standard 2010 Limited
Les Paul Standard Billy Gibbons 'Pearly Gates'
Les Paul Standard F
Les Paul Standard Faded
Les Paul Standard HP
Les Paul Standard Lite
Les Paul Standard Lite Limited Edition
Les Paul Standard Michael Bloomfield 1959
Les Paul Standard Mike McCready 1959
Les Paul Standard Music Zoo 25th Anniversary
Les Paul Standard Paul Kossoff 1959
Les Paul Standard Plus
Les Paul Standard Premium Plus
Les Paul Standard Raw Power
Les Paul Standard Rick Nielsen 1959
Les Paul Standard Robot
Les Paul Standard RSM 1959/RSM '59 Les
    Paul Standard
Les Paul Standard Showcase Edition
Les Paul Standard Sparkle
Les Paul Strings and Things Standard
Les Paul Tie Dye (St. Pierre)
Les Paul Tie Dye Custom Shop
Les Paul Traditional Pro/Pro II
Les Paul Traditional/Plus
Les Paul Ultima
Les Paul Ultra-Aged
Les Paul Warren Haynes
Les Paul Zebra Wood

Les Paul Studio
Following are Les Paul Studio models listed alphabetically.
Les Paul Studio
Les Paul Studio 120th Anniversary
Les Paul Studio '50s Tribute
Les Paul Studio '60s Tribute
Les Paul Studio '70s Tribute
Les Paul Studio Baritone
Les Paul Studio BFD
Les Paul Studio Custom
Les Paul Studio Deluxe '60s
Les Paul Studio Deluxe II
Les Paul Studio Faded Vintage Mahogany
Les Paul Studio Faded/Pro Faded
Les Paul Studio Gem
Les Paul Studio Gothic
Les Paul Studio Gothic Morte
Les Paul Studio Joe Bonamassa
Les Paul Studio Limited Edition
Les Paul Studio Lite
Les Paul Studio Lite Mark III/M3/M III

MODEL YEAR	FEATURES	EXC. COND. LOW	HIGH

Les Paul Studio MLB Baseball
Les Paul Studio Platinum
Les Paul Studio Platinum Plus
Les Paul Studio Plus
Les Paul Studio Premium Plus
Les Paul Studio Raw Power
Les Paul Studio Robot
Les Paul Studio Robot Limited Edition
Les Paul Studio Roland Synthesizer
Les Paul Studio Shred
Les Paul Studio Special
Les Paul Studio Special Limited Edition
Les Paul Studio Standard
Les Paul Studio Swamp Ash
Les Paul Studio USA Anniversary Flood

Les Paul Supreme
Les Paul Vixen
Les Paul Voodoo/Voodoo Les Paul
Les Paul XR-I / II / III
The Les Paul
The Paul
The Paul Firebrand Deluxe
The Paul II

'60 Les Paul Corvette
1995-1997. Custom Shop Les Paul, distinctive Chevrolet Corvette styling from '60, offered in 6 colors.

1995-1997		$5,000	$6,500

Les Paul 25/50 Anniversary
1978-1979. Split-block inlays, five- or seven- piece maple and walnut neck, gold and silver hardware, 2 humbuckers, coil splitter, TP-6 tailpiece, antique sunburst, natural, wine red, black, and white finishes offered, 8-digit SN followed by 4-digit limited edition number, 1,106 made in '78, 2,305 in '79.

1978-1979		$4,500	$6,000

Les Paul 40th Anniversary (from 1952)
1991-1992. Black finish, 2 soapbar P-100 pickups, gold hardware, stop tailpiece, 40th Anniversary inlay at 12th fret.

1991-1992		$2,750	$3,500

Les Paul (All Maple)
1984. Limited run, all maple body, Super 400-style inlay, gold hardware.

1984		$2,750	$3,750

Les Paul Artisan and Artisan/3
1976-1982. Carved maple top, 2 or 3 humbuckers, gold hardware, hearts and flowers inlays on 'board and headstock, ebony, sunburst or walnut.

1976-1982	2 pickups	$5,500	$7,000
1976-1982	3 pickups	$5,500	$7,000

Les Paul Artist/L.P. Artist/ Les Paul Active
1979-1982. Two humbuckers (3 optional), active electronics, gold hardware, 3 mini-switches, multi-bound, Fireburst, ebony or sunburst.

1979-1982		$2,500	$3,250

Les Paul Classic
Following are Les Paul Classic models listed alphabetically.

MODEL YEAR	FEATURES	EXC. COND. LOW	HIGH

Les Paul Classic

1990-1998, 2000-2008, 2014-present. Early models have 1960 on pickguard, 2 exposed humbuckers, Les Paul Model on peghead until '93, Les Paul Classic afterwards. Limited run of Ebony finish in 2000, 2014 and 2015 have those years in the model name.

1990-2008	Various colors	$1,750	$2,500
2014-2023	Various colors	$1,500	$2,000

Les Paul Classic 1960 Mars Music

2000. All black.

2000		$1,500	$2,000

Les Paul Classic Antique Mahogany

2007. All mahogany body, exposed humbuckers, Guitar of the Week, limited run of 400 each of cherry (week 27) and sunburst (week 33).

2007		$2,000	$2,500

Les Paul Classic Custom

2007-2008, 2011-2012. Mahogany body with carved maple top, 2 exposed humbuckers in '07-'08, covered afterwards, various colors.

2007-2012		$2,000	$2,500

Les Paul Classic H-90

2008. Guitar of the Week, 400 made, gold hardware, H-90 soapbar pickups.

2008		$1,500	$2,000

Les Paul Classic Limited Edition

2000. Limited Edition logo on back of headstock, Les Paul Classic stencil logo, 3 exposed humbuckers, gold hardware, black finish.

2000		$2,000	$2,500

Les Paul Classic Mark III/MIII

1991-1993. Les Paul Classic features, no 'guard, exposed-coil humbuckers at neck and bridge and single-coil at middle position, 5-way switch, coil-tap.

1991-1993		$2,000	$2,500

Les Paul Classic Plus

1991-1996, 1999-2003. Les Paul Classic with fancier maple top, 2 exposed humbucker pickups. Price depends on top figure.

1991-2003		$2,000	$2,500

Les Paul Classic Premium Plus

1993-1996, 2001-2002. Les Paul Classic with AAA-grade flame maple top, 2 exposed humbucker pickups. Price depends on top figure.

1993-2002		$2,500	$3,500

Les Paul Classic Premium Plus (Custom Shop)

1994-1998. Custom Shop version, quilted maple top, Custom Shop logo, various colors.

1994-1998		$2,500	$3,500

Les Paul Classic Tom Morgan Limited Edition

2007. 400 made, custom finish top, black finish back/sides, Classic logo on truss rod cover.

2007		$2,250	$3,000

Les Paul Custom

Following are Les Paul Custom models listed alphabetically.

MODEL YEAR	FEATURES	EXC. COND. LOW	HIGH

Les Paul Custom

1953-1963 (renamed SG Custom late-1963), 1968-present (production moved to Custom Shop in 2004). Les Paul body shape except for SG body '61-'63, 2 pickups (3 humbuckers mid-'57-'63 and '68-'70, 3 pickups were optional various years after), '75 Price List shows a Les Paul Custom (B) model which is equipped with a Bigsby tailpiece versus a wraparound. By '80 offered as Les Paul Custom/Gold Parts and / Nickel Parts, because gold plating wears more quickly and is therefore less attractive there is no difference in price between an '80s Gold Parts and Nickel Parts instrument.

1953	Very early NSN model	$38,500	$55,000
1954-1957	Single coils	$38,500	$55,000
1954-1957	Single coils, factory Bigsby	$33,000	$41,500
1957-1961	Bigsby	$75,000	$95,000
1957-1961	Stoptail	$100,000	$150,000
1957-1961	Stoptail, only 2 pu	$200,000	$250,000
1961-1963	White, SG body, Maestro	$27,000	$33,500
1961-1963	White, SG body, side-pull vibrato	$20,000	$25,000
1962-1963	Black option, SG body, factory stop tail	$30,000	$37,500
1962-1963	Black option, SG body, side-pull vibrato	$20,000	$25,000
1962-1963	White, SG body, factory stop tail	$30,000	$37,500
1968	Black, 1-piece body	$21,500	$27,000
1969	Black, 1-piece body	$17,500	$22,000
1969	Black, 3-piece body	$13,000	$16,500
1970-1973	Various colors, 3 pu	$7,000	$9,500
1970-1974	Various colors, 2 pu	$7,000	$9,500
1974	Black, white, 3 pu	$7,000	$9,500
1974	Natural, cherry sunburst	$5,500	$7,500
1975-1976	Maple 'board, 2 pu	$5,500	$7,500
1975-1976	Maple 'board, 3 pu	$5,500	$7,500
1975-1978	Volute, 2 pu	$5,000	$6,500
1975-1978	Volute, 3 pu	$5,000	$6,500
1977	Maple 'board, black, 2 pu	$5,500	$7,000
1977-1978	Maple 'board, blond, 2 pu	$5,500	$7,000
1979	2 or 3 pickups	$5,000	$6,500
1979	Silverburst, 2 pu	$8,500	$11,000
1980-1984	Silverburst, 2 pu	$7,000	$9,000
1980-1986	2 or 3 pickups	$5,000	$6,500
1987-1989	Various colors	$5,000	$6,500
1990-1999	Limited Edition color series	$4,500	$6,000
1990-1999	Various colors	$4,000	$5,500
2000-2023	Various colors	$4,000	$5,500

2018 Gibson Classic Player Plus

Dan Lussier

1985 Gibson Les Paul Custom

Luis R Barrios

Gibson 1957 Les Paul
Custom Light Aged

Gibson Les Paul Custom
Adam Jones 1979

MODEL YEAR	FEATURES	EXC. COND. LOW	HIGH

Les Paul Custom 25
2007. Custom Shop Limited Edition run of 100, Les Paul "25" logo on truss rod cover, COA name Custom 25, triple-split block inlays, mahogany body with flame maple top, gold hardware, sunburst.

2007		$3,750	$5,000

Les Paul Custom '54
1972-1973. Reissue of 1954 Custom, black finish, Alnico V and P-90 pickups.

1972-1973		$8,500	$10,500

Les Paul Custom Historic '54
1991-2013. Custom Shop Historic Collection, 1954 appointments and pickup configuration, black, gold hardware.

1991-2013		$4,500	$5,500

Les Paul Custom Historic
'57 Black Beauty
1991-2013. Black finish, gold hardware, 2 or 3 humbucker pickups, part of Gibson's Historic Collection.

1991-2012	2 pickups	$3,500	$4,500
1991-2013	3 pickups	$3,500	$4,500
2007	Goldtop, 3 pu	$3,500	$4,500
2007	Murphy aged, 3 pu	$3,500	$4,500

1957 Les Paul Custom
(2-Pickup) Ultra Light Aged
2021-present. Custom Shop Murphy Lab Collection, Ebony finish.

2021-2023		$5,000	$6,500

1957 Les Paul Custom
(3-Pickup) Light Aged
2021-present. Custom Shop Murphy Lab Collection, with Bigsby vibrato, Ebony finish.

2021-2023		$6,000	$7,750

Les Paul Custom Historic '68
1999-2007. Custom Shop Historic Collection, flamed maple top, 2 pickups.

1999-2007	Flamed maple	$3,500	$4,500
2000	Black	$3,500	$4,500

1968 Les Paul Custom
Reissue (Custom Shop)
2020-present. Solid maple top, mahogany back, 2 humbucker pickups, gold hardware, Ebony gloss nitro finish. Limited slightly aged Silverburst in '20.

2020	Aged Silverburst	$5,500	$7,000
2020-2023	Ebony	$4,000	$5,000

1968 Les Paul Custom Ultra Light Aged
2021-2022. Custom Shop Murphy Lab Collection, Ebony finish.

2021-2022		$4,250	$5,500

20th Anniversary Les Paul Custom
1974. Regular 2-pickup Custom, with 20th Anniversary inlay at 15th fret, cherry sunburst, natural, black or white.

1974	Black, white	$6,000	$7,750
1974	Cherry Sunburst, natural	$4,500	$6,000

25th Anniversary (Guitar Center) Les Paul Custom
1977-1978. Guitar Center Silver Anniversary, 50 made, 'Les Paul Custom' logo on truss rod cover, special 'Les Paul Custom Made in USA' on back of headstock, silver finish.

1977-1978		$4,000	$5,000

MODEL YEAR	FEATURES	EXC. COND. LOW	HIGH

35th Anniversary Les Paul Custom
1989. Gold hardware, 3 pickups, carved, solid mahogany body and neck, 35th Anniversary inlay on headstock, black.

1989		$4,000	$5,000

120th Anniversary Les Paul Custom
2014. Custom Shop, 120th Anniversary neck inlay.

2014		$4,500	$5,500

120th Anniversary Les Paul Custom Lite
2014. Custom Shop, 120th Anniversary neck inlay.

2014		$2,250	$3,000

Les Paul Custom Ace Frehley "Budokan"
2012-2013. Custom Shop, limited edition of 50 hand-aged signed by Frehley, 100 hand-aged unsigned and 150 additional with VOS finish.

2012-2013	All options	$4,250	$5,500

Les Paul Custom Ace Frehley Signature
1997-2001. Ace's signature inlay at 15th fret, 3 humbuckers, sunburst.

1997	Pilot run, CS specs	$7,250	$9,500
1997-2001		$5,750	$7,500

Les Paul Custom Adam Jones 1979
2021-present. Custom Shop Limited Edition, recreates Jones' '79 LP Custom, 1st 79 aged and signed by Jones, Antique Silverburst VOS finish.

2021-2023	Signed	$6,750	$8,750
2021-2023	Unsigned	$4,500	$5,750

Les Paul Custom F (Custom Shop)
2014-2018. Figured maple top, various colors.

2014-2018		$4,500	$5,750

Les Paul Custom Jeff Beck 1954 Oxblood
2009. Custom Shop, limited run of 150, 1st 50 aged, hand-signed and played by Beck, next 100 VOS, mahogany body, carved maple top, rosewood 'board, Burstbucker humbucking pickups, Oxblood VOS finish.

2009		$5,500	$7,500

Les Paul Custom Jimmy Page
2008. Based on Page's '60 LP Custom with 3 pickups, stop tailpiece or Bigsby option, certificate of authenticity, black VOS finish.

2008		$7,500	$10,000

Les Paul Custom John Sykes 1978
2006. Custom Shop Limited Edition, run of 66, recreates Sykes' '78 LP Custom including mods he made, aged Ebony finish.

2006		$4,500	$5,750

Les Paul Custom Lite
1987-1990, 2013-2016. Carved maple top, ebony 'board, pearl block inlays, gold hardware, PAF pickups, bound neck, headstock and body. Reissue in '13 with new options and colors.

1987-1990	Floyd Rose, opaque	$2,250	$2,750
1987-1990	Other colors	$2,250	$2,750
1987-1990	Sunburst, mild figure	$2,250	$2,750
2013-2016		$2,250	$2,750

Les Paul Custom Lite (Show Case Edition)
1988. Showcase Edition, only 200 made, gold top.

1988		$2,500	$3,000

MODEL YEAR	FEATURES	EXC. COND. LOW	HIGH

Les Paul Custom Mick Ronson '68
2007. Custom Shop, includes certificate and other authentication material.

2007		$3,500	$4,500

Les Paul Custom Music Machine
2003. Custom run for dealer Music Machine with special serial number series, chambered body style for reduced body weight, quilt tops.

2003	Figured Brazilian	$9,500	$12,500
2003	Quilted	$3,500	$4,500

Les Paul Custom Peter Frampton Signature
2008. Limited Edition 3-pickup version of Frampton's LP Custom, PF serial number series, black.

2008		$4,500	$5,500

Les Paul Custom Plus
1991-1998. Regular Custom with figured maple top, sunburst finish or colors.

1991-1998		$3,500	$4,500

Les Paul Custom Showcase Edition
1988. Showcase Edition logo on back of headstock, goldtop, black hardware.

1988		$3,500	$4,500

Les Paul Custom Silverburst
2007-2014. Custom Shop Limited Edition.

2007-2014		$3,750	$4,750

Les Paul Custom Steve Jones 1974
2008. Custom Shop Limited Edition, recreates Jones' '74 LP Custom including pin-up girl stickers, aged white finish.

2008		$4,500	$5,500

Les Paul Custom Zakk Wylde Signature
1999, 2003-2016. Custom shop, black and antique-white bullseye graphic finish. Green Camo option.

1999-2016	Various options	$4,500	$6,000

Les Paul Dale Earnhardt
1999. 333 made, Dale's image and number 3 on front and headstock, signature script on fretboard, several pieces of literature and an original certificate are part of the overall package, a lower serial number may add value.

1999		$3,500	$4,500

Les Paul Dale Earnhardt Intimidator
2000. 333 made, Dale's 'Goodwrench' car on the front of the body, The Intimidator inlay on the fretboard, includes certificate, chrome hardware.

2000		$3,500	$4,500

Les Paul Dark Fire
2009. Limited edition, 1st run of Les Pauls with Robot 2 Chameleon tone Technology designed to produce various classic guitar tones, completely computer interactive, Burstbucker3 bridge pickup, P-90H neck pickup and 6 Piezo pickups.

2009		$2,000	$2,500

Les Paul Dark Knight Quilt Top
2019. Exclusive limited run made for Guitar Center, trans black satin finish over quilted maple top.

2019		$2,250	$2,750

Les Paul DC AA
2007. Double A flamed top.

2007		$2,000	$2,500

Les Paul DC Classic
1992-1993. Gold finish.

1992-1993		$1,750	$2,250

Les Paul DC Pro
1997-1998, 2006-2007. Custom Shop, body like a '59 Les Paul Junior, carved highly figured maple top, various options. Name revived in '06 but not a Custom Shop model.

1997-1998		$2,250	$2,750
2006-2007		$1,500	$2,000

Les Paul DC Standard (Plus)
1998-1999, 2001-2006. Offset double-cut, highly flamed maple top, translucent lacquer finishes in various colors, reintroduced as Standard Lite in '99 but without Les Paul designation on headstock or truss rod cover.

1998-1999		$1,750	$2,250
2001-2006		$1,750	$2,250

Les Paul DC Studio
1997-1999. DC Series double-cut like late '50s models, carved maple top, 2 humbucker pickups, various colors.

1997-1999		$1,125	$1,500

Les Paul Deluxe
Following are Les Paul Deluxe models listed alphabetically.

Les Paul Deluxe
1969-1985. In 1969, the Goldtop Les Paul Standard was renamed the Deluxe. Two mini-humbuckers (regular humbuckers optional in mid-'70s). Mid-'70s sparkle tops are worth more than standard finishes. The market slightly favors the Goldtop finish, but practically speaking condition is more important than finish, such that all finishes fetch about the same amount (with the exception of the sparkle finish). Initially, the Deluxe was offered only as a Goldtop and the first year models are more highly prized than the others. Cherry sunburst was offered in '71, cherry in '71-'75, walnut in '71-'72, brown sunburst in '72-'79, natural in '75, red sparkle in '73-'75 only, blue sparkle in '73-'77, wine red/see-thru red offered '75-'85. In '99, the Deluxe was reissued for its 30th anniversary.

1969	Goldtop	$9,000	$12,000
1970	Goldtop	$7,500	$9,500
1971-1975	Goldtop	$7,000	$8,750
1971-1975	Natural	$4,500	$6,000
1971-1975	Red (solid)	$4,500	$6,000
1971-1975	Sunburst	$4,500	$6,000
1971-1975	Wine	$4,500	$6,000
1973-1975	Red sparkle, few made	$7,500	$9,500
1973-1977	Blue sparkle, more made	$7,250	$9,000
1976-1979	All other colors	$4,000	$5,500
1976-1979	Goldtop	$5,500	$7,000
1976-1979	Natural	$4,250	$5,500
1976-1979	Sunburst	$4,250	$5,500
1980-1985	Various colors	$4,000	$5,250

Gibson Les Paul Dark Knight Quilt Top

1973 Gibson Les Paul Deluxe
Rich Goldman

GUITARS

1952 Gibson Les Paul Model

mrosenow2

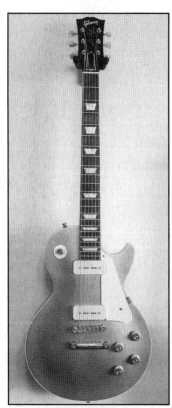

2006 Gibson '56 Les Paul Goldtop

Johnny Zapp

MODEL YEAR	FEATURES	EXC. COND. LOW	HIGH

Les Paul Deluxe 30th Anniversary
1999. Limited Edition logo on the lower back of the headstock, Deluxe logo on truss rod cover, Wine Red.

| 1999 | | $1,500 | $2,000 |

Les Paul Deluxe '69 Reissue
2000-2005. Mini-humbuckers, gold top

| 2000-2005 | | $1,750 | $2,250 |

Les Paul Deluxe Hall of Fame
1991. All gold finish.

| 1991 | | $2,000 | $2,500 |

Les Paul Deluxe Limited Edition
1999-2002. Limited edition reissue with Les Paul Standard features and Deluxe mini-humbuckers, black.

| 1999-2002 | | $1,750 | $2,250 |

Les Paul Deluxe Limited Edition AMS
2014. Limited edition chocolate finish, offered only by American Musical Supply.

| 2014 | | $550 | $725 |

Les Paul Deluxe Reissue
2012. Mini-humbuckers, chambered body.

| 2012 | | $2,250 | $3,000 |

Les Paul Deluxe #1 Pete Townshend
2006. Limited to 75, red.

| 2006 | | $7,000 | $9,000 |

Les Paul Deluxe #3 Pete Townshend
2006. Limited to 75, goldtop.

| 2006 | | $7,000 | $9,000 |

Les Paul Deluxe #9 Pete Townshend
2006. Limited to 75, cherry burst.

| 2006 | | $7,000 | $9,000 |

Les Paul Pro Deluxe
1978-1982. Chrome hardware, 2 P-90s, various colors. Les Pauls could vary significantly in weight during the '70s and '80s and lighter-weight examples may be worth up to 25% more than these values.

| 1978-1982 | | $2,625 | $3,500 |

Les Paul Dusk Tiger
Late-2009-2012. Limited edition, 1000 to be made, features Gibson's Robot Technology, Burstbucker bridge, P-90H neck and 6 Piezo pickups.

| 2009-2012 | | $2,000 | $2,500 |

Les Paul ES-Les Paul
2014-2018. Semi-hollow Les Paul body with f-holes, 3-ply maple/basswood/maple top and back, mahogany neck with maple spline, dark rosewood 'board, 2 pickups, light burst or black.

| 2014-2018 | | $2,250 | $3,000 |

Les Paul ES-Les Paul Custom
2015. Memphis Shop, limited run, semi-hollow maple/poplar/maple body, f-holes, high gloss Ebony finish.

| 2015 | | $3,750 | $4,750 |

Les Paul ES-Les Paul Standard
2016. Memphis Shop, limited run, semi-hollow, figured maple, various colors.

| 2016 | | $3,750 | $4,750 |

Les Paul ES-Les Paul Studio
2016. Memphis Shop, limited run, semi-hollow maple body, f-holes, Ginger Burst or Wine Red.

| 2016 | | $1,875 | $2,500 |

MODEL YEAR	FEATURES	EXC. COND. LOW	HIGH

Les Paul Florentine Plus
1997-2001. Custom Shop model, hollowbody with f-holes, higher-end appointments.

| 1997-2001 | | $3,500 | $4,500 |

Les Paul Supreme Florentine
2009-2015. Les Paul Standard with sharp Florentine cutaway, 350 made, Bigsby tailpiece, chambered mahogany body, highly figured maple top and back, Caribbean Blue finish.

| 2009-2015 | | $3,000 | $4,000 |

Les Paul Futura
2014-2015. Light weight, unbound, Min-Etune, various bright colors.

| 2014-2015 | | $900 | $1,250 |

Les Paul Goddess
2006-2007. Maple carved top, trapezoid inlays, smaller body, 2 humbuckers, 2 controls, tune-a-matic bridge.

| 2007 | | $1,250 | $1,750 |

Les Paul Goldtop
Following are Les Paul Goldtop models listed alphabetically.

Les Paul Model
1952-1958. The Goldtop, 2 P-90 pickups until mid-'57, humbuckers after, trapeze tailpiece until late-'53, stud tailpiece/bridge '53-mid-'55, Tune-o-matic bridge '55-'58, renamed Les Paul Standard in '58. All gold option add +10% if the neck retains 90% of the gold paint. All gold option with ugly green wear on the neck is equal to or below the value of a standard paint job. Some instruments had all mahogany bodies which did not have the maple cap. The all-mahogany version, although rarer, has a 10% lower value. A factory installed Bigsby tailpiece will reduce value by 30%. A non-factory installed Bigsby will reduce value up to 50%.

1952	1st made, unbound neck	$35,000	$45,000
1952	5/8" knobs, bound neck	$30,000	$40,000
1953	1/2" knobs, trapeze tailpiece	$30,000	$40,000
1953	Late-'53, 1/2" knobs, stud tailpiece	$45,000	$55,000
1954	Stud tailpiece, wrap-around	$45,000	$55,000
1955	Early-'55, stud tailpiece, wrap-around	$45,000	$55,000
1955	Late-'55, tune-o-matic tailpiece	$85,000	$100,000
1956	Tune-o-matic tailpiece	$85,000	$100,000
1957	Early-'57, P-90s	$85,000	$100,000
1957	PAFs, black plastic	$170,000	$245,000
1957-1958	PAFs, white plastic	$175,000	$250,000

MODEL YEAR	FEATURES	EXC. COND. LOW	HIGH

'52 Les Paul Goldtop
1997-2002. Goldtop finish, 2 P-90s, '52-style trapeze tailpiece/bridge.

1997-2002		$2,250	$3,000
1997-2002	Murphy aged	$2,500	$3,250

'52 Les Paul Tribute
2009. Recreation of '52 Les Paul Goldtop model, 564 made, special serialization, each guitar has 'prototype' impressed on back of headstock, Tribute designation logo on truss rod, includes COA booklet with serialized COA and tribute dates 1915-2009.

2009		$3,000	$4,000

'54 Les Paul Goldtop
1996-2013. Goldtop finish, 2 P-90s, '53-'54 stud tailpiece/bridge.

1996-2013		$3,000	$4,000
2003	Brazilian, COA	$6,000	$8,000

'54 Les Paul Wildwood
2012. Wildwood guitars special run, '54 specs, wrap-around tailpiece, 2 P-90 pickups, plaintop sunburst.

2012		$3,000	$4,000

1954 Les Paul Goldtop Heavy Aged
2021. Custom Shop Murphy Lab Collection, Double Gold finish.

2021		$4,750	$6,000

'55 Les Paul Goldtop Hot-Mod Wraptail
2010. Musician's Friend, based on '55 LP Humbucking Pickup Test Guitar, '55 specs, aged nitrocellulose gold finish, includes COA.

2010		$3,000	$4,000

'56 Les Paul Goldtop
1991-2016. Renamed from Les Paul Reissue Goldtop. Goldtop finish, 2 P-90 pickups, Tune-o-matic, now part of Gibson's Historic Collection, Custom Authentic aging optional from '01, Vintage Original Specs aging optional from '06.

1991-2016		$3,000	$4,000
2003	Brazilian	$6,500	$8,500

1956 Les Paul Goldtop "CME Spec"
2019-2020. Custom Shop special run for Chicago Music Exchange, Double Gold with VOS finish.

2019-2020		$4,000	$5,000

1956 Les Paul Goldtop Reissue
2020-present. Custom Shop, authentic replica parts, Double Gold nitro finish.

2020-2023		$3,500	$4,500

1956 Les Paul Goldtop Ultra Light Aged
2021-2022. Custom Shop Murphy Lab Collection, Double Gold finish.

2021-2022		$3,750	$4,750

'57 Les Paul Goldtop
1993-2018. Goldtop finish, 2 humbuckers, now part of Gibson's Historic Collection.

1993-2018		$3,000	$4,000
2003	Brazilian	$6,500	$8,500

'57 Les Paul Goldtop (R-7 wrap-around)
2007. Special run with wrap-around bar tailpiece/bridge similar to tailpiece on an original '54 Les Paul Goldtop.

2007		$3,000	$4,000

1957 Les Paul Goldtop Darkback Light Aged
2021-present. Custom Shop Murphy Lab Collection, Double Gold finish with dark back.

2021-2023		$4,750	$6,000

1957 Les Paul Goldtop Reissue
2020-present. Custom Shop, authentic replica parts, all Double Gold or Double Gold with dark back.

2020-2023		$3,500	$4,500

1957 Les Paul Goldtop Ultra Light/Ultra Heavy Aged
2021-present. Custom Shop Murphy Lab Collection, ultra light or heavy aged, Double Gold finish. Ultra light ended in '22.

2021-2023		$4,000	$5,000

Les Paul 30th Anniversary
1982-1984. Features of a 1958 Les Paul Goldtop, 2 humbuckers, 30th Anniversary inlay on 19th fret.

1982-1984		$3,500	$4,500

Les Paul 50th Anniversary 1956 Les Paul Standard Goldtop
2006. Custom Shop, '56 tune-o-matic P-90 specs.

2006		$3,500	$4,500

Les Paul 50th Anniversary 1957 Les Paul Standard Goldtop
2007. Custom Shop, limited run of 150, humbucker pickups, large gold 50th Anniversary headstock logo.

2007		$5,000	$6,500

Les Paul Billy F. Gibbons Goldtop
2014-2018. Custom Shop, mahogany neck with maple spline, rosewood 'board, holly headstock, 2 Duncan Pearly Gates pickups, Goldtop VOS or Goldtop Aged.

2014-2018		$6,250	$8,000

Les Paul Centennial ('56 LP Standard Goldtop)
1994. Guitar of the Month, limited edition of 100, Goldtop mahogany body, gold hardware, gold truss rod plate, gold medallion, engraved light-gold 'guard, with COA.

1994		$3,750	$5,000

Les Paul Dickey Betts Goldtop
2001-2003. Aged gold top.

2001-2003		$6,750	$8,750

Les Paul Joe Bonamassa Aged Goldtop
2008. Inspired By Series, LP Standard aged goldtop with black trim (including black pickup rings), serial number starts with BONAMASSA.

2008		$3,250	$4,500

Les Paul LP-295 Goldtop
2008. Guitar of the Month (April, '08), limited run of 1000, Les Paul body style, goldtop, 2 humbuckers, ES-295 appointments such as 'guard and fretboard markers, Bigsby tailpiece option.

2008		$2,500	$3,500

Les Paul Pro Showcase Edition
1988. Goldtop 1956 specs, Showcase Edition decal, 200 made.

1988		$3,250	$4,250

Les Paul Reissue Goldtop
1983-1991. Goldtop finish, 2 P-100 pickups, renamed '56 Les Paul Goldtop in '91.

1983-1991		$3,000	$4,000

1994 Gibson '57 Les Paul Goldtop
W. H. Stephens

Gibson Les Paul 50th Anniversary 1957 Les Paul Standard Goldtop
Matt Carleson

To get the most from this book, be sure to read "Using *The Guide*" in the introduction.

1961 Gibson Les Paul Junior

Michael Alonzi

2008 Gibson Les Paul
Junior John Lennon LTD

MODEL YEAR	FEATURES	EXC. COND. LOW	HIGH

Les Paul Slash Signature Goldtop
2008. Limited Edition, 1000 made, LP Standard model, Slash logo truss rod cover, Limited Edition logo back of headstock, certificate of authenticity.

2008		$3,750	$4,750

Les Paul Government Series II
2014-2018. 2 Dirty Fingers pickups, certificate of authenticity, Government Tan finish.

2013-2018		$1,250	$1,750

Les Paul GT
2007. Includes over/under dual truss rods, GT logo on truss rod cover, several specs designed to add durability during heavy professional use.

2007		$2,000	$2,500

Les Paul HD.6-X Pro Digital
2008-2009. Digital sound system, hex pickups.

2008-2009		$2,500	$3,000

Les Paul Indian Motorcycle
2002. 100 made, has Indian script logo on fretboard and chrome cast war bonnet on the body, crimson red and cream white.

2002		$5,000	$6,500

Les Paul Jumbo
1969-1970. Single rounded cutaway, flat-top dreadnought acoustic/electric, 1 pickup, rosewood back and sides, natural.

1969-1970		$3,500	$4,500

Les Paul Junior
Following are Les Paul Junior models listed alphabetically.

Les Paul Junior
1954-1963, 1986-1992, 2001-2002, 2005-2013. One P-90 pickup, single-cut solidbody '54-mid-'58, double-cut '58-early-'61, SG body '61-'63, renamed SG Jr. in '63, reintroduced as single-cut for '86-'92, reissued as the 1957 Les Paul Jr. Single Cutaway in '98. Headstock repair reduces the value by 40%-50%. Reinstalled tuners reduces the value by 5% to 10%. Replaced tuner buttons reduces the value by 5% to 10%.

1954-1958	Sunburst, single-cut	$11,500	$14,000
1958-1961	Cherry, double-cut	$10,500	$13,500
1961-1963	Cherry, SG body	$6,500	$8,500
1986-1992	Sunburst, single-cut, tune-o-matic	$1,500	$2,000
1998-2013	Sunburst, single-cut, stop tail	$1,500	$2,000

Les Paul Junior 3/4
1956-1961. One P-90 pickup, short-scale, single-cut solidbody '54-mid-'58, double-cut '58-early-'61.

1956-1958	Sunburst, single-cut	$5,500	$7,500
1958-1961	Cherry, double-cut	$4,750	$6,250

1957 Les Paul Junior (Single-Cut) Ultra Light Aged/Heavy Aged
2021-present. Custom Shop Murphy Lab Collection, ultra light or heavy aged, TV Yellow finish on both.

2021-2023	Heavy aged	$4,250	$5,500
2021-2023	Ultra Light aged	$3,000	$4,000

1957 Les Paul Junior (Single-Cut) VOS
1998-2014. Custom Shop, nickel-plated hardware, Vintage Original Spec aging optional from '06.

1998-2014		$2,500	$3,250

1958 Les Paul Junior (Double-Cut) VOS
1998-2013. Custom Shop, nickel plated hardware, Vintage Original Spec aging optional from '06.

1998-2013		$2,500	$3,250

'60 Les Paul Junior
1992-2003. Historic Collection reissue.

1992-2003		$2,250	$3,000

1960 Les Paul Junior (Double-Cut) Ultra Heavy Aged
2021. Custom Shop Murphy Lab Collection, Ebony finish.

2021		$5,500	$7,250

Les Paul J / LPJ
2013-2018. Mahogany body with carved maple top, '50s profile maple neck, rosewood 'board, 2 Modern Classics humbucking pickups, various finishes.

2013-2018		$650	$850

Les Paul Junior Billie Joe Armstrong Signature
2006-2013. 1956 LP Junior specs.

2006-2013		$1,250	$1,625

Les Paul Junior DC Hall of Fame
1990-1992. Part of Hall of Fame Series, limited run of LP Junior Double Cutaway but with P-100 pickup.

1990-1992		$1,125	$1,500

Les Paul Junior Double Cutaway
1986-1992, 1995-1996. Copy of '50s double-cut Jr., cherry or sunburst, reissued as the 1958 Les Paul Jr. Double Cutaway in '98.

1986-1989		$1,125	$1,500

Les Paul Junior Faded
2010-2012. Single-cut, faded cherry finish.

2010-2012		$775	$1,000

Les Paul Junior John Lennon LTD
2008. Custom Shop Inspired By series, 300 made, Charlie Christian neck pickup and P-90 bridge as per Lennon's modified Junior, aged-relic finish, certificate, book and New York t-shirt.

2008		$4,750	$6,250

Les Paul Junior Lite
1999-2002. Double-cut, Tune-o-matic, 2 P-100 pickups, stop tail, mini-trapezoid markers, burnt cherry gloss finish.

1999-2002		$875	$1,125

Les Paul Junior Special
1999-2004. LP Jr. single-cut slab body with 2 P-90s (making it a Special) instead of the standard single P-90, double pickup controls, cherry, tinted natural or sunburst.

1999-2004		$950	$1,250

Les Paul Junior Special Robot
2008. P-90s, TV Yellow.

2008		$1,125	$1,500

Les Paul Junior Tenor/Plectrum
Late-1950s. Four string neck on Junior body, cherry.

1959		$4,750	$6,250

MODEL YEAR	FEATURES	EXC. COND. LOW	HIGH

Les Paul TV
1954-1959. Les Paul Jr. with limed mahogany (TV Yellow) finish, single-cut until mid-'59, double-cut after, renamed SG TV (see that listing for more) in late-'59.

| 1954-1959 | Single-cut | $16,500 | $25,000 |
| 1958-1959 | Double-cut | $15,500 | $20,000 |

Les Paul TV 3/4
1954-1957. Limed mahogany (TV Yellow) Les Paul Jr. 3/4, short-scale, single-cut.

| 1954-1957 | | $8,500 | $10,500 |

Les Paul TV Junior
2001-2016. Custom Shop, TV Yellow.

| 2001-2016 | | $2,250 | $3,000 |

Les Paul Limited Run 2016 Series
Various Les Paul limited edition models released in 2016.

2016-2018	Fort Knox	$4,000	$5,000
2016-2018	Mahogany Limited	$4,000	$5,000
2016-2018	Pete Townshend Deluxe	$4,000	$5,000
2016-2018	Redwood	$4,000	$5,000
2016-2018	Standard Figured Walnut	$4,000	$5,000
2016-2018	Sunken Treasure	$4,000	$5,000

Les Paul Lou Pallo Signature
2010. Maple top, mahogany back and neck, rosewood 'board, 2 pickups, ebony finish.

| 2010 | | $2,250 | $2,750 |

Les Paul Marc Bolan
2011. Artist model with certificate of authenticity, limited run of 100 hand aged and 350 VOS, Bolan Chablis finish.

| 2011 | | $5,000 | $6,500 |

Les Paul Menace
2006-2007. Carved mahogany body, 2 humbucker pickups.

| 2006-2007 | | $750 | $975 |

Les Paul Old Hickory
1998 only. Limited run of 200, tulip poplar body wood from The Hermitage, Custom-style trim.

| 1998 | | $4,500 | $6,000 |

Les Paul Personal
1969-1972. Two angled, low impedance pickups, phase switch, gold parts, walnut finish.

| 1969-1972 | | $2,500 | $3,250 |

Les Paul Professional
1969-1971, 1977-1979. Single-cut, 2 angled, low impedance pickups, carved top, walnut or white.

| 1969-1971 | Walnut | $2,750 | $3,500 |
| 1969-1971 | White | $2,750 | $3,500 |

Les Paul Recording
1971-1979. Two angled, low impedance pickups, high/low impedance selector switch, walnut '71-'77, white added '75, natural, ebony and sunburst added '78.

1971-1977	Walnut	$2,750	$3,500
1975-1979	White	$3,750	$4,750
1978-1979	Black, Natural, Sunburst	$3,250	$4,250

Les Paul Richard Petty LTD
2003. Richard Petty's image on front and back, 'The King' inlay on fretboard.

| 2003 | | $3,500 | $4,500 |

Les Paul Signature/L.P. Signature
1973-1978. Thin semi-hollowbody, double-cut, 2 low impedance pickups, f-holes, various colors. The Price List refers to it as L.P. Signature.

| 1973-1978 | | $4,250 | $5,500 |

Les Paul Silver Streak
1982. Custom Shop decal, silver finish.

| 1982 | | $3,500 | $4,500 |

Les Paul SM
1980. Solid mahogany, single-cut with coil-tap, Les Paul SM truss rod logo, burgundy or silverburst finish.

| 1980 | | $2,250 | $3,000 |

Les Paul SmartWood Exotic
1998-2001. Full-depth Les Paul-style built with eco-friendly woods, Muiracatiara (or Muir) top, mahogany back, Preciosa 'board, pearloid dots.

| 1998-2001 | | $1,250 | $1,625 |

Les Paul SmartWood Standard
1996-2002. Smartwood Series, figured maple top, mahogany body, Smartwood on truss rod cover, antique natural.

| 1996-2002 | | $1,250 | $1,625 |

Les Paul SmartWood Studio
2002-2006. Muiracatiara (Muir) top and mahogany back, Preciosa (Prec) 'board, Studio appointments including pearl-style dot markers.

| 2002-2006 | | $1,125 | $1,500 |

Les Paul special
Following are Les Paul Special models listed alphabetically.

Les Paul Special
1955-1959. Slab solidbody, 2 pickups (P-90s in '50s, P-100 stacked humbuckers on later version), single-cut until end of '58, double in '59, renamed SG Special in late-'59.

1955-1958	TV Yellow, single-cut	$16,500	$22,000
1959	Cherry, double-cut	$12,000	$15,000
1959	TV Yellow, double-cut	$20,000	$25,000

Les Paul 55
1974, 1976-1981. Single-cut Special reissue, 2 pickups. By '78 the catalog name is Les Paul 55/78.

1974-1981	Sunburst	$2,250	$3,000
1974-1981	TV Yellow (limed)	$2,500	$3,250
1976-1981	Wine	$2,250	$3,000

'60 Les Paul Special
1998-2012. Historic Collection reissue, limited edition, single-cut or double-cut.

| 1998-2012 | | $2,500 | $3,250 |
| 2007 | Murphy aged | $2,750 | $3,500 |

Les Paul Special (Reissue)
1989-1998, 2002-2006. Briefly introduced as Les Paul Junior II but name changed to Special in the first year, single-cut, 2 P-100 stacked humbuckers, TV

Gibson Les Paul TV Junior
Bill Miller

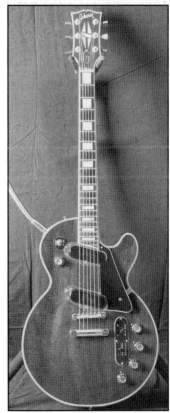

1969 Gibson Les Paul Personal
Frank Manno

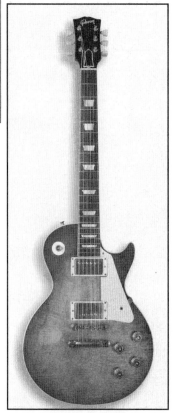

1958 Gibson Les Standard
Gary's Classic Guitars

1959 Gibson Les Paul Standard
Gordon Kennedy

MODEL YEAR	FEATURES	EXC. COND. LOW	HIGH

Yellow, in '90 there was a run of 300 with LE serial number, renamed Special SL in '98.

| 1989-1998 | P-100s | $975 | $1,250 |
| 2002-2006 | Humbuckers | $975 | $1,250 |

Les Paul Special 100/100 Special
2015-2016. Reissue double-cut slab body, 2 P-90s, 'Les Paul 100' birthday signature on headstock.

| 2015-2016 | | $975 | $1,250 |

Les Paul Special 3/4
1959. Slab solidbody, 2 P-90 pickups, double-cut, short-scale, cherry finish, renamed SG Special 3/4 in late-'59.

| 1959 | | $6,500 | $8,500 |

Les Paul Special Centennial
1994 only. 100 made, double-cut, cherry, 100 year banner at the 12th fret, diamonds in headstock and in gold-plated knobs, gold-plated Gibson coin in back of headstock.

| 1994 | | $4,000 | $5,000 |

Les Paul Special Double Cutaway
1976-1979, 1993-1994. Double-cut, 2 P-90s, 1990s version was made in Custom Shop and was reintroduced as the '60 Les Paul Special Historic in '98.

| 1976-1979 | | $2,500 | $3,250 |
| 1993-1994 | Custom Shop | $1,500 | $2,000 |

Les Paul Special Faded
2005-2012. Double- or single-cut, dot markers, 2 P-90s, Special logo on truss rod cover, faded TV limed mahogany or cherry finish.

| 2005-2012 | | $800 | $1,000 |

Les Paul Special New Century
2006-2008. Full-body mirror 'guard, 2 exposed humbuckers, single-cut LP Special body, mirror truss rod cover.

| 2006-2008 | | $1,250 | $1,750 |

Les Paul Special Robot
2008. Two P-90 pickups, various colors.

| 2008 | | $1,000 | $1,375 |

Les Paul Special Tenor
1959. Four-string electric tenor, LP Special body, TV Yellow.

| 1959 | | $5,750 | $7,500 |

Les Paul Special Worn Cherry
2003-2006. Single-cut, non-bound LP Special with 2 humbuckers.

| 2003-2006 | | $775 | $1,000 |

Les Paul Standard
Following are Les Paul Standard models, beginning with the original model, then listed alphabetically.

Les Paul Standard (Sunburst)
1958-1960, special order 1972-1975. Les Paul Sunbursts from '58-'60 should be individually valued based on originality, color and the amount and type of figure in the maple top, changed tuners or a Bigsby removal will drop the value. Approximately 15% came with the Bigsby tailpiece. The noted price ranges are guidance valuations. Each '58-'60 Les Paul Standard should be evaluated on a case-by-case basis. As is always the case, the low and high ranges are for an all original,

excellent condition, undamaged guitar. About 70% of the '58-'60 Les Paul Standards have relatively plain maple tops. The majority of '58-'60 Les Paul Standards have moderate or extreme color fade.

Wider fret wire was introduced in early-'59. White bobbins were introduced in early- to mid-'59. Double ring Kluson Deluxe tuners were introduced in late-'60. It has been suggested that all '58-'60 models have 2-piece centerseam tops. This implies that 1-piece tops, 3-piece tops and off-centerseam tops do not exist.

The terminology of the 'Burst includes: arching medullary grain, swirling medullary grain, ribbon-curl, chevrons, Honey-Amber, receding red aniline, pinstripe, bookmatched, double-white bobbins, zebra bobbins, black bobbins, fiddleback maple, sunburst finish, Honeyburst, lemon drop, quarter sawn, blistered figure, width of gradation, flat sawn, Teaburst, Bigsby-shadow, rift sawn, heel size, aged clear lacquer, 3-dimensional figure, intense fine flame, tag-shadow, red pore filler, Eastern maple fleck, medium-thick flame, shrunk tuners, wave and flame, flitch-matched, elbow discoloration, ambered top coat, natural gradation, grain orientation, script oxidation, asymmetrical figure Tangerineburst, Greenburst, and birdseye.

The bobbins used for the pickup winding were either black or white. The market has determined that white bobbin PAFs are the most highly regarded. Generally speaking, in '58 bobbins were black, in '59 the bobbin component transitioned to white and some guitars have 1 white and 1 black bobbin (aka zebra). In '60, there were zebras and double blacks returned.

Rather than listing separate line items for fade and wood, the Guide lists discounts and premiums as follows. The price ranges shown below are for instruments with excellent color, excellent wood, with the original guitar case. The following discounts and premiums should be considered.

An instrument with moderate or total color fade should be discounted about 10%.

One with a factory Bigsby should be discounted about 10%-15%.

Original jumbo frets are preferred over original small frets and are worth +10%.

1958	Highly figured	$450,000	$550,000
1958	Minor figured	$375,000	$475,000
1958	Plain top, no figuring	$275,000	$350,000
1959	Highly figured	$550,000	$750,000
1959	Minor figured	$450,000	$600,000
1959	Plain top, no figuring	$300,000	$400,000
1960	Early '60, fat neck, highly figured	$550,000	$750,000
1960	Early '60, fat neck, minor figured	$450,000	$600,000
1960	Early '60, fat neck, plain top	$300,000	$400,000

The Official Vintage Guitar magazine Price Guide 2025   **Gibson** Les Paul Std. (SG body) — '59 LP Flametop/Reissue/Std.   **183**

GUITARS

MODEL YEAR	FEATURES	EXC. COND. LOW	HIGH
1960	Late '60, flat neck, highly figured	$400,000	$500,000
1960	Late '60, flat neck, minor figured	$300,000	$400,000
1960	Late '60, flat neck, plain top	$250,000	$350,000

Les Paul Standard (SG body)

1961-1963 (SG body those years) Renamed SG Standard in late-'63

Year	Features	LOW	HIGH
1961-1963	Cherry, side vibrola, PAFs	$25,000	$30,000
1962	Cherry, Bigsby, 1 pat #, 1 PAF	$20,000	$25,000
1962-1963	Cherry, side vibrola, pat #	$18,000	$22,000
1962-1963	Ebony block, SG, PAFs, dlx vibrola	$25,000	$30,000
1962-1963	Ebony block, SG, pat #, dlx vibrola	$20,000	$25,000

Les Paul Standard (reintroduced then renamed)

1968-1969. Comes back as a goldtop with P-90s for '68-'69 (renamed Les Paul Deluxe, '69), available as special order Deluxe '72-'76.

Year	Features	LOW	HIGH
1968	P-90s, small hdsk, no volute	$22,000	$27,000
1968-1969	P-90s, large hdsk	$18,000	$24,000

Les Paul Standard (reintroduced)

1971-July 2008, 2012-2018. Available as special order Deluxe '72-'76, reintroduced with 2 humbuckers '76-present. The '75 Price List shows a Les Paul Standard (B) model which is equipped with a Bigsby tailpiece versus a wraparound, also shows a Les Paul Standard (B) with palm pedal. Replaced by Les Paul Standard 2008 in August '08. Name revived in '12 on chambered-body version with tapped Burstbucker pickups, available in AAA tops, black, Gold Top or Blue Mist finishes.

Year	Features	LOW	HIGH
1971	Early special order goldtop, P-90s	$13,500	$17,000
1972-1974	Special order goldtop, P-90s	$10,500	$13,500
1972-1974	Special order sunburst, P-90s	$8,000	$10,000
1974-1975	Special order, hums	$8,000	$10,000
1976	Sunburst, 4-piece pancake body	$5,000	$6,500
1976-1978	Other colors	$4,000	$5,500
1977-1978	Sunburst	$5,000	$6,500
1978-1979	Natural	$4,000	$5,500
1979	Brown Sunburst	$5,000	$6,500
1979	Cherry Sunburst	$5,000	$6,500
1979	Goldtop	$5,000	$6,500
1979	Wine Red	$4,000	$5,500
1980-1984	Other colors	$4,000	$5,500
1980-1984	Sunburst	$4,000	$5,500

MODEL YEAR	FEATURES	EXC. COND. LOW	HIGH
1980-1984	White (RRhoads)	$4,000	$5,500
1985-1989	Various colors	$3,500	$4,500
1985-1989	White (RRhoads)	$3,500	$4,500
1990-1993	Ltd Ed colors with sticker	$3,500	$4,500
1990-1999	White (RRhoads)	$3,000	$4,000
1990-2018	Figured top	$3,000	$4,000
1990-2018	Plain top	$2,500	$3,000
2000-2018	Opaque solid color	$2,500	$3,000

'50s Les Paul Standard

2005-present. Originally an AMS exclusive with AA (later AAA) maple top and various finishes. In '19, Gibson introduced a regular production model with the same name with standard maple top finished in Goldtop, Heritage Cherry Sunburst or Tobacco Burst.

Year	Features	LOW	HIGH
2005-2023	AA & AAA top	$2,500	$3,000

'58 Les Paul Figured Top

1996-2000, 2002-2003, 2009-2012. Custom Shop, less top figure than '59 Reissue, sunburst.

Year	Features	LOW	HIGH
1996-2000		$4,500	$5,500
2002-2012		$4,500	$5,500
2003	Brazilian	$12,500	$16,000

'58 Les Paul Plaintop (VOS)

1994-1999, 2003-2013. Custom Shop model, plain maple top version of '58 Standard reissue, sunburst, VOS model starts in '04. Replaced by the 1958 Les Paul Reissue with a non-chambered body.

Year	Features	LOW	HIGH
1994-1999	Non-VOS	$3,500	$4,500
2003-2013	VOS, non-chambered	$3,500	$4,500
2006-2013	VOS, chambered	$3,500	$4,500

1958 Les Paul Standard "CME Spec"

2019-2020. Custom Shop special run for Chicago Music Exchange, various colors with VOS finish.

Year	Features	LOW	HIGH
2019-2020		$4,000	$5,000

1958 Les Paul Standard Light Aged/Heavy Aged

2021-present. Custom Shop Murphy Lab Collection, light or heavy aged, Lemon Burst.

Year	Features	LOW	HIGH
2021-2023		$4,500	$5,750

1958 Les Paul Standard Ultra Light Aged

2021-2022. Custom Shop Murphy Lab Collection, Bourbon Burst or Washed Cherry Sunburst.

Year	Features	LOW	HIGH
2021-2022		$4,000	$5,000

'59 Les Paul Flametop/Reissue/Standard

1993-2016. Renamed from Les Paul Reissue Flametop, for 2000-'05 called the 1959 Les Paul Reissue, in '06 this model became part of Gibson's Vintage Original Spec series and is called the '59 Les Paul Standard VOS. Flame maple top, 2 humbuckers, thick '59-style neck, sunburst finish, part of Gibson's Historic Collection, the original certificate authenticity adds value, an instrument without the matching certificate has less value. By '98 Gibson guaranteed only AAA Premium grade maple tops would be used.

Collectors of Historic Collection instruments tend to buy and store these instruments, maintaining them in near mint to New Old Stock (NOS) mint condition. In recent years, NOS instruments that are up to five years old, but in like-new mint condition, have been sold at prices that are higher than instruments in

1962 Gibson Les Paul Standard

Gibson '50s Les Paul Standard

GUITARS

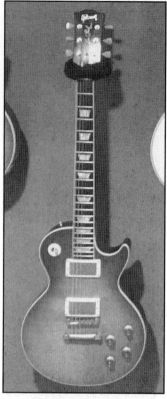

2009 Gibson '59 Les
Paul Burst Brothers

Anthony Perrotta

Gibson '60 Les Paul Flametop

Tyler Willison

MODEL YEAR	FEATURES	EXC. COND. LOW	HIGH

excellent condition, which is the usual condition that VG Price Guide values are given. Because of that trend, the prices shown here give consideration to the numerous NOS instruments that have sold. The inclusion of both excellent condition instruments and mint NOS instruments creates a wider than normal price range, but the high-side of the range is very realistic for NOS instruments.

MODEL YEAR	FEATURES	EXC. COND. LOW	HIGH
1993	Custom Shop decal, early '93	$7,250	$9,500
1993	Historic decal, late '93	$6,000	$7,750
1994-1995	Murphy aged	$6,000	$7,750
1994-1999	Aged, figured top	$6,000	$7,750
1996-1999	Figured top	$6,000	$7,750
2000-2016	Aged, figured top	$5,500	$7,250
2000-2016	Figured top	$5,000	$6,500
2003	Brazilian, aged, figured	$13,500	$17,500
2003	Brazilian, highly figured	$12,500	$16,500
2003	Brazilian, low figured	$11,000	$14,500

'59 Les Paul Burst Brothers

2009-2010. Limited edition created with Dave Belzer and Drew Berlin, sold through Guitar Center, wood-figure was selected to reflect the nature of a '50s LP Standard rather than using only AAA best-quality flame, 1st run of 34 (ser. # series BB 9 001-034) with dark Madagascar rosewood 'board, 2nd run had 37 (ser. # series BB 0 001-037).

2009	1st run, 34 made	$8,500	$11,000
2010	2nd run, 37 made	$7,250	$9,500

'59 Les Paul Korina Reissue

2008. Custom Shop Limited Edition, korina body and neck, quilted maple top, rosewood 'board, natural finish.

2008		$6,250	$8,250

'59 Les Paul Plaintop (VOS)

2006-2013. Custom Shop, very little or no-flame.

2006-2013		$3,500	$4,500

1959 Les Paul Standard "CME Spec"

2019-2020. Custom Shop special run for Chicago Music Exchange, various colors with VOS finish.

2019-2020		$6,500	$8,500

1959 Les Paul Standard Heavy Aged

2021-present. Custom Shop Murphy Lab Collection, Green Lemon Fade, Golden Poppy Burst or Slow Iced Tea Fade.

2021-2023		$6,500	$8,500

1959 Les Paul Standard Light Aged

2021-present. Custom Shop Murphy Lab Collection, Cherry Tea Burst, Lemon Burst or Royal Tea Burst.

2021-2023		$6,000	$7,750

1959 Les Paul Standard Reissue

2020-present. Custom Shop, authentic replica parts, Washed Cherry Sunburst, Iced Tea Burst or Dirty Lemon, all colors with VOS finish.

2020-2023		$4,750	$6,250

1959 Les Paul Standard Ultra Heavy Aged

2021-present. Custom Shop Murphy Lab Collection, Kindred Burst or Lemon Burst.

2021-2023		$7,750	$10,000

1959 Les Paul Standard Ultra Light Aged

2021-2022. Custom Shop Murphy Lab Collection, Factory Burst, Southern Fade Burst or Sunrise Teaburst.

2021-2022		$5,250	$7,000

True Historic 1959 Les Paul

2015-2018. Figured maple top, Indian rosewood 'board, certificate of authenticity, various vintage finishes including Murphy aged option.

2015-2018		$5,250	$7,000

'60s Les Paul Standard

2005-present. Originally an AMS exclusive with AA (later AAA) maple top and various finishes. In '19, Gibson introduced a regular production model with the same name with standard maple top finished in Ice Tea, Bourbon Burst, or Unburst.

2005-2023	AA & AAA top	$2,250	$3,000

'60 Les Paul Flametop/Standard '60s

1991-present. Renamed from Les Paul Reissue Flametop, flame maple top, 2 humbuckers, thinner neck, sunburst finish, part of Gibson's Historic Collection. In '06 this model became part of Gibson's Vintage Original Spec series and called '60 Les Paul Standard VOS, then in '17 the name changed to Les Paul Standard '60s.

1991-1999	Figured top	$6,000	$7,500
1994-1999	Aged, figured	$6,000	$7,500
2000-2016	Aged, figured	$5,000	$6,500
2000-2023	Figured top	$4,500	$5,750
2003	Brazilian, aged, figured	$13,250	$17,000
2003	Brazilian, figured	$12,750	$16,500

'60 Les Paul Plaintop (VOS)

2006-2010. Plain maple top version of '60 Standard reissue, certificate of authenticity, VOS cherry sunburst.

2006-2010		$3,500	$4,500

1960 Les Paul Standard Heavy Aged

2020-present. Custom Shop Murphy Lab Collection, heavy aged Tangerine Burst.

2020-2023		$6,500	$8,500

1960 Les Paul Standard Light Aged

2020-present. Custom Shop Murphy Lab Collection, light aged Tomato Soup Burst.

2020-2023		$6,000	$7,750

1960 Les Paul Standard Reissue

2020-present. Custom Shop, authentic reproduction, vintage-style appointments, various colors with VOS finish.

2020-2023		$4,750	$6,250

1960 Les Paul Standard Ultra Light Aged

2020-2022. Custom Shop Murphy Lab Collection, ultra light aged Orange Lemon Fade Burst or Wide Tomato Burst.

2020-2022		$5,250	$6,750

MODEL YEAR FEATURES	EXC. COND. LOW	HIGH

True Historic 1960 Les Paul
2015-2018. Figured maple top, Indian rosewood 'board, certificate of authenticity, various vintage finishes including Murphy aged option.

| 2015-2018 | $5,500 | $7,250 |

'82 Les Paul Standard
1982. Standard 82 on truss rod cover, made in Kalamazoo, Made in USA stamp on back of the headstock, generally quilted maple tops.

| 1982 | $3,250 | $4,250 |

Les Paul 10th Anniversary Chambered '58 Reissue
2014. Custom Shop, chambered mahogany body, carved maple top, '50s neck profile, rosewood 'board.

| 2014 | $3,500 | $4,500 |

Les Paul 40th Anniversary (from 1959)
1999. Reissue Historic, humbuckers, highly figured top, price includes 40th Anniversary Edition Certificate of Authenticity with matching serial number, a guitar without the certificate is worth less.

| 1999 | $5,000 | $6,500 |

Les Paul 50th Anniversary (Historic)
2002. From Gibson Custom Art & Historic Division, 50 made, carved figured koa top, figured maple back and sides, 3-piece figured maple neck, abalone cloud inlay markers, pearl split-diamond headstock inlay and pearl Gibson logo, Antique Natural.

| 2002 | $7,750 | $10,000 |

Les Paul 50th Anniversary 1956 Les Paul Standard
2006. Custom Shop, highly figured top, certificate of authenticity.

| 2006 | $3,000 | $4,000 |

Les Paul 50th Anniversary 1959 Les Paul Standard
2009-2011. Custom Shop, highly figured top, certificate of authenticity.

| 2009-2011 | $5,000 | $6,500 |

Les Paul 50th Anniversary 1960 Les Paul Standard
2010-2011. Limited Edition, offered in Heritage Cherry Sunburst, Heritage Dark Burst, Sunset Tea Burst and Cherry Burst.

| 2010-2011 | $5,000 | $6,500 |

Les Paul 50th Anniversary DaPra
2009. Limited run of 25 made for Vic DaPra of Guitar Gallery, '59 Historic R9.

| 2009 | $5,250 | $6,750 |

Les Paul 50th Anniversary Korina Tribute
2009. Custom Shop model, 100 made, single-cut Korina natural finish body, 3 pickups, dot markers, V-shaped Futura headstock, Custom logo on truss rod cover, slanted raised Gibson logo on headstock.

| 2009 | $6,000 | $7,750 |

Les Paul 50th Anniversary Les Paul Standard (Sweetwater)
2009. Custom Shop, limited run of 25 for Sweetwater Music, exclusive custom Ruby 'Burst finish.

| 2009 | $5,250 | $6,750 |

Les Paul 60th Anniversary 1960 Les Paul Standard "CME Spec"
2020. Custom Shop, special run for Chicago Music Exchange, Orange Lemon Fade or Tomato Soup Burst, with VOS finish.

| 2020 | $4,750 | $6,250 |

Les Paul 120th Anniversary
2014. Custom Shop, 120th Anniversary neck inlay, heavy quilted top.

| 2014 | $3,000 | $4,000 |

Les Paul Axcess Alex Lifeson
2011-2018. Custom Shop, push-pull volume pots, nitrocellulose lacquer finish in Royal Crimson or Viceroy Brown Sunburst, first 25 of each color signed by Lifeson with additional production unsigned, certificate of authenticity.

| 2011 | Signed | $5,000 | $6,500 |
| 2011-2018 | Unsigned | $3,750 | $4,750 |

Les Paul Axcess Dave Amato
2016. Custom Shop, figured maple top, mahogany back and neck, single '57 Classic Plus pickup, Floyd Rose tailpiece, TV yellow.

| 2016 | $4,750 | $6,250 |

Les Paul Axcess Standard
2009-present. Custom Shop, new neck joint carve allows access to high frets, Floyd Rose, slightly thinner body, nitro lacquer Iced Tea Burst or Gun Metal Gray. In '20 DC Rust (unique stain) only.

| 2009-2023 | $2,500 | $3,250 |

Les Paul BFG
2006-2008, 2018. Burstbucker 3 humbucker at bridge and P-90 at neck, 2 volume and 1 tone knobs, figured maple top over mahogany body. Reissued in '18.

| 2006-2008 | $1,250 | $1,625 |
| 2018 | $1,250 | $1,625 |

Les Paul Bird's-Eye Standard
1999. Birdseye top, gold hardware, 2 humbucking pickups, transparent amber.

| 1999 | $2,250 | $2,750 |

Les Paul Carved Series
2003-2005. Custom Shop Standards with relief-carved tops, one in diamond pattern, one with flame pattern.

| 2003-2005 | $2,250 | $3,000 |

Les Paul Catalina
1996-1997. Large Custom Shop logo on headstock.

| 1996-1997 | $2,750 | $3,500 |

Les Paul Centennial ('59 LP Special)
1994. Guitar of the Month, limited edition of 100, slab body Special-style configuration, gold hardware, P-90s, gold medallion, commemorative engraving in 'guard, cherry, with COA.

| 1994 | $3,500 | $4,500 |

Les Paul Class 5
2001-2017. Custom Shop, various woods, highly flamed or quilt top, or special finish, 1960 profile neck, weight relieved body, Burst Bucker humbucking pickups, several color options.

| 2001-2017 | All models | $3,500 | $4,500 |

Gibson Les Paul Custom Shop VOS 1960
Dudley Taft

2009 Gibson Les Paul Gary Moore BFG
James Magrini

1992 Gibson Les
Paul Heritage 80

Sam Gabriel

1996 Gibson Les Paul
Jimmy Page Signature

Tony Jones

MODEL YEAR	FEATURES	EXC. COND. LOW	HIGH

Les Paul Cloud 9 Series

2003-2006. Special lightweight Les Paul series run for three dealers, Music Machine, Dave's Guitar Shop, and Wildwood Guitars, '59 Les Paul body specs, CR serial series number, '59 or '60 neck profile options, various colors, other reissue models available.

2003-2006	All models	$3,500	$4,500

Les Paul Collector's Choice Series

2010-2018. Custom Shop models based on Gibson replicas of one-of-a-kind historic guitars.

2010-2018	All models	$5,500	$13,000

Les Paul Dickey Betts Red Top

2003. Transparent red, gold hardware.

2003		$5,000	$6,500

Les Paul Don Felder Hotel California 1959

2010. Custom Shop, '59 sunburst specs, 50 Murphy aged and signed by Felder, 100 aged, and 150 in VOS finish.

2010	Aged, signed	$8,000	$10,500
2010	Aged, unsigned	$7,500	$9,750
2010	VOS	$6,250	$8,250

Les Paul Duane Allman

2013. Custom Shop certificate, Murphy Aged or VOS, 150 made of each.

2013	Aged	$8,750	$11,500
2013	VOS	$6,750	$8,750

Les Paul Duane Allman Hot 'Lanta

2003. "DUANE" spelled out in fret wire on back, Custom Shop certificate, 55 made.

2003		$25,000	$30,000

Les Paul Elegant

1994-2004. Custom Shop, highly flamed maple top, abalone crown markers and Custom Shop headstock inlay.

1994-2004		$4,000	$5,000

Les Paul Eric Clapton 1960

2011. Nicknamed the Beano Burst, '60 thinner 'Clapton' neck profile, Custom Bucker pickups, nickel-plated Grover kidney button tuners, lightly figured maple cap, traditional 17-degree angled headstock, total of 500 made; 55 Murphy Aged and signed by Clapton, 95 unsigned Murphy Aged, 350 finished with Gibson's VOS treatment.

2011	Aged, signed	$22,000	$30,000
2011	Aged, unsigned	$9,250	$12,000
2011	VOS	$6,500	$8,500

Les Paul Gary Moore BFG

2009-2012. Plain appointment BFG specs, P-90 neck pickup and Burstbucker 3 bridge pickup.

2009-2012		$1,500	$2,000

Les Paul Gary Moore Signature

2000-2002. Signature Series model, Gary Moore script logo on truss rod cover, flamed maple top.

2000-2002		$3,000	$4,000

Les Paul Gary Rossington Signature

2002. GR serial number, replica of his '59 LP Standard, Custom Shop, aged finish, 250 made, includes display case with backdrop photo of Rossington, price includes certificate with matching serial number.

2002		$9,250	$12,000

Les Paul Guitar Trader Reissue

1982-1983. Special order flametop Les Paul by the Guitar Trader Company, Redbank, New Jersey. Approximately 47 were built, the first 15 guitars ordered received original PAFs, all were double black bobbins (except 1 Zebra and 1 double white), 3 of the guitars were made in the '60-style. The PAF equipped models were based on order date and not build date. The serial number series started with 9 1001 and a second serial number was put in the control cavity based upon the standard Gibson serial number system, which allowed for exact build date identification. Gibson's pickup designer in the early-'80s was Tim Shaw and the pickups used for the last 32 guitars have been nicknamed Shaw PAFs. After Gibson's short run for Guitar Trader, 10 non-Gibson replica Les Pauls were made. These guitars have a poorly done Gibson logo and other telltale issues.

1982-1983	Actual PAFs installed	$15,000	$20,000
1982-1983	Shaw PAFs, highly flamed	$7,500	$9,750
1982-1983	Shaw PAFs, low flame	$5,750	$7,500

Les Paul Heritage 80

1980-1982. Copy of '59 Les Paul Standard, curly maple top, mahogany body, rosewood 'board, nickel hardware, sunburst. In '80 cataloged as Les Paul Standard-80 without reference to Heritage, the catalog notes that the guitar has Heritage Series truss rod cover.

1980-1982	Figured top	$5,250	$6,750
1980-1982	Plain top	$4,000	$5,000

Les Paul Heritage 80 Award

1982. Ebony 'board, 1-piece mahogany neck, gold-plated hardware, sunburst.

1982	Figured	$6,000	$7,500
1982	Highly figured	$7,500	$9,750

Les Paul Heritage 80 Elite

1980-1982. Copy of '59 Les Paul Standard, quilted maple top, mahogany body and neck, ebony 'board, chrome hardware, sunburst. In '80 cataloged as Les Paul Standard-80 Elite without reference to Heritage, the catalog notes that the guitar has the distinctive Heritage Series truss rod cover.

1980-1982		$5,750	$7,500

Les Paul Heritage 80/Standard 80

1982. Based on '57 Les Paul Standard Goldtop, Heritage Series Standard 80 logo on truss rod cover.

1982		$4,250	$5,500

Les Paul Hot Rod Magazine '58 Standard

2008. Custom Shop, Hot Rod inspired flames over a figured-maple top, Hot Rod truss rod cover.

2008		$4,250	$5,500

Les Paul Jim Beam (Custom Shop)

Ca. 2002-2003. JBLP serial number series, several versions of Jim Beam logo art on top of guitar, award-ribbon-style B Bean logo on headstock, around 75 made.

2002-2003		$2,000	$2,500

The Official Vintage Guitar magazine Price Guide 2025 **Gibson** LP Jimmy Page "Number Two" — LP Music Machine Brazilian Stinger **187**

GUITARS

MODEL YEAR	FEATURES	EXC. COND. LOW	HIGH

Les Paul Jimmy Page "Number Two"
2009-2010. Custom Shop, 1st 25 aged and signed, 100 aged and unsigned, 200 VOS.

2009-2010		$12,500	$16,500

Les Paul Jimmy Page (Custom Authentic)
2004-2006. Custom Shop, includes certificate.

2004-2006		$8,750	$11,500

Les Paul Jimmy Page Signature
1995-1999. Jimmy Page signature on 'guard, mid-grade figured top, push-pull knobs for phasing and coil-tapping, Grover tuners, gold-plated hardware. This is not the '04 Custom Shop Jimmy Page Signature Series Les Paul (see separate listing).

1995	1st year, highly figured	$6,750	$8,750
1995	1st year, low figure	$5,500	$7,250
1995	1st year, moderate figure	$6,000	$7,750
1996-1999	Highly figured	$5,500	$7,250
1996-1999	Low figure	$3,750	$4,750
1996-1999	Moderate figure	$4,750	$6,250

Les Paul Jimmy Page Signature (Custom Shop)
2004. January '04 NAMM Show, 175 planned production, the first 25 were personally inspected, played-in, and autographed by Jimmy Page. Initial retail price for first 25 was $25,000, the remaining 150 instruments had an initial retail price of $16,400. Cosmetically aged by Tom Murphy to resemble Page's No. 1 Les Paul in color fade, weight, top flame, slab cut attribution on the edges, neck size and profile.

2004	1st 25 made	$21,500	$28,000
2004	Next 26-150	$15,500	$20,000

Les Paul Jimmy Wallace Reissue
1978-1997. Les Paul Standard '59 reissue with Jimmy Wallace on truss rod cover, special order by dealer Jimmy Wallace, figured maple top, sunburst.

1978-1982	Kalamazoo, low flame	$4,500	$5,750
1978-1983	Kalamazoo, high flame	$5,250	$6,750
1983-1997	Nashville-made	$4,250	$5,500

Les Paul Joe Bonamassa Bonabyrd
2015-2016. Limited Edition, 100 made each signed by Joe, plain maple top, retro Firebird headstock, Indian rosewood 'board, 2 Custom Bucker pickups, Antique Pelham Blue finish.

2015-2016		$6,250	$8,250

Les Paul Joe Bonamassa Skinnerburst 1959
2014. Custom Shop, recreation of '59 Les Paul, 150 Murphy aged (first 50 signed by Joe) and 150 VOS, faded Dirty Lemon finish.

2014	All options	$10,000	$13,000

Les Paul Joe Bonamassa 'Tomato Soup Burst' Limited Edition
2016. Limited run of 150, AAA flamed maple top, mahogany back and neck, rosewood 'board, Tomato Soup Burst finish.

2016		$4,500	$5,750

Les Paul Joe Perry 1959
2013. Custom Shop, recreation of '59 Les Paul, 150 Murphy aged (first 50 signed by Perry) and 150 VOS, faded Tobacco Sunburst finish.

2013		$13,500	$17,500

Les Paul Joe Perry Signature
1997-2001. Unbound slab body with push-pull knobs and Joe Perry signature below bridge, Bone-Yard logo model with typical Les Paul Standard bound body, configuration and appointments.

1997-2001	Bone-Yard option	$2,000	$2,500
1997-2001	Unbound standard	$2,000	$2,500

Les Paul KM (Kalamazoo Model)
1979. Regular Les Paul Standard with 2 exposed humbuckers, KM on headstock, sunburst, approximately 1500 were made in the Kalamazoo plant.

1979		$3,750	$4,750

Les Paul Korina
1999. Custom Shop logo on back of headstock, limited run with figured Korina top.

1999		$3,750	$4,750

Les Paul Leo's Reissue
1980-1985. Special order from Gibson's Nashville facility for Leo's Music, Oakland, California. Identified by serial number with L at the beginning, flamed maple top. About 800 guitars were made, with about 400 being exported to Japan. Kalamazoo-made Leo's have a 2nd serial number in the control cavity, Nashville-made Leo's do not have a 2nd serial number.

1980-1983	Kalamazoo, high flame	$5,250	$6,750
1980-1983	Kalamazoo, low flame	$4,250	$5,500
1983-1985	Nashville-made	$4,750	$6,250

Les Paul Limited Edition (3-tone)
1997. Limited Edition stamped on the back of the headstock, Les Paul Standard configuration with cloud inlay markers, 2-piece 3-tone sunburst finish over non-figured maple top.

1997		$2,500	$3,250

Les Paul Modern
2017-present. New light-weight features, mahogany body with maple top, back is natural finish, top with faded pelham blue, sparkling burgundy or graphite black.

2017-2023		$3,250	$4,250

Les Paul Music Machine 25th Anniversary
2002. Custom run for dealer Music Machine with special serial number series, 14 flame top and 14 quilt top instruments were produced, Music Machine 25th Anniversary logo on truss rod cover, special cherry sunburst finish.

2002	Flame top	$5,750	$7,500
2002	Quilt top	$5,250	$6,750

Les Paul Music Machine Brazilian Stinger
2003. Custom run for dealer Music Machine with special serial number series, Brazilian rosewood 'board, black stinger paint on back of neck-headstock, '59 or '60 reissue body and neck profile options, highly figured flame or quilt top options, other reissue options available.

2003	'54, '56 or '58, figured flame or quilt	$13,500	$17,500

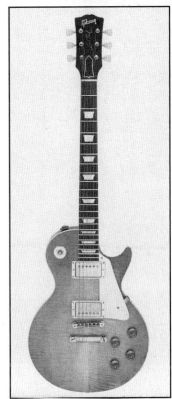

2014 Gibson Les Paul Joe Bonamassa Skinnerburst 1959

Imaged by Heritage Auctions, HA.com

Gibson Les Paul Modern

1983 Gibson Les Paul
Spotlight Special

Gibson Les Paul Standard Faded
Ted Mottor

MODEL YEAR	FEATURES	EXC. COND. LOW	HIGH
2003	'54, '56 or '58, goldtop	$10,000	$13,000
2003	'59 or '60, figured flame or quilt	$14,000	$18,500
2003	'59 or '60, plain top	$12,500	$16,500

Les Paul Music Rising Katrina
2005. Built for U2's Music Rising campaign to raise funds to replace instruments lost to hurricane Katrina. Multi-colored Mardi Gras motif, less than 300 made, no two finishes the same. Wood back plate, pickguard, toggle cover, and truss rod cover. Music Rising logo etched into pickguard.

2005		$2,750	$3,500

Les Paul Neal Schon Signature
2005. Custom Shop, 80 made, Floyd Rose tremolo, signature on truss rod cover, COA, black.

2005		$11,500	$15,000

Les Paul Peace
2014-2015. AA top, rosewood 'board, 2 pickups, various color finishes.

2014-2015		$2,000	$2,500

Les Paul Reissue Flametop
1983-1990. Flame maple top, 2 humbuckers, thicker '59-style neck, sunburst finish, renamed '59 Les Paul Flametop in '91.

1983-1990	Highly figured	$5,750	$7,500

Les Paul SG '61 Reissue
1993-2003. Renamed the Les Paul SG '61 Reissue from SG '62 Reissue, early '60s Les Paul Standard SG specs with small guard, trapezoid markers, heritage cherry finish, by 2003 the Les Paul script marking was not on the truss rod cover, renamed to SG '61 Reissue.

1993-2003	Stud tail	$2,000	$2,500

Les Paul SG Standard Authentic
2005. SG '61 specs, small guard, Les Paul truss rod logo, stud tailpiece.

2005		$2,500	$3,250

Les Paul SG Standard Reissue
2000-2004. Reissue of early-'60s specs including Deluxe Maestro vibrato with lyre tailpiece (stop bar tp offered), small 'guard, holly head veneer, standard color faded cherry, available in Classic White or TV Yellow, becomes the SG Standard Reissue by '05.

2000-2004	Maestro	$2,500	$3,250

Les Paul Signature "T"
2014-2018. Chambered solidbody, 2 exposed split-coil humbuckers, "Les Paul" signature on 'guard, Mini-Etune.

2014-2018		$2,250	$3,000

Les Paul Slash Appetite
2010-2012. Figured maple top, Slash artwork headstock logo, 2 Alnico II Pro Slash pickups, Appetite Amber finish.

2010-2012		$5,500	$7,250

Les Paul Slash Appetite For Destruction
2010-2011. Custom Shop, figured maple top, 2 Duncan Slash pickups, butterscotch finish available as VOS or Aged.

2010-2011	VOS	$10,500	$13,500

MODEL YEAR	FEATURES	EXC. COND. LOW	HIGH

Les Paul Slash Signature
2008. Slash logo on truss rod, Darkburst, SL serial number series.

2008		$3,750	$4,750

Les Paul Slash Signature VOS
2008-2010. Inspired By series, Slash hat logo on body and signature logo on guitar case, plain maple top with faded VOS finish.

2008-2010		$4,500	$5,750

Les Paul Slash Snakepit
1996-1997. Custom Art Historic, highly figured top, cobra inlay neck, snake and hat on body.

1996-1997		$30,000	$40,000

Les Paul Southern Rock Tribute 1959
2014-2018. Limited Edition, commemorative medallion on switch-cavity cover, first 50 aged and signed by Southern Rock Ambassadors (Dickey Betts, Charlie Daniels, Gary Rossington, Jimmy Hall), remainder are VOS, reverse burst finish.

2014-2016	Aged	$6,500	$8,500
2014-2018	VOS	$5,500	$7,250

Les Paul Spider-Man
2002. Custom Shop, superhero depicted on the body, red spider logo, gold hardware, Standard appointments. 15 guitars were produced as a Gibson/Columbia TriStar Home Entertainment/Tower Records promotion, while a larger batch was sold at retail.

2002		$3,750	$4,750

Les Paul Spotlight Special
1983-1984. Curly maple and walnut top, 2 humbuckers, gold hardware, multi-bound top, Custom Shop Edition logo, natural or sunburst.

1983-1984	Figured top	$7,250	$9,500

Les Paul Standard 100
2015. Les Paul 100 on headstock (facsimile of his actual signature) honoring his 100th birthday, Les Paul hologram back of headstock, G-Force tuning, various new colors with high gloss finish.

2015		$2,000	$2,500

Les Paul Standard 2008
August 2008-2012. 2008 added to name, chambered mahogany body, new asymmetrical neck profile, locking grovers, plain or AA flamed maple top, Ebony, Gold Top, various sunbursts.

2008-2012	Figured top	$2,750	$3,500
2008-2012	Gold top	$2,250	$3,000
2008-2012	Plain top	$2,250	$3,000

Les Paul Standard 2010 Limited
2010. Robot tuning technology, 2 pickups, scripted "Limited Edition" logo on headstock, Fireball Sunburst finish.

2010		$2,000	$2,500

Les Paul Standard Billy Gibbons 'Pearly Gates'
2009-2011. Aged - 50 made, Aged and signed - 50 made, V.O.S. - 250 made.

2009-2011	Aged	$11,500	$15,000
2009-2011	VOS	$10,500	$13,500

Les Paul Standard F
2010-2017. Custom Shop, also called LPS-F, 5A flame maple top, 2 Burstbucker pickups, various new

MODEL YEAR	FEATURES	EXC. COND. LOW	HIGH

colors with gloss nitro finish.

| 2010-2017 | | $3,250 | $4,250 |

Les Paul Standard Faded

2005-2008. Figured top, exposed humbuckers, faded satin finish.

| 2005-2008 | | $2,250 | $3,000 |

Les Paul Standard HP

2016-2018. Solidbody, figured maple top, mahogany back and sides, 2 humbucker pickups, G-Force automatic tuners, various colors with gloss nitro finish.

| 2016-2018 | | $2,250 | $3,000 |

Les Paul Standard Lite

1999-2001. DC body-style, renamed from DC Standard in '99, reintroduced as Les Paul Standard DC Plus in 2001, various translucent finishes, available in 2004 under this name also.

| 1999-2001 | | $1,500 | $2,000 |

Les Paul Standard Lite Limited Edition

2014. Thin body LP, Burstbuckers, 3 knobs, coil tap switch, "120th Anniversary" on 12th fret, highly figured flame top or plain top offered.

| 2014 | Plain top | $1,250 | $1,750 |

Les Paul Standard Michael Bloomfield 1959

2009-2011. Custom Shop, limited production of 100 Murphy-aged and 200 VOS, matching certificate of authenticity.

| 2009-2011 | | $8,250 | $10,500 |

Les Paul Standard Mike McCready 1959

2010-2016. Custom Shop, limited to 50 aged and signed, 100 VOS finish.

| 2010-2016 | Aged, signed | $8,250 | $10,500 |
| 2010-2016 | VOS | $7,250 | $9,500 |

Les Paul Standard Music Zoo 25th Anniversary

2019. Custom Shop special run for Music Zoo, styled from '59 LP Standard, figured maple top, mahogany body and neck, Indian rosewood 'board, VOS Orange Drop finish.

| 2019 | | $5,500 | $7,250 |

Les Paul Standard Paul Kossoff 1959

2012-2013. Custom Shop, 100 aged and 250 VOS, green lemon finish, certificate of authenticity.

| 2012-2013 | Aged | $6,250 | $8,250 |
| 2012-2013 | VOS | $5,750 | $7,500 |

Les Paul Standard Plus

1995-2012. Gibson USA model, figured maple top, Vintage Sunburst, Heritage Cherry Sunburst or Honeyburst finish.

| 1995-2012 | | $2,750 | $3,500 |

Les Paul Standard Premium Plus

1999-2007. Premium plus flamed maple top.

| 1999-2007 | | $2,750 | $3,500 |

Les Paul Standard Raw Power

2000-2001, 2006-2007. Natural gloss finish on maple top, appears to have been a Musician's Friend version in '06-'07.

| 2000-2001 | | $2,000 | $2,500 |

Les Paul Standard Rick Nielsen 1959

2016-2017. Custom Shop, first 50 aged and signed, figured maple top, mahogany back and neck, Indian

rosewood 'board, aged or vintage gloss finish.

| 2016-2017 | Signed | $8,750 | $11,500 |
| 2016-2017 | Unsigned | $6,500 | $8,500 |

Les Paul Standard Robot

2007. Blueburst finish, robot tuning.

| 2007 | | $1,250 | $1,750 |

Les Paul Standard RSM 1959 / RSM '59 Les Paul Standard

2018 and 2020. Custom Shop special run for Rumble Seat Music, recreation of the original 1959 LP Standard, limited run of 6 each year, highly flamed top, Brazilian rosewood 'board.

| 2018 | | $16,000 | $28,000 |
| 2020 | | $15,000 | $20,000 |

Les Paul Standard Showcase Edition

1988. Showcase Edition logo on back of neck, Guitar of the Month, silverburst.

| 1988 | | $4,500 | $5,750 |

Les Paul Standard Sparkle

2001. Sparkle holoflake top, reflective back, Standard logo on truss rod.

| 2001 | | $2,750 | $3,500 |

Les Paul Strings and Things Standard

1975-1978. Special order flamed maple top Les Paul Standard model, built for Chris Lovell, owner of Strings and Things, a Gibson dealer in Memphis, approximately 28 were built, sunburst. Authentication of a Strings and Things Les Paul is difficult due to no diffinitive attributes, valuation should be on a case-by-case basis.

1975-1978	Figured 2-piece top	$9,000	$11,500
1975-1978	Plain 2-piece top	$7,250	$9,000
1975-1978	Plain 3-piece top	$4,750	$6,250

Les Paul Tie Dye (St. Pierre)

1996-1997. Hand colored by George St. Pierre, just over 100 made.

| 1996-1997 | | $2,750 | $3,500 |

Les Paul Tie Dye Custom Shop

2002. Limited series of one-off colorful finishes, Custom Shop logo.

| 2002 | | $2,750 | $3,500 |

Les Paul Traditional Pro/Pro II

2010-2014. Exposed tapped coil humbuckers, sunbursts, goldtop, ebony or wine red.

| 2010-2014 | Various colors | $1,750 | $2,250 |

Les Paul Traditional/Plus

2008-2019. Traditional on truss rod, '80s styling with weight-relief holes in an unchambered body, standard appointments. Figured maple (Plus) or opaque color top.

2008-2014	Opaque	$2,000	$2,500
2008-2019	Plain sunburst	$2,000	$2,500
2008-2019	Plus, figured maple	$2,250	$3,000

Les Paul Ultima

1996-2007. Custom Shop, flame or quilt sunburst, abalone and mother-of-pearl tree of life, harp, or flame fingerboard inlay, multi abalone bound body.

| 1996-2007 | | $6,500 | $8,500 |

Les Paul Ultra-Aged

2011-2012. Custom Shop, '59 specs, Bigsby optional, aged by Tom Murphy.

| 2011-2012 | | $5,500 | $7,250 |

2011 Gibson Les Paul Standard Plus
Rivington Guitars

2017 Gibson Les Paul Traditional
Cream City Music

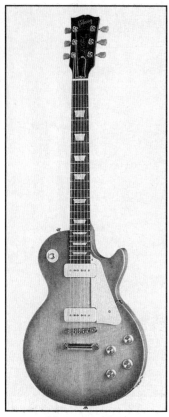

Gibson Les Paul
Studio '60s Tribute

2003 Gibson Les
Paul Studio Plus

MODEL YEAR	FEATURES	EXC. COND. LOW	HIGH

Les Paul Warren Haynes
2007. Custom Shop, Inspired by Artist series.

| 2007 | | $3,250 | $4,250 |

Les Paul Zebra Wood
2007. Zebrawood top, mahogany back and neck, rosewood 'board, 2 '57 Classic pickups, natural satin zebrawood finish.

| 2007 | | $2,250 | $3,000 |

Les Paul Studio
Following are Les Paul Studio models listed alphabetically.

Les Paul Studio
1983-present. Unbound mahogany body, (early models have alder body), 2 humbuckers, various colors.

1983-2009		$1,500	$2,000
2009-2012	Silverburst	$1,250	$1,625
2010-2019		$1,125	$1,500
2020-2023		$1,000	$1,375

Les Paul Studio 120th Anniversary
2014. Figured maple top, 120th Anniversary badge on 12th fret, vintage gloss finish on various colors.

| 2014 | | $1,250 | $1,750 |

Les Paul Studio '50s Tribute
2010-2016. '56 LP Goldtop specs, P-90s, '50s neck, Tune-o-matic, stopbar tailpiece, chambered unbound body.

| 2010-2016 | | $850 | $1,125 |

Les Paul Studio '60s Tribute
2011-2016. Similar to '50s Tribute except for '60 slim taper neck.

| 2011-2016 | | $850 | $1,125 |

Les Paul Studio '70s Tribute
2012-2016. Similar to '50s Tribute except for '70s neck profile with volute.

| 2012-2016 | | $850 | $1,125 |

Les Paul Studio Baritone
2004-2012. 28" baritone scale, maple top, mahogany back and neck, 2 pickups, nitro gloss honeyburst finish.

| 2004-2012 | | $1,500 | $2,000 |

Les Paul Studio BFD
2007. Studio specs but with BFD electronics.

| 2007 | | $775 | $1,000 |

Les Paul Studio Custom
1981-1985. 2 humbucking pickups, multi-bound top, gold-plated hardware, various colors.

| 1981-1985 | | $1,500 | $2,000 |

Les Paul Studio Deluxe '60s
2010-2012. Exposed pickups, Deluxe logo on truss rod cover, sunburst.

| 2010-2012 | | $1,250 | $1,625 |

Les Paul Studio Deluxe II
2008-2013. Carved flame maple top, mahogany back, 2 pickups, various colors.

| 2008-2013 | | $1,250 | $1,625 |

Les Paul Studio Faded Vintage Mahogany
2007-2010. Vintage mahogany with faded satin.

| 2007-2010 | | $825 | $1,125 |

Les Paul Studio Faded/Pro Faded
2005-2012. Faded sunburst tops. Name changes to Studio Pro Faded in '12, then ends production.

| 2005-2012 | | $825 | $1,125 |

MODEL YEAR	FEATURES	EXC. COND. LOW	HIGH

Les Paul Studio Gem
1996-1998. Limited edition with Les Paul Studio features, but using P-90 pickups instead of humbucker pickups, plus trapezoid markers and gold hardware.

| 1996-1998 | | $1,250 | $1,625 |

Les Paul Studio Gothic
2000-2001. Orville Gibson image on back of headstock, single Gibson crescent and star neck marker, Gothic Black with black hardware.

| 2000-2001 | | $950 | $1,250 |

Les Paul Studio Gothic Morte
2011-2012. All-mahogany body, African Obeche 'board, 2 humbuckers, satin ebony finish.

| 2011-2012 | | $950 | $1,250 |

Les Paul Studio Joe Bonamassa
2011-2013. Maple top, mahogany back and neck, 2 Alnico II pickups, goldtop finish.

| 2011-2013 | | $1,750 | $2,250 |

Les Paul Studio Limited Edition
1997. P-100 pickups, black.

| 1997 | | $950 | $1,250 |

Les Paul Studio Lite
1987-1998. Carved maple top, mahogany back and neck, 2 humbucker pickups, various colors.

| 1987-1998 | | $1,250 | $1,625 |

Les Paul Studio Lite Mark III/M3/M III
1991-1994. HSH pickup configuration, trans finishes.

| 1991-1994 | | $1,250 | $1,625 |

Les Paul Studio MLB Baseball
2008. Major League Baseball graphics on body, only 30 made, satin finish, dot markers.

| 2008 | | $1,750 | $2,250 |

Les Paul Studio Platinum
2004-2006. 2 Humbuckers, no position markers, brushed metal hardware, body, neck and headstock in satin platinum finish, matching platinum hardshell case.

| 2004-2006 | | $1,250 | $1,750 |

Les Paul Studio Platinum Plus
2004-2006. Same as Platinum but with trapezoid markers and black hardshell case.

| 2004-2006 | | $1,250 | $1,750 |

Les Paul Studio Plus
2002-2007. Two-piece AA flamed unbound top, gold hardware, Desert Burst or see-thru black.

| 2002-2007 | | $1,250 | $1,750 |

Les Paul Studio Premium Plus
2006-2008. AAA flamed-maple top.

| 2006-2008 | | $1,750 | $2,250 |

Les Paul Studio Raw Power
2009-2012. Unbound maple top, chambered maple body, 2 humbuckers, dots, satin finishes.

| 2009-2012 | | $1,250 | $1,750 |

Les Paul Studio Robot
2007-2011. Robot tuning, trapezoid inlays, silverburst, fireburst, wine red, black, red metallic, green metallic.

| 2007-2011 | All colors | $975 | $1,250 |

Les Paul Studio Robot Limited Edition
2012. 'Chameleon' tone circuit.

| 2012 | | $1,000 | $1,375 |

MODEL YEAR	FEATURES	EXC. COND. LOW	HIGH

Les Paul Studio Roland Synthesizer
1985. With Roland 700 synth.

1985		$1,000	$1,375

Les Paul Studio Shred
2012. Unbound body, trapazoid markers, 2 humbuckers. Floyd Rose, high-gloss ebony nitro finish.

2012		$1,250	$1,625

Les Paul Studio Special
2001. Solidbody, single-cut, 2 pickups, various colors.

2001-2020		$1,250	$1,625

Les Paul Studio Special Limited Edition
2019-2020. Limited Edition, nitro finish in Lemon Burst or Desert Burst.

2019-2020		$1,000	$1,375

Les Paul Studio Standard
1984-1987. Cream top and neck binding, dots.

1984-1987		$1,750	$2,250

Les Paul Studio Swamp Ash
2004-2012. Studio model with swamp ash body.

2004-2012		$1,250	$1,750

Les Paul Studio USA Anniversary Flood
2011. Commemorating the Nashville flood of May, 2010, blue or green swirl.

2011		$1,250	$1,750

Les Paul Supreme
2003-2018. Highly figured AAAA maple top and back on translucent finishes only, custom binding, deluxe pearl markers, chambered mahogany body, globe logo or "Supreme" on headstock, solid colors available by '06.

2003-2018	Various tops & colors	$3,500	$4,500

Les Paul Vixen
2006-2007. Les Paul Special single-cut slab body, dot markers, 2 humbuckers, 2 controls, wrap-around bridge.

2006-2007	Various colors	$1,250	$1,625

Les Paul Voodoo/Voodoo Les Paul
2004-2005. Single-cut, swamp ash body, 2 exposed humbuckers, black satin finish.

2004-2005		$1,750	$2,250

Les Paul XR-I / II / III
1981-1983. No frills model with Dirty Finger pickups, dot markers, Les Paul stencil logo on headstock, goldburst, silverburst and cherryburst finishes.

1981-1983	All models	$1,625	$2,000

The Les Paul
1976-1979. Figured maple top, 2 humbuckers, gold hardware, rosewood binding, 'guard, 'board, knobs, cover plates, etc., natural or rosewood finishing, natural only by '79.

1976-1979	Natural or rosewood	$11,500	$15,000

The Paul
1978-1982. Offered as The Paul Standard with solid walnut body and The Paul Deluxe with solid mahogany body, 2 exposed humbuckers.

1978-1982	Walnut or mahogany	$1,250	$1,750

The Paul Firebrand Deluxe
1980-1982. Single-cut mahogany solidbody, Gibson branded in headstock, 2 exposed humbuckers, black, Pelham Blue or rough natural finish.

1980-1982	All colors	$1,500	$2,000

The Paul II
1996-1998. Mahogany body, 2 humbucking pickups, rosewood dot neck, renamed The Paul SL in '98.

1996-1998		$775	$1,000

LG-0
1958-1974. Flat-top acoustic, mahogany, bound body, rosewood bridge '58-'61 and '68-'74, plastic bridge '62-'67, natural.

1958-1961	Rosewood bridge	$1,500	$1,875
1962-1964	Plastic bridge	$1,250	$1,500
1965	Plastic bridge	$1,125	$1,500
1966	Plastic bridge	$950	$1,125
1967-1969	Rosewood bridge	$950	$1,125
1970-1974		$850	$1,000

LG-1
1943-1968. Flat-top acoustic, spruce top, mahogany back and sides, bound body, rosewood bridge '43-'61, plastic bridge after, examples seen to '74, sunburst.

1943-1945		$3,500	$4,500
1946-1949		$3,500	$4,500
1950-1959	Rosewood bridge	$3,000	$4,000
1960-1961	Rosewood bridge	$2,500	$3,500
1962-1964	Plastic bridge	$2,250	$3,000
1965		$2,000	$2,500
1966-1968		$2,000	$2,500

LG-2
1942-1962. Flat-top acoustic, spruce top, mahogany back and sides (some with maple '43-'46), banner headstock '42-'46, bound body, X-bracing, sunburst finish, replaced by B-25 in '62.

1942-1945	Banner, mahogany	$5,000	$6,500
1942-1945	Banner, spruce	$6,500	$8,500
1946-1949	Sitka	$5,500	$7,500
1950-1959		$5,000	$6,500
1960-1961	Rosewood bridge	$3,500	$4,500
1962	Adjustable bridge	$3,500	$4,500

LG-2 3/4
1949-1962. Short-scale version of LG-2 flat-top, wood bridge, sunburst.

1949	Rosewood bridge	$3,000	$4,000
1950-1959	Rosewood bridge	$2,875	$3,750
1960-1961	Rosewood bridge	$2,500	$3,500
1962	Adjustable bridge	$2,500	$3,500

LG-2 3/4 Arlo Guthrie
2003, 2005-2018. Vintage replica finish.

2003-2018		$1,750	$2,250

LG-2 American Eagle
2013-2018. Sitka top, mahogany back and sides, L.R. Baggs.

2013-2018		$1,500	$2,000

LG-2 Banner
2013. All mahogany, only 50 made.

2013		$2,000	$2,500

1964 Gibson LG-1
Johnny Zapp

1946 Gibson LG-2
David Stone

1983 Gibson Map Guitar
James Seldin

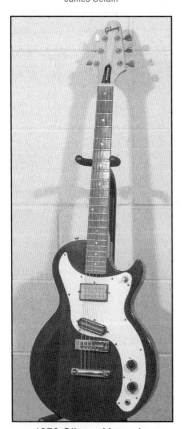

1976 Gibson Marauder
Tom Pfeifer

MODEL YEAR	FEATURES	EXC. COND. LOW	HIGH
LG-2 H			
1945-1955. Flat-top, Hawaiian, natural or sunburst.			
1944-1945		$5,000	$6,500
1946-1949		$4,000	$5,000
1950-1955		$3,500	$4,500
LG-3			
1942-1964. Flat-top acoustic, spruce top, mahogany back and sides, bound body, natural finish, replaced by B-25 N.			
1942-1945	Banner	$6,500	$8,500
1946-1949		$6,000	$7,500
1950-1959		$4,500	$5,500
1960-1961	Last wood bridge	$4,000	$5,000
1962-1964	Plastic bridge	$3,750	$4,750
Longhorn Double Cutaway			
2008. Guitar of the Month for July '08, AA figured maple top, 2 active pickups, piezo pickup, sunburst or transparent finishes.			
2008		$1,750	$2,250
M III Series			
1991-1996, 2013-2018. Double-cut solidbody with extra long bass horn, six-on-a-side tuners on a reverse pointy headstock, dot markers, reverse Gibson decal logo. Reissued in '13 with natural finish on 'board and choice of Cosmic Cobalt, Electric Lime, Vibrant Red, or Orange Glow.			
1991-1992	Deluxe	$1,625	$2,125
1991-1996	Standard	$1,625	$2,125
2013-2018	Reissue	$1,125	$1,500
M IV Series			
1993-1995. M III with Steinberger vibrato.			
1993-1995	S Deluxe	$1,500	$2,000
1993-1995	S Standard	$1,375	$1,750
Mach II			
1990-1991. Renamed from U-2, offset double-cut, 2 single coils and 1 humbucking pickup.			
1990-1991		$1,000	$1,375
Map Guitar			
1983, 1985. Body cutout like lower 48, 2 humbuckers, limited run promotion, '83 version in natural mahogany or red, white and blue, '85 version red, white and blue stars and stripes on a white background. This model can often be found in better than excellent condition because the instrument is as much a show piece as it is a player guitar, and the price range reflects that.			
1983	Natural	$4,500	$5,500
1983	Red, white & blue	$5,000	$6,500
Marauder			
1975-1980. Single-cut solidbody, pointed headstock, 2 pickups, bolt-on neck, various colors.			
1975-1980		$1,250	$1,750
Marauder Custom			
1976-1977. Marauder with 3-way selector switch, bound 'board, block markers, bolt-on neck, Marauder logo on truss rod cover, sunburst.			
1976-1977		$1,750	$2,250
Melody Maker			
1959-1971, 1986-1993. Slab solidbody, 1 pickup, single-cut until '61, double '61-'66, SG body '66-'71, reintroduced as single-cut in '86-'93. A single-cut Les Paul Melody Maker was offered from '03-'06.			

MODEL YEAR	FEATURES	EXC. COND. LOW	HIGH
1959-1961	Sunburst, single-cut	$2,250	$3,000
1962-1964	Sunburst, cherry, double-cut	$1,875	$2,500
1965-1966	Cherry, double cut	$1,750	$2,250
1966-1971	Various colors, SG body	$2,250	$2,750
1986-1993	Reintroduced as single-cut	$900	$1,250
Melody Maker 3/4			
1959-1963. Short-scale version.			
1959-1963		$1,875	$2,500
Melody Maker D			
1960-1970. Two pickup version of Melody Maker, reintroduced as Melody Maker Double in '77.			
1960-1961	Sunburst, single-cut	$2,875	$3,750
1961-1964	Sunburst, cherry, double-cut	$2,625	$3,250
1965-1966	Sunburst, cherry, double-cut	$2,125	$2,750
1966-1970	Various colors, SG body	$2,250	$2,750
Melody Maker Double			
1977-1983. Reintroduction of Melody Maker D, double-cut solidbody, 2 pickups, cherry or sunburst.			
1977-1983	Bolt-on	$1,125	$1,500
1977-1983	Set-neck	$1,250	$1,750
Melody Maker III			
1967-1971. SG-style double-cut solidbody, 3 pickups, various colors.			
1967-1971		$2,625	$3,500
Melody Maker 12			
1967-1971. SG-style solidbody, 12 strings, 2 pickups, red, white or Pelham Blue.			
1967-1971		$2,375	$3,000
Melody Maker Faded			
2003. Les Paul Jr. styling, single-cut, 1 P-90 style pickup, Nashville tune-o-matic bridge, black satin finish.			
2003		$500	$650
Les Paul Melody Maker			
2003-2008. Slab single-cut solidbody, one P-90, tune-o-matic bridge, dot markers, 2 knobs. Revised in '07 with 1 single-coil (2 also offered), wrap around tailpiece, 1 knob, pickguard mounted jack.			
2003-2006	1 pickup	$550	$750
2007-2008	1 pickup, revised specs	$550	$750
2007-2008	2 pickup option	$550	$750
Les Paul Melody Maker 120th Anniversary			
2014. Custom Shop, 120th Anniversary neck inlay, maple top, mahogany back, Charcoal, TV Yellow, Wine Red or Manhattan Midnight, all with satin finish.			
2014		$900	$1,125
Melody Maker Joan Jett Signature			
2008-2012. Double-cut, worn-white (til '11), 1 Burstbucker 3. Blackheart version in black with red dots starts '10.			
2008-2012		$1,250	$1,625
Midnight Special			
1974-1975. L-6S body style, maple 'board, dot markers, 2 humbucker pickups, custom colors.			
1974-1975		$1,625	$2,125

MODEL YEAR	FEATURES	EXC. COND. LOW	HIGH

Midtown Custom
2012-2014. 335-style semi-hollow, 2 humbuckers, block markers.

| 2012-2014 | | $1,750 | $2,250 |

Midtown Kalamazoo
2013-2015. Limited run of 600, maple top, mahogany back and sides, 2 pickups, 165-style tailpiece, Vintage Sunburst.

| 2013-2015 | | $1,500 | $2,000 |

Midtown Standard P-90
2011-2014. Like Midtown Custom but with P-90s.

| 2011-2014 | | $1,500 | $2,000 |

MK-35
1975-1978. Mark Series flat-top acoustic, mahogany back and sides, black-bound body, natural or sunburst, 5226 made.

| 1975-1978 | | $950 | $1,250 |

MK-53
1975-1978. Mark Series flat-top acoustic, maple back and sides, multi-bound body, natural or sunburst, 1424 made.

| 1975-1978 | | $1,000 | $1,375 |

MK-72
1975-1978. Mark Series flat-top acoustic, rosewood back and sides, black-bound body, chrome tuners, natural or sunburst, 1229 made.

| 1975-1978 | | $1,125 | $1,500 |

MK-81
1975-1978. Mark Series flat-top acoustic, rosewood back and sides, multi-bound body, gold tuners, high-end appointments, natural or sunburst, 431 made.

| 1975-1978 | | $1,500 | $2,000 |

Moderne
2012. Limited run, mahogany body and neck, dual '57 Classic humbuckers, trans amber or ebony finish.

| 2012 | | $2,250 | $3,000 |

Moderne Heritage
1981-1983. Limited edition, korina body, 2 humbucking pickups, gold hardware, natural, black or white.

| 1981-1983 | Black or white | $8,000 | $11,000 |
| 1981-1983 | Natural | $10,000 | $15,000 |

Nick Lucas / Gibson Special
1926-1941. Though they were shipped into '41, the last year of production was '37. Mahogany 13 ½" L-1 body ('26-'29), 14 ¾" L-00 body ('30-'41), parallel bracing '26-'27, X-braced '28-'41, 12 frets early (13 and 14 later), banjo tuners early (guitar style later), black (rare) or sunburst finish. Reintroduced in '91.

| 1926-1941 | Various specs | $25,000 | $60,000 |

Nick Lucas Reissue Limited Edition
1991-1992. 100 made, label signed by Ren Ferguson.

| 1991-1992 | | $2,500 | $3,250 |

Nick Lucas Tenor
1928-1938. 14 3/4", 12-fret, early models have mahogany, later maple, The Gibson headstock logo.

| 1928-1930 | Mahogany | $7,500 | $10,000 |
| 1931-1938 | Maple | $7,500 | $10,000 |

Nick Lucas Elite
1999-2002. Ebony 'board, abalone inlay and inlays.

| 1999-2002 | | $3,500 | $4,500 |
| 2001 | Elite Custom | $3,500 | $4,500 |

Nick Lucas Grande
2015-2016. Limited Edition of 50, Sitka spruce top, English walnut back and sides, COA, Honeyburst finish.

| 2015-2016 | | $3,250 | $4,250 |

Nick Lucas Koa Elite
2015. Limited to 50, Adirondack and koa, COA.

| 2015 | | $3,250 | $4,250 |

Nick Lucas Supreme
2015. Limited to 40, Adirondack red spruce top, AAA flame koa back and sides, abalone trim, certificate of authenticity, Honeyburst finish.

| 2015 | | $3,500 | $4,500 |

Nighthawk 2009 Limited
2009. Limited series, AAA figured maple top, mahogany body, Translucent Amber finish.

| 2009 | | $1,625 | $2,125 |

Nighthawk Custom
1993-1998. Flame maple top, ebony 'board, gold hardware, fireburst, single/double/mini pickups.

| 1993-1998 | | $1,750 | $2,500 |

Nighthawk Special
1993-1998. Single-cut solidbody, figured maple top, double-coil and mini-pickup or with additional single-coil options, dot marker inlay, cherry, ebony or sunburst.

| 1993-1998 | | $1,500 | $2,000 |

Nighthawk Standard
1993-1998. Single-cut solidbody, figured maple top, 2 or 3 pickups, double-parallelogram inlay, amber, fireburst or sunburst.

| 1993-1998 | | $1,625 | $2,125 |

Nighthawk Standard 2010 Limited
2010-2012. Limited Run series, AAA quilted maple top, chambered poplar body, 3 pickups, Memphis Mojo, St. Louis Sauce or Chicago Blue finishes.

| 2010-2012 | | $1,625 | $2,125 |

Nighthawk Studio
2011-2012. AAA quilted maple top, dots.

| 2011-2012 | | $900 | $1,250 |

Nouveau NV6T-M
1986-1987. Hybrid USA/Japan, a line of Gibson flat-tops with imported parts assembled and finished in the U.S., acoustic dreadnought, bound maple body, natural.

| 1986-1987 | | $525 | $700 |

NR-336F
2012. Custom Shop, 25 made, double-cut, non-reverse (NR) Firebird headstock, flamed maple top, rosewood 'board, antique sunburst top, cherry back.

| 2012 | | $3,000 | $4,000 |

OP-25
1991-1992. Acoustic-electric, limited production run, synthetic back.

| 1991-1992 | | $800 | $1,125 |

Original Jumbo (Custom Shop)
2003. 16" jumbo body, Adirondack top, mahogany sides and back, butterbean tuner buttons, deep sunburst finish on complete body, Custom Art Historic.

| 2003 | | $3,000 | $4,000 |

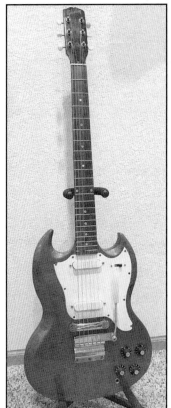
1967 Gibson Melody Maker D
Tim McClutchy

1936 Gibson Nick Lucas
M. Mattingly

1972 Gibson SG II
Rivington Guitars

2006 Gibson SG '61 Reissue

MODEL YEAR	FEATURES	EXC. COND. LOW	HIGH

Pat Martino Custom/Signature
1999-2006. Sharp single-cut thinline, f-holes, 2 humbuckers, flamed cherry sunburst maple top, small snakehead style headstock, Pat Martino logo on truss rod cover.

| 1999-2006 | | $3,000 | $4,000 |

PG-00
1932-1937. Plectrum neck, flat-top.

| 1932-1937 | | $2,000 | $2,500 |

PG-1
1928-1938. Plectrum neck, flat-top.

| 1929 | | $2,000 | $2,500 |

PG-175
1950. Acoustic/electric with ES-175 bobdy and 4-string plectrum neck, bow-tie markers, sunburst.

| 1950 | | $3,750 | $4,750 |

Q-100
1985-1986. Offset double-cut solidbody, Kahler trem, 6-on-a-side tuners, 1 humbucker, black hardware.

| 1985-1986 | | $1,000 | $1,375 |

Q-200/Q2000
1985-1986. Like Q-100, but with 1 single and 1 hum, black or chrome hardware. Name changed to 2000 late '85.

| 1985-1986 | | $1,125 | $1,500 |

Q-300/Q3000
1985-1986. Like Q-100, but with 3 single-coils, black or chrome hardware. Name changed to 3000 late '85.

| 1985-1986 | | $1,250 | $1,625 |

Q-3000 Custom Shop
1985. Limited Custom production, 3 single-coil pickups.

| 1985 | | $1,750 | $2,250 |

Q-4000/Q400
Late-1985-1987. Limited custom production, like Q-100, but with 2 singles and 1 hum, black hardware, Name changed to 400 late '85. Ferrari Red or Pink Panther finish as 4000, ebony as 400.

| 1985-1987 | | $1,750 | $2,250 |

RD Artist CMT
1981. Figured top.

| 1981 | | $3,250 | $4,250 |

RD Artist/77
1980. The 77 model has a 25.5" scale versus 24.75".

| 1980 | | $2,500 | $3,250 |

RD Artist/79
1978-1982. Double-cut solidbody, 2 humbuckers, TP-6 tailpiece, active electronics, ebony 'board, block inlays, gold-plated parts, various colors, called just RD (no Artist) in '81 and '82.

| 1978-1982 | | $3,000 | $3,750 |

RD Custom
1977-1979. Double-cut solidbody, 2 humbuckers, stop tailpiece, active electronics, dot inlays, maple 'board, chrome parts, natural or walnut.

| 1977-1979 | | $2,500 | $3,250 |

RD Standard
1977-1979. Double-cut solidbody, 2 humbuckers, stop tailpiece, rosewood 'board, dot inlays, chrome parts, natural, sunburst or walnut.

| 1977-1979 | | $2,500 | $3,250 |

MODEL YEAR	FEATURES	EXC. COND. LOW	HIGH

RD Standard Reissue
2007, 2009, 2011. 400 Silverburst made in '07. Black or Trans Amber Red versions offered as limited run in '09 in Japan and in U.S. in '11.

| 2007-2011 | Various colors | $2,000 | $2,500 |

Roy Smeck Radio Grande Hawaiian
1934-1939. Dreadnought acoustic flat-top, rosewood back and sides, bound body and neck, natural.

| 1934-1939 | Brazilian, Spanish converted | $20,000 | $25,000 |
| 1934-1939 | Brazilian, unconverted | $15,000 | $20,000 |

Roy Smeck Radio Grande Hawaiian Limited
1994. Centennial Guitar of the Month in '94, 100 made, Indian rosewood.

| 1994 | | $2,500 | $3,250 |

Roy Smeck Radio Grande Hawaiian Reissue
1996. Part of SmartWood Series, Grenadillo back and sides.

| 1996 | | $2,500 | $3,250 |

Roy Smeck Stage Deluxe Hawaiian
1934-1942. Dreadnought acoustic flat-top, mahogany back and sides, bound body, natural.

| 1934-1942 | Spanish converted | $11,000 | $14,000 |
| 1934-1942 | Unconverted | $8,000 | $10,000 |

S-1
1976-1980. Single-cut solidbody, pointed headstock, 3 single-coil pickups, similar to the Marauder, various colors.

| 1976-1980 | | $1,750 | $2,250 |

SG
Following are models, listed alphabetically, bearing the SG name.

SG I
1972-1978. Double-cut, mahogany body, 1 mini-humbucker (some with SG Jr. P-90), wraparound bridge/tailpiece, cherry or walnut.

| 1972-1978 | | $1,250 | $1,500 |

SG II
1972-1979. SG I with 2 mini-humbuckers (some in '75 had regular humbuckers), 2 slide switches, cherry or walnut.

| 1972-1979 | | $1,500 | $2,000 |

SG III
1972-1977. SG II with sunburst and tune-o-matic.

| 1972-1977 | | $1,375 | $1,750 |

SG-3
2007-2008. SG styling, SG Standard appointments, 3 gold humbuckers or 3 single coils, 1 rotor switch, 2 knobs, stop tail.

| 2007-2008 | 3 humbuckers | $1,125 | $1,500 |
| 2007-2008 | 3 single coils | $1,000 | $1,375 |

SG '61 Reissue
2003-2015. Renamed from Les Paul SG '61 Reissue, no Les Paul script on truss rod, small 'guard, stop bar tailpiece (no Deluxe Maestro vibrato), '60 slim-taper neck profile.

| 2003-2015 | | $1,750 | $2,250 |

MODEL YEAR	FEATURES	EXC. COND. LOW	HIGH

SG '62 Reissue/SG Reissue
1986-1991. Trapezoid markers, stop bar, 2 humbuckers, called SG Reissue '86-'87, SG '62 Reissue '88-'91. Reintroduced as Les Paul SG '61 Reissue for '93-'03 and SG '61 Reissue '03-present, cherry.

1986-1991		$1,750	$2,250

SG '62 Reissue Showcase Edition
1988. Guitar of the Month, bright blue opaque finish, 200 made.

1988		$1,750	$2,250

Les Paul '63 Corvette Sting Ray
1995-1997. Custom Shop SG-style body carved to simulate split rear window on '63 Corvette, Sting Ray inlay, 150 made, offered in black, white, silver or red.

1995-1997		$5,500	$7,000

SG-90 Double
1988-1990. SG body, updated electronics, graphite reinforced neck, 2 pickups, cherry, turquoise or white.

1988-1990		$925	$1,250

SG-90 Single
1988-1990. SG body, updated electronics, graphite reinforced neck, 1 humbucker pickup, cherry, turquoise or white.

1988-1990		$850	$1,125

SG-100
1971-1972. Double-cut solidbody, 1 pickup, cherry or walnut.

1971-1972	Melody Maker pu	$1,250	$1,750
1971-1972	P-90 pu option	$1,250	$1,750
1971-1972	Sam Ash model	$1,250	$1,750

SG-200
1971-1972. Two pickup version of SG-100 in black, cherry or walnut finish, replaced by SG II.

1971-1972	2 Melody Makers	$1,500	$2,000

SG-250
1971-1972. Two-pickup version of SG-100 in cherry sunburst, replaced by SG III.

1971-1972	2 Melody Makers	$1,250	$1,500

SG-400/SG Special 400
1985-1987. SG body with 3 toggles, 2 knobs (master volume, master tone), single-single-humbucker pickups, available with uncommon opaque finishes.

1985-1987		$1,250	$1,500

SG Angus Young
2010-2016. Like Angus Signature but with small guard, stop tailpiece and tune-o-matic, Aged Cherry.

2010-2016		$2,000	$2,500

SG Angus Young Signature
2000-2009. Late-'60s Std specs with large 'guard, Deluxe Maestro lyre vibrato with Angus logo, aged cherry finish.

2000-2009		$2,000	$2,500

SG Baritone
2013-2016. Longer 27" scale, 2 exposed humbuckers, ebony 'board, Alpine White finish.

2013-2016		$1,500	$2,000

SG Carved Top - Autumn Burst
2009. Limited run of 350, highly flamed carved maple top, rosewood 'board, certificate of authenticity.

2009		$2,000	$2,500

SG Classic/SG Classic Faded
1999-2001, 2003-2013. Late '60s SG Special style, Classic on truss rod cover, large 'guard, black soap-bar single-coil P-90s, dot markers, stop bar tailpiece, cherry or ebony stain.

1999-2013		$1,000	$1,375

SG Custom
1963-1980. Renamed from Les Paul Custom, 3 humbuckers, vibrato, made with Les Paul Custom plate from '61-'63 (see Les Paul Custom), white finish until '68, walnut and others after.

1963-1964	White, pat #, Maestro	$25,000	$30,000
1965	Early '65, white, large neck	$16,500	$20,000
1965	Late '65, white, small neck	$15,500	$19,500
1966-1968	White, large 'guard	$11,500	$14,500
1969	Walnut, lyre, 1-piece neck	$7,125	$9,000
1969	Walnut, lyre, 3-piece neck	$5,250	$6,500
1969	White, lyre, 1 piece neck	$7,125	$9,000
1969	White, lyre, 3 piece neck	$5,750	$7,125
1970	Walnut, lyre	$4,500	$5,750
1970	White, lyre	$4,500	$5,750
1970-1973	Walnut, Bigsby	$3,500	$4,500
1970-1973	White option, Bigsby	$4,500	$5,750
1974-1975	Brown, dark cherry	$3,125	$4,000
1974-1975	White option	$3,750	$4,750
1976-1979	Brown, dark cherry	$2,750	$3,500
1976-1979	White option	$3,500	$4,500
1980	Various colors	$2,500	$3,250

SG Custom '67 Reissue/
Les Paul SG '67 Custom
1991-1993. The SG Custom '67 Reissue has a wine red finish, the Les Paul SG '67 Custom ('92-'93) has a wine red or white finish.

1991-1993		$2,750	$3,500

SG Custom Elliot Easton Signature
2006-2007. Custom Shop, SG Custom specs, Maestro deluxe vibrola, Pelham Blue or white, includes Certificate of Authenticity.

2006-2007		$3,500	$4,500

SG Deluxe
1971-1972, 1981-1985, 1998-1999, 2013-2018. The '70s models were offered in cherry, natural or walnut finishes, reintroduced in '98 with 3 Firebird mini-humbucker-style pickups in black, red or Ice Blue finishes, in 2013 with 3 '57 Classic humbuckers in Cobalt Fade, Lime Burst, Orange Burst or Red Fade.

1971-1972	Cherry	$2,250	$2,875
1971-1972	Natural, walnut	$2,250	$2,875
1981-1985	Various colors	$2,000	$2,500
1998-1999	Various colors	$1,500	$1,875
2013-2018	New specs, all colors	$2,000	$2,500

1971 Gibson SG-200
Imaged by Heritage Auctions, HA.com

1972 Gibson SG Custom
Tom Allen

2014 Gibson SG
Government Series

2012 Gibson SG Jeff
Tweedy Signature

Matt Carleson

MODEL YEAR	FEATURES	EXC. COND. LOW	HIGH

SG Diablo
2008. Guitar of the Month for Dec. '08, 1,000 made, '61 specs, metallic silver finish with matching headstock, 1 volume, 1 tone knob, 3-way toggle, 24 frets.

2008		$1,500	$2,000

SG Diablo Premium Plus
2012-2013. AAA maple top.

2012-2013		$1,500	$2,000

SG Diablo Tremolo
2012-2013. Diablo with Floyd Rose.

2012-2013		$1,500	$2,000

SG Dickey Betts
2012. Custom Shop, 75 hand-aged include a leather certificate of authenticity signed by Betts, 250 VOS include unsigned COA, Vintage Red finish.

2012	Aged, signed	$6,000	$8,000
2012	VOS, unsigned	$4,000	$5,000

SG Elegant
2004-2013. Custom Shop, quilt maple top, gold hardware, Blue Burst, Firemist and Iguana Burst finishes.

2004-2013		$3,000	$4,000

SG Elite
1987-1989. SG Custom specs, 3 humbuckers, gold hardware, ebony 'board, various colors.

1987-1989		$2,250	$3,000

SG Exclusive
1979. SG with humbuckers, coil-tap and rotary control knob, block inlay, pearl logo (not decal), black/ebony finish.

1979		$2,000	$2,500

SG Firebrand
1980-1982. Double-cut mahogany solidbody, rough natural finish, Gibson branded in headstock, 2 exposed humbuckers, Firebrand logo on The SG (Standard) model.

1980-1982		$1,125	$1,500

SG Frank Zappa "Roxy"
2013. 400 offered, Maestro vibrola, 2 exposed-coil humbuckers.

2013		$2,250	$3,000

SG Futura
2013-2014. Mahogany body, maple neck, rosewood 'board, 2 pickups, various colors.

2013-2014		$975	$1,250

SG Goddess
2007. SG Goddess logo on truss rod cover, only 2 control knobs versus standard 4, exposed humbuckers.

2007		$975	$1,250

SG Gothic
2000-2003. SG Special with satin black finish, moon and star marker on 12th fret, black hardware.

2000-2003		$975	$1,250

SG Gothic Morte
2011-2012. Solid mahogany body, African Obeche 'board, 2 pickups, satin ebony finish

2011-2012		$775	$1,000

SG Government Series
2013-2016. Made from guitar bodies, necks and 'boards returned from Federal Government after '11 raid on Gibson, with Certificate of Authenticity.

2013-2016		$1,250	$1,625

SG GT
2006-2007. '61 specs with racing stripes paint job and removable tailpiece hood scoop, locking tuners, Candy Apple Red, Daytona Blue, or Phantom Black.

2006-2007		$3,000	$4,000

SG Jeff Tweedy Signature
2012. SG Standard with Maestro vibrola, mahogany body and neck, rosewood 'board, Blue Mist.

2012		$2,750	$3,500

SG Judas Priest Signature
2003. Custom Shop, 30 made, dot markers, exposed '57 classic humbucker and EMG58 pickups, black, large chrome metal 'guard, also sold as a set with Flying V Judas Priest, includes certificate of authenticity.

2003		$2,500	$3,250

SG Judas Priest Signature Set With Flying V
2003. Custom Shop, 30 sets made.

2003		$5,000	$6,500

SG Junior
1963-1971, 1991-1994. One pickup, solidbody. Prices are for an unfaded finish, cherry finish faded to brown reduces the value by 30%.

1963-1964	Cherry	$5,500	$7,000
1964	White	$6,000	$7,500
1965	Early-'65, cherry	$5,000	$6,500
1965	Late-'65, cherry	$3,750	$5,000
1965	Pelham Blue	$7,500	$10,000
1965	White	$5,000	$6,500
1966-1969	Cherry	$3,500	$4,500
1966-1969	White	$4,500	$6,000
1970-1971	Cherry or walnut	$3,000	$4,000
1991-1994	Various colors	$1,250	$1,625

SG Junior (Reintroduced)
2018-present. Gibson Original series, '60s design, mahogany body, P-90 single-coil pickup, Vintage Cherry gloss nitro finish.

2018-2023		$1,125	$1,500

SG Junior Limited
2018. Double-cut, mahogany body and neck, rosewood 'board, 1 single-coil pickup, Vintage Cherry.

2018		$1,125	$1,500

SG Junior P-90
2006-2007. Single P-90 pickup, large 'guard, stop tail, cherry finish.

2006-2007		$950	$1,250

SG Kirk Douglas Signature
2019-2023. Mother-of-pearl headstock logo, 3 BurstBucker pickups, ebony or Inverness Green.

2019-2023		$2,000	$2,500

SG Les Paul '61 Custom
1997-2005. 1961 specs, SG body style, 3 humbuckers, Deluxe Maestro vibrato or stud with tune-o-matic bridge, white or silver option.

1997-2005		$2,750	$3,500

SG Les Paul '62 Custom
2003. Custom Shop, Maestro vibrato, small 'guard, white.

1986-1990		$2,750	$3,500

SG Les Paul '62 Custom (Custom Shop)
2003. Custom Shop, Maestro vibrato, small 'guard, white.

2003		$2,750	$3,500

The Official Vintage Guitar magazine Price Guide 2025   **Gibson** SG Les Paul '90 Custom — SG Special Faded (3 pickups)   **197**

GUITARS

MODEL YEAR	FEATURES	EXC. COND. LOW	HIGH

SG Les Paul '90 Custom
1990-1992. 1962 specs, 3 humbuckers.

1990-1992		$2,750	$3,500

SG Les Paul Custom 30th Anniversary
1991. SG body, 3 humbuckers, gold hardware, TV Yellow finish, 30th Anniversary on peghead.

1991		$3,000	$4,000

SG Menace
2006-2007. Carved mahogany body, 2 exposed humbuckers, flat black finish, black hardware, single brass knuckle position marker, gig bag.

2006-2007		$1,000	$1,375

SG Music Machine Stinger
2003. Custom run for dealer Music Machine, special serial number series, SG Custom with 2 pickups and SG Standard models available, black stinger paint job on neck/headstock, various colors.

2003	SG Custom	$3,000	$4,000
2003	SG Standard	$3,000	$4,000

SG Original
2013-2019. Mahogany body, slim '60s neck profile, Lyre vibrato, '57 classic pickups, Vintage Cherry. Replaced by SG Standard '61 Maestro Vibrola in '19.

2013-2019		$1,750	$2,250

SG Pete Townshend Signature
2001. Signature on back of headstock.

2001		$1,875	$2,500

SG Pete Townshend Signature (Custom Shop)
2000. Custom Shop Limited Edition, 250 made, SG Special with '69 specs, large 'guard, 2 cases, cherry red, COA.

2000		$1,875	$2,500

SG Platinum
2005. A mix of SG Special and SG Standard specs, platinum paint on the body, back of neck, and head-stock, no crown inlay, Gibson stencil logo, exposed humbucker pickups, large plantium-finish 'guard, special plantinum colored Gibson logo guitar case.

2005		$1,375	$1,750

SG Pro
1971-1974. Tune-o-matic bridge, vibrato, 2 P-90 pickups, cherry, mahogany or walnut.

1971-1974		$1,750	$2,250

SG R1/SG Artist
1980-1982. Active RD-era electronics. SG style but thicker body, no 'guard, ebony 'board, black finish, dot markers, renamed SG Artist in '81.

1980	SG-R1	$1,500	$2,000
1981-1982	SG Artist	$1,500	$2,000

SG Raw Power
2009-2012. All maple body, neck and 'board, 2 exposed-coil humbuckers, offered in 9 satin finishes, including natural.

2009-2012		$1,250	$1,750

SG Select
2007. Made in Nashville, TN, carved solid book-matched AAA flame maple, 3-piece flamed maple neck, described as the most exquisite SG offered to date, 2 humbuckers, gold hardware.

2007		$3,000	$4,000

MODEL YEAR	FEATURES	EXC. COND. LOW	HIGH

SG Special
1960-1978. Rounded double-cut for '60, switched to SG body early-'61, 2 P-90s '59-'71, 2 mini-humbuckers '72-'78, 2 regular humbuckers on current version, redesigned in '85. Prices are for an unfaded finish, cherry finish faded to brown reduces the value by 20%-30%. Instruments with stop tailpieces vs. Maestro tailpiece have the same value.

1960	Cherry, slab, low neck pu	$10,000	$12,500
1961-1962	Cherry, SG body	$7,500	$9,500
1961-1962	TV Yellow, SG body	$25,000	$30,000
1962	White, SG body	$8,500	$11,000
1963-1964	Cherry, Maestro or stop	$7,500	$9,500
1963-1964	White	$8,500	$10,500
1965	Cherry, Maestro or stop	$5,000	$6,500
1965	White	$6,500	$8,500
1966	Cherry, large 'guard	$4,500	$5,500
1966	Cherry, small 'guard	$4,500	$5,500
1966	White, large 'guard	$5,500	$7,000
1966	White, small 'guard	$6,000	$7,500
1967	Cherry, large 'guard	$4,500	$5,500
1967	White, large 'guard	$5,500	$7,000
1968-1969	Cherry, large 'guard	$4,500	$5,500
1970-1971	Cherry	$4,000	$5,000
1972-1978	Mini-hums	$2,000	$2,500

SG Special (redesigned)
1985-1996. In mid-'85 Gibson introduced a redesigned SG Special model with 2 control knobs (1 pickup) or 3 control knobs (2 pickups) versus the previously used 4-knob layout.

1985-1986	1 pu, 2 knobs	$775	$1,000
1985-1989	2 pus, 3 knobs	$875	$1,125
1990-1996	2 pus, 3 knobs	$775	$1,000

SG Special (reintroduced)
1996-present. In '96 Gibson reintroduced the original 4-knob layout, 2 humbucker pickups, dot markers.

1996-2023		$775	$1,000

SG Special 3/4
1961. Only 61 shipped.

1961		$3,000	$4,000

SG Special '60s Tribute
2011-2018. '60s specs including small guard, dot markers, dual P-90s, Slim Taper '60s neck profile, 4 worn-finish options.

2011-2018		$775	$1,000

1963 SG Special Ultra Light Aged
2021. Custom Shop Murphy Lab Collection, Classic White finish.

2021		$3,250	$4,250

SG Special Faded (3 pickups)
2007. Made in Nashville, TN, 3 exposed 490 humbuckers, dot markers, stop tail, SG initials on truss rod cover, 2 knobs and 6-position selector switch, hand-worn satin finish.

2007		$750	$975

1965 Gibson SG Junior
Tim Fleck

1969 Gibson SG Special
Landon Furlong

1984 Gibson SG Standard

Rivington Guitars

1969 Gibson SG Standard

W. H. Stephens

MODEL YEAR	FEATURES	EXC. COND. LOW	HIGH

SG Special Faded/Faded SG Special
2002-2018. Aged worn cherry finish.

2002-2005	Half moon markers	$725	$950
2003-2018	Dot markers	$725	$950

SG Special I
1983-1985. Dot markers, 1 exposed-coil humbucker pickup with 2 knobs, called by various names including Gibson Special ('83), Special I, and SG Special I.

1983-1985		$725	$950

SG Special II
1983-1985. Dot markers, 2 exposed-coil humbucker pickups with 3 knobs, called by various names including Gibson Special ('83), Special II, SG Special II.

1983-1985		$850	$1,125

SG Special II EMG
2007. EMG humbucker pickups, no position markers, standard 4-knob and 3-way toggle switch SG format, black satin finish over entire guitar, black hardware.

2007		$850	$1,125

SG Special New Century
2006-2008. Full-body mirror 'guard, 2 exposed humbuckers, SG body, mirror truss rod cover.

2006-2008		$1,125	$1,500

SG Special Robot
2008-2012. Dot markers, robot tuning.

2008-2012		$1,125	$1,500

SG Special Robot Limited
2008. Limited run with trapezoid markers, robot tuning.

2008		$1,250	$1,625

SG Special Robot Limited Silverburst
2008. Limited run of 400.

2008		$1,500	$2,000

SG Special VOS Reissue
2006-2013. Custom Shop, mahogany body and neck, bound rosewood 'board, dot inlays, 2 P-90s, certificate, white, TV yellow, or faded cherry finish.

2006-2013		$2,500	$3,500

SG Standard
1963-1981, 1983-present. Les Paul Standard changes to SG body, 2 humbuckers, some very early models have optional factory Bigsby. Prices are for an unfaded finish, a cherry finish faded to brown reduces the value by 30% or more.

1963-1964	Cherry, sm 'guard, dlx vibr or Bigsby	$20,000	$25,000
1964	Pelham Blue, sm 'guard, dlx vibr	$26,500	$33,500
1965	Cherry, sm 'guard, dlx vibr, lg neck	$16,500	$20,500
1965	Cherry, sm 'guard, dlx vibr, sm neck	$15,500	$20,000
1965	Pelham Blue, sm 'guard, dlx vibr	$25,000	$32,500
1966	Early '66, cherry, vibr, sm 'guard, dlx vibrato	$11,000	$13,500
1966	Late '66, cherry, lg 'guard	$8,500	$10,500
1967	Burgundy Metallic	$9,000	$11,500

MODEL YEAR	FEATURES	EXC. COND. LOW	HIGH
1967	Cherry	$8,250	$10,500
1967	White	$10,000	$12,500
1968	Cherry, engraved lyre	$7,000	$8,500
1969	Engraved lyre, 1-piece neck	$7,000	$8,500
1969	Engraved lyre, 3-piece neck	$5,500	$7,000
1970	Engraved lyre, 3-piece neck	$5,000	$6,500
1970	Walnut, non-lyre tailpiece	$3,500	$4,500
1970-1971	Cherry, non-lyre tailpiece	$3,500	$4,500
1971	Engraved lyre, 3-piece neck	$4,500	$5,500
1972-1979	Blocks, mini 'guard, top mount	$3,000	$4,000
1980-1986	New colors, sm blocks	$2,250	$2,750
1992-1999	New specs	$1,375	$1,750
2000-2023	Standard colors	$1,375	$1,750
2006-2012	Silverburst	$1,625	$2,000

SG Standard '61 Reissue
2004-2008. Small 'guard, stop tail, Nashville tune-o-matic bridge, Gibson Deluxe Keystone tuners, standard Gibson logo and crown inlay, no Les Paul logo, Vintage Original Spec aging optional from '06. Reintroduced in '19.

2004-2008		$2,000	$2,500

SG Standard '61
2019-present. Classic '61 design, 3 models offered - Maestro vibrola, Sideways or Stop Bar, mahogany body and neck, rosewood 'board, vintage cherry finish.

2019-2023	Maestro vibrola	$2,000	$2,500
2019-2023	Sideways vibrola	$2,000	$2,500
2019-2023	Stop Bar vibrola	$2,000	$2,500

1964 SG Standard (Maestro Vibrola) Murphy Lab Aged
2021-present. Custom Shop Murphy Lab Collection, heavy aged (Faded Cherry), light aged (Pelham Blue) and ultra light (Cherry Red or Pelham Blue).

2021-2023	Heavy aged	$5,000	$6,500
2021-2023	Light aged	$5,000	$6,500
2021-2022	Ultra Light aged	$3,750	$5,000

SG Standard 24 50th Anniversary
2011. Limited run, mother-of-pearl Gibson logo with gold 50th Anniversary silkscreen, 2 '57 classic pickups, antique ebony finish.

2011		$1,500	$2,000

SG Standard (Etune)
2014-2018. Min-Etune robot tuners, Etune logo on truss rod.

2014-2018		$1,125	$1,500

SG Standard Brian Ray '63 (Custom Shop)
2015. Silver Fox finish, Bigsby, certificate of authenticity.

2015		$3,750	$5,000

MODEL YEAR FEATURES	EXC. COND. LOW	HIGH

SG Standard Celebrity Series
1991-1992. SG Standard with large 'guard, gold hardware, black finish.

1991-1992	$2,250	$2,750

SG Standard Gary Rossington Signature
2004. '63-'64 SG Standard specs with Deluxe Maestro vibrola, '60 slim taper neck, limited edition, faded cherry aged by Tom Murphy.

2004	$6,000	$8,000

SG Standard HP (High Performance)
2016-2019. Solid mahogany body and neck, AA figured maple top, 2 pickups, different colors offered each year.

2016-2019	$1,500	$2,000

SG Standard Korina (Custom Shop)
2008-2009. Custom Shop limited reissue of '60s SG Standard, 2 BurstBucker pickups, black.

2008-2009	$2,750	$3,500

SG Standard Korina Limited Edition
1993-1994. Korina version of SG Standard, limited run, natural.

1993-1994	$3,500	$4,500

SG Standard Korina/SG Standard K (Custom Shop)
2001-2008. Custom Shop serial number, large 'guard, no SG logo on truss rod, CS logo back of headstock, natural finish.

2001-2008	$4,500	$5,750

SG Standard Limited Edition
2000. Limited Edition logo back of headstock, 2 humbuckers, large pearloid guard, gold hardware, dark opaque finish.

2000	$1,250	$1,750

SG Standard Limited Edition (3 pickups)
2007. Guitar of the Week, 400 made, 3 single-coil blade pickups, 6-position rotator switch with chickenhead knob, SG logo on truss rod cover, large 'guard, satin finish.

2007	$1,250	$1,750

SG Standard Reissue
2004-2018. Reissue of near '63-'64 specs with Deluxe Maestro lyre vibrato and small 'guard, also offered with stop bar tailpiece, cherry finish, '60 slim taper neck, smooth neck heel joint, trapezoid markers, unmarked truss rod cover without Les Paul designation, formerly called Les Paul SG Standard Reissue, by 2005 part of Gibson's 'Vintage Original Spec' Custom Shop series, certificate of authenticity.

2004-2007	VOS, Maestro	$3,000	$4,000
2007-2018	VOS, stoptail	$3,000	$4,000
2008-2009	Maestro, LP logo	$3,000	$4,000

SG Standard VOS Historic
2003-2014. Custom Shop, Vintage Original Specs.

2003-2014	$3,000	$4,000

SG Standard Robby Krieger
2009. Custom Shop model, Inspired By series, based on Krieger's '67 SG, limited run of 150 with 50 aged and signed, 100 with V.O.S. finish treatment, certificate of authenticity.

2009	Aged, signed	$4,500	$5,750
2009	VOS	$4,000	$5,250

SG Standard Robby Krieger 50th Anniversary
2012. Mahogany body and neck, rosewood 'board, 2 '57 classic Alnico II pickups, Maestro tailpiece, Heritage Cherry finish.

2012	$2,000	$2,500

SG Supreme
2004-2007. '57 humbuckers, flamed maple top, split-diamond markers, various colors.

2004-2007	$2,250	$3,000

SG Tony Iommi Signature (Historic/Custom Shop)
2001-2003. Custom Shop Historic Collection, higher-end, signature humbuckers without poles, cross inlays, ebony or Wine Red.

2001-2003	$6,500	$8,500

SG Tony Iommi Signature (Production)
2002-2003. Standard production model.

2002-2008	$2,500	$3,250

SG TV
1961-1963. Name changed from Les Paul TV, SG body, 1 pickup, white finish. In '64 called SG Junior White.

1961-1963	$5,500	$7,250

SG Voodoo/Voodoo SG
2002-2004. Carved top, black hardware, voodoo doll inlay at 5th fret, Juju finish (black with red wood filler).

2002-2004	$1,250	$1,750

SG-X
1998-2000. Previously part of the All American series, SG body with single bridge humbucker, various colors.

1998-2000	$750	$975

SG-X Tommy Hilfiger
1998. Hilfiger logo on front, dot markers, plain headstock like a SG Special, dark blue finish, 100 made.

1998	$650	$850

SG Zoot Suit
2007-2010. Body of individual dyed strips of birch.

2007-2010	$1,750	$2,250

SG-Z
1998. Z-shaped string-thru tailpiece, 2 humbuckers, split diamond markers.

1998	$1,625	$2,125

The SG
1979-1983. Offered as The SG Standard (walnut body) and The SG Deluxe (mahogany), ebony 'board, 2 humbuckers, 'The SG' truss rod logo.

1979-1983	Walnut or mahogany	$1,000	$1,500

Sheryl Crow Country Western Supreme
2019-2022. Artist series, aged Sitka spruce top, mahogany back and sides, Antique Cherry finish.

2019-2022	$3,250	$4,250

Sheryl Crow Signature
2001-2018. Artist Series, based on Sheryl Crow's 1962 Country and Western with Hummingbird influences.

2001-2018	$2,500	$3,250

Gibson 1964 SG Standard
(Maestro Vibrola)
Murphy Lab Aged

Gibson Sheryl Crow Country
Western Supreme

GUITARS

1960 Gibson SJ
David Stone

Gibson SJ Woody Guthrie
Bill Miller

MODEL YEAR	FEATURES	EXC. COND. LOW	HIGH

Sheryl Crow Southern Jumbo Special Edition

2013-2018. Adirondack red spruce top, mahogany back and sides, rosewood 'board, with signed certificate of authenticity, Montana Sunsetburst finish. Limited production in '13.

2013-2018		$3,250	$4,250

SJ (Southern Jumbo)

1942-1969,1991-1996. Flat-top, sunburst standard, natural optional starting in '54 (natural finish version called Country-Western starting in '56), round shoulders (changed to square in '62), catalog name changed to SJ Deluxe in '70, refer to that listing.

1942-1944	Banner, Adirondack	$20,000	$25,000
1942-1944	Banner, mahogany	$15,500	$20,000
1945	Script, Sitka	$16,500	$20,500
1946	Script, Sitka	$14,500	$20,000
1947	Script, Sitka	$13,500	$16,500
1948-1949	Script, Sitka	$12,000	$15,000
1950-1953		$8,000	$10,500
1954-1956	Natural option	$8,000	$10,500
1954-1959	Sunburst	$8,000	$10,500
1960-1962	Round shoulder (ends)	$7,000	$9,000
1962-1964	Square shoulder (begins)	$6,500	$8,500
1965	Cherry Sunburst	$4,500	$6,000
1965	Tobacco Sunburst	$5,500	$7,000
1966	Tobacco Sunburst	$5,000	$6,500
1966-1968	Cherry Sunburst	$4,500	$6,000
1969	Below belly bridge	$3,500	$4,500

SJ Deluxe (Southern Jumbo)

1970-1978. SJ name changed to SJ Deluxe in catalog, along with a series of engineering changes.

1970-1971	Non-adj saddle	$2,500	$3,500
1972-1973	Unbound 'board	$2,500	$3,500
1974-1978	4-ply to binding	$2,500	$3,500

SJN (Country-Western)

1956-1969. Flat-top, natural finish version of SJ, round shoulders '56-'62, square shoulders after, called the SJN in '60 and '61, the SJN Country Western after that, catalog name changed to SJN Deluxe in '70, refer to that listing.

1956-1959		$8,000	$10,500
1960-1962	Round shoulder (ends)	$7,500	$10,000
1962-1964	Square shoulder (begins)	$7,000	$9,000
1965		$5,000	$6,500
1966-1968		$4,500	$6,000
1969	Below belly bridge	$3,500	$4,500

SJN Deluxe (Country-Western Jumbo)

1970-1978. SJN name changed to SJN Deluxe in catalog, along with a series of engineering changes.

1970-1971	Non-adj saddle	$2,750	$3,500
1972-1973	Unbound 'board	$2,750	$3,500
1974-1978	4-ply to binding	$2,750	$3,500

SJ 1942 Reissue (Southern Jumbo)

2000. Custom Shop, mahogany back and sides, '42 SJ appointments, 'Only A Gibson is Good Enough' banner logo.

2000		$3,000	$4,000

SJ Reissue (Southern Jumbo)

2003-2007. Sunburst.

2003-2007		$3,000	$4,000

SJ Hank Williams Jr. Hall of Fame

1997. Custom Shop, mahogany back and sides, SJ appointments.

1997		$3,000	$4,000

SJ Hank Williams Sr.

1993. Custom Shop, 25 offered.

1993		$4,500	$6,000

SJ Kristofferson

2009-2012. Limited run of 300, AAA Sitka top, mahogany back and sides, Indian rosewood 'board, aged vintage sunburst.

2009-2012		$2,500	$3,000

SJ True Vintage

2007-2008. "Only A Gibson Is Good Enough" headstock banner, Sitka spruce top, dark mahogany back and sides, dual parallelogram markers.

2007-2008		$2,750	$3,500

SJ Woody Guthrie

2003-2018. Single-bound round shoulder body, mahogany back and sides, parallelogram inlays.

2003-2018		$2,500	$3,000

SJ-100

2008. Jumbo body, dot markers, crown headstock inlay, inlaid Gibson logo, natural.

2008		$1,500	$2,000

1939 SJ-100 Centennial

1994. Acoustic flat-top, limited edition, sunburst.

1994		$2,500	$3,000

1941 SJ-100

2013-2018. Sitka spruce top, mahogany back, sides and neck, rosewood 'board, Vintage Sunburst or Antique Natural.

2013-2018		$2,500	$3,000

SJ-150

Listed with J-150.

SJ-200

Listed with J-200.

1957 SJ-200 (Custom Shop)

2020-present. Aged Sitka spruce top, flamed maple back and sides, 4 bar moustach bridge, VOS finish, Antique Natural or Vintage Sunburst.

2020-2023		$4,250	$5,500

SJ-200 Bob Dylan Autographed Collector's Edition

2015-2018. Exact replica of Dylan's personal highly-customized SJ-200, Indian rosewood, Sitka spruce, Dylan eye logo inlaid on headstock, abalone inlay on 'guard, label signed by Bob Dylan, 175 made, case with embroidered eye logo.

2015-2018		$12,000	$15,500

SJ-200 Bob Dylan Player's Edition

2015-2018. Adirondack red spruce, flamed maple, eye logo headstock inlay, LR Baggs Anthem pickup.

2015-2018		$5,500	$7,000

The *Vintage Guitar Price Guide* shows values for all-original, excellent condition instruments and, where applicable, with original case.

MODEL YEAR FEATURES	EXC. COND. LOW	HIGH

SJ-200 Centennial Limited Edition
1994. Made in Bozeman, Montana, 100 made, 'guard specs based on '38 design, inside label "Gibson 100 Years 1894-1994", includes certificate of authenticity.

1994	$3,750	$4,750

SJ-200 Custom Rosewood
2007. Custom shop, certificate of authenticity.

2007	$4,500	$6,000

SJ-200 Deluxe (Custom Shop)
2020-present. Sitka spruce top, rosewood back and sides, mother-of-pearl crown inlays, Rosewood Burst finish.

2020-2023	$5,000	$6,500

SJ-200 Elite
1998-2007. Gibson Custom Shop Bozeman, maple sides and back.

1998-2007	$4,000	$5,000

SJ-200 Elite Custom Koa
2004. Figured koa, ebony board with abalone crown inlays, Antique Natural.

2004	$4,500	$6,000

SJ-200 Elvis Presley
2007. Custom Shop, 250 made, kings crown logo and facsimile signature of Presley on truss rod cover, certificate of authenticity, black finish.

2007	$4,500	$6,000

SJ-200 Pete Townshend Limited
2004-2012. Gibson Custom Shop Bozeman, maple sides and back.

2004	Signed, 1st 50 made	$6,000	$7,750
2004-2012		$3,750	$4,750

SJ-200 Ray Whitley/J-200 Custom Club
1994-1995. Based on Ray Whitley's late-1930s J-200, including engraved inlays and initials on the truss rod cover, only 37 made, one of the limited edition models the Montana division released to celebrate Gibson's 100th anniversary.

1994-1995	$16,500	$21,500

SJ-200 Ron Wood
Listed with J-200 Ron Wood.

SJ-200 Sea Green Limited Edition
2016. Bozeman Custom Shop, 40 made, Sitka spruce top, AAA flamed maple back and sides, mother-of-pearl crown inlays.

2016	$4,500	$5,500

SJ-200 Standard
2015-present. AAA flamed maple body, on-board electronics, Wine Red or Autumnburst.

2015-2023	$3,750	$4,750

SJ-200 Summer Jam Koa
2006. Custom Shop, only 6 made, offered to attendees of Gibson Guitar Summer Jam, highly figured koa back/sides.

2006	$5,500	$7,000

SJ-200 True Vintage/SJ-200 Vintage
2007-2019. AAA Adirondack red spruce top, AAA Eastern curly maple back and sides, rosewood 'board, tortoise 'guard, nitro finish. True dropped from name in '19.

2007-2019	$4,500	$5,750

SJ-200 Vine
2002-2018. Custom Shop, Sitka spruce top, Eastern curly maple back/sides, abalone vine inlay in 'board, abalone body trim. Limited Edition in '15, 30 made.

2002-2018	$6,750	$8,750

SJ-250 Monarch
Listed with J-250 Monarch.

SJ-300
2007-2010. Super Jumbo with Indian rosewood back and sides, ebony 'board, abalone crown inlays and rosette, gold imperial tuners, active transducer.

2007-2010	$3,500	$4,500

SJ-1000
Listed with J-1000.

Sonex Artist
1981-1985. Active electronics, 3 mini switches, 2 humbuckers.

1981-1985	$850	$1,125

Sonex-180 Custom
1980-1982. Two Super humbuckers, coil-tap, maple neck, ebony 'board, single-cut, body of Multi-Phonic synthetic material, black or white.

1980-1982	$800	$1,125

Sonex-180 Deluxe
1980-1984. Hardwood neck, rosewood 'board, single-cut, body of Multi-Phonic synthetic material, 2 pickups, no coil-tap, various colors.

1980-1984	Various colors	$800	$1,125
1982-1984	Silverburst	$1,000	$1,500

Sonex-180 Standard
1980. Dirty-fingers pickups, rosewood 'board, ebony finish.

1980	$800	$1,125

Songbird Deluxe
1999-2002. Solid rosewood back, sides and 'board, on-board electronics. Renamed Songwriter Deluxe.

1999-2002	$1,500	$2,000

Songwriter
2003-2020. Sitka spruce top, rosewood back, sides and 'board, mahogany neck, Antique Natural or Rosewood Burst. Becomes Songwriter Standard in '20.

2003-2020	$2,250	$2,750

Songwriter 12-String Rosewood
2019-2020. Sitka spruce top, rosewood back and sides, Antique Natural or Rosewood Burst.

2019-2020	$2,250	$3,000

Songwriter Deluxe
2003-2011. Solid rosewood back and sides, trapezoid inlays, cutaway or non-cutaway, on-board electronics.

2003-2011	$1,750	$2,250

Songwriter Deluxe 12-String
2006-2022. 12-string version, non-cut.

2006-2022	$1,750	$2,250

Songwriter Deluxe Koa
2009. Custom Shop, all koa, cutaway.

2009	$2,750	$3,500

Songwriter Deluxe Standard
2009-2012. Solid rosewood back and sides, bound ebony 'board, diamond and arrows inlays, cutaway or non-cutaway.

2009-2012	$2,250	$3,000

1982 Gibson Sonex-180 Deluxe
Imaged by Heritage Auctions, HA.com

2019 Gibson Songwriter

GUITARS

1917 Gibson Style
U Harp Guitar

1940 Gibson Super 400N

Kevin

MODEL YEAR	FEATURES	EXC. COND. LOW	HIGH
Songwriter Deluxe Studio			
2009-2018. Like Standard, but with bound rosewood 'board and double parallelogram inlays, cutaway or non-cutaway.			
2009-2018		$1,750	$2,250
Songwriter Modern EC Mahogany			
2020-2021. Cutaway, Sitka spruce top, mahogany back, sides and neck, Light Cherry Burst with nitro finish.			
2020-2021		$1,750	$2,250
Songwriter Modern EC Rosewood			
2020-2021. Cutaway, Sitka spruce top, rosewood back and sides, mahogany neck, Rosewood Burst with nitro finish.			
2020-2021		$2,000	$2,500
Songwriter Special			
2007. Mahogany sides and back, dark opaque finish.			
2007		$1,625	$2,125
Songwriter Special Deluxe			
2003. Custom Shop, Brazilian rosewood.			
2003		$2,375	$3,250
Songwriter Standard EC Rosewood			
2020-present. Cutaway, Sitka spruce top, rosewood back and sides, Antique Natural or Rosewood Burst finish.			
2020-2023		$2,250	$3,000
Songwriter Standard Rosewood			
2020-present. Non-cut, Sitka spruce top, rosewood back and sides, Antique Natural or Rosewood Burst finish.			
2020-2023		$2,250	$3,000
Songwriter Studio			
2003-2019. Non-cutaway or cutaway.			
2003-2019		$2,000	$2,500
Special 400			
1985-1986. Double-cut SG body, exposed humbucker and 2 single-coils, Kahler locking tremolo, coil tap.			
1985-1986		$850	$1,250
Spirit I			
1982-1987. Double rounded cutaway, 1 pickup, chrome hardware, various colors.			
1982-1987		$1,375	$1,750
Spirit I XPL			
1985-1986. Spirit I with 6-on-a-side Explorer-style headstock.			
1985-1986		$1,375	$1,750
Spirit II			
1982-1987. Spirit I with 2 pickups, bound top.			
1982-1987		$1,625	$2,000
Spirit II XPL			
1985-1987. 2 pickup version.			
1985-1987		$1,750	$2,250
SR-71			
1987-1989. Floyd Rose tremolo, 1 humbucker, 2 single-coil pickups, various colors, Wayne Charvel designed.			
1987-1989		$1,750	$2,250
Star			
1992. Star logo on headstock, star position markers, single sharp cutaway flat-top, sunburst.			
1991-1992		$1,750	$2,250

MODEL YEAR	FEATURES	EXC. COND. LOW	HIGH
Starburst Standard/Flame			
1992-1994. Single-cut acoustic/electric, star inlays, figured maple back and sides.			
1992-1994		$2,000	$2,500
Style O			
1902-1925. Acoustic archtop, oval sound hole, bound top, neck and headstock, various colors.			
1902-1906	Paddle headstock	$7,000	$8,500
1902-1906	Paddle headstock, fancy	$8,500	$10,500
1906-1908	Slotted headstock	$8,500	$10,500
1908-1913	Solid headstock	$8,500	$10,500
1914-1921	Scroll variation	$8,500	$10,500
1922-1924	Loar era	$10,000	$12,500
1925	Scroll, truss rod	$9,000	$11,500
Style O-1			
1902. Acoustic archtop, celluloid binding.			
1902		$9,500	$11,500
Style O-2			
1902. Acoustic archtop, pearl/ebony binding.			
1902		$9,500	$12,000
Style O-3			
1902. Acoustic archtop, green/white binding.			
1902		$9,500	$12,000
Style R Harp Guitar			
1902-1907. Acoustic 6-string, with 6 sub-bass strings, walnut back and sides, bound sound hole.			
1902-1907		$6,000	$7,500
Style R-1 Harp Guitar			
1902. Style R with fancier pearl and ivory rope pattern binding.			
1902		$6,000	$7,500
Style U Harp Guitar			
1902-1939. Acoustic 6-string, with 10 or 12 sub-bass strings, walnut (until about '07) or birch back and sides, bound sound hole, black.			
1902-1939		$6,250	$8,500
Style U-1 Harp Guitar			
1902-1907, 1915, 1917. Slightly fancier Style U.			
1902-1917		$7,000	$8,750
Super 300			
1948-1955. Acoustic archtop, non-cut, bound body, neck and headstock, sunburst.			
1948-1955		$5,000	$6,250
Super 300 C			
1954-1958. Acoustic archtop, rounded cutaway, bound body, neck and headstock, sunburst with natural option.			
1954-1958	Sunburst	$5,500	$6,750
Super 400			
1935-1941, 1947-1955. Introduced early '35 as Super L-5 Deluxe. Acoustic archtop, non-cut, maple, multi-bound, f-holes, sunburst (see Super 400 N for natural version).			
1935	Early, L-5, highly flamed	$20,000	$25,000
1935	Early, L-5, plain	$17,500	$22,000
1935	Late, 400, highly flamed	$18,500	$23,500
1935	Late, 400, plain	$13,500	$16,500
1936-1941	Highly flamed	$15,000	$20,000

MODEL YEAR	FEATURES	EXC. COND. LOW	HIGH
1936-1941	Plain	$12,000	$15,000
1947-1949	Highly flamed	$9,500	$11,500
1947-1949	Plain	$7,500	$10,000
1950-1955		$7,000	$9,000

Super 400 N

1940, 1948-1955. Natural finish version of Super 400, highly flamed, non-cut, acoustic archtop.

1940		$20,000	$25,000
1948-1949		$15,000	$20,000
1950-1955		$12,000	$18,000

Super 400 P (Premier)

1939-1941. Acoustic archtop, single rounded cut-away, '39 model 'board rests on top, sunburst finish.

1939-1941		$25,000	$32,000

Super 400 PN (Premier Natural)

1939-1940. Rounded cutaway, '39 'board rests on top, natural finish.

1939-1940		$35,000	$45,000

Super 400 C

1948-1982. Introduced as Super 400 Premier, acoustic archtop, single-cut, sunburst finish (natural is called Super 400 CN).

1948-1949		$16,500	$22,000
1950-1959		$15,500	$20,000
1960-1964		$14,500	$18,500
1965		$10,000	$12,500
1966-1969		$8,500	$11,000
1970-1982		$6,500	$8,500

Super 400 CN

1950-1987. Natural finish version of Super 400 C.

1950-1959		$17,500	$22,000
1960-1964		$15,000	$18,500
1965		$14,000	$17,500
1966-1969		$12,500	$15,000

Super 400 CES

1951-2018. Electric version of Super 400 C, archtop, single-cut (round '51-'60 and '69-present, pointed '60-'69), 2 pickups (P-90s '51-'54, Alnico Vs '54-'57, humbuckers '57 on), sunburst (natural version called Super 400 CESN), now part of Gibson's Historic Collection.

1951-1953	P-90s	$22,000	$27,500
1954-1957	Alnico Vs	$22,000	$27,500
1957-1960	PAFs	$30,000	$37,500
1961-1962	PAFs, sharp cut	$26,500	$33,500
1963-1964	Pat #	$20,000	$25,000
1965		$13,500	$16,500
1966-1969		$12,000	$15,000
1970-1979		$10,000	$12,500
1980-2018		$10,000	$12,500

Super 400 CESN

1952-2016. Natural version of Super 400 CES, now part of Gibson's Historic Collection.

1952-1953	P-90s	$22,000	$27,500
1954-1956	Alnico Vs	$22,000	$27,500
1957-1960	PAFs	$30,000	$37,500
1961-1962	PAFs, sharp cut	$26,500	$33,500
1963-1964	Pat #	$20,000	$25,000
1965		$13,500	$16,500
1966-1969		$12,000	$15,000
1970-1979		$10,000	$12,500
1980-2016		$10,000	$12,500

Super 400 (Custom Shop)

2009. Non-cutaway, natural.

2009		$8,750	$11,500

'39 Super 400 Historic

1993-1997. Custom Shop Historic Collection, reissue of non-cut '39 version, various colors.

1993-1997		$7,500	$9,750

Super 4000 Chet Atkins

2000. Limited run of 25. AAA Sitka spruce carved top, highly figured carved maple back, antique natural and faded cherry sunburst.

2000		$21,500	$28,000

Super Jumbo 100

1939-1943. Jumbo flat-top, mahogany back and sides, bound body and neck, sunburst, reintroduced as J-100 with different specs in '84.

1939-1941	Early '41	$35,000	$45,000
1941-1943	Late '41	$30,000	$40,000

Super Jumbo/Super Jumbo 200

1938-1942. Initially called Super Jumbo in '38 and named Super Jumbo 200 in '39. Name then changed to J-200 (see that listing) by '47 (with maple back and sides) and SJ-200 by the '50s. Named for super large jumbo 16 7/8" flat-top body, double braced with rosewood back and sides, sunburst finish.

1938-1940		$125,000	$150,000
1941-1942		$115,000	$145,000

Super V BJB

1978-1983. A Super V CES but with a single floating pickup.

1978-1983		$6,000	$8,000

Super V CES

1978-1993. Archtop, L-5 with a Super 400 neck, 2 humbucker pickups, natural or sunburst.

1978-1993		$6,000	$8,000

Tal Farlow

1962-1971, 1993-2018. Full body, single-cut archtop, 2 humbuckers, triple-bound top, reintroduced '93 as part of Gibson's Historic Collection.

1962-1964	Viceroy Brown	$8,500	$10,500
1965	Viceroy Brown	$8,000	$10,000
1966-1971	Viceroy Brown	$7,500	$9,500
1993-2018	Various colors	$4,250	$5,500

TG-0

1927-1933, 1960-1974. Acoustic tenor based on L-0, mahogany body, light amber.

1927-1933		$2,250	$2,750
1960-1964		$1,250	$1,500
1965		$875	$1,125
1966-1969		$825	$1,125
1970-1974		$750	$950

TG-00

1932-1943. Tenor flat-top based on L-00.

1932-1943		$2,250	$2,750

TG-1/L-1 Tenor/L-4 Tenor

1927-1937. Acoustic flat-top, tenor or plectrum guitar based on L-1, mahogany back and sides, bound body, sunburst.

1927-1937		$2,500	$3,250
1928-1932	Rare Lucas/ Johnson body	$3,750	$4,750

1969 Gibson Super 400 CN
Loek Van Schooten

Gibson Super 400 CES

To get the most from this book, be sure to read "Using *The Guide*" in the introduction.

GUITARS

1965 Gibson Trini Lopez Standard

Matt Carleson

Giffin T Deluxe

MODEL YEAR	FEATURES	EXC. COND. LOW	HIGH

TG-2/L-2 Tenor
1929-1930. Acoustic tenor guitar.

1929-1930		$4,750	$6,250

TG-7
1934-1940. Tenor based on the L-7, sunburst.

1934-1940		$3,750	$4,750

TG-25/TG-25 N
1962-1970. Acoustic flat-top, tenor guitar based on B-25, mahogany back and sides, sunburst or natural (25 N).

1962-1964		$1,875	$2,500
1965		$1,375	$1,750
1966-1969		$1,250	$1,500
1970		$975	$1,250

TG-50
1934-1940, 1947-1961, 1963. Acoustic archtop, tenor guitar based on L-50, mahogany back and sides, sunburst.

1934-1940		$2,000	$2,500
1947-1963		$2,000	$2,500

Traveling Songwriter EC
2005-2015. Solid spruce top, solid mahogany sides and back, soft cutaway, on-board electronics and EQ.

2005-2015		$2,000	$2,500

Trini Lopez Standard
1964-1970. Double rounded cutaway, thinline archtop, 2 humbuckers, tune-o-matic bridge, trapeze tailpiece, single-bound, cherry, Sparkling Burgundy and Pelham Blue finishes.

1964	Cherry	$11,000	$14,000
1965	Cherry	$10,000	$13,000
1965	Pelham Blue	$15,000	$20,000
1965	Sparkling Burgundy	$11,000	$14,000
1966	Pelham Blue	$12,000	$15,000
1966-1970	Cherry	$9,000	$12,000
1966-1970	Sparkling Burgundy	$9,000	$12,000

Trini Lopez Standard (Custom Shop)
2010-2011. Custom Shop reissue of thinline Trini Lopez Standard, diamond f-holes, 6-on-a-side tuners, trapeze tailpiece, Certificate of Authenticity, cherry red.

2010-2011		$3,250	$4,250

Trini Lopez Deluxe
1964-1970. Double pointed cutaway archtop, 2 humbuckers, triple-bound, sunburst.

1964		$8,500	$11,000
1965		$8,000	$10,000
1966-1970		$7,500	$9,750

U-2
1987-1989. Double-cut, 1 humbucker and 2 single-coil pickups, ebony or red, renamed Mach II in '90-'91.

1987-1991		$1,250	$1,625

U-2 Showcase Edition
1988. November 1988 Guitar of the Month series, 250 made.

1988		$1,250	$1,625

US-1/US-3
1986-1991. Double-cut maple top with mahogany back, 3 humbucker pickups (US-1), or 3 P-90s (US-3), standard production and Custom Shop.

1986-1991		$1,250	$1,625

Vegas Standard
2006-2007. Flat-top semi-hollowbody thinline, slim neck, 2 humbuckers, f-holes, split diamond inlays.

2006-2007		$1,250	$1,625

Vegas High Roller
2006-2007. Upgraded version, AAA maple top, gold hardware and frets, block inlays.

2006-2007		$1,250	$1,625

Victory MV II (MV 2)
1981-1984. Asymetrical double-cut with long horn, 3-way slider, maple body and neck, rosewood 'board, 2 pickups.

1981-1984		$1,250	$1,625

Victory MV X (MV 10)
1981-1984. 3 humbuckers, 5-way switch, various colors.

1981-1984		$1,500	$2,000

WRC
1987-1988. Designed for Gibson by Wayne R. Charvel (WRC), earlier models had Kahler trem, later Floyd Rose, offered in red, black or white.

1987-1988		$975	$1,250

XPL Custom
1985-1986. Explorer-like shape, exposed humbuckers, locking tremolo, bound maple top, sunburst or white.

1985-1986		$1,500	$2,000

Y2K Dwight Yoakam Signature
2005. Limited run of 200, small body jumbo, spruce top, highly figured maple sides and back, 2-piece flamed maple neck, double 'guard, gloss natural finish.

2005		$2,250	$3,000

Zakk Wylde ZV Buzzsaw
2008. Custom Shop Inspired By series, limited run of 50, Flying V wings with SG horns, 2 humbuckers.

2008		$4,000	$5,250

Gibson Baldwin
2005-ca. 2013. Entry-level electric and acoustic guitars, basses, amps and accessories made in China for discount store market and sold under the Signature, Maestro, Echelon, and Genesis brand names. Models include Les Paul and SG copies. Guitars have Music - Gibson logo on neckplate and brand logo on headstock.

Giffin
1977-1988, 1997-present. Professional and premium grade, production/custom, hollow-, semi-hollow-, and solidbody guitars built by luthier Roger Giffin in West San Fernando Valley, California. For '77-'88, Giffin's shop was in London. From '88 to '93, he worked for the Gibson Custom Shop in California as a Master Luthier. In '97, Giffin set up shop in Sweden for a year, moving back to California in the Spring of '98. He also built small numbers of instruments during '67-'76 and '94-'96 (when he had a repair business).

MODEL YEAR FEATURES	EXC. COND. LOW	HIGH

Gigliotti

2000-present. Premium grade, production/custom, electric guitars with a metal plate top and tone chambers and designed by Patrick Gigliotti in Tacoma, Washington.

Gila Eban Guitars

Premium grade, custom, classical guitars built by luthier Gila Eban in Riverside, Connecticut, starting in 1979.

Gilbert Guitars

1965-present. Custom classical guitars by luthiers John Gilbert and William Gilbert in Paso Robles, California. Son William has handled all production since '91. John died early 2012.

Gilchrist

1977-present. Currently known more for his mandolins, luthier Steve Gilchrist, of Warrnambool, Australia, has also built premium and presentation grade, custom, guitars.

Acoustic Archtop

1990s-present. Very limited production.

1990s-2023	$20,000	$26,000

Gilet Guitars

1976-present. Luthier Gerard Gilet builds production/custom, premium grade, acoustic, classical, flamenco, and wooden bodied resonator guitars in Botany, Sydney, New South Wales, Australia. He also builds lap steels.

Girl Brand Guitars

1996-2012. Premium-grade, production/custom, guitars built by luthier Chris Larsen in Tucson, Arizona. Larson now builds under the Larsen Guitar Mfg. name.

Gitane

2003-present. Intermediate and professional grade, production, classic Selmer-Maccaferri style jazz guitars made in China for Saga.

Gittler

1974-ca.1985. Minimalistic electric guitar designed by Allan Gittler, consisting basically of a thin rod with frets welded to it. A total of 560 were built, with Gittler making the first 60 in the U.S. from '74 to the early '80s. The remainder were made around '85 in Israel by the Astron corporation under a licensing agreement. Three Gittler basses were also built. Gittler emigrated to Israel in the early '80s and changed his name to Avraham Bar Rashi. He died in 2002. A U.S.-made Gittler is the only musical instrument in the Museum of Modern Art in New York.

Metal Skeleton

1971-1982	$2,500	$3,250
1982-1999	$2,250	$3,000

Giulietti

1962-1965. The Giulietti Accordion Company, New York, offered guitars and amps in the '60s.

GJ2

Gold Jackson Enterprises LLC, a partnership between luthier Grover Jackson and Jon Gold, established 2012, builds professional and premium grade, production/custom, solidbody electric guitars in Laguna Hills, California.

Glendale

2004-present. Professional grade, production/custom, solidbody guitars built by luthier Dale Clark in Arlington, Texas.

GLF

1991-1997. Solidbody electric guitars built by luthier Kevin Smith in Minnesota. In '97 he started building his ToneSmith line of guitars.

Glick Guitars

Premium grade, production/custom, acoustic and electric archtop, and acoustic guitars built in Santa Barbara, California by luthier Mike Glick, starting in '96.

Global

Late-1960s-1970s. Budget copy models, not unlike Teisco, imported from Asia for the student market. They also offered amps.

Electric Solidbody

Late-1960s-1970s.

1968	$200	$500

GMP

1990-2005. Professional and premium grade solidbody electric guitars built by GM Precision Products, Inc. of San Dimas, California. Original owners were Gary and Cameron Moline, Dave Pearson and Glenn Matjezel. Many guitars featured fancy tops or custom graphics. They also made basses. Overall production is estimated at 1120 guitars and basses. GMP reopened in '10 under new ownership (see following).

GMP (Genuine Musical Products)

2010-present. The GMP brand was acquired by Dan and Kim Lawrence in '08. Since '10, Dan along with fellow luthiers Glenn Matjezel and William Stempke build professional and premium grade, production/custom, electric guitars in San Dimas, California. They also build basses.

GMW

1998-present. Professional grade, production/custom, solidbody guitars from Lee Garver's GMW Guitarworks of Glendora, California.

Gitane DG-255

Glendale

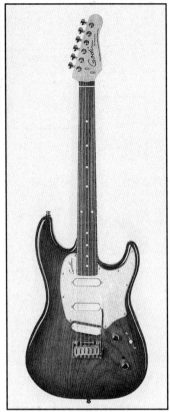

Godin Passion RG-3

Gold Tone Mastertone PBR-D

MODEL YEAR	FEATURES	EXC. COND. LOW	HIGH

Godin

1987-present. Intermediate and professional grade, production, solidbody electrics and nylon and steel string acoustic/electrics from luthier Robert Godin. They also build basses and mandolins. Necks and bodies are made in La Patrie, Quebec with final assembly in Berlin, New Hampshire. Godin is also involved in the Seagull, Norman, Richmond, Art & Lutherie, and Patrick & Simon brand of guitars. SA on Godin models stands for Synth Access.

5th Avenue Kingpin
2008-present. Full-size non-cut electric archtop, 1 or 2 P-90 pickups, plain or highly flamed top, premium price for highly flamed.

2008-2023		$750	$975

5th Avenue Uptown
2012-present. Archtop cutaway with Bigsby, f-holes, Canadian wild cherry top, back and sides, silver leaf maple neck, various colors.

2012-2023		$750	$975

A Series
1990s-present. Electric-acoustic nylon strings, single-cut, chambered body, 6-, 11-, 12-string, various wood and colors.

1990s-2023	A12, 12-string	$925	$1,250
1990s-2023	A6, 6-string	$600	$775
2000-2017	A11 Glissentar, 11-string	$850	$1,125

Acousticaster (6)
1987-2020. Thin line single-cut chambered maple body, acoustic/electric, maple neck, 6-on-a-side tuners, spruce top.

1987-2020		$550	$750

Acousticaster 6 Deluxe
1994-2008. Acousticaster 6 with mahogany body.

1994-2008		$625	$850

Artisan ST I/ST I
1992-1998. Offset double-cut solidbody, birdseye maple top, 3 pickups.

1992-1998		$725	$950

Flat Five X
2002-2004. Single-cut, semi-hollow with f-holes, 3-way pickup system (magnetic to transducer).

2002-2004		$925	$1,250

Freeway Classic/Freeway Classic SA
2004-2015. Offset double-cut solidbody, birdseye maple top on translucent finishes, hum-single-hum pickups.

2004-2015		$575	$750

G-1000/G-2000/G-3000
1993-1996. Offset double-cut solidbody, extra-large bass horn, various pickup options.

1993-1996		$350	$450

Jeff Cook Signature
1994-1995. Quilted maple top, light maple back, 2 twin rail and 1 humbucker pickups.

1994-1995		$600	$775

L.R. Baggs Signature
1990s. Single-cut chambered thinline electric, spruce top, mahogany body, EQ.

1990s		$600	$775

MODEL YEAR	FEATURES	EXC. COND. LOW	HIGH

LG/LGT
1995-2011. Single-cut carved slab mahogany body, 2 Tetrad Combo pickups ('95-'97) or 2 Duncan SP-90 pickups ('98-present), various colors, satin lacquer finish. LGT with tremolo.

1995-2011		$400	$550

LGX/LGXT/LGX-SA
1996-2018. Single-cut maple-top carved solidbody, 2 Duncan humbuckers, various quality tops offered. LGXT with tremolo.

1996-2018	Standard top	$725	$950
1997-2018	SA synth access	$950	$1,250
1998-2018	AA top	$1,125	$1,500
1998-2018	AAA top	$1,250	$1,750

Montreal Series
2004-present. Chambered body carved from solid mahogany, f-holes, 2 humbuckers, saddle transducer, stereo mixing output.

2004-2023		$850	$1,125

Multiac Series
1994-present. Single-cut, thinline electric with solid spruce top, RMC Sensor System electronics, available in either nylon string or steel string versions, built-in EQ, program up/down buttons.

1994-2023	Various models	$650	$1,750

Passion RG-3
2011-2022. Double-cut, 3 single-coil pickups, swamp ash body, rosewood neck (RN) or maple (MN), Indigo Burst finish with artic white pearloid 'guard.

2011-2022		$1,500	$1,875

Radiator
1999-2013. Single-cut, dual pickup, pearloid top, dot markers.

1999-2013		$325	$425

Redline Series
2007-2015. Maple body and neck, rosewood 'board, Redline 1 has 1 pickup, 2 and 3 have 2 pickups (3 has Floyd Rose), various colors.

2007-2011	Redline 1	$450	$575
2008-2015	Redline 2 & 3	$475	$625

SD Series
1990s-2012. Performance series, figured maple veneer top, maple neck, maple or rosewood 'board, various colors.

1990-2012	SD22, SD24	$350	$450

Solidac - Two Voice
2000-2009. Single-cut, 2-voice technology for electric or acoustic sound.

2000-2009		$425	$550

TC Signature
1987-1999. Single-cut, quilted maple top, 2 Tetrad Combo pickups.

1987-1999		$725	$950

Velocity
2007-2011. Offset double-cut, hum/single/single.

2007-2011		$650	$850

Gold Tone

1993-present. Wayne and Robyn Rogers build their intermediate and professional grade, production/custom guitars and basses in Titusville,

MODEL YEAR	FEATURES	EXC. COND. LOW	HIGH

Florida. They also build lap steels, mandolins, ukuleles, banjos and banjitars.

Goldbug Guitars
1997-present. Presentation grade, production/custom, acoustic and electric guitars built by luthier Sandy Winters in Delavan, Wisconsin.

Golden Hawaiian
1920s-1930s. Private branded lap guitar most likely made by one of the many Chicago makers for a small retailer, publisher, cataloger, or teaching studio.

Guitars

1920-1930s	Various models	$500	$650

Goldentone
1960s. Guitars made by Ibanez most likely in the mid to late '60s. Often have a stylized I (for Ibanez) on the tailpiece or an Ibanez logo on the headstock.

Goldon
German manufacturer of high-quality archtops and other guitars before and shortly after WW II. After the war, they were located in East Germany and by the late 1940s were only making musical toys.

Goodall
1972-present. Premium grade, custom flat-tops and nylon-strings, built by luthier James Goodall originally in California and, since '92, in Kailua-Kona, Hawaii.

Classical
1986. Brazilian and cedar.

1986	BC425	$6,500	$9,000

Concert Jumbo
1998-present. Various woods.

2007-2023	Red cedar/Indian rw	$3,500	$4,500
2007-2023	Sitka/figured Koa	$3,500	$4,500

Concert Jumbo Cutaway
2004-2018. Rosewood.

2004-2018		$3,750	$5,000

Jumbo KJ
1995-2011. Sitka, Koa.

1995-2011		$3,500	$4,500

RS Rosewood Standard
1989-1997. Indian rosewood back and sides.

1989-1997		$3,500	$4,500

Standard
1980s-present. Jumbo-style with wide waist, mahogany back and sides, Sitka spruce top.

1980s-2023		$3,250	$4,500

Goodman Guitars
1975-present. Premium grade, custom/production, archtop, flat-top, classical, and electric guitars built by luthier Brad Goodman in Brewster, New York. He also builds mandolins.

Goran Custom Guitars
1998-present. Luthier Goran Djuric builds his professional and premium grade, custom, electric guitars in Belgrade, Serbia. He also builds effects.

Gordon-Smith
1979-present. Intermediate and professional grade, production/custom, semi-hollow and solidbody guitars built by luthier John Smith in Partington, England.

Gower
1955-1960s. Built in Nashville by Jay Gower, later joined by his son Randy. Gower is also associated with Billy Grammer and Grammer guitars.

G-55-2 Flat-Top
1955-1968. Square shoulder-style flat-top, triple abalone rosette, abalone fretboard trim, dot markers, natural.

1955-1968		$1,250	$1,625

G-65 Flat-Top
1955-1968. Square shoulder-style flat-top, lower belly bridge with pearl dots on bridge, dot markers, sunburst.

1955-1968		$950	$1,250

G-100 Flat-Top

1955-1968	Brazilian rosewood	$1,500	$2,000

Goya
1952-1996. Brand initially used by Hershman Musical Instrument Company of New York City, New York, in mid-'50s for acoustic guitars made in Sweden by Levin, particularly known for its classicals. From '58 to '61 they imported Hagstrom- and Galanti-made electrics labeled as Goya; in '62 they offered electrics made by Valco. In '67 they again offered electrics, this time made by Zero Sette in Castelfidardo, Italy. By '63 the company had become the Goya Musical Instrument Corporation, marketing primarily Goya acoustics. Goya was purchased by Avnet, Inc., prior to '66, when Avnet purchased Guild Guitars. In '69, Goya was purchased by Kustom which offered the instruments until '71. Probably some '70s guitars were made in Japan. The brand name was purchased by C.F. Martin in '76, with Japanese-made acoustic guitars, solidbody electric guitars and basses, banjos and mandolins imported in around '78 and continuing into the '90s.

Classical
1955-1960s. Various models.

1955-1960s	G Series	$225	$1,250
1970s-80s	Japan	$450	$600

Flamenco
1955-1960s. Various models.

1955-1960s	FL Series	$225	$1,250

Folk
1950s-1980s. Various models.

1955-1960s	F Series	$225	$1,250

Model 80/Model 90
1959-1962. Single-cut body, replaceable modular pickup assembly, sparkle top.

1959-1962		$1,000	$1,500

Goodall Concert Jumbo

Goya G-13

Imaged by Heritage Auctions, HA.com

GUITARS

1966 Grammer

Bill Lawlor

Granata Resonator

MODEL		EXC. COND.	
YEAR	FEATURES	LOW	HIGH

Panther S-3
1967-1968. Double-cut solidbody, 3 pickups, Panther S-3 Goya logo, volume and tone knobs with 6 upper bass bout switches, bolt-on neck.

1967-1968		$1,000	$1,500

Rangemaster
1967-1968. Wide variety of models.

1967-1968		$925	$1,250

Steel
1955-1960s. Various models.

1955-1960s M and S Series		$150	$350

Graf
See listing under Oskar Graf Guitars.

Grammer
1965-1971. Acoustic guitars built in Nashville. Founded by country guitarist Bill Grammer, music store owner Clyde Reid and luthier J.W. Gower (who also built his own line). Grammer sold the company to Ampeg in '68 who sold it again in '71, but it quickly ceased business. Originally the Grammer headstock logo had an upper-case G, Ampeg-made instruments have a lower-case one.

G-10
1965-1970. Solid Brazilian rosewood back and sides, solid spruce top, large crown-shaped bridge, pearl dot markers, natural.

1965-1967	Grammer era	$2,500	$3,250
1968-1970	Ampeg era	$2,125	$2,750

G-20
1965-1970. Flamed maple, natural.

1965-1967	Grammer era	$2,250	$3,000
1968-1970	Ampeg era	$2,125	$2,750

G-30
1965-1970. Ribbon mahogany, natural.

1965-1967	Grammer era	$2,250	$3,000
1968-1970	Ampeg era	$2,125	$2,750

G-50
1965-1970. Top-of-the-line Grammer, Brazilian rosewood back and sides, Adirondack spruce top.

1965-1967	Grammer era	$3,000	$4,000
1968-1970	Ampeg era	$2,750	$3,500

S-30
1965-1970. Solid spruce top, solid ribbon mahogany back and sides.

1965-1967	Grammer era	$2,000	$2,500
1968-1970	Ampeg era	$1,750	$2,250

Granada
Late 1960s-1980s. Japanese-made acoustic, electric solid, semi-hollow and hollowbody guitars, many copies of classic American models. They also offered basses.

Acoustic
1970-1979. Import from Japan, various copy models.

1970-1979		$175	$275

Electric
1970-1979. Import from Japan, various copy models.

1970-1979		$250	$325

MODEL		EXC. COND.	
YEAR	FEATURES	LOW	HIGH

Granata Guitars
1989-present. Luthier Peter Granata builds his professional grade, custom, flat-top and resonator guitars in Oak Ridge, New Jersey.

Graveel
Production/custom, solidbody guitars built by luthier Dean Graveel in Indianapolis, Indiana.

Grazioso
1950s. Grazioso was a brand name used by Selmer in England on instruments made in Czechoslovakia. They replaced the brand with their Futurama line of guitars.

GRD
1978-1982. High-end acoustic and electric guitars produced in Charles Fox's Guitar Research & Design Center in Vermont. GRD introduced the original thin-line acoustic-electric guitar to the world at the '78 Winter NAMM show.

Great Divide Guitars
2009-2011. Budget and intermediate grade, production, flat-top guitars imported from China, designed by luthier Tom Bedell, Dan Mills and Sophia Yang. They also offer Bedell Guitars.

Greco
1960s-present. Brand name used in Japan and owned by Kanda Shokai. Fuji Gen Gakki, maker of many Hoshino/Ibanez guitars, also made many Greco models during the '70s; thus often Greco guitars are similar to Ibanez. During the '70s the company sold many high-quality copies of American designs, though by '75 they offered many weird-shaped original designs, including the Iceman and carved people shapes. By the late-'70s they were offering neck-through-body guitars. Currently offering solidbody, hollowbody and acoustic guitars and basses, including models licensed by Zemaitis.

Green, Aaron
1990-present. Premium and presentation grade, custom, classical and flamenco guitars built by luthier Aaron Green in Waltham, Massachusetts.

Greene & Campbell
2002-2005. Luthier Dean Campbell built his intermediate and professional grade, production/custom, solidbody guitars in Westwood, Massachusetts. Founding partner Jeffrey Greene left the company in '04; Greene earlier built guitars under his own name. In '05, Campbell changed the name to Campbell American Guitars.

Greene, Jeffrey
2000-2002. Professional grade, production/custom, electric solidbody guitars built by luthier Jeffrey Greene in West Kingston, Rhode Island. He went to work with Dean Campbell building the Greene & Campbell line of guitars.

MODEL YEAR	FEATURES	EXC. COND. LOW	HIGH

Greenfield Guitars

1996-present. Luthier Michael Greenfield builds his production/custom, presentation grade, acoustic steel string, concert classical and archtop guitars in Montreal, Quebec.

Gretsch

1883-present. Currently Gretsch offers intermediate, professional, and premium grade, production, acoustic, solidbody, hollowbody, double neck, resonator and Hawaiian guitars. They also offer basses, amps and lap steels. In 2012 they again started offering mandolins, ukuleles, and banjos.

Previous brands included Gretsch, Rex, 20th Century, Recording King (for Montgomery Ward), Dorado (Japanese imports). Founded by Friedrich Gretsch in Brooklyn, New York, making drums, banjos, tambourines, and toy instruments which were sold to large distributors including C. Bruno and Wurlitzer. Upon early death of Friedrich, son Fred Gretsch, Sr. took over business at age 15. By the turn of the century the company was also making mandolins. In the '20s, they were distributing Rex and 20th Century brands, some made by Gretsch, some by others such as Kay. Charles "Duke" Kramer joined Gretsch in '35. In '40 Gretsch purchased Bacon & Day banjos. Fred Gretsch, Sr. retired in '42 and was replaced by sons Fred, Jr., and Bill. Fred departs for Navy and Bill runs company until his death in '48, when Fred resumes control. After the war the decision was made to promote the Gretsch brand rather than selling to distributors, though some jobbing continues. Kramer becomes Chicago branch manager in '48. Gretsch's most successful innovations occurred during the Jimmie Webster era in the mid-50s. This would include straying from traditional sunburst finishes, marketing humbucking pickups, and employing a bridge that could be precisely intoned before Gibson or Fender.

The change from single-cut to double-cut bodies beginning in 1961 significantly lowers the value of most models.

In '67 Baldwin of Cincinnati bought Gretsch. During '70-'72 the factory relocated from Brooklyn to Booneville, Arkansas and company headquarters are moved to Cincinnati. A '72 factory fire drastically reduced production for next two years. In '78 Baldwin bought Kustom amps and sold Gretsch to Kustom's Charlie Roy, and headquarters are moved to Chanute, Kansas. Duke Kramer retired in '80. Guitar production ends '80-'81. Ca. '83 ownership reverted back to Baldwin and Kramer was asked to arrange the sale of the company. In '84 Fred Gretsch III was contacted and in '85 Gretsch guitars came back to the Gretsch family and Fred Gretsch Enterprises, Ltd (FGE). Initial Gretsch Enterprise models were imports made by Japan's Terada Company. In '95, some U.S.-made models were introduced. In 2003, Gretsch granted Fender the rights to develop, produce, market, and distribute Gretsch guitars worldwide, including development

of new products.

Binding rot can be a problem on 1950s models and prices shown are for fully original, unrestored bindings.

12-String Electric Archtop (6075/6076)

1967-1972. 16" double-cut, 2 Super Tron pickups, 17" body option available, sunburst (6075) or natural (6076).

1967-1972		$2,500	$3,250

12-String Flat-Top (6020)

1969-1972. 15 1/5" body, mahogany back and sides, spruce top, slotted headstock, dot markers.

1969-1972		$1,250	$1,625

Anniversary (6124/6125)

1958-1972, 1993-1999. Single-cut hollow body archtop, 1 pickup (Filtron '58-'60, Hi-Lo Tron '61 on), bound body, named for Gretsch's 75th anniversary. 6125 is 2-tone green with 2-tone tan an option, 6124 sunburst. Model numbers were revived in '90s.

1958-1959	Green 2-tone	$3,000	$5,000
1958-1959	Sunburst	$3,000	$5,000
1960-1961	Green 2-tone or tan	$3,000	$5,000
1960-1961	Sunburst	$3,000	$5,000
1962-1964	Green 2-tone or tan	$2,500	$3,500
1962-1964	Sunburst	$2,500	$3,500
1965-1966	Various colors	$1,750	$2,250
1967-1969	Various colors	$1,500	$2,000
1970-1972	Various colors	$1,375	$1,750

Anniversary Tenor (6124)

1958-1971. Gretsch offered many models with the 4-string tenor option and also made small batches of tenors, with the same colors and pickups as standard models.

1958-1971		$1,750	$2,250

Anniversary Reissue (6124/6125)

1993-1999. 1 pickup Anniversary reissue, 6124 in sunburst, 6125 2-tone green.

1993-1999		$1,500	$2,000

Anniversary Reissue (6117/6118)

1993-present. 2 pickup like Double Anniversary, 6118 in 2-tone green with (T) or without Bigsby, 6117 is sunburst.

1993-2015	6117	$1,500	$2,000
1993-2023	6118	$1,500	$2,000

Astro-Jet (6126)

1965-1967. Solid body electric, double-cut, 2 pickups, vibrato, 4/2 tuner arrangement, red top with black back and sides.

1965-1967		$2,000	$2,500

Atkins Axe (7685/7686)

1976-1980. Solid body electric, pointed single-cut, 2 pickups, ebony stain (7685) or red rosewood stain (7686), called the Super Axe with added on-board effects.

1976-1980		$1,375	$1,750

Atkins Super Axe (7680/7681)

1976-1981. Pointed single-cut solid body with built-in phaser and sustain, five knobs, three switches, Red Rosewood (7680) or Ebony (7681) stains.

1976-1981		$2,000	$2,500

1982 Greco Silverburst
Mike Greco

Greenfield Andy McKee Model

MODEL		EXC. COND.	
YEAR	FEATURES	LOW	HIGH

1961 Gretsch Bikini (6025)
Randy Barnett

Gretsch Brian Setzer
Hot Rod (6120SHx)

Bikini (6023/6024/6025)

1961-1962. Solid body electric, separate 6-string and bass neck-body units that slide into 1 of 3 body butterflies - 1 for the 6-string only (6023), 1 for bass only (6024), 1 for double neck (6 and bass - 6025). Components could be purchased separately.

1961-1962	6023/6024, single	$1,500	$2,000
1961-1962	6025, double	$3,500	$4,500

Billy-Bo Jupiter Thunderbird (6199)

2005-present. Billy Gibbons and Bo Diddley influenced, chambered mahogany body, laminate maple top, 2 pickups.

2005-2023		$2,250	$2,750

Black Falcon (6136BK/TBK/DSBK)

1992-1997, 2003-2015. Black version of Falcon, single-cut, 2.75" body, oversize f-holes, G tailpiece, DSBK with DynaSonic pickups replaces Filter'Tron BK in '06. Had the Limited Edition 1955 designation for '96-'97. Bigsby-equipped TBK offered '04-present.

1992-2015		$2,750	$3,500

Black Falcon (7594BK)

1992-1998. Black version of G7594 Falcon, double-cut, 2" thick body, Bigsby.

1992-1998		$2,750	$3,500

Black Falcon I (7593BK)

1993-1998, 2003-2005. G63136BK with Bigsby and standard f-holes. Came back in '03 as Black Falcon I with wire handle Gretsch Bigsby tailpiece.

1993-1998		$2,750	$3,500

Black Hawk (6100/6101)

1967-1972. Hollow body archtop, double-cut, 2 pickups, G tailpiece or Bigsby vibrato, bound body and neck, sunburst (6100) or black (6101).

1967-1972	6100, sunburst	$2,750	$3,500
1967-1972	6101, black	$2,750	$3,500

Black Penguin (6134B)

2003-2015. Jet black version.

2003-2015		$2,500	$3,125

Bo Diddley (1810/5810)

2000-2015. Korean-made version.

2000-2015		$275	$350

Bo Diddley (6138)

1999-present. Reproduction of rectangle-shaped, semi-hollow guitar originally made for Diddley by Gretsch, Firebird Red.

1999-2023		$1,500	$1,875

Broadkaster (Hollow Body)

1975-1980. Double-cut archtop, hollow body, 2 pickups, natural or sunburst. Red available '77-'80.

1975-1977	7603, Bigsby, natural	$1,250	$1,500
1975-1977	7604, Bigsby, sunburst	$1,250	$1,500
1975-1977	7607, G tailpiece, natural	$1,250	$1,500
1975-1977	7608, G tailpiece, sunburst	$1,250	$1,500
1977-1980	7609, red	$1,250	$1,500

Broadkaster (Solid Body)

1975-1979. Double-cut, maple body, 2 pickups, bolt-on neck, natural (7600) or sunburst (7601).

1975-1979	7600 and 7601	$1,250	$1,500

MODEL		EXC. COND.	
YEAR	FEATURES	LOW	HIGH

BST 1000 Beast

1979-1980. Single-cut solid body, bolt-on neck, mahogany body, available with 1 pickup in walnut stain (8210) or red stain (8216) or 2 pickups in walnut (7617, 8215, 8217) or red stain (8211).

1979-1980		$925	$1,125

BST 2000 Beast

1979. Symmetrical double-cut solid body of mahogany, 2 humbucking pickups, bolt-on neck, walnut stain (7620 or 8220) or red stain (8221).

1979		$925	$1,125

BST 5000 Beast

1979-1980. Asymmetrical double-cut solid body, neck-thru, walnut and maple construction, 2 humbucker pickups, stud tailpiece, natural walnut/maple (8250).

1979-1980		$1,000	$1,250

Burl Ives (6004)

1949-1955. Flat-top acoustic, mahogany back and sides, bound body, natural top (6004).

1949-1955		$1,000	$1,250

Chet Atkins Country Gentleman (6122/7670)

1958-1981. Hollow body, single-cut to late-'62 and double after, 2 pickups, painted f-holes until '72, real after, mahogany finish (6122). Model number changes to 7670 in '71. Guitars made during and after '64 might have replaced body binding which reduces the value shown by about 10% or more

1958-1959		$8,000	$11,000
1960		$7,000	$9,000
1961		$7,000	$9,000
1962-1963	George Harrison specs	$7,000	$9,000
1964		$3,500	$5,000
1965		$3,500	$5,000
1966-1970		$3,000	$4,000
1971-1981	7670	$3,000	$4,000

Chet Atkins Country Gentleman (6122-1958)

2007-2015. Single-cut reissue of '58.

2007-2015		$2,250	$3,000

Chet Atkins Country Gentleman (6122-1962)

2007-2015. Double-cut reissue of '62, double muffler (mutes) system, Filter'Trons.

2007-2015		$2,250	$3,000

Chet Atkins Hollow Body (6120)

1954-1966, 2007-2015. Archtop electric, single-cut to '61, double after, 2 pickups, vibrato, f-holes (real to '61 and fake after), cactus and cows engraved block inlays '54-early '56, G brand on top '54-'56, orange finish (6120). Renamed Chet Atkins Nashville in '67. Reissued single-cut in '07.

1954-1955	G brand, Western	$20,000	$25,000
1955-1956	Non-engraved, amber red	$15,000	$18,000
1957-1959	No G-brand	$10,000	$12,000
1960-1961	Single-cut	$8,000	$10,000
1961-1966	Double-cut	$5,000	$7,000
2007-2015	Single-cut	$2,000	$2,500

MODEL YEAR	FEATURES	EXC. COND. LOW	HIGH

Chet Atkins Nashville (6120/7660)
1967-1980. Replaced Chet Atkins Hollow Body (6120), electric archtop, double-cut, 2 pickups, amber red (orange). Renumbered 7660 in '72, reissued in '90 as the Model 6120 Nashville.

1967-1969	6120	$3,500	$4,500
1970-1971	6120	$2,500	$3,500
1972-1980	7660	$2,500	$3,500

Chet Atkins Nashville (6120DC)
2007-2016. Double-cut hollow body based on '62 model, gold plated 'guard with Atkin's signature.

2007-2016		$2,125	$2,750

Chet Atkins Hollow Body (6120W-1957)
2007-2009. Western Maple Stain, western block inlays, Bigsby.

2007-2009		$2,250	$3,000

Brian Setzer Black Phoenix (6136-SLBP)
2005-2015. Artist Signature Series, nitro gloss black.

2005-2015		$2,500	$3,500

Brian Setzer Hot Rod (6120SHx)
1999-present. Like SSL, but with only pickup switch and 1 master volume control, various colors.

1999-2020		$1,750	$2,500

Brian Setzer Nashville (6120SSL, etc.)
1993-present. Hollow body electric, double-cut, 2 Alnico PAF Filtertron pickups, based on the classic Gretsch 6120.

1993-2023	Western Orange	$2,500	$3,500

Chet Atkins Junior
1970. Archtop, single-cut, 1 pickup, vibrato, open f-holes, double-bound body, orange stain.

1970		$1,250	$1,625

Duane Eddy (6210DE)
1997-2003. 6120 style, 2 DeArmond single coils, Bigsby, orange.

1997-2003		$2,750	$3,500

Duane Eddy Signature Hollow Body (6120DE)
2011-present. Single-cut, Western Orange stain lacquer finish.

2011-2023		$2,250	$3,000

Eddie Cochran Signature Hollow Body (6120)
2011-present. Artist Signature Edition, maple body, rosewood 'board, Bigsby, Western maple stain.

2011-2023		$2,250	$3,000

Keith Scott Nashville (6120KS)
1999-2013. Hump-back inlays, gold hardware, metallic gold finish.

1999-2013		$2,125	$2,750

Nashville Double Neck 6/12 (6120)
1997-2002. Built in Japan, few made, all gold hardware, necks are maple with ebony 'boards, orange finish.

1997-2002		$3,000	$4,000

Nashville Jr. (6120-JR/JR2)
1998-2004. Orange, 2 pickups.

1998-2004		$1,250	$1,625

New Nashville (6120N)
2001-2003. Single-cut, humptop inlays, gold hardware.

2001-2003		$2,250	$3,000

Reverend Horton Heat (6120RHH)
2005-present. Cows and cactus inlays, TV jones pickups.

2005-2023		$2,250	$3,000

Chet Atkins Solid Body (6121)
1955-1963. Solid body electric, single-cut, maple or knotty pine top, 2 pickups, Bigsby vibrato, G brand until '57, multi-bound top, brown mahogany, orange finish (6121).

1955-1956	Full Western	$12,000	$14,000
1957	G brand	$10,000	$12,500
1957-1959	No G brand	$6,000	$8,000
1960	Single-cut	$6,000	$8,000
1961-1963	Double-cut	$5,000	$7,000

Chet Atkins Tennessean (6119/7655)
1958-1980. Archtop electric, single-cut, 1 pickup until early-'61 and 2 after, vibrato. Renumbered as the 7655 in '71.

1958-1960	1 Fil 'tron	$5,000	$6,500
1960-1961		$4,500	$6,000
1961-1964	2 Hi-Lo	$5,000	$6,000
1965-1967	2 pickups	$3,500	$4,500
1968-1970	2 pickups	$3,500	$4,500
1971-1980	7655	$3,250	$4,000

Chet Atkins Tennessee Rose (6119-1959, 1962)
1995-2015. Import, 16" maple body, maple neck, dual FilterTron pickups.

1995-2015	1959 and 1962	$2,000	$2,500

Clipper (6185/6186/6187/7555)
1958-1975. Archtop electric, single-cut, sunburst, 1 pickup (6186) until '72 and 2 pickups (6185) from '72-'75, also available in 1 pickup natural (6187) from '59-'61.

1958-1961	6186	$1,375	$1,750
1959-1961	6187	$1,500	$2,000
1962-1967	6186	$1,375	$1,750
1968-1971	6186	$1,250	$1,750
1972-1975	7555	$1,500	$2,000

Committee (7628)
1977-1980. Neck-thru electric solid body, double-cut, walnut and maple body, 2 pickups, 4 knobs, natural.

1977-1980		$1,000	$1,375

Constellation (6030/6031)
1955-1960. Renamed from Synchromatic 6030 and 6031, archtop acoustic, single-cut, G tailpiece, humped block inlay.

1955-1960		$2,250	$3,000

Convertible (6199)
1955-1958. Archtop electric, single-cut, 1 pickup, multi-bound body, G tailpiece, renamed Sal Salvador in '58.

1955-1958		$2,750	$3,500

Corsair
1955-1960. Renamed from Synchromatic 100, archtop acoustic, bound body and headstock, G tailpiece, available in sunburst (6014), natural (6015) or burgundy (6016).

1955-1960	6014, 6015, 6016	$1,250	$1,625

1956 Gretsch Chet Atkins
Hollow Body 6120
Jim Hilmar

1962 Gretsch Chet Atkins
Tennessean (6119/7655)
Matt Carleson

1963 Gretsch Country Club

Geoff Barker

1964 Gretsch Double
Anniversary Mono (6117/6118)

Guitar Maniacs

MODEL YEAR	FEATURES	EXC. COND. LOW	HIGH

Corvette (Hollow Body)

1955-1959. Renamed from Electromatic Spanish, archtop electric, 1 pickup, f-holes, bound body, Electromatic on headstock, non-cut, sunburst (6182), Jaguar Tan or natural (6184), and ivory with rounded cutaway (6187).

1955-1959	6182, sunburst	$1,250	$1,625
1955-1959	6184, Jaguar Tan	$1,625	$2,500
1955-1959	6184, natural	$2,000	$2,500
1957-1959	6187, ivory	$2,375	$3,000

Corvette (Solid Body)

1961-1972, 1976-1978. Double-cut slab solid body. Mahogany 6132 and cherry 6134 1 pickup for '61-'68. 2 pickup mahogany 6135 and cherry 7623 available by '63-'72 and '76-'78. From late-'61 through '63 a Twist option was offered featuring a red candy stripe 'guard. Platinum Gray 6133 available for '61-'63 and the Gold Duke and Silver Duke sparkle finishes were offered in '66.

1961-1962	Mahogany, cherry	$1,250	$1,625
1961-1963	Platinum Gray	$1,875	$2,500
1961-1963	Twist 'guard	$1,875	$2,500
1963-1965	Custom color, 1 pu	$1,875	$2,500
1963-1965	Custom color, 2 pu	$2,125	$2,750
1963-1965	Mahogany, cherry, 1 pu	$1,000	$1,500
1963-1965	Mahogany, cherry, 2 pu	$1,375	$1,750
1966	Gold Duke	$1,875	$2,500
1966	Silver Duke	$1,875	$2,500
1966-1968	Mahogany, cherry, 1 pu	$1,125	$1,500
1966-1968	Mahogany, cherry, 2 pu	$1,250	$1,625
1969-1972	Mahogany, cherry, 2 pu	$1,250	$1,625
1976-1978	7623, 2 pu	$1,125	$1,500

Corvette/CVT (5135)

2006-2018. Like double-cut solid body Corvette, 2 Mega'Tron pickups, Bigsby, becomes the CVT in '10.

2006-2018		$650	$850

Country Classic I/II (6122 Reissue)

1989-2006. Country Gentleman reissue with '58 (I) and '62 (II) specs. Also cataloged as G6122-1958 and G6122-1962 Country Classic.

1989-2006	'58, single-cut	$2,250	$3,000
1989-2006	'62, double-cut	$2,250	$3,000

Country Classic II Custom Edition (6122)

2005. Reissue of George Harrison's 2nd 6122 Country Gentleman, the Custom Edition has TV Jones Filtertron pickups.

2005		$2,250	$3,000

Country Club

1954-1981. Renamed from Electro II Cutaway, archtop electric, single-cut, 2 pickups (Filter Trons after '57), G tailpiece, multi-bound, various colors.

1954-1958	Sunburst	$5,000	$6,500
1954-1959	Cadillac Green	$6,000	$7,500
1954-1959	Natural	$5,000	$6,500
1959	Sunburst	$6,000	$7,500
1960-1964	Cadillac Green	$5,500	$7,000
1960-1964	Sunburst	$4,500	$6,000
1961-1962	Natural	$4,500	$6,000
1965-1969	Sunburst or walnut	$3,500	$4,500
1970-1981	Various colors	$3,000	$4,000

Country Club 1955 (6196-1955) (FGE)

1995-1999. U.S.-made reissue of Country Club, single-cut, 2 DeArmond pickups, hand-rubbed lacquer finish.

1995-1999		$2,250	$3,000

Country Club (6196, etc.)

2001-present. Includes Cadillac Green (G6196, '01-present), sunburst (G6192, '03-'08), amber natural (G6193,'03-'08), Bamboo Yellow (G6196TSP-BY, '09-'13), and smoky gray and violet 2-tone (G6196TSP-2G, '09-'12), G6196T-59GE Golden Era Edition ('16-present), T means Bigsby.

2001-2023	Cadillac Green	$2,250	$3,000
2009-2013	Bamboo Yellow	$2,250	$3,000

Country Roc (7620)

1974-1978. Single-cut solid body, 2 pickups, belt buckle tailpiece, western scene fretboard inlays, G brand, tooled leather side trim.

1974-1978		$2,500	$3,000

Custom (6117)

1964-1968. Limited production, smaller thinner version of Double Anniversary model, 2 pickups, cat's eye sound holes, red or black finish.

1964		$3,750	$5,000
1965-1966		$3,250	$4,500
1967-1968		$3,250	$4,500

Deluxe Chet (7680/7681)

1972-1974. Electric archtop with rounded cutaway, Autumn Red (7680) or brown walnut (7681) finishes.

1972-1974		$2,500	$3,500

Deluxe Flat-Top (7535)

1972-1978. 16" redwood top, mahogany back and sides.

1972-1978		$2,250	$3,000

Double Anniversary Mono (6117/6118)

1958-1976. Archtop electric, single-cut, 2 pickups, stereo optional until '63, sunburst (6117) or green 2-tone (6118). Reissued in '93 as the Anniversary 6117 and 6118.

1958-1959	Green 2-tone	$5,000	$7,000
1958-1959	Sunburst	$5,000	$7,000
1960-1961	Green 2-tone	$4,000	$5,000
1960-1961	Sunburst	$4,000	$5,000
1962-1964	Green 2-tone or tan	$3,000	$4,000
1962-1964	Sunburst	$2,500	$3,250
1965-1966	Various colors	$1,750	$2,250
1967-1969	Various colors	$1,500	$2,000
1970-1976	Various colors	$1,350	$1,750

Double Anniversary Stereo (6111/6112)

1961-1963. One stereo channel/signal per pickup, sunburst (6111) or green (6112).

1961-1963	Green	$3,000	$4,000
1961-1963	Sunburst	$2,500	$3,500

Duo-Jet (6128)

1953-1971. Solid body electric, single-cut until '61, double after, 2 pickups, block inlays to late '56, then humptop until early '58, then thumbprint inlays, black

MODEL YEAR	FEATURES	EXC. COND. LOW	HIGH

(6128) with a few special-order Cadillac Green, sparkle finishes were offered '63-'66, reissued in '90.

1953	Black, single-cut, script logo	$8,000	$10,000
1955-1956	Black, blocks	$6,000	$8,000
1956-1958	Black, humptop	$8,000	$10,000
1957	Cadillac Green	$15,000	$18,000
1958-1960	Black, thumbprint	$6,000	$8,000
1961-1964	Black, double-cut	$5,000	$6,000
1963-1966	Sparkle, double-cut	$10,000	$12,000
1965-1971	Black	$4,000	$5,000

Duo-Jet (6128TCG)
2005-2016. Cadillac Green, gold hardware, Bigsby.

2005-2016		$2,250	$3,000

Duo-Jet Reissue (6128/6128T)
1990-2017. Reissue of the '50s solid body, optional Bigsby (G6128T). Replaced by Vintage Select Edition series.

1990-2017		$1,750	$2,250

Duo-Jet Tenor (6127)
1954-1960. Electric tenor, 4 strings, block inlays, black.

1954-1960		$3,500	$4,500

Duo-Jet Vintage Select Edition '59 (6128T-59)
2017-present. Bigsby, TV Jones Filter 'Trons, black.

2017-2023		$2,250	$3,000

Elliot Easton Signature Duo-Jet (6128TEE)
2000-2005. Bigsby, gold hardware, Cadillac Green (TEE), red (TREE), black (TBEE).

2000-2005		$2,250	$3,000

Eldorado (6040/6041)
1955-1970, 1991-1997. This is the larger 18" version, renamed from Synchromatic 400, archtop acoustic, single-cut, triple-bound fretboard and peghead, sunburst (6040) or natural (6041). Reintroduced in '91, made by Heritage in Kalamazoo, as the G410 Synchromatic Eldorado in sunburst or natural (G410M).

1955-1959	Natural	$3,250	$4,250
1955-1959	Sunburst	$2,625	$3,500
1960-1963	Natural	$2,500	$3,250
1960-1963	Sunburst	$2,250	$3,000
1964	Natural	$2,000	$2,625
1964	Sunburst	$1,875	$2,500
1965-1997	Natural, sunburst	$1,750	$2,250

Eldorado (6038/6039)
1959-1968. The smaller 17" version, named Fleetwood from '55 to '58, sunburst (6038) or natural (6039), also available as a full body non-cutaway.

1959-1964	Natural, sunburst	$1,500	$2,000
1965-1968	Natural, sunburst	$1,375	$1,750

Electro Classic (6006/6495)
1969-1973. Classical flat-top with piezo pickup.

1969-1970	6006	$800	$1,125
1971-1973	6495	$800	$1,125

Electro II Cutaway (6192/6193)
1951-1954. Archtop electric, single-cut, Melita bridge by '53, 2 pickups, f-holes, sunburst (6192) or natural (6193). Renamed Country Club in '54.

1951-1954	6192, sunburst	$4,250	$5,500
1951-1954	6193, natural	$4,750	$6,125

Electro II Non-Cutaway (6187/6188)
1951-1954. 16" electric archtop, 2 DeArmonds, large f-holes, block markers, 6187 sunburst, 6188 natural, label is Model 6187-8, vertical Electromatic logo on headstock.

1951-1954	6187, sunburst	$3,750	$5,000
1951-1954	6188, natural	$3,750	$5,000

Electromatic (5420T)
2013-present. Hollow body, single-cut, Bigsby.

2013-2023		$550	$750

Electromatic (5422-12)
2013-present. 12-string 5422.

2013-2023		$550	$750

Electromatic (5422T)
2013-present. Hollow body, double-cut, Bigsby.

2013-2023		$550	$750

Electromatic Hollow Body (5120/5125-29/5420)
2005-2020. Single-cut, 2 dual-coils, Bigsby, black, Aspen Green, sunburst or orange. With Filter'Tron pickups in '13 (5420).

2005-2020		$550	$750

Electromatic Hollow Body (5122/5422)
2009-2014. Double-cut version of G5120, 2 dual-coils, Bigsby, black, trans red or walnut. With Filter'Tron pickups in '13 (5422). Replaced with G5422T.

2009-2014		$550	$750

Tim Armstrong Signature Electromatic (5191BK-TA)
2010-present. Hollow body, single-cut, gold hardware.

2010-2023		$750	$975

Electromatic Spanish (6185/6185N)
1940-1955. Hollow body, 17" wide, 1 pickup, sunburst (6185) or natural (6185N). Renamed Corvette (hollowbody) in '55.

1940-1949	Sunburst	$1,625	$2,125
1950-1955	Natural	$1,625	$2,125
1950-1955	Sunburst	$1,500	$2,000

Fleetwood (6038/6039)
1955-1958. Named Synchromatic prior to '55, single-cut, sunburst (6038) or natural (6039). Renamed Eldorado in '59, available by custom order.

1955-1958	Natural	$3,750	$5,000
1955-1958	Sunburst	$3,000	$4,000

Folk/Folk Singing (6003/7505/7506)
1963-1975. Lower-model of Gretsch flat-tops, 14 1/4", mahogany back and sides. Renamed from Jimmie Rodgers model, renamed Folk Singing in '63.

1963-1964		$875	$1,125
1965-1969		$750	$975
1970-1975		$650	$850

Golden Classic (Hauser/6000)
1961-1969. Grand Concert body size, nylon-string classical, 14 1/4" spruce top, mahogany back and sides, multiple inlaid sound hole purfling, inlaid headstock.

1961-1969		$575	$750

Grand Concert (6003)
1955-1959. Lower-model of Gretsch flat-tops, 14 1/4", mahogany back and sides. Renamed from Model 6003 and renamed Jimmie Rodgers in '59.

1955-1959		$900	$1,250

1955 Gretsch Eldorado (6040/6041)

2015 Gretsch Electromatic (5422T)
David Mullins

2019 Gretsch Malcom Young
Signature Jet (6131-MY)

1955 Gretsch New Yorker
Tim Fleck

MODEL YEAR	FEATURES	EXC. COND. LOW	HIGH

Guitar-Banjo
1920s. 6-string guitar neck on banjo body, slotted headstock, open back.

1920s		$675	$900

Jet 21
Late-1940s. 16" acoustic archtop, Jet 21 engraved logo on headstock, bound top and back, white 'guard, jet black finish.

1947-1948		$850	$1,125

Jet Firebird (6131)
1955-1971. Solid body electric, single-cut until '61, double '61-'71, 2 pickups, black body with red top, block inlays to late '56, then humptop until early '58, then thumbprint inlays.

1955-1956	Single-cut	$8,000	$10,000
1957-1958	Single-cut	$8,500	$10,000
1959-1960	Single-cut	$6,000	$8,000
1961-1964	Double-cut	$5,000	$6,500
1965-1967		$4,000	$5,500
1968-1971	Super Trons	$4,000	$5,500

Jet Firebird Reissue/Power Jet Firebird (6131/6131T)
1989-1997, 2003-2019. Single-cut '58 specs, red top, 2 FilterTrons, thumbprint markers, gold hardware for '91-'05, currently chrome. Bigsby available (T). Non-Bigsby 6131 ends in '05. DynaSonic-equipped TDS starts in '05 and TV Jones PowerTrons (TVP) in '06.

2003-2019		$1,750	$2,250

Jet/Pearl Jet/Blue Pearl Jet (6129/6129T)
1996-2011. Chambered mahogany body with maple top, unique Pearl or Blue Pearl finish.

1996-2011		$1,875	$2,500

Jimmie Rodgers (6003)
1959-1962. 14" flat-top with round hole, mahogany back and sides, renamed from Grand Concert and renamed Folk Singing in '63.

1959-1962		$900	$1,250

Jumbo Synchromatic (125F)
1947-1955. 17" flat-top, triangular sound hole, bound top and back, metal bridge anchor plate, adjustable wood bridge, natural top with sunburst back and sides or optional translucent white-blond top and sides.

1947-1955	Natural	$2,500	$3,250
1947-1955	White-blond	$2,750	$3,500

Malcom Young Signature Jet (6131-MY)
2018-present. Professional Collection series, double-cut mahogany body, maple top, aged white binding, semi-gloss natural finish.

2018-2023		$2,500	$3,250

Model 25 (Acoustic)
1933-1939. 16" archtop, no binding on top or back, dot markers, sunburst.

1933-1939		$775	$1,000

Model 30 (Acoustic)
1939-1949. 16" archtop, top binding, dot markers, sunburst.

1939-1949		$850	$1,125

Model 35 (Acoustic)
1933-1949. 16" archtop, single-bound top and back, dot markers, sunburst.

1933-1949		$1,000	$1,500

Model 40 Hawaiian (Acoustic)
1936-1949. Flat-top, bound top and neck, diamond inlays.

1936-1949		$1,000	$1,500

Model 50/50R (Acoustic)
1936-1949. Acoustic archtop, f-holes. Model 50R ('36-'39) has round sound hole.

1936-1939	TG-50 Tenor	$800	$1,125
1936-1949	50/50R	$1,250	$1,625

Model 65 (Acoustic)
1933-1939. Archtop acoustic, bound body, amber.

1933-1939		$1,250	$1,625

Model 75 Tenor (Acoustic)
1933-1949. 4-string tenor.

1933-1949		$850	$1,125

Model 6003
1951-1955. 14 1/4", mahogany back and sides, renamed Grand Concert in '55.

1951-1954		$1,000	$1,500

Monkees
Late 1966-1968. Hollow body electric, double-cut, 2 pickups, Monkees logo on 'guard, bound top, f-holes and neck, vibrato, red.

1966-1968		$3,000	$4,000

New Yorker
Ca.1949-1970. Archtop acoustic, f-holes, sunburst.

1949-1959		$750	$975
1960-1964		$700	$950
1965-1969		$600	$800
1970		$500	$650

New Yorker Tenor (6050)
1950s. 4-string tenor version.

1950s		$500	$650

Ozark/Ozark Soft String (6005)
1965-1968. 16" classical, rosewood back and sides.

1965-1968		$500	$650

Princess (6106)
1963. Corvette-type solid body double-cut, 1 pickup, vibrato, gold parts, colors available were white/grape, blue/white, pink/white, or white/gold, often sold with the Princess amp.

1963		$3,000	$4,000

Rally (6104/6105)
1967-1969. Archtop, double-cut, 2 pickups, vibrato, racing stripe on truss rod cover and pickguard, Rally Green (6104) or Bamboo Yellow (6105).

1967-1969	6104 or 6105	$2,750	$3,500

Rambler (6115)
1957-1961. Small body electric archtop, single-cut, 1 DeArmond pickup '57-59, then 1 Hi-Lo 'Tron '60-'61, G tailpiece, bound body and headstock.

1957-1959	DeArmond	$3,000	$4,000
1960-1961	Hi-Lo 'Tron	$2,375	$3,000

Rancher
1954-1980. Flat-top acoustic, triangle sound hole, Western theme inlay, G brand until '61 and '75 and after, Golden Red (orange), reissued in '90.

1954-1957	G brand	$6,000	$8,000
1958-1961	G brand	$5,500	$7,500
1962-1964	No G brand	$4,500	$5,750
1965-1969	No G brand	$3,500	$4,500

The Official Vintage Guitar magazine Price Guide 2025 **Gretsch** Roc I/Roc II (7635/7621) — Streamliner Center Block Jr. (2655T) **215**

GUITARS

MODEL YEAR	FEATURES	EXC. COND. LOW	HIGH
1970-1974	No G brand	$3,000	$4,000
1975-1980	G brand	$3,000	$4,000

Roc I/Roc II (7635/7621)

1974-1976. Electric solid body, mahogany, single-cut, Duo-Jet-style body, 1 pickup (7635) or 2 pickups (7621), bound body and neck.

1974-1976	Roc I	$1,500	$2,000
1974-1977	Roc II	$1,625	$2,125

Roc Jet

1970-1980. Electric solid body, single-cut, 2 pickups, adjustamatic bridge, black, cherry, pumpkin or walnut.

1970-1980		$1,875	$2,500

Round-Up (6130)

1954-1960. Electric solid body, single-cut, 2 pickups, G brand, belt buckle tailpiece, maple, pine, knotty pine or orange. Reissued in '90.

1954-1956	Knotty pine (2 knots)	$15,000	$20,000
1954-1956	Knotty pine (4 knots)	$20,000	$25,000
1954-1956	Mahogany (few made)	$12,000	$15,000
1954-1956	Pine	$15,000	$18,000
1957-1960	Orange	$8,000	$10,000

Round-Up Reissue (6121/6121W)

1989-1995, 2003-2006. Based on the '50s model, Bigsby, Western Orange.

1989-2006		$2,000	$2,500

Round-Up Western Leather Trim (6130)

2006-2007. Higher-end reissue of '55 Round-Up, G brand, tooled leather trim around edge, cactus and cows inlays.

2006-2007		$2,500	$3,250

Round-Up Knotty Pine (6130KPW)

2008-2010. Like '06 6130 but with belt buckle tailpiece and knotty pine top.

2008-2010		$3,250	$4,250

Sal Fabraio (6117)

1964-1968. Double-cut thin electric archtop, distinctive cats-eye f-holes, 2 pickups, sunburst, ordered for resale by guitar teacher Sal Fabraio.

1964-1968		$2,250	$3,000

Sal Salvador (6199)

1958-1968. Electric archtop, single-cut, 1 pickup, triple-bound neck and headstock, sunburst.

1958-1959		$2,500	$3,250
1960-1962		$2,250	$3,000
1963-1964		$2,000	$2,500
1965-1968		$1,750	$2,250

Sho Bro (Hawaiian/Spanish)

1969-1978. Flat-top acoustic, multi-bound, resonator, Lucite fretboard, Hawaiian version non-cut, square neck and Spanish version non- or single-cut, round neck.

1969-1978	Hawaiian	$1,250	$1,500
1969-1978	Spanish	$1,125	$1,375

Sierra Jumbo (3700)

1999-2005. Historic series, single-cut jumbo body, triangular sound hole, sunburst finish.

1999-2005		$450	$600

Silver Classic (Hauser/6001)

1961-1969. Grand Concert body size, nylon-string classical. Similar to Golden Classic but with less fancy appointments.

1961-1969		$500	$650

Silver Falcon (6136SL) (1955) (T)

1995-1999, 2003-2005. Black finish, silver features, single cut, G tailpiece available until '05, T for Bigsby available starting '05. Had the 1955 designation in the '90s.

1995-1999		$2,250	$3,000

Silver Falcon (7594SL)

1995-1999. Black finish and silver features, double-cut, 2" thick body.

1995-1999		$2,250	$3,000

Silver Jet (6129)

1954-1963. Solid body electric, single-cut until '61, double '61-'63, 2 pickups, Duo-Jet with silver sparkle top, reissued in '89. Optional sparkle colors were offered but were not given their own model numbers; refer to Duo-Jet listing for optional colors.

1954-1956	Single-cut	$8,000	$10,000
1957-1958	Single-cut	$8,000	$10,000
1959-1960	Single-cut	$8,000	$10,000
1961-1963	Double-cut	$7,500	$9,500
1961-1963	Double-cut, Burgandy	$13,000	$15,500

Silver Jet 1957 Reissue (6129-1957)

1989-2019. Reissue of single-cut '50s Silver Jet, silver sparkle. '1957' added to name in '94.

1989-2019		$1,500	$2,000

Silver Jet 1962 Reissue (6129-1962)

1996-2009. Reissue of '60s double-cut Silver Jet, silver sparkle.

1996-2009		$1,500	$2,000

Songbird (Sam Goody 711)

1967-1968. Standard body thinline double-cut with G sound holes, offered by Sam Goody of New York.

1967-1968		$3,500	$4,500

Southern Belle (7176)

1983. Electric archtop, walnut, parts from the late-'70s assembled in Mexico and U.S., 5 made with all original parts, several others without pickguard and case.

1983		$1,250	$1,625

Sparkle Jet (6129/6129T/6129TG)

1995-2019. Duo-Jet with sparkle finishes other than Silver, single-cut, 2 pickups. Many different colors offered over the years.

1995-2019		$1,500	$2,000

Streamliner Single Cutaway (6189/6190/6191)

1955-1959. Electric archtop, single-cut, maple top, G tailpiece, 1 pickup, multi-bound, Jaguar Tan (6189), sunburst (6190), or natural (6191). Name reintroduced as a double-cut in '68.

1955-1959	6189, Jaguar Tan	$3,000	$3,750
1955-1959	6190, Sunburst	$2,750	$3,500
1955-1959	6191, Natural	$3,500	$4,250

Streamliner Center Block Jr. (2655T)

2016-present. Double-cut, spruce center block, Bigsby, black, walnut stain or Golddust.

2016-2023		$450	$600

1970 Gretsch Sho Bro

Gretsch Streamliner Center Block Jr. (G2655T)

1988 Gretsch Traveling
Wilburys (TW300T)
Ted Wulfers

1955 Gretsch Syncromatic
Pete Mann

MODEL YEAR	FEATURES	EXC. COND. LOW	HIGH

Streamliner Double Cutaway (6102/6103)
1968-1973. Reintroduced from single-cut model, electric archtop, double-cut, 2 pickups, G tailpiece, cherry or sunburst.

| 1968-1973 | | $2,000 | $2,500 |

Sun Valley (6010/7515/7514)
1959-1977. Flat-top acoustic, laminated Brazilian rosewood back and sides, multi-bound top, natural or sunburst.

1959-1964	6010	$1,250	$1,625
1965-1970	6010	$1,000	$1,375
1971-1972	7515	$900	$1,125
1973-1977	7514	$900	$1,125

Super Chet (7690/7690-B/7691/7691-B)
1972-1980. Electric archtop, single rounded cutaway, 2 pickups, gold hardware, mini control knobs along edge of 'guard, Autumn Red or walnut.

| 1972-1980 | | $3,000 | $4,000 |

Supreme (7545)
1972-1978. Flat-top 16", spruce top, mahogany or rosewood body options, gold hardware.

| 1972-1978 | Mahogany | $3,750 | $5,000 |
| 1972-1979 | Rosewood | $3,750 | $5,000 |

Synchromatic (6030/6031)
1951-1955. 17" acoustic archtop, becomes Constellation in '55.

| 1951-1955 | 6030 or 6031 | $1,500 | $2,000 |

Synchromatic (6038/6039)
1951-1955. 17" acoustic archtop, single-cut, G tailpiece, multi-bound, sunburst (6038) or natural (6039), renamed Fleetwood in '55.

| 1951-1955 | 6038 or 6039 | $1,750 | $2,250 |

Synchromatic 75
1939-1949. Acoustic archtop, f-holes, multi-bound, large floral peghead inlay. Tenor available.

| 1939-1949 | | $1,000 | $1,500 |
| 1939-1949 | Tenor | $700 | $950 |

Synchromatic Jr. (3900)
1990-2003. Historic Series, 15" single-cut archtop acoustic.

| 1990-2003 | | $1,000 | $1,375 |

Synchromatic 100 (6014/6015)
1939-1955. Renamed from No. 100F, acoustic archtop, double-bound body, amber, sunburst (6014) or natural (6015), renamed Corsair in '55.

1939-1949	Natural	$1,125	$1,500
1939-1949	Sunburst	$900	$1,125
1950-1955	Natural	$950	$1,250

Synchromatic 160 (6028/6029)
1939-1943, 1947-1951. Acoustic archtop, cats-eye sound holes, maple back and sides, triple-bound, natural or sunburst.

1939-1943	Sunburst	$1,500	$2,000
1947-1951	Sunburst	$1,250	$1,625
1948-1951	Natural	$1,500	$2,000

Synchromatic 200
1939-1949. Acoustic archtop, cats-eye sound holes, maple back and sides, multi-bound, gold-plated hardware, amber or natural.

| 1939-1949 | | $1,500 | $2,000 |

MODEL YEAR	FEATURES	EXC. COND. LOW	HIGH

Synchromatic 300
1939-1955. Acoustic archtop, cats-eye sound holes until '51 and f-holes after, multi-bound, natural or sunburst.

1939-1949	Natural	$2,750	$3,500
1939-1949	Sunburst	$2,500	$3,250
1950-1955	Natural	$2,500	$3,250
1950-1955	Sunburst	$2,250	$3,000

Synchromatic 400
1940-1955. Acoustic archtop, cats-eye sound holes until '51 and f-holes after, multi-bound, gold hardware, natural or sunburst.

1940-1949	Natural	$5,750	$7,500
1940-1949	Sunburst	$5,250	$6,750
1950-1955	Natural	$5,250	$6,750
1950-1955	Sunburst	$6,250	$8,000

Synchromatic 400F/6042 Flat-Top
1947-1955. 18" flat-top, renamed 6042 in the late '40s.

| 1947-1948 | 400F | $5,750 | $7,500 |
| 1949-1955 | 6042 | $5,750 | $7,500 |

Synchromatic G400/400C
1990-2008. Acoustic archtop, full-body, non-cut (400) or single-cut (C), sunburst.

| 1990-2008 | G400 | $1,125 | $1,500 |
| 1990-2008 | G400C | $1,125 | $1,500 |

Synchromatic Limited (G450/G450M)
1997. Acoustic archtop, hand carved spruce (G450) or maple (G450M) top, floating pickup, sunburst, only 50 were to be made.

| 1997 | Maple | $1,250 | $1,625 |
| 1997 | Spruce | $1,125 | $1,500 |

Synchromatic Sierra
1949-1955. Renamed from Synchromatic X75F (see below), acoustic flat-top, maple back and sides, triangular sound hole, sunburst.

| 1949-1955 | | $1,750 | $2,250 |

Synchromatic X75F
1947-1949. Acoustic flat-top, maple back and sides, triangular sound hole, sunburst, renamed Synchromatic Sierra in '49.

| 1947-1949 | | $1,750 | $2,250 |

TK 300 (7624/7625)
1977-1981. Double-cut maple solid body, 1 humbucker, bolt-on neck, six-on-a-side tuners, hockey stick headstock, Autumn Red or natural.

| 1977-1981 | | $1,375 | $1,750 |

Town and Country (6021)
1954-1959. Renamed from Jumbo Synchromatic 125 F, flat-top acoustic, maple back and sides, triangular sound hole, multi-bound.

| 1954-1959 | | $3,500 | $4,500 |

Traveling Wilburys (TW300T)
1988-1990. Promotional guitar, solid body electric, single-cut, 1 and 2 pickups, 6 variations, graphics.

| 1988-1990 | | $550 | $750 |

Van Eps 6-String (6081/6082)
1968-1971. Electric archtop, single-cut, 2 pickups, 6 strings.

| 1968-1971 | | $3,500 | $4,500 |

The *Vintage Guitar Price Guide* shows values for all-original, excellent condition instruments and, where applicable, with original case.

MODEL YEAR	FEATURES	EXC. COND. LOW	HIGH

Van Eps 7-String (6079/6080/7580/7581)

1968-1978. 7-string version, sunburst (6079) or walnut (6080), model numbers change to 7580 (sunburst) and 7581 (walnut) in '72.

1968-1971	6079 or 6080	$3,500	$4,500
1972-1978	7580 or 7581	$3,250	$4,250

Viking

1964-1975. Archtop, double-cut, 2 pickups, vibrato, sunburst (6187), natural (6188) or Cadillac Green (6189). Re-designated 7585 (sunburst) and 7586 (natural) in '72.

1964	Cadillac Green	$6,000	$7,500
1964	Natural	$5,250	$6,500
1964	Sunburst	$4,000	$5,000
1965-1971	Cadillac Green	$4,500	$5,500
1965-1971	Natural	$4,500	$5,500
1965-1971	Sunburst	$3,250	$4,000
1972-1975	Sunburst, natural	$3,000	$3,750

Wayfarer Jumbo (6008)

1969-1971. Flat-top acoustic dreadnought, non-cut, maple back and sides, multi-bound, Wayfarer and sailing ship logo on 'guard.

1969-1971		$1,250	$1,625

White Falcon Mono (6136/7594)

1955-1981. Includes the single-cut 6136 of '55-'61, the double-cut 6136 of '62-'70, and the double-cut 7594 of '71-'81.

1955	6136, single-cut, gold leaf	$50,000	$65,000
1956-1961	6136, single-cut, sparkle binding	$45,000	$55,000
1962-1964	6136, double-cut	$25,000	$30,000
1965-1969		$15,000	$20,000
1970		$10,000	$12,500
1971-1972	7594	$7,500	$9,500
1973-1981	7594	$7,250	$9,000

White Falcon Stereo (6137)

1958-1964. Features Project-O-Sonic Stereo, gold sparkle trim.

1958-1961	Single-cut	$45,000	$60,000
1962-1964	Double-cut	$25,000	$30,000

White Falcon (Import)

1989-2021. Various imported models.

1989-2021	Various models	$2,500	$3,250

White Falcon Custom U.S.A. (6136-1955)

1995-1999. U.S.-made, single-cut, DynaSonic pickups, gold sparkle appointments, rhinestone embedded knobs, white. In '04, Current U.S. model called G6136CST is released. The import White Falcon has sometimes been listed with the 1955 designation and is not included here.

1995-1999		$4,500	$6,000

White Penguin (6134)

1955-1962. Electric solid body, single-cut until '61, double '61-'62, 2 pickups (DeArmond until '58 then Filter Tron), fewer than 100 made, white, gold sparkle bound, gold-plated parts. More than any other model, there seems a higher concern regarding forgery.

1956-1962		$150,000	$175,000

White Penguin (G6134)

1993, 2003-2018. White, single-cut, metalflake binding, gold hardware, jeweled knobs, Cadillac G tailpiece.

2003-2018		$2,750	$3,500

Greven

1969, 1975-2021. Luthier John Greven builds his premium grade, production/custom, acoustic guitars in Portland, Oregon.

Grez

2009-present. Production/custom, professional and premium grade, electric solid body, semi-hollowbody, archtop and acoustic guitars, built by Barry Grzebik in Petaluma, California.

Griffin String Instruments

1976-present. Luthier Kim Griffin builds his professional and premium grade, production/custom, parlor, steel-string, and classical guitars in Greenwich, New York.

Grimes Guitars

1972-present. Premium and presentation grade, custom, flat-tops, nylon-strings, archtops, semi-hollow electrics made by luthier Steve Grimes originally in Port Townsend, Washington, and since '82 in Kula, Hawaii. He also made mandolins early on.

Grinnell

Late 1930s-early 1940s. Private brand made by Gibson for Grinnell Music of Detroit and Southeast Michigan, which at the time, was the largest music chain in the Detroit area.

KG-14

1940. Gibson-made L-00 flat-top style with maple sides and back, tortoise-style binding on top and back, ladder bracing.

1940		$2,250	$3,000

Groehsl

1890-1921. Chicago's Groehsl Company made guitars for Wards and other mass-marketers. In 1921 the company became Stromberg-Voisinet, which in turn became the Kay Musical Instrument Company.

Groove Tools

2002-2004. Korean-made, production, intermediate grade, 7-string guitars that were offered by Conklin Guitars of Springfield, Missouri. They also offered basses.

Grosh

1993-present. Professional and premium grade, production/custom, solid and semi-hollow body guitars and basses built by luthier Don Grosh originally in Santa Clarita, California and, since '05 in Broomfield, Colorado. He also builds basses. Grosh worked in production for Valley Arts from '84-'92. Guitars generally with bolt necks until '03 when set-necks were added to the line.

Grez Guitars OM-1C

Grimes Custom Archtop

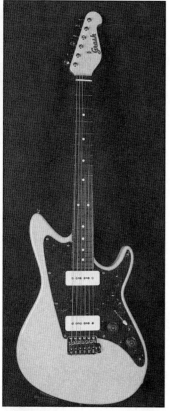

Grosh ElectraJet Custom

1967 Gruggett

MODEL		EXC. COND.	
YEAR	FEATURES	LOW	HIGH

Classical Electric

1990s. Single-cut solidbody with nylon strings and piezo-style hidden pickup, highly figured top.

1990s		$1,500	$2,000

Custom S Bent Top/Bent Top Custom

2003-2019. Offset double-cut, figured maple carved top, 2 pickups.

2003-2019		$1,500	$2,000

Custom T Carve Top

2003-2012. Single-cut, figured maple carved top, 2 pickups.

2003-2012		$1,500	$2,000

ElectraJet Custom

2009-present. Modified offset double-cut, 2 P-90s, 2 hums, or single-single-hum pickups.

2009-2023		$1,500	$2,000

Retro Classic

1993-present. Offset double-cut, 3 pickups.

1993-2023		$1,500	$2,000

Retro Classic Vintage T

1993-present. Single-cut, black 'guard.

1993-2023		$1,500	$2,000

Gruen Acoustic Guitars

Luthier Paul Gruen builds professional grade, custom steel-string guitars, starting in 1999, in Chapel Hill, North Carolina.

Gruggett

Mid 1960s-2012. In the 1960s, luthier Bill Gruggett worked with Mosrite and Hallmark guitars as well as building electric guitars under his own name in Bakersfield, California. He continued to make his Stradette model for Hallmark guitars until his death in October 2012.

Guernsey Resophonic Guitars

Production/custom, resonator guitars built by luthier Ivan Guernsey in Marysville, Indiana, starting in 1989.

Guild

1952-present. Professional and premium grade, production/custom, acoustic and acoustic/electric guitars. They have built solid, hollow and semi-hollowbody guitars in the past. Founded in New York City by jazz guitarist Alfred Dronge, employing many ex-Epiphone workers. The company was purchased by Avnet, Inc. in '66 and the Westerly, Rhode Island factory was opened in '68. Hoboken factory closed in '71 and headquarters moved to Elizabeth, New Jersey. The company was in bankruptcy in '88 and was purchased by Faas Corporation, New Berlin, Wisconsin. The brand was purchased by Fender in '95 and production was moved from Westerly to the Fender plant in Corona, California in 2001. In '05, Fender moved Guild production to their newly acquired Tacoma plant in Washington. In '08, production moved to the Ovation/Hamer plant in New Hartford, Connecticut.

With the 2001 move to the Fender Corona plant, Bob Benedetto and Fender veteran Tim Shaw (who previously ran the Nashville-based custom shop) created a line of Guild acoustic guitars that were primarily based on vintage Guild Hoboken designs.

Designs of Tacoma-built Guild product were nothing like Tacoma guitars. The new Guilds were dovetail neck based with nitrocellulose finishes. Later, FMIC Guild introduced the Contemporary Series giving the Tacoma factory another line in addition to the vintage-based F and D model Traditional Series. In '14 Fender sold Guild to Cordoba Music Group, manufacturer of Cordoba acoustic guitars who moved production to Oxnard, California.

A-50

1994-1996. Original A-50 models can be found under the Cordoba A-50 listing, the new model drops the Cordoba name, size 000 flat-top, spruce top, Indian rosewood body.

1994-1996		$1,250	$1,625

Aragon F-30

1954-1986. Acoustic flat-top, spruce top, laminated maple arched back (mahogany back and sides by '59), reintroduced as just F-30 in '98.

1954-1959		$2,750	$3,500
1960-1969		$2,500	$3,125
1970-1986		$2,250	$2,750

Aragon F-30 NT

1959-1985. Natural finish version of F-30.

1959-1969		$2,750	$3,500
1970-1985		$2,500	$3,250

Aragon F-30 R

1973-1995. Rosewood back and sides version of F-30, sunburst.

1973-1979		$2,500	$3,250

Aristocrat M-75

1954-1963. Electric archtop, routed semi-hollow single-cut body, 2 pickups, sunburst, natural (added '59) or cherry (added '61), reintroduced as Bluesbird M-75 in '67.

1954-1959		$5,000	$6,250
1960-1963		$4,625	$5,750

Aristocrat M-75 Tenor

Mid-late 1950s. Tenor version of 6-string Aristocrat electric, dual soapbar pickups, 4 knobs.

1950s		$3,000	$4,000

Artist Award

1961-1999. Renamed from Johnny Smith Award, single-cut electric archtop, floating DeArmond pickup (changed to humbucker in '80), multi-bound, gold hardware, sunburst or natural.

1961-1969		$7,500	$9,500
1970-1999		$6,000	$7,750

Bluegrass D-25/D-25M

1968-1999. Flat-top, mahogany top until '76, spruce after, mahogany back and sides, various colors, called Bluegrass D-25 M in late-'70s and '80s, listed as D-25 in '90s.

1968-1969		$950	$1,250
1970-1999		$925	$1,125

The *Vintage Guitar Price Guide* shows values for all-original, excellent condition instruments and, where applicable, with original case.

Bluegrass D-25-12

1987-1992, 1996-1998. 12-string version of D-25.

MODEL YEAR	FEATURES	EXC. COND. LOW	HIGH
1987-1998		$775	$975

Bluegrass D-35

1966-1988. Acoustic flat-top, spruce top and mahogany back and sides, rosewood 'board and bridge, natural.

MODEL YEAR	FEATURES	EXC. COND. LOW	HIGH
1966-1969		$1,500	$1,875
1970-1988		$1,500	$1,875

Bluegrass F-40/Valencia F-40

1954-1963, 1973-1983. Acoustic flat-top, spruce top, maple back and sides, rosewood 'board and bridge, natural or sunburst.

MODEL YEAR	FEATURES	EXC. COND. LOW	HIGH
1954-1963	Valencia F-40	$4,500	$5,750
1973-1983	Bluegrass F-40	$1,875	$2,375

Bluegrass F-47

1963-1976. 16" narrow-waist style, mahogany sides and back, acoustic flat-top, spruce top, mahogany back and sides, bound rosewood 'board and bridge, natural.

MODEL YEAR	FEATURES	EXC. COND. LOW	HIGH
1963-1969	Horses-art 'guard	$3,375	$4,250
1970-1976		$3,250	$4,000

Bluegrass Jubilee D-40

1963-1992. Acoustic flat-top, spruce top, mahogany back and sides, rosewood 'board and bridge, natural. Has been reissued.

MODEL YEAR	FEATURES	EXC. COND. LOW	HIGH
1963-1969		$2,625	$3,250
1970-1992		$2,250	$2,875

Bluegrass Jubilee D-40C

1975-1991. Acoustic flat-top, single Florentine cutaway, mahogany back and sides, rosewood 'board and bridge, natural.

MODEL YEAR	FEATURES	EXC. COND. LOW	HIGH
1975-1991		$2,250	$2,875

Bluegrass Jubilee D-44

1965-1972. Acoustic flat-top, spruce top, pearwood back and sides, ebony 'board, rosewood bridge.

MODEL YEAR	FEATURES	EXC. COND. LOW	HIGH
1965-1969		$2,375	$3,000
1970-1972		$2,250	$2,875

Bluegrass Jubilee D-44M

1971-1985. Acoustic flat-top, spruce top, maple back & sides, ebony fingerboard, rosewood bridge.

MODEL YEAR	FEATURES	EXC. COND. LOW	HIGH
1971-1985		$2,250	$2,875

Bluegrass Special D-50

1963-1993. Acoustic flat-top, spruce top, rosewood back and sides, ebony fretboard, multi-bound. Reissued in '99.

MODEL YEAR	FEATURES	EXC. COND. LOW	HIGH
1963-1968	Brazilian rosewood	$6,250	$7,875
1969-1979	Indian rosewood	$2,625	$3,250
1980-1993	Indian rosewood	$2,625	$3,250

Bluegrass Special D-50 (Reissue)/D-50

1999-2004. Also available with pickup system, initially listed as D-50. Reintroduced in '06.

MODEL YEAR	FEATURES	EXC. COND. LOW	HIGH
1999-2004		$1,750	$2,250

Blues 90

2000-2002. Bluesbird single-cut, chambered body, unbound rosewood 'board, dots, 2 Duncan P-90s.

MODEL YEAR	FEATURES	EXC. COND. LOW	HIGH
2000-2002		$1,375	$1,750

Bluesbird M-75 (Hollow Body)

1967-1970. Reintroduced from Aristocrat M-75, thinbody electric archtop of maple, spruce ('67) or mahogany, single-cut, 2 pickups, Deluxe has gold hardware, Standard chrome. A solidbody Bluesbird
was also introduced in '70.

MODEL YEAR	FEATURES	EXC. COND. LOW	HIGH
1967-1970		$2,875	$3,500

Bluesbird M-75 (Solid Body)

1970-1978. Solid body version of Bluesbird M-75, mahogany body, rounded cutaway, 2 pickups, CS with plain top and chrome hardware, GS flamed top and gold hardware.

MODEL YEAR	FEATURES	EXC. COND. LOW	HIGH
1970-1978	CS	$2,750	$3,500
1970-1978	GS	$3,500	$4,375

Bluesbird M-75 (Solid Body) Reintroduced

1984-1988. Various pickups; 3 single-coil ('84-'85), 3 EMG ('86), 3 DiMarzio ('87-'88).

MODEL YEAR	FEATURES	EXC. COND. LOW	HIGH
1984-1985	Single-coil	$1,500	$2,000
1986	EMG	$1,500	$2,000
1987-1988	DiMarzio	$1,500	$2,000

Bluesbird (Reintroduced)

1994-2003. Single-cut chambered solid body, 2 humbuckers, block inlays, available with AAA flamed maple top.

MODEL YEAR	FEATURES	EXC. COND. LOW	HIGH
1994-2003		$1,500	$2,000
2001	Fender CS	$2,500	$3,250

Bluesbird

2011-2012. Single-cut solid body, Chesterfield headstock logo, flame maple top, block markers, 2 humbuckers, natural finish.

MODEL YEAR	FEATURES	EXC. COND. LOW	HIGH
2011-2012		$1,500	$2,000

Brian May BHM-1

1984-1987. Electric solid body, double-cut, vibrato, 3 pickups, bound top and back, red or green, Brian May Pro, Special and Standard introduced in '94.

MODEL YEAR	FEATURES	EXC. COND. LOW	HIGH
1984-1987		$4,250	$5,250

Brian May Pro

1994-1995. Electric solid body, double-cut, vibrato, 3 pickups, bound top and back, various colors.

MODEL YEAR	FEATURES	EXC. COND. LOW	HIGH
1994-1995		$4,250	$5,250

Brian May Signature Red Special

1994. Signature initials on truss rod cover, script signature on back of headstock, BM serial number, dot markers, custom Duncan pickups, custom vibrola, red special finish.

MODEL YEAR	FEATURES	EXC. COND. LOW	HIGH
1994		$4,250	$5,250

CA-100 Capri

1956-1973. Acoustic archtop version of CE-100, sharp Florentine cutaway, solid spruce top, laminated maple back and sides, rosewood 'board and bridge, nickel-plated metal parts, natural or sunburst.

MODEL YEAR	FEATURES	EXC. COND. LOW	HIGH
1956-1959		$2,375	$3,000
1960-1973		$2,250	$2,875

Capri CE-100

1956-1985. Electric archtop, single Florentine cutaway, 1 pickup (2 pickups by '83), maple body, Waverly tailpiece, sunburst, in '59-'82 CE-100 D listed with 2 pickups.

MODEL YEAR	FEATURES	EXC. COND. LOW	HIGH
1956-1959		$2,500	$3,125
1960-1985		$2,375	$3,000

Capri CE-100D

1956-1982. Electric archtop, single Florentine cutaway, 2 pickups, maple body, sunburst, Waverly tailpiece (D dropped, became the Capri CE-100 in '83).

MODEL YEAR	FEATURES	EXC. COND. LOW	HIGH
1956-1959		$2,750	$3,500
1960-1982		$2,625	$3,250

1973 Guild Bluesbird M-75
Cream City Music

1995 Guild Brian May Pro
Rivington Guitars

GUITARS

Guild D4-12

Imaged by Heritage Auctions, HA.com

1968 Gretsch Guild D-25

Imaged by Heritage Auctions, HA.com

MODEL YEAR	FEATURES	EXC. COND. LOW	HIGH

Capri CE-100T Tenor
1950s. Electric-archtop Capri 4-string tenor guitar, sunburst.

| 1956 | | $2,250 | $2,875 |

CO-1/CO-1C
2006-2008. Contemporary series, F-30 style, red cedar top, solid mahogany neck/back/sides, rosewood 'board, natural. CO-1C with soft cutaway.

| 2006-2008 | CO-1 | $975 | $1,250 |
| 2006-2008 | CO-1C | $1,125 | $1,500 |

CO-2/CO-2C
2008. Contemporary series, as CO-1 but with red spruce top, ebony 'board, and offered in blonde, Antique Burst or Ice Tea Burst. CO-2C with soft cutaway.

| 2008 | CO-2 | $975 | $1,250 |
| 2008 | CO-2C | $1,125 | $1,500 |

Cordoba A-50
1961-1972. Acoustic archtop, lowest-end in the Guild archtop line, named Granada A-50 prior to '61.

| 1961-1965 | | $1,375 | $1,750 |
| 1966-1972 | | $1,250 | $1,500 |

Cordoba T-50 Slim
1961-1973. Thinbody version of Cordoba X-50.

1961-1965		$1,375	$1,750
1966-1969		$1,375	$1,750
1970-1972		$1,250	$1,500

Cordoba X-50
1961-1970. Electric archtop non-cut, laminated maple body, rosewood 'board, 1 pickup, nickel-plated parts.

| 1961-1965 | | $1,500 | $2,000 |
| 1966-1970 | | $1,375 | $1,750 |

CR-1 Crossroads Single E/Double E
1993-2000. Single-cut solid body acoustic, humbucker (S2 in '93) neck pickup and Piezo bridge, 97 single necks (Single E, '93-'97) and very few 6/12 double necks (Double E, '93, '98-'00) made by Guild custom shop.

| 1993-1997 | Single neck | $1,750 | $2,250 |
| 1993-2000 | Double neck | $4,250 | $5,500 |

Custom F-412 12-String
1968-1986. Special order only from '68-'74, then regular production, 17" wide body 12-string version of F-50 flat-top, spruce top, maple back and sides, arched back, 2-tone block inlays, gold hardware, natural finish.

| 1968-1969 | | $2,500 | $3,250 |
| 1970-1986 | | $2,125 | $2,750 |

Custom F-512 12-String
1968-1986, 1990. Indian rosewood back and sides version of F-412. See F-512 for reissue.

1968-1969		$3,000	$4,000
1970-1979		$2,750	$3,500
1980-1986		$2,500	$3,250

Custom F-612 12-String
1972-1973. Acoustic 12-string, similar to Custom F-512, but with 18" body, fancy mother-of-pearl inlays, and black/white marquee body, neck and headstock binding.

| 1972-1973 | Brazilian rosewood | $4,500 | $6,000 |
| 1972-1973 | Indian rosewood | $2,875 | $3,750 |

MODEL YEAR	FEATURES	EXC. COND. LOW	HIGH

Custom Shop 45th Anniversary
1997. Built in Guild's Nashville Custom Shop, all solid wood, spruce top, maple back and sides, high-end appointments, gold hardware, natural.

| 1997 | | $2,750 | $3,500 |

CV-1/CV-1C
2006-2008. Contemporary Vintage series, F-40 style, solid Indian rosewood back/sides, rosewood 'board. CV-1C with sharp cutaway.

| 2006-2008 | CV-1 | $1,000 | $1,375 |
| 2006-2008 | CV-1C | $1,125 | $1,500 |

CV-2/CV-2C
2008. Contemporary Vintage series, as CV-1 but with flamed maple back/sides, ebony 'board. CV-2C with sharp cutaway.

| 2008 | CV-2 | $1,125 | $1,500 |
| 2008 | CV-2C | $1,125 | $1,500 |

D-4 Series
1991-2002. Dreadnought flat-top, mahogany sides, dot markers.

| 1991-2002 | 6-String | $700 | $875 |
| 1992-1999 | 12-String | $700 | $875 |

D-6 (D-6E/D-6HG/D-6HE)
1992-1995. Flat-top, 15 3/4", mahogany back and sides, natural satin non-gloss finish, options available.

| 1992-1995 | | $675 | $900 |

D-15 Mahogany Rush
1983-1988. Dreadnought flat-top, mahogany body and neck, rosewood 'board, dot inlays, stain finish.

| 1983-1988 | | $700 | $875 |

D-15 12-String
1983-1985. 12-string version of Mahogany Rush D-15.

| 1983-1985 | | $700 | $875 |

D-16 Mahogany Rush
1984-1986. Like D-15, but with gloss finish.

| 1984-1986 | | $850 | $1,125 |

D-17 Mahogany Rush
1984-1988. Like D-15, but with gloss finish and bound body.

| 1984-1988 | | $850 | $1,125 |

D-25/D-25M
2003. Solid mahogany body. Refer to Bluegrass D-25 for earlier models. Reintroduced in '06 as GAD-25.

| 2003 | | $850 | $1,125 |

D-26 (Guitar Center)
1995. Made for Guitar Center, spruce top, mahogany back and sides, natural finish.

| 1995 | | $850 | $1,125 |

D-30
1987-1999. Acoustic flat-top, spruce-top, laminated maple back and solid maple sides, rosewood 'board, multi-bound, various colors.

| 1987-1999 | | $1,375 | $1,750 |

D-40
1999-2007. Solid spruce top, mahogany back and sides, rosewood 'board. See earlier models under Bluegrass Jubilee D-40.

| 1999-2007 | | $1,500 | $1,875 |

MODEL YEAR	FEATURES	EXC. COND. LOW	HIGH

D-40 Bluegrass Jubilee
2006-2014. Indian rosewood, red spruce top, mahogany back and sides, 3-piece neck (mahogany/walnut/mahogany).

2006-2014	No pickup	$1,500	$2,000
2006-2014	With Duncan D-TAR	$1,375	$1,750

D-40 Richie Havens
2003-2014. Richie Havens signature logo on truss rod cover, mahogany sides and back, Fishman Matrix, natural.

2003-2014		$1,500	$2,000

D-40C NT
1975-1991. Pointed cutaway version.

1975-1991		$1,750	$2,250

D-46
1980-1985. Dreadnought acoustic, ash back, sides and neck, spruce top, ebony 'board, ivoroid body binding.

1980-1985		$1,250	$1,500

D-50
See Bluegrass Special Model.

D-55
See TV Model.

D-55 50th Anniversary
2003. Brazilian rosewood, 1953-2003 Anniversary logo.

2003		$5,000	$6,500

D-60
1987-1990, 1998-2000. Renamed from D-66, rosewood back and sides ('87-'90), maple ('98-'00), scalloped bracing, multi-bound top, slotted diamond inlay, G shield logo.

1987-1990	Rosewood	$2,625	$3,250
1998-1999	Maple	$2,625	$3,250

D-64
1984-1986. Maple back and side, multi-bound body, notched diamond inlays, limited production.

1984-1986		$2,625	$3,250

D-66
1984-1987. Amber, rosewood back and sides, 15 3/4", scalloped bracing, renamed D-60 in '87.

1984-1987		$2,625	$3,250

D-70
1981-1985. Dreadnought acoustic, spruce top, Indian rosewood back and sides, multi-bound, ebony 'board with mother-of-pearl inlays.

1981-1985		$3,875	$5,000

D-70-12E
1981-1985. Only 2 made, 12-string version, Fishman electronics.

1981-1985		$4,000	$5,000

D-80
1983-1987. Non-carved heel.

1983-1987		$4,000	$5,000

D-100
1990-1998. Top-of-the-line dreadnought-size acoustic, spruce top, rosewood back and sides, scalloped bracing.

1990-1998		$4,000	$5,000

D-125
2011-2014. All mahogany with Indian rosewood 'board, natural or cherry red.

2011-2014		$475	$600

D-212 12-String/D-25-12/D-212
1981-1983, 1987-1992, 1996-2022. 12-string version of D-25, laminated mahogany back and sides, natural, sunburst or black. Renamed D-25-12 for '87-'92, reintroduced as D-212 '96.

1981-1983		$800	$1,125

D-412 12-String
1990-1997. Dreadnought, 12 strings, mahogany sides and arched back, satin finished, natural.

1990-1997		$1,375	$1,750

DC-130
1994-1995. US-made, limited run, D-style cutaway, flamed maple top/back/sides.

1994-1995		$3,250	$4,000

DCE True American
1993-2000. Cutaway flat-top acoustic/electric, 1 with mahogany back and sides, 5 with rosewood.

1993-2000	DC-1, DCE-1 True Amer	$725	$950
1994-2000	DCE-5	$800	$1,000

Del Rio M-30
1959-1964. Flat-top, 15", all mahogany body, satin non-gloss finish.

1959		$2,500	$3,250
1960-1964		$2,250	$3,000

Detonator
1987-1990. Electric solid body, double-cut, 3 pickups, bolt-on neck, Guild/Mueller tremolo system, black hardware.

1987-1990		$650	$850

DK-70 Peacock Limited Edition
1995-1996. Limited run of 50, Koa, peacock 'guard.

1995-1996		$4,000	$5,250

Duane Eddy Deluxe DE-500
1962-1974, 1984-1987. Electric archtop, single rounded cutaway, 2 pickups (early years and '80s version have DeArmonds), Bigsby, master volume, spruce top with maple back and sides, available in blond (BL) or sunburst (SB).

1962-1964	Natural	$7,500	$9,500
1962-1964	Sunburst	$6,000	$7,500
1965	Natural	$6,250	$8,000
1965	Sunburst	$5,500	$6,750
1966	Natural	$5,750	$7,500
1966	Sunburst	$5,250	$6,500
1967-1969	Various colors	$5,250	$6,500
1970-1974	Various colors	$4,750	$6,000
1984-1987	Various colors	$3,750	$5,000

Duane Eddy Standard DE-400
1963-1974. Electric archtop, single rounded cutaway, 2 pickups, vibrato, natural or sunburst, less appointments than DE-500 Deluxe.

1963	Cherry (option)	$5,250	$6,500
1963	Natural	$5,250	$6,500
1963	Sunburst	$4,250	$5,250
1964	Cherry (option)	$4,750	$6,000
1964	Natural	$4,750	$6,000

1971 Guild D-40
Richard Potter

1963 Guild Duane Eddy DE-300
Earl Ward

GUITARS

Guild DV-6

1958 Guild Freshman M-65

Charlie Apicella

MODEL YEAR	FEATURES	EXC. COND. LOW	HIGH
1964	Sunburst	$4,250	$5,500
1965	Natural	$4,250	$5,500
1965	Sunburst	$3,500	$4,500
1966	Natural	$3,750	$5,000
1966	Sunburst	$3,250	$4,000
1967-1969	Various colors	$3,250	$4,000
1970-1974	Various colors	$2,750	$3,500

DV Series

1992-2001, 2007-2011. Acoustic flat-tops, mahogany or rosewood back and sides, ebony or rosewood 'board, satin or gloss finish.

1992-2001	DV-52S	$1,500	$2,000
1993-1994	DV-76	$3,500	$4,500
1993-1995	DV-62	$1,500	$2,250
1994-1995	DV-72	$3,000	$4,000
1994-1995	DV-73	$3,000	$4,000
1995-1996	DV-74 Pueblo	$3,500	$4,500
1995-1999	DV-6	$800	$1,000
1999-2000	DV-25	$1,125	$1,375
1999-2001	DV-4	$625	$850

Economy M-20

1958-1965, 1969-1973. Mahogany body, acoustic flat-top, natural or sunburst satin finish.

1958-1959	$2,375	$3,000
1960-1969	$2,250	$2,875
1970-1973	$2,000	$2,500

F-4CEHG

1992-2002. High Gloss finish, single-cut flat-top, acoustic/electric.

1992-2002	$700	$875

F-5CE

1992-2001. Acoustic/electric, single-cut, rosewood back and sides, dot inlays, chrome tuners.

1992-2001	$700	$875

F-30

1990-2001. Formerly the Aragon F-30, made in Westerly, Rhode Island.

1990-2001	$1,500	$2,000

F-30R-LS

1990s. Custom Shop, limited production, bearclaw spruce top, rosewood sides and back.

1990s	$1,625	$2,000

F-44

1984-1987. Acoustic flat-top, maple, designed by George Gruhn.

1984-1987	$2,250	$3,000

F-45CE

1983-1992. Acoustic/electric, single-cut, mahogany or maple back and sides, rosewood 'board, on-board electronics, natural. Early '87 model was named GF-45CE (flamed maple), by mid '87 it was back to F-45CE.

1983-1984	Laminated mahogany	$1,000	$1,250
1985-1986	Flamed maple	$1,250	$1,500
1987	Early '87, GF-45CE	$1,250	$1,500
1987-1992	Mid '87, F-45CE	$1,250	$1,500

F-46

1984. Jumbo body style flat-top, designed for Guild by George Gruhn.

1984	$3,000	$3,750

MODEL YEAR	FEATURES	EXC. COND. LOW	HIGH

F-47M/F-47MC

2007-2016. Made in the USA, solid flamed maple sides and back, MC with cutaway.

2007-2016	F-47M	$2,000	$2,500
2007-2016	F-47MC	$2,000	$2,500

F-47R/F-47RC

2008-2014. Solid rosewood sides and back, available with electronics, RC with cutaway.

2008-2014	$2,000	$2,500

F-47RCE Grand Auditorium

1999-2003. Cutaway acoustic/electric, rosewood back and sides, block inlays.

1999-2003	$2,000	$2,500

F-50/F-50R

2002-2016. Jumbo, solid spruce top, solid maple sides, arched laminated maple back, abalone rosette. See Navarre F-50/F-50R for earlier models.

2002-2016	F-50, maple	$2,250	$2,875
2002-2016	F-50R, rosewood	$2,250	$2,875

F-65CE

1992-2001. Acoustic/electric, single-cut, rosewood back and sides, block inlay, gold tuners.

1992-2001	$2,250	$2,750

F-212 12-String/F-212XL

1964-1986, 1998-2000. Acoustic flat-top jumbo, 12 strings, spruce top, mahogany back and sides, 16" body. Named F-212XL in '66, then XL dropped from name in '98.

1964-1965	F-212	$1,500	$1,875
1966-1986	F-212XL	$1,500	$1,875
1998-2000	F-212	$1,000	$1,375

F-312 Artist 12-String

1964-1973. Flat-top, rosewood back and sides, spruce top, no board inlay (but some in '72 may have dots).

1964-1968	Brazilian rosewood	$5,000	$6,500
1969-1973	Indian rosewood	$2,250	$2,875

F-412

2002-2016. Solid spruce top, solid maple back and sides, block inlays, 12-string. See Custom F-412 for earlier models.

2002-2016	$2,000	$2,500

F-512

2002-present. Solid spruce top, rosewood back and sides, 12-string. See Custom F-512 for earlier models.

2002-2023	$2,250	$2,875

Freshman M-65

1958-1973. Electric archtop, single-cut, mahogany back and sides, f-holes, 1 single-coil (some with 2), sunburst or natural top.

1958-1959	$2,250	$2,875
1960-1969	$1,750	$2,125
1970-1973	$1,625	$2,000

Freshman M-65 3/4

1958-1973. Short-scale version of M-65, 1 pickup.

1958-1959	$1,875	$2,375
1960-1969	$1,500	$1,875
1970-1973	$1,500	$1,875

FS-20CE

1986-1987. Solid body acoustic, routed mahogany body.

1986-1987	$825	$1,125

The *Vintage Guitar Price Guide* shows values for all-original, excellent condition instruments and, where applicable, with original case.

MODEL YEAR	FEATURES	EXC. COND. LOW	HIGH

FS-46CE
1983-1986. Flat-top acoustic/electric, pointed cutaway, mahogany, black, natural or sunburst.

1983-1986		$975	$1,250

G-5P
1988-ca.1989. Handmade in Spain, cedar top, gold-plated hardware.

1988-1989		$1,375	$1,750

G-37
1973-1986. Acoustic flat-top, spruce top, laminated maple back and sides, rosewood 'board and bridge, sunburst or natural top.

1973-1986		$1,375	$1,750

G-41
1974-1978. Acoustic flat-top, spruce top, mahogany back and sides, rosewood 'board and bridge, 20 frets.

1975-1978		$1,375	$1,750

G-45 Hank Williams Jr.
1982-1986, 1993-1996. Hank Williams Jr. logo on 'guard, flat-top.

1982-1996		$1,500	$1,875

G-75
1975-1977. Acoustic flat-top, 3/4-size version of D-50, spruce top, rosewood back and sides, mahogany neck, ebony 'board and bridge.

1975-1977		$1,375	$1,750

G-212 12-String
1974-1983. Acoustic flat-top 12-string version of D-40, spruce top, mahogany back and sides, natural or sunburst.

1974-1983		$1,375	$1,750

G-212XL 12-String
1974-1983. 17" version of G-212 12-String.

1974-1983		$1,375	$1,750

G-312 12-String
1974-1987. Acoustic flat-top 12-string version of the D-50, spruce top, rosewood back and sides. Renamed D-50-12 in '87.

1974-1987		$1,375	$1,750

GAD (Guild Acoustic Design) Series
2004-2014. Imported, all models begin with GAD, various woods, some with electronics (E).

2004-2014 Various models		$500	$1,250

George Barnes AcoustiLectric
1962-1972. Electric archtop, single-cut, solid spruce top, curly maple back and sides, multi-bound, 2 humbuckers, gold-plated hardware, sunburst or natural finish.

1962-1972		$5,000	$6,500

George Barnes Guitar in F
1963-1973. Smaller electric archtop at 13.5", 2 humbuckers, chrome hardware.

1963-1973		$5,000	$6,500

GF-25
1987-1992. Acoustic flat-top, mahogany back and sides.

1987-1992		$850	$1,125

GF-25C
1988-1991. Cutaway GF-25.

1988-1991		$1,125	$1,375

GF-30
1987-1991. Acoustic flat-top, maple back/sides/neck, multi-bound.

1987-1991		$1,250	$1,625

GF-40
1987-1991. Mahogany back and sides, multi-bound.

1987-1991		$1,375	$1,750

GF-50
1987-1991. Acoustic flat-top, rosewood back and sides, mahogany neck, multi-bound.

1987-1991		$1,500	$2,000

GF-55
1990-1991. Jumbo acoustic, spruce top, rosewood back and sides, natural.

1990-1991		$2,000	$2,500

GF-60
1987-1989. Jumbo size, rosewood or maple sides and back, diamond markers. Cutaway version available.

1987-1989	GF-60C, cutaway	$2,500	$3,250
1987-1989	GF-60M, maple	$2,500	$3,250
1987-1989	GF-60R, rosewood	$2,500	$3,250

Granada A-50 (Acoustic Archtop)
1956-1960. Lowest-end acoustic archtop in the Guild line, renamed Cordoba A-50 in '61.

1956-1960		$1,500	$2,000

Granada X-50
1954-1961. Electric archtop, non-cut, laminated all maple body, rosewood 'board and bridge, nickel-plated metal parts, 1 pickup, sunburst. Renamed Cordoba X-50 in '61.

1954-1959		$1,750	$2,250
1960-1961		$1,500	$2,000

GV (Guild Vintage) Series
1993-1995. Flat-top, rosewood back and sides, various enhancements.

1993-1995	GV-52, rw, gloss	$1,375	$1,750
1993-1995	GV-52, rw, satin	$1,125	$1,375
1993-1995	GV-70, abalone, gloss	$1,375	$1,750
1993-1995	GV-72, herringbone, gloss	$1,375	$1,750

Jet Star S-50
1963-1970. Electric solid body, double-cut, mahogany or alder body, 1 pickup, vibrato optional by '65, asymmetrical headstock until '65. Reintroduced as S-50 in '72-'78 with body redesign.

1963-1965	3-on-side	$2,125	$2,625
1966-1969	6-in-line	$1,625	$2,000
1970	6-in-line	$1,625	$2,000

JF-4NT
1992-1995. Jumbo flat-top, mahogany, natural.

1992-1995		$950	$1,250

JF-30
1987-2004. Jumbo 6-string acoustic, spruce top, laminated maple back, solid maple sides, multi-bound. Becomes GAD-JF30 in '04.

1987-2004		$1,500	$2,000

JF-30-12
1987-2004. 12-string version of the JF-30.

1987-2004		$1,500	$2,000

Guild George Barnes
AcoustiLectric

1993 Guild JF-30

Imaged by Heritage Auctions, HA.com

To get the most from this book, be sure to read "Using *The Guide*" in the introduction.

1958 Guild Johnny Smith Award
Richard Sarmento

1975 Guild Mark III
Rivington Guitars

MODEL YEAR	FEATURES	EXC. COND. LOW	HIGH

JF-30E
1994-2004. Acoustic/electric version.

1994-2004		$1,500	$2,000

JF-50R
1987-1988. Jumbo 6-string acoustic, rosewood back and sides, multi-bound.

1987-1988		$1,500	$2,000

JF-55
1989-2000. Jumbo flat-top, spruce top, rosewood body.

1989-2000		$2,000	$2,500

JF-55-12
1991-2000. 12-string JF-55.

1991-2000		$2,000	$2,500

JF-65
1987-1994. Renamed from Navarre F-50, Jumbo flat-top acoustic, spruce top, R has rosewood back and sides and M has maple.

1987-1994	JF-65M, maple	$2,500	$3,250
1987-1994	JF-65R, rosewood	$2,500	$3,250

JF-65-12
1987-2001. 12-string, version of JF-65.

1987-2001	JF-65M-12, maple	$2,500	$3,250
1987-2001	JF-65R-12, rosewood	$2,500	$3,250

JF-100
1992-2000. Jumbo, maple top, rosewood back and sides, abalone trim, natural. Carved heel available '94-'00.

1992-1995		$3,500	$4,500

JF-100-12
1992-2000. Jumbo 12-string version, non-carved or carved heel.

1994-2000	Carved heel	$3,500	$4,500

Johnny Smith Award
1956-1961. Single-cut electric archtop, floating DeArmond pickup, multi-bound, gold hardware, sunburst or natural, renamed Artist Award in '61.

1956-1961		$8,000	$10,000

Johnny Smith Award - Benedetto
2004-2006. Only 18 custom made under the supervision of Bob Benedetto, signed by Johnny Smith, with certificate of authenticity signed by Smith and Benedetto.

2004-2006	18 made	$6,000	$7,500

JV-72
1993-1999. Jumbo acoustic, custom turquoise inlay.

1993-1999		$2,500	$3,250

Liberator Elite
1988. Limited Edition, set-neck, offset double-cut solid body, figured maple top, mahogany body, rising-sun inlays, 3 active pickups, last of the Guild solidbodies.

1988		$1,250	$1,625

M-80CS/M-80
1975-1984. Solidbody, double-cut, 2 pickups, introduced as M-80CS with bound rosewood 'board and block inlays, shortened to M-80 in '80 with unbound ebony 'board and dots.

1975-1980		$1,625	$2,125

MODEL YEAR	FEATURES	EXC. COND. LOW	HIGH

Manhattan X-170 (Mini-Manhattan X-170)
1985-2002. Called Mini-Manhattan X-170 in '85-'86, electric archtop hollow body, single rounded cutaway, maple body, f-holes, 2 humbuckers, block inlays, gold hardware, natural or sunburst.

1985-2002		$2,250	$3,000

Manhattan X-175 (Sunburst)
1954-1985. Electric archtop, single rounded cutaway, laminated spruce top, laminated maple back and sides, 2 pickups, chrome hardware, sunburst. Reissued as X-160 Savoy.

1954-1959		$2,500	$3,250
1960-1969		$2,125	$2,750
1970-1985		$2,000	$2,500

Manhattan X-175 B (Natural)
1954-1976. Natural finish X-175.

1954-1959		$2,500	$3,250
1960-1969		$2,125	$2,750
1970-1976		$2,125	$2,750

Mark I
1961-1972. Classical, Honduras mahogany body, rosewood 'board, slotted headstock.

1961-1969		$475	$625
1970-1973		$400	$525

Mark II
1961-1987. Like Mark I, but with spruce top and body binding.

1961-1969		$700	$925
1970-1979		$500	$650
1980-1987		$400	$525

Mark III
1961-1987. Like Mark II, but with Peruvian mahogany back and sides and floral sound hole design.

1961-1969		$725	$950
1970-1979		$625	$825
1980-1987		$500	$650

Mark IV
1961-1985. Like Mark III, but with flamed pearwood back and sides (rosewood offered in '61, maple in '62).

1961-1969	Pearwood	$775	$1,000
1970-1979	Pearwood	$700	$950
1980-1985	Pearwood	$575	$750

Mark V
1961-1987. Like Mark III, but with rosewood back and sides (maple available for '61-'64).

1961-1968	Brazilian rw	$1,750	$2,250
1969-1979	Indian rw	$750	$975
1980-1987	Indian rw	$600	$775

Mark VI
1962-1973. Rosewood back and sides, spruce top, wood binding.

1962-1968	Brazilian rw	$2,500	$3,250
1969-1973	Indian rw	$1,000	$1,375

Mark VII Custom
1968-1973. Special order only, spruce top, premium rosewood back and sides, inlaid rosewood bridge, engraved gold tuners.

1962-1968	Brazilian rw	$2,750	$3,500
1969-1973	Indian rw	$1,250	$1,625

Navarre F-48
1972-1975. 17", mahogany, block markers.

1972-1975		$1,875	$2,500

MODEL		EXC. COND.	
YEAR	FEATURES	LOW	HIGH

Navarre F-50/F-50

1954-1986, 1994-1995. Acoustic flat-top, spruce top, curly maple back and sides, rosewood 'board and bridge, 17" rounded lower bout, laminated arched maple back, renamed JF-65 M in '87. Reissued in '94 and again in '02 as the F-50.

1954-1956		$6,000	$7,750
1957-1962	Pearl block markers	$6,000	$7,750
1963-1969	Ebony 'board	$5,500	$7,250
1970-1995		$2,750	$3,500

Navarre F-50R/F-50R

1965-1987. Rosewood back and side version of F-50, renamed JF-65 R in '87. Reissued in '02 as F-50R.

1965-1968	Brazilian rw	$7,750	$10,000
1969-1987	Indian rw	$3,500	$4,500

Nightbird

1985-1987. Single-cut solid body, tone chambers, 2 pickups, multi-bound, black or gold hardware, renamed Nightbird II in '87.

1985-1987		$2,375	$3,000

Nightbird I

1987-1988. Like Nightbird but with chrome hardware, less binding and appointments.

1987-1988		$2,375	$3,000

Nightbird II

1987-1992. Renamed from Nightbird, with black hardware, renamed Nightbird X-2000 in '92.

1987-1992		$2,375	$3,000

Nightbird X-2000

1992-1996. Renamed from Nightbird II.

1992-1996		$2,375	$3,000

Park Ave X-180

2005. Cutaway acoustic archtop, 2 pickups, block markers.

2005		$1,500	$2,000

Peregrine

1999-2005. Solid body acoustic, cutaway, Fishman.

1999-2005	Custom	$1,125	$1,500
1999-2005	Flamed maple	$1,250	$1,625
1999-2005	S7CE, (CS)	$1,250	$1,625
1999-2005	S7CE, (CS), quilted	$1,250	$1,625
1999-2005	Standard	$1,000	$1,375

Polara S-100

1963-1970. Double-cut mahogany or alder solid body, rosewood 'board, 2 single coils, built-in stand until '70, asymmetrical headstock, in '70 Polara dropped from title (see S-100), renamed Polara S-100 in '97.

1963-1970	2 or 3 pickups	$2,000	$2,500

Roy Buchanan T-200

1986. Single-cut solid body, 2 pickups, pointed six-on-a-side headstock, poplar body, bolt-on neck, gold and brass hardware.

1986		$700	$900

S-50

1972-1978. Double-cut solid body, 1 single-coil (switched to humbucker in '74), dot inlay.

1972-1978		$1,250	$1,625

S-60/S-60D

1976-1981. Double-cut solid body with long bass horn, 1 humbucker (60) or 2 single-coils (60D), mahogany body, rosewood 'board.

1976-1981		$1,125	$1,500

S-65D

1980-1981. S-60 but with 1 DiMarzio Super Distortion pickup.

1980-1981		$1,125	$1,500

S-70D/S-70AD

1979-1981. Solid body (mahogany D, ash AD), rosewood 'board, 3 single-coils.

1979-1981	S-70AD	$1,375	$1,750
1979-1981	S-70D	$1,375	$1,750

S-90

1972-1977. Double-cut SG-like body, 2 humbuckers, dot inlay, chrome hardware.

1972-1977		$1,375	$1,750

S-100

1970-1978, 1994-1996. S-100 Standard is double-cut solid body, 2 humbuckers, block inlays. Deluxe of '72-'75 had added Bigsby. Standard Carved '74-'77 has acorns and oakleaves carved in the top.

1970-1978	Standard	$2,250	$3,000
1972-1975	Deluxe	$2,250	$3,000
1974-1977	Standard Carved	$2,250	$3,000

S-100 Reissue

1994-1997. Renamed Polara in '97.

1994-1997		$850	$1,125

S-250

1981-1983. Double-cut solid body, 2 humbuckers.

1981-1983		$600	$800

S-261

Ca.1985. Double-cut, maple body, black Kahler tremolo, 1 humbucker and 2 single-coil pickups, rosewood 'board.

1985		$600	$800

S-270 Runaway

1985. Offset double-cut solid body, 1 humbucker, Kahler.

1985		$600	$800

S-271 Sprint

1986. Replaced the S-270.

1986		$600	$800

S-275

1982-1983. Offset double-cut body, 2 humbuckers, bound figured maple top, sunburst or natural.

1982-1983		$600	$800

S-280 Flyer

1983-1984. Double-cut poplar body, 2 humbuckers or 3 single-coils, maple or rosewood neck, dot markers.

1983-1984		$600	$800

S-281 Flyer

1983-1988. Double-cut poplar body S-280 with locking vibrato, optional pickups available.

1983-1988		$600	$800

S-284 Starling/Aviator

1984-1988. Starling (early-'84) and Aviator (late-'84-'88), double-cut, 3 pickups.

1984	Starling	$600	$800
1984-1988	Aviator	$600	$800

S-285 Aviator

1986. Deluxe Aviator, bound 'board, fancy inlays.

1986		$600	$800

1963 Guild S-50
Rivington Guitars

1979 Guild S-70D

To get the most from this book, be sure to read "Using *The Guide*" in the introduction.

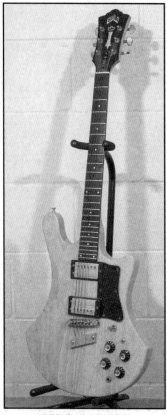

1978 Guild S-300A
Tom Pfeifer

1962 Guild Slim Jim T-100D
Brian Chambers

MODEL YEAR	FEATURES	EXC. COND. LOW	HIGH

S-300 Series
1976-1983. Double-cut mahogany solid body with larger bass horn and rounded bottom, 2 humbuckers. S-300 A has ash body, D has exposed DiMarzio humbuckers.

1976-1983	S-300	$1,250	$1,625
1977-1982	S-300D	$1,250	$1,625
1977-1983	S-300A	$1,250	$1,625

S-400/S-400A
1980-1981. Double-cut solid body, mahogany (400) or ash (400A), 2 humbuckers.

1980-1981		$1,125	$1,500

Savoy A-150
1958-1973, 2013-present. Acoustic archtop version of X-150, available with floating pickup, natural or sunburst finish. Reissued in '13, part of Newark St. Collection.

1958-1961	Natural	$2,500	$3,250
1958-1961	Sunburst	$2,250	$3,000
2013-2023		$1,375	$1,750

Savoy X-150
1954-1965. Electric archtop, rounded single-cut, spruce top, maple back and sides, rosewood 'board and bridge, 1 single-coil pickup, sunburst, blond or sparkling gold finish. Reissued in '98 as X-150 Savoy.

1954	Sunburst	$3,000	$4,000
1955-1959	Sunburst	$2,750	$3,500
1960-1965	Sunburst	$2,500	$3,250

Slim Jim T-100
1958-1973. Electric archtop thinline, single-cut, laminated all-maple body, rosewood 'board and bridge, Waverly tailpiece, 1 pickup, natural or sunburst.

1958-1959		$2,500	$3,250
1960-1964		$2,375	$3,000
1965-1969		$2,125	$2,750
1970-1973		$2,000	$2,500

Slim Jim T-100D
1958-1973. Semi-hollow body electric, single Florentine cutaway, thinline, 2-pickup version of the T-100, natural or sunburst.

1958-1959		$2,625	$3,500
1960-1964		$2,500	$3,250
1965-1969		$2,375	$3,000
1970-1973		$2,125	$2,750

Songbird S Series
1984-1991. Designed by George Gruhn, flat-top, mahogany back, spruce top, single pointed cutaway, pickup with preamp, multi-bound top, black, natural or white. Renamed S-4 later in run.

1984-1991		$1,125	$1,500

Standard (STD) Series
2010-2014. Imported flat-top acoustics based on various classic Guild models.

2010-2014		$1,250	$1,625

Standard F-112 12-String
1968-1982. Acoustic flat-top, spruce top, mahogany back, sides and neck.

1968-1969		$1,250	$1,625
1970-1982		$1,000	$1,375

MODEL YEAR	FEATURES	EXC. COND. LOW	HIGH

Starfire I
1960-1964. Electric archtop, single-cut thinline, laminated maple or mahogany body, bound body and neck, 1 pickup, Starfire Red finish.

1960-1961		$1,625	$2,125
1962-1964		$1,625	$2,125

Starfire II
1960-1976, 1997-2001. Electric archtop, single-cut thinline, laminated maple or mahogany body, bound body and rosewood neck, 2 pickups, various colors.

1960-1961	Sunburst	$2,625	$3,500
1962	Emerald Green	$2,625	$3,500
1962-1966	Special color options	$2,875	$3,500
1962-1966	Sunburst, Starfire Red	$2,625	$3,500
1967-1969	Sunburst, Starfire Red	$2,375	$3,000
1970-1976	Sunburst, Starfire Red	$2,250	$3,000
1997-2001	Reissue	$1,500	$2,000

Starfire III
1960-1974, 1997-2005, 2013-present. Electric archtop, single-cut thinline, laminated maple or mahogany body, bound body and rosewood neck, 2 pickups, Guild or Bigsby vibrato, Starfire Red. Reissued in '13, part of Newark St. Collection.

1960-1966		$3,375	$4,375
1967-1974		$3,125	$4,000
1997-2005	Reissue	$1,500	$2,000
2013-2023	Newark St	$1,000	$1,375

Starfire IV
1963-1987, 1991-2005. Thinline, double-cut semi-hollow body, laminated maple or mahogany body, f-holes, 2 humbuckers, rosewood 'board, cherry or sunburst.

1963-1966		$3,375	$4,375
1967-1975		$3,125	$4,000
1976-1987		$2,625	$3,375
1991-2005	Reissue	$1,500	$2,000

Starfire IV Special (Custom Shop)
2001-2002. Nashville Custom Shop.

2001-2002		$2,000	$2,500

Starfire V
1963-1973, 1999-2001. Same as Starfire IV but with block markers, Bigsby and master volume, natural or sunburst finish, reissued in '99.

1963-1966		$3,375	$4,375
1967-1973		$3,125	$4,000
1999-2001	Reissue	$1,500	$2,000

Starfire VI
1964-1979. Same as Starfire IV but with higher appointments such as ebony 'board, pearl inlays, Guild/Bigsby vibrato, natural or sunburst.

1964-1966		$3,375	$4,375
1967-1975		$3,125	$4,000
1976-1979		$2,625	$3,375

Starfire XII
1966-1973. Electric archtop, 12-string, double-cut, maple or mahogany body, set-in neck, 2 humbuckers, harp tailpiece.

1966-1969		$2,375	$3,000
1970-1973		$2,375	$3,000

MODEL YEAR	FEATURES	EXC. COND. LOW	HIGH
Stratford A-350			
1956-1973. Acoustic archtop, rounded single-cut, solid spruce top with solid curly maple back and sides, rosewood 'board and bridge (changed to ebony by '60), sunburst.			
1956-1959		$3,375	$4,375
1960-1965		$3,125	$4,000
1966-1969		$2,625	$3,500
1970-1973		$2,625	$3,375
Stratford A-350B			
1956-1973. A-350 in blond/natural finish option.			
1956-1959		$3,625	$4,750
1960-1965		$3,375	$4,375
1966-1969		$3,125	$4,000
1970-1973		$2,875	$3,750
Stratford X-350			
1954-1965. Electric archtop, rounded single-cut, laminated spruce top with laminated maple back and sides, rosewood 'board, 6 push-button pickup selectors, sunburst finish (natural finish is X-375).			
1954-1959		$4,250	$5,500
1960-1965		$3,750	$5,000
Stratford X-375/X-350B			
1953-1965. Natural finish version of X-350, renamed X-350B in '58.			
1953-1958	X-375	$4,500	$5,750
1959-1965	X-350B	$3,750	$4,750
Stuart A-500			
1956-1969. Acoustic archtop single-cut, 17" body, A-500 sunburst, available with Guild logo, floating DeArmond pickup.			
1956-1959		$3,750	$4,750
1960-1965		$3,750	$4,750
1966-1969		$3,500	$4,500
Stuart A-550/A-500B			
1956-1969. Natural blond finish version of Stuart A-500, renamed A-500B in '60.			
1956-1959		$4,000	$5,250
1960-1965		$3,750	$4,750
1966-1969		$3,500	$4,500
Stuart X-500			
1953-1995. Electric archtop, single-cut, laminated spruce top, laminated curly maple back and sides, 2 pickups, sunburst.			
1953-1959		$4,500	$5,750
1960-1965		$4,250	$5,500
1966-1969		$4,000	$5,250
1970-1995		$3,500	$4,500
Stuart X-550/X-500B			
1953-1995. Natural blond finish Stuart X-550, renamed X-500B in '60.			
1953-1959		$4,500	$5,750
1960-1964		$4,250	$5,500
1965-1969		$4,000	$5,250
1970-1995		$3,500	$4,500
Studio 301/ST301			
1968-1970. Thinline, semi-hollow archtop Starfire-style but with sharp horns, 1 single-coil pickup, 2 humbuckers in '70, dot inlays, cherry or sunburst.			
1968-1969	1 single-coil	$1,375	$1,750
1970	2 humbuckers	$1,625	$2,125

MODEL YEAR	FEATURES	EXC. COND. LOW	HIGH
Studio 302/ST302			
1968-1970. Like Studio 301, but with 2 pickups.			
1968-1969	2 single-coils	$1,875	$2,500
1970	2 humbuckers	$1,875	$2,500
Studio 303/ST303			
1968-1970. Like Studio 301, but with 2 pickups and Guild/Bigsby.			
1968-1969	2 single-coils	$2,125	$2,750
1969-1970	2 humbuckers	$2,125	$2,750
Studio 402/ST402			
1969-1970. Inch thicker body than other Studios, 2 pickups, block inlays.			
1969-1970	2 humbuckers	$2,625	$3,500
1969-1970	2 single-coils	$2,625	$3,500
T-250			
1986-1988. Single-cut body and pickup configuration with banana-style headstock.			
1986-1988		$650	$850
Thunderbird S-200			
1963-1968. Electric solid body, offset double-cut, built-in rear guitar stand, AdjustoMatic bridge and vibrato tailpiece, 2 humbucker pickups, changed to single-coils in '66.			
1963-1965	Humbuckers	$5,000	$6,500
1966-1968	Single-coils	$4,500	$6,000
Troubadour F-20			
1956-1987. Acoustic flat-top, spruce top with maple back and sides (mahogany '59 and after), rosewood 'board and bridge, natural or sunburst.			
1956-1959		$2,500	$3,250
1960-1964		$2,250	$3,000
1965-1969		$2,250	$3,000
1970-1979		$1,750	$2,250
1980-1987		$1,500	$2,000
TV Model D-55/D-65/D-55			
1968-1987, 1990-present (special order only for 1968-1973). Dreadnought acoustic, spruce top, rosewood back and sides, scalloped bracing, gold-plated tuners, renamed D-65 in '87. Reintroduced as D-55 in '90.			
1968-1969		$2,500	$3,250
1970-1987		$2,500	$3,250
1988-1989	D-65	$2,500	$3,250
1990-1999	D-55	$2,500	$3,250
2000-2023	D-55	$2,500	$3,250
Willy Porter Signature			
2007-2008. AAA Sitka spruce top, solid flamed maple sides and back, special appointments, Fishman Ellipse system.			
2007-2008		$1,250	$1,625
X-79 Skyhawk			
1981-1986. Four-point solid body, 2 pickups, coil-tap or phase switch, various colors. Custom graphics available '84-'86.			
1981-1986		$1,125	$1,500
X-80 Skylark/Swan			
1982-1985. Solid body with 2 deep cutaways, banana-style 6-on-a-side headstock, renamed Swan in '85.			
1982-1985		$1,125	$1,500

1975 Standard F-112
Rivington Guitars

1965 Guild Starfire III

1985 Guild X-100 Bladerunner
Rivington Guitars

1970 Gurian J-M
Imaged by Heritage Auctions, HA.com

MODEL YEAR	FEATURES	EXC. COND. LOW	HIGH

X-82 Nova/Starfighter
1981-1986. Solid body, XR-7 humbuckerss, also available with 3 single-coil pickups, Quick Change SP-6 tailpiece, Adjusto-Matic bridge, Deluxe tuning machine.

1981-1983	Nova	$1,125	$1,500
1984-1986	Starfighter	$1,125	$1,500

X-88 Flying Star Motley Crue
1984-1986. Pointy 4-point star body, rocket ship meets spearhead headstock on bolt neck, 1 pickup, optional vibrato.

1984-1986		$1,125	$1,500

X-88D Star
1984-1987. 2 humbucker version X-88.

1984-1987		$1,125	$1,500

X-92 Citron
1984. Electric solid body, detachable body section, 3 pickups.

1984		$1,000	$1,375

X-100/X-110
1953-1954. Guild was founded in 1952, so this is a very early model, 17" non-cut, single-coil soapbar neck pickup, X-100 sunburst, X-110 natural blond.

1953-1954	X-100	$2,125	$2,750
1953-1954	X-110	$2,375	$3,000

X-100 Bladerunner
1985-1987. 4-point body with large cutouts, 1 humbucker, Kahler, script Guild logo on body, cutout headstock.

1985-1987		$2,750	$3,500

X-150 Savoy/X-150D Savoy
1998-2013. Replaces Savoy X-150, 1 pickup, D has 2 pickups.

1998-2005	X-150	$1,250	$1,625
1998-2013	X-150D	$1,375	$1,750

X-160 Savoy
1989-1993. No Bigsby, black or sunburst.

1989-1993		$1,750	$2,250

X-161 Savoy/X-160B Savoy
1989-1994. X-160 Savoy with Bigsby, sunburst or black.

1989-1994		$1,750	$2,250

X-200/X-220
1953-1954. Electric archtop, spruce top, laminated maple body, rosewood 'board, non-cut, 2 pickups. X-200 is sunburst and X-220 blond.

1953-1954	X-200	$2,375	$3,000
1953-1954	X-220	$2,625	$3,250

X-300/X-330
1953-1954. No model name, non-cut, 2 pickups, X-300 is sunburst and X-330 blond. Becomes Savoy X-150 in '54.

1953-1954	X-300	$2,375	$3,000
1953-1954	X-330	$2,625	$3,250

X-400/X-440
1953-1954. Electric archtop, single-cut, spruce top, laminated maple body, rosewood 'board, 2 pickups, X-400 in sunburst and X-440 in blond. Becomes Manhattan X-175 in '54.

1953-1954	X-400	$3,125	$4,000
1953-1954	X-440	$3,500	$4,500

X-600/X-660
1953. No model name, single-cut, 3 pickups, X-600 in sunburst and X-660 in blond. Becomes Stratford X-350 in '54.

1953	X-600	$4,250	$5,500
1953	X-660	$4,750	$6,125

X-700
1994-1999. Rounded cutaway, 17", solid spruce top, laminated maple back and sides, gold hardware, natural or sunburst.

1994-1999		$2,250	$3,000

Guillermo Roberto Guitars
Professional grade, solidbody electric bajo quintos made in San Fernando, California starting in the year 2000.

Guitar Company of America
1971-2015. Professional grade, custom, acoustic guitars and mandolins built by luthier Dixie Michell. Originally built in Tennessee, then Missouri and finally in Tulsa, Oklahoma. Michell died in '15.

Guitar Mill
2006-2011. Luthier Mario Martin built his production/custom, professional grade, semi-hollow and solidbody guitars and basses in Murfreesboro, Tennessee. He also built basses. In '11, he started branding his guitars as Mario Martin.

Gurian
1965-1981. Luthier Michael Gurian started making classical guitars on a special-order basis, in New York City. In '69, he started building steel-string guitars as well. 1971 brought a move to Hinsdale, Vermont, with increased production. In February, '79 a fire destroyed his factory, stock, and tools. He reopened in West Swanzey, New Hampshire, but closed the doors in '81. Around 2,000 Gurian instruments were built. The guitars have unusual neck joint construction and can be difficult, if not impossible, to repair. Dealers have reported that '70s models sometimes have notable wood cracks which require repair.

CL Series
1970-1981. Classical Series, mahogany (M), Indian rosewood (R), or Brazilian rosewood (B).

1970-1981	CLB, Brazilian rw	$3,500	$4,500
1970-1981	CLM, mahogany	$1,500	$2,000
1970-1981	CLR, Indian rw	$1,750	$2,250

FLC
1970-1981. Flamenco guitar, yellow cedar back and sides, friction tuning pegs.

1970-1981		$2,000	$2,500

JB3H

1970-1981	Brazilian rosewood	$3,500	$4,500

JM/JMR
1970-1981. Jumbo body, mahogany (JM) or Indian rosewood (JMR), relatively wide waist (versus D-style or SJ-style).

1970-1981	JM	$1,750	$2,250
1970-1981	JMR	$1,750	$2,250

The Official Vintage Guitar magazine Price Guide 2025   **Gurian** JR3H — **Hagstrom** Model III/F-300 Futura/H III   **229**

GUITARS

MODEL YEAR	FEATURES	EXC. COND. LOW	HIGH

JR3H

1970-1981. Jumbo, Indian rosewood sides and back, 3-piece back, herringbone trim.

1970-1981		$2,250	$3,000

S2B3H

1970-1981	Brazilian rosewood	$3,750	$4,750

S2M

1970-1981. Size 2 guitar with mahogany back and sides.

1970-1981		$1,750	$2,250

S2R/S2R3H

1970-1981. Size 2 with Indian rosewood sides and back, R3H has 3-piece back and herringbone trim.

1970-1981	S2R	$1,750	$2,250
1970-1981	S2R3H	$1,750	$2,250

S3B3H

1981	Brazilian rosewood	$3,750	$4,750

S3M

1970-1981	Mahogany	$1,750	$2,250

S3R/S3R3H

1970-1981. Size 3 with Indian Rosewood, S3R3H has 3-piece back and herringbone trim.

1970-1981	S3R	$1,750	$2,250
1970-1981	S3R3H	$1,750	$2,250

Guyatone

1933-present. Made in Tokyo by Matsuki Seisakujo, founded by Hawaiian guitarists Mitsuo Matsuki and Atsuo Kaneko (later of Teisco). Made Guya brand Rickenbacker lap steel copies in '30s. After a hiatus for the war ('40-'48), Seisakujo resumes production of laps and amps as Matsuki Denki Onkyo Kenkyujo. In '51 the Guyatone brand was first used on guitars and basses, and in '52 they changed the company name to Tokyo Sound Company. Guyatones are among the earliest U.S. imports, branded as Marco Polo, Winston, Kingston and Kent. Other brand names included LaFayette and Bradford. Production and exports slowed after '68.

Hagenlocher, Henner

1996-present. Luthier Henner Hagenlocher builds his premium grade, custom, nylon-string guitars in Granada, Spain.

Hagstrom

1958-1983, 2004-present. Intermediate, professional, and premium grade, production/custom, solidbody, semi-hollowbody and acoustic guitars made in the U.S. and imported. Founded by Albin Hagström of Älvdalen, Sweden, who began importing accordions in 1921. Electric guitar and bass production began in '58 with plastic-covered hollowbody De Luxe and Standard models. The guitars were imported into the U.S. by Hershman Music of New York as Goya 90 and 80 from '58-'61. Bass versions were imported in '61. Following a year in the U.S., Albin's son Karl-Erik Hagström took over the company as exclusive distributor of Fender in Scandinavia; he changed the U.S. importer to Merson Musical Instruments of New York (later Unicord in '65), and redesigned the line. The company closed its doors in '83. In 2004 American Music & Sound started manufacturing and distributing the Hagstrom brand under license from A.B. Albin Hagstrom. In 2009 U.S. Music became involved via its acquisition of JAM, and the 'new' Hagstrom established a Swedish office. A new line of instruments under the Vintage Series (made in China) included classic '60s models. Later the Northen series was introduced with instruments made entirely in Europe.

Corvette/Condor

1963-1967. Offset double-cut solidbody, 3 single-coils, multiple push-button switches, spring vibrato, called the Condor on U.S. imports.

1963-1967		$1,250	$1,500

D'Aquisto Jimmy

1969-1975, 1976-1979. Designed by James D'Aquisto, electric archtop, f-holes, 2 pickups, sunburst, natural, cherry or white. The '69 had dot inlays, the later version had blocks. From '77 to '79, another version with an oval soundhole (no f-holes) was also available.

1969-1975	1st design	$1,500	$1,875
1976-1979	2nd design	$1,375	$1,750

Deluxe 90

1958-1962. Carved single-cut mahogany body, set-neck, 2 humbuckers, sparkle tops or sunburst.

1958-1962	Sparkle top	$1,500	$2,000

F Series

2004-2015. Made in China, offset double-cut basswood body, 2 or 3 pickups.

2004-2015	Various models	$200	$350

H-12 Electric/Viking XII

1965-1967. Double-cut, 2 pickups, 12 strings.

1965-1967		$625	$775

H-22 Folk

1965-1967. Flat-top acoustic.

1965-1967		$375	$475

Impala

1963-1967. Two-pickup version of the Corvette, sunburst.

1963-1967		$900	$1,125

Kent

1962-1967. Offset double-cut solidbody, 2 pickups.

1962-1967		$625	$775

Model I

1965-1971. Small double-cut solidbody, 2 single-coils, early models have plastic top.

1965-1971		$850	$1,125

Model II/F-200 Futura/H II

1965-1972, 1975-1976. Offset double-cut slab body with beveled edge, 2 pickups, called F-200 Futura in U.S., Model II elsewhere, '75-'76 called H II. F-200 reissued in 2004.

1965-1976		$900	$1,125

Model III/F-300 Futura/H III

1965-1972, 1977. Offset double-cut slab body with beveled edge, 3 pickups, called F-300 Futura in U.S., Model III elsewhere, '77 called H III.

1965-1969		$950	$1,250
1970-1977		$525	$650

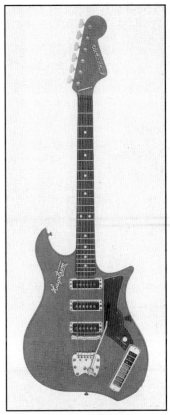

Hagstrom Corvette

Imaged by Heritage Auctions, HA.com

1965 Hagstrom Model I

Rivington Guitars

1972 Hagstrom Swede
Rivington Guitars

Hahn Model 112

MODEL YEAR	FEATURES	EXC. COND. LOW	HIGH
Swede			

1970-1982, 2004-present. Bolt-on neck, single-cut solidbody, black, cherry or natural, '04 version is set-neck.

1979-1982		$1,000	$1,250
Super Swede			

1979-1983, 2004-present. Glued-in neck upgrade of Swede, '04 version is maple top upgrade of Swede.

1979-1983		$1,000	$1,250
1979-1983	Custom color	$1,375	$1,750
2004-2020	Reissue	$450	$575
Viking/V1			

1965-1975, 1978-1979, 2004-present. Double-cut thinline, 2 f-holes, 2 pickups, chrome hardware, dot inlays, also advertised as the V-1. '60s had 6-on-side headstock, '70s was 3-and-3, latest version back to 6-on-side.

1965-1979		$1,125	$1,500
2004-2023	Reissue	$400	$500
Viking Deluxe/V2			

1967-1968, 2004-present. Upscale version, gold hardware, block inlays, bound headstock and f-holes. Current version upgrades are blocks and flame maple.

1967-1968		$1,250	$1,500
2004-2023	Reissue	$400	$500

Hahn

2007-present. Professional and premium grade, custom electric guitars built by luthier Chihoe Hahn in Garnerville, New York.

Haight

1989-present. Premium and presentation grade, production/custom, acoustic (steel and classical) guitars built in Scottsdale, Arizona by luthier Norman Haight. He also builds mandolins.

Halfling Guitars and Basses

Luthier Tom Ribbecke builds premium grade, production/custom, pin bridge, thinline and jazz guitars and basses, starting in 2003, in Healdsburg, California.

Hallmark

1965-1967, 2004-present. Imported and U.S.-made, intermediate and premium grade, production/custom, guitars and basses from luthiers Bob Shade and Bill Gruggett, and located in Greenbelt, Maryland. They also make basses. The brand was originally founded by Joe Hall in Arvin, California, in '65. Hall had worked for Semie Moseley (Mosrite) and had also designed guitars for Standel in the mid-'60s. Bill Gruggett, who also built his own line of guitars, was the company's production manager. Joe Hall estimates that less than 1000 original Hallmark guitars were built. The brand was revived by Shade in '04.

Sweptwing

1965-1967, 2000s. Pointed body, sorta like a backwards Flying V.

1965-1967		$3,500	$4,375
2000s	Reissue	$650	$850

Hamblin Guitars

Luthier Kent Hamblin built his premium grade, production/custom, flat-top acoustic guitars in Phoenix, Arizona and Telluride, Colorado, and presently builds in Colorado Springs. He began building in 1996.

Hamer

1974-2012, 2017-present. Intermediate grade, production, electric guitars. Hamer previously made basses and the Slammer line of instruments. Founded in Arlington Heights, Illinois, by Paul Hamer and Jol Dantzig. Prototype guitars built in early-'70s were on Gibson lines, with first production guitar, the Standard (Explorer shape), introduced in '75. Hamer was puchased by Kaman Corporation (Ovation) in '88. The Illinois factory was closed and the operations were moved to the Ovation factory in Connecticut in '97. On January 1, '08, Fender acquired Kaman Music Corporation and the Hamer brand. In '90, they started the Korean-import Hamer Slammer series which in '97 became Hamer Import Series (no Slammer on headstock). In '05 production was moved to China and name changed to XT Series (in '07 production moved to Indonesia). The U.S.-made ones have U.S.A. on the headstock. The less expensive import Slammer brand (not to be confused with the earlier Slammer Series) was introduced in '99 (see that listing). Fender suspended production of the Hamer brand at the end of 2012, later selling KMC (and Hamer brand) to Jam Industries, which relaunched Hamer in '17.

Archtop P-90

Solidbody double-cut, archtop sloping on top, P-90 pickups.

1993		$1,250	$1,750
Artist/Archtop Artist/Artist Custom			

1995-2012. U.S.-made, similar to Sunburst Archtop with semi-solid, f-hole design, sunburst, named Archtop Artist, then renamed Artist (with stop tailpiece)/Artist Custom in '97.

1995-2012	Higher-end specs	$2,000	$2,500
1995-2012	Standard specs	$1,500	$2,000
Artist 25th Anniversary Edition			

1998. Made in USA, 25th Anniversary Edition script logo on headstock.

1998		$1,500	$2,000
Artist Korina			

2001-2012. Double-cut, bass f-hole, korina (limba) body and neck, 2 P-90s or 2 humbuckers (HB), natural gloss finish.

2001-2012		$2,000	$2,500
Artist Ultimate			

1998-2012. Figured maple top, deluxe binding, gold hardware.

1998-2012		$2,500	$3,250
Blitz			

1982-1984 (1st version), 1984-1990 (2nd version). Explorer-style body, 2 humbuckers, 3-on-a-side peghead, dot inlays, choice of tremolo or fixed bridge, second version same except has angled 6-in-line peghead and Floyd Rose tremolo.

MODEL YEAR	FEATURES	EXC. COND. LOW	HIGH
1982-1984	3-on-a-side	$2,500	$3,125
1984-1990	6-in-line	$1,750	$2,250

Californian
1987-1997. Made in the USA, solidbody double cut, bolt neck, 1 humbucker and 1 single-coil, Floyd Rose tremolo.

1987-1989	Various features	$2,500	$3,500
1990-1997	Various features	$2,250	$3,000

Californian Custom
1987-1997. Made in the USA, downsized contoured body, offset double-cut, neck-thru-body, optional figured maple body, Duncan Trembucker and Trem-single pickups.

1987-1989		$2,500	$3,500
1990-1997		$2,250	$3,000

Californian Elite
1987-1997. Made in the USA, downsized contoured body, offset double-cut, optional figured maple body, bolt-on neck, Duncan Trembucker and Trem-single pickups.

1987-1989		$2,500	$3,500
1990-1997		$2,250	$3,000

Centaura
1989-1995. Alder or swamp ash offset double-cut, bolt-on neck, 1 humbucker and 2 single-coils, Floyd Rose, sunburst.

1989-1995		$1,500	$2,000

Chaparral
1985-1987 (1st version), 1987-1994 (2nd version). Offset double-cut, glued neck, angled peghead, 1 humbucker and 2 single-coils, tremolo, second version has bolt neck with a modified peghead.

1985-1987	Set-neck	$2,000	$3,000
1987-1994	Bolt-on neck	$1,500	$2,000

Daytona
1993-1997. Offset double-cut, bolt neck, dot inlay, 3 single-coils, Wilkinson tremolo.

1993-1997		$1,375	$1,750

Diablo/Diablo II
1992-1997. Offset double-cut, bolt neck, rosewood 'board, dot inlays, reversed peghead '92-'94, 2 pickups, tremolo. Diablo II has 3 pickups.

1992-1997		$1,250	$1,625

DuoTone
1993-2003. Semi-hollowbody, double-cut, bound top, glued-in neck, rosewood 'board, 2 humbuckers, EQ.

1993-2003		$950	$1,250

Echotone/Echotone Custom
2000-2002. Thinline semi-hollow archtop, f-holes, 2 humbuckers, trapezoid inlays, gold hardware.

2000-2002		$500	$650

Eclipse
1994-1996. Asymmetrical double-cut slab mahogany body, glued neck, rosewood 'board, 2 Duncan Mini-Humbuckers, cherry.

1994-1996		$950	$1,250

Eclipse (Import)
1997-1999. Import version.

1997-1999		$350	$500

Eclipse 12-String
1994-1996. 12-string version of Eclipse.

1995		$900	$1,250

FB I
1986-1987. Reverse Firebird-style body, glued-in neck, reverse headstock, 1 pickup, rosewood 'board with dot inlays, also available in non-reverse body.

1986-1987		$3,000	$4,000

FB II
1986-1987. Reverse Firebird-style, glued-in neck, ebony 'board with boomerang inlays, angled headstock, 2 humbuckers, Floyd Rose tremolo, also available as a 12-string.

1986-1987		$3,500	$4,500

Korina Standard
1995-1996. Limited run, 100 made, Korina Explorer-type body, glued-in neck, angled peghead, 2 humbuckers.

1995-1996		$4,000	$5,000

Korina V
1995-1996. Limited run, 72 made, Korina Explorer-type body, 2 humbuckers.

1995-1996		$4,500	$6,000

Maestro
1990. Offset double-cut, 7 strings, tremolo, bolt-on maple neck, 3 Seymour Duncan rail pickups.

1990		$1,500	$2,000

Mirage
1994-1998. Double-cut carved figured Koa wood top, transparent flamed top, initially with 3 single-coil pickups, dual humbucker option in '95.

1994-1998		$1,500	$2,000

Monaco III
2003-2007. Single-cut semi-hollow, 3 P90 pickups.

2003-2007		$2,000	$2,500

Newport Series
1999-2012. USA, double-cut thinline, center block, f-holes, 2 humbuckers (Newport 90 has P-90s), wrap-around bridge tailpiece.

1999-2012	Newport	$1,500	$2,000
1999-2012	Newport Pro	$1,500	$2,000

Phantom A5
1982-1884, 1985-1986 (2nd version). Offset double-cut, glued neck, 3-on-a-side peghead, 1 triple-coil and 1 single-coil pickup, second version same but with 6-in-line peghead and Kahler.

1982-1984		$1,500	$2,250

Phantom GT
1984-1986. Contoured body, offset double-cut, glued-in fixed neck, 6-in-line peghead, 1 humbucker, single volume control.

1984-1986		$1,500	$2,000

Prototype
1981-1985. Contoured mahogany body, double-cut with 1 splitable triple-coil pickup, fixed bridge, three-on-a-side peghead, Prototype II has extra pickup and tremolo.

1981-1985		$1,500	$2,500

Scarab I
1984-1986. Multiple cutaway body, 6-in-line peghead, 1 humbucker, tremolo, rosewood or ebony 'board, dot inlays.

1984-1986		$2,000	$2,500

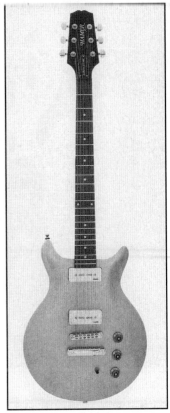

Hamer Archtop P-90
Imaged by Heritage Auctions, HA.com

Hamer Artist Korina

1993 Hamer Special
Paul Johnson

1982 Hamer Standard
Bo Belaski

MODEL YEAR	FEATURES	EXC. COND. LOW	HIGH

Scarab II
1984-1986. Two humbucker version of the Scarab.

| 1984-1986 | | $2,000 | $2,500 |

Scepter
1986-1990. Futuristic-type body, ebony 'board with boomerang inlays, angled 6-in-line peghead, Floyd Rose tremolo.

| 1986-1990 | | $3,500 | $5,000 |

Slammer Series
1990-1997. Various models imported from Korea, not to be confused with Hamer's current Slammer budget line started in '98.

| 1990-1997 | | $350 | $450 |

Special Series
1980-1983 (1st version), 1984-1985 (Floyd Rose version), 1992-1997 (2nd version), 2017-present. Double-cut solidbody, flame maple top, glued neck, 3-on-a-side peghead, 2 humbuckers, Rose version has mahogany body with ebony 'board, the 2nd version is all mahogany and has tune-o-matic bridge, stop tailpiece and Duncan P-90s, cherry red.

1980-1983	1st version	$2,250	$3,000
1984-1985	With Floyd Rose	$2,250	$3,000
1992-1997	2nd version	$1,750	$2,500
2017-2023	Reissue	$1,750	$2,500

Standard
1974-1985, 1995-2005. Futuristic body, maple top, bound or unbound body, glued neck, angled headstock, either unbound neck with dot inlays or bound neck with crown inlays, 2 humbuckers. Reissued in '95 with same specs but unbound mahogany body after '97. Higher dollar Standard Custom still available.

1974-1975	Pre-production, 20 made	$20,000	$25,000
1975-1977	Production, 50 made, PAFs	$15,000	$20,000
1977-1979	Dimarzio PAF-copy	$12,000	$15,000
1980-1985		$9,000	$11,500
1995-1999		$5,000	$6,500
2000-2005	USA, flamed top	$3,000	$4,000

Standard (Import, XT)
1998-2012. Import version, 2 humbuckers.

| 1998-2012 | | $400 | $600 |

Standard Custom GSTC
2007-2012. Made in the USA, flamed maple top, mahogany neck, rosewood 'board.

| 2007-2012 | | $4,500 | $5,500 |

Stellar 1
1999-2000. Korean import, double-cut, 2 humbuckers.

| 1999-2000 | | $200 | $250 |

Steve Stevens I
1984-1992. Introduced as Prototype SS, changed to Steve Stevens I in '86, contoured double-cut, 6-in-line headstock, dot or crown inlays, 1 humbucker and 2 single-coil pickups.

| 1984-1992 | | $2,000 | $2,500 |

Steve Stevens II
1986-1987. One humbucker and 1 single-coil version.

| 1986-1987 | | $2,000 | $2,500 |

Studio
1993-2012. Double-cut, flamed maple top on mahogany body, 2 humbuckers, cherry or natural.

| 1993-2012 | | $1,250 | $1,625 |

Studio Custom
1997-2012. Carved figured maple, humbuckers, tune-o-matic bridge, stop tailpiece, sunburst.

| 1997-2012 | | $1,750 | $2,250 |

Sunburst
1977-1979, 1990-1992. Double-cut bound solidbody, flamed maple top, glued-in neck, bound neck and crown inlays optional, 3-on-a-side headstock, 2 humbuckers.

1977	1st 100, thin body	$5,000	$6,500
1978-1979		$3,000	$4,500
1990-1992		$2,000	$2,500

Sunburst (Import, XT)
1997-2012. Import version of Sunburst, flat-top or archtop, 2 pickups.

| 1997-2012 | | $300 | $450 |

Sunburst Archtop
1991-1997. Sunburst model with figured maple carved top, 2 humbuckers, offered under various names: Standard - unbound neck and dot inlays, tune-o-matic and stop tailpiece '91-'93 (replaced by the Studio). Custom - bound neck and crown inlays '91-'93, which became the Archtop for '94-'97 (replaced by the Studio Custom). Archtop GT - Gold top with P-90 soapbar-style pickups '93-'97.

| 1991-1997 | Various models | $2,000 | $2,500 |

T-51
1993-1997. Classic single-cut southern ash body, 2 single-coils.

| 1993-1997 | | $1,000 | $1,500 |

T-62
1991-1995. Classic offset double-cut solidbody, tremolo, pau ferro 'board, Lubritrak nut, locking tuners, 3-band active EQ, various colors.

| 1991-1995 | | $1,000 | $1,500 |

TLE
1986-1992. Single-cut mahogany body, maple top, glued neck, 6-in-line headstock, rosewood 'board, dot inlays, 3 pickups.

| 1986-1992 | | $2,500 | $3,500 |

TLE Custom
1986-1992. Bound, single-cut solidbody with maple top, glued-in neck, angled headstock, ebony 'board with boomerang inlays, 3 pickups.

| 1986-1992 | | $2,500 | $3,500 |

Vector
1982-1985. V-style body (optional flame maple top), 3-on-a-side peghead, rosewood 'board, 2 humbuckers, Sustain Block fixed bridge (Kahler or Floyd Rose tremolos may also be used).

| 1982-1985 | | $1,500 | $2,500 |

Vector Limited Edition Korina
1997. 72 built in Hamer's Arlington Heights, Illinois shop, price includes original Hamer certificate of authenticity with matching serial number, Flying-V Vector style body, gold hardware, natural finish.

| 1997 | | $4,000 | $5,000 |

MODEL		EXC. COND.	
YEAR	FEATURES	LOW	HIGH

Hanson

2009-present. Founders John and Bo Pirruccello import intermediate grade, electric guitars which are set up in Chicago, Illinois.

Harden Engineering

1999-present. Professional grade, custom, solid-body guitars built by luthier William Harnden in Chicago, Illinois. He also builds effects pedals.

Harmony

1892-1976, late 1970s-present. Huge, Chicago-based manufacturer of fretted instruments, mainly budget models under the Harmony name or for many other American brands and mass marketers. Harmony was at one time the largest guitar builder in the world. In its glory days, Harmony made over one-half of the guitars built in the U.S., with '65 being their peak year. But by the early-'70s, the crash of the '60s guitar boom and increasing foreign competition brought an end to the company. The Harmony brand appeared on Asian-built instruments starting in the late '70s to the '90s with sales mainly through mass-retail stores. In 2000, the Harmony brand was distributed by MBT International. In '02, former MBT marketing director Alison Gillette launched Harmony Classic Reissue Guitars and Basses and in '09 the trademark was acquired by Westheimer Corporation. Many Harmony guitars have a factory order number on the inside back of the guitar which often contains the serial number. Most older Harmony acoustics and hollowbodies have a date ink-stamped inside the body. DeArmond made most of the electronic assemblies used on older Harmony electrics, and they often have a date stamped on the underside.

Amplifying Resonator Model 27
1930s. Dobro-licensed with Dobro metal resonator, wood body.

1930s		$750	$950

Cremona
1930s-1952. Full-size archtop line, Harmony and Cremona logo on headstock, natural. Cutaways became available in '53.

1940-1952		$300	$400

D Series (Electric)
Late-1980s-Early-1990s. Classic electric copy models including offset double- and single-cut solidbody and double-cut thin hollowbody (D720), 1 to 3 pickups. All models begin with D, some models part of Harmony Electric series and others the Harmony Igniter series.

1980s-90s	Various models	$95	$175

H/HG Series (Electric)
Late-1980s-Early-1990s. Classic electric copy models including offset double-cut, single-cut and double-cut semi-hollow, 1 to 3 pickups, with or without tremolo. All models begin with H or HG, some models part of Harmony Electric series and others the Harmony Igniter series.

1980s-90s	Various models	$100	$175

H14/H15 Bob Kat
1968. Replaces Silhouette solidbody, H14 has single pickup and 2 knobs, H15 has 2 pickups. When vibrato is added it becomes the H16 model.

1968	H14	$500	$650
1968	H15	$625	$775

H14/H15/H17 Silhouette
1963-1967. Double-cut solidbody, H14 single pickup, H15 dual pickup, H17 dual with vibrato (offered until '66).

1963-1967	H14	$450	$650
1963-1967	H15	$550	$750
1963-1967	H17	$650	$850

H19 Silhouette De Luxe Double
1965-1969. Double-cut solidbody, deluxe pickups, block markers, advanced vibrato, sunburst.

1965-1969		$775	$975

H37 Hollywood
1960-1961. Electric archtop, auditorium size 15.75" body, 1 pickup, Harmony and Hollywood logo on headstock, 2-tone gold metallic finish.

1960-1961		$500	$650

H39 Hollywood
1960-1965. Like H37 but with sunburst.

1960-1965		$400	$550

H41 Hollywood
1960-1965. Like H37 but with 2 pickups, sunburst.

1960-1965		$600	$775

H42/1 and H42/2 Stratotone Newport
1957-1958. Brightly colored, single-cut, Newport headstock logo, 1 single-coil. 42/1 in sunshine yellow, /2 in metallic green.

1957-1958		$1,500	$2,000

H44 Stratotone
1953-1957. First edition models had small bodies and rounded cutaway, 1 pickup with plain cover using 2 mounting rivets, sometimes called Hershey Bar pickup, '60s models had slightly larger bodies and sharp cutaways, some with headstock logo Harmony Stratotone with atomic note graphic.

1953-1957		$1,625	$2,000

H45/H46 Stratotone Mars Electric
1958-1968. Single-cut, tone chamber construction, sunburst finish, H45 with 1 pickup, H46 with 2 pickups.

1960s	H45	$725	$900
1960s	H46	$950	$1,250

H47/48 Stratotone Mercury Electric
1958-1968. Single-cut, tone chamber construction, H47 with 1 pickup, block inlay and curly maple sunburst top, H48 is the same with a blond top.

1960s	H47	$950	$1,250
1960s	H48	$950	$1,250

H49 Stratotone Deluxe Jupiter
1958-1965. Single-cut, tone chamber construction, 2 pickups, bound spruce top, curly maple back and 6 control knobs, blond finish.

1958-1965		$1,250	$1,500

H53 Rocket I
1959-1973. Single-cut, f-holes, 1 pickup, trapeze, 2-tone brown sunburst ('59-'62) or red sunburst ('63 on).

1959-1969		$525	$650
1970-1973		$425	$550

1968 Harmony Bob Kat H15
Tom Pfeifer

1967 Harmony Silhouette De Luxe Double H19
Tom Pfeifer

Harmony H72 Double
Cutaway Hollowbody
Tom Pfeifer

1967 Harmony H79 Double
Cutaway Hollowbody 12-string
Bill Ruxton

MODEL YEAR	FEATURES	EXC. COND. LOW	HIGH
H54 Rocket II			
1959-1973. Same as H53 but with 2 pickups.			
1959-1969		$850	$1,125
1970-1973		$525	$650
H59 Rocket III			
1960-1973. Same as H53 but with 3 pickups.			
1960-1969		$1,250	$1,625
1970-1973		$1,125	$1,500
H59 Rocket Reissue			
2000s. Import, double-cut, 3 pickups, 6 knobs.			
2000s		$550	$750
H60 Double Cutaway Hollowbody			
1968-1970. Thinline double-cut, 2 pickups, trapeze tailpiece, sunburst.			
1968-1970		$1,000	$1,375
H62 Blond			
1950s-1965. Thin body, dual pickup archtop, curly maple back and sides, spruce top, block markers, blond.			
1950s-1965		$2,000	$2,500
H62VS (Reissue)			
2000s. H62 with sunburst finish.			
2000s		$900	$1,125
H63 Espanada			
1950s-1965. Thick body, single-cut, jazz-style double pickups, black finish with white appointments, by early '60s 'Espanada' logo on lower bass bout.			
1950s-1965		$1,500	$2,000
H64 Double Cutaway Electric			
1968-1970. Double-cut electric, factory Bigsby, dot markers, sunburst.			
1968-1970		$1,250	$1,625
H65 Modern Trend			
1956-1960. Short-scale electric thin body archtop, 1 single-coil, block inlays, Sherry Blond finish on curly maple grain.			
1956-1960		$1,125	$1,500
H66 Vibra-Jet			
1962-1966. Thinline single-cut, 2 pickups, built-in tremolo circuit and control panel knobs and selection dial, sunburst.			
1962-1966		$1,500	$2,000
H68 Deep Body Electric			
1968-1971. Full-body single-cut electric archtop, 2 pickups, trapeze bridge, block markers.			
1968-1971		$1,375	$1,750
H70/H71 Meteor			
1958-1966. Single rounded cutaway 2" thin body, 2 pickups, 3-part f-holes, block inlays, bolt neck, H70 sunburst, H71 natural (ended '65), lefty offered '65-'66, reintroduced as H661 and H671 (without Meteor name) in '72-'74.			
1958-1965	H71, natural	$1,500	$2,000
1958-1966	H70, sunburst	$1,500	$2,000
H72/H72V Double Cutaway Hollowbody			
1966-1971. Multiple bindings, 2 pickups, cherry red, H72V has Bigsby.			
1966-1971		$1,375	$1,750
H73 Roy Smeck			
1963-1964. Electric hollowbody, single neck silver bar-style pickup or 2 Harmony pickups.			
1963-1964		$1,375	$1,750

MODEL YEAR	FEATURES	EXC. COND. LOW	HIGH
H74 Neo-Cutaway			
1961-1967. Modified double-cut, 2 pickups, Bigsby, 3-part F-holes, dot inlays.			
1961-1967		$1,500	$2,000
H75 Double Cutaway Hollowbody			
1960-1970. Three pickups, multi-bound body, 3-part f-holes, block inlays, bolt neck, brown sunburst.			
1960-1970		$1,500	$2,000
H76 Double Cutaway Hollowbody			
1960-1962. H75 with Bigsby.			
1960-1962		$1,500	$2,000
H77 Double Cutaway Hollowbody			
Late-1960s. Same as H75, but in cherry sunburst.			
1960s		$1,500	$2,000
H78 Double Cutaway Hollowbody			
Late-1960s. H77 with Bigsby.			
1960s		$1,500	$2,000
H79 Double Cutaway Hollowbody 12-String			
1966-1970. Unique slotted headstock, cherry finish.			
1966-1970		$1,500	$2,000
H81 Rebel			
1968-1971. Single pickup version of Rebel, brown sunburst.			
1968-1971		$450	$600
H82/H82G Rebel			
Listed as a new model in 1971. Thin body, hollow tone chamber, double-cut, 2 pickups, H82 sunburst, H82G greenburst avacado shading (renumbered as H682 and H683 in '72).			
1970s	H82	$650	$800
1970s	H82G	$650	$800
H88 Stratotone Doublet			
1954-1957. Basically 2-pickup H44.			
1954-1957		$1,375	$1,750
H150 Student			
1963-1969. Parlor-size acoustic.			
1963-1969		$175	$250
H162 Folk			
1950s-1971. Grand concert size acoustic, spruce top, mahogany body.			
1950s-1971		$450	$575
H165 Grand Concert			
1948-1957. Flat-top, all mahogany body. Body changed to square-shoulder in '58 (see Folk H165).			
1948-1957		$400	$500
H165/H6365 Folk			
1958-1974. Square-shouldered flat-top, all mahogany body. Renamed the H6365 in '72.			
1958-1974		$425	$550
H169 Buck Owens			
1969. Acoustic flat-top, red, white and blue. The price shown is for a guitar that has an unblemished finish, paint wear will reduce the price, prices vary considerable due to the condition of the finish.			
1969		$2,500	$3,500
H600 Roy Rogers			
1954-1958. 3/4 size, stencil, sold through Sears.			
1954-1958		$375	$475

The *Vintage Guitar Price Guide* shows values for all-original, excellent condition instruments and, where applicable, with original case.

MODEL YEAR	FEATURES	EXC. COND. LOW	HIGH

H910 Classical
1970s. Beginner guitar, natural.

1970s		$75	$95

H945 Master
1965-1966. 15" Auditorium-sized acoustic archtop, block markers, music note painted logo on headstock, sunburst.

1965-1966		$300	$400

H950/H952/H1325/H1456/H1457/H6450
1930s-1974. Line of Auditorium and Grand Auditorium acoustic archtop models.

1950s	H950 Monterey	$325	$450
1950s	H952 Colorama	$450	$550
1950s-60s	Other models	$300	$500
1970s	H6450	$175	$250

H954 Broadway
1930s-1971. 15-3/4" body, acoustic archtop, dot markers, sunburst.

1930s-1971		$250	$500

H1057 Singing Cowboys
1950s. Western chuck-wagon scene stencil top, Singing Cowboys stenciled on either side of upper bouts, brown background versus earlier Supertone version that had black background.

1950s		$350	$500

H1200 Auditorium Series
1948-1975. Acoustic archtop, treble-clef artwork on headstock, model 1213 & 1215 (shaded brown sunburst) and 1214 (blond ivory, ends in '64). Model 1215 was renamed H6415 in '72 and lasted until '75.

1948-1975	Various models	$275	$500

H1203 Sovereign Western Special Jumbo
1960s-1970s. 15" wide body, 000-style.

1960s		$600	$750

H1215 Archtone
1950-1960s. Lower-end archtop, 6-string, sunburst.

1950-60s		$400	$500

H1215 Archtone Tenor
1950-1960s. Lower-end archtop tenor, 4-string, sunburst.

1950-60s		$350	$450

H1250 Roy Smeck Vita Standard
1928-1931. Pear shaped body, seal-shaped sound holes.

1928-1931		$950	$1,250

H1252 Professional Hawaiian
1940. Hawaiian acoustic jumbo, high-end appointments, Professional logo on headstock, figured Koa or mahogany back and sides, spruce top, Brazilian rosewood fretboard, various-shaped fretboard markers.

1940		$2,250	$3,000

H1260 Sovereign Jumbo
1960s-1970s. Jumbo shape, 16" wide body, natural.

1960s		$675	$850
1970s		$500	$625

H1265 Sovereign Jumbo Deluxe
1965-1969. Jumbo D-style, 16" fancy.

1965-1969		$1,250	$1,500

H1266 Sovereign Jumbo Deluxe
Late-1960s-1970s. Jumbo nearly D-style, 16" wide body with out-sized 'guard, natural.

1960s		$1,375	$1,750
1970s		$725	$900

H1270 Flat-Top 12-String
1965. 16" deluxe acoustic 12-string flat-top, spruce top, mahogany sides and back, dot markers.

1965		$750	$1,250

H1310 Brilliant Cutaway
1953-1973. Grand Auditorium acoustic archtop, single rounded cutaway, block inlays, sunburst. Called H6510 in '72.

1953-1973		$625	$800

H1311 Brilliant Cutaway
1953-1962. As H1310, but in blond.

1953-1963		$875	$1,125

H1407/H1414/H1418 Patrician
1932-1973. Model line mostly with mahogany bodies and alternating single/double dot markers (later models with single dots), introduced as flat-top, changed to archtop in '34. In '37 line expanded to 9 archtops (some with blocks) and 1 flat-top. Flat-tops disappeared in the '40s, with various archtops offered up to '73.

1932-1973		$375	$500

H1442 Roy Smeck Artiste
1939-ca. 1942. Grand auditorium acoustic archtop, Roy Smeck Artiste logo on headstock, split rectangle markers, black with white guard.

1939-1942		$600	$750

H4101 Flat-Top Tenor
1950s-1970s. Mahogany body, 4-string.

1950s-70s		$400	$500

Holiday Rocket
Mid-1960s. Similar to H59 Rocket III but with push-button controls instead of rotary selector switch, 3 Goldentone pickups, pickup trim rings, Holiday logo on 'guard, higher model than standard Rocket.

1960s		$1,125	$1,500

Igniter Series (D/H/HG)
Late-1980s to early-1990s. Pointy-headstock electric copy models, offset double-cut, all models begin with D, H, or HG.

1980s-90s	Various models	$110	$250

Lone Ranger
1950-1951. Lone Ranger headstock stencil, Lone Ranger and Tonto stencil on brown body. This model was first introduced in 1936 as the Supertone Lone Ranger with the same stencil on a black body.

1950-1951		$325	$450

TG1201 Tenor
1950s. Spruce top, two-on-a-side tuners, Sovereign model tenor, natural.

1950s		$350	$450

Harptone

1893-ca. 1975. The Harptone Manufacturing Corporation was located in Newark, New Jersey. They made musical instrument cases and accessories and got into instrument production from 1934 to '42, making guitars, banjos, mandolins, and tiples. In '66 they got back into guitar production, making the Standel line from '67 to '69. Harptone offered flat-tops and archtops under their own brand until the mid-'70s when the name was sold to the Diamond S company, which owned Micro-Frets.

1969 Harmony H954 Broadway
Edward Sparks

1963 Harmony H1215
Auditorium
Douglas Morissette

1988 Heartfield RR9
Tom Pfeifer

Hendrick Generator

MODEL YEAR	FEATURES	EXC. COND. LOW	HIGH
Acoustic			
1966-mid-1970s. Various models.			
1966-1970s	Deluxe/Custom	$1,500	$2,000
1966-1970s	Standard	$1,125	$1,500
Electric			
1966-mid-1970s. Various models.			
1966-1970s		$1,500	$2,000

Harrison Guitars

1992-present. Luthier Douglas Harrison builds premium grade, production/custom, archtop and semi-hollowbody jazz guitars in Toronto, Ontario.

Harwood

Harwood was a brand introduced in 1885 by Kansas City, Missouri instrument wholesalers J.W. Jenkins & Sons (though some guitars marked Harwood, New York). May have been built by Jenkins until circa 1905, but work was later contracted out to Harmony.

Parlor

1890s. Slotted headstocks, most had mahogany bodies, some with Brazilian rosewood body, considered to be well made.

1890s	Brazilian rosewood	$1,000	$1,500
1890s	Mahogany	$600	$775

Hascal Haile

Late 1960s-1986. Luthier Hascal Haile started building acoustic, classical and solidbody guitars in Tompkinsville, Kentucky, after retiring from furniture making. He died in '86.

Hauver Guitar

2001-present. Professional and premium grade, custom, acoustic guitars, built in Sharpsburg, Maryland by luthier Michael S. Hauver.

Hayes Guitars

Professional and premium grade, production/custom, steel and nylon string guitars made by luthier Louis Hayes in Paonia, Colorado. He began building in 1993.

Hayman

1970-1973. Solid and semi-hollowbody guitars and basses developed by Jim Burns and Bob Pearson for Ivor Arbiter of the Dallas Arbiter Company and built by Shergold in England.

Haynes

1865-early 1900s. The John C. Haynes Co. of Boston also made the Bay State brand.

Heartfield

1989-1994. Founded as a joint venture between Fender Musical Instrument Corporation (U.S.A.) and Fender Japan (partnership between Fender and distributors Kanda Shokai and Yamano Music) to build and market more advanced designs (built by Fuji Gen-Gakki). First RR and EX guitar series and

DR Bass series debut in '90. Talon and Elan guitar series and Prophecy bass series were introduced in '91. The brand was dead by '94.

Electric Solidbody

1989-1994	Various models	$725	$950

Heiden Stringed Instruments

1974-present. Luthier Michael Heiden builds his premium grade, production/custom, flat-top guitars in Chilliwack, British Columbia. He also builds mandolins.

Heit Deluxe

Ca. 1967-1970. Imported from Japan by unidentified New York distributor. Many were made by Teisco, the most famous being the Teisco V-2 Mosrite copy. They also had basses.

Acoustic

1967-1970	Various models	$225	$300

Electric

1967-1970	Various models	$375	$500

Hembry Guitars

2002-present. Professional grade, production/custom, solidbody electric guitars built by luthier Scott Hembry in Shelton, Washington. He also builds basses.

Hemken, Michael

1993-2021. Luthier Michael Hemken built his premium grade, custom, archtops in St. Helena, California. He died January 2021.

HenBev

Premium grade, production, solid and hollow body electric guitars and basses built by luthier Scotty Bevilacqua in Oceanside, California, starting in 2005.

Henderson Guitars

Luthier Wayne C. Henderson builds premium and presentation grade, custom acoustic guitars in Rugby, Virginia. He produces around 20 guitars per year and has also made mandolins, banjos and fiddles.

Hendrick

1982-1985. Solidbody guitars built by luthier Kurt Hendrick in Texas, Ohio and Michigan. Less than 100 built, the most popular model was the Generator. Hendrick also worked with Schecter, Fender, Jackson and Epiphone.

Henman Guitars

2010-present. Owners Graham and Paris Henman offer premium grade, production/custom, solidbody and chambered electric guitars and basses built by luthier Rick Turner in Santa Cruz, California.

MODEL YEAR	FEATURES	EXC. COND. LOW	HIGH

Heritage

1985-present. Professional, premium, and presentation grade, production/custom, hollow, semi-hollow, and solidbody guitars built in Kalamazoo, Michigan. They have also made banjos, mandolins, flat-tops, and basses in the past.

Founded by Jim Deurloo, Marvin Lamb, J.P. Moats, Bill Paige and Mike Korpak, all former Gibson employees who did not go to Nashville when Norlin closed the original Gibson factory in '84. In 2007, Vince Margol bought out Paige. In '16, a private group of local Kalamazoo investors bought the business with Deurloo, Lamb and Paige remaining active in the company.

Eagle
1986-2009. Single rounded cut semi-hollowbody, mahogany body and neck, bound body, 1 jazz pickup, f-holes, sunburst or natural.

1986-2009		$2,500	$3,125

Eagle Classic
1992-present. Standard Collection, Eagle with maple body and neck, bound neck and headstock, gold hardware, sunburst or natural.

1992-2023		$3,250	$4,000

Gary Moore
1989-1991. Single-cut solidbody, 2 pickups, chrome hardware, sunburst.

1989-1991		$2,250	$2,875

Golden Eagle
1985-2019. Single-cut hollowbody, back inlaid with mother-of-pearl eagle and registration number, multi-bound ebony 'board with mother-of-pearl cloud inlays, bound f-holes, gold-plated parts, ebony bridge inlaid with mother-of-pearl, mother-of-pearl truss rod cover engraved with owner's name, 1 Heritage jazz pickup, multi-bound curly maple 'guard.

1985-2019	Floating pickup	$3,250	$4,000
1985-2019	Mounted pickup	$3,250	$4,000

Groove Master
2004-2018. 16" hollow-body, single rounded cutaway, neck pickup, sunburst.

2004-2018		$1,875	$2,375

H-137
1980s-2021. Standard Collection, single-cut solidbody, 2 P-90s, sunburst, natural lime (early) or TV yellow (later).

1980s-2018	Sunburst or natural lime	$1,250	$1,500
2019-2021	Sunburst or TV yellow	$1,375	$1,750

H-137 AA
2018-2021. Artisan Aged Collection, sunburst or TV yellow with aged finish.

2018-2021		$1,375	$1,750

H-140/H-140 CM
1985-2005, 2007-2016. Single pointed cutaway solidbody, bound curly maple ('85-'04) or solid gold top ('94-'05), 2 humbuckers, chrome parts.

1985-1996	Black	$1,250	$1,625
1985-2004	CM, curly maple	$1,250	$1,625
1994-2005	Goldtop	$1,250	$1,625
2001	CM, flamed maple	$1,250	$1,625
2007-2016	2nd edition, goldtop	$1,250	$1,625

H-147
1990-1991. Single-cut solidbody, 2 humbuckers, mahogany body, mother-of-pearl block inlays, black with black or gold hardware.

1990-1991		$1,250	$1,500

H-150
1990s-present. Standard Collection, solid carved figured maple top, mahogany back, various colors.

1990s-2023	Cherry Sunburst	$2,000	$2,500
1990s-2023	Ebony	$2,000	$2,500
1990s-2023	Goldtop	$2,000	$2,500
1990s-2023	Sunburst	$2,000	$2,500

H-150 AA
2018-2023. Artisan Aged Collection, sunburst, ebony, various colors with aged finish.

2018-2023		$2,000	$2,500

H-150 C/H-150 CM
1985-2018. Single rounded cutaway solidbody, curly maple top, 2 pickups, chrome parts, cherry sunburst.

1985-2018	Flamed	$2,000	$2,500
1985-2018	Goldtop	$1,750	$2,250

H-150 Deluxe Limited Edition
1992. 300 made.

1992		$1,750	$2,250

H-157
1989-2004. Mahogany body with maple top, natural, sunburst or black.

1989-2004		$2,000	$2,500

H-157 Ultra
1993-1994. Single-cut solidbody, large block markers, highly figured maple top.

1993-1994		$2,000	$2,500

H-160
1986, 2007. Limited production.

1986		$1,000	$1,500
2007	2nd Edition	$1,000	$1,500

H-170
1980s-1997. Double-cut solidbody, 2 humbuckers, bound carved top, was also a later curly maple top version (H-170CM).

1980s-1997		$1,250	$1,625

H-204 DD
1986-1989. Single-cut solidbody of mahogany, curly maple top, 1-piece mahogany neck, 22-fret rosewood 'board.

1986-1989		$650	$850

H-207 DD
1986-1989. Double-cut solidbody of mahogany, curly maple top, 1-piece mahogany neck, 22-fret rosewood 'board.

1986-1989		$650	$850

H-357
1989-1994. Asymmetrical solidbody, neck-thru.

1989-1994		$2,250	$3,000

H-516 Thin
1999-2015. Single-cut, thin all maple body, mahogany neck, 2 humbucking pickups, various colors.

1999-2015		$2,000	$2,500

1986 Heritage H-140
Carter Vintage Guitars

Heritage H-150
Cream City Music

GUITARS

Heritage H-535

Heritage H-575

MODEL		EXC. COND.	
YEAR	FEATURES	LOW	HIGH

H-530
2016-present. Standard Collection, double-cut hollowbody, sunburst, trans cherry or antique natural.

2016-2023		$2,125	$2,750

H-535
1987-present. Standard Collection, double-cut semi-hollowbody, curly maple top and back, 2 pickups, various colors.

1987-2018		$2,125	$2,750
2019-2023		$2,125	$2,750

H-535 AA
2018-2021. Artisan Aged Collection, various colors with aged finish.

2018-2021		$2,000	$2,500

H-537
1990. Single-cut, thinline, dots.

1990		$1,500	$2,000

H-550
1990-2018. Single-cut hollowbody, laminated maple top and back, multiple bound top, white bound 'guard, f-holes, 2 humbuckers.

1990-2018		$2,250	$3,000

H-555
1989-2018. Like 535, but with maple neck, ebony 'board, pearl and abalone inlays, gold hardware.

1989-2018		$2,250	$3,000

H-575
1987-present. Standard Collection, sharp single-cut hollowbody, solid maple top and back, cream bound top and back, wood 'guard, f-holes, 2 humbuckers.

1987-2019		$2,750	$3,500
2020-2023		$2,750	$3,500

H-575 AA
2018-2020. Artisan Aged Collection, various colors with aged finish.

2018-2020		$2,750	$3,500

H-576
1990-2004. Single rounded cut hollowbody, laminated maple top and back, multiple bound top, single bound back and f-holes and wood 'guard, 2 humbuckers.

1990-2004		$2,000	$2,500

Henry Johnson (HJ) Signature
2005-2018. Pointed single cut curly maple back and sides hollowbody, 2 humbuckers, block inlays, multi-bound.

2005-2018		$1,750	$2,250

HFT-445
1987-2000. Flat-top acoustic, mahogany back and sides, spruce top, maple neck, rosewood 'board.

1987-2000		$850	$1,125

Johnny Smith
1989-2001. Custom hand-carved 17" hollowbody, single-cut, f-holes, 1 pickup, various colors.

1989-2001	Various options	$3,500	$4,500

Kenny Burrell (KB) Groove Master
2004-2018. Single-cut 16" hollow body, 1 humbucker, gold hardware, block inlays.

2004-2018		$2,250	$3,000

MODEL		EXC. COND.	
YEAR	FEATURES	LOW	HIGH

Millennium Eagle 2000
2000-2009. Single-cut semi-solidbody, multiple bound curly maple top, single-bound curly maple back, f-holes, 2 humbuckers, block inlays.

2000-2009		$2,000	$2,500

Millennium Eagle Custom
2000-2009. Like ME 2000 but with curlier maple, multiple bound neck, split block inlays.

2000-2009		$2,750	$3,500

Millennium SAE
2000-2009. Single-cut semi-solidbody, laminated arch top, single cream bound top and back, f-holes, 2 humbuckers.

2000-2009		$1,250	$1,625

Millennium Ultra/Standard Ultra
2004-2016. Single-cut, ultra curly maple top, mahogany back and sides, 1-piece mahogany neck, f-holes, mother-of-pearl block inlays.

2004-2016		$1,750	$2,250

Parsons Street
1989-1992. Offset double-cut, curly maple top on mahogany body, single/single/hum pickups, pearl block markers, sunburst or natural.

1989-1992		$825	$1,000

Roy Clark
1992-2018. Thinline, single-cut semi-hollow archtop, gold hardware, 2 humbuckers, block markers, cherry sunburst.

1992-2018		$2,500	$3,250

SAE Custom
1992-2000. Single-cut maple semi-hollowbody, f-holes, 2 humbuckers and 1 bridge pickup.

1992-2000		$1,375	$1,750

Super Eagle
1988-2018. 18" body, single-cut electric archtop, 2 humbuckers.

1989-2018		$3,125	$4,000

Super KB Kenny Burrell
2005-2011. Carved spruce top, tiger-flame maple back and sides, 2 pickups, natural or Antique Sunburst.

2005-2011		$6,000	$7,750

Sweet 16
1987-2018. Single-cut maple semi-hollowbody, spruce top, 2 pickups, pearl inlays.

1987-2018		$3,000	$4,000

Hermann Hauser

Born in 1882, Hauser started out building zithers and at age 23 added classical guitars and lutes, most built in his shop in Munich, Germany. He died in 1952. Hermann I instruments are linked with Andres Segovia. Hermann II Era instruments with modern players like Julian Bream. Hermann III builds Segovia style and custom-made instruments. Kathrin Hauser, daughter of Hermann III, is a fourth-generation builder. The original Hauser shop in Munich was destroyed during the war in 1946 and was moved to Reisbach. Labels often stipulate the city of construction as well as the Hermann Hauser name. Labels are easily removed and changed, and an original instrument should be authenticated.

MODEL YEAR	FEATURES	EXC. COND. LOW	HIGH

Beautiful violin-like clear varnish finish ends in '52, approximately 400 instruments were made by Hermann I. Under Hermann II nitrocellulose lacquer spray replaces varnish in '52, bracing patterns change in the '60s. He built 500-600 instruments from '52 to '88. Hermann III took over the business upon the death of his father in '88. Instruments should be evaluated on a case-by-case basis.

Hess

1872-ca. 1940. Located in Klingenthal, Germany, Hess built acoustic and harp guitars, as well as other stringed instruments and accordians.

Hewett Guitars

1994-present. Luthier James Hewett builds his professional and premium grade, custom/production, steel string, archtop jazz, solidbody and harp guitars in Panorama Village, Texas.

Hill Guitar Company

1972-1980, 1990-present. Luthier Kenny Hill builds his professional and premium grade production/custom, classical and flamenco guitars in Felton, California and Michoacan, Mexico.

Hirade Classical

1968-present. Professional grade, production, solid top, classical guitars built in Japan by Takamine. The late Mass Hirade was the founder of the Takamine workshop. He learned his craft from master luthier Masare Kohno. Hirade represents Takamine's finest craftsmanship and material.

HML Guitars

Introduced in 1997, Howard Leese custom-designs, premium grade, electric guitars, built by luthier Jack Pimentel in Puyallup, Washington.

Hoffman Guitars

1971-present. Premium grade, custom flat-tops and harp guitars built by luthier Charles Hoffman in Minneapolis, Minnesota.

Höfner

1887-present. Budget, intermediate, professional and premium grade, production, solidbody, semi-hollow, archtop, acoustic, and classical guitars built in Germany and the Far East. They also produce basses and bowed instruments. Founded by Karl Höfner in Schonbach, Germany. The company was already producing guitars when sons Josef and Walter joined the company in 1919 and '21 and expanded the market worldwide. They moved the company to Bavaria in '50 and to Hagenau in '97. The S in Hofner model names usually denotes cutaway.

Beatle Electric Model 459TZ

1966-1967. Violin-shaped 500/1 body, block-stripe position markers, transistor-powered flip-fuzz and treble boost, sunburst.

1966-1967		$1,750	$2,500

Beatle Electric Model 459VTZ

1966-1967. Same as Model 459TZ except with vibrato tailpiece, brown (standard) or blond option.

1966-1967	Blond option	$2,000	$2,500
1966-1967	Brown	$1,750	$2,250

Beatle Electric Model G459TZ Super

1966-1967. Deluxe version of Model 459TZ, flamed maple sides, narrow grain spruce top, gold hardware, elaborate inlays and binding, natural blond.

1966-1967		$2,000	$2,500

Beatle Electric Model G459VTZ Super

1966-1967. Same as G459TZ Super but with vibrato tailpiece.

1966-1967		$2,000	$2,500

Club Model 40

1959-1962. Lowest-level of the Club Series, single-cut, 2 pickups, sunburst.

1959-1962		$2,500	$3,500

Club Model 40 John Lennon Limited Edition

2008. Limited run of 120, single-cut, spruce top, maple back and sides, neck pickup, vertical Höfner logo on headstock, Lennon signature on 'guard.

2008		$1,750	$2,250

Club Model 50

1959-1962. Mid level of the 'Club Series', single-cut, 2 pickups, sunburst.

1959-1962		$2,000	$2,500

Club Model 60

1959. Highest model of 'Club Series', single-cut, 2 black bar pickups, 2 knobs and 2 slider switches on control panel, high-end split-diamond style markers, natural blond finish.

1959-1962		$2,250	$2,750

Club Model 126

1954-1970. Mid-sized single-cut solidbody, dot markers, flamed maple back and sides, spruce top, sunburst. Listed with Höfner Professional Electric Series.

1954-1970		$1,500	$2,000

Committee Model 4680 Thin Electric

1961-1968. Thinline single-cut archtop, 2 pickups, split-arrowhead markers, no vibrato, sunburst.

1961-1968		$1,750	$2,500

Deluxe Model 176

1964-1983. Double-cut, 3 pickups, polyester varnished sunburst finish, vibrola tailpiece, similar to Model 175 polyester varnished red and gold version.

1964-1966		$1,125	$1,500
1967-1969		$850	$1,125
1970-1983		$650	$850

Galaxy Model 175

1963-1966. Double-cut, 3 pickups, red and gold vinyl covering, fancy red-patch 'guard, vibrola, similar to Model 176 polyester varnished sunburst version.

1963-1966		$1,125	$1,500

Golden Höfner

1959-1963. Single-cut archtop, blond, 2 pickups, f-holes.

1959-1963		$6,750	$8,500

Hoffman Small Jumbo

1965 Höfner Deluxe Model 176

1961 Höfner 173 II S
Imaged by Heritage Auctions, HA.com

1969 Hofner Model 457/12
12-String Electric
Imaged by Heritage Auctions, HA.com

MODEL YEAR	FEATURES	EXC. COND. LOW	HIGH

Jazzica Custom
2000-2010. Full body, single soft cutaway, acoustic/ electric archtop, carved German spruce top, sunburst.

2000-2010		$1,750	$2,250

Model 165
1975-1976. Offset double-cut, S-style body, 2 single-coil pickups, bolt-on neck.

1975-1976		$450	$575

Model 171
1975-1976. Copy of Tele-Thinline.

1975-1976		$400	$500

Model 172 II (R) (S) (I)
1962-1963. Double-cut body, polyester varnished wood (S) or scuff-proof red (R) or white (I) vinyl, 2 pickups, vibrato.

1962-1963		$500	$625

Model 173 II (S) (I)
1962-1963. Double-cut body, polyester varnished wood (S) or scuff-proof vinyl (I), 3 pickups, vibrato.

1962-1963		$550	$675

Model 178
1967-ca. 1969. Offset double-cut solidbody, 2 pickups with an array of switches and push button controls, fancy position markers, vibrola, sunburst. 178 used on different design in the '70s.

1967-1969		$550	$675

Model 180 Shorty Standard
1982. Small-bodied travel guitar, single-cut, solid-body, 1 pickup. The Shorty Super had a built-in amp and speaker.

1982		$300	$375

Model 450S Acoustic Archtop
Mid-1960s. Economy single-cut acoustic archtop in Hofner line, dot markers, Höfner logo on 'guard, sunburst.

1960s		$500	$625

Model 455S Acoustic Archtop
1950s-1970. Archtop, single-cut, block markers.

1950s-1970		$750	$950

Model 456 Acoustic Archtop
1950s-1962. Full body acoustic archtop, f-holes, laminated maple top, sides, back, large pearloid blocks, two color pearloid headstock laminate.

1950s-1962		$700	$900

Model 457 President
1959-1972. Single-cut thinline archtop, 2 pickups, non-vibrato.

1959-1972		$800	$1,000

Model 457/12 12-String Electric
1969-1970. Comfort-thin cutaway archtop, shaded brown.

1969-1970		$700	$975

Model 462 Acoustic Archtop
Ca. 1952-1960s. Single-cut archtop, bound cat's-eye soundholes, 3-piece pearloid headstock overlay, 3-piece large block inlays. Also offered with fingerboard mounted pickup with no controls (EG) and by mid '50s with 1, 2, or 3 pickups with volume and tone knobs/ switches (462S/E1, 2, or 3).

1952-1960s 462S		$650	$825
1952-1960s 462SEG		$950	$1,250

Model 463 Electric Archtop
1958-1960. Archtop electric, 2 or 3 pickups.

1958-1960		$1,250	$1,500

Model 470SE2 Electric Archtop
1961-1994. Large single rounded cutaway electric archtop on Höfner's higher-end they call "superbly flamed maple (back and sides), carved top of best spruce," 2 pickups, 3 control knobs, gold hardware, pearl inlay, natural finish only.

1961-1994		$850	$1,125

Model 471SE2 Electric Archtop
1969-1977. Large single pointed cutaway electric archtop, flamed maple back and sides, spruce top, black celluloid binding, ebony 'board, pearl inlays, sunburst version of the 470SE2.

1969-1977		$850	$1,125

Model 490 Acoustic Flat-Top
Late 1960s. 16" body, 12-string, spruce top, maple back and sides, dot markers, natural.

1960s		$300	$375

Model 490E Electric Flat-Top
Late 1960s. Flat-top 12-string with on-board pickup and 2 control knobs.

1960s		$400	$500

Model 491 Acoustic Flat-Top
1960s-1970s. Slope shoulder body style, spruce top, mahogany back and sides, shaded sunburst.

1970s		$400	$500

Model 492 Acoustic
Late-1960s. 16" body, 12-string, spruce top, mahogany back and sides, dot markers.

1960s		$350	$450

Model 492E Acoustic Electric
Late 1960s. Flat-top 12-string with on-board pickup and 2 control knobs.

1960s		$325	$400

Model 496 Jumbo Flat-Top
1960s. Jumbo-style body, selected spruce top, flamed maple back and sides, gold-plated hardware, vine pattern 'guard, sunburst.

1960s		$550	$675

Model 514-H Classical Concert
1960s. Concert model, lower end of the Höfner classical line, natural.

1960s		$175	$225

Model 4500 Thin Electric
Late-1960s-early-1970s. Thinline archtop, single-cut, 3 options, laminated maple top and back, dot markers, top mounted controls, brown sunburst.

1960s-70s E1, 1 pickup		$550	$700
1960s-70s E2, 2 pus		$650	$850
1960s-70s V2, 2 pus, vibrato		$650	$850

Model 4560 Thin Electric
Late-1960s-early-1970s. Thinline archtop, single-cut, 2 options, laminated maple top and back, 2-color headstock, large block markers, top mounted controls, brown sunburst.

1960s-70s E2		$725	$1,000
1960s-70s V2, vibrato		$775	$1,125

MODEL YEAR	FEATURES	EXC. COND. LOW	HIGH

Model 4574VTZ Extra Thin
Late-1960s-early-1970s. Extra thinline acoustic, 2 pickups, vibrato arm, treble boost and flip-fuzz.

| 1960s-70s | | $825 | $1,125 |

Model 4575VTZ Extra Thin
Late-1960s-early-1970s. Extra-thinline acoustic, double-cut with shallow rounded horns, 3 pickups, vibrato arm, treble boost and flip-fuzz.

| 1960s-70s | | $1,125 | $1,500 |

Model 4578TZ President
1959-1970. Double-cut archtop. 'President' dropped from name by late-'60s and renamed Model 4578 Dual Cutaway, also added sharp horns.

| 1959-1965 | | $850 | $1,125 |
| 1966-1970 | | $750 | $950 |

Model 4600 Thin Electric
Late-1960s-early-1970s. Thinline acoustic, double-cut, 2 pickups, dot markers, sunburst, V2 with vibrato.

| 1960s-70s | E2 | $650 | $850 |
| 1960s-70s | V2, vibrato | $700 | $875 |

Model 4680 Thin Electric
Late-1960s-early-1970s. Single-cut thinline electric, 2 pickups, 3-in-a-line control knobs, ornate inlays, spruce top, brown sunburst, V2 with vibrato.

| 1960s-70s | E2 | $1,000 | $1,250 |
| 1960s-70s | V2, vibrato | $1,125 | $1,500 |

Model 4700 Thin Electric
Late-1960s-early-1970s. Deluxe version of Model 4680, gold plated appointments and natural finish, V2 with vibrato.

| 1960s-70s | E2 | $1,125 | $1,500 |
| 1960s-70s | V2, vibrato | $1,250 | $1,625 |

Senator Acoustic Archtop
1958-1960s. Full body archtop, floating pickup option available, f-holes, made for Selmer, London.

| 1958-1960 | | $575 | $725 |

Senator E1
1961. Senator full body archtop jazz, single top mounted pickup and controls.

| 1961 | | $725 | $1,000 |

Verythin Standard
2001-2008. Update of the 1960s Verythin line, 2 humbuckers, f-holes, dot inlays.

| 2001-2008 | | $825 | $1,125 |

Hohner

1857-present. Budget and intermediate grade, production, acoustic and electric guitars and basses. They also have mandolins, banjos and ukuleles. Matthias Hohner, a clockmaker in Trossingen, Germany, founded Hohner in 1857, making harmonicas. Hohner has been offering guitars and basses at least since the early '70s. HSS was founded in 1986 as a distributor of guitars and other musical products. By 2000, Hohner was also offering the Crafter brands of guitars.

Alpha Standard
1987. Designed by Klaus Scholler, solidbody, stereo outputs, Flytune tremolo.

| 1987 | | $275 | $350 |

G 2T/G 3T Series
1980s-1990s. Steinberger-style body, 6-string, neck-thru, locking tremolo.

| 1980s-90s | | $350 | $450 |

Jacaranda Rosewood Dreadnought
1978. Flat-top acoustic.

| 1978 | | $850 | $1,250 |

Jack
1987-1990s. Mate for Jack Bass. Headless, tone circuit, tremolo, 2 single-coils and 1 humbucker.

| 1987-1992 | | $350 | $450 |

L 59/L 75 Series
Late-1970s-1980s. Classic single-cut solidbody, 2 humbuckers, glued neck, sunburst, 59 has upgrade maple body with maple veneer top.

| 1970s-80s | | $350 | $450 |

Mad Cat
1972-1973. Tele-style, associated with Prince, walnut strip in the middle, leopard print 'guard.

| 1972-1973 | | $10,000 | $12,000 |

Miller Beer Guitar
1985. Solidbody, shaped like Miller beer logo.

| 1985 | | $275 | $350 |

Professional
1980s. Single-cut solidbody, maple neck, extra-large 'guard, natural.

| 1980s | | $350 | $450 |

Professional Series - TE Custom
1980s-1990s. Single-cut solidbody, bolt neck.

| 1980s-90s | | $850 | $1,125 |

Professional Series - TE Prinz
Late 1980s-early 1990s. Based on Prince's No. 1 guitar, 2 single-coils, bolt neck, Professional The Prinz headstock logo, natural.

| 1989-1990 | | $850 | $1,125 |

SE 35
1989-mid-1990s. Semi-hollow thinline, 2 humbuckers, natural.

| 1989 | | $350 | $450 |

SG Lion
1980s-1990s. Offset double-cut, pointy headstock, glued neck.

| 1980s-90s | | $275 | $350 |

ST Series
1986-1990s. Includes the bolt neck ST 57, ST Special, ST Special S, Viper I, Viper II (snakeskin finish option), ST Victory, ST Metal S, and the ST Custom.

| 1986-1992 | | $325 | $400 |

Standard Series - EX Artist
1970s-1980s. Solidbody, 2 humbuckers, gold hardware, neck-thru, solid maple body, rosewood 'board, tremolo.

| 1970s-80s | | $325 | $400 |

Standard Series - RR Custom
1970s-1980s. Randy Rhoads V body, 2 humbuckers, chrome hardware, glued neck, mahogany body, rosewood 'board, tremolo.

| 1970s-80s | | $325 | $400 |

Standard Series - SR Heavy
1970s-1980s. Hybrid body, 2 humbuckers, neck-thru, solid maple body, rosewood 'board, tremolo.

| 1970s-80s | | $325 | $400 |

1966 Höfner 4570 E2
Heinz Rebellius

1950s Höfner Senator
Acoustic Archtop
Paul Johnson

Hollingworth Guitars

Early-'80s Hondo
Deluxe 748 Mark II

Jim Gleason

MODEL YEAR	FEATURES	EXC. COND. LOW	HIGH

Holiday
1960s. Electric, acoustic and bass guitars sold by Aldens, a Chicago catalog company. Most models built by Harmony. They also offered mandolins and banjos.

Silhouette Bobcat
1964-1967. Solidbody electric made by Harmony, similar to Harmony Silhouette, offset double-cut, 2 pickups, 4-in-a-row control knobs.

1964-1967		$475	$600

Hollenbeck Guitars
1970-2008. Luthier Bill Hollenbeck built his premium grade, production/custom, hollow and semi-hollow body acoustics and electric guitars in Lincoln, Illinois. Bill passed away in '08.

Hollingworth Guitars
1995-present. Luthier Graham Hollingworth builds his production/custom, premium grade, electric, acoustic and archtop guitars in Mermaid Beach, Gold Coast, Queensland, Australia. He also builds lap steels.

Holman
1966-1968. Built by the Holman-Woodell guitar factory in Neodesha, Kansas. The factory was started to build guitars for Wurlitzer, but that fell through by '67.

Holst
1984-present. Premium grade, custom, archtop, flat-top, semi-hollow, and classical guitars built in Creswell, Oregon by luthier Stephen Holst. He also builds mandolins. Until '01 he was in Eugene, Oregon.

Holzapfel (Holzapfel & Beitel)
1898-1930s. Carl C. Holzapfel and Clemence Beitel built guitars, banjos, and mandolins in Baltimore, but are best-known as early innovators of the 12-string guitar. Beitel left the company in 1905 and Holzapfel continued to build instruments up to the depression. He, and later his son, Carl M., mainly repaired instruments after that (up to 1988), but still would do custom builds.

Hondo/Hondo II
1969-1987, 1991-2005. Budget grade, production, imported acoustic, classical and electric guitars. They also offered basses, banjos, and mandolins. Originally imported by International Music Corporation (IMC) of Fort Worth, Texas, founded by Jerry Freed and Tommy Moore and named after a small town near San Antonio, Texas. Early pioneers of Korean guitar making, primarily targeted at beginner market. Introduced their first electrics in '72. Changed brand to Hondo II in '74. Some better Hondos made in Japan '74-'82/'83. In '85 IMC purchased major interest in Jackson/Charvel, and

MODEL YEAR	FEATURES	EXC. COND. LOW	HIGH

the Hondo line was supplanted by Charvels. 1987 was the last catalog before hiatus. In '88 IMC was sold and Freed began Jerry Freed International and in '91 he revived the Hondo name. Acquired by MBT International in '95, currently part of Musicorp.

Acoustic Flat-Top
1969-1987, 1991-2005.

1969-2005		$115	$150

Electric Hollowbody
1969-1987, 1991-2005.

1969-2005		$200	$600

Electric Solidbody
1969-1987, 1991-2005.

1969-1987		$200	$600
1991-1999		$200	$600
2000-2005		$100	$200

Hondo Chiquita Travel Guitar
See Chiquita brand.

Longhorn
Ca. 1978-1980s. Copy of Danelectro Long Horn guitar, Dano Coke bottle-style headstock, brown-copper.

1978-80s		$500	$650

Longhorn 6/12 Doubleneck
Ca. 1978s-1980s. Copy of Danelectro Longhorn 6/12 Doubleneck guitar, Dano coke bottle-style headstock, white sunburst.

1978s-80s		$750	$1,000

M 16 Rambo-Machine Gun
1970s-1980s. Machine gun body-style, matching machine gun-shaped guitar case, black or red. Price includes original case with form-fit interior; deduct as much as 40% less for non-original case.

1970s-80s		$500	$650

Hopf
1906-present. Intermediate, professional, premium, and presentation grade, production/custom, classical guitars made in Germany. They also make basses, mandolins and flutes.

The Hopf family of Germany has a tradition of instrument building going back to 1669, but the modern company was founded in 1906. Hopf started making electric guitars in the mid-'50s. Some Hopf models were made by others for the company. By the late-'70s, Hopf had discontinued making electrics, concentrating on classicals.

Explorer Standard
1960s. Double-cut semi-hollow, sharp horns, center block, 2 mini-humbuckers.

1960s		$1,000	$1,500

Saturn Archtop
1960s. Offset cutaway, archtop-style sound holes, 2 pickups, white, says Saturn on headstock.

1960s		$1,250	$1,750

Super Deluxe Archtop
1960s. Archtop, 16 3/4", catseye sound holes, carved spruce top, flamed maple back and sides, sunburst.

1960s		$1,500	$2,000

MODEL YEAR	FEATURES	EXC. COND. LOW	HIGH

Hopkins
1998-present. Luthier Peter Hopkins builds his presentation grade, custom, hand-carved archtop guitars in British Columbia.

Horabe
Classical and Espana models made in Japan.
Classical
1960-1980s Various models	$400	$800

Hottie
In 2009, amp builders Jean-Claude Escudie and Mike Bernards added production/custom, professional and premium grade, solidbody electric guitars built by luthier Saul Koll in Portland, Oregon.

House Guitars
2004-present. Luthier Joshua House builds his production/custom, premium grade, acoustic guitars and guitar-bouzoukis in Goderich, Ontario.

Howe-Orme
1897-ca. 1910. Elias Howe and George Orme's Boston-based publishing and distribution buisness offered a variety of mandolin family instruments and guitars and received many patents for their designs. Many of their guitars featured detachable necks.

Hoyer
1874-present. Intermediate grade, production, flat-top, classical, electric, and resonator guitars. They also build basses. Founded by Franz Hoyer, building classical guitars and other instruments. His son, Arnold, added archtops in the late-1940s, and solidbodies in the '60s. In '67, Arnold's son, Walter, took over, leaving the company in '77. The company changed hands a few times over the following years. Walter started building guitars again in '84 under the W.A. Hoyer brand, which is not associated with Hoyer.
Acoustic
1960s. Acoustic archtop or flat-top.
1960s	$500	$650
Junior
Early-1960s. Solidbody with unusual sharp horn cutaway, single neck pickup, bolt-on neck, dot markers, Arnold Hoyer logo on headstock, shaded sunburst.
1960s	$650	$850
Soloist Electric
1960-1962. Single-cut acoustic-electric archtop, 2 pickups, teardrop f-holes, sunburst.
1960-1962	$650	$850
Special 24
1950s-1960s. Single-cut acoustic archtop, Hoyer Special script logo on headstock, pickups added in '60s. SL was the deluxe version.
1950s-60s	$2,000	$2,500

Huerga
Introduced in 1995, professional to presentation grade, production/custom, archtop, flat-top, and metal-front solidbody electric guitars built by luthier Diego Huerga in Buenos Aires, Argentina.

Humming Bird
1947-ca.1975. Japanese manufacturer offering acoustics and electrics. By 1968 making pointy Mosrite inspirations. Probably not imported into the U.S.
Electric Solidbody
1950s	$225	$300

Humphrey, Thomas
1970-2008. Premium and presentation grade, custom, nylon-string guitars built by luthier Thomas Humphrey in Gardiner, New York. In 1996 Humphrey began collaborating with Martin Guitars, resulting in the Martin C-TSH and C-1R. Often the inside back label will indicate the year of manufacture. Humphrey died in April 2008.
Classical
1976-1984. Brazilian or Indian rosewood back and sides, spruce top, traditionally-based designs evolved over time with Millenium becoming a benchmark design in 1985, values can increase with new designs. Valuations depend on each specific instrument; each instrument should be evaluated on a case-by-case basis.
1976-1984	$6,000	$7,500
Millennium (Classical)
1985-2008. Professional performance-grade high-end classical guitar with innovative taper body design and elevated 'board, tops are generally spruce (versus cedar) with rosewood back and sides.
1995-2008	$11,000	$15,000
Steel String
1974. D-style, only 4 made.
1974	$3,500	$4,500

Huss and Dalton Guitar Company
1995-present. Luthiers Jeff Huss and Mark Dalton build their professional and premium grade flat-tops and banjos in Staunton, Virginia.

Hutchins
2006-present. Gary Hutchins in Sussex, U.K. imports intermediate and professional grade, production, acoustic and electric guitars and basses from China, Germany and Korea.

Ian A. Guitars
1991-present. In the early 1990s luthier Ian Anderson built guitars under his name, in 2005 he began using the Ian A. brand. He builds premium grade, production/custom, solidbody electric guitars in Poway, California.

1963 Hopf Saturn
Dudley Taft

Hopkins Contessa

MODEL YEAR	FEATURES	EXC. COND. LOW	HIGH

Ibanez AM-225 Artist
Imaged by Heritage Auctions, HA.com

1981 Ibanez DT50 Destroyer II
Imaged by Heritage Auctions, HA.com

Ibanez

1932-present. Budget, intermediate, and professional grade, production/custom, acoustic and electric guitars. They also make basses, amps, mandolins, and effects.

Founded in Nagoya, Japan, by Matsujiro Hoshino as book and stationary supply, started retailing musical instruments in 1909, importing them by '21. The company's factories were destroyed during World War II, but the business was revived in '50. The Ibanez name was in use by 1957. Junpei Hoshino, grandson of founder, became president in '60; a new factory opened called Tama Seisakusho (Tama Industries). Brand names by '64 included Ibanez, Star, King's Stone, Jamboree and Goldentone, supplied by 85 factories serving global markets. Sold acoustic guitars to Harry Rosenblum of Elger Guitars ('59-ca.'65) in Ardmore, Pennsylvania, in early-'60s. Around '62 Hoshino purchased a 50% interest in Elger Guitars, and ca. '65 changed the name to Ibanez.

Jeff Hasselberger headed the American guitar side beginning '73-'74, and the company headquarters were moved to Cornwells Heights, Pennsylvania in '74. By '75 the instruments were being distributed by Chesbro Music Company in Idaho Falls, Idaho, and Harry Rosenblum sells his interest to Hoshino shortly thereafter. Ca. '81, the Elger Company becomes Hoshino U.S.A. An U.S. Custom Shop was opened in '88.

Most glued-neck guitars from '70s are fairly rare. Dating: copy guitars begin ca. '71. Serial numbers begin '75 with letter (A-L for month) followed by 6 digits, the first 2 indicating year, last 4 sequential (MYYXXXX). By '88 the month letter drops off. Dating code stops early-'90s; by '94 letter preface either F for Fuji or C for Cort (Korean) manufacturer followed by number for year and consecutive numbers (F4XXXX=Fuji, C4XXXX=Cort, 1994).

Pickups on Asian import electric guitars from the '50s-'70s are often considered to be the weakest engineering specification on the instrument. Old Ibanez pickups can become microphonic and it is not unusual to see them replaced.

AE (Acoustic Electric) Series
1983-present. Flat-top models include AE, AEF, AEG, AEL, AES, (no archtops).
| 1983-2023 Various models | $175 | $550 |

AH10 Allan Holdsworth
1985-1987. Offset double-cut solidbody, bolt neck, bridge humbucker, dots, various colors.
| 1985-1987 1 pickup | $1,125 | $1,375 |

AH20 Allan Holdsworth
| 1986 2 pickups | $1,250 | $1,500 |

AM (Archtop) Series
1985-1991. Small body archtops, models include AM70, 75, 75T, 100, 225. Becomes Artstar in '92.
| 1985-1991 Various models | $1,000 | $2,000 |

AM Stagemaster Series
1983-1984, 1989-1990. Made in Japan, small double-cut semi-hollow body, 2 humbuckers, models include AM50, 100, 205, 255. Model name used again, without Stagemaster in '89-'90.
| 1983-1984 Various models | $1,000 | $2,000 |

Artcore Series
2002-present. Made in China, hollowbody electric, models include AF, AG, AK, AM, AS, AWD, FWD, and TM.
| 2002-2023 Various models | $250 | $800 |

Artist AR50 (Jr. Artist)
1979-1983. Double-cut solidbody, dot markers, 2 humbuckers.
| 1979-1983 | $950 | $1,250 |

Artist AR100
1979-1984. Double-cut solidbody, set neck, maple top, 2 humbuckers.
| 1979-1984 | $1,250 | $1,625 |

Artist AR300
1979-1982. Symmetrical double-cut, carved maple top.
| 1979-1982 | $1,750 | $2,125 |

Artist AR500
1979-1982. 2 humbuckers, EQ.
| 1979-1982 | $1,250 | $1,625 |

Artist AS50
1980-1981. Made in Japan, semi-acoustic.
| 1980-1981 | $750 | $975 |

Artist AS100
1979-1981. Set neck, gold hardware.
| 1979-1981 | $1,250 | $1,500 |

Artist AS200
1979-1986. Double-cut semi-acoustic, flamed maple, block markers, gold hardware, 2 humbuckers, replaced Artist 2630. Artist dropped from name when model becomes hollowbody archtop in '82.
| 1979-1986 | $1,750 | $2,125 |

Artstar AS50
1998-1999. Laminated maple body, bound rosewood 'board, dot inlays, 2 humbuckers.
| 1998-1999 | $750 | $975 |

Artstar AS80
1994-2002. Double-cut semi-hollow body, dots, 2 humbuckers.
| 1994-2002 | $750 | $975 |

Artstar AS180
1997-1999. Double-cut semi-hollow body, plain top, dots, 2 humbuckers.
| 1997-1999 | $950 | $1,250 |

Artstar AS200
1992-2000. Flame maple top, gold hardware, 2 humbuckers, block inlays.
| 1992-2000 | $1,500 | $2,000 |

Artwood Series
1979-present. Electric-acoustics, various AW, AC models.
| 1979-2023 Various models | $250 | $600 |

Blazer Series
1980-1982, 1997-1998. Offset double-cut, 10 similar BL models in the '80s with different body woods and electronic configurations. Series name returns on 3 models in late '90s.
| 1980-1998 Various BL models | $350 | $750 |

MODEL		EXC. COND.	
YEAR	FEATURES	LOW	HIGH

Bob Weir (2681)
1975-1980, 1995. Double-cut ash solidbody, ebony 'board, tree-of-life inlay, gold-plated pickups, limited numbers. Reintroduced as a limited run in '95.

| 1975-1980 | | $2,250 | $3,000 |

Bob Weir Standard (2680)
1976-1980. Standard production model of 2681.

| 1976-1980 | | $1,500 | $2,000 |

Bob Weir Model One BWM1 (Cowboy Fancy)
2005. Limited run of 30, double-cut swamp ash solidbody, ebony 'board, pearl vine inlay down neck and part way around body.

| 2005 | | $5,000 | $7,000 |

Challenger (2552ASH)
1977-1978. T-style ash solidbody.

| 1977-1978 | | $500 | $650 |

CN100 Concert Standard
1978-1979. Double-cut solidbody, set neck, 2 humbuckers, chrome hardware, dot markers.

| 1978-1979 | | $500 | $650 |

CN200 Concert Custom
1978-1979. Carved maple top, mahogany body, 7 layer black/white binding, bolt-on neck, gold hardware, block inlays, 2 Super 80 pickups.

| 1978-1979 | | $650 | $850 |

CN250 Concert
1978-1979. Like CN200 but with vine inlay.

| 1978-1979 | | $800 | $1,250 |

DG350 Destroyer II
1986-1987. X Series, modified X-shaped basswood body, flame maple top, 2 humbuckers, trem.

| 1986-1987 | | $700 | $875 |

DT50 Destroyer II
1980-1982. Modified alder Explorer body, 6-in-line headstock, bolt neck, 2 humbuckers, thick paint.

| 1980-1982 | | $800 | $1,000 |

DT150 Destroyer II
1982-1984. Like DT50 but birch/basswood, 1 humbucker.

| 1982-1984 | | $800 | $1,000 |

DT155 Destroyer II
1982-1984. Like DT150 but with 3 humbuckers.

| 1982-1984 | | $1,125 | $1,500 |

DT350 Destroyer II
1984-1985. X Series, opaque finish, 1 humbucker, trem.

| 1984-1985 | | $700 | $875 |

DT400 Destroyer II
1980-1982. Modified mahogany Explorer body, flame maple top, 6-in-line headstock, set-neck, 2 humbuckers, cherry sunburst. Model changed to DT500 in '82.

| 1980-1982 | | $800 | $1,000 |

DT500 Destroyer II
1982-1984. Replaced the DT400, flame maple top.

| 1982-1984 | | $800 | $1,000 |

DT555 Destroyer II Phil Collen
1983-1987. Bound basswood solidbody, 3 humbuckers, vibrato, black.

| 1983-1987 | | $2,500 | $3,250 |

DTX120 Destroyer
2000-2004. X Series, known as the Millennium Destroyer, 2 humbuckers.

| 2000-2004 | | $350 | $450 |

EX Series
1988-1993. Double-cut electric solidbodies with long thin horns.

| 1988-1993 | Various models | $180 | $400 |

FA/FG (Full Acoustic) Series
1973-1987. Single-cut full body jazz-style.

| 1973-1987 | Various models | $1,250 | $2,500 |

Flash (I, II, III)
1975. The Iceman was first introduced as the Flash at the Frankfurt Trade Show in West Germany in '75, it was renamed the Iceman prior to its introduction in the U.S. See Iceman 2663 listing.

1FR1620/Prestige FR1620
2008-2014. Ash body, maple/walnut neck, rosewood 'board, 2 pickups, Prestige logo on headstock, black or red finish.

| 2008-2014 | | $750 | $975 |

GAX Series
1998-2009. Symmetrical double-cut (Gibson SG style) with 2 humbuckers, lower cost of the AX line.

| 1998-2009 | Various models | $110 | $250 |

George Benson GB10
1977-present. Single-cut, laminated spruce top, flame maple back and sides, 2 humbuckers, 3-piece set-in maple neck, ebony 'board, sunburst or blond.

1977-1989		$2,000	$2,500
1990-1999		$1,750	$2,250
2000-2023		$1,500	$2,000

George Benson GB15
2006-2010. Like GB10, but with 1 humbucker.

| 2006-2010 | | $2,000 | $2,500 |

George Benson GB20
1978-1982. Larger than GB10, laminated spruce top, flame maple back and sides.

| 1978-1982 | | $2,750 | $3,500 |

George Benson GB100 Deluxe
1993-1996. GB-10 with flamed maple top, pearl binding, sunburst finish 'guard, pearl vine inlay tailpiece, gold hardware.

| 1993-1996 | | $3,000 | $4,000 |

GSA Series
2000-2011. Offset double-cut body.

| 2000-2011 | GSA20/GSA60 | $150 | $250 |

Iceman 2663/2663TC/2663SL
1975-1978. The original Iceman Series models, called the Flash I, II and III respectively, I has 2 humbuckers, II (TC) and III (SL) have 1 triple-coil pickup.

| 1975-1978 | | $4,000 | $5,500 |

Iceman PS10 Paul Stanley
1978-1981. Limited edition Paul Stanley model, abalone trim, Stanley's name engraved at 21st fret, reissued in '95 with upgraded model names.

| 1978-1981 | Korina finish | $2,500 | $3,500 |
| 1978-1981 | Sunburst or black | $2,000 | $2,500 |

Iceman PS10 II Paul Stanley
1995-1996. Reissue of original PS-10.

| 1995-1996 | Black | $2,250 | $3,000 |

1993 Ibanez EX160

Imaged by Heritage Auctions, HA.com

Ibanez George Benson GB10

GUITARS

1979 Ibanez Iceman IC400
Eric Van Gansen

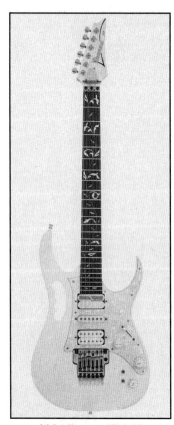

2004 Ibanez JEM 77
Imaged by Heritage Auctions, HA.com

MODEL YEAR	FEATURES	EXC. COND. LOW	HIGH
Iceman PS10LTD Paul Stanley			
1995-1996. Limited edition, gold mirror appointments, gold hardware, black pearl metalflake finish.			
1995-1996		$2,750	$3,500
Iceman Series			
1975-2010. Ibanez unique body styles with hooked lower treble horn body.			
1978-1979	IC250	$1,125	$1,500
1978-1979	IC300 (Korina)	$1,125	$1,500
1978-1980	IC210	$1,125	$1,500
1978-1982	IC400	$1,250	$1,625
1978-1990	IC200	$950	$1,250
1979-1980	IC50	$950	$1,250
1981-1982	IC400 CS	$1,000	$1,375
1994	IC500	$1,000	$1,375
1994-2003	IC300	$375	$500
1995-1996	IC350	$375	$500
IMG-2010 Guitar Controller MIDI			
1985-1987. Similar to Roland GR-707, slim triangle-wedge body with treble horn.			
1985-1987	Guitar only	$650	$850
JEM7 Series			
1988-2010. Basswood or alder body, various models, alder 7V offered until '10.			
1988-2010	Various models	$2,000	$2,500
JEM77 Series			
1988-1999, 2003-2010. Basswood body, monkey grip handle, 3 pickups, 'board with tree of life or pyramids inlay, finishes include floral pattern or multicolor swirl. Current version has dot inlays and solid finish. The JEM 77BRMR Bad Horsie was introduced in '05 with a mirror finish.			
1980-2010	Various models	$3,000	$3,500
JEM555			
1994-2000. Basswood, dots and vine inlay, 3 pickups.			
1994-2000		$600	$800
JEM777 Series			
1987-1996. Basswood body, monkey grip 3 pickups, pyramids or vine inlay.			
1987-1996	Various models	$5,000	$8,000
JEM 10th Anniversary			
1996. Limited Edition signature Steve Vai model, bolt neck, vine metal 'guard, vine neck inlays and headstock art.			
1996		$6,000	$8,000
JEM 20th Anniversary			
2007. Steve Vai 20th Anniversary JEM model, green acrylic illuminating body, celebrates the 20th year (1987-2007) of the Ibanez JEM series, limited edition.			
2007		$6,000	$8,000
JEM 90th Anniversary			
1997. Limited Edition signature Steve Vai model, textured silver finish, chrome 'guard.			
1997		$3,500	$4,500
JEM Y2KDNA (Limited Edition)			
2000. Red Swirl marble finish using Steve Vai's blood in the paint.			
2000		$10,000	$12,000

MODEL YEAR	FEATURES	EXC. COND. LOW	HIGH
Joe Pass JP20			
1981-1990. Full body, single-cut, 1 pickup, abalone and pearl split block inlay, JP inlay on headstock.			
1981-1990	Sunburst	$1,750	$2,250
Joe Satriani JS1			
1993. Limited production, JS Series headstock logo.			
1993		$1,500	$2,000
Joe Satriani JS2 Chrome Boy			
1990. Extremely rare.			
1990		$7,500	$9,500
Joe Satriani JS3 Donnie Hunt			
1990. Limited to 300, hand painted by Donnie Hunt.			
1990		$7,500	$9,500
Joe Satriani JS4 Electric Rainbow			
1992. Only 22 made, hand painted by Joan Satriani.			
1992		$7,500	$9,500
Joe Satriani JS5 Rain Forrest			
1995. Limited production, rain forrest graphic.			
1995		$7,500	$9,500
Joe Satriani JS6			
1993. Limited production, lightweight mahogany body, non-gloss stained oil finish, JS Series headstock logo.			
1993		$1,750	$2,500
Joe Satriani JS100			
1994-2014. Offset double cut basswood body, 2 humbuckers, vibrato, red, black, white or custom finish.			
1994-2014	Custom finish	$575	$750
1994-2014	Standard finish	$425	$550
Joe Satriani JS1000			
1994-1996, 1998-2012. 2 DiMarzio humbuckers, lightweight body.			
1994-2012	Various colors	$950	$2,000
Joe Satriani JS1200			
2004-2016. Candy Apple Red.			
2004-2016		$1,000	$1,375
Joe Satriani JS 10th Anniversary			
1998. Chrome-metal body, Satriani Anniversary script on back cover plate.			
1998		$3,750	$5000
Joe Satriani JS 20th Anniversary			
2008. Opaque finish with alien surfer graphic.			
2008		$3,750	$5,000
Joe Satriani Y2K			
2000. Clear see-thru plexi-style body.			
2000		$3,750	$5,000
John Petrucci JPM100 P2			
1996. Offset double-cut solidbody, 2 pickups, multicolor graphic.			
1996		$2,250	$3,000
John Petrucci JPM100 P3			
1997. As P2 but with same graphic in black and white.			
1997		$2,250	$3,000
John Petrucci JPM100 P4			
1998. As P2 but with same graphic in camo colors.			
1998		$2,250	$3,000
John Scofield JSM100			
2001-present. Double-cut semi hollow body, 2 humbuckers, ebony 'board, gold hardware.			
2001-2023		$2,250	$3,000

The *Vintage Guitar Price Guide* shows values for all-original, excellent condition instruments and, where applicable, with original case.

MODEL YEAR	FEATURES	EXC. COND. LOW	HIGH

Lee Ritenour LR10

1981-1987. Flame maple body, bound set neck, Quick Change tailpiece, 2 pickups, dark red sunburst, foam-filled body to limit feedback.

| 1981-1987 | | $2,000 | $2,500 |

M310

1982. D-size flat-top, maple back and sides, rosewood 'board.

| 1982 | | $200 | $275 |

M340

1978-1979. D-size flat-top, flamed maple back and sides, maple 'board.

| 1978-1979 | | $300 | $400 |

Maxxas

1987-1988. Solidbody (MX2) or with internal sound chambers (MX3, '88 only), 2 pickups, all-access neck joint system.

| 1987-1988 | MX2 | $1,000 | $1,500 |
| 1988 | MX3 | $1,250 | $1,750 |

MC Musician Series

1978-1982. Solidbodies, various models.

1978-1980	MC500, carved top	$1,500	$2,000
1978-1980	Neck-thru body	$1,250	$1,750
1978-1982	Bolt-neck	$975	$1,250

Mick Thompson MTM-1

2006. Seven logo on fretboard, MTM1 logo on back of headstock.

| 2006 | | $975 | $1,250 |

Model 600 Series

1974-1978. Copy era acoustic flat-tops with model numbers in the 600 Series, basically copies of classic American square shoulder dreadnoughts. Includes the 683, 684, 693 and the 6-in-line 647; there were 12-string copies as well.

| 1974-1978 | Various models | $775 | $900 |

Model 700 Series

1974-1977. Upgraded flat-top models such as the Brazilian Scent 750, with more original design content than 600 Series.

| 1974-1977 | Various models | $775 | $900 |

Model 900 Series

1963-1964. Offset double-cut solidbody with sharp curving horns, Burns Bison copy.

| 1963-1964 | 901, 1 pickup | $400 | $525 |
| 1963-1964 | 992, 2 pickups | $425 | $550 |

Model 1453

1971-1973. Copy of classic single-cut hollowbody, replaced by Model 2355 in '73.

| 1971-1973 | | $1,500 | $2,000 |

Model 1800 Series

1962-1963. Offset double-cut solidbody (Jazzmaster-style), models came with bar (stud) or vibrato tailpiece, and 2, 3 or 4 pickups.

| 1962-1963 | Various models | $375 | $500 |

Model 1912

1971-1973. Double-cut semi-hollow body, sunburst finish.

| 1971-1973 | | $1,000 | $1,375 |

Model 2020

1970. Initial offering of the copy era, offset double-cut, 2 unusual rectangular pickups, block markers, raised nailed-on headstock logo, sunburst.

| 1970 | | $825 | $1,000 |

Model 2240M

Early 1970s. Thick hollowbody electric copy, single pointed cutaway, double-parallelogram markers, 2 humbuckers, natural finish.

| 1971-1973 | | $1,625 | $2,250 |

Model 2336 Les Jr.

1974-1976. Copy of classic slab solidbody, TV Lime.

| 1974-1976 | | $600 | $775 |

Model 2340 Deluxe '59er

1974-1977. Copy of classic single-cut solidbody, Hi-Power humbuckers, opaque or flametop.

| 1974-1977 | Flametop | $800 | $1,000 |
| 1974-1977 | Opaque | $800 | $1,000 |

Model 2341 Les Custom

1974-1977. Copy of classic single-cut solidbody.

| 1974-1977 | | $750 | $975 |

Model 2342 Les Moonlight/ Sunlight Special

1974-1977. Copy of classic slab solidbody, black (Moonlight) or ivory (Sunlight).

| 1974-1977 | | $750 | $975 |

Model 2343 FM Jr.

1974-1976. Copy of LP TV Jr.

| 1974-1976 | | $750 | $975 |

Model 2343 Jr.

1974-1976. Copy of classic Jr., cherry mahogany.

| 1974-1976 | | $750 | $975 |

Model 2344

1974-1976. Copy of classic double-cut solidbody.

| 1974-1976 | | $475 | $625 |

Model 2345

1974-1976. Copy of classic sharp double-cut solidbody, set neck, walnut or white, vibrato, 3 pickups.

| 1974-1976 | | $750 | $975 |

Model 2346

1974. Copy of classic sharp double-cut solidbody, vibrato, set neck, 2 pickups.

| 1974 | | $750 | $975 |

Model 2347

1974-1976. Copy of classic sharp double-cut solidbody, set-neck, 1 pickup.

| 1974-1976 | | $600 | $775 |

Model 2348 Firebrand

1974-1977. Copy of classic reverse solidbody, mahogany body, bolt neck, 2 pickups.

| 1974-1977 | | $950 | $1,250 |

Model 2350 Les

1971-1977. Copy of classic single-cut solidbody, bolt neck, black, gold hardware, goldtop version (2350G Les) also available. A cherry sunburst finish (2350 Les Custom) was offered by '74.

| 1971-1977 | | $850 | $1,125 |

Model 2351 Les

1974-1977. Copy of classic single-cut solidbody, gold top, 2 pickups.

| 1974-1977 | | $900 | $1,250 |

Model 2351DX

1974-1977. Copy of classic single-cut solidbody, gold top, 2 mini-humbuckers.

| 1974-1977 | | $750 | $975 |

1979 Ibanez M340
Tom Pfeifer

1978 Ibanez MC Musician
Rivington Guitars

GUITARS

1976 Ibanez 2355
Stoeffu Vogt

Ibanez Model 2404 Double Axe
Greg Perrine

MODEL YEAR	FEATURES	EXC. COND. LOW	HIGH
Model 2351M Les			
1974-1977. LP Standard style, sunburst.			
1974-1977		$750	$975
Model 2352 Telly			
1974-1978. Copy of early classic single-cut solidbody, 1 bridge pickup, white finish.			
1974-1978		$750	$975
Model 2352CT			
1974-1978. Copy of classic single-cut solidbody, single-coil bridge and humbucker neck pickup.			
1974-1978		$750	$975
Model 2352DX Telly			
1974-1978. Copy of classic single-cut solidbody, 2 humbuckers.			
1974-1978		$750	$975
Model 2354			
1974-1977. Copy of classic sharp double-cut solidbody, 2 humbuckers, vibrato.			
1974-1977		$750	$975
Model 2354S			
1972-1977. Stop tailpiece version of 2354.			
1972-1977		$750	$975
Model 2355/2355M			
1973-1977. Copy of classic single-cut hollowbody, sunburst or natural maple (M).			
1973-1977		$1,375	$1,750
Model 2356			
1973-1975. Copy of classic double pointed cutaway hollowbody, bowtie markers, sunburst. There was another Model 2356 in '74, a copy of a different hollowbody.			
1973-1975		$1,250	$1,625
Model 2363R			
1973-1974. Cherry finish copy of classic varitone double-cut semi-hollow body.			
1973-1974		$1,250	$1,625
Model 2364 Ibanex			
1971-1973. Dan Armstrong see-thru Lucite copy, 2 mounted humbuckers.			
1971-1973		$950	$1,250
Model 2368 Telly			
1973-1978. Copy of classic single-cut thinline, chambered f-hole body, single coil pickup, mahogany body.			
1974-1978		$750	$975
Model 2368F			
1973-1974. Classic single-cut black 'guard copy.			
1973-1974		$750	$975
Model 2370			
1972-1977. Sunburst version of Model 2363R.			
1972-1977		$1,250	$1,625
Model 2372 Les Pro/2372DX Les Pro			
1972-1977. Copy of classic single-cut solidbody, bolt neck, low impedance pickups, DX with gold hardware available for '73-'74.			
1972-1977		$750	$975
Model 2374 Crest			
1974-1976. Copy of classic double-cut semi-hollow body, walnut finish.			
1974-1976		$1,250	$1,625
Model 2375 Strato			
1971-1978. Strat copy, 3 single-coils, sunburst.			
1971-1978		$750	$975
Model 2375 Strato 6/12			
1974-1975. Double neck, 6 and 12 strings.			
1974-1975		$1,750	$2,250
Model 2375ASH Strato			
1974-1978. 2375 with ash body.			
1974-1978		$750	$975
Model 2375WH/N/BK Strato			
1974-1978. 2375 in white (WH), natural (N), and black (BK) finishes.			
1974-1978		$1,000	$1,375
Model 2377			
1974-1975. Copy of classic double sharp-cut solidbody, short production run, dot markers.			
1974-1975		$650	$850
Model 2380			
1973-1977. Copy of LP Recording, single-cut solidbody, low impedence pickups, small block markers.			
1973-1977		$750	$975
Model 2383			
1974-1976. Copy of classic double sharp cut solidbody, white or walnut, 3 humbuckers, gold hardware.			
1974-1976		$750	$975
Model 2384 Telly			
1974-1976. Copy of classic single-cut, f-holes, 2 humbuckers, ash body.			
1974-1976		$750	$975
Model 2387 Rocket Roll/Rocket Roll Sr.			
1975-1977. V copy, bolt-neck (2387) or set-neck (2387DX/2387CT), dot markers, gold-covered pickups.			
1975-1977 All models		$4,500	$6,500
Model 2390			
1974-1976. Copy of classic double-cut semi-hollow body, maple 'board, walnut finish.			
1974-1976		$1,250	$1,625
Model 2394			
Ca. 1974-ca. 1976. SG style, 2 humbuckers, maple 'board, black block inlays.			
1974-1976		$750	$975
Model 2395			
1974-1976. Natural finished 2390.			
1974-1976		$1,250	$1,625
Model 2397			
1974-1976. Double-cut semi-hollow body, low impedance electronics, trapezoid markers, goldtop.			
1974-1976		$1,250	$1,625
Model 2399DX Jazz Solid			
1974-1976. Single-cut solidbody, sunburst, set-neck, gold hardware.			
1974-1976		$1,250	$1,625
Model 2401 Signature			
1974-1976. Double-cut semi-hollow archtop, gold top, bolt neck.			
1974-1976		$1,250	$1,625
Model 2402/2402DX Double Axe			
1974-1977. Double sharp cut solidbody 6/12 doubleneck, cherry or walnut, DX model has gold hardware and white finish.			
1974-1977 All models		$2,000	$2,750

MODEL YEAR	FEATURES	EXC. COND. LOW	HIGH

Model 2404 Double Axe
1974-1977. Double sharp cut solidbody guitar/bass doubleneck copy, walnut, white available '75 only.
1974-1977 $2,000 $2,500

Model 2405 Custom Agent
1974-1977. Single-cut solidbody, set neck, scroll headstock, pearl body inlay, 2 humbuckers.
1974-1977 $2,000 $2,500

Model 2406 Double Axe
1974-1977. Double sharp cut solidbody doubleneck, two 6-strings, cherry or walnut.
1974-1977 $1,500 $2,000

Model 2407 Stratojazz 4/6
1974-1975. Half Strat, half Jazz bass, all rock and roll!
1974-1975 $1,500 $2,000

Model 2451
1974-1977. Single-cut solidbody, maple 'board, black or natural, set neck.
1974-1977 $1,250 $1,625

Model 2453 Howie Roberts
1974-1977. Single-cut archtop, round soundhole, maple body, set neck, rosewood 'board, block markers, 1 pickup, gold hardware, burgundy or sunburst.
1974-1977 $1,500 $2,000

Model 2454
1974-1977. Copy of classic double-cut semi-hollow body, set-neck, small block markers, cherry finish over ash.
1974-1977 $1,250 $1,625

Model 2455
1974-1977. L-5 copy, sharp single-cut archtop, blocks, natural.
1974-1977 $2,250 $3,000

Model 2459 Destroyer
1975-1977. Korina finished mahogany body.
1975-1977 $5,500 $8,000

Model 2460
1975-1977. L-5 copy, rounded cut laminated archtop, blocks, natural.
1975-1977 $2,250 $3,000

Model 2461
1975-1977. Copy of classic single-cut archtop, laminated spruce top, curly maple body, set-neck, ebony 'board, pearl blocks, 2 pickups, gold hardware, sunburst or natural.
1975-1977 $2,250 $3,000

Model 2464
1975-1977. Byrdland copy, rounded single-cut, blocks, natural.
1975-1977 $2,250 $3,000

Model 2469 Futura
1976-1977. Korina finished futuristic model copy.
1976-1977 $2,750 $3,500

Model 2601 to 2604 Artist
1976-1978. Upgrade acoustic flat-tops, higher end than 600 and 700 series, less of a copy model, original headstock decal.
1976-1978   All models $525 $675

Model 2612 Artist
1974-1975. Rounded double-cut solidbody, black finish, birch top, gold hardware, bound rosewood 'board, 2 humbuckers, fleur-de-lis inlay.
1974-1975 $1,250 $1,625

Model 2613 Artist
1974-1975. Natural version of 2612.
1974-1975 $1,250 $1,625

Model 2616 Artist Jazz
1974-1975. Single-cut curly maple hollow body, f-holes, fleur-de-lis, 2 humbuckers.
1974-1975 $2,250 $3,000

Model 2617 Artist
1976-1980. Pointed double-cut natural ash solidbody, set-neck, German carved top, spilt block inlays, bound ebony 'board, 2 humbuckers, later would evolve into the Professional model.
1976-1980 $1,750 $2,250

Model 2618 Artist
1976-1979. Like 2617, but with maple and mahogany body and dot markers. Becomes AR200 in '79.
1976-1979 $1,500 $1,875

Model 2619 Artist
1976-1979. Like 2618, but with split block markers. Becomes AR300 in '79.
1976-1979 $1,500 $1,875

Model 2622 Artist EQ
1977-1979. EQ, Steve Miller model. Becomes AR500 in '79.
1977-1979 $1,500 $2,000

Model 2630 Artist Deluxe
1976-1979. Double cut semi-hollow body, sunburst, name changed to AS200 in '79.
1976-1979 $1,875 $2,375

Model 2640 Artist/AR1200 Doubleneck
1977-1984. Double-cut solidbody, set 6/12 necks, 4 humbuckers, gold hardware. Called 2640 until '79 when changed to AR1200.
1977-1984 $1,750 $2,250

Model 2662 Super Cutaway
1974-1976. Solidbody, set neck, 2 dramatic cutaways, block inlays, 2 humbuckers.
1974-1976 $1,750 $2,250

Model 2671 Randy Scruggs
1976-1978. Single-cut solidbody, tree-of-life inlay, German-carve top.
1976-1978 $1,500 $2,000

Model 2700 Artist Custom
1977-1978. Cutaway, dot markers, gold hardware, natural, black, antique violin or dark satin finish.
1977-1978 $2,000 $2,500

Model 2710 Artist Custom
1978. Like Model 2700 with exotic wood and Anvil case.
1978 $2,000 $2,500

Model 2800 Andorra Series
1974-1979. Classical nylon-string guitars, part of Ibanez Andorra Series, all with 2800-2899 model numbers.
1974-1979   Various models $425 $550

1976 Ibanez Model
2405 Custom Agent

Ibanez Model 2671
Randy Scruggs

Greg Perrine

Ibanez Pat Metheny PM200

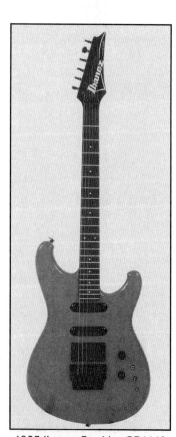

1985 Ibanez Pro Line PR1440

Imaged by Heritage Auctions, HA.com

MODEL YEAR	FEATURES	EXC. COND. LOW	HIGH

Model 2900 Andorra Professional Series
1974-1979. Steel-string dreadnought models with solid spruce tops, all with 2909-2912 model numbers.

| 1974-1979 | Various models | $425 | $550 |

Pat Metheny PM
1996-present. Acoustic-electric archtops, single or single/half cutaway, 1 or 2 humbuckers.

1996-2010	PM100	$1,750	$2,250
1997-1999	PM20	$1,250	$1,750
2000-2015	PM120	$2,000	$2,500

Paul Gilbert PGM
1992-2011. Superstrat body style, painted f-holes, appointments vary with model numbers.

1997-2011	PGM300 WH	$1,500	$2,000
1998	PGM 90th	$1,750	$2,250
1998	PGM200 FB	$1,750	$2,250

PF Performer Series Acoustics
1987-present. Mostly dreadnought size flat-tops.

| 1987-2023 | Various models | $100 | $500 |

PF100 Performer Standard
1978-1979. Single-cut solidbody, plain birch top, mahogany body, bolt neck, dot inlays, 2 humbuckers.

| 1978-1979 | | $500 | $750 |

PF200 Performer Custom
1978-1979. Maple top PF100.

| 1978-1979 | | $650 | $800 |

PF300 Performer
1978-1980. Single-cut solidbody, maple top, mahogany body, set neck, 2 humbuckers, Tri-Sound.

| 1978-1980 | | $650 | $800 |

PF400 Performer
1978-1979. Single cut solidbody, flame maple top, alder body, set neck, block inlays, 2 humbuckers, Tri-Sound.

| 1978-1979 | | $700 | $900 |

PL Pro Line Series
1985-1987. Pro Line models begin with PL or PR.

| 1985-1987 | Various models | $450 | $1,250 |

PR Pro Line Series
1985-1987. Pro Line models begin with PL or PR.

| 1985-1987 | Various models | $450 | $1,250 |

Reb Beach Voyager RBM1
1991-1996. Unusual cutaway lower bout, extreme upper bout cutaways, RBM Series logo on headstock.

| 1991-1996 | | $1,500 | $2,000 |

RG/RS Roadster/Roadstar Series
1979-present. A large family of guitars whose model identification starts with prefix RS ('79-'81) or RG ('82-present), includes the Roadstar Standard, Roadstar Deluxe and Roadstar II models.

1979-2023	Higher-range	$650	$950
1979-2023	Highest-range	$950	$1,750
1979-2023	Low to mid-range	$325	$450
1979-2023	Lower-range	$250	$350
1979-2023	Mid-range	$450	$650

Rocket Roll II RR550
1982-1984. Flying V body, six-on-side headstock, pearloid blocks, cherry sunburst, maple top, set neck.

| 1982-1984 | | $1,500 | $2,000 |

RT Series
1992-1993. Offset double-cut, bolt neck, rosewood 'board, dot markers.

| 1992-1993 | Various models | $350 | $650 |

RX Series
1994-1997. Offset double-cut, solidbodies.

| 1994-1997 | Various models | $150 | $350 |

S Models
1987-present. In '87 Ibanez introduced a new line of highly tapered, ultra-thin body, offset double-cut guitars that were grouped together as the S Models. Initially the S Models were going to be called the Sabre models but that name was trademarked by Music Man and could not be used. The S models will carry an S suffix or S prefix in the model name.

| 1987-2023 | Various models | $450 | $1,250 |

ST Studio Series
1978-1982. Double-cut solidbodies, lots of natural finishes, various models, even a doubleneck.

| 1979-1981 | Various models | $375 | $800 |
| | STW Double | | |

1999. Double neck with 7-string and 6-string neck, limited edition.

| 1999 | | $2,250 | $3,000 |

TC/TV Talman Series
1994-1998. Softer double-cut solidbodies.

| 1994-1998 | Various models | $275 | $675 |

USRG U.S.A. Custom Series
1994-1995. RG style guitars built in the U.S. by PBC Guitar Technology.

| 1994-1995 | Various models | $1,250 | $1,750 |

UV7PBK Steve Vai Universe
1990-1994. Black, green dot inlays.

| 1990-1994 | | $2,000 | $3,000 |

UV7PWH Steve Vai Universe
1990-1993. White, pyramid inlays.

| 1990-1993 | | $2,000 | $3,500 |

UV77MC Steve Vai Universe
1990-1997. Multi-colored.

| 1990-1997 | | $5,000 | $12,000 |

UV777BK Steve Vai Universe
1998-2000s. Black, mirrored 'guard.

| 1998-2000s | | $1,500 | $2,500 |

UV777GR Steve Vai Universe
1998-2000s. Green, pyramid inlays.

| 1998-2000s | | $4,000 | $7,000 |

V300 Vintage Series
1978-1991. Vintage Series acoustic dreadnought, spruce top, mahogany back and sides, sunburst or various colors.

| 1978-1991 | | $200 | $300 |

Xiphos Series
2007-2015. Part of the X Series, various XP and XPT models, X-shaped solidbody electric, neck-thru construction. Replaced by Iron Label (XPIR) series in '15.

| 2007-2015 | Various models | $975 | $1,250 |

XV500
1985-1987. Sharply pointed X-body with scalloped bottom.

| 1985-1987 | | $950 | $1,250 |

MODEL		EXC. COND.	
YEAR	FEATURES	LOW	HIGH

Ibanez, Salvador

1875-1920. Salvador Ibanez was a Spanish luthier who operated a small guitar-building workshop. In the early 1900s he founded Spain's largest guitar factory. In 1929 Japan's Hoshino family began importing Salvador Ibanez guitars. Demand for the Salvador Ibanez guitars became so great that the Hoshino family began building their own guitars, which ultimately became known as the Ibanez brand. Guitars from 1875-1920 were mostly classical style and often can be identified by a label on the inside back which stipulates Salvador Ibanez.

Ignacio Rozas

1987-2008. Luthier Ignacio M. Rozas built his classical and flamenco guitars in Madrid, Spain. He also offered factory-made guitars built to his specifications. He retired in '08.

Illusion Guitars

1992-present. Luthier Jeff Scott builds his premium grade, production/custom, solidbody guitars in Fallbrook, California.

Imperial

Ca.1963-ca.1970. Imported by the Imperial Accordion Company of Chicago, Illinois. Early guitars made in Italy by accordion builder Crucianelli. By ca. '66 switched to Japanese guitars. They also made basses.

Imperial (Japan)

1957-1960. Early, budget grade, Japanese imports from the Hoshino company which was later renamed Ibanez.

Infeld

2003-2005. Solidbody guitars and basses offered by string-maker Thomastik-Infeld of Vienna.

Infinox

1980s. Infinox by JTG, of Nashville, offered a line of 'the classic shapes of yesterday and the hi-tech chic of today', including copies of many classic American solidbody designs with special metallic grafteq paint finish, space-age faux graphite-feel neck, Gotoh tuning machines, Gotoh locking nut tremolo with fine tuners, all models with 1 or 2 humbuckers.

Interdonati

1920s-1930s. Guitars built by luthier Philip Interdonati, in New York City, originally professional grade. He also built mandolins.

Isana

1951-1974. Acoustic and electric archtop guitars built by luthier Josef Sandner in Nauheim, Germany. Elvis played one while in the army in Germany.

Acoustic Archtop

1951-1974	Various models	$500	$1,500

Island Instruments

2010-present. Luthier Nic Delisle builds professional and premium grade, production/custom, small-bodied acoustic and electric guitars in Montreal, Quebec. He also builds basses.

Italia

1999-present. Intermediate grade, production, solid, semi-solid, and hollow body guitars and basses designed by Trevor Wilkinson and made in Korea.

J Backlund Design

2008-present. Professional and premium grade, custom, electric guitars and basses designed by J. Backlund in Hixson, Tennessee, starting in 2008. He also imports Korean-made guitars under the Retronix brand.

J Burda Guitars

Flat-top guitars built by luthier Jan Burda in Berrien Springs, Michigan.

J. Frog Guitars

1978-present. Professional and premium grade, production/custom, solidbody guitars made by Ed Roman Guitars.

J.B. Player

1980s. Budget and intermediate grade, production, imported acoustic, acoustic/electric, and solidbody guitars and basses. They also offer banjos and mandolins. Founded in United States. Moved production of guitars to Korea but maintained a U.S. Custom Shop. MBT International/Musicorp took over manufacture and distribution in '89, then Kamen acquired MBT in 2005.

J.R. Zeidler Guitars

1977-2002. Luthier John Zeidler built premium and presentation grade, custom, flat-top, 12-string, and archtop guitars in Wallingford, Pennsylvania. He also built mandolins. He died in '02 at age 44.

J.S. Bogdanovich

1996-present. Production/custom, premium grade, classical and steel string guitars built by luthier John S. Bogdanovich in Swannanoa, North Carolina.

J.T. Hargreaves Basses & Guitars

1995-present. Luthier Jay Hargreaves builds his premium grade, production/custom, classical and steel string guitars and basses in Seattle, Washington.

Jack Daniel's

2004-2017. Acoustic and electric guitars and basses, some with Jack Daniel's artwork on the body and headstock, built by Peavey for Jack Daniel's Distillery. There is also an amp model.

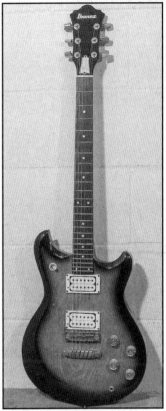

1980 Ibanez Studio ST-55
Tom Pfeifer

1979 Ibanez V302
Peter Busch

1994 Jackson JSX94

Imaged by Heritage Auctions, HA.com

**Jackson Phil Collen
PC1 (U.S.A.)**

MODEL YEAR	FEATURES	EXC. COND. LOW	HIGH

Jackson

1980-present. Currently Jackson offers intermediate, professional, and premium grade, production, electric guitars. They also offer basses. In '78 Grover Jackson bought out Charvel Guitars and moved it to San Dimas. Jackson made custom-built bolt-on Charvels. In '82 the pointy, tilt-back Jackson headstock became standard. The Jackson logo was born in '80 and used on a guitar designed as Randy Rhoad's first flying V. Jacksons were neck-through construction. The Charvel trademark was licensed to IMC in '85. IMC moved the Jackson factory to Ontario, California in '86.

Grover Jackson stayed with Jackson/Charvel until '89 (see Charvel). On October 25, 2002, Fender Musical Instruments Corp (FMIC) took ownership of Jackson/Charvel Manufacturing Inc.

Dinky Reverse DR2
1996-1998. US-made, reverse headstock, no inlay, 2 Duncan humbuckers, ebony 'board.

1996-1998		$950	$1,500

Dinky Reverse DR3/DR5
1992-2001. Import, reverse headstock, 2 humbuckers, dots (DR5) or sharkfin inlays (DR3), locking trem.

1992-1997	Dots	$450	$650
1995-2001	Sharkfin	$550	$750

DX Series
2000-2007. Standard offset double-cut body, reverse headstock.

2000-2007		$300	$400

Fusion Pro
Late 1980s-early 1990s. Import from Japan.

1980s-90s		$600	$800

Fusion U.S.A.
1992-1994. Jackson with Made In USA logo on headstock, graphics.

1992-1994		$2,000	$2,500

Jenna II RX10D Rhoads
2009. Limited production, Rhoads body style, named after performer Jenna Jameson.

2009		$800	$1,250

JSX94
1994-1995. Offset double-cut solidbody, single/single/hum, rosewood 'board, dot markers.

1994-1995		$350	$450

JTX
1993-1995. Partial offset double-cut, single-coil neck pickup, humbucker bridge pickup, Jackson-Rose double lock vibrato, bolt-on neck, dot markers on maple fretboard, JTX truss rod cover logo.

1993-1995		$450	$600

Kelly Custom
1984-early 1990s. Solidbody, Kahler tremolo, 2 humbuckers, ebony 'board with shark's tooth inlays, bound neck and headstock.

1984-1993		$4,000	$5,000

Kelly Pro
1994-1995. Pointy-cut solidbody, neck-thru, 2 humbuckers, bound ebony 'board, sharkfin inlays.

1994-1995		$3,000	$4,000

Kelly Standard
1993-1995. Pointy cutaway solidbody, bolt neck, 2 humbuckers, dot markers.

1993-1995		$2,000	$3,000

Kelly U.S.A. (KE2)
1998-2021. Alder solidbody, flame maple top, neck-thru.

1998-2021		$2,000	$3,000

Kelly XL
1994-1995. Pointy cutaway solidbody, bolt neck, 2 humbuckers, bound rosewood 'board, sharkfin inlays.

1994-1995		$675	$900

King V Dave Mustaine (KV1)
1998. Dave Mustaine (Megadeth) signature, sharkfin inlays, 2 pickups.

1998		$3,000	$3,500

King V (KV2)
2003-present. King V Pro reissue, neck-thru, sharkfin markers, Floyd Rose, U.S.-made.

2003-2023		$1,000	$1,500

King V Pro
1993-1995. Soft V-shaped neck-thru solidbody, sharkfin markers, 2 humbuckers.

1993-1995		$675	$950

King V STD
1993-1995. Bolt neck version of King V.

1993-1995		$350	$500

Phil Collen
1989-1991, 1993-1995. Offset double-cut maple neck-thru solidbody, 6-in-line tuners, 1 volume, bound ebony 'board, U.S.-made, early version has poplar body, 1 humbucker; later version with basswood body, 1 single-coil and 1 humbucker.

1989-1995		$3,000	$4,000

Phil Collen PC1 (U.S.A.)
1996-present. Quilt maple top, bolt-on maple neck, maple board, koa body '96-'00, mahogany body '01-present, 1 humbucker and 1 single coil '96-'97, humbucker, stacked humbucker, and single coil '98-present.

1996-2023		$2,500	$3,000

Phil Collen PC3 (Import)
1996-2001. Downscale version of Collen model, poplar body, bolt neck, humbucker\single\single.

1996-2001		$575	$750

PS Performers Series
1994-2003. Some with PS model number on truss rod cover.

1994-2003	Various models	$350	$500

Randy Rhoads (Import)
1992-2011. Bolt neck import version.

1992-2011		$500	$650

Randy Rhoads Limited Edition
1992 only. Shark fin-style maple neck-thru body, gold hardware, white with black pinstriping, block inlays, 6-in-line tuners, U.S.-made, only 200 built.

1992		$6,000	$10,000

Randy Rhoads Pro Series RR3 and RR5
1995-2012. Made in Japan, various finishes.

1995-2012	RR3, bolt-on	$1,250	$3,000
2001-2011	RR5, neck-thru	$1,250	$3,000

The *Vintage Guitar Price Guide* shows values for all-original, excellent condition instruments and, where applicable, with original case.

The Official Vintage Guitar magazine Price Guide 2025   **Jackson** Randy Rhoads Relic Tribute — **Jackson-Guldan**   **253**

GUITARS

MODEL YEAR	FEATURES	EXC. COND. LOW	HIGH

Randy Rhoads Relic Tribute
2009. Custom Shop limited edition to celebrate the 30th anniversary of the Randy Rhoads Concorde, 60 made, exacting dimension and design of Rhoads' original custom-made Concorde guitar, relic-treatment to mimic the original.

2009		$7,500	$12,000

Randy Rhoads Roswell
1996-1999. Mother-of-pearl crop circle inlays.

1996-1999		$10,000	$12,000

Randy Rhoads U.S.A.
1983-present. V-shaped (also referred to as Concorde-shaped) neck-thru solidbody, 2 humbuckers, originally made at San Dimas plant, serial numbers RR 0001 to RR 1929, production moved to the Ontario plant by '87, serial numbers RR 1930 to present in sequential order.

1983	Early serial #, no trem	$7,500	$10,000
1983	Mid serial #, no trem	$6,500	$8,500
1983-1986	Late serial #, Kahler trem	$5,000	$6,500
1983-1986	Rose trem or string-thru	$4,500	$6,000
1987-1989	Early Ontario-built	$3,500	$4,500
1990-1992	Early '90s vintage	$3,000	$4,000
1993-2002		$3,000	$4,000
2003-2019	RR5	$2,500	$3,500
2003-2023	RR1	$3,500	$4,500

RX Series
2000-2011. Bolt-on, shark fin inlays.

2000-2008	RX10D Rhoads	$300	$400

San Dimas Serialized Plated
1980-1982. Various custom-built solidbody models, values vary depending on each individual instrument. The values are true for so-called "Serialized Plated" "with Jackson neck plate, Jackson logo and serial number.

1980-1982		$6,000	$7,500

Soloist Custom
1993-1995. U.S.-made, double-cut, neck-thru solidbody, 1 humbucker and 2 single-coils, bound ebony 'board, shark's tooth inlays.

1993-1995		$3,500	$4,500

Soloist Pro
1990-1995. Imported version of Soloist, with, shark's tooth inlays.

1990-1995		$800	$1,125

Soloist Shannon
1998. Shark fin inlays, single-single-hum pickups, Rose, signed by Mike Shannon.

1998		$3,500	$4,500

Soloist Student J1 (U.S.A.)
1984-1999. Double-cut neck-thru solidbody, Seymour Duncan single-single-hum pickups, rosewood 'board, dot inlays, no binding.

1984-1986	San Dimas-built	$2,500	$3,500
1986-1999	Ontario-built	$2,500	$3,500

Soloist/Soloist USA/X Series
1984-present. U.S.-made, double-cut, neck-thru, string-thru solidbody, 2 humbuckers, bound rosewood 'board, standard vibrato system on Soloist is Floyd Rose locking vibrato, a guitar with Kahler vibrato is worth less. Replaced by the Soloist USA in '90, then X Series in 2023.

1984-1986	Custom order, Floyd Rose	$6,000	$7,500
1984-1986	Custom order, Kahler	$4,000	$5,500
1984-1986	San Dimas-built, Floyd Rose	$5,000	$6,000
1984-1986	San Dimas-built, Kahler	$4,000	$5,500
1986-1990	Custom order features	$4,000	$5,500
1986-1990	Ontario-built	$3,000	$4,000
1990-2023	Various models, includes SL1 & SL2	$2,500	$3,500

Stealth EX
1992-late 1990s. Offset double-cut, pointed headstock, H/S/S pickups, offset dot markers, tremolo, Jackson Professional logo.

1990s		$500	$650

Stealth HX
1992-1995. 3 humbucker version of Stealth, string-thru body.

1992-1995		$500	$650

Stealth XL
1993. Stealth XL truss rod cover logo, 1 humbucker, 2 single-coils, left edge dot markers.

1993		$500	$650

Surfcaster SC1
1998-2001. Jackson logo on headstock, Charvel Surfcaster styling.

1998-2001		$1,250	$1,750

Warrior Pro (Import)
1990-1992. Japanese version.

1990-1992		$400	$550

Warrior U.S.A.
1990-1992. Four-point neck-thru solidbody, 1 humbucker and 1 single-coil, triangle markers, active electronics, U.S.-made, the Warrior Pro was Japanese version.

1990-1992	Red	$1,000	$1,500

Y2KV Dave Mustaine Signature
2000-2002. V-shaped body, shark tooth markers, neck-thru, 2 humbuckers.

2000-2002		$5,000	$6,500

Jackson-Guldan/ Jay G Guitars
1920s-1960s. The Jackson-Guldan Violin Company, of Columbus, Ohio, mainly built inexpensive violins, violas, cellos, etc. but also offered acoustic guitars in the 1950s and early '60s, some of which were distributed by Wards. Their sales flyers from that era state - Made in America by Jackson-Guldan Craftsman. Very similar to small (13"-14") Stella economy flat-tops. Jay G name with quarter-note logo is sometimes on the headstock. They also offered lap steels and small tube amps early on.

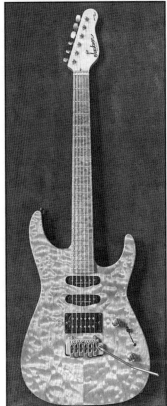

1997 Jackson PC3 (U.S.A.)
Ian Vatet

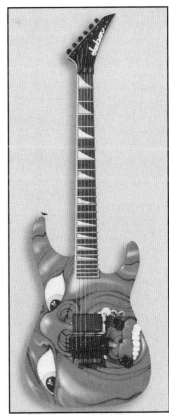

1987 Jackson Soloist
John DeSilva

**2005 James Trussart
Steel Deville**
Rivington Guitars

James Tyler Studio Elite HD
Frank Manno

Jacobacci

1930s-1994. Founded in France by Italian Vincent Jacobacci and originally building basso-guitars, banjos, and mandolins. Sons Roger and Andre joined the company and encouraged pop to add lapsteels and electric and regular acoustic guitars around '52. The guitars are sometimes labeled Jaco and, from ca. '54 to ca. '66, as Jaco Major. In '58 the company introduced aluminum neck models, and in '59 their first solidbodies. In the '60s they also made instruments branded Royal, Texas, Ohio, Star and made instruments for Major Conn and other companies. By the mid '60s, they were producing mainly jazz style guitars.

Jamboree

1960s. Guitar brand exported by Japan's Hoshino (Ibanez).

James Einolf Guitars

1964-2017. Production/custom, professional grade, flat-top guitars built first in Denver, then Castle Rock, Colorado by luthier James Einolf.

James R. Baker Guitars

1996-present. Luthier James R. Baker builds his premium grade, custom, archtops in Shoreham, New York.

James Trussart

1980-present. Luthier James Trussart builds his premium grade, custom/production, solid and semi-hollow body electric guitars and basses in Los Angeles, California.

James Tyler

Early 1980s-present. Luthier James Tyler builds his professional and premium grade, custom/production, solidbody guitars and basses in Van Nuys, California, and also has a model built in Japan.

Janofsky Guitars

Production classical and flamenco guitars built by luthier Stephen Janofsky in Amherst, Massachusetts starting in 1978.

Jaros

Beginning in 1995 these professional and premium grade, production/custom, solidbody and acoustic/electric guitars were originally built by father and son luthiers Harry and Jim Jaros in Rochester, Pennsylvania. In '01 Ed Roman in Las Vegas, bought the brand. He sold it in '04 to Dave Weiler in Nashville. Serial numbers under 1000 were made by the Jaros', numbers 1001-2000 were made by Ed Roman, over 2000 made by Dave Weiler.

Jasmine

1994-2019. Budget and intermediate grade, production, steel and classical guitars offered by Takamine Jasmine or Jasmine by Takamine. Student level instruments.

Jason Z. Schroeder Guitars

1994-present. Luthier Jason Schroeder builds professional and premium grade, production/custom, electric guitars in Redding, California.

Jay Turser

1997-present. Budget and intermediate grade, production, imported acoustic, acoustic/electric, electric and resonator guitars and basses. They also have amps. Designed and developed by Tommy Rizzi for Music Industries Corp.

JBG (Joe Bochar Guitars)

2009-present. Production/custom, professional grade, solidbody electric guitars built by luthier Joe Bochar in Santa Clarita, California.

JD Bluesville

John Schappell and luthier Davis Millard build their professional grade, custom/production, solidbody electric guitars in Allentown, Pennsylvania. They began in 2005.

Jeff Traugott Guitars

1991-present. Premium and presentation grade, custom, flat-top, nylon-string, and acoustic/electric guitars built by luthier Jeff Traugott, in Santa Cruz, California.

Jeremy Locke Guitars

Premium grade, production/custom, classical and flamenco guitars built by luthier Jeremy Locke in Coomera, South East Queensland, Australia, starting in 1985.

Jeronimo Pena Fernandez

1967-2002. Luthier Jeronimo Pena Fernandez started building classical guitars in Marmolejo, Spain, in the '50s. In '67, he went full-time and soon became well-known for his fine work. He is now retired, but still builds a few guitars a year. Prices can vary depending on model specs, each instrument should be evaluated on a case-by-case basis.

Jerry Jones

1981-2011. Intermediate grade, production, semi-hollowbody electric guitars and sitars from luthier Jerry Jones, built in Nashville, Tennessee. They also built basses. Jones started building custom guitars in '81 and launched his Danelectro-inspired line in '87. He retired in 2011.

Electric

Various models include Baritone 6-string ('89-'11); Electric Sitar ('90-'11) with buzz-bar sitar bridge, individual pickup for sympathetic strings and custom color gator finish; Longhorn Guitarlin ('89-'00, '05-'11) with large cutaway Guitarlin-style body, 24 frets in '89 and 31 after; and the Neptune 12-string ('81-'11) single-cut with 3 pickups.

MODEL YEAR	FEATURES	EXC. COND. LOW	HIGH
1981-2011	Neptune 12-string	$2,000	$3,000
1981-2011	Neptune 6/12		
	Double Neck	$3,000	$4,000

MODEL YEAR	FEATURES	EXC. COND. LOW	HIGH
1989-2011	Baritone 6-string	$2,000	$3,000
1989-2011	Longhorn Guitarlin	$2,000	$3,000
1989-2011	Neptune, baritone 6-string	$2,500	$3,500
1990-2011	Baby Sitar	$2,000	$2,500
1990-2011	Shorthorn	$2,000	$2,500
1990-2011	Sitar	$2,000	$2,500
1990-2011	U-3, 3 pickups	$2,000	$2,500

Jersey Girl
1991-present Premium grade, production/custom, solidbody guitars made in Japan. They also build effects.

JET
1998-present. Premium grade, custom/production, chambered solidbody electric guitars built by luthier Jeffrey Earle Terwilliger in Raleigh, North Carolina.

Jewel
1920s. Instruments built by the Oscar Schmidt Co. and possibly others. Most likely a brand made for a distributor.

JG Guitars
1991-present. Luthier Johan Gustavsson builds his premium and presentation grade, production/custom, solidbody electric guitars in Malmö, Sweden.

Jim Dyson
1972-2015. Intermediate, professional and premium grade, production/custom electric guitars and basses built by luthier Jim Dyson in Torquay, Southern Victoria, Australia. He also built lap steels.

Jim Redgate Guitars
1992-present. Luthier Jim Redgate builds his premium grade, custom, nylon-string classical guitars in Belair, Adelaide, South Australia.

John Le Voi Guitars
1970-present. Production/custom, gypsy jazz, flat-top, and archtop guitars built by luthier John Le Voi in Lincolnshire, United Kingdom. He also builds mandolin family instruments.

John Page Guitars and John Page Classic
2006-present. Luthier John Page builds his custom, premium grade, chambered and solidbody electric guitars in Sunny Valley, Oregon.

John Price Guitars
Custom classical and flamenco guitars built by luthier John Price, starting in 1984, in Australia.

Johnson
Mid-1990s-present. Budget, intermediate, and professional grade, production, acoustic, classical, acoustic/electric, resonator and solidbody guitars and basses imported by The Music Link, Brisbane, California. Johnson also offers amps, mandolins, ukuleles and effects.

Jon Kammerer Guitars
1997-present. Luthier Jon Kammerer builds his professional and premium grade, custom/production, solidbody, chambered, hollowbody, and acoustic guitars and basses in Keokuk, Iowa.

Jones
See TV Jones listing.

Jordan
1981-present. Professional and premium grade, custom, flat-top and archtop guitars built by luthier John Jordan in Concord, California. He also builds electric violins and cellos.

Jose Oribe
1962-present. Presentation grade, production, classical, flamenco, and steel-string acoustic guitars built by luthier Jose Oribe in Vista, California.

Jose Ramirez
See listing under Ramirez, Jose.

Juliett
1960s. Guitars built by Zerosette (or Zero-Sette), an accordion builder near Castelfidardo, Italy.

JY Jeffrey Yong Guitars
2003-present. Professional and premium grade, production/custom, classical, acoustic and electric guitars and basses and harp guitars built by Jeffrey Yong in Kuala Lumpur, Malaysia.

K & S
1992-1998. Hawaiian-style and classical guitars distributed by George Katechis and Marc Silber and handmade in Paracho, Mexico. A few 16" wide Leadbelly Model 12-strings were made in Oakland, California by luthier Stewart Port. K & S also offered mandolins, mandolas and ukes. In '98, Silber started marketing guitars under the Marc Silber Guitar Company brand and Katechis continued to offer instruments under the Casa Montalvo brand.

Kakos, Stephen
Luthier Stephen Kakos builds his premium grade, production/custom, classical guitars in Mound, Minnesota starting in 1972.

Kalamazoo
1933-1942, 1965-1970. Budget brand built by Gibson. Made flat-tops, solidbodies, mandolins, lap steels, banjos, and amps. Name revived for a line of amps, solidbodies and basses in '65-'67. Playability and string tension will affect values of '60s electrics.

Jason Z. Schroeder
The Chopper TL

Jeffery Yong JJ Special
Model 2017

GUITARS

1940 Kalamazoo KG-12
David Stone

1941 Kalamazoo KGN-32 Oriole
David Stone

MODEL YEAR	FEATURES	EXC. COND. LOW	HIGH

KG-1/KG-1A

1965-1969. Offset double-cut (initial issue) or SG-shape (second issue), 1 pickup, Model 1A with spring vibrato, red, blue, or white.

| 1965-1969 | | $575 | $725 |

KG-2/KG-2A

1965-1970. Offset double-cut (initial shape) or SG-shape, 2 pickups, Model 2A with spring vibrato, red, blue, or white.

| 1965-1970 | | $625 | $775 |

KG-11

1933-1941. Flat-top, all mahogany, 14" with no 'guard, sunburst.

| 1933-1941 | | $1,875 | $2,375 |

KTG-11 Tenor

1936-1940. Tenor version of 11.

| 1936-1940 | | $850 | $1,125 |

KG-12

1940-1941. Rare model, L-00, sunburst.

| 1940-1941 | | $2,875 | $3,500 |

KG-14/KG-14N

1936-1940. Flat-top L-0-size, mahogany back and sides, with 'guard, sunburst or natural (N).

| 1936-1940 | | $2,875 | $3,500 |

KTG-14 Tenor

1936-1940. Tenor version of 14.

| 1936-1940 | | $1,375 | $1,750 |

KG-16

1939-1940. Gibson-made archtop, small body, f-hole.

| 1939-1940 | | $1,375 | $1,750 |

KG-21

1936-1941. Early model 15" archtop (bent, not curved), dot markers, bound top, sunburst.

| 1936-1941 | | $1,375 | $1,750 |

KTG-21 Tenor

1935-1939. Tenor version of 21.

| 1935-1939 | | $775 | $975 |

KG-22

1940-1942. Early model 16" archtop.

| 1940-1942 | | $1,500 | $1,875 |

KG-31

1935-1940. Archtop L-50-size, 16" body, non-carved spruce top, mahogany back and sides.

| 1935-1940 | | $1,500 | $1,875 |

KG-32

1939-1942. Archtop, 16" body.

| 1939-1942 | | $1,875 | $2,375 |

KG Senior

1933-1934. Senior Model logo, fire stripe guard, bound top and bottom, rope rose.

| 1933-1934 | | $2,625 | $3,250 |

KG Sport

1937-1942. Small body, ¾ size, Sport Model logo.

| 1937-1942 | | $2,625 | $3,250 |

KGN-12 Oriole

1940-1941. Flat-top, same body as KG-14, but with maple back and sides, stencil Oriole picture on headstock, natural.

| 1940-1941 | | $2,875 | $3,500 |

KGN-32 Oriole

1940-1941. Archtop, maple back and sides, stencil Oriole picture on headstock, natural.

| 1940-1941 | | $2,875 | $3,500 |

KHG Series

1936-1941. Acoustic Hawaiian guitar (HG), some converted to Spanish set-up.

| 1936-1940 | KHG-11 | $1,875 | $2,375 |
| 1936-1941 | KHG-14 | $2,875 | $3,500 |

Kamico

1947-1951. Flat-top acoustic guitars. Low-end budget brand made by Kay Musical Instrument Company and sold through various distributors. They also offered lap steel and amp sets.

K Stratotone Thin Single

1950-1951. Similar to Kay Stratotone-style neck-thru solidbody, single slim-tube pickup.

| 1950-1951 | | $1,000 | $1,500 |

Kapa

Ca. 1962-1970. Begun by Dutch immigrant and music store owner Koob Veneman in Hyattsville, Maryland whose father had made Amka guitars in Holland. Kapa is from K for Koob, A for son Albert, P for daughter Patricia, and A for wife Adeline. Crown shield logo from Amka guitars. The brand included some Hofner and Italian imports in '60. Ca. '66 Kapa started offering thinner bodies. Some German Pix pickups ca. '66. Thinlines and Japanese bodies in '69. Kapa closed shop in '70 and the parts and equipment were sold to Micro-Frets and Mosrite. Later Veneman was involved with Bradley copy guitars imported from Japan. Approximately 120,000 Kapa guitars and basses were made.

Electric

1962-1970. Various models include Challenger with 3-way toggle from '62-'66/'67 and 2 on/off switches after; Cobra with 1 pickup; Continental and Continental 12-string; Minstrel and Minstrel 12-string with teardrop shape, 3 pickups; and the Wildcat, mini offset double-cut, 3 pickups and mute.

| 1962-1970 | Various models | $400 | $775 |

Karol Guitars

2001-present. Luthier Tony Karol builds his custom, premium grade, acoustic and electric guitars in Mississauga, Ontario.

Kasha

1967-1997. Innovative classical guitars built by luthier Richard Schneider in collaboration with Dr. Michael Kasha. Schneider also consulted for Gibson and Gretsch. Schneider died in '97.

Kathy Wingert Guitars

1996-present. Luthier Kathy Wingert builds her premium grade, production/custom, flat-tops in Rancho Palos Verdes, California.

MODEL YEAR	FEATURES	EXC. COND. LOW	HIGH

Kawai

1927-present. Kawai is a Japanese piano and guitar maker. They started offering guitars around '56 and they were imported into the U.S. carrying many different brand names, including Kimberly and Teisco. In '67 Kawai purchased Teisco. Odd-shaped guitars were offered from late-'60s through the mid-'70s. Few imports carrying the Kawai brand until the late-'70s; best known for high quality basses. By '90s they were making plexiglass replicas of Teisco Spectrum 5 and Kawai moon-shaped guitar. Kawai quit offering guitars and basses around 2002.

Acoustic

1956-2002		$350	$500

Electric

1956-2002	Common model	$375	$500
1956-2002	Rare model	$600	$2,500

Kay

Ca. 1931 (1890)-present. Originally founded in Chicago, Illinois as Groehsl Company (or Groehsel) in 1890, making bowl-backed mandolins. Offered Groehsl, Stromberg, Kay Kraft, Kay, Arch Kraft brand names, plus made guitars for S.S.Maxwell, Old Kraftsman (Spiegel), Recording King (Wards), Supertone (Sears), Silvertone (Sears), National, Dobro, Custom Kraft (St.Louis Music), Hollywood (Shireson Bros.), Oahu and others.

In 1921 the name was changed to Stromberg-Voisinet Company. Henry Kay "Hank" Kuhrmeyer joined the company in '23 and was secretary by '25. By the mid-'20s the company was making many better Montgomery Ward guitars, banjos and mandolins, often with lots of pearloid. First production electric guitars and amps are introduced with big fanfare in '28; perhaps only 200 or so made. Last Stromberg instruments seen in '32. Kuhrmeyer becomes president and the Kay Kraft brand was introduced in '31, probably named for Kuhrmeyer's middle name, though S-V had used Kay brand on German Kreuzinger violins '28-'36. By '34, if not earlier, the company is changed to the Kay Musical Instrument Company. A new factory was built at 1640 West Walnut Street in '35. The Kay Kraft brand ends in '37 and the Kay brand is introduced in late-'36 or '37.

Violin Style Guitars and upright acoustic basses debuted in '38. In '40 the first guitars for Sears, carrying the new Silvertone brand, were offered. Kamico budget line introduced in '47 and Rex flat-tops and archtops sold through Gretsch in late-'40s. Kuhrmeyer retires in '55 dies a year later. A new gigantic factory in Elk Grove Village, Illinois opens in '64. Seeburg purchased Kay in '66 and sold it to Valco in '67. Valco/Kay went out of business in '68 and its assets were auctioned in '69. The Kay name went to Sol Weindling and Barry Hornstein of W.M.I. (Teisco Del Rey) who began putting Kay name on Teisco guitars. By '73 most Teisco guitars are called Kay. Tony Blair, president of Indianapolis-based A.R. Musical Enterprises Inc.

(founded in '73) purchased the Kay nameplate in '79 and currently distributes Kay in the U.S. Currently Kay offers budget and intermediate grade, production, acoustic, semi-hollow body, solidbody, and resonator guitars. They also make amps, basses, banjos, mandolins, ukes, violins.

K11/K8911 Rhythm Special

1953-1961. Single-cut 17" acoustic archtop, "eighth note" headstock logo, large position markers, white 'guard, became K8911 in '57, sunburst or blond (B).

1953-1961	Blond	$1,125	$1,500
1953-1961	Sunburst	$1,000	$1,250

K20 Super Auditorium

1939-1942. 16" archtop, solid spruce top, maple back and sides, sunburst.

1939-1942		$350	$450

K20T

1970s. Japanese-made solidbody, 2 pickups, tremolo, model number on neck plate, circle-capital K logo on headstock.

1970s		$175	$250

K21/K21B Cutaway Professional

1952-1956. Single-cut 17" acoustic archtop, split block markers, sunburst or blond (B).

1952-1956	Blond	$1,375	$1,750
1952-1956	Sunburst	$1,375	$1,750

K22 Artist Spanish

1947-1956. Flat-top similar to Gibson J-100 17", spruce top, mahogany back and sides.

1947-1956		$700	$875

K26 Artist Spanish

1947-1951. Flat-top, block markers, natural.

1947-1951		$775	$975

K27 Jumbo

1952-1956. 17" Jumbo flat-top, fancy appointments.

1952-1956		$1,375	$1,750

K37T Spanish Tenor

1952-1956. Mahogany bodied archtop, tenor.

1952-1956		$300	$375

K39 Super Grand Auditorium

1947-1951. Full size acoustic archtop, faux rope binding on top, Kay script logo.

1947-1951		$450	$575

K44 Artist Archtop

1947-1951. Non-cut archtop, solid spruce top, 17" curly maple veneered body, block markers, sunburst.

1947-1951		$650	$825

K45 Professional Master Size Archtop

1952-1954. Non-cut archtop, 17" body, engraved tortoiseshell-celluloid headstock, large block markers, natural.

1952-1954		$650	$825

K45 Travel Guitar

1981. Made in Korea, known as the 'rifle guitar', 'travel guitar', or 'Austin-Hatchet copy', circle K logo.

1981		$425	$550

K46 Artist Master Size Archtop

1947-1951. Non-cut archtop, solid spruce top, 17" curly maple-veneered body, double-eighth note headstock inlay, sunburst.

1947-1951		$625	$775

1953 Kay K11
John Neff

1950s Kay K-21
Donald DiLoreto

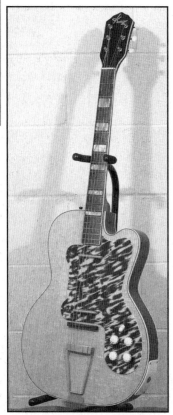

1953 Kay K161 Thin Twin
Tom Pfeifer

1963 Kay K300
Richard Kregear

MODEL YEAR	FEATURES	EXC. COND. LOW	HIGH

K48 Artist Master Size Archtop
1947-1951. Non-cut archtop, 17" solid spruce top with figured maple back and sides, split block inlays, sunburst or black.

1947-1951		$950	$1,250

K48/K21 Jazz Special
Late-1960s. Slim solidbody with 3 reflective pickups, garden spade headstock, fancy position Circle K headstock logo, white.

1968		$550	$725

K100 Vanguard
1961-1966. Offset double-cut slab solidbody, genuine maple veneered top and back over hardwood body, sunburst.

1961-1966		$350	$450

K102 Vanguard
1961-1966. Double pickup version of the K100, sunburst.

1961-1966		$400	$550

K136 (aka Stratotone)
1955-1957. Small single-cut slab solidbody electric, similar to Harmony Stratotone style, set neck, 1 pickup, trapeze tailpiece, triangle paint graphic in Spring Green and White Mist, matching green headstock, attractive finish adds value to this otherwise lower-end student model.

1955-1957		$1,125	$1,500

K142 (aka Stratotone)
1955-1957. Small slab solidbody, introduced in '55 along with the K136, offered with 1 pickup or 2 pickups (more rare), trapeze tailpiece, copper finish.

1955-1957	1 pickup	$1,125	$1,500
1955-1957	2 pickups	$1,125	$1,500

K161 Thin Twin/Jimmy Reed
1952-1958. Single-cut semi-hollow body, 2 pickups.

1952-1958		$1,125	$1,750

K161V/VB Thin Twin
2009-present. Vintage Reissue series, single-cut hollowbody, 2 pickups.

2009-2023		$875	$1,250

K300 Double Cutaway Solid Electric
1962-1966. Two single-coils, block inlays, some with curly maple top and some with plain maple top, natural.

1962-1966		$550	$675

K360 Apollo/K365 Apollo II
1965-1968. Solidbody, 2 pickups, block inlays, vibrato.

1965-1968		$1,125	$1,500

K535 Double Cutaway Thinline
1961-1965. Thinline double-cut, 2 pickups, vibrato, sunburst.

1961-1965		$625	$775

K550 Dove
1970s. Square shoulder D-style, 2 Dove-style 'guards, capital K logo.

1970s		$150	$200

K571/K572/K573 Speed Demon
1961-1965. Thinline semi-acoustic/electric, single pointed cutaway, some with Bigsby vibrato, with 1 (K571), 2 (K572) or 3 (K573) pickups. There was also a Speed Demon solidbody.

1961-1965	571, 1 pickup	$450	$575
1961-1965	572, 2 pickups	$525	$650
1961-1965	573, 3 pickups	$550	$675

K580 Galaxy
1961-1966. Thinline, single-cut, 1 pickup.

1961-1966		$575	$725

K592 Double Cutaway Thinline
1962-1966. Thinline semi-acoustic/electric, double Florentine cut, 2 or 3 pickups, Bigsby vibrato, pie-slice inlays, cherry.

1962-1966		$575	$725

K672/K673 Swingmaster
1961-1965. Single rounded cutaway semi-hollowbody, with 2 (K672) or 3 (K673) pickups.

1961-1965	672, 2 pickups	$1,125	$1,500
1961-1965	673, 3 pickups	$1,250	$1,625

K682 Galaxie II
1966-1968. Hollowbody, 2 pickups, vibrato tailpiece.

1966-1968		$600	$750

K775/K776 Jazz II
1961-1966. Electric thinline archtop, double-cut, standard Bigsby vibrato, 2 Gold K pickups, 4 knobs with toggle controls. Replaces Barney Kessel series as top-of-the-line model.

1961-1966	775, shaded	$1,500	$2,000
1961-1966	776, blond	$1,500	$2,000

K797 Acoustic Archtop
1930s. Full size student-intermediate acoustic archtop, 3-on-a-strip tuners, dot markers, sunburst.

1935-1937		$325	$400

K1160 Standard
1957-1964. Small 13" (standard) flat-top, laminated construction.

1957-1964		$60	$75

K1452 Aristocrat
1952. Acoustic-electric archtop, 2 pickups, sunburst.

1952		$900	$1,250

K1700/K1701 Barney Kessel Pro
1957-1960. 13" hollowbody, single-cut, Kelvinator headstock, ebony 'board with pearl inlays, white binding, 1 (K1701) or 2 (K1700) pickups, sunburst.

1957-1960	1700, 2 pickups	$2,125	$2,625
1957-1960	1701, 1 pickup	$1,875	$2,500

K1961/K1962/K1963 Value Leader
1960-1965. Part of Value Leader line, thinline single-cut, hollowbody, identified by single chrome-plated checkered, body-length guard on treble side, laminated maple body, maple neck, dot markers, sunburst, with 1 (K1961), 2 (K1962) or 3 (K1963) pickups.

1960-1965	1961, 1 pickup	$475	$600
1960-1965	1962, 2 pickups	$500	$625
1960-1965	1963, 3 pickups	$575	$725

K1982/K1983 Style Leader/Jimmy Reed
1960-1965. Part of the Style Leader mid-level Kay line. Sometimes dubbed Jimmy Reed of 1960s. Easily identified by the long, brushed copper dual guard plates on either side of the strings. Brown or gleaming golden blond (natural) finish, laminated curly maple body, simple script Kay logo, with 2 (K1982) or 3 (K1983) pickups.

1960-1965	1982, 2 pickups	$625	$825
1960-1965	1983, 3 pickups	$750	$975

MODEL YEAR FEATURES	EXC. COND. LOW	HIGH

K3500 Studio Concert
1966-1968. 14 1/2" flat-top, solid spruce top, laminated maple back and sides.

1966-1968	$100	$150

K5113 Plains Special
1968. Flat-top, solid spruce top, laminated mahogany back and sides.

1968	$200	$250

K5160 Auditorium
1957-1965. Flat-top 15" auditorium-size, laminated construction.

1957-1965	$200	$250

K6100 Country
1950s-1960s. Jumbo flat-top, spruce x-braced top, mahogany back and sides, natural.

1957-1962	$475	$600

K6116 Super Auditorium
1957-1965. Super Auditorium-size flat-top, laminated figured maple back and sides, solid spruce top.

1957-1965	$275	$350

K6120 Western
1960s. Jumbo flat-top, laminated maple body, pinless bridge, sunburst.

1962	$250	$325

K6130 Calypso
1960-1965. 15 1/2" flat-top with narrow waist, slotted headstock, natural.

1960-1965	$325	$400

K6533/K6535 Value Leader
1961-1965. Value Leader was the budget line of Kay, full body archtop, with 1 (K6533) or 2 (K6535) pickups, sunburst.

1961-1965	6533, 1 pickup	$425	$550
1961-1965	6535, 2 pickups	$475	$600

K6700/K6701 Barney Kessel Artist
1956-1960. Single-cut, 15 1/2" body, 1 (K6701) or 2 (K6700) pickups, Kelvinator headstock, sunburst or blond.

1956-1960	6700, 2 pickups	$3,000	$3,750
1956-1960	6701, 1 pickup	$2,750	$3,500

K6878 Style Leader
1966-1968. Full size (15.75) acoustic archtop, circle K logo on 'guard, sunburst.

1966-1968	$275	$350

K7000 Artist
1960-1965. Highest-end of Kay classical series, fan bracing, spruce top, maple back and sides.

1960-1965	$375	$475

K7010 Concerto
1960-1965. Entry level of Kay classical series.

1960-1965	$115	$150

K7010 Maestro
1960-1965. Middle level of Kay classical series.

1960-1965	$250	$325

K8110 Master
1957-1960. 17" master-size flat-top which was largest of the series, laminated construction.

1957-1960	$200	$250

K8127 Solo Special
1957-1965. Kay's professional grade flat-top, narrow waist jumbo, block markers.

1957-1965	$500	$625

K8700/K8701 Barney Kessel Jazz Special
1956-1960. Part of the Gold K Line, top-of-the-line model, 17" single-cut archtop, 1 (K8701) or 2 (K8700) pickups, 4 controls and toggle, Kelvinator headstock with white background, natural or shaded sunburst, Barney Kessel signature logo on acrylic scalloped 'guard, no signature logo on '60 model.

1956-1960	8700, 2 pickups	$3,000	$3,750
1956-1960	8701, 1 pickup	$2,625	$3,250

K8990/K8995 Upbeat
1956/1958-1960. Less expensive alternative to Barney Kessel Jazz Special, 2 (K8990) or 3 (K8995) pickups, Gold K Line, Kelvinator headstock, sunburst.

1956-1960	8990, 2 pickups	$1,625	$2,000
1958-1960	8995, 3 pickups	$1,750	$2,125

Wood Amplifying Guitar
1934. Engineered after Dobro/National metal resonator models except the resonator and chamber on this model are made of wood, small production.

1934	$1,875	$2,250

Kay Kraft
1927-1937. First brand name of the Kay Musical Instrument Company as it began its transition from Stromberg-Voisinet Company to Kay (see Kay for more info).

Recording King

1931-1937	$675	$850

Venetian Archtop
1930s. Unique Venetian cutaway body style, acoustic with round soundhole, flower-vine decal art on low bout.

1930s	$1,375	$1,750

KB
1989-present. Luthier Ken Bebensee builds his premium grade, custom, acoustic, and electric guitars and basses in North San Juan, California. He was in San Luis Obispo from '89-'01. He also builds mandolins.

Kel Kroydon (by Gibson)
1930-1933. Private branded budget level instruments made by Gibson. They also had mandolins and banjos. The name has been revived on a line of banjos by Tom Mirisola and made in Nashville.

KK-1
1932. 14 3/4" L-0 sytle body, colorful parrot stencils on body.

1932	$4,500	$6,000

Keller Custom Guitars
Professional grade, production/custom, solidbody guitars built by luthier Randall Keller in Mandan, North Dakota. He began in 1994.

Keller Guitars
1975-2022. Premium grade, production/custom, flat-tops made by luthier Michael L. Keller in Rochester, Minnesota.

1961 Kay K776 Jazz II
Jim Bame

1963 Kay K6535 Value Leader
Rivington Guitars

GUITARS

Kelly Guitar

Kiesel Jason Becker Yin Yang

MODEL		EXC. COND.	
YEAR	FEATURES	LOW	HIGH

Kelly Guitars

1968-present. Luthier Rick Kelly builds professional grade, custom, solidbody electric guitars in New York, New York.

Ken Franklin

2003-present. Luthier Ken Franklin builds his premium grade, production/custom, acoustic guitars and ukuleles in Ukiah, California.

Kendrick

1989-present. Premium grade, production/custom, solidbody guitars built in Texas. Founded by Gerald Weber in Pflugerville, Texas and currently located in Kempner, Texas. Mainly known for their handmade tube amps, Kendrick added guitars in '94 and also offers speakers and effects.

Kenneth Lawrence Instruments

1986-present. Luthier Kenneth Lawrence builds his premium grade, production/custom, electric solidbody and chambered guitars and basses in Arcata, California.

Kent

1961-1969. Imported from Japan by Buegeleisen and Jacobson of New York, New York. Manufacturers unknown but many early guitars and basses were made by Guyatone and Teisco.

Acoustic Flat-Top
1962-1969. Various models.

1962-1969		$200	$350

Acoustic/Electric
1962-1969. Various models.

1962-1969		$275	$400

Electric 12-String
1965-1969. Thinline electric, double pointy cutaways, 12 strings, slanted dual pickup, sunburst.

1965-1969		$450	$600

Semi-Hollow Electric
1962-1969. Thinline electric, offset double pointy cutaways, slanted dual pickups, various colors.

1962-1969		$450	$600

Solidbody Electric
1962-1969. Models include Polaris I, II and III, Lido, Copa and Videocaster.

1962-1969	Common model	$275	$400
1962-1969	Rare model	$450	$600

Kevin Ryan Guitars

1989-present. Premium grade, custom, flattops built by luthier Kevin Ryan in Westminster, California.

KeyKord

Ca. 1929-mid 1930s. Keykord offered guitars, ukes and banjos that had a push-button mechanism mounted over the fingerboard that "fin gered" a different chord for each button. The guitars were built by Chicago's Stromberg-Voisinet (Kay).

MODEL		EXC. COND.	
YEAR	FEATURES	LOW	HIGH

Tenor
1920s-1930s. Venetian mahogany body, 4-string, pearloid headstock overlay.

1920s-30s		$550	$700

Kiesel

1946-present. Founded by Lowell C. Kiesel in '46. Refer to Carvin listing for more info regarding the early years. Prior to his death in 2009, L.C. had turned the business over to his sons and it was located in several different California cities over the years.

In 2015, son Mark and grandson Jeff Kiesel began the new independent Kiesel Custom Guitars. They build professional and premium grade, acoustic and electric guitars and basses in Escondido, California.

Kimbara

1970s-1980s. Japanese line of guitars and basses mainly imported into the U.K. Models were the same as the Fresher brand.

Kimberly

Late-1960s-early-1970s. Private branded import made in the same Japanese factory as Teisco. They also made basses.

Longhorn
1960s. S-style, deep double-cut, 2 pickups.

1960s		$500	$650

May Queen
1960s. Same as Teisco May Queen with Kimberly script logo on headstock and May Queen Teisco on the 'guard.

1960s		$600	$800

Kinal

1969-present. Production/custom, professional and premium grade, solid body electric and archtop guitars and basses built and imported by luthier Michael Kinal in Vancouver, British Columbia.

King's Stone

1960s. Guitar brand exported by Japan's Hoshino (Ibanez).

Kingsley

1960s. Early Japanese imports, Teisco-made.

Soldibody Electric
1960s. Four pickups with tremolo.

1960s		$350	$500

Kingslight Guitars

1980-2015. Luthier John Kingslight built his premium grade, custom/production, steel string guitars and basses in Portage, Michigan (in Taos, New Mexico for '80-'83).

Kingston

Ca. 1958-1967. Guitars and basses imported from Japan by Jack Westheimer and Westheimer Importing Corporation of Chicago, Illinois. Early

MODEL YEAR	FEATURES	EXC. COND. LOW	HIGH

examples made by Guyotone and Teisco. They also offered mandolins and banjos.

Electric

1958-1967. Various models include B-1, soldibody, 1 pickup; B-2T/B-3T/B-4T, solidbodies, 2/3/4 pickups and tremolo; SA-27, thin hollowbody, 2 pickups, tremolo.

1958-1967	Common model	$350	$450
1958-1967	Rare model	$600	$850

Kinscherff Guitars

1990-present. Luthier Jamie Kinscherff builds his premium grade, production/custom, flat-top guitars in Austin, Texas.

Kleartone

1930s. Private brand made by Regal and/or Gibson.

Small Flat-Top

1930s		$550	$750

Klein Acoustic Guitars

First produced in 1972, luthiers Steve Klein and Steven Kauffman build their production/custom, premium and presentation grade flat-tops and basses outside Sonoma, California.

Klein Electric Guitars

1988-2007. Steve Klein added electrics to his line in '88. In '95, he sold the electric part of his business to Lorenzo German, who continued to produce professional grade, production/custom, solidbody guitars and basses in Linden, California.

K-Line Guitars

2005-present. Professional grade, production/custom, T-style and S-style guitars and basses built by luthier Chris Kroenlein in St. Louis, Missouri. He also builds basses.

Klira

1887-1980s. Founded by Johannes Klira in Schoenbach, Germany, mainly made violins, but added guitars in the 1950s. The guitars of the '50s and '60s were original designs, but by the '70s most models were similar to popular American models. The guitars of the '50s and '60s were aimed at the budget market, but workmanship improved with the '70s models. They also made basses.

Electric

1950s-60s	Common model	$450	$800
1950s-60s	Rare model	$850	$1,500

Knaggs

2010-present. Luthiers Joseph Knaggs and Peter Wolf build premium and presentation grade, production/custom, acoustic and electric guitars and basses in Greensboro, Maryland.

Knox

Early-mid-1960s. Budget grade guitars imported from Japan, script Knox logo on headstock.

Electric Solidbody

1960s. Student models, 2 pickups, push buttons.

1960s	Various models	$375	$500

Knutsen

1890s-1920s. Luthier Chris J. Knutsen of Tacoma and Seattle, Washington, experimented with and perfected Hawaiian and harp guitar models. He moved to Los Angeles, California around 1916. He also made steels, mandolins and ukes. Dealers state the glue used on Knutsen instruments is prone to fail and instruments may need repair.

Convertible

1909-1914. Flat-top model with adjustable neck angle that allowed for a convertible Hawaiian or Spanish setup.

1909-1914		$4,500	$5,500

Harp Guitar

1900s. Normally 11 strings with fancy purfling and trim.

1900-1910		$4,000	$5,000

Knutson Luthiery

1981-present. Professional and premium grade, custom, archtop and flat-top guitars built by luthier John Knutson in Forestville, California. He also builds basses, lap steels and mandolins.

Kohno

1960-present. Luthier Masaru Kohno built his classical guitars in Tokyo, Japan. When he died in '98, production was taken over by his nephew, Masaki Sakurai.

Koll

1990-present. Professional and premium grade, custom/production, solidbody, chambered, and archtop guitars and basses built by luthier Saul Koll, originally in Long Beach, California, and since '93, in Portland, Oregon.

Kona

1910s-1920s. Acoustic Hawaiian guitars sold by C.S. Delano and others, with later models made by the Herman Weissenborn Co. Weissenborn appointments are in line with style number, with thicker body and solid neck construction. Kona name is currently used on an import line offered by M&M Merchandisers.

Style 2

1927-1928		$2,750	$3,500

Style 3

1920s	Koa	$3,750	$5,000

Style 4

1920s	Hawaiian	$3,750	$5,000
1920s	Spanish	$3,750	$5,000

Knaggs Chena Tier 2

Knutson Luthiery Classic

Kramer the 84

1978 Kramer 450-G Deluxe

Carter Vintage Guitars

MODEL YEAR	FEATURES	EXC. COND. LOW	HIGH

Kona Guitar Company

2000-present. Located in Fort Worth, Texas, Kona imports budget and intermediate grade, production, nylon and steel string acoustic and solid and semi-hollow body electric guitars and basses. They also offer amps, mandolins and ukes.

Koontz

1970-late 1980s. Luthier Sam Koontz started building custom guitars in the late '50s. Starting in '66 Koontz, who was associated with Harptone guitars, built guitars for Standel. In '70, he opened his own shop in Linden, New Jersey, building a variety of custom guitars. Koontz died in the late '80s. His guitars varied greatly and should be valued on a case-by-case basis.

Kopp String Instruments

Located in Republic, Ohio from 2000-2004, luthier Denny Kopp presently builds his professional and premium grade, production/custom, semi-hollow archtop electric and hand-carved archtop jazz guitars in Catawba Island, Ohio. He started in 2000.

Kopy Kat

1970s. Budget copy-era solidbody, semi-hollow body and acoustic guitars imported from Japan. They also made basses and mandolins.

Acoustic

1970s	J-200 copy	$250	$325

Kragenbrink

Premium grade, production/custom, steel string acoustic guitars built by luthier Lance Kragenbrink in Vandercook Lake, Michigan, starting in the year 2001.

Kramer

1976-1990, 1995-present. Currently Kramer offers budget and intermediate grade, production, imported acoustic, acoustic/electric, semi-hollow and solidbody guitars. They also offer basses, amps, and effects.

Founded by New York music retailer Dennis Berardi, ex-Travis Bean partner Gary Kramer and ex-Norlin executive Peter LaPlaca. Initial financing provided by real estate developer Henry Vaccaro. Parent company named BKL Corporation (Berardi, Kramer, LaPlaca), located in Neptune City, New Jersey. The first guitars were designed by Berardi and luthier Phil Petillo and featured aluminum necks with wooden inserts on the back to give them a wooden feel. Guitar production commenced in late-'76. Control passed to Guitar Center of Los Angeles for '79-'82, which recommended a switch to more economical wood necks. Most wooden necks from Kramer's Golden Era (1981-1986) we made in Japan by ESP and shipped to the U.S.A. for final guitar assembly. Aluminum necks were phased out during the early-'80s and were last produced in '85. In '84 they added their first import models, the Japanese-

MODEL YEAR	FEATURES	EXC. COND. LOW	HIGH

made Focus line, followed by the Korean-made Striker line. By 1986 Kramer was the top American electric guitarmaker. In '89, a new investment group was brought in with James Liati as president, hoping for access to Russian market, but the company went out of business in late-'90. In '95 Henry Vaccaro and new partners revived the company and designed several new guitars in conjunction with Phil Petillo. However, in '97 the Kramer brand was sold to Gibson. In '98, Henry Vaccaro released his new line of aluminum-core neck, split headstock guitars under the Vacarro brand. From 1997 to 2009, sales of Kramer instruments were only through Gibson's MusicYo website. In 2010, Gibson began to distribute the brand through traditional music retail channels with new issues and 1980s legacy models. Non-U.S.-made models include the following lines: Aerostar, Ferrington, Focus, Hundred (post-'85 made with 3 digits in the 100-900), Showster, Striker, Thousand (post-'85 made with 4 digits in the 1000-9000), XL (except XL-5 made in '80s).

Serial numbers for import models include:

Two alpha followed by 4 numbers: for example AA2341 with any assortment of letters and numbers.

One alpha followed by 5 numbers: for example B23412.

Five numbers: for example 23412.

Model number preceding numbers: for example XL1-03205.

The notation "Kramer, Neptune, NJ" does indicate U.S.A.-made production.

Most post-'85 Kramers were ESP Japanese-made guitars. American Series were ESP Japanese components that were assembled in the U.S.

The vintage/used market makes value distinctions between U.S.-made and import models.

Headstock and logo shape can help identify U.S. versus imports as follows:

Traditional or Classic headstock with capital K as Kramer: U.S.A. '81-'84.

Banana (soft edges) headstock with all caps KRAMER: U.S.A. American Series '84-'86.

Pointy (sharp cut) headstock with all caps KRAMER: U.S.A. American Series '86-'87.

Pointy (sharp cut) headstock with downsized letters Kramer plus American decal: U.S.A. American Series '87-'94.

Pointy (sharp cut) headstock with downsized letters Kramer but without American decal, is an import.

1984 Reissue

2003-2007. Made in the U.S., based on EVH's Kramer, single Gibson humbucker, Rose tremolo, various colors.

2003-2007		$650	$850

The 84 (Original Collection)

2019-present. Alder body, maple neck, Seymour Duncan pickup, Floyd Rose trem, various colors with gloss finish.

2019-2023		$600	$800

MODEL YEAR	FEATURES	EXC. COND. LOW	HIGH

250-G Special
1977-1979. Offset double-cut, tropical woods, aluminum neck, dot markers, 2 pickups.

1977-1979		$800	$1,125

350-G Standard
1976-1979. Offset double-cut, tropical woods, aluminum neck, tuning fork headstock, ebonol 'board, zero fret, 2 single coils, dot inlays. The 350 and 450 were Kramer's first models.

1976-1979		$1,250	$1,750

450-G Deluxe
1976-1980. Like 350-G, but with block inlays, 2 humbuckers. Became the 450G Deluxe in late '77 with dot inlays.

1976-1980		$1,250	$1,750

650-G Artist
1977-1980. Aluminum neck, ebonol 'board, double-cut solidbody, 2 humbuckers.

1977-1980		$1,500	$2,000

Assault 220FR/Assault 220 (Modern Collection)
2010-present. Mahogany body, 2 humbucker pickups, Floyd Rose trem, white or black gloss finish. FR dropped from name in '20.

2010-2019	FR	$400	$550
2020-2023		$300	$400

Assault Plus (Modern Collection)
2020-present. Mahogany body with flame maple veneer top, reverse headstock, 2 Seymour Duncan pickups, Floyd Rose trem, Bengal Burst or Trans Purple Burst.

2020		$500	$650

Baretta
1984-1990. Offset double-cut, banana six-on-a-side headstock, 1 pickup, Floyd Rose tremolo, black hardware, U.S.A.-made.

1984-1985		$2,500	$3,500
1986-1987		$2,000	$2,500
1988-1990	Standard opaque	$850	$1,250
1988-1990	With graphics	$1,000	$1,500
1988-1990	More desirable graphics	$4,000	$6,000
1990	Baretta III hybrid	$750	$1,000

Baretta '85 Reissue
2006. Made in the U.S., based on 1985 banana headstock model, Rose tremolo.

2006		$800	$1,125

Baretta II/Soloist
1986-1990. Soloist sleek body with pointed cutaway horns.

1986-1990		$800	$1,125

Baretta (Original Collection)
2020-present. Maple body and neck, Seymour Duncan pickup, Floyd Rose trem, Pewter Gray or Ruby Red.

2020-2023		$500	$650

Baretta Special (Original Collection)
2020-present. Mahogany body, maple neck, Alnico humbucker pickup, traditional trem, gloss finish in Candy Blue, Ruby Red or Purple.

2020-2023		$130	$175

Classic Series
1986-1987. Solidbody copies of the famous Southern California builder, including offset contoured double-cut (Classic I) and slab body single-cut designs (Classic II and Classic III).

1986-1987	Classic I	$600	$800
1986-1987	Classic II	$850	$1,250
1986-1987	Classic III	$850	$1,250

Condor
1985-1986. Futuristic 4-point body with large upper bass horn and lower treble horn.

1985-1986		$850	$1,250

DMZ Custom Series
1978-1981. Solidbody double-cut with larger upper horn, bolt-on aluminum T-neck, slot headstock, models include the 1000 (super distortion humbuckers), 2000 (dual-sound humbuckers), 3000 (3 SDS single-coils), 6000 (dual-sound humbuckers, active DBL).

1978-1981	DMZ-1000	$1,500	$2,500
1978-1981	DMZ-2000	$1,500	$2,500
1978-1981	DMZ-3000	$1,750	$2,500
1978-1981	DMZ-6000	$2,000	$3,000

Duke Custom/Standard
1981-1982. Headless aluminum neck, 22-fret neck, 1 pickup, Floyd Rose tremolo.

1981-1982		$550	$750

Duke Special
1982-1985. Headless aluminum neck, two pickups, tuners on body.

1982-1985		$550	$750

Elliot Easton Pro I
1987-1988. Designed by Elliot Easton, offset double-cut, six-on-a-side headstock, Floyd Rose tremolo, 2 single-coils and 1 humbucker.

1987-1988		$900	$1,250

Elliot Easton Pro II
1987-1988. Same as Pro I, but with fixed-bridge tailpiece, 2 single-coils.

1987-1988		$800	$1,125

Ferrington
1985-1990. Acoustic-electric, offered in single- and double-cut, bolt-on electric-style neck, transducers, made in Korea.

1985-1990		$500	$650

Floyd Rose Signature Edition
1983-1984. Four pointed-bout body with deep cutawaybelow tremolo assembly, Floyd Rose vibrato system.

1983-1984		$900	$1,125

Focus/F Series (Import)
1983-1989. Kramer introduced the Focus series as import copies of their American-made models like the Pacer, Baretta, Vanguard (Rhoads-V), and Voyager (star body). Model numbers were 1000-6000, plus the Focus Classic I, II, and III. Most models were offset, double-cut solidbodies. In '87 the Focus line was renamed the F-Series. In '88 a neck-through body design, which is noted as NT, was introduced for a short time. The Classic series was offered with over a dozen color options.

1983-1989	Various models	$350	$900

1979 Kramer DMZ-3000

Late-'80s Kramer Ferrington
Imaged by Heritage Auctions, HA.com

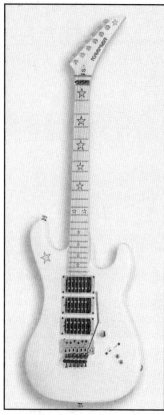

Kramer Jersey Star

1988 Kramer Nightswan

Jamie Wetsch

MODEL YEAR	FEATURES	EXC. COND. LOW	HIGH

Gene Simmons Axe
1980-1981. Axe-shaped guitar, aluminum neck, 1 humbucker, slot headstock, stop tailpiece, 25 were made.

| 1980-1981 | | $6,000 | $8,000 |

Gorky Park (Import)
1986-1989. Triangular balalaika, bolt-on maple neck, pointy droopy six-on-a-side headstock, 1 pickup, Floyd Rose tremolo, red with iron sickle graphics, tribute to Russian rock, reissued in late-'90s.

| 1986-1989 | | $500 | $650 |

Hundred Series
1988-1990. Import budget line, most with offset double-cut 7/8th solidbody.

| 1988-1990 | Various models | $200 | $400 |

Jersey Star
2004-2007. A reissue of the Richie Sambora model.

| 2004-2007 | | $900 | $1,250 |

Jersey Star (Original Collection)
2020-present. Alder body, maple neck, mother-of-pearl Jersey Star logo, 3 pickups, Floyd Rose trem, Candy Apple Red or Alpine White.

| 2020 | | $750 | $1,000 |

Liberty '86 Series
1986-1987. Offset double cut arched-top solidbody, pointy head, 2 humbuckers, black, white or flame-maple bound body.

| 1986-1987 | Black or white | $3,500 | $4,500 |
| 1986-1987 | Flame maple | $4,000 | $5,000 |

Metalist/Showster Series
1989-1990. Korean-made offset double-cut solidbody, metal trim in body design, pointy droopy six-on-a-side headstock, various pickup options, Floyd Rose.

| 1989-1990 | | $550 | $750 |

Night Rider
2000-2007. Inexpensive import double-cut semi-hollow, 2 humbuckers.

| 2000-2007 | | $100 | $150 |

Nightswan
1987-1990. Offset double-cut, six-on-a-side headstock, 2 Duncan humbuckers, Floyd Rose tremolo, blue metallic.

1987-1990		$1,625	$2,250
1987-1990	Custom color/ finish	$2,000	$3,000
1987-1990	More desirable graphics	$4,000	$10,000

Nightswan (Original Collection)
2020-present. Mahogany body, maple neck, 2 pickups, Floyd Rose trem, jet black metallic, vintage white with Aztec graphic or black with blue polka dots.

| 2020-2023 | | $600 | $750 |

Night-V (Modern Collection)
2020-present. Mahogany body, maple neck, 2 pickups, Floyd Rose trem, satin black finish.

| 2020-2023 | | $300 | $400 |

Night-V Plus (Modern Collection)
2020-present. Mahogany body, maple neck, 2 pickups, Floyd Rose trem, Alpine white.

| 2020-2023 | | $500 | $650 |

MODEL YEAR	FEATURES	EXC. COND. LOW	HIGH

Pacer (Original Collection)
2020-present. Double-cut offset maple body, 2 Seymour Duncan pickups, Floyd Rose trem, pearl white or orange tiger finish.

| 2020-2023 | | $550 | $750 |

Pacer Carrera
1982-1986. Offset double-cut, wood neck, classic six-on-a-side headstock, ebonized 22-fret rosewood 'board, 2 pickups, 3-way switch, black Rockinger, restyled body with Floyd Rose in '83, banana headstock in '85.

| 1982-1985 | | $925 | $1,250 |
| 1986 | | $825 | $1,125 |

Pacer Custom
1983-1987. Offset double-cut, bolt-on maple neck with maple cap, 2 humbuckers, translucent finish, gold hardware.

| 1983-1985 | | $1,375 | $1,750 |
| 1986-1987 | | $950 | $1,250 |

Pacer Custom I
1987-1989. Custom with slanted hum and 2 single coils, various colors.

| 1987-1989 | | $950 | $1,250 |

Pacer Custom II
1987-1989. Custom with hum and 2 single coils, various colors.

| 1987-1989 | | $950 | $1,250 |

Pacer Deluxe
1983-1987. Offset double-cut, six-on-a-side headstock, hum/single/single pickups, bolt-on maple neck.

| 1983-1985 | | $1,000 | $1,500 |
| 1986-1987 | | $950 | $1,250 |

Pacer Imperial
1981-1989. Offset double cut, bolt-on maple neck with maple cap, 2 humbuckers.

| 1981-1985 | | $1,000 | $1,500 |
| 1986-1989 | | $950 | $1,250 |

Pacer Special
1981-1985. Various headstocks, 1 humbucker pickup, EVH trem.

| 1981-1985 | | $1,000 | $1,500 |

The Pacer
1982-1985. Pacer with 3 single coils.

| 1982-1985 | | $1,000 | $1,500 |

Paul Dean
1986-1988. Offset double cut, neck-thru, hum/single/single pickups, droopy pointy head.

| 1986-1988 | | $950 | $1,250 |

ProAxe (U.S.A.)
1989-1990. U.S.A.-made, offset double-cut, sharp pointy headstock, dot markers, 2 or 3 pickups, smaller 7/8ths size body, 3 models offered with slightly different pickup options. The model was discontinued when Kramer went out of business in 1990.

1989-1990	Deluxe	$1,250	$1,750
1989-1990	Special	$1,250	$1,750
1989-1990	Standard	$1,250	$1,750

Richie Sambora
1987-1989. Designed by Sambora, mahogany offset double-cut, maple neck, pointy droopy 6-on-a-side headstock, gold hardware, Floyd Rose, 3 pickups, 2 coil-taps.

| 1987-1989 | | $1,500 | $2,000 |

The *Vintage Guitar Price Guide* shows values for all-original, excellent condition instruments and, where applicable, with original case.

MODEL YEAR	FEATURES	EXC. COND. LOW	HIGH

Ripley RSG-1

1984-1987. Offset double-cut, banana six-on-a-side headstock, 22 frets, hexophonic humbucking pickups, panpots, dual volume, Floyd Rose tremolo, black hardware, stereo output, pointy droopy headstock in '87.

| 1984-1985 | | $1,000 | $1,500 |
| 1986-1987 | | $900 | $1,250 |

Savant/Showster Series

1989-1990. Offset double-cut solidbody, pointy headstock, various pickup options.

| 1989-1990 | Various models | $900 | $1,250 |

SM-1 (Original Collection)

2020-present. Double-cut mahogany body, 3 pickups, Floyd Rose trem, gloss finish in Orange Crush, Candy Blue or Maximum Steel.

| 2020-2023 | | $750 | $1,000 |

Stagemaster Series

1983-1987. Offset double-cut neck-thru solidbody models, smaller 7/8th body.

| 1983-1987 | Various models | $1,000 | $3,500 |

Striker Series

1984-1989. Offset double-cut, various pickup options, series included Striker 100, 200, 300, 400, 600 and 700 Bass.

| 1984-1989 | Various models | $250 | $400 |

Sustainer

1989. Offset double-cut solidbody, reverse pointy headstock, Floyd Rose tremolo.

| 1989 | | $1,000 | $1,500 |

Triax

1986. Rare, odd shape, 2 humbuckers, Floyd Rose trem, Pearlescent Red.

| 1986 | | $3,000 | $4,000 |

Vanguard Series

1981-1986. U.S.-made or American Series (assembled in U.S.). V shape, 1 humbucker, aluminum (Special '81-'83) or wood (Custom '81-'83) neck. Added for '83-'84 were the Imperial (wood neck, 2 humbuckers) and the Headless (alum neck, 1 humbucker). For '85-'86, the body was modified to a Jackson Randy Rhoads style V body, with a banana headstock and 2 humbuckers. In '99 this last design was revived as an import.

| 1981-1986 | Various models | $950 | $1,500 |

Vanguard (Reissue)

1999-2014. Pointy headstock, 2 humbuckers, licensed Floyd Rose.

| 1999-2014 | | $450 | $600 |

Voyager

1982-1985. Wood neck, classic headstock, rosewood 'board, 1 pickup (2 optional), Floyd Rose tremolo, black.

| 1982-1985 | | $1,250 | $1,625 |

XKG-10

1980-1981. Aluminum neck, V-shaped body.

| 1980-1981 | | $1,000 | $1,500 |

XKG-20

1980-1981. More traditional double-cut body with small horns.

| 1980-1981 | | $1,000 | $1,500 |

XL Series

1980-1981, 1987-1990. The early-'80s U.S.-made models had aluminum necks and were completely different than the late-'80s wood neck models, which were inexpensive imports.

| 1980-1981 | Aluminum neck | $1,000 | $1,500 |
| 1987-1990 | Wood neck | $300 | $400 |

ZX Aero Star Series

1986-1989. Offset double-cut solidbodies, pointy six-on-a-side headstock. Models include the 1 humbucker ZX-10, 2 humbucker ZX-20, 3 single coil ZX-30, and hum/single/single ZX-30H.

| 1986-1989 | | $150 | $250 |

Kramer-Harrison, William

Luthier William Kramer-Harrison began building in 1977, premium grade, custom, classical, and flat-top guitars in Kingston, New York.

KSM

Luthier Kevin S. Moore, starting in 1988, premium grade, custom/production, solidbody electric guitars in Logan, Utah.

Kubicki

1973-present. Kubicki is best known for their Factor basses but did offer a few guitar models in the early '80s. See Bass section for more company info.

Kustom

1968-present. Founded by Bud Ross in Chanute, Kansas, and best known for the tuck-and-roll amps, Kustom also offered guitars from '68 to '69. See Amp section for more company info.

Electric Hollowbody

1968-1969. Hollowed-out 2-part bodies; includes the K200A (humbucker, Bigsby), the K200B (single-coils, trapeze tailpiece), and the K200C (less fancy tuners), various colors.

| 1968-1969 | | $1,375 | $1,750 |

Kwasnycia Guitars

1997-present. Production/custom, premium grade, acoustic guitars built by luthier Dennis Kwasnycia in Chatham, Ontario.

Kyle, Doug

Premium grade, custom, Selmer-style guitars made by luthier Doug Kyle in the U.K., starting in 1990.

L Benito

Professional grade, steel and nylon string acoustics from luthier Lito Benito and built in Chile starting in 2001.

La Baye

1967. Designed by Dan Helland in Green Bay, Wisconsin and built by the Holman-Woodell factory in Neodesha, Kansas. Introduced at NAMM and folded when no orders came in. Only 45 prototypes were made. A few may have been sold later as 21st Century. They also had basses.

Kramer Night V

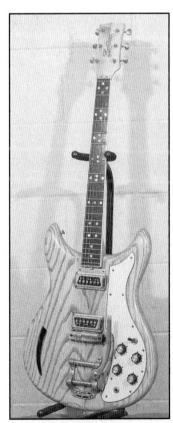

1968 Kustom K200A

Tom Pfeifer

GUITARS

Lace Cybercaster Standard

1987 Langejans 12-string

Rivington Guitars

MODEL		EXC. COND.	
YEAR	FEATURES	LOW	HIGH

2x4 6-String
1967. Narrow plank body, controls on top, 2 pickups, tremolo, 12-string version was also made.

1967		$2,500	$3,500

La Mancha
Professional and premium grade, production/custom, classical guitars made in Mexico under the supervision of Kenny Hill and Gil Carnal and distributed by Jerry Roberts of Nashville, Tennessee. They began in 1996.

La Patrie
Production, classical guitars. Founded by luthier Robert Godin, who also has the Norman, Godin, Seagull, and Patrick & Simon brands of instruments.

La Scala
Ca. 1920s-1930s. La Scala was another brand of the Oscar Schmidt Company of New Jersey, and was used on guitars, banjos, and mandolins. These were often the fanciest of the Schmidt instruments. Schmidt made the guitars and mandolins; the banjos were made by Rettberg & Lang.

Lace Music Products
1979-present. Intermediate and professional, production, electric guitars from Lace Music Products of Cypress, California, a division of Actodyne General Inc. which was founded by Don Lace Sr., inventor of the Lace Sensor Pickup. In '96, Lace added amplifiers, followed by guitars in 2001 and Rat Fink guitars in '02.

Lacey Guitars
1974-present. Luthier Mark Lacey builds his premium and presentation archtops and flat-tops in Nashville, Tennessee.

Lado
1973-present. Founded by Joe Kovacic, Lado builds professional and premium grade, production/custom, solidbody guitars and basses in Lindsay, Ontario. Some model lines are branded J. K. Lado.

Lafayette
Ca. 1963-1967. Sold through Lafayette Electronics catalogs. Early Japanese-made guitars and basses from pre-copy era, generally shorter scale beginner instruments. Many made by Guyatone, some possibly by Teisco.
Electric
1963-1967. Various models.

1963-1967		$550	$750

Laguna
2008-present. Guitar Center private label, budget and intermediate grade, production, imported electric and acoustic guitars price range.

MODEL		EXC. COND.	
YEAR	FEATURES	LOW	HIGH

Lakeside (Lyon & Healy)
Early-1900s. Mainly catalog sales of guitars and mandolins from the Chicago maker. Marketed as a less expensive alternative to the Lyon & Healy Washburn product line.
Harp Guitar
Early-1900s. Spruce top, rosewood finished birch back and sides, two 6-string necks with standard tuners, 1 neck is fretless without dot markers, rectangular bridge.

1900s		$2,250	$3,000

Parlor
Early-1900s. Spruce top, oak back and sides, cedar neck.

1900s		$600	$800

Lakewood
1986-present. Luthier Martin Seeliger builds his professional and premium grade, production/custom, steel and nylon string guitars in Giessen, Germany. He has also built mandolins.

Langdon Guitars
Luthier Jeff Langdon, began in 1997, builds professional and premium grade, production/custom, flat-top, archtop, and solidbody guitars in Eureka, California.

Langejans Guitars
1971-2016. Premium grade, production/custom, flat-top, 12-string, and classical guitars built by luthier Delwyn Langejans in Holland, Michigan. He retired in '16.

Larrivee
1968-present. Professional and premium grade, production/custom, acoustic, acoustic/electric, and classical guitars built in Vancouver, British Columbia and, since '01, in Oxnard, California. They also offered several acoustic and a few electric basses over the years as well as ukes. Founded by Jean Larrivee, who apprenticed under Edgar Monch in Toronto. He built classical guitars in his home from '68-'70 and built his first steel string guitar in '71. Moved company to Victoria, BC in '77 and to Vancouver in '82. In '83, he began building solidbody electric guitars until '89, when focus again returned to acoustics.

Up to 2002, Larrivee used the following model designations: 05 Mahogany Standard, 09 Rosewood Standard, 10 Deluxe, 19 Special, 50 & 60 Standard (unique inlay), 70 Deluxe, and 72 Presentation. Starting in '03 designations used are: 01 Parlor, 03 Standard, 05 Select Mahogany, 09 Rosewood Artist, 10 Rosewood Deluxe, 19 California Anniv. Special Edition Series, 50 Traditional Series, 60 Traditional Series, E = Electric, R = Rosewood.

Larrivee also offers Limited Edition, Custom Shop, and Custom variations of standard models although the model name is the same as the standard model. These Custom models are worth more than the values shown.

MODEL YEAR	FEATURES	EXC. COND. LOW	HIGH
0-60			
2005. Small fancy rosewood.			
2005		$2,250	$3,000
00-05			
1996. 14.25", all mahogany.			
1996		$1,375	$1,750
00-09			
2000s		$1,500	$2,000
00-10			
2000s. 00-size 14" lower bout, spruce top, rosewood back and sides, gloss finish.			
2000s		$1,750	$2,250
000-40R			
2014-present. Legacy series, sitka spruce top, Indian rosewood back and sides, satin finish.			
2014-2023		$1,375	$1,750
000-50			
2008-present. Mahogany back and sides.			
2008-2023		$1,625	$2,500
000-60			
2006-present. Traditional Series, Indian rosewood.			
2006-2023		$1,750	$2,250
000-60K			
Traditional Series, figured koa.			
2012		$3,000	$4,000
C-10 Deluxe			
Late-1980s-1990s. Sitka spruce top, Indian rosewood back and sides, sharp cutaway, fancy binding.			
1980s		$2,000	$2,500
C-72 Presentation			
1990s. Spruce top, Indian rosewood back and sides, non-cut Style D, ultra-fancy abalone and pearl hand-engraved headstock.			
1990s	Jester headstock	$3,500	$4,500
C-72 Presentation Cutaway			
1990s. Spruce top, Indian rosewood back and sides, sharp cutaway, ultra-fancy abalone and pearl hand-engraved headstock.			
1990s	Mermaid headstock	$3,500	$4,500
D-02/D-02E			
1998-2013. Sitka spruce top, mahogany back and sides, satin finish, E with electronics.			
1998-2013		$650	$850
D-03E			
2008-present. Solid mahogany back and sides, spruce top, satin finish, electronics.			
2008-2023		$850	$1,250
D-03R			
2002-present. Rosewood.			
2002-2023		$1,125	$1,625
D-03RE			
2010-present. Rosewood, on-board electronics.			
2010-2023		$1,125	$1,625
DV-03K			
Venetian cutaway, koa back and sides.			
2000s		$1,875	$2,250
D-04E			
2000-2004, 2013-2014. Mahogany, on-board electronics.			
2000-2014		$1,375	$1,750

MODEL YEAR	FEATURES	EXC. COND. LOW	HIGH
D-05-12E			
2008-2013	12 strings	$1,375	$1,750
D-09			
2001-present. Rosewood, spruce top, gloss finish.			
2001-2012	Indian or walnut	$1,750	$2,250
2001-2023	Brazilian	$3,500	$4,500
D-10 Deluxe			
1995-present. Sitka spruce top, Indian rosewood back and sides, abalone top and sound hole trim.			
1995-2023		$2,250	$3,000
D-50			
2003-present. Traditional Series, mahogany back and sides.			
2003-2023		$1,750	$2,250
D-60			
2003-present. Brazilian or Indian rosewood back and sides.			
2000s	Brazilian	$3,500	$4,500
2003-2023	Indian	$1,750	$2,250
D-70			
1992-1995. Horsehead headstock inlay, ebony 'board, rosewood back and sides.			
1992-1995		$2,250	$3,000
D-Style Classical			
1970s. Rosewood body, unicorn inlays.			
1970s		$2,000	$2,500
J-05-12			
2000s. Jumbo acoustic-electric 12-string, spruce top, mahogany back and sides.			
2000s		$1,750	$2,250
J-09			
2002-2009. Jumbo, rosewood back and sides, Sitka spruce top.			
2002-2009		$1,875	$2,500
J-09-12K			
Jumbo 12-string, rosewood back and sides.			
2000s		$2,500	$3,000
J-70			
1990s. Jumbo, Sitka spruce top, solid Indian rosewood back and sides, presentation grade fancy appointments, limited production.			
1990s		$2,250	$3,000
JV-05 Mahogany Standard			
Mahogany back and sides, Venetian cutaway.			
2000s		$1,500	$2,000
L Series			
1980s-present. Various models, mahogany or rosewood (R) back and sides, some with on-board electronics (E).			
1990s	L-50	$1,875	$2,500
1990s-2023	L-72 (Presentation)	$3,500	$4,500
2000s	L-30 (Classical)	$1,500	$2,000
L-0 Standard Series			
1983-present. Various models, 6- or 12-string, mahogany, rosewood (R) or Koa (K), some with on-board electronics (E), satin or gloss finish.			
1983-2023	L-03/03E	$950	$1,250
1983-2023	L-05/05E	$1,500	$2,000
1983-2023	L-09/09E	$1,500	$2,000
2000s	L-01	$775	$1,000
2000s	L-04	$1,000	$1,375

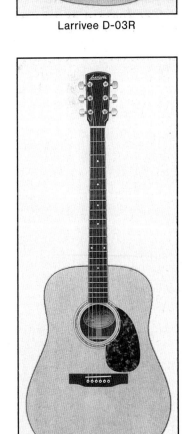

Larrivee D-03R

Larrivee D-09

Larrivee OM-10
Tim Page

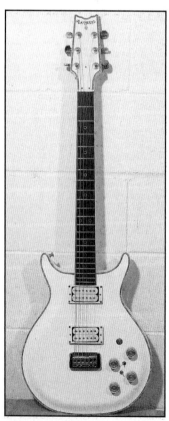

1985 Lotus
Tom Pfeifer

MODEL YEAR	FEATURES	EXC. COND. LOW	HIGH
2008-2012	L-03K, Koa	$1,375	$1,750
2008-2023	L-03R, rosewood	$1,125	$1,500
2008-2023	L-03R-12, 12-string	$975	$1,250
2008-2023	L-03RE	$1,125	$1,500

LS Series
1990s-2011. Various models.

1990s-2011	LS-05, mahogany	$1,500	$2,000
2008-2011	LS-03R, rosewood	$1,500	$2,000

LV Series
1990s-present. Various models.

1990s-2023	LV-05/05E	$1,625	$2,125
1990s-2023	LV-09/09E	$1,750	$2,250
2002	LV-19 Special Vine	$4,000	$5,500
2007-2023	LV-03/03E	$1,500	$2,000
2007-2023	LV-10/10E	$2,750	$3,500

OM Series
1990s-present. Various models.

1990-2000s	OM-02	$1,125	$1,500
1990-2000s	OM-09R, rosewood	$1,625	$2,125
1990s-2023	OM-03/03E	$1,250	$1,625
1990s-2023	OM-10 Deluxe	$2,500	$3,250
1999-2023	OM-05/05E	$1,625	$2,125
2000-2023	OM-03R, rosewood	$1,250	$1,625
2000-2023	OM-40/40E	$1,875	$2,500
2000-2023	OM-50/50E	$1,625	$2,125
2000s	OM-09K, Koa	$2,250	$3,000
2008-2023	OM-60/60E	$1,750	$2,250

OMV Series
1990s-present. Various models.

2000s-2023	OMV-09/09E	$1,625	$2,125
2000s-2023	OMV-50/50E	$2,125	$2,750
2009-2023	OMV-60/60E	$2,250	$3,000

Parlor Walnut
Early-2000s. Spruce top, solid walnut back and sides.

2000s		$825	$1,125

PV Series
2007-present. Various Parlor models.

2007	PV-09, maple	$1,625	$2,125
2007-2023	PV-09/09E, rosewood	$3,250	$4,250

RS-2 Ventura
2010-2015. Mahogany solidbody, rosewood 'board, 1 or 2 pickups, satin finish various colors.

2010-2015		$1,125	$1,500

RS-4 CM Carved Top
1988-1989. Carved top solidbody, curly maple top, single-single-humbucker pickups, sunburst or trans-lucent finishes.

1988-1989		$1,625	$2,125

SD Series
2008-present. Various models.

2008-2012	SD-03R	$1,625	$2,125
2008-2023	SD-50/50E	$2,125	$2,750
2008-2023	SD-60/60E	$1,750	$2,250

Larry Alan Guitars

2003-present. Professional and premium grade, production/custom, acoustic and electric guitars and basses, built by luthier Larry Alan Daft in Lansing, Michigan. He also builds effects pedals.

Larson Brothers

1900-1944. Chicago's Carl and August Larson bought Maurer & Company in 1900 where they built guitars and mandolin family instruments until 1944. Their house brands were Maurer, Prairie State and Euphonon and they also built for catalog companies Wm. C. Stahl and W. J. Dyer & Bro., adding brands like Stetson, a house brand of Dyer. See brand listings for more information.

Laskin

1973-present. Luthier William "Grit" Laskin builds his premium and presentation grade, custom, steel-string, classical, and flamenco guitars in Toronto, Ontario. Many of his instruments feature extensive inlay work.

Laurie Williams Guitars

1983-present. Luthier Laurie Williams builds his premium and presentation grade, custom/production, steel string, classical and archtop guitars on the North Island of New Zealand. He also builds mandolins.

Leach Guitars

1980-present. Luthier Harvey Leach builds his professional and premium grade, custom, flat-tops, archtops, and solidbody electrics, travel guitars and basses in Cedar Ridge, California.

Lehmann Stringed Instruments

1971-present. Luthier Bernard Lehmann builds his professional and premium grade, production/custom, flat-top, archtop, classical and Gypsy guitars in Rochester, New York. He also builds lutes, vielles and rebecs.

Lehtela

1993-present. Professional and premium grade, custom/production, acoustic, acoustic/electric, archtop, and solidbody guitars and basses built by luthier Ari Lehtela in Newell, North Carolina.

Lentz

1975-present. Luthier Scott Lentz builds his professional, premium, and presentation grade, custom/production, solidbody electric guitars in San Marcos, California.

Les Stansell Guitars

1980-present. Luthier Les Stansell builds his premium grade, custom, nylon-string guitars in Pistol River, Oregon.

Levin

1900-1973. Founded by Herman Carlson Levin and located in Gothenburg, Sweden, Levin was best known for their classical guitars, which they also built for other brands, most notably Goya from ca. 1955 to the mid '70s. They also built mandolins and ukes.

Levy-Page Special

1930s. Acoustic guitars likely built by Gibson, having many features of Kalamzoo guitars of the era. Possibly made for a distributor.

Lewis

1981-present. Luthier Michael Lewis builds his premium and presentation grade, custom/production, archtop guitars in Grass Valley, California. He also builds mandolins. He also built guitars under the D'Angelico name.

Linc Luthier

1991-present. Professional and premium grade, custom/production, electric and acoustic guitars, basses and double-necks built by luthier Linc Luthier in Upland, California.

Lindberg

Ca. 1950s. Line of guitars produced by Hoyer for Germany's Lindberg music store.

Lindert

1986-2002. Luthier Chuck Lindert made his intermediate and professional grade, production/custom, Art Deco-vibe electric guitars in Chelan, Washington.

Line 6

1996-present. Professional grade, production, imported solidbody and acoustic modeling guitars able to replicate the tones of a variety of instruments. Line 6 also builds effects and amps.

Lion

1960s. One of the brand names of guitars built for others by Egmond in Holland.

Lipe Guitars USA

1983-1989, 2000-2018. Luthier Michael Lipe built custom, professional grade, guitars and basses in Sun Valley, California. Lipe died Dec. '18.

Liscombe

1992-2013. Professional grade, production and limited custom, chambered electric guitars built by luthier Ken Liscombe in Burlington, Ontario.

Loar (The)

2005-present. Professional grade, production, imported archtop acoustic guitars designed by Greg Rich for The Music Link, which also has Johnson and other brands of instruments. They also offer mandolins.

Lollar

1979-present. Luthier Jason Lollar builds his premium grade, production/custom, solidbody and archtop guitars in Vashon, Washington.

Lopez, Abel Garcia

Luthier Abel Garcia Lopez builds his premium grade, custom, classical guitars in Mexico starting in 1985.

MODEL YEAR	FEATURES	EXC. COND. LOW	HIGH

Loprinzi

1972-present. Professional and premium grade, production/custom, classical and steel-string guitars built in Clearwater, Florida. They also build ukes. Founded by Augustino LoPrinzi and his brother Thomas in New Jersey. The guitar operations were taken over by AMF/Maark Corp. in '73. LoPrinzi left the company and again started producing his own Augustino Guitars, moving his operations to Florida in '78. AMF ceased production in '80, and a few years later, LoPrinzi got his trademarked name back.

Classical

1970s. Various models.

1970s	Brazilian rosewood	$2,000	$2,500
1970s	Indian rosewood	$1,250	$1,625
1970s	Mahogany	$1,125	$1,500

Lord

Mid-1960s. Acoustic and solidbody electric guitars imported by Halifax.

Acoustic or Electric Solidbody

1960s	Various models	$250	$350

Lotus

Late-1970s-2004. Budget grade acoustic and electric guitars and basses imported originally by Midco International, of Effingham, Illinois, and most recently by Musicorp. They also offered banjos and mandolins.

Louis Panormo

Early to mid-1800s. Spanish guitars made in London, England by luthier Louis (Luis) Panormo. He was born in Paris in 1784, and died in 1862.

Lowden

1973-present. Luthier George Lowden builds his premium and presentation grade, production/custom, steel and nylon string guitars in Downpatrick, Northern Ireland. From '80 to '85, he had some models made in Japan.

Flat-Top

1980s-present. Standard models include D, F, O, and S sizes and models 10 through 32.

1980s-2023	Premium models	$4,500	$11,000
1980s-2023	Standard models	$2,250	$4,500

LsL Instruments

2008-present. Luthier Lance Lerman builds his production, professional grade, solidbody electric guitars and basses in Los Angeles, California.

LSR Headless Instruments

1988-present. Professional and premium grade, production/custom, solidbody headless guitars and basses made by Ed Roman Guitars.

LTD

1995-present. Intermediate grade, production, Korean-made solidbody guitars and basses offered by ESP.

LSL Instruments Del Rey

LTD SN-1000HT

Luttrell Guitars

1953 Maccaferri Islander

Steve Bauman

Lucas Custom Instruments

1989-present. Premium and presentation grade, production/custom, flat-tops built by luthier Randy Lucas in Columbus, Indiana.

Lucas, A. J.

1990-present. Luthier A. J. Lucas builds his production/custom, classical and steel string guitars in Lincolnshire, England.

Luis Feu de Mesquita

2000-present. Professional and premium grade, custom, acoustic and flat-top guitars including Spanish, classical and flamenco built in Toronto, Ontario by luthier Luis Feu de Mesquita.

Luna Guitars

2005-present. Located in Tampa, Florida, Yvonne de Villiers imports her budget to professional grade, production, acoustic and electric guitars and basses from Japan, Korea and China. She also added ukuleles in '09 and amps in '10.

Luttrell Guitars

1993-present. Professional and premium grade, production/custom, acoustic, electric and resonator guitars built by luthier Ralph H. Luttrell in Sandy Springs, Georgia.

Lyle

Ca. 1969-1980. Imported by distributor L.D. Heater of Portland, Oregon. Generally higher quality Japanese-made copies of American designs by unknown manufacturers, but some early ones, at least, were made by Arai and Company. They also had basses and mandolins.

Lyon & Healy

1864-present. Founded by George Washburn Lyon and Patrick Joseph Healy, Lyon & Healy was an industry giant, operating a chain of music stores, and manufacturing harps (their only remaining product), pianos, Washburn guitars and a line of brass and wind instruments. See Washburn, American Conservatory, Lakeside, and College brands.

Lyon by Washburn

1990s-2000s. Budget grade, production, solidbody guitars and basses sold by mass merchandisers such as Target.

Lyra

1920s. Instruments built by the Oscar Schmidt Co. and possibly others. Most likely a brand made for a distributor.

Lyric

Luthier John Southern started building his professional and premium grade, custom, semi-hollow and solidbody and bass guitars in Tulsa, Oklahoma in 1996.

M. Campellone Guitars

See listing under Campellone Guitars.

MODEL		EXC. COND.	
YEAR	FEATURES	LOW	HIGH

M.Zaganin and N.Zaganin

1989-present. Luthier Márcio Zaganin began his career using the M.Zaganin brand, in 2004 it was changed to N. He builds professional and premium grade, production/custom, semi-hollow and solidbody electric guitars in São Paulo, Brazil. He also builds basses.

Maccaferri

1923-1990. Built by luthier and classical guitarist Mario Maccaferri (b. May 20, 1900, Cento, Italy; d. 1993, New York) in Cento, Italy; Paris, France; New York, New York; and Mount Vernon, New York. Maccaferri was a student of Luigi Mozzani from '11 to '28. His first catalog was in '23 and included a cutaway guitar. He also made mandolins. His Europe-era instruments are very rare. He designed Selmer guitars in '31. Maccaferri invented the plastic clothespin during World War II and used that technology to produce plastic ukes starting in '49 and Dow Styron plastic guitars in '53. He made several experimental plastic electrics in the '60s and plastic violins in the late-'80s.

Plastic (Dow Styron)

1950s. Plastic construction, models include Deluxe (archtop, crown logo), Islander (Islander logo), TV Pal (4-string cutaway) and Showtime (Showtime logo).

1950s	Deluxe	$200	$350
1950s	Islander	$200	$400
1950s	Romancer	$200	$350
1950s	Showtime	$200	$350
1950s	TV Pal	$150	$300

Madeira

1973-ca. 1984, ca. 1990. Imported budget and intermediate grade acoustic and electric guitars distributed by Guild. The Japanese-made electrics were basically copies of Gibson, Fender, and Guild models, the acoustics originally copies of Martin. The electrics were only offered first year or so during the '70s run. Name revived again around '90 on imported acoustics and electrics. They also offered mandolins and banjos.

Madrid

1996-present. Luthier Brandon Madrid builds his production/custom, professional and premium grade, acoustic and solidbody electric guitars, in San Diego, California. Prior to 2009 he built in Portland, Oregon.

Maestro

1950s-1970s, 2001-2012, 2022-present. Maestro is a brand name Gibson first used on 1950s accordion amplifiers. The first Maestro effects were introduced in the early-'60s and they used the name until the late-'70s. In 2001, Gibson revived the name for a line of effects, banjos and mandolins. Those were dropped in '09, when imported budget and intermediate, production, acoustic and electric guitars and amps were added. By '12 the brand was

MODEL		EXC. COND.	
YEAR	FEATURES	LOW	HIGH

no longer listed but was reintroduced on a line of Gibson effects in '22. Since '04, the brand has also been used on an unrelated line of acoustic guitars and ukes built in Singapore.

Electric
2009-2012. Various student models, Maestro head-stock logo, 'By Gibson' logo on truss rod cover.

2009-2012		$85	$155

Magnatone
Ca.1937-1971, 2013-present. Founded as Dickerson Brothers in Los Angeles, California and known as Magna Electronics from '47, with Art Duhamell president. Brands include Dickerson, Oahu (not all), Gourley, Natural Music Guild, Magnatone. In '59 Magna and Estey merged and in '66 the company relocated to Pennsylvania. In '71, the brand was taken over by a toy company. Between 1957 and '67, the company produced four different model lines of Spanish electrics. In 2013, Ted Kornblum revived the Magnatone name on a line of tube amps built in St. Louis, Missouri.

Cyclops
1930s. Dobro-made resonator guitar.

1930s	Round neck	$1,500	$2,000
1930s	Square neck	$1,500	$2,000

Mark Artist Series

1959-1961	More common	$1,125	$1,500
1959-1961	Rare	$1,500	$2,000

Mark Series
1955-1960. Solidbody series made by Paul Bigsby in small quantities, then taken over by Paul Barth at Magnatone in '59.

1955-1959	Mark II	$2,000	$2,500
1955-1959	Mark III	$2,000	$2,500
1955-1959	Mark IV	$2,500	$3,000
1955-1959	Mark V	$2,500	$3,000

Model Series

1962	Model 100	$450	$600
1962	Model 150	$450	$600
1962	Model 200, 2 pus	$450	$600

X-5 Zephyr
1965-1966. Double-cut with 2 DeArmond single-coil pickups, vibrato, metallic finish.

1965-1966		$700	$950

X-15 Tornado
1965-1966. Offset double-cut body, 2 pickups, various options.

1965-1966		$975	$1,250

X-20 Typhoon
1965-1966. Double-cut solidbody, 3 pickups, various options.

1965-1966		$1,125	$1,500

Magno-Tone
1930s. Brand most likely used by a music studio (or distributor) on instruments made by others, including Regal-built resonator instruments.

Mai Kai
1910s. Line of Hawaiian guitars built in Los Angeles, California by the Shireson Brothers.

MODEL		EXC. COND.	
YEAR	FEATURES	LOW	HIGH

Mako
1985-1989. Line of budget to lower-intermediate solidbody guitars from Kaman (Ovation, Hamer). They also offered basses and amps.

Solidbody

1985-1989	Various models	$150	$500

Mal n' Sal
See listing for Alternative Guitar and Amplifier Company.

Malinoski
1986-present. Luthier Peter Malinoski builds his production/custom, professional and premium grade, solidbody electric guitars and basses in Hyattsville, Maryland.

Mann
Ca. 1971-ca. 1985. A brand name used in Canada by Japan's Hoshino company on some of the same acoustic and electric models as their Ibanez guitars.

Manne
1987-present. Professional and premium grade, production/custom, semi-acoustic and electric guitars and basses built by luthier Andrea Ballarin in Italy.

Manson Guitar Works
1979-present. Premium grade, production/custom, electric guitars built by luthiers Hugh Manson and Adrian Ashton in Exeter, Devon UK. They also offer a line of professional grade, guitars crafted in the Czech Republic and assembled in UK. They also build basses.

Manuel & Patterson
1993-present. Luthiers Joe Manuel and Phil Patterson build professional, premium and presentation grade, production/custom, flat-top, archtop and solidbody electric guitars in Abita Springs, Louisiana. They also offer mandolins.

Manuel Contreras
1962-1994. Luthier Manuel Gonzalez Contreras worked with José Ramírez III, before opening his own shop in Madrid, Spain, in '62.

Manuel Contreras II
1986-present. Professional grade, production/custom, nylon-string guitars made in Madrid, Spain, by luthier Pablo Contreras, son of Manuel.

Manuel Ramirez
See listing under Ramirez, Manuel.

Manuel Rodriguez and Sons, S.L.
1905-present. Professional, premium, and presentation grade, custom flat-top and nylon-string guitars from Madrid, Spain.

Maestro 12-String
Rivington Guitars

1957 Magnatone Mark IV
Michael Wright

Manson META Series MBM-1

Marchione 16" Archtop

Manuel Velázquez

1933-2014. Luthier Manuel Velázquez (d. 2014) built his classical guitars in Puerto Rico ('72-'82), New York City, Virginia, and Florida. His son Alfredo continues to build guitars.

Manzanita Guitars

1993-present. Custom, steel-string, Hawaiian, and resonator guitars built by luthiers Manfred Pietrzok and Moritz Sattler in Rosdorf, Germany.

Manzer Guitars

1976-present. Luthier Linda Manzer builds her premium and presentation grade, custom, steel-string, nylon-string, and archtop guitars in Toronto, Ontario.

Maple Lake

2003-present. Intermediate grade, production, flat-top and acoustic/electric imported guitars from luthier Abe Wechter. Wechter also builds guitars under his own name.

MapleTree Guitars Canada

2011-present. Steve Maric, owner and luthier from Toronto, Canada, works with luthier Fulu Wang, Beijing, China to build production/custom, professional grade, acoustic guitars.

Mapson

1995-present. Luthier James L. Mapson builds his premium and presentation grade, production/custom, archtops in Santa Ana, California.

Marc Silber Guitar Company

1998-present. Intermediate and professional grade, production, flat-top, nylon-string, and Hawaiian guitars designed by Marc Silber and made in Mexico. These were offered under the K & S Guitars and/or Silber brands for 1992-'98. Silber also has ukuleles.

Marchione Guitars

1993-present. Premium and presentation grade, custom, archtops and solidbodies built by Stephen Marchione originally in New York City, but currently in Houston, Texas.

Marcia

1920s. Instruments built by the Oscar Schmidt Co. and possibly others. Most likely a brand made for a distributor.

Marco Polo

1960-ca. 1964. Imported from Japan by Harry Stewart and the Marco Polo Company of Santa Ana, California. One of the first American distributors to advertise inexpensive Japanese guitars and basses. Manufacturers unknown, but some acoustics by Suzuki, some electrics by Guyatone.

MODEL YEAR	FEATURES	EXC. COND. LOW	HIGH
Acoustic Hollowbody			
1960-1964	Various models	$125	$300

Mario Martin Guitars

2011-present. Luthier Mario Martin builds his production/custom, professional grade, semi-hollow and solidbody guitars and basses in Murfreesboro, Tennessee. From 2006 to '11, he built guitars under the Guitar Mill brand name.

Mark Wescott Guitars

Premium grade, custom, flat-tops, built by luthier Mark Wescott, starting in 1980, in Somers Point, New Jersey.

Marling

Ca. 1975. Budget line guitars and basses marketed by EKO of Recanati, Italy; probably made by them, although possibly imported.

Acoustic

1975. Includes the steel-string S.110, and the dreadnoughts W.354 Western, and W.356 Western.

1975		$125	$300

Electric Soldibody

1975. Includes the E.400 (semi-acoustic/electric), E.490 (solidbody), E.480 (single-cut), and the 460 (Manta-style).

1975		$125	$300

Martelle

1934. Private brand attributed to Gibson and some to Kay.

De Luxe

1934. Gibson 12-fret round shoulder Jumbo construction, laminate maple or mahogany back and sides, sunburst, Hawaiian or Spanish option.

1934		$10,000	$12,000

Martin

1833-present. Intermediate, professional, premium, and presentation grade, production/custom, acoustic, acoustic/electric, archtop and resonator guitars. Founded in New York City by Christian Frederick Martin, former employee of J. Staufer in Vienna, Austria. Moved to Nazareth, Pennsylvania in 1839. Early guitars were made in the European style, many made with partners John Coupa, Charles Bruno and Henry Schatz. Scalloped X-bracing was introduced in the late-1840s. The dreadnought was introduced in 1916 for the Oliver Ditson Company, Boston; and Martin introduced their own versions in 1931.

Martin model size and shape are indicated by the letter prefix (e.g., 0, 00, 000, D, etc.); materials and ornamentation are indicated by number, with the higher the number, the fancier the instrument (e.g., 18, 28, 35, etc.). Martin offered electric thinline guitars from '61-'68 and electric solidbodies from '78-'82. The Martin Shenandoah was made in Asia and assembled in U.S. Japanese Martin Sigma ('72-'73) and Korean Martin Stinger ('85 on) imported solidbodies.

Most Martin flat-top guitars, particularly Style 18 and above, came with a standard natural finish, therefore Martin guitar finish coloring is generally not mentioned because it is assumed to be see-through natural. Conversely, Gibson's standard finish for their flat-tops during their Golden Era was sunburst. Martin introduced their shaded (sunburst) finish as an option on their Style 18 in 1934 and their Style 28 in 1931. Values for a shaded finish should be considered on a case-by-case basis. Braced for steel strings specifications described under certain models are based on current consensus information and data provided by the late Martin employee-historian Mike Longworth and is for guidance only. Variations from these specs have been found, so "bracing" should be considered on a case-by-case basis.

0-15

1935, 1940-1943, 1948-1961. Maple or birch in '35, all mahogany after, unbound rosewood 'board, slotted peghead and 12-fret neck until '34, solid peghead and 14-fret neck thereafter, natural mahogany.

1935	Maple or birch	$3,750	$5,000
1940-1949	Mahogany begins	$3,750	$5,000
1950-1959		$3,500	$4,500
1960-1961		$3,000	$4,000

0-15H

1940. Hawaiian neck, all mahogany.

1940	$4,000	$5,250

0-15M Elderly Instruments 40th Anniversary

2011-2012. Limited Edition, 10 made, solid mahogany body and neck, special appointments, inside label signed by Elderly Instruments president Stan Werbin and Martin CEO Chris Martin.

2011-2012	$1,125	$1,500

0-15T

1960-1963. Tenor with Style 15 appointments, natural mahogany.

1960-1963	$1,375	$1,750

0-16

1961 only. Six made.

1961	$3,000	$4,000

0-16NY

1961-1977, 1979-1992, 1994. Mahogany back and sides, 12 frets, slotted peghead, unbound extra-wide rosewood 'board, natural.

1961-1969	$3,500	$4,500
1970-1979	$3,000	$4,000
1980-1989	$2,500	$3,250
1990-1994	$2,500	$3,250

0-17

1906-1917, 1929-1948, 1966-1968. The first version has mahogany back and sides, 3 black sound hole rings, rosewood bound back, unbound ebony 'board, 12 frets, slotted peghead. The second version ('29 and on) is all mahogany, 3 white-black-white sound hole rings, top bound until '30, thin black backstripe, 12 frets and slotted peghead until '34, solid peghead and 14 frets beginning in '33, natural mahogany.

1906-1917	Gut	$3,500	$4,500
1929-1933	Steel, 12-fret	$4,500	$5,000

1933-1934	Flat natural, 14-fret	$5,500	$7,000
1934-1938	Gloss dark, 14-fret	$5,500	$7,000
1939	Early '39, 175 neck	$5,500	$7,000
1939	Late '39, 168 neck	$5,500	$7,000
1940-1946		$5,250	$6,500
1947-1948		$4,500	$5,500
1966-1968	Special order	$4,000	$5,000

0-17H

1930, 1935-1940. Hawaiian, mahogany back and sides, 12 frets clear of body, natural.

1930	12-fret	$5,000	$6,500
1935-1940	14-fret	$5,500	$7,000

0-17S

Early 1930s. Limited production style 17 with spruce top, unique 'guard.

1931	$7,000	$9,000

0-17T

1932-1960. Mahogany back and sides, tenor, natural.

1932-1933	$1,500	$2,000
1934-1939	$2,250	$3,000
1940-1947	$1,750	$2,250
1948-1949	$1,500	$2,000
1950-1960	$1,500	$2,000

0-18

1898-1994, 2017-present. Rosewood back and sides until 1917, mahogany back and sides after, Adirondack spruce top until 1946, slotted peghead and 12 frets until 1934, solid peghead and 14 frets after 1934, braced for steel strings in 1923, improved neck in late-1934, non-scalloped braces appear late-'44, natural. Reintroduced '17, Sikta spruce, mahogany.

1898-1917	Brazilian	$5,500	$7,000
1918-1922	Mahogany, gut	$4,500	$5,500
1923-1934	12-fret, steel	$7,500	$9,500
1932-1938	14-fret	$8,500	$11,000
1939	Early '39, 175 neck	$8,500	$11,000
1939	Later '39, 168 neck	$7,500	$9,500
1940-1944		$7,000	$9,000
1945-1946		$6,000	$7,500
1947-1949		$5,500	$7,000
1950-1959		$5,000	$6,500
1960-1964		$4,750	$6,000
1965		$4,500	$5,750
1966-1969		$4,000	$5,000
1970-1979		$3,500	$4,500
1980-1989		$3,00	$3,750
1990-1994		$3,000	$3,750
2017-2023	Reintroduced	$2,500	$3,125

0-18G

1960s. Special order classical nylon-string model, natural.

1961	$2,250	$2,750

0-18K

1918-1935. Hawaiian, all Koa wood, T-frets and steel T-bar neck in late-1934, natural.

1918-1933	$6,500	$8,500
1934-1935	$7,500	$9,500

0-18KH

1927-1928. Hawaiian, Koa.

1927-1928	$7,500	$9,500

1941 Martin 0-15

Imaged by Heritage Auctions, HA.com

1919 Martin 0-18

David Stone

To get the most from this book, be sure to read "Using *The Guide*" in the introduction.

1926 Martin 0-21

Imaged by Heritage Auctions, HA.com

Martin 0-X1E

MODEL YEAR	FEATURES	EXC. COND. LOW	HIGH
0-18T			
1929-1932, 1936-1989, 1991-1992, 1994-1995. Mahogany body, spruce top, tenor, natural.			
1929-1939		$2,750	$3,500
1940-1946		$2,375	$3,000
1947-1949		$2,125	$2,750
1950-1959		$2,000	$2,500
1960-1969		$1,875	$2,500
1970-1979		$1,500	$2,000
1980-1989		$1,250	$1,625
1991-1995		$1,250	$1,625
0-18T Nick Reynolds			
2010-2011. Custom Artist Edition, mahogany.			
2010-2011		$2,500	$3,250
0-18TE			
1959, 1962. Only 2 made, tenor, 1 pickup.			
1959, 1962		$6,500	$8,500
0-18VS Elderly Instruments 40th Anniversary Limited Edition			
2012-2014. Mahogany body, Sikta spruce top, slotted headstock, 12-fret neck, inside label signed by C. F. Martin IV and Elderly founder Stan Werbin.			
2012-2014		$2,250	$3,000
0-20			
1850-1859		$6,500	$8,500
0-21			
1898-1931, 1934-1938, 1941, 1944, 1946-1948. Rosewood back and sides, Adirondack spruce top until 1946, 12 frets, T-frets and steel T-bar neck in late-1934, non-scalloped braces in late-1944, natural.			
1898-1926	Gut	$9,000	$11,500
1927-1929	Steel	$11,000	$15,000
1930	14-fret (only year)	$11,000	$15,000
1930	Belly bridge	$11,000	$15,000
1931-1938		$11,000	$15,000
1941		$10,500	$13,500
1944	Non-scalloped	$10,000	$12,500
1946	Adirondack	$8,000	$10,000
1947-1948	Sikta	$7,750	$9,500
0-21K			
1919-1929. Koa top, back and sides.			
1919-1929		$10,000	$12,500
0-21T			
1929-1930, 1935, 1961.			
1929-1935		$5,000	$6,500
1961		$2,750	$3,500
0-26			
1895. Only 1 made, rosewood back and sides, ivory-bound top, rope-style purfling.			
1895		$8,000	$11,000
0-27			
1850s-1890s. Rosewood back and sides, ivory-bound top.			
1850s	Antique market value	$12,000	$15,000
1860s-90s		$9,500	$12,000
0-28			
1874-1931, 1937 (6 made), 1969 (1 made). Brazilian rosewood back and sides, herringbone binding until 1937, natural.			
1874-1895		$10,500	$15,000

MODEL YEAR	FEATURES	EXC. COND. LOW	HIGH
1896-1897	Dark orange (rare)	$10,500	$15,000
1898-1923		$10,500	$15,000
1924-1927	Gut	$10,500	$15,000
1925-1927	Steel option	$15,000	$20,000
1928-1929	Steel (standard)	$15,000	$20,000
1930-1931	Belly bridge, 12-fret	$18,000	$22,500
1937	Belly bridge, 14-fret	$22,000	$27,500
1969	Brazilian	$9,500	$12,000
0-28H			
1927-1928. One made each year, Hawaiian, Koa.			
1927-1928		$12,000	$15,000
0-28IA Ian Anderson			
2004. Limited Edition 87 made, Adirondack spruce top, Indian rosewood sides and back, slotted headstock, can be converted from nylon to light steel strings.			
2004		$4,000	$5,000
0-28K			
1917-1931, 1935. Hawaiian, all Koa wood, braced for steel strings in '23, natural.			
1917-1924		$11,500	$15,000
1925-1929		$12,500	$15,500
1930-1935		$13,500	$18,000
0-28T			
1930-1931, 1941. Tenor neck.			
1930-1931	Steel option	$6,000	$7,750
1941		$4,750	$6,250
0-28VS			
2009-2019. Rosewood back and sides, slotted head, 12 fret neck.			
2009-2019		$3,000	$4,000
0-30			
1899-1921. Brazilian rosewood back and sides, ivory-bound body, neck and headstock.			
1899-1921		$10,000	$12,500
0-34			
1885, 1898-1899, 1907. Brazilian rosewood.			
1885-1907		$9,500	$12,000
0-40			
1860s-1898, 1912-1913. Indian rosewood.			
1880-1913		$12,000	$15,000
0-42			
1870s-1924, 1926-1930, 1 each in '34, '38,'42. Brazilian rosewood back and sides, 12 frets, natural.			
1890-1924		$22,500	$30,000
1926-1927	Gut	$22,500	$30,000
1928-1942	Steel	$35,000	$45,000
0-44 Soloist/Olcott-Bickford Artist			
1911-1931. Vahdah Olcott-Bickford Artist Model, run of 17 style-44 guitars made, Brazilian rosewood, ivory or faux-ivory-bound ebony 'board.			
1911-1931		$30,000	$40,000
0-45			
1904-1908, '11, '13, '15, '17-'20, '22-'24, '26-'30, '39. Brazilian rosewood back and sides, natural, special order only for '31-'39.			
1904-1927	Gut	$45,000	$60,000
1927-1939	Steel	$65,000	$85,000
0-45JB Joan Baez			
1998. Indian rosewood, 59 made.			
1998		$5,000	$6,500

MODEL YEAR	FEATURES	EXC. COND. LOW	HIGH

0-45S Stephen Stills
2007. Madagascar rosewood sides and back, Adirondack spruce top, 91 made.

2007		$10,000	$12,500

0-X1E
2020-2023. Concert size, figured mahogany laminate, Fishman electronics.

2020-2023		$450	$550

00-1
1995-2002. Grand Concert, mahogany.

1995-2002		$800	$1,000

00-1R
1995-1999. Rosewood version.

1995-1999		$800	$1,000

00-15
1999-2010. Sapele/mahogany.

1999-2010		$975	$1,250

00-15E Retro
2017-2018. Solid mahogany top, back and sides, electronics.

2017-2018		$1,500	$2,000

00-15M
2009-present. All mahogany.

2009-2023		$975	$1,250

00-15M Custom Elderly Instruments
2010-2014. All mahogany, diamond and square inlays, custom-made for Elderly Instruments, about 10 offered each year.

2010-2014		$1,125	$1,500

00-15M Elderly Instruments 40th Anniversary Limited Edition
2012. Only 12 made, mahogany body and neck, label signed by Elderly's president Stan Werbin and Martin CEO Chris Martin.

2012		$1,125	$1,500

00C-15AE
2000-2002. Built-in electronics, natural finish.

2000-2002		$1,125	$1,500

00-16C
1962-1977, 1980-1981. Classical, mahogany back and sides, 5-ply bound top, satin finish, 12 frets, slotted peghead, natural.

1962-1969		$2,250	$2,750
1970-1977		$1,750	$2,125
1980-1981	2 made	$1,375	$1,750

00-16DBFM
2006. Women and Music series, deep body (DB), flamed maple (FM), slotted headstock.

2001-2003		$1,500	$2,000

00-16DBM
2000-2005. Women and Music series, deep body (DB), mahogany (M), slotted headstock, gloss finish.

2000-2005		$1,500	$2,000

00-16DBR
1998-2000. Women and Music series, deep body (DB), rosewood, 14-fret slotted headstock, gloss natural finish.

1998-2000		$1,500	$2,000

00C-16DB
1999-2002. Women in Music series, cutaway, deep body (DB), mahogany, slotted headstock.

1999-2002		$1,750	$2,250

00C-16DBRE
2005-2007. Women and Music series, rounded cutaway, deep body (DB), rosewood (R), electronics (E).

2005-2007		$1,750	$2,250

00-17
1908-1917, 1930-1960, 1982-1988, 2001-2004. Mahogany back and sides, 12 frets and slotted headstock until '34, solid headstock and 14 frets after '34, natural mahogany, reissued in 2001 with a high gloss finish.

1908-1917	Gut strings	$4,500	$5,500
1930-1933	Steel, 12-fret	$6,500	$8,000
1934	14-fret, flat natural	$7,000	$8,500
1935-1938	14-fret, gloss dark	$7,000	$8,500
1939	Early '39, 175 neck	$7,000	$8,500
1939	Later '39, 168 neck	$6,500	$8,000
1940-1944		$6,500	$8,000
1945-1946		$6,000	$7,500
1947-1949		$5,500	$7,000
1950-1960		$5,000	$6,500
1982-1988		$2,500	$3,500
2001-2004	Reissue	$2,000	$2,500

00-17 Authentic 1931
2018-2020. Mahogany top, back and sides, Brazilian rosewood 'board, vintage gloss finish.

2018-2020		$3,500	$4,500

00-17H
1934-1935. Hawaiian set-up, mahogany body, no binding.

1934-1935		$7,000	$8,500

00-17S Black Smoke/Whiskey Sunset
2015-2020. Sikta spruce top, mahogany back and sides, rosewood 'board and bridge, on-board electronics (E) optional.

2015-2020	No electronics	$1,250	$1,625
2016-2020	With electronics	$1,500	$2,000

00-17SO Sing Out! 50th Anniversary
2000. Limited Edition, 50 made for 50th anniversary of Sing Out! Magazine, folk era logo inlays, SING OUT inlay on 20th fret, mahogany body.

2000		$1,625	$2,125

00-18
1898-1995, 2016-present. Rosewood back and sides until 1917, mahogany after, braced for steel strings in '23, improved neck in late-'34, war-time design changes '42-'46, non-scalloped braces in late-'44, Adirondack spruce top until '46, natural. Reissued 2016 with Sikta spruce top and mahogany back and sides.

1898-1917	Brazilian	$7,500	$9,500
1918-1922	Mahogany	$7,500	$9,500
1923-1929		$10,000	$12,500
1930-1932	12-fret	$15,000	$20,000
1933	14-fret, bar fret	$20,000	$25,000
1934-1937	14-fret	$20,000	$25,000
1938	175 neck	$20,000	$25,000
1939	Early '39, 175 neck	$20,000	$25,000
1939	Late '39, 168 neck	$18,000	$22,500
1940-1941		$18,000	$22,500
1942-1944	Scalloped	$18,000	$22,500
1944-1946	Non-scalloped	$12,500	$15,500
1947-1949		$10,000	$12,500
1950-1953		$5,500	$7,000

1952 Martin 00-18
Billy White Jr.

1937 Martin 00-18
Ross Hamilton

GUITARS

1963 Martin 00-18E
Greg Perrine

1947 Martin 00-21
Imaged by Heritage Auctions, HA.com

MODEL YEAR	FEATURES	EXC. COND. LOW	HIGH
1954-1959		$5,500	$7,000
1960-1964		$4,750	$6,000
1965		$4,500	$5,500
1966-1969		$4,000	$5,000
1970-1979		$3,500	$4,500
1980-1989		$3,000	$4,000
1990-1995		$2,875	$3,500
2016-2023		$2,000	$2,500

00-18 Authentic 1931
2016-2018. Adirondack spruce top, mahogany back and sides, ebony 'board, Vintage Tone System (VTS), natural finish.

2016-2018	$4,500	$6,000

00-18 Custom
2008. Custom Shop run of 75 or more made.

2008	$2,500	$3,250

00-18 Gruhn Limited Edition
1995. Sikta spruce top, C-shaped neck profile, 25 made.

1995	$2,500	$3,250

00-18 Tim O'Brien Signature
2008-2011. Limited Edition, 25.5" scale, label signed by O'Brien.

2008-2011	$4,250	$5,500

00-18C
1962-1995. Renamed from 00-18 G in '62, mahogany back and sides, classical, 12 frets, slotted headstock, natural.

1962-1969	$2,375	$3,000
1970-1979	$1,750	$2,250
1980-1995	$1,500	$1,875

00-18CTN Elizabeth Cotton
2001. Commemorative Edition, 76 made.

2001	$2,500	$3,250

00-18E
1959-1964. Flat-top Style 18, single neck pickup and 2 knobs, heavier bracing, natural.

1959-1964	$6,500	$8,000

00-18G
1936-1962. Mahogany back and sides, classical, natural, renamed 00-18 C in '62.

1936-1939	$3,500	$4,500
1940-1949	$2,500	$3,500
1950-1959	$2,500	$3,500
1960-1962	$2,500	$3,500

00-18H
1935-1941. Hawaiian, mahogany back and sides, 12 frets clear of body, natural. The Price Guide is generally for all original instruments. The H conversion is an exception, because converting from H (Hawaiian-style) to 00-18 specs is considered by some to be a favorable improvement and something that adds value.

1935-1941	$11,500	$15,000

00-18H Geoff Muldaur
2006-2011. Solid Adirondack spruce top, solid mahogany sides and back, sunburst.

2006-2011	$3,250	$4,250

00-18K
1918-1925, 1934. All Koa.

1918-1921	$5,000	$6,500
1922-1925	$7,500	$9,500
1934	$8,000	$10,000

00-18S John Mellencamp
2009-2010. Slotted, 12-fret.

2009-2010	$4,000	$5,000

00-18SH Steve Howe
1999-2000. Limited edition run of 250.

1999-2000	$3,000	$4,000

00-18T
1931, 1936, 1938-1940. Tenor version.

1931-1940	$3,500	$4,500

00-18V
1984, 2003-2015. Vintage Series, mahogany back and sides, spruce top.

1984	9 made	$2,500	$3,500
2003-2015		$2,250	$3,000

00-18V/VS Elderly Instruments 40th Anniversary
2012-2013. Limited Edition, solid (V) or slotted (VS) headstock, 12-fret, low profile.

2012-2013	V	$2,125	$2,750
2013	VS	$2,125	$2,750

00-21
1898-1996. Brazilian rosewood back and sides, changed to Indian rosewood in 1970, dark outer binding, unbound ebony 'board until 1947, rosewood from 1947, slotted diamond inlays until '44, dot after, natural.

1898-1926	Gut bracing	$9,500	$12,000
1927-1939	Steel bracing	$17,500	$22,000
1940-1943	Scalloped	$17,500	$22,000
1944-1947	Non-scalloped	$13,500	$16,500
1948-1949		$12,500	$15,500
1950-1959		$11,500	$14,500
1960-1964		$9,500	$12,000
1965		$7,000	$9,000
1966-1969	Brazilian	$6,250	$8,000
1970-1979	Indian	$4,000	$5,000
1980-1989	Indian	$4,000	$5,000
1990-1996	Indian	$4,000	$5,000

00-21 Custom
2005-2006. Custom order size 00 style 21, Brazilian rosewood sides and back.

2005-2006	$4,250	$5,500

00-21 Kingston Trio LTD
2007. 50th Anniversary of the Kingston Trio, inspired by Dave Guard's 00-21, 100 made, 12-fret, Indian rosewood, Kingston Trio label and notation "In Memory of Dave Guard 1934-1991".

2008-2009	$3,625	$4,750

00-21G
1937-1938. Gut string, Brazilian rosewood sides and back.

1937-1938	$4,000	$5,000

00-21GE Golden Era

1998-2000	$3,000	$4,000

00-21H
Hawaiian, special order, limited production.

1914	1 made	$9,000	$11,500
1934		$18,500	$23,500
1952, 1955	1 made each year	$12,500	$15,500

MODEL YEAR	FEATURES	EXC. COND. LOW	HIGH

00-21LE
1987. Guitar of the Month, Limited Edition, 19 made.

1987		$2,500	$3,250

00-21NY
1961-1965. Brazilian rosewood back and sides, no inlay, natural.

1961-1964		$8,000	$10,000
1965		$7,000	$9,000

00-21S
1968. Slotted headstock, Brazilian rosewood sides and back.

1968		$5,500	$7,500

00-21T
1934. Tenor, Brazilian rosewood back and sides, only 2 made.

1934		$5,500	$7,500

00-25K
1980, 1985, 1988. Spruce top, Koa back and sides.

1980-1988		$3,000	$4,000

00-25K2
1980, 1982-1984, 1987-1989. Koa top, back and sides.

1980-1989		$3,000	$4,000

00-28
Mid-1880s-1931, 1934, 1936-1941, 1958 (1 made), 1977 (1 made), 1984 (2 made), 2017-present. Brazilian rosewood back and sides, changed to Indian rosewood in 1977, herringbone purfling through 1941, white binding and unbound 'board after 1941, no inlays before 1901, diamond inlays from 1901-'41, dot after, natural. Reintroduced 2017, Sikta spruce top, modified low oval neck.

1880s-1924	Gut	$15,000	$18,500
1925-1931	Steel	$30,000	$37,500
1934	Few made	$40,000	$50,000
1936-1941	Few made	$40,000	$50,000
1958	Special order	$16,500	$20,500
1977	Special order	$4,000	$5,000
1984	Special order	$3,500	$4,500
2017-2023	Reissue	$2,500	$3,250

00-28C
1966-1995. Renamed from 00-28 G, Brazilian rosewood back and sides, changed to Indian rosewood in '70, classical, 12 frets, natural.

1966-1969	Brazilian	$4,250	$5,250
1970-1979	Indian	$2,250	$2,875
1980-1989		$1,750	$2,125
1990-1995		$1,750	$2,125

00-28G
1936-1962. Brazilian rosewood back and sides, classical, natural, reintroduced as 00-28 C in '66.

1936-1946		$6,500	$8,500
1947-1949		$5,500	$7,000
1950-1959		$4,750	$6,000
1960-1962		$4,500	$5,750

00-28K
1919-1921, 1926, 1928-1931, 1933. Hawaiian, Koa back and sides.

1919-1921	34 made	$15,500	$20,000
1926-1933	1 made per year	$25,000	$32,000

00-28T
1931, 1940. Tenor, Brazilian rosewood back and sides, tenor 4-string neck, only 2 made.

1931, 1940		$8,000	$10,500

00-28VS
2009-2019. Rosewood back and sides.

2009-2019		$3,000	$4,000

00-28VS Custom Shop
2009-2013. Various Custom Shop options.

2009-2013		$3,500	$4,500

00-30
1890s-1921. Rosewood.

1899-1921		$17,000	$21,500

00-34
1898-1899. 6 made.

1898-1899		$20,000	$25,000

00-37K2 Steve Miller
2001. Flamed Koa back and sides, solid Engelmann spruce top, limited run of 68.

2001		$5,500	$7,500

00-40
1913, 1917. 4 made.

1913	Brazilian	$35,000	$45,000
1917	Koa	$35,000	$45,000

00-40 Martin Stauffer
1997. Rosewood/spruce, 35 made.

1997		$6,500	$8,500

00-40H
1928-1939. Hawaiian, Brazilian rosewood back and sides, 12 frets clear of body, natural. H models are sometimes converted to standard Spanish setup, in higher-end models this can make the instrument more valuable to some people.

1928-1929	Pyramid bridge	$30,000	$40,000
1930-1939	Belly bridge	$30,000	$40,000

00-40K
Few were made (only 6), figured Koa, natural.

1918	1 made	$30,000	$40,000
1930	5 made	$30,000	$40,000

00-41 Custom
2005. Custom Shop model, parlor size.

2005		$5,000	$6,500

00-42
1898-1943, 1973 (1 made). Brazilian rosewood back and sides, Indian rosewood in 1973, pearl top borders, 12 frets, ivory bound peghead until 1918, ivoroid binding after 1918, natural.

1898-1927	Pyramid bridge	$35,000	$45,000
1927-1943	Steel bracing	$55,000	$75,000
1973	1 made	$5,500	$7,500

00-42 Linda Ronstadt Limited Edition
2009-2010. Madagascar rosewood, slotted headstock.

2009-2010		$7,000	$9,000

00-42G
1936-1939. Gut string slotted headstock classical, only 3 made.

1936-1939	3 made	$12,500	$15,500

1983 Martin 00-25K

1925 Martin 00-28
Izzy Miller

2015 Martin 00-DB Jeff Tweedy
Rodger Reed

Martin 000-10E

MODEL YEAR	FEATURES	EXC. COND. LOW	HIGH

00-42JM-C John Mayer Crossroads
2019. Limited run of 50 for Guitar Center, designed by John Mayer to benefit Crossroads Centre in Antigua, Sikta spruce top, Cocobolo back and sides, gloss finish.

2019		$7,000	$8,500

00-42K
1919. Koa body, only 1 made.

1919	1 made	$50,000	$65,000

00-42K2 Robbie Robertson
2008-2009. Limited Edition, all Koa body (K2), 00-12 fret style, high-end appointments.

2008-2009		$5,750	$7,500

00-42SC John Mayer
2012-2019. Sikta spruce top, cocobolo back, sides and headplate, ebony 'board.

2012-2019		$5,500	$7,500

00-44 Soloist/Olcott-Bickford Artist
1913-1939. Custom-made in small quantities, Brazilian rosewood, ivory or faux-ivory-bound ebony 'board.

1913-1939	6 made	$45,000	$60,000

00-44G
1938. Set up with gut strings, 1 made.

1938	1 made	$35,000	$45,000

00-45
1904-1929, 1970-1982, 1984-1987, 1989-1990, 1992-1993. Brazilian rosewood back and sides, changed to Indian rosewood in '70, 12 frets and slotted headstock until '34 and from '70 on 14 frets, and solid headstock from '34-'70, natural.

1904-1927	Gut	$55,000	$75,000
1927-1929	Steel	$100,000	$125,000
1970-1979	Reintroduced	$7,500	$9,500
1980-1993		$6,500	$8,500

00-45K
1919. Koa body, 1 made.

1919		$75,000	$95,000

00-45S
1970. Slotted headstock.

1970		$7,000	$9,000

00-45S Limited Edition
2002. 1902 vintage-pattern with fancy inlays, 00 size style 45, 50 made.

2002		$12,500	$16,500

00-45SC John Mayer
2012-2013. Limited Edition, 25 made, slotted headstock, cocobolo.

2012-2013		$12,000	$16,000

00-45ST Stauffer Commemorative
1997-1998. Limited Edition, 25 made, six-on-a-side headstock, 45-style appointments, 00 body, Sikta top, Brazilian rosewood back and sides.

1997-1998		$12,000	$16,000

00-55
1935. 12 made for Rudnick's Music of Akron, Ohio.

1935		$13,500	$18,000

00CMAE
1999-2001. Single-cut acoustic-electric flat-top, laminate back and sides, made in U.S.

1999-2001		$650	$850

00CXAE
2000-2013. Single-cut acoustic-electric flat-top, composite laminate back and sides, made in U.S.

2000-2013	Various colors	$500	$650

00L Earth
2021-2023. Dedicated to climate control, 100% FSC-certified and 100% plastic-free, graphic art by Robert Goetzl, gig bag made from hemp.

2021-2023		$1,500	$2,000

00L Fly Fishing
2019-2021. Limited Edition, run of 100, artwork by William Matthews, Sikta spruce top, Goncalo Alves back and sides, gloss finish.

2019-2021		$1,750	$3,500

00L-17 Black Smoke/Whiskey Sunset
2016-2019. Sikta spruce top, mahogany back and sides, on-board electronics optional.

2016-2019	17, No electronics	$1,250	$1,625
2016-2019	17E, Electronics	$1,375	$1,750

00L-X1AE

2017-2019		$450	$600

00L-X2E
2020-2022. Sikta spruce top, figured mahogany laminate back and sides, Fishman electronics, natural finish.

2020-2022		$550	$750

00-DB Jeff Tweedy Signature
2011-2019. Custom Shop Signature Edition with solid FSC Certified Mahogany and mahogany burst finish.

2011-2019		$2,000	$2,500

00-X1AE

2015-2019		$375	$500

00-X2E
2020-present. Sikta spruce top, figured mahogany laminate back and sides, Fishman electronics, natural finish.

2020-2023		$525	$700

000-1
1994-2005. Solid spruce top with laminated mahogany back and sides.

1994-2005		$800	$1,000

000-1E
1994-2005. 000-1 with electronics.

1994-2005		$875	$1,125

000-1R
1994-2003. 000-1 with Indian rosewood back and sides.

1994-2003		$800	$1,000

000-10E
2019-present. Road Series, updated version of 000RS1, sapele top, back and sides, Fishman electronics, satin finish.

2019-2023		$575	$725

000-12E Koa
2019-present. Road Series, Sikta spruce top, Koa veneer back and sides, Fishman electronics, gloss finish.

2019-2023		$1,250	$1,500

000-13E
2017-2018. Road Series, updated version of 000RSG, Sikta spruce top, siris back and sides, Fishman electronics, natural gloss.

2017-2018		$775	$975

MODEL YEAR	FEATURES	EXC. COND. LOW	HIGH

000-15/000-15S
1999-2009. Mahogany body, headstock is solid or slotted (S, first offered in '00). Renamed 000-15M with solid headstock in '10.

1999-2009	000-15	$1,125	$1,500
2000-2009	000-15S	$1,250	$1,500

000-15M
2010-present. All mahogany, satin finish.

2010-2023		$950	$1,125

000-15M Burst
2016-2018. Solid mahogany, 14-fret, satin finish with added burst to top.

2016-2018		$1,125	$1,500

000-15M Elderly Instruments 40th Anniversary
2011-2012. 10 made, mahogany body and neck, label signed by Elderly Instruments president Stan Werbin and Martin CEO Chris Martin

2011-2012		$1,125	$1,500

000-15M StreetMaster
2017-present. Same specs as 000-15M but with distressed mahogany satin finish.

2017-2023		$1,125	$1,500

000-15SM
2011-present. Solid mahogany, slotted headstock, 12-fret neck, satin finish.

2011-2023		$1,125	$1,500

000-16 Series
1989-present. Mahogany back and sides, diamonds and squares inlay, sunburst, name changed to 000-16 T Auditorium with higher appointments in '96, in 2000-2005 slotted (000-16 S) and gloss finish (000-16 SGT) were offered. Various models continue to be added to this series.

1989	000-16M	$1,125	$1,500
1989-1995	000-16	$1,250	$1,625
1989-2023	000-16GT	$1,000	$1,375
1995-1998	000-16T	$1,125	$1,500
1996	000-16TR	$975	$1,250
1996-2002	000-16R	$1,125	$1,500
2001-2005	000-16RGT	$975	$1,250
2002-2003	000-16SRGT	$1,125	$1,500
2003-2004	000-16SGT	$1,125	$1,500
2019-2023	000-16E	$1,500	$2,000

000-17
1911, 1952. Mahogany back and sides, 1 made in 1911, 25 more in '52.

1911		$10,000	$13,000
1952		$4,500	$6,000

000-17 Black Smoke/Whiskey Sunset
2016-2023. Sikta spruce top, mahogany back and sides, rosewood 'board and bridge, on-board electronics (000-17E) optional.

2016-2023	17, No electronics	$1,125	$1,500
2016-2023	17E, Electronics	$1,250	$1,625

000-17S
2002-2004. All mahogany, slotted headstock, 12 fret neck.

2002-2004		$1,375	$1,750

000-17SM
2013-2015. Sikta spruce top, mahogany back and sides, East Indian rosewood headplate, vintage slotted headstock.

2013-2015		$1,375	$1,750

000-18
1906, 1911-present (none in 1932-1933). Maple back and sides in '06, then rosewood until '17, and mahogany since, longer scale in '24-'34, 12-fret neck until '33, changed to 14 in '34. Improved neck late-'34, war-time changes '41-'46, non-scalloped braces in late-'44, switched from Adirondack spruce to Sikta spruce top in '46 (though some Adirondack tops in '50s and '60s), natural. Now a part of the Standard Series.

1906	Maple	$15,000	$18,500
1911-1917	Rosewood	$15,000	$18,500
1920-1922	Gut, mahogany	$13,500	$16,500
1923-1931	Steel	$22,500	$30,000
1934	Early '34, long scale	$35,000	$40,000
1934-1938	14-fret	$35,000	$40,000
1939	Early '39 175 neck	$23,500	$30,000
1939	Late '39, 168 neck	$18,500	$25,000
1940-1941		$17,500	$22,000
1942-1943	Scalloped braces	$17,500	$22,000
1944	Scalloped braces	$15,000	$20,000
1944-1947	Non-scalloped	$11,500	$15,000
1948-1949		$9,500	$12,000
1950-1953		$9,000	$11,500
1954-1959		$7,500	$9,500
1960-1964		$6,000	$7,500
1965		$5,500	$7,000
1966-1969		$4,500	$6,000
1970-1979		$3,125	$4,000
1980-1989		$2,500	$3,250
1990-1999		$2,500	$3,250
2000-2013		$2,250	$3,000
2014-2023	Standard Series	$2,250	$3,000

000-18 Authentic 1937
2008-2011. Natural or sunburst, high-X bracing.

2008-2011		$4,500	$5,750

000-18 Kenny Sultan Signature
2007-2009. Flamed mahogany sides, diamond and squares inlays, label signed by Sultan.

2007-2009		$3,000	$4,000

000-18 Norman Blake Signature
2006-2011. 12 fret neck on 14-fret body.

2006-2011		$3,000	$4,000

000-18E Retro
2012-2019. Sikta spruce top, mahogany back and sides.

2012-2019		$2,000	$2,500

000-18G
1955. Classical, 1 made.

1955		$4,500	$6,000

000-18GE Golden Era 1934 Special Edition
2007. Adirondack red spruce top, scalloped and forward shifted X-bracing, 14-fret V-shaped mahogany neck, 20-fret ebony 'board, old style decal logo.

2007		$3,125	$4,000

Martin 000-17 Black Smoke

1936 Martin 000-18
M. Mattingly

GUITARS

1948 Martin 000-21
Carter Vintage Guitars

Martin 000-28 Modern Deluxe

MODEL YEAR	FEATURES	EXC. COND. LOW	HIGH

000-18GE Golden Era 1937 Special Edition
2006-2014. Natural or sunburst. 1937 dropped from name in '12.

2006-2014	Natural or sunburst	$3,125	$4,000

000-18GE Golden Era Sunburst
2006-2014. Sunburst version, Adirondack.

2006-2014		$3,125	$4,000

000-18P
1930. Plectrum neck.

1930		$6,500	$8,500

000-18S
1976-1977. Slotted, 12-fret.

1976-1977		$3,500	$4,500

000-18T
1930, '34, '36, '38, '41. Tenor.

1930		$7,000	$9,000
1934-1938		$12,500	$15,500
1941		$7,500	$9,500

000-18V/VS Elderly Instruments 40th Anniversary
2012-2013. Limited Edition, solid (V) or slotted (VS) headstock, Sikta top, label signed by C.F. Martin IV and Stan Werbin, includes matching wood guitar stand.

2012-2013	V	$2,750	$3,500
2013	VS	$2,750	$3,500

000-18WG Woody Guthrie
1999. Signed label including artwork and model identification.

1999		$3,000	$4,000

000-21
1902-1923 (22 made over that time), 1931(2), 1938-1959, 1965 (1), 1979 (12). Brazilian rosewood back and sides, changed to Indian rosewood in '79, natural.

1902-1923		$20,000	$25,000
1931	12-fret	$24,000	$30,000
1938-1939	Early '39, 175 neck	$36,000	$45,000
1939	Late '39, 168 neck	$30,000	$38,000
1940-1941		$24,000	$30,000
1942-1943		$22,000	$27,500
1944-1945		$20,000	$25,000
1946		$14,000	$17,500
1947-1949		$11,500	$14,500
1950-1954		$11,250	$14,000
1955-1959		$11,000	$13,500
1965	Last Brazilian	$10,000	$12,500
1979	Indian	$4,000	$5,000

000-21 10-String/Harp Guitar
1902. Only 2 made, 10 strings, Brazilian rosewood back and sides.

1902		$6,500	$8,500

000-28
1902-present. Brazilian rosewood back and sides, changed to Indian rosewood in '70, herringbone purfling through '41, white binding and unbound 'board after '41, no inlays before '01, slotted diamond inlays from '01-'44, dot after, 12 frets until '32, 14 frets '31 on (both 12 and 14 frets were made during '31-'32), natural through '93, sunburst or natural after.

1902-1927	Gut	$25,000	$32,000
1925-1927	Steel	$45,000	$60,000
1928		$45,000	$60,000
1929	Pyramid bridge	$45,000	$60,000
1930	Belly bridge	$45,000	$60,000
1931-1933		$45,000	$60,000
1934	Early '34, long scale	$75,000	$95,000
1934-1937	Not long scale	$70,000	$90,000
1938-1939	Early '39, 175 neck	$65,000	$85,000
1939	Late '39, 168 neck	$60,000	$75,000
1940-1941		$50,000	$65,000
1942-1944	Scalloped, herringbone	$50,000	$65,000
1944-1946	Non-scalloped, herringbone	$35,000	$45,000
1947-1949	Non-herringbone	$20,000	$25,000
1950-1952		$16,500	$20,000
1953-1955	Kluson	$16,500	$20,000
1956-1958	Kluson	$15,000	$18,500
1958-1959	Late '58, Grover	$15,000	$18,500
1960-1962		$12,000	$15,000
1964		$11,500	$14,500
1965		$9,000	$11,500
1966-1969	Early '66, Tortoise 'guard	$9,000	$11,500
1970-1979		$4,250	$5,500
1980-1989		$3,500	$4,500
1990-1999		$3,250	$4,000
2000-2023		$3,000	$3,750

000-28 Martin/Mandolin Brothers 25th Anniversary
1997-1998. Limited Edition, 25 made, mandolin 12th fret inlay, signed label.

1997-1998		$3,500	$4,500

000-28 Modern Deluxe
2019-present. Sikta spruce top, Vintage Tone System, Indian rosewood back and sides. Electronics are optional (000-28E).

2019-2023	28, No electronics	$2,500	$3,250
2019-2023	28E, Electronics	$4,000	$5,250

000-28 Norman Blake
2004-2008. Signature Edition, 12-fret neck on 14-fret body, B version is Brazilian rosewood.

2004-2008	Brazilian	$8,500	$11,000
2004-2008	Indian	$4,000	$5,250

000-28 Perry Bechtel
2007. East Indian rosewood back and sides, 29 made.

2007		$3,750	$5,000

000-28C
1962-1967. Classical, Brazilian rosewood back and sides, slotted peghead, natural.

1962-1967		$6,000	$7,500

000-28EC
1996-present. Custom Signature Edition, Eric Clapton specs, Sikta spruce top, Indian rosewood back and sides, herringbone trim, natural or sunburst.

1996-2023	Natural	$3,000	$4,000
1996-2023	Sunburst	$2,750	$3,500

MODEL YEAR	FEATURES	EXC. COND. LOW	HIGH

000-28EC Eric Clapton Crossroads Madagascar

2013. Limited to 150 in collaboration with Guitar Center, sound hole label hand-signed by Clapton and Chris Martin, Crossroads symbol inlaid (mother-of-pearl) into bridge, Clapton signature between 19th-20th frets, Clapton signature case and strap.

2013		$6,000	$7,500

000-28ECB Eric Clapton

2002-2003. Limited edition, EC 000-28 with Brazilian rosewood, certificate of authenticity, label hand-signed by Eric Clapton and Chris Martin.

2002-2003		$9,000	$12,000

000-28F

1964-1967. Folk, 12-fret, slotted.

1964		$8,750	$11,500
1965		$7,500	$9,500
1966-1967		$7,000	$9,000

000-28G

1937, 1939-1940, 1946-1947, 1949-1950, 1955. Special order classical guitar, very limited production.

1937-1940		$10,000	$12,500
1946		$9,250	$11,500
1947, 1949		$7,500	$9,500
1950, 1955		$6,500	$8,500

000-28GE Golden Era

1996 only. Sikta spruce top, rosewood back and sides, scalloped braces, herringbone trim, 12-fret model, natural.

1996		$4,750	$6,000

000-28H

2000-2017. Herringbone top trim, production model for '00-'02, Custom Shop model made for Elderly Instruments after that (stamped Custom on neck block).

2000-2002		$2,500	$3,250
2003-2017	Custom Shop	$2,750	$3,500

000-28HB Brazilian 1937 Reissue

1997. Pre-war specs including scalloped bracing, Brazilian rosewood.

1997		$7,500	$9,750

000-28K

1921. Non-catalog special order model, only 2 known to exist, Koa top, back and sides.

1921	Rare model	$50,000	$65,000

000-28K Authentic 1921

2014-2015. Slotted, 12-fret, highly figured Koa body.

2014-2015		$5,500	$7,500

000-28LSH/LSH Custom

2008. Large sound hold (LSH), style 28 appointments, wild grain East Indian sides and back.

2008		$3,000	$4,000

000-28M Eric Clapton

2009. Limited Edition run of 461, Madagascar rosewood back and sides, Carpathian spruce top, signature between 19th and 20th frets, interior label hand-signed by Clapton, natural or sunburst.

2009		$5,500	$7,000

000-28NY

1962. 2 made.

1962		$9,000	$11,500

000-28S

1974-1977. Slotted headstock, 12-fret neck.

1974-1977		$4,000	$5,000

000-28SO Sing Out! 40th Anniversary

1990. Limited Edition, 40 made for 40th Anniversary of Sing Out! Magazine.

1990		$2,500	$3,500

000-28VS

1999-2019. Vintage Series, spruce top with aging toner, scalloped bracing, rosewood sides and back, slotted diamond markers, herringbone top trim.

1999-2019		$3,000	$4,000

000-30 Authentic 1919

2017-2018. Adirondack spruce top, Vintage Tone System, Madagascar rosewood back and sides.

2017-2018		$5,000	$6,500

000-38

1980. Rosewood back and sides, 3 made.

1980		$3,000	$4,000

000-40

1909. Ivoroid bound top and back, snowflake inlay, 1 made.

1909		$40,000	$50,000

000-40Q2GN Graham Nash

2003. Limited edition of 147 guitars, quilted mahogany top/back/sides, flying-heart logo on headstock, Graham Nash signature on frets 18-20.

2003		$4,000	$5,000

000-40SPR Peter Rowan "Midnight Moonlight" Signature

2001-2002. Limited run of 87, Sikta spruce top, mahogany back and sides, phases of the moon inlays.

2001-2002		$3,500	$4,500

000-41

1975, 1996. Custom shop style 000-41.

1975		$5,000	$6,500
1996		$3,875	$5,000

000-42

1918, 1921-1922, 1925, 1930, 1932, 1934, 1938-1943, 2004-present. Brazilian rosewood back and sides, natural. The 1918-1934 price range is wide due to the variety of specifications.

1918-1925	Limited production	$55,000	$70,000
1930, 1932	2 made, 14 fret	$90,000	$112,500
1934	1 made	$112,000	$140,000
1938	27 made	$100,000	$125,000
1939	Early '39, 175 neck	$100,000	$125,000
1939	Late '39, 168 neck	$95,000	$120,000
1940-1943	Last pearl border	$100,000	$125,000
2004-2023		$5,500	$7,500

000-42 Authentic 1939

2017-2019. Adirondack spruce top with Vintage Tone System (VTS), Madagascar rosewood back and sides, ebony 'board and bridge.

2017-2019		$9,750	$12,000

000-42 Marquis

2007-2009. Indian rosewood.

2007-2009		$5,500	$7,250

Martin 000-28EC

Martin 000-42 Authentic 1939

1936 Martin 000-45

Imaged by Heritage Auctions, HA.com

Martin 000C12-16E Nylon

MODEL YEAR	FEATURES	EXC. COND. LOW	HIGH

000-42EC Eric Clapton
1995. Style 45 pearl-inlaid headplate, ivoroid bindings, Eric Clapton signature, 24.9" scale, flat-top, sunburst top price is $8320 ('95 price), only 461 made; 433 natural, 28 sunburst.

1995		$9,000	$11,000

000-42ECB Eric Clapton
2000-2001. With Brazilian rosewood, 200 made.

2000-2001		$16,000	$20,000

000-42EC-Z Eric Clapton Crossroads
2019-2021. Ziricote back and sides, 50 made to benefit Crossroads Centre.

2019-2021		$13,000	$17,000

000-42M Eric Clapton Limited Edition
2008-2009. Limited Edition, 250 made, Madagascar rosewood sides and back, Carpathian spruce top.

2008-2009		$8,500	$11,000

000-42SB
2004. 1935 style with sunburst finish, Indian rosewood back and sides.

2004		$4,750	$6,000

000-44 Soloist/Olcott-Bickford Artist
1917-1919. Style 44 guitars were made for guitarist Vahdah Olcott-Bickford, rosewood back and sides, 3 made.

1917-1919		$50,000	$65,000

000-45
1906, 1911-1914, '17-'19, '22-'29, '34-'42, '70-'94. Brazilian rosewood back and sides, changed to Indian rosewood in '70, 12-fret neck and slotted headstock until '34 (but 7 were made in '70 and 1 in '75), 14-fret neck and solid headstock after '34, natural.

1906-1919		$85,000	$110,000
1922-1927	Gut	$85,000	$110,000
1926-1929	Steel	$165,000	$200,000
1930-1931	000-45 designated	$165,000	$200,000
1934	Early '34, long scale	$250,000	$325,000
1934	Late '34, short scale	$225,000	$300,000
1935-1937	14 fret, CFM inlay	$225,000	$300,000
1938	Early '38	$225,000	$300,000
1938	Late '38	$200,000	$250,000
1940-1942		$165,000	$200,000
1970-1977		$10,000	$12,500
1980-1989		$8,500	$10,500
1990-1994		$7,500	$9,500

000-45 7-String
1911, 1929, 1931. 1 made each year.

1911-1931		$50,000	$62,500

000-45B
1985. Brazilian rosewood, 2 made.

1985		$16,000	$20,000

000-45EC Eric Clapton Crossroads Brazilian
2013. Limited to 18 in collaboration with Guitar Center, Brazilian rosewood, Crossroads symbol inlaid both ends of bridge, Crossroads case and strap.

2013		$40,000	$52,000

000-45EC Eric Clapton Crossroads Madagascar
2013. Limited to 55 in collaboration with Guitar Center, Crossroads symbol inlaid both ends of bridge, Crossroads case and strap.

2013		$11,500	$15,000

000-45H
1937. Brazilian rosewood, Hawaiian, 2 made.

1937		$225,000	$375,000

000-45JR Jimmie Rodgers
1997-1998. Adirondack spruce top, Brazilian rosewood back and sides, scalloped high X-braces, abalone trim, natural, 52 made. Sometimes referred to as Blue Yodel.

1997-1998		$15,000	$20,000

000-45S
1974-1976. 12-fret.

1974-1976		$9,000	$12,000

000-45S Stephen Stills
2005. Only 91 made, Indian rosewood.

2005		$12,000	$15,000

000C David Gray Custom
2005-2006. Custom Artist Edition, 000-size cutaway, Italian spruce top, mahogany back and sides, interior label signed by David Gray.

2005-2006		$3,250	$4,000

000C Nylon
2012-2018. Cutaway, 12-fret, Sikta spruce top, sapele back and sides, slotted headstock, Fishman.

2012-2018		$1,375	$1,750

000C Steve Miller Pegasus
2005-2006. Cutaway, mahogany back and sides, Pegasus logo.

2005-2006		$3,500	$4,500

000C12-16E Nylon
2020-present. Gloss Sikta spruce top, satin mahogany back and sides, Fishman electronics.

2020-2023		$1,500	$2,000

000C-15E
1999-2002. Cutaway, mahogany back and sides, Fishman.

1999-2002		$1,000	$1,375

000C-16 (T Auditorium)
1990-1998. Cutaway acoustic, mahogany back and sides, diamonds and squares inlay, name changed to 000-C16T Auditorium in '96.

1990-1998		$1,250	$1,625

000C-16GTE
1999-2003. Cutaway, mahogany.

1999-2003		$1,375	$1,750

000C-16GTE Premium
2003-2009. Mahogany back and sides.

2003-2009		$1,375	$1,750

000C-16RB (Baby Face)
2000-2002. Cutaway acoustic, East Indian rosewood back and sides.

2000-2002		$1,750	$2,250

000C-16RGTE
2000-2010. Cutaway, rosewood back and sides.

2000-2010		$1,125	$1,500

MODEL YEAR	FEATURES	EXC. COND. LOW	HIGH

000C-16SGTNE
2003-2006. Classical electric, nylon string, cutaway, mahogany body, 12-fret cedar neck, slotted headstock.

2003-2006		$1,250	$1,625

000C-16SRNE
2003-2005. Classical cutaway, rosewood body, 12-fret cedar neck, slotted headstock.

2003-2005		$1,250	$1,625

000C-16T
1996-1997. Sikta spruce top, mahogany back, sides and neck, rosewood 'board.

1996-1997		$1,125	$1,500

000C-1E Auditorium
1997-1999. Cutaway, mahogany back and sides, transducer pickup.

1997-1999		$900	$1,125

000C-28 Andy Summers
2006. Cutaway, rosewood back and sides, Buddhist Mudra inlays.

2006		$4,000	$5,000

000C-28SMH Merle Haggard
2001-2002. Cutaway, 12-fret neck, Blue Yodel No. 13 inlay.

2001 2002		$4,500	$5,750

000CDB Dion The Wanderer
2002. Cutaway acoustic/electric, 57 made, scalloped bracing, mahogany sides and back, slotted diamond and square markers, Dion logo on headstock, gloss black finish.

2002		$4,750	$6,125

000CDG Doug Greth Commemorative Edition
2011. Nylon string cutaway, slotted headstock, mahogany back and sides, 48 made.

2011		$1,750	$2,250

000CJR-10E
2019-2022. Junior Series, 000JR-10 model with Fishman electronics.

2019-2022		$500	$650

000CME
1999-2002. Laminate back and sides, on-board electronics, satin finish.

1999-2002		$775	$1,000

000CXE Black
2003-2013. Acoustic-electric, cutaway, laminated body, black finish.

2003-2013		$550	$700

000E Black Walnut Ambertone
2020. Limited Edition, run of 125, Sikta spruce top with gloss amber burst finish, satin black walnut back and sides, Fishman electronics.

2020		$1,625	$2,125

000-ECHF Bellezza Bianca
2005-2006. Eric Clapton and Hiroshi Fujiwara White Beauty model, Engleman spruce top, flamed Pacific big-leaf maple back and sides, model name logo on 20th fret, white finish, all-white case, 410 made.

2005-2006		$5,000	$6,500

000-ECHF Bellezza Nera
2004-2005. Eric Clapton and Hiroshi Fujiwara Black Beauty Model, 476 made, Italian Alpine spruce top, Indian rosewood back and sides, black finish.

2004-2005		$6,500	$8,500

000-JBP Jimmy Buffett Pollywog
2003. Model name and number on label inside back, 168 made.

2003		$3,500	$4,500

000JR-10
2019-present. Junior Series, Sikta spruce top, sapele back and sides, satin finish.

2019-2023		$475	$600

000-M
1997-2009. Road Series, mahogany or sapele back and sides.

1997-2009		$650	$850

000-MMV Custom
2005-2018. Guitar Center model, spruce, rosewood, gloss finish.

2005-2018		$1,500	$2,000

000RS1
2014-2018. Road Series, made in Mexico, sapele top, back and sides, Fishman Sonitone electronics. Replaced by 000-10E in '19.

2014-2018		$550	$750

000RS2
2014-2015. Road Series as above with spruce top.

2014-2015		$550	$750

000RS25 Navojoa 25th Anniversary
2014-2016. Made in Mexico, celebrates 25th Anniversary of Martin's Navojoa facility, headstock Anniversary logo, Sikta spruce top, sapele back and sides, East Indian rosewood 'board.

2014-2016		$575	$750

000X Hippie
2007. Limited Edition of 200, celebrates the 40th Anniversary of the 'Summer of Love'.

2007		$1,500	$2,000

000X1
2000-2010. Mahogany grained HPL (high pressure laminate) back and sides, solid spruce top.

2000-2010		$400	$550

000X1AE
2010-2019. 000X1 with electronics. Replaced by 000-X2E in '20.

2010-2019		$450	$600

000-X2E
2020-present. X Series, Sikta spruce top, figured mahogany laminate back and sides, Fishman electronics.

2020-2023		$575	$750

000XE Black
2002-2005. Black satin finish.

2002-2005		$450	$600

000XM Auditorium
1999-2002. Spruce top, Indian rosewood back and sides, natural finish.

1999-2002		$450	$600

0000-1
1997-2001. 0000-size, mahogany.

1997-2001		$850	$1,125

Martin 000Jr-10

Martin 000-X2E

1890s Martin 2-24
Cody Lindsey

1880s Martin 2 1/2-21
Imaged by Heritage Auctions, HA.com

MODEL YEAR	FEATURES	EXC. COND. LOW	HIGH

0000-18 Custom/Custom 0000-18 (Gruhn 35th Anniversary)
2005-2009. Commissioned for Gruhn Guitars 35th Anniversary, 1st year models have signed Anniversary labels, 16" lower bout, high X-brace, mahogany back and sides.

2005-2009		$3,000	$4,000

0000-21S Custom (Gruhn 45th Anniversary)
2015. Commissioned for Gruhn Guitars 45th Anniversary, label signed by CF Martin IV and George Gruhn, Adirondack spruce top, Cocobolo or Guatemalan rosewood back and sides.

2015		$5,500	$7,250

0000-28 Series
1997-2011. Several models, jumbo-size 0000 cutaway body, models include H (herringbone trim, Sikta spruce top), Custom (Indian rosewood, Sikta), H-AG (Arlo Guthrie 30th anniversary, Indian rosewood, only 30 made), HA (herringbone trim, Adirondack).

1997-2000	0000-28H	$2,500	$3,500
1998-2006	0000-28 Custom	$2,500	$3,500
1999	0000-28H-AG	$2,500	$3,500
2011	0000-28HA	$2,500	$3,500

0000-38 (M-38)
1997-1998. Called M-38 in '77-'97 and '07-present (see that listing), 0000-size, Indian rosewood back and sides, multi-bound.

1997-1998		$3,500	$4,500

1-17
1906-1917 (1st version), 1931-1934 (2nd version). The first version has spruce top, mahogany back and sides, second version has all mahogany with flat natural finish.

1906-1934		$4,000	$5,000

1-17P
1928-1931, 1939. Mahogany back and sides, plectrum neck, 272 made.

1928-1939		$2,000	$2,500

1-18
1899-1903, 1906-1907, 1909-1921, 1923-1927. Brazilian rosewood or mahogany back and sides.

1899-1917	Brazilian	$5,000	$6,500
1918-1927	Mahogany	$3,500	$4,500

1-18H
1918. Hawaiian, only 3 made.

1918		$3,500	$4,500

1-18K
1917-1919. Koa.

1917-1919		$5,500	$7,000

1-18P
1929. 5-string plectrum, 1 made.

1929		$2,750	$3,500

1-18T
1927. Tenor 5-string, only 3 made.

1927		$2,500	$3,250

1-20
1860s. Parlor guitar, rosewood back and sides.

1867		$6,500	$8,500

1-21
1860s-1907, 1911, 1913-1921, 1925-1926. Initially offered in size 1 in the 1860s, ornate sound hole rings. A beautiful crack-free instrument is worth twice as much as a worn model with repaired cracks.

1860s-1926		$6,500	$8,500

1-21P
1930. Plectrum.

1930		$3,125	$4,000

1-22
1850s. Antique market value.

1850s		$10,000	$12,500

1-26
1855, 1874, 1890, 1903. Rosewood back and sides, ivory-bound top, rope-style purfling, antique market value.

1855-1903		$10,000	$12,500

1-27
1880s-1907, 1911, 1913-1921, 1925-1926. Antique market value.

1880-1926		$10,000	$12,500

1-28
1880s-1904, 1906-1907, 1909, 1911-1920, 1923. Style 28 appointments including Brazilian rosewood back and sides, antique market value.

1880s-1923		$10,000	$12,500

1-28P
1928-1930. Plectrum.

1928-1930		$4,000	$5,000

1-30
1860s-1904, 1906-1907, 1911-1914, 1916-1917, 1919. Size 1 Style 30 with pearl sound hole trim, cedar neck, antique market value.

1860s-1919		$8,500	$10,500

1-42
1858-1919. Rosewood back and sides, ivory-bound top and 'board.

1858-1919		$13,500	$17,500

1-45
1904-1905, 1911-1913, 1919. Only 6 made, slotted headstock and Style 45 appointments.

1904-1919		$30,000	$35,000

1/4 - 28
1973, 1979. 14 made.

1973, 1979		$6,500	$8,500

2-15
1939-1964. All mahogany body, dot markers.

1939-1964		$2,750	$3,500

2-17
1910, 1922-1934, 1936-1938. The 1910 version has spruce top, mahogany back and sides. '22 on, all mahogany body, no body binding after '30.

1867		$3,250	$4,000
1910		$3,000	$3,750
1922-1938		$3,000	$3,750

2-17H
1927-1929, 1931. Hawaiian, all mahogany, 12 frets clear of body.

1927-1931		$3,000	$3,750

2-17T
1927-1928. Tenor, 45 made.

1927-1928		$1,500	$2,000

MODEL YEAR	FEATURES	EXC. COND. LOW	HIGH

2-18

1857-1900, 1902-1903, 1907, 1925, 1929, 1934, 1938. Rosewood back and sides, changed to mahogany from 1917, dark outer binding, black back stripe, no dot inlay until 1902.

| 1857-1938 | | $4,250 | $5,500 |

2-18T

1928-1930. Tenor.

| 1928-1930 | | $2,500 | $3,250 |

2-20

1855-1897. Rare style only offered in size 2.

| 1855-1897 | | $5,000 | $6,250 |

2-21

1850s-1900, 1903-1904, 1909, 1925, 1928-1929. Rosewood back and sides, herringbone sound hole ring.

| 1885-1929 | | $4,000 | $5,000 |

2-21T

1928. Tenor.

| 1928 | | $1,875 | $2,500 |

2-24

1857-1898. Antique market value.

| 1857-1898 | | $7,000 | $8,750 |

2-27

1857-1880s, 1898-1900, 1907. Brazilian rosewood back and sides, pearl ring, zigzag back stripe, ivory bound ebony 'board and peghead.

| 1857-1907 | | $8,000 | $10,000 |

2-28

Brazilian rosewood back and sides, slot head.

| 1880 | | $8,000 | $10,000 |

2-28T

1928-1929. Tenor neck, Brazilian rosewood back and sides, herringbone top purfling.

| 1928-1929 | | $4,000 | $5,000 |

2-30

1874, 1902-1904, 1909-1910, 1921. Similar to 2-27, only 7 made.

| 1874-1921 | | $8,500 | $10,500 |

2-34

1850s-1898. Similar to 2-30.

| 1850s-1898 | | $9,000 | $11,500 |

2-40

1850s-1898, 1909.

| 1850s-1898 | | $9,500 | $12,000 |

2-42

1858-1900.

| 1874 | | $11,000 | $13,500 |

2-44

1930. Style 44, Olcott-Bickford Soloist custom order, only 4 made.

| 1930 | | $18,500 | $23,500 |

2-45T

1927-1928. Tenor style 45, 2 made.

| 1927-1928 | | $8,750 | $11,500 |

2 1/2-17

1856-1897, 1909, 1911-1914. The first Style 17s were small size 2 1/2 and 3, these early models use Brazilian rosewood.

| 1856-1914 | | $4,000 | $5,500 |

2 1/2-18

1865-1898, 1901, 1909-1914, 1916-1923. Parlor-size body with Style 18 appointments.

| 1865-1917 | Brazilian | $4,000 | $5,500 |
| 1918-1923 | Mahogany | $3,500 | $4,500 |

2 1/2-21

1880s, 1909, 1911-1913, 1917-1921. Brazilian rosewood back and sides.

| 1880s-1921 | | $4,500 | $6,500 |

2 1/2-42

1880s, 1911. Style 42 size 2 1/2 with Brazilian rosewood. Only 1 made 1911.

| 1880s-1911 | | $11,500 | $15,000 |

3-17

1856-1897, 1908 (1 made). The first Style 17s were small size 2 1/2 and 3. The early models use Brazilian rosewood, spruce top, bound back, unbound ebony 'board.

| 1856-1870s | Brazilian | $3,125 | $4,000 |
| 1880s-1908 | Mahogany | $3,000 | $3,750 |

3-21

1885. Brazilian rosewood.

| 1885 | | $4,000 | $5,000 |

3-24

1860. Brazilian rosewood.

| 1860 | | $6,500 | $8,500 |

3-34

1860. Brazilian rosewood.

| 1860 | | $8,500 | $10,500 |

5-15

2003-2007. Sapele or mahogany body, shorter scale.

| 2003-2007 | | $1,250 | $1,750 |

5-15T

1949-1963. Tenor neck, all mahogany, non-gloss finish.

| 1927-1930 | | $2,250 | $3,000 |
| 1949-1963 | | $1,750 | $2,500 |

5-16

1962-1963. Mahogany back and sides, unbound rosewood 'board.

| 1962-1963 | | $3,125 | $4,000 |

5-17

1912-1914, 1916, 1927-1928, 1930-1931, 1933-1943. Special order 1912-'36, standard production '37-'43.

1912-1916		$3,000	$4,000
1927-1928		$4,500	$5,500
1930-1939		$3,500	$4,500
1940-1943		$3,000	$4,000

5-17T

1949-1958. Tenor neck, all mahogany.

| 1949-1958 | | $1,500 | $2,000 |

5-18

1898-1899, 1912-1914, 1917, 1919-1921, 1923-1924, 1926-1932, 1934-1937, 1940-1941, 1943-1962, 1965, 1968-1977, 1979-1981, 1983-1989. Rosewood back and sides (changed to mahogany from 1917 on), 12 frets, slotted headstock.

1898-1917		$4,500	$6,000
1919-1921		$3,500	$4,500
1923-1937		$6,500	$8,500
1940-1946		$6,000	$7,500

1950 Martin 5-18
David Stone

1950 Martin 5-15 T
David Stone

GUITARS

1967 Martin 5-18
Imaged by Heritage Auctions, HA.com

Martin Bentley Snowflake First Edition

MODEL YEAR	FEATURES	EXC. COND. LOW	HIGH
1948-1949		$5,500	$7,000
1950-1959		$5,000	$6,250
1960-1962		$4,000	$5,000
1965		$3,750	$4,750
1966-1969		$3,250	$4,000
1970-1979		$3,000	$3,750
1980-1989		$2,500	$3,500

5-18 Marty Robbins
2009-2011. Custom Edition, 12-fret, Adirondack top, mahogany back and sides.

2009-2011		$2,250	$3,000

5-18T
1940, 1954, 1960-1961. Tenor, only 1 made each year.

1940		$1,750	$2,250
1954		$1,500	$2,000
1960-1961		$1,250	$1,625

5-21
1890s, 1902, 1912-1914, 1916-1920, 1927, 1977. Rosewood back and sides.

1890s-1977		$5,000	$6,250

5-21T
1927-1928. Tenor guitar with 21-styling.

1927-1928		$2,250	$3,000

5-28
1901-1902, 1904, 1918, 1920-1921, 1923, 1935, 1939, 1969-1970, 1977, 1980-1981, 1988, 2001-2002. Special edition, 1/2-size parlor guitar, rosewood back and sides.

1901-1923		$3,875	$5,000
1935-1939		$6,625	$8,750
1969-1988		$5,375	$7,000
2001-2002		$2,625	$3,500

7-28
1980-1995, 1997-2002. 7/8-body-size of a D-model, Style 28 appointments.

1980-1989		$2,625	$3,500
1990-2002		$2,250	$3,000

7-37K
1980-1987. 7/8-size baby dreadnought acoustic, Koa back and sides, spruce top, oval sound hole.

1980-1987		$2,500	$3,250

Alternative II Resophonic
2004-2007. Textured aluminum top, matching headstock overlay, high pressure laminate sides and back, spun aluminum cone resonator, Fishman pickup.

2004-2007		$650	$850

Alternative X
2001-2013. OO-Grand Concert body shape, textured aluminum top, matching headstock overlay, spun aluminum cone resonator, Fishman pickup.

2001-2013		$650	$850

Alternative X Midi
2003-2004. Roland GK Midi pickup with 13-pin output, additional Fishman Prefix Pro pickup and preamp system, requires Roland GA-20 interface.

2003-2004		$675	$900

Alternative XT
2002-2005. Alternative with DiMarzio humbucker, volume & tone controls, coil tap, Bigsby.

2003-2005		$650	$850

MODEL YEAR	FEATURES	EXC. COND. LOW	HIGH

America's Guitar 175th Anniversary
2008. D-style, 14-fret, Adirondack spruce top, Madagascar rosewood sides and back, 175 made, 'America's Guitar' headstock inlay, '175th Anniversary 1833-2008'.

2008		$5,000	$6,500

ASD-41 Australian Series
2005. Tasmanian Blackwood sides and back, Sikta spruce top, Australian theme appointments and label.

2005		$4,000	$5,250

Backpacker
1992-present. Small-bodied travel guitar, nylon called Classical Backpacker.

1992-2023	Steel strings	$150	$250
1994-2021	Nylon strings	$145	$200

Backpacker 25th Anniversary
2017 only. Sapele.

2017		$250	$350

Bentley Snowflake First Edition
2021-present. Custom Shop Limited Edition, Sikta spruce top, Madagascar rosewood back and sides, exclusive Wilson A. Bentley (photomicrography) snowflake images for neck and pickguard inlays.

2021-2023		$10,000	$13,000

Bigsby/Martin D-28 Bigsby
2018-2019. Martin partnered with Gretsch to build, Merle Travis inspired, Sikta spruce top, East Indian rosewood back and sides, Bigsby headstock, natural finish.

2018-2019		$2,750	$3,500

C-1
1931-1942. Acoustic archtop, mahogany back and sides, spruce top, round hole until '33 (449 made), f-holes appear in '32 (786 made), bound body, sunburst.

1931-1933	Round hole	$3,000	$3,750
1932-1942	F-hole	$3,000	$3,750

C-1-12
1932. Only 1 made, 12-string version.

1932		$3,000	$3,750

C-1P
1931-1933, 1939. Archtop, plectrum.

1931-1933	Round hole	$2,250	$3,750
1939	F-hole	$2,250	$3,000

C-1R Humphrey
1997-2000. Solid cedar top, laminated rosewood back and sides, satin finish.

1997-2000		$1,125	$1,500

C-1T
1931-1934, 1936-1938. Archtop, tenor, round hole (71 made) or f-hole (83 made).

1931-1933	Round hole	$2,250	$3,000
1933-1938	F-hole	$2,250	$3,000

C-2
1931-1942. Acoustic archtop, Brazilian rosewood back and sides, carved spruce top, round hole until '33 (269 made), f-holes appear in '32 (439 made), zigzag back stripe, multi-bound body, slotted-diamond inlay, sunburst.

1931-1933	Round hole	$4,000	$5,000
1932-1942	F-hole	$3,500	$4,500

C-2-12
1932. Only 1 made, 12-string version.

1932		$3,375	$4,250

MODEL		EXC. COND.	
YEAR	FEATURES	LOW	HIGH

C-2P
1931. Archtop, plectrum, round hole, 2 made.
| 1931 | | $3,125 | $4,000 |

C-2T
1931-1936. Archtop, tenor, round or f-hole.
| 1931-1934 | Round hole | $3,000 | $3,750 |
| 1934-1936 | F-hole | $2,250 | $3,000 |

C-3
1931-1934. Archtop, Brazilian rosewood back and sides, round sound hole until early '33 (53 made), f-holes after (58 made).
| 1931-1933 | Round hole | $6,500 | $8,500 |
| 1933-1934 | F-hole | $5,000 | $6,500 |

C-3T
1933. Archtop, tenor, 1 made.
| 1933 | | $4,250 | $5,500 |

Car Talk Special Edition
2008-2010. D-size, East Indian rosewood back and sides, car parts and tools inlay, Car Talk credits on 'guard.
| 2008-2010 | | $4,500 | $6,000 |

CEO Series
1997-present. Chief Executive Officer (C.F. Martin IV), Special Edition (CEO-1 through CEO-6) and Custom Signature Edition (CEO-7 through CEO-9), various woods and specs. CEO-1/1R ('97-'98), 2 ('98), 3 ('99-'00), 4 ('01-'04), 4R ('02-'10), 5 ('01-'04), 6 ('11-'13), 7 ('15-present), 8 ('15-'17), 8.2/E ('17-'18), 9 ('19-present).
1997-2016	CEO-1 to CEO-6	$2,000	$2,500
2014-2023	CEO-7	$2,000	$2,500
2015-2017	CEO-8	$3,125	$4,000
2017-2018	CEO-82	$4,250	$5,500
2017-2018	CEO-82E	$2,875	$3,750

CF-1 American Archtop
2004-2009. 17", solid maple sides, laminated maple back, ebony 'board, dot markers, 1 pickup, sunburst, natural or black.
| 2004-2009 | | $2,500 | $3,250 |

CF-2 American Archtop
2004-2009. CF-1 with 2 humbuckers, sunburst, natural or black.
| 2004-2009 | | $2,500 | $3,250 |

Claire's Guitar
2005-2006. Made to celebrate the birth of Claire Frances Martin, limited to 100, small parlor size, Sikta spruce top, Brazilian rosewood back and sides, fancy appointments, comes with pink-lined hard case.
| 2005-2006 | | $6,000 | $7,750 |

Concept III
2003. U.S.-made, solid spruce top, solid mahogany back and sides, cutaway, on-board electronics, sparkle-mist finish.
| 2003 | | $2,000 | $2,500 |

**Cowboy 2015 Limited Edition/
LE Cowboy 2015**
2015. Limited to number sold in '15, 000, 12-fret, Sikta spruce top, solid Goncalo Alves back and sides, cowboy on horse artwork by William Matthews.
| 2015 | | $3,250 | $4,250 |

**Cowboy 2016 Limited Edition/
LE Cowboy 2016**
2016. Limited to number sold in '16, auditorium, 12-fret, Sikta spruce top, mahogany back and sides, cowboy on bucking bronco artwork by William Matthews.
| 2016 | | $3,250 | $4,250 |

Cowboy Series
2000-2009. Models include Cowboy X (2000, 250 made), Cowboy II ('01, 500 made), Cowboy III ('03, 750 made), and Cowboy IV ('05-'06, 250 made), Cowboy V ('06-'09, 500 made).
| 2001-2009 | Various models | $750 | $1,500 |

CS-21-11
2011. Limited Edition, 171 made, Madagascar rosewood.
| 2011 | | $4,000 | $5,250 |

CS-Bluegrass-16
2016-2020. Limited to 100, Adirondack spruce top, Guatemalan rosewood back and sides, vintage gloss finish.
| 2016-2020 | | $4,500 | $6,000 |

CS-CF Martin Outlaw-17
2017-2020. Limited to 100 made, Adirondack spruce top, mahogany back and sides, natural gloss finish.
| 2017-2020 | | $4,250 | $5,500 |

CSN (Gerry Tolman Tribute)
2007-2009. Crosby, Stills & Nash, CSN logo on headstock, D-style, high-end appointments, East Indian rosewood back and sides. Tolman was CSN's longtime manager and was killed in car wreck in '06.
| 2007-2009 | | $2,500 | $3,250 |

C-TSH (Humphrey/Martin)
1997-2002. Designed by classical guitar luthier Thomas Humphrey, based on his Millenium model, arched Englemann spruce top, rosewood back and sides.
| 1997-2002 | | $2,500 | $3,250 |

Custom 15
1991-1994. Renamed HD-28V Custom 15 in ca. 2001.
| 1991-1994 | | $2,750 | $3,500 |

Custom D Classic Mahogany
2006-2014. D body, spruce top, mahogany back and sides.
| 2006-2014 | | $800 | $1,125 |

Custom D Classic Rosewood
2006-2011. D body, spruce top, rosewood back and sides.
| 2006-2011 | | $800 | $1,125 |

Custom Shop 18 Style 0000
2019-2020. Adirondack, Sinker mahogany back and sides, Sinker is old growth from 1900-1920, specs can vary.
| 2019-2020 | | $2,750 | $3,500 |

Custom Shop 18 Style Dreadnought
2019-2020. Adirondack, Sinker mahogany back and sides, specs can vary.
| 2019-2020 | | $2,750 | $3,500 |

Custom Shop 18 Style OM
2020. Adirondack, Sinker mahogany back and sides, 14-fret, specs can vary.
| 2020 | | $2,500 | $3,500 |

Martin CS-Bluegrass-16

CS-CF Martin Outlaw-17

GUITARS

Martin D-10E

Martin D-13E

| MODEL | | EXC. COND. | |
YEAR	FEATURES	LOW	HIGH

Custom Shop 28 Style Dreadnought
2020. Adirondack, Indian rosewood back and sides.

| 2020 | | $3,250 | $4,250 |

Custom Shop 28 Style OM
2020. Adirondack, Indian rosewood back and sides, sunburst or natural.

| 2020 | | $3,000 | $4,000 |

D-1
1992-2005, 2009. Current model with mahogany body, A-frame bracing, available as an acoustic/electric.

| 1992-2005 | | $800 | $1,125 |
| 2009 | Reintroduced | $800 | $1,125 |

D12-1
1996-2001. Mahogany, satin finish, 12-string.

| 1996-2001 | | $775 | $1,000 |

D-1 Authentic 1931
2016-2019. Adirondack spruce top, dark mahogany back and sides, Vintage Gloss finish.

| 2016-2019 | | $4,750 | $6,000 |

D-1E
1994-1998, 2009. Acoustic/electric version, current model solid Sikta with sapele.

| 1994-1998 | | $850 | $1,125 |
| 2009 | | $850 | $1,125 |

D-1GT
2011-2014. Double bound body, gloss finish top, satin back and sides.

| 2011-2014 | | $775 | $1,000 |

D-1R
1994-2003, 2012. D-1 with laminated rosewood back and sides.

| 1994-2003 | | $775 | $1,000 |
| 2012 | Reintroduced | $775 | $1,000 |

D-1RE
1994-1995, 1998. D-1R with various electronics.

| 1994-1998 | | $850 | $1,125 |

D-2
1931-1932, 1934. Earliest version of the D-28, Brazilian rosewood.

| 1931-1934 | | $250,000 | $328,000 |

D-2R
1996-2002. Style 28 appointments, laminated rosewood back and sides, natural satin finish.

| 1996-2002 | | $775 | $1,000 |

D-3-18
1991. Limited Edition, run of 80, Sikta spruce top, 3-piece mahogany back.

| 1991 | | $1,750 | $2,250 |

D-3R
1996-2002. Style 35 appointments, laminated rosewood back and sides, natural satin finish.

| 1996-2002 | | $850 | $1,125 |

D-10E
2019-present. Road Series, updated version of DSR1/DSR2, Sikta spruce or sapele top, sapele back and sides, Fishman electronics, satin finish.

| 2019-2023 | | $500 | $650 |

D-11E
2019. Road Series, Sikta spruce top, solid sapele back and sides, Fishman.

| 2019 | | $650 | $850 |

D-12E
2019-present. Sikta spruce top, sapele back and sides, Fishman.

| 2019-2023 | | $875 | $1,250 |

D-12E Koa
2020. Sikta spruce top, Koa veneer back and sides, gloss finish.

| 2020 | | $1,125 | $1,500 |

D12 David Crosby
2009-2011. D-size 12-string, quilted mahogany body, Carpathian spruce top.

| 2009-2011 | | $4,000 | $5,000 |

D-13E
2019-present. Updated version of DRSG, Sikta spruce top, siris back and sides, Fishman.

| 2019-2023 | | $850 | $1,125 |

D-15/D-15M
1997-present. The body is all mahogany up to 2002, mahogany or sapele (which is like mahogany) up to '10. Becomes the all-mahogany D-15M in '11.

| 1997-2010 | | $1,000 | $1,375 |
| 2011-2023 M | | $1,000 | $1,375 |

D-15M Burst
2015-2018. Shaded mahogany top, back and sides, satin finish.

| 2015-2018 | | $1,125 | $1,500 |

D-15M Elderly Instruments 40th Anniversary
2012. Only 10 made, solid mahogany body, special appointments, label signed by Elderly president Stan Werbin and Chris Martin.

| 2012 | | $1,125 | $1,500 |

D-15M StreetMaster
2017-present. Distressed mahogany satin finish.

| 2017-2023 | | $975 | $1,250 |

D-15S
2001-2009. Slotted headstock D-15, body is solid sapele or mahogany.

| 2001-2009 | | $975 | $1,250 |

D-16 Adirondack
2009-2013. Adirondack spruce top, mahogany back and sides.

| 2009-2013 | | $1,675 | $2,125 |

D-16 Lyptus
2003-2005. Lyptus back and sides.

| 2003-2005 | | $1,125 | $1,500 |

D-16A
1987-1990. North American ash back and sides, scalloped bracing.

| 1987-1990 | | $1,375 | $1,750 |

D-16E Burst
2019-2021. Mahogany burst ovangkol gloss top, satin ovangkol back and sides, Fishman electronics.

| 2019-2021 | | $1,625 | $2,125 |

D-16E Rock The Vote
2019-2021. Special Edition, designed by David Crosby, custom artwork by Robert F. Goetzl, Sikta spruce gloss top, satin sycamore back and sides, Fishman electronics.

| 2019-2021 | | $2,000 | $2,500 |

MODEL YEAR	FEATURES	EXC. COND. LOW	HIGH
D-16E Rosewood			
2019-2021. Gloss Sitka spruce top, satin East Indian rosewood back and sides, Fishman electronics.			
2019-2021		$1,500	$2,000
D-16E/D-16E Mahogany			
2017-present. Gloss Sitka spruce top, satin sycamore back and sides, Fishman electronics. Mahogany in '20.			
2017-2020		$1,500	$2,000
2020-2023	Mahogany	$1,500	$2,000
D-16GT			
1999-2019. D-16 with gloss top.			
1999-2019		$975	$1,250
D-16GTE			
1999-2015. D-16GT with Fishman electronics.			
1999-2015		$1,125	$1,500
D-16H (1991, 1992, 1993)			
1990-1994. D-16 with herringbone sound hole ring, replaced by D-16T in '94.			
1990-1994		$1,250	$1,625
D-16K Koa			
1986. Koa back and sides.			
1986		$1,625	$2,125
D-16M Mahogany			
1986-1990. Mahogany back and sides.			
1986-1990		$1,125	$1,500
D-16O Oak			
1999. Red oak or white oak, 4 made.			
1999		$1,125	$1,500
D-16R 50th Anniversary			
2010. Adirondack spruce top, rosewood back and sides, natural.			
2010		$2,000	$2,500
D-16R/D-16TR/D-16TRG			
1995-2009. Spruce top, Indian rosewood back and sides, satin finish (R), gloss (TR) or full gloss (TRG).			
1995-2009		$975	$1,250
D-16RGT			
1999-2019. D-16 T specs with rosewood back and sides, gloss finish.			
1999-2019		$975	$1,250
D-16RGT Ryman Auditorium			
2007. Custom designed by George Gruhn, oak 'guard, headplate and fret markers made from original Ryman Auditorium pews, laser-etched image of Ryman on headplate, spruce top, Indian rosewood back and sides, special Ryman label.			
2007		$3,000	$4,000
D-16T/D-16TG			
1994-1998. Mahogany back and sides, satin finish (T) or gloss (TG).			
1994-1998	T	$1,000	$1,375
1995-1997	TG	$975	$1,250
D-16W Walnut			
1987, 1990. Walnut back and sides.			
1987, 1990		$975	$1,250
D-17			
2001-2005. All solid mahogany back, sides and top, natural brown mahogany finish.			
2001-2005		$975	$1,250

MODEL YEAR	FEATURES	EXC. COND. LOW	HIGH
D-17E			
2002-2003. With on-board electronics.			
2002-2003		$1,125	$1,500
D-17M			
2013-2016. Shaded spruce top, solid mahogany back and sides.			
2013-2016		$975	$1,250
D-18			
1931-present. Standard Series, mahogany back and sides, spruce top, black back stripe, 12-fret neck, changed to 14 frets in '34.			
1931-1934	12-fret	$90,000	$110,000
1934	14-fret, dark top	$140,000	$175,000
1934-1937	14-fret	$80,000	$100,000
1938	Early '38, Advanced X	$75,000	$95,000
1938	Late '38, Rear X	$55,000	$75,000
1939	Early '39, 175 neck	$50,000	$65,000
1939	Late '39, 168 neck	$40,000	$50,000
1940-1941		$40,000	$50,000
1942-1944	Scalloped	$35,000	$45,000
1944-1946	Non-scalloped	$25,000	$30,000
1947-1949		$12,000	$15,000
1950-1959		$9,000	$11,500
1960-1964		$6,500	$8,500
1965		$6,000	$7,500
1966-1969		$4,250	$5,500
1970-1979		$3,000	$4,000
1980-1989		$2,500	$3,250
1983	50th Ann. 1833-1983	$2,500	$3,250
1990-1999		$2,500	$3,250
2000-2023		$2,250	$3,000
D12-18			
1973-1995. Mahogany back and sides, 12 strings, 14 frets clear of body, solid headstock.			
1973-1979		$2,000	$2,500
1980-1989		$1,750	$2,250
1990-1995		$1,750	$2,250
CS-D18-12			
2012-2014. Custom Shop, based on 1929 Ditson 111 (12-string), 75 made, 12-fret mahogany neck, Adirondack spruce top, Madagascar rosewood binding.			
2012-2014		$4,000	$5,000
D-18 1955 CFM IV			
2010. Celebrates C. F. Martin IV birthday, 55 made.			
2010		$3,375	$4,250
D-18 75th Anniversary Edition			
2009. '75th Anniversary Edition 1934-2009' noted on label and headstock stencil.			
2009		$3,500	$4,500
D-18 Andy Griffith			
2003. Bear claw spruce top, Andy's script signature on 18th fret.			
2003		$2,750	$3,500
D-18 Authentic 1937			
2006-present. Authentic pre-war specs, Adirondack spruce, forward X-brace and scalloped Adirondack bracing, 14-fret neck.			
2006-2023		$5,000	$6,500

1947 Martin D-18
Folkway Music

Martin D-18 Authentic 1937

1968 Martin D-12-20
W. H. Stephens

1956 Martin D-21
David Stone

MODEL			EXC. COND.	
YEAR		FEATURES	LOW	HIGH

D-18 Authentic 1939

2013-present. Adirondack spruce top, mahogany back, sides and neck, ebony 'board, vintage gloss finish.

2013-2019		$5,000	$6,500
2019-2023	VTS	$5,000	$6,500

D-18 Authentic 1939 Aged

2020-present. New design, Torrefied Adirondack.

2020-2023	$4,000	$5,250

D-18 Custom Adirondack

2016. Adirondack spruce top, mahogany back and sides.

2016	$2,750	$3,500

D-18 Del McCourey 50th Anniversary

2008. Adirondack spruce top, mahogany sides and back, interior label signed by Del McCourey, 50 made.

2008	$3,500	$4,750

D-18 Modern Deluxe

2019-present. Sikta spruce top with Vintage Tone System (VTS), mahogany back and sides, gloss finish.

2019-2023	$2,125	$2,750

D-18 Special

1989. Guitar of the Month, 28 made, first Martin to use rosewood for binding, heel cap and endpiece since 1932, scalloped top, mahogany back and sides, slotted-diamond markers.

1989	$2,500	$3,250

D-18CW Clarence White Commemorative Edition

2001. Rare Appalachian spruce top, 2-piece quilted mahogany back and sides, Clarence White's signature between 19th - 20th frets, aged gloss lacquer finish.

2001	$3,000	$4,000

D-18D

1975. Frap pickup.

1975	$2,250	$3,000

D-18DC David Crosby

2002. David Crosby signature at 20th fret, Engel-mann spruce top, quilted mahogany back and sides, 250 made.

2002	$5,000	$6,500

D-18E

1958-1959. D-18 factory built with DeArmond pickups which required ladder bracing (reducing acoustic volume and quality).

1958-1959	$9,500	$12,000

D-18E 2020

2020. Limited Edition, 2,020 offered, Sikta spruce top, mahogany back and sides, electronics, gloss finish.

2020	$2,500	$3,250

D-18E Modern Deluxe

2020-2021. Torrified Sikta spruce top, Fishman electronics.

2020-2021	$2,750	$3,500

D-18E Retro

2012-2019. Sikta spruce top, mahogany back and sides.

2012-2019	$2,125	$2,750

D-18GE Golden Era

1995, 2000-2016. The 1995 version is a copy of a '37 D-18, 272 made. The current model is based on '34 model, natural or sunburst.

1995	$3,250	$4,000
2000-2016	$3,250	$4,000

MODEL			EXC. COND.	
YEAR		FEATURES	LOW	HIGH

D-18GE Golden Era 1934 Special Edition

1999-2012. Specs from '34 D-18, red Adirondack spruce top, mahogany back and sides, aged finish.

1999-2012	$3,125	$4,000

D-18H

1934-1935. Hawaiian.

1934-1935	$90,000	$125,000

D-18H Huda

1966. Huda wood, Hawaiian, 2 made.

1966	$4,000	$5,250

D-18LE

1986-1987. Limited Edition, quilted or flamed mahogany back and sides, scalloped braces, gold tuners with ebony buttons.

1986-1987	$3,125	$4,000

D-18MB

1990. Limited Edition Guitar of the Month, flame maple binding, Engelmann spruce top signed by shop foremen, X-brace, total of 99 sold.

1990	$2,500	$3,250

D-18P

2010-2011. Fishman electronics.

2010-2011	$2,250	$3,000

D-18S

1967-1994. Mahogany back and sides, 12-fret neck, slotted headstock, majority of production before '77, infrequent after that.

1967-1969	$5,000	$6,500
1970-1979	$4,000	$5,000
1980-1989	$3,000	$4,000
1990-1994	$3,000	$4,000

D-18SS

2009-2012. 24.9" short scale.

2009	$2,250	$3,000

D-18V/D-18 Vintage

1985 (V), 1992 (Vintage). Low-profile neck, scalloped braces, bound, total of 218 sold, Guitar of the Month in '85, Vintage Series in '92.

1985	V	$2,625	$3,500
1992	Vintage	$2,625	$3,500

D-18VE

2004-2007. D-18 V with Fishman Ellipse.

2004-2007	$2,750	$3,500

D-18VM/D-18V/D-18VO

1995-2011. Vintage Series, 14-fret, mahogany (M) back and sides, tortoise binding, V-neck. M dropped from name in '99. Natural finish. 48 sunburst (D-18VO) made in '95.

1995	VO	$2,750	$3,500
1995-1998	VM	$2,750	$3,500
1999-2011	V	$2,750	$3,500

D-18VMS/D-18VS

1996-2011. Vintage Series, 12-fret version of D-18 VM/V, M dropped from name in '99.

1996-1999	VMS	$2,750	$3,500
2000-2011	VS	$2,750	$3,500

D-19

1977-1988. Deluxe mahogany dreadnought, optional mahogany top, multi-bound but unbound rosewood 'board.

1977-1979	$3,000	$4,000
1980-1988	$2,500	$3,250

MODEL YEAR	FEATURES	EXC. COND. LOW	HIGH
D12-20			

1964-1991. Mahogany back and sides, 12 strings, 12 frets clear of body, slotted headstock.

MODEL YEAR	FEATURES	EXC. COND. LOW	HIGH
1964-1969		$2,250	$3,000
1970-1979		$2,000	$2,500
1980-1991		$1,750	$2,250

D-21

1955-1969. Brazilian rosewood back and sides, rosewood 'board, chrome tuners.

1955-1959		$12,000	$15,000
1960-1964		$10,500	$13,500
1965		$9,000	$11,500
1966-1969		$8,000	$10,000

D-21 Special/D-21S

2008-2020. Sikta spruce top, Indian rosewood back and sides, herringbone sound hole.

2008-2020		$2,150	$2,875

D-21JC Jim Croce Signature

1999-2000. Jim Croce signature and 1973 dime inlaid on neck, Indian rosewood back and sides, 73 made.

1999-2000		$4,500	$6,000

D-21JCB Jim Croce Limited Edition

1999-2001. Same as above but with Brazilian rosewood back and sides.

1999-2001		$10,000	$13,000

D-21LE

1985. Limited Edition, 75 made.

1985		$2,500	$3,250

D-25K

1980-1989. Dreadnought-size, Koa back and sides, spruce top.

1980-1989		$2,750	$3,500

D-25K2

1980-1989. Same as D-25K, but with Koa top and black 'guard.

1980-1989		$2,750	$3,500

D-28

1931-present. Brazilian rosewood back and sides (changed to Indian rosewood in '70), '36 was the last year for the 12-fret model, '44 was the last year for scalloped bracing, '47 was the last year herringbone trim was offered, natural. Ultra high-end D-28 Martin guitar (pre-'47) valuations are very sensitive to structural and cosmetic condition. Finish wear and body cracks for ultra high-end Martin flat-tops should be evaluated on a case-by-case basis. Small variances within the 'excellent condition' category can lead to notable valuation differences.

1931-1936	12-fret	$300,000	$350,000
1934-1937	14-fret, dark top	$225,000	$275,000
1934-1937	14-fret	$175,000	$225,000
1938	Early '38, Advanced X	$175,000	$225,000
1938	Late '38, Rear X	$165,000	$215,000
1939	Early '39, 175 neck	$165,000	$215,000
1939	Late '39, 168 neck	$150,000	$175,000
1940-1941		$115,000	$150,000
1942	Scalloped	$115,000	$150,000
1943	Scalloped	$100,000	$125,000
1944	Scalloped,		

MODEL YEAR	FEATURES	EXC. COND. LOW	HIGH
	herringbone	$95,000	$120,000
1944-1945	Herringbone, non-scalloped	$50,000	$65,000
1946-1947	Early '47, herring- bone, non- scalloped	$45,000	$55,000
1947-1949	Late '47, non- herringbone	$21,500	$28,500
1950-1952		$15,000	$20,000
1953-1957	Kluson	$15,000	$20,000
1958-1959	Grover	$15,000	$20,000
1960-1962		$10,000	$12,500
1963-1964		$9,500	$12,500
1965		$8,500	$11,000
1966-1969	Brazilian	$8,000	$10,000
1970-1979	Indian	$4,000	$5,000
1980-1989		$3,000	$4,000
1990-1999		$2,750	$3,500
2000-2009		$2,500	$3,000
2010-2017	Standard X	$2,500	$3,000
2018-2023	Forward-shifted X	$2,500	$3,000

D12-28

1970-2018. Indian rosewood back and sides, 12 strings, 14 frets clear of body, solid headstock.

1970-1979		$2,500	$3,250
1980-1989		$2,250	$3,000
1990-1999		$2,250	$3,000
2000-2018		$2,250	$3,000

D-28 1935 Special

1993. Guitar of the Month, 1935 features, Indian rosewood back and sides, peghead with Brazilian rosewood veneer.

1993		$3,000	$4,000

D-28 1955 CFM IV

2009-2010. Limited Edition, 55 made celebrating Chris Martin IV birthyear 1955, Madagascar rosewood.

2009-2010		$5,000	$6,500

D-28 50th Anniversary

1983. Stamped inside '1833-1983 150th Anniversary', Indian rosewood back and sides.

1983		$2,500	$3,250

D-28 75th Anniversary

2009 only. Limited production celebrating 1934 to 2009, Madagascar rosewood back and sides, Adirondack spruce top.

2009		$5,250	$7,000

D-28 75th Anniversary Brazilian

1983. Brazilian rosewood back and sides.

1983		$9,000	$12,000

D-28 150th Anniversary

1983-1985. Limited production of 268, only '83 vintage have the anniversary stamp, Brazilian rosewood sides and back.

1983	150th stamp	$9,000	$12,000
1984-1985	No stamp	$9,000	$12,000

D-28 Authentic 1931

2013-2015. Adirondack spruce top, Madagascar rosewood back and sides, authentic '31 appointments, vintage gloss finish.

2013-2015		$6,000	$7,500

1947 Martin D-28
Terry White

1971 Martin D-28
Tim Carroll

MODEL YEAR	FEATURES	EXC. COND. LOW	HIGH

D-28 Authentic 1937
2007-2009, 2014-present. '37 specs, 50 made of first Brazilian rosewood batch. Reintroduced '14 with Madagascar rosewood and Vintage Tone System (VTS).

2007-2009	Brazilian	$20,000	$25,000
2014-2023	Madagascar	$6,500	$8,500
2020-2023	VTS aged	$6,000	$7,500

D-28 Authentic 1941
2013-2016. Adirondack, Madagascar rosewood.

2013-2016	$6,250	$8,000

D-28 Custom
1984. Guitar of the Month Nov. '84, double bound D-body, multi-ring rosette, rosewood back/sides, spruce top, 43 made.

1984	$3,500	$4,500

D-28 Dan Tyminski
2010-2013. Custom Artist limited edition, Indian rosewood back and sides, Adirondack spruce top, other bracing specs.

2010-2013	$3,250	$4,250

D-28CW/CWB Clarence White
2003-2014. CW has Indian rosewood back and sides, the CWB Brazilian, only 150 CWBs were to be built.

2003-2004	CWB	$7,500	$9,750
2003-2014	CW	$3,750	$5,000

D-28D
1975. Frap pickup.

1975	$3,250	$4,500

D-28DM Del McCourey Signature
2003. Limited edition of 115, natural.

2003	$3,500	$4,500

D-28E
1959-1964. Electronics, Brazilian rosewood back and sides, 2 DeArmond pickups, natural.

1959-1964	$9,000	$11,500

D-28E Modern Deluxe
2020-2021. Sikta spruce VTS aged top, East Indian rosewood back and sides, Fishman electronics, gloss finish.

2020-2021	$3,750	$4,750

D-28 Elvis Presley
2008-2010. Carpathian spruce top, East Indian rosewood back and sides.

2008-2010	$4,500	$5,500

D-28 Elvis Presley CVR
2008-2010. Carpathian spruce top, East Indian rosewood back and sides, tooled leather cover.

2008-2010	$5,500	$7,250

D-28 John Lennon
2017-2018. Custom Signature Edition, Sikta spruce top with Vintage Tone System, East Indian rosewood back and sides, back inlaid with a peace sign, Lennon's self-portrait illustration beneath Martin logo on headstock.

2017-2018	$3,000	$4,000

D-28 John Lennon 75th Anniversary
2016. Limited Edition to commemorate Lennon's 75th birthday (10/9/2015), 75 made, Adirondack spruce top, Madagascar rosewood back and sides, headplate includes Lennon's famous self-portrait illustration.

2016	$9,000	$12,000

Martin D-28 Authentic 1937

Martin D-28 Modern Deluxe

D-28 John Prine
2017-2020. Custom Signature Edition, only 70 offered, Engelmann spruce top, Madagascar rosewood back and sides, inlaid pearl angel wings on headstock.

2017-2020	$4,250	$5,500

D-28 Louvin Brothers
2015-2020. Limited run of 50, Sikta spruce top, East Indian rosewood back and sides, printed Louvin Brothers artwork from "Satan is Real" album.

2015-2020	$2,500	$3,500

D-28 Marquis
2004-2017. Golden Era appointments, Adirondack top, Indian rosewood, natural or sunburst.

2004-2017	Natural	$3,250	$4,500
2004-2017	Sunburst	$3,250	$4,500
2007-2009	Madagascar option	$3,250	$4,500

D-28 Modern Deluxe
2019-present. Sikta spruce top with Vintage Tone System (VTS), East Indian rosewood back and sides, gloss finish.

2019-2023	$2,500	$3,250

D-28 Museum Edition 1941
2009-2012. Based on '41 model located in Martin's PA museum, Adirondack spruce top, Madagascar rosewood back and sides, natural finish.

2009-2012	$5,500	$7,000

D-28 Rich Robinson
2022-present. Custom Signature Edition, styled from Robinson's '54 D-28, Sikta spruce top, East Indian rosewood back and sides, aged vintage gloss finish.

2022-2023	$5,000	$6,500

D-28GE Golden Era
1999-2005. GE Golden Era, Brazilian rosewood, herringbone trim.

1999-2005	$10,000	$13,000

D-28HW Hank Williams
1998. Limited Edition, 150 made, replica of Hank Williams' 1944 D-28, Brazilian rosewood sides and back, scalloped braces, herringbone.

1998	$7,500	$10,000

D-28KTBS Bob Shane
2003. Bob Shane of the Kingston Trio, Signature Edition with 51 offered, Sikta spruce top, East Indian rosewood back and sides, The Kingston Trio logo between 11th-13th frets, Shane's pearl signature 19th-20th frets.

2003	$4,000	$5,250

D-28LF Lester Flatt
1998. Limited Edition, 50 made, Brazilian rosewood.

1998	$7,500	$10,000

D-28LSH
1991. Guitar of the Month, Indian rosewood back and sides, herringbone trim, snowflake inlay, zigzag back stripe.

1991	$2,750	$3,500

D-28LSV
1999-2005. Large sound hole model.

1999-2005	$2,500	$3,250

MODEL YEAR	FEATURES	EXC. COND. LOW	HIGH

D-28M Elvis Presley
2008-2010. Limited Edition, 175 made, Madagascar rosewood back and sides, Adirondack top, tooled leather cover.

2008-2010		$7,000	$9,000

D-28M Merle Travis
2008-2010. 100 made, Adirondack top, Madagascar rosewood back and sides, curly maple neck, 6-on-a-side Bigsby-style headstock, heart-diamond-spade-club inlays.

2008-2010		$5,000	$6,500

D-28M The Mamas and The Papas
2012-2014. Custom Artist, 100 made, Madagascar rosewood back and sides.

2012-2014		$3,000	$4,000

D-28P
1988-1990, 2011-2012. P indicates low-profile neck, Indian rosewood back and sides. Reintroduced 2011 with high performance neck.

1988-1990		$2,250	$3,000
2011-2012		$2,250	$3,000

D-28S
1954-1994. Rosewood back and sides, 12-fret neck.

1954-1959	Special order	$20,000	$25,000
1960-1965	Special order	$15,000	$20,000
1966-1969	Brazilian	$13,500	$18,000
1970-1979	Indian	$3,750	$5,000
1980-1989		$2,750	$3,500
1990-1994		$2,750	$3,500

D-28SW Wurlitzer
1962-1965, 1968. Made for the Wurlitzer Co.

1962-1965		$9,000	$12,000
1968		$9,000	$12,000

D-28V
1983-1985. Limited Edition, Brazilian rosewood back and sides, herringbone trim, slotted diamond inlay.

1983-1985		$7,000	$9,000

D-35
1965-present. Brazilian rosewood sides and 3-piece back, changed to Brazilian wings and Indian center in '70, then all Indian rosewood in '71, natural with sunburst option. For a brief time, on the back side, the center panel was Brazilian and the two side panels were Indian.

1965	Brazilian	$10,000	$12,500
1966-1970	Brazilian	$9,500	$12,000
1970	Center panel only	$4,500	$5,500
1970-1979	Indian	$4,000	$5,000
1980-1989		$3,500	$4,500
1983	150th center strip	$3,500	$4,500
1990-1999		$3,000	$3,750
2000-2023		$3,000	$3,750
2015	50th Anniv Label	$3,000	$3,750

D12-35
1965-1995. Brazilian rosewood back and sides, changed to Indian rosewood in '70, 12 strings, 12 frets clear of body, slotted headstock.

1965-1969	Brazilian	$6,500	$8,500
1970-1979	Indian	$3,250	$4,000
1980-1989		$3,000	$3,750
1990-1995		$3,000	$3,750

D12-35 50th Anniversary Limited Edition
2015-2016. Limited to 183 (the quantity of 1st production run in '65), European spruce top, 3-piece East Indian rosewood back and sides, natural gloss finish.

2015-2016		$4,500	$6,000

D-35 30th Anniversary
1995. Limited Edition, 207 made, D-35 with '1965-1995' inlay on 20th fret, gold hardware.

1995		$4,000	$5,250

D-35 Bicentennial
1975-1976. Limited Edition, 197 made, Sikta spruce top, 3-piece Indian rosewood back, eagle inlay on headstock, 13 star inlay on 'board.

1975-1976		$3,750	$5,000

D-35 Ernest Tubb
2003. Indian rosewood back and sides, special inlays, 90 built.

2003		$3,500	$4,500

D-35 Seth Avett
2013-2019. Swiss spruce top, East Indian rosewood/flamed Koa back, copper snowflake inlay.

2013-2019		$2,750	$3,500

D-35E Retro
2012-2019. Sikta spruce top, East Indian rosewood back and sides.

2012-2019		$2,500	$3,500

D-35JC Johnny Cash
2006-present. Rosewood back and sides.

2006-2023		$3,750	$5,000

D-35MP
2011-2012. Madagascar rosewood back and sides, high performance neck.

2011-2012		$2,500	$3,250

D-35P
1986-1990. P indicates low-profile neck.

1986-1990		$2,500	$3,250

D-35S
1966-1993. Brazilian rosewood back and sides, changed to Indian rosewood in '70, 12-fret neck, slotted peghead.

1966-1969	Brazilian	$11,500	$14,500
1970-1979	Indian	$4,500	$5,500
1980-1989		$3,750	$4,750
1990-1993		$3,000	$3,750

D-35SW Wurlitzer
1966, 1968. Made for the Wurlitzer Co., Brazilian rosewood.

1966, 1968		$10,000	$13,000

D-35V
1984. Limited Edition, 10 made, Brazilian rosewood back and sides.

1984		$7,250	$9,500

D-37K
1980-1994. Dreadnought-size, Koa back and sides, spruce top.

1980-1994		$3,000	$4,000

D-37K2
1980-1994. Same as D-37 K but has a Koa top and black 'guard.

1980-1994		$3,000	$4,000

1974 Martin D12-35
Peter Van Wagner

1968 Martin D-35S
David Stone

Martin D-41

2000 Martin D-42
Rivington Guitars

MODEL YEAR	FEATURES	EXC. COND. LOW	EXC. COND. HIGH
D-37W Lucinda Williams			
2003. Only 4 made, never put into production, Aztec pearl inlay favored by Lucinda Williams, quilted mahogany sides and back.			
2003		$4,000	$5,250
D-40			
1997-2005. Indian rosewood back and sides, hexagon inlays.			
1997-2005		$2,500	$3,250
D-40BLE			
1990. Limited Edition Guitar of the Month, Brazilian rosewood back and sides, pearl top border except around 'board.			
1990		$8,000	$10,500
D-40DM Don McLean			
1998. Only 50 made, Englemann spruce top.			
1998		$6,250	$8,000
D-40FMG			
1995-1996. Figured mahogany back and sides, 150 made.			
1995-1996		$4,500	$5,750
D-40FW Limited Edition			
1996. Figured claro walnut sides and back, 'Limited Edition D-40FW' label, 148 made.			
1996		$3,000	$4,000
D-40QM Limited Edition			
1996. Limited Edition, 200 made, quilted maple body.			
1996		$3,000	$4,000
D-41			
1969-present. Brazilian rosewood back and sides for the first ones in '69 then Indian rosewood, bound body, scalloped braces, natural.			
1969	Brazilian	$30,000	$37,500
1970-1979	Indian	$5,000	$6,500
1980-1989		$4,500	$5,500
1990-1999		$4,500	$5,500
2000-2009		$4,500	$5,500
2010-2023		$4,500	$5,500
D12-41			
1970-1994. Very few made, special order after '93, 12-string, 14-fret.			
1970-1994		$5,000	$6,500
D-41 Porter Wagoner			
2008-2011. Custom Artist series, Indian rosewood back and sides.			
2008-2011		$3,000	$4,000
D-41 Special			
2004-2011. D-41 with snowflake inlays.			
2004-2011		$3,500	$4,500
D-41A Turbo Mandolin Brothers			
2011, 2013. Two Custom Shop models made for Mandolin Bros., Adirondack top. Similar except 10 40th Anniversary models which have abalone and pearl mandolin 12th-fret inlay and label signed by Stan Jay and Chris Martin.			
2011		$3,500	$4,500
D-41BLE			
1989. Limited Edition Guitar of the Month, Brazilian rosewood back and sides, pearl top border except around 'board.			
1989		$7,500	$9,750

MODEL YEAR	FEATURES	EXC. COND. LOW	EXC. COND. HIGH
D-41DF Dan Fogelberg			
2001. 141 made, East Indian rosewood back and sides, hexagon 'board inlays, pearl snowflakes inlaid on bridge.			
2001		$5,500	$7,500
D-41E			
1971. Indian rosewood.			
1971		$4,250	$5,500
D-41GJ George Jones			
2001. Style 41 appointments, limited edition of 100, label signed by the Opossum.			
2001		$4,000	$5,000
D-41K Purple Martin			
2013-2020. Limited to 50 with labels signed by C.F. Martin IV, highly flamed Koa back and sides, purple martin-inspired inlay on 'board, bridge, and 'guard.			
2013-2020		$10,000	$12,500
D-41S/SD-41S			
1970-1994. Sunburst, Indian rosewood, 12-fret neck, slotted peghead.			
1970-1979		$5,000	$6,500
1980-1994		$4,500	$5,500
D-42			
1973-1988, 1995-present. Limited production '73-'88, Indian rosewood back and sides, spruce top, pearl rosette and inlays, snowflake 'board inlays, gold tuners, gloss finish.			
1973-1988		$5,500	$7,000
1995-2023		$5,000	$6,250
D-42E			
1996-2008. With Fishman Ellipse VT pickup system.			
1996-2008		$4,500	$6,000
D-42 Amazon Rosewood Limited Edition			
2007. Limited to 35, Amazon rosewood is similar to Brazilian rosewood but a different species.			
2007		$5,000	$6,500
D-42 Flamed Mahogany			
2006. Adirondack, figured mahogany, 30 made with tree-of-life inlay.			
2006		$7,000	$9,000
D-42 Peter Frampton			
2006-2007. Indian rosewood back and sides, Style 45 features.			
2006-2007		$5,500	$7,250
D-42 Purple Martin Flamed Myrtle			
2018-2021. Flamed myrtle back and sides, limited to 100 made.			
2018-2021		$10,000	$12,500
D-42AR (Amazon Rosewood)			
2002-2003. Limited to 30 made, Amazon rosewood is similar to Brazilian rosewood but a different species.			
2002-2003		$4,500	$6,000
D-42JC Johnny Cash			
1997. Rosewood back and sides, gloss black lacquer on body and neck, Cash signature inlaid at 19th fret, have label signed by Cash and C.F. Martin IV, 80 sold.			
1997		$6,000	$8,000
D-42K Limited Edition			
1998. Limited production, highly flamed Koa back and sides, Sitka top with aging toner, high X-brace design, 45-style abalone snowflake inlays.			
1998		$4,500	$6,000

The Vintage Guitar Price Guide shows values for all-original, excellent condition instruments and, where applicable, with original case.

MODEL YEAR	FEATURES	EXC. COND. LOW	HIGH

D-42K/D-42K2

1998-2006. K has Koa back and sides, the all Koa body K2 was discontinued in '05.

| 1998-2006 | D-42K | $4,500 | $6,000 |
| 2000-2005 | D-42K2 | $4,500 | $6,000 |

D-42LE

1988 only. Limited Edition (75 sold), D-42-style, scalloped braces, low profile neck.

| 1988 | | $4,500 | $6,000 |

D-42SB

2006-2007. Sunburst finish, Sikta spruce top, 45-style appointments.

| 2006-2007 | | $4,500 | $6,000 |

D-42V

1985. Vintage Series, 12 made, Brazilian rosewood, scalloped braces.

| 1985 | | $8,000 | $11,000 |

D-45

1933-1942 (96 made), 1968-present. Brazilian rosewood back and sides, changed to Indian rosewood during '69. The pre-WW II D-45 is one of the holy grails. A pre-war D-45 should be evaluated on a case-by-case basis. The price ranges are for all-original guitars in excellent condition and are guidance pricing only. These ranges are for a crack-free guitar. Unfortunately, many older acoustics have a crack or two and this can make ultra-expensive acoustics more difficult to evaluate than ultra-expensive solidbody electrics. Technically, a repaired body crack makes a guitar non-original, but the vintage market generally considers a professionally repaired crack to be original. Crack width, length and depth can vary, therefore extra attention is suggested.

1936-1938		$550,000	$675,000
1939	Early, wide neck	$550,000	$675,000
1939	Late, thin neck	$500,000	$600,000
1940-1942		$450,000	$550,000
1968	European spruce, Brazilian	$55,000	$70,000
1969	Sikta, Brazilian	$50,000	$65,000
1970-1979		$9,500	$12,000
1980-1989		$9,500	$12,000
1990-1999		$9,000	$11,500
2000-2017		$9,000	$11,500
2018-2023	New specs	$9,000	$11,500

D12-45

1970s-1987. Special order instrument, not a standard catalog item, with D-45 appointments, Indian rosewood.

| 1970-1979 | | $7,500 | $9,500 |
| 1980-1987 | | $7,000 | $9,000 |

D-45 100th Anniversary Limited Edition

1996. Label reads '1896-1996 C.F. Martin Commemorative Anniversary Model'.

| 1996 | | $7,000 | $9,500 |

D-45 150th Anniversary

1983. Brazilian rosewood back and sides, Sikta spruce top, '150th' logo stamp.

| 1983 | | $14,000 | $18,000 |

D-45CFMB CMR Sr. (200th Anniversary, Brazilian)

1996. Commemorating the 200th Anniversary of C.F. Martin Sr. birthday, Brazilian rosewood back and sides, style 45 Deluxe pearl bordering, fossilized ivory nut and saddle, 14-fret neck, gold hardware.

| 1996 | | $14,000 | $18,000 |

D-45CFM CMR Sr. (200th Anniversary, East Indian)

1996. Commemorating the 200th Anniversary of C.F. Martin Sr. birthday, East Indian rosewood back and sides, style 45 pearl bordering, bone nut and saddle, 14-fret neck, gold hardware.

| 1996 | | $7,000 | $9,000 |

D-45 (1939 Reissue Mandolin Brothers)

1990. Commissioned by Mandolin Brothers, 5 made, figured Brazilian rosewood. Original name "The Reissue 1939 Martin D-45." Said to be the first reissue of the era and the seed for the '90s Martin Custom Shop.

| 1990 | | $14,000 | $18,000 |

D-45 (1939 Reissue)

1992. High-grade spruce top, figured Brazilian rosewood back and sides, high X and scalloped braces, abalone trim, natural, gold tuners.

| 1992 | | $14,000 | $18,000 |

D-45 Celtic Knot

2004-2005. Brazilian rosewood, Celtic knot 'board inlays, 30 built.

| 2004-2005 | | $22,000 | $28,000 |

D-45 Custom Shop

1984, 1991-1992. Various options and models, Indian rosewood back and sides in '84, then Brazilian rosewood.

| 1984 | Indian | $7,250 | $9,500 |
| 1991-1992 | Brazilian | $15,500 | $20,000 |

D-45 Deluxe

1993 only. Guitar of the Month, Brazilian rosewood back and sides, figured spruce top, inlay in bridge and 'guard, tree-of-life inlay on 'board, pearl borders and back stripe, gold tuners with large gold buttons, total of 60 sold.

| 1993 | | $18,000 | $23,000 |

D-45 Deluxe CFM Sr. (200th Anniversary, Brazilian)

1996. Commemorating the 200th Anniversary of C.F. Martin Sr. birthday, 91 made, Brazilian rosewood back and sides, style 45 Deluxe pearl bordering, fossilized-ivory nut and saddle, 14-fret neck, gold hardware.

| 1996 | | $14,500 | $19,000 |

D-45 Gene Autry

1994 only. Gene Autry inlay (2 options available), natural.

| 1994 | Gene Autry 'board | $20,000 | $26,000 |
| 1994 | Snowflake 'board option | $20,000 | $26,000 |

D-45 Marquis

2006-2008. Rosewood back and sides.

| 2006-2008 | | $8,000 | $10,000 |

D-45 Mike Longworth Commemorative Edition

2004-2006. East Indian rosewood back and sides, Adirondack spruce top, 91 made, label signed by Mike's wife Sue and C.F. Martin IV.

| 2004-2006 | | $8,500 | $11,000 |

Martin D-42 Purple
Martin Flamed Myrtle

1968 Martin D-45
Wayne Stephens

GUITARS

Martin D-45S Authentic 1936

Martin DJr-10E StreetMaster

MODEL YEAR	FEATURES	EXC. COND. LOW	HIGH
D-45 Woodstock 50th Anniversary			
2019-2020. Limited Edition, run of 50, East Indian rosewood back and sides, abalone inlay, Woodstock dove on headstock, '1969-2019' on 'board, peace sign on heelcap.			
2019-2020		$9,500	$12,500
D-45B Brazilian			
1994. Brazilian rosewood.			
1994		$13,000	$16,000
D-45E Aura			
2010. With Fishman Electronics Ellipse Aura technology.			
2010		$6,750	$8,750
D-45E Retro			
2013-2019. East Indian rosewood, Fishman.			
2013-2019		$7,500	$9,750
D-45GE Golden Era			
2001-2004. 167 made, '37 specs, Brazilian rosewood.			
2001-2004		$25,000	$32,500
D-45K			
2006-2008. Flamed Koa back and sides.			
2006-2008		$7,500	$9,500
D-45KLE			
1991. Limited Edition Koa, Engelmann, bear claw, 54 made.			
1991		$9,500	$12,000
D-45LE			
1987. Limited Edition, 44 made, Guitar of the Month, September '87.			
1987		$15,000	$20,000
D-45S Authentic 1936			
2013-present. Adirondack spruce top, Vintage Tone System, Brazilian rosewood back and sides, '36 style appointments and specs.			
2013-2023		$42,000	$55,000
D-45S Deluxe			
1992. Limited Edition, 50 made, Indian rosewood, spruce top, high-end appointments.			
1992		$8,000	$10,500
D-45S/SD-45S			
1969-1994. Brazilian rosewood back and sides in '69, Indian rosewood after, 12-fret neck, S means slotted peghead, only 50 made.			
1969	Brazilian	$50,000	$65,000
1970-1979	Indian	$10,000	$12,500
1980-1994	Indian	$9,500	$12,000
D-45SS Steven Stills			
1998. Brazilian rosewood back and sides, 91 made.			
1998		$30,000	$37,500
D-45V Brazilian			
1983. Brazilian rosewood back and sides, scalloped braces, snowflake inlay, natural.			
1983		$15,000	$20,000
D-45VR/D-45V			
1997-2020. Vintage specs, Indian rosewood back and sides, vintage aging toner, snowflake inlay. Name changed to D-45V in '99 (not to be confused with Brazilian rosewood D-45V of the '80s).			
1997-1998	VR	$7,500	$9,750
1999-2020	V	$7,500	$9,750

MODEL YEAR	FEATURES	EXC. COND. LOW	HIGH
D-50 Deluxe/D-50DX			
2001-2003. Deluxe limited edition, 50 made, one of the most ornate Martin models ever made, Brazilian rosewood back and sides, highly ornate pearl inlay.			
2001-2003		$40,000	$50,000
D-50K Deluxe/D-50K2 Deluxe			
2003-2006. As D-50 Deluxe with ornate pearl inlay and highly flamed Koa back and sides (K, 45 made) or highly flamed Koa top, back and sides (K2, 5 made).			
2003-2006	K Deluxe	$35,000	$45,000
2003-2006	K2 Deluxe	$35,000	$45,000
D-60			
1989-1995. Birdseye maple back and sides, snowflake inlays, tortoiseshell binding and 'guard.			
1989-1995		$2,500	$3,500
D-62			
1987-1995. Flamed maple back and sides, chrome-plated enclosed Schaller tuners.			
1987-1995		$2,500	$3,500
D-62LE			
1986. Limited Edition, Guitar of the Month October '86, flamed maple back and sides, spruce top, snowflake inlays, natural.			
1986		$2,500	$3,500
D-64			
1985-1995. Flamed maple top, low profile neck.			
1985-1995		$2,500	$3,500
D-76 Bicentennial Limited Edition			
1975-1976. Limited to 200 made in '75 and 1,976 made in '76, Indian rosewood back and sides, 3-piece back, herringbone back stripe, pearl stars on 'board, eagle on peghead.			
1975-1976		$5,000	$6,500
D-93			
1993. Mahogany, spruce, 93 pertains to the year, not a style number.			
1993		$2,500	$3,250
D-100 Deluxe			
2004. Limited Edition, guitars have the first 50 sequential serial numbers following the millionth Martin guitar (1,000,001 to 1,000,050), fancy pearl inlay on back, 'guard, headstock, 'board and bridge. Herringbone top and rosette inlay, Adirondack spruce top, Brazilian rosewood back and sides.			
2004		$50,000	$62,500
D-200 Deluxe			
2017-present. Celebration of Martin's two-millionth serial number, limited to 50 offered, watch-themed highly decorative, comes with renowned watchmaker Roland G Murphy watch with matching serial no., premium case has built-in hygrometer.			
2017-2023		$95,000	$120,000
D-222 100th Anniversary			
2016. Commemorates 100th anniversary of the dreadnought, limited to 100, Sikta spruce top, mahogany back and sides, ivoroid binding, slotted headstock.			
2016		$3,500	$4,500
D-420			
2017-2019. Top with custom legal weed illustration by artist Robert Goetzl, mahogany back and sides.			
2017-2019		$2,500	$3,250

MODEL YEAR	FEATURES	EXC. COND. LOW	HIGH

DJr / DJrE

2015-2018. Dreadnought Junior, Sikta spruce top, sapele back and sides. DJrE with Fishman electronics.

| 2015-2018 | No electronics | $325 | $450 |
| 2015-2018 | With electronics | $375 | $500 |

DJr-10 / DJr-10E

2020-present. Dreadnought Junior, thinner 000-sized body, Sikta spruce or sapele top, satin sapele back and sides. Fishman electronics available (DJr-10E).

| 2020-2023 | No electronics | $350 | $450 |
| 2020-2023 | With electronics | $400 | $550 |

DJr-10E StreetMaster

2021-present. Dreadnought Junior with thinner body and tapered neck, Fishman electronics, dark mahogany finish.

| 2021-2023 | | $475 | $625 |

DC Series

1980s-2021. Dreadnought cutaway versions, E models have electronics, GT is gloss top, R indicates rosewood back and sides. Replaced by DC-X Series starting in '20.

1981-1997	DC-28	$2,750	$3,500
1996-2000	DC-1	$675	$875
1996-2010	DC-1E	$775	$1,000
1997-2000	DCM	$650	$850
1997-2005	DC-1M	$650	$850
1997-2006	DCME	$700	$950
1998	DCXM	$500	$650
1998-2001	DCXME	$500	$650
1998-2010	DC-15E	$775	$1,000
1999-2000	DC-1R	$675	$875
2000	DCRE	$700	$950
2000-2013	DCX1E	$500	$650
2001-2005	DCXE Black	$500	$650
2002-2003	DC-16RE	$800	$1,125
2003-2005	DC-16GTE Premium	$1,250	$1,625
2003-2016	DC-16GTE	$1,125	$1,500
2003-2019	DC-16E	$1,125	$1,500
2004-2013	DCX1KE	$500	$650
2004-2013	DCX1RE	$500	$650
2005	DC Trey Anastasio	$5,000	$6,500
2005	DC-16RE Aura	$850	$1,125
2005	DC-16RGTE Aura	$1,125	$1,500
2005-2007	DC-16E Koa	$1,125	$1,500
2005-2008	DC-16RGTE	$1,125	$1,500
2005-2010	DC-Aura	$2,500	$3,250
2006-2019	DC-28E	$2,375	$3,125
2009-2016	DCPA1/ DCPA1 Plus	$2,125	$2,750
2011	DCPA2/DCPA3	$1,125	$1,500
2011-2016	DCPA4 Shaded	$1,125	$1,500
2011-2017	DCPA4 Rosewood	$1,250	$1,625
2013-2016	DCPA5	$500	$650
2013-2016	DCPA5 Black	$500	$650
2013-2016	DCPA5K Koa	$500	$650
2016-2019	DC-15ME	$775	$1,000
2016-2019	DC-35E	$2,500	$3,250
2017-2018	DCRSG	$875	$1,125
2017-2019	DC-18E	$2,250	$3,000

MODEL YEAR	FEATURES	EXC. COND. LOW	HIGH
2017-2019	DCPA4	$1,125	$1,500
2017-2019	DCX1AE/ DCX1AE Macassar	$475	$625
2017-2019	DCX1RAE	$500	$650
2019-2021	DC-13E	$650	$850

DC-X Series

2020-present. Replaces the DC Series, dreadnought models with various woods, some with electronics.

| 2020-2022 | DC-X2E | $625 | $850 |

Ditson Dreadnaught 111

2007-2009. Based on 1929 Ditson 111, 12-fret neck, slot head, mahogany back and sides, Brazilian rosewood binding.

| 2007-2009 | | $4,250 | $5,500 |

DM

1996-2009. Solid Sikta spruce top, laminated mahogany back and sides, dot markers, natural satin.

| 1996-2009 | | $600 | $800 |

DM-12

1996-2009. 12-string DM.

| 1996-2009 | | $600 | $800 |

DM3MD Dave Matthews

1999-2001. Three-piece back of Indian rosewood, African padauk center wedge, Englemann spruce top, high-end appointments.

| 1999-2001 | | $5,000 | $6,500 |

Doobie-42 Tom Johnston

2007. Signature Edition, D-42 style, 35 made, solid Indian rosewood back and sides, abalone and catseye markers, other special appointments.

| 2007 | | $5,000 | $6,500 |

DR

1997-2008. Road Series Dreadnought, rosewood back and sides.

| 1997-2008 | | $650 | $850 |

DR Centennial LE

2016-2020. Limited Edition celebrates '100 Years of the Dreadnought', Adirondack, East Indian rosewood, antique white binding, satin finish.

| 2016-2020 | | $2,000 | $2,500 |

DRS1 (Road/1 Series)

2011-2019. D-size, sapele top, back and sides, satin finish, Fishman. Replaced by D-10E in '19.

| 2011-2019 | | $550 | $725 |

DRS2 (Road/1 Series)

2012-2018. DRS1 with spruce top. Replaced by D-10E in '19.

| 2012-2018 | | $625 | $850 |

DRSG

2017-2018. Sikta spruce top, siris back and sides, Fishman Sonitone. Replaced by D-13E in '19.

| 2017-2018 | | $800 | $1,000 |

DRSGT

2014-2015. Sikta spruce top, sapele back and sides, Fishman with USB port.

| 2014-2015 | | $650 | $850 |

DSR Sugar Ray

2003. Limited Edition of 57 made, D-17 style, all mahogany, signed by C.F. Martin IV and all members of Sugar Ray band.

| 2003 | | $4,250 | $5,500 |

Martin DC-X2E

Martin DR Centennial LE

Martin DSS-17

2002 Martin DX121

Johnny Zapp

MODEL YEAR	FEATURES	EXC. COND. LOW	HIGH

DSS-17

2018-present. Slope-shoulder dreadnought, Sikta spruce top, mahogany back and sides with antique white binding, satin Black Smoke or Whiskey Sunset Burst.

2018-2019	Black Smoke	$1,125	$1,500
2019-2023	Whiskey Sunset	$1,125	$1,500

DVM Veterans

2002-2008. D-style, spruce top, rosewood back and sides, special veterans' ornamentation.

2002-2008		$2,250	$3,000

Dwight Yoakam DD28

2017-2018. Custom Signature Edition, Sikta spruce top, East Indian rosewood back and sides, inlaid mother-of-pearl and recon stone playing cards.

2017-2018		$3,500	$4,500

DX 175th Anniversary

2008. Rosewood HPL back and sides, founder's picture on top.

2008		$400	$550

DX Johnny Cash

2019-present. D-sized, Jett black HPL top, back and sides, custom 'board inlaid with stars and CASH logo, Cash's signature on rosette and label, Fishman electronics.

2019-2023		$475	$650

DX Series

1996-2020. D-size, high pressure wood laminate (HPL) backs and sides, exterior wood-grain image with gloss finish. M is for mahogany woodgrain, R rosewood and K Koa. A 1 indicates a solid spruce top with Series 1 bracing, otherwise the top is wood-patterned HPL. C indicates cutaway and E Fishman Presys Plus and AE Fishman Sonitone. Replaced by D-X Series starting in '20.

1996-2009	DXM / DMX	$400	$550
1998-2012	DXME	$400	$550
1999-2000	D12XM 12-String	$400	$550
1999-2019	DXMAE	$400	$550
2000-2014	DX1 / DX1E	$350	$450
2000-2019	DX1AE	$400	$550
2001-2009	DX1R	$400	$550
2002-2009	DXK2	$400	$550
2004-2009	DX1K	$400	$550
2008-2010	D12X1 12-String	$400	$550
2010-2020	DX1KAE	$400	$550
2011-2019	D12X1AE 12-String	$425	$575
2014-2019	DXAE Black	$400	$550
2014-2020	DXK2AE	$400	$550
2015-2019	DX1RAE	$400	$550
2017	DX420	$850	$1,125
2017-2019	DX2AE Macassar	$400	$550

D-X Series

2020-present. New spec dreadnought models to replace the DX Series. Various options, woods and finishes.

2020-2023	D-X1E	$425	$575
2020-2023	D-X2E	$475	$650
2020-2023	D-X2E 12-String	$475	$650

MODEL YEAR	FEATURES	EXC. COND. LOW	HIGH

E-18

1979-1983. Offset double-cut, maple and rosewood laminate solidbody, 2 DiMarzio pickups, phase switch, natural.

1979-1983		$1,750	$2,250

E-28

1980-1983. Double-cut electric solidbody, carved top, ebony 'board, 2 humbuckers.

1980-1983		$1,875	$2,500

EM-18

1979-1983. Offset double-cut, maple and rosewood laminate solidbody, 2 exposed-coil humbucking pickups, coil split switch.

1979-1983		$1,750	$2,250

EMP-1

1998-1999. Employee series designed by Martin employee team, cutaway solid spruce top, ovangkol wood back and sides with rosewood middle insert (D-35-style insert), on-board pickup.

1998-1999		$2,000	$2,500

EMP-2 Limited Edition

1999. D size, tzalam body, flying saucer inlays.

1999		$2,000	$2,500

F-1

1940-1942. Archtop, mahogany back and sides, carved spruce top, multi-bound, f-holes, sunburst, 91 made.

1940-1942		$4,000	$5,000

F-1-12

1941. F-1 12 string.

1941		$3,500	$4,500

F-2

1940-1942. Carved spruce top, maple or rosewood back and sides, multi-bound, f-holes, 46 made.

1940-1942		$4,500	$6,500

F-5

1940. 2 made.

1940		$7,500	$9,500

F-7

1935-1939, 1941-1942. Brazilian rosewood back and sides, f-holes, carved top, back arched by braces, multi-bound, sunburst top finish.

1935-1938		$10,000	$12,500
1941-1942		$9,500	$12,000

F-9

1935-1942. Highest-end archtop, Brazilian rosewood, Martin inlaid vertically on headstock, 7-ply top binding, 45-style back strip, sunburst.

1935-1942		$20,000	$25,000

F-50

1961-1965. Single-cut thinline archtop with laminated maple body, 1 pickup.

1961-1965		$2,000	$2,500

F-55

1961-1965. Single-cut thinline archtop with laminated maple body, 2 pickups.

1961-1965		$3,500	$4,500

F-65

1961-1965. Electric archtop, double-cut, f-holes, 2 pickups, square-cornered peghead, Bigsby, sunburst.

1961-1965		$3,500	$4,500

MODEL YEAR	FEATURES	EXC. COND. LOW	HIGH

Felix The Cat
2004-2010. Felix the Cat logo art, Don Oriolo logo, red body, Felix gig bag.

2004	Felix I, 756 made	$550	$750
2005-2006	Felix II, 625 made	$550	$750
2007-2010	Felix III, 1000 made	$550	$750

GCD-16CP (Guitar Center)
1998. 15 5/8" Style D.

1998		$1,750	$2,250

GPC Series
2010-present. Standard Series (GPC-), Performing Artist (GPCPA) and X Series (GPCX), Grand Performance size, cutaway, acoustic/electric, various woods.

2010-2016	GPCPA1/Plus	$2,125	$2,750
2011	GPCPA2	$1,375	$1,750
2011-2012	GPCPA3	$1,375	$1,750
2012-2016	GPCPA5K Koa	$475	$650
2013-2016	GPCPA4	$1,125	$1,500
2013-2016	GPCPA5	$475	$650
2013-2016	GPCPA5 Black	$475	$650
2013-2019	GPC12PA4 12-string	$1,125	$1,500
2013-2019	GPCPA4 Rosewood	$1,125	$1,500
2013-2019	GPCPA4 Sapele	$1,375	$1,750
2016-2018	GPC-35E	$2,500	$3,250
2016-2020	GPC-18E	$2,250	$3,000
2016-2020	GPC-28E	$2,500	$3,250
2017-2018	GPC-15ME	$1,125	$1,500
2017-2018	GPCRSG	$825	$1,125
2017-2018	GPCRSGT	$650	$850
2017-2018	GPCXAE Black	$425	$550
2017-2019	GPCX1RAE	$450	$600
2017-2021	GPCX1AE	$450	$600
2017-2021	GPCX2AE Macassar	$450	$600
2017-2023	GPC-X2E	$575	$750
2019-2023	GPC-11E	$775	$1,000
2019-2023	GPC-13E	$900	$1,125
2020-2021	GPC-16E Rosewood	$1,500	$2,000
2020-2023	GPC-16E	$1,500	$2,000

Grand J12-40E Special
2009-2011. J12-40 with D-TAR Multi-source electronics.

2009-2011		$3,000	$4,000

Grand J-28LSE
2011-2014. Baritone.

2011-2014		$2,500	$3,250

Grand J-35E
2009-2011. Grand jumbo size, rosewood back and sides.

2009-2011		$2,500	$3,250

Grand Ole Opry/HDO Grand Ole Opry
1999-2007. Custom Shop Limited Edition, 650 made, 'Grand Ole Opry 75th Anniversary' on neck block, WSM microphone headstock logo, off-white Micarta fingerboard, Sikta spruce top, East Indian rosewood back and sides.

1999-2007		$3,000	$4,000

Gruhn 50th Anniversary 0000 (Custom Shop)
2020. Celebrates Gruhn Guitar 50 years in business, interior label signed by George Gruhn, 12- or 14-fret, limited to 50 each in natural or sunburst.

2020		$5,500	$7,250

GT-70
1965-1966. Electric archtop, bound body, f-holes, single-cut, 2 pickups, tremolo, burgundy or black finish.

1965-1966		$2,500	$3,500

GT-75
1965-1967. Electric archtop, bound body, f-holes, double-cut, 2 pickups, tremolo, burgundy or black finish. There is also a 12-string version.

1965-1967		$3,000	$4,000

Hawaiian X
2002-2004. Hawaiian scene painted on top, similar to the Cowboy guitar model, limited edition of 500.

2002-2004		$750	$975

HD-7 Roger McGuinn
2005-2008. Rosewood back and sides, herringbone top trim, 7-string with double G.

2005-2008		$3,250	$4,250

HD12-28
2018-present. Sikta spruce top, East Indian rosewood back and sides, natural.

2018-2023		$2,375	$3,000

HD-16R Adirondack
2008-2016. Rosewood back and sides, Adirondack top.

2010-2016		$1,750	$2,250

HD-16R LSH
2007-2013. Indian rosewood (R), large sound hole (LSH).

2007-2013		$1,750	$2,250

HD-18JB Jimmy Buffett
1998. 424 made, solid mahogany back and sides, herringbone trim, palm tree headstock logo, Style 42 markers, Buffett pearl signature.

1998		$5,500	$7,000

HD-18LE
1987. Indian rosewood.

1987		$2,375	$3,000

HD-28
1976-present. Standard Series, Indian rosewood back and sides, scalloped bracing, herringbone purfling, sunburst. Ambertone added in '22.

1976-1979		$3,500	$4,500
1980-1989		$2,625	$3,500
1990-1999		$2,500	$3,250
2000-2017	Last Standard X	$2,500	$3,250
2018-2023	Forward X	$2,500	$3,250

HD-28 1935 Special
1993. 'HD-28 1935 Special' model name on label.

1993		$2,750	$3,500

HD-28 2R
1991, 1993-1997. 2R specification for 2 herringbone sound hole rings, larger sound hole.

1991-1997		$2,500	$3,250

Martin GPC-13E

Martin HD12-28

GUITARS

Martin HD-28 VR

2002 Martin HD-28LSV

MODEL YEAR FEATURES	EXC. COND. LOW	HIGH

HD-28 Custom 150th Anniversary
1983. 150th Anniversary, Martin Custom Shop, Indian rosewood sides and back, '1833-1983 150th Year' stamped on inside backstrip.

1983	$2,875	$3,750

HD-28 Custom/Custom HD-28
1994. Custom Shop model.

1994-1995	$2,625	$3,500

HD-28AWB Custom
2008-2013. Elderly Instruments Custom model, Adirondack spruce top, rosewood back and sides, white-bound body, gloss natural finish.

2008-2013	$3,000	$4,000

HD-28BLE
1990. Guitar of the Month, 100 made, Brazilian rosewood back and sides, herringbone sound hole ring, low profile neck (LE), chrome tuners, aging toner finish.

1990	$6,625	$8,750

HD-28BSE
1987-1999. Brazilian rosewood, 93 made.

1987-1999	$6,625	$8,750

HD-28CTB
1992. Guitar of the Month, herringbone top trim/ back stripe, fancy peghead inlay, tortoise binding, gold hardware, label signed by CF Martin IV.

1992	$2,625	$3,500

HD-28E Retro
2013-2019. Solid Sikta spruce top, East Indian rosewood back and sides.

2013-2019	$2,375	$3,000

HD-28GM
1989. Grand Marquis, Guitar of the Month, scalloped braced Sikta spruce top with 1930s-era bracing pattern that replaced the X-brace below the sound hole, herringbone top purfling, sound hole ring and back stripe, gold tuners.

1989	$3,500	$4,500

HD-28GM LSH
1994. Grand Marquis, Guitar of the Month, rosewood back and sides, large sound hole with double herringbone rings, snowflake inlay in bridge, natural (115 made) or sunburst (36 made).

1994	$2,875	$3,750

HD-28KM Keb Mo
2001-2002. Signature Edition, Hawaiian Koa back and sides, 252 made.

2001-2002	$3,000	$4,000

HD-28LE
1985. Limited Edition, Guitar of the Month, rosewood back and sides, scalloped bracing, herringbone top purfling, diamonds and squares 'board inlay, V-neck.

1985	$3,375	$4,500

HD-28LSV
1997-2005. Vintage Series, large sound hole, patterned after Clarence White's modified '35 D-28.

1997-2005	$2,750	$3,500

HD-28M
1988. Standard profile.

1988	$2,500	$3,250

HD-28MP
1990-1991, 2011-2012. Bolivian rosewood back and sides, herringbone top trim, low profile neck. Reissued in 2011 with Madagascar rosewood and modern-style neck.

1990-1991	$2,125	$2,750
2011-2012	$2,125	$2,750

HD-28P
1987-1989. Rosewood back and sides, scalloped braces, herringbone, low profile neck (P), zigzag back stripe.

1987-1989	$2,125	$2,750

HD-28PSE
1988. Signature Edition, Guitar of the Month, rosewood back and sides, signed by C.F. Martin IV and foremen, scalloped braces, herringbone top purfling, low profile neck, squared peghead, ebony tuner buttons.

1988	$2,500	$3,250

HD-28S Custom
1995. Slotted headstock.

1995	$2,875	$3,750

HD-28SB/HD-28 Ambertone/ HD-28SB-AMB
2016-2022. Sikta, East Indian rosewood, natural, sunburst or ambertone. SB and Ambertone dropped from name in '22 and ambertone finish added to HD-28.

2016-2022	$2,500	$3,250

HD-28SE
1986-1987. Signature Edition, rosewood back and sides, signed by C. F. Martin and foremen/supervisors, '87 model was a Guitar of the Month with Brazilian rosewood.

1986		$2,875	$3,750
1987	Brazilian	$6,250	$8,250

HD-28SO Sing Out!
1996. Limited edition, 45 made, Indian rosewood back and sides.

1996	$3,000	$4,000

HD-28V Custom
2007-2012. Indian rosewood back and sides, Adirondack top, wide nut, Elderly Instruments special issue.

2007-2012	$3,375	$4,500

HD-28V/HD-28VR
1996-2019. 14-fret, Indian rosewood body, R dropped from name in '99.

1996-1999	HD-28VR	$2,750	$3,500
2000-2019	HD-28V	$2,750	$3,500

HD-28VE
2004-2006. HD-28 V with Fishman Ellipse Blend system.

2004-2006	$3,000	$4,000

HD-28VS
1996-2016. Slotted headstock, 12-fret, spruce top with aging toner, Indian rosewood sides and back.

1996-2016	$3,125	$4,000

HD-35
1978-present. Indian rosewood back and sides, herringbone top trim, zipper back stripe.

1978-1979	$3,500	$4,500
1980-1999	$2,750	$3,500
2000-2023	$2,500	$3,125

MODEL		EXC. COND.	
YEAR	FEATURES	LOW	HIGH

HD-35 CFM IV 60th
2016-2020. Celebrates C.F. Martin IV's 60th birthday, limited to 60, European spruce top, 3-piece back of siris wings and East Indian rosewood wedge, personally signed label.

2016-2020		$6,500	$8,500

HD-35 Custom
2009. Custom Designed on neck block, Adirondack spruce top, East Indian rosewood sides and back.

2009		$2,875	$3,750

HD-35 Nancy Wilson
2006-2007. Englemann spruce top, 3-piece back with bubinga center wedge, 101 made.

2006-2007		$3,500	$4,500

HD-35P
1987-1989. HD-35 with low profile neck.

1987-1989		$2,500	$3,250

HD-35SJC Judy Collins
2002. 50 made, Collins signature headstock logo, wildflower headstock inlay, East Indian rosewood, 3-piece back with figured maple center.

2002		$3,375	$4,500

HD-40 Tom Petty Signature Edition
2004-2006. Limited run of 274, Indian rosewood sides and back, high-end appointments, inside label with signature.

2004-2006		$5,750	$7,500

HD-40MK Mark Knopfler
2001-2002. Limited Edition of 251 made, Mark Knopfler signature inlay 20th fret, herringbone trim, fancy marquetry sound hole rings.

2001-2002		$4,375	$5,750

HD-40MS Marty Stuart
1996. Indian rosewood, 250 made, pearl/abalone inlay.

1996		$4,375	$5,750

HD-282R
1992-1996. Large sound hole with 2 herringbone rings, zigzag backstripe.

1992-1996		$2,500	$3,250

HD Dierks Bentley
2013-2014. Rosewood.

2013-2014		$3,875	$5,000

HD Elliot Easton Custom Edition
2006-2008. Limited Edition, Adirondack spruce top with aging tone, Fishman Ellipse Aura pickup available on HDE.

2006-2008		$3,125	$4,000

HDN Negative Limited Edition
2003. Limited to 135 made, unusual appointments include pearloid headstock and black finish, HDN Negative Limited Edition notation on the inside label.

2003		$3,500	$4,500

HJ-28
1992, 1996-2000. Limited Edition Guitar of the Month in '92, regular production started in '96. Jumbo, non-cut, spruce top, Indian rosewood sides and back, herringbone top purfling, with or without on-board electronics.

1992	Limited Edition	$2,625	$3,500
1996-2000		$2,500	$3,250

HJ-28M
1994. Mahogany/spruce, herringbone top purfling, Guitar of the Month, 72 made.

1994		$2,625	$3,500

HJ-38 Stefan Grossman
2008-2011. Custom Edition, Madagascar rosewood back and sides.

2008-2011		$3,625	$4,750

HM Ben Harper
2008-2009. Special Edition, M-style width, 000-style depth, solid Adirondack spruce top, solid East Indian rosewood sides and back, onboard Fishman Ellipse Matrix Blend.

2008-2009		$3,625	$4,750

HOM-35
1989. Herringbone Orchestra Model, Guitar of the Month, scalloped braces, 3-piece Brazilian rosewood back, book matched sides, 14-fret neck, only 60 built.

1989		$5,250	$6,875

HPD-41
1999-2001. Like D-41, but with herringbone rosette, binding.

1999-2001		$3,750	$4,875

HTA Kitty Wells 'Honky Tonk Angel'
2002. D-size with 000-size depth, Indian rosewood back and sides, Queen of Country Music inlay logo on headstock (no Martin headstock logo).

2002		$2,500	$3,250

J-1 Jumbo
1997-2001. Jumbo body with mahogany back and sides.

1997-2001		$900	$1,125

J12-15
2000-2008. 12-string version of J-15.

2000-2008		$900	$1,125

J12-16GT
2000-2013. 16" jumbo 12-string, satin solid mahogany back and sides, gloss solid spruce top.

2000-2013		$1,000	$1,375

J12-16GTE
2014-2015. Jumbo 12-string, Fishman.

2014-2015		$1,000	$1,375

J12-40/J12-40M
1985-1996. Called J12-40M from '85-'90, rosewood back and sides, 12 strings, 16" jumbo size, 14-fret neck, solid peghead, gold tuners.

1985-1990	J12-40M	$2,500	$3,250
1991-1996	J12-40	$2,500	$3,250

J12-65
1985-1995. Called J12-65M for '84-'90, 12-string, figured maple back and sides.

1985-1995		$2,000	$2,500

J-15
1999-2010. Jumbo 16" narrow-waist body, solid mahogany top, sides, and back, satin finish.

1999-2010		$1,000	$1,375

J-15E
2000-2001. Acoustic/electric J-15.

2000-2001		$1,125	$1,500

J-16E 12-String
2021-present. Grand 14-fret, Sitka spruce top, rosewood back and sides.

2021-2023		$1,500	$2,000

Martin HD-40 MS Marty Stuart
Imaged by Heritage Auctions, HA.com

Martin J-16E 12-String

GUITARS

Martin J-40

Martin LX1R

MODEL YEAR	FEATURES	EXC. COND. LOW	HIGH

J-18/J-18M
1987-1996. Called J-18M for '87-'89, J-size body with Style 18 appointments, natural.

| 1987-1989 | J-18M | $2,125 | $2,750 |
| 1990-1996 | J-18 | $2,125 | $2,750 |

J-21/J-21M
1985-1996. Called J-21M prior to '90, Indian rosewood back and sides, black binding, rosewood 'board, chrome tuners.

| 1985-1989 | J-21M | $1,875 | $2,500 |
| 1990-1996 | J-21 | $1,875 | $2,500 |

J-21MC
1986. J cutaway, oval sound hole, Guitar of the Month.

| 1986 | | $2,000 | $2,500 |

J-40
1990-present. Called J-40M from '85-'89, Jumbo, Indian rosewood back and sides, triple-bound 'board, hexagonal inlays.

| 1990-2023 | | $2,375 | $3,000 |

J-40 Custom
1993-1996. J-40 with upgrades including abalone top trim and rosette.

| 1993-1996 | | $2,375 | $3,000 |

J-40BK
1990-1997. Black finish and 'guard, gold hardware.

| 1990-1997 | | $2,375 | $3,000 |

J-40M/J-40MBK
1985-1989. Jumbo, Indian rosewood back and sides, triple-bound 'board, hexagonal inlays, MBK ('88-'89) indicates black, name changed to J-40 in '90.

| 1985-1989 | J-40M | $2,375 | $3,000 |
| 1988-1989 | J-40MBK | $2,375 | $3,000 |

J-40MBLE
1987. Brazilian rosewood, Style 45 snowflakes, 17 made.

| 1987 | | $4,875 | $6,250 |

J-40MC
1987-1989. Rounded Venetian cutaway version of J-40 M, oval sound hole, gold-plated enclosed tuners. Becomes JC-40 in '90.

| 1987-1989 | | $2,500 | $3,250 |

J-41 Special
2004-2007. East Indian rosewood back and sides, Style 45 snowflake inlays.

| 2004-2007 | | $3,125 | $4,000 |

J-45M Deluxe
1986. Guitar of the Month, East Indian rosewood back and sides, tortoise-colored binding, mother-of-pearl and abalone, gold tuners with ebony buttons.

| 1986 | | $4,000 | $5,250 |

J-65 Custom/J-65FM
1993-1996. White binding, herringbone. Available with MEQ electronics.

| 1993-1996 | | $2,375 | $3,000 |
| 1993-1996 | With MEQ | $2,375 | $3,000 |

J-65/J-65E/J-65M
1985-1995. Jumbo, maple back and sides, gold-plated tuners, scalloped bracing, ebony 'board, tortoise shell-style binding.

| 1985-1995 | | $2,250 | $3,000 |

MODEL YEAR	FEATURES	EXC. COND. LOW	HIGH

JC Buddy Guy Signature
2006-2007. Only 36 made, rosewood back and sides.

| 2006-2007 | | $3,125 | $4,000 |

JC-1E
1999-2002. Jumbo, mahogany, cutaway, pickup.

| 1999-2002 | | $950 | $1,250 |

JC-16GTE
2000-2003. Jumbo, cutaway, mahogany back and sides, gloss top, Fishman.

| 2000-2003 | | $1,125 | $1,500 |

JC-16GTE Premium
2003-2005. Fishman Prefix Stereo Blender pickup system.

| 2003-2005 | | $1,250 | $1,625 |

JC-16KWS Kenny Wayne Shepherd Signature
2001-2002. Cutaway, blue lacquer top, back and sides in gloss black, on-board electronics, 198 made.

| 2001-2002 | 198 made | $1,375 | $1,750 |

JC-16ME Aura
2006-2009. JC-16 with maple back and sides, Fishman Aura.

| 2006-2009 | | $1,625 | $2,125 |

JC-16RE Aura
2006-2011. Like ME, but with rosewood back and sides.

| 2006-2011 | | $1,625 | $2,125 |

JC-16RGTE Aura
2000-2003. Like RE Aura, but with gloss top.

| 2000-2003 | | $1,250 | $1,625 |

JC-16WE

| 2002-2003 | | $1,125 | $1,500 |

JC-40
1990-1997. Renamed from J-40 MC, cutaway flat-top, oval sound hole.

| 1990-1997 | | $2,500 | $3,250 |

JSO Sing Out! 60th Pete Seeger
2011. Triangular sound hole, Sikta top, East Indian rosewood back and sides, 2 'guards, 120 made. There was also a 12-string model (J12SO!).

| 2011 | | $3,125 | $4,000 |

LE-HMSD 2015 (HMS Dreadnought Battleship)
2015. Limited Edition, HMS Dreadnought Battleship (British Royal Navy) illustrated by artist Robert Goetzl is printed on the Sikta spruce top, dark mahogany back and sides, ebony 'board.

| 2015 | | $2,625 | $3,500 |

LX Series
2003-present. The LX series is the Little Martin models, featuring small bodies with high pressure wood laminate (HPL) backs and sides with an exterior wood-grain image with a gloss finish. M is for mahogany woodgrain, R for rosewood and K for Koa. They are also offered in all solid colors. A 1 indicates a HPL spruce top, 2 is HPL Koa top. E indicates electronics.

2003-2019	LXM	$225	$300
2004-2023	LX1	$225	$300
2004-2023	LXK2	$225	$300
2009	LX Elvis Presley	$400	$550
2009-2021	LX1E	$300	$400

GUITARS

MODEL YEAR	FEATURES	EXC. COND. LOW	HIGH
2013-2014	LX1E Ed Sheeran	$400	$550
2013-2019	LXME	$275	$400
2017-2023	LX Black	$225	$300
2019-2021	LX1RE	$375	$500
2019-2023	LX1R	$325	$450

M2C-28

1988. Double-cut, Guitar of the Month, 22 made.

1988		$2,125	$2,750

M-3H Cathy Fink

2005. M 0000-size body, gloss finish, rosewood sides, 3-piece back with flamed Koa center panel, torch headstock inlay, herringbone top trim, no Martin logo on headstock.

2005		$2,625	$3,500

M-3M George Martin

2005-2006. M Model, Style 40 appointments with Style 42 snowflake inlays, 127 made.

2005-2006		$4,375	$5,750

M-3SC Shawn Colvin

2002-2003. M 0000-size body, 120 made, mahogany sides, 3-piece mahogany/rosewood back, Fishman, Shawn Colvin & C.F.M. III signed label.

2002-2003		$2,500	$3,250

M-16GT

2001-2003. M-size single cut, gloss top, mahogany sides and back.

2001-2003		$1,000	$1,375

M-18

1984-1988. M size, mahogany.

1984-1988		$2,375	$3,000

M-21

December 1984. Guitar of the Month, low profile neck M-Series, Indian rosewood back and sides, special ornamentation.

1984		$2,250	$3,000

M-21 Steve Earle

2008-2011. Custom Edition, East Indian rosewood back and sides, Italian Alpine spruce top.

2008-2011		$3,000	$4,000

M-30 Jorma Kaukonen

2010-2013. Custom Artist Edition, M 0000-size body, Style 30 appointments, East Indian rosewood back and sides, Maltese diamond/square inlays, optional electronics.

2010-2013		$4,750	$6,250

M-35/M-36

1978-1997, 2007-present. First 26 labeled as M-35, Indian rosewood back and sides, bound 'board, low profile neck, multi-bound, white-black-white back stripes.

1978	M-35, 26 made	$3,000	$4,000
1978-1979		$2,875	$3,750
1980-1989		$2,375	$3,000
1990-2023		$2,250	$3,000
2008	175th Anniv	$2,250	$3,000

M-36B

1985. Brazilian rosewood.

1985		$4,625	$6,000

M-38 (0000-38)

1977-1997, 2007-2011. Called 0000-38 (see that listing) in '97-'98, 0000-size, Indian rosewood back

and sides, multi-bound.

1977-1979		$3,125	$4,000
1980-1997		$3,000	$4,000
2007-2011		$3,000	$4,000

M-38 Koa Special

2009-2010. Sikta spruce top, highly flamed Koa back and sides.

2009-2010		$3,000	$4,000

M-38B

1985. Brazilian rosewood.

1985		$5,875	$7,750

M-42 David Bromberg

2005-2006. 0000-14 body, rosewood back and sides, snowflakes, 83 made.

2005-2006		$4,375	$5,750

M-64

1985-1996. Flamed maple back and sides, tortoise-shell-style 'guard and binding. The 11 made in '85 were labeled M-64R.

1985-1996		$2,375	$3,000

MC12-41 Richie Sambora

2006. 12-string version of OMC-41 Richie Sambora, planned 200 combined models made.

2006		$4,250	$5,500

MC-16GTE

2002-2004. M-16 GT with single-cut and Fishman.

2002-2004		$975	$1,250

MC-16GTE Premium

2003-2005. Fishman Prefix Stereo Blender pickup system.

2003-2005		$1,250	$1,625

MC-28

1981-1996. Rosewood back and sides, single-cut, oval sound hole, scalloped braces.

1981-1996		$2,500	$3,250

MC-37K

1981-1982, 1987-1994. Cutaway, Koa back and sides.

1981-1994		$2,625	$3,500

MC-38 Steve Howe

2009-2011. Indian rosewood back and sides, cut-away, slot headstock.

2009-2011		$5,250	$6,875

MC-68/MC-68R/MC-68+

1985-1996. Auditorium-size, single-cut, maple back and sides, scalloped bracing, vertical logo, natural or sunburst. In '85 it was called the MC-68 R (for adjustable truss-rod), 7 with sunburst shaded top option called MC-68+.

1985	MC-68R	$3,000	$4,000
1986-1996	MC-68	$3,000	$4,000
1986-1996	MC-68+	$3,250	$4,250

MC-DSM

2007-2010. Limited Edition of 100, cutaway, designed by District Sales Manager (DSM), spruce top, figured Koa back and sides.

2007-2010		$3,250	$4,250

Mini-Martin Limited Edition

1999-2009. Size 5 Terz body, solid Sikta spruce top, rosewood sides and back, vintage style Martin Geib case with green interior.

1999-2009		$1,875	$2,500

Martin M-36

1979 Martin M-38
Gantt Kushner

1933 Martin OM-18
Jet City Guitars

1930 Martin OM-28
Jet City Guitars

MODEL YEAR	FEATURES	EXC. COND. LOW	HIGH
MMV			
2008-2012. D-style, rosewood sides and back, nitro finish.			
2008-2012		$1,250	$1,625
Model America 1			
2018. Limited Edition D-body, United States sourced woods, Adirondack spruce top, sycamore back and sides, cherry neck, black walnut 'board, gloss finish.			
2018		$2,500	$3,250
MTV-1 Unplugged			
1996. The body is 1/2 rosewood and 1/2 mahogany, scalloped bracing, MTV logo on headstock, gloss (588 sold) or satin (73 sold) finish.			
1996	Gloss finish	$2,250	$3,000
1996	Satin finish	$2,000	$2,500
MTV-2 Unplugged			
2003-2004. The body is 1/2 rosewood and 1/2 maple, scalloped bracing, MTV logo on headstock.			
2003-2004		$1,625	$2,125
N-10			
1968-1993. Classical, mahogany back and sides, fan bracing, wood marquetry sound hole ring, unbound rosewood 'board, 12-fret neck and slotted peghead from '70.			
1968-1970	Short-scale	$4,000	$5,000
1970-1979	Long-scale	$3,500	$4,500
1980-1993	Long-scale	$3,250	$4,000
N-20			
1968-1992. Classical, Brazilian rosewood back and sides (changed to Indian rosewood in '69), multi-bound, 12-fret neck, solid headstock (changed to slotted in '70), natural.			
1968-1969	Brazilian, short-scale	$12,500	$20,000
1969	Prismatone pu & Baldwin C-1 Amp	$13,500	$22,000
1970	Indian, short-scale	$5,500	$7,500
1970-1979	Indian, long-scale	$5,500	$7,500
1980-1992	Long-scale	$5,500	$7,500
N-20B			
1985-1986. Brazilian rosewood N-20.			
1985-1986		$10,000	$13,000
N-20WNB 'Trigger'			
1998-1999. Designed after Willie Nelson's famous N-20 he named Trigger, 100 made, Brazilian rosewood (30) or Indian (70).			
1998-1999	Brazilian	$12,000	$15,000
1998-1999	Indian	$5,500	$7,000
OM-1			
1999-2002, 2009-2010. Sikta spruce top, sapele back and sides, East Indian rosewood 'board, natural satin finish.			
1999-2010		$750	$950
OM-1GT			
2011-2014. OM-1 with gloss top.			
2011-2014		$750	$950
CS-OM-13			
2013. Custom Shop Limited Edition, 80 made, Swiss spruce top, Madagascar rosewood back and sides, gloss natural finish.			
2013		$3,125	$4,000

MODEL YEAR	FEATURES	EXC. COND. LOW	HIGH
OM-15			
2001-2003. Mahogany body, cutaway.			
2001-2003		$1,125	$1,500
OM-15M			
2015. All mahogany, natural satin finish.			
2015		$1,125	$1,500
OM-16GT			
2001-2005. Spruce top, mahogany back, sides and neck, natural gloss finish.			
2001-2005		$1,125	$1,500
OM-18			
1930-1934. Orchestra Model, mahogany back and sides, 14-fret neck, solid peghead, banjo tuners (changed to right-angle in '31).			
1930-1931	Banjo tuners, small 'guard	$45,000	$55,000
1931	Standard tuners, small 'guard	$37,500	$50,000
1932-1933	Standard tuners, large 'guard	$27,500	$35,000
OM-18 Authentic 1933			
2013-2019. Period-correct (1933) appointments, Vintage Tone System, vintage gloss finish.			
2013-2019		$4,500	$5,750
OM-18 Special			
2012. Custom Shop model.			
2012		$2,750	$3,500
OM-18GE Golden Era			
2003-2009. Mahogany back and sides, Brazilian rosewood purfling and binding.			
2003-2009		$3,500	$4,500
OM-18P			
1930-1931. Plectrum.			
1930-1931		$8,500	$10,500
OM-18V			
1999-2009. Vintage features.			
1999-2009		$3,000	$3,750
OM-18VLJ Laurence Juber			
2002, 2008-2009. Cutaway, Adirondack spruce top.			
2002-2009		$4,000	$5,000
OM-21			
1994-present. Indian rosewood back and sides, herringbone back stripe and sound hole ring, 14-fret neck, chrome tuners, natural or sunburst.			
1994-1999		$2,250	$2,875
2000-2023		$2,250	$2,875
OM-21 Special			
1991, 2007-2011. Upgrade to ebony 'board, rosewood bindings.			
1992-2011		$2,875	$3,750
OM-21 Special Limited Edition			
1991. Custom Shop, prototype to '92 production.			
1991	36 made	$2,875	$3,750
OM-28			
1929-1933, 1990-1997, 2015-present. Brazilian rosewood back and sides, 14-fret neck, solid peghead, banjo tuners (changed to right-angle in '31), reintroduced with Indian rosewood for '90-'97 and again in 2015.			
1929	Banjo pegs, small 'guard, pyramid end bridge	$135,000	$175,000

MODEL YEAR	FEATURES	EXC. COND. LOW	HIGH
1930	Early '30, banjo tuners, small 'guard, pyramid bridge	$125,000	$150,000
1930	Late '30, banjo tuners, small 'guard, belly bridge	$100,000	$125,000
1931	Early '31, banjo tuners, small 'guard, belly bridge	$100,000	$125,000
1931	Late '31, standard tuners, large 'guard	$85,000	$110,000
1931	Mid '31, banjo tuners, large 'guard	$100,000	$125,000
1932-1933	Standard tuners, full-size 'guard	$85,000	$110,000
1990-1997		$3,000	$3,750
2015-2023		$2,500	$3,250

OM-28 Authentic 1931

2015-2019. Adirondack spruce top, Madagascar rosewood back and sides, Vintage Tone System (VTS).

2015-2019		$5,750	$7,500

OM-28 Marquis

2005-2015. Pre-war appointments, Adirondack top, East Indian rosewood back, sides and headplate.

2005-2015		$3,500	$4,500

OM-28 Marquis Adirondack

2011-2013. Adirondack spruce top.

2011-2013		$3,500	$4,500

OM-28 Marquis Madagascar

2007-2008. Madagascar rosewood.

2007-2008		$3,500	$4,500

OM-28 Modern Deluxe

2019-present. Sikta spruce top with Vintage Tone System (VTS), East Indian rosewood back and sides, '30s style script logo on headstock, gloss finish. Electronics available (OM-28E).

2019-2023		$2,750	$3,500
2019-2023	OM-28E	$4,500	$5,500

OM-28E Retro

2012-2019. Sikta top, Indian rosewood back and sides, herringbone binding, Fishman.

2012-2019		$2,750	$3,500

OM-28GE Golden Era

2003-2004. Brazilian rosewood back and sides, Adirondack spruce top.

2003-2004		$10,000	$13,000

OM-28GE Golden Era Guatemalan Rosewood

2015. Custom Shop model, Guatemalan rosewood back and sides.

2015		$4,750	$6,125

OM-28JM John Mayer

2003. Limited Edition, 404 made.

2003		$8,000	$11,000

OM-28LE

1985. Limited Edition only 40 made, Guitar of the Month, Indian rosewood back and sides, herringbone top binding, V-neck.

1985		$3,500	$4,500

OM-28M Roseanne Cash

2008. Signature Edition, Madagascar rosewood back and sides, 100 made.

2008		$5,000	$6,500

OM-28PB Perry Bechtel

1993. Guitar of the Month, signed by Perry Bechtel's widow Ina, Indian rosewood back and sides, zigzag back stripe, chrome tuners, V-neck, 50 made.

1993		$5,000	$6,500

OM-28SO Sing Out! 35th Anniversary

1985. For Sing Out! Magazine's 35th anniversary, label signed by Pete Seeger.

1985		$3,500	$4,500

OM-28V Custom Shop (Brazilian/Adirondack)

2000-2001. Brazilian rosewood back and sides, Adirondack "red" spruce top, ca. 1933 prewar features including Martin gold headstock decal logo.

2000-2001		$8,000	$10,000

OM-28VR/OM-28V

1984-1990, 1999-2014. VR suffix until '99, then just V (Vintage Series), rosewood back and sides.

1984-1999	OM-28VR	$3,125	$4,000
1999-2014	OM-28V	$3,125	$4,000

OM-35

2003-2007. 000-size body, Indian rosewood sides and 3-piece back, spruce top, gloss natural finish.

2003-2007		$2,250	$3,000

OM-40 Rory Block

2004. Limited Edition, 38 made, 000-size, Indian rosewood back and sides, Englemann spruce top, 'the road' inlay markers, vintage-auto inlay on headstock.

2004		$3,500	$4,500

OM-40BLE

1990. Limited Edition, 50 made, Brazilian rosewood back and sides.

1990		$8,500	$11,000

OM-40LE

1994. Limited Edition, Guitar of the Month, Indian rosewood back and sides, double pearl borders, snowflake inlay on 'board, gold tuners, natural (57 sold) or sunburst (29 sold).

1994		$4,250	$5,500

OM-41 Special

2005-2006. Rosewood back and sides, Style 45 snowflake inlays.

2005-2006		$3,500	$4,500

OM-42

1930, 1999-present. Indian rosewood back and sides, Style 45 snowflake inlays, there were 2 guitars labeled OM-42 built in 1930.

1930	2 made	$125,000	$165,000
1999-2023		$4,000	$5,250

OM-42 Flamed Mahogany

2006. Limited Edition, 30 made, flamed mahogany back and sides, vines.

2006		$7,250	$9,500

Martin OM-28E Retro

1998 Martin OM-28VR

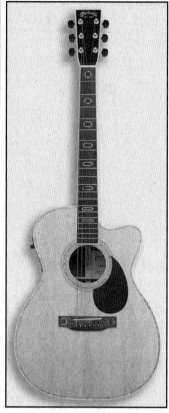

2008 Martin OMC Aura

Martin OMC-16 E Burst

MODEL YEAR	FEATURES	EXC. COND. LOW	HIGH

OM-42 Koa
2005-2008. Koa sides and back.

| 2006-2008 | | $6,000 | $8,000 |

OM-42PS Paul Simon
1997. Book matched Sikta spruce top, Indian rosewood back and sides, 42- and 45-style features, low profile PS neck, 500 planned but only 223 made.

| 1997 | | $4,500 | $6,000 |

OM-45
1930-1933. OM-style, 45 level appointments. Condition is critically important on this or any ultra high-end instrument, minor flaws are critical to value.

1930	Banjo pegs	$500,000	$625,000
1931	Right-angle tuners	$350,000	$450,000
1932-1933		$350,000	$450,000

OM-45/SOM-45/Special OM-45
1977-1994. First batch labeled SOM-45, 2 labeled OM-45N in '94 that had square tube bar in neck and without scalloped braces.

1977-1979		$7,750	$10,000
1980-1989		$7,500	$9,750
1990-1994		$6,875	$9,000
1994	OM-45 N option	$6,875	$9,000

OM-45 Custom Deluxe
1998-1999. Limited custom shop run of 14, Adirondack spruce and typical Style 45 appointments.

| 1998-1999 | | $17,500 | $23,000 |

OM-45 Deluxe
1930. Only 14 made, Brazilian rosewood back and sides, zipper pattern back stripe, pearl inlay in 'guard and bridge. Condition is critically important on this or any ultra high-end instrument, minor flaws are critical to value.

| 1930 | | $450,000 | $550,000 |

OM-45 Deluxe (Special)
1999. 4 made on special order, highly figured Brazilian rosewood.

| 1999 | | $22,500 | $30,000 |

OM-45 Deluxe Golden Era
1998. Brazilian, few made.

| 1998 | | $22,500 | $30,000 |

OM-45 Tasmanian Blackwood
2005. Limited Edition, 29 made, Tasmanian Blackwood (Koa-family) back and sides with curly grain, 000-size, OM and 45 style appointments.

| 2005 | | $7,875 | $10,500 |

OM-45/OM-45B Roy Rogers
2006. Limited Edition, based on Roy's 1930 OM-45 Deluxe, Indian rosewood (84 made) or Brazilian rosewood (45B, 14 made).

| 2006 | OM-45, Indian | $10,000 | $13,000 |
| 2006 | OM-45B, Brazilian | $24,000 | $30,000 |

OM-45GE Golden Era
1999, 2001-2005. Red spruce top, Brazilian rosewood.

| 1999-2005 | | $22,500 | $30,000 |

OM 1833 Custom Shop Limited Edition
2006. Italian alpine spruce top, flamed claro walnut back and sides, 000-size, low profile 14-fret neck, fancy

MODEL YEAR	FEATURES	EXC. COND. LOW	HIGH

inlay and appointments, natural gloss finish.

| 2006 | | $4,000 | $5,250 |

OM Chris Hillman
2009-2010. Adirondack top, Indian rosewood back and sides, sunburst.

| 2009-2010 | | $3,125 | $4,000 |

OM Jeff Daniels
2012-2013. Based on Daniels 1934 C-2 archtop conversion, Adirondack, Madagascar rosewood back and sides, sunburst.

| 2012-2013 | | $2,500 | $3,250 |

OM Negative
2007-2008. Limited Edition, 60 made, black body and white 'board, black inside label signed Dick Boak, gloss finish.

| 2007-2008 | | $3,625 | $4,750 |

OM True North-16/CS-OM True North-16
2016. Custom Shop Limited Edition, 50 made, Adirondack spruce top, figured Koa back and sides, back features a compass design inlaid with flamed jarrah, Claro walnut, waterfall bubinga and Paua pearl, ebony headplate has True North design inlaid with mother of pearl.

| 2016 | | $10,500 | $13,500 |

OMC Aura
2004-2011. OM size, cutaway, rosewood back and sides, Fishman Aura.

| 2004-2011 | | $2,500 | $3,250 |

OMC Cherry
2008-2013. Sustainable wood program, solid cherry back and sides, solid rescued spruce top, 000 body, cutaway, Fishman electronics.

| 2008-2013 | | $2,500 | $3,250 |

OMC Fingerstyle 1
2005-2008. Cutaway, Spanish cedar back and sides, no inlays.

| 2005-2008 | | $2,500 | $3,250 |

OMC Red Birch
2005-2009. Sustainable Series, rescued spruce top, solid red birch back and sides, Fishman electronics.

| 2005-2009 | | $2,125 | $2,750 |

OMC-1E
2009-2010. Style 28 appointments, cutaway, onboard Fishman.

| 2009-2010 | | $850 | $1,125 |

OMC-15E
2001-2007. All solid mahogany body.

| 2001-2007 | | $1,125 | $1,500 |

OMC-15ME
2016-2022. Mahogany top, back and sides, East Indian rosewood 'board, Fishman electronics.

| 2016-2022 | | $1,125 | $1,500 |

OMC-16E Burst
2019-2022. Mahogany burst ovangkol gloss top, satin ovangkol back and sides, Fishman electronics.

| 2019-2022 | | $1,500 | $2,000 |

OMC-16E Koa
2005-2009. Koa back and sides, on-board electronics.

| 2005-2009 | | $1,500 | $2,000 |

MODEL YEAR	FEATURES	EXC. COND. LOW	HIGH

OMC-16E Maple
2005-2009. Maple, on-board electronics.

2005		$1,500	$2,000

OMC-16E/E Premium
2003-2007, 2017-2019. Sikta spruce top, sapele back and sides, on-board electronics. Premium model with Prefix Premium Blend electronics. Reintroduced '17 with cherry back and sides and Fishman® Matrix VT.

2003-2007		$1,500	$2,000
2017-2019	16E, Reintroduced	$1,500	$2,000

OMC-16GTE
2010-2013. Gloss top, satin sapele back and sides.

2010-2013		$1,250	$1,625

OMC-16RE Aura
2005-2009. East Indian rosewood back and sides, gloss body.

2005-2009		$1,500	$2,000

OMC-16RE/RE Premium
2003-2005. Solid rosewood back and sides, on-board electronics.

2003-2005		$1,375	$1,750

OMC-16WE
2002-2003. Walnut back and sides.

2002-2003		$1,375	$1,750

OMC-18 Laurence Juber Custom Edition
2008. Venetian cutaway 000 body, Adirondack spruce top, gloss natural finish.

2008		$2,500	$3,250

OMC-18E
2017-2019. Sikta spruce top, mahogany back and sides, ebony 'board, Fishman electronics.

2017-2019		$1,375	$1,750

OMC-18LJ Laurence Juber
2008-2010. Cutaway 000, Adirondack spruce top.

2008-2010		$3,125	$4,000

OMC-28
1990. Guitar of the Month, 81 made, Indian rosewood, low profile neck, label signed by C.F. Martin IV.

1990		$3,000	$4,000

OMC-28 Laurence Juber
2004-2005. OM size, cutaway, Indian rosewood.

2004-2005		$3,875	$5,000

OMC-28BLJ Laurence Juber
2004. Brazilian rosewood, 50 made.

2004		$8,000	$10,500

OMC-28E
2006-2009, 2017-2019. OMC-28 with Fishman Ellipse. Reintroduced '17 with Fishman Aura.

2006-2009		$2,500	$3,250
2017-2019		$2,500	$3,250

OMC-28M Laurence Juber
2006-2011. Madagascar rosewood.

2006-2011		$3,875	$5,000

OMC-35E
2016-2017. Sikta spruce top, East Indian rosewood back & sides, ebony 'board and 'guard, Fishman electronics.

2016-2017		$2,500	$3,250

OMC-41 Richie Sambora
2006-2009. Madagascar rosewood sides and back, combination Style 45 and 41 appointments, 12-string is MC12-41 Richie Sambora, planned 200 made combined models.

2006-2009		$5,000	$6,500

OMC-LJ Pro Laurence Juber
2013. Custom Shop Artist Edition, Adirondack spruce top, flamed maple back and sides.

2013		$3,250	$4,500

OMCPA Series
2010-2019. Performing Artist Series, OM size, cutaway, acoustic/electric, various woods.

2010-2016	OMCPA1/1 Plus	$2,125	$2,750
2011	OMCPA2	$1,375	$1,750
2011-2013	OMCPA3	$1,375	$1,750
2011-2019	OMCPA4 Sapele	$1,375	$1,750
2012-2019	OMCPA4 Rosewood	$1,125	$1,500

OMCRE
2008-2009. Carpathian spruce top, East Indian rosewood sides and back, Babicz adjustable neck joint, Fishman, gloss finish.

2008-2009		$2,125	$2,750

OMC-X1E Black
2020-2023. Replaces OMCXAE Black. Jett black HPL top, back and sides, Fishman electronics.

2020-2023		$475	$650

OMCXK2E
2006-2009. Hawaiian Koa HPL (high pressure laminate) textured finish.

2006-2009		$550	$750

OMJM John Mayer
2003-present. Indian rosewood sides and back.

2003-2023		$2,750	$3,500

OMM
2000-2003. Solid spruce top, mahogany back and sides.

2000-2003		$750	$975

OMM John Renbourne
2011-2013. Madagascar rosewood sides and back.

2011-2013		$3,500	$4,500

OMXAE Black
2014-2019. Black HPL back and sides, black Richlite 'board.

2014-2019		$375	$500

Philadelphia Folk Festival 40th Anniversary
2002. Commemorating 40th Anniversary of Martin Philly Folk Festival, 85 made, 0000-14 fret, Englemann spruce top, Indian rosewood back and sides, PFF logo inlays, one label signed by CF Martin IV and David Baskin, one signed by festival participants, blue denim-covered hard case.

2002		$2,750	$3,500

POW MIA
2006-2010. POW MIA logo position marker lettering on fretboard, D-style body, dark finish.

2006-2010		$2,500	$3,250

PS2 Paul Simon Signature
2003. Paul Simon signature logo at bottom of fretboard, 200 made.

2003		$3,000	$4,000

R-15
1934. Archtop, sunburst.

1934	2 made	$2,500	$3,500

Martin OMCPA4

Martin OMJM John Mayer

GUITARS

1937 Martin R-18
Frank Manno

Martin SC-10E

R-17
1934-1942. All mahogany, arched top and back, 3-segment f-holes (changed to 1-segment in '37).
1934-1942 — $2,500 — $3,500

R-18P
1934-1936. Only 4 made, plectrum neck.
1934-1936 — $2,500 — $3,500

R-18S/R-18
1932-1942. Spruce arched top (carved top by 1937), mahogany back and sides, bound top, sunburst.
1932-1942 — $3,250 — $4,000

R-18T
1934-1941. Tenor archtop, 14 3/8" lower bout, 2 f-holes, dot markers, sunburst.
1934-1941 — $2,000 — $2,500

R-21
1938. 000 body archtop, 1 made.
1938 — $6,250 — $7,500

SC Series
2020-present. Road Series, patented Sure Align® neck system, Sikta spruce top with various wood back and sides, 10E/13E (Koa), 13E Special (ziricote), CS-SC-2022 (Custom Shop, rosewood).
2020-2023 SC-13E — $1,250 — $1,625
2022 CS-SC-2022 — $6,000 — $8,000
2022-2023 SC-10E — $925 — $1,250
2022-2023 SC-13E Special — $1,375 — $1,750
2022-2023 SC-13E Special Burst — $1,500 — $2,000

Schoenberg Soloist by C.F. Martin
1987-1994. Designed by Eric Schoenberg with help from luthier Dana Bourgeois, OM body, Brazilian rosewood back and sides.
1987-1994 — $6,500 — $8,500

Shenandoah Series
1983-1993. Bodies and necks were built in Japan with final assembly and finishing in Nazareth and a Thinline piezo added, styled after U.S. models with a 32 added to the model name.
1983-1993 Various models — $1,000 — $1,625

SP000 Series
1996-2002. Special Edition 000-size, spruce top with aging toner, scalloped bracing, rosewood or mahogany body.
1996-1997 SP000C-16TR — $1,375 — $1,750
1996-2002 SP000-16 — $1,250 — $1,625
1996-2002 SP000-16R — $1,250 — $1,625
1996-2002 SP000-16T — $1,250 — $1,625
1996-2002 SP000-16TR — $1,250 — $1,625
1997-2002 SP000C-16R — $1,375 — $1,750
1999-2002 SP000C-16 — $1,375 — $1,750
1999-2002 SP000C-16E — $1,375 — $1,750
2003 SP000C-16R (CS) — $2,250 — $3,000

SP00-16RST Stauffer
2000-2002. Stauffer 6-on-a-side headstock, 12-fret neck, rosewood back and sides.
2000-2002 — $1,500 — $2,000

SPD12-16R
1997-2004. 12-string, solid rosewood body, abalone sound hole ring, Style-45 backstripe.
1999-2000 — $1,500 — $2,000

SPD-16 Series
1997-2004. D-16 Series Special models.
1996-1999 SPD-16TR — $1,500 — $2,000
1997-2004 SPD-16 — $1,375 — $1,750
1997-2004 SPD-16T — $1,375 — $1,750
1999-2001 SPD-16B Black — $1,375 — $1,750
1999-2002 SPD-16M Maple — $1,250 — $1,625
1999-2002 SPD-16W Walnut — $1,250 — $1,625
2000 SPD-16E — $1,500 — $2,000
2000-2002 SPD-16R — $1,500 — $2,000
2000-2005 SPD-16K — $1,750 — $2,250
2000-2005 SPD-16K2 — $1,750 — $2,250

SPDC-16 Series
1997-2001. Cutaway version of SPD-16.
1997-1999 SPDC-16TR — $1,500 — $2,000
1997-2001 SPDC-16RE Rosewood — $1,500 — $2,000
2000-2002 SPDC-16R — $1,500 — $2,000

SPJC-16RE
2000-2003. Single-cut, East Indian rosewood body, 000-size, on-board electronics.
2000-2003 — $1,500 — $2,000

SPOM-16
1999-2001. Mahogany.
1999-2001 — $1,500 — $2,000

SS-0041GB-17
2017-2020. Limited Edition of 50, Grand Concert 12-fret, European spruce top with Vintage Tone System (VTS), Guatemalan rosewood back and sides, gloss finish.
2017-2020 — $6,000 — $7,750

SS-00L41-16
2016-2020. Limited Edition, Adirondack spruce top with Vintage Tone System (VTS), moabi back and sides, mahogany neck, hand-rubbed finish.
2016-2020 — $3,625 — $4,750

SS-OMVine-16
2016. Limited Edition of 35, NAMM show special, figured English walnut, aluminum vine inlay on ebony 'board.
2016 — $9,000 — $12,000

Stauffer
1830s-ca.1850s. One of C.F. Martin's earliest models, distinguished by the scrolled, six-on-a-side headstock, ornamentation varies. Each instrument should be evaluated on a case-by-case basis, those in truly original excellent condition may be worth more than the values shown.
1835 Fancy (2nd highest) — $45,000 — $60,000
1835 Fancy (highest) — $150,000 — $175,000
1835 Mid-level — $30,000 — $40,000
1835 Plain (2nd lowest) — $25,000 — $30,000
1835 Plain (lowest) — $18,000 — $25,000

Sting Mini
2006. 100 made, Size 5, Western red cedar top, Solomon padauk body.
2005-2006 — $2,625 — $3,500

Stinger
1980s-1990s. Import copy offset S-style electric solidbody.
1980s-90s — $250 — $350

The *Vintage Guitar Price Guide* shows values for all-original, excellent condition instruments and, where applicable, with original case.

MODEL YEAR	FEATURES	EXC. COND. LOW	HIGH

SW00-D8 Machiche
2006-2007. Smartwood Limited Edition, 125 made, rescued solid spruce top, sustainable machiche sides and back.

2006-2007		$1,500	$2,000

SWC
1998. Smartwood 'The Sting Signature Classical Model', machiche wood body.

1998		$1,500	$2,000

SWD
1998-2001. Smartwood D-size, built from wood material certified by the Forest Stewardship Council, Sikta top, cherry back and sides, natural satin finish.

1998-2001		$1,250	$1,625

SWD Red Birch
2003-2005. Red Birch.

2003-2005		$1,250	$1,625

SWDGT
2001-2016. Gloss top SWD.

2001-2016		$1,250	$1,625

SWDTG
2000-2007. Cherry back and sides, gloss finish.

2000-2007		$1,250	$1,625

SWMGT
2002-2003. M size, cherry back and sides, gloss finish.

2002-2003		$1,250	$1,625

SWOM
2000-2001. Sustainable Woods Series.

2000-2001		$1,250	$1,625

SWOMGT
2001-2018. Smartwood OM, rescued solid Sikta spruce top, sustainable cherry sides and back, gloss finish.

2001-2018		$1,250	$1,625

Yuengling 180th Anniversary Custom
2008. Celebrating 180th company anniversary, limited production, large company logo on top of body, fancy D-41 style appointments, certificate.

2008		$4,000	$5,000

Maruha

1960s-1970s. Japanese-made acoustic, classical, archtop and solidbody guitars, often copies of American brands. Probably not imported into the U.S.

Marvel

1950s-mid-1960s. Brand name used for budget guitars and basses marketed by Peter Sorkin Company in New York, New York. Sorkin manufactured and distributed Premier guitars and amplifiers made by its Multivox subsidiary. Marvel instruments were primarily beginner-grade. Brand disappears by mid-'60s. The name was also used on archtop guitars made by Regal and marketed by the Slingerland drum company in the 1930s to early 1940s.

Electric

1950s-60s	Various models	$250	$550

Marveltone by Regal

1925-1930. Private branded by Regal, Marveltone pearl style logo on headstock.

Guitar
1925-1930. 14" Brazilian rosewood.

1925-1930		$2,500	$3,250

Masaki Sakurai

See Kohno brand.

Mason

1936-1939. Henry L. Mason on headstock, wholesale distribution, similar to Gibson/Cromwell, pressed wood back and sides.

Student/Intermediate Student
1936-1939. Various flat-top and archtop student/budget models.

1936-1939		$550	$1,000

Mason Bernard

1990-1991. Founded by Bernie Rico (BC Rich founder). During this period BC Rich guitars were licensed and controlled by Randy Waltuch and Class Axe. Most Mason models were designs similar to the BC Rich Assassin, according to Bernie Rico only the very best materials were used, large MB logo on headstock. Around 225 guitars were built bearing this brand.

Maton

1946-present. Intermediate and professional grade, production/custom, acoustic, acoustic/electric, hollowbody and solidbody guitars built in Box Hill, Victoria, Australia. Founded by Bill May and his brother Reg and still run by the family. Only available in USA since '82.

Matsuda Guitars

See listing for Michihiro Matsuda.

Matsuoka

1970s. Ryoji Matsuoka from Japan built intermediate grade M series classical guitars that often featured solid tops and laminated sides and back.

Matt Pulcinella Guitars

1998-present. Production/custom, professional grade, electric guitars and basses built in Chadds Ford, Pennsylvania by luthier Matt Pulcinella.

Mauel Guitars

Luthier Hank Mauel builds his premium grade, custom, flat-tops in Auburn, California. He began in 1995.

Maurer

Late 1880s-1944. Robert Maurer built guitars and mandolins in the late 1880s under the Maurer and Champion brands in his Chicago shop. Carl and August Larson bought the company in 1900 and retained the Maurer name. The Larsons also built under the Prairie State, Euphonon, W. J. Dyer and Wm. C. Stahl brands.

1987 Martin Stinger SSX-10

1962 Maton EG240SE

1930s May Bell
Imaged by Heritage Auctions, HA.com

Late-'70s MCI B-35 Guitorgan
Tom Pfeifer

Max B
Luthier Sebastien Sulser builds professional grade, production/custom, electric guitars and basses, starting in 2000, in Kirby, Vermont.

May Bell
1923-1940s. Brand of flat-top guitars, some with fake resonators, marketed by the Slingerland Company. Most were made by Regal.

Maya
See El Maya.

McAlister Guitars
1997-present. Premium grade, custom, flat-tops built by luthier Roy McAlister in Watsonville, California.

McCollum Guitars
1994-2009. Luthier Lance McCollum builds his premium grade, custom, flat-top and harp guitars in Colfax, California. McCollum died in 2009.

McCurdy Guitars
1983-present. Premium grade, production/custom, archtops built by luthier Ric McCurdy originally in Santa Barbara, California and, since '91, New York, New York.

McElroy
1995-present. Premium grade, custom, classical and flat-top steel string acoustic guitars built by luthier Brent McElroy in Seattle, Washington.

McGill Guitars
1976-present. Luthier Paul McGill builds his premium grade, production/custom, classical, resonator, and acoustic/electric guitars in Nashville, Tennessee.

McGlincy
Ca. 1974-ca. 1978. Custom flat-tops built by luthier Edward McGlincy in Toms River, New Jersey. Only 12 instruments made, and owners included Gordon Lightfoot and David Bromberg. He later offered uke and guitar kits. He also operated Ed's Musical Instruments. McGlincy died in '97.

McGlynn Guitars
2005-2007. Luthier Michael J. McGlynn built his premium and presentation grade, custom, solidbody guitars in Henderson, Nevada. McGlynn died in '07.

McGowan Guitars
Luthier Brian McGowan builds his production/custom, premium grade, steel-string acoustic guitars in Hampton, Virginia. He began in 2004.

MCI, Inc
1967-1988. MusiConics International (MCI), of Waco, Texas, introduced the world to the GuitOrgan, invented by Bob Murrell. Later, they also offered effects and a steel guitar. In the '80s, a MIDI

MODEL YEAR	FEATURES	EXC. COND. LOW	HIGH

version was offered. MCI was also involved with the Daion line of guitars in the late '70s and early '80s. MCI also built a double-neck lap steel.

GuitOrgan B-35
1970s (ca. 1976-1978?). Duplicated the sounds of an organ and more. MCI bought double-cut semi-hollow body guitars from others and outfitted them with lots of switches and buttons. Each fret has 6 segments that correspond to an organ tone. There was also a B-300 and B-30 version, and the earlier M-300 and 340.

1970s	Fully functional	$1,500	$2,000

McInturff
1996-present. Professional and premium grade, production/custom, solidbody guitars built by luthier Terry C. McInturff originally in Holly Springs, North Carolina, and since '04, in Moncure, North Carolina. McInturff spent 17 years doing guitar repair and custom work before starting his own guitar line.

McKnight Guitars
1992-present. Luthier Tim McKnight builds his custom, premium grade, acoustic steel string guitars in Morral, Ohio.

McPherson Guitars
1981-present. Premium grade, production, flat-tops built by luthier Mander McPherson in Sparta, Wisconsin.

Mean Gene
1988-1990. Heavy metal style solidbodies made by Gene Baker, who started Baker U.S.A. guitars in '97, and Eric Zoellner in Santa Maria, California. They built around 30 custom guitars. Baker currently builds b3 guitars.

Megas Guitars
1989-present. Luthier Ted Megas builds his premium grade, custom, archtop and solidbody guitars, originally in San Franciso, and currently in Portland, Oregon.

Melancon
Professional and premium grade, custom/production, solid and semi-hollow body guitars and basses built by luthier Gerard Melancon, beginning in 1995, in Thibodaux, Louisiana.

Mello, John F.
1973-present. Premium grade, production/custom, classical and flat-top guitars built by luthier John Mello in Kensington, California.

Melophonic
1960s. Brand built by the Valco Company of Chicago, Illinois.

Resonator
1965		$1,000	$1,375

MODEL		EXC. COND.	
YEAR	FEATURES	LOW	HIGH

Melville Guitars

1988-present. Luthier Christopher Melville builds his premium grade, custom, flat-tops in Milton, Queensland, Australia.

Memphis

One of the many guitar brands built by Japan's Matsumoku company.

Mercurio

2002-2005. Luthier Peter Mercurio built his custom/production solidbody guitars, featuring his interchangeable PickupPak system to swap pickups, in Chanhassen, Minnesota.

Mermer Guitars

Luthier Richard Mermer, started building in 1983, premium grade, production/custom, steel-string, nylon-string, and Hawaiian guitars in Sebastian, Florida.

Merrill Brothers

Premium grade, production/custom, steel-string and harp guitars built by luthiers Jim and Dave Merrill in Williamsburg, Virginia, starting in 1998.

Mesrobian

1995-present. Luthier Carl Mesrobian builds his professional and premium grade, custom, archtop guitars in Salem, Massachusetts.

Messenger

1967-1968. Built by Musicraft, Inc., originally of 156 Montgomery Street, San Francisco, California. The distinguishing feature of the Messengers is a metal alloy neck which extended through the body to the tailblock, plus mono or stereo outputs. Sometime before March '68 the company relocated to Astoria, Oregon. Press touted "improved" magnesium neck, though it's not clear if this constituted a change from '67. Brand disappears after '68. They also made basses.

Electric Hollowbody Archtop

1967-1968. Symmetrical double-cut body shape, metal neck with rosewood 'boards, stereo.

1967-1968		$2,750	$3,500

Metropolitan

1995-2008. Professional and premium grade, production/custom, retro-styled solidbodies designed by David Wintz reminiscent of the '50s National Res-o-glas and wood body guitars. They featured full-scale set-neck construction and a wood body instead of Res-o-glas. Wintz also made Robin and Alamo brand instruments.

Electric Solidbody

1995-2008	Various models	$2,000	$2,500

Meyers Custom Guitars

Professional grade, custom, solidbody electric guitars built by luthier Donald Meyers in Houma, Louisiana, beginning 2005.

Miami

1920s. Instruments built by the Oscar Schmidt Co. and possibly others. Most likely a brand made for a distributor.

Michael Collins Custom Guitars

Premium grade, custom/production, classical, flamenco and steel string guitars built in Argyle, New York, by luthier Michael Collins, starting in 1975.

Michael Collins Guitars

Luthier Michael Collins builds his professional and premium grade, custom, Selmer style, archtop and flat-top guitars, starting in 2002, in Keswick, Ontario. He also builds mandolins.

Michael Cone

1968-present. Presentation grade, production/custom, classical guitars built previously in California and currently in Kihei Maui, Hawaii by luthier Michael Cone. He also builds ukuleles.

Michael Dunn Guitars

Luthier Michael Dunn begins in 1968, builds production/custom Maccaferri-style guitars in New Westminster, British Columbia. He also offers a harp uke and a Weissenborn- or Knutsen-style Hawaiian guitar and has built archtops.

Michael Kelly

1999-present. Founded by Tracy Hoeft and offering intermediate and professional grade, production, acoustic, solidbody and archtop guitars. The brand was owned by the Hanser Music Group from 2004-'15. They also offer mandolins and basses.

Michael Lewis Instruments

1992-present. Luthier Michael Lewis builds his premium and presentation grade, custom, archtop guitars in Grass Valley, California. He also builds mandolins.

Michael Menkevich

Luthier Michael Menkevich builds his professional and premium grade, production/custom, flamenco and classical guitars in Elkins Park, Pennsylvania, starting in 1970.

Michael Silvey Custom Guitars

2003-ca. 2007. Solidbody electric guitars built by Michael Silvey in North Canton, Ohio.

Michael Thames

1972-present. Luthier Michael Thames builds his premium grade, custom/production, classical guitars in Taos, New Mexico.

Michael Tuttle

2003-present. Professional and premium grade, custom, solid and hollowbody guitars and basses built by luthier Michael Tuttle in Saugus, California.

1997 Metropolitan Glendale
Imaged by Heritage Auctions, HA.com

Michael Kelly Hybrid Special
Cream City Music

Microfrets Plainsman
Michael Kellum

Modulus Blackknife
Joseph Fradella

MODEL YEAR	FEATURES	EXC. COND. LOW	HIGH

Michihiro Matsuda

1997-present. Presentation grade, production/custom, steel and nylon string acoustic guitars built by luthier Michihiro Matsuda in Oakland, California. He also builds harp guitars.

Microfrets

1967-1975, 2004-2005. Professional grade, production, electric guitars built in Myersville, Maryland. They also built basses. Founded by Ralph S. Jones, Sr. in Frederick, Microfrets offered over 20 models of guitars that sported innovative designs and features, with pickups designed by Bill Lawrence. The brand was revived, again in Frederick, by Will Meadors and Paul Rose in '04.

Serial numbers run from about 1000 to about 3800. Not all instruments have serial numbers, particularly ones produced in '75. Serial numbers do not appear to be correlated to a model type but are sequential by the general date of production.

Instruments can be identified by body styles as follows; Styles 1, 1.5, 2, and 3. An instrument may be described as a Model Name and Style Number (for example, Covington Style 1). Style 1 has a wavey-shaped pickguard with control knobs mounted below the guard and the 2-piece guitar body has a particle board side gasket. Style 1.5 has the same guard and knobs, but no side body gasket. Style 2 has an oblong pickguard with top mounted control knobs and a pancake style seam between the top and lower part of the body. Style 3 has a seamless 2-piece body and a Speedline neck.

Baritone Signature
1971. Baritone version of Signature Guitar, sharply pointed double-cut, with or without f-holes, single- or double-dot inlays.

1971		$1,500	$2,000

Baritone Stage II
1971-ca. 1975. Double-cut, 2 pickups.

1971-1975		$1,500	$2,000

Calibra I
1969-1975. Double-cut, 2 pickups, f-hole.

1969-1975		$1,250	$1,625

Covington
1967-1969. Offset double-cut, 2 pickups, f-hole.

1967-1969		$1,750	$2,250

Golden Comet
1969. Double-cut, 2 pickups, f-hole, name changed to Wanderer.

1969		$1,750	$2,250

Golden Melody
1969, 2004-2005. Offset double-cut, 2 pickups, f-hole, name changed to Stage II in '69.

1969-1971		$1,750	$2,250

Huntington
1969-1975. Double-cut, 2 pickups.

1969-1975		$2,000	$2,500

Orbiter
1967-1969. Odd triple cutaway body, thumbwheel controls on bottom edge of 'guard.

1967-1969		$2,000	$2,500

Plainsman
1967-1969. Offset double-cut, 2 pickups, f-hole, thumbwheel controls on bottom edge of 'guard.

1967-1969		$2,000	$2,500

Signature
1967-1969. Double-cut, 2 pickups.

1967-1969		$2,000	$2,500

Spacetone
1969-1971, 2004-2005. Double-cut semi-hollow body, 2 pickups.

1969-1971		$2,000	$2,500

Stage II
1969-1975. Renamed from Golden Melody, offset double-cut, 2 pickups.

1969-1975		$1,750	$2,250

Swinger
1971-1975. Offset double-cut, 2 pickups.

1971-1975		$1,750	$2,250

Voyager/The Voyager
1967-1968. Early model, less than a dozen made, Voyager headstock logo (no Microfrets logo), 2 DeArmond-style single-coils, offset double-cut body, FM transmitter on upper bass bout facilitates wireless transmission to Microfrets receiver or FM radio.

1967-1968		$3,125	$4,000

Wanderer
1969-1971. Renamed from Golden Comet, double-cut, 2 pickups.

1969-1971		$1,750	$2,250

Mike Lull Custom Guitars

1995-present. Professional and premium grade, production/custom, guitars and basses built by luthier Mike Lull in Bellevue, Washington.

Milburn Guitars

1990-present. Luthiers Orville and Robert Milburn build their premium grade, custom, classical guitars in Sweet Home, Oregon.

Miller

1960s. One of the brand names of guitars built for others by Egmond in Holland.

Minarik

2002-present. Luthier M.E. Minarik builds his professional and premium grade, custom/production, solid and chambered body guitars in Van Nuys, California.

Minerva

1930s. Resonator and archtop guitars sold through catalog stores, likely made by one of the big Chicago builders of the era.

Mirabella

1997-present. Professional and premium grade, custom archtops, flat-tops, hollowbody, and solid-body guitars and basses built by luthier Cristian Mirabella in Babylon, New York. He also builds mandolins and ukes.

Miranda Guitars

Owner Phil Green uses components made by various shops in California to assemble and set-up, professional grade, full-size travel/silent-practice guitars in Palo Alto, California. He started in 2002.

Mitre

1983-1985. Bolt neck, solidbody guitars and basses made in Aldenville (or East Longmeadow), Massachusetts, featuring pointy body shapes, 2 humbuckers, active or passive electronics.

MJ Guitar Engineering

1993-present. Professional and premium grade, production/custom, hollowbody, chambered and solidbody guitars and basses built by luthier Mark Johnson in Rohnert Park, California.

Mobius Megatar

2000-2019. Professional grade, production, hybrid guitars designed for two-handed tapping, built in Mount Shasta, California. Founded by Reg Thompson, Henri Dupont, and Traktor Topaz in '97, they released their first guitars in '00.

Modulus

1978-2013. Founded by Geoff Gould in the San Francisco area, and later built in Novato, California. Modulus built professional grade, production/custom, solidbody electric guitars up to '05.

Genesis 2/2T

1996-2005. Double-cut, extended bass horn alder body, bolt-on carbon fiber/red cedar neck, hum-single-single pickups, locking vibrato (2T model).

1996-2005	$1,750	$2,250

Moll Custom Instruments

1996-present. Luthier Bill Moll builds his professional and premium grade, archtops in Springfield, Missouri. He has also built violins, violas and cellos.

Monrad, Eric

1993-present. Premium, custom, flamenco and classical guitars built by luthier Eric Monrad in Healdsburg, California.

Monroe Guitars

Luthier Matt Handley builds his custom, professional grade, solidbody electric guitars and basses in State Center, Iowa. He started in 2004.

Montalvo

See the listing under Casa Montalvo.

Montaya

Late 1970s-1980s. Montaya Hyosung 'America' Inc., Korean acoustic and electric import copies.

Monteleone

1976-present. Presentation grade, production/custom, archtop guitars built by Luthier John Monteleone in Islip, New York. He also builds mandolins. Instruments should be evaluated on a case-by-case basis.

MODEL YEAR	FEATURES	EXC. COND. LOW	HIGH

Eclipse

1990s. Very rare archtop.

1990s		$50,000	$65,000

Montgomery Ward

The mail-order and retail giant offered a variety of instruments and amps from several different U.S. and overseas manufacturers.

Model 8379/H44 Stratotone

Mid-1950s. Private branded Harmony Stratotone, some without logo but with crown-style stencil/painted logo on headstock, many with gold-copper finish, 1 pickup.

1950s	Various models	$1,000	$1,500

Monty

1980-present. Luthier Brian Monty builds his professional, premium and presentation grade, production/custom, archtop, semi-hollow, solidbody, and chambered electric guitars originally in Lennoxville, Quebec, and currently in Anne de Prescott, Ontario.

Moog

1964-present. Moog introduced its premium grade, production, Harmonic Control System solidbody guitar in 2008. They also offer guitar effects.

Moon (Japan)

1979-present. Professional and premium grade, production/custom, guitars and basses made in Japan.

Moon (Scotland)

1979-present. Intermediate, professional and premium grade, production/custom, acoustic and electric guitars built by luthier Jimmy Moon in Glasgow, Scotland. They also build mandolin family instruments.

Moonstone

1972-2020. Professional, premium, and presentation grade production/custom flat-top, solid and semi-hollow electric guitars, built by luthier Steve Helgeson in Eureka, California. He also built basses. Higher unit sales in the early-'80s. Some models have an optional graphite composite neck built by Modulus. Steve passed away in June 2020.

Earth Axe

1974-1976. Limited production, solidbody, natural finish.

1974-1976		$6,000	$8,000

Eclipse Deluxe

1979-1983. Figured birdseye maple body, offset double-cut, neck-thru, gold hardware, diamond markers, natural finish.

1979-1983		$3,000	$4,500

Eclipse Standard

1979-1983. Figured wood body, offset double-cut, neck-thru, standard maple neck, dot markers, natural finish, 12-string (XII) available.

1979-1983		$2,500	$3,500
1979-1983	XII	$2,500	$3,500

Moll Custom Instruments

1957 Montgomery Ward
Donald Kuntze

1968 Mosrite Combo
Dave Mullikin

1968 Mosrite Joe Maphis Mark XVIII
Mathew A. Dirjish

MODEL YEAR	FEATURES	EXC. COND. LOW	HIGH

Exploder
1980-1983. Figured wood solidbody, neck-thru, standard maple neck, natural finish.

1980-1983		$2,500	$3,500

Flaming V
1980-1984. Figured wood body, V-shaped, neck-thru, standard maple neck, natural finish.

1980-1984		$2,500	$3,500

M-80
1980-1984. Figured wood double-cut semi-hollow body, standard maple or optional graphite neck, natural finish.

1980s	Maple or graphite	$3,000	$3,500

Vulcan Deluxe
1979-1983. Figured maple carved-top body, offset double-cut, diamond markers, standard maple or optional graphite neck, natural finish.

1979-1983	Maple or graphite	$3,000	$3,500

Vulcan Standard
1979-1983. Mahogany carved-top body, offset double-cutaway, dot markers, standard maple or optional graphite neck, natural finish.

1979-1983	Maple or graphite	$3,000	$3,500

Morales
Ca.1967-1968. Guitars and basses made in Japan by Zen-On, not heavily imported into the U.S., if at all.

Solidbody Electric
1967-1968	Various models	$150	$400

More Harmony
1930s. Private branded by Dobro for Dailey's More Harmony Music Studio. Private branding for catalog companies, teaching studios, publishers, and music stores was common for the Chicago makers. More Harmony silk-screen logo on the headstock.

Dobro
1930s. 14" wood body with upper bout f-holes and metal resonator, sunburst.

1930s		$1,000	$1,500

Morgaine Guitars
1994-2004. Luthier Jorg Tandler built his professional and premium grade, production/custom electrics in Germany, until 2004. He started using Tandler name in '05.

Morgan Monroe
Intermediate grade, production, acoustic, acoustic/electric and resonator guitars and basses made in Korea and distributed by SHS International of Indianapolis, Indiana. They also offer mandolins and banjos.

Morris
1967-present. Intermediate, professional and premium grade, production, acoustic guitars imported by Moridaira of Japan. Morris guitars were first imported into the U.S. from the early '70s to around '90. They are again being imported into the U.S. starting in 2001. They also offered mandolins in the '70s.

000 Copy
1970s. Brazilian rosewood laminate body.

1970s		$1,000	$1,500

Acoustic-Electric Archtop
1970s	Various models	$1,000	$1,500

D-45 Copy
1970s. Brazilian rosewood laminate body.

1970s		$1,000	$2,000

Mortoro Guitars
1992-present. Luthier Gary Mortoro builds his premium grade, custom, archtop guitars in Miami, Florida.

Mosrite
The history of Mosrite has more ups and downs than just about any other guitar company. Founder Semie Moseley had several innovative designs and had his first success in 1954, at age 19, building doubleneck guitars for super picker Joe Maphis and protégé Larry Collins. Next came The Ventures, who launched the brand nationally by playing Mosrites and featuring them on album covers. At its '60s peak, the company was turning out around 1,000 guitars a month. The company ceased production in '69, and Moseley went back to playing gospel concerts and built a few custom instruments during the '70s.

In the early-'80s, Mosrite again set up shop in Jonas Ridge, North Carolina, but the plant burned down in November '83, taking about 300 guitars with it. In early-'92, Mosrite relocated to Booneville, Arkansas, producing a new line of Mosrites, of which 96% were exported to Japan, where the Ventures and Mosrite have always been popular. Semie Moseley died, at age 57, on August 7, '92 and the business carried on until finally closing its doors in '93. The Mosrite line has again been revived, offering intermediate and premium grade, production, reissues.

Throughout much of the history of Mosrite, production numbers were small and model features often changed. As a result, exact production dates are difficult to determine.

Balladeer
1964-1965. Mid-size flat-top, slope shoulder, natural or sunburst.

1964-1965		$1,500	$2,000

Brass Rail
1970s. Double-cut solidbody, has a brass plate running the length of the 'board.

1970s		$1,375	$1,750

Celebrity 1
Late-1960s-1970s. Thick hollowbody, 2 pickups, sunburst.

1960s-70s		$1,375	$1,750

MODEL YEAR	FEATURES	EXC. COND. LOW	HIGH

Celebrity 2 Standard
Late-1960s-1970s. Thin hollowbody, 2 pickups, in the '70s, it came in a Standard and a Deluxe version.

1960s-70s		$1,500	$2,000

Celebrity 3
Late-1960s-1970s. Thin hollowbody, double-cut, 2 pickups, f-holes.

1960s-70s		$1,375	$1,750

Combo Mark 1
1966-1968. Bound body, 1 f-hole.

1966-1968		$2,000	$2,500

Custom-Built
1952-1962. Pre-production custom instruments hand built by Semie Moseley, guidance pricing only, each instrument will vary. A wide variety of instruments were made during this period. Some were outstanding, but others, especially those made around '60, could be very basic and of much lower quality. Logos would vary widely and some '60 logos looked especially homemade.

1952-1959	Rare, high-end	$10,500	$15,000
1960-1962	Common, low-end	$1,750	$2,500

D-40 Resonator
1960s. Symmetrical double-cut thinline archtop-style body with metal resonator in center of body, 2 pickups, 2 control knobs and toggle switch.

1960s		$1,500	$2,000

D-100 Californian
1960s. Double-cut, resonator guitar with 2 pickups.

1967		$1,500	$2,000

Gospel
1967. Thinline double-cut, f-hole, 2 pickups, vibrato, Gospel logo on headstock.

1967	Sunburst	$1,750	$2,250
1967	White	$2,500	$3,250

Joe Maphis Doubleneck
1963-1968. Limited Edition reissue of the guitar Semie Moseley made for Maphis, with the smaller octave neck, sunburst.

1963-1968	Octave 6/standard 6	$4,000	$5,000
1963-1968	Standard 6/12	$4,000	$5,000

Joe Maphis Mark 1
1959-1972. Semi-hollow double-cut, 2 single-coils, spruce top, walnut back, rosewood 'board, natural.

1959-1972		$2,500	$3,500

Joe Maphis Mark XVIII
1960s. 6/12 doubleneck, double-cut, 2 pickups on each neck, Moseley tremolo on 6-string.

1960s		$4,000	$5,000

Mosrite 1988
1988-early-1990s. Has traditional Mosrite body styling, Mosrite pickups and bridge.

1988		$650	$850

Octave Guitar
1963-1965. 14" scale, 1 pickup, Ventures Mosrite body style, single neck pickup, very few made.

1963-1965		$4,500	$5,500

Stereo 350
1974-1975. Single-cut solidbody, 2 outputs, 2 pickups, 4 knobs, slider and toggle, black.

1974-1975		$1,250	$1,750

Ventures Model
1963-1968. Double-cut solidbody, triple-bound body '63, no binding after, Vibramute for '63-'64, Moseley tailpiece '65-'68.

1963	Blue or red, bound	$7,500	$9,500
1963	Sunburst, bound	$6,000	$8,000
1964	Blue or red, Vibramute	$5,500	$7,000
1964	Sunburst, Vibramute	$6,000	$8,000
1965	Moseley (2 screws)	$3,500	$5,000
1965	Vibramute, (3 screws)	$4,500	$6,000
1966-1968	Moseley	$3,000	$4,000

Ventures (Jonas Ridge/Boonville)
1982-1993. Made in Jonas Ridge, NC or Booneville, AR, classic Ventures styling.

1982-1993		$1,750	$2,250

Ventures Mark V
1963-1967. Double-cut solidbody.

1963-1967		$1,750	$2,250

Ventures Mark XII
1966-1967. Double-cut solidbody, 12 strings.

1966-1967		$3,000	$4,000

Mossman

Professional and premium grade, production/custom, flat-top guitars built in Sulphur Springs, Texas, starting in 1965. They have also built acoustic basses. Founded by Stuart L. Mossman in Winfield, Kansas. In '75, fire destroyed one company building, including the complete supply of Brazilian rosewood. They entered into an agreement with C.G. Conn Co. to distribute guitars by '77. 1200 Mossman guitars in a Conn warehouse in Nevada were ruined by being heated during the day and frozen during the night. A disagreement about who was responsible resulted in cash flow problems for Mossman. Production fell to a few guitars per month until the company was sold in '86 to Scott Baxendale. Baxendale sold the company to John Kinsey and Bob Casey in Sulphur Springs in '89.

Flint Hills
1970-1979. Flat-top acoustic, East Indian rosewood back and sides.

1970-1979	Indian rosewood	$2,000	$2,500

Flint Hills Custom

1970-1979	Indian rosewood	$3,000	$3,500

Golden Era
1970-1977. D-style, vine inlay and other high-end appointments, Brazilian rosewood back and sides until '76, then Indian rosewood.

1970-1975	Brazilian rosewood	$5,000	$6,500
1976-1977	Indian rosewood	$3,500	$4,500

Golden Era Custom

1970-1975	Brazilian rosewood	$7,000	$9,000

Great Plains
1970-1979. Flat-top, Brazilian rosewood until '75 then Indian rosewood, herringbone trim.

1970-1975	Brazilian rosewood	$3,500	$4,500
1976-1979	Indian rosewood	$2,500	$3,500

1976 Mossman Flint Hills
Allen Boudreaux

1975 Mossman Great Plains
David Stone

GUITARS

1976 Mossman Southwind

Musicman Sabre II

Tom Pfeifer

MODEL YEAR	FEATURES	EXC. COND. LOW	HIGH
Great Plains Custom			
1970-1975	Brazilian rosewood	$5,500	$7,500
Southwind			
1976-ca. 1986, mid-1990s-2002. Flat-top, abalone trim top.			
1976-1979	Indian rosewood	$3,000	$4,000
Tennessee			
1972-1979. D-style, spruce top, mahogany back and sides, rope marquetry purfling, rope binding.			
1972-1979		$2,000	$2,500
Tennessee 12-String			
1975-1979	Mahogany	$2,000	$2,500
Timber Creek			
1976-1979. D-style, Indian rosewood back and sides, spruce top.			
1976-1979	Indian rosewood	$2,500	$3,500
Winter Wheat			
1976-1979, mid-1990s-2000s. Flat-top, Indian rosewood back and sides, abalone trim, natural finish.			
1976-1979	Indian rosewood	$3,000	$4,000
Winter Wheat 12-String			
1976-1979. 12-string version of Winter Wheat, natural.			
1976-1979	Indian rosewood	$3,000	$4,000

MotorAve Guitars

2002-present. Luthier Mark Fuqua builds his professional and premium grade, production, electric guitars originally in Los Angeles, California, and currently in Durham, North Carolina.

Mouradian

1983-present. Luthiers Jim and Jon Mouradian build their professional and premium grade, production/custom, electric guitars and basses in Winchester, Massachusetts. Jim died in 2017.

Mozart

1930s. Private brand made by Kay.

Hawaiian (Square Neck)

1930s. Spruce top, solid mahogany sides and back, pearloid overlay on peghead with large Mozart inscribed logo, small jumbo 15 1/2" body.

1935-1939		$1,250	$1,750

Mozzani

Built in shops of Luigi Mozzani (b. March 9, 1869, Faenza, Italy; d. 1943) who opened lutherie schools in Bologna, Cento and Rovereto in 1890s. By 1926 No. 1 and 2 Original Mozzani Model Mandolin (flat back), No. 3 Mandola (flat back), No. 4 6-String Guitar, No. 5 7-, 8-, and 9-String Guitars, No. 6 Lyre-Guitar.

M-Tone Guitars

2009-present. Professional and premium grade, production/custom, solidbody electric guitars built in Portland, Oregon by luthier Matt Proctor.

Muiderman Guitars

1997-present. Custom, premium grade, steel string and classical guitars built by luthier Kevin Muiderman currently in Grand Forks, North Dakota, and previously in Beverly Hills, Michigan, 1997-2001, and Neenah, Wisconsin, '01-'07. He also builds mandolins.

Murph

1965-1967. Mid-level electric semi-hollow and solidbody guitars built by Pat Murphy in San Fernado, California. Murph logo on headstock. They also offered basses and amps.

Electric Solidbody

1965-1967		$1,250	$1,625

Electric XII

1965-1967		$1,250	$1,625

Music Man

1972-present. Professional grade, production, solidbody guitars built in San Luis Obispo, California. They also build basses. Founded by ex-Fender executives Forrest White and Tom Walker in Orange County, California. Music Man originally produced guitar and bass amps based on early Fender ideas using many former Fender employees. They contracted with Leo Fender's CLF Research to design and produce a line of solidbody guitars and basses. Leo Fender began G & L Guitars with George Fullerton in '80. In '84, Music Man was purchased by Ernie Ball and production was moved to San Luis Obispo.

Albert Lee Signature

1993-present. Swamp ash body, figured maple neck, 3 pickups, white pearloid 'guard, Pinkburst.

1993-1996	Pinkburst	$1,500	$2,250
1996-2019	Tremolo option	$1,250	$1,750

Axis

1996-present. Offset double-cut solidbody, figured maple top, basswood body, 2 humbucker pickups, Floyd Rose.

1996-2023		$1,250	$1,750

Axis Sport

1996-2002. Two P-90s.

1996-2002		$1,250	$1,750

Axis Super Sport

2003-present. Figured top.

2003-2023		$1,500	$2,250

Edward Van Halen

1991-1996. Basswood solidbody, figured maple top, bolt-on maple neck, maple 'board, binding, 2 humbuckers, named changed to Axis.

1991-1996	6,000 made	$5,500	$7,500
1991-1996	Rare color (purple & black)	$8,000	$10,000

John Petrucci 6/JP-6

2008-2021. Standard model, basswood body, maple neck, rosewood 'board, various colors with high gloss finish.

2008-2021		$1,750	$2,250

MODEL		EXC. COND.	
YEAR	FEATURES	LOW	HIGH

John Petrucci BFR
2011-2020. Ball Family Reserve (BFR).

2011-2020		$2,000	$2,500

Reflex
2011-2017. Referred to as The Game Changer, patent-pending pickup switching system, maple or rosewood neck with matching headstock, black finish.

2011-2017		$1,500	$2,000

S.U.B 1
2004-2006. Offset double-cut solidbody.

2004-2005		$600	$750

Sabre I
1978-1982. Offset double-cut solidbody, maple neck, 2 pickups, Sabre I comes with a flat 'board with jumbo frets.

1978-1982		$1,250	$1,750

Sabre II
1978-1982. Same as Sabre I, but with an oval 7 1/2" radius 'board.

1978-1982		$1,250	$1,750

Silhouette
1986-present. Offset double-cut, contoured beveled solidbody, various pickup configurations.

1986-2023		$1,250	$1,750
2006	20th Anniversary	$1,250	$1,750

Silhouette 6/12 Double Neck
2009-2014. Alder body, maple or rosewood 'boards, 4 humbuckers.

2009-2014		$2,000	$2,500

Silhouette Special
1995-present. Silhouette with Silent Circuit.

1995-2023		$1,250	$1,750

Steve Morse Signature
1987-present. Solidbody, 4 pickups, humbuckers in the neck and bridge positions, 2 single-coils in the middle, special pickup switching, 6-bolt neck mounting, maple neck.

1987-2023		$1,750	$2,250

Stingray I
1976-1982. Offset double-cut solidbody, flat 'board radius.

1976-1982		$1,250	$1,750

Stingray II
1976-1982. Offset double-cut solidbody, rounder 'board radius.

1976-1982		$1,250	$1,750

Musicvox
1996-2001, 2011-present. Intermediate grade, production, imported retro-vibe guitars and basses from Matt Eichen of Cherry Hill, New Jersey.

Myka
2003-present. Luthier David Myka builds his professional and premium grade, custom/production, solidbody, semi-hollowbody, hollowbody, archtop, and flat-top guitars in Seattle, Washington. Until '07 he was located in Orchard Park, New York.

Nady
1976-present. Wireless sound company Nady

Systems offered guitars and basses with built-in wireless systems for 1985-'87. Made by Fernandes in Japan until '86, then by Cort in Korea.

Lightning/Lightning II
1985-1987. Double-cut, neck-thru, solidbody, 24 frets, built-in wireless, labeled as just Lightning until cheaper second version (bolt-neck) came out in '86.

1985-1987		$375	$500

Napolitano Guitars
1993-2010. Luthier Arthur Napolitano built professional and premium grade, custom, archtop guitars in Allentown, New Jersey.

NashGuitars
2001-present. Luthier Bill Nash builds his professional grade, production/custom, aged solidbody electric guitars and basses in Olympia, Washington.

Nashville Guitar Company
1985-present. Professional and premium grade, custom, flat-top guitars built by luthier Marty Lanham in Nashville, Tennessee. He has also built banjos.

National
Ca. 1927-present. Founded in Los Angeles as the National String Instrument Corporation by John Dopyera, George Beauchamp, Ted Kleinmeyer and Paul Barth. In '29 Dopyera left to start the Dobro Manufacturing Company with Rudy and Ed Dopyera and Vic Smith. The Dobro company competed with National until the companies reunited. Beauchamp and Barth then left National to found Ro-Pat-In with Adolph Rickenbacker and C.L. Farr (later becoming Electro String Instrument Corporation, then Rickenbacher). In '32 Dopyera returns to National and National and Dobro start their merger in late-'33, finalizing it by mid-'34. Throughout the '30s, National and Dobro maintained separate production, sales, and distribution. National Dobro moved to Chicago in '36 where archtop and flat-top bodies are built primarily by Regal and Kay; after '37 all National resonator guitar bodies made by Kay. L.A. production is maintained until around '37, although some assembly of Dobros continued in L.A. (primarily for export) until '39 when the L.A. offices are finally closed. By ca. '39 the Dobro brand disappears.

In '42, the company's resonator production ceased, and Victor Smith, Al Frost and Louis Dopyera buy the company and change name to Valco Manufacturing Company. Post-war production resumed in '46. Valco was purchased by treasurer Robert Engelhardt in '64. In '67, Valco bought Kay, but in '68 the new Valco/Kay company went out of business. In the Summer of '69 the assets, including brand names, were auctioned off and the National and Supro names were purchased by Chicago-area distributor/importer Strum 'N Drum (Noble, Norma brands). The National brand is used

Music Man Steve Morse Signature

1976 Music Man Stingray II
Cream City Music

GUITARS

National Don Style 1

Imaged by Heritage Auctions, HA.com

National Model 1105 Glenwood

Mike Newton

MODEL			EXC. COND.	
YEAR		FEATURES	LOW	HIGH

on copies in the early- to mid-'70s, and the brand went into hiatus by the '80s.

In '88 National Resophonic Guitars is founded in San Luis Obispo, California, by Don Young, with production of National-style resonator guitars beginning in '89 (see following). In the '90s, the National brand also resurfaces on inexpensive Asian imports.

National Resonator guitars are categorized by materials and decoration (from plain to fancy): Duolian, Triolian, Style 0, Style 1, Style 2, Style 3, Style 4, Don #1, Style 97, Don #2, Don #3, Style 35.

National guitars all have serial numbers which provide clues to date of production. This is a complex issue. This list combines information included in George Gruhn and Walter Carter's Gruhn's Guide to Vintage Guitars, which was originally provided by Bob Brozman and Mike Newton, with new information provided by Mike Newton.

Pre Chicago numbers:
A101-A450 1935-1936.

Chicago numbers:
A prefix (some may not have the prefix) 1936-mid-1997. B prefix Mid-1937-1938. C prefix Late-1938-1940. G prefix up to 200 Ea. 1941-ea. 1942. G suffix under 2000 Ea. 1941-ea. 1942. G suffix 2000-3000s (probably old parts) 1943-1945. G suffix 4000s (old parts) Late 1945-mid-1947.

V100-V7500 1947. V7500-V15000 1948. V15000-V25000 1949. V25000-V35000 1950. V35000-V38000 1951. X100-X7000 1951. X7000-X17000 1952. X17000-X30000 1953. X30000-X43000 1954. X43000-X57000 1955. X57000-X71000 1956. X71000-X85000 1957. X85000-X990001958.

T100-T5000 1958. T5000-T25000 1959. T25000-T50000 1960. T50000-T75000 1961. T75000-T90000 1962. G100-G5000 1962. T90000-T99000 1963. G5000-G15000 1963. G15000-G40000 1964. 1 prefix 1965-ea. 1968. 2 prefix Mid-1968.

Aragon De Luxe
1939-1942. Archtop with resonator (the only archtop resonator offered), spruce top and maple back and sides, light brown.

1939-1942			$9,500	$12,000

Big Daddy LP-457-2
1970s. Strum & Drum import, single-cut, LP-style, 2 pickups, gold hardware, black.

1970s			$350	$450

Bluegrass 35
1963-1965. Acoustic, non-cut single-cone resonator, Res-O-Glas body in Arctic White.

1963-1965			$2,000	$2,500

Bobbie Thomas
Ca.1967-1968. Double-cut thinline hollowbody, bat-shaped f-holes, 2 pickups, Bobbie Thomas on 'guard, vibrato.

1967-1968			$1,500	$2,000

MODEL			EXC. COND.	
YEAR		FEATURES	LOW	HIGH

Cameo
1957-1958. Renamed from Model 1140 in '57, full-body acoustic archtop with carved top.

1957-1958			$975	$1,250

Collegian
1942-1943. Metal body resonator similar to Duolian, 14-fret round or square neck, yellow.

1942-1943			$1,750	$2,250

Don Style 1
1934-1936. Plain body with engraved borders, pearl dot inlay, 14 frets, single-cone, silver (nickel-plated).

1934-1936			$10,000	$12,500

Don Style 2
1934-1936. Geometric Art Deco body engraving, 14 frets, single-cone, fancy square pearl inlays and pearl-oid headstock overlay, silver (nickel-plated).

1934-1936			$11,500	$14,500

Don Style 3
1934-1936. Same as Style 2 but more elaborate floral engravings, fancy pearl diamond inlays, 14 frets, single-cone, silver (nickel-plated), only a very few made.

1934-1936			$20,000	$25,000

Duolian
1930-1939. Acoustic steel body, frosted paint finish until '36, mahogany-grain paint finish '37-'39, round neck, square neck available in '33, 12-fret neck until '34 then 14-fret.

1930-1934	Round neck		$3,750	$4,500

EG 685 Hollow Body Electric
1970s. Strum & Drum distributed, double-cut hollowbody copy, 2 pickups.

1970s			$550	$700

El Trovador
1933 only. Wood body, 12 frets.

1933			$3,500	$4,500

Electric Spanish
1935-1938. 15 1/2" archtop with Pat. Appl. For bridge pickup, National crest logo, fancy N-logo 'guard, black and white art deco, sunburst, becomes New Yorker Spanish '39-'58.

1935-1938			$2,500	$3,000

Estralita
1934-1942. Acoustic with single-cone resonator, f-holes, multi-bound, 14-fret, mahogany top and back, shaded brown.

1934-1942			$1,500	$1,875

Glenwood 95
1962-1964. Glenwood 98 without third bridge-mount pickup, Vermillion Red or Flame Red.

1962-1964			$4,000	$5,000

Glenwood 98
1964-1965. USA map-shaped solidbody of molded Res-O-Glas, 2 regular and 1 bridge pickup, vibrato, 3 tailpiece options, Pearl White.

1964-1965			$4,000	$5,000

Glenwood 99
1962-1965. USA map-shaped solidbody of molded Res-O-Glas, 2 regular and 1 bridge pickups, butterfly inlay.

1962-1963	Snow White		$4,000	$5,000
1964-1965	Green/Blue		$10,000	$15,000

MODEL YEAR	FEATURES	EXC. COND. LOW	HIGH

Glenwood Deluxe

1959-1961. Renamed from Glenwood 1105, Les Paul-shaped solidbody, wood body, not fiberglass, multibound, 2 pickups, factory Bigsby, vibrato, natural.

1959-1961		$2,500	$3,500

Havana

1938-1942. Natural spruce top, sunburst back and sides.

1938-1942	Round neck	$1,500	$2,000
1938-1942	Square neck	$850	$1,125

Model 1100 California

1949-1955. Electric hollowbody archtop, multibound, f-holes, trapeze tailpiece, 1 pickup, natural.

1949-1955		$1,000	$1,500

Model 1103 Del-Mar

1954-1957. Electric archtop, 2 pickups, adjustable bridge, sunburst finish.

1954-1957		$1,250	$1,625

Model 1104 Town and Country

1954-1958. Model just below Glenwood 1105, dots, 2 or 3 pickups, plastic overlay on back, natural finish.

1954-1958	2 pickups	$1,875	$2,500
1954-1958	3 pickups	$2,125	$2,750

Model 1105 Glenwood

1954-1958. Les Paul-shaped solidbody, wood body, not fiberglass, single-cut, multi bound, 2 pickups, natural, renamed Glenwood Deluxe with Bigsby in '59.

1954-1958		$2,750	$3,500

Model 1106 Val-Trol Baron

1959-1960. Single-cut solidbody, 2 pickups, 1 piezo, block inlays, black.

1959-1960		$1,750	$2,125

Model 1107 Debonaire

1953-1960. Single rounded-cutaway full-depth 16" electric archtop, single neck pickup, Debonaire logo on 'guard (for most models), large raised National script logo on headstock, sunburst.

1953-1960		$1,125	$1,500

Model 1109/1198 Bel-Aire

1953-1960. Single pointed cut archtop, 2 (1109) pickups until '57, 3 (1198) after, master tone knob and jack, bound body, sunburst.

1953-1957	1109, 2 pickups	$1,750	$2,125
1958-1960	1198, 3 pickups	$2,000	$2,500

Model 1110/1111 Aristocrat

1941-1954. Electric full body non-cut archtop, 1 pickup, 2 knobs, early model with triple backslash markers, later with block markers, National-crest headstock inlaid logo, natural finish only until model numbers added to name in '48, shaded sunburst finish (1110) and natural (1111).

1941-1948	Natural	$950	$1,250
1948-1955	1110, sunburst	$1,125	$1,500
1948-1955	1111, natural	$1,125	$1,500

Model 1120 New Yorker

1954-1958. Renamed from New Yorker Spanish, 16.25" electric archtop, 1 pickup on floating 'guard, dot markers, blond.

1954-1958		$1,250	$1,500

Model 1122 Cosmopolitan

1954-1957. Small wood non-cutaway solidbody, dot markers, 1 pickup, 2 knobs on mounted 'guard.

1954-1957		$1,000	$1,250

Model 1122 Val-Trol Junior

1959-1960. Single-cut solidbody, 1 pickup and 1piezo, dot inlays, ivory.

1959-1960		$1,250	$1,625

Model 1123 Bolero

1954-1957. Les Paul-shape, control knobs mounted on 'guard, single pickup, trapeze tailpiece, sunburst.

1954-1957		$950	$1,125

Model 1124/1124B/1134 Avalon

1954-1957. Small wood solidbody, 2 pickups, 4 control knobs and switch on top-mounted 'guard, block markers, short trapeze bridge, sunburst (1124) or blond (1124B).

1954-1957	1124, sunburst	$1,250	$1,625
1954-1957	1124B/1134, blond	$1,375	$1,750

Model 1125 Dynamic

1951-1959. Full body 15.5" acoustic-electric archtop, sunburst version of New Yorker 1120 with some appointments slightly below the New Yorker, dot markers, 1 pickup, sunburst.

1951-1959		$900	$1,125

Model 1135 Acoustic Archtop

1948-1954. 17.25" full body acoustic archtop, carved top, split pearl markers.

1948-1954		$1,500	$2,000

Model 1140 Acoustic Archtop

1948-1957. 15.5" full body acoustic archtop, carved top, dot markers.

1948-1957		$900	$1,125

Model 1150 Flat-Top Auditorium

1951-1958. Auditorium-size flat-top, 14.25" narrow-waist, dot markers.

1951-1958		$900	$1,125

Model 1155/1155E /N-66 Jumbo

1948-1961. Flat-top acoustic with Gibson Jumbo body, mahogany back and sides, bolt-on neck.

1947	N-66	$2,750	$3,500
1948-1961	1155/1155E	$2,750	$3,500

Model 1170 Club Combo

1952-1955, 1959-1961. Electric hollowbody archtop, 2 pickups, rounded cutaway.

1952-1961		$1,500	$2,000

N600 Series

1968. Offset double-cut solidbody, 1, 2, and 3 pickup models, with and without vibrato.

1968	N624, 1 pickup	$525	$775
1968	N634, 2 pus, vibrato	$625	$825
1968	N644, 3 pus, vibrato	$825	$1,125
1968	N654, 12-string	$625	$825

N700 Series

1968. Flat-top, 700/710 dreadnoughts, 720/730 jumbos.

1968	N700 Western	$625	$825
1968	N710	$375	$500
1968	N720 Western	$425	$575
1968	N730 Deluxe	$600	$800

1954 National Model N-66/1155
Imaged by Heritage Auctions, HA.com

1968 National N634

GUITARS

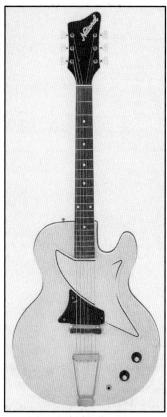

1962 National Studio 66
Imaged by Heritage Auctions, HA.com

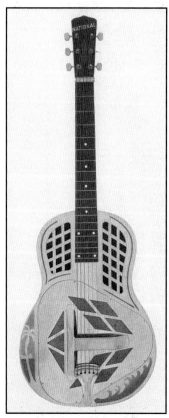

1936 National Style 97
Imaged by Heritage Auctions, HA.com

MODEL YEAR	FEATURES	EXC. COND. LOW	HIGH
N800 Series			
1968. Double-cut semi-hollow body, various models with or without Bigsby.			
1968	No Bigsby	$625	$825
1968	With Bigsby	$725	$950
New Yorker Spanish			
1939-1953. Electric archtop, 15.5" body until '47 then 16.25", 1 neck pickup, dot-diamond markers, sunburst or natural. Renamed New Yorker 1120 in '54.			
1939-1946	15.5"	$2,250	$2,875
1947-1949	1625"	$2,000	$2,500
1950-1953	16.25"	$1,625	$2,000
Newport 82			
1963-1965. Renamed from Val-Pro 82, USA map-shaped Res-O-Glas, 1 pickup, Pepper Red finish.			
1963-1965		$2,500	$3,500
Newport 84			
1963-1965. Renamed from Val-Pro 84, USA map-shaped Res-O-Glas, 1 regular and 1 bridge pickup, Sea Foam Green finish.			
1963-1965		$4,000	$5,000
Newport 88			
1963-1965. Renamed from Val-Pro 88, USA map-shaped Res-O-Glas, 2 regular and 1 bridge pickup, Raven Black finish.			
1963-1965		$3,000	$4,000
Reso-phonic			
1956-1964. Pearloid-covered, single-cut semi-solidbody acoustic, single resonator, maroon or white, also a non-cut, square neck version was offered, which is included in these values.			
1956-1964	Round neck, common finish	$1,875	$2,500
1956-1964	Round neck, rare finish	$2,000	$2,500
1956-1964	Square neck	$1,500	$2,000
Rosita			
1933-1939. Plywood body by Harmony, plain metal resonator, plain appointments.			
1933-1939		$1,250	$1,500
Silvo (Electric Hawaiian)			
1937-1941. Nickel-plated metal body flat-top, small upper bout, f-holes, square neck, multiple straight line body art over dark background, Roman numeral parallelogram markers, National badge headstock logo, Silvo name on coverplate.			
1937-1941	Silver	$3,375	$4,250
Studio 66			
1961-1964. Electric solidbody of Res-O-Glas, single-cut, 1 pickup, renamed Varsity 66 in '65.			
1961-1962	Sand Buff, bridge pu	$1,500	$2,000
1963-1964	Jet Black, neck pu	$1,500	$2,000
Style 0			
1930-1942. Acoustic single-cone brass body (early models had a steel body), Hawaiian scene etching, 12-fret neck '30-'34, 14-fret neck '35 on, round (all years) or square ('33 on) neck.			
1930-1934	Round neck, 12-fret, common etching	$3,750	$5,000
1930-1934	Round neck, 12-fret, rare etching	$5,000	$8,500

MODEL YEAR	FEATURES	EXC. COND. LOW	HIGH
1933-1942	Square neck, common etching	$1,750	$2,500
1933-1942	Square neck, rare etching	$3,250	$4,000
1935-1942	Round, 14-fret (Knopfler assoc)	$7,500	$9,500
1935-1942	Round, 14-fret, common etching	$3,250	$4,000
1935-1942	Round, 14-fret, rare etching	$4,750	$6,000
Style 0 Tenor			
1929-1930. Tenor, 4 strings, single-cone brass body, Hawaiian scene etching.			
1929-1930		$975	$1,250
Style 1 Tricone			
1927-1943. German silver body tricone resonator, ebony 'board, mahogany square (Hawaiian) or round (Spanish) neck, plain body, 12-fret neck until '34, 14-fret after.			
1927-1943	Round neck	$6,500	$8,500
1928-1943	Square neck	$4,250	$5,500
Style 1 Tricone Plectrum			
1928-1935. 26" scale versus the 23" scale of the tenor.			
1928-1935		$2,125	$2,750
Style 1 Tricone Tenor			
1928-1935. Tenor, 4 strings, 23" scale, square neck is Hawaiian, round neck is Spanish.			
1928-1935		$2,125	$2,750
Style 1.5 Tricone			
1930s. A "1/2" style like the 1.5 represents a different engraving pattern.			
1930s	Round neck	$9,750	$12,500
1930s	Square neck	$3,250	$4,250
Style 2 Tricone			
1927-1942. German silver body tricone resonator, wild rose engraving, square (Hawaiian) or round (Spanish) neck, 12-fret neck until '34, 14-fret after.			
1927-1942	Round neck	$12,500	$15,500
1927-1942	Square neck	$4,000	$5,000
Style 2 Tricone Plectrum			
1928-1935. 26" scale versus the 23" scale of the tenor.			
1928-1935		$1,750	$2,250
Style 2 Tricone Tenor			
1928-1935. Tenor.			
1928-1935		$2,000	$3,000
Style 2.5 Tricone			
1927-1928. Collector term for Style 2 with additional rose engravings on coverplate, bound ebony fretboard.			
1927-1928		$9,500	$12,500
Style 3 Tricone			
1928-1941. German silver body tricone resonator, lily-of-the-valley engraving, square (Hawaiian) or round (Spanish) neck, 12-fret neck until '34, 14-fret after, reintroduced with a nickel-plated brass body in '94.			
1928-1939	Round neck	$15,000	$20,000
1928-1941	Square neck	$5,500	$7,250
Style 3 Tricone Plectrum			
1928-1935. 26" scale versus the 23" scale of the tenor.			
1928-1935		$3,500	$4,500

MODEL YEAR	FEATURES	EXC. COND. LOW	HIGH
Style 3 Tricone Tenor			
1928-1939. Tenor version.			
1928-1939		$3,250	$4,250
Style 4 Tricone			
1928-1940. German silver body tricone resonator, chrysanthemum etching, 12-fret neck until '34, 14-fret after, reissued in '95 with same specs.			
1928-1940	Round neck	$20,000	$25,000
1928-1940	Square neck	$5,500	$7,500
Style 35			
1936-1942. Brass body tricone resonator, sandblasted minstrel and trees scene, 12 frets, square (Hawaiian) or round (Spanish) neck.			
1936-1942	Round neck	$35,000	$45,000
1936-1942	Square neck	$11,500	$15,000
Style 97			
1936-1940. Nickel-plated brass body tricone resonator, sandblasted scene of female surf rider and palm trees, 12 frets, slotted peghead.			
1936	Early '36, square neck	$11,500	$15,000
1936	Late '36, square neck, different 'board	$8,000	$10,000
1936-1940	Round neck	$30,000	$40,000
Style N			
1930-1931. Nickel-plated brass body single-cone resonator, plain finish, 12 frets.			
1930-1931		$5,500	$7,500
Triolian			
1928-1941. Single-cone resonator, wood body replaced by metal body in '29, 12-fret neck and slotted headstock '28-'34, changed to 14-fret neck in '35 and solid headstock in '36, round or square ('33 on) neck available.			
1928-1936	Various colors	$3,500	$4,500
1936-1937	Fake rosewood grain	$3,250	$4,250
Triolian Tenor			
1928-1936. Tenor, metal body.			
1928-1936		$1,250	$1,500
Trojan			
1934-1942. Single-cone resonator wood body, f-holes, bound top, 14-fret round neck.			
1934-1942		$1,500	$2,000
Val-Pro 82			
1962-1963. USA map-shaped Res-O-Glas, 1 pickup, Vermillion Red finish, renamed Newport 82 in '63.			
1962-1963		$1,625	$2,000
Val-Pro 84			
1962-1963. USA map-shaped Res-O-Glas, 1 regular and 1 bridge pickup, snow white finish, renamed Newport 84 in '63.			
1962-1963		$1,875	$2,375
Val-Pro 88			
1962-1963. USA map-shaped Res-O-Glas, 2 regular and 1 bridge pickup, black finish, renamed Newport 88 in '63.			
1962-1963		$2,625	$3,250

MODEL YEAR	FEATURES	EXC. COND. LOW	HIGH
Varsity 66			
1964-1965. Renamed from Studio 66 in '64, molded Res-O-Glas, 1 pickup, 2 knobs, beige finish.			
1964-1965		$1,375	$1,750
Westwood 72			
1962-1964. USA map-shaped solid hardwood body (not fiberglass), 1 pickup, Cherry Red.			
1962-1964		$2,125	$2,750
Westwood 75			
1962-1964. USA map-shaped solid hardwood body (not fiberglass), 1 regular and 1 bridge pickup, cherry-to-black sunburst finish.			
1962-1964		$2,125	$2,750
Westwood 77			
1962-1965. USA map-shaped solid hardwood body (not fiberglass), 2 regular and 1 bridge pickup.			
1962-1965	Blond-Ivory	$2,125	$2,750

National Reso-Phonic

1989-present. Professional and premium grade, production/custom, single cone, acoustic-electric, and tricone guitars (all with resonators), built in San Luis Obispo, California. They also build basses, mandolins, and ukuleles. McGregor Gaines and Don Young formed the National Reso-Phonic Guitar Company with the objective of building instruments based upon the original National designs. Replicon is the aging process to capture the appearance and sound of a vintage National.

MODEL YEAR	FEATURES	EXC. COND. LOW	HIGH
Collegian			
2010-2020. Thin gauge steel body, 9.5" cone, biscuit bridge, aged ivory finish.			
2010-2020		$1,500	$2,000
Delphi			
1993-2010. Single cone, steel body.			
1993-2010		$1,750	$2,250
Dueco			
2012-2020. Gold or Silver crystalline finish.			
2012-2020		$2,250	$3,000
El Trovador			
2010-present. Wood body Dobro-style, single cone, biscuit bridge.			
2010-2023		$2,375	$3,000
Estralita Deluxe			
2006-2021. Single cone, walnut body, figured maple top, Koa offered in '03.			
2006-2021	Maple or Koa	$2,500	$3,250
Estralita Harlem Slim			
2010. Laminate maple.			
2010		$1,375	$1,750
Model 97			
2002-2009. Nickel-plated tricone resonator, female surf rider and palm trees scene.			
2002-2009		$3,000	$4,000
Model D			
2003-2010. Laminate wood body, spruce top, walnut back and sides, spun cone and spider bridge. Replaced by Smith and Young Model 1 (metal body) and Model 11 (wood body).			
2003-2010		$1,625	$2,125

1964 National Varsity 66
Rivington Guitars

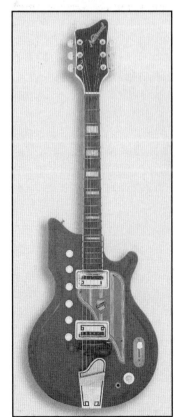

National Westwood 77

GUITARS

New Orleans Custom JB16

Nik Huber Dolphin II

MODEL			EXC. COND.	
YEAR	FEATURES		LOW	HIGH

NRP Steel
2009-present. Steel body with rubbed nickel finish, Honduran mahogany neck, slotted headstock.

2009-2023			$2,375	$3,000

Resoelectric Jr./Jr. II
2005-2010. Basic model of ResoLectric with painted body, Jr. with P-90, Jr. II with Lollar lipstick-tube. Replaced by the ResoTone.

2005-2010			$900	$1,125

Resolectric
1992-present. Single-cut electric resonator, maple (flamed maple since '96), single biscuit, 1 regular pickup (lipstick-tube up to '95, P-90 since) and 1 under-saddle.

1992-1995	Lipstick pickup		$1,875	$2,500
1996-2023	P-90 pickup		$1,750	$2,250

ResoRocket
2005-present. Single-cut steel body, Tricone style grill.

2005-2023			$2,750	$3,500

ResoRocket N
2009-present. Highly polished nickel-plated finish.

2009-2023			$2,750	$3,500

Style M-1/M-2
1990-1994, 2003-2010. Bound mahogany body single-cone, M-1 with ebony 'board, M-2 with bound rosewood 'board.

1990-2010			$1,750	$2,250

Style N
1993-2005. Nickel-plated brass body single-cone resonator, plain mirror finish, 12 fret neck.

1993-2005			$2,750	$3,500

Style O/O Deluxe/O Replicon 14-Fret
1992-present. Nickel-plated brass body, Hawaiian palm tree etched. Deluxe has upgrades like figured-maple neck and mother-of-pearl diamond inlays. Replicon 14-Fret is a replica of Mark Knopfler model.

1992-2023	O		$2,750	$3,500
1992-2023	O Deluxe		$3,125	$4,000
1992-2023	O Replicon		$3,000	$4,000

Tricone
1994-present. Nickel-plated brass body, bound ebony 'board.

1994-2023	Style 1		$2,375	$3,000
1994-2023	Style 15		$2,875	$3,750
1995-2004	Style 3, Lily of the Valley		$5,000	$6,500

Triolian
2009-present. Steel body with f-holes, sieve-hole coverplate, maple neck, 12 or 14 fret neck, ivoroid-bound rosewood 'board, mother-of-pearl markers, hand painted walnut-burst.

2009-2023	12 fret		$1,750	$2,250
2009-2023	14 fret		$1,750	$2,250

Navarro Custom
1986-present. Professional and premium grade, production/custom, electric guitars and basses built in San Juan, Puerto Rico by luthier Mike Navarro.

Neubauer
1966-1990s. Luthier Helmut Neubauer built his acoustic and electric archtop guitars in Bubenreuth, Germany.

New Era Guitars
See listing under ARK - New Era Guitars.

New Orleans Guitar Company
1992-present. Luthier Vincent Guidroz builds his premium grade, production/custom, solid and semi-hollow body guitars in New Orleans, Louisiana.

Nickerson Guitars
1983-present. Luthier Brad Nickerson builds his professional and premium grade, production/custom, archtop and flat-top guitars in Northampton, Massachusetts.

Nielsen
2004-present. Premium grade, custom/production, archtop guitars built by luthier Dale Nielsen in Duluth, Minnesota.

Nik Huber Guitars
1997-present. Premium grade, production/custom, electric guitars built in Rodgau, Germany by luthier Nik Huber.

Nioma
1932-1952. NIOMA, the National Institute of Music and Arts, was founded in Seattle but soon had schools across the western U.S. and Canada. By '35 they added guitar instruction, offering their own branded Spanish, resonator and lap steel (with matching amps) guitars, made by Regal, Harmony, Dickerson.

Noble
Ca. 1950-ca. 1969. Instruments made by others and distributed by Don Noble and Company of Chicago. Plastic-covered guitars made by EKO debuted in '62. Aluminum-necked Wandré guitars were added to the line in early-'63. By ca. '65-'66 the brand is owned by Chicago-area importer and distributor Strum 'N Drum and used mainly on Japanese-made solidbodies. Strum 'N Drum bought the National brand name in '69 and imported Japanese copies of American designs under the National brand and Japanese original designs under Norma through the early '70s.

The Noble brand disappears at least by the advent of the Japanese National brand, if not before. They also offered amps.

NoName Guitars
1999-present. Luthier Dan Kugler builds his production/custom, professional and premium grade, acoustic guitars and basses in Conifer, Colorado.

Nordy (Nordstrand Guitars)
2003-present. Professional and premium grade, production/custom, electric guitars and basses built by luthier Carey Nordstrand in Yucaipa, California.

The Official Vintage Guitar magazine Price Guide 2025

Norma – Oahu **323**

MODEL YEAR	FEATURES	EXC. COND. LOW	HIGH

Norma

Ca.1965-1970. Imported from Japan by Strum 'N Drum, Inc. of Chicago (see Noble brand info). Early examples were built by Tombo, most notably sparkle plastic covered guitars and basses.

Electric Solidbody

1965-1970. Type of finish has effect on value. Various models include; EG-350 (student double-cut, 1 pickup), EG-403 (unique pointy cutaway, 2 pickups), EG-400 (double-cut, 2 pickups), EG-450 (double-cut, 2 split-coil pickups), EG-421 (double-cut, 4 pickups), EG-412-12 (double-cut, 12-string).

1965-1968	Blue, red, gold sparkle	$350	$700
1965-1970	Non-sparkle	$250	$400

Norman

1972-present. Intermediate grade, production, acoustic and acoustic/electric guitars built in LaPatrie, Quebec. Norman was the first guitar production venture luthier Robert Godin was involved with. He has since added the Seagull, Godin, and Patrick & Simon brands of instruments.

Normandy Guitars

2008-present. Jim Normandy builds professional grade, production, aluminum archtop and electric guitars and basses, first in Salem and currently in Portland, Oregon.

Northworthy Guitars

Professional and premium grade, production/ custom, flat-top and electric guitars and basses built by luthier Alan Marshall in Ashbourne, Derbyshire, U.K., starting in 1987. He also builds mandolins.

Norwood

1960s. Budget guitars imported most likely from Japan.

Electric Solidbody

1960s. Offset double-cut body, 3 soapbar-style pickups, Norwood label on headstock.

1960s		$200	$300

Novax Guitars

1989-present. Luthier Ralph Novak builds his fanned-fret professional and premium grade, production/custom, solidbody and acoustic guitars and basses, originally in San Leandro, California, and since May '06, in Eugene, Oregon.

Noyce

Luthier Ian Noyce, started in 1974, builds production/custom, professional and premium grade, acoustic and electric guitars and basses in Ballarat, Victoria, Australia.

Nyberg Instruments

1993-present. Professional grade, custom, flat-top and Maccaferri-style guitars built by luthier Lawrence Nyberg in Hornby Island, British Columbia. He also builds mandolins, mandolas, bouzoukis and citterns.

Oahu

1926-1985, present. The Oahu Publishing Company and Honolulu Conservatory, based in Cleveland, Ohio was active in the sheet music and student instrument business in the '30s. An instrument, set of instructional sheet music, and lessons were offered as a complete package. Lessons were often given to large groups of students. Instruments, lessons, and sheet music could also be purchased by mail order. The Oahu Publishing Co. advertised itself as The World's Largest Guitar Dealer. Most '30s Oahu guitars were made by Kay with smaller numbers from the Oscar Schmidt Company.

Guitar Models from the Mid-'30s include: 71K (jumbo square neck), 72K (jumbo roundneck), 68B (jumbo, vine body decoration), 68K (deluxe jumbo square neck), 69K (deluxe jumbo roundneck), 65K and 66K (mahogany, square neck), 64K and 67K (mahogany, roundneck), 65M (standard-size, checker binding, mahogany), 53K (roundneck, mahogany), 51 (black, Hawaiian scene, pearlette 'board), 51K (black, pond scene decoration), 52K (black, Hawaiian scene decoration), 50 and 50K (student guitar, brown).

The brand has been revived on a line of tube amps.

Graphic Body

1930s. 13" painted artwork bodies, includes Styles 51 and 52 Hawaiian scene.

1930s	Floral, etc	$425	$550
1930s	Hawaiian scenes	$425	$550

Round Neck 14" Flat-Top

1930s. Spruce top, figured maple back and sides, thin logo.

1932		$1,125	$1,500

Style 50K Student

1930s. Student-size guitar, brown finish.

1935		$175	$250

Style 52K

1930s. 13" with fancy Hawaiian stencil, slotted headstock.

1930s		$400	$500

Style 65M

1933-1935. Standard-size mahogany body, checker binding, natural brown.

1933-1935		$675	$850

Style 68K De Luxe Jumbo

1930s. Hawaiian, 15.5" wide, square neck, Brazilian back and sides, spruce top, fancy pearl vine inlay, abalone trim on top and soundhole, rosewood pyramid bridge, fancy pearl headstock inlay, butterbean tuners, ladder-braced, natural. High-end model made for Oahu by Kay.

1934-1935		$4,500	$5,500

Style 71K Hawaiian

1930s. Hawaiian, gold vine pattern on bound sunburst top, dot inlays.

1930s		$1,375	$1,750

Novax Charlie Hunter 8-String

1930s Oahu
Bernunzio Uptown Music

MODEL YEAR	FEATURES	EXC. COND. LOW	HIGH

1954 Old Kraftsman Model K1
John Neff

Optek Fretlight

Ochoteco Guitars

1979-present. Production/custom steel- and nylon-stringed guitars built by luthier Gabriel Ochoteco in Germany until '84 and in Brisbane, Australia since.

Odessa

1981-1990s. Budget guitars imported by Davitt & Hanser (BC Rich). Mainly acoustics in the '90s, but some electrics early on.

O'Hagan

1979-1983. Designed by clarinetist and importer Jerol O'Hagan in St. Louis Park, Minnesota. Primarily neck-thru construction, most with German-carved bodies. In '81 became Jemar Corporation and in '83 it was closed by the I.R.S., a victim of recession.

SN=YYM(M)NN (e.g., 80905, September '80, 5th guitar); or MYMNNN (e.g., A34006, April 1983, 6th guitar). Approximately 3000 total instruments were made with the majority being NightWatches (approx. 200 Twenty Twos, 100-150 Sharks, 100 Lasers; about 25 with birdseye maple

Shark
1979-1983. Explorer-looking solidbody, maple body, 2 Shaller humbucker pickups, 3-piece maple/walnut laminate neck, natural.

1979-1983		$950	$1,250

Ohio

1959-ca. 1965. Line of electric solidbodies and basses made by France's Jacobacci company, which also built under its own brand. Sparkle finish, bolt-on aluminum necks, strings-thru-body design.

Old Kraftsman

Ca. 1930s-ca. 1960s. Brand name used by the Spiegel catalog company for instruments made by other American manufacturers, including Regal, Kay and even Gibson. The instruments were of mixed quality, but some better grade instruments were comparable to those offered by Wards.

Archtop
1930s-1960s. Various models.

1930s-40s		$450	$575
1950s-60s		$350	$450

Flat-Top
1930s-1960s. Various models.

1950s	Prairie Ramblers (stencil)	$350	$450

Jazz II K775
1960-1963. Kay 775 with Old Kraftsman logo on large headstock, small double-cut thinline, 2 pickups, Bigsby, natural.

1960-1963		$1,250	$1,500

Sizzler K4140
1959. Single-cut, single neck pickup, Sizzler logo on body with other art images.

1959		$550	$700

Thin Twin Jimmy Reed

1952-1958		$1,250	$2,000

Value Leader
1961-1965. Electric single-cut semi-solid, 1 pickup, Kay Value Leader series.

1961-1965		$425	$550

OLP (Officially Licensed Product)

2001-2009. Intermediate grade, production, imported guitars and basses based on higher dollar guitar models officially licensed from the original manufacturer. OLP logo on headstock.

Olson Guitars

1977-present. Luthier James A. Olson builds his presentation grade, custom, flat-tops in Circle Pines, Minnesota.

Olympia by Tacoma

1997-2006. Import acoustic guitars and mandolins from Tacoma Guitars.

OD Series

1997-2006	Various models	$125	$350

Omega

1996-2010. Luthier Kevin Gallagher built his premium grade, custom/production acoustic guitars in East Saylorsburg, Pennsylvania. He died in '10.

Oncor Sound

1980-ca. 1981. This Salt Lake City, Utah-based company made both a guitar and a bass synthesizer.

Optek

1980s-present. Intermediate grade, production, imported Fretlight acoustic/electric and electric guitars. Located in Reno, Nevada.

Fretlight
1989-present. Double-cut, 126 LED lights in fretboard controlled by a scale/chord selector.

1989-2023		$375	$475

Opus

1972-Mid 1970s. Acoustic and classical guitars, imported from Japan by Ampeg/Selmer. In '75-'76, Harmony made a line of acoustics with the Opus model name.

Original Senn

2004-present. Luthier Jeff Senn builds his professional and premium grade, production/custom, solidbody electric guitars and basses in Nashville, Tennessee.

Ormsby Guitars

2003-present. Luthier Perry Ormsby builds his custom, professional and premium grade, solid and chambered electric guitars in Perth, Western Australia.

MODEL YEAR	FEATURES	EXC. COND. LOW	HIGH

Orpheum

1897-1942, 1944-late 1960s, 2001-2006. Intermediate grade, production, acoustic and resonator guitars. They also offered mandolins. Orpheum originally was a brand of Rettberg and Lange, who made instruments for other companies as well. William Rettberg and William Lange bought the facilities of New York banjo maker James H. Buckbee in 1897. Lange went out on his own in '21 to start the Paramount brand. He apparently continued using the Orpheum brand as well. He went out of business in '42. In '44 the brand was acquired by New York's Maurice Lipsky Music Co. who used it primarily on beginner to medium grade instruments, which were manufactured by Regal, Kay, and United Guitar (and maybe others). In the early '60s Lipsky applied the brand to Japanese and European (by Egmond) imports. Lipsky dropped the name in the early '70s. The brand was revived from '01 to '06 by Tacoma Guitars.

Auditorium Archtop 835/837
1950s. Acoustic archtop, auditorium size, dot markers, Orpheum shell headpiece, white celluloid 'guard, model 835 with spruce top/back/sides, 837 with mahogany.

1950s		$400	$500

Orpheum Special
1930s. Made by Regal, slot head, Dobro-style wood body, metal resonator, sunburst.

1930s		$1,000	$1,250

President
1940s. 18" pro-level acoustic archtop, Orpheum block logo and President script logo on headstock, large split-block markers, sunburst.

1940s		$1,875	$2,500

Style B
1940s. Acoustic archtop, Style B logo on headstock, block markers, sunburst.

1940s		$775	$1,000

Thin Twin Jimmy Reed 865E
1950s. Model 865E is the Orpheum version of the generically named Thin Twin Jimmy Reed style electric Spanish cutaway thin solidbody, hand engraved shell celluloid Orpheum headpiece, described as #865E Cutaway Thin Electric Guitar in catalog.

1950s		$1,500	$2,000

Ultra Deluxe Professional 899
1950s. 17" cutaway, 2 pickups, 2 knobs, maple back and sides, top material varies, dot markers, finishes as follows: E-C copper, E-G gold, E-G-B gold-black sunburst, E-B blond curly maple, E-S golden orange sunburst.

1950s		$1,500	$2,000

Orville

1984-1993. Orville by Gibson and Orville guitars were made by Japan's Fuji Gen Gakki for Gibson. See following listing for details. Guitars listed here state only Orville (no By Gibson) on the headstock.

Electric

1984-1993	CE Atkins	$1,125	$1,500

1984-1993	ES-335	$1,500	$2,000
1984-1993	LP Custom	$1,250	$1,625
1984-1993	LP Standard	$1,250	$1,625

Orville by Gibson

1984-1993. Orville by Gibson and Orville guitars were made by Japan's Fuji Gen Gakki for Gibson. Basically, the same models except the Orville by Gibson guitars had real Gibson USA PAF '57 Classic pickups and a true nitrocellulose lacquer finish. The Orville models used Japanese electronics and a poly finish. Prices here are for the Orville by Gibson models.

Acoustic-Electric
1984-1993. On-board electronics.

1984-1993	Dove	$1,750	$2,250
1984-1993	J-160E	$1,750	$2,250
1984-1993	J-200NE	$1,750	$2,250

Electric
1984-1993. Various models.

1984-1993	ES-175	$1,750	$2,500
1984-1993	ES-335	$1,750	$2,500
1984-1993	Explorer	$1,750	$2,500
1984-1993	Firebird V	$1,500	$2,000
1984-1993	Firebird VII	$1,500	$2,000
1984-1993	Flying V	$1,750	$2,500
1984-1993	Les Paul Custom	$1,750	$2,500
1984-1993	Les Paul Jr	$875	$1,125
1984-1993	LP Standard	$1,750	$2,500
1984-1993	LP Studio JP	$1,250	$1,625
1984-1993	MM/Les Paul Jr	$725	$950
1984-1993	SG LP Custom	$1,250	$1,625
1984-1993	SG LP Standard	$1,250	$1,625

Osborne Sound Laboratories

Late 1970s. Founded by Ralph Scaffidi and wife guitarist Mary Osborne; originally building guitar amps, they did also offer solidbody guitars.

Oscar Schmidt

1879-1938, 1979-present. Budget and intermediate grade, production, acoustic, acoustic/electric, and electric guitars and basses distributed by U.S. Music Corp. (Washburn, Randall, etc.). They also offer mandolins, banjos, ukuleles and the famous Oscar Schmidt autoharp.

The original Oscar Schmidt Company, Jersey City, New Jersey, offered banjo mandolins, tenor banjos, guitar banjos, ukuleles, mandolins and guitars under their own brand and others (including Sovereign and Stella). By the early 1900s, the company had factories in the U.S. and Europe producing instruments producing instruments under their own brand as well as other brands for mail-order and other distributors. Oscar Schmidt was also an early contributor to innovative mandolin designs and the company participated in the '00-'30 mandolin boom. The company hit hard times during the Depression and was sold to Harmony by the end of the '30s. In '79, Washburn acquired the brand and it is now part of U.S. Music.

1993 Orville by Gibson ES-335
Steve Soest

1993 Orville Les Paul Standard
Stoeffu Vogt

GUITARS

2001 Ovation Adamas 1598-MEII Melissa Etheridge

Imaged by Heritage Auctions, HA.com

1981 Ovation Adamas II

Rivington Guitars

Oskar Graf Guitars

1970-present. Premium and presentation grade, custom, archtop, acoustic and classical guitars and basses built in Clarendon, Ontario, by luthier Oskar Graf. He also builds lutes.

Otwin

1950s-1960s. A brand used on electric guitars made by the Musima company of East Germany. Musima also produced guitars under their own brand.

Outbound Instruments

1990-2002. Intermediate grade, production, travel-size acoustics from the Boulder, Colorado-based company.

Ovation

1966-present. Intermediate and professional grade, production, acoustic and acoustic/electric guitars. They also build basses and mandolins. Until 2014, they also had U.S. production.

Helicopter manufacturer Kaman Corporation, founded in 1945 by jazz guitarist and aeronautical engineer Charles Huron Kaman in Bloomfield, Connecticut, decided to use their helicopter expertise (working with synthetic materials, spruce, high tolerances) and designed, with the help of employee and violin restorer John Ringso, the first fiberglass-backed (Lyracord) acoustic guitars in '65. Production began in '66 and the music factory moved to New Hartford, Connecticut, in '67. Early input was provided by fingerstyle jazz guitarist Charlie Byrd, who gave Kaman the idea for the name Ovation. Kaman Music purchased Hamer Guitars in '88, and Trace Elliot amplifiers (U.K.) in '90. In '08, Fender acquired Kaman Music Corporation and the Ovation brand; in '14 U.S. production ceased, and the brand was sold to Drum Workshop, Inc., who re-opened the Hartford, CT plant in late '15.

Adamas 1581-KK Kaki King

2011-2014. Deep bowl cutaway, rosewood 'board, 12th-fret crown inlay, OP-Pro preamp, Kaki personally signs the label on each guitar.

2011-2014	$3,000	$4,000

Adamas 1587

1979-1998. Carbon top, walnut, single-cut, bowl back, binding, mini-soundholes.

1979-1998 Black Sparkle	$1,750	$2,250

Adamas 1597

1998-2003. Carbon birch composite top, on-board electronics.

1998-2003 Black	$1,000	$1,300

Adamas 1598-MEII Melissa Etheridge

2001-2014. Mid-depth cutaway, ebony 'board, 'ME' maple symbol at 12th fret, OP-Pro preamp, Melissa personally signs the label on each guitar.

2001-2014 12-string	$1,500	$2,000

Adamas 1687

1977-1998. Acoustic/electric, carbon top, non-cut, bowl back, mini-sound holes.

1977-1998 Sunburst	$1,750	$2,250

Adamas CVT W591

2000. Crossweave fiber top, mid-depth body, on-board electronics.

2000	$1,000	$1,500

Adamas II 1881 NB-2

1993-1998. Acoustic/electric, single-cut, shallow bowl, brown.

1993-1998	$1,500	$2,000

Adamas Millenium

2000. Limited edition, 75 made, planet inlays, Cobalt Blue.

2000	$2,500	$3,500

Anniversary Electric 1657

1978. Deep bowl, abalone inlays, gold-plated parts, for Ovation's 10th anniversary. They also offered an acoustic Anniversary.

1978	$475	$650

Balladeer 1111

1968-1983, 1993-2000. Acoustic, non-cut with deep bowl, bound body, natural top, later called the Standard Balladeer.

1976-1983	$450	$575

Balladeer Artist 1121

1968-1990. Acoustic, non-cut with shallow bowl, bound body.

1968-1969 Early production	$600	$775
1970-1990	$450	$600

Balladeer Classic 1122

1970s. Classical shallow-bowl version of Concert Classic, nylon strings, slotted headstock.

1970s	$450	$575

Balladeer Custom 1112

1976-1990. Acoustic, deep bowl, diamond inlays.

1976-1990	$550	$750

Balladeer Custom Electric 12-String 1655/1755

1982-1994. 12-string version of Balladeer Custom Electric.

1982-1994	$500	$650

Balladeer Custom Electric 1612/1712

1976-1990. Acoustic/electric version of Balladeer Custom, deep bowl.

1976-1990	$600	$800

Balladeer Standard 1561/1661/1761/1861

1982-2000. Acoustic/electric, deep bowl, rounded cutaway.

1982-2000	$575	$775

Balladeer Standard 1771 LX

2008-2010. Acoustic/electric, mid-depth bowl, rosewood, Sitka spruce top.

2008-2010	$650	$850

Balladeer Standard 12-String 6751 LX

2008-2010. Acoustic/electric, 12 strings, rosewood, spruce top.

2008-2010	$775	$1,000

Breadwinner 1251

1971-1983. Axe-like shaped single-cut solidbody, 2 pickups, textured finish, black, blue, tan or white.

1971-1983	$1,000	$1,375

MODEL YEAR	FEATURES	EXC. COND. LOW	HIGH

Celebrity CC-48
2007-2013. Acoustic/electric, super shallow, laminated spruce top, white bound rosewood 'board with abalone dot inlays.

2007-2013		$325	$450

Celebrity CC-57
1990-1996. Laminated spruce top, shallow bowl, mahogany neck.

1990-1996		$325	$450

Celebrity CC-63
1984-1996. Classical, deep bowl, piezo bridge pickup.

1984-1996		$325	$450

Celebrity CK-057
2002-2004. Acoustic/electric rounded cutaway, shallow back.

2002-2004		$400	$550

Celebrity CS-257
1992-2005, 2010. Made in Korea, super shallow bowl back body, single-cut, Adamas sound holes, alternating dot and diamond markers.

1992-2005	Celebrity	$475	$650
2010	Celebrity Deluxe	$550	$750

Classic 1613/1713
1971-1993. Acoustic/electric, non-cut, deep bowl, no inlay, slotted headstock, gold tuners, natural.

1971-1993		$575	$750

Classic 1663/1763
1982-1998. Acoustic/electric, single-cut, deep bowl, cedar top, EQ, no inlay, slotted headstock, gold tuners.

1982-1998		$675	$875

Classic 1863
1989-1998. Acoustic/electric, single-cut, shallow bowl, no inlay, cedar top, EQ, slotted headstock, gold tuners.

1989-1998		$675	$875

Collectors Series
1982-2008. Limited edition, different model featured each year and production limited to that year only, the year designation is marked at the 12th fret, various colors (each year different).

1982-2008	Common models	$575	$800
1982-2008	Rare models	$775	$1,000

Concert Classic 1116
1974-1990. Deep-bowl nylon string classical, slotted headstock.

1974-1990		$400	$550

Contemporary Folk Classic Electric 1616
1974-1990. Acoustic/electric, no inlay, slotted headstock, natural or sunburst.

1974-1990		$400	$550

Country Artist Classic Electric 6773
1995-2011. Classic electric, soft-cut, solid spruce top, slotted headstock, Ovation pickup system.

1995-2011		$625	$825

Country Artist Electric 1624
1971-1990. Nylon strings, slotted headstock, standard steel-string sized neck to simulate a folk guitar, on-board electronics.

1971-1990		$675	$875

Custom Ballader 1762
1992. Rounded cutaway, higher-end specs.

1992		$875	$1,125

Custom Elite Guitar Center 30th Anniversary

1994	50 made	$1,500	$2,000

Custom Legend 1117
1970s. non-electric 2nd generation Ovation, higher-end with abalone inlays and gold hardware, open V-bracing pattern. Model 1117-4, natural.

1970s		$900	$1,125

Custom Legend 1569
1980s. Rounded cutaway acoustic/electric, super shallow bowl, gloss black finish.

1980s		$750	$975

Custom Legend 1619/1719
1970s. Acoustic/electric 2nd generation Ovation, electric version of model 1117, higher-end with abalone inlays and gold hardware, open V-bracing pattern.

1970s		$850	$1,125

Custom Legend 1759
1984-2004. Single-cut acoustic/electric, 12-string.

1984-2004		$850	$1,125

Custom Legend 1769
1982, 1993, 1996-1999 Single-cut acoustic/electric.

1982-1999		$1,250	$1,625

Custom Legend 1869
1994, 2003. Acoustic/electric, cutaway, super shallow bowl.

1994, 2003		$950	$1,250

Custom Legend 6759

2003		$1,875	$2,500

Deacon 1252
1973-1980. Axe-shaped solidbody electric, active electronics, diamond fret markers.

1973-1980		$1,250	$1,625

Deacon 12-String 1253
1975. Axe-shaped solidbody, diamond inlay, 2 pickups. only a few made.

1975		$1,250	$1,625

Eclipse
1971-1973. Thinline double cut acoustic-electric archtop, 2 pickups.

1971-1973		$950	$1,250

Elite 1718
1982-1997. Acoustic/electric, non-cut, deep bowl, solid spruce top, Adamas-type sound hole, volume and tone controls, stereo output.

1982-1997		$950	$1,250

Elite 1758
1990-1998. Acoustic/electric, non-cut, deep bowl.

1990-1998		$950	$1,250

Elite 1768
1990-1998. Acoustic/electric, cutaway, deep bowl.

1990-1998		$775	$1,000

Elite 1858 12-String
1993-2004. 12-string acoustic/electric, ebony 'board and bridge.

1993-2004		$950	$1,250

Ovation Concert Classic 1116
Sam Stathakis

Ovation Custom Legend 1619
Imaged by Heritage Auctions, HA.com

Ovation Glen Campbell 1118
Imaged by Heritage Auctions, HA.com

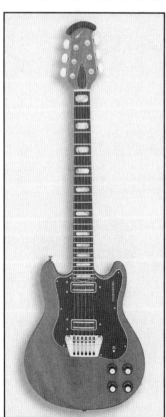

1977 Ovation Preacher

MODEL YEAR	FEATURES	EXC. COND. LOW	HIGH

Elite 1868
1983-2004. Acoustic/electric, cutaway, shallow bowl.
| 1983-2004 | | $725 | $950 |

Elite 5858
1991. Super shallow bowl, single cutaway, Adamas-style sound hole, gold hardware, on-board factory OP24 pickup.
| 1991 | | $775 | $1,000 |

Elite Doubleneck
1989-1990s. Six- and 12-string necks, can be ordered with a variety of custom options.
| 1989 | | $1,000 | $1,300 |

Elite Standard 6868
1994-1999. Elite Standard with cutaway shallow bowl.
| 1994-1999 | | $750 | $975 |

Elite T/TX 1778
2002-2018. Acoustic/electric, cutaway, U.S. T replaced by import TX in '08.
| 2002-2008 | T, original version | $950 | $1,250 |
| 2008-2018 | TX, Import | $350 | $500 |

Folklore 1614
1972-1983. Acoustic/electric, 12-fret neck on full-size body, wide neck, on-board electronics.
| 1972-1983 | | $675 | $900 |

GCXT
2008. Acoustic-electric made for Guitar Center, single-cut, flamed paint graphic.
| 2008 | | $775 | $1,000 |

Glen Campbell 12-String 1118 (K-1118)
1968-1982. Acoustic, 12 strings, shallow bowl version of Legend, gold tuners, diamond inlay.
| 1968-1982 | | $750 | $975 |

Glen Campbell Artist 1627
2006. Glen Campbell 40th Anniversary model, diamond inlay, gold tuners.
| 2006 | | $1,250 | $1,625 |

Glen Campbell Artist Balladeer 1127
1968-1990. Acoustic, shallow bowl, diamond inlay, gold tuners, natural.
| 1968-1990 | | $750 | $975 |

Hurricane 12-String K-1120
1968-1969. ES-335-style electric semi-hollowbody, double-cut, 12 strings, f-holes, 2 pickups.
| 1968-1969 | | $925 | $1,250 |

Josh White 1114
1967-1970, 1972-1983. Wide 12-fret neck, dot markers, classical-style tuners.
| 1967-1970 | | $775 | $1,000 |
| 1972-1983 | | $675 | $900 |

Legend 1117
1972-1999. Deep bowl acoustic, 5-ply top binding, gold tuners, various colors (most natural).
| 1972-1999 | | $600 | $800 |

Legend 1567/1867
1984-2004. Acoustic/electric, shallow bowl, single-cut, gold tuners.
| 1984-2004 | | $650 | $850 |

Legend 12-String 1866
1989-2007. Acoustic/electric, cutaway, 12 strings, shallow bowl, 5-ply top binding, black.
| 1989-2007 | | $650 | $850 |

Legend 1717
1990-2008. Acoustic/electric, 5-ply top binding, various colors.
| 1990-2008 | | $625 | $825 |

Legend 1767
1990s. Acoustic/electric, deep bowl, single-cut, black.
| 1990s | | $625 | $850 |

Legend Cutaway 1667
1982-1996. Acoustic/electric, cutaway, deep bowl, abalone, gold tuners.
| 1982-1996 | | $675 | $900 |

Legend Electric 1617
1972-1998. Acoustic/electric, deep bowl, abalone, gold tuners, various colors.
| 1972-1998 | | $600 | $800 |

Pacemaker 12-String 1115/1615
1968-1982. Originally called the K-1115 12-string, Renamed Pacemaker in '72.
| 1968-1982 | | $650 | $850 |

Patriot Bicentennial
*1976. Limited run of 1776 guitars, Legend Custom model with drum and flag decal and 1776*1976 decal on lower bout.*
| 1976 | | $1,250 | $1,625 |

Pinnacle
1990-1992. Spruce or sycamore top, broad leaf pattern rosette, mahogany neck, piezo bridge pickup, sunburst.
| 1990-1992 | | $575 | $750 |

Pinnacle Shallow Cutaway
1990-1994. Pinnacle with shallow bowl body and single-cut, sunburst.
| 1990-1994 | | $575 | $750 |

Preacher 1281
1975-1982. Solidbody, mahogany body, double-cut, 2 pickups.
| 1975-1982 | | $900 | $1,125 |

Preacher Deluxe 1282
1975-1982. Double-cut solidbody, 2 pickups with series/parallel pickup switch and mid-range control.
| 1975-1982 | | $900 | $1,125 |

Preacher 12-String 1285
1975-1983. Double-cut solidbody, 12 strings, 2 pickups.
| 1975-1983 | | $900 | $1,125 |

Thunderhead 1460
1968-1972. Double-cut, 2 pickups, gold hardware, phase switch, master volume, separate tone controls, pickup balance/blend control, vibrato.
| 1968-1972 | Natural or rare color | $1,625 | $2,250 |
| 1968-1972 | Sunburst | $1,250 | $1,625 |

Tornado 1260
1968-1973. Same as Thunderhead without phase switch, with chrome hardware.
| 1968-1973 | | $875 | $1,125 |

UK II 1291
1980-1982. Single-cut solidbody, 2 pickups, body made of Urelite on aluminum frame, bolt-on neck, gold hardware.
| 1980-1982 | | $1,000 | $1,300 |

MODEL YEAR	FEATURES	EXC. COND. LOW	HIGH

Ultra GS/GP Series
1984. Korean solidbodies and necks assembled in U.S., DiMarzio pickups, offset double-cut (GS) with 1 hum, or hum/single/single or LP style (GP) with 2 humbuckers. There was also a bass.

1984		$475	$650

Ultra Series
1970s-2000s. Various Ultra model acoustic/ electrics.

1970-2000s		$350	$800

Viper 1271
1975-1982. Single-cut, 2 single-coil pickups.

1975-1982		$825	$1,125

Viper EA 68
1994-2008. Thin acoustic/electric, single-cut mahogany body, spruce top over sound chamber with multiple upper bout sound holes, black.

1994-2008		$575	$750

Viper III 1273
1975-1982. Single-cut, 3 single-coil pickups.

1975-1982		$825	$1,125

VXT Hybrid
2007-2009. Single-cut solidbody, 2 Seymour Duncan '59 humbuckers, Fishman Power Bridge.

2007-2009		$875	$1,125

Overture Guitars

Luthier Justin Hoffman began building in the year 2008, professional to presentation grade, custom/production, solidbody guitars and basses in Morton, Illinois.

P. W. Crump Company

1975-present. Luthier Phil Crump builds his custom flat-top guitars in Arcata, California. He also builds mandolin-family instruments.

Palen

1998-present. Premium grade, production/custom, archtop guitars built by luthier Nelson Palen in Beloit, Kansas.

Palmer

Budget and intermediate grade, production acoustic, acoustic/electric and classical guitars imported from Europe and Asia, starting in the early 1970s. They also have offered electrics.

Panache

2004-2008. Budget grade, production, solidbody electric and acoustic guitars imported from China.

PANaramic

1961-1963. Guitars and basses made in Italy by the Crucianelli accordion company and imported by PANaramic accordion. They also offered amps made by Magnatone.

Acoustic-Electric Archtop
1961-1963. Full body cutaway, 2 pickups.

1961-1963		$1,125	$1,500

Paolo Soprani

Early 1960s. Italian plastic covered guitars with pushbutton controls made by the Polverini Brothers.

Paramount

1921-1942, Late 1940s. The William L. Lange Company began selling Paramount banjos, guitar banjos and mandolin banjos in the early 1920s, and added archtop guitars in '34. The guitars were made by Martin and possibly others. Lange went out of business by '42; Gretsch picked up the Paramount name and used it on acoustics and electrics for a time in the late '40s.

GB
1920s-1930s. Guitar banjo.

1920s-30s		$1,125	$1,500

Style C
1930s. 16" acoustic archtop, maple back and sides.

1930s		$550	$750

Style L
1930s. Made by Martin, limited to about 36 instruments, small body with resonator, Brazilian rosewood.

1930s	Spanish 6-string	$7,250	$9,500
1930s	Tenor 4-string	$5,250	$7,000

Parker

1992-2016. U.S.-made and imported intermediate, professional, and premium grade, production/custom, solidbody guitars featuring a thin skin of carbon and glass fibers bonded to a wooden guitar body. In '05, they added wood body acoustic/electrics. They also build basses. Originally located northwest of Boston, Parker was founded by Ken Parker and Larry Fishman (Fishman Transducers). Korg USA committed money to get the Fly Deluxe model into production in July '93. Parker added a Custom Shop in '03 to produce special build instruments and non-core higher-end models that were no longer available as a standard product offering. In early '04, Parker was acquired by U.S. Music Corp. and moved USA production from the Boston area to Chicago. U.S. Music was acquired by Jam Industries in '09 and production of Parker Guitars was ceased in '16.

Concert
1997 only. Solid Sitka spruce top, only piezo system pickup, no magnetic pickups, transparent butterscotch.

1997		$2,125	$2,625

Fly
1993-1994. There are many Parker Fly models, the model simply called Fly is similar to the more common Fly Deluxe, except it does not have the Fishman piezo pickup system.

1993-1994		$2,125	$2,625

Fly Artist
1998-1999. Solid Sitka spruce top, vibrato, Deluxe-style electronics, transparent blond finish.

1998-1999		$2,375	$3,000

Fly Classic
1996-1998, 2000-2011. One-piece Honduras mahogany body, basswood neck, electronics same as Fly Deluxe.

1996-2011		$2,125	$2,625

Ovation Viper 1271
Rivington Guitars

Palen Archtop

Parker NiteFly
Imaged by Heritage Auctions, HA.com

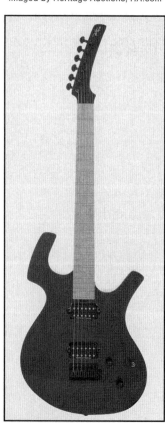

2008 Parker Fly P-42 Pro

MODEL YEAR	FEATURES	EXC. COND. LOW	HIGH

Fly Classic Maple
2000. Classic with maple body (vs. mahogany), transparent butterscotch.

2000		$2,125	$2,625

Fly Deluxe
1993-2016. Poplar body, basswood neck, 2 pickups, Fishman bridge transducer, '93-'96 models were offered with or without vibrato, then non-vibrato discontinued. The Deluxe normally came with a gig bag, but also offered with a hardshell case, which would add about $50 to the values listed.

1993-2016		$2,125	$2,625

Fly Supreme
1996-1999. One-piece flame maple body, electronics same as the Fly Deluxe, highly flamed butterscotch, includes hard molded case.

1996-1999		$2,875	$3,500

MaxxFly PDF Series
2013-2016. PDF is import line of more traditionally-shaped Maxx solidbodies, various models.

2013-2016	PDF30	$400	$500
2013-2016	PDF60	$450	$675
2013-2016	PDF70	$550	$675

Mojo
2003-2010. Fly either single-cut or double-cut.

2003-2007	Single-cut	$1,375	$1,750
2003-2010	Double-cut	$1,875	$2,375

NiteFly Series
1996-2009. Two single-coil and 1 humbucker pickup NiteFly, Fishman piezo system, bolt neck, maple body for '96-'98, ash for '99-present. Called the NiteFly in '96, NiteFly NFV2 ('97-'98), NiteFly NFV4 ('98), NiteFly NFV6 ('99), NiteFly SA ('00-present).

1996-2009	Various models	$1,250	$4,000

P Series
2000-2009. Various acoustic and solidbody electric models.

2000-2009		$400	$800

Tulipwood Limited Edition
1998. Limited build of 35, standard Deluxe features with tulipwood body.

1998		$2,000	$2,500

Parkwood
2007-present. Intermediate grade, acoustic and acoustic-electric guitars, Parkwood logo on headstock.

Patrick Eggle Guitars
1991-present. Founded by Patrick Eggle and others in Birmingham, England, building solid and semi-solidbody electric guitars and basses. In '95, Eggle left the company to build acoustics.

Patrick James Eggle
2001-present. Eggle co-founded the Patrick Eggle Guitar company in '91 building solidbodies. In '95, he left to do repairs and custom work. In '01 he opened a new workshop in Bedforshire, England, building professional and premium grade, production/custom, archtop and flatop guitars. For

a short time he relocated to Hendersonville, North Carolina, but in '05 returned to England and opened a shop in Oswestry.

Paul Berger
1972-2015. Acoustic guitars built by luthier Paul Berger in St. Augustine, Florida. He died in '15.

Paul H. Jacobson
1974-present. Premium grade, production/custom, classical guitars built by luthier Paul H. Jacobson in Cleveland, Missouri.

Paul Reed Smith
1985-present. Intermediate, professional, and premium grade, production/custom, solid, semi-hollow body, and acoustic guitars made in the U.S. and imported. They also build basses. Paul Reed Smith built his first guitar in '75 as an independent study project in college and refined his design over the next 10 years building custom guitars. After building two prototypes and getting several orders from East Coast guitar dealers, Smith was able to secure the support necessary to start PRS in a factory on Virginia Avenue in Annapolis, Maryland. In '95, they moved to their current location on Kent Island in Stevensville. In 2001 PRS introduced the Korean-made SE Series. Acoustics were added in '08.

10th Anniversary
1995. 200 made, mother-of-pearl inlays, abalone purfling, gold pickups, either wide-fat or wide-thin neck, 10th Anniversary logo, price includes certificate of authenticity.

1995	With certificate	$5,500	$7,500

305
2010-2013. Alder body, maple neck and 'board, birds, 3 single-coils.

2010-2013		$1,500	$2,000

305 25th Anniversary
2010. 305 made, 3 single-coils, wide-fat or wide-thin, 25th Anniversary logo.

2010		$1,500	$2,000

513 Rosewood
Dec.2003-2006. Brazilian rosewood neck, newly developed PRS pickup system with 13 sound settings, hum-single-hum pickups.

2003-2006		$4,000	$5,500

513 Swamp Ash
2010. Figured ash, natural.

2010		$2,000	$2,500

513 25th Anniversary
2010. Carved figured maple top, 25th Anniversary shadow birds inlay.

2010		$2,000	$2,500

Al Di Meola Prism
2008-2014. Curly maple 10 top, 22-fret, prism multicolor finish.

2008-2014		$3,500	$4,500

Angelus Cutaway
2009-2015. Flat-top, on-board electronics, European spruce top, figured mahogany back and sides, flamed

MODEL		EXC. COND.	
YEAR	FEATURES	LOW	HIGH

maple binding. Listed under Private Stock in '20, with select wood options.

| 2009-2015 | | $4,000 | $5,500 |

Artist/Artist I/Artist 24
1991-1994. Carved maple top, offset double-cut, 24-fret neck, bird markers, less than 500 made. A different Custom 24 Artist package was subsequently offered in the 2000s.

| 1991-1994 | | $3,500 | $4,500 |

Artist II/Artist 22
1993-1995. Curly maple top, maple purfling on rosewood 'board, inlaid maple bound headstock, abalone birds, 22 frets, gold hardware, short run of less than 500.

| 1993-1995 | | $3,000 | $4,000 |

Artist III
1996-1997. Continuation of the 22-fret neck with some changes in materials and specs, figured maple tops, short run of less than 500 instruments.

| 1996-1997 | | $3,000 | $4,000 |

Artist IV
1996. Continuation of the 22-fret neck with some upgrades in materials and specs, short run of less than 70 instruments.

| 1996 | | $4,000 | $5,000 |

Artist Limited
1994-1995. Like the Artist II with 14-carat gold bird inlays, abalone purfling on neck, headstock and truss rod cover, Brazilian rosewood 'board, 165 made.

| 1994-1995 | | $4,000 | $5,000 |

CE 22
1994-2000, 2005-2008. Double-cut carved alder body (1995), mahogany '96-'00 and '05-'07, back to alder in '08, bolt-on maple neck with rosewood 'board, dot inlays, 2 humbuckers, chrome hardware, translucent colors, options include vibrato and gold hardware and custom colors.

1994-1995	Alder	$1,000	$1,500
1996-2000	Mahogany	$1,000	$1,500
2005-2008	Reintroduced	$1,000	$1,500

CE 22 Maple Top
1994-2008. CE 22 with figured maple top, upgrade options included gold hardware, custom colors or 10 top.

| 1994-2008 | | $1,250 | $1,625 |

CE 24 (Classic Electric, CE)
1988-2000, 2005-2008. Double-cut, alder body to '95, mahogany '96-'00 and '05-'07, back to alder in '08, carved top, 24-fret bolt-on maple neck, 2 humbuckers, dot inlays, upgrade options included gold hardware, custom colors or 10 top.

| 1988-1991 | Rosewood 'board | $1,500 | $2,000 |
| 1992-2008 | | $1,500 | $2,000 |

CE 24 Maple Top (CE Maple Top)
1989-2008. CE 24 with figured maple top, upgrade options may include any or all the following: gold hardware, custom colors or 10 top.

| 1989-2008 | | $1,500 | $2,000 |

Chris Henderson Signature
2007-2012. Single-cut, 3 exposed humbucker pickups, carved flame maple top on mahogany body, wide flat neck profile, 22 frets.

| 2007-2012 | | $2,000 | $2,500 |

Corvette
2005-2006. Custom 22 with Velcity Yellow finish, Standard 22 red finish, Z06 inlays, Corvette logo on body.

| 2005 | Custom 22, yellow | $2,000 | $2,500 |
| 2006 | Standard 22, red | $2,000 | $2,500 |

Custom (Custom 24/PRS Custom)
1985-present. Double-cut solidbody, curly maple top, mahogany back and neck, pearl and abalone moon inlays, 24 frets, 2 humbuckers, tremolo, options include quilted or 10 Top, bird inlays, and gold hardware. 1985 Customs should be evaluated on a case-by-case basis.

1985		$12,000	$20,000
1986		$6,500	$9,000
1987		$4,500	$6,500
1988		$4,000	$6,000
1989		$3,000	$5,000
1990-2023	Wood Library adds $1,000	$3,000	$4,000

Custom 22
1993-2009, 2013-2023. Custom 22 with flamed or quilted maple top on mahogany body, 22-fret set-neck, upgrade option is gold hardware, normally the quilt top is higher than flamed top. Listed under Private Stock in '21, with select wood options.

| 1993-2023 | | $1,625 | $2,125 |

Custom 22 (Brazilian)
2003-2004. Limited run of 500 with Brazilian rosewood 'board, figured 10 top, pearl bird inlays.

| 2003-2004 | | $2,500 | $3,500 |

Custom 22 20th Anniversary
2005. Abalone 20th Anniversary birds inlay, 20th engraved on truss rod cover.

| 2005 | | $1,875 | $2,500 |

Custom 22 30th Anniversary "Vine"
2015. Limited run of 100, Mother of Pearl 30th Anniversary vine with Paua/Paua heart vine inlay.

| 2015 | | $2,000 | $2,500 |

Custom 22 Soapbar
1998-2002. 3 Seymour Duncan soapbar single-coils.

| 1998-2002 | | $1,500 | $2,000 |

Custom 22/12
December 2003-2009. 12-string version, flame or quilt maple top, hum/single/hum pickups.

| 2003-2009 | | $2,500 | $3,000 |

Custom 24 (Brazilian)
2003-2004. Limited run with Brazilian rosewood 'board, figured 10 top, pearl bird inlays.

| 2003-2004 | | $4,000 | $6,500 |

Custom 24 (Walnut)
1992. Seamless matched walnut over mahogany, 3 made.

| 1992 | | $2,500 | $3,250 |

Custom 24 20th Anniversary
2005. Abalone 20th Anniversary birds inlay, 20th engraved on truss rod cover.

| 2005 | | $2,000 | $2,500 |

Custom 24 25th Anniversary
2010. Carved figured maple top, 25th Anniversary shadow birds inlay.

| 2010 | | $2,000 | $2,500 |

Patrick James Eggle
Macon Junior

PRS Angelus Cutaway

GUITARS

PRS Dragon 2000

PRS Mark Tremonti Signature

MODEL YEAR	FEATURES	EXC. COND. LOW	HIGH

Dave Navarro Signature
2005-2014. Carved maple top, bird inlays, tremolo, white.

| 2005-2014 | | $1,500 | $2,000 |

DC3
2010-2013. Double-cut contoured body, bolt-on neck, 3 special single-coils.

| 2010-2013 | | $1,125 | $1,500 |

DGT David Grissom Trem
2007-present. Based on the McCarty Tremolo model with an added volume control, a nitro topcoat, vintage colors, large frets designed for .011-gauge strings.

| 2007-2023 | | $2,500 | $3,500 |

Dragon I
1992. Fingerboard inlay of a dragon made of 201 pieces of abalone, turquoise and mother-of-pearl, gold hardware, 50 made. The Dragon model collector requires an instrument to be truly mint and pristine with no play wear. The values shown here are for pristine instruments. Any issue whatsoever may dramatically reduce the high-side price shown. Price includes the certificate of authenticity.

| 1992 | Amber quilt, amber flame | $35,000 | $40,000 |
| 1992 | Teal black | $30,000 | $38,000 |

Dragon II
1993. Fingerboard inlay of a dragon made of 218 pieces of gold, coral, abalone, malachite, onyx and mother-of-pearl, 100 made.

| 1993 | | $14,000 | $18,000 |

Dragon III
1994. Fingerboard inlay of a dragon made of 438 pieces of gold, red and green abalone, mother-of-pearl, mammoth ivory, and stone, 100 made.

| 1994 | | $14,000 | $18,000 |

Dragon 2002
2002. Limited edition of 100 guitars, ultra-inlay work depicting dragon head on the guitar body.

| 2002 | | $18,000 | $25,000 |

Dragon 25th Anniversary
2009-2010. Multi-material dragon fingerboard inlay, green ripple abalone Modern Eagle headstock, body shape and electronics are modeled after an early company PRS guitar, 60 made.

| 2009-2010 | | $12,000 | $16,000 |

Dragon Doubleneck
2005. Limited edition 20th Anniversary model, about 50 made.

| 2005 | | $30,000 | $48,000 |

Dragon Millenium/Dragon 2000
1999-2000. Three-D dragon inlay in body versus neck inlay of previous models, limited production of 50 guitars.

| 1999-2000 | Black cherry | $18,000 | $25,000 |
| 1999-2000 | Rare color | $22,000 | $30,000 |

EG II
1991-1995. Double-cut solidbody, bolt-on neck, 3 single-coils, single-single-hum, or hum-single-hum pickup options, opaque finish.

| 1991-1995 | | $850 | $1,125 |

EG II Maple Top
1991-1995. EG II with flamed maple top, chrome hardware.

| 1991-1995 | | $1,125 | $1,500 |

EG 3
1990-1991. Double-cut solidbody, bolt-on 22-fret neck, 3 single-coil pickups.

1990-1991	Flamed 10 top	$1,125	$1,500
1990-1991	Opaque finish	$850	$1,125
1990-1991	Plain top, sunburst	$850	$1,125

EG 4
1990-1991. Similar to EG 3 with single-single-hum pickup configuration, opaque finish.

| 1990-1991 | | $850 | $1,125 |

Golden Eagle
1997-1998. Very limited production, eagle head and shoulders carved into lower bouts, varied high-end appointments.

| 1997-1998 | | $5,000 | $7,000 |

John Mayer Silver Sky
2018-present. Alder body, maple neck, rosewood or maple 'board, 3 single-coil pickups, various colors available.

| 2018-2023 | | $1,250 | $1,625 |

John Mayer Silver Sky Limited Edition
2020-2021. Lunar Ice color with unique polychromatic finish.

| 2020-2021 | | $4,000 | $5,500 |

Johnny Hiland
2006-2009. Maple fretboard.

| 2006-2009 | | $1,500 | $2,000 |

KL-33 Korina
2008. Double-cut solid korina body, rosewood 'board, PRS Mira pickups, limited run of 100.

| 2008 | | $1,500 | $2,000 |

KQ-24 Custom 24 (Killer Quilt)
2009. Limited Edition of 120, quilted maple top over korina body, 24 frets.

| 2009 | | $1,625 | $2,250 |

Limited Edition
1989-1991, 2000. Double-cut, semi-hollow mahogany body, figured cedar top, gold hardware, less than 300 made. In '00, single-cut, short run of 5 antique white and 5 black offered via Garrett Park Guitars.

| 1989-1991 | | $3,000 | $4,000 |
| 2000 | | $3,000 | $4,000 |

Limited Edition Howard
Leese Golden Eagle
2009. Private Stock, curly maple top, old style mother of pearl birds, 100 made.

| 2009 | | $4,000 | $5,000 |

LTD Experience (Limited Experience)
2007. 200 built to commemorate PRS 2007 Experience Open House, 24 frets, matching headstock, maple top with mahogany body.

| 2007 | | $1,625 | $2,250 |

Mark Tremonti Model
2001-2007. Single-cut, 2 humbuckers, black or platinum finish.

| 2001-2007 | | $1,500 | $2,000 |

MODEL YEAR	FEATURES	EXC. COND. LOW	HIGH

Mark Tremonti Signature

2007-present. Single-cut, 2 humbuckers, figured maple top (10 top upgrade offered), various finishes.

| 2007-2023 | 10 top upgrade | $1,875 | $2,500 |
| 2007-2023 | Figured maple top | $1,625 | $2,250 |

Mark Tremonti Tribal

2004-2006. With Tribal artwork, 100 made.

| 2004-2006 | | $1,750 | $2,500 |

McCarty Model

1994-2007. Mahogany body with figured maple top, upgrade options may include a 10 top, gold hardware, bird inlays. Replaced by McCarty II.

| 1994-2007 | | $1,750 | $2,250 |

McCarty II

2008-2009. Replaced the McCarty, featured new MVC (Mastering Voice Control) circuitry for switching between a single-coil voice to a heavy-metal voice, opaque finish.

| 2008-2009 | | $1,750 | $2,250 |

McCarty 1957/2008 Limited

2008. "1957/2008" logo on truss rod cover, 08 serial number series, 150 made.

| 2008 | | $2,250 | $3,000 |

McCarty 58/MC-58

2009-2011. "MC-58" logo on truss rod cover, similar to other McCarty models except for new neck shape, 57/08 humbucker pickups and V12 finish.

| 2009-2011 | | $2,375 | $3,000 |

McCarty 594

2016-present. Figured maple top, mahogany back, bird inlays, various colors.

| 2016-2023 | | $3,500 | $6,500 |

McCarty Archtop (Spruce)

1998-2000. Deep mahogany body, archtop, spruce top, 22-fret set-neck.

| 1998-2000 | | $2,125 | $2,750 |

McCarty Archtop Artist

1998-2002. Highest grade figured maple top and highest appointments, gold hardware.

| 1998-2002 | | $3,250 | $4,250 |

McCarty Archtop II (Maple)

1998-2000. Like Archtop but with figured maple top.

| 1998-2000 | Flamed or quilt | $2,375 | $3,000 |

McCarty Hollowbody I/Hollowbody I

1998-2009. Medium deep mahogany hollowbody, maple top, 22-fret set-neck, chrome hardware. McCarty dropped from name in '06.

| 1998-2009 | | $2,750 | $3,500 |

McCarty Hollowbody II/Hollowbody II

1998-2017. Like Hollowbody I but with figured maple top and back. McCarty dropped from name in '06.

| 1998-2017 | | $3,500 | $5,000 |

McCarty Hollowbody/Hollowbody Spruce

2000-2009. Similar to Hollowbody I with less appointments, spruce top. McCarty dropped from name in '06.

| 2000-2009 | | $2,000 | $3,000 |

McCarty Model/McCarty Brazilian

2003-2004. Limited run of 250, Brazilian rosewood 'board, Brazilian is printed on headstock just below the PRS script logo.

| 1999 | | $5,500 | $6,500 |
| 2003-2004 | | $5,000 | $6,000 |

McCarty Rosewood

2004-2005. PRS-22 fret with Indian rosewood neck.

| 2004-2005 | | $2,250 | $3,000 |

McCarty Soapbar (Korina)

2008-2009. Korina body, 2 Duncan soapbar pickups.

| 2008-2009 | | $1,750 | $2,250 |

McCarty Soapbar (Maple)

1998-2007. Soapbar with figured maple top option, nickel hardware.

| 1998-2007 | | $1,750 | $2,250 |

McCarty Soapbar Standard

1998-2009. Solid mahogany body, P-90-style soapbar pickups, 22-fret set-neck, nickel-plated hardware, upgrade options may include gold hardware and bird inlays.

| 1998-2009 | | $1,625 | $2,125 |

McCarty Standard

1994-2006. McCarty Model with carved mahogany body but without maple top, nickel-plated hardware, upgrade options may include gold hardware and bird inlays.

| 1994-2006 | | $1,625 | $2,125 |

Metal Bud Davis

1985-1986. Solid mahogany body with custom 2-color striped body finish and graphics, 24-fret set-neck, nickel hardware, 2 humbuckers.

| 1985-1986 | | $11,500 | $15,000 |

Metal '85 Reissue (Private Stock)

2008. With certificate of authenticity.

| 2008 | | $3,500 | $4,500 |

Mira

2007-2013. 2 exposed-coil humbuckers, abalone moon inlays, various opaque finishes. Replaced by S2 Mira in '14.

| 2007-2013 | | $775 | $1,000 |

Mira 25th Anniversary

2010. 2 soapbar single-coils, shadow bird inlays.

| 2010 | | $775 | $1,000 |

Mira Korina

2007-2009. Korina body and neck version, natural.

| 2007-2009 | | $900 | $1,250 |

Mira Maple Top (MT)

2008-2009. Figured maple, moon or bird inlays.

| 2008-2009 | | $1,000 | $1,500 |

Modern Eagle

2004-2007. Higher-end model based on Private Stock innovations, satin nitrocellulose finish, Brazilian rosewood neck.

| 2004-2007 | | $5,500 | $7,500 |

Modern Eagle II/MEII

2008-2009. Curly maple top, black rosewood neck and 'board.

| 2008-2009 | | $3,500 | $4,500 |

Modern Eagle Quatro/ME Quatro

2010-2012. Updated version of Modern Eagle, 53/10 humbucker pickups, select upgraded woods.

| 2010-2012 | | $2,500 | $3,000 |

NF3

2010-2013. 3 Narrowfield pickups on top-mounted 1-piece assembly, double-cut contoured body, bolt-on neck.

| 2010-2013 | | $1,250 | $1,625 |

PRS McCarty 594

PRS Metal

Ian Gilmour

PRS Paul's Guitar

PRS SE Santana

MODEL YEAR	FEATURES	EXC. COND. LOW	HIGH

P22
2012-2016. Carved figured maple top, birds, rosewood 'board, 10-top flame optional.

2012-2016		$3,500	$4,500

P245
2015. Semi-hollow electric, single-cut, 2 humbuckers and a piezo.

2015		$2,250	$3,000

Paul's Dirty 100
2010. Private Stock run of 100, highly figured curly maple top, moon inlays, 'Paul's Dirty 100' logo on back of headstock, black gold finish, paisley hard case.

2010		$6,000	$8,000

Paul's Guitar
2013-present. Carved figured maple top, mahogany back and neck, Honduran rosewood 'board with brushstroke birds, various colors. Artist package and other options offered.

2013-2023		$2,500	$3,250

Private Stock Program
April 1996-present. Custom instruments based around existing PRS models. Values may be somewhat near regular production equivalent models or higher. The Private Stock option was reintroduced by 2003. That year a standard production offering might retail at about $7,500, but a '03 Santana I Private Stock might retail at over $15,000, so each guitar should be evaluated on a case-by-case basis.

1996-2023	Various models	$5,500	$9,500

PRS Guitar
1975-1985. About 75 to 100 guitars were built by Paul Smith himself or with a team of others, from '75 to '85, before he formed the current PRS company. Each guitar from this era should be evaluated on a case-by-case basis and the values shown are for guidance only. Authentication is highly recommended; these guitars do not have a PRS serial number. Some of these went to celebrity players and, as such, may command values higher than shown here because of that connection.

1975-1983	Mahogany	$9,000	$50,000
1975-1983	Maple	$15,000	$46,000
1984-1985	Preproduction with provenance	$10,000	$26,000
1985-1986	Team-built	$6,000	$10,000

Rosewood Limited
1996. Mahogany body with figured maple top, 1-piece rosewood neck with ultra-deluxe tree-of-life neck inlay, gold hardware.

1996		$7,500	$10,000

Santana
1995-1998, 2011-present. Limited production special order, figured maple top, 24-fret, symmetric Santana headstock, unique body purfling, chrome and nickel-plated hardware, yellow is the most popular color, followed by orange, quality of top will affect price.

1995	1st 100 signed	$7,000	$9,000
1995-1998		$4,000	$5,500

Santana II
1998-2007. Three-way toggle replaces former dual mini-switches, special order, Brazilian 'board.

1998-2007		$6,000	$8,000

Santana III
2001-2006. Less ornate version of Santana II.

2001-2006		$2,250	$3,000

Santana (Brazilian)
2003. Quilted or flamed maple top, Brazilian rosewood neck and fretboard, eagle inlay on headstock, Santana Brazilian logo on back cover plate, 200 made.

2003-2004		$7,500	$10,000

Santana 25th Anniversary Santana II
2010. Figured maple top, rosewood 'board, eagle inlay on headstock, 25th Anniversary shadow birds.

2010		$2,500	$3,500

SC 58 Artist
2011-2012. Artist grade figured maple top, rosewood 'board, MOP/Paua birds.

2011-2012		$2,250	$3,000

SC 245
2007-2010. Single-cut 22-fret, 2 humbuckers, bird markers, SC 245 logo on truss rod cover.

2007	Flamed top, Brazilian 'board	$2,500	$3,500
2007-2010	Solid color top	$2,000	$2,500

SC 250
2007-2010. Figured maple top, 2 humbuckers, 25" scale and locking tuners.

2007-2010		$1,500	$2,000

SC-J Thinline
2008. Large full-scale single-cut hollowbody, originally part of Private Stock program until made in limited run of 300, select grade maple top and back over a mahogany middle body section, SC-J logo on truss rod cover.

2008		$3,750	$5,000

SE Series
2001-present. PRS import line, solidbody and semi-hollow.

2001-2023	Higher-end models	$525	$900
2001-2023	Most models	$325	$500

Signature/PRS Signature
1987-1991. 1,000 made, solid mahogany body, figured maple top, hand-signed signature on headstock, Vintage Yellow is most valuable color and will fetch more, orange is second, quilt top is more valuable than flametop. Each guitar should be evaluated on a case-by-case basis.

1987	Various colors	$3,500	$10,000
1988-1991	Various colors	$3,000	$5,000

Signature (Private Stock)
2011. Limited run by Private Stock, 100 made, 408 humbucker pickups (8 tonal configurations), special signature headstock and fretboard inlays.

2011		$6,500	$10,000

Singlecut
2000-2004, 2005-early 2008. Single-cut mahogany body, maple top, 22-fret 'board, upgrade options include 10 top flamed maple, gold hardware, bird inlays. Replaced by SC 245 and SC 250.

2000-2007	Various specs	$1,500	$2,000
2001	Brazilian neck/'board	$2,125	$2,750

The Official Vintage Guitar magazine Price Guide 2025 **PRS** Singlecut Hollowbody II CB 25th Ann. — **Peavey** Cropper Classic **335**

GUITARS

MODEL YEAR	FEATURES	EXC. COND. LOW	HIGH
2006-2007	Artist 20th Anniv, Brazilian	$2,125	$2,750
2006-2007	Standard 20th Anniv, Indian	$1,375	$1,750
2007-2008	Ltd Ed, Indian	$1,500	$2,000

Singlecut Hollowbody II CB 25th Anniversary

2010. Semi-hollow (CB means center block), f-holes, 10 maple top, bird inlays.

2010		$1,875	$2,500

Singlecut Hollowbody Standard

2008-2009. Mahogany body.

2008-2009		$1,875	$2,500

Singlecut Standard Satin

2006-2007. Thinner solid mahogany body, thin nitro cellulose finish, humbuckers or soapbars.

2006-2007		$1,125	$1,500

Special

1987-1990, 1991-1993. Similar to Standard with upgrades, wide-thin neck, 2 HFS humbuckers. From '91-'93, a special option package was offered featuring a wide-thin neck and high output humbuckers.

1987-1990	Solid color finish	$2,500	$3,250
1991-1993	Special order only	$2,750	$3,500

Standard

1987-1998. Set-neck, solid mahogany body, 24-fret 'board, 2 humbuckers, chrome hardware. Originally called the PRS Guitar from '85-'86 (see that listing), renamed Standard 24 from '98.

1987-1989	Sunburst & optional colors	$5,500	$7,000
1990-1991	Last Brazilian 'board	$3,000	$4,000
1992-1995		$1,500	$2,000
1995-1998	Stevensville	$1,500	$2,000

Standard 22

1994-2009. 22-fret Standard.

1994-1995		$1,500	$2,000
1995-1999	Stevensville	$1,500	$2,000
2000-2009		$1,500	$2,000

Standard 24

1998-2009. Renamed from Standard, solid mahogany body, 24-fret set-neck.

1998-2009		$1,500	$2,000

Starla

2008-2013. Single-cut solidbody with retro-vibe, glued neck, 2 chrome humbuckers. Replaced by S2 Starla in '14.

2008-2013		$900	$1,125

Studio

1988-1991, 2011-2013. Standard model variant, 24-fret set-neck, chrome and nickel hardware, single-single-hum pickups. The Studio package of pickups was offered until '96 on other models. Reissued in '11 with 22 frets, flamed maple top.

1988-1991		$1,625	$2,250
2011-2013	Reintroduced	$1,625	$2,250

Studio Maple Top

1990-1991. Mahogany solidbody, bird inlays, 2 single-coils and 1 humbucker, tremolo, transparent finish.

1990-1991		$1,625	$2,250

MODEL YEAR	FEATURES	EXC. COND. LOW	HIGH

Super Eagle

2016. Private Stock collaboration with John Mayer (Dead & Company), 100 made.

2016		$18,000	$23,000

Super Eagle II

2016-2017. Private Stock collaboration with John Mayer, 120 made.

2016-2017		$25,000	$40,000

Swamp Ash Special

1996-2009. Solid swamp ash body, 22-fret bolt-on maple neck, 3 pickups, upgrade options available.

1996-2009		$1,250	$1,625

Swamp Ash Special 25th Anniversary

2010. Swamp ash body, bolt-on neck, 25th Anniversary shadow bird inlays.

2010		$1,250	$1,625

Tonare Grand

2009-2016. Full-body flat-top, European/German spruce top, rosewood back and sides, optional Adirondack red spruce top or AAAA grade top, onboard Acoustic Pickup System.

2009-2016		$4,000	$5,500

West Street/1980 West Street Limited

2008. 180 made for the US market, 120 made for export market, faithful replica of the model made in the original West Street shop, Sapele top.

2008		$2,125	$2,750

Pawar

1999-2010. Founded by Jay Pawar, Jeff Johnston and Kevin Johnston in Willoughby Hills, Ohio, Pawar built professional and premium grade, production/custom, solidbody guitars.

PBC Guitar Technology

See Bunker Guitars for more info.

Pearl

1971-ca.1974. Acoustic and electric guitars sold by Pearl Musical Instrument Co. (Pearl drums), and built by other Japanese builders.

Peavey

1965-present. Headquartered in Meridan, Mississippi, Peavey builds budget, intermediate, professional, and premium grade, production/custom, acoustic and electric guitars. They also build basses, amps, PA gear, effects, and drums. Hartley Peavey's first products were guitar amps. He added guitars to the mix in '78.

Axcelerator/AX

1994-1998. Offset double-cut swamp ash or poplar body, bolt-on maple neck, dot markers, AX with locking vibrato, various colors.

1994-1998		$425	$550

Cropper Classic

1995-2005. Single-cut solidbody, 1 humbucker and 1 single coil, figured maple top over thin mahogany body, transparent Onion Green.

1995-2005		$425	$550

2007 PRS Singlecut Standard
Rivington Guitars

PRS Swamp Ash Special
Imaged by Heritage Auctions, HA.com

GUITARS

2000 Peavey EVH
Wolfgang Special

Willie Moseley

Peavey Hydra Doubleneck

MODEL YEAR	FEATURES	EXC. COND. LOW	HIGH

Defender
1994-1995. Double-cut, solid poplar body, 2 humbuckers and 1 single-coil pickup, locking Floyd Rose tremolo, metallic or pearl finish.

| 1994-1995 | | $190 | $250 |

Destiny
1989-1992. Double-cut, mahogany body, maple top, neck-thru-bridge, maple neck, 3 integrated pickups, double locking tremolo.

| 1989-1992 | | $400 | $550 |

Destiny Custom
1989-1992. Destiny with figured wood and higher-end appointments, various colors.

| 1989-1992 | | $550 | $725 |

Detonator AX
1995-1998. Double-cut, maple neck, rosewood 'board, dot markers, hum/single/hum pickups, black.

| 1995-1998 | | $250 | $350 |

EVH Wolfgang
1996-2004. Offset double-cut, arched top, bolt neck, stop tailpiece or Floyd Rose vibrato, quilted or flamed maple top upgrade option.

1996	Pat pending early production	$3,250	$4,000
1997-1998	Pat pending	$2,500	$3,125
1999-2004	Flamed maple top	$2,250	$2,875
1999-2004	Standard top	$1,625	$2,000

EVH Wolfgang Special
1997-2004. Offset double-cut lower-end Wolfgang model, various opaque finishes, flamed top optional.

1996-2004	Standard top, D-Tuna	$950	$1,500
1997-2004	Flamed maple top	$1,000	$1,250
1997-2004	Standard basswood	$900	$1,125

EVH Wolfgang Special EXP
2002-2004. Made in Korea.

| 2002-2004 | | $850 | $1,125 |

Falcon/Falcon Active/Falcon Custom
1987-1992. Double-cut, 3 pickups, passive or active electronics, Kahler locking vibrato.

| 1987-1992 | Custom color | $400 | $500 |
| 1987-1992 | Standard color | $300 | $400 |

Firenza
1994-1999. Offset double-cut, bolt-on neck, single-coil pickups.

| 1994-1999 | | $350 | $450 |

Firenza AX
1994-1999. Upscale Firenza Impact with humbucking pickups.

| 1994-1999 | | $400 | $550 |

Generation Custom EX
2006-2008. Single-cut solidbody, 2 humbuckers, 5-way switch.

| 2006-2008 | | $250 | $350 |

Generation S-1/S-2/S-3
1988-1994. Single-cut, maple cap on mahogany body, bolt-on maple neck, six-on-a-side tuners, active single/hum pickups, S-2 with locking vibrato system.

| 1988-1994 | | $450 | $575 |

Horizon/Horizon II
1983-1985. Extended pointy horns, angled lower bout, maple body, rear routing for electronics, 2 humbucking pickups. Horizon II has added blade pickup.

| 1983-1985 | | $400 | $500 |

HP Special USA
2008-2011. Offset cutaway, 2 humbuckers.

| 2008-2011 | | $750 | $1,250 |

Hydra Doubleneck
1985-1989. Available as a custom order, 6/12-string necks each with 2 humbuckers, 3-way pickup select.

| 1985-1989 | | $800 | $1,000 |

Impact 1/Impact 2
1985-1987. Offset double-cut, Impact 1 has higher-end synthetic 'board, Impact 2 with conventional rosewood 'board.

| 1985-1987 | | $350 | $500 |

Liberator JT-85 A435 John Taylor
2007. Models by John Taylor and Juicy Couture, basswood body, maple neck, 1 humbucker and 2 single-coils, black with graphics, certificate of authenticity.

| 2007 | 100 made | $700 | $900 |

Mantis
1984-1989. Hybrid X-shaped solidbody, 1 humbucking pickup, tremolo, laminated maple neck.

| 1984-1989 | | $350 | $500 |

Milestone 12-String
1985-1986. Offset double-cut, 12 strings.

| 1985-1986 | | $250 | $350 |

Milestone/Milestone Custom
1983-1986. Offset double-cut solidbody.

| 1983-1986 | | $225 | $325 |

Mystic
1983-1989. Double-cut, 2 pickups, st p tailpiece initially, later Power Bend vibrato, maple body and neck.

| 1983-1989 | | $400 | $500 |

Nitro I Active
1988-1990. Active electronics.

| 1988-1990 | | $350 | $450 |

Nitro I/II/III
1986-1989. Offset double-cut, banana-style headstock, 1 humbucker (I), 2 humbuckers (II), or single/single/hum pickups (III).

1986-1989	Nitro I	$250	$350
1986-1989	Nitro II	$350	$500
1986-1989	Nitro III	$400	$550

Odyssey
1990-1994. Single-cut, figured carved maple top on mahogany body, humbuckers.

| 1990-1994 | | $600 | $750 |

Odyssey 25th Anniversary
1990. Single-cut body, limited production.

| 1990 | | $750 | $950 |

Omniac JD USA
2005-2010. Designed by Jerry Donahue, single-cut solidbody, 2 single-coils.

| 2005-2010 | | $825 | $1,125 |

Patriot
1983-1987. Double-cut, single bridge humbucker.

| 1983-1987 | | $300 | $400 |

MODEL YEAR	FEATURES	EXC. COND. LOW	HIGH
Patriot Plus			
	1983-1987. Double-cut, 2 humbucker pickups, bi-laminated maple neck.		
1983-1987		$400	$500
Patriot Tremolo			
	1986-1990. Double-cut, single bridge humbucker, tremolo, replaced the standard Patriot.		
1986-1990		$400	$500
Predator Plus 7ST			
	2008-2010. 7-string.		
2008-2010		$400	$500
Predator Series			
	1985-1988, 1990-2016. Double-cut poplar body, 2 pickups until '87, 3 after, vibrato.		
1985-2016		$250	$350
Raptor Series			
	1997-present. Offset double-cut solidbody, 3 pickups.		
1997-2023		$100	$125
Razer			
	1983-1989. Double-cut with arrowhead point for lower bout, 2 pickups, 1 volume and 2 tone controls, stop tailpiece or vibrato.		
1983-1989		$400	$550
Reactor			
	1993-1999. Classic single-cut style, 2 single-coils.		
1993-1999		$350	$450
Rockmaster II Stage Pack			
	2000s. Student solidbody Rockmaster electric guitar and GT-5 amp pack.		
2000		$95	$125
Rotor Series			
	2004-2010. Classic futuristic body, elongated upper treble bout/lower bass bout, 2 humbuckers.		
2004-2008	Rotor EXP	$300	$400
2004-2010	Rotor EX	$275	$375
T-15			
	1981-1983. Offset double-cut, bolt-on neck, dual ferrite blade single-coil pickups, natural. Amp-in-case available.		
1981-1983	Amp-in-case	$425	$600
1981-1983	Guitar only	$350	$500
T-25			
	1979-1985. Synthetic polymer body, 2 pickups, cream 'guard, sunburst finish.		
1979-1985		$500	$600
T-25 Special			
	1979-1985. Same as T-25, but with super high output pickups, phenolic 'board, black/white/black 'guard, ebony black finish.		
1979-1985		$500	$600
T-26			
	1982-1986. Same as T-25, but with 3 single-coil pickups and 5-way switch.		
1982-1986		$450	$550
T-27			
	1981-1983. Offset double-cut, bolt-on neck, dual ferrite blade single-coil pickups.		
1981-1983		$550	$650

MODEL YEAR	FEATURES	EXC. COND. LOW	HIGH
T-30			
	1982-1985. Short-scale, 3 single-coil pickups, 5-way select, by '83 amp-in-case available.		
1982-1985	Guitar only	$500	$650
1983-1985	Amp-in-case	$600	$750
T-60			
	1978-1988. Contoured offset double-cut, ash body, six-in-line tuners, 2 humbuckers, thru-body strings, by '87 maple bodies, various finishes.		
1978-1988		$650	$950
T-1000 LT			
	1992-1994. Double-cut, 2 single-coils and humbucker with coil-tap.		
1992-1994		$350	$450
Tracer Custom			
	1989-1990. Tracer with 2 single humbuckers and extras.		
1989-1990		$350	$450
Tracer/Tracer II			
	1987-1994. Offset scooped double-cut with extended pointy horns, poplar body, 1 pickup, Floyd Rose.		
1987-1994		$350	$450
Vandenberg Quilt Top			
	1989-1992. Vandenberg Custom with quilted maple top, 2 humbuckers, glued-in neck, mahogany body and neck.		
1989-1992		$1,500	$2,500
Vandenberg Signature			
	1988-1992. Double-cut, reverse headstock, bolt-on neck, locking vibrato, various colors.		
1988-1992		$850	$1,500
Vortex I/Vortex II			
	1986. Streamlined Mantis with 2 pickups, 3-way, Kahler locking vibrato. Vortex II has Randy Rhoads Sharkfin V.		
1986		$400	$500
V-Type Series			
	2004-2007. Offset double-cut solidbody, pointed reverse 6-on-a-side headstock, 2 humbuckers.		
2004-2007		$350	$475
Wolfgang Special			
	1996-1997. Peavy logo on headstock (not EVH), curly maple quilt top, various colors.		
1996-1997		$2,000	$3,000

Pederson Custom Guitars

2009-present. Luthier Kevin Pederson builds his premium grade, production/custom, hollowbody and solidbody guitars in Forest City, Iowa. From 1997-2009 he produced guitars under the Abyss brand name.

Pedro de Miguel

1991-present. Luthiers Pedro Pérez and Miguel Rodriguez build their professional and premium grade, custom/production, classical guitars in Madrid, Spain. They also offer factory-made instruments built to their specifications.

1983 Peavey T-15 Red
Rivington Guitars

1978 Peavey T-60
Tom Pfeifer

1976 Penco
Reese Shellman

Pensa MK1

MODEL		EXC. COND.	
YEAR	FEATURES	LOW	HIGH

Pedulla

1975-2019. Known for basses, Pedulla did offer a few solidbody guitar models into the early 1980s.

MVP

1981-1984. Double-cut solidbody, 2 humbuckers, dot markers, 4 knobs with main toggle and 3 mini-toggle switches, stencil Pedulla logo, MVP serial number series.

1981-1984		$2,000	$2,500

Peekamoose

1983-present. Production/custom, premium grade, solidbody, chambered, and archtop electric guitars built in New York City, New York by luthier Paul Schwartz.

Pegasus Guitars and Ukuleles

1977-present. Premium grade, custom steel-string guitars built by luthier Bob Gleason in Kurtistown, Hawaii, who also builds ukulele family instruments.

Penco

Ca. 1974-1978. Generally high-quality Japanese-made copies of classic American acoustic, electric and bass guitars. Imported by Philadelphia Music Company of Limerick, Pennsylvania during the copy era. Includes dreadnought acoustics with laminated woods, bolt-neck solidbody electric guitars and basses, mandolins, and banjos.

Acoustic Flat-Top

1974-1978	Various models	$150	$400

Electric

1974-1978	Solidbody	$350	$600
1974-1978	Thinline Archtop	$350	$600
1977	E-72 Howard Roberts	$950	$1,500

Penn

1950s. Archtop and acoustic guitars built by made by United Guitar Corporation in Jersey City, New Jersey, which also made Premier acoustics. Penn was located in L.A.

Pensa (Pensa-Suhr)

1982-present. Premium grade, production/custom, solidbody guitars and basses built in the U.S. Rudy Pensa, of Rudy's Music Stop, New York City, New York, started building Pensa guitars in '82. In '85 he teamed up with John Suhr to build Pensa-Suhr instruments. Name changed back to Pensa in '96.

Classic

1992-Ca. 1998. Offset double-cut, 3 single-coils, gold hardware.

1992-1998	Various models	$2,500	$3,500

MK 1 (Mark Knopfler)

1985-2018. Offset double-cut solidbody, carved flamed maple bound top, 3 pickups, gold hardware, dot markers, bolt-on neck.

1985-2018		$3,000	$4,500

Suhr Custom

1985-1989. Two-piece maple body, bolt-on maple neck with rosewood 'board, custom order basis with a variety of woods and options available.

1985-1989	Various options	$3,000	$4,500

Suhr Standard

1985-1991. Double-cut, single/single/hum pickup configuration, opaque solid finish normally, dot markers.

1985-1991		$2,500	$3,500

Perlman Guitars

1976-present. Luthier Alan Perlman builds his premium grade, custom, steel-string and classical guitars in San Francisco, California.

Perri Ink.

Custom, professional grade, solidbody electric guitars built by luthier Nick Perri in Los Angeles, California, starting in 2009.

Perry Guitars

1982-present. Premium grade, production/custom, classical guitars built by luthier Daryl Perry in Winnipeg, Manitoba. He also builds lutes.

Petillo Masterpiece Guitars

1965-present. Intermediate, professional and premium grade, custom, steel-string, nylon-string, 12-string, resonator, archtop, and Hawaiian guitars in Ocean, New Jersey, originally by father and son luthiers Phillip J. "Doc" and David Petillo. Doc died in August 2010.

Petros Guitars

1992-present. Premium grade, production/custom, flat-top, 12-string, and nylon-string guitars built by father and son luthiers Bruce and Matthew Petros in Kaukauna, Wisconsin.

PH Guitars

2006-present. Luthier Paul A. Hartmann builds professional and premium grade, custom, acoustic archtop and electric guitars in Hyde Park, New York.

Phantom Guitar Works

1992-present. Intermediate grade, production/custom, classic Phantom, and Teardrop shaped solid and hollowbody guitars and basses assembled in Clatskanie, Oregon. They also offer the Mando-Guitar. Phantom was established by Jack Charles, former lead guitarist of the band Quarterflash. Some earlier guitars were built overseas.

Pheo

Luthier Phil Sylvester, began building in 1996, unique premium grade, production/custom, electric and acoustic guitars in Portland, Oregon.

MODEL YEAR	FEATURES	EXC. COND. LOW	HIGH

Phoenix Guitar Company

1994-present. Luthiers George Leach and Diana Huber build their premium grade, production/custom, archtop and classical guitars in Scottsdale, Arizona.

Pieper

Premium grade, custom, solidbody guitars and basses built by luthier Robert Pieper in New Haven, Connecticut starting in 2005.

Pignose

1972-present. The original portable amp company also offers intermediate grade, production, dreadnaught and amplified electric guitars. They also offer effects. Refer to Amps section for more company info.

Pilgrim

1970's-late-1980s, 2010-present. Built in the U.K., luthier Paul Tebbutt introduced the brand back in the '70s and his guitars were available until late '80s. His designs are now used on intermediate grade, production, electric acoustic guitars, built in the Far East and distributed by John Hornby Skewes & Co. Ltd. They also offer mandolins, ukuleles and banjos.

Pimentel and Sons

1951-present. Luthiers Lorenzo Pimentel and sons build their professional, premium and presentation grade, flat-top, jazz, cutaway electric, and classical guitars in Albuquerque, New Mexico.

Player

1984-1985. Player guitars featured interchangeable pickup modules that mounted through the back of the guitar. They offered a double-cut solidbody with various options and the pickup modules were sold separately. The company was located in Scarsdale, New York.

Pleasant

Late 1940s-ca.1966. Solidbody electric guitars, obviously others, Japanese manufacturer, probably not imported into the U.S.

Electric Solidbody
1940s-1966. Various models.

1940s-1966		$250	$350

Potvin

2003-present. Production/custom, professional and premium grade, chambered, hollowbody and solidbody electric guitars built by luthier Mike Potvin in Ontario.

Prairie State

1927-ca. 1940. A Larson Brothers brand, basically a derivative of Maurer & Company. The Prairie State models were slightly more expensive than the equivalent Maurer models. They featured a patented steel rod mechanism to strengthen the body, which ran from the end block to the neck block. The model

usually had Brazilian rosewood back and sides, laminated necks and X-bracing. Some later models were built with figured maple.

Prairiewood

Luthier Robert Dixon of Fargo, North Dakota, began in 2005, builds professional grade, production/custom, hollowbody archtop and solidbody guitars.

Premier

Ca.1938-ca.1975, 1990s-2010. Brands originally offered by Premier include Premier, Multivox, Marvel, Belltone and Strad-O-Lin. Produced by Peter Sorkin Music Company in Manhattan, New York City, New York, who began in Philadelphia, relocating to NYC in '35. First radio-sized amplifiers and stick-on pickups for acoustic archtops were introduced by '38. After WWII, they set up the Multivox subsidiary to manufacture amplifiers ca. '46. The first flat-top with pickup appeared in '46.

Most acoustic instruments were made by United Guitar Corporation in Jersey City, New Jersey. Ca. '57 Multivox acquires Strad-O-Lin. Ca.'64-'65 their Custom line guitars are assembled with probably Italian bodies and hardware, Japanese electronics, possibly Egmond necks from Holland. By ca. '74-'75, there were a few Japanese-made guitars, then Premier brand goes into hiatus. The brand reappears on Asian-made budget and intermediate grade, production, solidbody guitars and basses beginning in the '90s.

Bantam Custom
1950s-1960s. Single-cut archtop, dots, earlier with white potted pickups, then metal-covered pickups, and finally Japanese-made pickups (least valued).

1950s-60s		$1,000	$1,500

Bantam Deluxe
1950s-1960s. Single-cut archtop, fully bound, sparkle knobs, earlier with white potted pickups, then metal-covered pickups, and finally Japanese-made pickups (least valued), block markers, 1 or 2 pickups (deduct $100 for 1 pickup).

1950s-60s	Blond, sunburst	$2,000	$2,500

Bantam Special
1950s-1960s. Single-cut archtop, dots, early models with white potted pickups, then metal-covered pickups, and finally Japanese-made pickups (least valued), 1 or 2 pickups (deduct $100 for 1 pickup).

1950s-60s		$975	$1,250

Custom Solidbody
1958-1970. Notable solidbody bass scroll cutaway, various models with various components used, finally import components only.

1958-1970	1 pickup	$625	$825
1958-1970	2 pickups	$725	$950
1958-1970	3 pickups	$975	$1,250

Deluxe Archtop
1950s-1960s. Full body 17 1/4" archtop, square block markers, single-cut, early models with white potted pickups, later '60s models with metal pickups.

1950s-60s		$1,750	$2,250

Petillo Archtop

1959 Premier A-300
Rivington Guitars

GUITARS

Prestige Heritage
Elite Spalt Maple

1996 R.C. Allen Leader

MODEL YEAR	FEATURES	EXC. COND. LOW	HIGH

E-727

1958-1962. E-scroll style solidbody with scroll bass bout, 3 single-coil pickups, Premier headstock logo, made by the Multivox factory in New York.

1958-1962		$1,250	$1,500

Semi-Pro 16" Archtop

1950s-early-1960s. Thinline electric 16" archtop with 2 1/4" deep body, acoustic or electric.

1950s-60s	Acoustic	$875	$1,125
1950s-60s	Electric	$975	$1,250

Semi-Pro Bantam Series

1960s. Thinline electric archtop with 2 3/4" deep body, offered in cutaway and non-cut models.

1960s		$400	$550

Special Archtop

1950s-1960s. Full body 17 1/4" archtop, less fancy than Deluxe, single-cut, early models with white potted pickups, '60s models with metal pickups.

1950s-60s		$1,125	$1,500

Studio Six Archtop

1950s-early-1960s. 16" wide archtop, single pickup, early pickups white potted, changed later to metal top.

1950s-60s		$675	$875

Prenkert Guitars

1980-present. Premium and presentation grade, production/custom, classical and flamenco guitars built in Sebastopol, California by luthier Richard Prenkert.

Prestige

2003-present. Intermediate, professional, and premium grade, production/custom, acoustic, solidbody and hollowbody guitars and basses from Vancouver, British Columbia.

PST Guitars

Ca. 2000-present. Professional and premium grade, custom, electric guitars and basses, built by luthier P. Scott Tucker, in King George, Virginia. He has also built acoustic guitars.

Queen Shoals Stringed Instruments

1972-ca. 2010. Luthier Larry Cadle builds his production/custom, flat-top, 12-string, and nylon-string guitars in Clendenin, West Virginia.

Queguiner, Alain

1982-present. Custom flat-tops, 12 strings, and nylon strings built by luthier Alain Queguiner in Paris, France.

Quest

1982-ca. 1986. Originally labeled Quest by Vantage, these solidbody guitars and basses were built in Japan, mostly by Chushin Gakki.

R.C. Allen

1951-2014. Luthier R. C. "Dick" Allen built professional and premium grade, custom hollow-body and semi-hollowbody guitars in El Monte, California. He has also built solidbody guitars. He passed away in '14.

Rahan

1999-present. Professional grade, production/custom, solidbody guitars built by luthiers Mike Curd and Rick Cantu in Houston, Texas.

Rahbek Guitars

2000-present. Professional and premium grade, production/custom, solidbody electrics built by luthier Peter Rahbek in Copenhagen, Denmark.

Raimundo

1970s-present. Intermediate, professional and premium grade flamenco and classical guitars made in Valencia, Spain, by luthiers Antonio Aparicio and Manual Raimundo.

RainSong

1991-2023. Professional grade, production, all-graphite and graphite and wood acoustic guitars built originally in Maui, and currently in Woodinville, Washington. Developed by luthier engineer John Decker with help from luthier Lorenzo Pimentel, engineer Chris Halford, and sailboard builder George Clayton.

RAM Guitars

2007-present. Luthier Ron Mielzynski builds his professional grade, production/custom, solidbody, chambered and archtop electric guitars in Fox River Grove, Illinois.

Rambler

See Strobel Guitars listing.

Ramirez, Jose

1882-present. Professional, premium, and presentation grade, custom/production, classical guitars built in Madrid, Spain. Founded by Jose Ramirez (1858-1923) who was an apprentice at the shop of Francisco Gonzales. Jose opened his own workshop in 1882 working with his younger brother, Manuel. Manuel split with Jose and opened his own, competing workshop. Jose's business was continued by Jose's son Jose Ramirez II (1885-1957), grandson Jose III (1922-1995), and great grandchildren Jose IV (1953-2000) and Amalia Ramirez. In the 1930's a larger body instrument with improved fan bracing was developed to meet the need for more power and volume. Other refinements were developed and the Ramirez 1A Tradicional was soon introduced which found favor with Andres Segovia. The Ramirez company has produced both student and professional instruments, but in the classical guitar field, like the old-master violin business, a student model is often a very fine instrument that is now valued at $2,000 or more. In the 1980s Ramirez offered the E Series student guitar line that was built for, but not by, Ramirez. In 1991 the company offered the even more affordable R Series which was offered for about

MODEL		EXC. COND.	
YEAR	FEATURES	LOW	HIGH

$1,300. As is typically the case, Ramirez classical guitars do not have a name-logo on the headstock. The brand is identified by a Ramirez label on the inside back which also may have the model number listed.

A/1A
1960s-2000s. Classical, Brazilian or Indian rosewood.

1960s-70s	Brazilian, cedar	$8,500	$12,000
1970s-80s	Indian	$3,750	$5,000
1980s	Brazilian	$6,750	$8,750
1990-2000s	Indian	$3,500	$4,500

A/2A
1970s-80s	Indian	$3,750	$5,000

AE Estudio
2004		$2,000	$2,500

De Camera
1980s. Classical, cedar top, Brazilian rosewood back and sides.

1980s		$3,000	$4,000

E/1E/Estudio
1988-1990s. Intermediate level.

1988-1990s		$1,500	$2,000

E/2E
1990s-2000s. Red cedar top, Indian rosewood back and sides, Spanish cedar neck, ebony 'board.

1990-2000s		$1,500	$2,000

E/3E/Estudio
1990s. Cedar, rosewood.

1990s		$1,725	$2,500

E/4E/Estudio
1980s-2000s. Top of the E Series line, solid red cedar top, solid Indian rosewood back and sides.

1980-2000s		$2,250	$3,000

Flamenco
1920s-1979. European spruce top, cypress back and sides.

1920s-50s		$4,500	$6,000
1960-1969		$3,250	$4,500
1970-1979		$3,250	$4,500

R1
1991-2014. Red cedar top, mahogany sides and back, Spanish cedar neck, ebony 'board. Replaced by RA series in '14.

1991-2014		$600	$750

R2
1991-2014. Red cedar top, Indian rosewood back and sides, cedar neck, ebony 'board. Replaced by RA series in '14.

1991-2014		$1,000	$1,500

R3
1998. Cedar, rosewood.

1998		$1,000	$1,500

R4 Classical
1995-2014. All solid wood, Western red cedar top, rosewood back and sides. Replaced by RB series in '14.

1995-2014		$1,500	$2,000

S/S1
2005-2007. Solid German spruce top, African mahogany sides and back, most affordable in Estudio line.

2005-2007		$700	$950

MODEL		EXC. COND.	
YEAR	FEATURES	LOW	HIGH

Segovia
Cedar, Indian rosewood.

1966		$7,000	$9,000
1974-1978		$5,000	$6,500

SP Series
2002-2018. Semi-professional level designed to be between the company's 'concert/professional' series and 'student' series.

2002-2018		$5,000	$6,500

Ramirez, Manuel
1890-1916. Brother of Jose Ramirez, and a respected professional classical guitar builder from Madrid, Spain. His small shop left no heirs, so the business was not continued after Manuel's death in 1916. Manuel was generally considered to be more famous during his lifetime than his brother Jose, and while his business did not continue, Manuel trained many well-known Spanish classical guitar luthiers who prospered with their own businesses. During Manuel's era his shop produced at least 48 different models, with prices ranging from 10 to 1,000 pesetas, therefore vintage prices can vary widely. Guitars made prior to 1912 have a label with a street address of Arlaban 10, in 1912 the shop moved to Arlaban 11.

Randy Reynolds Guitars
1996-2018. Luthier Randy Reynolds builds his premium grade, production/custom classical and flamenco guitars in Colorado Springs, Colorado. Reynolds announced his retirement on January 1, 2019.

Randy Wood Guitars
1968-present. Premium grade, custom/production, archtop, flat-top, and resonator guitars built by luthier Randy Wood in Bloomingdale, Georgia. He also builds mandolins.

Rarebird Guitars
1978-present. Luthier Bruce Clay builds his professional and premium grade, production/custom, guitars and basses, originally in Arvada, Colorado, and currently in Hoehne, Colorado.

Rat Fink
2002-2005. Lace Music Products, the makers of the Lace Sensor pickup, offered the intermediate grade, production, guitars and basses, featuring the artwork of Ed "Big Daddy" Roth until '05.

Rayco
2002-present. Professional and premium grade, custom, resonator and Hawaiian-style acoustic guitars built in British Columbia, by luthiers Mark Thibeault and Jason Friesen.

Rahbek Cos-T

Randy Wood Custom

GUITARS

MODEL YEAR	FEATURES	EXC. COND. LOW	HIGH

Recco

1960s. Electric guitar imports made by Teisco, pricing similar to Teisco models, Recco logo on headstock, upscale solidbodies can have four pickups with several knobs and four switches.

Electric Solidbody

1960s	4 pickups	$500	$650

Recording King

1929-1943. Brand name used by Montgomery Ward for instruments made by various American manufacturers, including Kay, Gibson and Gretsch. Generally mid-grade instruments. M Series are Gibson-made archtops.

Carson Robison/Model 1052

1938-1939. Made by Gibson, flat-top, 16", sunburst.

1938-1939		$2,625	$3,250

Kay 17" Flat-Top

1940-1941		$1,125	$1,500

M-2

1936-1941. Gibson-made archtop with carved top and f-holes, maple back and sides.

1936-1941		$800	$1,125

M-3

1936-1941. Gibson-made archtop, f-holes, maple back and sides, carved top.

1936-1941		$900	$1,250

M-4

1937-1940. Gibson-made archtop, f-holes, maple back and sides, rope-checkered binding, flying bat wing markers.

1937-1940		$1,125	$1,500

M-5

1936-1941. Gibson-made archtop with f-holes, maple back and sides, trapeze tailpiece, checkered top binding.

1936-1938	16" body	$1,625	$2,000
1939-1941	17" body	$1,625	$2,000

M-6

1938-1939. M-5 with upgraded gold hardware.

1938-1939		$1,625	$2,000

Model 681

Mid-1930s. Small flat top by Gibson, ladder braced.

1930s		$1,625	$2,000

Model 1124

1937. 16" acoustic archtop, body by Gibson, attractive higher-end appointments, block-dot markers, sunburst.

1937		$2,125	$2,500

Ray Whitley

1939-1940. High-quality model made by Gibson, round shoulder flat-top, mahogany (Model 1028) or Brazilian rosewood (Model 1027) back and sides, 5-piece maple neck, Ray Whitley stencil script peghead logo, pearl crown inlay on peghead, fancy inlaid markers.

1939-1940	Brazilian	$25,000	$30,000
1939-1940	Mahogany	$12,500	$16,000

Roy Smeck

1938-1940. 16.25" electric archtop, large Recording King badge logo, Roy Smeck stencil logo, bar pickup, 2 control knobs on upper bass bout, dot markers.

1938-1940		$1,500	$2,000

1939 Recording King Carson Robinson/Model 1052

Jet City Guitars

Redentore Psalmist

MODEL YEAR	FEATURES	EXC. COND. LOW	HIGH

Recording King (TML)

2005-present. Budget grade, production, acoustic cowboy stenciled guitars designed by Greg Rich for The Music Link, which also offers Johnson and other brand instruments. They also have banjos and ukes.

Redentore

2007-present. Luthier Mark Piper builds professional and premium grade, production/custom, archtop jazz, acoustic flat-top, carve-top and semi-hollow electric guitars in Columbia, Tennessee.

RedLine Acoustics and RedLine Resophonics

2007-present. Professional and premium grade, production, acoustic and resophonic guitars built in Hendersonville, Tennessee by luthiers Steve Smith, Jason Denton, Christian McAdams and Ryan Futch. They also build mandolins and plan to add lap steels.

Regal

Ca. 1895-1966, 1987-present. Intermediate and professional grade, production, acoustic and wood and metal body resonator guitars and basses. Originally a mass manufacturer founded in Indianapolis, Indiana, the Regal brand was first used by Emil Wulschner & Son. After 1900, new owners changed the company name to The Regal Manufacturing Company. The company was moved to Chicago in '08 and renamed the Regal Musical Instrument Company. Regal made brands for distributors and mass merchandisers as well as marketing its own Regal brand. Regal purchased the Lyon & Healy factory in '28. Regal was licensed to co-manufacture Dobros in '32 and became the sole manufacturer of them in '37 (see Dobro for those instruments). Most Regal instruments were beginner-grade; however, some very fancy archtops were made during the '30s. The company was purchased by Harmony in '54 and absorbed. From '59 to '66, Harmony made acoustics under the Regal name for Fender. In '87 the Regal name was revived on a line of resonator instruments by Saga.

Acoustic Hawaiian

1930s. Student model, small 13" body, square neck, glued or trapeze bridge.

1930s	Faux grain painted finish	$500	$650
1930s	Plain sunburst, birch, trapeze	$300	$400

Concert Folk H6382

1960s. Regal by Harmony, solid spruce top, mahogany back and sides, dot markers, natural.

1960s		$350	$450

Deluxe Dreadnought H6600

1960s. Regal by Harmony, solid spruce top, mahogany back and sides, bound top and back, rosewood 'board, dot markers, natural.

1960s		$350	$450

MODEL YEAR	FEATURES	EXC. COND. LOW	HIGH

Dreadnought 12-String H1269
1960s. Regal by Harmony, solid spruce top, 12-string version of Deluxe, natural.

1960s		$350	$450

Esquire
1940s. 15 1/2" acoustic archtop, higher-end appointments, fancy logo art and script pearl Esquire headstock logo and Regal logo, natural.

1940s		$1,375	$1,750

Meteor
1960s. Single-cut acoustic-electric archtop, 2 pickups.

1960s		$1,375	$1,750

Model 27
1933-1942. Birch wood body, mahogany or maple, 2-tone walnut finish, single-bound top, round or square neck.

1933-1942		$1,125	$1,500

Model 45
1933-1937. Spruce top and mahogany back and sides, bound body, square neck.

1933-1937		$1,875	$2,500

Model 46
1933-1937. Round neck.

1933-1937		$1,875	$2,250

Model 55 Standard
1933-1934. Regal's version of Dobro Model 55 which was discontinued in '33.

1933-1934		$1,125	$1,500

Model 75
1939-1940. Metal body, square neck.

1939-1940		$2,125	$2,625

Model TG 60 Resonator Tenor
1930s. Wood body, large single cone biscuit bridge resonator, 2 upper bout metal ports, 4-string tenor.

1930s		$1,625	$2,000

Parlor
1920s. Small body, slotted headstock, birch sides and back, spruce top.

1920s		$350	$550

Prince
1930s. High-end 18" acoustic archtop, fancy appointments, Prince name inlaid in headstock along with Regal script logo and strolling guitarist art.

1930s		$2,000	$2,500

Spirit Of '76
1976. Red-white-blue, flat-top.

1976		$500	$650

Reliance
1920s. Instruments built by the Oscar Schmidt Co. and possibly others. Most likely a brand made for a distributor.

Relixx
2001-2013. Intermediate and professional grade, production/custom, aged vintage-style solidbody guitars built in Sanborn, New York by luthier Nick Hazlett. He discontinued complete guitars in '13 and now offers only vintage parts.

Renaissance
1978-1980. Plexiglass solidbody electric guitars and basses. Founded in Malvern, Pennsylvania, by John Marshall (designer), Phil Goldberg and Daniel Lamb. Original partners gradually leave, and John Dragonetti takes over by late-'79. The line is redesigned with passive electronics on guitars, exotic shapes, but when deal with Sunn amplifiers falls through, company closes. Brand name currently used on a line of guitars and basses made by Rick Turner in Santa Cruz, California.

Fewer than 300 of first series made, plus a few prototypes and several wooden versions; six or so prototypes of second series made. SN=M(M) YYXXXX: month, year, consecutive number.

Electric Plexiglas Solidbody
1978-1980. Models include the SPG ('78-'79, DiMarzio pickups, active electronics), T-200G ('80, Bich-style with 2 passive DiMarzio pickups), and the S-200G ('80, double-cut, 2 DiMarzio pickups, passive electronics).

1978-1980		$1,000	$1,500

Renaissance Guitars
1994-present. Professional grade, custom, semi-acoustic flat-top, nylon-string and solidbody guitars and basses built by luthier Rick Turner in Santa Cruz, California. He also builds ukes.

Repiso
Late-1950s-early-1970s. Spanish-born luthier Sergio Repiso Villarruel made professional and premium grade, Gypsy-style jazz and solidbody electric guitars, mostly in Argentina. It is estimated that throughout his life he produced about 1,000 instruments.

Republic Guitars
2006-present. Intermediate grade, production, reso-phonic and Weissenborn-style guitars imported by American Folklore, Inc. of Austin, Texas. They also offer mandolins and ukes.

Retronix
2013-present. Korean-made solidbody guitars designed and imported by J. Backlund. They also build J. Backlund guitars.

Reuter Guitars
1984-present. Professional and premium grade, custom, flat-top, 12-string, resonator, and Hawaiian guitars built by luthier John Reuter, the Director of Training at the Roberto-Venn School of Luthiery, in Tempe, Arizona.

Reverend
1996-present. Intermediate grade, production, guitars and basses, designed by luthier and founder Joe Naylor, manufactured in South Korea, and setup by Reverend originally in Warren, Livonia, Michigan, and currently in Toledo, Ohio. There were also earlier U.S. production guitars built in Warren. Reverend has built amps and effects in

1978 Renaissance SPG
Rivington Guitars

2004 Reverend Wolfman
Thomas Whitty

Reverend Rick Vito Soulshaker
Rick Vito

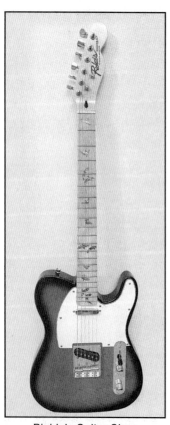

Richie's Guitar Shop

MODEL YEAR	FEATURES	EXC. COND. LOW	HIGH

the past. In 2010, Ken and Penny Haas purchased the company with Naylor continuing with design. Naylor also founded Naylor Amps, Armor Gold Cables, Stringdog, and Railhammer Pickups.

Electric

1996-present. Solid and semi-solid bodies, bolt or set-neck, various pickups.

1996-2023	Various models	$450	$2,000

Rex

1920s-1940s, 1950s-1960s. Generally, beginner-grade guitars made by Kay and sold through Fred Gretsch distributors. In the '50s and '60s, the Lamberti Brothers Company in Melbourne, Australia built electrics bearing the Rex brand that were not distributed by Gretsch. They also had built amps.

Ribbecke Guitars

Premium and presentation grade, custom thinline, flat-top, and archtop guitars built by luthier Tom Ribbecke, starting in 1973, in Healdsburg, California.

Rice Custom Guitars

1998-present. Father and son luthiers, Richard Rice and Christopher Rice, build professional and premium grade, custom, solidbody, semi-hollow and hollowbody electric guitars and basses in Arlington Heights, Illinois.

Rich and Taylor

1993-1996. Custom acoustic and electric guitars, mandolins and banjos from luthiers Greg Rich and Mark Taylor (Crafters of Tennessee).

Richard Schneider

1960s-1997. Luthier Richard Schneider built his acoustic guitars in Washington state. Over the years, he collaborated with Dr. Michael A. Kasha on many guitar designs and innovations. Originally from Michigan, he also was involved in designing guitars for Gretsch and Gibson. He died in early '97.

Richie's Guitar Shop

Intermediate and professional grade, custom, electric guitars and basses, built by luthier Richard 'Richie' Baxt, in New York City, New York. He began in 1983.

Richmond

Luthiers Robert Godin (Godin Guitars) and Daniel Fiocco build intermediate and professional grade, production, chambered and solidbody electric guitars in Richmond, Quebec. Richmond is one of several brands used by Godin.

Richter Mfg.

1930s. One of many Chicago makers of the era, the company allegedly bought already-made guitars from other manufacturers, painted and decorated them to their liking and resold them.

Rick Hayes Instruments

2006-present. Owned by Rick and Lyn Hayes and offering professional and premium grade, production/custom, dreadnought acoustic and electric guitars, and mandolins built by Rick and Steve Hogsed in Goshen, Ohio.

Rick Turner

1979-1981, 1990-present. Rick Turner has a long career as a luthier, electronics designer and innovator. He also makes the Renaissance line of guitars in his shop in Santa Cruz, California. The guitars and basses built in 1979-'81 were numbered sequentially in the order they were completed and shipped with the second part of the serial number indicating the year the instrument was built. Turner estimates that approximately 200 instruments were made during that period.

Rickenbacker

1931-present. Professional and premium grade, production/custom, acoustic and electric guitars built in California. They also build basses. Founded in Los Angeles as Ro-Pat-In by ex-National executives George Beauchamp, Paul Barth and National's resonator cone supplier Adolph Rickenbacher. Rickenbacher was born in Basel, Switzerland in 1886, emigrated to the U.S. and moved to Los Angeles in 1918, opening a tool and die business in '20.

In the mid-'20s, Rickenbacher began providing resonator cones and other metal parts to George Beauchamp and Louis Dopyera of National String Instrument Corporation and became a shareholder in National. Beauchamp, Barth and Harry Watson came up with wooden "frying pan" electric Hawaiian lap steel for National in '31; National was not interested, so Beauchamp and Barth joined with Rickenbacher as Ro-Pat-In (probably for ElectRO-PATent-INstruments) to produce Electro guitars. Cast aluminum frying pans were introduced in '32. Some Spanish guitars (flat-top, F-holes) with Electro pickups were produced beginning in '32. Ro-Pat-In changes their name to Electro String Instrument Corporation in '34, and brand becomes Rickenbacher Electro, soon changed to Rickenbacker, with a "k." Beauchamp retires in '40. There was a production hiatus during World War II.

In '53, Electro was purchased by Francis Cary Hall (born 1908), owner of Radio and Television Equipment Company (Radio-Tel) in Santa Ana, California (founded in '20s as Hall's Radio Service, which began distributing Fender instruments in '46). The factory was relocated to Santa Ana in '62 and the sales/distribution company's name changed from Radio-Tel to Rickenbacker Inc. in '65.

1950s serial numbers have from 4 to 7 letters and numbers, with the number following the letter indicating the '50s year (e.g., NNL8NN would be from '58). From '61 to '86 serial numbers indicate month and year of production with initial letter A-Z for the year A=1961, Z=1986) followed by letter for the month A-M (A=January) plus numbers as before followed by a number 0-9 for the year (0=1987; 9=1996). To avoid

MODEL YEAR	FEATURES	EXC. COND. LOW	HIGH

confusion, we have listed all instruments by model number. For example, the Combo 400 is listed as Model 400/Combo 400. OS and NS stands for Old Style and New Style. On the 360, for example, Ric changed the design in 1964 to their New Style with more rounded body horns and rounded top edges and other changes. But they still offered the Old Style with more pointed horns and top binding until the late 1960s. Ric still sometimes uses the two designations on some of their vintage reissues.

Electro ES-16
1964-1971. Double-cut, set neck, solidbody, 3/4 size, 1 pickup. The Electro line was manufactured by Rickenbacker and distributed by Radio-Tel. The Electro logo appears on the headstock.

1964-1971		$1,375	$1,750

Electro ES-17
1964-1975. Cutaway, set neck, solidbody, 1 pickup.

1964-1975		$1,500	$2,000

Electro Spanish (Model B Spanish)
1935-1943. Small guitar with a lap steel appearance played Spanish-style, hollow black bakelite body augmented with 5 chrome plates (white enamel in '40), 1 octagon knob (2 round-ridged in '38), called the Model B ca. '40.

1935-1937	Chrome, 1 knob	$4,000	$5,000
1935-1937	Tenor 4-string, 1 knob	$4,000	$5,000
1938-1939	Chrome, 2 knobs	$4,000	$5,000
1940-1943	White, 2 knobs	$3,500	$4,500

Electro-Spanish Ken Roberts
1935-1939. Mahogany body, f-holes in lower bout, horseshoe pickup, Kauffman vibrato.

1935-1939		$5,000	$6,500

Model 220 Hamburg
1992-1997. Solidbody.

1992-1997		$1,250	$1,500

Model 230 GF Glenn Frey
1992-1997. Glenn Frey Limited Edition, solidbody, 2 high output humbuckers, black hardware, chrome 'guard.

1992-1997		$2,250	$2,750

Model 230 Hamburg
1983-1991. Solidbody, offset double-cut, 2 pickups, dot inlay, rosewood 'board, chrome-plated hardware.

1983-1991		$1,375	$1,750

Model 250 El Dorado
1983-1991. Deluxe version of Hamburg, gold hardware, white binding.

1983-1991		$1,125	$1,500

Model 260 El Dorado
1992-1997. Replaces 250.

1992-1997		$1,125	$1,500

Model 310
1959-1969, 1981-1985. Two-pickup version of Model 320.

1959-1960	Capri, thick body	$15,000	$20,000
1964-1969	Thinner body	$6,500	$8,500
1981-1985	Reintroduced	$2,000	$2,500

Model 315
1959-1974. Two-pickup version of Model 325.

1959-1960	Capri, thick body	$15,000	$20,000
1964-1969	Thinner body	$8,000	$10,000
1974		$3,500	$4,500

Model 320
1964-1992. Short-scale hollowbody, 3 pickups, f-holes optional in '61 and standard in '64 and optional again in '79.

1964-1969	Fireglo	$6,500	$8,500
1966-1969	Mapleglo	$6,000	$7,500
1974-1979		$3,500	$4,500
1980-1992		$2,750	$3,500

Model 320/12V63
1986. Short run for Japanese market.

1986		$3,000	$4,000

Model 325
1958-1979, 1985-1992. This was a low production model, with some years having no production. In the mid-'60s, the 325 was unofficially known as the John Lennon Model due to his guitar's high exposure on the Ed Sullivan Show and in the Saturday Evening Post.

1958	Early, solid top, John Lennon, 6 made	$100,000	$250,000
1958	Late, Capri, thick body, F-hole	$40,000	$50,000
1959-1960		$30,000	$38,000
1964-1970	Fireglo or Jetglo	$6,500	$8,500
1966-1970	Mapleglo	$6,000	$7,500
1974-1979		$3,500	$4,500

Model 325/12
1985-1986, 1999. Based on John Lennon's one-of-a-kind '64 325/12.

1985-1986		$3,500	$4,500
1999		$3,500	$4,500

Model 325B
1983-1984. Reissue of early '60s model.

1983-1984		$3,000	$4,000

Model 325C58
2002-2014. Copy of the '58 model that John Lennon saw in Germany.

2002-2014		$3,000	$4,000

Model 325C64
2002-present. Copy of the famous '64 model.

2002-2019		$3,000	$4,000

Model 325JL (John Lennon)
1989-1993. John Lennon Limited Edition, 3 vintage Ric pickups, vintage vibrato, maple body; 3/4-size rosewood neck, a 12-string and a full-scale version are also available.

1989-1993		$3,500	$4,500

Model 325S
1964-1967. F-holes.

1964-1967		$8,000	$12,000

Model 325V59
1984-2001. Reissue of John Lennon's modified '59 325, 3 pickups, short-scale.

1984-2001		$3,250	$4,250

Rick Hayes

Rick Turner Model 1

Rickenbacker Model 330 75th
Ron O'Keefe

1966 Rickenbacker Model 335
Jeffrey Phelps

MODEL YEAR	FEATURES	EXC. COND. LOW	HIGH

Model 325V63
1984-2001. Reissue of John Lennon's '63 325.

1984-2001		$3,250	$4,250

Model 330
1958-present. Thinline hollowbody, 2 pickups, slash soundhole, natural or sunburst.

1958-1960	Capri, thick body	$9,000	$12,000
1965-1969	Thinner body	$4,000	$6,500
1970-1976	21 frets	$2,500	$4,000
1977-1983	Small hdstk, Jetglo or Burgundyglo	$2,500	$4,000
1984-2023		$2,000	$3,250

Model 330/12
1965-present. Thinline, 2 pickups, 12-string version of Model 300.

1965-1969	330-style body	$4,500	$6,500
1970-1976	21 frets	$3,000	$4,500
1980-1989		$2,500	$3,500
1990-1999		$2,250	$3,000
2000-2023		$2,000	$2,500

Model 330F
1958-1973. F-style.

1958-1960	Thick version	$12,500	$14,000
1968-1973	Thin version	$8,000	$12,000

Model 330S/12
1964 (1 made)-1965 (2 made). Rare, total of 3 made.

1964-1965		$25,000	$35,000

Model 331 Light Show
1970-1975. Model 330 with translucent top with lights in body that lit up when played, needed external transformer. The first offering's design, noted as Type 1, had heat problems and a fully original one is difficult to find. The 2nd offering's design, noted as Type 2, was a more stable design and is more highly valued in the market.

1970-1971	Type 1 1st edition	$10,000	$15,000
1971-1975	Type 2 2nd edition	$12,000	$16,000

Model 335
1958-1976. Thinline, 330-style body, 2 pickups, vibrato, Fireglo. Called the 330VB from '85-'97.

1958-1960	Capri, thick body	$9,000	$12,000
1965-1969	Thinner body	$4,000	$6,500
1970-1976	21 frets	$2,500	$4,000

Model 335F
1958-1969. F-style.

1958-1961	Thick version	$12,500	$14,000
1961-1969	Thin version	$8,000	$12,000

Model 335S
1964-1967. Rose Morris model, 2 or 3 pickups.

1964-1967		$6,500	$9,000

Model 336/12
1966-1969. Like 300-12, but with 6-12 converter comb, 330-style body.

1966-1969		$5,500	$7,000

Model 340
1958-2014. Thin semi-hollowbody, thru-body maple neck, 2 single-coil pickups, sharp point horns, very limited production '58-'65, with first notable volume of 45 units starting in '66.

1958-1960	Capri, thick body	$9,000	$12,000
1965-1969	Thinner body	$4,000	$6,500
1970-1976	21 frets	$3,500	$5,500
1974-1979	24 frets	$2,500	$3,500
1980-2014		$2,000	$3,250

Model 340/12
1980-2014. 12-string version, 330-style body.

1980-2014		$2,500	$3,500

Model 340F
1958-1960. F-style.

1958-1960	Thick version	$12,500	$14,000

Model 345
1958-1979. Thinline 330-345 series, version with 3 pickups and vibrato tailpiece.

1958-1960	Capri, thick body	$9,000	$12,500
1965-1969	Thinner body	$4,000	$7,500
1970-1976	21 frets	$3,500	$5,500
1974-1979	24 frets	$2,500	$3,500

Model 345 Reissue
2002. Low production, 3 pickups.

2002		$2,750	$3,500

Model 345F
1958-1960. F-style.

1958-1960	Thick version	$12,500	$14,000

Model 350 Liverpool
1983-1997. Thinline, 3 pickups, vibrato, no sound hole.

1983-1997		$2,750	$3,500

Model 350/12V63 Liverpool
1994-2014. Vintage Series, 12-string 350V63.

1994-2014		$3,000	$4,000

Model 350SH (Susanna Hoffs)
1988-1990. Susanna Hoffs Limited Edition.

1988-1990		$4,500	$6,000

Model 350V59
1988. Very low production.

1988		$3,000	$4,000

Model 350V63 Liverpool
1994-present. Vintage Series, like 355 JL, but without signature.

1994-2023		$3,000	$4,000

Model 355/12JL (John Lennon)
1989-1993. 12-string 355 JL, limited production.

1989-1993		$4,000	$5,000

Model 355JL (John Lennon)
1989-1993. John Lennon model, signature and drawing on 'guard.

1989-1993		$4,000	$5,000

Model 360 Tuxedo
1987 only. Tuxedo option included white body, white painted fretboard, and black hardware.

1987		$2,500	$3,500

Model 360/12
1964-present. Deluxe double-cut thinline, 2 pickups, triangle inlays. The 360/12 was offered in both the Old Style (OS) body with double-bound body and pointed horns, and the New Style (NS) body with rounded top edges and rounder horns. George Harrison's original 360/12 had the OS body in a Fireglo finish. Production of the OS and NS bodies overlapped.

1964-1969	NS, Fireglo, rounded horns	$6,500	$8,500

MODEL YEAR	FEATURES	EXC. COND. LOW	HIGH
1964-1969	NS, Mapleglo, rounded horns	$6,500	$8,500
1964-1969	OS, Mapleglo, pointed horns	$20,000	$25,000
1965-1969	OS, Fireglo, pointed horns	$25,000	$35,000
1970-1973	21 frets, '60s features	$4,500	$6,500
1974-1979	24 frets	$3,500	$5,000
1980-2009		$3,000	$4,000
2010-2023		$2,500	$3,500

Model 360/12 RCA
1992. Limited edition made for RCA Nashville as gifts for their artists, has RCA dog-and-gramophone logo on pickguard.

1992		$3,000	$4,000

Model 360/12 Tuxedo
1987 only. 12-string version of 360 Tuxedo.

1987		$3,000	$4,000

Model 360/12C63
2004-present. More exact replica of the Harrison model.

2004-2023		$2,750	$4,000

Model 360/12CW (Carl Wilson)
2000. Carl Wilson, 12-string version of 360 CW.

2000		$3,000	$4,000

Model 360/12V64
1985-2003. Deluxe thinline with '64 features, 2 pickups, 12 strings, slanted plate tailpiece.

1985-2003		$3,000	$4,000

Model 360/12VP
2004. VP is vintage pickup.

2004		$3,000	$4,000

Model 360/12WB
1984-1998. 12-string version of 360WB.

1984-1998		$3,000	$4,000

Model 360
1958-1991, 2000-present. Deluxe thinline, 2 pickups, slash sound hole, bound body until '64.

1958-1960	Capri, thick body	$12,000	$15,000
1961-1963	New Capri, bound body	$8,000	$12,000
1964-1969	New style body	$5,500	$7,000
1965-1970	OS body	$7,500	$9,500
1970-1973	360, no vibrato, 21 frets	$4,000	$5,000
1974-1984	360VB, vibrato, 24 frets	$3,000	$4,000
1985-2023	360VB, vibrato	$2,000	$3,500

Model 360CW (Carl Wilson)
2000. Carl Wilson Limited Edition, 6-string, includes certificate, 500 made.

2000		$3,500	$4,500

Model 360DCM 75th Anniversary
2006. 360 with 75th Anniversary dark cherry metallic finish, 75 made.

2006		$3,500	$4,500

Model 360F
1959-1969. F-style.

1959-1960	Thick version	$12,000	$15,000
1968-1969	Thin version	$8,000	$12,000

Model 360F/12
1968-1969. F-style, 12-string.

1968-1969		$11,500	$14,000

Model 360SF
1968-ca. 1972. Slanted frets (SF), standard on some models, an option on others.

1968-1972		$7,500	$9,000

Model 360V64
1991-2003. Reissue of '64 Model 360 old style body without vibrola, has binding with full length inlays.

1991-2003		$3,000	$4,000

Model 360WB
1984-1998. Double bound body, 2 pickups, vibrato optional (VB).

1984-1990		$2,750	$4,000
1991-1998	WB no vibrato	$2,500	$3,500
1991-1998	WBVB, vibrato	$2,750	$4,000

Model 362/12
1975-1992. Doubleneck 6 & 12, 360 features.

1975-1992		$7,000	$9,000

Model 365
1958-1973. Deluxe thinline, 2 pickups, vibrato, called Model 360 WBVB from '84-'98.

1958-1960	Capri, thick body	$12,000	$15,000
1961-1963	New Capri, bound body	$8,000	$12,000
1964-1970	New style body, 21 frets	$5,500	$7,000
1965-1970	OS body	$7,500	$9,500
1970-1973		$5,500	$7,000

Model 365F
1959-1969. Thin full-body (F designation), 2 pickups, Deluxe features.

1959-1960	Capri, thick body	$12,000	$15,000
1968-1969	Thin version	$10,000	$12,000

Model 366/12 Convertible
1967-1970. Two pickups, 12 strings, comb-like device that converts it to a 6-string, production only noted in '68, perhaps available on custom order basis.

1967-1970	New style body	$5,500	$7,500
1967-1970	OS, double bound	$10,000	$12,500

Model 370
1958-1990, 1994-2007. Deluxe thinline, 3 pickups. Could be considered a dealer special order item from '58-'67 with limited production.

1958-1960	Capri, thick body	$12,000	$15,000
1961-1963	New Capri, bound body	$8,000	$12,000
1964-1970	New style body, 21 frets	$5,500	$7,000
1965-1970	OS body	$7,500	$9,500
1974-1979	24 frets	$3,000	$3,500
1980-1989		$2,500	$3,000
2000-2007		$2,500	$3,000

Model 370/12
1964-1972, 1974-2023. Not regular production until '80, deluxe thinline, 3 pickups, 12 strings. Could be considered a dealer special order item in the '60s and '70s with limited production.

1964-1972		$7,000	$10,000
1974-2023	24 frets	$3,000	$4,000

1958 Rickenbacker
Model 335 Capri
Imaged by Heritage Auctions, HA.com

1960 Rickenbacker 360F

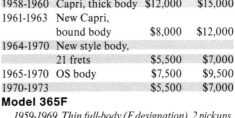

GUITARS

Rickenbacker Model 375 Capri

Ron O'Keefe

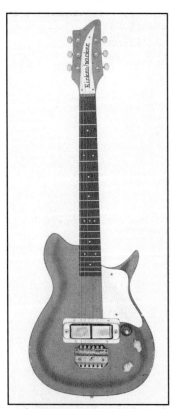

1954 Rickenbacker Model
600/Combo 600

Imaged by Heritage Auctions, HA.com

Model 370/12RM (Roger McGuinn)
1988-1990. Limited Edition Roger McGuinn, 1000 made, higher-quality appointments.

MODEL YEAR	FEATURES	EXC. COND. LOW	HIGH
1988-1990		$5,000	$6,500

Model 370F
1959-1969. F-style, 3 pickups, Deluxe features.

1959-1961	Thick version	$12,000	$15,000
1968-1969	Thin version	$10,000	$12,000

Model 370VP
2006-2007. Limited run with special specs including vintage toaster pickups (VP).

2006-2007		$3,000	$4,000

Model 370WB
1984-1998. Double bound body, 3 pickups, vibrato optional (VB).

1984-1998		$3,000	$4,000

Model 375
1958-1974. Deluxe thinline, 3 pickups, vibrato, called Model 370 WBVB from '84-'98.

1958-1960	Capri, thick body	$12,000	$15,000
1961-1963	New Capri, bound body	$8,000	$12,000
1961-1969	New style body, 21 frets	$5,500	$7,000
1965-1970	OS body	$7,500	$9,500
1970-1974	21 frets	$5,500	$7,000

Model 375F
1959-1969. F-style, 2 pickups.

1959-1960	Thick version	$12,000	$15,000
1968-1969	Thin version	$10,000	$12,000

Model 380L Laguna
1996-2005. Semi-hollow, oil-finished walnut body, Maple neck and 'board, 2 humbuckers, PZ saddle pickups optional.

1996-2005		$2,500	$3,500
1996-2005	PZ option	$2,500	$3,500

Model 381
1969-1974. Double-cut archtop, 2 pickups, slash sound hole.

1969-1974	Various colors, some rare	$7,000	$9,500

Model 381/12V69
1987-2023. Reissue of 381/12, deep double-cut body, sound body cavity, catseye sound hole, triangle inlays, bridge with 12 individual saddles. Finishes include Fireglo, Mapleglo and Jetglo.

1987-2023	Figured top	$3,000	$4,000

Model 381JK (John Kay)
1988-1997. Limited Edition, 250 made, 2 humbucking pickups, active electronics, stereo and mono outputs, Jetglo black.

1988-1997		$3,000	$4,000

Model 381V69
1991-2023. Reissue of vintage 381.

1987-2023		$3,000	$4,000

Model 400/Combo 400
1956-1958. Double-cut tulip body, neck-thru, 1 pickup, gold anodized 'guard, 21 frets, replaced by Model 425 in '58. Available in black (216 made), blue

turquoise (53), Cloverfield Green (53), Montezuma Brown (41), and 4 in other custom colors.

MODEL YEAR	FEATURES	EXC. COND. LOW	HIGH
1956-1958		$6,000	$8,000

Model 420
1965-1983. Non-vibrato version of Model 425, single pickup.

1965-1968		$2,250	$2,875
1969-1983		$1,750	$2,250

Model 425/Combo 425
1958-1973. Double-cut solidbody, 1 pickup, sunburst.

1958-1959	425 Cresting Wave	$4,000	$5,000
1960		$3,000	$3,750
1961-1964		$2,250	$2,750
1965-1968		$2,000	$2,500
1969-1973		$1,750	$2,250

Model 425/12V63
1999-2000. 136 made.

1999-2000		$2,000	$2,500

Model 425V63
1999-2000. Beatles associated model, 145 JG black made, 116 BG burgundy transparent made, originally custom ordered by Rickenbacker collectors and they were not part of Rickenbacker's sales literature in the late '90s.

1999-2000		$2,000	$2,500

Model 430
1971-1982. Style 200 body, natural.

1971-1982		$1,000	$1,375

Model 450/Combo 450
1957-1984. Replaces Combo 450, 2 pickups (3 optional '62-'77), tulip body shape '57-'59, cresting wave body shape after.

1957-1958	450 Tulip body (Combo)	$5,500	$7,000
1958-1959	450 Cresting Wave	$4,000	$5,000
1960	Cresting Wave, flat body	$3,000	$3,750
1961-1966	Cresting Wave, super slim	$2,500	$3,250
1970-1979	Includes rare color	$2,250	$3,000
1980-1984		$1,500	$2,000

Model 450/12
1964-1985. Double-cut solidbody, 12-string version of Model 450, 2 pickups.

1964-1966		$3,000	$3,750
1967-1969		$2,750	$3,500
1970-1979	Includes rare color	$2,250	$2,750
1980-1985		$1,875	$2,375

Model 450V63
1999-2001. Reissue of '63 450.

1999-2001		$1,750	$2,250

Model 456/12 Convertible
1968-1978. Double-cut solidbody, 2 pickups, comb-like device to convert it to 6-string.

1968-1969		$3,500	$4,500
1970-1978		$3,000	$4,000

Model 460
1961-1985. Double-cut solidbody, 2 pickups, neck-thru-body, deluxe trim.

1961-1965		$3,500	$4,500
1966-1969		$3,000	$3,750

MODEL YEAR	FEATURES	EXC. COND. LOW	HIGH
1970-1979	Includes rare color	$2,500	$3,250
1980-1985		$1,750	$2,250

Model 480

1973-1984. Double-cut solidbody with long thin bass horn in 4001 bass series style, 2 pickups, cresting wave body and headstock, bolt-on neck.

1973-1979		$2,750	$3,625
1980-1984		$2,625	$3,500

Model 481

1973-1983. Cresting wave body with longer bass horn, 2 humbuckers (3 optional), angled frets.

1973-1979		$2,750	$3,625
1980-1983		$2,625	$3,500

Model 483

1973-1983. Cresting wave body with longer bass horn, 3 humbuckers.

1973-1979		$3,000	$4,000
1980-1983		$2,625	$3,500

Model 600/Combo 600

1954-1958. Modified double-cut, horseshoe pickup.

1954-1957	Blond/white	$6,000	$8,000
1956-1958	OT/Blue Turquoise	$6,000	$8,000

Model 610

1985-1991. Cresting-wave cutaway solidbody, 2 pickups, trapeze R-tailpiece, Jetglo.

1985-1991		$1,250	$1,625

Model 610/12

1988-1997. 12-string version of Model 610.

1988-1997		$1,500	$2,000

Model 615

1962-1966, 1969-1977. Double-cut solidbody, 2 pickups, vibrato.

1962-1965		$2,750	$3,500
1966-1977		$2,500	$3,125

Model 620

1974-present. Double-cut solidbody, deluxe binding, 2 pickups, neck-thru-body.

1974-1979		$2,250	$3,000
1980-2023		$2,000	$2,500

Model 620/12

1981-2023. Double-cut solidbody, 2 pickups, 12 strings, standard trim.

1981-2023		$2,000	$2,500

Model 625

1962-1977. Double-cut solidbody, deluxe trim, 2 pickups, vibrato.

1962-1963		$4,500	$6,000
1965-1969		$4,500	$5,500
1970-1977		$3,000	$4,000

Model 650/Combo 650

1957-1959. Standard color, 1 pickup.

1957-1959		$5,000	$6,500

Model 650A Atlantis

1992-2003. Double cut cresting wave solidbody, maple body wings, neck-thru, 2 pickups, chrome hardware, turquoise.

1992-2003		$1,500	$2,000

Model 650C Colorado

1993-2017. Like Atlantis but with black finish.

1993-2017		$1,500	$2,000

Model 650D Dakota

1993-2017. Like Atlantis but with walnut body wings and oil-satin finish.

1993-2017		$1,500	$2,000

Model 650E Excalibur/F Frisco

1991-2003. Like Atlantis but with brown vermilion body wings and gold hardware. Name changed to Frisco in '95.

1991-2003		$1,500	$2,000

Model 650S Sierra

1993-2017. Like Dakota but with gold hardware.

1993-2017		$1,500	$2,000

Model 660

1998-present. Cresting wave maple body, triangle inlays, 2 pickups.

1998-2023		$2,250	$3,000

Model 660/12

1998-present. 12-string 660.

1998-2023		$3,000	$4,000

Model 660/12TP (Tom Petty)

1991-1998. Tom Petty model, 12 strings, cresting wave body, 2 pickups, deluxe trim, limited run of 1000, certificate of authenticity.

1991-1998	With certificate	$5,750	$7,500

Model 660DCM 75th Anniversary

2006-2007. 75th 1931-2006 Anniversary pickguard logo.

2006-2007		$2,500	$3,500

Model 800/Combo 800

1954-1959. Offset double-cut, 1 horseshoe pickup until late-'57, second bar type after.

1954-1957	Blond/white, 1 pickup	$7,500	$9,500
1954-1957	Blue or green, 1 pickup	$7,500	$9,500
1957-1959	Blond/white, 2 pickups	$7,500	$9,500
1957-1959	Blue or green, 2 pickups	$7,500	$9,500

Model 850/Combo 850

1957-1959. Extreme double-cut, 1 pickup until '58, 2 after, various colors, called Model 850 in the '60s.

1957-1959	Various colors	$7,500	$9,500

Model 900/Combo 900

1957-1980. Double-cut tulip body shape, 3/4 size, 1 pickup. Body changes to cresting wave shape in '69.

1957-1966		$2,500	$3,500

Model 950/Combo 950

1957-1980. Like Model 900, but with 2 pickups, 21 frets. Body changes to cresting wave shape in '69.

1957-1964		$3,000	$4,000
1965-1980		$2,250	$2,750

Model 1000

1956-1970. Like Model 900, but with 18 frets, 1 pickup, black and white. Body does not change to cresting wave shape.

1956-1966		$2,000	$2,500
1967-1970		$2,000	$2,500

1983 Rickenbacker 620
Jeff DiPaola

Rickenbacker 660
Ron O'Keefe

1964 Rickenbacker Model 950
Rivington Guitars

Rigaud Acoustics Parlor

MODEL YEAR	FEATURES	EXC. COND. LOW	HIGH

Model 1993/12RM (Rose-Morris)
1964-1967. Export 'slim-line' 12-string model made for English distributor Rose-Morris of London, built along the lines of the U.S. Model 360/12 but with small differences that are considered important in the vintage guitar market.

July 1964	Flat tailpiece (stubby), 25 made	$25,000	$35,000
1964-1967	R tailpiece, 75 made	$22,000	$30,000

Model 1995RM (Rose-Morris)
1964-1967. Rose-Morris import.

1964-1967		$3,500	$5,000

Model 1996RM (Rose-Morris)
1964-1967. Rose-Morris import, 3/4 size built similarly to the U.S. Model 325.

1964-1967		$8,000	$12,000

Model 1996RM Reissue
2006. Reissue of the Rose-Morris version of Model 325, this reissue available on special order in 2006.

2006		$3,000	$4,000

Model 1997PT (Pete Townshend)
1987-1988. Pete Townshend Signature Model, semi-hollowbody, single f-hole, maple neck, 21-fret rosewood 'board, 3 pickups, Firemist finish, limited to 250 total production.

1987-1988		$3,000	$4,000

Model 1997RM (Rose-Morris)
1964-1967. Export 'slim-line' model made for English distributor Rose-Morris of London, built along the lines of the U.S. Model 335, but with small differences that are considered important in the vintage guitar market, 2 pickups, vibrola tailpiece. Rose-Morris export models sent to the USA generally had a red-lined guitar case vs. the USA domestic blue-lined guitar case.

1964-1967		$6,500	$9,000

Model 1997RM Reissue
1987-1995. Reissue of '60s Rose-Morris model, but with vibrola (VB) or without.

1987-1995		$2,500	$3,250

Model 1997SPC
1993-2002. 3 pickup version of reissue.

1993-2002		$2,000	$2,500

Model 1998RM (Rose-Morris)
1964-1967. Export 'slim-line' model made for English distributor Rose-Morris of London, built along the lines of a U.S. Model 345 but with small differences that are considered important in the vintage guitar market, 3 pickups, vibrola tailpiece.

1964-1967		$6,500	$9,000

Rickenbacker Spanish/Spanish/SP
1946-1949. Block markers.

1946-1949		$2,250	$2,875

S-59
1940-1942. Arch top body built by Kay, horseshoe magnet pickup.

1940-1942		$2,000	$2,500

Rigaud Guitars
1978-present. Luthier Robert Rigaud builds his premium grade, custom, parlor to jumbo acoustic guitars in Greensboro, North Carolina. He also builds ukuleles under the New Moon brand.

Ritz
1989. Solidbody electric guitars and basses produced in Calimesa, California, by Wayne Charvel, Eric Galletta and Brad Becnel, many of which featured cracked shell mosiac finishes.

RKS
Professional and premium grade, production/custom, electric hollowbody and solidbody guitars and basses designed by Ravi Sawhney and guitarist Dave Mason and built in Thousand Oaks, California. They began in 2003.

Robert Cefalu
Luthier Robert Cefalu built his professional grade, production/custom, acoustic guitars in Buffalo, New York. The guitars have an RC on the headstock.

Robert Guitars
1981-present. Luthier Mikhail Robert builds his premium grade, production/custom, classical guitars in Summerland, British Columbia.

Robertson Guitars
1995-present. Luthier Jeff Robertson builds his premium grade, production/custom flat-top guitars in South New Berlin, New York.

Robin
1982-2010. Professional and premium grade, production/custom, guitars from luthier David Wintz and built in Houston, Texas. Most guitars were Japanese made until '87; American production began in '88. Most Japanese Robins were pretty consistent in features, but the American ones were often custom-made, so many variations in models exist. They also made Metropolitan ('96-'08) and Alamo ('00-'08) brand guitars.

Avalon Classic
1994-2010. Single-cut, figured maple top, 2 humbuckers.

1994-2010	Various options	$1,625	$2,000

Medley Pro
1990s. Solidbody with 2 extreme cutaway horns, hum-single-single.

1990s	US-made	$1,125	$1,500

Medley Special
1992-1995. Ash body, maple neck, rosewood 'board, 24 frets, various pickup options.

1992-1995		$725	$900

Medley Standard
1985-2010. Offset double-cut swamp ash solidbody, bolt neck, originally with hum-single-single pickups, but now also available with 2 humbuckers.

1985-1987	Japan-made	$600	$750
1988-2010	US-made	$1,250	$1,500

The Vintage Guitar Price Guide shows values for all-original, excellent condition instruments and, where applicable, with original case.

MODEL YEAR	FEATURES	EXC. COND. LOW	HIGH

Octave

1982-1990s. Tuned an octave above standard tuning, full body size with 15 1/2" short-scale bolt maple neck. Japanese-made production model until '87, U.S.-made custom shop after.

1990s	With original case	$775	$1,000

Raider I/Raider II/Raider III

1985-1991. Double-cut solidbody, 1 humbucker pickup (Raider I), 2 humbuckers (Raider II), or 3 single-coils (Raider III), maple neck, either maple or rosewood 'board, sunburst.

1985-1991	1 pickup	$500	$625
1985-1991	2 pickups	$550	$675
1985-1991	3 pickups	$600	$750

Ranger

1982. First production model with 2 single-coil pickups in middle and neck position, reverse headstock, dot markers.

1982		$1,125	$1,500

Ranger Custom

1982-1986, 1988-2010. Swamp ash bound body, bolt-on maple neck, rosewood or maple 'board, 2 single coils and 1 humbucker, orange, made in Japan until '86, U.S.-made after.

1982-1986	Japan-made	$600	$750
1988-2010	US-made	$1,125	$1,500

RDN-Doubleneck Octave/Six

1982-1985. Six-string standard neck with 3 pickups, 6-string octave neck with 1 pickup, double-cut solidbody.

1982-1985	With original case	$1,375	$1,750

Savoy Deluxe/Standard

1995-2010. Semi-hollow thinline single cut archtop, 2 pickups, set neck.

1996-2010		$1,625	$2,000

Soloist/Artisan

1982-1986. Mahogany double-cut solidbody, carved bound maple top, set neck, 2 humbuckers. Renamed Artisan in '85. Only about 125 made in Japan.

1982-1986		$850	$1,125

Wedge

1985-ca. 1988. Triangle-shaped body, 2 humbuckers, Custom with set neck and triangle inlays, Standard with bolt neck and dots, about 200 made.

1980s		$1,250	$1,625

Wrangler

1995-2002. Classic '50s single-cut slab body, 3 Rio Grande pickups, opaque finish.

1995-2002		$850	$1,125

Robinson Guitars

2002-present. Premium and presentation grade, custom/production, steel string guitars built by luthier Jake Robinson first in Kalamazoo, and since '08 in Hoxeyville, Michigan.

RockBeach Guitars

2005-present. Luthier Greg Bogoshian builds his custom, professional grade, chambered electric guitars and basses in Rochester, New York.

Rockinbetter

2011-2014. Intermediate grade, production electric guitars and basses, copies of Rickenbacker models, made in China.

Rocking F

See listing under Fox.

Rockit Guitar

Luthier Rod MacKenzie builds his premium grade, custom, electric guitars and basses in Everett, Washington, starting in 2006.

Rogands

Late 1960s. Produced by France's Jacobacci company and named after brothers Roger and Andre. Short-lived brand; the brothers made instruments under several other brands as well.

Roger

Guitars built in Germany by luthier Wenzel Rossmeisl and named for his son Roger. Roger Rossmeisl would go on to work at Rickenbacker and Fender.

Rogue

2001-present. Budget and intermediate grade, production, acoustic, resonator, electric and sitar guitars and basses. They also offer mandolins, banjos, ukuleles, and lap steels. They previously offered effects and amps. Fender offered instruments branded Rogue by Squire for a short period starting in '99.

Roland

Best known for keyboards, effects, and amps, Roland offered synthesizer-based guitars and basses from 1977 to '97.

Rolando

1916-ca. 1919. Private branded instruments made for the Southern California Music Company of Los Angeles, by Martin. There were three models.

00-28K/1500

1916-1919		$10,000	$13,000

Rolf Spuler

1981-2014. Presentation grade, custom, hybrid electric-acoustic guitars, built by luthier Rolf Spuler in Gebenstorf, Switzerland. He also built basses. He passed away in '14.

Roman & Lipman Guitars

1989-2000. Production/custom, solidbody guitars and basses made in Danbury, Connecticut by Ed Roman Guitars.

Roman Abstract Guitars

1989-present. Professional and premium grade, production/custom, solidbody guitars made by Ed Roman Guitars.

Robin Octave
Allen Eagles

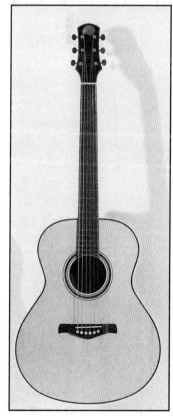

Robinson Small Jumbo

RS Guitarworks Slab
Blackguard

S. Walker Custom
The Revelator

MODEL		EXC. COND.	
YEAR	FEATURES	LOW	HIGH

Roman Centurion Guitars

2001-present. Premium and presentation grade, custom guitars made by Ed Roman Guitars.

Roman Pearlcaster Guitars

1999-present. Professional and premium grade, production/custom, solidbody guitars made by Ed Roman Guitars.

Roman Quicksilver Guitars

1997-present. Professional and premium grade, production/custom, solid and hollow-body guitars made by Ed Roman Guitars.

Roman RVC Guitars

1999-present. Professional and premium grade, production/custom, solidbody guitars made by Ed Roman Guitars.

Roman Vampire Guitars

2004-2020. Professional and premium grade, production/custom, solidbody guitars made by Ed Roman Guitars. Special orders only about '13-'20.

Rono

In 1967 luthier Ron Oates began building professional and premium grade, production/custom, flattop, jazz, Wiesenborn-style, and resonator guitars and basses in Boulder, Colorado. He also built mandolins.

Ro-Pat-In

See Rickenbacker.

Rosetti

1950s-1960s. Guitars imported into England by distributor Rosetti, made by Holland's Egmond, and maybe others.

Solid 7

1960s. Symmetrical cutaway electric semi-hollow, large 'guard with top-mounted dual pickups, 4 control knobs, value is associated with Paul McCartney's use in '60, value dependent on completely original McCartney specs.

1960s	McCartney model	$2,250	$3,000
1960s	Various other	$650	$850

Roudhloff

1810s-1840s. Luthier Francois Roudhloff built his instruments in France. Labels could state F. Roudhloff-Mauchand or Roudhloff Brothers. Valuation depends strongly on condition and repair. His sons built guitars under the D & A Roudhloff label.

Rowan

Professional and premium grade, production/custom, solidbody and acoustic/electric guitars built by luthier Michael Rowan in Garland, Texas.

Royal

Ca. 1954-ca. 1965. Line of jazz style guitars made by France's Jacobacci company, which also built under its own brand.

Royal (Japan)

1957-1960s. Early budget level instruments made by Tokyo Sound Company and Gakki and exported by Japan's Hoshino (Ibanez).

Royden Guitars

Professional grade, production/custom, flat-tops and solidbody electrics built by luthier Royden Moran in Peterborough, Ontario, starting in 1996.

RS Guitarworks

1994-present. Professional grade, production/custom, solid and hollowbody guitars built by luthier Roy Bowen in Winchester, Kentucky.

Rubio, German Vasquez

1993-present. Luthier German Vasquez Rubio builds his professional and premium grade, production/custom classical and flamenco guitars in Los Angeles, California.

Ruck, Robert

1966-2018. Premium grade, custom classical and flamenco guitars built by luthier Robert Ruck originally in Kalaheo, Hawaii, then in Eugene, Oregon. Ruck died in '18.

Running Dog Guitars

1994-present. Luthier Rick Davis builds his professional and premium grade, custom flat-tops in Seattle, Washington. He was originally located in Richmond, Vermont.

Ruokangas

1995-present. Luthier Juha Ruokangas builds his premium and presentation grade, production/custom, solidbody and semi-acoustic electric guitars in Hyvinkaa, Finland.

Rustler

1993-ca. 1998. Solidbody electrics with hand-tooled leather bound and studded sides and R branded into the top, built by luthier Charles Caponi in Mason City, Iowa.

RWK

1991-present. Luthier Bob Karger builds his intermediate grade, production/custom, solidbody electrics and travel guitars in Highland Park, Illinois.

Ryder

1963. Made by Rickenbacker, the one model with this brand was the same as their solidbody Model 425.

S. Walker Custom Guitars

2002-present. Luthier Scott Walker builds his premium grade, production/custom, solid and semi hollow body electric guitars in Santa Cruz, California.

S. Yairi

Ca. 1960-1980s. Steel string folk guitars and classical nylon string guitars by master Japanese

MODEL		EXC. COND.	
YEAR	FEATURES	LOW	HIGH

luthier Sadao Yairi, imported by Philadelphia Music Company of Limerick, Pennsylvania. Early sales literature called the brand Syairi. Most steel string models have dreadnought bodies and nylon-string classical guitars are mostly standard grand concert size. All models are handmade. Steel string Jumbos and dreadnoughts have Syairi logo on the headstock, nylon-classical models have no logo. The Model 900 has a solid wood body, others assumed to have laminate bodies.

S.B. Brown Guitars

Custom flat-tops made by luthier Steve Brown in Fullerton, California.

S.B. MacDonald Custom Instruments

1988-present. Professional and premium grade, custom/production, flat-top, resonator, and solid-body guitars built by luthier Scott B. MacDonald in Huntington, New York.

S.D. Curlee

1975-1982. Founded in Matteson, Illinois by music store owner Randy Curlee, after an unsuccessful attempt to recruit builder Dan Armstrong. S.D. Curlee guitars were made in Illinois, while S.D. Curlee International instruments were made by Matsumoku in Japan. The guitars featured mostly Watco oil finishes, often with exotic hardwoods, and unique neck-thru-bridge construction on American and Japanese instruments. These were the first production guitars to use a single-coil pickup at the bridge with a humbucker at the neck, and a square brass nut. DiMarzio pickups. Offered in a variety of shapes, later some copies. Approximately 12,000 American-made basses and 3,000 guitars were made, most of which were sold overseas. Two hundred were made in '75-'76; the first production guitar numbered 518.

Electric Solidbody

1975-1982. Models include the '75-'81 Standard I, II and III, '76-'81 International C-10 and C-11, '80-'81 Yankee, Liberty, Butcher, Curbeck, Summit, Special, and the '81-'82 Destroyer, Flying V.

1975-1982		$500	$650

S.L. Smith Guitars

Professional grade, production/custom, acoustic guitars built by Steven Smith in Brant Lake, New York beginning in 2007.

S.S. Stewart

The original S.S. Stewart Company (1878-1904), of Philadelphia, Pennsylvania is considered to be one of the most important banjo manufacturers of the late 19th century. Samuel Swaim Stewart died in 1888 and his family was out of the company by the early 1900s, and the brand was soon acquired by Bugellsein & Jacobsen of New York. The brand name was used on guitars into the 1960s.

Flat-Top

1930s. Gibson L-2 style body.

1932		$9,500	$12,000

S101

Budget and intermediate grade, production, classical, acoustic, resonator, solid and semi-hollow body guitars and basses imported from China by America Sejung Corp. They also offer mandolins, and banjos.

Sadowsky

1980-present. Professional and premium grade, production/custom, solidbody, semi-hollowbody, archtop, and electric nylon-string guitars built by luthier Roger Sadowsky in Brooklyn, New York. He also builds basses and amps. In '96, luthier Yoshi Kikuchi started building Sadowsky Tokyo instruments in Japan.

Saga

Saga Musical Instruments, of San Francisco, California distributes a wide variety of instruments and brands, occasionally including their own line of solidbody guitars called the Saga Gladiator Scrics (1987-'88, '94-'95). In the 2000s, Saga also offered component kits ($90-$130) that allowed for complete assembly in white wood.

Sahlin Guitars

Luthier Eric Sahlin hs built his premium grade, custom, classical and flamenco guitars in Spokane, Washington since 1975.

Samick

1958-2001, 2002-present. Budget, intermediate and professional grade, production, imported acoustic and electric guitars and basses. They also offer mandolins, ukes and banjos and distribute Abilene and Silvertone brand instruments.

Samick started out producing pianos, adding guitars in '65 under other brands. In '88 Samick greatly increased their guitar production. The Samick line of 350 models was totally closed out in 2001. A new line of 250 models was introduced January 2002 at NAMM. All 2002 models have the new compact smaller headstock and highly styled S logo.

Sammo

1920s. Labels on these instruments state they were made by the Osborne Mfg. Co. with an address of Masonic Temple, Chicago, Illinois. High quality and often with a high degree of ornamentation. They also made ukes and mandolins.

Sand Guitars

Luthier Kirk Sand opened the Guitar Shoppe in Laguna Beach, California in 1972 with James Matthews. By '79, he started producing his own line of premium grade, production/custom-made flat-tops.

Sadowsky SS-15

Saga Blueridge

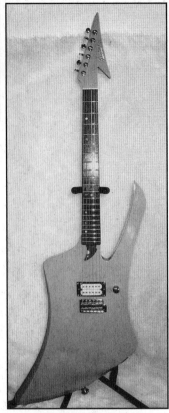

Sandoval Flamingo

1992 Santa Cruz OM

Marshall Fleisher

MODEL		EXC. COND.	
YEAR	FEATURES	LOW	HIGH

Sandoval Engineering

1979-present. Luthier Karl Sandoval builds his premium grade, custom, solidbody guitars in Santa Fe Springs, California.

Sano

1944-ca. 1970. Sano was a New Jersey-based accordion company that imported Italian-made solid and semi-hollow body guitars for a few years, starting in 1966; some, if not all, made by Zero Sette. They also built their own amps and reverb units.

Santa Cruz

1976-present. Professional, premium and presentation grade, production/custom, flat-top, 12-string, and archtop guitars from luthier Richard Hoover in Santa Cruz, California. They also build a mandocello and ukuleles. Founded by Hoover, Bruce Ross and William Davis. Hoover became sole owner in '89. Custom ordered instruments with special upgrades may have higher values than the ranges listed here. Other models offer "build-your-own" options on woods and features and this means larger value ranges on those instruments.

00 12-Fret

1997-present. Indian rosewood, Brazilian offered in 2006.

1997-2023	Indian rosewood	$3,500	$4,500
2006	Brazilian rosewood	$8,500	$12,000

000 12-Fret

1994-present. 000 size, 12-fret body, Indian rosewood back and sides, ebony 'board, ivoroid binding.

1994-2023	Indian rosewood	$3,500	$4,500
2011	Brazilian rosewood	$8,500	$12,000

Archtop

Early 1980s-2010. Originally the FJZ, by mid-'90s, called the Archtop, offering 16", 17" and 18" cutaway acoustic/electric models, often special order. Curly maple body, ebony 'board, floating pickup, f-holes, sunburst or natural. Many custom options are available.

1980s-90s		$4,250	$5,500

Bob Brozman Baritone

1998-2019. Flat-top acoustic, mahogany body, spruce top.

1998-2019		$4,250	$5,500

D 12-Fret

1994-present. 12-fret neck, slotted headstock, round shoulders, mahogany back and sides, notch diamond markers, herringbone trim. Special orders vary in value and could exceed the posted range.

1994-2023		$3,750	$4,750

D Koa

1980s-1990s. Style D with Koa back and sides.

1980s-90s		$3,750	$4,750

D/HR

Style D with Indian rosewood back and sides, Brazilian rosewood headstock overlay.

2000		$3,750	$4,750

D/PW Pre-War

2001-present. Pre-war D-style. "Build-your-own" options cause a wide value range.

2001-2023	Various models	$3,500	$4,500

MODEL		EXC. COND.	
YEAR	FEATURES	LOW	HIGH

Eric Skye 00

Signature model, Cocobolo/Adirondack.

2020		$5,500	$7,000

F

1979-present. 15 7/8" scale with narrow waist, Sitka spruce top, Indian rosewood back and sides, natural.

1979-2023		$4,000	$5,500

F46R

1980s. Brazilian rosewood, single-cut.

1980s		$4,750	$6,250

Firefly

2009-present. Premium quality travel/parlor guitar, cedar top, flamed maple sides and back.

2009-2023		$3,500	$4,500

FS (Finger Style)

1988-present. Single-cut, cedar top, Indian rosewood back and sides, mahogany neck, modified X-bracing.

1988-2023		$3,750	$4,750

H

1977-present. Parlor size, originally a 13-fret neck, but soon changed to 14, Indian rosewood back and sides. The H A/E ('92-'04) added electronics and cutaway.

1977-2023	Indian rosewood	$3,750	$4,750
1994	Flamed Koa	$4,750	$6,250
2005	Brazilian rosewood	$8,500	$12,000

H/13

2004-present. Like H, but with 13-fret neck, mahogany back and sides and slotted headstock.

2004-2023	Mahogany	$4,000	$5,000
2005	Flamed Koa	$4,750	$6,250

H91

1990s. 14 5/8", flamed Koa.

1990s		$4,750	$6,250

Model 1929 00

2010-present. 00-size, all mahogany, 12-fret neck.

2010-2023		$3,500	$4,500

OM (Orchestra Model)

1987-present. Orchestra model acoustic, Sitka spruce top, Indian rosewood (Brazilian optional) back and sides, herringbone rosette, scalloped braces.

1987-2023	Brazilian rosewood	$7,500	$9,500
1987-2023	Indian rosewood	$3,750	$4,750
1995	Koa	$4,750	$6,250
2002	German spruce	$5,500	$7,000
2010	Italian spruce	$6,000	$7,750
2012	Figured mahogany	$6,750	$8,750

OM/PW Pre-War

1999-present. Indian rosewood, advanced X and scalloped top bracing.

1999-2023		$3,750	$4,750

PJ

1990s-present. Parlor-size, Indian rosewood back and sides, 24" scale, 12-fret neck.

1990s-2023		$3,750	$4,750

Style 1

Indian rosewood standard, various other woods optional.

2014	Brazilian, Adirondack	$10,000	$15,000

The *Vintage Guitar Price Guide* shows values for all-original, excellent condition instruments and, where applicable, with original case.

MODEL		EXC. COND.	
YEAR	FEATURES	LOW	HIGH

Tony Rice

1976-present. Dreadnought, Indian rosewood body (Brazilian optional until Tony Rice Professional model available), Sitka spruce top, solid peghead, zigzag back stripe, pickup optional.

1976-2023		$4,500	$5,500

Tony Rice Professional

1997-present. Brazilian rosewood back and sides, carved German spruce top, zigzag back stripe, solid peghead.

1997-2023		$8,500	$12,000

Vintage Artist (VA)

1992-present. Mahogany body, Sitka spruce top, zigzag back stripe, solid peghead, scalloped X-bracing, pickup optional.

1992-2023		$3,750	$4,750

Vintage Artist Custom

1992-2004. Martin D-42 style, mahogany body, Indian rosewood back and sides, Sitka spruce top, zigzag back stripe, solid peghead, scalloped X-bracing, pickup optional.

1992-2004		$3,750	$4,750

Vintage Jumbo (VJ)

2000-present. 16" scale, round shouldered body, Sitka spruce, figured mahogany back and sides, natural.

2000-2023		$3,750	$4,750

Vintage Southerner (VS)

2007-present. Sitka spruce top standard, various other woods optional.

2007-2023		$5,750	$7,500

Santos Martinez

Ca. 1997-present. Intermediate grade, production, acoustic and electro-acoustic classical guitars, imported from China by John Hornby Skewes & Co. in the U.K.

Sardonyx

1978-1979. Guitars and basses built by luthier Jeff Levin in the back of Matt Umanov's New York City guitar shop, industrial looking design with 2 aluminum outrigger-style tubes extended from the rectangle body. Very limited production.

Saturn

1960s-1970s. Imported, most likely from Japan, solid and semi-hollow body electric guitars and basses. Large S logo with Saturn name inside the S. Many sold through Eaton's in Canada.

Saturn

1960s-1970s. Solidbody, 4 pickups.

1960s		$550	$750
1970s		$500	$650

Sawchyn Guitars

1972-2023. Professional and premium grade, production/custom, flat-top and flamenco guitars and mandolins built by luthier Peter Sawchyn in Regina, Saskatchewan.

Schaefer

1997-2014. Premium grade, production/custom, flat-top acoustic guitars built by luthier Edward A. Schaefer in Austin, Texas. He previously built archtops, basses and mandolins. He retired in '14.

Schecter

1976-present. Intermediate, professional and premium grade, production/custom, acoustic and electric guitars and basses. Guitar component manufacturer founded in California by four partners (David Schecter's name sounded the best), started offering complete instruments in '79. The company was bought out and moved to Dallas, Texas in the early '80s. By '88 the company was back in California and in '89 was purchased by Hisatake Shibuya. Schecter Custom Shop guitars are made in Burbank, California and their intermediate grade Diamond Series is made in South Korea.

Scheerhorn

1989-present. Professional and premium grade, custom, resonator and Hawaiian guitars built by luthier Tim Scheerhorn in Kentwood, Michigan. Around 2010, Scheerhorn becomes a division of National Reso-Phonic.

Schoenberg

1986-present. Premium grade, production/custom, flat-tops offered by Eric Schoenberg of Tiburon, California. From '86-'94 guitars were made to Schoenberg's specifications by Martin. From '86-'90 constructed by Schoenberg's luthier and from '90-'94 assembled by Martin but voiced and inlaid in the Schoenberg shop. Current models made to Schoenberg specs by various smaller shops.

Schon

1986-1991. Designed by guitarist Neal Schon, early production by Charvel/Jackson building about 200 in the San Dimas factory. The final 500 were built by Larrivee in Canada. Leo Knapp also built custom Schon guitars from '85-'87, and '90s custom-made Schon guitars were also available.

Standard (Canada)

1987-1991. Made in Canada on headstock.

1987-1991		$750	$1,000

Standard (U.S.A.)

1986 only. Made in U.S.A. on headstock, San Dimas/Jackson model, single-cut, pointy headstock shape.

1986		$1,750	$2,250

Schramm Guitars

1990-present. Premium grade, production/custom, classical and flamenco guitars built by luthier David Schramm in Clovis, California.

Schroder Guitars

Luthier Timothy Schroeder (he drops the first e in his name on the guitars) builds premium grade, production/custom, archtops in Northbrook, Illinois. He began in 1993.

Schechter Blackjack
SLS Avenger
Michael Mitchell

Schoenberg Standard

GUITARS

Seagull Maritime SWS
Concert Hall SG

Sheppard Guitars

MODEL		EXC. COND.	
YEAR	FEATURES	LOW	HIGH

Schulte
1950s-2000. Luthier C. Eric Schulte made solid-body, semi-hollow body, hollowbody and acoustic guitars, both original designs and copies, covering a range of prices, in the Philadelphia area.

Custom Copy
1982. Single-cut solidbody, figured maple top.

1982		$900	$1,125

Schulz
Ca. 1903-1917. Luthier August Schulz built harp guitars and lute-guitars in Nuremberg, Germany.

Harp Guitar

1906		$1,250	$1,625

Schwartz Guitars
1992-present. Premium grade, custom, flat-top guitars built by luthier Sheldon Schwartz in Concord, Ontario.

ScoGo
Professional and premium grade, production/custom, solidbody guitars built by luthier Scott Gordon in Parkesburg, Pennsylvania starting in 2001.

Scorpion Guitars
1998-2014. Professional and premium grade, custom, solidbody guitars made by Ed Roman Guitars.

Scott French
2004-present. Professional grade, production/custom, electric guitars and basses built by luthier Scott French in Auburn, California. In '12 he discontinued offering custom built.

Scott Walker Custom Guitars
Refer to S. Walker Custom Guitars.

SeaGlass Guitars USA
2011-present. Professional grade, production/custom, electric guitars, built by luthier Roger Mello in Groton, Massachusetts.

Seagull
1982-present. Intermediate grade, production, acoustic and acoustic/electric guitars built in Canada. Seagull was founded by luthier Robert Godin, who also has the Norman, Godin, and Patrick & Simon brands of instruments.

Sebring
1980s-mid-1990s. Entry level Korean imports distributed by V.M.I. Industries.

Seiwa
Early 1980s. Entry-level to mid-level Japanese electric guitars and basses, logo may indicate Since 1956.

MODEL		EXC. COND.	
YEAR	FEATURES	LOW	HIGH

Sekova
Mid-1960s-mid-1970s. Entry level instruments imported by the U.S. Musical Merchandise Corporation of New York.

Selmer
1932-1952. France-based Selmer & Cie was primarily a maker of wind instruments when they asked Mario Maccaferri to design a line of guitars for them. The guitars, with an internal sound chamber for increased volume, were built in Mantes-la-Ville. Both gut and steel string models were offered. Maccaferri left Selmer in '33, but guitar production continued, and the original models are gradually phased out. In '36, only the 14 fret oval model was built. Production stopped for WWII and resumed in '46, finally stopping in '52. Less than 900 guitars are built in total.

Classique
1942. Solid Rosewood back and sides, no cutaway, solid spruce top, round sound hole, classical guitar size, possibly only 2 built.

1942		$5,500	$7,500

Concert
1932-1933. For gut strings, cutaway, laminated Indian rosewood back and sides, internal resonator, spruce top with D hole, wide walnut neck, ebony 'board, only a few dozen built.

1932		$12,000	$16,000
1933		$16,500	$22,000

Eddie Freeman Special
1933. For steel strings, 4 strings, laminated Indian rosewood back and sides, cutaway, no internal resonator, solid spruce top, D hole, black and white rosette inlays, walnut 12 fret neck, ebony 'board, 640mm scale, approx. 100 made.

1933		$6,000	$7,500

Espagnol
1932. For gut strings, laminated Indian rosewood back and sides, no cutaway, internal resonator, solid spruce top, round soundhole, wide walnut neck, ebony 'board, only a few made.

1932		$8,500	$11,500

Grand Modele 4 Cordes
1932-1933. For steel strings, 4 string model, laminated back and sides, cutaway, internal resonator, solid spruce top, D hole, walnut neck, ebony 'board, 12 fret, 640mm scale, 2 or 3 dozen made.

1932-1933		$12,500	$16,500

Harp Guitar
1933. For gut strings, solid mahogany body, extended horn holding 3 sub bass strings, 3 screw adjustable neck, wide walnut neck, ebony 'board, only about 12 built.

1933		$12,500	$16,500

Hawaienne
1932-1934. For steel strings, 6 or 7 strings, laminated back and sides, no cutaway, internal resonator, solid spruce top, D hole, wide walnut neck, ebony 'board, 2 or 3 dozen built.

1932-1934		$25,000	$33,000

Modele Jazz
1936-1942, 1946-1952. For steel strings, laminated Indian rosewood back and sides (some laminated or

MODEL YEAR	FEATURES	EXC. COND. LOW	HIGH

solid mahogany), cutaway, solid spruce top, small oval soundhole, walnut neck, ebony 'board (latest ones with rosewood necks), 14 fret to the body, 670mm scale. Production interrupted for WWII.

| 1936-1952 | | $33,000 | $45,000 |

Modeles de Transition

1934-1936. Transition models appearing before 14 fret oval hole model, some in solid maple with solid headstock, some with round soundhole and cutaway, some 12 fret models with oval hole.

| 1934-1936 | | $20,000 | $25,000 |

Orchestre

1932-1934. For steel strings, laminated back and sides, cutaway, internal resonator, solid spruce top, D hole, walnut neck, ebony 'board, about 100 made.

| 1932-1934 | | $35,000 | $45,000 |

Tenor

1932-1933. For steel strings, 4 strings, laminated back and sides, internal resonator, solid spruce top, D hole, walnut neck, ebony 'board, 12 fret, 570mm scale, 2 or 3 dozen built.

| 1932-1933 | | $5,000 | $6,500 |

Serenghetti

2007-present. Luthier Ray Patterson builds professional and premium grade, production/custom, 1-piece and neck-thru guitars and basses in Ocala, Florida.

Serge Guitars

1995-present. Luthier Serge Michaud builds his production/custom, classical, steel-string, resophonic and archtop guitars in Breakeyville, Quebec.

Series 10

1980s. Budget grade electric guitars, Series 10 by Bently on headstock.

Sexauer Guitars

1967-present. Premium and presentation grade, custom, steel-string, 12-string, nylon-string, and archtop guitars built by luthier Bruce Sexauer in Petaluma, California.

Shadow

1990s. Made in Europe, copy models such as the classic offset double cutaway solidbody, large Shadow logo on headstock, Shadow logo on pickup cover, student to intermediate grade.

Shanti Guitars

1985-2019. Premium and presentation grade, custom, steel-string, 12-string, nylon-string and archtop guitars built by luthier Michael Hornick in Avery, California. He made a few more guitars after retiring in '19.

Shelley D. Park Guitars

1991-present. Luthier Shelley D. Park builds her professional grade, custom, nylon- and steel-string guitars in Vancouver, British Columbia.

Shelton-Farretta

1967-present. Premium grade, production/custom, flamenco, and classical guitars built by luthiers John Shelton and Susan Farretta originally in Portland, Oregon, and since '05 in Alsea, Oregon.

Sheppard Guitars

1993-present. Luthier Gerald Sheppard builds his premium grade, production/custom, steel-string guitars in Kingsport, Tennessee.

Shergold

1968-1992. Founded by Jack Golder and Norman Houlder, Shergold originally made guitars for other brands like Hayman and Barnes and Mullins. In '75, they started building guitars and basses under their own name. By '82, general guitar production was halted but custom orders were filled through '90. In '91, general production was again started but ended in '92 when Golder died.

Sherwood

Late 1940s-early 1950s. Archtop and lap steel guitars made for Montgomery Ward by Chicago manufacturers such as Kay. There were also Sherwood amps made by Danelectro. Value ranges are about the same as Kay model equivalent.

Shifflett

1990-present. Luthier Charles Shifflett builds his premium grade, production/custom, flat-top, classical, flamenco, resophonic, and harp guitars and basses in High River, Alberta. He also builds banjos.

Sho-Bro

1969-1978. Spanish and Hawaiian style resonator guitars made by Sho-Bud in Nashville, Tennessee and distributed by Gretsch. Designed by Shot Jackson and Buddy Emmons.

7-String Dobro

| 1972-1978 | | $1,500 | $2,000 |

Grand Slam

1978. Acoustic, spruce top, mahogany neck, jacaranda sides and back, and mother-of-pearl inlays, abalone sound hole purfling.

| 1970s | | $750 | $950 |

Resonator

1972-1978. Flat-top style guitar with metal resonator with 2 small circular grilled sound holes.

| 1972-1978 | | $1,250 | $1,625 |

Siegmund Guitars & Amplifiers

Luthier Chris Siegmund builds his professional, premium, and presentation grade, custom/production, archtop, solidbody, and resonator guitars in Los Angeles, California. He founded the company in Seattle in 1993, moving to Austin, Texas for '95-'97. He also builds amps and effects pedals.

Sherwood Deluxe
Donald DiLoreto

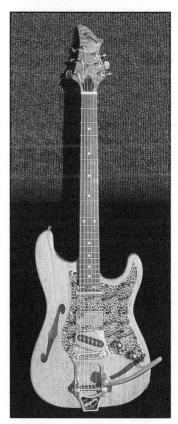

Siegmund Outcaster

Silvertone Espanada
Mercedes Girard

1960 Silvertone Model 1423L Jupiter
Tom Pfeifer

MODEL YEAR	FEATURES	EXC. COND. LOW	HIGH

Sierra
Budget level imports by Musicorp, starting in 2006. There is an unrelated brand of Sierra steels and lap steels.

Sigma
1970-2007. Budget and intermediate grade, production, import acoustic and electric guitars and basses distributed by C.F. Martin Company. They also offered mandolins and banjos. Japanese-made for 1970-'72; lower-end model production moved to Korea in '73; most of remaining Japanese production moved to Korea in '83; most production moved to Taiwan and Indonesia in '96.

Acoustic/Acoustic Electric/Electric
1970-2007	Various models	$275	$975

Signature
2005-ca. 2013. See listing under Gibson Baldwin.

Signature Guitar Company (Canada)
1987-1990. Intermediate/professional grade, electric guitars and basses built in Ontario, Canada. Mother of pearl inlaid on 21st fret with model name and, as an option, you could custom order any model with your name inlaid on the 12th fret.

Odyssey
1987-1990. Flat-top, figured maple top, 3 pickups.
1987-1990		$2,000	$2,500

Oracle
1987-1990. Flat-top, figured maple top, 3 pickups.
1987-1990		$2,000	$2,500

Signet
1972-Mid 1970s. Acoustic flat-top guitars, imported from Japan by Ampeg/Selmer.

Silber
1992-1998. Solid wood, steel-string guitars designed by Marc Silber, made in Paracho, Mexico, and distributed by K & S Music. Silber continues to offer the same models under the Marc Silber Music brand.

Silver Street
1979-1986. Founded by brothers Bruce and Craig Hardy, production of solidbody electric guitars built in Elkhart, Indiana and later in Shelby, Michigan. Original TAXI model prototypes built by luthier Richard Schneider. Later models included Spitfire, Cobra, MX, Nightwing, Tommy Shaw and Elite, all offered with various pickups, custom paint and optional hardware. Total production is estimated to be 550 units.

Various Models
1979-1986	Early small models	$675	$900
1979-1986	Larger models	$1,000	$1,250

Silvertone
1941-ca. 1970, present. Brand of Sears instruments which replaced their Supertone brand in '41. The Silvertone name was used on Sears phonographs, records and radios as early as the 'teens, and on occasional guitar models. When Sears divested itself of the Harmony guitar subsidiary in '40 it turned to other suppliers including Kay. In '40 Kay-made archtops and Hawaiian electric lap steels appeared in the catalog bearing the Silvertone brand, and after '41-'42, all guitars, regardless of manufacturer, were called Silvertone.

Sears offered Danelectro-made solidbodies in the fall of '54. Danelectro hollowbodies appeared in '56. By '65, the Silvertones were Teisco-made guitars from W.M.I., but never sold through the catalog. The first imports shown in the catalog were in '69. By '70, most guitars sold by Sears were imports and did not carry the Silvertone name.

Currently, Samick offers a line of acoustic and electric guitars, basses and amps under the Silvertone name.

Amp-In-Case
1962-1968. The black, sharp double cutaway, 1-pickup 1448, introduced in '62, came with a smaller wattage amp without tremolo. The black, 2-pickup 1449, introduced in '63, came with a higher-watt amp with tremolo and better-quality Jensen speaker and was replaced by the red burst 1457 in '64. Gray tolex covered the guitar-amp case. In '66 they were replaced with the black 1451 and 1452 with soft, rounded cutaway horns.
1962-1966	1448, 1 pu, black	$700	$900
1963-1966	1449, 2 pus, black	$900	$1,250
1964-1966	1457, 2 pus, red burst	$900	$1,250
1966-1968	1451, 1 pu, round cut	$700	$900
1966-1968	1452, 2 pus, round cut	$900	$1,250

Belmont
1958. Single-cut solidbody, 2 pickups, black.
1958		$1,000	$1,375

Black Beauty 1384L
1956-1958. Called 'The Black Beauty' in Sears catalog, large body acoustic-electric archtop, cutaway, 2 pickups, block markers, white binding, spruce top, mahogany sides and back, black lacquer finish.
1956-1958		$1,250	$1,750

Black Beauty 1385
1957. Basically the same as model 1384L.
1957		$1,250	$1,750

Espanada
1960s. Bigsby, 2 pickups, black.
1960s		$1,500	$2,000

Estrelita
1960s. Semi-hollowbody archtop, 2 pickups, black, Harmony-made.
1960s		$1,375	$1,750

F-66
1964. Similar to Harmony Rocket III, single-cut, thinline electric, 3 pickups, Bigsby.
1964		$1,000	$1,500

MODEL YEAR	FEATURES	EXC. COND. LOW	HIGH

Gene Autry Melody Ranch
1941-1955. 13" Harmony-made acoustic, Gene Autry signature on belly, cowboy roundup stencil, same as earlier Supertone Gene Autry Roundup.

1941-1955		$375	$500

H1214
1951. Full-size acoustic archtop, script Silvertone headstock logo, dot markers, blond with simulated grain finish.

1951		$575	$750

H1260 Sovereign Jumbo
1968. Silvertone's version of Harmony's Sovereign jumbo flat-top, dot markers, sunburst.

1968		$725	$950

H1434 Rocket
1965. Similar to Harmony Rocket H59, sold by Sears, 3 pickups, Bigsby vibrato.

1965		$1,000	$1,500

Meteor
1955. Single-cut, 1 pickup, sunburst.

1955		$500	$650

Model 623
Late-1950s. Large-body acoustic archtop, dot markers, white 'guard, black finish, painted white binding to give a black and white attractive appearance.

1950s		$250	$325

Model 1300/Model 1302
1958-1959. Single-cut, 1 lipstick pickup, dot markers, 3-on-a-side symmetric headstock, bronze (1300) or black (1302).

1958-1959	1300	$725	$950
1958-1959	1302	$725	$950

Model 1301/Model 1303
1958-1959. 1300 with 2 lipstick pickups, bronze (1301) or black (1303).

1958-1959	1301	$975	$1,250
1958-1959	1303	$975	$1,250

Model 1305
1958-1959. Single-cut, 3 lipstick pickups, dot markers, 3-on-a-side symmetric headstock, white and black finish.

1958-1959		$1,500	$2,000

Model 1317
1957. Single-cut solidbody, 1 lipstick pickup, dot markers, 3-on-a-side symmetric headstock, bronze finish.

1957		$575	$750

Model 1381/Model 1382
1954-1957. Kay-made (many '50s Silvertones were made by Danelectro), slim-style electric similar to Thin Twin/Jimmy Reed, 2 lipstick pickups, 4 knobs, crown-crest logo on 'guard under strings, bolt neck, block markers, sunburst, sold without (Model 1381) and with a case (1382).

1954-1957	1381	$600	$775
1954-1957	1382	$1,000	$1,500

Model 1413
1962-1964. Double-cut slab body, single pickup, 2 control knobs, dot markers.

1962-1964		$250	$350

Model 1415/Model 1417
1960-1962. Single-cut, 1 lipstick pickup, 6-on-a-side dolphin headstock, dot markers, bronze (1415) or black (1417).

1960	1417	$575	$750
1961-1962	1415	$575	$750

Model 1420
1959-1963. Single-cut extra thin solidbody, bolt neck, 2 pickups, natural shaded or black finish.

1959-1963		$575	$750

Model 1423L
1960. Single-cut solidbody, 2 pickups, 5 control knobs with rotator switch, block markers, gleaming gold-color splatter-effect over black finish.

1960		$600	$775

Model 1429L
1962-1963. Harmony-made and similar to Harmony's H-75, single-cut thinline electric, 3 pickups, trapeze tailpiece, 3 toggles, 6 knobs, block marker, sunburst.

1962-1963		$1,000	$1,500

Model 1445L
1960s. Teisco-made solidbody, 3 pickups.

1960s		$825	$1,125

Model 1446
1962-1966. Single-cut thin acoustic archtop, 2 pickups, original factory Bigsby tailpiece, black lacquer finish with white 'guard.

1962-1966		$1,500	$2,000

Model 1454
1962-1966. Single-cut thin acoustic archtop, 3 pickups, original factory Bigsby tailpiece, red lacquer finish.

1962-1966		$1,500	$2,000

Model 1476/Model 1477
1964-1966. Offset double-cut solidbody, 2 pickups, dot markers. 4 control knobs, tremolo, black (1476) or sunburst (1477).

1964-1966	1476	$575	$750
1964-1966	1477	$575	$750

Model 1478/Model 1488 Silhouette
1964-1967. Offset double-cut, rectangular pickups, tremolo, bound 'board, block markers.

1964-1967	1478, 1 pickup	$400	$600
1964-1967	1478, 2 pickups	$475	$650
1964-1967	1488, 3 pickups	$725	$950

Model S1352
1955		$725	$850

Model S1453 Rebel
1968. Two sharp cutaway, single f-hole, 2 pickups, vibrato.

1968		$575	$750

Student-level 13" Flat-Top
1960s. Harmony-made, 13" lower bout.

1960s		$40	$60

Student-level 15.5" Flat-Top
1960s. Harmony-made, 15.5" lower bout.

1960s	Model S621	$175	$250

Simon & Patrick
1985-present. Intermediate and professional grade, production, acoustic and acoustic/electric guitars built in Canada. Founded by luthier

Silvertone Model H1446
Tom Pfeifer

1965 Silvertone Model 1476 Bobkat
Ray Hammond

SMK Music Works

Spalt Instruments
Purpleheart Special

MODEL YEAR	FEATURES	EXC. COND. LOW	HIGH

Robert Godin and named after his sons. He also produces the Seagull, Godin, and Norman brands of instruments.

Sims Custom Shop
2007-present. Custom, professional and premium grade, electric guitars built in Chattanooga, Tennessee by luthier Patrick Sims.

Singletouch
Luthier Mark Singleton builds his professional and premium grade, custom/production, solid and semi-hollow body guitars and basses in Phillips Ranch, California.

Skylark
1981. Solidbody guitars made in Japan and distributed by JC Penney. Two set-neck models and one bolt-neck model were offered. Most likely a one-time deal as brand quickly disappeared.

Slammer
1998-2009. Budget and intermediate grade, production, guitars and basses imported from Indonesia by Hamer. Not to be confused with Hamer's Korean-made series of guitars from 1990-'97 called Hamer Slammer.

Slammer Series (Import)

MODEL YEAR	FEATURES	EXC. COND. LOW	HIGH
1998-2009	Various models	$225	$300

Slingerland
Ca. 1914-2019. Henry Slingerland opened a music school in Chicago, Illinois, in 1914 where he supplied instruments made by others to students who took his course. That grew into the Slingerland Manufacturing Company, then Slingerland Banjo and Drum Company in '28, selling banjos, guitars and ukes, built by them and others into the '40s. They also marketed the May Bell brand. Many of the guitars were made by other companies, including Regal. Slingerland ownership changed multiple times in the 1970s-80s until it was acquired by Gibson (from Gretsch) in 1994. The current owner, Drum Workshop (DW), acquired Slingerland in 2019.

Nitehawk
1930s. 16" archtop, Nitehawk logo on headstock, fancy position neck markers.

1930s		$975	$1,375

Songster Archtop/Flat-Top

1930s	Archtop	$800	$1,125
1930s	Flat-Top	$1,375	$1,750

Songster Tenor
1930s. Archtop.

1930s		$550	$725

Smart Fine Instruments
1986-present. Luthier A. Lawrence Smart builds his professional and premium grade, custom, flat-top guitars first in McCall and now Hailey, Idaho. He also builds mandolin-family instruments.

Smith, George
1959-2020. Custom classical and flamenco guitars built by luthier George Smith in Portland, Oregon.

Smith, Lawrence K.
1989-present. Luthier Lawrence Smith builds his professional and premium grade, production/ custom, flat-top, nylon-string, and archtop guitars in Thirrow, New South Wales, Australia. He also builds mandolins.

SMK Music Works
2002-present. Luthier Scott Kenerson builds production/custom, professional grade, solidbody electric guitars and basses in Waterford, Michigan.

Smooth Stone Guitar
2007-present. Luthier R. Dale Humphries builds his professional and premium grade, production/ custom, acoustic and electric guitars and basses in Pocatello, Idaho.

Solomon Guitars
1995-present. Luthier Erich Solomon builds his premium and presentation grade, production/custom, archtop, flat-top, classical and electric guitars in Epping, New Hampshire. Prior to '99 he was in Anchorage, Alaska.

Somervell
Luthier Douglas P. Somervell built premium and presentation grade, production/custom, classical and flamenco guitars in Brasstown, North Carolina.

Somogyi, Ervin
1971-present. Luthier Ervin Somogyi builds his presentation grade, production/custom, flat-top, flamenco, and classical guitars in Oakland, California.

Sonata
1960s. Private brand Harmony-made, Sonata brand logo on headstock and pickguard.

Superior
1965. Grand Auditorium acoustic archtop, block markers, celluloid bound edges, similar to Harmony 1456, Superior logo on headstock.

1965		$550	$725

SonFather Guitars
1994-2016. Luthier David A. Cassotta built his production/custom, flat-top, 12-string, nylon-string and electric guitars in Rocklin, California.

Sorrentino
1930s. Private brand made by Epiphone and distributed by C.M.I. Quality close to similar Epiphone models.

Arcadia
1930s. Lower-end f-hole acoustic archtop similar to Epiphone Blackstone.

1930s		$625	$825

MODEL		EXC. COND.	
YEAR	FEATURES	LOW	HIGH

Sorrento

1960s. Electric guitar imports made by Teisco, pricing similar to Teisco models, Sorrento logo on headstock, upscale solidbodies can have four pickups with five knobs and four switches.

Electric Solidbody

1960s	4 pickups	$400	$550

Southwell Guitars

1983-present. Premium grade, custom, nylon-string guitars built by luthier Gary Southwell in Nottingham, U.K.

Sovereign

Ca. 1899-1938. Sovereign was originally a brand of The Oscar Schmidt Company of Jersey City, New Jersey, and used on guitars, banjos and mandolins starting in the very late 1800s. In the late '30s, Harmony purchased several trade names from the Schmidt Company, including Sovereign and Stella. Sovereign then ceased as a brand, but Harmony continued using it on a model line of Harmony guitars.

Spalt Instruments

2002-present. Professional and premium grade, production/custom, electric solidbody and hollowbody guitars and basses built by luthier Michael Spalt, originally in Los Angeles, California and since '11 in Vienna, Austria.

Sparrow Guitars

Guitars manufactured in China are dismantled and "overhauled" in Vancouver, British Columbia, starting in '04. From these imports, luthier Billy Bones builds his intermediate and professional grade, production/custom solidbody and hollowbody electric guitars.

Specht Guitars

1991-present. Premium grade, production/custom, acoustic, baritone, parlor, jazz and classical guitars and basses built by luthier Oliver Specht in Vancouver, British Columbia.

Specimen Products

1984-present. Luthier Ian Schneller builds his professional and premium grade, production/custom, aluminum and wood body guitars and basses in Chicago, Illinois. He also builds ukes and amps.

Spector/Stuart Spector Design

1975-1990 (Spector), 1991-1998 (SSD), 1998-present (Spector SSD). Known mainly for basses, Spector offered U.S.-made guitars during '75-'90 and '96-'99, and imports for '87-'90 and '96-'99. Since 2003, they again offer U.S.-professional grade, production, solidbody guitars. See Bass Section for more company info.

MODEL		EXC. COND.	
YEAR	FEATURES	LOW	HIGH

SPG

2006-2009. Originally professional grade, custom, solidbody and chambered guitars built by luthier Rick Welch in Farmingdale, Maine and Hanson, Massachusetts. He also built lapsteels. Currently brand is used on imported line.

Squier

See models listed under Squier in Fender section.

St. Blues

1980-1989, 2005-present. Intermediate and professional grade, production/custom, solidbody guitars and basses imported and built in Memphis, Tennessee. The original '80s line was designed by Tom Keckler and Charles Lawing at Memphis' Strings & Things.

St. George

Mid to late 1960s. Early Japanese brand imported possibly by Buegeleisen & Jacobson of New York, New York.

Electric Solidbody

1960s. Early Japanese import duplicate of Zim Gar model, top mounted controls, 3 pickups, bolt-on neck.

1960s	Sunburst	$650	$850

St. Moritz

1960s. Guitars and basses imported from Japan by the Manhattan Novelty Corp. Manufacturer unknown, but some appear to be Fuji Gen Gakki products. Generally shorter scale beginner guitars, some with interesting pickup configurations.

Stahl

1900-1941. William C. Stahl, of Milwaukee, Wisconsin, ran a publishing company, taught stringed instrument classes and sold instruments to his students as well as by mail order across America. His label claimed that he was the maker but most of his products were built by the Larson brothers of Maurer & Co. of Chicago, with the balance mostly from Washburn. The most commonly found Larson-built models are the Style 6 and 7 as seen in the ca. 1912 Stahl catalog. Jimi Hendrix was the proud owner of a Style 8. The Style 6 is a moderately trimmed 15" Brazilian rosewood beauty that is much like the highly sought Maurer Style 551. The Style 7 and 8 are pearl trimmed 13 ½" concert size Brazilians comparable to the Maurer Style 562 ½. The 1912 Stahl catalog Styles 4, 5 and 9 were built by Washburn.

Stambaugh

1995-present. Luthier Chris Stambaugh builds his professional grade, custom/production, solidbody guitars basses in Stratham, New Hampshire.

Starcaster
Bernunzio Uptown Music

Steinegger D-45
Carter Vintage Guitars

GUITARS

1969 Standel
Jerry Amend

1968 Stella
Edward Sparks

MODEL YEAR	FEATURES	EXC. COND. LOW	HIGH

Standel

1952-1974, 1997-present. Amp builder Bob Crooks offered instruments under his Standel brand 3 different times during the '60s. In '61 Semie Moseley, later of Mosrite fame, made 2 guitar models and 1 bass for Standel, in limited numbers. Also, in '61, Standel began distributing Sierra steels and Dobro resonators, sometimes under the Standel name. In '65 and '66 Standel offered a guitar and a bass made by Joe Hall, who also made the Hallmark guitars. In '66 Standel connected with Sam Koontz, who designed and produced the most numerous Standel models (but still in relatively small numbers) in Newark, New Jersey. These models hit the market in '67 and were handled by Harptone, which was associated with Koontz. By '70 Standel was out of the guitar biz. See Amp section for more company info.

Custom Deluxe 101/101X

1967-1968. Custom solidbody with better electronics, 101X has no vibrato, sunburst, black, pearl white and metallic red.

1967-1968		$1,500	$2,000

Custom Deluxe 102/102X

1967-1968. Custom thin body with better electronics, 102X has no vibrato, offered in sunburst and 5 solid color options.

1967-1968		$1,500	$2,000

Custom 201/201X

1967-1968. Solidbody, 2 pickups, vibrola, 2 pointed cutaways, headstock similar to that on Fender XII, 201X has no vibrato, sunburst, black, pearl white and metallic red.

1967-1968		$1,250	$1,625

Custom 202/202X

1967-1968. Thin body, headstock similar to that on Fender XII, 202X has no vibrato, offered in sunburst and 5 solid color options.

1967-1968		$1,250	$1,625

Custom 420S

1967-1968. Custom thin body with 2 pickups.

1967-1968		$1,500	$2,000

Star

1957-1960s. Early budget level instruments made by Tokyo Sound Company and Gakki and exported by Japan's Hoshino (translates to Star) company which also has Ibanez.

Starcaster

2000s. Budget brand from Fender that has been used on acoustic, electric and bass guitars, effects, amps and drums and sold through mass retailers such as Costco, Target and others. See Fender listing for guitar values.

Starfield

1992-1993. Solidbody guitars from Hoshino (Ibanez) made in the U.S. and Japan. U.S. guitars are identified as American models; Japanese ones as SJ models. Hoshino also used the Star Field name on a line of Japanese guitars in the late '70s. These Star Fields had nothing to do with the '90s versions and were not sold in the U.S.

Starforce

Ca. 1989. Import copies from Starforce Music/Starforce USA.

Stars

Intermediate grade, production, solidbody guitars made in Korea.

Status Graphite

1981-present. Professional grade, production/custom, solidbody guitars and basses built in Colchester, Essex, U.K. Status was the first English company to produce a carbon fiber instrument.

Stauffer

1800s. Old World violin and guitar maker, Georg Stauffer. Valid attributions include signed or labeled by the maker indicating the guitar was actually made by Stauffer, as opposed to attributed to Stauffer or one of his contemporaries. See Martin for listing.

Stefan Sobell Musical Instruments

1982-present. Premium grade, production/custom, flat-top, 12-string, and archtop guitars built by luthier Stefan Sobell in Hetham, Northumberland, England. He also builds mandolins, citterns and bouzoukis.

Steinberger

1979-present. Currently Steinberger offers budget, intermediate, and professional grade, production, electric guitars. They also offer basses. Founded by Ned Steinberger, who started designing NS Models for Stuart Spector in '76. In '79, he designed the L-2 headless bass. In '80, the Steinberger Sound Corp. was founded. Steinberger Sound was purchased by the Gibson Guitar Corp. in '87, and in '92, Steinberger relocated to Nashville, Tennessee.

Headless model codes for '85-'93 are:
First letter is X for bass or G for guitar.
Second letter is for body shape: M is regular offset double-cut guitar body; L is rectangle body; P is mini V shaped body.
Number is pickup designation: 2 = 2 humbuckers, 3 = 3 single coils, 4 = single/single/humbucker.
Last letter is type of tremolo: S = S-Trem tremolo; T = Trans-Trem which cost more on original retail.

GL

1979-1984. Headless, rectangle body, 2 pickups.

1979-1984		$5,500	$10,000

Steinegger

1976-2021. Premium grade, custom steel-string flat-top guitars built by luthier Robert Steinegger in Portland, Oregon. He retired in March, 2021.

MODEL		EXC. COND.	
YEAR	FEATURES	LOW	HIGH

Stella

Ca. 1899-1974, 2000s. Stella was a brand of the Oscar Schmidt Company which started using the brand on low-mid to mid-level instruments in the very late 1800s. Oscar Schmidt produced all types of stringed instruments and was very successful in the 1920s. Company salesmen reached many rural areas and Stella instruments were available in general stores, furniture stores, and dry goods stores, ending up in the hands of musicians such as Leadbelly and Charlie Patton. Harmony acquired the Stella brand in '39 and built thousands of instruments with that name in the '50s and '60s. Harmony dissolved in '74. The Stella brand was reintroduced in the 2000s by MBT International.

00 Style

1900-1930. Oak body flat-top.

1900-1930		$575	$750

Flat-Top 15" 12-String

1920s-1930s. Associated with early blues and folk musicians, top of the line for Stella.

1920s-30s		$8,250	$10,000

Flat-Top by Harmony

1950s-1960s. The low end of the Harmony-built models, US-made until the end of the '60s, student level, Stella logo on headstock, playing action can often be very high which makes them difficult to play.

1950s-60s	13", student	$75	$200
1950s-60s	14", 12-string	$100	$150
1950s-60s	Sundale (colors)	$400	$550
1950s-60s	Tenor 4-string	$75	$200

Harp Guitar

Early-1900s.

1900s		$2,250	$3,000

Singing Cowboy

2000s. Copy of Supertone (black background)/Silvertone/Harmony Singing Cowboy, import with laminated wood construction and ladder bracing.

2000s	Stencil over black	$55	$75

Stetson

1884-ca. 1924. Stetson was a house brand of William John Dyer's St. Paul, Minnesota, music store. They started advertising this brand as early as 1894, but those built by the Larson brothers of Maurer & Co. date from ca. 1904-c. 1924. Most Stetsons were made by the Larsons. Others were built by Harmony (early ones), Washburn and three are credited to the Martin Co.

Stevenson

1999-present. Professional grade, production/custom, solidbody electric guitars and basses built by luthier Ted Stevenson in Lachine, Quebec. He also builds amps.

Stiehler

Production/custom, professional and premium grade, acoustic electric and electric solidbody guitars and basses, built by luthier Bob Stiehler, first in Wellington and since '11 in Carson City, Nevada. He started in 2005.

MODEL		EXC. COND.	
YEAR	FEATURES	LOW	HIGH

Stonebridge

1981-present. Czech Republic luthier Frantisek Furch builds professional and premium grade, production/custom, acoustic guitars. He also builds mandolins.

Stonetree Custom Guitars

1996-present. Luthier Scott Platts builds his professional and premium grade, custom/production, solidbody and chambered electric guitars and basses in Saratoga, Wyoming.

Strad-O-Lin/Stradolin

Ca.1920s-ca.1960s. The Strad-O-Lin company was operated by the Hominic brothers in New York, primarily making mandolins for wholesalers. Around '57 Multivox/Premier bought the company and also used the name on electric and acoustic guitars, basses and amps. Premier also marketed student level guitars under the U.S. Strad brand.

Electric

1960s	Various models	$400	$550

Stratosphere

1954-1958. Solidbody electrics made in Springfield, Missouri by brothers Claude and Russ Deaver, some featuring fanned frets. They also made an odd double neck called the Stratosphere Twin with a regular 6-string neck and a 12-string tuned in minor and major thirds. The brothers likely made less than 200 instruments.

Electric

1954-1958		$1,000	$1,500

Strobel Guitars

2003-present. Luthier Russ Strobel builds custom, professional grade, electric travel guitars and basses in Boca Raton, Florida. He also offers a production, intermediate grade, travel guitar built in Asia.

Stromberg

1906-1955, 2001-present. Intermediate and professional grade, production, archtop guitars imported by Larry Davis.

Founded in Boston by master luthier Charles Stromberg, a Swedish immigrant, building banjos and drums. Son Harry joined the company in 1907and stayed until '27. Son Elmer started in 1910 at age 15. The shop was well known for tenor banjos, but when the banjo's popularity declined, they began building archtop orchestra model guitars. The shop moved to Hanover Street in Boston in '27 and began producing custom order archtop guitars, in particular the 16" G-series and the Deluxe. As styles changed the G-series was increased to 17 3/8" and the 19" Master 400 model was introduced in '37. Stromberg designs radically changed around '40, most likely when Elmer took over guitar production. Both Charles and Elmer died within a few months of each other in '55. Most of the interest in vintage

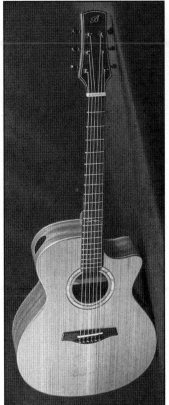

Stonebridge Bridgeport
200 Series AC-CM

Stonetree Roscoecaster

Stromberg-Voisinet
Hawaiian Parlor

David Stone

Suhr Pete Thorn Signature

MODEL YEAR	FEATURES	EXC. COND. LOW	HIGH

Strombergs comes out of the Boston area.

Larry Davis of WD Music Products revived the Stromberg name and introduced a series of moderately priced jazz guitars in June 2001. The models are crafted by a small Korean shop with component parts supplied by WD.

Deluxe

1927-1955. Non-cut, 16" body to '34, 17 3/8" body after '35, also sometimes labeled Delux.

1927-1939	2 parallel 3 ladder	$3,500	$4,500
1940-1947	2 braces	$4,500	$6,000
1948-1955	1 brace	$15,000	$20,000

G-1

1927-1955. Non-cut, 16" body to '35, 17 3/8" body after '35, sunburst.

1927-1935	2 parallel 3 ladder	$3,500	$5,000
1936-1947	2 braces	$4,500	$6,000
1948-1955	1 brace	$15,000	$20,000

G-3

Early 1930s. Archtop, 16 3/8", 3 segment F-holes, ladder bracing, gold hardware, engraved tailpiece, 8-ply 'guard, 5-ply body binding, laminate maple back, fancy engraved headstock with Stromberg name, less total refinement than higher-end Stromberg models.

1927-1935	2 parallel 3 ladder	$3,500	$5,000

G-5

1952-1955. 17" cutaway.

1952-1955	1 brace	$20,000	$30,000

Master 300

1937-1955. 19" non-cut.

1937-1947	2 braces, natural	$5,000	$6,500
1937-1947	2 braces, sunburst	$5,500	$6,500
1948-1955	1 brace, natural	$10,000	$20,000
1948-1955	1 brace, sunburst	$10,000	$20,000

Master 400

1937-1955. 19" top-of-the-line non-cut, the most common of Stromberg's models.

1937-1947	2 braces, natural	$10,000	$12,500
1937-1947	2 braces, sunburst	$10,000	$12,500
1948-1955	1 brace, natural	$20,000	$40,000
1948-1955	1 brace, sunburst	$20,000	$40,000

Master 400 Cutaway

1949, 1953. Only 7 cutaway Strombergs are known to exist.

1949, 1953	1 brace, natural	$40,000	$60,000

Stromberg-Voisinet

1921-ca.1932. Marketed Stromberg (not to be confused with Charles Stromberg of Boston) and Kay Kraft brands, plus guitars of other distributors and retailers. Stromberg was the successor to the Groehsl Company (or Groehsel) founded in Chicago, Illinois in 1890; and the predecessor to the Kay Musical Instrument Company. In 1921, the name was changed to Stromberg-Voisinet Company. Henry Kay "Hank" Kuhrmeyer joined the company in '23 and was secretary by '25. By the mid-'20s, the company was making many better Montgomery Ward guitars, banjos and mandolins, often with lots of pearloid.

Joseph Zorzi, Philip Gabriel and John Abbott

left Lyon & Healy for S-V in '26 or '27, developing a 2-point Venetian shape, which was offered in '27. The first production of electric guitars and amps was introduced with big fanfare in '28; perhaps only 200 or so were made. The last Stromberg acoustic instruments were seen in '32. The Kay Kraft brand was introduced by Kuhrmeyer in '31 as the company made its transition to Kay (see Kay).

Acoustic

1921-1932. Various art and colors.

1921-1932	Various models	$350	$1,500

Stroup

Luthier Gary D. Stroup builds his intermediate and professional grade, production/custom, archtop and flat-top guitars in Eckley, Colorado, starting in 2003.

Stuart Custom Guitars

Professional and premium grade, production/custom, solid and semi-hollow body guitars built by luthier Fred Stuart, starting the year 2004, in Riverside, California. Stuart was a Senior Master Builder at Fender. He also builds pickups.

Suhr Guitars

1997-present. Luthier John Suhr builds his professional and premium grade, production/custom, solidbody electrics guitars and basses in Lake Elsinore, California. He also builds amps. He previously built Pensa-Suhr guitars with Rudy Pensa in New York.

Electric Solidbody

1997-2023	Various models	$2,750	$3,750

Sunset

2010-present. Luthier Leon White builds professional and premium grade, production/custom, electric solidbody, chambered and hollowbody guitars in Los Angeles, California.

Superior Guitars

1987-present. Intermediate grade, production/custom Hawaiian, flamenco, and classical guitars made in Mexico for George Katechis Montalvo of Berkeley Musical Instrument Exchange. They also offer lap steels and mandolin-family instruments.

Supersound

1952-1974. Founded by England's Alan Wootton, building custom amps and radios. In 1958-'59 he worked with Jim Burns to produce about 20 short scale, single-cut solidbodies bearing this name. They also built a bass model. The firm continued to build amps and effects into the early '60s.

Supertone

1914-1941. Brand used by Sears, Roebuck and Company for instruments made by various American manufacturers, including especially its own subsidiary Harmony (which it purchased in 1916). When

MODEL YEAR	FEATURES	EXC. COND. LOW	HIGH

Sears divested itself of Harmony in '40, instruments began making a transition to the Silvertone brand. By '41 the Supertone name was gone.

Acoustic Flat-Top (High-End Appointments)

MODEL YEAR	FEATURES	EXC. COND. LOW	HIGH
1920s	Pearl trim 00-42 likeness	$1,750	$2,250
1920s	Pearl trim, Lindbergh model	$1,750	$2,250

Acoustic Flat-Top 13"

| 1920s-30s | Non-stencil, plain top | $225 | $300 |
| 1920s-30s | Stencil top | $350 | $450 |

Gene Autry Roundup

1932-1939. Harmony made acoustic, Gene Autry signature on belly, cowboy roundup stencil, 13" body until '35, then 14".

| 1932-1939 | | $425 | $550 |

Lone Ranger

1936-1941. Black with red and silver Lone Ranger and Tonto stencil, silver-painted fretboard, 13 1/2" wide. "Hi-Yo Silver" added in '37, changed to "Hi-Ho Silver" in '38.

| 1936-1941 | | $425 | $550 |

Robin Hood

1930s. 13" flat-top similar to Singing Cowboys, but with green and white art showing Robin Hood and his men against a black background.

| 1933 | | $425 | $550 |

Singing Cowboys

1938-1943. Stencil of guitar strumming cowboys around chuck wagon and campfire, branded Silvertone after '41.

| 1938-1943 | | $425 | $550 |

Supertone Wedge

1930s. Triangle-shaped wedge body, laminate construction, blue-silver Supertone label inside sound chamber, art decals on body.

| 1930s | | $350 | $450 |

Supro

1935-1968, 2004-present. Budget brand of National Dobro Company and Valco. Some Supro models also sold under the Airline brand for Montgomery Ward. In '42 Victor Smith, Al Frost and Louis Dopyera bought National and changed the name to Valco Manufacturing Company. Valco Manufacturing Company name changed to Valco Guitars, Inc., in '62. Company treasurer Robert Engelhardt bought Valco in '64. In '67 Valco bought Kay and in '68 Valco/Kay went out of business. In the summer of '69, Valco/Kay brands and assets were sold at auction and the Supro and National names purchased by Chicago-area importer and distributor Strum N' Drum (Norma, Noble). In the early-'80s, ownership of the Supro name was transferred to Archer's Music, Fresno, California. Some Supros assembled from new-old-stock parts.

Amp builder Bruce Zinky revived the Supro name for a line of guitars built in the U.S. by luthier John Bolin and others. He also offers amps. In 2013, Absara Audio, LLC acquired the Supro trademark and started releasing amps and guitars in July 2014.

Arlington

1967-1967. Jazzmaster-style, wood body, 6 buttons, 4 knobs, vibrato, 2 pickups.

| 1966-1967 | Various colors | $1,375 | $1,750 |

Atlas

1958. Rare model, Atlas logo, semi-single cutaway, 2 pickups plus bridge-tailpiece pickup, blond finish.

| 1958 | | $1,875 | $2,500 |

Belmont

1955-1964. For '55-'60, 12" wide, single-cut, 1 neck pickup, 2 knobs treble side in 'guard, reverse-stairs tailpiece, No-Mar plastic maroon-colored covering. For '60, size increased to 13 1/2" wide. For '62-'64, Res-o-glas fiberglass was used for the body, a slight cutaway on bass side, 1 bridge pickup, 2 knobs on opposite sides, Polar White.

| 1955-1962 | Black or white No-Mar | $1,250 | $1,625 |
| 1961-1964 | Polar White Res-o-glas | $1,375 | $1,750 |

Bermuda

1962 only. Slab body (not beveled), double pickups, dot markers, cherry glass-fiber finish.

| 1962 | | $1,500 | $2,000 |

Collegian Spanish

1939-1942. Metal body, 12 frets. Moved to National line in '42.

| 1939-1942 | | $1,250 | $1,625 |

Coronado/Coronado II

1961-1967, 2017-2021. Listed as II in '62 15 1/2" scale, single-cut thinline, 2 pickups, natural blond spruce top. Changed to slight cutaway on bass side in '62 when renamed II. Reintroduced 2017, Americana series.

1961-1962	Blond, spruce top	$1,750	$2,250
1963-1967	Black fiberglass	$1,875	$2,500
2017-2021	II, Americana Series	$600	$800

Dual-Tone

1954-1966, 2004-2014. The Dual Tone had several body style changes, all instruments had dual pickups. '54, 11 1/4" body, No Mar Arctic White plastic body ('54-'62). '55, 12" body. '58, 13" body. '60, 13 1/2" body. '62, Res-o-glas Ermine White body, light cutaway on bass side.

| 1954-1961 | Arctic White No-Mar | $1,500 | $2,000 |
| 1962-1964 | Ermine White Res-o-glas | $1,625 | $2,125 |

El Capitan

1948-1955. Archtop, 1 single-coil pickup.

| 1948-1955 | | $700 | $950 |

Folk Star/Vagabond

1964-1967. Molded Res-o-glas body, single-cone resonator, dot inlays, Fire Engine Red. Name changed to Vagabond in '66.

| 1964-1967 | | $1,000 | $1,500 |

Jamesport

2017-2021. Island Series, electric solidbody, '60s-era design, alder body, maple neck, rosewood 'board, Gold Foil pickup, antique white or jet black.

| 2017-2021 | | $400 | $550 |

Supertone Lone Ranger
Imaged by Heritage Auctions, HA.com

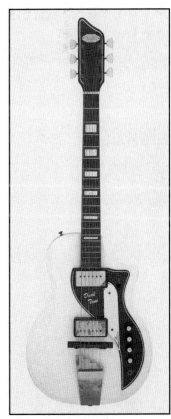

1960 Supro Dual Tone
Imaged by Heritage Auctions, HA.com

Supro Lexington
Rivington Guitars

Tacoma DM-10
Imaged by Heritage Auctions, HA.com

MODEL YEAR	FEATURES	EXC. COND. LOW	HIGH

Kingston
1962-1963. Double-cut slab body, bridge pickup, glass-fiber sand finish, similar to same vintage Ozark.

| 1962-1963 | | $1,125 | $1,500 |

Lexington
1967. Double-cut, wood body.

| 1967 | | $725 | $950 |

Martinique (Val-Trol)
1962-1967. Single-cut, 13 1/2" wide, 2 standard and 1 bridge pickups, block markers, Val-Trol script on 'guard, Bigsby, blue or Ermine White Polyester Glas. Collectors sometimes call this Val-Trol, referring to the 6 mini tone and volume controls. Not to be confused with Silverwood model which also has 6 mini-knobs.

| 1962-1967 | | $2,500 | $3,500 |

N800 Thinline Electric
1967-1968. Thin body, symmetrical double-cut, 2 pickups, copy model, similar to National N800 series models.

| 1967-1968 | | $650 | $850 |

Ozark
1952-1954, 1958-1967, 2004-2013. Non-cut, 1 pickup, dot inlay, white pearloid body, name reintroduced in '58 as a continuation of model Sixty with single-cut, Dobro tailpiece.

1952-1954	White pearloid	$1,125	$1,500
1958-1961	Red	$1,125	$1,500
1962-1967	Jet Black or Fire Bronze	$1,125	$1,500

Ranchero
1948-1960. Full body electric archtop, neck pickup, dot markers, bound body, sunburst.

| 1948-1960 | | $750 | $1,000 |

Rhythm Master (Val-Trol)
1959. Val-Trol 'guard.

| 1959 | | $2,000 | $2,500 |

S710 Flat-Top
1967-1968. Jumbo-style 15.5" flat-top, block markers, asymmetrical headstock, natural.

| 1967-1968 | | $450 | $600 |

Sahara/Sahara 70
1960-1967. 13 1/2" body-style similar to Dual-Tone, single pickup, 2 knobs, Sand-Buff or Wedgewood Blue, Sahara until '63, Sahara 70 after.

| 1960-1967 | | $1,250 | $1,625 |

Silverwood (Val-Trol)
1960-1962, 2019-2021. Single-cut, 13 1/2" wide, 2 standard and 1 bridge pickups, block markers, natural blond, Val-Trol script on 'guard, renamed Martinique in '62. Collectors sometimes call this Val-Trol, referring to the guitar's 6 mini tone and volume controls. The Martinique also has the Val-Trol system but the knobs are not in a straight line like on the Silverwood. Reintroduced 2019, mahogany or ash body, maple neck, 2 Gold Foil pickups, Daphne Blue, Ash Natural, British Racing Green and Transparent Red.

| 1960-1962 | | $2,125 | $2,750 |
| 2019-2021 | | $800 | $1,125 |

Sixty
1955-1958. Single-cut, single pickup, white No-Mar, became Ozark in '58.

| 1955-1958 | | $950 | $1,250 |

Special 12
1958-1960. Single-cut, replaces Supro Sixty, neck pickup 'guard mounted.

| 1958-1960 | | $950 | $1,250 |

Stratford
1968. ES-335-style double-cut, 3 pickups, 3 switches, 6 knobs, vibrato.

| 1968 | | $750 | $975 |

Strum 'N Drum Solidbody
1970s. Student-level import, 1 pickup, large Supro logo on headstock.

| 1970s | Higher-end | $500 | $650 |
| 1970s | Lower-end | $400 | $525 |

Super
1958-1964. 12" wide single-cut body style like mid-'50s models, single bridge pickup, short-scale, ivory.

| 1958-1964 | | $700 | $950 |

Super Seven
1965-1967. Offset double-cut solidbody, short scale, middle pickup, Calypso Blue.

| 1965-1967 | | $700 | $950 |

Suprosonic 30
1963-1967. Introduced as Suprosonic, renamed Suprosonic 30 in '64, double-cut, single neck pickup, vibrato tailpiece, more of a student model, Holly Red.

| 1963-1967 | | $650 | $850 |

Tremo-Lectric
1965. Fiberglas hollowbody, 2 pickups, unique built-in electric tremolo (not mechanical), Wedgewood Blue finish, multiple controls associated with electric tremolo.

| 1965 | | $1,500 | $2,000 |

Tri Tone
Reintroduced 2019-2021. Single-cut mahogany body, maple neck, 3 pickups, black.

| 2019-2021 | | $1,125 | $1,500 |

Westbury
Reintroduced 2017-2021. Island Series, alder body, maple neck, 2 Gold Foil pickups, black, white, turquoise, or tobacco burst.

| 2017-2021 | | $450 | $550 |

Westwood 1580A
1955-1958. Single-cut archtop solidbody, 1 pickup.

| 1955-1958 | | $1,125 | $1,500 |

White Holiday/Holiday
1963-1967, 2018-2021. Introduced as Holiday, renamed White Holiday in '64, fiberglas double-cut, vibrato tailpiece, single bridge pickup, Dawn White. Reintroduced 2018, Americana Series, mahogany body and neck, 2 pickups.

| 1963-1967 | | $1,250 | $1,625 |
| 2018-2021 | | $575 | $750 |

Suzuki Takeharu
See listing for Takeharu.

SX
See listing for Essex.

MODEL YEAR	FEATURES	EXC. COND. LOW	HIGH

Szlag

2000-present. Luthier John J. Slog builds his professional and premium grade, custom carved, guitars and basses in Bethlehem, Pennsylvania.

T.D. Hibbs

Production/custom, professional grade, steel string and classical guitars built in Cambridge, Ontario by luthier Trevor Hibbs.

T.H. Davis

1976-2008. Professional and premium grade, custom, steel string and classical guitars built by luthier Ted Davis in Loudon, Tennessee. He also built mandolins. Davis died in '08.

T.J. Thompson

Luthier T.J. Thompson began in the 1980's building presentation grade, custom, steel string guitars in West Concord, Massachusetts.

Tacoma

1995-2009. Intermediate, and professional grade, production, acoustic guitars produced in Tacoma, Washington and New Hartford, Connecticut. They also built acoustic basses and mandolins. In October, '04, Fender acquired Tacoma and in '09 ceased production.

BM6C Thunderhawk Baritone

2004-2009. Single-cut acoustic baritone.

2004-2009		$1,500	$2,000

C-1C/C-1CE Chief

1997-2009. Cutaway flat-top with upper bass bout sound hole, solid cedar top, mahogany back and sides, rosewood 'board. Sides laminated until 2000, solid after, CE is acoustic/electric.

1997-2009		$500	$750
1997-2009	Fishman electronics	$600	$800

DM Series

1997-2006. Dreadnought, solid spruce top, mahogany back and sides, satin finish, natural, C suffix indicates cutaway.

1997-2006	Various models	$350	$1,250

DR Series

1997-2006. Dreadnought, solid Sitka spruce top, rosewood back and sides, natural. Models include DR-20 (non-cut, herringbone trim, abalone rosette), DR-20E (with on-board electronics), DR-8C (cutaway), and DR-38.

1997-2006	Various models	$350	$1,250

EM Series

1999-2008. Little Jumbo series, spruce top, mahogany back and sides, C suffix indicates cutaway.

1999-2008	Various models	$600	$800

JM Series

1997-2006. Jumbo series, spruce top, mahogany back and sides.

1997-2006		$950	$1,250

JR-14C Jumbo Rosewood

Late-1990s. Jumbo cutaway, 16 5/8" lower bout, gloss spruce top, satin rosewood body.

1990s		$1,000	$1,500

JR-50CE4 Jumbo Koa

1997-2003. Jumbo cutaway, 17" lower bout, Sitka spruce top, figured Koa back and sides.

1997-2003		$1,000	$1,375

P-1/P-2 Papoose

1995-2009. Travel-size mini-flat-top, all solid wood, mahogany back and sides (P-1), with on-board electronics (P-1E) or solid rosewood (P-2), cedar top, natural satin finish.

1995-2000	P-2	$450	$600
1995-2009	P-1	$350	$450
1995-2009	P-1E	$450	$600

Parlor Series

1997-2003. Smaller 14 3/4" body, solid spruce top, various woods for back and sides.

1997-2003	PK-30 Koa	$800	$1,125
1997-2003	PK-40 Rosewood	$800	$1,125

PM Series

1997-2003. Full-size, standard sound hole.

1997-2003	Various models	$450	$1,000

Takamine

1962-present. Intermediate and professional grade, production, steel- and nylon-string, acoustic and acoustic/electric guitars and basses. Takamine is named after a mountain near its factory in Sakashita, Japan. Mass Hirade joined Takamine in '68 and revamped the brand's designs and improved quality. In '75, Takamine began exporting to other countries, including U.S. distribution by Kaman Music (Ovation). In '78, Takamine introduced acoustic/electric guitars. They offered solidbody electrics and some archtops for '83-'84.

Takeharu (by Suzuki)

Mid-1970s. Classical guitars offered by Suzuki as part of their internationally known teaching method (e.g., Violin Suzuki method), various sized instruments designed to eliminate the confusion of size that has been a problem for classroom guitar programs.

Taku Sakashta Guitars

1994-2010. Premium and presentation grade, production/custom, archtop, flat-top, 12-sting, and nylon-string guitars, built by luthier Taku Sakashta in Sebastopol, California. He died in February 2010.

Tama

Ca. 1959-1967, 1974-1979. Hoshino's (Ibanez) brand of higher-end acoustic flat-tops made in Japan. Many of the brand's features would be transferred to Ibanez's Artwood acoustics.

Tamura

1970s. Made in Japan by Mitsura Tamura, the line includes intermediate grade solid wood classical guitars.

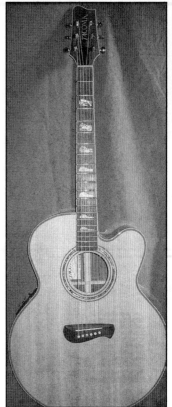

Tacoma JK50-CE
Vic Hines

2012 Takamine Ef508Kc
50th Anniversary Koa
Cream City Music

To get the most from this book, be sure to read "Using *The Guide*" in the introduction.

Taylor 110e

2016 Taylor 150e

MODEL YEAR	FEATURES	EXC. COND. LOW	HIGH

Tanglewood Guitar Company UK

1991-present. Owners Dirk Kommer and Tony Flatt in Biggin Hill, U.K. import intermediate and professional grade, production, acoustic, classical, resonator and electric guitars and basses from China. They also offer mandolins, banjos, ukuleles and amps.

Taylor

1974-present. Intermediate, professional, premium, and presentation grade, production/custom, steel- and nylon-string, acoustic, acoustic/electric, semi-hollow, and solidbody guitars built in El Cajon, California and Tecate, Mexico. They have also built basses. Founded by Bob Taylor, Steve Schemmer and Kurt Listug in Lemon Grove, California, the company was originally named the Westland Music Company, but was soon changed to Taylor (Bob designed the guitars and it fit on the logo). Taylor and Listug bought out Schemmer in '83. Bob Taylor was the first commercially successful guitar maker to harness CAD/CAM CNC technology for acoustic guitars and in '91 introduced the 410 Model, the first all-solid wood American-made guitar with a list price under $1,000. The plain-appointment model using CNC technology was a major innovation combining quality and price. They added semi-hollowbodies in '05 and solidbodies in '07. In '08, they added the Build To Order custom shop. In '18, they added their new V-Class bracing to most every steel-string model in the 300 Series and above. V-Class braced Taylors have a black graphite nut vs the white one on standard braced models.

Understanding Taylor's Model Numbering System:
The first digit or letter identifies the series (100 Series to 900 Series, PS-Presentation and K-Koa Series) and most models within each series share the same back and side woods and appointment package.
The second digit: 1=6-string with softwood (spruce) top; 2=6-string with hardwood top; 5=12-string with softwood top; 2=12-string with hardwood top.
The third digit is body shape: 0=Dreadnought; 2=Grand Concert; 4=Grand Auditorium; 6=Grand Symphony; 7=Grand Pacific; 8=Grand Orchestra.
A "c" at the end of the number indicates cutaway, an "e" onboard electronics, and a "N" nylon-string.

110 Series
2003-present. Dreadnought, sapele back and sides, Sitka spruce top, e and ce begin '08.

2003-2016	110	$500	$650
2008-2019	110ce	$625	$800
2008-2023	110e	$550	$750

114 Series
2007-present. Grand Auditorium, sapele back and sides, Sitka spruce top.

2007-2016	114	$500	$650
2008-2023	114ce	$625	$800
2008-2023	114e	$550	$750

150 Series
2016-present. Dreadnought 12-string, Sitka spruce top, walnut back and sides.

2016-2023	150e	$600	$750

210 Series
2005-present. Dreadnought, sapele or Indian rosewood back and sides, Sitka spruce top.

2005-2016	210	$600	$800
2005-2016	210e	$650	$850
2008-2023	210ce	$725	$900

214 Series
2004-present. Grand Auditorium, sapele or Indian rosewood back and sides, Sitka spruce top.

2004-2016	214	$550	$750
2004-2016	214c	$600	$750
2005-2016	214e	$600	$750
2008-2023	214ce	$675	$850
2012-2017	214ce-N Classic	$800	$1,000
2014-2023	214ce-K DLX (Koa)	$850	$1,250
2020	214ce DLX	$975	$1,250
2020	214ce-SB DLX	$1,125	$1,375

224ce-K DLX
2016-present. Grand Auditorium, solid Koa top, laminated Koa back and sides.

2016-2023		$1,250	$1,500

254ce
2018-present. Venetian cutaway, Sitka spruce top, rosewood back and sides.

2018-2023		$675	$850

310 Series
1998-2018. Dreadnought, mahogany or sapele back and sides, Sitka spruce top. The non-cut 310 discontinued '07-'12, then reappeared in '13 along with 310e version.

1998-2006	310	$775	$1,000
1998-2018	310ce	$925	$1,125

310ce-L30
2004. Limited Edition 30th Anniversary, myrtlewood leaf inlays, Koa rosette, 30th Anniversary headstock logo.

2004		$1,000	$1,375

312 Series
1998-present. Grand Concert, Venetian cutaway, mahogany or sapele back and sides, Sitka spruce top. Non-cut 312 and 312e versions were offered in 2013. V-Class introduced '20.

1998-2019	312ce	$1,500	$1,875
2019-2023	312ce V-Class	$1,625	$2,000

314 Series
1998-2006, 2013-present. Mid-size Grand Auditorium, mahogany or sapele back and sides, Sitka spruce top. Non-cut offered again in '13 along with 314e version. V-Class introduced '20.

1998-2006	314	$1,250	$1,625
1998-2019	314ce	$1,375	$1,750
2000	314ce-K (Koa)	$1,625	$2,000
2019-2023	314ce V-Class	$1,625	$2,000

314ce-LTD
2012-2018. Hawaiian Koa back and sides, Indian rosewood headstock. Also offered with nylon strings (N).

2012-2018		$1,500	$2,000

MODEL YEAR	FEATURES	EXC. COND. LOW	HIGH

315 Series
1998-2011. Jumbo, mahogany or sapele back and sides, Sitka spruce top.

| 1998-2011 | 315ce | $1,125 | $1,375 |

316 Series
2012-2019. Grand Symphony, Sitka spruce top, sapele back and sides.

2012-2019	316ce	$1,250	$1,500
2013-2016	316	$1,000	$1,375
2013-2016	316e	$1,250	$1,500
2018	316e Baritone-8 LTD	$1,625	$2,125

320e Baritone SLTD
2014. Limited Edition Dreadnought, mahogany top and body, Expression electronics.

| 2014 | | $1,500 | $2,000 |

322 Series
2019-present. Grand Concert, non-cut, blackwood/mahogany top.

| 2019-2023 | 322ce V-Class | $1,500 | $2,000 |
| 2020 | 322e | $1,500 | $2,000 |

324 Series
2015-present. Grand Auditorium, mahogany top, African sapele back and sides.

2015-2020	324e	$1,250	$1,625
2019-2023	324ce V-Class	$1,625	$2,000
2020-2023	324	$1,125	$1,500

326ce Baritone
2015-present. Grand Symphony, special edition, 6- or 8-string, mahogany top.

| 2015-2023 | | $1,500 | $2,000 |

352 Series
2019-present. Grand Concert 12-string, Sitka spruce top, sapele back and sides, natural.

| 2019-2023 | 352ce V-Class | $1,500 | $2,000 |

354ce
2004-2011. Grand Auditorium 12-string, cutaway, mahogany back and sides, Expression system.

| 2004-2011 | | $1,500 | $2,000 |

355 Series
1998-2011. Jumbo 12-string, mahogany or sapele back and sides, Sitka spruce top.

| 1998-2006 | 355 | $1,125 | $1,500 |
| 1998-2011 | 355ce | $1,375 | $1,750 |

356 Series
2014-2019. Grand Symphony 12-string, Sitka spruce top, sapele back and sides, non-cut, cutaway, or ce cutaway electric.

| 2014-2019 | 356ce | $1,375 | $1,750 |

362 Series
2019-present. Grand Concert 12-string, mahogany top, blackwood back and sides.

| 2019-2023 | 362ce V-Class | $1,500 | $2,000 |

363 Series

| 2020 | 363ce V-Class | $1,500 | $2,000 |

410 Series
1991-2018. Dreadnought, mahogany back and sides until '98, ovangkol after '98, Sitka spruce top. Non-cut offered again in '13 along with 410e version.

1991-2006	410	$1,000	$1,375
1991-2018	410ce	$1,375	$1,750
2000	410-MA, maple	$1,250	$1,625

412 Series
1991-present. Grand Concert, mahogany back and sides until '98, ovangkol after, Sitka spruce top. Cutaway electric version replaced the 412 in '98. Non-cut offered again in '13 along with 412e version.

1991-1998	412	$1,500	$2,000
1996	412-K (Koa)	$1,625	$2,125
1998-2020	412ce	$1,750	$2,125
1998-2023	412ce-R	$1,750	$2,125

414 Series
1998-present. Grand Auditorium, ovangkol back and sides, Sitka spruce top. Non-cut offered again in '13 along with 414e version.

1998	414-K (Koa)	$1,625	$2,125
1998-2006	414	$1,500	$2,000
1998-2023	414ce	$1,750	$2,250
2019-2023	414ce-R V-Class	$1,750	$2,125

414ce-LTD
2013. Limited Edition, Sitka spruce top, tropical mahogany neck.

| 2013 | | $1,375 | $1,750 |

414-L10
2005. Limited Edition, rosewood sides and back, gloss spruce top, satin finish.

| 2005 | | $1,250 | $1,625 |

414-L30
2004. Limited Edition 30th Anniversary, Hawaiian Koa back and sides, Engelmann spruce top, pearl and gold 30th Anniversary inlay.

| 2004 | | $1,250 | $1,625 |

415 Series
1998-2006. Jumbo, ovangkol back and sides, Sitka spruce top.

| 1998-2006 | 415ce | $1,375 | $1,750 |

416 Series
2011-2019. Grand Symphony, ovangkol back and sides, Sitka spruce top.

| 2011-2019 | 416ce | $1,375 | $1,750 |

418 Series
2015-2019. Grand Orchestra, ovangkol back and sides, Sitka spruce top.

| 2015-2019 | 418e | $1,375 | $1,750 |

420
1990-1997. Dreadnought, Indian rosewood back and sides, Sitka spruce top.

| 1990-1997 | | $1,250 | $1,750 |

422 Series
1991-1998. Grand Concert, solid maple construction.

| 1991-1998 | 422-K (Koa) | $1,500 | $2,000 |
| 1997 | 422-R (Rosewood) | $1,500 | $2,000 |

426ce-LTD
2008. Limited Edition, Tasmanian blackwood top, back and sides.

| 2008 | | $1,625 | $2,125 |

450
1996-1997. Dreadnought 12-string, mahogany back and sides, spruce top.

| 1996-1997 | | $1,125 | $1,500 |

Taylor 324e

Taylor 414ce

GUITARS

Taylor 552ce

Taylor 618e

MODEL YEAR	FEATURES	EXC. COND. LOW	HIGH
454ce			
2004-2011. Grand Auditorium 12-string, Ovangkol back and sides, Sitka spruce top.			
2004-2011		$1,375	$1,750
455 Series			
2001-2011. Jumbo 12-string, Ovangkol back and sides, Sitka spruce top.			
2001-2006	455	$1,250	$1,625
2001-2011	455ce	$1,375	$1,750
455ce-LTD			
2001-2003. Limited Edition, imbuia back and sides.			
2001-2003		$1,625	$2,000
456 Series			
2012-2016. Grand Symphony 12-string.			
2012-2016	456e and 456ce	$1,750	$2,125
458e			
2016-2019. Grand Orchestra 12-string.			
2016-2019		$1,625	$2,125
510 Series			
1978-2017. Dreadnought, mahogany back and sides, spruce top. Non-cut offered again in '13 along with 510e version.			
1978-2006	510	$1,250	$1,625
1978-2017	510ce	$1,500	$1,875
510ce-AB 25th Anniversary			
1999. Limited Edition, 25th Anniversary on headstock, spruce top, mahogany back, sides and neck.			
1999		$2,000	$2,500
510-LTD			
2002. Limited Edition, mahogany back and sides, Sitka spruce top.			
2002		$1,375	$1,750
512 Series			
1978-present. Grand Concert, mahogany back and sides, red cedar top. Non-cut offered again in '13-'16 along with 512e version.			
1978-2000	512	$1,250	$1,625
1978-2000	512c	$1,375	$1,750
1978-2023	512ce	$1,625	$2,000
2012-2016	512ce-N	$1,625	$2,000
512ce-L10			
2005. Limited Edition, American mahogany body and neck, abalone sound hole rosette, pearl diamond inlays, gold tuners.			
2005		$1,500	$2,000
512-NG Nanci Griffith			
1996-1997. 512ce with sunburst finish.			
1996-1997		$2,000	$2,500
514 Series			
1990-present. Grand Auditorium, mahogany back and sides, Engelmann or Sitka spruce top. Western red cedar top on 514c and ce. Non-cut offered again in '13-'16 along with 514e version. V-Class introduced '20.			
1990-1998	514	$1,625	$2,125
1996-1998	514c	$1,750	$2,250
1998-2023	514ce	$1,875	$2,375
515-LTD			
1981. Limited Edition, mahogany back and sides, black binding, tortoise 'guard.			
1981		$1,625	$2,125

MODEL YEAR	FEATURES	EXC. COND. LOW	HIGH
516 Series			
2008-2019. Grand Symphony, mahogany back and sides, Engelmann spruce top. Non-cut 516 offered in '13 along with 516e version.			
2008-2019	516ce	$1,750	$2,125
516ce-LTD			
2010. Spring Limited Editions, Tasmanian blackwood back and sides, Sitka spruce top.			
2010		$2,375	$3,000
518 Series			
2012-2014. Grand Orchestra, tropical mahogany back and sides, Sitka spruce top, tortoise 'guard.			
2012-2014	518/518e	$1,625	$2,125
522 Series			
2013-2023. Grand Concert, all tropical mahogany. V-Class introduced '20.			
2013-2018	522	$1,625	$2,125
2013-2019	522e	$1,625	$2,125
2013-2023	522ce	$1,750	$2,125
524ce-LTD			
2018. Grand Auditorium, all walnut.			
2018		$2,250	$3,000
554 Series			
2004-2005. Grand Auditorium 12-string, mahogany.			
2004-2005	554	$2,000	$2,500
555 Series			
1978-2006. Jumbo 12-string, mahogany back and sides, Sitka spruce top, higher-end appointments.			
1994-2006	555	$1,625	$2,125
1994-2006	555ce	$1,875	$2,375
562 Series			
2019-2022. Grand Concert 12-strings, V-Class bracing, mahogany top.			
2019-2022	562ce	$1,875	$2,375
610 Series			
1978-2017. Dreadnought, big leaf maple back and sides, Sitka spruce top. Non-cut offered again in '13 along with 610e version.			
1978-1998	610	$1,875	$2,500
1998-2017	610ce	$2,125	$2,625
2013-2017	610e	$2,000	$2,500
612 Series			
1984-present. Grand Concert, big leaf maple back and sides, Sitka spruce top. Non-cut offered again in '13 along with 612e version. V-Class introduced '20.			
1984-1998	612	$1,875	$2,500
1998-2023	612ce	$2,125	$2,625
2013-2016	612e	$2,000	$2,500
614 Series			
1978-present. Grand Auditorium, big leaf maple back and sides, Sitka spruce top. Non-cut offered again in '13 along with 614e version. V-Class introduced '20.			
1978-1998	614	$1,875	$2,500
1998-2023	614ce	$2,125	$2,625
2013-2016	614e	$2,000	$2,500
615 Series			
1981-2011. Jumbo, big leaf maple back and sides, Sitka spruce top.			
1981-1998	615	$1,875	$2,500
1981-1998	615e	$2,000	$2,500
1998-2011	615ce	$2,125	$2,625

MODEL YEAR	FEATURES	EXC. COND. LOW	HIGH

616 Series
2008-2019. Grand Symphony, big leaf maple back and sides, Sitka spruce top. Non-cut 616 offered in '13-'16 along with 616e version.

2008-2019	616ce	$2,375	$3,000
2013-2016	616e	$2,000	$2,500

618 Series
2013-present. Grand Orchestra, Sitka spruce top, big leaf maple back and sides.

2013-2023	618e	$2,125	$2,625

654 Series
2004-2011. Grand Auditorium 12-string, big leaf maple back and sides, Sitka spruce top.

2004-2011	654ce	$2,125	$2,625

655 Series
1978-1991, 1996-2011. Jumbo 12-string, big leaf maple back and sides, Sitka spruce top.

1978-2006	655	$1,875	$2,500
1998-2011	655ce	$2,250	$2,875

656 Series
2008-2019. Grand Symphony 12-string, big leaf maple back and sides.

2018-2019	656ce	$2,125	$2,625

710 Series
1977-2017. Dreadnought, Indian rosewood back and sides, Englemann or Sitka spruce top. Non-cut offered again in '13 along with 710e version.

1977-2006	710 (Spruce)	$1,750	$2,250
1990s	710-BR (Brazilian)	$2,750	$3,500
1998-2006	710 (Cedar)	$1,750	$2,250
1998-2017	710ce (Cedar)	$2,250	$2,875

710-B 25th Anniversary
1999. Limited Edition, 25th Anniversary on headstock, spruce top, abalone rosette, Brazilian rosewood sides and back, mahogany neck.

1999		$2,750	$3,500

710ce-L30
2004. Limited Edition 30th Anniversary, Englemann top, Indian rosewood body, 30th Anniversary inlay.

2004		$1,625	$2,000

712 Series
1984-2023. Grand Concert, Indian rosewood back and sides, Englemann or Sitka spruce top. Non-cut offered again in '13 along with 712e version. V-Class introduced '20.

1984-2006	712	$1,875	$2,500
2000-2023	712ce	$2,125	$2,625
2013-2019	712e	$2,000	$2,500

714 Series
1996-2023. Grand Auditorium, Indian rosewood back and sides, red cedar top. Non-cut offered again in '13-'16 along with 714e version. V-Class introduced '20.

1996-2006	714	$1,875	$2,500
1998-2019	714ce	$2,125	$2,625
2020-2023	714ce, V-Class	$2,250	$2,875

714-BRZ
1997. Brazilian rosewood, cedar, fancy.

1997		$4,250	$5,500

714ce-L1
2003-2004. Limited Edition, Western red cedar top, grafted walnut sides and back, pearl inlay, Hawaiian Koa rosette.

2003-2004		$2,125	$2,750

714ce-S-LTD
2015. Limited Edition Grand Auditorium, Sitka spruce top, blackheart sassafras back and sides.

2015		$2,125	$2,750

716ce
2007-2019. Grand Symphony, lutz spruce, Indian rosewood.

2007-2019		$2,125	$2,750

716ce-LTD
2009. Limited Edition, Sitka spruce top, Madagascar rosewood back and sides.

2009		$2,125	$2,750

750
1990-2000s. Dreadnought 12-string, spruce top.

1990-2000s		$2,000	$2,500

755
1990-1998. Jumbo 12-string, rosewood back and sides.

1990-1998		$2,000	$2,500

810 Series
1975-2017. Classic Dreadnought, Indian rosewood back and sides, Sitka spruce top. Non-cut offered again in '13 along with 810e version.

1975-2006	810	$1,875	$2,500
1975-2006	810e	$2,000	$2,500
1993-1998	810c	$2,000	$2,500
1996-2016	810ce-BR (Brazilian)	$3,250	$4,000
1996-2017	810ce	$2,125	$2,625

810-L30
2004. Limited Edition 30th Anniversary, maple leaf inlays, sound hole rosette, 30th Anniversary logo.

2004		$2,250	$3,000

810ce-LTD
2010. Limited Edition, Venetian cutaway, Madagascar rosewood back and sides, solid Sitka spruce top.

2010		$2,500	$3,000

812 Series
1985, 1993-present. Grand Concert, Indian rosewood back and sides, Sitka spruce top. Non-cut offered again in '13-'16 along with 812e version. V-Class introduced '20.

1985	812	$1,875	$2,500
1993-1998	812c	$2,000	$2,500
1998-2019	812ce	$2,125	$2,625
2013-2016	812e	$2,000	$2,500
2019-2023	812ce V-Class	$2,625	$3,250

814 Series
1993-present. Grand Auditorium, Indian rosewood back and sides, Sitka spruce top. Non-cut offered again in '13 along with 814e version. V-Class introduced '20.

1993-1998	814	$2,375	$3,000
1996-1998	814c	$2,500	$3,250
1998-2019	814ce	$2,500	$3,250
2000	814-BE (Brazilian/ Englemann)	$3,250	$4,000
2020-2023	814ce V-Class	$2,625	$3,250

2001 Taylor 710ce
Jeff Mangan

2000 Taylor 814ce
Cream City Music

2003 Taylor 910
Cream City Music

Taylor 914ce

MODEL YEAR	FEATURES	EXC. COND. LOW	HIGH
814ce-LTD			
2012. Spring Limited Edition, cocobolo back and sides, Sitka spruce top.			
2012		$2,500	$3,250
815 Series			
1970s-2011. Jumbo, Indian rosewood back and sides, Sitka spruce top.			
1970s-2006	815	$2,250	$3,000
1993-1998	815c	$2,500	$3,250
1997	815c-BR		
	(Brazilian)	$3,250	$4,000
1998-2011	815ce	$2,625	$3,250
816 Series			
2008-2019. Grand Symphony, Sitka spruce top, Indian rosewood back and sides.			
2008-2014	816e	$2,500	$3,250
2008-2019	816ce	$2,625	$3,250
2013-2016	816	$2,250	$3,000
818 Series			
2014-present. Grand Orchestra, Sitka spruce, Indian rosewood. V-Class introduced '20.			
2014-2019	818e	$2,500	$3,250
854ce-LTD			
2002. Grand Auditorium 12-string, Indian rosewood back and sides, Sitka spruce top.			
2002		$2,500	$3,250
855 Series			
1981-2011. Jumbo 12-string, Indian rosewood back and sides, Sitka spruce top.			
1981-2011	855	$2,000	$2,500
2004-2011	855ce	$2,250	$2,875
856 Series			
2012-2019. Grand Symphony 12-string, Sitka spruce, Indian rosewood.			
2012-2018	856e	$2,000	$2,500
2013-2019	856ce	$2,125	$2,625
910 Series			
1977-2017. Dreadnought, maple back and sides, changed to Brazilian rosewood in '86, wide abalone-style rosette. Non-cut offered again in '13 along with 910e version, Indian rosewood back and sides, Sitka spruce top.			
1977-1985	910 Maple	$2,875	$3,750
1986-2006	910 Brazilian	$5,375	$6,750
1998-2016	910ce	$3,250	$4,000
912 Series			
1993-present. Grand Concert, Indian rosewood back and sides, Engelmann spruce top, abalone. Non-cut offered in '13 along with 912e version. V-Class introduced '20.			
1993-2002	912c	$3,000	$4,000
1993-2019	912ce	$3,125	$4,000
2020-2023	912ce V-Class	$3,375	$4,250
914 Series			
1990s-present. Grand Concert, Indian rosewood back and sides, Engelmann spruce top. Non-cut offered in '13 along with 914e version. V-Class introduced '20.			
2002-2019	914ce	$3,125	$4,000
2020-2023	914ce V-Class	$3,375	$4,250

MODEL YEAR	FEATURES	EXC. COND. LOW	HIGH
914ce-L1			
2003. Fall Limited Edition, Indian rosewood back and sides, Engelmann spruce top, abalone leaf and vine inlays.			
2003		$3,000	$4,000
914ce-L7			
2004. Sitka spruce top, Brazilian rosewood and sides, abalone rosette.			
2004		$5,000	$6,250
916 Series			
2010-2019. Grand Symphony, Florentine cutaway, Indian rosewood back and sides.			
2010-2019	916ce	$3,000	$4,000
918 Series			
2013-2014. Grand Orchestra, Sitka spruce top, Indian rosewood back and sides.			
2013-2014	918e	$3,000	$4,000
955			
1996-2000. Jumbo 12 string, rosewood back and sides, spruce top.			
1996-2000		$3,000	$4,000
Academy Series			
2017-present. Designed for beginner guitar players, 10 is D-size and 12 is 000-size, e indicates on-board electronics.			
2017-2023	10	$400	$550
2017-2023	10e	$450	$600
2017-2023	12e	$450	$600
2017-2023	12e-N	$450	$600
American Dream Series (AD)			
2020-present. Grand Pacific body style, wood pairings include sapele/mahogany and ovangkol/spruce, V-Class bracing, e indicates on-board electronics.			
2020-2023	AD17	$900	$1,125
2020-2023	AD17e	$1,125	$1,500
2020-2023	AD27e	$1,125	$1,500
2020-2023	AD28e	$1,125	$1,500
Baby Taylor			
1996-present. 3/4-size Dreadnought, mahogany laminated back and sides until '99, sapele laminate after, various tops.			
1996-2023	BT1, Sitka spruce	$250	$350
1998-2023	BT2, mahogany	$250	$350
2000-2003	BT3, maple	$250	$350
2010-2023	TSBT Taylor Swift	$250	$350
2016-2023	BTe-Koa	$300	$400
Baby Rosewood			
2000-2003. Laminated Indian rosewood back and sides Baby.			
2000-2003		$250	$350
Baritone 6			
2010-2013. Grand Symphony 6-string baritone, Indian rosewood or mahogany back and sides.			
2010-2013		$2,250	$3,000
Baritone 8/GT-8 Baritone			
2010-2013. Grand Symphony 8-string baritone, Indian rosewood or mahogany back and sides.			
2010-2013		$2,625	$3,500
Big Baby BBT			
2000-present. 15/16-size Dreadnought, sapele laminate back and sides, Sitka spruce top.			
2000-2023		$325	$450

MODEL YEAR	FEATURES	EXC. COND. LOW	HIGH

Builder's Edition

2018-present. New designs from master builders, premium features. All models have 'Builder's Edition' in the model name.

2019-2023	517	$2,250	$2,875
2019-2023	717	$2,250	$2,875
2020-2023	324ce	$2,125	$2,625
2020-2023	614ce	$2,875	$3,625
2020-2023	652ce	$2,875	$3,625
2020-2023	816ce	$2,750	$3,500
2020-2023	K-14ce Koa, vine inlay	$3,625	$4,500
2020-2023	K-24ce Koa	$3,625	$4,500

Builder's Reserve (BR)

A series of special limited guitars built using Taylor's private wood reserves accumulated 30-plus years.

2008	BR VII	$2,250	$3,000

CPSM Chris Proctor Signature

2000-2001. Limited edition, 100 made, Indian rosewood body, Engelmann spruce top.

2000-2001		$2,000	$2,500

CUJO-10/CUJO-14

1997. Dreadnought (CUJO-10) or Grand Auditorium (CUJO-14), made from 100+ year old black walnut tree appearing in famous Stephen King movie "Cujo"(1983). Robert Taylor purchased the tree when it was dying of old age. The DN has spruce top, GA has cedar, both have elaborate appointments and are signed by Taylor and King. Only 125 made of each.

1997		$1,750	$2,250

Custom Shop

2008-present. Custom shop models - some are one-offs, others are series ordered by specific dealers. Previously called Taylor's Build To Order program.

Custom Dreadnought/Custom DN

2008-2017	AA+ Indian/ Adirondack	$2,750	$3,500

Custom Grand Auditorium

2008-2017	Adirondack/ mahogany	$3,250	$4,000
2008-2023	Figured Koa	$4,250	$5,500
2008-2023	Spruce/maple	$3,500	$4,500

Custom Grand Concert

2008-2017	Various woods	$3,500	$4,500

Custom TF

2011. Acoustic-electric, slotted headstock, rosewood, Taylor Build To Order program.

2011		$2,750	$3,750

DCSM Dan Crary Signature

1986-2000. Dreadnought, Venetian cutaway, thin spruce top, Indian rosewood back and sides, Crary signature on headstock.

1986-2000		$1,875	$2,500

DDAD Doyle Dykes Signature Anniversary

2005. Indian rosewood back and sides, soft cutaway, on-board transducer.

2005		$3,000	$4,000

DDSM Doyle Dykes Signature

2000-2012. Grand auditorium cutaway acoustic/ electric, figured maple body.

2000-2012		$3,000	$4,000

MODEL YEAR	FEATURES	EXC. COND. LOW	HIGH

DDSM-LTD Doyle Dykes Desert Rose Edition

2000-2003. Grand Auditorium, Limited Edition, 72 offered, Sitka spruce, flamed maple, on-board electronics.

2000-2003		$3,125	$4,000

DMSM Dave Matthews Signature

2010-2012. Limited Edition based on 914ce, Taylor Expression pickup system.

2010-2012		$4,250	$5,500

DN Series

2007-2012. Dreadnought Series, various woods.

2007-2011	DNK (Koa)	$2,000	$2,500
2007-2012	DN3	$900	$1,125
2007-2012	DN5	$1,500	$2,000
2007-2012	DN8	$1,500	$2,000

E14ce Limited Edition

2018-2019. Grand Auditorium, Venetian cutaway, V-Class bracing, spruce top, African ebony back and sides, natural finish.

2018-2019		$2,250	$3,000

GA Limited Editions

1995. Grand Auditorium Limited Editions. GA-BE has Brazilian rosewood back and sides with Engelmann spruce top, KC has Koa/cedar, KS Koa/spruce, MC mahogany/cedar, RS Indian rosewood/spruce, and WS walnut/spruce.

1995	GABE (Brazilian)	$4,500	$5,500
1995	GAKC (Koa)	$3,000	$4,000
1995	GAMC (Cedar)	$2,500	$3,250
1995	GARS (Indian)	$2,500	$3,250
1995	GAWS (Walnut)	$2,625	$3,500

GA Series

2007-2012. Grand Auditorium Series, various woods.

2007-2012	GA3, Sitka/sapele	$900	$1,125
2007-2012	GA3-12	$900	$1,125
2007-2012	GA4, Sitka/ ovangkol	$1,000	$1,375
2007-2012	GA5, cedar/ mahogany	$1,500	$2,000
2007-2012	GA6, Sitka/ flamed maple	$1,500	$2,000
2007-2012	GA6-12	$1,500	$2,000
2007-2012	GA7, cedar/r osewood	$1,500	$2,000
2007-2012	GA8, Sitka/ rosewood	$1,500	$2,000
2008-2012	GA-K-12, cedar/Koa	$2,250	$3,000
2012	GACE (Fall LE)	$2,125	$2,750
2013	GAMC (Fall LE)	$2,125	$2,750

GC Series

2007-2012. Grand Concert Series, various woods.

2007-2012	GC3, Sitka/sapele	$900	$1,125
2007-2012	GC4, Sitka/ ovangkol	$1,000	$1,375
2007-2012	GC5, cedar/ mahogany	$1,500	$2,000
2007-2012	GC6, Sitka/maple	$1,500	$2,000

Taylor AD27e

Taylor Builder's Edition 652ce

GUITARS

Taylor GT K21e

Taylor T-5
Charlie Brown

MODEL YEAR	FEATURES	EXC. COND. LOW	HIGH
2007-2012	GC7, cedar/rosewood	$1,500	$2,000
2007-2012	GC8, Sitka/rosewood	$1,500	$2,000
2011	GC-LTD, all mahogany	$1,500	$2,000

GS Series
2006-present. Grand Symphony Series, various woods.

MODEL YEAR	FEATURES	EXC. COND. LOW	HIGH
2007	GS4E-LTD	$1,625	$2,000
2007-2012	GS3, Sitka/sapele	$900	$1,125
2007-2012	GS5, cedar/mahogany	$1,625	$2,000
2007-2012	GS5-12, cedar/mahogany	$1,625	$2,000
2007-2012	GS6, Sitka/maple	$1,625	$2,000
2007-2012	GS7, cedar/rosewood	$1,625	$2,000
2007-2012	GS8, Sitka/rosewood	$1,625	$2,000
2007-2012	GS8-12, Sitka/rosewood	$1,625	$2,000
2011-2023	GS Mini	$400	$500
2019-2023	GS Mini-e Koa	$600	$750
2019-2023	GS Mini-e Mahogany	$525	$650
2019-2023	GS Mini-e Plus	$700	$875

GT Series
2020-present. Grand Theater Series, various woods, e indicates on-board electronics.

MODEL YEAR	FEATURES	EXC. COND. LOW	HIGH
2020-2023	GT, Sitka/ash	$975	$1,250
2020-2022	GT811e, Sitka/Indian	$2,250	$2,875
2020-2023	GTe, Sitka/ash	$1,250	$1,500
2020-2022	GTK21e, all Koa	$3,375	$4,250

Hot Rod Limited Edition HR14-LTD/HR15-LTD
2003. Grand Auditorium (HR14) or Jumbo (HR15), 32 of each made, natural finish with red-stained back and sides or gloss black with transparent black.

MODEL YEAR	FEATURES	EXC. COND. LOW	HIGH
2003		$2,500	$3,250

K Series
1983-present. Koa Series, various models with Hawaiian Koa. V-Class introduced '20.

MODEL YEAR	FEATURES	EXC. COND. LOW	HIGH
1983-1992	K20	$2,125	$2,750
1983-2006	K10	$2,000	$2,500
1992-2002	K20c	$2,250	$3,000
1995-1998	K65, 12-string	$2,875	$3,750
1998-2000	K22	$2,250	$3,000
1998-2002	K14c	$2,000	$2,500
1998-2012	K14ce	$2,000	$2,500
2001-2006	K55, 12-string	$2,500	$3,250
2001-2016	K20ce	$2,500	$3,250
2003-2023	K22ce	$2,500	$3,250
2007-2011	K54ce	$3,000	$4,000
2007-2012	K10ce	$2,000	$2,500
2007-2023	K24ce	$2,750	$3,500
2008-2022	K26ce	$2,750	$3,500
2020-2023	K24ce V-Class	$2,750	$3,500

LKSM-6/12 Leo Kottke Signature
1981-2012. Jumbo 17" body, 6- or 12-string, rounded cutaway, Sitka spruce top, mahogany back and sides, gloss finish, Leo Kottke signature.

MODEL YEAR	FEATURES	EXC. COND. LOW	HIGH
1981-2012	12-string	$2,500	$3,250
1981-2012	6-string	$2,500	$3,250

LTG Liberty Tree L.E.
2002. Limited Edition includes DVD and certificate which are important to instrument's value, solid wood grand concert body, high-end art and appointments. Around 400 made.

MODEL YEAR	FEATURES	EXC. COND. LOW	HIGH
2002		$5,500	$7,000

NS Series
2002-2011. Nylon Strung series, various models and woods, models include NS24e/NS24ce (Indian rosewood/spruce), NS32ce/NS34ce (mahogany/spruce), NS42ce/NS44ce (ovangkol), NS52ce/NS54ce (mahogany), NS62ce/NS64ce (maple/Engelmann) and NS72ce/NS74ce (Indian rosewood/cedar). All models were cutaway electric (ce) by '04, until '10 when NS24e was offered.

MODEL YEAR	FEATURES	EXC. COND. LOW	HIGH
2002-2006	NS42ce	$900	$1,250
2002-2006	NS44/NS44ce	$1,125	$1,500
2002-2006	NS52ce	$1,125	$1,500
2002-2006	NS54ce	$1,250	$1,625
2002-2011	NS32ce	$900	$1,125
2002-2011	NS62ce	$1,625	$2,125
2002-2011	NS64ce	$1,625	$2,125
2002-2011	NS72ce	$1,750	$2,250
2002-2011	NS74/NS74ce	$2,000	$2,500
2004-2011	NS34ce	$900	$1,250
2010-2011	NS24e/NS24ce	$625	$850

PS Series
1996-present. Presentation Series, various models, Hawaiian Koa with Engelmann spruce used early on, followed by Brazilian rosewood, by '07 a variety of woods were offered, values vary depending on specs and appointments.

MODEL YEAR	FEATURES	EXC. COND. LOW	HIGH
1996-2023	Various options	$5,000	$10,000

Solidbody Classic
2008-2014. Single- or double-cut, ash body, 2 humbuckers or single-coils, pearl 'guard.

MODEL YEAR	FEATURES	EXC. COND. LOW	HIGH
2008-2014		$900	$1,250

Solidbody Custom
2008-2010. Single- or double-cut, Koa top with Tasmanian blackwood body in '08 and mahogany after or walnut top with sapele body, 2 humbuckers, diamond inlays, ivoroid binding.

MODEL YEAR	FEATURES	EXC. COND. LOW	HIGH
2008-2010		$1,500	$2,000

Solidbody Standard
2008-2014. Single- or double-cut, Tamo ash top ('08-'09) and maple after, sapele body (08-'10) and mahogany after, 2 exposed coil humbuckers, ivoroid binding.

MODEL YEAR	FEATURES	EXC. COND. LOW	HIGH
2008-2014		$800	$1,000

T3 Series
2009-2020. Semi-hollow thinline, single-cut, figured maple. T3/B with Bigsby.

MODEL YEAR	FEATURES	EXC. COND. LOW	HIGH
2009-2020	T3, T3/B	$2,000	$2,500

T5/T5z Series
2005-2020. T5 '05-'19 and T5z introduced '20, semi-hollow thinline body, sapele back and sides, spruce, maple, or Koa tops, Custom models have gold hardware and Artist inlays, Standard is chrome with micro-dots. Prices will vary depending on type of figured-wood used, figured maple and Koa will be more than plain tops.

MODEL YEAR	FEATURES	EXC. COND. LOW	HIGH
2005-2020	12-string	$2,000	$2,500
2005-2020	6-string	$2,000	$2,500

MODEL		EXC. COND.	
YEAR	FEATURES	LOW	HIGH

Walnut/W Series
1998-2006. Highly figured claro walnut backs and sides with spruce, cedar, or walnut tops. Ivoroid, ebony, gold and abalone accents.

1998-2000	W12c	$2,000	$2,500
1998-2006	W10	$2,000	$2,500
2000-2006	W14ce	$2,000	$2,500

WHCM Windham Hill
2003. Commemorative Model, D-size, spruce top, rosewood sides and back, fancy appointments with Windham Hill logo inlay.

2003		$2,000	$2,500

XX 20th Anniversary Series
1994. Limited Edition, grand auditorium, "XX" solid 18 karat gold inlay, mother-of-pearl inlay, abalone rosette, available either mahogany back and sides with cedar top (XX-MC) or Indian rosewood with spruce (XX-RS).

1994	XX-MC	$2,625	$3,500
1994	XX-RS	$2,625	$3,500

XXV 25th Anniversary
1999-2000. Dreadnought (XXV-DR) and grand auditorium (XXV-GA) models, various woods.

1999-2000	Both models	$2,000	$2,500

XXX 30th Anniversary Series
2004-2005. Limited Edition, grand concert, "XXX" solid 18 karat gold inlay, fancy appointments, XXX-BE has Brazilian rosewood back and sides with Engelmann spruce top, KE has Koa/Engelmann spruce, MS maple/spruce and RS Indian rosewood/spruce.

2004-2005	XXX-BE	$4,250	$5,500
2004-2005	XXX-KE	$2,625	$3,500
2004-2005	XXX-MS	$2,500	$3,250
2004-2005	XXX-RS	$2,500	$3,250

XXXV 35th Anniversary Series
2009. Limited Edition, various models and woods, "35" between the 11th and 12th frets. Models include DN (Dreadnought), GC (Grand Concert), GS (Grand Symphony), P (Parlor), TF (12-Fret), 9-string, plus more.

2009	All models	$2,500	$3,250

Taylor/R. Taylor Guitars
2006-2011. Bob Taylor set up the R. Taylor studio with a small group of elite luthiers to handcraft a limited amount of guitars each year, using higher grade materials and offered in a few body styles - essentially custom made models. Each style has a number of options.

Style 1

2006-2009	Various options	$3,125	$4,000

Teisco
Founded in 1946 in Tokyo, Japan by Hawaiian and Spanish guitarist Atswo Kaneko and electrical engineer Doryu Matsuda, the original company name was Aoi Onpa Kenkyujo; Teisco was the instrument name. Most imported into U.S. by Jack Westheimer beginning ca. '60 and Chicago's W.M.I. Corporation beginning around '64, some early ones for New York's Bugeleisen and Jacobson. Brands made by the company include Teisco, Teisco Del Rey, Kingston, World Teisco, Silvertone, Kent, Kimberly and Heit Deluxe.

In '56, the company's name was changed to Nippon Onpa Kogyo Co., Ltd., and in '64 the name changed again to Teisco Co., Ltd. In January '67, the company was purchased by Kawai. After '73, the brand was converted to Kay in U.S.; Teisco went into hiatus in Japan until being beifly revived in the early-'90s with plexiglas reproductions of the Spectrum 5 (not available in U.S.). Some older Teisco Del Rey stock continued to be sold in U.S. through the '70s.

Electric

1966-1969	1 pickup	$250	$325
1966-1969	2 pickups	$350	$450
1966-1969	3 pickups	$475	$625
1966-1969	4 pus or sparkle	$700	$925
1966-1969	Spectrum V	$850	$1,125
1968-1969	May Queen, black	$850	$1,125
1968-1969	May Queen, red	$850	$1,125
1968-1969	Phantom	$850	$1,125

Tele-Star
1965-ca.1972. Imported from Japan by Tele-Star Musical Instrument Corporation of New York, New York. Primarily made by Kawai, many inspired by Burns designs, some in cool sparkle finishes. They also built basses.

Electric

1966-1969	1, 2, 3 pickups	$475	$625
1966-1969	4 pus or sparkle	$550	$675
1966-1969	Amp-in-case	$450	$600
1969-1970	Double neck 6/4	$800	$1,125

Tempo
1950s-1970s. Solid and semi-hollow body electric and acoustic guitars, most likely imported by Merson Musical Products from Japan. They also offered basses and amps.

Terada
Japanese guitar manufacturer began producing semi-acoustic and acoustic guitars in the year 1912. They have made guitars for Ibanez, Orville by Gibson, Epiphone Japan, Gretsch, and other well-known brands. At their peak (late '70s to early '90s), they were producing around 10,000 guitars a month using 3 factories.

Teuffel
1988-present. Luthier Ulrich Teuffel builds his production/custom, premium and presentation grade electric solidbody guitars in Neu-Ulm, Bavaria, Germany.

Texas
1959-ca. 1965. Line of aluminum neck electric solidbodies and basses made by France's Jacobacci company, which also built under its own brand. One, two, or three pickups.

Teisco Del Rey ET-230
Tom Pfeifer

Ca. 1970s Teisco ET-110
Jim Edwards

GUITARS

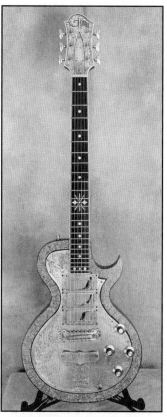

2006 Teye Electric Gypsy

Late-'90s Tobias

Greg Perrine

MODEL YEAR	FEATURES	EXC. COND. LOW	HIGH

Teye

2006-present. Luthier Teye Wijterp builds his premium and presentation grade, production/custom, solid and chambered body guitars in Austin, Texas. Some instruments are branded as Electric Gypsy guitars.

Thomas

1960s-1970s. Single, double and triple-neck electrics made by luthier Harvey Thomas in Midway, Washington. Best known for his Maltese cross shaped models, he also offered several other unique shaped designs and one-offs.

Thomas Rein

1972-present. Luthier Thomas Rein builds his premium grade, production/custom, classical guitars in St. Louis, Missouri.

Thompson Guitars

1980-present. Luthier Ted Thompson builds his professional and premium grade, production/custom, flat-top, 12-string, and nylon-string guitars in Vernon, British Columbia.

Thorell Fine Guitars

1994-present. Premium grade, custom/production, archtop, flattop and classical guitars built by luthier Ryan Thorell in Logan, Utah.

Thorn Custom Guitars

2000-present. Professional and premium grade, custom/production, solid and hollowbody electrics built by luthiers Bill Thorn and his sons Bill, Jr. and Ron in Glendale, California. They started Thorn Custom Inlay in the early '90s to do custom inlay work for other builders. In '00, they added their own line of guitars.

Thornward

Ca. 1901-ca. 1910. Line of guitars sold by the Montgomery Ward company and built by others including Lyon & Healy. The name is from a combination of the last names of company founder Aaron Montgomery Ward and company manager George Thorne.

Threet Guitars

1990-present. Premium grade, production/custom, flat-tops built by luthier Judy Threet in Calgary, Alberta.

Tilton

1850s-late 1800s. Built by William B. Tilton, of New York City, New York. He was quite an innovator and held several guitar-related patents. He also built banjos.

Parlor

1850s-1890s. Parlor guitar with various woods.

MODEL YEAR	FEATURES	EXC. COND. LOW	HIGH
1850s-80s	Brazilian, fancy binding	$2,125	$2,750
1890s	Diagonal grain spruce, Brazilian	$1,750	$2,250
1890s	Pearl trim, Brazilian	$3,125	$4,000
1890s	Standard grain spruce, Brazilian	$900	$1,250

Tim Reede Custom Guitars

2004-present. Luthier Tim Reede builds his professional and premium grade, production/custom, archtop, flat-top and electric guitars in Minneapolis, Minnesota.

Timeless Instruments

1980-present. Luthier David Freeman builds his professional, premium and presentation grade, custom, flattop, 12-string, nylon-string, and resonator guitars in Tugaske, Saskatchewan. He also builds mandolins and dulcimers.

Timm Guitars

Professional grade, custom, flat-top, resonator and travel guitars built by luthier Jerry Timm in Auburn, Washington. He started in 1997.

Timtone Custom Guitars

1993-2006. Luthier Tim Diebert built his premium grade, custom, solidbody, chambered-body and acoustic guitars and basses in Grand Forks, British Columbia. He also built lap steels.

Tippin Guitar Co.

1978-present. Professional, premium and presentation grade, production/custom, flat-top guitars built by luthier Bill Tippin in Marblehead, Massachusetts.

Tobias

1977-2019. Known mainly for basses, Tobias did offer guitar models in the '80s. See Bass Section for more company info.

TogaMan GuitarViol

2003-present. Premium grade, production/custom, bow-playable solidbody guitars built by luthier Jonathan Wilson in Sylmar, California.

Tokai

1947-present. Japan's Tokai Company started out making a keyboard harmonica that was widely used in Japanese schools. In '65, they started producing acoustic guitars, followed shortly by electrics. In the late '60s, Tokai hooked up with Tommy Moore, a successful instrument merchandiser from Fort Worth, Texas, and by '70 they were producing private label and OEM guitars, sold in the U.S. under the brands of various importers. By the '70s, the Tokai name was being used on the instruments. Today Tokai continues to offer electrics, acoustics, and electric basses made in Japan and Korea.

MODEL YEAR	FEATURES	EXC. COND. LOW	HIGH

ASD-403 Custom Edition
1980s. Strat copy, single-single-hum pickups, locking tremolo.

1980s		$725	$950

AST Series
Early 1980s. Strat copies, maple board (AST-56) or slab rosewood (AST-62), 3 single-coils.

1980s	AST-56	$850	$1,250
1980s	AST-62	$850	$1,250

ATE Series
Early 1980s. Tele copies, blond (ATE-52) and pink paisley (ATE-67), 2 single-coils.

1980s	ATE-52	$875	$1,250
1980s	ATE-67	$875	$1,250

Blazing Fire
1982-1984. Hybrid-shaped solidbody with 2 medium-short pointy horns, cast aluminum body.

1982-1984		$725	$950

Breezy Sound
1977-1984. Copy of '60s rosewood board Tele.

1977-1984		$850	$1,250

CE-180W Cat's Eyes
Late-1970s-Early-1980s. D-style flat-top, made by Tokai Gakki, Nyatoh sides and back.

1979-1980s		$375	$475

CE-250 Cat's Eyes
Late-1970s-Early-1980s. D-style flat-top.

1979-1980s		$375	$475

CE-300 Cat's Eyes
Late-1970s-Early-1980s. D-style flat-top, made by Tokai Gakki, rosewood sides and back.

1979-1980s		$525	$675

CE-400 Cat's Eyes
Late-1970s-Early-1980s. D-style flat-top, made by Tokai Gakki, rosewood sides and back.

1979-1980s		$725	$950

CE-600 Cat's Eyes
1979-1980. D-style flat-top, rosewood sides and back.

1979-1980		$725	$950

FV48
1980s. Flying V copy.

1980s		$825	$1,000

Goldstar Sound
1984. Replica that replaced the Springy Sound, new less pointy headstock shape.

1984		$725	$1,250

J-200N
1979-1980. Gibson J-200 natural copy.

1979-1980		$725	$950

Les Paul Reborn
1976-1985. LP copy with Gibson-style Tokai headstock logo and Les Paul Reborn script logo instead of Les Paul Model, renamed Reborn Old in '82, becomes Love Rock in mid-'80s.

1976-1982	Les Paul Reborn	$1,750	$2,250
1982-1985	Reborn Old	$1,750	$2,250

Love Rock/LS Series
1980s-2000s. Various LP Std copy models (LC are LP Custom copies), 2 humbuckers, sunburst, gold top, black, figured tops at the high end, Love Rock in script logo on headstock.

MODEL YEAR	FEATURES	EXC. COND. LOW	HIGH
1980s		$1,125	$1,500
2003	LS 75 Love Rock	$1,125	$1,500
2003	LS 80 Love Rock	$1,125	$1,500

SC Series
Tele copies.

2000s	SC-1	$525	$675

Silver Star
1977-1984. Copy of post-CBS large headstock Strat.

1977-1984		$725	$1,250

Springy Sound/ST-60
1977-1984. Strat copy, original high-end nitro-finish.

1977-1979	With skunk stripe	$1,375	$1,750
1979-1984	No skunk stripe	$1,375	$1,750

Vintage Series EX-55
1980s. Vintage Series, Explorer copies, bolt neck, 1 or 2 humbuckers.

1980s	1 pickup	$700	$900
1980s	2 pickups	$775	$1,000

Vintage Series TST
Early-1980s. Copy of maple neck (TST-56) and rosewood slab board (TST-62) Strats, 4-bolt neck plate with serial number.

1980s	TST-56	$850	$1,125
1980s	TST-62	$850	$1,125

Tom Anderson Guitarworks
1984-present. Professional and premium grade, production/custom, solidbody, semi-solidbody and acoustic guitars built by luthier Tom Anderson in Newbury Park, California.

Solidbody Electric
1984-present. Various models.

1984-2023	Most models	$2,250	$3,500

TommyHawk
1993-2005. Acoustic travel guitars built by luthier Tom Barth in Succasunna, New Jersey. They also offered a full-scale acoustic/electric model. Barth died in '05.

Toneline
1950s. Student-level private brand built by Chicago builders (Kay, Harmony). Typical '50s Stella brand specs like birch body with painted binding and rosette, pointed Toneline script logo on headstock.

Tonemaster
1960s. Guitars and basses, made in Italy by the Crucianelli Company, with typical '60s Italian sparkle plastic finish and push-button controls, bolt-on neck. Imported into the U.S. by The Imperial Accordion Company. They also offered guitar amps.

Rhythm Tone
1960-1963. Tonemaster headstock logo, Rhythm Tone logo on 'guard, single neck pickup, 3-in-line control knobs, bolt-on neck, black finish.

1960-1963		$925	$1,250

1983 Tokai Goldstar
Rivington Guitars

Tom Anderson Hollow T
Curtis Hill

GUITARS

Tony Vines CX

Traveler Acoustic AG-105

MODEL		EXC. COND.	
YEAR	FEATURES	LOW	HIGH

ToneSmith

1997-present. Luthier Kevin Smith builds his professional and premium grade, production/custom, semi-hollow body guitars and basses in Rogers, Minnesota. He previously built GLF brand guitars and built the line of Vox USA guitars from '98-'01.

Tony Nobles

Professional and premium grade, custom, acoustic and electric guitars built by luthier Tony Nobles in Wimberley, Texas starting in 1990.

Tony Vines Guitars

Luthier Tony Vines began in 1989, builds premium and presentation grade, custom/production, steel string guitars in Kingsport, Tennessee.

Torres (Antonio de Torres Jurado)

19th Century luthier most often associated with the initial development of the Classical Spanish guitar.

Tosca

1950s. Private economy brand made by Valco, possibly for a jobber, mail-order catalog or local department store.

Bolero 1123

1954-1957. Small three-quarter size electric similar to National (Valco) model 1123, single-cut, 1 neck pickup, guard mounted controls.

1954-1957		$900	$1,125

Toyota

1972-1970s. Imported from Japan by Hershman of New York, New York. At least 1 high-end acoustic designed by T. Kurosawa was ambitiously priced at $650.

Traphagen, Dake

1972-present. Luthier Dake Traphagen builds his premium grade, custom, classical and steel-string guitars in Bellingham, Washington.

Traugott Guitars

1991-present. Premium grade, production/custom, flat-top and acoustic/electric guitars built by luthier Jeff Traugott in Santa Cruz, California.

Traveler Guitar

1992-present. Intermediate grade, production, travel size electric, acoustic, classical, and acoustic/electric guitars and basses made in Redlands, California.

Travis Bean

1974-1979, 1999. Aluminum-necked solidbody electric guitars and basses. The company was founded by motorcycle and metal-sculpture enthusiast Travis Bean and guitar repairman Marc McElwee in Southern California; soon joined by

MODEL		EXC. COND.	
YEAR	FEATURES	LOW	HIGH

Gary Kramer (see Kramer guitars). Kramer left Travis Bean in '75 and founded Kramer guitars with other partners. Guitar production began in mid-'76. The guitars featured carved aluminum necks with three-and-three heads with a T cutout in the center and wooden 'boards. Some necks had bare aluminum backs; some were painted black. A total of about 3,650 instruments were produced. Travis Bean guitar production was stopped in the summer of '79.

Serial numbers were stamped on headstock and were more-or-less consecutive. Original retail prices were $895 to $1195.

The company announced renewed production in '99 with updated versions of original designs and new models, but it evidently never got going.

TB-500

1975-1976. Aluminum neck, T-slotted headstock, double-cut, 2 single coils mounted in 'guard, 2 controls, dot markers, white.

1975-1976		$7,500	$9,500

TB-1000 Artist

1974-1979. Aluminum neck, T-slotted headstock, double-cut archtop, 2 humbuckers, 4 controls, block inlays.

1974-1979		$8,000	$10,000
1974-1979	Rare colors	$9,500	$12,000

TB-1000 Standard

1974-1979. Similar to TB-1000 Artist, but with dot inlays.

1974-1979		$9,000	$11,500

TB-3000 Wedge

1976-1979. Aluminum neck with T-slotted headstock, triangle-shaped body, 2 humbucking pickups, 4 controls, block markers on 'board.

1976-1979		$12,000	$15,000

Tregan Guitars

2007-present. Solidbody electrics including Bison-style sharp curved horns body style, plus other less traditional styles, student and intermediate grade.

Tremblett Archtops

Luthier Mark Tremblett started in the year 2006, he builds professional grade, custom, archtop guitars in Pouch Cove, Newfoundland.

Tremcaster

Luthier John Mosconi, along with Robert Gelley and Jeff Russell, started in 2008, build professional grade, production/custom, electric and acoustic guitars in Akron, Ohio.

Trenier

1998-present. Premium grade, production/custom, archtop guitars built by luthier Bryant Trenier in Seattle, Washington. From '02 to '04 he was located in Prague, Czech Republic.

MODEL YEAR	FEATURES	EXC. COND. LOW	HIGH

Triggs

1992-present. Luthiers Jim Triggs and his son Ryan build their professional and premium grade, production/custom, archtop, flat-top, and solidbody guitars originally in Nashville Tennessee, and, since '98, in Kansas City, Kansas. They also build mandolins.

Acoustic/Electric Archtop

1992-present. Various archtop cutaway models.

YEAR	FEATURES	LOW	HIGH
1992-2009	Byrdland 17"	$2,750	$3,500
1992-2009	Excel 17"	$4,000	$5,000
1992-2009	Jazzmaster	$2,250	$3,000
1992-2009	New Yorker 18"	$5,500	$7,000
1992-2010	Stromberg Master 400	$5,500	$7,000
1997	Trinity 18"	$5,500	$7,000
2006	San Salvador	$3,500	$4,500

Trinity River

Located in Fort Worth, Texas, luthiers Marcus Lawyer and Ross McLeod import their production/custom, budget and intermediate grade, acoustic and resonator guitars and basses from Asia. They started in 2004 and also import mandolins and banjos.

True North Guitars

1994-present. Luthier Dennis Scannell builds his premium grade, custom, flat-tops in Waterbury, Vermont.

True Tone

1960s. Guitars, basses and amps retailed by Western Auto, manufactured by Chicago guitar makers like Kay. The brand was most likely gone by '68.

Double Cutaway (K300 Kay)

1962-1966. Made by Kay and similar to their K300, double-cut solidbody, dual pickups and vibrola arm, red.

1962-1966		$525	$675

Double Cutaway Electric Archtop (K592 Kay)

1960s. Made by Kay and similar to their K592 double-cut thinline acoustic, 2 pickups, Bigsby tailpiece, burgundy red.

1960s		$600	$775

Fun Time

Early- to mid-1960s. Student 13" flat-top, painted 5-point 'guard, red sunburst finish.

1960s		$95	$125

Imperial Deluxe

Mid-1960s. Harmony-made (Rocket), 3 pickups, trapeze tailpiece, 6 control knobs, block markers, sunburst.

1960s		$700	$925

Jazz King (K573 Kay)

1960s. Kay's K573 Speed Demon, 3 pickups, thinline archtop electric with f-hole, eighth note art on 'guard, sunburst.

1960s		$525	$675

Rock 'n Roll Electric (K100 Kay)

1960s. Kay's K100, slab body, single pickup, but with a bright red multiple lacquer finish.

1960s		$425	$575

Speed Master (K6533 Kay)

1960s. Made by Kay and similar to their K6533 full-body electric archtop Value Leader line, eighth note art 'guard, sunburst.

1960s		$450	$600

Western Spanish Auditorium

Early- to mid-1960s. 15" flat-top, laminate construction, celluloid 'guard, sunburst.

1960s		$200	$275

Tsunami

Custom, intermediate grade, one-off solidbody electric guitars built by luthier Paul Brzozowski, starting in 2009, in Cleveland, Tennessee.

Tucker

Founded by John N. "Jack" Tucker, John Morrall, and David Killingsworth in 2000, Tucker builds professional and premium grade, production/custom, albizzia wood solidbody guitars and basses in Hanalei, Hawaii.

Tuscany Guitars

2008-2013. Intermediate grade, production, classic model electric guitars imported from Asia and finished by luthier Galeazzo Frudua in San Lazzaro di Savena, Italy.

Tut Taylor

Line of professional and premium grade, production/custom, resophonic guitars built by luthier Mark Taylor of Crafters of Tennessee in Old Hickory, Tennessee. Brand named for his father, dobro artist Tut Taylor. Taylor also builds the Tennessee line of guitars, mandolins and banjos and was part of Rich and Taylor guitars for '93-'96.

TV Jones

1993-present. Professional and premium grade, production/custom, hollow, chambered, and solid body guitars built by luthier Thomas Vincent Jones originally in California, now in Poulsbo, Washington. The instruments have either Jones or TV Jones inlaid on the headstock. He also builds pickups.

U. A. C.

1920s. Instruments built by the Oscar Schmidt Co. and possibly others. Most likely a brand made for a distributor.

Unique Guitars

2003-ca. 2007. Professional and premium grade, production/custom, solidbody guitars and basses built by luthier Joey Rico in California. Joey is the son of Bernie Rico, the founder of BC Rich guitars.

Truetone Speed Master
Tom Pfeifer

TV Jones Spectra
Sonic Supreme

GUITARS

Univox Hi Flier
Charlie Brown

1958 Valco Supro Thunderstick
Rivington Guitars

MODEL YEAR	FEATURES	EXC. COND. LOW	HIGH

Univox

1964-1978. Univox started out as an amp line and added guitars around '68. Guitars were imported from Japan by the Merson Musical Supply Company, later Unicord, Westbury, New York. Many if not all supplied by Arai and Company (Aria, Aria Pro II), some made by Matsumoku. Univox Lucy ('69) first copy of lucite Ampeg Dan Armstrong. Generally mid-level copies of American designs.

Acoustic Flat-Top
1969-1978. Various models.

1970s		$250	$650

Bicentennial
1976. Offset double-cut, heavily carved body, brown stain, 3 humbucker-style pickups.

1976		$1,125	$1,500

Deep Body Electric

1960s-70s	ES-175 style	$625	$850

GuitOrgan FSB C-3000
1970s. Double-cut semi-hollow body, multiple controls, GuitOrgan logo on headstock, foot pedal.

1970s	Fully functional	$1,250	$1,625

Solid Body Electric
1960s-1970s. Includes Flying V, Mosrite and Hofner violin-guitar copies.

1960s-70s	Hi Flier	$850	$1,250
1960s-70s	Various models	$750	$975
1970s	Effector	$650	$750

Thin Line (Coily)

1960s-70s	12-string	$550	$750
1960s-70s	6-string	$550	$750

USA Custom Guitars

1999-2020. Professional and premium grade, custom/production, solidbody electric guitars built in Tacoma, Washington. They also did work for other luthiers. In late '20, USA was acquired by MJT Aged Guitar Finishes in Carthage, Missouri.

Vaccaro

1997-2002. Founded by Henry Vaccaro, Sr., one of the founders of Kramer Guitars. They offered intermediate and professional grade, production/custom, aluminum-necked guitars and basses designed by Vaccaro, former Kramer designer Phil Petillo, and Henry Vaccaro, Jr., which were made in Asbury Park, New Jersey.

Val Dez

Early-1960s-early-1970s. Less expensive guitars built by Landola in Sweden or Finland; they also made the Espana brand.

Valco

1942-1968. Valco, of Chicago, was a big player in the guitar and amplifier business. Their products were private branded for other companies like National, Supro, Airline, Oahu, and Gretsch. In '42, National Dobro ceased operations and Victor Smith, Al Frost and Louis Dopyera bought the company and changed the name to Valco Manufac-

MODEL YEAR	FEATURES	EXC. COND. LOW	HIGH

turing Company. Post-war production resumed in '46. Valco was purchased by treasurer Robert Engelhardt in '64. In '67, Valco bought Kay, but in '68 the new Valco/Kay company went out of business.

Valencia

1985-present. Budget grade, production, classical guitars imported first by Rondo Music of Union, New Jersey and presently distributed by others.

Valley Arts

Ca. 1977-2010. Professional and premium grade, production/custom, semi-hollow and solidbody guitars and basses built in Nashville, Tennessee. Valley Arts originally was a Southern California music store owned by partners Al Carness and Mike McGuire where McGuire taught and did most of the repairs. Around '77, McGuire and Valley Arts started making custom instruments on a large scale. By '83, they opened a separate manufacturing facility to build the guitars. In '92 Samick acquired half of the company with McGuire staying on for a year as a consultant. Samick offered made-in-the-U.S. production and custom models under the Valley Arts name. In '02, Valley Arts became a division of Gibson Guitar Corp., which built the guitars in Nashville. Founders Carness and McGuire were once again involved with the company. They reintroduced the line in January, '03. The brand has been inactive since '10.

Vantage

1977-1998. Budget and intermediate grade, production, acoustic and electric guitars and basses from Japan '77-'90 and from Korea '90-'98.

Vega

1889-1980s, 1989-present. Founded in Boston by the Nelson family, Vega was big in the banjo market into the 1930s, before adding guitars to their line. The company was purchased by C.F. Martin in '70 who built Vega banjos and starting in '76 they also used the brand on imported guitars, first from the Netherlands and later from Japan, with the Japanese Vegas being of higher quality. In '79, Martin sold the Vega trademark to Korea's Galaxy Trading Company. The Deering Banjo Company, in Spring Valley, California acquired the brand in '89 and uses it (and the star logo) on a line of banjos.

C Series (Archtop)
1933-1950s. Carved-top archtops, '30's models are the 14 5/8" mahogany body C-20 and C-40, 16 1/8" maple body C-60, and the C-70/C75 Vehaphone with rosewood body and gold parts, and the figured-maple body C-80 with deluxe appointments. By '40 the line was the 14-16" C-19, -26, -46, and -56, and the 17" Professional Series C-66 Professional, C-71 Soloist, C-76 Artist, and C-86 Deluxe. Optional blond finish available by '40.

1933-1939	C-20	$1,125	$1,500
1933-1939	C-40	$1,125	$1,500

MODEL YEAR	FEATURES	EXC. COND. LOW	HIGH
1933-1939	C-60	$1,625	$2,125
1933-1939	C-70	$1,875	$2,500
1933-1939	C-80	$2,125	$2,750
1938	C-75	$3,125	$4,000
1940-1949	C-19, C-26, C-46	$950	$1,250
1940-1949	C-56	$1,750	$2,250
1940-1949	C-66 Professional	$1,875	$2,500
1940-1949	C-71 Soloist	$1,875	$2,500
1940-1949	C-76 Artist	$2,125	$2,750
1940-1949	C-86 Deluxe	$2,125	$2,750

Duo-Tron Series (Electric Archtop)

1947-late 1950s. Various mid-level large body cutaway and non-cut carved-top archtops, 1, 2 or 3 (rare) floating pickups, dot or block markers, natural or sunburst.

1947-50s	High-end models	$2,625	$3,500
1947-50s	Low-end models	$800	$1,125
1947-50s	Mid-range models	$1,125	$1,500

E-201 Electric Archtop

1959. One pickup, sunburst.

1959		$1,875	$2,500

FT-90 Flat-Top

1960s. 15" body with narrow waist, dot markers, Vega logo, natural.

1960s		$450	$600

G-30

1968-ca. 1970. D-style with solid spruce top and solid mahogany sides and back, Vega logo with star on headstock, dot markers, natural finish.

1968-1970		$350	$500

O'Dell

1950s. Full body, single cut, acoustic-electric, 1 pickup, tailpiece controls.

1950s	Sunburst	$1,125	$1,500

Parlor

Early-1900s-1920s. Small parlor-sized instrument, styles and appointment levels, including binding, purfling and inlays, vary.

1900s	Mahogany	$475	$650
1910s	Brazilian	$1,125	$1,500
1910s-20s	Brazilian, fancy	$4,000	$5,250

Profundo Flat-Top

1930s-1950s. Flat-top D-style body, spruce top, mahogany or rosewood back and sides.

1930s-50s	Mahogany	$1,750	$2,250
1940s-50s	Rosewood	$2,500	$3,500

Solidbody Electric (Import)

1970s-1980s. Solidbody copies of classic designs, Vega script logo on headstock, bolt-on necks.

1970s		$300	$400

Vega Electric Archtop

1939. Full-body electric archtop, figured maple, 1 pickup, 2 control knobs, trapeze bridge, diamond markers, large Vega and star headstock logo, blond.

1939		$1,375	$1,750

Vega, Charles

1993-2010. Luthier Charles Vega built his premium, production/custom, nylon-string guitars in Baltimore, Maryland.

Veillette

1991-present. Luthiers Joe Veillette (of Veillette-Citron fame) and Martin Keith build their professional grade, production/custom, acoustic, acoustic/electric, electric 6- and 12-string and baritone guitars and basses in Woodstock, New York. They also build mandolins.

Veillette-Citron

1975-1983. Founded by Joe Veillette and Harvey Citron who met at the New York College School of Architecture in the late '60s. Joe took a guitar building course from Michael Gurian and by the Summer of '76, he and Harvey started producing neck-thru solidbody guitars and basses. Veillette and Citron both are back building instruments.

Velázquez

1948-1972. Manuel Velázquez, New York, New York, gained a reputation as a fine repairman in the late 1940s. He opened his 3rd Avenue guitar building shop in the early 1950s. By the mid-1950s he was considered by some as being the finest American builder of classical guitars. Velázquez left New York in 1972 and moved to Puerto Rico. He continued building guitars for the Japanese market. He returned to the United States in 1982. By the 2000s he built instruments with his son and daughter.

Veleno

1967, 1970-1977, 2003-2018. Premium and presentation grade, production/custom, all-aluminum electric solidbody guitars built by luthier John Veleno in St. Petersburg, Florida. First prototype in '67. Later production begins in the late '70s and lasts until '75 or '76. The guitars were chrome or gold-plated, with various anodized colors. The Traveler Guitar was the idea of B.B. King; only 10 were made. Two Ankh guitars were made for Todd Rundgren in '77. Only one bass was made. Approximately 185 instruments were made up to '77 and are sequentially numbered. In 2003, John Veleno reintroduced his brand, he died in '18.

Original (Aluminum Solidbody)

1973-1976. V-headstock, chrome and aluminum.

1973-1976	Rare color	$20,000	$25,000
1973-1976	Standard	$15,000	$20,000

Traveler

1973-1976. Limited production of about a dozen instruments, drop-anchor-style metal body.

1973-1976		$12,000	$15,000

Vengeance Guitars & Graphix

2002-present. Luthier Rick Stewart builds his professional and premium grade, custom/production, solidbody guitars and basses in Arden, North Carolina.

1938 Vega C-75 Vegaphone
Michael J. Scanlon

Veillette Swift

Ventura Bruno VS III
W. H. Stephens

Vintage V100 M
Thomas Booth

MODEL YEAR	FEATURES	EXC. COND. LOW	HIGH

Ventura

1970s. Acoustic and electric guitars imported by C. Bruno Company, mainly copies of classic American models. They also offered basses.

Acoustic Flat-Top

1970s		$500	$650

Guitorgan

1970s. Based on MCI Guitorgan, converts standard electric guitar into a Guitorgan through the addition of electronic organ components, multiple switches, large Barney Kessel sharp-horned acoustic-electric style body.

1970s		$1,125	$1,500

Hollowbody Electric

1970s		$725	$950

Solidbody Electric

1970s		$725	$950

Verri

Premium grade, production/custom, archtop guitars built by luthier Henry Verri in Little Falls, New York starting in 1992.

Versoul, LTD

1989-present. Premium grade, production/custom steel-string flat-top, acoustic/electric, nylon-string, resonator, solidbody, and baritone guitars, basses and sitars built by luthier Kari Nieminen in Helsinki, Finland.

VibraWood

2012-present. Luthier John J. Slog builds custom, professional and premium grade, vintage-style guitars and basses in Bethlehem, Pennsylvania.

Vicente Tatay

1894-late 1930s. Classical guitars built by luthier Vicente Tatay and his sons in Valencia, Spain.

Victor Baker Guitars

1998-present. Professional and premium grade, custom, carved archtop, flat-top and solidbody electric guitars built by luthier Victor Baker in Philadelphia, Pennsylvania. In '10 he relocated to Brooklyn, New York and is currently in Astoria.

Victor Guitars

2002-2008. Luthiers Edward Victor Dick and Greg German built their premium grade, production/custom, flat-top guitars in Denver, Colorado.

Victoria

Ca. 1902-1920s. Brand name for New York distributor Buegeleisen & Jacobson. Instruments built by the Oscar Schmidt Co. and possibly others. Most likely a brand made for a distributor.

Vigier

1980-present. Luthier Patrice Vigier builds high-end electric guitars and basses near Paris, France.

MODEL YEAR	FEATURES	EXC. COND. LOW	HIGH

Electric Solidbody

1980-present. Various models.

1980	Arpege	$2,250	$2,875
2000-2006	Expert	$2,250	$2,875
2005-2023	Excalibur Shawn Lane	$2,250	$2,875
2020-2023	Excalibur Special	$2,625	$3,250
2020-2023	Excalibur Supra 7	$2,125	$2,625
2020-2023	Excalibur Thirteen	$2,250	$2,875
2020-2023	Excalibur Ultra Blues	$2,500	$3,125
2021-2023	Texas Blues	$2,000	$2,500

Viking Guitars

2003-present. Premium grade, solidbody guitars made by Ed Roman Guitars. Production was '03-'04, custom only since.

Vinetto

2003-present. Luthier Vince Cunetto builds his professional grade, production/custom, solid, chambered and semi-hollow body guitars in St. Louis, Missouri.

Vintage

Ca. 1993-present. Intermediate grade, production, solidbody and semi-hollow acoustic, electro-acoustic and resonator guitars and basses, imported from China, Korea and Vietnam by John Hornby Skewes & Co. in the U.K. They also offer folk instruments.

Vintique

Luthier Jay Monterose built premium grade, custom/production, electric guitars in Suffern, New York. Vintique also manufactured guitar hardware.

Vivi-Tone

1932-1938. Founded in Kalamazoo, Michigan, by former Gibson designer Lloyd Loar, Walter Moon and Lewis Williams, Vivi-Tone built acoustic archtop guitars as well as some of the earliest electric solidbodies. They also built basses and mandolins and offered amps built by Webster Electric. A Vivi-Tone instrument must be all original. Any missing part makes this instrument practically unsellable in the vintage-market.

Various Models

1932-1938	Rare models	$3,500	$4,500
1932-1938	Standard models	$2,625	$3,500
1932-1938	Tenor, 4-string	$2,125	$2,750

Vox

1954-present. Name introduced by Jennings Musical Instruments (JMI) of England. First Vox products was a volume pedal, amplifiers were brought to the market in late '57 by Tom Jennings and Dick Denny. Guitars were introduced in '61, with an Echo Unit starting the Vox line of effects in '63.

Guitars and basses bearing the Vox name were offered from '61-'69 (made in England and Italy),

MODEL YEAR	FEATURES	EXC. COND. LOW	HIGH

'82-'85 (Japan), '85-'88 (Korea), '98-2001 (U.S.), and they introduced a limited-edition U.S.-made teardrop guitar in '07 and the semi-hollow Virage guitars in '08.

Ace/Super Ace
1963-1968. Offset double cut solidbody, 2 single-coils. Super Ace has 3 pickups.

1963-1968	Ace	$700	$950
1963-1968	Super Ace	$925	$1,250

Apache
1960s. Modified teardrop body, 3 pickups, vibrato.

1966		$900	$1,125

Apollo
1967-1968. Single sharp cutaway, 1 pickup, distortion, treble and bass booster, available in sunburst or cherry

1967-1968		$900	$1,125

Bobcat
1963-1968. Double-cut semi-hollowbody style, block markers, 3 pickups, vibrato, 2 volume and 2 tone controls.

1963-1965	England	$1,250	$1,625
1966-1968	Italy	$925	$1,250

Bossman
1967-1968. Single rounded cutaway, 1 pickup, distortion, treble and bass booster, available in sunburst or cherry.

1967-1968		$775	$1,000

Bulldog
1966. Solidbody double-cut, 3 pickups.

1966		$1,250	$1,625

Delta
1967-1968. 5-sided Phantom shaped solidbody, 2 pickups, distortion, treble and bass boosters, vibrato, 1 volume and 2 tone controls, available in white only.

1967-1968		$1,625	$2,125

Folk XII
1966-1969. Dreadnought 12-string flat-top, large 3-point 'guard, block markers, natural.

1966-1969		$500	$650

Guitar-Organ
1966. Standard Phantom with oscillators from a Continental organ installed inside. Plays either organ sounds, guitar sounds, or both. Weighs over 20 pounds. Prices vary widely due to operating issues with this model.

1966	Fully functional	$2,750	$4,000
1966	Functional 'board	$1,750	$3,000
1966	Partial function	$825	$1,250

Harlem
1965-1967. Offset double-cut solidbody, 2 extended range pickups, sunburst or color option. Values vary widely due to operating issues with this model.

1965-1967		$900	$1,125

Hurricane
1965-1967. Double-cut solidbody, 2 pickups, spring action vibrato, sunburst or color option.

1965-1967		$775	$1,000

Invader (V262)
1966-1967. Solidbody double-cut, 2 pickups, on-board effects, sunburst. Must have fully functional electronics.

1966-1967		$2,250	$3,000

Mando Guitar
1966. Made in Italy, 12-string mandolin thing.

1966		$1,375	$1,750

Mark III (U.S.A)
1998-2001. Teardrop reissue, made in U.S.A., 2 single-coils, fixed bridge or Bigsby. A limited model was introduced in '08.

1998-2001		$1,000	$1,300

Mark III 50th Anniversary
2007. Only 100 made, teardrop body, 2 pickups, white finish.

2007		$1,250	$1,625

Mark III Limited Edition
2008. Custom Shop USA model, white hardwood body, maple neck, rosewood 'board.

2008		$2,000	$2,500

Mark III/Phantom Mark III
1963-1964. Made in England, teardrop body, 2 pickups, 2 controls, Marvin Bigsby, guitar version of Mark IV bass, while it is called a Phantom Mark III it does not have a Phantom shape.

1963-1964		$3,500	$4,500

Mark IX
1965-1966. Solidbody teardrop-shaped, 9 strings, 3 pickups, vibrato, 1 volume and 2 tone controls.

1965-1966		$1,625	$2,125

Mark VI
1965-1967. Teardrop-shaped solidbody, 3 pickups, vibrato, 1 volume and 2 tone controls.

1964-1965	England, white, Brian Jones	$4,000	$5,000
1965-1967	Italy, sunburst	$2,250	$3,000

Mark VI Reissue
1998-2001. Actually, this is a reissue of the original Phantom VI (Vox couldn't use that name due to trademark reasons), made in U.S.A.

1998-2001		$925	$1,250

Mark XII
1965-1967. Teardrop-shaped solidbody, 12 strings, 3 pickups, vibrato, 1 volume and 2 tone controls, sunburst. Reissued for '98-'01.

1965-1967		$1,875	$2,500

Meteor/Super Meteor
1965-1967. Solidbody double-cut, 1 pickup, Super Meteor with vibrato.

1965-1967	Meteor	$550	$750
1965-1967	Super Meteor	$600	$800

New Orleans
1966. Thin double-cut acoustic electric similar to ES-330, 2 pickups, a scaled down version of the 3-pickup Bobcat model.

1966		$875	$1,125

Phantom VI
1962-1967. Five-sided body, 6 strings, 3 pickups, vibrato, 1 volume and 2 tone controls.

1962-1964	English-made	$3,750	$4,500
1965-1967	Italian-made	$2,500	$3,500

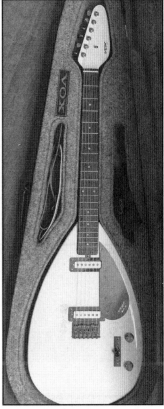

1998 Vox Mark III
Frank Quarracino

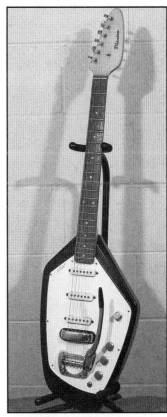

1965 Vox Phantom VI
Tom Pfeifer

1969 Vox V221 Phantom
XII 12-String
Craig Brody

Vox Ultrasonic
Imaged by Heritage Auctions, HA.com

MODEL YEAR	FEATURES	EXC. COND. LOW	HIGH
Phantom XII			
1964-1967. 12 string version of VI.			
1964	English-made	$3,750	$4,500
1965-1967	Italian-made	$2,500	$3,500
Phantom XII Stereo			
1966. Phantom XII with 3 special offset stereo pickups making 6 pickup combinations, 3 separate pickup mode selectors, color option.			
1966		$2,750	$3,500
Shadow			
1965. Solidbody double-cut, 3 pickups, tremolo tailpiece, sunburst.			
1965	English-made	$1,000	$1,500
Spitfire			
1965-1967. Solidbody double-cut, 3 pickups, vibrato.			
1965-1967		$925	$1,250
Starstream			
1967-1968. Teardrop-shaped hollowbody, 2 pickups, distortion, treble and bass boosters, wah-wah, vibrato, 1 volume and 2 tone controls, 3-way pickup selector, available in cherry or sandburst.			
1967-1968		$2,000	$2,500
Starstream XII			
1967-1968. 12 string version.			
1967-1968		$2,000	$2,500
Stroller			
1961-1966. Made in England, solidbody, single bridge pickup, Hurricane-style contoured body, dot markers, red.			
1961-1966		$575	$750
Student Prince			
1965-1967. Made in Italy, mahogany body thinline archtop electric, 2 knobs, dot markers.			
1965-1967		$550	$750
Super Lynx			
1965-1967. Similar to Bobcat but with 2 pickups and no vibrola, double-cut, 2 pickups, adjustable truss rod, 2 bass and 2 volume controls.			
1965-1967		$925	$1,250
Super Lynx Deluxe			
1965-1967. Super Lynx with added vibrato tailpiece.			
1965-1967		$950	$1,375
Tempest XII			
1965-1967. Solidbody double-cut, 12 strings, 3 pickups.			
1965-1967		$925	$1,250
Thunder Jet			
1960s-style with single pickup and vibrato arm.			
1960s		$700	$950
Tornado			
1965-1967. Thinline archtop, single pickup, dot markers, sunburst.			
1965-1967		$500	$650
Typhoon			
1965-1967. Hollowbody single-cut, 2 pickups, 3-piece laminated neck.			
1965-1967		$575	$750
Ultrasonic			
1967-1968. Hollowbody double-cut, 2 pickups, distortion, treble and bass boosters, wah-wah, vibrato,			

MODEL YEAR	FEATURES	EXC. COND. LOW	HIGH
1 volume and 2 tone controls, 3-way pickup selector, available in sunburst or cherry.			
1967-1968	12-string	$2,500	$3,500
1967-1968	6-string	$2,500	$3,500
Viper			
1968. Double-cut, thinline archtop electric, built-in distortion.			
1968		$1,500	$2,000
Virage/Virage II			
2008-2014. Semi-hollowbody made in Japan, single-cut or double (II), 2 triple-coil pickups.			
2008-2014		$2,000	$2,500
Wildcat			
1965-1967. Single-cut acoustic-electric archtop, 1 pickup, Wildcat and Vox logos on 'guard, dot markers.			
1965-1967		$550	$750

W. J. Dyer

See listing under Dyer.

Wabash

1950s. Acoustic and electric guitars distributed by the David Wexler company and made by others, most likely Kay. They also offered lap steels and amps.

Walden Guitars

Luthier Jonathan Lee of Portland, Oregon imports production, budget to professional grade, acoustic, acoustic-electric and classical guitars from Lilan, China. He began in 1996.

Walker

1994-present. Premium and presentation grade, production/custom, flat-top and archtop guitars built by luthier Kim Walker in North Stonington, Connecticut.

Walker (Kramer)

1981. Kramer came up with idea to offer this brand to produce wood-neck guitars and basses; they didn't want to dilute the Kramer aluminum-neck market they had built up. The idea didn't last long, and few, if any, of these instruments were produced, but prototypes exist.

Wandre (Davoli)

Ca. 1956/57-1969. Solidbody and thinline hollowbody electric guitars and basses created by German-descended Italian motorcycle and guitar enthusiast, artist, and sculptor from Milan, Italy, Wandre Pioli. Brands include Wandre (pronounced Vahn-dray), Davoli, Framez, JMI, Noble, Dallas, Avalon, Avanti I and others. Until '60, they were built by Pioli himself; from '60-'63 built in Milan by Framez; '63-'65 built by Davoli; '66-'69 built in Pioli's own factory.

The guitars originally used Framez pickups, but from '63 on (or earlier) they used Davoli pickups. Mostly strange shapes characterized by neck-thru-tailpiece aluminum neck with plastic back and

MODEL		EXC. COND.	
YEAR	FEATURES	LOW	HIGH

rosewood 'board. Often multi-color and sparkle finishes, using unusual materials like linoleum, fiberglass and laminates, metal bindings. Often the instruments will have numerous identifying names but usually somewhere there is a Wandre blob logo.

Distributed early on in the U.K. by Jennings Musical Industries, Ltd. (JMI) and in the U.S. by Don Noble and Company. Model B.B. dedicated to Brigitte Bardot. Among more exotic instruments were the minimalist Krundaal Bikini guitar with a built-in amplifier and attached speaker, and the pogo stick Swedenbass. These guitars are relatively rare and highly collectible. In '05, the brand was revived on a line of imported intermediate grade, production, solidbodies from Eastwood guitars.

Electric
1956-1969	Common models	$5,000	$10,000
1956-1969	Rare models	$10,000	$20,000

Warren
2005-present. Luthier Don Warren builds his professional and premium grade, custom/production, solidbody electric guitars in Latham, New York.

Warrior
1995-present. Professional, premium, and presentation grade, production/custom, acoustic and solidbody electric guitars and basses built by luthier J.D. Lewis in Rossville, Georgia.

Washburn
1962-present. Budget, intermediate, professional, and premium grade, production/custom, acoustic and electric guitars and basses made in the U.S., Japan, and Korea. They also make amps, banjos and mandolins.

Originally a Lyon & Healy brand, the Washburn line was revived on a line of imports in '62 by Roland who sold it to Beckman Musical Instruments in '74/'75. Beckman sold the rights to the Washburn name to Fretted Instruments, Inc. in '76. Guitars originally made in Japan and Korea, but production moved back to U.S. in '91. Currently Washburn is part of U.S. Music.

Washburn (Lyon & Healy)
1880s-ca.1949. Washburn was founded in Chicago as one of the lines for Lyon & Healy to promote high quality stringed instruments, ca. 1880s. The rights to manufacture Washburns were sold to J.R. Stewart Co. in '28, but rights to Washburn name were sold to Tonk Brothers of Chicago. In the Great Depression (about 1930), J.R. Stewart Co. was hit hard and declared bankruptcy. Tonk Brothers bought at auction all Stewart trade names, then sold them to Regal Musical Instrument Co. Regal built Washburns by the mid-'30s. The Tonk Brothers still licensed the name. These Washburn models lasted until ca. '49. In '62 the brand resurfaced on a line of imports from Roland.

MODEL		EXC. COND.	
YEAR	FEATURES	LOW	HIGH

Washington
Washington was a brand manufactured by Kansas City, Missouri instrument wholesalers J.W. Jenkins & Sons. First introduced in 1895, the brand also offered mandolins.

Waterloo
2014-present. Professional grade, production, acoustic guitars based on Depression-era models, built by Bill Collings in Austin, Texas. Waterloo was the original city name of Austin.

WL-12
2014-present. Parlor size, vintage-style sunburst finish.
2014-2023		$2,000	$2,500

WL-14 Scissortail
2014-present. Solid spruce top, maple back and sides, X-bracing.
2014-2023		$2,000	$2,500

WL-14LTR
2014-present. Acoustic 14.75", solid headstock, ladder bracing (L).
2014-2023		$1,750	$2,250

WL-14MH
2014-present. Parlor size, all mahogany.
2014-2023		$2,000	$2,500

WL-14X
2014-present. Acoustic 14.75", solid headstock, X bracing (X).
2014-2023		$2,000	$2,500

WL-JK
2014-present. Nick-named 'Jumbo King', 15.75" body, X-bracing. Optional East Indian rosewood back and sides.
2014-2023		$1,750	$2,250

WL-JK Deluxe
2014-present. Ornate appointments.
2014-2023		$2,500	$3,250

WL-K
2014-present. Lightweight 14.75", '30s Kel Kroyden inspired, optional hand-painted "Southwest" scene.
2014-2023		$2,000	$2,500

WL-S
2014-present. Slotted headstock 14", '30s Stella inspired, solid cherry wood back and sides, iced tea sunburst.
2014-2023		$2,000	$2,500

WL-S Deluxe
2014-present. Ornate appointments.
2014-2023		$2,500	$3,250

Waterstone
2003-present. Intermediate and professional grade, production/custom, electric solid and semi-hollowbody and acoustic guitars and basses imported from Korea by Waterstone Musical Instruments, LLC of Nashville, Tennessee.

Walden Madera

Waterloo WL-14 Scissortail

GUITARS

1962 Watkins Rapier
Rivington Guitars

Wechter
Benjamin E. Rios

MODEL		EXC. COND.	
YEAR	FEATURES	LOW	HIGH

Watkins/WEM

1957-present. Watkins Electric Music (WEM) was founded by Charlie Watkins. Their first commercial product was the Watkins Dominator (wedge Gibson stereo amp shape) in '57. They made the Rapier line of guitars and basses from the beginning. Watkins offered guitars and basses up to '82. They currently build accordion amps.

Wayne

1998-present. Professional and premium grade, production/custom, solidbody guitars built by luthiers Wayne and Michael (son) Charvel in Paradise, California. They also build lap steels.

Webber

1988-2020. Professional grade, production/custom flat-top guitars built by luthier David Webber in North Vancouver, British Columbia. Webber retired in '20.

Weber

1996-present. Premium grade, production/custom, carved-top acoustic and resonator guitars built by luthier Bruce Weber and his Sound To Earth, Ltd. company, originally in Belgrade, Montana, in '04 moving to Logan, Montana. They also build mandolins. In '12, Two Old Hippies (Breedlove, Bedell) acquired the brand, moving production in '13 to Oregon where Bruce Weber oversees development.

Webster

1940s. Archtop and acoustic guitars, most likely built by Kay or other mass builder.

Model 16C Acoustic Archtop

1940s		$700	$900

Wechter

1984-present. Intermediate, professional and premium grade, production/custom, flat-top, 12-string, resonator and nylon-string guitars and basses from luthier Abe Wechter in Paw Paw, Michigan. The Elite line is built in Paw Paw, the others in Asia. Until '94 he built guitars on a custom basis. In '95, he set up a manufacturing facility in Paw Paw to produce his new line and in '00 he added the Asian guitars. In '04, he added resonators designed by Tim Scheerhorn. Wechter was associated with Gibson Kalamazoo from the mid-'70s to '84. He also offers the Maple Lake brand of acoustics. In '08 he moved his shop to Fort Wayne, Indiana.

Weissenborn

1910s-1937, present. Hermann Weissenborn was well-established as a violin and piano builder in Los Angeles by the early 1910s. Around '20, he added guitars, ukes and steels to his line. Most of his production was in the '20s and '30s until his death in '37. He made tenor, plectrum, parlor, and Spanish guitars, ukuleles, and mandolins, but is best remembered for his Koa Hawaiian guitars that caught the popular wave of Hawaiian music. That

MODEL		EXC. COND.	
YEAR	FEATURES	LOW	HIGH

music captivated America after being introduced to the masses at San Francisco's Panama Pacific International Exposition which was thrown in '15 to celebrate the opening of the Panama Canal and attended by more than 13 million people. He also made instruments for Kona and other brands. Most of his instruments were most likely sold before the late 1920s. The Weissenborn brand has been revived on a line of reissue style guitars.

Spanish Acoustic

1920s. High-end Spanish set-up, rope binding, Koa top, sides and back, limited production.

1920s		$2,500	$3,500

Style #1 Hawaiian

1920-1930s. Koa, no binding, 3 wood circle sound hole inlays.

1920s-30s		$3,500	$5,000

Style #2 Hawaiian

1920-1930s. Koa, black celluloid body binding, white wood 'board binding, rope sound hole binding.

1920s-30s		$4,000	$5,500

Style #2 Spanish

1920s. Spanish set-up, Style 2 features.

1920s		$2,750	$4,000

Style #3 Hawaiian

1920-1930s. Koa, rope binding on top, 'board, and sound hole.

1920s-30s		$5,000	$7,500

Style #4 Hawaiian

1920-1930s. Koa, rope binding on body, 'board, headstock and sound hole.

1920s-30s		$6,000	$8,000

Teardrop

Late 1920s-1930s. Teardrop/spoon shaped, Style 1 features.

1930s		$925	$1,250

Tenor

1920-1927		$1,250	$1,625

Welker Custom

Professional and premium grade, production/custom, archtop and flat-top guitars built by luthier Fred Welker in Nashville, Tennessee.

Welson

1960s-1970s. Models made by Quagliardi, an accordion maker in Italy, ranging from acoustics to solidbodies, thinlines, archtops and basses. Some acoustic Welsons were sold in the U.S. by Wurlitzer. By the '70s, they had jumped on the copy-guitar bandwagon.

Electric

1960s	Various models	$350	$1,250

Wendler

1999-present. Intermediate and professional grade, production/custom, solidbody, electro-acoustic guitars and basses from luthier Dave Wendler of Ozark Instrument Building in Branson, Missouri. He also builds amps. In '91, Wendler patented a pickup system that became the Taylor ES system.

MODEL		EXC. COND.	
YEAR	FEATURES	LOW	HIGH

Westbury-Unicord

1978-ca. 1983. Imported from Japan by Unicord of Westbury, New York. High quality original designs, generally with 2 humbuckers, some with varitone and glued-in necks. They also had basses.

Westminster

One of the many guitar brands built by Japan's Matsumoku company.

Westone

1970s-1990, 1996-2001. Made by Matsumoku in Japan and imported by St. Louis Music. Around '81, St. Louis Music purchased an interest in Matsumoku and began to make a transition from its own Electra brand to the Westone brand previously used by Matsumoku. In the beginning of '84, the brand became Electra-Westone with a phoenix bird head surrounded by circular wings and flames. By the end of '84 the Electra name was dropped, leaving only Westone and a squared-off bird with W-shaped wings logo. Electra, Electra-Westone and Westone instruments from this period are virtually identical except for the brand and logo treatment. Many of these guitars and basses were made in very limited runs and are relatively rare.

From '96 to '01, England's FCN Music offered Westone branded electric and acoustic guitars. The electrics were built in England and the acoustics in Korea. Matsumoku-made guitars feature a serial number in which the first 1 or 2 digits represent the year of manufacture. Electra-Westone guitars should begin with either a 4 or 84.

Weymann

1864-1933. H.A. Weymann & Sons was a musical instrument distributor located in Philadelphia that marketed various stringed instruments, but mainly known for banjos. Some guitar models were made by Regal and Vega, but they also built their own instruments.

Large Models

1890-1928	Most w/Brazilian	$4,500	$6,500
1928-1932	Most w/Brazilian	$5,500	$7,500

Small Models/Standard

1890-1928	Brazilian	$3,500	$5,000
1890-1928	Mahogany	$850	$1,500
1928-1932	Brazilian	$4,500	$6,000
1928-1932	Mahogany	$1,000	$1,500

Jimmie Rodgers Signature Edition

1929-1932		$8,000	$10,000

White Guitars and Woodley White Luthier

1992-present. Premium grade, custom, classical, acoustic and electric guitars, built by luthier Woodley White, first in Portland, Oregon and since 2008 in Naalehu, Hawaii.

Wicked

2004-present. Production/custom, intermediate and professional grade, semi-hollow and electric solidbody guitars and basses built by luthier Nicholas Dijkman in Montreal, Quebec.

Widman Custom Electrics

2008-present. Professional and premium grade, custom, electric guitars built in Arden, North Carolina by luthier John Widman.

Wilkanowski

Early-1930s-mid-1940s. W. Wilkanowski primarily built violins. He did make a few dozen guitars which were heavily influenced by violin design concepts and in fact look very similar to a large violin with a guitar neck.

Wilkat Guitars

1998-2013. Professional grade, custom, electric guitars and basses built by luthier Bill Wilkat in Montreal, Quebec. He retired in '13.

Wilkins

1984-present. Custom guitars built by luthier Pat Wilkins in Van Nuys, California. Wilkins also does finish work for individuals and a variety of other builders.

William C. Stahl

See listing under Stahl.

William Hall and Son

William Hall and Son was a New York City based distributor offering guitars built by other luthiers in the mid to late 1800s.

William Jeffrey Jones

2006-present. Luthier William Jeffrey Jones builds his ornately carved, professional and premium grade, production/custom, solidbody and semi-hollow electric guitars in Neosho, Missouri.

Wilson

1960s-1970s. One of the brand names of guitars built in the 1960s for others by Egmond in Holland. Also, a brand name used by the U.K.'s Watkins WEM in the 1960s and '70s.

Wilson Brothers Guitars

2004-present. Intermediate and professional grade, production, imported electric and acoustic guitars and basses. Founded by Ventures guitarist Don Wilson. VCM and VSP models made in Japan; VM electrics in Korea; VM acoustic in China.

Windsor

Ca. 1890s-ca. 1914. Brand used by Montgomery Ward for flat-top guitars and mandolins made by various American manufacturers, including Lyon & Healy and, possibly, Harmony. Generally, beginner-grade instruments.

Westminster Archtop
W. H. Stephens

Wilson Brothers VMCC-60
Ventures Custom Classic PW

1966 Wurlitzer Gemini
Tom Pfeifer

Yamaha FG-180
Kris Nocula

MODEL		EXC. COND.	
YEAR	FEATURES	LOW	HIGH

Winston

Ca. 1963-1967. Imported from Japan by Buegeleisen and Jacobson of New York. Manufacturers unknown, but some are by Guyatone. Generally shorter scale beginner guitars and basses.

Worland

1997-present. Luthier Jim Worland builds professional through presentation grade, production/custom, acoustic flat-top guitars and harp guitars in Rockford, Illinois. He also builds under the Worlatron brand.

Worlatron

2010-present. Professional grade, production/custom, hollowbody electric-acoustic guitars and basses built by luthier Jim Worland in Rockford, Illinois.

WRC Music International

1989-mid-1990s. Guitars by Wayne Richard Charvel, who was the original founder of Charvel Guitars. He now builds Wayne guitars with his son Michael.

Wright Guitar Technology

1993-present. Luthier Rossco Wright builds his unique intermediate and professional grade, production, travel/practice steel-string and nylon-string guitars in The Dalles, Oregon. Basses were added in 2009.

Wurlitzer

Wurlitzer had full-line music stores in several major cities and marketed a line of American-made guitars in the 1920s. They also offered American- and foreign-made guitars starting in '65. The American ones were built from '65-'66 by the Holman-Woodell guitar factory in Neodesha, Kansas. In '67, Wurlitzer switched to Italian-made Welson guitars.

00-18

1920s		$5,750	$7,500

Model 2077 (Martin 0-K)
1920s. Made by Martin, size 0 with Koa top, back and sides, limited production of about 28 instruments.

1920s	Natural	$4,500	$5,750

Model 2090 (Martin 0-28)
1920s. Made by Martin, size 0 with appointments similar to a Martin 0-28 of that era, limited production of about 11 instruments, Wurlitzer branded on the back of the headstock and on the inside back seam, Martin name also branded on inside seam.

1920s	Natural	$6,500	$8,500

Wild One Stereo
1960s. Two pickups, various colors.

1960s		$750	$975

Xaviere

Budget and intermediate grade, production, solid and semi-hollow body guitars from Guitar Fetish, which also has GFS pickups and effects.

Xotic Guitars

1996-present. Luthier Hiro Miura builds his professional grade, production/custom guitars and basses in San Fernando, California. The Xotic brand is also used on a line of guitar effects.

XOX Audio Tools

2007-present. U.S. debut in '08 of premium grade, production/custom, carbon fiber electric guitars built by luthier Peter Solomon in Europe.

Xtone

2003-2014. Semi-hollow body electric, acoustic and acoustic/electric guitars from ESP. Originally branded Xtone on headstock, in '10 the instruments were marketed as a model series under LTD (ESP's other brand) and stated as such on the headstock.

XXL Guitars

2003-present. Luthier Marc Lupien builds his production/custom, professional grade, chambered electric guitars in Montreal, Quebec.

Yamaha

1946-present. Budget, intermediate, professional, and presentation grade, production/custom, acoustic, acoustic/electric, and electric guitars. They also build basses, amps, and effects. The Japanese instrument maker was founded in 1887. Began classical guitar production around 1946. Solidbody electric production began in '66; steel string acoustics debuted sometime after that. They began to export guitars into the U.S. in '69. Production shifted from Japan to Taiwan (Yamaha's special-built plant) in the '80s, though some high-end guitars still made in Japan. Some Korean production began in '90s.

Serialization patterns:
Serial numbers are coded as follows:
H = 1, I = 2, J = 3, etc., Z = 12
To use this pattern, you need to know the decade of production.
Serial numbers are ordered as follows:
Year/Month/Day/Factory Order
Example: NL 29159 represents a N=1987 year, L=5th month or May, 29=29th day (of May), 159=159th guitar made that day (the factory order). This guitar was the 159 guitar made on May 29, 1987.

AE Series (Archtop)
1966-2011. Various archtop models.

1966-2011	Higher-end	$1,250	$2,500
1966-2011	Lower-end	$250	$700
1966-2011	Mid-level	$700	$1,250

AES Series (Semi-Hollowbody)
1990-2011. Various semi-hollowbody models.

1990-2011	Higher-end	$1,250	$2,500
1990-2011	Lower-end	$250	$350
1990-2011	Mid-level	$700	$1,250

MODEL YEAR	FEATURES	EXC. COND. LOW	HIGH

AEX-1500
1995-2011. Full-body archtop electric, set neck, humbucker and piezo, EQ, multi-bound.
| 1995-2011 | | $950 | $1,250 |

APX Series (Acoustic-Electric)
1987-present. Acoustic-electric, various features.
1987-2023	Higher-end	$950	$1,250
1987-2023	Lower-end	$250	$650
1987-2023	Mid-level	$650	$850

CG Series (Classical)
1984-present. Various classical models.
1984-2023	Higher-end	$400	$550
1984-2023	Lower-end	$125	$175
1984-2023	Mid-level	$250	$350

DW Series (Dreadnought)
1999-2002. Dreadnought flat-top models, sunburst, solid spruce top, higher-end appointments like abalone rosette and top purfling.
1999-2002	Higher-end	$375	$550
1999-2002	Lower-end	$110	$250
1999-2002	Mid-level	$225	$400

EG Series (Electric Solidbody)
2000-2009. Various electric solidbody models.
| 2000-2009 | | $110 | $350 |

Eterna Series (Folk Acoustic)
1983-1994. Folk-style acoustics, there were 4 models.
| 1983-1994 | | $110 | $300 |

FG Series (Flat-Top)
1970s-present. Economy market flat-top models, laminated sides and back, a 12 suffix indicates 12-string, CE indicates on-board electronics, many models are D-style bodies.
1970-2023	Higher-end	$650	$1,125
1970-2023	Highest-end	$1,125	$1,500
1970-2023	Lower-end	$80	$250
1970-2023	Mid-level	$300	$500

G Series (Classical)
1981-2000. Various Classical models.
| 1981-2000 | | $900 | $1,125 |

GC Series (Classical)
1970s-present. Classical models, '70s made in Japan, '80s made in Taiwan.
1970s-2023	Higher-end	$1,500	$2,500
1970s-2023	Lower-end	$250	$750
1970s-2023	Mid-level	$750	$1,500

Image Custom
1988-1992. Electric double-cut, Brazilian rosewood 'board, maple top, 2 humbuckers, active circuitry, LED position markers, script Image logo on truss rod cover. The Image was called the MSG in the U.K.
| 1988-1992 | | $1,250 | $1,625 |

L Series (Flat-Top)
1984-present. Custom hand-built flat-top models, solid wood.
1984-2023	Higher-end	$1,250	$5,000
1984-2023	Lower-end	$600	$1,000
1984-2023	Mid-level	$1,000	$1,500

PAC Pacifica Series
1989-present. Offset double-cut with longer horns, dot markers, large script Pacifica logo and small block Yamaha logo on headstock, various models.
| 1989-2023 | | $200 | $600 |

RGX Series
1988-2011. Bolt-on neck for the 600 series and neck-thru body designs for 1200 series, various models include 110 (1 hum), 211 (hum-single), 220 (2 hums), 312 (hum-single-single), 603 (3 singles), 612 (hum-single-single), 620 (2 hums), 1203S (3 singles), 1212S (hum-single-single), 1220S (2 hums).
1988-2011	Higher-end	$400	$600
1988-2011	Lower-end	$85	$200
1988-2011	Mid-level	$225	$350

RGZ Series
1989-1994. Double-cut solidbodies, various pickups.
1989-1994	Higher-end	$400	$600
1989-1994	Lower-end	$85	$200
1989-1994	Mid-level	$225	$350

SA (Super Axe) Series
1966-1994. Super Axe series, full-size and thinline archtop models.
1966-1994	Higher-end	$1,250	$1,875
1966-1994	Highest-end	$1,750	$2,250
1966-1994	Lower-end	$550	$750
1966-1994	Mid-level	$950	$1,250

SBG Series (Solidbody)
1983-1992. Solidbody models, set necks, model name logo on truss rod cover.
1983-1992	Higher-end	$1,250	$1,750
1983-1992	Highest-end	$1,750	$3,500
1983-1992	Lower-end	$550	$1,000
1983-1992	Mid-level	$950	$1,250

SE Series (Solidbody Electric)
1986-1992. Solidbody electric models.
1986-1992	Higher-end	$500	$650
1986-1992	Lower-end	$250	$350
1986-1992	Mid-level	$400	$500

SF (Super Flighter) Series
1977-early 1980s. Super Flighter series, double-cut solidbody electrics, 2 humbuckers.
| 1977-80s | Various models | $775 | $1,250 |

SG-3
1965-1966. Early double-cut solidbody with sharp horns, bolt neck, 3 hum-single pickup layout, large white guard, rotor controls, tremolo.
| 1965-1966 | | $1,250 | $1,750 |

SG-5/SG-5A
1966-1971. Asymmetrical double-cut solidbody with extended lower horn, bolt neck, 2 pickups, chrome hardware.
| 1966-1971 | | $1,750 | $2,250 |

SG-7/SG-7A
1966-1971. Like SG-5, but with gold hardware.
| 1966-1971 | | $3,000 | $4,000 |
| 1993-1996 | 7A | $2,000 | $2,500 |

SG-7A 20th Anniversary
| 1986 | | $2,250 | $3,000 |

SG-20
1972-1973. Bolt-on neck, slab body, single-cut, 1 pickup.
| 1972-1973 | | $600 | $800 |

SG-30/SG-30A
1973-1976. Slab katsura wood (30) or slab maple (30A) solidbody, bolt-on neck, 2 humbuckers, dot inlays.
| 1973-1976 | | $650 | $850 |

1966 Yamaha SA-15
Brian Goff

1985 Yamaha SA2100
Craig Brody

GUITARS

1973 Yamaha SG-85

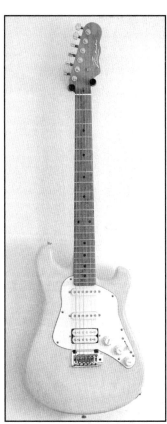

Zanini Villano

MODEL YEAR	FEATURES	EXC. COND. LOW	HIGH

SG-35/SG-35A
1973-1976. Slab mahogany (35) or slab maple (35A) solidbody, bolt-on neck, 2 humbuckers, parallelogram inlays.

1973-1976		$700	$900

SG-40
1972-1973. Bolt-on neck, carved body, single-cut.

1972-1973		$700	$900

SG-45
1972-1976. Glued neck, single-cut, bound flat-top.

1972-1976		$725	$950

SG-50
1974-1976. Slab katsura wood solidbody, glued neck, 2 humbuckers, dot inlays, large 'guard.

1974-1976		$725	$950

SG-60
1972 only. Bolt-on neck, carved body, single-cut.

1972		$725	$950

SG-60T
1973 only. SG-60 with large cast vibrato system.

1973		$725	$950

SG-65
1972-1976. Glued neck, single-cut, bound flat-top.

1972-1976		$875	$1,125

SG-70
1974-1976. Slab maple solidbody, glued neck, 2 humbuckers, dot inlays, large 'guard.

1974-1976		$900	$1,250

SG-80
1972 only. Bolt-on neck, carved body, single-cut.

1972		$725	$950

SG-80T
1973. SG-60 with large cast vibrato system.

1973		$800	$1,125

SG-85
1972-1976. Glued neck, single-cut, bound flat-top.

1972-1976		$900	$1,250

SG-90
1974-1976. Carved top mahogany solidbody, glued neck, elevated 'guard, bound top, dot inlays, chrome hardware.

1974-1976		$1,125	$1,500

SG-175
1974-1976. Carved top mahogany solidbody, glued neck, elevated 'guard, abalone bound top, abalone split wing or pyramid inlays, gold hardware.

1974-1976		$1,250	$1,625

SG-500
1976-1978. Carved unbound maple top, double pointed cutaways, glued neck, 2 exposed humbuckers, 3-ply bound headstock, bound neck with clay split wing inlays, chrome hardware. Reissued as the SBG-500 (800S in Japan) in '81.

1976-1978		$800	$1,125

SG-700
1976-1978. Carved unbound maple top, double pointed cutaways, glued neck, 2 humbuckers, 3-ply bound headstock, bound neck with clay split wing inlays, chrome hardware.

1976-1978		$1,125	$1,500

SG-700S
1999-2001. Set neck, mahogany body, 2 humbuckers with coil tap.

1999-2001		$1,000	$1,500

SG-800S
1981-1984. Eastern mahogany with maple top, set neck, 2 pickups, blue, tobacco burst or cherry sunburst.

1981-1984		$1,000	$1,500

SG-1000/SBG-1000
1976-1983 ('84 in Japan), 2007-2013. Carved maple top, double pointed cutaways, glued neck, 2 humbuckers, 3-ply bound headstock, unbound body, bound neck with clay split wing inlays, gold hardware. Export model name changed to SBG-1000 in '80. SBG-1000 reissued in '07.

1976-1979	SG-1000	$1,500	$2,500
1980-1983	SBG-1000	$1,500	$2,500

SG-1500
1976-1979. Carved maple top, double pointed cutaways, laminated neck-thru-body neck, laminated mahogany body wings, 2 humbuckers, 5-ply bound headstock and body, bound neck with dot inlays, chrome hardware. Name used on Japan-only model in the '80s.

1976-1979		$1,250	$2,000

SG-2000/SG-2000S
1976-1980 (1988 in Japan). Maple top, double pointed cutaways, neck-thru-body, mahogany body wings, 2 humbuckers, 5-ply bound headstock and body, bound neck with abalone split wing inlays, gold hardware. In '80, the model was changed to the SBG-2000 in the U.S., and the SG-2000S everywhere else except Japan (where it remained the SG-2000). Export model renamed SBG-2100 in '84.

1976-1980		$1,750	$2,500

SG-2100S
1983. Similar to SG-2000 with upgrades such as the pickups.

1983		$1,875	$2,500

SG-3000/SBG-3000/Custom Professional
1982-1992. SG-2000 upgrade with higher output pickups and abalone purfling on top.

1982-1992		$2,500	$3,500

SGV-300
2000-2006. 1960s SG model features.

2000-2006		$600	$800

SHB-400
1981-1985. Solidbody electric, set-in neck, 2 pickups.

1981-1985		$600	$800

SJ-180
1983-1994. Student Jumbo, entry level Folk Series model, laminated top.

1983-1994		$300	$400

SJ-400S
1983-1994. Student Jumbo Folk Series model, solid wood top.

1983-1994		$350	$450

SL (Studio Lord) Series
1977-1981. LP-style copy models.

1977-1981	Various models	$650	$1,500

MODEL		EXC. COND.	
YEAR	FEATURES	LOW	HIGH

SR (Super Rock'n Roller) Series
1977-1981. Strat copy models.

1977-1981	Various models	$575	$750

SSC Series (Solidbody Electric)
1983-1992. Solidbody electric models.

1983-1992	SSC-400/SC-400	$600	$800
1983-1992	SSC-500	$550	$725
1983-1992	SSC-600/SC-600	$750	$975

Weddington Classic
1989-1992. Electric solidbody, redesigned set-in neck/body joint for increased access to the higher frets.

1989-1992		$950	$1,250

Yanuziello Stringed Instruments

1980-present. Production/custom resonator and Hawaiian guitars built by luthier Joseph Yanuziello, in Toronto, Ontario.

Yosco

1900-1930s. Lawrence L. Yosco was a New York City luthier building guitars, round back mandolins and banjos under his own brand and for others.

Zachary

1996-present. Luthier Alex Csiky builds his professional grade, production, solidbody electric guitars and basses in Windsor, Ontario.

Zanini

2007-2020. Premium grade, production, electric guitars designed by Luca Zanini of Italy and built in the U.S.

Zaukus Guitars

2011-present. Luthier Joseph Zaukus builds his premium grade, production/custom, solidbody electric guitars in Antioch, Tennessee.

Zeiler Guitars

1992-present. Custom flat-top, 12-string, and nylon-string guitars built by luthier Jamonn Zeiler in Aurora, Indiana.

Zemaitis

1960-1999, 2004-present. Professional, premium, and presentation grade, custom/production, electric and acoustic guitars. Tony Zemaitis (born Antanus Casimere Zemaitis) began selling his guitars in 1960. He emphasized simple light-weight construction and was known for hand engraved metal front guitars. The metal front designs were originally engineered to reduce hum, but they became popular as functional art. Each hand-built guitar and bass was a unique instrument. Ron Wood was an early customer and his use created a demand for them. Approximately 6 to 10 instruments were built each year. Tony retired in '99 and passed away in '02 at the age of 67. In '04, Japan's Kanda Shokai Corporation, with the endorsement of Tony Zemaitis, Jr., started building the guitars again. KSC builds the higher priced ones

and licenses the lower priced guitars to Greco.

Celebrity association with Zemaitis is not uncommon. Validated celebrity provenance may add 25% to 100% (or more) to a guitar's value. Tony Zemaitis also made so-called student model instruments for customers with average incomes. These had wood tops instead of metal or pearl. Some wood top instruments have been converted to non-Zemaitis metal tops, which are therefore not fully original Zemaitis instruments.

Acoustic instruments are valued more as collectibles and less so for their acoustic sound. Originality and verifiable, documented provenance are required in the Zemaitis market as fake instruments can be a problem.

Zen-On

1946-ca.1968. Japanese manufacturer. By '67 using the Morales brand name. Not heavily imported into the U.S., if at all (see Morales).

Acoustic Hollowbody

1946-1968	Various models	$200	$350

Electric Solidbody

1946-1968	Various models	$200	$600

Zerberus

2002-present. Professional and premium grade, production/custom, electric guitars built in Speyer, Germany by luthier Frank Scheucher.

Zeta

1982-2010. Zeta made solid, semi-hollow and resonator guitars, many with electronic and MIDI options, and mandolins in Oakland, California over the years, but mainly offered upright basses, amps and violins.

Ziegenfuss Guitars

2006-present. Luthier Stephen Ziegenfuss builds his professional and premium grade, custom, acoustic and solidbody electric guitars and basses in Jackson, Michigan.

Zim-Gar

1960s. Imported from Japan by Gar-Zim Musical Instrument Corporation of Brooklyn, New York. Manufacturers unknown. Generally shorter scale beginner guitars.

Electric Solidbody

1960s		$200	$600

Zimnicki, Gary

1980-present. Luthier Gary Zimnicki builds his professional and premium grade, custom, flat-top, 12-string, nylon-string, and archtop guitars in Allen Park, Michigan.

Zion

1980-present. Professional and premium grade, production/custom, semi-hollow and solidbody guitars built by luthier Ken Hoover, originally in Greensboro, North Carolina, currently in Raleigh.

Zen-On W100
Bruce Hughes

Zion
Kirby Velarde

Zuni

Zolla

Professional grade, production/custom, electric guitars and basses built by luthier Bill Zolla in San Diego, California starting in 1979.

Zon

1981-present. Currently luthier Joe Zon only offers basses, but he also built guitars from '85-'91. See Bass Section for more company info.

Zuni

1993-present. Premium grade, custom, solidbody electric guitars built by luthier Michael Blank in Alto Pass, Illinois and Amasa, Michigan.

ZZ Ryder

Solidbody electric guitars and basses from Stenzler Musical Instruments of Ft. Worth, Texas.

BASSES

BASSES

1962 Airline Pocket
Robbie Keene

**2004 Alembic Mark
King Signature**
Imaged by Heritage Auctions, HA.com

MODEL YEAR	FEATURES	EXC. COND. LOW	HIGH

A Basses

1976-2002. Luthier Albey Balgochian built his professional grade, solidbody basses in Waltham, Massachusetts. Sports the A logo on headstock.

Solidbody

1976-2002		$1,250	$1,625

Acoustic

Ca. 1965-ca. 1987, 2001-2005, 2008-present. Mainly known for solidstate amps, the Acoustic Control Corp. of Los Angeles, did offer guitars and basses from around '69 to late '74. The brand was revived in '01 by Samick for a line of amps.

Black Widow AC600/AC650

1969-1970, 1972-1974. The AC600 featured a black double-cut body, German carve, Ebonite 'board, 2 pickups, and a protective "spider design" pad on back. The AC650 is short-scale. The '72-'74 versions had a rosewood 'board and 1 pickup. Acoustic outsourced the production of the basses, possibly to Japan, but at least part of the final production was by Semie Moseley.

1969-1970		$1,250	$1,625
1972-1974		$1,125	$1,500

Airline

1958-1968, 2004-present. Brand for Montgomery Ward. Built by Kay, Harmony and Valco. In '04, the brand was revived on a line of reissues from Eastwood guitars.

Electric Solidbody

1958-1968	Various models	$725	$1,250

Pocket 3/4 (Valco/National)

1962-1968. Airline brand of double-cut Pocket Bass, short-scale, 2 pickups, 1 acoustic bridge and 1 neck humbucker, sunburst and other colors.

1962-1968		$825	$1,500

Alamo

1947-1982. Founded by Charles Eilenberg, Milton Fink, and Southern Music, San Antonio, Texas. Distributed by Bruno & Sons.

Eldorado (Model 2600)

1965-1966. Solidbody, 1 pickup, angular offset shape, double cut.

1965-1966		$475	$625

Titan

1963-1970. Hollowbody, 1 pickup, angular offset shape.

1963-1970		$475	$625

Alembic

1969-present. Professional, premium, and presentation grade, production/custom, 4-, 5-, and 6-string basses built in Santa Rosa, California. They also build guitars. Established in San Francisco as one of the first handmade bass builders. Alembic basses come with many options concerning woods (examples are maple, bubinga, walnut, vermilion, wenge, zebrawood), finishes, inlays, etc., all of which affect the values listed here. These dollar amounts should be used as a baseline guide to values for Alembic.

MODEL YEAR	FEATURES	EXC. COND. LOW	HIGH

Distillate

1981-1991. One of Alembic's early lower-cost models, early ones with 1 pickup, 2 pickups by '82, exotic woods, active electronics.

1981-1991	Distillate 4	$4,000	$5,000
1981-1991	Distillate 5	$4,000	$5,000

Elan

1985-1996. Available in 4-, 5-, 6- and 8-string models, 3-piece thru-body laminated maple neck, solid maple body, active electronics, solid brass hardware, offered in a variety of hardwood tops and custom finishes.

1985-1996	Elan 4	$4,000	$5,250
1985-1996	Elan 5	$4,250	$5,500
1985-1996	Elan 6	$4,500	$5,750

Epic

1993-2015. Mahogany body with various tops, extra-large pointed bass horn, maple/walnut veneer set-neck, available in 4-, 5-, and 6-string versions.

1993-2015	4-string	$2,500	$3,250
1993-2015	5-string	$2,500	$3,250
1993-2015	6-string	$3,000	$4,000

Essence

1991-present. Mahogany body with various tops, extra-large pointed bass horn, walnut/maple laminate neck-thru.

1991-2023	Essence 4	$2,750	$3,500
1991-2023	Essence 5	$3,000	$4,000
1991-2023	Essence 6	$3,250	$4,250

Europa

1992-present. Mahogany body with various tops, ebony 'board, available as 4-, 5-, and 6-string.

1992-2023		$4,000	$5,500

Excel

1999-present. Solidbody 5-string, set neck, several wood options.

1998-2023		$2,500	$4,500

Exploiter

1980s. Figured maple solidbody 4-string, neck-thru, transparent finish.

1984-1988		$3,500	$8,000

Mark King Signature

1989-2019. Standard or Deluxe models.

1989-2008		$6,000	$7,500

Orion

1996-present. Offset double cut solidbody, various figured-wood top, 4, 5, or 6 strings.

1996-2023		$3,250	$5,000

Persuader

1983-1991. Offset double-cut solidbody, 4-string, neck-thru.

1983-1991		$3,250	$5,000

Rogue

1996-present. Double-cut solidbody, extreme long pointed bass horn.

1996-2023		$3,000	$4,500

Series I

1971-present. Mahogany body with various tops, maple/purpleheart laminate neck-thru, active electronics, available in 3 scale lengths and with 4, 5 or 6 strings.

1971-1979	All scales	$5,500	$6,500
1980-1989	All scales	$5,500	$6,500
1990-2023	Highly figured	$6,000	$7,500

MODEL YEAR	FEATURES	EXC. COND. LOW	HIGH

Series II

1971-present. Generally custom-made option, each instrument valued on a case-by-case basis, guidance pricing only.

1971-1979		$8,500	$12,000
1980-2023		$8,500	$16,000

Spoiler

1981-1999. Solid mahogany body, maple neck-thru, 4, 5 or 6 strings, active electronics, various high-end wood options.

1981-1986	6-string	$4,000	$5,000
1981-1989	5-string	$4,000	$5,000
1981-1999	4-string	$3,500	$4,500

Stanley Clarke Signature Deluxe

1990-present. Neck-thru-body, active electronics, 24-fret ebony 'board, mahogany body with various wood and laminate tops, 4-, 5-, and 6-string versions.

1990-2023	All scales	$7,500	$11,000

Stanley Clarke Signature Standard

1990-present. Neck-thru-body, active electronics, 24-fret ebony 'board, mahogany body with various wood and laminate tops, 4-, 5-, and 6-string versions.

1990-2023	All scales	$6,500	$10,000

Alleva-Coppolo Basses and Guitars

1995-present. Professional and premium grade, custom/production, solidbody electric guitars and basses built by luthier Jimmy Coppolo in Dallas Texas for '95-97, in New York City for '98-2008, Upland, CA for "99-'21 and in Gadsden AL 2021-present.

Alvarez

1965-present. Imported by St. Louis Music, they offered electric basses from '90 to '02 and acoustic basses in the mid-'90s.

American Showster

1986-2004, 2010-2011. Established by Bill Meeker and David Haines, Bayville, New Jersey. They also made guitars.

AS-57-B Classic

1987-1997. Bass version of AS-57 with body styled like a '57 Chevy tail fin.

1987-1997		$3,500	$5,500

Ampeg

1949-present. Ampeg was founded on a vision of an amplified bass peg, which evolved into the Baby Bass. Ampeg has sold basses on and off throughout its history. In '08 they got back into basses with the reissue of the Dan Armstrong Plexi Bass.

AEB-1

1966-1967. F-holes through the body, fretted, scroll headstock, pickup in body, sunburst. Reissued as the AEB-2 for '97-'99.

1966-1967		$5,500	$7,500

ASB-1 Devil/AUSB-1 Devil

1966-1967. Long-horn body, fretted (ASB-1) or fretless (AUSB-1), triangular f-holes through the body, fireburst.

1966-1967		$5,500	$7,500

AUB-1

1966-1967. Same as AEB-1, but fretless, sunburst. Reissued as the AUB-2 for '97-'99.

1966-1967		$4,500	$5,500

BB-4 Baby (4-string)

1962-1971. Electric upright slim-looking bass that is smaller than a cello, 4-string, available in sunburst, white, red, black, and a few turquoise. Reissued as the ABB-1 Baby Bass for '97-'99.

1962-1971	Solid color	$3,250	$4,500
1962-1971	Sunburst	$2,750	$3,500

BB-5 Baby (5-string)

1964-1971. Five-string version.

1964-1971	Solid color	$3,500	$4,750
1964-1971	Sunburst	$3,000	$4,000

Dan Armstrong Lucite

1969-1971. Clear solid lucite body, did not have switchable pickups like the Lucite guitar.

1969-1971	Clear	$2,500	$3,500
1969-1971	Smoke	$3,000	$5,000

Dan Armstrong Lucite Reissue/ADA4

1998-2001, 2008-2009. Lucite body, Dan Armstrong Ampeg block lettering on 'guard. Reissue in '08 as the ADA4.

1998-2001		$1,125	$1,750
2008-2009	Reintroduced	$1,125	$1,500

EB-1 Wild Dog

1963-1964. Made by Burns of London, along with the Wild Dog Guitar, offset double cut solidbody, 3 pickups.

1963-1964		$1,250	$1,625

GEB-101 Little Stud

1973-1975. Import from Japan, offset double-cut solidbody, two-on-a-side tuners, 1 pickup.

1973-1975		$750	$975

GEB-750 Big Stud

1973-1975. Import from Japan, similar to Little Stud, but with 2 pickups.

1973-1975		$750	$975

SSB

1967-1968. Short scale, fretted, 4-string.

1967-1968		$3,000	$4,500

SSUB

1967-1968. Short scale, fretless, 4-string.

1967-1968		$3,000	$4,500

Andreas

1995-2004. Aluminium-necked, solidbody guitars and basses built by luthier Andreas Pichler in Dollach, Austria.

Angelica

1967-1975. Student and entry-level basses and guitars imported from Japan.

Electric Solid Body

1970s. Japanese imports.

1970s	Various models	$175	$400

Apollo

Ca. 1967-1972. Entry-level basses imported from Japan by St. Louis Music. They also had guitars and effects.

1966 Ampeg AEB-1
Imaged by Heritage Auctions, HA.com

Ampeg Dan Armstrong Lucite
Imaged by Heritage Auctions, HA.com

1980 Aria Pro II
Imaged by Heritage Auctions, HA.com

1965 Baldwin Baby Bison
Rivington Guitars

MODEL YEAR	FEATURES	EXC. COND. LOW	HIGH
Electric Hollow Body			
1967-1972. Japanese imports.			
1967-1972		$500	$700

Arbor

1983-ca. 2013. Budget grade, production, solid body basses imported by Musicorp (MBT). They also offered guitars.

Electric

1983-2013	Various models	$250	$400

Aria/Aria Pro II

1956-present. Budget and intermediate grade, production, acoustic, acoustic/electric, solidbody, hollowbody and upright basses. They also make guitars, mandolins, and banjos. Originally branded as Aria; renamed Aria Pro II in '75; both names used over the next several years; in '01, the Pro II part of the name was dropped altogether.

Electric

1980s	Various models	$300	$2,000

Austin Hatchet

Mid-1970s-mid-1980s. Trademark of distributor Targ and Dinner, Chicago, Illinois.

Hatchet

1981	Travel bass	$750	$1,250

B.C. Rich

1966-present. Budget, intermediate, and premium grade, production/custom, import and U.S.-made basses. They also offer guitars. Many B.C. Rich models came in a variety of colors. For example, in '88 they offered black, Competition Red, metallic red, GlitteRock White, Ultra Violet, and Thunder Blue. Also in '88, other custom colors, graphic features, paint-to-match headstocks, and special inlays were offered.

Bich

1978-1998. Solidbody, neck-thru, 2 pickups.

1978-1979	USA	$7,000	$9,500
1980-1985		$2,500	$3,250
1986-1989		$1,750	$2,250
1989-1993	Class Axe era	$1,750	$2,250
1994-1998	2nd Rico-era	$1,750	$2,250

Bich Supreme 8-String

Late-1970s-early-1980s.

1978-1982	Painted wood	$7,000	$9,500
1978-1982	Translucent wood	$8,000	$10,000

Eagle (U.S.A.)

1977-1996. Curved double-cut, solidbody, natural.

1977-1979	Translucent wood	$4,000	$5,500
1977-1996	Painted wood	$3,750	$5,000
1980-1996	Translucent wood	$3,500	$4,500

Gunslinger

1987-1999. Inverted headstock, 1 humbucker.

1987-1989		$1,500	$2,000
1989-1993	Class Axe era	$1,500	$2,000
1994-1999		$1,250	$1,625

Ironbird

1984-1998. Kind of star-shaped, neck-thru, solid-

MODEL YEAR	FEATURES	EXC. COND. LOW	HIGH
body, 2 pickups, active electronics, diamond inlays.			
1984-1989		$1,500	$2,000
1989-1993	Class Axe era	$1,500	$2,000
1994-1998	2nd Rico era	$1,250	$1,625

Mockingbird

1976-2009. US-made, short horn until '78, long horn after.

1976	Painted	$4,000	$5,500
1976	Translucent	$4,500	$6,000
1977-1978	Painted	$3,750	$5,000
1977-1978	Translucent	$4,000	$5,500
1979-1983	Painted	$4,000	$5,500
1979-1983	Translucent	$4,000	$5,500
1984-1985	End 1st Rico-era	$3,500	$4,500
1986-1989	End 1st Rico era	$2,500	$3,500
1994-2009	New Rico-era	$2,500	$3,500

Mockingbird Heritage Classic

2007-2015. 4-string, neck-thru, quilted maple top, cloud inlay.

2007-2015		$500	$750

Nighthawk

1980-1982. Bolt-neck.

1980-1982		$2,250	$3,000

NJ Series

1983-2006. Various mid-level import models include Beast, Eagle, Innovator, Mockingbird, Virgin and Warlock. Replaced by NT Series.

1983-1984	Early, Japan	$600	$2,000
1985-1986	Japan	$600	$2,000
1987-2006		$600	$2,000

Platinum Series

1986-2006. Lower-priced import versions including Eagle, Mockingbird, Beast, Warlock.

1986-1999	Various models	$450	$650

Seagull

1973-1975. Solidbody, single cut, changed to Seagull II in '76.

1973		$4,000	$5,500
1974-1975		$3,500	$4,500

Seagull II

1976-1977. Double-cut version.

1976-1977		$3,000	$4,000

Son Of A Rich

1980-1981. Double-cut, 4-string.

1980-1981		$1,500	$2,000

ST-III

1987-1998. Bolt or set neck, black hardware, P-Bass/J-Bass pickup configuration, ebony 'board.

1987-1989	Bolt-on	$850	$1,125
1987-1989	Neck-thru	$925	$1,250
1989-1993	Class Axe-era	$850	$1,125
1994-1998	New Rico-era	$925	$1,250

Warlock (U.S.A.)

1981-2015. Bolt neck, maple body, rosewood 'board, Badass II low profile bridge by '88.

1981-1985		$2,500	$3,500
1986-1989		$2,000	$2,750

Wave

Early 1980s. Double-cut, cresting wave, neck-thru, solid body, 2 pickups, active electronics.

1983		$4,000	$5,000

MODEL YEAR	FEATURES	EXC. COND. LOW	HIGH

B.C. Rico

1978-1982. B.C. Rich's first Japan-made guitars and basses were labeled B.C. Rico.

Eagle

1978-1982		$3,000	$4,000

Baldwin

1965-1970. The giant organ company got into guitars and basses in '65 when it bought Burns Guitars of England and sold those models in the U.S. under the Baldwin name.

Baby Bison

1965-1970. Scroll head, 2 pickups, black, red or white finishes.

1965-1966		$1,750	$2,250
1966-1970	Model 560	$1,250	$1,625

Bison

1965-1970. Scroll headstock, 3 pickups, black or white finishes.

1965-1966		$1,625	$2,125
1966-1970	Model 516	$1,125	$1,500

G.B. 66

1965-1966. Bass equivalent of G.B. 66 guitar, covered bridge tailpiece.

1965-1966		$1,125	$1,500

Jazz Split Sound

1965-1970. Offset double-cut solidbody, 2 pickups, red sunburst.

1965-1966	Long-scale	$1,375	$1,750
1966-1970	Short-scale	$1,250	$1,625

Nu-Sonic

1965-1966. Bass version of Nu-Sonic.

1965-1966		$1,250	$1,625

Shadows/Shadows Signature

1965-1970. Named after Hank Marvin's backup band, solidbody, 3 slanted pickups, white finish.

1965-1966	Shadows	$2,250	$3,000
1966-1970	Shadows Signature	$2,000	$2,500

Vibraslim

1965-1970. Thin body, scroll head, 2 pickups, sunburst.

1965-1966		$2,000	$2,500
1966-1970	Model 549	$1,750	$2,250

Barclay

1960s. Generally shorter-scale, student-level imports from Japan. They also made guitars.

Bass Collection

1985-1992. Mid-level imports from Japan, distributed by Meisel Music of Springfield, New Jersey. Sam Ash Music, New York, sold the remaining inventory from '92 to '94.

Black Jack

1960s. Entry-level and mid-level imports from Japan. They also offered guitars.

Bradford

1960s. House brand of W.T. Grant department store, often imported. They also offered guitars.

Brian Moore

1992-present. Brian Moore added basses in '97. Currently they offer professional grade, production, solidbody basses. They also build guitars and mandolins.

i2000 Series

2000-present. Offset double-cut solidbody with extended bass horn, 2 pickups, 4- (i4) or 5-string (i5), options include piezo (p), fretless (-f), Bartolini pickups (B), and 13-pin mid (.13).

2000-2023		$950	$1,250

Brice

1985-present. Budget grade, production, electric and acoustic basses imported by Rondo Music of Union, New Jersey.

BSX Bass

1990-present. Luthier Dino Fiumara builds his professional and premium grade, production/custom, acoustic, solidbody, semi-solid upright basses in Aliquippa, Pennsylvania.

Burns

1960-1970, 1974-1983, 1992-present. Intermediate and professional grade, production, basses built in England and Korea. They also build guitars.

Baby Bison

1965-1968. Early version had "V" headstock and long Rez-O-Tube vibrato. Later short Rezo-Tube tailpiece.

1965-1968		$1,250	$1,625

Bison

1965-1968. Double-cut, long scale, 4-string.

1965-1968		$2,000	$2,625

Nu-Sonic

1964-1965, 2011-2020. Offset double-cut solidbody, 2 pickups.

1964-1965		$1,375	$1,750

Scorpion

Introduced 1979, 2003-2009. Double-cut scorpion-like solidbody.

2003-2009		$675	$875

Cameo

1960s-1970s. Japanese- and Korean-made electric basses. They also offered guitars.

Electric

1960s-70s		$400	$550

Charvel

1976-present. U.S.-made from '78 to '85 and a combination of imports and U.S.-made post-'85. They also build guitars.

Pre-Pro

1980-1981. Pre-mass production basses made Nov. '80 to '81. Refer to Charvel guitar section for details.

1980-1981	All models	$2,500	$3,500

850 XL

1988-1991. Four-string, neck-thru, active.

1988-1991		$925	$1,250

Brian Moore i2000 Series
Richard Memmel

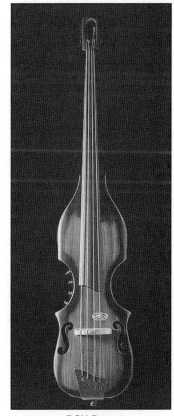

BSX Bass

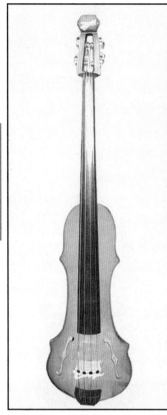

Clevinger Concerto Grande

1968 Coral Firefly

Imaged by Heritage Auctions, HA.com

MODEL YEAR	FEATURES	EXC. COND. LOW	HIGH
CX-490			
1991-1994. Double-cut, 4-string, bolt neck, red or white.			
1991-1994		$325	$425
Eliminator			
1990-1991. Offset double-cut, active electronics, bolt neck.			
1990-1991		$500	$650
Fusion			
1989-1991. Active circuitry, 4- and 5-string models.			
1989-1991	IV	$650	$850
1989-1991	V	$725	$950
Model 1			
1986-1988. Double-cut, bolt neck, 1 pickup.			
1986-1988		$525	$675
Model 2			
1986-1988. Double-cut, bolt neck, 2 pickups.			
1986-1988		$550	$725
Model 3			
1986-1988. Neck-thru, 2 single-coils, active, master volume, bass and treble knobs.			
1986-1988		$650	$850
Model 4			
1986-1988. Like Model 3, but with bolt neck.			
1986-1988		$750	$975
Model 5			
1986-1989. Double-cut, P/J pickups.			
1986-1989		$750	$975
San Dimas Serialized Plated			
1981-1982. Soft headstock early models.			
1981-1982		$3,500	$4,500
SB-4			
1990s. Offset double cut solid, long bass horn, 2 pickups.			
1990s		$550	$725
Star			
1980-1981. Unique 4-point solidbody, 1 pickup, considered by Charvel collectors to be Charvel's only original early design.			
1980-1981		$4,500	$6,000
Surfcaster			
1991-1994. Semi-hollow, lipstick tube pickups.			
1991-1994		$1,375	$1,750

Cipher

1960s. Student market basses imported from Japan. They also made guitars.

Electric Solid Body

1960s. Japanese imports.

1960s		$400	$525

Clevinger

Established in 1982 by Martin Clevinger, Oakland, California. Mainly specializing in electric upright basses but has offered bass guitars as well.

College Line

One of many Lyon & Healy brands, made during the era of extreme design experimentation.

Monster (Style 2089)

Early-1900s. 22" lower bout, flat-top guitar/bass, natural.

1915		$3,000	$4,000

Conrad

Ca.1968-1978. Student and mid-level copy basses imported by David Wexler, Chicago, Illinois. They also offered guitars, mandolins and banjos.

Electric

1970s	Various models	$425	$550

Professional Bison

1970s. Solidbody, 2 pickups.

1970s		$500	$650

Coral

1967-1969. In '66 MCA bought Danelectro and in '67 introduced the Coral brand of guitars, basses and amps. The line included several solid and semi-solidbody basses.

Deluxe D2N4

1967-1969. Offset double-cut, 2 pickups.

1967-1969	Black	$1,500	$2,000
1967-1969	Sunburst	$1,500	$2,000

Fiddle FB2B4

1967-1969. Violin bass hollow body, 2 pickups.

1967-1969		$1,500	$2,000

Firefly F2B4

1968-1969. 335-style semi-hollow, 2 pickups.

1968-1969	Red	$1,250	$1,500
1968-1969	Sunburst	$1,250	$1,500

Long Horn

1968-1969. Standard neck (L2B4) or extended neck (L2LB4), 4 strings.

1968	L2LB4	$2,500	$3,000
1968-1969	L2B4	$2,000	$2,500

Wasp

1967-1969. 4-string (2B4) or 6-string (2B6), black, red or sunburst.

1967-1969	2B4, black or red	$1,500	$2,000
1967-1969	2B4, sunburst	$1,500	$2,000
1967-1969	2B6, black or red	$1,500	$2,000
1967-1969	2B6, sunburst	$1,500	$2,000

Crestwood

1970s. Imported by La Playa Distributing Company of Detroit. Product line includes copies of the popular classical guitars, flat-tops, electric solidbodies and basses of the era.

Electric

1970s. Includes models 2048, 2049, 2079, 2090, 2092, 2093, and 2098.

1970s		$325	$450

Crown

1960s. Violin-shaped hollowbody electrics, solidbody electric guitars and basses, possibly others. Imported from Japan.

Electric Solidbody

1960s	Import	$325	$450

Custom Kraft

Late-1950s-1968. A house brand of St. Louis Music Supply, instruments built by Valco and others. They also offered guitars and amps.

MODEL YEAR	FEATURES	EXC. COND. LOW	HIGH

Bone Buzzer Model 12178
Late 1960s. Symmetrical double-cut thin hollow body, lightning bolt f-holes, 4-on-a-side tuners, 2 pickups, sunburst or emerald sunburst.

1960s		$675	$900

D'Agostino
1976-early 1990s. Import company established by Pat D'Agostino. Solidbodies imported from EKO Italy '77-'82, Japan '82-'84, and in Korea for '84 on. Overall, about 60% of guitars and basses were Japanese, 40% Korean.

Electric Solidbody

1970s	Various models	$850	$1,125

Daion
1978-1984. Higher quality copy basses imported from Japan. Original designs were introduced in '80s. They also had guitars.

Electric

1978-1984	Higher-end	$1,125	$1,500
1978-1984	Lower-end	$650	$850

Danelectro
1946-1969, 1997-present. Danelectro offered basses throughout most of its early history. In '96, the Evets Corporation, of San Clemente, California, introduced a line of Danelectro effects; amps, basses and guitars, many reissues of earlier instruments, soon followed. In early '03, Evets discontinued the guitar, bass and amp lines, but revived the guitar and bass line in '05. Danelectro also built Coral brand instruments (see Coral).

Dane A Series
1967. Solidbody, 2 pickups, 4-string.

1967		$1,000	$1,250

Dane C Series
1967. Semi-solidbody 4- or 6-string, 2 pickups.

1967	4-string	$1,250	$1,500
1967	6-string	$1,500	$2,000

Dane D Series
1967. Solidbody, 2 pickups, 4- or 6-string.

1967	4-string	$1,250	$1,500
1967	6-string	$1,500	$2,000

Dane E Series
1967. Solidbody, 2 pickups, 4-string.

1967		$1,500	$2,000

Hawk
1967. Solidbody, 4-string, 1 pickup.

1967		$1,500	$2,000

Model 1444L
Ca.1958-ca.1964. Masonite body, single-cut, 2 pickups, copper finish.

1958-1964		$1,500	$2,000

Model 3412 Standard (Shorthorn)
1959-1966. Coke bottle headstock, 4- or 6-string, 1 pickup, kidney 'guard through '60, seal 'guard after, copper finish.

1959-1960	Kidney 'guard, 4-string	$1,000	$1,500

MODEL YEAR	FEATURES	EXC. COND. LOW	HIGH
1959-1960	Kidney 'guard, 6-string	$1,500	$2,000
1961-1966	Seal 'guard, 4-string	$1,000	$1,500
1961-1966	Seal 'guard, 6-string	$1,500	$2,000

Model 3612 Standard (Shorthorn)
1959-1966. 6-string version.

1959-1962	Kidney 'guard	$1,250	$1,500
1961-1966	Seal 'guard	$1,250	$1,500

'58 Shorthorn Reissue
1997-2003. Reissues of classic Shorthorn bass.

1997-2003		$400	$550

Model 4423 Longhorn 4-String
1959-1966. Coke bottle headstock, 4-string, 2 pickups, tweed case '59, gray tolex after.

1959	Tweed case	$2,500	$3,000
1960-1966	Gray tolex case	$2,500	$3,000

Model 4623 Longhorn 6-String
1959-1966, 1969-1970. 6-string version.

1959	Tweed case	$3,000	$3,500
1960-1966	Gray tolex case	$3,000	$3,500
1969-1970		$2,000	$2,500

'58 Longhorn Reissue/Longhorn Pro
1997-2010. Reissues of classic Longhorn bass.

1997-2010		$300	$400

UB-2 6-String
1956-1958. Single-cut, 2 pickups, black, bronze or ivory.

1956-1958		$2,000	$2,500

David J King
1987-present. Production/custom, professional and premium grade, electric basses built by luthier David King first in Amherst, Massachusetts and since '92 in Portland, Oregon.

Dean
1976-present. Intermediate and professional grade, production, solidbody, hollowbody, acoustic, and acoustic/electric, basses made overseas. They also offer guitars, banjos, mandolins, and amps.

Baby ML
1982-1986. Downsized version of ML.

1982-1986	Import	$550	$750

Mach V
1985-1986. U.S.-made pointed solidbody, 2 pickups, rosewood 'board.

1985-1986		$2,000	$2,500

ML
1977-1986, 2001-2010. Futuristic body style, fork headstock.

1977-1983	US-made	$4,500	$6,000
1984-1986	Korean import	$1,250	$1,625

Rhapsody Series (USA)
2001-2004. Scroll shaped offset double-cut, various models.

2001-2004	12-string	$1,000	$1,500
2001-2004	8-string	$1,000	$1,500
2001-2004	HFB fretless	$650	$850

Custom Kraft Bone Buzzer
Rivington Guitars

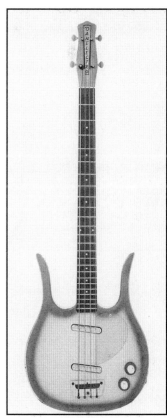

1964 Danelectro 4423 Longhorn

BASSES

Dingwall D-Roc

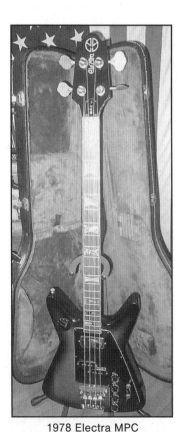

1978 Electra MPC
X-620 Outlaw
Rivington Guitars

MODEL YEAR	FEATURES	EXC. COND. LOW	HIGH

DeArmond

1999-2004. Electric basses based on Guild models and imported from Korea by Fender. They also offered guitars.

Electric

1999-2004. Various imported models.

1999-2004		$550	$725

Dingwall

1988-present. Luthier Sheldon Dingwall, Saskatoon, Saskatchewan, started out producing guitar bodies and necks, eventually offering complete guitars and basses. Currently Dingwall offers professional to premium grade, production/custom 4-, 5-, and 6-string basses featuring the Novax Fanned-Fret System.

Domino

Ca. 1967-1968. Imported from Japan by Maurice Lipsky Music of New York, mainly copies, but some original designs. They also offered guitars.

Electric

1967-1968. Includes the Beatle Bass and Fireball Bass, a Vox Phantom IV copy.

1967-1968		$450	$600

Dorado

Ca. 1972-1973. Name used briefly by Baldwin/Gretsch on a line of Japanese guitar and bass imports.

Electric Solidbody

1970s	Import	$350	$450

Earthwood

1972-1985. Acoustic designs by Ernie Ball with input from George Fullerton and made in Newport Beach, California. One of the first to offer acoustic basses.

Acoustic

1972-1985. Big bodied acoustic bass alternative between Kay double bass and solidbody Fender bass.

1972-1985		$3,000	$4,000

EKO

1959-1985, 2000-present. Built by the Oliviero Pigini Company, Italy. Original importers included LoDuca Brothers, Milwaukee, Wisconsin. Since about 2000, production, acoustic and electric EKO basses are again available and made in Italy and China. They also make guitars and amps.

Barracuda

1967-1978. Offset double-cut semi-hollow, 2 pickups.

1967-1978		$650	$900

Cobra II

1967-ca.1969. Offset double-cut solidbody, 2 pickups.

1967-1969		$550	$750

Kadett

1967-1978. Red or sunburst.

1967-1978		$550	$750

Model 995/2 Violin

1966-ca.1969.

1966-1969		$850	$1,250

MODEL YEAR	FEATURES	EXC. COND. LOW	HIGH

Model 1100/2

1961-1966. Jaguar-style plastic covered solidbody, 2 pickups, sparkle finish.

1961-1966		$750	$950

Rocket IV/Rokes

1967-early-1970s. Rocket-shape design, solidbody, says Rokes on the headstock, the Rokes were a popular English band that endorsed EKO guitars. Marketed as the Rocket IV in the U.S. and as the Rokes in Europe. Often called the Rok. Sunburst, 1 pickup.

1967-1971		$1,250	$1,750

Electra

1970-1984, 2013-present. Originally basses imported from Japan by St. Louis Music. They also offered guitars. Currently U.S.-made in Tampa, Florida.

Electric Solidbody

1970s. Japanese imports, various models.

1970s		$650	$850

MPC Outlaw

1970s. Symmetric solidbody with large straight horns, 2 separate plug-in modules for different effects, MPC headstock logo, bowtie markers, sunburst.

1970s		$950	$1,250

Emperador

1966-1992. Student-level basses imported by Westheimer Musical Instruments. Early models appear to be made by either Teisco or Kawai; later models were made by Cort. They also had guitars.

Electric Solidbody

1960s. Japanese imports, various models.

1960s	Beatle Violin Bass	$350	$550
1960s	Various models	$200	$300

Engelhardt

Engelhardt specializes in student acoustic basses and cellos and is located in Elk Grove Village, Illinois.

Epiphone

1928-present. Epiphone didn't add basses until 1959, after Gibson acquired the brand. The Gibson Epiphones were American made until '69, then all imports until into the '80s, when some models were again made in the U.S. Currently Epiphone offers intermediate and professional grade, production, acoustic and electric basses.

B-1 Acoustic Viol

1940-1949. Maple back and sides, cherry sunburst.

1940-1949		$2,000	$2,500

B-2 Acoustic Viol

1940-1949. Mid-level maple back and sides.

1940-1949		$2,250	$3,000

B-3 Acoustic Viol

1940-1949. Higher-level maple back and sides.

1940-1949		$2,250	$3,000

B-4 Acoustic Viol

1940-1964. Highly figured maple back and sides.

1940-1964		$3,000	$4,000

BASSES

MODEL YEAR	FEATURES	EXC. COND. LOW	HIGH

B-5 Artist Acoustic Viol
1941-1964. Highly figured maple back and sides.

1941-1964		$3,500	$4,500

EA/ET/ES Series (Japan)
1970-1979. Production of the Epiphone brand was moved to Japan in '70. Models included the EA (electric thinline) and ET (electric solidbody).

1970-1975	Various models	$650	$850

EB-0/EB-1/EB-3/EBM-4
1991-2019. EB-0 ('98-'19), EB-1 ('98-'00), EB-3 ('99-'19) and EBM-4 ('91-'98).

1991-2019	Various models	$250	$600

Elitist Series
2003-2005. Higher-end appointments such as set-necks and USA pickups.

2003-2005	Various models	$850	$1,250

Embassy Deluxe
1963-1969. Solidbody, double-cut, 2 pickups, tune-o-matic bridge, cherry finish.

1963-1964		$6,000	$7,500
1965		$6,000	$7,250
1966-1969		$5,500	$7,000

Explorer Korina
2000-2001. Made in Korea, Gibson Explorer body style, genuine korina body, set neck, gold hardware.

2000-2001		$650	$850

Genesis
1979-1980. Double-cut solidbody, 2 humbuckers, Made in Taiwan.

1979-1980		$1,250	$1,625

Jack Cassady Signature
1997-present. Maple body, mahogany neck, rosewood 'board, 1 pickup, metallic gold or ebony finish.

1997-2023		$750	$975

Les Paul Special
1997-2013. LP Jr.-style slab body, single-cut, bolt neck, 2 humbuckers.

1997-2013		$350	$450

Newport EB-6

1962-1964	6-String	$7,000	$9,000

Newport EBD
1960-1970. Double-cut solidbody, 1 pickup (2 pickups optional until '63), 2-on-a-side tuners until '63, 4-on-a-side after that, cherry.

1960-1964		$3,000	$4,000
1965		$2,500	$3,500
1966		$2,000	$2,500
1967-1970		$2,000	$2,500

Newport EB-SF
1962-1963. Newport with added built-in fuzz, cherry.

1962-1963		$3,000	$4,000

Ripper
1998-2000, 2006-2008. Offset double-cut, 1 humbucker pickup, black or natural.

1998-2000		$750	$975

Rivoli (1 Pickup)
1959-1961, 1964-1970, 1994-2000. ES-335-style semi-hollowbody bass, 2-on-a-side tuners, 1 pickup (2 in '70).

1959-1960	Banjo tuners, natural	$8,000	$10,500
1959-1960	Banjo tuners, sunburst	$6,500	$8,500
1961	Standard tuners, natural	$4,500	$6,000
1961	Standard tuners, sunburst	$4,000	$5,000
1964		$3,500	$4,500
1965		$3,000	$4,000
1966-1969		$3,000	$4,000
1967	Sparkling Burgundy	$4,000	$5,000
1970		$3,000	$4,000

Rivoli (2 Pickups)
1970 only. Double pickup Epiphone version of Gibson EB-2D.

1970		$3,000	$4,000

Rivoli II Reissue
1995-2000. Made in Korea, set neck, blond.

1995-2000		$850	$1,250

Thunderbird IV
1997-2019. Reverse-style mahogany body, 2 pickups, sunburst.

1997-2019		$550	$750

Thunderbird IV (Non-Reverse)
1995-1998. Non-reverse-style mahogany body, 2 pickups, 5-string optional.

1995-1998		$550	$750

Viola
1995-present. Beatle Bass 500/1 copy, sunburst.

1995-2023		$450	$600

ESP
1975-present. Intermediate, professional, and premium grade, production/custom, electric basses. Japan's ESP (Electric Sound Products) made inroads in the U.S. market with mainly copy styles in the early '80s, mixing in original designs over the years. In the '90s, ESP opened a California-based Custom Shop. They also build guitars.

Electric
1980s-1990s. Various factory production models.

1980s-90s		$800	$1,250

Essex (SX)
1985-present. Budget grade, production, electric basses imported by Rondo Music of Union, New Jersey. They also offer guitars.

Estrada
1960s-1970s. Line of classical, acoustic and electric guitars and basses imported from Japan.

Violin

1960s	Import	$500	$650

Fender
1946-present. Intermediate, professional, and premium grade, production/custom, electric and acoustic basses made in the U.S. and overseas. Leo Fender is the father of the electric bass. The introduction of his Precision Bass in late '51 changed forever how music was performed, recorded and heard. Leo followed with other popular models

1966 Epiphone Newport
Imaged by Heritage Auctions, HA.com

1997 Epiphone Rivoli 1 Pickup
Angelo Guarini

BASSES

1964 Fender Bass VI

David Swartz

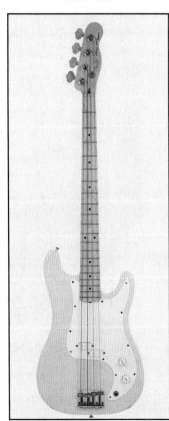

1982 Fender Bullet Deluxe

Imaged by Heritage Auctions, HA.com

MODEL YEAR	FEATURES	EXC. COND. LOW	HIGH

of basses that continue to make up a large part of Fender's production. Please note that all the variations of the Jazz and Precision Basses are grouped under those general headings.

The Precision Bass first left the Fender factory painted blond (same color as the Telecaster). It changed to a 2-color sunburst in mid-1955 (same color as Stratocaster). Some blond Precision basses were shipped after 1955. They are typically worth 50% more. The Jazz Bass standard color is sunburst. All Fender basses could be shipped in a custom DuPont Duco or DuPont Lucite color. Some custom colors are rarer than others. Below is a list of the custom colors offered in 1960 by Fender. They are sorted in ascending order with the most valuable color, Shell Pink, listed last. In the 1960 list, Black and Blond are the least valuable and Shell Pink is the most valuable. A Fiesta Red is typically worth 12% more than a Black or Blond. In the rare color group, a Foam Green is normally worth 8% more than a Shoreline Gold. The two very rare colors are often worth 30% more than a Shoreline Gold. In our pricing information we will list the standard color, then the relative value of a common custom color, and then the value of a rare custom color. Remember that the amount of fade also affects the price. These prices are for factory original custom colors with slight or no fade. Fade implies a lighter color, but with custom colors a faded example can also be much darker in color due to the yellowing of the nitrocellulose clearcoat. Blue can fade to dark green. White can fade to deep yellow.

The Price Guide lists the standard color, plus the value of a Common Color and the value of a Rare Color. The list below defines which group a color falls into for 1960, and it is in ascending order so, for example, a Daphne Blue should be considered more valuable than a Lake Placid Blue, assuming they are in equal condition.

Common Colors: Black, Blond, Candy Apple Red, Olympic White, Lake Placid Blue, Dakota Red, Daphne Blue, Fiesta Red

Rare Colors: Shoreline Gold, Inca Silver, Burgundy Mist, Sherwood Green, Sonic Blue, Foam Green

Rare (Very Rare) Pastel Colors: Surf Green, Shell Pink

Ashbory

2003-2006. Unique-shaped travel bass, Ashbory logo on body, Fender logo on back of headstock, previously sold under Fender's DeArmond brand.

2003-2006		$250	$350

Bass V

1965-1970. Five strings, double-cut, 1 pickup, dot inlay '65-'66, block inlay '66-'70. Please refer to the beginning of the Fender Bass Section for details on Fender color options.

1965	Common color	$5,500	$8,500
1965	Rare color	$7,000	$10,000
1965	Sunburst	$4,250	$5,500
1966-1970	Common color	$5,000	$8,500
1966-1970	Rare color	$6,500	$10,000
1966-1970	Sunburst	$4,500	$5,500

MODEL YEAR	FEATURES	EXC. COND. LOW	HIGH

Bass VI

1961-1975. Six strings, Jazzmaster-like body, 3 pickups, dot inlay until '66, block inlay '66-'75. Reintroduced as Japanese-made Collectable model '95-'98. Please refer to the beginning of the Fender Bass Section for details on Fender color options.

1961-1962	Common color	$16,000	$25,000
1961-1962	Rare color	$21,000	$30,000
1961-1962	Sunburst	$9,000	$13,000
1963-1964	Common color	$15,000	$25,000
1963-1964	Rare color	$20,000	$30,000
1963-1964	Sunburst	$8,500	$12,000
1965	Common color	$13,500	$20,000
1965	Rare color	$17,500	$25,000
1965	Sunburst	$7,000	$10,000
1966-1969	Common color	$10,000	$15,000
1966-1969	Rare color	$12,500	$20,000
1966-1969	Sunburst	$6,500	$8,000
1970-1971	Custom color	$9,000	$12,000
1970-1971	Sunburst	$5,500	$7,500
1972-1974	Custom color	$8,500	$11,000
1972-1974	Natural	$5,500	$7,500
1972-1974	Sunburst	$5,500	$7,500
1972-1974	Walnut	$5,500	$7,500
1975	Black, blond, white	$5,500	$7,500
1975	Natural	$5,000	$7,000
1975	Sunburst	$5,000	$7,000
1975	Walnut	$5,000	$7,000

Bass VI Reissue (CS)

2006. Custom Shop, 3-tone sunburst, certificate of authenticity.

2006		$2,500	$3,500

Bass VI Reissue (Import)

1995-1998. Import, sunburst.

1995-1998		$1,250	$1,625

Bass VI Reissue (Japan)

Japanese market only, JD serial number.

2014		$1,250	$1,750

Bass VI Pawn Shop

2013-2014. Alder body, maple neck, rosewood 'board, 3-color sunburst.

2013-2014		$700	$900

BG Series

1995-2012. Acoustic flat-top basses, single-cut, two-on-a-side tuners, Fishman on-board controls.

1995-2012	Various models	$175	$250

Bullet (B30, B34, B40)

1982-1983. Alder body, 1 pickup, offered in short- and long-scale, red or walnut. U.S.-made, replaced by Japanese-made Squire Bullet Bass.

1982-1983		$850	$1,250

Bullet Deluxe

1982-1983. Fender logo with Bullet Bass Deluxe on headstock, E-series serial number, small Telecaster-style headstock shape.

1982-1983		$850	$1,250

Coronado I

1966-1970. Thinline, double-cut, 1 pickup, dot inlay, sunburst and cherry red were the standard colors, but custom colors could be ordered.

1966-1970	Various colors	$1,750	$2,500

MODEL YEAR	FEATURES	EXC. COND. LOW	HIGH

Coronado II
1966-1972. Two pickups, block inlay, sunburst and cherry red standard colors, but custom colors could be ordered. Only Antigua finish offered from '70 on.

1966-1969	Various colors	$2,250	$3,000
1966-1969	Wildwood option	$3,000	$4,500
1970-1972	Antigua only	$2,500	$3,500

Coronado Reissue
2014-2016. Reissue of the 2 pickup (Coronado II), block inlay.

2014-2016	$650	$825

Dimension
2004-2006. Made in Mexico, 4- or 5-string, P and J pickups.

2004-2006	$650	$1,000

HM
1989-1991. Japanese-made, 4 strings (IV) or 5 strings (V), basswood body, no 'guard, 3 Jazz Bass pickups, 5-way switch, master volume, master TBX, sunburst.

1989-1991	IV, 4-string	$850	$1,125
1989-1991	V, 5-string	$925	$1,250

Jaguar
1995, 2006-2010. Crafted in Japan, Jaguar Bass logo on headstock.

1995	$1,000	$1,375
2006-2010	$925	$1,250

Jaguar (Modern Player)
2012-2016. Made in China, koto body, maple neck and 'board, black.

2012-2016	$325	$425

Jaguar Baritone Custom
2007. Fender Jaguar Baritone Custom logo on headstock, 6-string.

2007	$1,125	$1,500

Deluxe Jaguar
2012-2014. Maple neck, rosewood 'board, 2 pickups, 3-color sunburst, Candy Apple Red, Cobalt Blue.

2012-2014	$600	$775

Troy Sanders Jaguar
2014-2023. Artist series, alder body, bolt-on maple neck, 2 pickups, silverburst.

2014-2023	$850	$1,125

Jazz Bass
The following are variations of the Jazz Bass. The first seven listings are for the main U.S.-made models. All others are listed alphabetically after that in the following order:

Jazz
Standard Jazz
American Standard Jazz
American Standard Jazz V
American Series Jazz
American Series Jazz V
American Professional/Professional II Jazz
50th Anniversary American Standard Jazz
50th Anniversary Jazz Limited Edition
'60 Custom Shop Limited Jazz
'60s Jazz (Custom Shop)
'60s Jazz (Import)

Road Worn '60s Jazz
Vintera '60s Jazz
60th Anniversary American Jazz
60th Anniversary Road Worn Jazz
'61 Journeyman Jazz
'62 Jazz (U.S.A.)
'64 Jazz (Custom Shop)
'64 Jazz (American Vintage)
'66 Jazz Special Limited Edition
'66 Journeyman Jazz
'74 Jazz (American Vintage)
'75 Jazz (American Vintage)
75th Anniversary Commemorative Jazz
75th Anniversary Jazz (Diamond Anniversary)
Aerodyne Jazz
American Deluxe Jazz/Jazz V
American Deluxe FMT Jazz
American Elite Jazz/Jazz V
American Ultra Jazz
Contemporary Jazz
Custom Classic Jazz/Jazz V
Deluxe Jazz/Jazz V (Active)
Deluxe Power Jazz
Flea Signature Jazz
Foto Flame Jazz
FSR Standard Special Edition Jazz
Geddy Lee Signature Jazz
Gold Jazz
Highway One Jazz
Jaco Pastorius Jazz
Jazz Plus IV/Jazz Plus V
Jazz Special (Import)
Marcus Miller Signature Jazz
Masterbuilt Custom Shop Jazz
Noel Redding Signature Jazz
Rarities Flame Ash Top Jazz
Reggie Hamilton Jazz
Roscoe Beck Jazz IV/Jazz V
Select Jazz
Standard Jazz (Import)
Standard Jazz Fretless (Import)
Steve Bailey Jazz VI
Ventures Limited Edition Jazz
Victor Baily Jazz

Jazz
1960-1981. Two stack knobs '60-'62, 3 regular controls '62 on. Dot markers '60-'66, block markers from '66 on. Rosewood 'board standard, but maple available from '68 on. With the introduction of vintage reissue models in '81, Fender started calling the American-made version the Standard Jazz Bass. That became the American Standard Jazz Bass in '88, the American Series Jazz Bass in '00, back to the American Standard Jazz Bass in '08, and currently the American Professional Jazz Bass. Post '71 Jazz Bass values are affected more by condition than color or neck option. The Jazz Bass was fitted with a 3-bolt neck or bullet rod in late-'74. Prices assume a 3-bolt neck starting in '75. Please refer to the beginning of the Fender Bass Section for details on Fender color options. Post '71 Jazz Bass values are affected more by condition than color or neck option. The Jazz Bass was fitted with a 3-bolt neck or bullet rod in late-'74. Prices assume a

1967 Fender Coronado II
Rivington Guitars

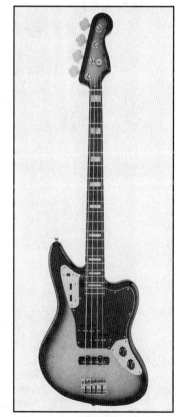

Fender Troy Sanders Jaguar

BASSES

1964 Fender Jazz
Ron Cascisa

1966 Fender Jazz
David Carlino

3-bolt neck starting in '75. Please refer to the beginning of the Fender Bass Section for details on Fender color options.

MODEL YEAR	FEATURES	EXC. COND. LOW	HIGH
1960	Common color	$35,000	$42,000
1960	Rare color	$45,000	$150,000
1960	Sunburst	$23,500	$31,500
1961-1962	Common color, stack knob	$35,000	$42,000
1961-1962	Rare color, stack knob	$45,000	$150,000
1961-1962	Sunburst, stack knob	$23,500	$31,500
1962	Common color, 3 knob, curved	$20,000	$30,000
1962	Common color, 3 knob, slab	$25,000	$35,000
1962	Rare color, 3 knob, curved	$25,000	$40,000
1962	Rare color, 3 knob, slab	$28,000	$45,000
1962	Sunburst, 3 knob, curved	$16,000	$21,000
1962	Sunburst, 3 knob, slab	$17,000	$23,000
1963	Common color	$18,000	$25,000
1963	Rare color	$20,000	$30,000
1963	Sunburst	$13,500	$17,500
1964	Common color	$18,000	$25,000
1964	Rare color	$20,000	$30,000
1964	Sunburst, early '64	$13,500	$17,500
1964	Sunburst, late '64	$12,000	$15,500
1965	Common color	$12,000	$16,000
1965	Rare color	$15,000	$25,000
1965	Sunburst	$10,000	$13,000
1966	Common color	$9,000	$15,000
1966	Rare color	$12,000	$20,000
1966	Sunburst, blocks	$8,000	$10,000
1966	Sunburst, dots	$8,500	$11,000
1967-1969	Custom color	$9,000	$15,000
1967-1969	Sunburst	$8,000	$10,500
1970	Custom color	$6,500	$9,000
1970	Sunburst	$5,000	$6,500
1971	Custom color	$5,500	$7,000
1971	Sunburst	$4,500	$5,500
1972	Custom color	$5,500	$7,000
1972	Natural, black block option	$4,000	$5,000
1972	Natural, standard markers	$4,250	$5,500
1972	Sunburst	$4,500	$6,000
1973	Custom color	$5,500	$7,000
1973	Natural	$4,000	$5,000
1973	Sunburst	$4,250	$5,500
1973	Walnut	$4,000	$5,000
1974	Black, blond, white, 3-bolt	$3,750	$4,750
1974	Black, blond, white, 4-bolt	$3,875	$5,000
1974	Natural, 3-bolt	$3,000	$4,000
1974	Natural, 4-bolt	$3,500	$4,500
1974	Sunburst, 3-bolt,		

MODEL YEAR	FEATURES	EXC. COND. LOW	HIGH
	late-'74	$3,250	$4,000
1974	Sunburst, 4-bolt	$3,500	$4,500
1974	Walnut, 3-bolt	$3,250	$4,000
1974	Walnut, 4-bolt	$3,625	$4,750
1975-1977	All colors	$3,375	$4,000
1978-1980	All Colors	$2,750	$3,750
1981	Black & Gold	$2,625	$3,250
1981	Black, white, wine	$2,375	$3,000
1981	International colors	$2,500	$3,500
1981	Sunburst	$2,250	$2,875

Standard Jazz
1981-1984. Replaced Jazz Bass ('60-'81) and replaced by the American Standard Jazz Bass in '88. Name now used on import version. Please refer to the beginning of the Fender Bass Section for details on Fender color options.

1981-1984		$1,250	$2,000

American Standard Jazz
1988-2000, 2008-2016. Replaced Standard Jazz Bass ('81-'88) and replaced by the American Series Jazz Bass in '00, back to American Standard in Jan. '08.

1988-2016		$1,000	$1,500

American Standard Jazz V
1998-2000, 2008-2016. 5-string version.

1998-2016		$1,000	$1,375

American Series Jazz
2000-2007. Replaces American Standard Jazz Bass. Renamed American Standard in '08.

2000-2007		$1,000	$1,375

American Series Jazz V
2000-2007. 5-string version.

2000-2007		$1,000	$1,375

American Professional/ Professional II Jazz
2017-present. Redesign includes V-Mod pickups, narrow-tall frets, 'deep C' neck profile, various colors. Also available left-hand model. Renamed American Professional II in '20.

2017-2023		$1,250	$1,625

50th Anniversary American Standard Jazz
1996. Regular American Standard with gold hardware, 4- or 5-string, gold Fender's 50th Anniversary commemorative neck plate, rosewood 'board, sunburst.

1996	IV	$1,375	$1,750
1996	V	$1,375	$1,750

50th Anniversary Jazz Limited Edition
2010. 50th anniversary of the Jazz Bass, nitro Candy Apple Red with matching headstock, mix of vintage and modern specs, rosewood 'board, block markers, 50th Anniversary neck plate.

2010		$1,500	$2,500

'60 Custom Shop Limited Jazz
2020. Limited Edition, heavy relic.

2020		$3,000	$4,000

'60s Jazz (Custom Shop)
1994-1998. Early '60s specs, relic for 1996-1998. Replaced by the CS '64 Jazz Bass. Early Relic work was

MODEL YEAR	FEATURES	EXC. COND. LOW	HIGH

done outside of Fender by Vince Cunetto or his staff.

1994-1995		$3,000	$4,000
1996	Relic (Cunetto)	$3,000	$4,000
1997-1998	Relic (Cunetto staff)	$3,000	$4,000

'60s Jazz (Import)

1991-1994, 2001-2019. Classic series, '60s features, rosewood 'board, Japan-made for first years, Mexico after.

| 1991-1994 | Japan | $625 | $850 |
| 2001-2019 | Mexico | $550 | $725 |

Road Worn '60s Jazz

2009-2019. Rosewood 'board, aged finish.

| 2009-2019 | | $600 | $825 |

Vintera '60s Jazz

2020-present. Vintage style appointments, 3-Color Sunburst, Daphne Blue or Firemist Gold.

| 2020-2023 | | $650 | $850 |

60th Anniversary American Jazz

2006. Rosewood 'board, 3-tone sunburst.

| 2006 | | $1,500 | $2,000 |

60th Anniversary Road Worn Jazz

2020-2021. Road Worn lacquer finish, 3-color sunburst, Firemist Silver or Olympic White.

| 2020-2021 | | $850 | $1,125 |

'61 Journeyman Jazz

2020. Heavy relic.

| 2020 | | $3,000 | $4,000 |

'62 Jazz (U.S.A.)

1982-1984, 1986-2012. U.S.A.-made, American Vintage series, reissue of '62 Jazz Bass. Please refer to the beginning of the Fender Bass Section for details on Fender color options.

1982-1984		$3,500	$5,000
1986-1999		$1,500	$2,500
2000-2012		$1,250	$2,000

'64 Jazz (Custom Shop)

1998-2009. Alder body, rosewood 'board, tortoise shell 'guard. From June '95 to June '99 Relic work was done outside of Fender by Vince Cunetto and included a certificate noting model and year built, a bass without the certificate is valued less than shown.

1998-1999	Relic (Cunetto)	$3,000	$4,000
2000-2009	Closet		
	Classic option	$3,000	$4,000
2000-2009	NOS option	$3,000	$4,000
2000-2009	Relic option	$3,000	$4,000

'64 Jazz (American Vintage)

2013-2017. American Vintage series, dot inlays.

| 2013-2017 | | $1,500 | $2,000 |

'66 Jazz Special Limited Edition

2013. Japan, made for retailer Sweetwater, aged Oly White, 132 made for North American distribution.

| 2013 | | $1,125 | $1,500 |

'66 Journeyman Jazz

2020. Relic.

| 2020 | | $3,000 | $4,000 |

'74 Jazz (American Vintage)

2013-2017. American Vintage series, block inlays.

| 2013-2017 | | $1,500 | $2,000 |

'75 Jazz (American Vintage)

1994-2012. American Vintage series, maple neck with black block markers.

| 1994-2012 | | $1,500 | $2,000 |

75th Anniversary Commemorative Jazz

2021. Limited Edition, gold 75th ingot back of headstock and 75th anniversary neck plate, gold hardware, 2-color Bourbon Burst.

| 2021 | | $1,000 | $1,500 |

75th Anniversary Jazz (Diamond Anniversary)

2021. Diamond Anniversary metallic finish with matching painted headstock, 75th engraved silver neck plate.

| 2021 | | $550 | $775 |

Aerodyne Jazz

2003-present. Bound basswood body, P/J pickups, Deluxe Series.

| 2003-2023 | | $825 | $1,125 |

American Deluxe Jazz/Jazz V

1998-2016. U.S., 4 (IV) or 5-string (V), active electronics, alder or ash body. Alder body colors - sunburst or transparent red, ash body colors - white, blond, transparent teal green or transparent purple.

| 1998-2016 | IV or V | $1,250 | $1,625 |

American Deluxe FMT Jazz

2001-2006. Flame maple top version (FMT), active EQ, dual J pickups.

| 2001-2006 | | $1,500 | $2,000 |

American Elite Jazz/Jazz V

2016-2019. Compound radius 'board, 4 (IV) or 5-string (V), Noiseless pickups, onboard preamp, various colors.

| 2016-2019 | IV or V | $1,250 | $1,625 |

American Ultra Jazz

2019-present. Alder or ash body, 2 Noiseless Vintage pickups, redesigned active/passive preamp, 4- (IV) or 5-string (V), various colors with satin finish.

| 2019-2023 | IV or V | $1,375 | $1,875 |

Contemporary Jazz

1987. Made in Japan.

| 1987 | | $600 | $775 |

Custom Classic Jazz/Jazz V

2001-2009. Custom Shop, slightly slimmer waist, deeper cutaways, maple or rosewood 'board, block inlays, 4 (IV) or 5-string (V).

| 2001-2009 | IV or V | $2,250 | $3,000 |

Deluxe Jazz/Jazz V (Active)

1995-2021. Made in Mexico, active electronics, 4 (IV) or 5-string (V), various colors.

| 1995-2021 | IV or V | $475 | $625 |

Deluxe Power Jazz

2006. Part of Deluxe Series with Fishman piezo power bridge.

| 2006 | | $750 | $975 |

Flea Signature Jazz

2019-present. Flea logo neck plate, Road Worn Faded Shell Pink lacquer finish.

| 2019-2023 | | $950 | $1,250 |

Foto Flame Jazz

1994-1996. Japanese import, alder and basswood body with Foto Flame figured wood image.

| 1994-1996 | | $750 | $975 |

Fender 50th Anniversary Jazz
Rivington Guitars

Fender Flea Signature Jazz

BASSES

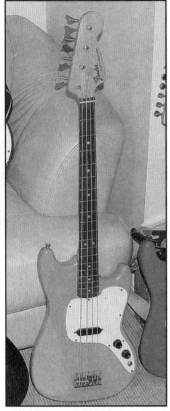

Fender Musicmaster
John Lento

Fender Parallel Universe
'51 Telecaster PJ

MODEL YEAR	FEATURES	EXC. COND. LOW	HIGH

FSR Standard Special Edition Jazz
2007-2009. Made in Mexico, Fender Special Edition logo on back of headstock, ash body with natural finish.

2007-2009		$525	$675

Geddy Lee Signature Jazz
1998-present. Limited run import in '98, now part of Artist Series, black.

1998-2023		$800	$1,125

Gold Jazz
1981-1984. Gold finish and gold-plated hardware.

1981-1984		$2,500	$3,500

Highway One Jazz
2003-2011. U.S.-made, alder body, satin lacquer finish.

2003-2011		$750	$975

Jaco Pastorius Jazz
1999-present. Artist Series, standard production model made in Corona, '62 3-color sunburst body without pickup covers.

1999-2000	Fretted	$2,500	$4,000
1999-2023	Fretless	$2,500	$4,000

Jazz Plus IV/Jazz Plus V
1990-1994. Alder body, 4-string (IV) or 5-string (V), 2 Lace Sensors, active electronics, rotary circuit selector, master volume, balance, bass boost, bass cut, treble boost, treble cut, various colors.

1990-1994	Various colors	$1,000	$1,375

Jazz Special (Import)
1984-1991. Japanese-made, Jazz/Precision hybrid, Precision-shaped basswood body, Jazz neck (fretless available), 2 P/J pickups, offered with active (Power) or passive electronics.

1984-1991		$650	$850

Marcus Miller Signature Jazz
1998-2014. Artist series.

1998-2004	Import	$950	$1,250
2005-2014	US Custom Shop	$2,000	$2,750

Masterbuilt Custom Shop Jazz
2003-present. Various models and builders.

2003-2023		$4,000	$10,000

Noel Redding Signature Jazz
1997. Limited Edition import, artist signature on 'guard, sunburst, rosewood 'board.

1997		$1,250	$1,625

Rarities Flame Ash Top Jazz
2019-2021. Two-piece alder body with flame ash top, Plasma Red Burst finish.

2019-2021		$1,750	$2,375

Reggie Hamilton Jazz
2002-2016. Custom Artist series, alder body, passive/active switch and pan control.

2002-2016		$600	$775

Roscoe Beck Jazz IV/Jazz V
1997-2009. 5-string version offered '97-'06, 4-string '04-'09.

1997-2006	V, 5-string	$1,625	$2,250
2004-2009	IV, 4-string	$1,625	$2,250

Select Jazz
2012-2013. US-made, figured top, rear-headstock 'Fender Select' medallion.

2012-2013		$2,000	$2,625

Standard Jazz (Import)
1985-2018. Standard series, Japan-made into '90, Mexico after. Not to be confused with '81-'84 American-made model with the same name. Replaced by Player Series.

1985-1990	Japan	$1,000	$1,500
1991-2018	Mexico	$425	$550

Standard Jazz Fretless (Import)
1994-2018. Standard series, fretless version. Replaced by Player Series.

1994-2018	IV or V	$425	$550

Steve Bailey Jazz VI
2009-2011. USA, 6-string, fretless or fretted, sunburst or black.

2009-2011		$1,750	$2,250

Ventures Limited Edition Jazz
1996. Made in Japan, part of Ventures guitar and bass set, dark purple.

1996		$1,250	$1,625

Victor Baily Jazz
2002-2011. Artist series, koa, rosewood and mahogany body, fretless with white fret markers.

2002-2011		$1,375	$1,750

JP-90
1990-1994. Two P/J pickups, rosewood fretboard, poplar body, black or red.

1990-1994		$650	$850

Kingman
2011-present. Acoustic, solid spruce top, mahogany back and sides.

2011-2023		$450	$600

MB IV/MB V
1994-1995. Made in Japan, offset double-cut, 1 P- and 1 J-style pickup, 4-string (IV) or 5-string (V).

1994-1995	IV or V	$500	$650

Musicmaster
1970-1983. Shorter scale, solidbody, 1 pickup. various colors.

1970-1983		$1,125	$1,500

Mustang
1966-1982. Shorter scale, solidbody, 1 pickup, offered in standard colors and, for '69-'73, Competition Red, Blue and Orange with racing stripes on the body (with matching headstock for '69-'70).

1966-1969		$5,000	$6,000
1969-1970	Competition	$4,500	$5,500
1970-1979		$4,500	$5,500
1978-1980	Antigua finish	$4,000	$5,000
1980-1982		$2,750	$3,500

Mustang (Import)
2002-2018. First made in Japan, later Mexico (ca. 2015), alder body, '60s features.

2002-2018		$750	$950

Parallel Universe '51 Telecaster PJ
2018. Limited edition, authentic '51 style, mixes elements from both Jazz and Precision Basses.

2018		$1,500	$2,000

Performer
1985-1986. Swinger-like body style, active electronics, various colors.

1985-1986		$1,500	$2,000

MODEL YEAR	FEATURES	EXC. COND. LOW	HIGH

Postmodern

2015-2019. Custom Shop, P-Bass body, Jazz Bass neck, at times offered in Relic, Journeyman Relic, NOS, and Lush Closet Classic finishes.

2015-2019	Various options	$2,500	$3,500

Precision Bass

The following are variations of the Precision Bass. The first six listings are for the main U.S.-made models. All others are listed alphabetically after that in the following order:

Precision
Standard Precision
American Standard Precision
American Series Precision
American Series Precision V
American Professional/Professional II Precision
40th Anniversary Precision (Custom Shop)
50th Anniversary American Standard Precision
50th Anniversary Precision
'50s Precision
Road Worn '50s Precision
'51 Precision
'55 Precision (Custom Shop)
'57 Precision
'57 Precision (Custom Shop)
'57 Precision (Import)
'59 Precision (Custom Shop)
60th Anniversary Precision (Mexico)
60th Anniversary Precision (USA)
'61 Precision (Custom Shop)
'62 Precision
'62 Precision (Import)
'63 Precision (U.S.A.)
75th Anniversary Commemorative Precision
75th Anniversary Precision (Diamond Anniversary)
Adam Clayton Signature Precision
Aerodyne Classic Precision Special
American Deluxe Precision
American Ultra Precision
Big Block Precision
Cabronita Precision
California Precision Special
Deluxe Active Precision Special
Elite/Gold Elite Precision Series
Foto Flame Precision
Highway One Precision
Magnificent Seven LE American Standard PJ
Mark Hoppus Signature Precision
Mike Dirnt Road Worn Precision
Nate Mendel Precision
Pino Palladino Signature Precision
Precision Jr.
Precision Lyte
Precision Special (Mexico)
Precision Special (U.S.A.)
Precision U.S. Plus/Plus
Precision U.S. Deluxe/Plus Deluxe
Roger Waters Precision
Select Precision
Standard/Player Precision (Import)

Sting Precision
Tony Franklin Precision
Walnut Elite Precision
Walnut Precision Special

Precision

1951-1981. Slab body until '54, 1-piece maple neck standard until '59, optional after '69, rosewood 'board standard '59 on (slab until mid-'62, curved after), blond finish standard until '54, sunburst standard after that (2-tone '54-'58, 3-tone after '58). Became the Standard Precision Bass in '81-'85, the American Standard Precision for '88-'00, the American Series Precision Bass in '00-'08, and the American Standard Precision again for '08-'16. Currently called the American Professional Precision Bass. Unlike the Jazz and Telecaster Basses, the Precision was never fitted with a 3-bolt neck or bullet rod. Please refer to the beginning of the Fender Bass Section for details on Fender color options.

YEAR	FEATURES	LOW	HIGH
1951	Blond, slab	$25,000	$33,000
1952-1954	Blond, slab	$17,000	$23,000
1955	Blond, contour	$14,000	$18,000
1956	Blond, contour	$14,000	$18,000
1956	Sunburst, contour	$12,000	$16,000
1957	Blond	$14,000	$18,000
1957	Blond, anodized guard	$25,000	$35,000
1957	Sunburst, anodized guard	$20,000	$22,000
1958	Blond	$25,000	$35,000
1958	Sunburst, anodized guard	$16,000	$25,000
1959	Blond	$25,000	$35,000
1959	Sunburst, anodized guard	$16,000	$25,000
1959	Sunburst, tortoise guard	$14,000	$16,500
1960	Blond	$18,500	$23,500
1960	Custom color	$18,500	$50,000
1960	Sunburst	$13,500	$17,500
1961	Custom color	$16,000	$45,000
1961	Sunburst	$13,500	$17,500
1962	Custom color, curved	$15,500	$45,000
1962	Custom color, slab	$19,000	$50,000
1962	Sunburst, curved	$13,000	$16,000
1962	Sunburst, slab	$14,000	$17,500
1963	Custom color	$13,000	$36,000
1963	Sunburst	$11,500	$15,000
1964	Custom color	$12,000	$35,000
1964	Sunburst, early '64, spaghetti logo, green guard	$11,000	$13,500
1964	Sunburst, late '64	$10,500	$13,500
1965	Custom color	$12,000	$23,000
1965	Sunburst	$10,000	$12,500
1966	Custom color	$9,000	$20,000
1966	Sunburst	$7,000	$9,500
1967-1969	Custom color	$8,250	$14,000
1967-1969	Sunburst	$6,250	$9,000
1970	Custom color	$7,500	$10,000
1970	Sunburst	$4,000	$5,000

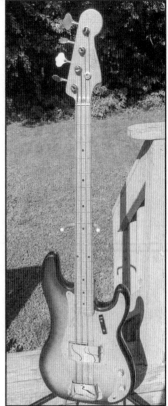

1958 Fender Precision
Phil Avelli

1959 Fender Precision
Charlie Faucher

BASSES

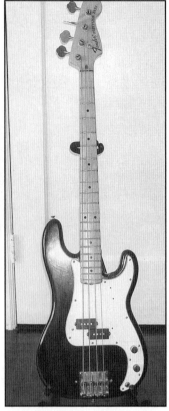

1973 Fender Precision

KC Cormack

1988 Fender '62 Precision

Jonathan Bell

MODEL YEAR	FEATURES	EXC. COND. LOW	HIGH
1971	Custom color	$6,000	$7,500
1971	Sunburst	$4,000	$5,000
1972	Custom color	$5,500	$7,000
1972	Sunburst	$3,500	$5,000
1973	Custom color	$4,000	$5,000
1973	Natural, sunburst, walnut	$3,250	$4,500
1974	All colors	$3,250	$4,250
1975-1977	All colors	$3,250	$4,000
1978-1979	All colors	$2,500	$3,500
1980	Color with matching hdstk, gold hw	$2,250	$3,000
1980	International colors	$2,250	$3,000
1980	Other colors	$2,125	$2,750
1981	Black & gold	$2,250	$3,000
1981	International colors	$2,375	$3,000
1981	Other colors	$1,500	$2,250

Standard Precision

1981-1984. Replaces Precision Bass, various colors. Replaced by American Standard Precision '88-'00. The Standard name is used on import Precision model for '88-present.

1981-1984		$1,250	$2,000

American Standard Precision

1988-2000, 2008-2016. Replaces Standard Precision Bass, replaced by American Series Precision in '00, back to American Standard in Jan. '08.

1988-1989	Blond, gold hw	$1,250	$1,750
1988-2016	Various colors	$1,250	$1,750

American Series Precision

2000-2007. Replaces American Standard Precision Bass, various colors. Renamed American Standard in '08.

2000-2007		$1,250	$1,500

American Series Precision V

2000-2007. 5-string version.

2000-2007		$1,250	$1,500

American Professional/ Professional II Precision

2017-present. Redesign includes V-Mod pickups, '63 P Bass neck profile, narrow-tall frets, various colors. Also available left-hand model. Renamed American Professional II in '20.

2017-2023		$1,250	$1,625

40th Anniversary Precision (Custom Shop)

1991. 400 made, quilted amber maple top, gold hardware.

1991		$3,000	$4,000

50th Anniversary American Standard Precision

1996. Regular American Standard with gold hardware, 4- or 5-string, gold 50th Anniversary commemorative neck plate, rosewood 'board, sunburst.

1996		$1,375	$1,750

50th Anniversary Precision

2001. Commemorative certificate with date and serial number, butterscotch finish, ash body, maple neck, black 'guard.

2001	With certificate	$1,375	$1,750

'50s Precision

1992-1996, 2006-2019. First run made in Japan, currently in Mexico, 1 split-coil, maple neck.

1992-1996	Japan	$800	$1,250
2006-2019	Mexico	$550	$725

Road Worn '50s Precision

2009-2019. Mexico, 1 split-coil, maple neck, aged finish.

2009-2019		$600	$825

'51 Precision

1994-1997, 2003-2010. Import from Japan, no pickup or bridge covers, blond or sunburst. Offered in Japan in the '90s.

1994-1997	Japan only	$1,125	$1,500
2003-2010		$1,125	$1,500

'55 Precision (Custom Shop)

2003-2011. 1955 specs, including oversized 'guard, 1-piece maple neck/fretboard, preproduction bridge and pickup covers, single-coil pickup. Offered in N.O.S., Closet Classic or highest-end Relic.

2003-2006	NOS	$3,000	$4,000
2003-2006	Relic	$3,000	$4,000
2003-2011	Closet Classic	$3,000	$4,000

'57 Precision

1982-1984, 1986-2012. U.S.-made reissue, American Vintage series, various colors.

1982-1984		$3,000	$4,500
1986-1999		$2,000	$2,625
2000-2012		$1,750	$2,500

'57 Precision (Custom Shop)

2013	Heavy relic	$3,000	$4,000

'57 Precision (Import)

1984-1986	Black	$2,000	$3,000

'59 Precision (Custom Shop)

2003-2010. Custom Shop built with late-'59 specs, rosewood 'board.

2003-2008	Closet Classic	$3,000	$4,000
2003-2010	NOS	$3,000	$4,000
2003-2010	Relic	$3,000	$4,000

60th Anniversary Precision (Mexico)

2011. Made in Mexico, with 60th Anniversary gig bag.

2011		$500	$650

60th Anniversary Precision (USA)

2011. 1951-2011 Anniversary date label.

2011		$1,500	$2,000

'61 Precision (Custom Shop)

2010-2013. Made for Musician's Friend and Guitar Center.

2010-2013	Closet Classic	$3,000	$4,000
2010-2013	NOS	$3,000	$4,000
2010-2013	Relic	$3,000	$4,000

'62 Precision

1982-1984, 1986-2012. American Vintage series, alder body. No production in '85. Limited run Mary Kaye Blond (gold hardware) in '90.

1982-1984		$2,750	$4,375
1986-1999		$1,750	$2,500
1990	Mary Kaye Blond	$1,500	$2,250
2000-2012		$1,250	$2,000

The *Vintage Guitar Price Guide* shows values for all-original, excellent condition instruments and, where applicable, with original case.

MODEL YEAR	FEATURES	EXC. COND. LOW	HIGH

'62 Precision (Import)
1984-1986. Foreign-made, black.

1984-1986		$1,000	$1,375

'63 Precision (U.S.A.)
2013-2017. American Vintage series.

2013-2017		$1,500	$2,000

75th Anniversary Commemorative Precision
2021. Limited Edition, gold 75th ingot back of headstock and 75th anniversary neck plate, gold hardware, 2-color Bourbon Burst.

2021		$1,250	$1,750

75th Anniversary Precision (Diamond Anniversary)
2021. Diamond Anniversary metallic finish with matching painted headstock, 75th engraved silver neck plate.

2021		$625	$825

Adam Clayton Signature Precision
2011. Custom Shop Limited Edition.

2011		$3,250	$4,500

Aerodyne Classic Precision Special
2006. Made in Japan, labeled Precision and Aerodyne P Bass, figured maple top, matching headstock, P-J pickup.

2006		$825	$1,125

American Deluxe Precision
1998-2016. U.S., active electronics, 4 (IV) or 5-string (V), alder or ash body. Alder body colors - sunburst or transparent red. Ash body colors - white blond, transparent teal green or transparent purple.

1998-2016	IV or V	$1,250	$1,625

American Ultra Precision
2019-present. Alder or ash body, 2 Noiseless Vintage pickups, 4-string, various colors with gloss finish.

2019-2023		$1,375	$1,875

Big Block Precision
2005-2009. Made in Mexico, pearloid block markers, black finish with matching headstock, 1 double Jazz Bass humbucker, bass and treble boost and cut controls.

2005-2009		$725	$950

Cabronita Precision
2014-2015. One Fideli'Tron pickup, 2 knobs.

2014-2015		$350	$525

California Precision Special
1997. California Series, assembled and finished in Mexico and California, P/J pickup configuration.

1997		$700	$925

Deluxe Active Precision Special
1995-2021. Made in Mexico, P/J pickups, Jazz Bass neck.

1995-2021		$475	$625

Elite/Gold Elite Precision Series
1983-1985. Active electronics, noise-cancelling pickups, Elite I (ash body, 1 pickup), Elite II (2 pickups), Gold Elite I (gold-plated hardware, 1 pickup), Gold Elite II (2 pickups), various colors.

1983-1985	Various models	$2,000	$2,750

Foto Flame Precision
1994-1996. Made in Japan, simulated woodgrain finish, natural or sunburst.

1994-1996		$750	$975

Highway One Precision
2003-2011. U.S.-made, alder body, satin lacquer finish.

2003-2011		$750	$975

Magnificent Seven LE American Standard PJ
2016. U.S., Limited Edition, P-bass body with Jazz neck, 500 made.

2016		$1,000	$1,375

Mark Hoppus Signature Precision
2002-2016. Mark Hoppus engraved on neck plate.

2002-2016	Mexico serial no	$600	$825

Mike Dirnt Road Worn Precision
2014-present. '51 era P-Bass style, ash body, maple or rosewood 'board.

2014-2023		$850	$1,125

Nate Mendel Precision
2013-present. Ash body, rosewood 'board.

2013-2023		$700	$950

Pino Palladino Signature Precision
2006-present. Custom Shop Artist series, based on '62 used by Palladino, certificate of authenticity, Fiesta Red.

2006-2023		$3,000	$4,000

Precision Jr.
2004-2006. 3/4 size.

2004-2006		$600	$800

Precision Lyte
1992-2001. Japanese-made, smaller, lighter basswood body, 2 pickups, sunburst.

1992-2001		$875	$1,125

Precision Special (Mexico)
1997-1998. Chrome hardware, 1 P- and 1 J-pickup.

1997-1998		$625	$825

Precision Special (U.S.A.)
1980-1982. Gold hardware, matching headstock, active electronics, CA Red, LP Blue, Oly White or walnut (see separate listing).

1980-1982	Rare color	$2,000	$3,000
1980-1982	Standard color	$1,500	$2,500

Precision U.S. Plus/Plus
1989-1992. P-style bass with P- and J-bass pickups.

1989-1992	Rare color	$1,125	$1,500
1989-1992	Standard color	$1,000	$1,375

Precision U.S. Deluxe/Plus Deluxe
1991-1994. P-style bass with P- and J-bass pickups, active electronics, no 'guard models available.

1991-1994	Rare color	$1,125	$1,500
1991-1994	Standard color	$1,000	$1,375

Roger Waters Precision
2010-2019. Alder body, maple neck, black.

2010-2019		$775	$1,000

Select Precision
2012. Alder body, flamed maple top, rear headstock 'Fender Select' medallion.

2012		$2,000	$2,625

Fender Nate Mendel Precision

1981 Fender Precision Special (U.S.A.)
Willie Moseley

BASSES

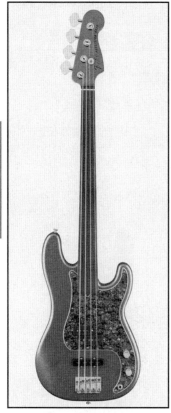

Fender Tony Franklin Precision

Fender Squier Bronco

Standard/Player Precision (Import)

1985-present. Made in Japan into '90, and Mexico after. Not to be confused with '81-'84 American-made model with the same name. Also available left-handed. Replaced by Player Series in 18.

MODEL YEAR	FEATURES	EXC. COND. LOW	HIGH
1985-1990	Japan	$1,000	$1,375
1991-2023	Mexico	$450	$600
2016	Mexico, Custom Art Series	$450	$600

Sting Precision

2001-2013. Made in Japan, 2-tone sunburst, 1 single-coil, Sting's signature.

2001-2013		$1,000	$1,375

Tony Franklin Precision

2007-present. Fretless, P and J pickups, 3-way selector, lacquer finish.

2007-2023		$1,500	$1,750

Walnut Elite Precision

1983-1985. The Elite Series features active electronics and noise-cancelling pickups, walnut body, 1 pickup (Elite I) or 2 (Elite II), rosewood 'board, natural.

1983-1985	Elite I	$2,000	$2,500
1983-1985	Elite II	$2,000	$2,500

Walnut Precision Special

1980-1982. Precision Bass Special with a walnut body, natural.

1980-1982		$2,000	$2,500

Prodigy Active

1992-1995. U.S.-made, poplar body, 1 J- and 1 P-style pickup, active.

1992-1995		$1,000	$1,375

Rhodes Piano

1962. Electric keyboard in bass register, Fender-Rhodes sticker, Piano Bass logo, various colors.

1962		$2,250	$3,000

Squier Affinity Jazz

1997-present. Affinity is the lower priced series made in China.

1997-2023		$115	$150

Squier Bronco

1998-present. The lowest priced Squier bass, single coil plastic cover pickup, 3/4 body.

1998-2023		$125	$175

Squier Bullet

1983-1990. Japanese-made, Squier-branded, replaces Bullet Bass, black.

1983-1990		$450	$550

Squier Classic Vibe Series

2009-present. Various models.

2009-2023		$265	$350

Squier HM/HM V

1989-1993 Korean-made, 5-string also offered

1989-1993		$265	$350

Squier Jazz Standard

1983-2010. Jazz bass import, without cover plates, various colors.

1983-1984	1st logo	$400	$550
1985-1989	2nd logo	$375	$500
1990-1999		$185	$250
2000-2010		$175	$225

Squier Katana

1985-1986. Made in Japan, wedge-shaped, arrow headstock.

MODEL YEAR	FEATURES	EXC. COND. LOW	HIGH
1985-1986		$950	$1,250

Squier Precision Special

1998-2010. Agathis body, P/J pickups, 4-string (IV) or 5-string (V).

1998-2010	IV or V	$115	$150

Squier Precision Standard

1983-1984	1st logo	$400	$550
1985-1989	2nd logo	$375	$500
1990-1999	Some from Mexico	$185	$250
2000-2006	Indonesia	$135	$175

Squier Vintage Modified Series

2007-2019. Includes Jaguar, Jazz and Precision models.

2007-2019	Various models	$175	$230

Stu Hamm Urge (U.S.A.)

1992-1999. Contoured Precision-style body with smaller wide treble cutaway, J and P pickups, 32"scale.

1992-1999		$1,500	$2,000

Stu Hamm Urge II (U.S.A.)

1999-2009. J and P pickups, 34" scale.

1999-2009		$1,500	$2,000

Telecaster

1968-1979. Slab solidbody, 1 pickup, fretless option '70, blond and custom colors available (Pink Paisley or Blue Floral '68-'69). Please refer to the beginning of the Fender Bass Section for details on Fender color options.

1968	Black, nitro	$6,000	$7,500
1968	Black, poly	$6,000	$7,500
1968	Blond, nitro	$4,500	$5,500
1968	Blond, poly	$4,500	$5,500
1968	Blue Floral Paisley	$18,000	$25,000
1968	Lake Placid Blue	$6,000	$7,500
1968	Pink Paisley	$17,000	$20,500
1969-1972	4-bolt, single-coil	$4,500	$5,500
1973-1974	3-bolt, hum, rare color	$3,250	$4,500
1973-1974	3-bolt, humbucker	$2,750	$4,000
1975-1979	3-bolt, humbucker	$2,750	$4,000

Zone (American Deluxe)

2001-2006. Smaller lightweight offset double-cut, active humbuckers, exotic tone woods, U.S.-made.

2001-2006		$1,500	$2,000

Fodera

1983-present. Luthiers Vinnie Fodera and Joseph Lauricella build their professional and premium grade, production/custom, solidbody basses in Brooklyn, New York.

High-level

1983-2023	4, 5, 6 strings	$9,000	$12,000

Mid-level

1983-2023	4, 5, 6 strings	$8,000	$11,000

Low-level

1983-2023	4, 5, 6 strings	$5,000	$6,500

Framus

1946-1975, 1996-present. Professional and premium grade, production/custom, basses made in Germany. They also build guitars and amps.

MODEL YEAR	FEATURES	EXC. COND. LOW	HIGH

Atlantic Model 5/140

1960s. Single-cut thinline with f-holes, 2 pickups, sunburst or blackrose.

1960s		$750	$975

Atlantic Model 5/143

1960s. Offset double-cut thinbody with f-holes, 2 pickups, 4-on-a-side keys.

1960s		$750	$975

Atlantic Model 5/144

1960s. Double-cut thinbody with f-holes, ES-335 body style, 2 pickups. Becomes Model J/144 in the '70s.

1960s		$750	$975

Charavelle 4 Model 5/153

1960s. Double-cut thinline with f-holes, 335-style body, 2 pickups, sunburst, cherry red or Sunset.

1960s		$800	$1,125

De Luxe 4 Model 5/154

1960s. Double-cut thinline, sharp horns and f-holes, 2 pickups, mute, sunburst or natural/blond.

1960s		$800	$1,125

Electric Upright

1950s. Full-scale neck, triangular body, black.

1958		$2,250	$3,000

Star Series (Bill Wyman)

1959-1968. Early flyer says, Bill Wyman of the Rolling Stones prefers the Star Bass. The model's name was later changed to Framus Stone Bass. Single-cut semi-hollow body, 5/149 (1 pickup) and 5/150 (2 pickups), sunburst.

1959-1965	Model 5/150	$1,125	$1,500
1960s	Model 5/149	$1,125	$1,500

Strato De Luxe Star Model 5/165

Ca. 1964-ca. 1972. Offset double-cut solidbody, 2 pickups, sunburst. There was also a gold hardware version (5/165 gl) and a 6-string (5/166).

1960s		$850	$1,125

Strato Star Series

Ca. 1963-ca. 1972. Double-cut solidbody, 5/156/50 (1 pickup) or 5/156/52 (2 pickups), beige, cherry or sunburst.

1960s	Model 5/156/50	$850	$1,125
1960s	Model 5/156/52	$850	$1,125

T.V. Star

1960s. Offset double-cut thinbody with f-holes, 2 pickups, short-scale, sunburst or cherry red. Most expensive of the '60s Framus basses, although not as popular as the Bill Wyman 5/150 model.

1960s		$850	$1,125

Triumph Electric Upright

1956-1960. Solidbody bean pole electric bass, small body, long neck, slotted viol peghead, gold or black.

1956-1960		$2,250	$3,000

Fresher

1973-1985. Japanese-made, mainly copies of popular brands and not imported into the U.S., but they do show up at guitar shows. They also made guitars.

Solidbody Electric

1970s		$500	$650

G&L

1980-present. Intermediate and professional grade, production/custom, electric basses made in the U.S. In '03, G&L introduced the Korean-made G&L Tribute Series. A Tribute logo is clearly identified on the headstock. They also build guitars.

ASAT

1989-2020. Single-cut, solidbody, active and passive modes, 2 humbuckers, various colors.

1989-1991	About 400 made	$1,625	$2,125
1992-2020		$1,500	$2,000

ASAT Commemorative

1991-1992. About 150 made, 4-string ASAT commemorating Leo Fender's life.

1991-1992		$1,875	$2,500

ASAT Semi-Hollow

2001-2020. Semi-hollowbody style on ASAT bass.

2001-2020		$1,250	$1,625

Climax

1992-1996. Single active humbucker MFD.

1992-1996		$1,125	$1,500

El Toro

1983-1989. Double-cut, solidbody, 2 active, smaller, humbuckers, sunburst.

1983-1987		$1,375	$1,750
1988-1989		$1,250	$1,625

Interceptor

1984-1991. Sharp pointed double-cut, solidbody, 2 active, smaller humbuckers, sunburst.

1984-1986		$2,875	$3,750
1988-1991	Body signature	$1,625	$2,125

JB-2

2001-2018. Alder body, 2 Alnico V pickups.

2001-2018		$1,125	$1,500

Kiloton

2016-present. Single MFD humbucker pickup, custom options and finishes.

2016-2023	Standard top	$1,250	$1,875
2020-2023	Premium figured	$1,500	$2,500

L-1000

1980-1994, 2008. Offset double-cut, solidbody, 1 pickup, various colors. Limited run in '08.

1980-1985	Ash	$1,250	$1,625
1980-1985	Mahogany	$1,250	$1,625
1980-1985	Maple	$1,250	$1,625
1986-1991		$1,250	$1,625
1992-1999	3-bolt	$1,250	$1,625
2008	4-bolt	$1,250	$1,625

L-1500

1997-2018. Offset double-cut solidbody, 1 MFD humbucker.

1997-2018		$1,250	$1,625

L-1500 Custom

1997	Only year made	$1,250	$1,625

L-1505

1998-2018. Five-string version, single MFD humbucker.

1998-2018		$1,750	$2,250

1983 Fender Squier Precision Standard

Rivington Guitars

1968 Fender Telecaster Bass

Robbie Keene

BASSES

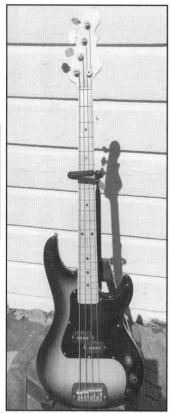

1991 G&L SB-1
KC Cormack

1969 Gibson EB-0
Cream City Music

MODEL YEAR	FEATURES	EXC. COND. LOW	HIGH
L-2000			
1980-present. Offset double-cut solidbody, 2 pickups, active electronics. Originally, the L-2000 was available with active (L-2000E) or passive (L-2000) electronics.			
1980-1985	Ash	$1,750	$2,250
1986		$1,500	$2,000
1987-1991	Leo signature	$1,500	$2,000
1992-2023		$1,500	$2,000
L-2000 30th Anniversary			
2010. Pearl Frost with matching headstock.			
2010		$1,625	$2,250
L-2000 40th Anniversary			
2020. Ruby Red finish.			
2020		$2,250	$3,000
L-2000 C.L.F. Centennial			
2009-2010. Swamp ash body, blonde, black hardware, planned run of 50, Certificate of Authenticity.			
2009-2010	COA, CD	$1,750	$2,250
L-2000 Custom			
1997. Ash top, wood-grain binding upgrade.			
1997		$1,500	$2,000
L-2000 Fretless			
1980-1998. Fretless version.			
1980-1982		$1,750	$2,250
L-2000E			
1980-1982. Offset double-cut, solidbody, 2 pickups, active electronics. Originally, the L-2000 was available with active (L-2000E) or passive (L-2000) electronics.			
1980-1982		$1,750	$2,250
L-2500			
1997-present. Dual MFD humbuckers, 5-string, figured tops can vary.			
1997-2023		$1,500	$2,000
L-2500 Custom			
1997. Ash top, wood-grain binding upgrade.			
1997		$1,500	$2,000
L-5000			
1988-1993. Offset double-cut, solidbody, G&L Z-shaped split-humbucker, 5 strings, approximately 400 made.			
1988-1992		$1,125	$1,500
L-5500			
1993-1997		$1,125	$1,500
L-5500 Custom			
1997. Ash top, wood-grain binding upgrade.			
1997		$1,125	$1,500
LB-100			
1993-present. Follow-up to earlier Legacy Bass.			
1993-2023		$1,125	$1,500
Legacy			
1992-1993. Offset double-cut solidbody, 1 split-coil, renamed LB-100 in '93.			
1992-1993		$1,125	$1,500
Lynx			
1984-1991. Offset double-cut, solidbody, 2 single-coils, black.			
1984-1991		$1,125	$1,500
M-2500			
2012-2022. Dual MFD humbuckers, 5-string, options and finishes.			
2012-2022		$1,500	$2,000

MODEL YEAR	FEATURES	EXC. COND. LOW	HIGH
SB-1			
1982-2000, 2014-present. Solidbody, maple neck, body and 'board, split-humbucker, 1 tone and 1 volume control. Reappears in '14 as Fullerton Deluxe SB-1.			
1982-2000		$1,000	$1,500
SB-2			
1982-present. Maple neck with tilt adjustment, 1 split-coil humbucker and 1 single-coil.			
1982-2023		$1,125	$1,625
Tribute Series			
2003-present. Various models, options and finishes.			
2003-2023	Various models	$400	$1,000

Garage by Wicked

2004-2010. A line of basses imported from China by luthier Nicholas Dijkman (Wicked) of Montreal, Quebec.

Gibson

1890s (1902)-present. Professional grade, production, U.S.-made electric basses. Gibson got into the electric bass market with the introduction of their Gibson Electric Bass in '53 (that model was renamed the EB-1 in '58 and reintroduced under that name in '69). Many more bass models followed. Gibson's custom colors can greatly increase the value of older instruments. Custom colors offered from '63 to '69 are Cardinal Red, Ember Red, Frost Blue, Golden Mist Metallic, Heather Metallic, Inverness Green, Kerry Green, Pelham Blue Metallic, Polaris White, Silver Mist Metallic.

MODEL YEAR	FEATURES	EXC. COND. LOW	HIGH
20/20			
1987-1988. Designed by Ned Steinberger, slim-wedge Steinberger style solidbody, 2 humbucker pickups, 20/20 logo on headstock, Luna Silver or Ferrari Red finish.			
1987-1988		$1,125	$1,375
Electric (EB-1)			
1953-1958. Introduced as Gibson Electric Bass in '53 but was called the EB-1 by Gibson in its last year of '58, thus, the whole line is commonly called the EB-1 by collectors, reissued in '69 as the EB-1 (see EB-1 listing), brown.			
1953-1958		$5,500	$8,000
EB			
1970, 2013-2019. Renamed from Melody Maker Bass, SG body, 1 humbucker pickup. Reintroduced in '13, 4- or 5-string, 2 pickups.			
1970		$3,500	$4,500
2013-2019	Reintroduced	$525	$750
EB-0			
1959-1979. Double-cut slab body with banjo-type tuners in '59 and '60, double-cut SG-type body with conventional tuners from '61 on, 1 pickup. Faded custom colors are of less value.			
1959-1960	Cherry, slab body	$4,750	$6,500
1961	Cherry, SG body	$2,875	$4,000
1962	Cherry	$2,875	$4,000
1963	Cherry	$2,875	$4,000
1964	Cherry, late '64 truss rod	$2,375	$3,500

MODEL YEAR	FEATURES	EXC. COND. LOW	HIGH
1964	Cherry, raised truss rod	$2,875	$3,500
1965-1966	Cherry	$2,000	$2,500
1965-1966	Pelham Blue	$3,875	$5,000
1967-1968	Cherry	$2,250	$2,875
1967-1968	Pelham Blue	$4,250	$6,000
1968	Black	$4,250	$5,000
1968	Burgundy Metallic	$3,000	$4,500
1969	Cherry, solid head	$2,000	$2,500
1969	Pelham Blue	$2,750	$4,000
1969-1974	Slotted head	$1,250	$1,875
1975-1979		$1,250	$1,875

EB-0 F
1962-1965. EB-0 with added built-in fuzz, cherry.

1962-1965		$3,250	$4,500

EB-0 L
1969-1979. 34.5-inch scale version of the EB-0, various colors.

1969-1979		$1,750	$2,500

EB-1
1969-1972. The Gibson Electric Bass ('53-'58) is often also called the EB-1 (see Electric Bass). Violin-shaped mahogany body, 1 pickup, standard tuners.

1969-1972		$3,500	$4,750

EB-2
1958 1961, 1964-1972. ES-335-type semi-hollowbody, double-cut, 1 pickup, banjo tuners '58-'60 and conventional tuners '60 on.

1958	Sunburst	$5,500	$7,500
1959	Natural	$6,500	$10,000
1959	Sunburst	$5,000	$7,000
1960	Natural	$6,500	$8,500
1960	Sunburst	$4,500	$6,000
1961	Sunburst, black pu	$4,250	$5,000
1961	Sunburst, brown pu	$4,500	$5,500
1964	Sunburst	$2,750	$3,500
1965	Sunburst	$2,500	$3,250
1966-1969	Cherry, sunburst	$2,250	$3,000
1967-1969	Sparkling Burgundy	$3,500	$4,250
1967-1969	Walnut	$3,250	$4,000
1970-1972	Sunburst	$2,750	$3,500

EB-2 D
1966-1972. Two-pickup version of EB-2, cherry, sunburst, or walnut.

1966-1969	Cherry, sunburst	$3,250	$5,500
1967-1969	Sparkling Burgundy	$3,000	$4,000
1967-1969	Walnut	$3,750	$4,750
1970-1972	Cherry, sunburst	$2,750	$3,750

EB-3
1961-1979. SG-style solidbody, 2 humbuckers, solid peghead '61-'68 and '72-'79, slotted peghead '69-'71, cherry to '71, various colors after.

1961-1964		$4,750	$7,000
1965	Early '65 version	$4,250	$6,250
1965	Late '65 version	$4,000	$5,000
1965	White (rare)	$7,000	$9,000
1966		$3,250	$4,250
1967-1968		$2,750	$3,500
1969	Early '69	$2,500	$3,250
1969	Late '69	$2,250	$3,000
1970		$2,250	$3,000

1971		$2,125	$2,750
1972-1979		$2,000	$2,500

EB-3 L
1969-1972. 34.5" scale version of EB-3, slotted headstock, EB-3L logo on truss rod cover, cherry, natural, or walnut.

1969-1972		$2,250	$3,000

EB-4 L
1972-1979. SG-style, 1 humbucker, 34.5" scale, cherry or walnut.

1972-1979		$1,500	$2,000

EB-6
1960-1966. Introduced as semi-hollowbody 335-style 6-string with 1 humbucker, changed to SG-style with 2 pickups in '62.

1960	Natural, 335-style	$8,000	$12,500
1960-1961	Sunburst, 335-style	$6,000	$8,750
1962-1964	Cherry, SG-style	$11,500	$15,000
1965-1966	Cherry, SG-style	$11,500	$15,000

EB-650
1991-1993. Semi-acoustic single cut, maple neck, laminated maple body with center block, 2 TB Plus pickups.

1991-1993	Blond	$4,500	$6,000
1991-1993	Blue	$4,250	$5,500
1991-1993	Other colors	$4,000	$5,250

EB-750
1991-1993. Like EB-650, but with Bartolini pickups and TCT active EQ.

1991-1993	Blond	$4,500	$6,000
1991-1993	Blue	$4,250	$5,500
1991-1993	Other colors	$4,000	$5,250

ES-335
2013. Sunburst or ebony.

2013		$1,375	$2,000

ES-Les Paul
2015-2018. Semi-solid, 3-ply maple/poplar/maple top, back and sides, rosewood 'board, mother-of-pearl inlay, faded darkburst or gold top finish.

2015-2018		$2,250	$3,000

Explorer
1984-1987, 2011-2012. Alder body, ebony 'board, dot inlays, 2 humbuckers, various colors. Limited run in '11 in sunburst or silverburst.

1984-1987	Various finishes	$1,750	$2,750
1985	Designer graphics	$1,750	$2,750
2011-2012	Silverburst	$2,000	$3,000
2011-2012	Sunburst	$1,500	$2,500

Flying V
1981-1982, 2011-2012, 2020-2021. Solidbody, Flying V body. Offered again in '20 with 2 Burstbucker pickups and Antique Natural finish.

1981-1982	Blue stain, ebony	$3,750	$5,000
1981-1982	Silverburst	$4,500	$6,000
2011-2012		$2,000	$2,500
2020-2021		$1,500	$2,000

Flying V B-2
2019-2020. Dirty Fingers humbucker pickups, satin ebony finish.

2019-2020		$1,000	$1,375

Gibson EB-1
Rivington Guitars

1982 Gibson Flying V
Russell Sutherland

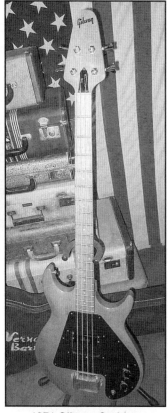

1974 Gibson Grabber
Rivington Guitars

1970 Gibson Les Paul
Jim Mathis

MODEL YEAR	FEATURES	EXC. COND. LOW	HIGH
Grabber			
1973-1982. Double-cut solidbody, 1 pickup, bolt maple neck, maple 'board, various colors.			
1973-1982		$2,000	$2,750
Grabber II			
2009-2011. Limited Run series, 350 offered, based on '73-'75 model, certificate of authenticity, black.			
2009-2011		$1,500	$2,000
Grabber III (G-3)			
1975-1982. Double-cut solidbody, 3 pickups, bolt maple neck, maple 'board, nickel-plated hardware, various colors.			
1975-1982		$1,750	$2,250
Gibson IV			
1986-1988. Mahogany body and neck, double-cut, 2 pickups, black chrome hardware, various colors.			
1986-1988		$1,500	$2,000
Gibson V			
1986-1988. Double-cut, 5 strings, 2 pickups.			
1986-1988		$1,250	$1,750
L9-S			
1973. Natural maple or cherry, renamed Ripper Bass in '74.			
1973		$2,375	$3,000
Les Paul			
1970-1971. Single-cut solidbody, 2 pickups, walnut finish, renamed Les Paul Triumph Bass '71-'79.			
1970-1971		$2,000	$2,750
Les Paul Money			
2007-2008. Solidbody offset double-cut, 2 humbuckers, dot markers, figured maple top over mahogany body, 400 made.			
2007-2008		$1,500	$2,000
Les Paul Signature			
1973-1979. Double-cut, semi-hollowbody, 1 pickup, sunburst or gold (gold only by '76). Name also used on LPB-3 bass in '90s.			
1973-1979	Sunburst or gold	$4,000	$5,500
Les Paul Special LPB-1			
1991-1998. 2 TB-Plus pickups, ebony 'board, dots, slab mahogany body, active electronics, also available as 5-string.			
1991-1998		$1,500	$2,000
Les Paul Deluxe Plus LPB-2			
1991-1998. Upgraded LPB-1, carved maple top, trapezoid inlays, active eq and Bartolini pickups. Flame maple top Premium version offered '93-'98.			
1991-1998		$1,500	$2,000
Les Paul Smartwood			
1998. 2 TB pickups, active electronics, trapezoid inlays.			
1998		$1,500	$2,000
Les Paul Special V			
1993-1996. Single-cut slab body, 5-string, 2 pickups, dot markers, black/ebony.			
1993-1996		$900	$1,250
Les Paul Standard			
1999-2018. Maple top, chambered mahogany body, trapezoid inlays, 2 pickups.			
1999-2018	Various colors	$2,000	$2,750

MODEL YEAR	FEATURES	EXC. COND. LOW	HIGH
Les Paul Standard LPB-3			
1991-1995. Like Les Paul Deluxe LPB-2 Bass, but with TB Plus pickups. Flame maple top Premium version offered '93-'95.			
1993-1995	Flamed top	$2,000	$2,750
Les Paul Triumph			
1971-1979. Renamed from Les Paul Bass.			
1971-1979	Various colors	$2,500	$3,250
1973-1974	Optional white	$3,500	$5,500
Melody Maker			
1967-1970. SG body, 1 humbucker pickup.			
1967-1970		$1,750	$3,000
Midtown Standard			
2012-2018. Semi-hollow body, double-cut, baked maple or rosewood board, 2 pickups.			
2012-2018		$1,625	$2,250
Nikki Sixx Blackbird/Thunderbird			
2000-2003, 2009-2010. Blackbird has black hardware and finish, iron cross inlays. '09 Thunderbird was flamed maple.			
2000-2003		$2,125	$2,750
Q-80			
1986-1988. Victory Series body shape, 2 pickups, bolt neck, black chrome hardware, renamed Q-90 in '88.			
1986-1988		$750	$1,250
Q-90			
1988-1992. Renamed from Q-80, mahogany body, 2 active humbuckers, maple neck, ebony 'board.			
1988-1992		$750	$1,250
RD Artist			
1977-1982. Double-cut solid maple body, laminated neck, 2 pickups, active electronics, string-thru-body, block inlays, various colors.			
1977-1982		$2,500	$3,250
RD Artist CMT			
1982. Flamed maple top.			
1982		$3,250	$4,250
RD Artist VI			
1980. Only 6 made, 6-string.			
1980		$4,500	$6,000
RD Standard			
1977-1979. Double-cut, solid maple body, laminated neck, 2 pickups, regular electronics, string-thru-body, dot inlays, various colors.			
1977-1979		$2,500	$3,250
Ripper			
1974-1982. Introduced as L-9 S Bass in '73, double-cut solidbody, glued neck, 2 pickups, string-thru-body, sunburst or natural maple until '76, sunburst only after. Black option '78-'79 and silverburst '80.			
1974-1976	Natural maple	$2,250	$2,750
1974-1982	Sunburst	$2,250	$2,750
1978-1979	Black option	$2,250	$2,750
1980	Silverburst option	$3,500	$5,000
Ripper II			
2009-2011. Solid maple body, 34" scale, 2 pickups, natural nitro lacquer.			
2009-2011		$1,000	$1,375

BASSES

MODEL YEAR	FEATURES	EXC. COND. LOW	HIGH

SB Series
1971-1978. In '71, oval pickups, replaced mid-model with rectangular pickups. Includes 300 and 350 (30" scale, 1 and 2 pickups), 350 (30", 2 pickups), 400 (34", 1 pickup), 450 (34", 2 pickups). The 450 was special order only.

1971-1973	SB-300, 400	$725	$1,000
1972-1974	SB-350, 450	$725	$1,000
1975-1978	SB-450 special order	$725	$1,000

SG Reissue/SG Standard
2005-present. Similar to '60s EB-3, 2 pickups, mahogany body, cherry or white. Renamed SG Standard in '08, various colors.

2005-2023	Various colors	$1,000	$1,375

SG Standard Faded
2013-2018. Solid mahogany body, baked maple 'board, worn cherry or ebony finish.

2013-2018		$625	$825

SG Supreme
2007-2008. Made in Nashville, SG body with AAA maple top, 2 pickups.

2007-2008		$1,250	$1,625

Thunderbird II
1963-1969. Reverse solidbody until '65, non-reverse solidbody '65-'69, 1 pickup, custom colors available, reintroduced with reverse body for '83-'84.

1963	Sunburst, reverse	$10,000	$14,000
1964	Pelham Blue, reverse	$15,000	$24,500
1964	Sunburst, reverse	$10,000	$14,000
1965	Cardinal Red, non-reverse	$9,500	$12,500
1965	Inverness Green, non-reverse	$9,500	$12,500
1965	Sunburst, non-reverse	$7,000	$9,500
1965	Sunburst, reverse	$10,000	$14,000
1966	Cardinal Red, non-reverse	$12,000	$15,500
1966	Pelham Blue	$12,000	$15,500
1966	Sunburst, non-reverse	$7,000	$10,000
1967	Cardinal Red, non-reverse	$12,000	$15,500
1967	Sunburst, non-reverse	$7,000	$9,500
1968	Cardinal Red, non-reverse	$12,000	$15,500
1968-1969	Sunburst, non-reverse	$7,000	$9,500

Thunderbird III
1979-1982. Reverse body, 2 pickups, Thunderbird logo on 'guard.

1979-1982		$3,000	$4,000

Thunderbird IV
1963-1969. Reverse solidbody until '64, non-reverse solidbody '65-'69, 2 pickups, custom colors available, reintroduced with reverse body for '86-present (see Thunderbird IV Bass Reissue).

1963	Sunburst, reverse	$11,500	$14,500
1964	Frost Blue, reverse	$23,500	$30,000

MODEL YEAR	FEATURES	EXC. COND. LOW	HIGH
1964	Pelham Blue, reverse	$23,500	$30,000
1964	Sunburst, reverse	$11,500	$15,000
1965	Cardinal Red, non-reverse	$11,000	$22,000
1965	Inverness Green, non-reverse	$11,000	$22,000
1965	Sunburst, reverse	$11,500	$14,500
1965-1966	Sunburst, non-reverse	$8,500	$11,500
1966	White, non-reverse	$14,000	$22,500
1967-1969	Sunburst, non-reverse	$8,500	$11,500

Thunderbird IV (Reissue)
1987-2016. Has reverse body and 2 pickups, various colors.

1987-2016	Various colors	$1,750	$2,250

Thunderbird IV Zebra Wood
2007. Guitar of the Week (week 11 of '07), limited run of 400, Zebrawood body.

2007		$1,875	$2,500

Thunderbird 50th Anniversary
2013-2018. Mahogany body and neck, rosewood 'board, Bullion Gold finish.

2013-2018		$2,250	$3,000

Thunderbird 76
1976 only. Reverse solidbody, 2 pickups, rosewood 'board, various colors.

1976		$3,500	$6,000

Thunderbird 79
1979 only. Reverse solidbody, 2 pickups, sunburst.

1979		$3,500	$6,000

Thunderbird Short Scale
2011-2013. 30.5" scale, 2 pickups, nitro satin ebony finish.

2011-2013		$1,125	$1,500

Thunderbird Studio/IV Studio
2005-2007. 4- or 5-string versions.

2005-2007		$1,250	$1,625

Victory Artist
1981-1985. Double-cut, solidbody, 2 humbuckers and active electronics, various colors.

1981-1985		$1,625	$2,125

Victory Custom
1982-1984. Double-cut, solidbody, 2 humbuckers, passive electronics, limited production.

1982-1984		$1,625	$2,125

Victory Standard
1981-1986. Double-cut, solidbody, 1 humbucker, active electronics, various colors.

1981-1986		$1,250	$1,625

Godin
1987-present. Intermediate and professional grade, production, solidbody electric and acoustic/electric basses from luthier Robert Godin. They also build guitars and mandolins.

A Series
1990s-present. Various acoustic/electric, 4- or 5-string.

1990s-2023	A-4, A-5	$475	$650

1982 Gibson The Ripper
Rivington Guitars

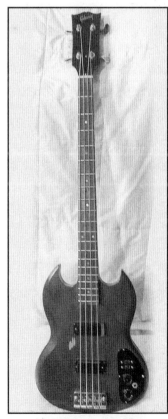
1972 Gibson SB-450
Richard Memmel

BASSES

BASSES

Gretsch 6119-B Broadkaster
Christophe Fié

Gretsch G2220
Electromatic Jr. Jet II

MODEL YEAR	FEATURES	EXC. COND. LOW	HIGH

Freeway A Series
2005-2012. Double-cut solidbodies, 4- or 5-string, passive or active.

2005-2012	Freeway A-4	$475	$650
2005-2012	Freeway A-5	$525	$700

Godlyke
2006-present. Professional and premium grade, production, solidbody basses from effects distributor Godlyke.

Goya
1955-1996. Originally imports from Sweden, brand later used on Japanese and Korean imports. They also offered guitars, mandolins, and banjos.

Electric Solidbody
1960s	Various models	$575	$850

Gretsch
1883-present. Intermediate and professional grade, production, solidbody, hollow body, and acoustic/electric basses. Gretsch came late to the electric bass game, introducing their first models in the early '60s. They also build guitars, amps and steels. In 2012 they again offered mandolins, ukes and banjos.

Broadkaster (6119-B)
1991-2013. Single-cut hollowbody, maple top, back and sides.

1991-2013		$1,750	$2,250

Broadkaster (7605/7606)
1975-1979. Double-cut solidbody, 1 pickup, bolt-on maple neck, natural (7605) or sunburst (7606).

1975-1979		$850	$1,125

Committee (7629)
1977-1980. Double-cut walnut and maple soldibody, neck-thru, 1 pickup, natural.

1977-1980		$850	$1,125

G2220 Electromatic Jr. Jet II
2012-present. Short scale, 2 pickups, various colors.

2012-2023		$300	$400

G5440LS Electromatic Long Scale Hollow Body
2012-2020. Single-cut, 2 pickups, "G" tailpiece, various colors.

2012-2020		$750	$1,000

G6072 Long Scale Hollow Body
1998-2006. Reissue of the '68 double-cut hollowbody, 2 pickups, sunburst, gold hardware.

1998-2006		$1,125	$1,500

G6136 White Falcon
2008. Single-cut hollowbody, 2 pickups, gold hardware.

2008		$2,500	$3,500

G6199 Billy-Bo Jupiter Thunderbird
2011. Double-cut solidbody, 2 pickups, gold hardware, black.

2011		$1,875	$2,500

Model 6070/6072
1963-1971 (1972 for 6070). Originally listed as the PX6070 Cello Bass, large thinline hollowbody double-cut archtop, fake f-holes, 1 pickup (6070) or 2 (6072), gold hardware.

1963-1964	6070, with endpin	$2,250	$3,000
1965-1972	6070, no endpin	$1,750	$2,250
1968-1971	6072, 2 pickups	$1,750	$2,250

Model 6071/6073
1968-1971 (1972 for 6071). Single-cut hollowbody, fake f-holes, 1 pickup (6071) or 2 (6073), padded back, red mahogany.

1968-1971	6073, 2 pickups	$2,250	$3,000
1968-1972	6071, 1 pickup	$1,750	$2,250

Model 7615
1972-1975. Offset double-cut solidbody, slotted bass horn (monkey grip), large, polished rosewood 'guard covering most of the body, 2 pickups, dot markers, brown mahogany finish. Only bass offered in Gretsch catalog for this era.

1972-1975		$1,125	$1,500

TK 300 (7626/7627)
1976-1981. Double-cut solidbody, 1 pickup, Autumn Red Stain or natural.

1976-1981		$750	$1,250

Guild
1952-present. Guild added electric basses in the mid-'60s and offered them until '02. New owner, Cordoba Music, reintroduced acoustic and electric basses to the line in '15.

Ashbory
1986-1988, 2009. 18" scale, total length 30", fretless, silicone rubber strings, active electronics, low-impedance circuitry.

1986-1988		$550	$700
2009	Fender Guild reissue	$250	$350

B-4 E
1993-2000. Acoustic/electric single-cut flat-top, mahogany sides with arched mahogany back, multi-bound, gold hardware until '95, chrome after.

1993-2000		$600	$800

B-30 E
1987-1999. Single-cut flat-top acoustic/electric, mahogany sides, arched mahogany back, multi-bound, fretless optional.

1987-1999		$1,250	$1,750

B-50 Acoustic
1975-1987. Acoustic flat-top, mahogany sides with arched mahogany back, spruce top, multi-bound, renamed B-30 in '87.

1975-1987		$1,250	$1,750

B-301/B-302
1976-1981. Double-cut solidbody, chrome-plated hardware. Models include B-301 (mahogany, 1 pickup), B-301A (ash, 1 pickup), B-302 (mahogany, 2 pickups), B-302A (ash, 2 pickups), and B-302AF (ash, fretless).

1976-1981	B-301, B-301A	$1,000	$1,500
1976-1981	B-302, B-302A	$1,000	$1,500
1977-1981	B-302AF	$1,000	$1,500

B-401/B-402
1980-1983. Model 401 with active circuit, 1 pickup. Model 402 passive and active, 2 pickups. A for ash body.

1980-1981	B-401, B-401A	$1,000	$1,500
1980-1983	B-402, B402A	$1,000	$1,500

MODEL YEAR	FEATURES	EXC. COND. LOW	HIGH

B-500 C Acoustic
1992-1993. Acoustic/electric flat-top, round soundhole, single-cut, solid spruce top, maple back and sides, dark stain, limited production.

1992-1993		$1,375	$1,750

FS-46
1983. Acoustic-electric flat-top, single-cut, sharp horn fretless.

1983		$800	$1,125

Jet Star
1964-1970 (limited production '68-'70). Offset double-cut solidbody, short treble horn, 1 pickup, 2-on-a-side tuners '64-'66 and 4 in-line tuners '66-'70.

1964-1966	2-on-side tuners	$1,750	$2,500
1966-1970	4 in-line tuners	$1,750	$2,500

JS I/JS II
1970-1977. Double-cut solidbody, 30" scale, 1 pickup (JS I or 1) or 2 (JS II or 2), carved-top oak leaf design available for '72-'76. 34" long scale (LS) versions offered fretted and fretless for '74-'75.

1970-1977	JS I	$1,750	$2,500
1970-1977	JS II	$1,750	$2,500
1974-1976	JS I, carved	$1,750	$2,500
1974-1976	JS II, carved	$1,750	$2,500

M-85 I/M-85 II
1967-1972. Single-cut semi-hollowbody, 1 pickup (M-85 I) or 2 (M-85 II).

1967-1972	M-85 I	$1,750	$2,500
1967-1972	M-85 II	$1,750	$2,500

M-85 I/M-85 II BluesBird
1972-1976. Single-cut solidbody archtop, Chesterfield headstock inlay, cherry mahogany, 1 humbucker pickup (I) or 2 (II).

1972-1973	M-85 I	$1,875	$2,500
1972-1976	M-85 II	$1,875	$2,500

MB-801
1981-1982. Double-cut solidbody, 1 pickup, dot inlays.

1981-1982		$800	$1,125

SB-201/SB-202/SB-203
1982-1983. Double-cut solidbody, 1 split coil pickup (201), 1 split coil and 1 single coil (202), or 1 split coil and 2 single coils (203).

1982-1983	SB-201	$900	$1,125
1982-1983	SB-202	$950	$1,250
1983	SB-203	$1,000	$1,375

SB-502 E
1984-1985. Double-cut solidbody, 2 pickups, active electronics.

1984-1985		$1,000	$1,375

SB-600/Pilot Series
1983-1993. Offset double-cut solidbody, bolt-on neck, poplar body. Models include SB-601 (1 pickup), SB-602 (2 pickups or fretless), SB-602 V (2 pickups, 5-string), SB-604 (2 pickups, offset peghead) and SB-605 (5-string, hipshot low D tuner). Models 604 and 605 are replaced in '93 with Pro4 and Pro5 Pilot.

1983-1989	SB-601	$650	$850
1983-1989	SB-602	$750	$1,000
1983-1989	SB-602, fretless	$750	$1,000
1983-1989	SB-602V	$750	$1,000

1986-1988	SB-604 Pilot	$750	$1,000
1986-1993	SB-605	$750	$1,000

SB-608 Flying Star Motley Crue
1984-1985. Pointy 4-point star body, 2 pickups, E version had EMG pickups.

1984-1985		$1,250	$1,625

Starfire
1965-1975. Double-cut semi-hollow thinbody, 1 pickup, mahogany neck, chrome-plated hardware, cherry or sunburst.

1965-1969	Single-coil	$2,500	$3,500
1970-1975	Humbucker	$2,500	$3,500

Starfire II
1967-1978. Two-pickup version of Starfire Bass. Single-coils until '69, humbuckers after, sunburst, cherry or very rare black. Starfire II Bass Special had gold hardware.

1967-1969	2 single-coils	$2,500	$3,500
1967-1969	Black	$3,000	$4,000
1970-1978	2 humbuckers	$2,500	$3,500

Starfire II Reissue
1997-present. Reissue of 2 humbucker version.

1997-2023		$1,000	$1,500

X-100 Blade Runner
1985-1986. Poplar body and neck, ebony 'board, 1 pickup.

1985-1986		$3,000	$4,000

X-701/X-702
1982-1984. Body with 4 sharp horns with extra-long bass horn, 1 pickup (X-701) or 2 (X-702), various metallic finishes.

1982-1984	X-701	$1,250	$1,500
1982-1984	X-702	$1,250	$1,500

GW Basses & Luthiery
2004-present. Professional and premium grade, production/custom, basses built by luthier Grandon Westlund in West Lafayette, Indiana.

Hagstrom
1921-1983, 2004-present. This Swedish guitar company first offered electric basses in '61.

Concord II Deluxe
1967-1970. Bass version of V-IN guitar, 335-style body, 2 pickups, sunburst.

1967-1970		$1,625	$2,250

Coronado IV
1963-1970. Offset double cut, Bi-Sonic pickups.

1963-1970		$1,125	$1,500

H-8
1967-1969. Double-cut solidbody, 8 strings, 2 pickups, various colors.

1967-1969		$2,250	$3,000

Kent
1963-1964. 2 single-coils, 4 sliders.

1962-1966		$725	$950

Model I B/F-100 B
1965-1973. Offset double-cut solidbody, 2 single-coils, 5 sliders, 30" scale, red, black, white or blue.

1965-1973		$775	$1,000

1967 Guild Starfire
Jay Pilzer

1968 Hagstrom H-8
Willie Moseley

BASSES

1970 Hagstrom Model II
Robbie Keene

Harmony H-25
Tom Pfeifer

MODEL YEAR	FEATURES	EXC. COND. LOW	HIGH

Model II B/F-400
1965-1970. Like Model I, but with 30.75" scale, red, black, white or blue. Called F-400 in U.S., II B elsewhere.

1965-1970		$775	$1,000

Swede 2000 (With Synth)
1977. Circuitry on this Swede bass connected to the Ampeg Patch 2000 pedal so bass would work with various synths.

1977		$1,125	$1,500

Swede
1971-1976, 2004-present. Single-cut solidbody, block inlays, bolt neck, 2 humbuckers, 30.75" scale, cherry or black

1971-1976		$975	$1,250

Super Swede
1979-1983, 2004-present. Like Swede, but with neck-thru body, 32" scale, sunburst, mahogany or black.

1979-1983		$975	$1,250

Hamer
1975-2012, 2017-present. Founded in Arlington Heights, Illinois, by Paul Hamer and Jol Dantzig, Hamer was purchased by Kaman in '88. They also built guitars. Fender acquired Hamer in '08 and suspended production in '12. The brand was reintroduced in '17 by Jam Industries.

8-String Short-Scale
1978-1993. Double cut solidbody, 1 or 2 pickups, 30.5" scale.

1978-1993		$2,250	$3,000

12-String Acoustic
1985-2010. Semi-hollow, long scale, single cut, sound hole, 2 pickups. Import XT model added in the 2000s.

1985-2010		$2,750	$3,500

12-String Short-Scale
1978-1996. Four sets of 3 strings - a fundamental and 2 tuned an octave higher, double cut maple and mahogany solidbody, 30.5" scale.

1978-1996		$2,250	$3,000

Blitz
1982-1990. Explorer-style solidbody, 2 pickups, bolt-on neck.

1982-1990		$1,750	$2,500

Chaparral
1986-1995, 2000-2008. Solidbody, 2 pickups, glued-in neck, later basses have bolt-on neck.

1986-1987	Set-neck	$1,750	$2,500
1987-1995	Bolt-on neck	$1,750	$2,500

Chaparral 5-String
1987-1995. Five strings, solidbody, 2 pickups, glued-in neck, later basses have 5-on-a-side reverse peghead.

1987-1995		$1,750	$2,500

Chaparral 12-String
1992-2012. Long 34" scale 12-string, offset double cut. Import XT model added in '01.

1992-2012	USA	$2,250	$3,000
2000-2012	Import	$500	$650

Chaparral Max
1986-1995. Chaparral Bass with figured maple body, glued-in neck and boomerang inlays.

1986-1995		$1,000	$1,500

Cruise
1982-1990, 1995-1999. J-style solidbody, 2 pickups, glued neck ('82-'90) or bolt-on neck ('95-'99), also available as a 5-string.

1982-1990	Set-neck	$1,000	$1,500
1995-1999	Bolt-on neck	$1,000	$1,500

Cruise 5
1982-1989. Five-string version, various colors.

1982-1989		$1,250	$1,625

FBIV
1985-1987. Reverse Firebird shape, 1 P-Bass Slammer and 1 J-Bass Slammer pickup, mahogany body, rosewood 'board, dots.

1985-1987		$1,250	$1,625

Monaco 4
2002-2012. Flamed maple top, rosewood 'board, Tobacco Burst or '59 Burst finish.

2002-2012		$2,500	$3,250

Standard
1975-1984, 2001. US-made, Explorer-style headstock, 2 humbuckers. Imported in '01.

1975-1979	Flamed top, bound	$7,500	$10,000
1975-1984	Plain top, unbound	$4,500	$6,000
1980-1984	Flamed top, bound	$6,000	$8,000
2001	Import	$500	$650

Velocity 5
2002-2012. Offset double-cut, long bass horn, active, 1 humbucker.

2002-2012		$500	$650

Harmony
1892-1976, late 1970s-present. Harmony once was one of the biggest instrument makers in the world, making guitars and basses under their own brand and for others.

H Series
Late-1980s-early-1990s. F-style solidbody copies, 1 or 2 pickups, all models begin H.

1980s-90s		$200	$250

H-22
1959-1972. Single-cut hollowbody, 2-on-a-side, 1 pickup.

1959-1969		$1,500	$2,000
1970-1972		$1,250	$1,625

H-22 Reissue
2000s. Imported reissue, 1 pickup.

2000s		$400	$550

H-25/Silhouette
1963-1967. Offset double-cut solidbody, 1 pickup (H-25) or 2 (Silhouette).

1963-1967	H-25	$850	$1,125
1963-1967	Silhouette	$850	$1,125

H-27
1968-1972. Double-cut hollowbody, 4-on-a-side, 2 pickups.

1968-1972		$850	$1,125

Hartke
Hartke offered a line of wood and aluminum-necked basses from 2000 to '03.

BASSES

MODEL YEAR	FEATURES	EXC. COND. LOW	HIGH

Heartfield

1989-1994. Distributed by Fender, imported from Japan. They also offered guitars.

Electric

1989-1994. Double-cut solidbody, graphite reinforced neck, 2 single-coils, available in 4-, 5- and 6-string models.

1989-1994		$300	$400

Heritage

1985-present. Mainly a builder of guitars, Kalamazoo, Michigan's Heritage has offered a few basses in the past.

HB-1

1987. P-style body, limited production, single-split pickup, 4-on-a-side tuners, figured maple body, bolt-on neck.

1987		$725	$950

Höfner

1887-present. Professional grade, production, basses. They also offer guitars and bowed instruments. Höfner basses, made famous in the U.S. by one Paul McCartney, are made in Germany.

G5000/1 Super Beatle (G500/1)

1968-2011. Bound ebony 'board, gold-plated hardware, natural finish, the version with active circuit is called G500/1 Super Beatle, reissued in '94.

1968-1979	LH	$2,750	$3,500
1968-1979	RH	$2,250	$3,000

Icon Series

2007-2011. Chinese versions of classic Höfners, often sold without a case or gig bag.

2007-2011		$225	$300

Model 172 Series

1968-1970. Offset double-cut, 6-on-a-side tuners, 2 pickups, 2 slide switches, dot markers, 172/S shaded sunburst, 172/R red vinyl covered body, 172/I vinyl covered with white top and black back.

1968-1970	172/I, white	$1,000	$1,375
1968-1970	172/R, red	$1,000	$1,375
1968-1970	172/S, sunburst	$1,000	$1,375

Model 182 Solid

1962-1985. Offset double-cut solidbody, 2 pickups.

1962-1965		$1,000	$1,375

Model 185 Solid

1962-ca. 1970. Classic offset double-cut solidbody, 2 double-coil pickups.

1962-1970		$1,000	$1,375

Model 500/1 Beatle

1956-present. Semi-acoustic, bound body in violin shape, glued-in neck, 2 pickups, right- or left-handed, sunburst. Listed as 500/1 Vintage '58, '59, '62 and '63 in '90s through 2014. Currently named 500/1 Violin Bass.

1956-1959	LH or RH	$7,500	$10,000
1960	LH, McCartney	$6,500	$8,500
1960	RH	$5,500	$7,000
1961	LH	$6,500	$8,500
1961	LH, McCartney	$11,000	$14,500
1961	RH	$5,500	$7,500

1962-1963	LH	$5,500	$7,500
1962-1963	RH	$5,500	$7,500
1964	LH	$5,500	$7,500
1964	LH, McCartney	$8,500	$12,000
1964	RH	$5,500	$7,500
1964	RH, McCartney	$5,000	$6,000
1965	LH	$3,500	$5,000
1965	RH	$3,375	$4,500
1966	LH	$3,375	$4,500
1966	RH	$3,375	$4,500
1967	LH	$3,375	$4,500
1967	RH	$3,000	$4,000
1968-1973	LH	$3,000	$4,000
1968-1973	RH	$2,500	$3,500
1974-1979	LH or RH	$2,500	$3,500

'58 Model 500/1 Beatle Reissue

2008-2013. Right- or left-handed.

2008-2013		$1,875	$2,500

'62 Model 500/1 Beatle Reissue

1990s-2014. Right- or left-handed.

1990s-2014		$1,875	$2,500

'63 Model 500/1 Beatle Reissue

1994-2010. Right- or left-handed.

1994-2010		$1,875	$2,500

'64 Model 500/1 Beatle Reissue

2015-2016. Right- or left-handed.

2015-2016		$1,875	$2,500

Model 500/1 1964-1984 Reissue

1984. '1964-1984' neckplate notation.

1984		$1,875	$2,500

Model 500/1 40th Anniversary

1995-1996. Only 300 made.

1995-1996		$3,000	$4,000

Model 500/1 50th Anniversary

2006. Pickguard logo states '50th Anniversary Höfner Violin Bass 1956-2006', large red Höfner logo also on 'guard, 150 made.

2006		$3,000	$4,000

Model 500/1 Cavern

2005. Limited run of 12, includes certificate.

2005		$1,875	$2,500

Model 500/1 Cavern Music Ground

1993. UK commissioned by Music Ground, said to be one of the first accurate reissues, 40 made.

1993		$1,875	$2,500

Model 500/1 Contemporary

2007-2008. Contemporary Series.

2007-2008		$700	$950

Model 500/2 and Club

1965-1970, 2015-present. Similar to the 500/1, but with 'club' body Höfner made for England's Selmer, sunburst. Club Bass has been reissued in various colors.

1965-1970		$2,125	$2,750
2015-2023		$2,125	$2,750

Model 500/3 Senator

1962-1964. Single-cut thin body, f-holes, 1 511b pickup, sunburst.

1962-1964		$1,875	$2,500

1964 Höfner 500/1 Beatle
Steve Lee

1963 Höfner 500/2 Club
Larry Wassgren

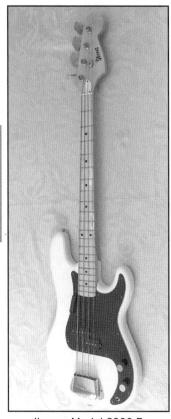

Ibanez Model 2366 B

Michael Burns

1984 Ibanez RS Roadstar II

Brian Chambers

BASSES

MODEL		EXC. COND.	
YEAR	FEATURES	LOW	HIGH

Model 500/5
1959-1963. Single-cut body with Beatle Bass-style pickups, sunburst. Becomes President Bass in '63.

| 1959-1963 | | $4,000 | $5,500 |

Model 500/6
Late-1960s. Introduced in '67, semi-acoustic, thinline, soft double-cut, 2 pickups, 4 control knobs, dot markers, sunburst.

| 1967 | | $2,125 | $2,750 |

Model 500/8BZ / B500/8BZ
Late-1960s. Semi-acoustic, thinline, sharp double-cut, multiple-line position markers, built in flip-fuzz and bass boost, sunburst or natural.

| 1967 | 500/8BZ, sunburst | $2,125 | $2,750 |
| 1967 | B500/8BZ, natural | $2,125 | $2,750 |

President
1963-1972. Made for England's Selmer, single-cut archtop, 2 Beatle Bass-style pickups, sunburst.

1963-1965		$2,750	$3,500
1966-1969		$2,125	$2,750
1970-1972		$2,125	$2,750

Hondo/Hondo II
1969-1987, 1991-2005. Budget grade, production, imported acoustic and electric solidbody basses. They also offered guitars, banjos and mandolins.

Electric Solidbody
1969-1987, 1991-2005. Various models.

| 1969-1999 | Rare models | $425 | $1,125 |
| 1969-1999 | Standard models | $150 | $300 |

Hoyer
1874-present. Intermediate grade, production, electric basses. They also build guitars.

Electric

| 1960s | Various models | $650 | $850 |

Ibanez
1932-present. Intermediate and professional grade, production, solidbody basses. They also have guitars, amps, and effects.

AXB Axstar Series
1986-1987. Various headless solidbody models.

| 1986-1987 | | $450 | $600 |

BTB Series
1999-present. Various models.

| 1999-2023 | | $325 | $450 |

Challenger
1977-1978. Offered as P-bass or J-bass style, and with ash body option.

| 1977-1978 | | $550 | $750 |

DB Destroyer II X Series
1984-1986. Futuristic-style body, P- and J-style pickups, dot markers, bolt neck.

| 1984-1986 | Various models | $550 | $750 |

DT Destroyer II Series
1980-1985. Futuristic-style body.

| 1983-1986 | Various models | $700 | $950 |

MODEL		EXC. COND.	
YEAR	FEATURES	LOW	HIGH

ICB Iceman
1994-1996, 2011. Iceman body, basswood (300) or mahogany (500) body. 300 reissued in '11.

| 1994 | ICB500, black | $600 | $850 |
| 1994-1996 | ICB300, white | $600 | $850 |

Jet King
2009-2010. Retro offset double-cut solidbody, bolt neck.

| 2009-2010 | | $300 | $400 |

MC Musician Series
1978-1988. Various models, solidbody, neck-thru.

| 1978-1988 | | $1,125 | $1,500 |

Model 2030
1970-1973. First copy era bass, offset double-cut, sunburst.

| 1970-1973 | | $850 | $1,125 |

Model 2353
1974-1976. Copy model, offset double-cut, 1 pickup, black.

| 1974-1976 | | $750 | $975 |

Model 2364B
1971-1973. Dan Armstrong see-thru Lucite copy with 2 mounted humbucker pickups, clear finish.

| 1971-1973 | | $1,000 | $1,375 |

Model 2365
1974-1975. Copy model, Offset double-cut, rosewood 'board, pearloid block markers, sunburst.

| 1974-1975 | | $850 | $1,125 |

Model 2366B/2366FLB
1974-1975. Copy model, offset double-cut, 1 split-coil pickup, sunburst, FLB fretless model.

| 1974-1975 | | $800 | $1,125 |

Model 2385
1974-1975. Copy model, offset double-cut, 1 pickup, ash natural finish.

| 1974-1975 | | $800 | $1,125 |

Model 2388B
1974-1976. Ric 4001 copy.

| 1974-1976 | | $800 | $1,125 |

Model 2452
1975. Ripper copy.

| 1975 | | $800 | $1,125 |

Model 2459B Destroyer
1974-1977. Laminated ash body, copy of Korina Explorer-style.

| 1974-1977 | | $3,000 | $4,000 |

Model 2537 DX
1974-1975. Hofner Beatle copy.

| 1974-1975 | | $800 | $1,125 |

Model 2609B Black Eagle
1974-1976. Burns-like bass, offset double-cut solidbody, sharp curving horns.

| 1974-1976 | | $1,500 | $2,000 |

PL Pro Line Series
1986-1987. Offset double cut solidbody.

| 1986-1987 | Various models | $550 | $750 |

RB/RS Roadstar Series
1983-1987. Solidbody basses, various models and colors.

| 1983-1987 | | $400 | $650 |

The *Vintage Guitar Price Guide* shows values for all-original, excellent condition instruments and, where applicable, with original case.

MODEL YEAR	FEATURES	EXC. COND. LOW	HIGH

Rocket Roll
1974-1976. Korina solidbody, V-shape, natural.
1974-1976 $2,250 $3,000

S/SB Solidbody Series
1990-1992. Various ultra slim solidbody basses.
1990-1992 $350 $450

SR Sound Gear Series
1987-present. Sleek, lightweight designs, active electronics, bolt necks. Model numbers higher than 1000 are usually arched-top, lower usually flat body.
1987-2023   Various models $300 $400

ST-980 Studio
1979-1980. Double cut, 8-string, bolt-on neck, walnut-maple-mahogany body.
1979-1980 $750 $1,000

Imperial

Ca.1963-ca.1970. Imported by the Imperial Accordion Company of Chicago, Illinois. Early guitars and basses made in Italy, but by ca. '66 Japanese-made.

Electric Hollowbody
1960s   Various models $250 $350

Electric Solidbody
1960s   Various models $250 $350

Jackson

1980-present. Intermediate, professional, and premium grade, production, solidbody basses. They also offer guitars. Founded by Grover Jackson, who owned Charvel.

Concert C5P 5-String (Import)
1998-2000. Bolt neck, dot inlay, chrome hardware.
1998-2000 $200 $250

Concert Custom (U.S.A.)
1984-1995. Neck-thru Custom Shop bass.
1984-1989 $1,500 $3,000
1990-1995 $1,000 $1,375

Concert EX 4-String (Import)
1992-1995. Bolt neck, dot inlay, black hardware.
1992-1995 $300 $400

Concert V 5-String (Import)
1992-1995. Bound neck, shark tooth inlay.
1992-1995 $400 $550

Concert XL 4-String (Import)
1992-1995. Bound neck, shark tooth inlay.
1992-1995 $350 $450

Kelly Pro
1994-1995. Pointy-cut bouts, neck-thru solidbody, shark fin marker inlays, includes Standard and Custom models.
1994-1995 $800 $1,125

Piezo
1986. Piezo bridge pickup, neck-thru, shark tooth inlays. The Student model has rosewood 'board, no binding. Custom Model has ebony 'board and binding.
1986 $1,500 $2,000

Soloist
1996. Pointy headstock, 4-string.
1996 $800 $1,125

Surfcaster SC1
1998-2001. Tube and humbucker pickups.
1998-2001 $1,125 $1,500

Jerry Jones

1981-2011. Intermediate grade, production, semi-hollow body electric basses from luthier Jerry Jones, and built in Nashville, Tennessee. They also build guitars and sitars. Jones retired in 2011.

Neptune Longhorn 4
1988-2011. Based on Danelectro longhorn models, 4-string, 2 lipstick-tube pickups, 30" scale.
1988-2011 $2,000 $3,000

Neptune Longhorn 6
1988-2011. 6-string version.
1988-2011 $2,500 $3,500

Neptune Shorthorn 4
1988-2011. Danelectro Coke bottle headstock, short horns double cut, 2 pickups.
1988-2011 $2,000 $3,000

Juzek

Violin maker John Juzek was originally located in Prague, Czeckoslovakia, but moved to West Germany due to World War II. Prague instruments are considered by most to be more valuable. Many German instruments were mass produced with laminate construction and some equate these German basses with the Kay laminate basses of the same era. Juzek still makes instruments.

Kalamazoo

1933-1942, 1965-1970. Kalamazoo was a brand Gibson used on one of their budget lines. They also used the name on electric basses, guitars and amps from '65 to '67.

Electric
1965-1970   Various models $500 $650

Kapa

Ca. 1962-1970. Kapa was founded by Koob Veneman in Maryland and offered basses and guitars.

Electric
1962-1970   Various models $250 $750

Kawai

1927-present. Japanese instrument manufacturer Kawai started offering guitars under other brand names around '56. There were few imports carrying the Kawai brand until the late-'70s; best known for high quality basses. Kawai quit offering guitars and basses around 2002.

Electric
1960s-80s   Various models $300 $800

Kay

Ca. 1931-present. Currently, budget and intermediate grade, production, imported solidbody basses. They also make amps, guitars, banjos, mandolins, ukes, and violins. Kay introduced upright acoustic laminate basses and 3/4 viols in '38 and electric basses in '54.

Ibanez ST-980 Studio
Willie Moseley

Jackson Concert Professional
Ken Kraynak

BASSES

BASSES

Kay Solidbody

Imaged by Heritage Auctions, HA.com

Klira Electric Solidbody

Rivington Guitars

MODEL YEAR	FEATURES	EXC. COND. LOW	HIGH

C1 Concert String
1938-1967. Standard (3/4) size student bass, laminated construction, spruce top, figured maple back and sides, shaded light brown.

1938-1949		$2,000	$2,500
1950-1959		$2,000	$2,500
1960-1967		$2,000	$2,500

K-160 Electronic
1955-1956. Same as K-162, but with plain white plastic trim.

1955-1956		$1,000	$1,500

K-162 Electronic
1955-1956. Bass version of K-161Thin Twin "Jimmy Reed," single-cut, 1 tube-style pickup.

1955-1956		$1,000	$1,500

K-5965 Pro
1954-1965. Single-cut, 1 pickup. named K-5965 Pro by 1961.

1954-1965		$1,000	$1,500

K-5970 Jazz Special
1960-1964. Double-cut, pickup, Kelvinator headstock, black or blond.

1960-1964		$2,500	$3,500

M-1 (Maestro) String
1952-late-1960s. Standard (3/4) size bass, laminated construction, spruce top and curly maple back and sides. Model M-3 is the Junior (1/4) size bass, Model M-1 B has a blond finish, other models include the S-51 B Chubby Jackson Five-String Bass and the S-9 Swingmaster.

1952-1967		$2,500	$3,500

M-5 (Maestro) String
1957-late-1960s. Five strings.

1957-1967		$3,000	$4,000

Semi-hollowbody
1954-1966. Various models, single or double cut, 1 or 2 pickups.

1954-1966	1 pickup	$400	$550
1954-1966	2 pickups	$450	$600

Solidbody
1965-1968. Various models, single or double cut, 1 or 2 pickups.

1965-1968	1 pickup	$400	$550
1965-1968	2 pickups	$450	$600

Ken Smith
See listing under Smith.

Kent
1961-1969. Guitars and basses imported from Japan by Buegeleisen and Jacobson of New York, New York. Manufacturers unknown but many early instruments by Guyatone and Teisco.

Electric
1962-1969. Import models include 628 Newport, 634 Basin Street, 629, and 635.

1961-1969	Common model	$250	$350
1961-1969	Rare model	$550	$800

Kimberly
Late-1960s-early-1970s. Private branded import made in the same Japanese factory as Teisco. They also made guitars.

Violin

1960s		$450	$600

Kingston
Ca. 1958-1967. Imported from Japan by Westheimer Importing Corp. of Chicago. Early examples made by Guyatone and Teisco. They also offered guitars, mandolins and banjos.

Electric

1960s	Common model	$150	$400
1960s	Rare model	$400	$750

Klira
Founded 1887 in Schoenbach, Germany, mainly making violins, but added guitars and basses in the 1950s. The instruments of the '50s and '60s were aimed at the budget market, but workmanship improved with the '70s models.

Electric

1960s	Common model	$400	$800
1960s	Rare model	$800	$1,500

Kramer
1976-1990, 1995-present. Budget grade, production, imported solidbody basses. They also offer guitars. Kramer's first guitars and basses featured aluminum necks with wooden inserts on the back. Around '80 they started to switch to more economical wood necks and aluminum necks were last produced in '85. Gibson acquired the brand in '97.

250-B Special
1977-1979. Offset double-cut, aluminum neck, Ebonol 'board, zero fret, 1 single-coil, natural.

1977-1979		$800	$1,125

350-B Standard
1976-1979. Offset double-cut, aluminum neck, Ebonol 'board, tropical woods, 1 single-coil, dots. The 350 and 450 were Kramer's first basses.

1976-1979		$1,000	$1,500

450-B Deluxe
1976-1980. As 350-B, but with 2 single-coils and blocks.

1976-1980		$1,000	$1,500

650-B Artist
1977-1980. Double-cut, birdseye maple/burled walnut, aluminum neck, zero fret, mother-of-pearl crowns, 2 humbuckers.

1977-1980		$1,750	$2,500

Deluxe 8
1980. Multi-piece body, aluminum neck.

1980		$1,500	$2,000

DMB 2000
1979. Bolt-on aluminum neck, slot headstock.

1979		$1,125	$1,750

DMZ 4000
1978-1982. Bolt-on aluminum neck, slot headstock, double-cut solidbody, active EQ and dual-coil humbucking pickup, dot inlay.

1978-1981		$850	$1,125
1982	Bill Wyman-type	$850	$1,125

The Vintage Guitar Price Guide shows values for all-original, excellent condition instruments and, where applicable, with original case.

MODEL YEAR	FEATURES	EXC. COND. LOW	HIGH

DMZ 4001
1979-1980. Aluminum neck, slot headstock, double-cut solidbody, 1 dual-coil humbucker pickup, dot inlay.
| 1979-1980 | | $1,250 | $1,750 |

DMZ 5000
1979-1980. Double-cut solidbody, aluminum neck, slotted headstock, 2 pickups, crown inlays.
| 1979-1980 | | $1,125 | $1,500 |

DMZ 6000B
1979-1980. Double-cut, aluminum neck, slotted headstock, 2 pickups, crown inlays.
| 1979-1980 | | $1,250 | $2,000 |

Duke Custom/Standard
1981-1983. Headless, aluminum neck, 1 humbucker.
| 1981-1983 | | $450 | $600 |

Duke Special
1982-1985. Headless, aluminum neck, 2 pickups, with frets or fretless.
| 1982-1985 | | $500 | $650 |

Ferrington KFB-1/KFB-2 Acoustic
1987-1990. Acoustic/electric, bridge-mounted active pickup, tone and volume control, various colors. KFB-1 has binding and diamond dot inlays; the KFB-2 has no binding and dot inlays. Danny Ferrington continued to offer the KFB-1 after Kramer closed in '90.
| 1987-1990 | | $350 | $500 |

Focus Series
1984-1987. Made in Japan, double-cut solidbody, 1 or 2 pickups, various models.
| 1984-1987 | | $250 | $800 |

Forum Series
1987-1990. Made in Japan, double-cut solidbody, 2 pickups, neck-thru (I & III) or bolt-neck (II & IV).
| 1987-1990 | | $350 | $550 |

Gene Simmons Axe
1980-1981. Axe-shaped body, aluminum neck.
| 1980-1981 | | $3,500 | $7,000 |

Hundred Series
1988-1990. Import budget line, 7/8th solidbody, various models.
| 1988-1990 | | $200 | $350 |

Pacer Series
1982-1984. Offset double-cut solidbody, various models.
| 1982-1984 | | $600 | $1,500 |

Pioneer Series
1981-1986. Various models, first wood neck basses, offset double-cut, JBX or PBX pickups, dots, '81-'84 models with soft headstocks, later '84 on with banana headstocks.
| 1981-1986 | | $450 | $1,000 |

Ripley
1984-1987. Offset double-cut, 4 (IV) or 5 (V) strings, stereo, pan pots for each string, front and back pickups for each string, active circuitry.
| 1984-1987 | IV and V | $700 | $950 |

Stagemaster Custom (Import)
1982-1985, 1987-1990. First version had an aluminum neck (wood optional). Later version was neck-thru-body, bound neck, either active or passive pickups.
1982-1985	Imperial	$1,000	$1,500
1982-1985	Special	$1,000	$1,500
1982-1985	Standard	$1,000	$1,500

Stagemaster Deluxe (U.S.A.)
1981. Made in USA, 8-string, metal neck.
| 1981 | | $1,250 | $1,750 |

Striker 700
1985-1989. Korean import, offset double-cut, 1 pickup until '87, 2 after. Striker name was again used on a bass in '99.
| 1985-1989 | | $200 | $300 |

Vanguard
1981-1983. V-shaped body, Special (aluminum neck) or Standard (wood neck).
| 1981-1982 | Special | $900 | $1,250 |
| 1983-1984 | Standard | $900 | $1,250 |

Voyager
1982-1983. X-body, headless.
| 1982-1983 | | $900 | $1,250 |

XKB-10 (Wedge)
1980-1981. Wedge-shaped body, aluminum neck.
| 1980-1981 | | $900 | $1,250 |

XKB-20
1981. 2nd version, more traditional double cut body.
| 1981 | | $1,000 | $1,375 |

XL Series
1980-1981. Odd shaped double-cut solidbody, aluminum neck, various models.
1980-1981	XL-24, 4-string	$1,250	$2,000
1980-1981	XL-8, 8-string	$1,500	$2,500
1980-1981	XL-9, 4-string	$1,250	$2,000

ZX Aero Star Series (Import)
1986-1989. Various models include ZX-70 (offset double-cut solidbody, 1 pickup).
| 1986-1989 | | $150 | $300 |

KSD
2003-present. Intermediate grade, production, imported bass line designed by Ken Smith (see Smith listing).

Kubicki
1973-present. Professional and premium grade, production/custom, solidbody basses built by luthier Phil Kubicki in Santa Barbara, California. Kubicki began building acoustic guitars when he was 15. In '64 at age 19, he went to work with Roger Rossmeisl at Fender Musical Instrument's research and development department for acoustic guitars. Nine years later he moved to Santa Barbara, California, and established Philip Kubicki Technology, which is best known for its line of Factor basses and also builds acoustic guitars, custom electric guitars, bodies and necks, and mini-guitars and does custom work, repairs and restorations. Phil Kubicki died in '13.

Kustom
1968-present. Founded by Bud Ross in Chanute, Kansas, and best known for the tuck-and-roll amps, Kustom also offered guitars and basses from '68 to '69.

1981 Kramer DMZ 6000B
Imaged by Heritage Auctions, HA.com

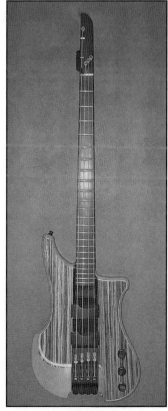

Kubicki Factor

BASSES

2020 Lakland Skyline Series
Cream City Music

Martin BCPA4
Kris Nocula

MODEL		EXC. COND.	
YEAR	FEATURES	LOW	HIGH

Electric Hollowbody
| 1968-1969 | Various models | $1,500 | $2,000 |

La Baye

1967. Short-lived brand out of Green Bay, Wisconsin and built by the Holman-Woodell factory in Neodesha, Kansas. There was also a guitar model.

Model 2x4 II
1967. Very low production, dual pickups, long-scale, small rectangle solidbody, sometimes referred to as the Bass II.
| 1967 | | $2,000 | $3,000 |

Model 2x4 Mini
1967. Short-scale, 1 pickup, small rectangle solidbody.
| 1967 | | $2,000 | $3,000 |

Lakland

1994-present. Professional and premium grade, production/custom, solid and hollowbody basses from luthier Dan Lakin in Chicago, Illinois. Lakland basses are built in the U.S. and overseas (Skyline series).

Electric
1994-present. Various models.
1994-2002	4-63 Classic	$2,500	$3,500
1994-2002	4-63 Deluxe	$2,750	$3,750
1994-2002	4-63 Standard	$2,500	$3,500
1994-2002	4-94 / 44-94 Classic	$2,500	$3,500
1994-2023	4-94 / 44-94 Deluxe	$2,750	$3,750
1994-2023	4-94 / 44-94 Standard	$2,500	$3,500
1998-2003	Joe Osborn	$2,750	$3,750
2012-2023	Skyline 44-60	$1,250	$1,750

Lowrider Basses

2003-2018. Professional grade, production/custom, solidbody basses made by Ed Roman Guitars.

M Basses or Maghini

1998-present. Production/custom, professional and premium grade, solidbody electric basses built in Terryville, Connecticut by luthier Jon Maghini.

Magnatone

Ca. 1937-1971, 2013-present. Founded as Dickerson Brothers, known as Magna Electronics from '47. Produced instruments under own brand and for many others.

Mark VI/Artist Mark VI
1959. Designed by luthier Paul Barth for Magnatone, double-cut, 4-string, 1 pickup.
| 1959 | | $1,250 | $1,750 |

X-10 Hurricane
1965-1966. Offset double cut solidbody, 1 single-coil, 4-on-a-side tuners, Magnatone logo on guard and headstock, Hurricane logo on headstock.
| 1965-1966 | | $1,000 | $1,500 |

Mako

1985-1989. Line of solidbody basses from Kaman (Ovation, Hamer). They also offered guitars and amps.

Electric Solidbody
| 1985-1989 | Various models | $150 | $500 |

Marco Polo

1960-ca.1964. One of the first inexpensive Japanese brands to be imported into the U.S., they also offered guitars.

Solidbody
| 1960s | Various models | $100 | $300 |

Marleaux

1990-present. Luthier Gerald Marleaux builds his custom, premium grade, electric basses in Clausthal-Zellerfeld, Germany.

Marling

Ca. 1975. Budget line instruments marketed by EKO of Recanati, Italy; probably made by them, although possibly imported. They also had guitars.

Electric Solidbody
Models include the E.495 (copy of LP), E.485 (copy of Tele), and the E.465 (Manta-style).
| 1970s | Various models | $100 | $300 |

Martin

1833-present. Professional grade, production, acoustic basses made in the U.S. In 1978, Martin re-entered the electric market and introduced their solidbody EB-18 and EB-28 Basses. In the '80s they offered Stinger brand electric basses. By the late '80s, they started offering acoustic basses.

00C-16GTAE
2006-2011. Mahogany back and sides, Fishman electronics.
| 2006-2011 | | $1,000 | $1,500 |

B-1/B-1E Acoustic
2002-2006. Mahogany back and sides, E has Fishman electronics.
| 2002-2006 | | $1,000 | $1,500 |

B-40/B-40B Acoustic
1989-1996. Jumbo, rosewood back and sides, built-in pickup and volume and tone controls. The B-40B had a pickup.
| 1989-1996 | B-40B | $1,500 | $2,000 |
| 1989-1996 | No pickup | $1,500 | $2,000 |

B-65 Acoustic
1989-1993. Like B-40 but with maple back and sides, built-in pickup and volume and tone controls.
| 1989-1993 | | $1,500 | $2,000 |

BC-15E Acoustic
2000-2006. Single-cut, all mahogany, on-board electronics.
| 2000-2006 | | $1,250 | $1,750 |

BC-16E Acoustic-Electric
2020-2022. Solid sitka spruce top, East Indian rosewood back and sides, built-in Fishman electronics.
| 2020-2022 | | $1,750 | $2,250 |

BC-16GTE Acoustic
2009-2013. Jumbo, cutaway, mahogany back and sides.
| 2009-2013 | | $1,500 | $2,000 |

MODEL YEAR	FEATURES	EXC. COND. LOW	HIGH

BCPA4 Acoustic-Electric
2013-2020. Performing Artist series, single-cut, sitka spruce top, sapele back and sides.

2013-2020		$1,500	$2,000

EB-18
1979-1982. Electric solidbody, neck-thru, 1 pickup, natural.

1979-1982		$1,250	$1,750

EB-28
1980-1982. Electric solidbody.

1980-1982		$1,500	$2,000

SBL-10
1980s. Stinger brand solidbody, maple neck, 1 split and 1 bar pickup.

1980s		$200	$275

Marvel
1950s-mid-1960s. Brand used for budget guitars and basses marketed by Peter Sorkin Company in New York, New York.

Electric Solidbody

1950s-60s	Various models	$250	$550

Messenger
1967-1968. Built by Musicraft, Inc., Messengers featured a neck-thru metal alloy neck. They also made guitars.

Metal Neck
1967-1968. Metal alloy neck. Messenger mainly made guitars - they offered a bass, but it is unlikely many were built.

1967-1968		$2,000	$2,500

Messenger Upright
Made by Knutson Luthiery, see that listing.

Microfrets
1967-1975, 2004-2005. Professional grade, production, electric basses built in Myersville, Maryland. They also built guitars.

Husky
1971-1974/75. Double-cut, 2 pickups, 2-on-a-side tuners.

1971-1975		$1,250	$1,625

Rendezvous
1970. One pickup, orange sunburst.

1970		$1,250	$1,625

Signature
1969-1975. Double-cut, 2 pickups, 2-on-a-side tuners.

1969-1975		$1,875	$2,500

Stage II
1969-1975. Double-cut, 2 pickups, 2-on-a-side tuners.

1969-1975		$1,875	$2,500

Thundermaster
1967-1975. Double-cut, 2 pickups, 2-on-a-side tuners.

1967-1975		$1,875	$2,500

Modulus
1978-2013. Founded by aerospace engineer Geoff Gould, Modulus offered professional and premium

grade, production/custom, solidbody basses built in California. They also built guitars.

Electric
1978-2013. Various standard models.

1978-2013		$1,500	$3,500

Mollerup Basses
In 1984 luthier Laurence Mollerup began building professional grade, custom/production, electric basses and electric double basses in Vancouver, British Columbia. He has also built guitars.

Moonstone
1972-2020. Luthier Steve Helgeson built his premium grade, production/custom, acoustic and electric basses in Eureka, California. He also built guitars.

Eclipse Deluxe
1980-1984. Double-cut solidbody.

1980-1984		$2,000	$3,500

Exploder
1980-1983. Figured wood body, Explorer-style neck-thru-body.

1980-1983		$2,000	$3,500

Vulcan
1982-1984. Solidbody, flat-top (Vulcan) or carved top (Vulcan II), maple body, gold hardware.

1982-1984		$2,000	$3,500

Morales
Ca.1967-1968. Guitars and basses made in Japan by Zen-On and not heavily imported into the U.S.

Electric Solidbody

1967-1968	Various models	$150	$400

Mosrite
Semie Moseley's Mosrite offered various bass models throughout the many versions of the Mosrite company.

Brut
Late-1960s. Assymetrical body with small cutaway on upper treble bout.

1960s		$700	$950

Celebrity
1965-1969. ES-335-style semi-thick double-cut body with f-holes, 2 pickups.

1965-1966	Custom color	$950	$1,250
1965-1967	Sunburst	$850	$1,125
1968-1969	Red	$800	$1,125
1969	Sunburst	$800	$1,125

Combo
1966-1968. Hollowbody, 2 pickups.

1966-1968		$1,500	$2,000

Joe Maphis
1966-1969. Ventures-style body, hollow without f-holes, 2 pickups, natural.

1966-1969		$1,750	$2,250

Ventures
1965-1972. Various colors, 1 or 2 pickups.

1965	1 pickup	$2,000	$2,500
1965	2 pickups	$2,250	$3,000

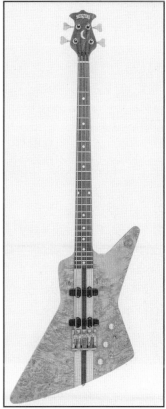

1982 Moonstone Exploder
Imaged by Heritage Auctions, HA.com

1966 Mosrite Celebrity
Rivington Guitars

BASSES

1979 Music Man StingRay

Imaged by Heritage Auctions, HA.com

1962 National Valpro 85

Imaged by Heritage Auctions, HA.com

MODEL YEAR	FEATURES	EXC. COND. LOW	HIGH
1966	1 pickup	$1,625	$2,125
1966	2 pickups	$2,000	$2,500
1967-1968	1 pickup	$1,500	$2,000
1967-1968	2 pickups	$1,625	$2,125
1969	1 pickup	$1,375	$1,750
1969	2 pickups	$1,625	$2,125
1970-1972	1 pickup	$1,500	$2,000
1970-1972	2 pickups	$1,500	$2,000

V-II

1973-1974. Ventures-style, 2 humbuckers, sunburst.

1973-1974		$1,750	$2,250

MTD

1994-present. Intermediate, professional, and premium grade, production/custom, electric basses built by luthier Michael Tobias (who founded Tobias Basses in '77) in Kingston, New York. Since '00, he also imports basses built in Korea to his specifications.

Murph

1965-1967. Mid-level electric solidbody basses built by Pat Murphy in San Fernado, California. Murph logo on headstock. They also offered guitars and amps.

Solidbody

1965-1967		$875	$1,125

Music Man

1972-present. Intermediate and professional grade, production, electric basses. They also build guitars.

Bongo

2003-present. Double cut solidbody, squared-off horns, 2 pickups, 4-, 5- and 6-string.

2003-2023	Bongo 4	$1,500	$2,000
2003-2023	Bongo 5	$1,625	$2,250
2003-2023	Bongo 6	$1,750	$2,500

Cutlass I/Cutlass II

1982-1987. Ash body, graphite neck, string-thru-body.

1982-1984	I, CLF era	$3,000	$5,000
1982-1984	II, CLF era	$2,500	$4,000
1984-1987	I, Ernie Ball era	$1,750	$2,250
1984-1987	II, Ernie Ball era	$2,000	$2,500

S.U.B. Series

2003-2007. Offset double-cut, 4- or 5-string, 1 humbucker.

2003-2007	IV Bass	$500	$650
2003-2007	V Bass	$600	$800

Sabre

1978-ca.1991. Double-cut solidbody bass, 3-and-1 tuning keys, 2 humbucking pickups, on-board preamp, natural.

1978-1984	CLF era	$3,000	$4,000
1984-1991	Ernie Ball era	$2,000	$2,500

Sterling

1993-present. Rosewood, 1 pickup, EQ, pearl blue. In '05, additional pickup options available. 5-string introduced in '08.

1993-2023	4-string	$1,500	$2,000
2008-2023	5-string	$1,500	$2,000

MODEL YEAR	FEATURES	EXC. COND. LOW	HIGH

StingRay

1976-present. Offset double-cut solidbody, 1 pickup, 3-and-1 tuners, string-thru until '80, various colors. 5-string introduced in '87. In '05, additional pickup options are available.

1976-1979	CLF era	$4,000	$6,000
1980-1984	CLF era	$3,000	$4,000
1984-1989	Ernie Ball era	$2,000	$3,000
1987-2023	5-string	$2,000	$2,500
1990-2023	4-string	$2,000	$2,500

StingRay 20th Anniversary

1996. 1400 made, flamed maple body.

1996		$2,000	$2,750

StingRay 30th Anniversary

2003. 800 made.

2003		$1,875	$2,500

StingRay Classic

2010-2019. Ash body, birds-eye or flame maple neck, 4- or 5-string.

2010-2019		$1,500	$2,500

National

Ca. 1927-present. National offered electric basses in the '60s when Valco owned the brand.

Beatle (Violin)

1970s. Strum & Drum era import, National script logo on headstock, 2 pickups, shaded brown finish.

1970s		$600	$775

EG 700V-2HB German Style

1970s. Strum & Drum era import, Beatle-style violin body, 2 humbuckers, bolt neck.

1970s		$600	$775

N-850

1967-1968. Semi-hollow double-cut, art deco f-holes, 2 pickups, block markers, bout control knobs, sunburst.

1967-1968		$825	$1,125

Val-Pro 85

1961-1962. Res-O-Glas body shaped like the U.S. map, 2 pickups, snow white, renamed National 85 in '63.

1961-1962		$1,125	$1,500

National Reso-Phonic

1988-present. Professional grade, production/custom, acoustic and acoustic/electric resonator basses built in San Luis Obispo, California. They also build guitars, mandolins and ukuleles.

New York Bass Works

1989-present. Luthier David Segal builds his professional and premium grade, production/custom, electric basses in New York.

Norma

Ca.1965-1970. Guitars and basses imported from Japan by Chicago's Strum and Drum.

Electric Solidbody

1960s	Various models	$165	$600

O'Hagan

1979-1983. Designed by Jerol O'Hagan in St. Louis Park, Minnesota. He also offered guitars.

MODEL YEAR	FEATURES	EXC. COND. LOW	HIGH

Electric Solidbody
1979-1983. Models include the Shark Bass, Night-Watch Bass, NightWatch Regular Bass, and the Twenty Two Bass.

1979-1983		$650	$850

Old Kraftsman
1930s-1960s. Brand used by the Spiegel Company. Guitars and basses made by other American manufacturers.

Electric Solidbody

1950s	Various models	$400	$550

Orville by Gibson
1984-1993. Orville by Gibson and Orville guitars were made by Japan's Fuji Gen Gakki for Gibson. Basically the same models except the Orville by Gibson guitars had real Gibson USA pickups and a true nitrocellulose lacquer finish. The Orville models used Japanese electronics and a poly finish. Prices here are for the Orville by Gibson models.

Thunderbird

1984-1993		$1,250	$1,625

Ovation
1966-present. Intermediate and professional grade, production, acoustic/electric basses. Ovation offered electric solidbody basses early on and added acoustic basses in the '90s. They also offer guitars and mandolins.

B768/Elite B768
1990. Single-cut acoustic-electric bass, Elite body style with upper bout soundholes.

1990		$900	$1,250

Celebrity Series
1990s-2013. Deep bowl back, cutaway, acoustic/electric.

1990s-2013	Various models	$400	$550

Magnum Series
1974-1980. Magnum I is an odd-shaped mahogany solidbody, 2 pickups, mono/stereo, mute, sunburst, red or natural. Magnum II has battery-powered preamp and 3-band EQ. Magnum III and IV had a new offset double-cut body.

1974-1980	Various models	$1,500	$2,000

NSB778 Elite T Nikki Sixx Limited Edition
2005-2013. Made in USA, acoustic-electric 4-string, 1 pickup, solid spruce top, ebony 'board, custom iron cross inlays, red or gray flame finish.

2005-2013		$1,500	$2,000

Typhoon II/Typhoon III
1968-1971. Ovation necks, but bodies and hardware were German imports. Semi-hollowbody, 2 pickups, red or sunburst. Typhoon II is 335-style and III is fretless.

1968-1971	Typhoon II	$900	$1,250
1968-1971	Typhoon III	$900	$1,250

Ultra
1984. Korean solidbodies and necks assembled in U.S., offset double-cut with 1 pickup.

1984		$500	$650

PANaramic
1961-1963. Guitars and basses made in Italy by the Crucianelli accordion company and imported by PANaramic accordion. They also offered amps made by Magnatone.

Electric Hollowbody
1961-1963. Double-cut hollowbody, 2 pickups, dot markers, sunburst.

1961-1963		$1,000	$1,500

Parker
1992-2016. Premium grade, production/custom, solidbody electric basses. They also built guitars.

Fly
2002-2011. Offered in 4- and 5-string models.

2002-2011		$1,750	$2,500

Paul Reed Smith
1985-present. PRS added basses in '86, but by '92 had dropped the models. In 2000 PRS started again offering professional and premium grade, production, solidbody electric basses. Bird inlays can add $100 or more to the values of PRS basses listed here.

Bass-4
1987-1991, 2007. Mahogany, set neck, 3 single-coil pickups, hum-cancelling coil, active circuitry, 22-fret Brazilian rosewood 'board. Reintroduced (OEB Series) in 2000s.

1987		$2,250	$3,000
1988-1991		$2,000	$2,750
2007		$2,000	$2,750

Bass-5
1987-1991. Mahogany, 5-string, set-neck, rosewood 'board, 3 single-coil pickups, active electronics. Options include custom colors, bird inlays, fretless 'board.

1987		$2,500	$3,500
1988-1991		$2,000	$3,000

CE Bass-4
1990-1991. Solidbody, 4-string, alder or maple body, bolt-on neck, rosewood 'board.

1990-1991	Alder	$1,125	$1,500
1990-1991	Maple	$1,125	$1,500

CE Bass-5
1990-1991. Solidbody, 5-string, alder or maple body, bolt-on neck, rosewood 'board.

1990-1991	Alder	$1,250	$1,750
1990-1991	Maple	$1,500	$2,000

Curly Bass-4
1987-1991. Double-cut solidbody, curly maple top, set maple neck, Brazilian rosewood 'board (ebony on fretless), 3 single-coil and 1 hum-cancelling pickups, various grades of maple tops, moon inlays.

1987		$3,000	$5,000
1988-1991		$2,000	$3,000

Curly Bass-5
1987-1991. Five-string version of Curly Bass-4.

1987		$3,000	$4,500
1988-1991		$2,000	$3,000

Electric
2000-2007. Bolt neck 4-string, offered in regular and maple top versions.

2000-2007	Maple	$1,500	$2,000
2000-2007	Plain	$1,000	$1,500

Ovation Magnum I
Imaged by Heritage Auctions, HA.com

1969 Ovation Typhoon II
Rivington Guitars

BASSES

BASSES

Peavey Milestone 4

Peavey T-40

MODEL YEAR	FEATURES	EXC. COND. LOW	HIGH
Private Stock Program			
2010-present. Custom instruments based around existing PRS models.			
2010-2023		$4,000	$8,000
SE Series			
2014-present. Various models, i.e., SE Kestrel and Kingfisher.			
2014-2023	Higher models	$550	$750
2014-2023	Most models	$450	$600

Peavey

1965-present. Intermediate and professional grade, production/custom, electric basses. They also build guitars and amps. Hartley Peavey's first products were guitar amps and he added guitars and basses to the mix in '78.

MODEL YEAR	FEATURES	EXC. COND. LOW	HIGH
Axcelerator			
1994-1998. Offset double-cut, long thin horns, 2 humbuckers, stacked control knobs, bolt neck, dot markers.			
1994-1998		$400	$650
Cirrus Series			
1998-2012. Offset double-cut, active electronics, in 4-, 5-, 6-string, and custom shop versions.			
1998-2009	Cirrus 5	$800	$1,500
1998-2012	Cirrus 4	$750	$1,250
1998-2012	Cirrus 6	$850	$1,750
Dyna-Bass			
1987-1993. Double-cut solidbody, active electronics, 3-band EQ, rosewood 'board, opaque finish.			
1987-1993		$425	$650
Dyna-Bass Limited			
1987-1990. Neck-thru-body, ebony 'board, flamed maple neck/body construction, purple heart strips, mother-of-pearl inlays.			
1987-1990		$600	$775
Forum			
1994-1995. Double-cut solidbody, rosewood 'board, dot inlays, 2 humbuckers.			
1994-1995		$300	$400
Forum Plus			
1994. Forum Bass with added active electronics.			
1994		$300	$400
Foundation			
1984-2002. Double-cut solidbody, 2 pickups, maple neck.			
1984-2002		$300	$400
Foundation S			
1986-1991. Two split-coil pickups, maple body, rosewood 'board, black hardware, black painted headstock.			
1986-1991		$300	$400
Foundation S Active			
1987-1991. Similar to Foundation S Bass with added active circuitry, provides low-impedance output, 2 pickups.			
1987-1991		$300	$400
Fury			
1983-1999. Double-cut solidbody, rosewood 'board, 1 split-coil humbucker.			
1983-1999		$300	$400

MODEL YEAR	FEATURES	EXC. COND. LOW	HIGH
Fury Custom			
1986-1993. Fury Bass with black hardware and narrow neck.			
1986-1993		$300	$400
Fury VI			
2001-2003. 6-string, active electronics, quilt top.			
2001-2003		$375	$500
G-Bass V			
1999-2002. Offset double-cut 5-string, humbucker, 3-band EQ.			
1999-2002		$750	$1,000
Grind Series			
2001-2020. Offset double-cut, neck-thru, long bass horn, 2 pickups, 4, 5, or 6 strings.			
2001-2020	Various models	$225	$300
Liberator JT-84 John Taylor			
2007. 2 humbuckers, black with graphics.			
2007		$1,250	$1,625
Milestone Series			
1994-present. Import offset double cut, Milestone I ('94) replaced by 1 P-style pickup II ('95-'01), split humbucker IV ('99-'04); 2 single-coil III ('99-present) now just called Milestone.			
1994-2023		$125	$350
Millenium Series			
2001-2020	Various models	$150	$1,000
Patriot			
1984-1988. General J-Bass styling with larger thinner horns, 1 single-coil, maple neck.			
1984-1988		$200	$450
Patriot Custom			
1986-1988. Patriot with rosewood neck, matching headstock.			
1986-1988		$200	$450
RJ-IV Randy Jackson			
1990-1993. Randy Jackson Signature model, neck-thru-body, 2 split-coil active pickups, ebony 'board, mother-of-pearl position markers.			
1990-1993		$400	$1,000
Rudy Sarzo Signature			
1989-1993. Double-cut solidbody, active EQ, ebony 'board, 2 pickups.			
1989-1993		$500	$750
T-20FL			
1980s. Fretless double-cut solidbody, 1 pickup, also available as the fretted T-20 ('82-'83).			
1980s		$250	$350
T-40/T-40FL			
1978-1987. Double-cut solidbody, 2 pickups. T-40FL is fretless.			
1978-1987	T-40	$550	$1,000
1978-1987	T-40FL	$550	$1,000
T-45			
1982-1986. T-40 with 1 humbucking pickup, and a mid-frequency roll off knob.			
1982-1986		$550	$1,000
TL Series			
1988-1998. Neck-thru-body, gold hardware, active humbuckers, EQ, flamed maple neck and body, 5-string (TL-Five) or 6 (TL-Six).			
1988-1998	TL-Five	$625	$850
1989-1998	TL-Six	$675	$900

MODEL YEAR	FEATURES	EXC. COND. LOW	HIGH

Void IV
2012. Maple neck, 2 pickups, gloss finish in red, white or black.

2012		$250	$350

Zodiac
2006-2012. Solid alder body, maple neck, 2 pickups.

2006-2012		$250	$350

Pedulla
1975-2019. Professional and premium grade, production/custom, electric basses made in Rockland, Massachusetts. Founded by Michael Pedulla, and which offered various upscale options that affect valuation, so each instrument should be evaluated on a case-by-case basis. Unless specifically noted, the following listings have standard to mid-level features. High-end options are specifically noted; if not, these options will have a relatively higher value than those shown here. Pedualla announced his retirement in '19.

Buzz-4/Buzz-5
1980-2008. Double-cut neck-thru solidbody, fretless, long-scale, maple neck and body wings, 2 pickups, preamp, some with other active electronics, various colors, 4-, 5-, 6-, 8-string versions.

1980-1999		$1,750	$2,500

Interceptor
1980s. Double-cut, maple/walnut laminated neck-thru.

1980s		$1,500	$2,000

MVP Series
1984-2019. Fretted version of Buzz Bass, standard or flame top, 4-, 5-, 6-, 8-string versions, MVP II is bolt-on neck version.

1980s	MVP-6	$2,000	$2,500
1984-1990s	MVP-4, flame top	$1,750	$2,500
1984-1990s	MVP-4, standard top	$1,500	$2,000
1984-1990s	MVP-5	$1,500	$2,000
1990s	MVP II	$1,000	$1,500

Orsini Wurlitzer 4-String
Mid-1970s. Body style similar to late-'50s Gibson double-cut slab body SG Special, neck-thru, 2 pickups, natural. Sold by Boston's Wurlitzer music store chain.

1970s		$1,500	$2,500

Quilt Limited
Neck-thru-body with curly maple center strip, quilted maple body wings, 2 Bartolini pickups, available in fretted or fretless 4- and 5-string models.

1987		$2,000	$3,000

Rapture Series
1995-2019. Solidbody with extra-long thin bass horn and extra short treble horn, 4- or 5-string, various colors.

1995-2019	Rapture 4	$1,500	$2,000
1995-2019	Rapture 5	$1,750	$2,500

Series II
1987-1992. Bolt neck, rosewood 'board, mother-of-pearl dot inlays, Bartolini pickups.

1987-1992		$1,500	$2,000

Thunderbass Series
1993-2019. Solidbody with extra-long thin bass horn and extra short treble horn, 4-, 5- or 6-string, standard features or triple A top.

1993-1999	4, AAA top	$2,250	$3,000
1993-1999	4, Standard	$1,750	$2,500
1993-1999	5, AAA top	$2,250	$3,000
1993-1999	5, Standard	$1,750	$2,500
1993-1999	6, AAA top	$2,250	$3,000
1993-1999	6, Standard	$2,000	$2,500
2000-2019	4, AAA top	$2,000	$2,500
2000-2019	5, AAA top	$2,250	$3,000
2000-2019	6, AAA top	$2,250	$3,000

Thunderbolt Series
1994-2019. Similar to Thunderbass Series but with bolt necks, 4-, 5- or 6-string, standard AA or AAA maple or optional 5A or exotic wood (ET) tops.

1994-2019	Various models	$1,750	$2,500

Penco
Ca. 1974-1978. Generally high-quality Japanese-made copies of classic American bass guitars. They also made guitars, mandolins and banjos.

Electric

1974-1978	Various models	$150	$400

Premier
Ca.1938-ca.1975, 1990s-2010. Originally American-made instruments, but by the '60s imported parts were being used. 1990s instruments were Asian imports.

Bantam
1950-1970. Small body, single-cut short-scale archtop electric, torch headstock inlay, sparkle 'guard, sunburst.

1950-1970		$800	$1,500

Electric Solidbody

1960s	Various models	$400	$1,250

Renaissance
1978-1980. Plexiglass solidbody electric guitars and basses made in Malvern, Pennsylvania.

Plexiglas
1978-1980. Plexiglas bodies and active electronics, models include the DPB bass (double-cut, 1 pickup, '78-'79), SPB (single-cut, 2 pickups, '78-'79), T-100B (Bich-style, 1 pickup, '80), S-100B (double-cut, 1 pickup, '80), and the S-200B (double-cut, 2 pickups, '80).

1978-1980	Various models	$750	$1,500

Rickenbacker
1931-present. Professional grade, production/custom, electric basses. They also build guitars. Rickenbacker introduced their first electric bass in '57 and has always been a strong player in the bass market.

Electric Upright
1936. Cast aluminum neck and body, horseshoe pickup, extension pole.

1936		$4,000	$5,500

1987 Pedulla Buzz-4
Imaged by Heritage Auctions, HA.com

1979 Renaissance SPB
Craig Brody

1976 Rickenbacker 3001

Imaged by Heritage Auctions, HA.com

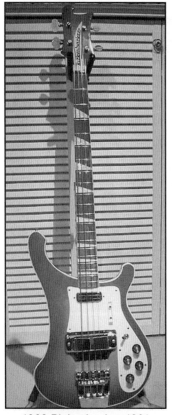

1968 Rickenbacker 4001

Richard Memmel

MODEL		EXC. COND.	
YEAR	FEATURES	LOW	HIGH

Model 1999 (Rose-Morris)
1964-1967. Export made for English distributor Rose-Morris of London, built along the lines of the U.S. Model 4000 Bass but with small differences that are considered important in the vintage guitar market.

1964-1966		$16,500	$21,500
1967		$9,500	$12,500

Model 2030 Hamburg
1984-1997. Rounded double-cut, 2 pickups, active electronics.

1984-1997		$2,000	$2,625

Model 2030GF (Glenn Frey)
1992-1995. Limited Edition, double-cut, 2 humbuckers, Jetglo finish.

1992-1995		$2,000	$3,000

Model 2050 El Dorado
1984-1992. Gold hardware, 2 pickups, active.

1984-1992		$2,000	$2,500

Model 2060 El Dorado
1992-1997. Gold hardware, 2 pickups, active, double-bound body.

1992-1997		$2,000	$2,500

Model 3000
1975-1984. Rounded double-cut, 30" scale, 1 pickup, brown sunburst.

1975-1984		$1,875	$2,500

Model 3001
1975-1984. Same as Model 3000 but with longer 33-1/2" scale, Wine Red.

1975-1984		$1,875	$2,500

Model 3261 (Rose-Morris Slim-Line)
1967. Export model made for English distributor Rose-Morris, built along the lines of a U.S. equivalent Model 4005 Bass.

1967		$10,500	$14,500

Model 4000
1958-1985. Cresting wave body and headstock, 1 horseshoe pickup (changed to regular pickup in '64), neck-thru-body.

1958-1962	Plank style	$14,500	$19,500
1963-1966		$12,500	$16,500
1967-1969		$9,500	$12,500
1970-1972		$3,500	$4,500
1973-1985		$2,875	$3,750

Model 4001
1961-1986. Fancy version of 4000, 1 horseshoe magnet pickup (changed to regular pickup in '64) and 1 bar magnet pickup, triangle inlays, bound neck.

1961-1963	Fireglo	$18,000	$23,500
1963-1966	Mapleglo	$16,000	$21,000
1964-1966	Fireglo	$18,000	$23,500
1967-1969	Various colors	$8,875	$12,000
1970-1972	Various colors	$5,500	$7,000
1973	Early '73 features	$4,500	$6,500
1973	Late '73 features	$3,750	$5,000
1974-1979	Various colors	$3,250	$4,250
1980-1986	Various colors	$2,750	$3,500

Model 4001C64S
2001-2014. Recreation of Paul McCartney's 4001 featuring changes he made like a reshaped body and zero-fret 'board.

2001-2014		$2,875	$3,750

MODEL		EXC. COND.	
YEAR	FEATURES	LOW	HIGH

Model 4001CS (Chris Squire)
1991-1997. Chris Squire signature model, with certificate.

1991-1997		$5,000	$7,500

Model 4001FL
1968-1986. Fretless version of 4001 Bass, special order in '60s, various colors.

1968-1986		$2,750	$5,000

Model 4001S
1964-1985. Same as Model 4000, but with 2 pickups, export model.

1980-1985		$2,000	$2,625

Model 4001V63
1984-2000. Vintage '63 reissue of Model 4001S, horseshoe-magnet pickup, Mapleglo.

1984-2000		$2,875	$3,750

Model 4002
1977-1984. Cresting wave body and headstock, 2 humbuckers, black 'guard, checkerboard binding.

1977-1984		$11,500	$13,500

Model 4003
1979-present. Similar to Model 4001, split 'guard, deluxe features.

1979-2023		$1,750	$2,500

Model 4003FL
1979-2017. Fretless version.

1979-2017		$1,750	$2,500

Model 4003 Shadow
1986. About 60 made for Guitar Center, all black 'board, inlays and hardware, Jetglo finish.

1986		$3,500	$5,500

Model 4003S
1986-2003, 2012-present. Standard feature version of 4003, 4 strings. Reissued in '12.

1986-2003		$1,750	$2,500
2012-2023	Reissue	$1,500	$2,000

Model 4003S Redneck
1988. Red body, 'board and headstock, black hardware.

1988		$3,500	$5,500

Model 4003S Tuxedo
1987. White body with black 'guard and hardware. 100 made.

1987		$3,500	$5,500

Model 4003S/5
1986-2003. Model 4003S with 5 strings.

1986-2003		$3,750	$4,500

Model 4003S/8
1986-2003. Model 4003S with 8 strings.

1986-2003		$3,500	$5,000

Model 4003S/SPC Blackstar
1989. Back finish, board, knobs, and hardware. Also offered as 5-string.

1989		$4,500	$5,500

Model 4003SW
2014-present. Solid walnut body, dot markers, satin natural finish.

2014-2023		$1,750	$2,375

Model 4003W
2013-present. Solid walnut body, deluxe triangle markers, satin natural finish.

2013-2023		$1,500	$2,000

MODEL YEAR	FEATURES	EXC. COND. LOW	HIGH

Model 4004C Cheyenne/4004Cii Cheyenne II
1993-2019. Cresting wave, maple neck-thru-body with walnut body and head wings, gold hardware, dot inlay. Replaced by maple top 4004Cii Cheyenne II in '00.

1993-1999	Cheyenne	$2,250	$2,750
2000-2019	Cheyenne II	$2,250	$2,750

Model 4004L Laredo
1993-2022. Like Cheyenne but without walnut wings.

1993-2022		$2,250	$2,750

Model 4005
1965-1984. New style double-cut semi-hollowbody, 2 pickups, R tailpiece, cresting wave headstock.

1965-1966	Fireglo	$10,500	$14,000
1965-1966	Jetglo	$9,500	$12,000
1965-1966	Mapleglo	$10,500	$13,000
1967-1969	Fireglo	$10,000	$12,500
1967-1969	Jetglo	$8,000	$10,500
1967-1969	Mapleglo	$9,500	$12,500
1970-1979	Various colors	$6,500	$8,500
1980-1984	Various colors	$6,000	$8,000

Model 4005-6
1965-1977. Model 4005 with 6 strings.

1965-1969		$10,500	$13,500
1970-1977		$7,000	$9,500

Model 4005-8
Late-1960s. Eight-string Model 4005, Fireglo or Mapleglo.

1968-1969		$10,000	$13,000

Model 4005L (Lightshow)
1970-1975. Model 4005 with translucent top with lights in body that lit up when played, needed external transformer.

1970-1971	1st edition	$17,000	$30,000
1972-1975	2nd edition	$20,000	$25,000

Model 4005WB
1966-1983. Old style Model 4005 with white-bound body, Fireglo.

1966		$10,000	$13,000
1967-1969		$9,000	$11,500
1970-1979		$5,500	$7,500
1980-1983		$5,000	$6,500

Model 4008
1975-1983. Eight-string, cresting wave body and headstock.

1975-1979		$4,500	$5,500
1980-1983		$4,500	$5,500

Model 4080 Doubleneck
1975-1992. Bolt-on 6- and 4-string necks, Jetglo or Mapleglo.

1975-1979		$10,000	$14,000
1980-1992		$10,000	$14,000

Ritter Royal Instruments
Production/custom, solidbody basses built by luthier Jens Ritter in Wachenheim, Germany.

Rob Allen
1997-present. Professional grade, production/custom, lightweight basses made by luthier Robert Allen in Santa Barbara, California.

MODEL YEAR	FEATURES	EXC. COND. LOW	HIGH

Robin
1982-2010. Founded by David Wintz and located in Houston, Texas, Robin built basses until 1997. Most basses were Japanese made until '87; American production began in '88. They also built guitars and also made Metropolitan ('96-'08) and Alamo ('00-'08) brand guitars.

Freedom I
1984-1986. Offset double-cut, active treble and bass EQ controls, 1 pickup.

1984-1986		$750	$1,000

Freedom I Passive
1986-1989. Non-active version of Freedom Bass, 1 humbucker. Passive dropped from name in '87.

1986-1989		$750	$1,000

Medley
1984-1997. Offset deep cutaways, 2 pickups, reverse headstock until '89, then split headstock, back to reverse by '94. Japanese-made until '87, U.S. after.

1984-1987	Japan	$550	$750
1988-1997	USA	$1,250	$1,750

Ranger
1984-1997. Vintage style body, dot markers, medium scale and 1 pickup from '84 to '88 and long scale with P-style and J-style pickup configuration from '89 to '97.

1984-1987	Japan	$550	$750
1988-1997	USA	$1,000	$1,375

Rock Bass
2002-2015. Chinese-made, intermediate and professional grade, production, bolt neck solidbody basses from the makers of Warwick basses.

Roland
Best known for keyboards, effects, and amps, Roland offered synthesizer-based guitars and basses from 1977 to '86.

GR-33B (G-88) Bass Guitar Synthesizer
Early-mid 1980s. Solidbody bass with synthesizer in the guitar case, G-88 deluxe bass.

1983-1985		$2,000	$3,000

Roman & Blake Basses
1977-2003. Professional grade, production/custom, solidbody bass guitars made by Ed Roman Guitars.

Roman USA Basses
Professional grade, production/custom, solidbody basses made by Ed Roman Guitars starting in 2000.

Roscoe Guitars
Early 1980s-present. Luthier Keith Roscoe builds his production/custom, professional and premium grade, solidbody electric basses in Greensboro, North Carolina.

S.D. Curlee
1975-1982. S.D. Curlee guitars and basses were made in Illinois; S.D. Curlee International instruments were made in Japan.

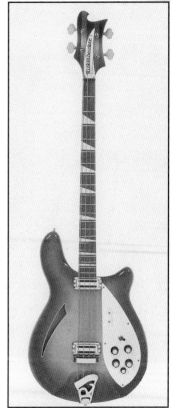

1966 Rickenbacker 4005

Robin Freedom II

Sadowsky NYC Custom 21-Fret

1965 Silvertone Model 1444
Erick Warner

MODEL YEAR	FEATURES	EXC. COND. LOW	HIGH
Electric Solidbody			
1970s	Various models	$500	$1,500

Sadowsky
1980-present. Professional and premium grade, production/custom, solidbody basses built by luthier Roger Sadowsky in Brooklyn, New York. He also builds guitars and amps.

Serenader
Mainly known for lap steels this Seattle, Washington brand also built a solidbody bass.

Silvertone
1941-ca.1970, present. Brand used by Sears. Instruments were U.S.-made and imported. Currently, Samick offers a line of acoustic and electric guitars, basses and amps under the Silvertone name.

Model 1373L/1376L			
1956-1959		$1,500	$2,000

Model 1442 Standard
1966-1968. Solidbody 30" standard size, 1 pickup, dot markers, shaded brown.

1966-1968		$750	$1,125

Model 1443 Extra Long
1966-1968. Solidbody 34" size, 2 pickups, dot markers, red sunburst.

1966-1968		$1,000	$1,500

Model 1443 Hornet
1950s-1960s. Made by Danelectro, 34" scale, red/black sunburst.

1950s-60s		$750	$1,125

Model 1444 Electric
1959-1965. Bass version of 6-string electric guitar Model 1415 (bronze) and 1416 (black), 4-on-a-side replaces the prior year coke-bottle headstock, 1 pickup on single-cut U-1 style body, black finish.

1959-1965		$1,000	$1,500

Model 1452
1966-1967. Made by Danelectro, 2 lipstick pickups, red/black sunburst.

1966-1967		$450	$650

Simmons
Luthier David L. Simmons, began in 2002, builds professional grade, production/custom, 4- and 5-string basses in Hendersonville, North Carolina.

Sinister
2003. A short run of intermediate grade, solidbody basses built for Sinister Guitars by luthier Jon Kammerer.

Smith
1978-present. Professional and premium grade, production/custom, electric basses built by luthier Ken Smith in Perkasie, Pennsylvania. Earlier models had Ken Smith on the headstock, recent models have a large S logo. He also designs the imported KSD line of basses.

MODEL YEAR	FEATURES	EXC. COND. LOW	HIGH
American-Made			
1978-2023	Various models	$3,500	$4,500
Imported			
1990s	Various models	$700	$1,000

Soundgear by Ibanez
SDGR Soundgear by Ibanez headstock logo, intermediate grade, production, solidbody electric basses, made in Japan, Korea and Indonesia, starting in 1987.

Spector/Stuart Spector Design
1975-1990 (Spector), 1991-1998 (SSD), 1998-present (Spector SSD). Imtermediate, professional, and premium grade, production/custom, basses made in the U.S., the Czech Republic, Korea, and China. Stuart Spector's first bass was the NS and the company quickly grew to the point where Kramer acquired it in '85. After Kramer went out of business in '90, Spector started building basses with the SSD logo (Stuart Spector Design). In '98 he recovered the Spector trademark.

Squier
See models listed under Squier in Fender section.

Standel
1952-1974, 1997-present. Amp builder Bob Crooks offered instruments under his Standel brand name three different times during the '60s. See Guitar section for production details. See Amp section for more company information.

Custom Deluxe Solidbody 401
1967-1968. Custom with higher appointments, various colors.

1967-1968		$1,250	$1,750

Custom Deluxe Thinbody 402
1967-1968. Custom with higher appointments, various colors.

1967-1968		$1,250	$1,750

Custom Solidbody 501
1967-1968. Solidbody, 1 pickup, various colors.

1967-1968		$1,000	$1,500

Custom Thinbody 502
1967-1968. Thin solidbody, 2 pickups, various colors.

1967-1968		$1,000	$1,500

Steinberger
1979-present. Steinberger offers budget and intermediate grade, production, electric basses. They also offer guitars.

H Series
1979-1982. Reinforced molded plastic wedge-shaped body, headless neck, 1 (H1) or 2 (H2) high impedence pickups, black, red or white.

1979-1982	H1, black	$3,500	$5,000
1979-1982	H1, red or white	$5,000	$6,500
1979-1982	H2, black	$3,500	$5,000
1979-1982	H2, red or white	$5,000	$6,500

MODEL YEAR	FEATURES	EXC. COND. LOW	HIGH

L Series
1979-1984. Reinforced molded plastic wedge-shaped body, headless neck, 1 (L1) or 2 (L2) low impedence active pickups, black, red or white. Evolved into XL series.

1979-1984	L1, black	$3,000	$4,000
1979-1984	L1, black, fretless	$3,000	$4,000
1979-1984	L1, red or white	$4,500	$6,000
1979-1984	L2, black	$3,000	$4,000
1979-1984	L2, black, fretless	$3,000	$4,000
1979-1984	L2, red or white	$4,500	$6,000

Q-4
1990-1991. Composite neck, Double Bass system, headless with traditional-style maple body, low-impedance pickups.

1990-1991		$2,500	$3,000

Q-5
1990-1991. Five-string version of Q Bass.

1990-1991		$2,500	$3,000

XL-2
1984-1993. Rectangular composite body, 4-string, headless, 2 pickups.

1984-1989		$3,000	$4,000
1990-1993		$3,000	$4,000

XL-2GR
1985-1990. Headless, Roland GR synthesizer controller.

1985-1990		$3,000	$4,000

XM-2
1986-1992. Headless, double-cut maple body, 4-string, 2 low-impedance pickups, optional fretted, lined fretless or unlined fretless, black, red or white.

1986-1992		$3,000	$4,000

XT-2/XZ-2 Spirit
1995 present. Headless, rectangular XL body, import.

1995-2023		$400	$600

Stewart Basses
2000-ca. 2009. Luthier Fred Stewart built his premium grade, custom/production, solidbody basses in Charlton, Maryland. He also built guitars starting in '94.

Stinger
See Martin listing.

Supro
1935-1968, 2004-present. Supro was a budget brand for the National Dobro Company. Supro offered only two bass models in the '60s. The brand name was revived in '04.

Pocket
1960-1968. Double-cut, neck pickup and bridge mounted pickup, semi-hollow, short-scale, black.

1960-1968		$850	$1,250

Taurus
1967-1968. Asymmetrical double-cut, neck pickup and bridge mounted pickup.

1967-1968		$750	$1,000

SX
See listing for Essex.

Tacoma
1995-2009. Professional grade, production, acoustic basses produced in Tacoma, Washington. They also built acoustic guitars and mandolins.

Thunderchief
1998-2009. 17 3/4 flat-top, solid spruce top, solid mahogany back, laminated mahogany sides, rounded cutaway, bolt-on neck, dot markers, natural satin finish.

1998-2009	Various models	$900	$1,750

Taylor
1974-present. Professional and premium grade, production, acoustic basses built in El Cajon, California. They are currently building guitars.

AB1
1996-2003. Acoustic/electric, sitka spruce top, imbuia walnut back and sides, designed for 'loose' woody sound.

1996-2003		$1,500	$2,000

AB2
1996-2003. Acoustic/electric, all imbuia walnut body.

1996-2003		$1,750	$2,500

AB3
1998-2003. Acoustic/electric, sitka spruce top, maple back and sides.

1998-2003		$2,000	$2,500

GS Series
2006-present. Grand Symphony, the GS Mini is scaled-down version.

2006-2023	Various models	$600	$800

Teisco
The Japanese Teisco line started offering basses in the '60s.

Electric
1968-1969. EB-100 (1 pickup, white 'guard), EB-200 (solidbody), EB-200B (semi-hollowbody) and Violin bass.

1968-1969	EB-100	$250	$350
1968-1969	EB-200	$800	$1,000
1968-1969	EB-200 B	$800	$1,000
1968-1969	Violin	$800	$1,000

Tele-Star
1965-ca.1972. Guitars and basses imported from Japan by Tele-Star Musical Instrument Corporation of New York. Primarily made by Kawai, many inspired by Burns designs, some in cool sparkle finishes.

Electric Solidbody

1960s	Various models	$200	$450

Tobias
1977-2019. Founded by Mike Tobias in Orlando, Florida. Moved to San Francisco for '80-'81, then to Costa Mesa, eventually ending up in Hollywood. In '90, he sold the company to Gibson which moved

Teisco Spectrum-Styl

Taylor GS Mini-e

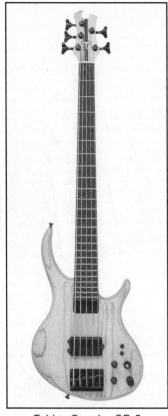

Tobias Growler GR-5

Imaged by Heritage Auctions, HA.com

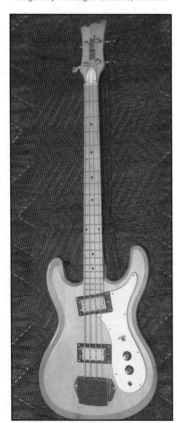

1974 Univox Hi Flier

Greg Boschert

it to Burbank. The first Tobias made under Gibson ownership was serial number 1094. The instruments continued to be made by the pre-Gibson crew until '92, when the company was moved to Nashville. The last LA Tobias/Gibson serial number is 2044. Mike left the company in '92 and started a new business in '94 called MTD where he continues to make electric and acoustic basses. In '99, production of Tobias basses was moved overseas. In late '03, Gibson started again offering U.S.-made Tobias instruments; they are made in Conway, Arkansas, in the former Baldwin grand piano facility. Currently Tobias offers imported and U.S.-made, intermediate and professional grade, production, acoustic and electric basses.

Basic Series
1984-1999. 30", 32", or 34" scale, neck-thru-body in alder, koa or walnut, 5-piece laminated neck.

MODEL YEAR	FEATURES	EXC. COND. LOW	HIGH
1984-1999	Basic B-4	$2,250	$3,000
1984-1999	Basic B-5	$2,250	$3,000

Classic C-4
1978-1999. One or 2 pickups, active or passive electronics, 2-octave rosewood 'board, available in short-, medium-, and long-scale models.

1978-1999		$2,250	$3,000

Classic C-5
1985-1999. 30", 32" or 34" scale, alder, koa or walnut body, book matched top, ebony or phenolic 'board, hardwood neck.

1985-1999		$2,250	$3,000

Classic C-6
Ca. 1986-1999. Flamed maple and padauk neck, alder body, padauk top, ebony 'board, active electronics, 32" or 34" scale.

1986-1999		$2,500	$3,500

Growler GR-5
1996-1999. 5-string, offset double-cut, bolt neck, various colors.

1996-1999		$750	$1,000

Growler Limited
2009. Limited run, natural finish swamp ash body, set neck.

2009		$900	$1,250

Killer Bee
1991-1999. Offset double-cut, swamp ash or lacewood body, various colors.

1991-1999	KB-4	$2,000	$2,750
1991-1999	KB-5	$2,250	$3,000
1991-1999	KB-6	$2,250	$3,000

Model T
1989-1991. Line of 4- and 5-string basses, 3-piece maple neck-thru-body, maple body halves, active treble and bass controls. Fretless available.

1989-1991		$1,750	$2,250

Renegade
1998-2001. Offset double-cut, 1 single-coil and 1 humbucker.

1998-2001		$1,875	$2,500

Signature S-4
1978-1999. Available in 4-, 5-, and 6-string models, chrome-plated milled brass bridge.

1978-1990	Tobias-Burbank	$3,250	$4,500
1990-1992	Gibson-Burbank	$2,875	$4,000

Standard ST-4
1992-1995. Japanese-made, 5-piece maple neck-thru, swamp ash body wings.

MODEL YEAR	FEATURES	EXC. COND. LOW	HIGH
1992-1995		$1,375	$1,750

Toby Deluxe TD-4
1994-1996. Offset double-cut, bolt neck.

1994-1996		$600	$775

Toby Deluxe TD-5
1994-1996. 5-string version.

1994-1996		$650	$850

Toby Pro 5
1994-1996. Solidbody 5-string, Toby Pro logo on truss rod cover, neck-thru body.

1994-1996		$600	$800

Toby Pro 6
1994-1996. Solidbody 6-string, Toby Pro logo on truss rod cover, neck-thru body.

1994-1996		$700	$900

Tokai
1947-present. Tokai started making guitars and basses around '70 and by the end of that decade they were being imported into the U.S. Today Tokai offers electrics, acoustics, and electric basses made in Japan and Korea.

Vintage
1970s-1980s. Tokai offered near copies of classic U.S. basses.

1970s-80s	Copy models	$550	$1,500

Tonemaster
1960s. Guitars and basses, imported from Italy, with typical '60s Italian sparkle plastic finish and push-button controls, bolt-on neck.

Electric

1960s	Various models	$550	$1,000

Traben
Intermediate grade, production, solidbody basses imported by Elite Music Brands of Clearwater, Florida, starting in 2004.

Travis Bean
1974-1979, 1999. The unique Travis Bean line included a couple of bass models. Travis Bean announced some new instruments in '99, but general production was not resumed.

TB-2000
1974-1979. Aluminum neck, T-slotted headstock, longer horned, double-cut body, 2 pickups, 4 controls, dot markers, various colors.

1974-1979		$7,000	$9,000

TB-4000 (Wedge Vee)
1974-1979. Bass version of Bean's Wedge guitar, few made.

1974-1979		$9,000	$11,000

True Tone
1960s. Western Auto retailed this line of basses, guitars and amps which were manufactured by Chicago builders like Kay. The brand was most likely gone by '68.

MODEL YEAR	FEATURES	EXC. COND. LOW	HIGH

Electric

| 1960s | Various models | $250 | $500 |

Univox

1964-1978. Univox started out as an amp line and added guitars and basses around '69. Guitars were imported from Japan by the Merson Musical Supply Company, later Unicord, Westbury, New York. Generally mid-level copies of American designs.

Badazz
1971-ca. 1975. Based on the Guild S-100.

| 1971-1975 | | $500 | $650 |

Bicentennial
1976. Carved eagle in body, matches Bicentennial guitar (see that listing), brown stain, maple 'board.

| 1976 | | $900 | $1,250 |

Hi Flier
1969-1977. Mosrite Ventures Bass copy, 2 pickups, rosewood 'board.

| 1969-1977 | | $600 | $800 |

Model 1970F 'Lectra
1969-ca. 1973. Violin bass, walnut.

| 1969-1973 | | $750 | $1,000 |

Model 3340 Semi-Hollow
1970-1971. Copy of Gibson EB-0 semi-hollow bass.

| 1970-1971 | | $600 | $800 |

Precisely
1971-ca. 1975. Copy of Fender P-Bass.

| 1971-1975 | | $600 | $800 |

Stereo
1976-1977. Rickenbacker 4001 Bass copy, model U1975B.

| 1976-1977 | | $600 | $800 |

Thin Line
1960s. EB-2 style, f-holes, 2 pickups.

| 1960s | | $600 | $800 |

Ventura

1970s. Import classic bass copies distributed by C. Bruno (Kaman). They also had guitars.

Vintage Electric

| 1970s | Copy models | $600 | $800 |

Vox

1954-present. Guitars and basses bearing the Vox name were offered from 1961-'69 (made in England, Italy), '82-'85 (Japan), '85-'88 (Korea), '98-2001 (U.S.), with a limited-edition teardrop bass offered in late '07. Special thanks to Jim Rhoads of Rhoads Music in Elizabethtown, Pennsylvania, for help on production years of these models.

Apollo IV
1967-1969. Single-cut hollowbody, bolt maple neck, 1 pickup, on-board fuzz, booster, sunburst.

| 1967-1969 | | $900 | $1,250 |

Astro IV
1967-1969. Violin-copy bass, 2 pickups.

| 1967-1969 | | $1,000 | $1,500 |

Bassmaster
1961-1965. Offset double-cut, 2 pickups, 2 knobs.

| 1961-1965 | | $800 | $1,125 |

Clubman
1961-1966. Double-cut 2-pickup solidbody, red.

| 1961-1966 | | $550 | $750 |

Constellation IV
1967-1968. Teardrop-shaped body, 2 pickups, 1 f-hole, 1 set of controls, treble, bass and distortion boosters.

| 1967-1968 | | $1,500 | $2,000 |

Cougar
1963-1967. Double-cut semi-hollow body, 2 f-holes, 2 pickups, 2 sets of controls, sunburst.

| 1963-1967 | | $1,000 | $1,500 |

Delta IV
1967-1968. Five-sided body, 2 pickups, 1 volume and 2 tone controls, distortion, treble and bass boosters.

| 1967-1968 | | $3,000 | $4,000 |

Guitar-Organ
1966. The 4-string bass version of the Guitar-Organ, Phantom-style body, white.

| 1966 | Excellent cond | $3,000 | $4,000 |
| 1966 | Functional | $2,000 | $2,500 |

Mark IV
1963-1969. Made in England first (white), then Italy (sunburst), teardrop-shaped body, 2 pickups, 1 set of controls.

| 1963-1965 | England | $2,750 | $3,750 |
| 1965-1969 | Italy | $2,000 | $2,500 |

Panther
1967-1968. Double-cut solidbody, 1 slanted pickup, rosewood 'board, sunburst.

| 1967-1968 | | $750 | $1,000 |

Phantom IV
1963-1969. Made in England first, then Italy, 5-sided body, 2 pickups, 1 set of controls.

| 1963-1964 | England | $3,000 | $4,000 |
| 1965-1969 | Italy | $2,000 | $2,500 |

Saturn IV
1967-1968. Single-cut, 2 f-holes, 1 set of controls, 1 pickup.

| 1967-1968 | | $750 | $1,000 |

Sidewinder IV (V272)
1967-1968. Double-cut semi-hollow body, 2 f-holes, 2 pickups, 1 set of controls, treble, bass, and distortion boosters.

| 1967-1968 | | $1,250 | $1,750 |

Stinger
1968. Teardrop-shaped, boat oar headstock.

| 1968 | | $900 | $1,250 |

Violin
1966. Electro-acoustic bass with violin shaped body, 2 extended range pickups, sunburst.

| 1966 | | $1,250 | $1,750 |

Wyman
1966. Teardrop-shaped body, 2 pickups, 1 f-hole, 1 set of controls, sunburst.

| 1966 | | $1,500 | $2,500 |

1965 Vox Phantom IV
Craig Brody

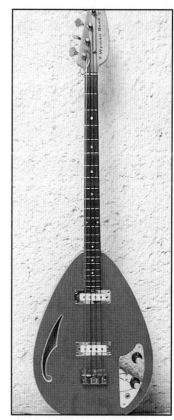

1966 Vox Wyman
Jorge Franco Avila

Wal Pro (Mark I)

MODEL YEAR	FEATURES	EXC. COND. LOW	HIGH

Wal

1976-present. Founded in England by luthier Ian Waller and his partner Peter Stevens, forming the company under the name Electric Wood in '78. Waller died in '88, Stevens enlists help of luthier Paul Herman, and in 2000s Stevens retires and Herman takes over. In the early years, the Mark designation was used generically. Newer contemporary models are named Mk1, Mk2 and Mk3. Prices shown will increase 5% with LED option, or 10% with rare top, but no value difference between fretted and fretless. MIDI electronics does not increase the value.

Custom (IV)

1980s-1990s. 4-string, active, no guard, generally highly figured front and back.

MODEL YEAR	FEATURES	EXC. COND. LOW	HIGH
1980s-90s	Mark I	$8,500	$12,000
1980s-90s	Mark II	$8,500	$12,000
1980s-90s	Mark III	$8,500	$12,000

Custom (V)

1980s-1990s. 5-string, active, no guard, generally highly figured front and back.

1980s-90s	Mark II	$10,500	$15,000
1980s-90s	Mark III	$10,500	$15,000

Custom (VI)

1990s. 6-string, active, no guard, generally highly figured front and back.

1990s	Mark III	$12,500	$16,000

JG

1976-1978. 4-string, passive with either tooled leather (34 made), or leather guard.

1976-1978	Non-tooled	$8,500	$12,000
1976-1978	Tooled	$9,500	$13,000

MODEL YEAR	FEATURES	EXC. COND. LOW	HIGH

Pro

Late-1970s. Passive, black guard.

1970s	Pro I	$5,500	$7,500
1970s	Pro II	$5,500	$7,500

Wandre (Davoli)

Ca. 1956/57-1969. Italian-made guitars and basses.

Electric

1956-1969	Common models	$3,000	$5,000
1956-1969	Rare models	$7,500	$10,000

Warwick

1982-present. Professional and premium grade, production/custom, electric and acoustic basses made in Markneukirchen, Germany; founded by Hans Peter Wilfer, whose father started Framus guitars. They also build amps.

Welson

1960s. Italian-made copy model guitars and basses.

Electric

1960s	Copy models	$150	$400

Wurlitzer

Large music retailer Wurlitzer marketed a line of American-made guitars in the 1920s. They also offered American- and foreign-made guitars starting in '65. In '67, Wurlitzer switched to Italian-made Welson guitars.

Hollowbody Electric

1960s	Italian-made	$500	$750

Yamaha TRB-4

The *Vintage Guitar Price Guide* shows values for all-original, excellent condition instruments and, where applicable, with original case.

MODEL YEAR	FEATURES	EXC. COND. LOW	HIGH

Yamaha
1946-present. Budget, intermediate, professional and premium grade, production, electric basses. They also build guitars. Yamaha began producing solidbody instruments in '66.
Electric
1960-present. Wide variety of models.

1960-2023	Various models	$200	$1,500

Zemaitis
1960-1999, 2004-present. Tony Zemaitis began selling his guitars in '60 and he retired in '99. He emphasized simple lightweight construction, and his instruments are known for hand engraved metal fronts. Each hand-built custom guitar or bass was a unique instrument. Approximately 10 custom guitars were built each year. In '04, Japan's Kanda Shokai, with the endorsement of Tony Zemaitis, Jr., started building the guitars again.

Zen-On
1946-ca.1968. Japanese-made. By '67 using the Morales brand name. Not heavily imported into the U.S., if at all (see Morales).
Electric Solidbody
1950s	Various models	$150	$400

Zim-Gar
1960s. Japanese guitars and basses imported by Gar-Zim Musical Instrument Corporation of Brooklyn, New York.
Electric Solidbody
1960s	Various models	$150	$400

Zon
1981-present. Luthier Joe Zon builds his professional and premium grade, production/custom, solidbody basses in Redwood City, California. Zon started the brand in Buffalo, New York and relocated to Redwood City in '87. He has also built guitars.
Legacy Elite
1989-present. 34" scale carbon-fiber neck, Bartolini pickups, ZP-2 active electronics.
1989-2023	V, 5-string	$1,750	$2,250
1989-2023	VI, 6-string	$1,875	$2,500
Scepter
1984-1993. Offset body shape, 24 frets, 1 pickup, tremolo.
1984-1993		$1,750	$2,250
Sonus Custom
1990s-present. Offset swamp ash body, 2 pickups.
1990s-2023		$2,250	$3,000

Zorko
Late-1950s-early-1962. Original maker of the Ampeg Baby Bass (see that listing), sold to Ampeg in 1962, Zorko logo on scroll.
Baby
1950s-1962		$2,750	$3,500

BASSES

Zemaitis GZB-2500

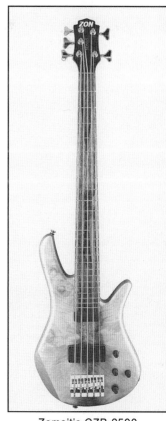
Zemaitis GZB-2500

AMPS

AMPS

3 Monkeys Sock Monkey 18

3rd Power Dragon 45 Combo

Acoustic 115

Rivington Guitars

MODEL YEAR	FEATURES	LOW	HIGH

The price of a vintage amp is affected by three things: the rarity of the amp, the historical significance of the amp, and the "wow" factor. The latter is the most important because the amp is responsible for shaping and coloring most of a purist's vintage tone.

Unlike a guitar, which generates a tiny signal and is usually pampered, the amplifier operates in a high-voltage, high-temperate environment. It was also likely manhandled most of its life. Thus, it's almost impossible to find rare and historically significant amps in excellent cosmetic condition. The only thing that matters to the tone purist is that these amps still function perfectly.

Two prices are shown in the guide. The first is the median value of an all-original amplifier that still functions perfectly. The vast majority of these amps will show signs of wear and tear. The marketplace accepts that these amps need to be regularly maintained. They will likely have grounded electrical plugs and non-original electrolytic capacitors. All other passive components in the electrical circuit should be original.

The second price shown is the premium paid for an all-original amp that functions perfectly and is in excellent cosmetic condition.

The prices shown do not include an original cloth cover. Having the original cover is highly desired.

Traditionally, recovering an amp will result in it losing half its value. A replaced output transformer will also result in lowering the value 40- to 50-percent. Non-original speakers will significantly reduce an amp's value. Alnico speaker replacement is more significant than ceramic speaker replacemen t. The marketplace no longer shuns re-coned speakers since the original paper cones have continuously deteriorated over time. Multi-speaker amps generally have matching speaker codes. Different speaker codes require explanation. Leather handles are often broken and replaced. A replacement handle drops the value of an amp. Grille cloths should have no tears or stains and a single tear can also drop the value of an amp.

3 Monkeys Amps

2007-present. Intermediate and professional grade, production/custom, amps and cabinets built by Greg Howard in Raleigh, North Carolina.

3rd Power

Mid-2009-present. Professional grade, production/custom, guitar amps built in Franklin, Tennessee by Jamie Scott.

65amps

Founded by Peter Stroud and Dan Boul in 2004, 65amps builds tube guitar head and combo amps and speaker cabs in Valley Village, California.

MODEL YEAR	FEATURES	LOW	HIGH

Ace Tone

Late-1960-1970s. Made by Sakata Shokai Limited of Osaka, Japan, early importer of amps and effects pedals. Later became Roland/Boss.

B-9
Late-1960s-early-1970s. Solid-state bass amp head.

| 1960s-70s | | $145 | $195 |

Mighty-5
Late-1960s-early-1970s. Tubes, 50-watt head.

| 1960s-70s | | $115 | $150 |

Solid A-5
Late-1960s-early-1970s. Solidstate 2x12 combo with vertical cab, reverb and tremolo, black tolex, silver grille.

| 1960s-70s | | $165 | $225 |

Acoustic

Ca.1965-ca.1987, 2001-2005, 2008-present. The Acoustic Control Corp., of Los Angeles, California, was mostly known for solidstate amplifiers. Heads and cabinets were sold separately with their own model numbers but were also combined (amp sets) and marketed under a different model number (for example, the 153 amp set was the 150b head with a 2x15" cabinet). The brand was revived by Samick in '01 for a line of amps. In '08 brand back again online of amps sold through Guitar Center and Musician's Friend.

114
Ca.1977-mid-1980s. Solidstate, 50 watts, 2x10", reverb, master volume.

| 1977-1984 | | $250 | $360 |

115
1977-1978. Solidstate, 1x12", 50 watts, reverb, master volume.

| 1977-1978 | | $250 | $360 |

116 Bass
1978-mid-1980s. Solidstate, 75 watts, 1x15", power boost switch.

| 1978-1984 | | $250 | $360 |

120 Head
1977-mid-1980s. Solidstate head, 125 watts.

| 1977-1984 | | $200 | $300 |

123
1977-1984. 1x12" combo.

| 1977-1984 | | $200 | $300 |

124
1977-mid-1980s. Solidstate, 4x10", 5-band EQ, 100 watts, master volume.

| 1977-1984 | | $275 | $400 |

125
1977-mid-1980s. Solidstate, 2x12", 5-band EQ, 100 watts, master volume.

| 1977-1984 | | $275 | $400 |

126 Bass
1977-mid-1980s. Solidstate, 100 watts, 1x15", 5-band EQ.

| 1977-1984 | | $275 | $400 |

134
1972-1976. Solidstate, 100-125 watts, 4x10" combo.

| 1972-1976 | | $275 | $400 |

MODEL YEAR FEATURES	LOW	HIGH

135
1972-1976. Solidstate, 125 watts, 2x12" combo, reverb, tremolo.

1972-1976	$275	$400

136
1972-1976. Solidstate, 125 watts, 1x15" combo.

1972-1976	$275	$400

140 Bass Head
1972-1976. Solidstate, 125 watts, 2 channels.

1972-1976	$200	$300

150 Head
1960s-1976. Popular selling model, generally many available in the used market. Solidstate, 110 watts until '72, 125 watts after.

1968-1976	$250	$350

150b Bass Head
1960s-1971. Bass amp version of 150 head.

1968-1971	$200	$300

153 Bass Set
1960s-1971. 150b head (bass version of 150) with 2x15" 466 cabinet, 110 watts.

1968-1971	$400	$600

165
1979-mid-1980s. All tube combo, switchable to 60 or 100 watts, brown tolex.

1979-1984	$350	$475

220 Bass Head
1977-1980s. Solidstate, 5-band EQ, either 125 or 160 watts, later models 170 or 200 watts, black tolex.

1977-1984	$250	$350

230 Head
1977-1980s. Solidstate head, 125/160 watts, 5-band EQ.

1977-1984	$250	$350

260 Head
1960s-1971. Solidstate, 275 watts, stereo/mono.

1968-1971	$550	$800

261 Head and Cabinet Set
1960s-1971. 275 watts with 2x15" cab.

1969-1971	$2,000	$3,000

270 Head
1970s. 400 watts.

1970s	$350	$500

320 Bass Head
1977-1980s. Solidstate, 5-band EQ, 160/300 watts, 2 switchable channels, black tolex.

1977-1984	$350	$500

360 Bass Head
1960s-1971. One of Acoustic's most popular models, 200 watts. By '72, the 360 is listed as a "preamp only."

1968-1971	$575	$850

370 Bass Head
1972-1977. Solidstate bass head, 365 watts early on, 275 later, Jaco Pastorius associated.

1972-1977 275 or 365 watt	$575	$850

402 Cabinet
1977-1980s. 2x15" bass cab, black tolex, black grille.

1977-1984	$225	$300

404 Cabinet
1970s. 6x10", Jaco Pastorius associated.

1970s	$400	$550

450 Head
1974-1976. 170 watts, 5-band EQ, normal and bright inputs.

1974-1976	$300	$425

455 Set
1974-1977. 170 watts, 450 head with 4x12" cabinet, black.

1974-1977	$575	$850

470 Head
1974-1977. 170 watts, dual channel.

1974-1977	$325	$450

AG15
2008-2016. Small combo, 15 watts.

2008-2016	$35	$45

B100 (MK II)
2008-2016. Classic style bass combo, 100 watts, 1x15.

2008-2016	$125	$175

B200 (MK II)
2009-2019. Bass combo, 200 watts, 1x15.

2009-2019	$175	$250

G20-110
1981-mid-1980s. Solidstate, 20 watts, 1x10". The G series was a lower-price d combo line.

1981-1985	$85	$125

G20-120
1981-mid-1980s. Solidstate, 20 watts, 1x12".

1981-1985	$85	$125

G60-112
1981-mid-1980s. Solidstate, 60 watts, 1x12".

1981-1985	$125	$175

G60-212
1981-mid-1980s. Solidstate, 60 watts, 2x12".

1981-1985	$150	$200

G60T-112
1981-1987. Tube, 60 watts, 1x12".

1981-1985	$250	$350

Tube 60
1986-1987. Combo, 60 watts, 1x12", spring reverb, bright switch, master volume control, effects loop.

1986-1987	$250	$350

ADA

1977-2002. ADA (Analog/Digital Associates) was located in Berkeley, California, and introduced its Flanger and Final Phase in '77. The company later moved to Oakland and made amplifiers, high-tech signal processors, and a reissue of its original Flanger.

Aguilar

1995-present. U.S.-made tube and solidstate amp heads, cabinets, and pre-amps from New York City, New York. They also made effect pedals.

Aiken Amplification

2000-present. Tube amps, combos, and cabinets built by Randall Aiken originally in Buford, Georgia, and since '05 in Pensacola, Florida.

1972 Acoustic 370 Bass
Imaged by Heritage Auctions, HA.com

AMPS

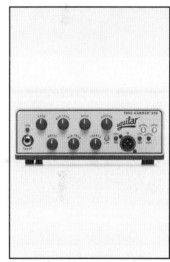

Aguilar Tone Hammer 350

Aiken

Airline Tremolo 2Reverb
Tom Pfeifer

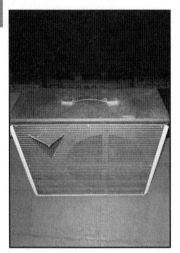

1965 Airline 62-9020A
Thunderbolt
Rivington Guitars

1967 Alamo Fury
Tom Pfeifer

MODEL YEAR	FEATURES	LOW	HIGH

Airline

Ca.1958-1968, 2004-present. Brand for Montgomery Ward, built by Danelectro, Valco and others. In '04, the brand was revived on a line of reissues from Eastwood guitars.

Tube Amp 1x6" Speaker

1958-1960s		$250	$400

Tube Amp 1x8" Speaker

1958-1960s		$350	$500

Tube Amp 1x10" Speaker

1958-1960s		$500	$750

Tube Amp 1x12" Speaker

1958-1960s		$725	$1,250

Tube Amp Higher-End

1958-1960s		$775	$1,250

Tube Amp Highest-End

1958-1960s		$1,000	$1,500

Alamo

1947-1982. Founded by Charles Eilenberg, Milton Fink, and Southern Music, San Antonio, Texas, and distributed by Bruno and Sons. Alamo started producing amps in '49 and the amps were all-tube until '73; solidstate preamp and tube output from '73 to ca. '80; all solidstate for ca. '80 to '82.

Bass Solidstate Preamp-Tube Output

1973-ca.1979. Solidstate preamp section with tube output section, 35 or 40 watts, 15" speakers, combo or piggyback. Models include the Paragon Bass, Paragon Bass Piggyback, Paragon Country Western Bass, Paragon Super Bass, and the Fury Bass.

1973-1979		$165	$225

Bass Tube

1960-1972. Leatherette covered, all tube, 20 to 35 watts, 15" speakers, combo or piggyback, some with Lansing speaker option. Models include the Paragon Special, Paragon Bass, Piggyback Band, Piggyback Bass, Fury Bass, and Paragon Bass (piggyback).

1960-1972		$400	$600

Birch "A" Combo

1949-1962. Birch wood cabinets with A-shaped grill cutout, 2 to 5 tubes. Models include the Embassy Amp 3, Jet Amp 4, Challenger Amp 2, Amp 5, and the Montclair.

1949-1962		$750	$1,500

Mid-Power Solidstate Preamp-Tube Output

1973-ca.1979. Solidstate preamp section with tube output section, 25 watts, 12" speaker, with reverb and tremolo. Models include the Montclair.

1973-1979		$165	$225

Mid-Power Tube

1960-1970. Leatherette covered, all tube, 15 to 30 watts, 12" or 15" speakers, some with tremolo and reverb, some with Lansing speaker option. Models include Montclair, Paragon, Paragon Band, Titan, and Futura.

1960-1970		$500	$750

Small Solidstate Preamp-Tube Output

1973-ca.1979. Solidstate preamp section with tube output section, 3 to 12 watts, 5" to 12" speaker, some

with reverb. Models include the Challenger, Capri, Special, Embassy, Dart, and Jet.

1973-1979		$165	$225

Small Tube

1960-1972. Leatherette covered, all tube, 3 to 10 watts, 6" to 10" speakers, some with tremolo. Models include the Jet, Embassy, Challenger, Capri, Fiesta, Dart, and Special.

1960-1972		$275	$450

Solidstate

Ca.1980-1982. All solidstate.

1980-1982		$45	$65

Twin Speaker Combo (Tube/Hybrid)

1973-ca.1979. Solidstate preamp section with tube output section, 20 or 70 watts, 10", 12" and 15" speaker configurations, some with reverb and tremolo. Models include the 70-watt Paragon Super Reverb Piggybacks, the 45-watt Futura 2x12, and the 20-watt Twin-Ten.

1973-1979		$275	$450

Twin Speaker Tube

1962-1972. Leatherette covered, all tube, up to 45 watts, 8", 10", 12" or 15" speaker configurations, some with tremolo and reverb, some with Lansing speaker option. Models include the Electra Twin Ten, Century Twin Ten, Futuramic Twin Eight, Galaxie Twin Twelve, Galaxie Twin Twelve Piggyback, Piggyback Super Band, Alamo Pro Reverb Piggyback, Futura, Galaxie Twin Ten, Twin-Ten, and Band Piggyback.

1962-1972		$525	$825

Alden

Small budget grade solidstate guitar and bass amps from Muse, Inc. of China.

Alesis

1992-present. Alesis has a wide range of products for the music industry, including digital modeling guitar amps. They also offer guitar effects.

Alessandro

1998-present. Tube amps built by George Alessandro in Huntingdon Valley, Pennsylvania. Founded in '94 as the Hound Dog Corporation, in '98 the company name was changed to Alessandro. The Redbone ('94) and the Bloodhound ('96) were the only models bearing the Hound Dog mark. Serial numbers are consecutive regardless of model (the earliest 20-30 did not have serial numbers). In '98 the company converted to exotic/high-end components and the name changed to Alessandro High-End Products. In '01, he added the Working Dog brand line of amps.

Allen Amplification

1998-present. Tube combo amps, heads and cabinets built by David Allen in Walton, Kentucky. He also offers the amps in kit form and produces replacement and upgrade transformers and a tube overdrive pedal.

The *Vintage Guitar Price Guide* shows values for an all-original condition amplifier, and where applicable, with original cover.

AMPS

MODEL			
YEAR	FEATURES	LOW	HIGH

Allston Amplifiers

2005-present. Professional and premium grade, custom, amps and cabinets built by Rob Lohr in Allston, Massachusetts.

Aloha

Late-1940s. Electric lap steel and amp Hawaiian outfits made for the Dallas-based Aloha.

Ampeg

1949-present. Ampeg was originally primarily known for their bass amps. In the eastern U.S., Ampeg was Fender's greatest challenger in the '60s and '70s bass amplifier market. Currently offering tube and solidstate heads, combos, and speaker cabinets. They have also built guitars.

Amp Covering Dates: Wood veneer 1946-1949, Smooth brown 1949-1952, Dot tweed 1952-1954, Tweed 1954-1955, Rough gray 1957-1958, Rough tan 1957-1958, Cream 1957-1958, Light blue 1958, Navy blue 1958-1962, Blue check 1962-1967, Black pebble 1967, Smooth black 1967-1980, Rough black 1967-1985.

AC-12
1970. 20 watts, 1x12", accordion amp that was a market failure and dropped after 1 year.

1970		$375	$550

AX-44 C
1990-1992. AX hybrid amp with solidstate power section and 1 preamp tube, 22 watts, 2x8 combo.

1990-1992		$175	$225

B-2 Bass
1994-2000. Solidstate, 200 watts, 1x15" combo or 4x8" combo, black vinyl, black grille, large A logo.

1994-2000	1x15"	$350	$500

B-2 R Bass Head
1994-2005. 200 watts, rackmount, replaced by 450-watt B2RE.

1994-2005		$250	$350

B-3
1995-2001. Solidstate head, 150 watts, 1x15".

1995-2001		$350	$475

B-4 Bass Head
1998-2008. Solidstate 1000-watt head, early models made in USA, then outsourced.

1998-2008		$275	$375

B-5 R Bass Head
2000-2005. 500 watts, 2-channel.

2000s		$275	$375

B-12 N Portaflex
1961-1965. 25 watts, 2x12", 2 6L6 power tubes.

1961-1965		$1,875	$2,375

B-12 X/B-12 XT Portaflex
1961-1969 Tube, 50 watts, 2x12", reverb, vibrato, 2x7027A power tubes

1961-1969		$2,000	$2,500

B-15 N (NB, NC, NF) Portaflex
1960-1970. Introduced as B-15 using 2 6L6 power tubes, B-15 N in '61, B-15 NB in '62, B-15 NC with rectifier tube in '64, B-15 NF with fixed-bias 2 6L6 power tubes and 30 watts in '67, 1x15".

1960-1965		$2,000	$2,500

1966-1970	1x15	$2,000	$2,500
1967-1968	2x15	$2,000	$2,500

B-15 R Portaflex (Reissue)
1997-2007. Reissue of '65 Portaflex 1x15", blue check, 60/100 watts.

1997-2007		$1,250	$1,625

B-15 S Portaflex
1971-1977. 60 watts, 2x7027A power tubes, 1x12".

1971-1977		$1,250	$1,625

B-18 N Portaflex
1964-1969. Bass, 50 watts, 1x18".

1964-1969		$1,875	$2,375

B-25
1969 only. 55 watts, 2 7027A power tubes, 2x15", no reverb, guitar amp.

1969		$1,125	$1,750

B-25 B Bass
1969-1980. Bass amp, 55 watts, 2 7027A power tubes, 2x15".

1969-1980		$1,125	$1,750

B-50 R Rocket Bass (Reissue)
1996-2005. 50 watts, 1x12" combo, vintage-style blue check cover.

1996-2005		$250	$400

B-100 R Rocket Bass (Reissue)
1996-2005. Solidstate, 100 watts, 1x15" combo bass amp, vintage-style blue check cover.

1996-2005		$250	$400

B-115
1973-1980. 120 watts, solidstate, 1x15" combo.

1973-1980		$300	$450

B-115 E Cabinet
2006-2017. Bass cab, 1x15".

2006-2017		$200	$300

B-410 Bass
1973-1980. Solidstate, 120 watts, 4x10", black vinyl, black grille.

1973-1980		$400	$575

BA Series
1999-2023. Solidstate bass combo amps, model number is speaker configuration.

1999-2023	Various models	$125	$350

BT-15
1966-1968. Ampeg introduced solidstate amps in '66, the same year as Fender. Solidstate, 50 watts, 1x15", generally used as a bass amp. The BT-15D has 2 1x15" cabinets. The BT-15C is a 2x15" column portaflex cabinet.

1966-1968		$400	$575

BT-18
1966-1968. Solidstate, 50 watts, 1x18", generally used as a bass amp. The BT-18D has dual 1x18" cabinets. The BT-18C is a 2x18" column portaflex cabinet.

1966-1968		$400	$575

Continental I
1956-1959. Single-channel version of Duette, 30 watts, 1x15".

1956-1959		$775	$1,125

1974 Alamo Montclair
Reverb 2565
Tom Pfeifer

1965 Ampeg B-12 X Portaflex
Tom Pfeifer

1969 Ampeg B-15 N
Imaged by Heritage Auctions, HA.com

Ampeg ET-2 Super Echo Twin
Imaged by Heritage Auctions, HA.com

1965 Ampeg GS-12-R
Reverberocket 2
Tom Pfeifer

1968 Ampeg GV-15 Gemini V
Ted Wulfers

Dolphin
1956-1960. Smallest combo offered during this era, 15 watts, 1x12", single-channel (I) and dual-channel (II) options.

		LOW	HIGH
1956-1959	Dolphin I	$550	$800
1956-1960	Dolphin II	$600	$875

Duette
1956-1958. Dual-channel, 3 combo models offered: Zephyr (20w, 1x15"), Continental (30w, 1x15") and Duette 50 D-50 (50w, 2x12", tremolo).

		LOW	HIGH
1956-1958	Continental Duette	$650	$950
1956-1958	Zephyr Duette	$650	$950
1957-1958	Duette 50 D-50	$950	$1,375

ET-1 Echo Twin
1961-1964. Tube, 30 watts, 1x12", stereo reverb.

	LOW	HIGH
1961-1964	$1,000	$1,500

ET-2 Super Echo Twin
1962-1964. Tube, 2x12", 30 watts, stereo reverb.

	LOW	HIGH
1962-1964	$1,125	$1,625

G-12 Gemini I
1964-1971. Tube, 1x12", 22 watts, reverb.

	LOW	HIGH
1964-1971	$750	$975

G-15 Gemini II
1965-1968. Tube, 30 watts, 1x15", reverb.

	LOW	HIGH
1965-1968	$750	$975

G-18
1977-1980. Solidstate, 1 channel, 10 watts, 1x8", volume, treble, and bass controls.

	LOW	HIGH
1977-1980	$80	$125

G-20 Gemini 20
1969-1970. Tubes, 35 watts, 2x10".

	LOW	HIGH
1968-1969	$750	$975

G-110
1978-1980. Solidstate, 20 watts, 1x10", reverb, tremolo.

	LOW	HIGH
1978-1980	$125	$200

G-115
1979-1980. Solidstate, 175 watts, 1x15" JBL, reverb and tremolo, designed for steel guitar.

	LOW	HIGH
1979-1980	$150	$250

G-212
1973-1980. Solidstate, 120 watts, 2x12".

	LOW	HIGH
1973-1980	$225	$325

GS-12 Rocket 2
1965-1968. This name replaced the Reverberocket 2 (II), 15 watts, 1x12".

	LOW	HIGH
1965-1968	$700	$1,125

GS-12-R Reverberocket 2
1965-1969. Tube, 1x12", 18 watts, reverb. Called the Reverberocket II in '68 and '69, then Rocket II in '69.

	LOW	HIGH
1965-1969	$700	$1,125

GS-15-R Gemini VI
1966-1967. 30 watts, 1x15", single channel, considered to be "the accordion version" of the Gemini II.

	LOW	HIGH
1966-1967	$700	$1,125

GT-10
1971-1980. Solidstate, 15 watts, 1x10", basic practice amp with reverb.

	LOW	HIGH
1971-1980	$150	$225

GV-15 Gemini V
1968-1971. Unimusic-era tube amp, 30 watts, 1x15" combo, reverb and tremolo.

	LOW	HIGH
1968-1971	$700	$1,125

GV-22 Gemini 22
Tube, 1x12", reverb, vibrato.

	LOW	HIGH
1969-1972	$800	$1,125

J-12 Jet
1958-1964, 1967-1972. 20 watts, 1x12", 6V6GT power tubes. The second addition, also known as the Jet II, was like the J-12 D Jet but with 12AX7s.

		LOW	HIGH
1958	Rough tan	$600	$775
1959	Blue	$575	$750
1960-1964	Blue	$450	$600
1967-1972	Model reappears	$325	$450

J-12 A Jet
1964. Jet Amp with 7591A power tubes.

	LOW	HIGH
1964	$450	$600

J-12 D Jet
1966. Jet Amp with new solidstate rectifier.

	LOW	HIGH
1966	$425	$550

J-12 R Reverbojet
1967-1970. Part of Golden Glo Series, nicknamed 'copper front', 18 watts, 1x12" combo, single channel, tremolo and reverb, printed circuit replaces point-to-point wiring.

	LOW	HIGH
1967-1970	$450	$600

J-12 T Jet
1965, 2006-2008. J-12 A with revised preamp.

	LOW	HIGH
1965	$450	$600

J-20 Jet
2007-2008. Tubes, 20 watts, 1x12.

	LOW	HIGH
2007-2008	$400	$550

Jet II/J-12 T
2007-2008. 15 watts, 1x12".

	LOW	HIGH
2007-2008	$275	$375

Jupiter
1956-1958. Part of Accordiamp Series, similar to Dolphin except preamp voiced for accordion, 15 watts, 1x12".

	LOW	HIGH
1956-1958	$450	$650

M-12 Mercury
1957-1965. 15 watts, 2 channels, Rocket 1x12".

	LOW	HIGH
1957-1965	$600	$875

M-15 Big M
1959-1965. 20 watts, 2x6L6 power, 1x15".

	LOW	HIGH
1959-1965	$700	$1,125

Model 815 Bassamp
1955. 15-watt combo, 1 channel. Ampeg Bassamp logo on control panel.

	LOW	HIGH
1955	$700	$1,125

Model 820 Bassamp
1956-1958. 20-watt combo, 1 channel.

	LOW	HIGH
1956-1958	$800	$1,250

Model 822 Bassamp
1957-1958. 2 channel 820.

	LOW	HIGH
1957-1958	$825	$1,375

Model 830 Bassamp
1956-1958. 30-watt combo.

	LOW	HIGH
1956-1958	$800	$1,250

Model 835 Bassamp
1959-1961. 35-watt 1x15" combo, 2 channels.

	LOW	HIGH
1959-1961	$800	$1,250

MODEL YEAR	FEATURES	LOW	HIGH

New Yorker
1956-1958. Part of Accordiamp Series, similar to Continental except preamp voiced for accordion, 30 watts, 1x15".

1956-1958		$600	$875

Portabass (PB) Series
2002-2008. Portabass (PB) amps and speaker cabs.

2002-2004	PB-122H Cab	$250	$350
2002-2008	PB-250 Head	$250	$350

Portaflex (PF) Series
2011-present. Portaflex (PF) ultra-compact amp heads offered with flip-top cabs, 350 watt or 500 watt head and 115, 210 or 410 cab options.

2011-2022	PF350 Head	$250	$300
2011-2022	PF500 Head	$250	$300

R-12 Rocket
1957-1963. 12 watts, 1x12", 1 channel.

1957-1963		$600	$875

R-12 B Rocket
1964. 12 watts, 1x12", follow-up to the R-12 Rocket.

1964		$600	$875

R-12 R Reverberocket
1961-1963. Rocket with added on-board reverb.

1961-1963		$775	$1,250

R-12 R Reverberocket (Reissue)
1996-2007. 50 watts, 2xEL34 power tubes, 1x12" (R-212R is 2x12").

1996-2007		$475	$750

R-12 R-B Reverberocket
1964. 7591A power tubes replace R-12-R 6V6 power tubes.

1964		$700	$1,125

R-12 R-T Reverberocket
1965. 7591A or 7868 power tubes, revised preamp.

1965		$700	$1,125

R-15 R Superbreverb (Supereverb)
1963-1964. 1x15 combo, originally called Super-everb, but Fender had a problem with that name.

1963-1964		$850	$1,250

R-50 H Reverberocket
1997-2003. 50-watt head usually sold with a 4x12" bottom, blue check covering.

1997-2003	Head and cab	$500	$750

R-212 R Reverberocket
Combo 50 (Reissue)
1996-2007. 50 watts, 2x12", all tube reissue, vintage-style blue check cover, vintage-style grille.

1996-2007		$500	$750

Rhapsody
1956-1958. Part of Accordiamp Series, similar to Zephyr except preamp voiced for accordion, 20 watts, 1x15".

1956-1958		$600	$875

SB-12 Portaflex
1965-1971. 22 watts, 1x12", designed for use with Ampeg's Baby Bass, black.

1965-1971		$1,125	$1,500

SBT
1969-1971. 120 watts, 1x15", bass version of SST Amp.

1969-1971		$850	$1,250

SE-412 Cabinet
1996-1999. 4x12" speakers.

1996-1999		$250	$400

SJ-12 R/RT Super Jet
1996-2007. 50 watts, tube, 1x12", SJ-12 RT has tremolo added.

1996-2007		$350	$550

SS-35
1987-1992. Solidstate, 35 watts, 1x12", black vinyl, black grille, large A logo.

1987-1992		$150	$225

SS-70
1987-1990. Solidstate, 70 watts, 1x12".

1987-1990		$175	$250

SS-70 C
1987-1992. Solidstate, 70 watts, 2x10", chorus, black vinyl.

1987-1992		$225	$325

SS-140 C
1987-1992. Solidstate, 2x12 combo, chorus and reverb.

1987-1992		$250	$325

SS-150 Head
1987-1992. Solidstate, 150 watts.

1987-1992		$500	$750

SS-412 Cabinet
1987-1992. Matching 4x12 cab for SS series heads.

1987-1992		$300	$450

Super Combo/Model 833 Combo/
Model 950C Super Combo
1956-1960. 30 watts, 3 channels. 950C is 50 watts with 2 15" speakers (very few made).

1956-1957	Super Combo	$775	$1,125
1958	Model 833	$775	$1,125
1959-1960	Model 950C	$775	$1,125

SVT Bass Cabinets
1969-1985. Two 8x10" cabs only.

1969		$1,750	$2,625
1970-1985		$1,625	$2,375

SVT Bass Head
1969-1985. 300-watt head only.

1969	Stones World-Tour Assoc	$2,500	$3,500
1970-1979		$2,125	$3,000
1980-1985		$1,875	$2,500

SVT-II Bass Head
1989-1994. Rackmount, 300 watts, tube.

1989-1994		$900	$1,375

SVT-2 Pro Bass Head
1993-2014. 300 watts, rackmount, tube preamp and power section, black metal.

1993-2014		$950	$1,375

SVT-III Bass Head
1991-1994. Mosfet, 275/450 watts.

1991-1994		$550	$775

SVT-3 Pro Bass Head
1993-present. Tube preamp and MOS-FET power section, 450 watts, rackmount, black metal.

1993-2023		$450	$650

Ampeg J-12 R Reverbojet
Tom Pfeifer

1955 Ampeg 815 Bassamp
Imaged by Heritage Auctions, HA.com

1968 Ampeg SB-12 Portaflex
Tom Pfeifer

AMPS

2008 Ampeg SVT
Micro 210AV Cab

Anderson 45 RT

Andrews Para-Dyne 25

MODEL YEAR	FEATURES	LOW	HIGH
SVT-4 Pro Bass Head			
1997-present. Rackmount, all tube preamp, MOS-FET power section yielding 1600 watts.			
1997-2023		$600	$875
SVT-5 Pro Bass Head			
2002-2005. Rackmount, all tube preamp, MOS-FET power section yielding 1350 watts.			
2002-2005		$600	$875
SVT-6 Pro Bass Head			
2005-2009. Rackmount, all tube preamp, MOS-FET power section yielding 1100 watts.			
2005-2009		$375	$550
SVT-7 Pro Bass Head			
2005-present. Rackmount, all tube preamp, MOS-FET power section yielding 1000 watts.			
2005-2023		$450	$600
SVT-15 E Bass Cabinet			
1994-2017. Compact 1x15.			
1994-2017		$325	$500
SVT-100 T Bass Combo			
1990-1992. Solidstate, ultra-compact bass combo, 100 watts, 2x8".			
1990-1992		$350	$550
SVT-120 Combo			
1990s. Solidstate, compact, 120 watts, 2x8".			
1990s		$225	$325
SVT-200 T Head			
1987 only. Solidstate, 200 watts to 8 ohms or 320 watts to 4 ohms.			
1987		$325	$500
SVT-210 AV Cabinet			
2010. Bass enclosure 2x10, 200 watts.			
2010		$250	$350
SVT-350 Head			
1995-2005. Solidstate head, 350 watts, graphic EQ.			
1995-2005		$400	$650
SVT-400 Head			
1987-1997. Solidstate, 2 200 watt stereo amps, rack-mountable head with advanced (in '87) technology.			
1987-1997		$400	$650
SVT-410 HE/HSVT-410 Bass Cabinet			
1994-present. 4x10, horn/driver. H added to model name in '24.			
1994-2023		$400	$650
SVT-450 H Head			
2007-2017. Solidstate head, 275/450 watts.			
2007-2017		$400	$650
SVT-610 HLF Cabinet			
2003-2023. 6x10, horn/driver.			
2003-2023		$400	$650
SVT-810 E/HSVT-810 Cabinet			
1994-present. 8x10, H added to model name in '24..			
1994-2023		$400	$650
SVT-AV Anniversary Edition			
300-watt head.			
2001		$725	$1,125
SVT-CL/HSVT-CL Classic Bass Head			
1994-present Tube, 300 watts H added to name in '24			
1994-2023		$825	$1,250

MODEL YEAR	FEATURES	LOW	HIGH
SVT-GS Gene Simmons Punisher Head			
1999. SVT-GS logo on front panel, Punisher logo and Simmon's signature also on front panel.			
1999		$1,125	$1,625
SVT-VR Head			
2007. All tube, 300 watts.			
2007		$1,125	$1,500
V-2 Cabinet			
1971-1980. 4x12" cab, black tolex.			
1971-1980		$600	$850
V-2 Head			
1971-1980. 60-watt tube head.			
1971-1980		$700	$1,125
V-3 Head			
1971-1972. 55-watt tube head.			
1971-1972		$750	$1,250
V-4 B Bass Head			
1972-1980. Bass version of V-4 without reverb.			
1972-1980 Head only		$1,000	$1,500
V-4 BH Bass Head			
2007. Reissue.			
2007 Head only		$750	$1,250
V-4 Cabinet			
1970s. Single 4x12" cabinet only.			
1970-1980		$600	$875
V-7 SC			
1981-1985. Tube, 100 watts, 1x12", master volume, channel switching, reverb.			
1981-1985		$625	$950
VH-70			
1991-1992. Varying Harmonics, 70 watts, 1x12" combo with channel switching.			
1991-1992		$300	$450
VH-140 C			
1992-1995. Varying Harmonics (VH) with Chorus (C), two 70-watt channel stereo, 2x12".			
1992-1995		$375	$550
VH-150 Head			
1991-1992. 150 watts, channel-switchable, reverb.			
1991-1992		$375	$450
VL-502			
1991-1995. 50 watts, channel-switchable, all tube.			
1991-1995		$450	$600
VL-1001 Head			
1991-1993. 100 watts, non-switchable channels, all tube.			
1991-1993		$375	$550
VL-1002 Head			
1991-1995. 100 watts, channel-switchable, all tube.			
1991-1995		$400	$575
VT-22			
1970-1980. 100-watt combo version of V-4, 2x12".			
1970-1980		$700	$975
VT-40			
1971-1980. 60-watt combo, 4x10".			
1971-1980		$700	$975
VT-60 Combo			
1989-1991. Tube, 6L6 power, 60 watts, 1x12".			
1989-1991		$325	$500

AMPS

MODEL YEAR	FEATURES	LOW	HIGH

VT-60 Head
1989-1991. Tube head only, 6L6 power, 60 watts.

1989-1991		$375	$550

VT-120 Combo
1989-1992. Tube, 6L6 power, 120 watts, 1x12", also offered as head only.

1989-1992		$375	$550

VT-120 Head
1989-1992. 120 watts, 6L6 tube head.

1989-1992		$375	$550

Zephyr I
1956-1959. Single-channel, 20 watts, 1x15".

1956-1959		$600	$800

Anderson Amplifiers

1993-present. Tube amps and combos built by Jack Anderson in Gig Harbor, Washington.

Andrews

2006-2022. Professional grade, production/custom, amps and cabinets built by Jeff Andrews first in Dunwoody, then Atlanta, Georgia.

ARACOM Amplifiers

1997-present. Jeff Aragaki builds his tube amp heads, combos, and cabinets in Morgan Hill, California.

Area 51

2003-present. Guitar amps made in Newaygo, Michigan (made in Texas until early '06), by Dan Albrecht. They also build effects.

Aria/Aria Pro II

1956-present. The Japanese instrument builder offered a range of amps from around '79 to '89.

Ariatone

1962. Another private brand made by Magnatone, sold by private music and accordion studios.

Model 810
1962. 12 watts, 1x8, tremolo, brown cover.

1962		$550	$800

Ark

Owners Matt Schellenberg and Bill Compeau, started in 2005, build professional and premium grade, production/custom amps in Farmington Hills, Michigan (cabinet shop), with all wiring done in Windsor, Ontario.

Ashdown Amplification

1999-present. Founded in England by Mark Gooday after he spent several years with Trace Elliot, Ashdown offers amps, combos, and cabinets.

Audio Guild

1960s-1974. Audio Guild was already making amps under such brands as Universal and Versatone and others when they launched their own brand in the '60s.

Grand Prix
1969-1974. Tube combo 1x12, reverb and tremolo, dual channel.

1969-1974		$625	$950

Ultraflex
1969-1974. All-tube, higher power combo, 2 speakers, reverb and tremolo.

1969-1974		$900	$1,375

Universal
1960s-1974. Universal was a brand of Audio Guild. Tube combo amp, reverb, tremolo.

1960s-1974		$700	$1,125

Versatone Pan-O-Flex
1960s-1974. Versatone was a brand of Audio Guild. Mid-power tube amp, 1x12" and 1x8" combo, high and low gain input, volume, bass, treble and pan-o-flex balance control knobs, black cover.

1960s-1974		$875	$1,375

Audiovox

Ca.1935-ca.1950. Paul Tutmarc's Audiovox Manufacturing, of Seattle, Washington, was a pioneer in electric lap steels, basses, guitars, and amps.

Auralux

2000-2011. Founded by Mitchell Omori and David Salzmann, Auralux built effects and tube amps in Highland Park, Illinois.

Austin

1999-present. Budget and intermediate grade, production, guitar and bass amps imported by St. Louis Music. They also offer guitars, basses, mandolins, ukes and banjos.

Bacino

Tube combo amps, heads and cabinets built by Mike Bacino in Arlington Heights, Illinois starting in 2002.

Backline Engineering

Gary Lee builds his tube amp heads, starting 2004, in Camarillo, California. He also builds guitar effects.

Bad Cat Amplifier Company

1999-present. Originally located in Corona, California, and now in Santa Ana, Bad Cat offers class A combo amps, heads, cabinets and effects.

Baer Amplification

2009-present. Professional grade, production, bass amps built in Palmdale, California by Roger Baer.

Baldwin

Piano maker Baldwin offered amplifiers from 1965 to '70. The amps were solidstate with organ-like pastel-colored pushbutton switches.

Aria Pro II Revolution II

Ashdown RM-C210T-500
EVO II Combo

Bad Cat Cub IV 15R
Handwired Series

AMPS

AMPS

BC Audio Amplifier No. 9

Behringer VT100FX

Blackwing Black Hawk 15

MODEL YEAR	FEATURES	LOW	HIGH

Exterminator
1965-1970. Solidstate, 100 watts, 2x15"/2x12"/2x7", 4' vertical combo cabinet, reverb and tremolo, Supersound switch and slide controls.

1965-1970		$675	$950

Model B1 Bass
1965-1970. Solidstate, 45 watts, 1x15"/1x12", 2 channels.

1965-1970		$375	$650

Model B2 Bass
1965-1970. Solidstate, 35 watts, 1x15", 2 channels.

1965-1970		$350	$450

Model C1 Custom (Professional)
1965-1970. Solidstate, 45 watts, 2x12", reverb and tremolo, Supersound switch and slide controls.

1965-1970		$500	$1,125

Model C2 Custom
1965-1970. Solidstate, 40 watts, 2x12", reverb and tremolo.

1965-1970		$500	$650

Model D1 Deluxe (Professional)
1965-1970. Solidstate, 30 watts, 1x12", reverb and tremolo, Supersound switch and slide controls.

1965-1970		$500	$1,125

Barcus-Berry
1964-present. Pickup maker Barcus-Berry offered a line of amps from '75 to '79.

Barth
1950s-1960s. Products of Paul Barth's Barth Musical Instrument Company. Barth was also a co-founder of Rickenbacker. He also produced guitars and lap steels.

Studio Deluxe 958
1950s-1960s. Small practice combo amp.

1950s-60s		$500	$650

Basson
Speaker cabinets for guitar, bass and PA made by Victor Basson in Carlsbad, California, starting in 2001.

BC Audio
2009-present. Bruce Clement builds his production/custom, professional grade, tube amps in San Francisco, California.

Bedrock
1984-1997. Tube amp company founded by Brad Jeter and Ron Pinto in Nashua, New Hampshire. They produced 50 amps carrying the brand name Fred before changing the company name to Bedrock in '86. Around '88, Jay Abend joined the company. In '90, Jeter left and, shortly after, Pinto and Abend moved the company to Framingham, Massachusetts. The company closed in '97.

Behringer
1989-present. Founded in Germany by Uli Behringer, offering a full line of professional audio products. In '98 they added tube, solidstate, and modeling amps. They also offer effects and guitars.

Beltone
1950s-1960s. Japan's Teisco made a variety of brands for others, including the Beltone line of amps. There were also guitars sold under this name made by a variety of builders.

Benson
1967-1974. Ron Benson designed and built amps in conjunction with jazz ace Howard Roberts who needed a more versatile amp for recording sessions. Some featured built-in fuzz and plug-in equalizer modules. Originally built in California, later in Seattle. Some 2,000 amps total production.

Big M
1966-1967, 1975-1976. The Marshall name in Germany was owned by a trumpet maker, so Jim Marshall marketed his amps and cabs there under the Big M Made in England brand name until the issue was resolved. A decade later, in a failed attempt to lower speaker cabinets prices in the U.S., Marshall's American distributor-built cabs, with Marshall's permission, on Long Island, mainly for sales with Marshall solidstate lead and bass heads of the time, and labeled them Big M. They were loaded with cheaper Eminence speakers, instead of the usual Celestions.

Cabinet
1975-1976. The M2412 with 4x12 for lead and the M2212F 2x12 bass cabs.

1975-1976	2x12	$425	$550
1975-1976	4x12	$775	$1,000

JTM-45 Head
1966-1967. Branded Big M.

1966-1967		$6,000	$7,750

BigDog Amps
2005-2007. Tube head and combo guitar and bass amps and speaker cabinets built in Galveston, Texas, by Steve Gaines.

Bird
Ca. 1959-1965. Bird built electronic organs in the U.K. and offered tubes amps from around '59 to '65.

Blackstar Amplification
2007-present. Intermediate and professional grade guitar amps and cabinets from Joel Richardson of Northampton, U.K. He also offers effects pedals.

Blackwing
2016-2018. Professional and premium grade head and combo amps, and cabinets built in Corona, California by James Heidrich. He died in '18.

Blankenship Amplification
2005-present. Roy Blankenship builds his tube head and combo amps and cabinets in Northridge, California. He also built amps under the Point Blank brand.

MODEL YEAR	FEATURES	LOW	HIGH

Bluetone Amplifiers

2002-present. Founded by Alex Cooper in Worcestershire, England, Bluetone offers professional grade, production amps employing their virtual valve technology.

Bogen

1932-present. Founded in New York City by David Bogen, this company has made a wide range of electronic products for consumers and industry including a few small guitar combo tube amps such as the GA-5 and GA-20 and tube PA equipment. The company name (David Bogen, New York) and model number are on the lower back panel. The '50s Bogen tube amps are well respected as tone-generating workhorses. In '56 he sold the company, and it was moved to New Jersey, and they continue to offer pro audio PA gear.

Bogner

1988-present. Tube combos, amp heads, and speaker cabinets from builder Reinhold Bogner of North Hollywood, California.

Bolt

Professional grade, production, tube amps and cabinets built in Salt Lake City, Utah starting in 2009. They also built the Morpheus brand effects.

Brand X

2004-2007. Small solidstate combo amps from Fender Musical Instruments Corporation.

Bronson

1930s-1950s. Private brand utilized by Detroit lap steel instructor George Bronson. These amps were often sold with a matching lap steel and were made by other companies.

Lap Steel

MODEL YEAR	FEATURES	LOW	HIGH
1930s-50s	Melody King	$500	$650
1930s-50s	Pearloid	$325	$425
1947	Supreme	$575	$750

Bruno (Tony)

1995-present. Tube combos, amp heads, and speaker cabinets from builder Tony Bruno of Cairo, New York.

Budda

1995-present. Amps, combos, and cabinets originally built by Jeff Bober and Scott Sier in San Francisco, California. In '09, Budda was acquired by Peavey, and they started building Budda products in their Meridian, Mississippi Custom Shop. They also produce effects pedals.

Bugera

2008-present. Uli Behringer builds his budget and intermediate grade, production, tube amps in China. He also offers the Behringer brand.

Burriss

2001-present. Bob Burriss builds custom and production guitar and bass tube amps, bass preamps and speaker cabinets in Lexington, Kentucky. He also builds effects.

Byers

2001-2010. Tube combo amps built by Trevor Byers, in Corona, California. His initial focus was on small early-Fender era and K&F era models.

Cage

1998-present. Production/custom, professional grade, amp heads and cabinets built in Damascus, Maryland by Pete Cage.

California

2004-present. Student/budget level amps and guitar/amp packs, imported by Eleca International.

Callaham

1989-present. Custom tube amp heads built by Bill Callaham in Winchester, Virginia. He also builds solidbody electric guitars.

Campbell Sound

Intermediate and professional grade, production/custom, guitar amps built by Walt Campbell in Roseville, California, starting in 1999.

Carl Martin

1993-present. In '05, the Denmark-based guitar effects company added tube combo amps.

Carlsbro

1959-present. Guitar, bass, and keyboard combo amps, heads and cabinets from Carlsbro Electronics Limited of Nottingham, U.K. They also offer PA amps and speaker cabinets.

Carol-Ann Custom Amplifiers

2003-2022. Premium grade, production/custom, tube guitar amps built by Alan Phillips in North Andover, Massachusetts.

Carr Amplifiers

1998-present. Steve Carr started producing amps in his Chapel Hill, North Carolina amp repair business in '98. The company is now located in Pittsboro, North Carolina, and makes tube combo amps, heads, and cabinets.

Artemus

2010-2015. Combo 1x12", 15/30 watts.

2010-2015		$1,500	$2,000

Bloke

2012-2015. 48 watts, 1x12".

2012-2015	1x12"	$1,250	$1,750

Hammerhead MK 1/MK 2

2000-2004 (MK 1), 2004-2008 (MK 2). 25 watts (28 for MK 2), head or combo, 1x12", 2x10" or 2x12".

2000-2004	2x12" combo	$1,000	$1,500

Bogner Mephisto

Budda Superdrive 30 Series II 212 Combo

Carlsbro 60TC

AMPS

Carr Amplifiers Impala

Carr Mercury V

Crate Vintage Club 5212

Imaged by Heritage Auctions, HA.com

MODEL YEAR	FEATURES	LOW	HIGH
Impala			
2013-present. Combo 1x12", 44 watts - max 55 watts, reverb.			
2013-2023		$1,750	$2,250
Imperial Combo			
2000-2004. 60 watts, with 1x15", 2x12" or 4x10".			
2000-2004 4x10"		$1,750	$2,500
Lincoln			
2016-2018. Combo 1x12", 6 watts - max 18 watts, 2 channels.			
2016-2018		$1,500	$2,000
Mercury Combo			
2002-2014. 1x12", tube, 8 watts, reverb, built-in attenuator.			
2002-2014		$1,625	$2,250
Mercury V			
2017-present. Combo 1x12", 16 watts, built in attenuator.			
2017-2023		$1,625	$2,250
Raleigh			
2008-present. Practice/studio amp, 1x10", 3 watts.			
2008-2023		$1,000	$1,500
Rambler			
1999-present. Class A, tubes, 28 watts pentode/14 watts triode, with 1x12", 2x10", 2x12" or 1x15" speakers.			
1999-2019 1x12"		$1,625	$2,000
1999-2023 2x12"		$1,875	$2,500
Skylark			
2014-present. 12 watts, 1x12" with built in attenuator.			
2014-2023		$1,875	$2,500
Slant 6V (Dual 6V6)			
1998-2023. 40 watts, 2 channel, combo amp, 2x12" or 1x15", also available as a head.			
1998-2023		$1,875	$2,500
Sportsman			
2011-present. Available in 1x12 and 1x10 combos and head, 16-19 watts.			
2011-2023 1x12"		$1,375	$2,000
Telstar			
2018-present. Combo 17-watt with built in attenuator.			
2018-2023		$1,625	$2,250
Viceroy			
2006-2018. Class A, tubes, 33 or 7 watts, 1x12" or 1x15".			
2006-2018		$1,625	$2,250

Carvin

1946-present. Founded in Los Angeles by Lowell C. Kiesel who sold guitars and amps under the Kiesel name until late-'49, when the Carvin brand was introduced. They added small tube amps to their product line in '47 and today offer a variety of models. They also build guitars, basses and mandolins.

Caswell Amplification

2006-present. Programmable tube amp heads built by Tim Caswell in California.

Chicago Blues Box/ Butler Custom Sound

Tube combo amps built by Dan Butler of Butler Custom Sound originally in Elmhurst, then Lombard, Illinois. He began in 2001.

Clark Amplification

1995-present. Tweed-era replica tube amplifiers from builder Mike Clark, of Cayce, South Carolina. He also makes effects.

Club Amplifiers

2005-present. Don Anderson builds intermediate to premium grade, custom, vacuum tube guitar amps and cabinets in Felton, California.

CMI

1976-1977. Amps made by Marshall for Cleartone Musical Instruments of Birmingham, U.K. Mainly PA amps, but two tube heads and one combo amp were offered.

CMI Electronics

Late-1960s-1970s. CMI branded amplifiers designed to replace the Gibson Kalamazoo-made amps that ceased production in '67 when Gibson moved the electronics lab to Chicago, Illinois.

MODEL YEAR	FEATURES	LOW	HIGH
Sabre Reverb 1			
Late-1960s-early-1970s. Keyboard amp, 1x15" and side-mounted horn, utilized mid- to late-'60s cabinets and grilles, look similar to mid-late '60s Gibson black tolex and Epiphone gray amp series, black or gray tolex and silver grille.			
1960s-70s		$350	$450

CMW Amps

2002-present. Chris Winsemius builds his premium grade, production/custom, guitar amps in The Netherlands.

Colby

2012-present. Professional and premium grade, production/custom, tube amp heads, combos and cabinets built by Mitch Colby in City Island, New York. He also builds Park amps.

Comins

1992-present. Archtop luthier Bill Comins, of Willow Grove, Pennsylvania, introduced a Comins combo amp, built in collaboration with George Alessandro, in '03.

Coral

1967-1969. In '66 MCA bought Danelectro and in '67 introduced the Coral brand of guitars, basses and amps. The amp line included tube, solidstate, and hybrid models ranging from small combo amps to the Kilowatt (1000 Watts of Peak Power!), a hybrid head available with two 8x12" cabinets.

MODEL YEAR	FEATURES	LOW	HIGH

Cornell/Plexi

Amps based on the '67 Marshall plexi chassis built by Denis Cornell in the U.K. Large Plexi logo on front.

Cosmosound

Italy's Cosmosound made small amps with Leslie rotating drums in the late '60s and '70s. They also made effects pedals.

Crafter USA

1986-present. Giant Korean guitar and bass manufacturer Crafter also builds an acoustic guitar amp.

Crate

Solidstate and tube amplifiers originally distributed by St. Louis Music, beginning in 1979. In '05 LOUD Technologies acquired SLM and the Crate brand.

CA Series
1995-2005. Crate Acoustic series.

1995-2005		$195	$450

Solidstate
1979-1990s. Various student to mid-level amps, up to 150 watts.

1979-90s		$75	$125

Vintage Club Series
1994-2001. Tube amps.

1994-2001	Various models	$300	$650

XT Series
2000s. Solid State series.

2000s	XT-120R	$80	$125

Cruise Audio Systems

1999-2003. Founded by Mark Altekruse, Cruise offered amps, combos, and cabinets built in Cuyahoga Falls, Ohio. It appears the company was out of business by '03.

Cruzer

Solidstate guitar amps built by Korea's Crafter Guitars. They also build guitars, basses and effects under that brand.

Custom Kraft

Late-1950s-1968. A house brand of St. Louis Music Supply, instruments built by others. They also offered basses and guitars.

Import Student

1960s	1x6 or 1x8	$75	$125

Valco-Made

1960s	1x12 or 1x15	$450	$575

Da Vinci

Late-1950s-early-1960s. Another one of several private brands (for example, Unique, Twilighter, Titano, etc.) that Magnatone made for teaching studios and accordion companies.

D60 Custom
1965. 2x12", reverb, vibrato.

1965		$1,500	$2,000

Model 250
1958-1962. Similar to Magnatone Model 250 with about 20 watts and 1x12".

1958-1962		$1,375	$1,750

Model 440A/D40 Custom
1964-1966. 1x12", reverb, vibrato.

1964-1966		$1,500	$2,000

Danelectro

1946-1969, 1997-present. Founded in Red Bank, New Jersey, by Nathan I. "Nate" or "Nat" Daniel. His first amps were made for Montgomery Ward in '47, and in '48 he began supplying Silvertone Amps for Sears. His own amps were distributed by Targ and Dinner as Danelectro and S.S. Maxwell brands. In '96, the Evets Corporation, of San Clemente, California, reintroduced the Danelectro brand on effects, amps, basses, and guitars. In early '03, Evets discontinued the amp line, but still offers guitars, basses, and effects.

DM-10
1965-1967. Combo 'large knobs' cabinet, 10 watts, 1x8", 2 control vibrato, 2 inputs, 1 volume, 1 tone, dark vinyl with light grille, DM-10 logo next to script Danelectro logo right upper front.

1965-1967		$300	$450

DM-25
1965-1967. Stow-away piggyback, 25 watts, 1x12", reverb, vibrato, 4 inputs, 9 control knobs, dark vinyl cabinet with light grille, DM-25 logo next to script Danelectro logo below control knobs.

1965-1967		$700	$1,125

DS-50
1965-1969. 75 watts, 3x10" stow-away piggyback cabinet, reverb and tremolo, suitable for bass accordion.

1965-1969		$850	$1,250

DS-100
1967-1969. 150 watts, stow-away piggyback cabinet, 6x10" Jensens, reverb, tremolo, suitable for bass accordion, 36x22x12" cabinet weighs 79 lbs.

1965-1969		$1,250	$1,750

DTR-40
1965. Solidstate combo, 40 watts, 2x10", vibrato, DTR-40 logo under control knobs.

1965		$400	$575

Model 68 Special
1954-1957. 20 watts, 1x12", light tweed-fabric cover, light grille, leather handle, script Danelectro plexi-plate logo.

1954-1957		$550	$800

Model 72 Centurion
1954-1957. Series D 1x12" combo, blond tweed, rounded front D cabinet.

1954-1957		$550	$800

Model 78A Artist
1954-1957. Artist Series D, 115 watts,

1954-1957		$550	$800

Model 88 Commando
1954-1957. Series D, 25 watts with 4x6V6 power, suitcase-style amp with 8x8" speaker, light beige cover.

1954-1957		$2,000	$3,000

Cruzer CR-15RG

Danelectro Cadet
Erick Warner

Danelectro 68
Erick Warner

AMPS

1961 Danelectro 142 Viscount
Rivington Guitars

DeArmond R-5T Studio
Imaged by Heritage Auctions, HA.com

Demeter TGA-2.1

MODEL YEAR	FEATURES	LOW	HIGH

Model 89 Challenger
1954-1957. Series D 1x15" combo, blond tweed, rounded front D cabinet.

1954-1957		$450	$625

Model 98 Twin 12
1954-ca.1957. Rounded front Series D 2x12", blond tweed-style cover, brown control panel, vibrato speed and strength.

1954-1957		$950	$1,375

Model 122 Cadet
1955-1969. A longstanding model name, offered in different era cabinets and coverings but all using the standard 3-tube 1x6" format. Models 122 and 123 had 6 watts. 1x6", 3 tubes, 1 volume, 1 control, 2 inputs, 16x15x6" 'picture frame' cabinet with light-colored cover, dark grille.

1955-1969	Various models	$225	$325

Model 132 Corporal
1962-1964. 2x8", 4 tubes, 3 inputs, 4 control knobs, 19x15x7" picture frame cabinet in light-colored material with dark grille.

1962-1964		$350	$500

Model 142 Viscount
Late-1950s. Combo amp, lower watts, 1x12", light cover, brown grille, vibrato.

1959		$550	$775

Model 143 Viscount
1962-1964. 12 watts, 1x12", 6 tubes, 2 control vibrato, 1 volume, 1 tone, 'picture frame' narrow panel cabinet, light-colored cover with dark grille.

1962-1964		$450	$650

Model 217 Twin-Fifteen
1962-1964. Combo amp, 60 watts, 2x15" Jensen C15P speakers, black cover, white-silver grille, 2 channels with tremolo.

1962-1964		$1,000	$1,500

Model 274 Centurion
1961-1962. 15 watts, 1x12", 6 tubes, 2 channels with separate volume, treble, bass controls, Vibravox electronic vibrato, 4 inputs, 20x20x9 weighing 25 lbs., 'picture frame' cabinet with black cover and light grille.

1961-1962		$475	$725

Model 275 Centurion
1963-1964. Reverb added in '63, 15 watts, 1x12", 7 tubes, Vibravox vibrato, 2 channels with separate volume, bass, treble, picture frame cabinet with black cover and light grille.

1963-1964		$600	$900

Model 291 Explorer
1961-1964. 30 watts, 1x15", 7 tubes, 2 channels each with volume, bass, and treble controls, Vibravox vibrato, square picture frame cabinet, black cover and light grille.

1961-1964		$575	$850

Model 300 Twin-Twelve
1962-1964. 30 watts, 2x12", reverb, 8 tubes, 2 channels with separate volume, bass, and treble, Vibravox vibrato, picture frame cabinet with black cover and light grille.

1962-1964		$900	$1,250

MODEL YEAR	FEATURES	LOW	HIGH

Model 354 Twin-Twelve
Early 1950s. Series C twin 12" combo with diagonal speaker baffle holes, brown cover with light gold grille, Twin Twelve script logo on front as well as script Danelectro logo, diagonally mounted amp chassis, leather handle.

1950s		$1,250	$1,750

Dean
1976-present. Acoustic, electric, and bass amps made overseas. They also offer guitars, banjos, mandolins, and basses.

Dean Markley
The string and pickup manufacturer added a line of amps in 1983. Distributed by Kaman, they now offer combo guitar and bass amps and PA systems.

K Series
1980s. All solidstate, various models include K-15 (10 watts, 1x6"), K-20/K-20X (10 to 20 watts, 1x8", master volume, overdrive switch), K-50 (25 watts, 1x10", master volume, reverb), K-75 (35 watts, 1x12", master volume, reverb), K-200B (compact 1x12 combo).

1980s	K-15, K20, K20X	$45	$60
1980s	K-200B	$135	$185
1980s	K-50	$45	$65
1980s	K-75	$75	$100

DeArmond
Pickup manufacturer DeArmond started building tube guitar amps in 1950s. By '63, they were out of the amp business. They also made effects. Fender revived the name for a line of guitars in the late '90s.

R-5T Studio
1959-1960. 1x10", low power, 1-channel, brown.

1959-1960		$3,000	$4,000

R-15
1959-1961. 1x12", 15 watts, 2 channels, no tremolo, tan.

1959-1961		$3,500	$4,500

R-15T/Model 112
1959-1961. 1x12", 15 watts, 2 channels, tremolo, tan.

1959-1961		$3,750	$5,000

Decca
Mid-1960s. Small student-level amps made in Japan by Teisco and imported by Decca Records. They also offered guitars and a bass.

Demeter
1980-present. James Demeter founded the company as Innovative Audio and renamed it Demeter Amplification in '90. Originally located in Van Nuys, in '08 they moved to Templeton, California. The first products were direct boxes and by '85, amps were added. Currently they build amp heads, combos, and cabinets. They also have pro audio gear and guitar effects.

Devilcat
2012-present. Professional grade, production/custom, tube amps built in Statesboro, Georgia by Chris Mitchell.

AMPS

MODEL YEAR	FEATURES	LOW	HIGH

Diaz

Cesar Diaz restored amps for many of rock's biggest names, often working with them to develop desired tones. By the early '80s he was producing his own line of professional and premium grade, high-end custom amps and effects. Diaz died in '02; his widow Maggie and longtime friend Peter McMahon resumed production in '04 under Diaz Musical Products.

Dickerson

1937-1947. Dickerson was founded by the Dickerson brothers in 1937, primarily for electric lap steels and small amps. Instruments were also private branded for Cleveland's Oahu company, and for the Gourley brand. By '47, the company changed ownership and was renamed Magna Electronics (Magnatone). Amps were usually sold with a matching lap steel.

Oasis

1940s. Blue pearloid cover, 1x10", low wattage, Dickerson silk-screen logo on grille with Hawaiian background.

1940s		$350	$475

Dime Amplification

2011-ca. 2014. Solidstate combo and head amps and cabinets from Dean Guitars, designed by Gary Sunda and Grady Champion.

Dinosaur

2004-2015. Student/budget level amps and guitar/amp packs, imported by Eleca International. They also offered effects.

Divided By Thirteen

Mid-1990s-present. Fred Taccone builds his tube amp heads and cabinets in the Los Angeles, California area. He also builds effects.

Dr. Z

1988-present. Mike Zaite started producing his Dr. Z line of amps in the basement of the Music Manor in Maple Heights, Ohio. The company is now located in its own larger facility in the same city. Dr. Z offers combo amps, heads and cabinets.

Drive

Ca. 2001-ca. 2011. Budget grade, production, import solidstate amps. They also offered guitars.

DST Engineering

2002-2014. Jeff Swanson and Bob Dettorre built their tube amp combos, heads and cabinets in Beverly, Massachusetts. They also built reverb units.

Duca Tone

The Duca Tone brand was distributed by Lo Duca Brothers, Milwaukee, Wisconsin, which also distributed EKO guitars in the U.S.

MODEL YEAR	FEATURES	LOW	HIGH

Tube

1950s. 12 watts, 1x12".

1950s		$625	$800

Dumble

1963-2022. Made by Howard Alexander Dumble, an early custom-order amp maker from California. Initial efforts were a few Mosrite amps for Semie Moseley. The first shop was in '68 in Santa Cruz, California. Early on, Dumble also modified other brands such as Fender and those Dumble-modified amps are also valuable, based on authenticated provenance. Top dollar goes for combos or heads with the cab. A head alone would be 10-20% lower. Higher values are considered for an amp that has not been modified in any way, unless the mod is certified as being done by Dumble. The used/vintage Dumble market is a sophisticated luxury-market for those musicians and collectors that are wealthy enough to afford these amps. Each amplifier's value should be considered on a case-by-case basis. Dealers have reported that some Dumble amplifiers will sell upwards from $150,000 to $250,000. Mr. Dumble died January 2022.

Dynamic Amps

2008-present. David Carambula builds production/custom, professional grade, combo amps, heads and cabinets in Kalamazoo, Michigan.

Dynamo

2010-present. Professional and premium grade, production/custom, amps and cabinets built by Ervin Williams in Lake Dallas, Texas.

Earth Sound Research

1970s. Earth Sound was a product of ISC Audio of Farmingdale, New York, and offered a range of amps, cabinets and PA gear starting in the '70s. They also made Plush amps.

2000 G Half-Stack

1970s. 100 watts plus cab.

1970s		$575	$750

Model G-1000 Head

1970s	Reverb	$300	$500

Original 2000 Model 340

1970s. Black Tolex, 400-watt head and matching 2x15" cab.

1970s		$575	$750

Producer Model 440

1970s. 700-watt head and matching 2x15" cab.

1970s		$575	$750

Revival

1970s. 2x12" tweed twin copy, with similar back mounted control panel, tweed covering, but with solid-state preamp section and 4x6L6 power.

1970		$575	$750

Super Bass/B-2000

1970s. Tuck & roll black cover, 2 channels - super and normal, volume, bass, mid range, and treble tone controls, no reverb or tremolo.

1970s	Cabinet	$275	$375
1970s	Head only	$300	$500

Devilcat Gussie Combo

Dr. Z Z-Lux

Dynamo GTS

AMPS

Egnater Rebel 30 MK2

Eleca California

Electro-Harmonix Dirt
Road Special

Traveler
1970s. Vertical cab solidstate combo amp, 50 watts, 2x12 offset, black tolex.

MODEL YEAR	FEATURES	LOW	HIGH
1977		$550	$750

EBS
1988-present. The EBS Sweden AB company builds professional grade, production bass amps and cabinets in Stockholm, Sweden. They also build effects.

EchoSonic
1950s. Tube combo amps with built-in tape echo built by Ray Butts in Cairo, Illinois, with the first in '53. Used by greats such as Chet Atkins, Scotty Moore and Carl Perkins, probably less than 70 were made. Butts also developed the hum bucking Filter'Tron pickup for Gretsch.

Eden
1976-2011. Founded by David Nordschow in Minnesota as a custom builder, Eden offered a full line of amps, combos, and cabinets for the bassist, built in Mundelein, Illinois. In '02, the brand became a division of U.S. Music Corp (Washburn, Randall), they also produce the Nemesis brand of amps. In '11 Eden was sold to Marshall.

Egnater
1980-present. Production/custom, intermediate and professional grade, tube amps, combos, preamps and cabinets built in Berkley, Michigan by Bruce Egnater. He also imports some models.

Rebel
2008-present. 20-watt head, 1x12" cabinet.

		LOW	HIGH
2008-2023		$500	$750

Renegade Head
2009-present. 65 watts, 2 channel head.

2009-2023		$500	$750

Tourmaster Series
2009-present. 100-watt, all-tube amp and combo.

2009-2023	Various models	$500	$750

Tweaker
2013-present. 15 to 88-watt tube heads and cabinets.

2013-2023	1x12 combo	$450	$700
2013-2023	40-watt head/1x12 cab	$500	$750

EKO
1959-1985, 2000-present. In '67 EKO added amps to their product line, offering three piggyback and four combo amps, all with dark covering, dark grille, and the EKO logo. The amp line may have lasted into the early '70s. Since about 2000, EKO Asian-made, solidstate guitar and bass amps are again available. They also make basses and guitars.

El Grande
1951-1953. Built by Chicago's Valco Manufacturing Co. and sold together with lap steels. El Grande logo on front, Valco logo on back chassis, all have burgundy and white covering.

Valco Spectator
1951-1953. Same as Supro Spectator, 1x8", 5 watts, volume and tone.

MODEL YEAR	FEATURES	LOW	HIGH
1951-1953		$400	$575

Eleca
2004-present. Student level imported combo amps, Eleca logo on bottom of grille. They also offer guitars, effects and mandolins.

Electar
1996-2008. The Gibson owned Electar brand offered tube and solidstate amps, PA gear and wireless systems. Though branded separately, Electar amps were often marketed with other Epiphone products, so see them listed there. Epiphone also had amp models named Electar in the 1930s.

Electro-Harmonix
1968-1981, 1996-present. Electro-Harmonix has offered a few amps to go with its line of effects.

Freedom Brothers
Introduced in 1977. Small AC/DC amp with 2x5 1/2" speakers. E-H has reissued the similar Freedom amp.

1977		$275	$400

Mike Matthews Dirt Road Special
1970s. 25 watts, 1x12" Celestion, built-in Small Stone phase shifter. A 40-watt version was released in 2019.

1977		$275	$400

Electromuse
1940s-1950s. Tube amps made by others, like Valco, and usually sold as a package with a lap steel. They also offered guitars.

Various Models
Late-1940s. Vertical cabinet with metal handle, Electromuse stencil logo on front of cab.

1948-1949	Lower power	$325	$450

Electrosonic Amplifiers
2002-2009. Intermediate and professional grade, production/custom, tube amps built by Josh Corn in Boonville, Indiana. He also builds effects.

Elk
Late-1960s. Japanese-made by Elk Gakki Co., Ltd. Many were copies of American designs. They also offered guitars and effects.

Custom EL 150L
Late-1960s. Piggyback set, all-tube with head styled after very early Marshall and cab styled after large vertical Fender cab.

1968		$400	$525

Guitar Man EB 105 (Super Reverb)
Late-1960s. All-tube, reverb, copy of blackface Super Reverb.

1968		$400	$525

Twin 60/Twin 50 EB202
Late-1960s. All-tube, reverb, copy of blackface Dual Showman set (head plus horizontal cab).

1968		$400	$525

MODEL YEAR	FEATURES	LOW	HIGH

Viking 100 VK 100
Late-1960s. Piggyback set, head styled after very early Marshall and cab styled after very large vertical Fender cab.

1968		$400	$525

Elmwood Amps
1998-2015. Jan Alm builds his production/custom, professional and premium grade, guitar tube amps and cabinets in Tanumshede, Sweden.

Elpico
1960s. Made in Europe, PA tube amp heads are sometimes used for guitar.

PA Power Tube
1960s. Tubes, 20-watt, metal case, 3 channels, treble and bass control, 2 speaker outs on front panel, Elpico logo on front, small Mexican characterization logo on front.

1960s		$425	$575

Emery Sound
1997-present. Founded by Curt Emery in El Cerrito, California, Emery Sound specializes in custom-made low wattage tube amps.

Emmons
1970s-present. Owned by Lashley, Inc. of Burlington, North Carolina. Amps sold in conjunction with their steel guitars.

Epiphone
1928-present. Epiphone offered amps into the mid-'70s and reintroduced them in '91 with the EP series. Currently they offer tube and solidstate amps.

Century
1939. Lap steel companion amp, 1x12" combo, lattice wood front with Electar insignia "E" logo.

1939		$525	$750

Cornet
1939. Lap steel companion amp, square shaped wood box, Electar insignia "E" logo.

1939		$425	$600

E-30B
1972-1975. Solidstate model offered similarly to Gibson G-Series (not GA-Series), 30 watts, 2x10", 4 knobs.

1972-1975		$175	$250

E-60
1972-1975. Solidstate, 30 watts, 1x10", volume and tone knobs.

1972-1975		$150	$200

E-60T
1972-1975. E-60 with tremolo, volume, tone, and tremolo knobs.

1972-1975		$150	$200

E-70T
1971-1975. Solidstate, tremolo, 1x10", 3 knobs.

1971-1975		$150	$200

E-1051
Ca. 1971-1974. Tube practice amp, 1x10".

1971-1974		$175	$250

EA-12 RVT Futura
1962-1967. 50 watts, originally 4x8" but 4x10" by at least '65, '60s gray tolex, light grille.

1962-1967		$650	$850

EA-14 RVT Ensign
1965-1969. Gray tolex, silver-gray grille, 50 watts, 2x10", split C logo.

1965-1969		$600	$850

EA-15 RVT Zephyr
1961-1965. 14 or 20 watts, 1x15", gray tolex, light grille, split C logo on panel, tremolo and reverb, script Epiphone logo lower right grille.

1961-1965		$600	$850

EA-16 RVT Regent
1965-1969. 25 watts, 1x12", gray vinyl, gray grille, tremolo, reverb. Called the Lancer in first year.

1965-1969		$500	$700

EA-22 RVT Mighty Mite
1964-1967. 1x12", mid-level power, stereo, reverb, vibrato, old style rear mounted control panel.

1964-1967		$1,125	$1,500

EA-26 RVT Electra
1965-1969. Gray tolex, reverb, tremolo, footswitch, 1x12".

1965-1969		$500	$700

EA-28 RVT Pathfinder
Mid-1960s. Similar to Gibson's GA-19 RVT, medium power, 1x12, reverb and tremolo.

1964-1966		$500	$700

EA-30 Triumph
1959-1961. Low-power, limited production, 1x12, light colored cover, 3 knobs.

1959-1961		$950	$1,250

EA-32 RVT Comet
1965-1967. 1x10", tremolo, reverb.

1965-1967		$500	$700

EA-33 RVT Galaxie
1963-1964. Gray tolex, gray grille, 1x10".

1963-1964		$500	$700

EA-35 Devon
1961-1963. 1x10" until '62, 1x12" with tremolo in '63.

1961-1963		$500	$700

EA-35T Devon
1963. Tremolo, 6 knobs.

1963		$500	$700

EA-50 Pacemaker
1961-1969. 1x8" until '62, 1x10" after. EA-50T with tremolo added in '63. Non-tremolo version dropped around '67.

1961-1965	1x8	$450	$650
1966-1969	1x10	$500	$700

EA-300 RVT Embassy
1965-1969. 90 watts, 2x12", gray vinyl, gray grille, tremolo, reverb.

1965-1969		$700	$950

EA-500T Panorama
1963-1967. 65 watts, head and large cabinet, tremolo, 1x15" and 1x10" until '64, 1x15" and 2x10" after.

1964-1967		$550	$750

Elmwood Bonneville 50

Epiphone EA-30 Triumph
Imaged by Heritage Auctions, HA.com

Epiphone EA-50 Pacemaker
Imaged by Heritage Auctions, HA.com

AMPS

Evans Custom
Amplifiers AE200

EVH 5150 III 50-Watt

E-Wave G-158R

MODEL YEAR	FEATURES	LOW	HIGH

EA-600 RVT Maxima
1966-1969. Solidstate Epiphone version of Gibson GSS-100, gray vinyl, gray grille, two 2x10" cabs and hi-fi stereo-style amp head.

1966-1969		$400	$550

Electar
1935-1939. All models have large "E" insignia logo on front, first model Electar in rectangular box with 1x8" speaker, 3 models introduced in '36 (Model C, Model M, and Super AC-DC), the Special AC-DC was introduced in '37, later models were 1x12" combos. Old Electar amps are rarely found in excellent working condition and the prices shown are for those rare examples.

1935	Electar	$550	$750
1936-1939	Model C	$750	$1,125
1936-1939	Model M	$750	$1,125
1936-1939	Super AC-DC	$875	$1,250
1937-1939	Special AC-DC	$875	$1,250

Electar Tube 10
1997-2004. These modern Electar amps were branded as Electar, not Epiphone, but since they were often marketed with other Epi products, they are included here. 10-watt combo, all tube, 8" speaker.

1997-2004		$125	$175

Electar Tube 30
1997-2004. 30-watt combo, all tube, 10" speaker, reverb added in 2002.

1997-2004		$125	$175

Model 100
1965-1967. Made in Kalamazoo, label with serial number, Model 100 logo on small 10" speaker, blue cover, 3 tubes, 3 knobs.

1965-1967		$500	$700

Zephyr
1939-1957. Maple veneer cabinet, 30 watts with 2x6L6 power, 1x12" until '54, 1x15" after, made by Danelectro using their typical designs, Dano D-style blond covering, large split "E" logo on front, brown grille cloth, large block Zephyr logo on back panel.

1939-1953	1x12	$850	$1,250
1953-1957	1x15	$1,000	$1,500

Zephyr Dreadnaught
1939. Similar to Zephyr amp but higher power and added microphone input.

1939		$850	$1,250

Esteban
2005-2007. Imported brand from China, student budget level compact amps.

Compact
2005-2007	$30	$50

Estey
Late-1960s. In 1959, Magnatone merged with the Estey Organ Company and in late '66/early '67 they introduced models branded Estey and based on their budget Magnatone Starlite series.

Model T12
Late-1960s. Based on Magnatone Starlite model 412.

1960s	$425	$650

Model T22
Late-1960s. Based on Magnatone Starlite model 422 but with larger 12" speaker.

1960s	$525	$675

Model T32
Late-1960s. Based on Magnatone Starlite model 432 with reverb and vibrato.

1960s	$600	$800

Model T42
Late-1960s. Based on Magnatone Starlite model 442 bass amp.

1960s	$600	$800

Evans Custom Amplifiers
1994-present. Professional grade, production, solidstate head and combo amps built by Scot Buffington in Burlington, North Carolina.

EVH
2007-present. Eddie Van Halen's line of professional and premium grade, production, tube amp heads and cabinets built by Fender. They also build guitars.

5150 III 50-Watt
2011-present. 50-watt head with 2x12 cab.

2011-2023	$1,125	$1,500

5150 III 100-Watt
2007-present. 100-watt head.

2007-2023	$1,250	$1,750

Evil Robot
2010-2014. Produced by David Brass and Fretted Americana, made in the U.S.A., initial product produced in limited quantities is based on the '59 Tonemaster (Magnatone) Troubadour amp. Production ceased in '14.

E-Wave Amplifiers
Built by Hangzhou Shengbei Sound Co. Ltd. in China, starting in 2004.

Excelsior
The Excelsior Company started offering accordions in 1924 and had a large factory in Italy by the late '40s. They started offering guitars and amps, uaually built by others including Valco and possibly Sano, around '62. By the early '70s they were out of the guitar business.

Americana Stereophonic High Fidelity
Late 1960s. 50 watts, 1x15", 2x8", 2x3x9" ovals, 2xEL34 power, tube rectifier, large Excelsior logo and small Excelsior The House of Music logo, guitar and accordion inputs, stereo reverb and vibrato.

1968-1969	$1,125	$1,625

Citation C-15
1962. Made by Sano, mid power with 2x6V6 power tubes, single speaker combo amp, large Citation by Excelsior logo on front panel.

1962	$750	$1,125

MODEL YEAR	FEATURES	LOW	HIGH

Fargen

1999-present. Benjamin Fargen builds his professional and premium grade, production/custom, guitar and bass tube amps in Sacramento, California. He also builds guitar effects.

Fender

1946-present. Leo Fender developed many groundbreaking instruments, but Leo's primary passion was amplifiers, and of all his important contributions to musicians, none exceeded those he made to the electric tube amplifier.

Tweed Fender amp circuits are highly valued because they define the tones of rock and roll. Blackface models remained basically the same until mid-'67. Some silverface circuits remained the same as the blackface circuits, while others were changed in the name of reliability.

Fender heads that are sold separately from their original cabinet are 75% of total value. Cabinets sold separately are 40% of the total value.

From 1953 to '67, Fender stamped a two-letter date code on the paper tube chart glued inside the cabinet. The first letter was the year (C='53, D='54, etc.) with the second the month (A=January, etc.).

The speaker code found on the frame of an original speaker will identify the manufacturer, and the week and year that the speaker was assembled. The speaker code is typically six (sometimes seven) digits. The first three digits represent the Electronics Industries Association (E.I.A.) source code which identifies the manufacturer. For example, a speaker code 220402 indicates a Jensen speaker (220), made in '54 (4) during the second week (02) of that year. This sample speaker also has another code stamped on the frame. ST654 P15N C4964 indicates the model of the speaker, in this case it is a P15N 15" speaker. The sample speaker also had a code stamped on the speaker cone, 4965 1, which indicates the cone number. All of these codes help identify the originality of the speaker.

Most Fender speakers from the '50s will be Jensens (code 220). By the late-'50s other suppliers were used. The supplier codes are Oxford (465), C.T.S. (137), Utah (328). JBL speakers were first used in the late-'50s Vibrasonic, and then in the Showman series, but JBL did not normally have a E.I.A. source code. An amp's speaker code should be reconciled with other dating info when the amp's original status is being verified.

General Production Eras: Diagonal tweed era, Brown tolex era, Blackface era, Silverface era with raised Fender logo with underlining tail, Silverface era with raised Fender logo without underlining tail, Silverface era with raised Fender logo with small MADE IN USA designation.

Nameplate and Logo Attribution: Fender nameplate with city but without model name (tweed era), Fender nameplate without city or model name (tweed era), Fender nameplate with model name noted (tweed era), Fender flat logo (brown era), Fender script raised logo (blackface era).

MODEL YEAR	FEATURES	LOW	HIGH
30			
1980-1981. Tube combo amp, 30 watts, 2x10" or 1x12".			
1980-1981	1x12	$550	$750
1980-1981	2x10	$600	$800
75			
1980-1982. Tube, 75 watts, offered as a 1x15" or 1x12" combo, or as head and 4x10" or 2x12" cab.			
1980-1982	1x15	$550	$725
1980-1982	2x12	$575	$750
1980-1982	4x10	$625	$850
85			
1988-1992. Solidstate, 85-watt 1x12" combo, black cover, silver grille.			
1988-1992		$275	$350
800 Pro Bass Head			
2004-2008. Rackmount, 800 watts, 5-band EQ.			
2004-2008		$350	$450
Acoustasonic 15			
2013-present. Student 1x6" amp, 15 watts.			
2013-2023		$60	$75
Acoustasonic 30/30 DSP			
2000-2011. Small combo, brown tolex, wheat grille. Upgrade model includes DSP (Digital Signal Processor) effects.			
2000-2005	30	$200	$250
2000-2011	30 DSP	$225	$300
Acoustasonic 100 Combo			
2012-2013. 100 watts, 1x8", horn.			
2012-2013		$275	$375
Acoustasonic 150 Combo			
2012-2017. 150 (2x75 stereo) watts, 2x8", piezo horn.			
2012-2017		$275	$375
Acoustasonic Junior/Junior DSP			
1998-2011. 2x40 watts, 2x8", Piezo horn.			
1998-2011		$225	$300
Acoustasonic SFX/SFX II			
1998-2011. SFX technology, 32 stereo digital presents, 2x80 watts, SFX is taller combo with one 10", a sideways mounted 8", and a horn. SFX II is a shorter cab with 8", sideways 6".			
1998-2003	SFX, tall cab	$275	$375
2003-2011	SFX II, short cab	$300	$400
Acoustasonic Ultralight			
2006-2009. Small 2x125-watt 2 channel head with 2x8 w/tweeters stereo cab.			
2006-2009		$600	$775
Acoustic Pro			
2016-2019. 200-watt digital combo, 12" and tweeter, natural blonde cab.			
2016-2019		$450	$600
Acoustic SFX			
2016-2019. 160-watt digital combo, 8" and 6.5" and tweeter, natural blonde cab.			
2016-2019		$450	$600
AmpCan			
1997-2008. Cylindrical can-shaped battery powered portable amp.			
1997-2008		$150	$200

Fargen MPMKIII

Fender Acoustic Pro

Fender Acoustasonic 15

AMPS

1964 Fender Bandmaster

Tom Pfeifer

Fender Bassbreaker 45 Combo

1963 Fender Bassman

Peter Guild

Automatic SE

1998-2000. Solidstate 25-watt, 1x10" (12" in 2000) combo, blackface cosmetics.

MODEL YEAR	FEATURES	LOW	HIGH
1998-2000		$95	$125

Bandmaster

1953-1975. Wide-panel 1x15" combo '53-'54, narrow-panel 3x10" combo '55-'60, tolex '60, brownface with 1x12" piggyback speaker cabinet '61, 2x12" '62, blackface '62-'67, silverface '68-'74.

MODEL YEAR	FEATURES	LOW	HIGH
1953-1954	Tweed, 1x15	$4,500	$5,500
1955-1958	Tweed, 3x10	$10,000	$13,000
1959-1960	Old style cab, pink brown tolex	$10,000	$13,000
1959-1960	Tweed, 3x10	$10,000	$13,000
1960	Brown tolex, 3x10	$5,250	$7,000
1960	Brown tolex, 3x10, reverse controls	$10,000	$12,000
1961	Rough white/ oxblood, 1x12	$3,500	$4,500
1961-1962	Rough white/ oxblood, 2x12	$3,000	$4,000
1963-1964	Smooth white/ gold, 2x12	$2,500	$3,500
1964-1967	Black tolex, 2x12	$1,500	$2,000
1964-1967	Black tolex, head only	$1,000	$1,500
1967-1968	Black, 2x12	$1,250	$1,625
1967-1969	Black, head only	$975	$1,250
1967-1969	Silverface, 2x12	$1,125	$1,500
1967-1970	Silverface, head only	$750	$975
1970-1974	Silverface, 2x12	$975	$1,250
1970-1975	Silverface, head only	$575	$750

Bandmaster Reverb

1968-1980. 45-watt silverface head with 2x12" cabinet.

MODEL YEAR	FEATURES	LOW	HIGH
1968-1972		$1,125	$1,500
1973-1980		$1,000	$1,375

Band-Master VM Set

2009-2012. Vintage Modified, 40 watts, piggyback, DSP reverb and effects.

MODEL YEAR	FEATURES	LOW	HIGH
2009-2012		$500	$650

Bantam Bass

1969-1971. 50 watts, large unusual 1x10" Yamaha speaker.

MODEL YEAR	FEATURES	LOW	HIGH
1969-1971	Original speaker	$700	$950

Bassbreaker 15

2015-present. Tube, 15 watts, 1x12" combo, master volume, gray tweed standard. Also offered in FSR limited editions.

MODEL YEAR	FEATURES	LOW	HIGH
2015-2021	Combo, gray tweed	$350	$450
2015-2023	Head, gray tweed	$300	$400
2017	Combo, LE Blonde Nubtex	$375	$525
2017	Combo, LE British Green	$375	$525

Bassbreaker 45

2015-2022. Head (until '18) or 2x12" combo, 45 watts, gray tweed.

MODEL YEAR	FEATURES	LOW	HIGH
2015-2018	Head	$625	$950
2016-2022	Combo	$675	$975

Bassman

1952-1971. Tweed TV front combo, 1x15" in '52, wide-panel '53-'54, narrow-panel and 4x10" '54-'60, tolex brownface with 1x12" in piggyback cabinet '61, 2x12" cabinet '61-'62, blackface '63-'67, silverface '67-'71, 2x15" cabinet '68-'71. Renamed the Bassman 50 in '72.

MODEL YEAR	FEATURES	LOW	HIGH
1952	TV front, 1x15	$3,500	$4,500
1953-1954	Wide panel, 1x15	$3,500	$4,500
1955-1957	Tweed, 4x10, 2 inputs	$8,000	$10,000
1957-1958	Tweed, 4x10, 4 inputs	$10,000	$13,000
1959-1960	Old style cab, pink brown tolex	$10,000	$13,000
1959-1960	Tweed, 4x10, 4 inputs	$10,000	$13,000
1961	White 1x12, 6G6, tube rectifier	$4,000	$5,500
1962	Late '62, white 2x12	$2,500	$3,500
1962	White 1x12, 6G6A, ss rectifier	$3,500	$4,500
1963-1964	Smooth whit 2x12, 6G6A/B	$3,000	$3,500
1964	Transition, black, white knobs	$2,000	$2,500
1965-1966	AA165/AB165, black knobs	$1,750	$2,250
1965-1966	AA165/AB165, head only	$1,250	$1,750
1967-1969	Silverface, vertical 2x15	$950	$1,250
1967-1969	Silverface, head only	$800	$1,000
1970-1971	Silverface, 2x15	$800	$1,125
1970-1971	Silverface, head only	$600	$775

'59 Bassman

1990-2003. Tube, 45 watts, 4x10", birch ply cab, solidstate rectifier.

MODEL YEAR	FEATURES	LOW	HIGH
1990-2003		$825	$1,125

'59 Bassman LTD

2004-present. Lacquered Tweed (LTD), tube, 45 watts, 4x10", solid pine cab, tube rectifier.

MODEL YEAR	FEATURES	LOW	HIGH
2004-2023		$1,000	$1,500

Bassman 10

1972-1982. 4x10" combo, silverface and 50 watts for '72-'80, blackface and 70 watts after.

MODEL YEAR	FEATURES	LOW	HIGH
1972-1980	50w	$625	$850
1981-1982	70w	$625	$850

Bassman 20

1982-1985. Tubes, 20 watts, 1x15".

MODEL YEAR	FEATURES	LOW	HIGH
1982-1985		$500	$650

Bassman 25

2000-2005. Wedge shape, 1x10", 25 watts, 3-band EQ.

MODEL YEAR	FEATURES	LOW	HIGH
2000-2005		$95	$125

Bassman 50

1972-1977. 50 watts, with 2x12" cab.

MODEL YEAR	FEATURES	LOW	HIGH
1972-1977		$700	$950

Bassman 60

1972-1976. 60 watts, 1x12".

MODEL YEAR	FEATURES	LOW	HIGH
1972-1976		$700	$950

The *Vintage Guitar Price Guide* shows values for an all-original condition amplifier, and where applicable, with original cover.

AMPS

MODEL YEAR	FEATURES	LOW	HIGH

Bassman 60 (later version)
2000-2005. Solidstate, 60 watts, 1x12".

| 2000-2005 | Combo | $95 | $125 |

Bassman 70
1977-1979. 70 watts, 2x15" cab.

| 1977-1979 | | $700 | $950 |

Bassman 100
1972-1977, 2000-2009. Tube, 100 watts, 4x12", name reused on solidstate combo amp.

| 1972-1977 | 4x12 | $700 | $950 |
| 2000-2009 | 1x15 combo | $200 | $275 |

Bassman 100 T
2012-2020. 100-watt head, master volume, '65 blackface cosmetics. Usually paired with Bassman NEO cabs.

| 2012-2020 | Head only | $975 | $1,375 |

Bassman 135
1978-1983. Tube, 135 watts, 4x10".

| 1978-1983 | | $725 | $975 |

Bassman 150 Combo
2005-2009. Solidstate 1x12" combo, 150 watts.

| 2005-2009 | | $225 | $300 |

Bassman 250 Combo
2005-2006. Import from Indonesia, 250 watts, 2x10".

| 2005-2006 | | $225 | $300 |

Bassman 300 Pro Head
2002-2012. All tube, 300 watts, 6x6550, black cover, black metal grille.

| 2002-2012 | | $900 | $1,250 |

Bassman 400
2000-2004. Solidstate, 350 watts with 2x10" plus horn, combo, black cover, black metal grille.

| 2000-2004 | Combo | $275 | $400 |
| 2000-2004 | Head | $250 | $350 |

Bassman Bassbreaker (Custom Shop)
1998-2003. Classic Bassman 4x10" configuration. Not offered by 2004 when the '59 Bassman LTD was introduced.

| 1998-2003 | 2x12 | $1,000 | $1,375 |
| 1998-2003 | 4x10 | $1,125 | $1,500 |

Bassman NEO Cabinet
2012-present. Cabinets used with Bassman 100 T head and Super Bassman head, standard '65 blackface cosmetics.

2012-2023	115	$425	$550
2012-2023	410	$530	$700
2012-2023	610	$625	$825
2012-2023	810	$725	$950

Bassman Solidstate
1968-1971. Small head, piggyback cab. The whole late 1960s Solidstate series was unreliable and prone to overheating, more of a historical novelty than a musical instrument.

| 1968-1971 | | $450 | $600 |

B-Dec 30
2006-2009. Bass version of the G-Dec, 30 watts, 1x10.

| 2006-2009 | | $125 | $175 |

Blues Deluxe
1993-2005. All tube, 40 watts, reverb, 1x12", tweed covering (blond tolex optional '95 only).

| 1993-2005 | Tweed | $525 | $700 |
| 1995 | Blond tolex | $525 | $700 |

Blues Deluxe Reissue
2006-present. All tube, tweed, 40 watts, reverb, 1x12".

| 2006-2023 | | $450 | $600 |

Blues DeVille
1993-1996. All tube Tweed Series, 60 watts, 4x10" (optional 2x12" in '94), reverb, high-gain channel, tweed cover (blond tolex optional '95 only).

| 1993-1996 | Tweed | $600 | $800 |
| 1995 | Blond tolex | $600 | $800 |

Blues DeVille Reissue
2006-2015. 60 watts, 4x10, tweed.

| 2006-2015 | | $600 | $800 |

Blues Junior (III) (IV)/LE
1995-present. Tube, 15 watts, 1x12", spring reverb, tweed in '95, black tolex with silver grille '96 on, blond '00-'09, brown '08, surf green '09. Woody Custom Shop (hardwood) in '02-'03. III update in '10, IV in '18. Limited Edition After the Gold Rush, Surf-Tone Green, Red Nova Two-Tone, Creamy Wine Two-Tone, Navy Blues, Silver Noir Two-Tone, and Chocolate Tweed offered in '12.

1995-2023	Black	$425	$550
2000-2009	Blond	$500	$650
2002-2003	Woody,		
	Custom Shop	$700	$900
2008	Brown	$500	$650
2009	Green	$500	$650
2010-2012	LE Colors	$500	$650
2015-2023	Lacquer tweed	$475	$625

Bronco
1967-1972, 1993-2001. 1x 8" speaker, all tube, 5 watts until '72, 6 watts for '72-'74, ('90s issue is 15 watts), solidstate, tweed covering (blond tolex was optional for '95 only).

| 1967-1972 | Tubes, 5w | $950 | $1,250 |
| 1993-2001 | Solidstate, 15w | $135 | $175 |

Bronco 40 Bass
2012-2018. 40 watts, 1x10", 12 effects.

| 2012-2018 | | $150 | $200 |

Bullet/Bullet Reverb
1994-2005. Solidstate, 15 watts, 1x8", with or without reverb.

| 1994-2005 | | $70 | $90 |

BXR Series Bass

| 1987-2000 | Various models | $75 | $100 |

Capricorn
1970-1972. Solidstate, 105 watts, 3x12".

| 1970-1972 | | $650 | $850 |

Champ
1953-1982. Renamed from the Champion 600. Tweed until '64, black tolex after, 3 watts in '53, 4 watts '54-'64, 5 watts '65-'71, 6 watts '72-'82, 1x6" until '57, 1x8" after.

| 1953-1954 | Wide panel, | | |
| | 1x6, 5C1 | $2,500 | $3,000 |

1964 Fender Bassman
Michael Butler

1975 Fender Bassman 100
Johnny Zapp

AMPS

2020 Fender Blues Junior IV
Cream City Music

1953 Fender Champion 600
Jeffrey Smith

1962 Fender Concert
KC Cormack

1955 Fender Deluxe
Jerome Pinkham

MODEL YEAR	FEATURES	LOW	HIGH
1955-1956	Narrow panel, 1x6, 5E1	$2,500	$3,500
1956-1964	Narrow panel, 1x8, 5F1	$3,500	$4,500
1964	New cab, black, AA764	$2,000	$2,500
1964	Old cab, black, 1x8, F51	$2,500	$3,500
1965-1967	New cab, black AA764	$1,500	$2,000
1968-1972	Silverface, 1x8	$850	$1,500
1973-1980	Silverface, 1x8	$750	$1,000
1981-1982	Blackface	$750	$1,000

Champ II
1982-1985. 18 watts, 1x10".

1982-1985		$700	$900

'57 Champ/'57 Custom Champ
2009-2011, 2016-present. Custom Series reissue, tweed, leather handle, 5 watts, 1x8". Custom added to model name in '16.

2009-2023		$750	$975

Champ 12
1986-1992. Tube, 12 watts, overdrive, reverb, 1x12".

1986-1992	Black	$350	$450
1986-1992	Other colors	$475	$625

Champ 25 SE
1992-1993. Hybrid solidstate and tube combo, 25 watts, 1x12".

1992-1993		$275	$350

Champion 20
2014-present. Solidstate, 20 watts, 1x8", black and silver.

2014-2023		$75	$100

Champion 30/30 DSP
1999-2003. Small solidstate combo, 30 watts, 1x8", reverb.

1999-2003		$95	$125

Champion 40
2014-present. Solidstate, 40 watts, 1x12".

2014-2023		$135	$175

Champion 100
2014-present. Solidstate, 100 watts, 2x12", 2 channels.

2014-2023		$200	$275

Champion 100XL
2019-2021. 100 watts, 2x12", 16 on-board effects, black.

2019-2021		$325	$450

Champion 110
1993-2000. Solidstate, 25 watts, 1x10", 2 channels.

1993-2000		$135	$175

Champion 300
2004-2007. 30-watt solidstate combo, Dyna-Touch Series, DSP effects.

2004-2007		$160	$200

Champion 600
1949-1953. Replaced the Champion 800, 3 watts, 1x6", 2-tone tolex, TV front. Replaced by the Champ.

1949-1953		$2,000	$3,000

Champion 600 (later version)
2007-2012. Small 5-watt combo.

2007-2012		$200	$275

MODEL YEAR	FEATURES	LOW	HIGH

Champion 800
1948. About 100 made, TV front, luggage tweed cover, 1x8, 3 tubes, becomes Champion 600 in '49.

1948		$2,500	$3,500

Concert
1960-1965. Introduced with 40 watts and 4x10", brown tolex until '63, blackface '63-'65. In '62 white tolex was ordered by Webbs Music (CA) instead of the standard brown tolex. A wide range is noted for the rare white tolex, and each amp should be valued on a case-by-case basis. In '60, the very first brown tolex had a pink tint but only on the first-year amps.

1960	Brown (pink) tolex	$3,000	$3,500
1960	Brown (pink) tweed	$3,000	$4,000
1961-1963	Brown tolex	$3,000	$3,500
1962	White tolex (Webbs Music)	$3,000	$3,500
1963-1965	Blackface	$2,500	$3,500

Concert (Pro Tube Series)
1993-1995. Tube combo, 60 watts, 1x12, blackface.

1993-1995		$675	$925

Concert Reverb (Pro Tube Series)
2002-2005. 4x10" combo, reverb, tremolo, overdrive.

2002-2005		$725	$950

Concert 112
1982-1985. Tube, 60 watts, 1x12", smaller Concert logo (not similar to '60s style logo).

1982-1985		$825	$1,125

Concert 210
1982-1985. Tube, 60 watts, 2x10".

1982-1985		$850	$1,125

Concert 410
1982-1985. Tube, 60 watts, 4x10".

1982-1985		$900	$1,125

Concert II Head
1982-1987. 60 watts, 2 channels.

1982-1987		$725	$975

Cyber Champ
2004-2005. 65 watts, 1x12", Cyber features, 21 presets.

2004-2005		$225	$300

Cyber Deluxe
2002-2005. 65 watts, 1x12", Cyber features, 64 presets.

2002-2005		$250	$350

Cyber-Twin (SE)
2001-2011. Hybrid tube/solidstate modeling amp, 2x65 watts, head or 2x12" combo, became the SE in '05.

2001-2003	Head only	$350	$450
2001-2004	Combo	$400	$550
2005-2011	SE, 2nd Edition	$400	$550

Deco-Tone (Custom Shop)
2000. Art-deco styling, 165 made, all tube, 15 watts, 1x12", round speaker baffle opening, uses 6BQ5/ES84 power tubes.

2000		$900	$1,250

Deluxe
1948-1966. Name changed from Model 26 ('46-'48). 10 watts (15 by '54 and 20 by '63), 1x12", TV front with tweed '48-'53, wide-panel '53-'55, narrow-panel '55-'60, brown tolex with brownface '61-'63,

AMPS

MODEL YEAR	FEATURES	LOW	HIGH
black tolex with blackface '63-'66.			
1948-1952	Tweed, TV front	$5,000	$6,000
1953-1954	Wide panel	$5,000	$6,000
1955	Narrow panel, small cab	$8,500	$12,000
1956-1960	Narrow panel, large cab	$8,500	$12,000
1961-1963	Brown tolex	$4,500	$5,500
1964-1966	Black tolex	$4,500	$5,500

Deluxe Reverb

1963-1981. 1x12", 20 watts, blackface '63-'67, silverface '68-'80, blackface with silver grille option introduced in mid-'80. Replaced by Deluxe Reverb II. Reissued as Deluxe Reverb '65 Reissue.

1963-1967	Blackface	$4,500	$6,500
1967-1968	Silverface	$2,500	$3,000
1969-1970	Silverface	$2,000	$2,750
1971-1980	Silverface	$1,500	$2,500
1980-1981	Blackface	$1,375	$2,000

Deluxe Reverb Solidstate

1966-1969. Part of Fender's early solidstate series.

1966-1969	$500	$675

'57 Deluxe/'57 Custom Deluxe

2007-2011, 2016-present. Custom Series reissue, hand-wired, 12 watts, 1x12" combo, tweed. Custom added to model name in '17. A '57 Deluxe head version was offered '16-'17 and Limited Editions in '18-'19.

2007-2011		$1,500	$2,000
2016-2017	Head only	$1,375	$1,750
2016-2023		$1,500	$2,000
2018	LE Blond	$1,500	$2,000

'57 Custom Deluxe Front Row

2019. Limited Edition, 5 offered, exotic wood cab made of century-old Alaskan yellow cedar, from Hollywood Bowl bench seats.

2019	LE Exotic Wood	$5,500	$7,250

'65 Deluxe Reverb

1993-present. Blackface reissue, 22 watts, 1x12".

1993-2023	$850	$1,125

'68 Custom Deluxe Reverb

2014-present. Vintage Modified silverface reissue with modified circuit, 1x12".

2014-2023	$825	$1,000

Deluxe Reverb II

1982-1986. Updated Deluxe Reverb with 2 6V6 power tubes, all tube preamp section, black tolex, blackface, 20 watts, 1x12".

1982-1986	$1,000	$1,375

Deluxe 85

1988-1993. Solidstate, 65 watts, 1x12", black tolex, silver grille, Red Knob Series.

1988-1993	$300	$400

Deluxe 90

1999-2003. Solidstate, 90 watts, 1x12" combo, DSP added in '02.

1999-2002		$200	$250
2002-2003	DSP option	$225	$300

Deluxe 112

1992-1995. Solidstate, 65 watts, 1x12", black tolex with silver grille.

1992-1995	$225	$300

Deluxe 112 Plus

1995-2000. 90 watts, 1x12", channel switching.

1995-2000	$225	$300

Deluxe 900

2004-2006. Solidstate, 90 watts, 1x12" combo, DSP effects.

2004-2006	$275	$350

Deluxe VM

2009-2013. Vintage Modified Series, 40 watts, 1x12", black.

2009-2013	$600	$800

MD20 Mini Deluxe

2007-present. One-watt, dual 2" speakers, headphone jack, 9V adapter jack.

2007-2023	$20	$25

The Edge Deluxe

2016-2019. 12-watts, 1x12" combo, tube, tweed. The Edge front panel badge.

2016-2019	$2,000	$2,500

Dual Professional

1994-2002. Custom Shop amp, all tube, point-to-point wiring, 100 watts, 2x12" Celestion Vintage 30s, fat switch, reverb, tremolo, white tolex, oxblood grille.

1994-2002	$1,500	$2,000

Dual Professional/Super

1947. V-front, early-'47 small metal name tag "Fender/Dual Professional/Fullerton California" tacked on front of cab, 2x10 Jensen PM10-C each with transformer attached to speaker frame, tube chart on inside of cab, late-'47 renamed Super and new metal badge "Fender/Fullerton"

1947	$7,500	$10,000

Dual Showman

1962-1969. Called the Double Showman for the first year. White tolex (black available from '64), 2x15", 85 watts. Reintroduced '87-'94 as solidstate, 100 watts, optional speaker cabs.

1962	Rough blond/ oxblood	$3,500	$4,500
1963	Smooth blond/ wheat	$3,000	$3,500
1964-1967	Black tolex, horizontal cab	$2,000	$2,500
1964-1967	Black tolex, head only	$1,250	$1,625
1968	Blackface, large vertical cab	$1,250	$2,000
1968	Blackface, head only	$1,000	$1,375
1968-1969	Silverface	$1,125	$1,500
1968-1969	Silverface, head only	$875	$1,125

Dual Showman Reverb

1968-1981. Black tolex with silver grille, silverface, 100 watts, 2x15".

1968-1972	$1,125	$1,500
1973-1981	$1,000	$1,375

Fender '57

2007. Only 300 made, limited edition combo, hand-wired, 1x12", retro styling.

2007	$1,500	$2,000

1962 Fender Deluxe
David Gant

1980 Fender Deluxe Reverb
Tom Pfeifer

1967 Fender Dual Showman
Imaged by Heritage Auctions, HA.com

AMPS

Fender G-DEC

1977 Fender Musicmaster Bass
Tom Pfeifer

Fender Mustang GTX50

MODEL YEAR	FEATURES	LOW	HIGH
FM Series			
2003-2010. Lower-priced solidstate amps, heads and combos.			
2003-2006	FM-212R, 2x12	$200	$250
2003-2010	FM-100 Head/Cab	$215	$275
Frontman Series			
1997-present. Student combo amps, models include 10G (10 watts, 1x6"), 15/15B/15G/15R (15 watts, 1x8"), 25R (25 watts, 1x10", reverb), 212R (100 watts, 2x12", reverb).			
1997-2004	15DSP,		
	15 FX selections	$50	$65
1997-2004	25DSP	$65	$90
1997-2006	65DSP	$125	$175
1997-2011	15/15B/15G/15R	$45	$60
1997-2011	65R	$85	$110
1997-2013	25R	$50	$65
2007-2013	212R	$170	$225
G-Dec			
2005-2012. Digital, amp and effects presets.			
2005-2009	G-Dec, small cab	$80	$100
2006-2009	G-Dec 30, larger cab	$125	$165
2007-2008	G-Dec Exec,		
	maple cab	$225	$300
2011-2012	G-Dec Jr, Champ cab	$65	$85
GE-112 Cabinet			
2003-2007. Extension cab, 1x12.			
2003-2007		$110	$150
H.O.T.			
1990-1996. Solidstate, 25 watts, 1x10", gray carpet cover (black by '92), black grille.			
1990-1996		$80	$100
Harvard Solidstate			
1980-1983. Reintroduced from tube model, black tolex with blackface, 20 watts, 1x10".			
1980-1983		$200	$250
Harvard Tube			
1956-1961. Tweed, 10 watts, 1x10", 2 knobs volume and roll-off tone, some were issued with 1x8". Reintroduced as a solidstate model in '80.			
1956-1961		$7,500	$9,000
Harvard Reverb			
1981-1982. Solidstate, 20 watts, 1x10", reverb, replaced by Harvard Reverb II in '83.			
1981-1982		$200	$250
Harvard Reverb II			
1983-1985. Solidstate, black tolex with blackface, 20 watts, 1x10", reverb.			
1983-1985		$200	$250
Hot Rod Blues Junior Limited			
2000s. Compact tube combo, rough blond tolex, dark tolex sides, wheat grille.			
2000s		$450	$600
Hot Rod Deluxe/Deluxe III/Deluxe IV			
1996-present. Updated Blues Deluxe, tube, 40 watts, 1x12", black tolex. Various covering optional by '98, also a wood cab in 2003. III added to name in '11 with various limited-edition colors. Renamed Deluxe IV in '20, offered in black.			
1996-2023	Various colors	$525	$700

MODEL YEAR	FEATURES	LOW	HIGH
Hot Rod DeVille 212			
1996-2011. Updated Blues DeVille, tube, 60 watts, black tolex, 2x12".			
1996-2011	Various colors	$600	$775
Hot Rod DeVille 410/DeVille 410 III			
1996-2018. Tube, 60 watts, black tolex, 4x10". III added to name in '11.			
1996-2018	Various colors	$600	$775
Hot Rod DeVille IV			
2018-present. Tube, 60 watts, black vinyl, 2x12".			
2018-2023		$550	$700
Hot Rod Pro Junior III			
2010-2018. Tube, 15 watts, black, 1x10".			
2010-2018		$525	$675
2011-2013	Red October LE	$325	$425
Hot Rod Pro Junior IV			
2018-present. Tube, 15 watts, lacquered tweed, 1x10". Hot Rod removed from name in '20.			
2018-2023		$350	$475
J.A.M.			
1990-1996. Solidstate, 25 watts, 1x12", 4 preprogrammed sounds, gray carpet cover (black by '92).			
1990-1996		$85	$125
Jazz King			
2005-2008. 140-watt solidstate 1x15" combo.			
2005-2008		$600	$800
Jazzmaster Ultralight			
2006-2011. 250-watt solidstate 1x12".			
2006-2011		$500	$650
KXR Series			
1995-2002. Keyboard combo amps, 50 to 200 watts, solidstate, 1x12" or 15".			
1995-2002	Various models	$200	$275
Libra			
1970-1972. Solidstate, 105 watts, 4x12" JBL speakers, black tolex.			
1970-1972		$600	$800
London 185			
1988-1992. Solidstate, 160 watts, black tolex.			
1988-1992	Head only	$275	$375
London Reverb			
1983-1985. Solidstate, 100 watts, 1x12" or 2x10", black tolex.			
1983-1985	1x12	$375	$500
1983-1985	2x10	$400	$525
1983-1985	Head	$275	$375
M-80 Series			
1989-1994. Solidstate, 90 watts, 1x12", also offered as head only, Bass (160w, 1x15"), Chorus (90w, 2x12") and Pro (90w, rackmount).			
1989-1993	M-80 Pro	$175	$225
1989-1994	M-80	$175	$225
1990-1994	M-80 Bass	$175	$225
1990-1994	M-80 Chorus	$175	$225
Machette			
2012-2013. 50 watts, 1x12" tube combo, inlaid white piping and gray vinyl accents on black tolex.			
2012-2013		$2,000	$2,500
Model 26			
1946-1947. Tube, 10 watts, 1x10", hardwood cabinet.			

AMPS

MODEL YEAR	FEATURES	LOW	HIGH

Sometimes called Deluxe Model 26, renamed Deluxe in '48.

| 1946-1947 | | $4,000 | $6,500 |

Montreux

1983-1985. Solidstate, 100 watts, 1x12", black tolex with silver grille.

| 1983-1985 | | $375 | $500 |

Musicmaster Bass

1970-1983. Tube, 12 watts, 1x12", black tolex.

| 1970-1980 | Silverface | $525 | $700 |
| 1981-1983 | Blackface | $525 | $700 |

Mustang Series

2010-present. Mustang I through V, modeling amp effects, small combo up to a half-stack. Mustang GTX and LT added in '20.

2010-2016	II, 40w, 1x12	$135	$175
2010-2019	I, 20w, 1x8	$75	$100
2011-2016	III, 100w, 1x12	$200	$275
2011-2016	IV, 150w, 2x12	$350	$450
2011-2016	V, 150w, 4x12	$400	$525

PA-100 Head

Early to mid-1970s. All tube head, 100 watts, 4 channels with standard guitar inputs, master volume.

| 1970s | | $500 | $650 |

PA-135 Head

Later 1970s. All tube head, 135 watts, 4 channels, master volume.

| 1970s | | $525 | $700 |

Pawn Shop Special Excelsior/ Excelsior Pro

2012-2013. Retro late-'40s vertical combo slate-grille cab, 13-watt 1x15" combo tube amp, tremolo, brown textured vinyl covering.

| 2012-2013 | | $300 | $400 |

Pawn Shop Special Greta

2012-2013. Mini tube tabletop amp, 2 watts, 1x4" vintage radio-style cab, red.

| 2012-2013 | | $150 | $200 |

Pawn Shop Special Ramparte

2014. Tube amp, 9 watts, 1x12", 2-tone chocolate and copper grille cloth with wheat.

| 2014 | | $300 | $400 |

Pawn Shop Special Vaporizer

2014. Tube amp, 12 watts, 2x10", Rocket Red, Slate Blue or Surf Green dimpled vinyl covering with silver grille cloth.

| 2014 | | $325 | $425 |

Performer 650

1993-1995. Solidstate hybrid amp with single tube, 70 watts, 1x12".

| 1993-1995 | | $225 | $300 |

Performer 1000

1993-1995. Solidstate hybrid amp with a single tube, 100 watts, 1x12".

| 1993-1995 | | $225 | $300 |

Princeton

1948-1979. Tube, 4.5 watts (12 watts by '61), 1x8" (1x10" by '61), tweed '48-'61, brown '61-'63, black with blackface '63-'69, silverface '69-'79.

| 1948 | Tweed, TV front | $3,500 | $4,500 |
| 1949-1953 | Tweed, TV front | $3,000 | $4,000 |

1953-1954	Wide panel	$3,000	$4,000
1955-1956	Narrow panel, small cab	$5,500	$6,500
1956-1961	Narrow panel, large cab	$5,500	$6,500
1961-1963	Brown, 6G2	$3,500	$4,500
1963-1964	Black, 6G2	$2,750	$4,250
1964-1966	Black, AA964, no grille logo	$2,500	$3,500
1966-1967	Black, AA964, raised grille logo	$2,000	$2,500
1968-1969	Silverface, alum grille trim	$1,500	$2,000
1969-1970	Silverface, no grille trim	$1,000	$1,500
1971-1979	Silverface, AB1270	$1,000	$1,500
1973-1975	Fender logo-tail	$1,000	$1,500
1975-1978	No Fender logo-tail	$1,000	$1,500
1978-1979	With boost pull-knob	$1,000	$1,500

Princeton Reverb

1964-1981. Tube, black tolex, blackface until '67, silverface after until blackface again in '80.

1964-1967	Blackface	$3,500	$4,500
1968-1972	Silverface, Fender logo-tail	$2,500	$3,500
1973-1979	Silverface, no Fender logo-tail	$2,000	$3,000
1980-1981	Blackface	$1,000	$1,500

Princeton Reverb II

1982-1985. Tube amp, 20 watts, 1x12", black tolex, silver grille, distortion feature.

| 1982-1985 | | $950 | $1,250 |

'65 Princeton Reverb

2009-present. Vintage Reissue series, includes various Limited-Edition colors.

| 2009-2023 | Various colors | $750 | $1,000 |

'68 Custom Princeton Reverb

2014-present. 12 watts, silver-and-turquoise front panel, aluminum grille cloth trim, black.

| 2014-2023 | | $625 | $850 |

Princeton Chorus

1988-1996. Solidstate, 2x10", 2 channels at 25 watts each, black tolex. Replaced by Princeton Stereo Chorus in '96.

| 1988-1996 | | $200 | $275 |

Princeton 65

1999-2003. Combo 1x2", reverb, blackface, DSP added in '02.

| 1999-2001 | | $150 | $200 |

Princeton 112/112 Plus

1993-1997. Solidstate, 40 watts (112) or 60 watts (112 Plus), 1x12", black tolex.

| 1993-1994 | 40 watts | $175 | $225 |
| 1995-1997 | 60 watts | $175 | $225 |

Princeton 650

2004-2006. Solidstate 65-watt 1x12" combo, DSP effects, black tolex.

| 2004-2006 | | $175 | $225 |

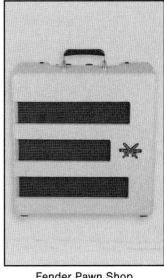

Fender Pawn Shop
Special Excelsior

1964 Fender Princeton
Scott Anderson

1964 Fender Princeton Reverb
Vern Juran

AMPS

1979 Fender Pro
Reverb Silverface
Rivington Guitars

2015 Fender Pro Junior III
Rivington Guitars

Fender Rumble 100

MODEL YEAR	FEATURES	LOW	HIGH
Princeton Recording			
2007-2009. Based on classic '65 Princeton Reverb, 15 watts, 1x10" combo, 2 on-board effects (overdrive/compression), 4-button footswitch, blackface cosmetics.			
2007-2009		$650	$900
Pro			
1946-1965. Called Professional '46-'48. 15 watts (26 by '54 and 25 by '60), 1x15", tweed TV front '48-'53, wide-panel '53-'54, narrow-panel '55-'60, brown tolex and brownface '60-'63, black and blackface '63-'65.			
1946-1953	Tweed, TV front	$4,000	$5,000
1953-1954	Wide panel	$4,250	$5,500
1955	Narrow panel, old chassis	$5,000	$6,000
1955-1959	Narrow panel, new chassis	$5,500	$6,500
1960	Pink/brown, tweed	$3,000	$4,000
1961-1962	Brown tolex	$2,500	$3,500
1963-1965	Black tolex	$2,500	$3,500
'57 Custom Pro			
2016-2019. Hand-wired, 26 watts, 1x15", lacquered tweed.			
2016-2019		$1,625	$2,250
Pro Reverb			
1965-1982. Tube, black tolex, 40 watts (45 watts by '72, 70 watts by '81), 2x12", blackface '65-'69 and '81-'83, silverface '69-'81.			
1965-1967	Blackface	$2,500	$3,500
1968	Silverface	$1,750	$2,500
1969-1970	Silverface	$1,500	$2,000
1971-1980	Silverface	$1,250	$1,500
1981-1982	Blackface	$1,250	$1,500
Pro Reverb Solidstate			
1967-1969. Fender's first attempt at solidstate design, the attempt was unsuccessful and many of these models will overheat and are known to be unreliable. 50 watts, 2x12", upright vertical combo cabinet.			
1967-1969		$550	$750
Pro Reverb Reissue (Pro Series)			
2002-2005. 50 watts, 1x12", 2 modern designed channels - clean and high gain.			
2002-2005		$850	$1,125
Pro 185			
1989-1991. Solidstate, 160 watts, 2x12", black tolex.			
1989-1991		$275	$375
Pro Junior (III/IV)			
1994-present. All tube, 2xEL84 tubes, 15 watts, 1x10" Alnico Blue speaker, tweed '94-'96, blonde in '95, black tolex '96-'17. Lacquered Tweed '18-present. III update in '10, IV in '18.			
1994-1996	Tweed	$475	$650
1995	Blonde	$350	$500
1996-2017	Black tolex	$300	$400
2018-2023	Lacquered Tweed	$375	$500
Pro Junior 60th Anniversary Woody			
2006. Recreation of original Fender model (1946-2006), 15 watts, 1x10, lacquered wood cab.			
2006		$675	$950
Pro Junior Masterbuilt (Custom Shop)			
Late-1990s. Transparent white-blond wood finish.			
1990s		$675	$950

MODEL YEAR	FEATURES	LOW	HIGH
Prosonic			
1996-2001. Custom Shop 2x10" combo or head/4x12" cab, 60 watts, 2 channels, 3-way rectifier switch, tube reverb, black, red or green.			
1996-2001	Cab	$400	$525
1996-2001	Combo	$850	$1,125
1996-2001	Head	$700	$950
Quad Reverb			
1971-1978. Black tolex, silverface, 4x12", tube, 100 watts.			
1971-1978		$1,000	$1,500
R.A.D.			
1990-1996. Solidstate, 20 watts, 1x8", gray carpet cover until '92, black after.			
1990-1996		$90	$125
R.A.D. Bass			
1992-1994. Solidstate, 25 watts, 1x10", renamed BXR 25.			
1992-1994		$90	$125
Roc-Pro 1000			
1997-2001. Hybrid tube combo or head, 100 watts, 1x12", spring reverb, 1000 logo on front panel.			
1997-2001	Combo	$250	$325
1997-2001	Half stack, head & cab	$350	$450
Rumble Bass			
1994-1998. Custom Shop tube amp, 300 watts, 4x10" cabs, blond tolex, oxblood grille. Not to be confused with later budget Rumble series.			
1994-1998	Cab	$800	$1,125
1994-1998	Head	$1,375	$1,750
1994-1998	Head & 2 cabs	$3,000	$4,000
Rumble Series			
2003-present. Solidstate bass amps, model number indicates watts, models include Rumble 15 (1x8"), 25 (1x10"), 30 (1x10"), 40 (1x10"), 60 (1x12"), 75 (1x12"), 100 (1x15" or 2x10"), 150 (1x15") and 350 (2x10"). Some models discontinued in '09 then restarted in '14.			
2003-2009	Rumble 60	$150	$200
2003-2013	Rumble 150	$175	$250
2003-2013	Rumble 150 Head	$135	$175
2003-2013	Rumble 30	$125	$175
2003-2013	Rumble 350 Combo	$280	$375
2003-2013	Rumble 350 Head	$175	$250
2003-2013	Rumble 75	$160	$200
2003-2023	Rumble 100	$175	$225
2003-2023	Rumble 15	$60	$75
2003-2023	Rumble 25	$75	$100
2003-2023	Rumble 40	$140	$175
Scorpio			
1970-1972. Solidstate, 56 watts, 2x12", black tolex.			
1970-1972		$600	$800
SFX Keyboard 200			
1998-1999. 2 stereo channels generate 80 watts per channel (160w).			
1998-1999		$150	$200
SFX Satellite			
1998-2000. 80 watts, 12" speaker.			
1998-2000		$125	$150

MODEL YEAR	FEATURES	LOW	HIGH
Showman 12			
1960-1966. Piggyback cabinet with 1x12", 85 watts, blond tolex (changed to black in '64), maroon grille '61-'63, gold grille '63-'64, silver grille '64-'67.			
1960-1962	Rough blonde/ oxblood	$4,500	$6,500
1963-1964	Smooth blonde/gold	$3,500	$5,000
1964-1966	Black	$2,500	$3,500
Showman 15			
1960-1968. Piggyback cabinet with 1x15", 85 watts, blonde tolex (changed to black in '64), maroon grille '61-'63, gold grille '63-'64, silver grille '64-'67.			
1960-1962	Rough blonde/ oxblood	$4,000	$6,000
1963-1964	Smooth blonde/ gold	$3,500	$5,000
1964-1967	Blackface	$2,000	$2,500
1964-1967	Blackface, head only	$1,125	$1,875
1967-1968	Silverface	$1,500	$2,000
1967-1968	Silverface, head only	$950	$1,250
Showman Solidstate			
1983-1987. Solidstate, 200 watts, 2 channels, reverb, EQ, effects loop, model number indicates size, models include; 112, 115, 210 and 212.			
1983-1987	Various models	$400	$500
Sidekick 10			
1983-1985. Small solidstate Japanese or Mexican import, 10 watts, 1x8".			
1983-1985		$60	$80
Sidekick Bass 30			
1983-1985. Combo, 30 watts, 1x12".			
1983-1985		$75	$100
Sidekick Reverb 15			
1983-1985. Small solidstate import, reverb, 15 watts.			
1983-1985		$85	$110
Sidekick Reverb 20			
1983-1985. Small solidstate Japanese or Mexican import, 20 watts, reverb, 1x10".			
1983-1985		$95	$125
Sidekick Reverb 30			
1983-1985. Small solidstate Japanese or Mexican import, 30 watts, 1x12", reverb.			
1983-1985		$100	$125
Sidekick Reverb 65			
1986-1988. Small solidstate Japanese or Mexican import, 65 watts, 1x12".			
1986-1988		$115	$150
Sidekick 100 Bass Head			
1986-1993. 100-watt bass head.			
1986-1993		$100	$125
Squier Champ 15			
1990s-2000s. 1x8, 15 watts, solidstate.			
1990s-00s		$50	$65
Squier SKX Series			
1990-1992. Solidstate, 15 watts, 1x8", model SKX15R with reverb. Model SKX25R is 25 watts, 1x10, reverb.			
1990-1992	15, no reverb	$50	$65

MODEL YEAR	FEATURES	LOW	HIGH
1990-1992	15R, reverb	$55	$75
1990-1992	25R, reverb	$60	$80
Squier SP10			
2003-2012. 10-watt solidstate, usually sold as part of a Guitar Pack.			
2003-2012		$50	$65
Stage 100/Stage 1000			
1999-2006. Solidstate, 1x12", combo or head only options, 100 watts, blackface. Head available until 2004.			
1999-2004	Head only	$250	$325
1999-2006	Combo	$325	$425
1999-2006	Combo stack, 2 cabs	$425	$550
Stage 112 SE			
2000s. Solidstate, 160 watts, 1x12" combo.			
2000s		$165	$225
Stage 185			
2000s. Solidstate, 150 watts, 1x12" combo.			
2000s		$180	$250
Stage 1000 Dyna-Touch III			
2000s. Solidstate, 100 watts, 1x12" combo.			
2000s		$325	$425
Stage 1600 DSP			
2004-2006. Solidstate, 160 watts, 2x12" combo, 16 digital effects (DSP).			
2004-2006		$350	$450
Stage Lead/Lead II			
1983-1985. Solidstate, 100 watts, 1x12", reverb, channel switching, black tolex. Stage Lead II has 2x12".			
1983-1985	1x12	$225	$300
1983-1985	2x12	$225	$300
Starcaster 15G by Fender			
2000s. Student economy pac amp, sold with a guitar, strap and stand, Starcaster by Fender logo. Sold in Costco and other discounters.			
2000s		$35	$45
Steel-King			
2004-2009. Designed for pedal steel, 200 watts, solidstate, 1x15".			
2004-2009		$625	$825
Studio 85			
1988. Studio 85 logo on upper right front of grille, solidstate, 1x12" combo, 65 watts, red knobs.			
1988		$225	$300
Studio Bass			
1977-1980. Uses Super Twin design, tube, 200-watt combo, 5-band eq, 1x15".			
1977-1980		$675	$900
Studio Lead			
1983-1986. Solidstate, 50 watts, 1x12", black tolex.			
1983-1986		$250	$350
Super			
1947-1963, 1992-1997. Introduced as Dual Professional in 1946, renamed Super '47, 2x10" speakers, 20 watts (30 watts by '60 with 45 watts in '62), tweed TV front '47-'53, wide-panel '53-'54, narrow-panel '55-'60, brown tolex '60-'64. Reintroduced '92-'97 with 4x10", 60 watts, black tolex.			
1947-1952	V-front	$7,500	$10,000
1953-1954	Tweed, wide panel	$5,000	$6,500

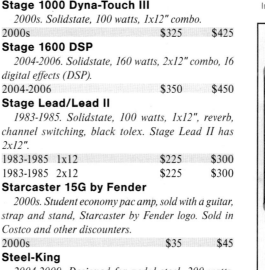

1963 Fender Showman
Imaged by Heritage Auctions, HA.com

Fender Sidekick Bass 30

1956 Fender Super
Rivington Guitars

1968 Fender Super Reverb
Michael Campbell

1958 Fender Tremolux
Scott Chapin

1962 Fender Twin
Jim Sheehan

MODEL YEAR	FEATURES	LOW	HIGH
1955	Tweed, narrow panel, 6L6	$7,500	$9,000
1956-1957	Tweed, narrow panel, 5E4, 6V6	$7,000	$8,500
1957-1960	Tweed, narrow panel, 6L6	$9,000	$12,000
1960	Pink, tweed-era grille	$3,500	$5,000
1960	Pink/brown, metal knobs	$3,500	$5,000
1960	Pink/brown, reverse knobs	$3,500	$5,000
1960-1962	Brown, oxblood grille, 6G4	$3,000	$4,500
1962-1963	Brown, tan/wheat grille, 6G4	$3,000	$4,500

Super 60
1989-1993. Red Knob series, 1x12", 60 watts, earlier versions with red knobs, later models with black knobs, offered in optional covers such as red, white, gray or snakeskin.

1989-1993	Combo	$350	$450
1989-1993	Head	$350	$450

Super 112
1990-1993. Red Knob series, 1x12", 60 watts, earlier versions with red knobs, later models with black knobs, originally designed to replace the Super60 but the Super60 remained until '93.

1990-1993		$400	$550

Super 210
1990-1993. Red Knob series, 2x10", 60 watts, earlier versions with red knobs, later models with black knobs.

1990-1993		$400	$550

Super 410
1992-1997. 60 watts, 4x10", black tolex, silver grille, blackface control panel.

1992-1997		$700	$950

Super Bassman Head
2012-present. 300-watt head, 6x6550 power tubes, master volume, standard '65 blackface cosmetics.

2012-2023		$1,125	$1,500

Super Champ
1982-1986. Black tolex, 18 watts, blackface, 1x10".

1982-1986		$1,000	$1,375

Super Champ Deluxe
1982-1986. Solid oak cabinet, 18 watts, upgrade 10" Electro-Voice speaker, see-thru brown grille cloth.

1982-1986		$1,125	$1,500

Super Champ XD
2008-2011. Tube amp with extra preamp voicing, 1x10" combo, blackface cosmetics. Replaced by X2 version.

2008-2011		$250	$350

Super Reverb
1963-1982. 4x10" speakers, blackface until '67 and '80-'82, silverface '68-'80.

1963-1964	Blackface, Fender Elec	$2,500	$4,500
1965-1967	Blackface, FMI	$2,500	$4,000
1968	Silverface, AB763	$1,500	$2,000
1969-1970	Silverface	$1,250	$1,750

MODEL YEAR	FEATURES	LOW	HIGH
1970-1972	Silverface, AA270	$1,125	$1,625
1972-1975	Int Master	$1,000	$1,500
1975-1980	MV with pull	$975	$1,250
1981-1982	Blackface	$975	$1,250

Super Reverb Solidstate
1967-1970. 50 watts, 4x10".

1967-1970		$525	$700

'65 Super Reverb
2001-present. 45 watts, all tube, 4x10", blackface cosmetics.

2001-2023		$975	$1,250

Super Showman XFL-1000/XFL-2000
1969-1971. Solidstate Super Showman head controlled 1 or more powered speaker cabs. The XFL-1000 was a 4x12" cab with 2 70-watt power amps, the 8x10" XFL-2000 had the same power amps.

1969-1971		$650	$850

Super Six Reverb
1970-1979. Large combo amp based on the Twin Reverb chassis, 100 watts, 6x10", black tolex.

1970-1979		$1,125	$1,500

Super Twin
1975-1980. 180 watts (6 6L6 power tubes), 2x12", distinctive dark grille.

1975-1976	Non-reverb	$850	$1,125
1976-1980	Reverb	$900	$1,250

Super-Sonic/60
2006-present. All tube, 60 watts, various options, 1x12" combo or 2x12" piggyback, blonde/oxblood or blackface. Straight and slant 4x12" cab added '11.

2006-2013	1x12, blonde/oxblood	$775	$1,000
2006-2014	1x12, blackface	$725	$950
2006-2015	2x12 piggyback, blonde	$1,000	$1,375

Super-Sonic 22 Combo Limited Edition "Black Gold" FSR
2012. 150 made, 1x12, 2-tone gold and black vinyl with white piping, black grille.

2012		$825	$1,125

Taurus
1970-1972. Solidstate, 42 watts, 2x10" JBL, black tolex, silver grille, JBL badge.

1970-1972		$500	$650

TB 600 Bass
2008-2019. Combo, 600 watts (4 ohms), 400 watts (8 ohms).

2008-2019		$350	$450

TB 1200 Bass Head
2013. Hybrid, 1200 watts (2 ohms), 800 watts (4 ohms), 550 watts (8 ohms), 4-button footswitch.

2013		$600	$775

Tone Master Set
1993-2002. Custom Shop, hand-wired head with Tonemaster 2x12" or 4x12" cabinet, blonde or oxblood.

1993-2002		$1,500	$2,000

Tone Master Deluxe Reverb
2019-present. 100-watt digital, reverb and tremolo, black or blonde.

2019-2023	Black	$625	$825
2019-2023	Blonde	$675	$875

The *Vintage Guitar Price Guide* shows values for an all-original condition amplifier, and where applicable, with original cover.

MODEL YEAR	FEATURES	LOW	HIGH

Tone Master Twin Reverb

2019-present. 200-watt digital, reverb and tremolo, black or blonde.

2019-2023	Black	$700	$925
2019-2023	Blonde	$725	$950

Tremolux

1955-1966. Tube, tweed, 1x12" '55-'60, white tolex with piggyback 1x10" cabinet '61-'62, 2x10" '62-'64, black tolex '64-'66.

1955-1960	Tweed, 1x12, narrow panel	$6,000	$7,500
1961	Rare 6G9 Ckt, EL84s	$5,500	$7,500
1961	Rough white/ oxblood, 1x10	$4,500	$5,500
1961-1962	Rough white/ oxblood, 2x10	$3,500	$4,500
1962-1963	Rough white/ wheat, 2x10	$3,000	$4,000
1963-1964	Smooth white/ gold, 2x10	$3,000	$4,000
1964-1966	Black tolex, 2x10	$2,500	$3,500
1964-1966	Black tolex, head only	$1,500	$2,000

EC Tremolux

2011-2016. Eric Clapton's variation on a '57, hand-wired, 12 watts, 1x12".

2011-2016		$1,375	$1,875

Twin

1952-1963, 1996-2010. Tube, 2x12"; 15 watts, tweed wide-panel '52-'55; narrow-panel '55-'60; 50 watts '55-'57; 80 watts '58; brown tolex '60; white tolex '61-'63. Reintroduced in '96 with black tolex, spring reverb and output control for 100 watts or 25 watts.

1952-1954	Tweed, wide panel	$9,500	$12,000
1955-1957	Tweed, 50w	$14,000	$18,000
1958-1959	Tweed, 80w	$20,000	$24,000
1960	Brown tolex, 80w	$15,000	$20,000
1960-1962	Rough white/ oxblood	$8,000	$10,000
1963	Smooth white/gold	$7,000	$9,000

'57 Twin/'57 Custom Twin

2004-2011, 2016-present. Custom Series reissue, tweed, 40 watts, 2x12". Custom added to model name in '16.

2004-2011		$1,625	$2,125
2016-2023		$1,875	$2,500

Twin Reverb

1963-1982. Black tolex, 85 watts (changed to 135 watts in '81), 2x12", blackface '63-'67 and '81-'82, silverface '68-'81, blackface optional in '80-'81 and standard in '82.

1963-1967	Blackface	$3,000	$4,000
1968	Silverface, no master vol	$1,500	$2,000
1969-1970	Silverface, no master vol	$1,250	$1,750
1971-1972	Silverface, no master vol	$1,000	$1,500
1973-1975	Silverface, master vol	$975	$1,250
1976-1980	Silverface, push/pull	$975	$1,250
1980-1982	Blackface	$975	$1,250

Twin Reverb Solidstate

1966-1969. 100 watts, 2x12", black tolex.

1966-1969		$550	$725

'65 Twin Reverb

1991-present. Black tolex, 2x12", 85 watts.

1991-2023		$950	$1,250

'65 Twin Custom 15

2009-2017. 85-watt Twin Reverb with 1x15".

2009-2017		$950	$1,250

'68 Custom Twin Reverb

2014-present. Vintage Modified silverface reissue, 1x12", 85 watts, modified all-tube circuitry.

2014-2023		$950	$1,250

Twin Reverb II

1983-1985. Black tolex, 2x12", 105 watts, channel switching, effects loop, blackface panel, silver grille.

1983-1985		$975	$1,250

Twin "The Twin"/"Evil Twin"

1987-1992. 100 watts, 2x12", red knobs, mostly black tolex, but white, red and snakeskin covers offered.

1987-1992		$750	$975

EC Twinolux

2011-2016. Eric Clapton's variation on a '57, hand-wired, 40 watts, 2x12".

2011-2016		$2,750	$3,500

Two Tone (Custom Shop)

2001-2003. Limited production, modern styling, slanted grille, 15 watts, 1x10" and 1x12", 2-tone blonde cab, based on modified Blues Deluxe circuit, Two Tone on name plate.

2001-2003		$1,125	$1,500

Ultimate Chorus DSP

1995-2001. Solidstate, 2x65 watts, 2x12", 32 built-in effect variations, blackface cosmetics.

1995-2001		$250	$350

Ultra Chorus

1992-1994. Solidstate, 2x65 watts, 2x12", standard control panel with chorus.

1992-1994		$250	$325

Vibrasonic

1959-1963. First amp to receive the new brown tolex and JBL, 1x15", 25 watts.

1959-1963		$2,500	$3,500

Vibrasonic Custom

1995-1997. Custom Shop designed for steel guitar and guitar, blackface, 1x15", 100 watts.

1995-1997		$900	$1,250

Vibrasonic Reverb

1972-1981. Black tolex, 100 watts, 1x15", silverface.

1972-1981		$900	$1,250

Vibro-Champ

1964-1982. Black tolex, 4 watts, (5 watts '69-'71, 6 watts '72-'80), 1x8", blackface '64-'68 and '82, silverface '69-'81.

1964-1967	Blackface, AA764	$1,500	$2,000
1968-1972	Silverface	$950	$1,250
1973-1981	Silverface	$900	$1,125
1982	Blackface	$850	$1,125

EC Vibro Champ

2011-2016. Eric Clapton's variation on a '57 Champ, hand-wired, 5 watts, 1x8".

2011-2016		$1,125	$1,500

1969 Fender Twin Reverb
Tom Pfeifer

AMPS

1970 Fender Vibro
Champ Silverface
Rivington Guitars

1960s Fender Vibrasonic
David Gant

1959 Fender Vibrolux
Ted Wulfers

1964 Fender Vibroverb
David Gant

Fryette Aether

MODEL YEAR	FEATURES	LOW	HIGH
Vibro-Champ XD			
2008-2011. Made in China, 5 watts, 1x8.			
2008-2011		$150	$200
Vibro-King Custom			
1993-2012. Custom Shop combo, 60 watts, 3x10", vintage reverb, tremolo, single channel, all tube, blond or black.			
1993-2012		$1,875	$2,500
Vibro-King 212 Cabinet			
1993-2012. Custom Shop extension cab, blond tolex, 2x12" Celestion GK80.			
1993-2012		$500	$725
Vibro-King Custom Limited Edition			
2012-2013. Limited Edition production of unique colors, Chocolate Crème Two-Tone, wheat grille (25 made) and Tequila Sunrise, 3-color sunburst on figured birdseye maple cab, oxblood grille.			
2012	Chocolate Crème	$2,000	$2,500
2013	Tequila Sunrise	$2,500	$3,500
Vibrolux			
1956-1964. Narrow-panel, 10 watts, tweed with 1x10" '56-'61, brown tolex and brownface with 1x12" and 30 watts '61-'62, black tolex and blackface '63-'64.			
1956-1961	Tweed, 1x10	$6,500	$7,500
1961-1962	Brown tolex, 1x12	$4,500	$5,500
1963-1964	Black tolex, 1x12	$4,000	$5,000
Vibrolux Reverb			
1964-1982. Black tolex, 2x10", blackface '64-'67 and '81-'82, silverface '70-'80. Reissued in '96 with blackface and 40 watts.			
1964-1967	Blackface	$4,000	$5,000
1968	Silverface	$2,500	$3,500
1969-1970	Silverface	$2,000	$2,500
1971-1980	Silverface	$1,500	$2,000
1981-1982	Blackface	$1,500	$2,000
Vibrolux Reverb Solidstate			
1967-1969. Fender CBS solidstate, 35 watts, 2x10", black tolex.			
1967-1969		$550	$725
Vibrolux Custom Reverb			
1995-2013. Part of Professional Series, Custom Shop designed, standard factory built, 40 watts, 2x10", tube, white knobs, blond tolex and tan grill for '95 only, black tolex, silver grille after. Does not say Custom on face plate.			
1995-2013	Various colors	$900	$1,250
'68 Custom Vibrolux Reverb			
2014-2020. Silverface-style, 35 watts, 2x10", black vinyl with silver-turquoise grille.			
2014-2020		$900	$1,250
Vibroverb			
1963-1964. Brown tolex with 35 watts, 2x10" and brownface '63, black tolex with 1x15" and blackface late '63-'64.			
1963	Brown tolex, 2x10	$8,000	$12,000
1963-1964	Black tolex, 1x15	$5,500	$9,000
'63 Vibroverb Reissue			
1990-1995. Reissue of 1963 Vibroverb, 40 watts, 2x10", reverb, vibrato, brown tolex.			
1990-1995		$1,375	$1,750

MODEL YEAR	FEATURES	LOW	HIGH
'64 Vibroverb (Custom Shop)			
2003-2008. Reissue of 1964 Vibroverb with 1x15" blackface specs.			
2003-2008		$1,375	$1,750
Yale Reverb			
1983-1985. Solidstate, black tolex, 50 watts, 1x12", silverface.			
1983-1985		$400	$525

FireBelly Amps
2008-present. Production/custom, professional and premium grade, vintage tube amps built by father/son, Steven and Scott Cohen, in Santa Monica, California.

Fishman
2003-present. Larry Fishman offers professional grade, production, amps that are designed and engineered in Andover, Massachusetts and assembled in China. They also build effects.

MODEL YEAR	FEATURES	LOW	HIGH
Loudbox 100			
2006-2013. 100 watts, 1x8" with dome.			
2006-2013		$275	$425
Loudbox Artist Pro-LBX-600			
2006-present. 120 watts,			
2006-2023		$300	$450
Loudbox Mini Pro-LBX-500			
2006-present. 60 watts.			
2006-2023		$200	$300
Loudbox Performer Pro-LBX-700			
2006-present. 180 watts.			
2006-2023		$400	$575

Flot-A-Tone
Ca.1946-early 1960s. Flot-A-Tone was in Milwaukee, Wisconsin, and made a variety of tube guitar and accordion amps. Most were distributed by the Lo Duca Brothers.

MODEL YEAR	FEATURES	LOW	HIGH
Large Models			
1960s. Four speakers.			
1946-60s		$775	$1,250
Smaller Models			
1960s. 1x8" speaker.			
1946-60s		$450	$725

Fortune
1978-1979. Created by Jim Kelley just prior to branding Jim Kelley Amplifiers in 1980, Fortune Amplifiers logo on front panel, specifications and performance similar to early Jim Kelley amplifiers, difficult to find in original condition, professional grade, designed and manufactured by Active Guitar Electronics company.

Fox Amps
Marc Vos builds professional grade, production/custom, guitar amps and cabinets, starting 2007, in Budel, Netherlands.

Framus
1946-1977, 1996-present. Tube guitar amp heads, combos and cabinets made in Markneukirchen,

MODEL YEAR	FEATURES	LOW	HIGH

Germany. They also build guitars, basses, mandolins and banjos. Begun as an acoustic instrument manufacturer, Framus added electrics in the mid-'50s. In the '60s, Framus instruments were imported into the U.S. by Philadelphia Music Company. The brand was revived in '96 by Hans Peter Wilfer, the president of Warwick, with production in Warwick's factory in Germany. Distributed in the U.S. by Dana B. Goods.

Fred

1984-1986. Before settling on the name Bedrock, company founders Brad Jeter and Ron Pinto produced 50 amps carrying the brand name Fred in Nashua, New Hampshire.

Frenzel

1952-present. Jim Frenzel built his first amp in '52 and began using his brand in '01. He offers intermediate and professional grade, production/custom, hand-wired, vintage tube, guitar and bass amps built in Mabank, Texas.

Frudua Guitar Works

1988-present. Intermediate grade, production, guitar and bass amps built by guitar luthier Galeazzo Frudua in Calusco d'Adda, Italy. He also builds guitars and basses.

Fryette

2009-present. Professional and premium grade amps, combos, and cabinets built by Steven M. Fryette, who also founded VHT amps. At the beginning of '09 AXL guitars acquired the VHT name to build their own product. Fryette continues to manufacture the VHT amp models under the Fryette brand in Burbank, California.

Fuchs Audio Technology

2000-present. Andy Fuchs started the company in '99 to rebuild and modify tube amps. In 2000 he started production of his own brand of amps, offering combos and heads from 10 to 150 watts. They also custom build audiophile and studio tube electronics. Originally located in Bloomfield, New Jersey, since '07 in Clifton, New Jersey.

Fulton-Webb

Steve Fulton and Bill Webb started in 1997, build tube amp heads, combos and cabinets in Austin, Texas, beginning.

Gabriel Sound Garage

2004-2014. Gabriel Bucataru built his tube amp heads and combos in Arlington Heights, Illinois.

Gallien-Krueger

1969-present. Gallien-Krueger has offered a variety of bass and guitar amps, combos and cabinets and is located in San Jose, California.

Garcia

Tube amp heads and speaker cabinets built by Matthew Garcia in Myrtle Beach, South Carolina, starting in 2004. He also built effects.

Garnet

Mid 1960s-1989. In the mid '60s, "Gar" Gillies started the Garnet Amplifier Company with his two sons, Russell and Garnet, after he started making PA systems in his Canadian radio and TV repair shop. The first PA from the new company was for Chad Allen & the Expressions (later known as The Guess Who). A wide variety of tube amps were offered, and all were designed by Gar, Sr. The company also produced the all-tube effects The Herzog, H zog, and two stand-alone reverb units designed by Gar in the late '60s and early '70s. The company closed in '89, due to financial reasons caused largely by a too rapid expansion. Gar repaired and designed custom amps up to his death in early 2007.

GDS Amplification

1998-present. Tube amps, combos and speaker cabinets from builder Graydon D. Stuckey of Fenton, Michigan. GDS also offers amp kits. In January, '09, GDS bought the assets of Guytron Amplification.

Genesis

Genesis was a 1980s line of student amps from Gibson.

B40

1984-late-1980s. Bass combo with 40 watts.

1984-1989		$110	$175

G Series

1984-late-1980s. Small combo amps.

1984-1989	G10, 10w	$70	$100
1984-1989	G25, 25w	$90	$150
1984-1989	G40R, 40w, reverb	$140	$200

Genz Benz

Founded by Jeff and Cathy Genzler in 1984 and located in Scottsdale, Arizona, the company offers guitar, bass, and PA amps and speaker cabinets. In late 2003, Genz Benz was acquired by Kaman (Ovation, Hamer, Takamine). On January 1, '08, Fender acquired Kaman Music Corporation and the Genz Benz brand.

George Dennis

1991-present. Founded by George Burgerstein, the original products were a line of effects pedals. In '96 they added a line of tube amps. The company is in Prague, Czech Republic.

Gerhart

2000-present. Production/custom, intermediate and professional grade, amps and cabinets from builder Gary Gerhart of West Hills, California. He also offers an amp in kit form.

Fuchs Lucky 7
Cream City Music

Garnet Gnome Reverb
John Maysenhoelder

Gerhart Gilmore

AMPS

Germino Club 40

1963 Gibson Atlas IV

Imaged by Heritage Auctions, HA.com

1953 Gibson BR-6

MODEL YEAR	FEATURES	LOW	HIGH

Germino
2002-present. Intermediate to professional grade tube amps, combos and cabinets built by Greg Germino in Graham, North Carolina.

Gibson
1890s (1902)-present. Gibson has offered a variety of amps since the mid-'30s to the present under the Gibson brandname and others. Many Gibson amps have missing or broken logos. The prices listed are for amps with fully intact logos. A broken or missing logo can diminish the value of the amp. Amps with a changed handle, power cord, and especially a broken logo should be taken on a case-by-case basis.

Atlas IV
1963-1967. Piggyback head and cab, introduced with trapezoid shape, changed to rectangular cabs in '65-'66 with black cover, simple circuit with 4 knobs, no reverb or tremolo, mid-power with 2 6L6, 1x15".

1963-1965	Brown	$650	$850
1966-1967	Black	$650	$850

Atlas Medalist
1964-1967. Combo version with 1x15".

1964-1967		$625	$800

B-40
1972-1975. Solidstate, 40 watts, 1x12".

1972-1975		$300	$400

BR-1
1946-1948. 15 watts, 1x12" field-coil speaker, brown leatherette cover, rectangular metal grille with large G.

1946-1948		$850	$1,250

BR-3
1946-1947. 12 watts, 1x12" Utah field-coil speaker (most BR models used Jensen speakers).

1946-1947		$850	$1,125

BR-4
1946-1948. 14 watts, 1x12" Utah field-coil speaker (most BR models used Jensen speakers).

1946-1948		$750	$1,000

BR-6
1946-1954. 10 to 12 watts, 1x10", brown leatherette, speaker opening split by cross panel with G logo, bottom mounted chassis with single on-off volume pointer knob.

1946-1947	Verticle cab	$750	$1,000
1948-1954	Horizontal cab	$750	$1,000

BR-9
1948-1954. Cream leatherette, 10 watts, 1x8". Originally sold with the BR-9 lap steel. Renamed GA-9 in '54.

1948-1954		$550	$750

Duo Metalist
1968-early 1970s. Upright vertical combo cab, tubes, faux wood grain panel, mid-power, 1x12".

1968-1970s		$575	$750

EH-100
1936-1942. Electric-Hawaiian companion amp, 1x10". AC/DC version called EH-110.

1936-1942		$950	$1,500

EH-125
1941-1942. 1x12", rounded shoulder cab, brown cover in '41 and dark green in '42, leather handle.

1941-1942		$1,125	$1,500

EH-126
1941. Experimental model, 6-volt variant of EH-125, about 5 made.

1941		$1,500	$2,500

EH-135
1941. Experimental model, alternating and direct current switchable, about 7 made.

1941		$1,500	$2,500

EH-150
1935-1942. Electric-Hawaiian companion amp, 1x12" ('35-'37) or 1x10" ('38-'42). AC/DC version called EH-160.

1935	13 3/4" square cab	$1,500	$2,500
1936-1937	14 3/4" square cab	$1,500	$2,500
1937-1942	15 3/8" round cab	$1,500	$2,500

EH-185
1939-1942. 1x12", tweed cover, black and orange vertical stripes, marketed as companion amp to the EH-185 Lap Steel. AC/DC version called EH-195.

1939-1942		$2,500	$3,250

EH-195
1939-1942. EH-185 variant with vibrato.

1939-1942		$2,250	$3,500

EH-250
1940. Upgraded natural maple cabinet using EH-185 chassis, only 2 made, evolved into EH-275.

1940		$2,500	$4,000

EH-275
1940-1942. Similar to EH-185 but with maple cab and celluloid binding, about 30 made.

1940-1942		$2,500	$4,000

Epoch Series
2000s. Solidstate student practice amps.

2000s	Various models	$30	$40

Falcon III F-3
Early 1970s. Solidstate, 1x12" combo, 65 watts, made in Chicago by CMI after Gibson ceased amp production in Kalamazoo ('67), black tolex, dark grille.

1970		$325	$425

Falcon Medalist (Hybrid)
1967. Transitional tube 1x12" combo amp from GA-19 tube Falcon to the solidstate Falcon, Falcon logo and Gibson logo on front panel, brown control panel, dark cover and dark grille, vertical combo cabinet.

1967		$375	$500

Falcon Medalist (Solidstate)
1968-1969. Solidstate combo, 15 watts, 1x12".

1968-1969		$400	$550

G-10
1972-1975. Solidstate, 10 watts, 1x10", no tremolo or reverb.

1972-1975		$150	$200

G-20
1972-1975. Solidstate with tremolo, 1x10", 10 watts.

1972-1975		$150	$200

G-25
1972-1975. 25 watts, 1x10".

1972-1975		$200	$300

G-35
1975. Solidstate, 30 watts, 1x12".

1975		$250	$350

MODEL YEAR	FEATURES	LOW	HIGH

G-40/G-40R
1972-1974. Solidstate with tremolo and reverb, 40 watts, 1x12" (G-40) and 2x10" (G-40 R).

1972-1974		$325	$450

G-50/G-50A/G-50B
1972, 1975. Solidstate with tremolo and reverb, models G-50 and 50 A are 1x12", 40 watts, model 50 B is a bass 1x15", 50 watts.

1972-1975		$350	$500

G-55
1975. 50 watts, 1x12".

1975		$325	$450

G-60
1972-1973. Solidstate with tremolo and reverb, 1x15", 60 watts.

1972-1973		$350	$450

G-70
1972-1973. Solidstate with tremolo and reverb, 2x12", 60 watts.

1972-1973		$400	$550

G-80
1972-1973. Solidstate with tremolo and reverb, 4x10", 60 watts.

1972-1973		$450	$600

G-100A/G-100B
1975. 100 watts, model 100 A is 2x12" and 100 B is 2x15".

1975		$450	$600

G-105
1974-1975. Solidstate, 100 watts, 2x12", reverb.

1974-1975		$450	$600

G-115
1975. 100 watts, 4x10".

1974-1975		$500	$650

GA-5 Les Paul Junior
1954-1957. Tan fabric cover (Mottled Brown by '57), 7" oval speaker, 4 watts. Renamed Skylark in '58.

1954-1957		$850	$1,500

GA-5 Les Paul Junior (Reissue)
2004-2008. Goldtone Series, class A, 5 watts, 1x8".

2004-2008		$400	$575

GA-5 Skylark
1958-1968. Gold cover (brown by '63 and black by '66), 1x8" (1x10" from '64 on), 4.5 watts (10 watts from '64 on), tremolo. Often sold with the Skylark Lap Steel.

1958-1959	Gold, 45w, 1x8	$650	$850
1960-1962	Gold, 45w, 1x8	$525	$800
1963	Brown, 45w, 1x8	$500	$750
1964	Brown, 10w, 1x10	$450	$700
1965-1967	Black, 10w, 1x10	$425	$650
1968	Skylark, last version	$300	$500

GA-5T Skylark
1960-1968. Tremolo, 4.5 watts early, 10 later, gold covering and 1x8" until '63, brown '63-'64, black and 1x10" after.

1960-1962	Gold, 45w, 1x8	$525	$750
1963	Brown, 45w, 1x8	$500	$725
1964	Brown, 10w, 1x10	$500	$725
1965-1967	Kalamazoo, black	$425	$575
1968	Norlin, vertical cab	$425	$575

MODEL YEAR	FEATURES	LOW	HIGH

GA-5W
Late-1960s. Norlin-era, post-Kalamazoo production, 15 watts, small speaker, volume and tone controls.

1969		$110	$140

GA-6
1956-1959. Replaced the BR-6, 8 to 12 watts, 1x12", has Gibson 6 above the grille. Renamed GA-6 Lancer in '60.

1956-1959		$1,250	$1,750

GA-6 Lancer
1960-1961. Renamed from GA-6, 1x12", tweed cover, 3 knobs, 14 watts.

1960-1961		$1,125	$1,500

GA-7 Les Paul TV Model
1954-1956. Basic old-style GA-5 with different graphics, 4 watts, small speaker.

1954-1956		$850	$1,125

GA-8 Discoverer
1962-1964. Renamed from GA-8 Gibsonette, gold fabric cover, 1x12", 10 watts.

1962-1964		$650	$950

GA-8 Gibsonette
1955-1962. Tan fabric cover (gold by '58), 1x10", 8 watts (9 watts by '58). See Gibsonette for 1952-'54. Name changed to GA-8 Discoverer in '62.

1955-1957	Gibsonette logo	$750	$975
1958-1959	Gibson logo	$650	$850
1960-1962	Gibson logo, tweed	$575	$800

GA-8T Discoverer
1960-1966. Tweed, 1x10", 9-watt, tremolo. Tan cover, 1x12", 15-watt '63-'64, black after.

1960-1962	Tweed, 9w, 1x10	$950	$1,500
1963-1964	Tan, 15w, 1x12	$750	$1,000
1965-1966	Black	$750	$1,000

GA-9
1954-1959. Renamed from BR-9, tan fabric cover, 8 watts, 1x10". Often sold with the BR-9 Lap Steel.

1954-1959	Gibson 9 logo	$750	$1,000

GA-14 Titan
1959-1961. About 15 watts using 2x6V6 power tubes, 1x10", tweed cover.

1959-1961		$925	$1,250

GA-15 RV Goldtone
1999-2004. 15 watts, Class A, 1x12", spring reverb.

1999-2004		$525	$750

GA-15 RVT Explorer
1965-1967. Tube, 1x10", tremolo, reverb, black vinyl.

1965-1967		$550	$750

GA-17 RVT Scout
1963-1967. Low power, 1x10", reverb and tremolo.

1963	Smooth brown	$600	$850
1964-1965	Textured brown	$600	$850
1966-1967	Black	$475	$650

GA-18 Explorer
1959. Tweed, tube, 14 watts, 1x10". Replaced in '60 by the GA-18 T Explorer.

1959		$1,500	$2,000

GA-18T Explorer
1960-1963. Tweed, 14 watts, 1x10", tremolo.

1960-1962	Tweed	$1,250	$1,750
1963	Brown	$950	$1,250

Gibson GA-5 Les Paul Junior

1964 Gibeon GA-5 T Skylark
Tom Pfeifer

1958 Gibson GA-9
Imaged by Heritage Auctions, HA.com

AMPS

1953 Gibson GA-20

Tom Pfeifer

1950 Gibson GA-30

Imaged by Heritage Auctions, HA.com

1954 Gibson GA-50 T

Imaged by Heritage Auctions, HA.com

MODEL YEAR	FEATURES	LOW	HIGH

GA-19 RVT Falcon

1961-1967. One of Gibson's best-selling amps. Initially tweed covered, followed by smooth brown, textured brown, and black. Each amp has a different tone. One 12" Jensen with deep-sounding reverb and tremolo.

1961-1962	Tweed	$1,000	$1,500
1962-1963	Smooth brown	$800	$1,250
1964	Textured brown	$725	$1,125
1965-1967	Black	$550	$850

GA-20

1950-1962. Brown leatherette (2-tone by '55 and tweed by '60), tube, 12 watts early, 14 watts later, 1x12". Renamed Crest in '60.

1950-1954	Brown, single G logo	$1,250	$1,500
1955-1958	2-tone salt/maroon	$1,500	$2,000
1959	2-tone blue/blond	$1,500	$2,000

GA-20 Crest

1960-1961. Tweed, tube, 14 watts, 1x12".

1960-1961		$1,375	$1,750

GA-20 RVT

2004-2007. 15 watts, 1x12", reverb, tremolo.

2004-2007		$700	$900

GA-20 RVT Minuteman

1965-1967. Black, 14 watts, 1x12", tube, reverb, tremolo.

1965-1967		$550	$775

GA-20T

1956-1959. Tube, 16 watts, tremolo, 1x12", 2-tone. Renamed Ranger in '60.

1956-1958	2-tone	$1,750	$2,500
1959	New 2-tone	$1,750	$2,500

GA-20T Ranger

1960-1961. Tube, 16 watts, tremolo, 1x12", tweed.

1960-1962		$1,625	$2,250

GA-25

1947-1948. Brown, 1x12" and 1x8", 15 watts. Replaced by GA-30 in '48.

1947-1948		$1,375	$1,875

GA-25 RVT Hawk

1963-1968. Reverb, tremolo, 1x15".

1963	Smooth brown	$875	$1,250
1964	Rough brown	$650	$1,000
1965-1967	Black	$650	$1,000
1968	Last version	$625	$950

GA-30/Invader

1948-1961. Brown until '54, 2-tone after, tweed in '60, 1x12" and 1x8", 14 watts. Renamed GA-30 Invader in '60.

1948-1954	Brown	$1,750	$2,500
1955-1959	2-tone salt/maroon	$1,750	$2,500
1960-1961	Invader, tweed	$1,750	$2,500

GA-30 RV Invader

1961. Tweed, 1x12" and 1x8", 14-16 watts, reverb but no tremolo.

1961		$1,500	$2,250

GA-30 RVH Goldtone Head

1999-2004. 30 watts, Class A head, reverb.

1999-2004		$900	$1,250

GA-30 RVS (Stereo) Goldtone

1999-2004. 15 watts per channel, Class A stereo,

2x12", reverb.

1999-2004		$1,125	$1,500

GA-30 RVT Invader

1962-1967. Updated model with reverb and tremolo, 25 watts, 1x12" and 1x10" speakers, first issue in tweed.

1962	Tweed	$1,750	$2,500
1963	Smooth brown	$950	$1,500
1964	Rough brown	$725	$1,250
1965-1967	Black	$650	$1,000

GA-35 RVT Lancer

1966-1967. Black, 1x12", tremolo, reverb.

1966-1967		$650	$850

GA-40 Les Paul

1952-1960. Introduced with the Les Paul Model guitar, 1x12" Jensen speaker, 14 watts earlier and 16 later, recessed leather handle using spring mounting (the handle is easily broken and replacement handle is more common than not). Two-tone leatherette covering, '50s checkerboard grille ('52-early-'55), Les Paul script logo on front of the amp ('52-'55), plastic grille insert with LP monogram, gold Gibson logo above grille. Cosmetics changed dramatically in early/mid-'55. Renamed GA-40 T Les Paul in '60.

1952-1955	Brown 2-tone, LP grille	$3,000	$4,000
1955-1957	2-tone salt/maroon	$3,000	$4,500
1958-1959	2-tone blue/blond	$3,000	$4,500

GA-40 RVT Limited Edition

2008-2011. GA-40RVT Limited Edition logo, 200 made, 2-tone brown/tan, front control panel, 30/15 switchable watts.

2008-2011		$775	$1,000

GA-40T Les Paul

1960-1962. Renamed from GA-40 Les Paul, 1x12", 16 watts, tremolo. Renamed Mariner in '62-'67.

1960-1961	Tweed	$2,750	$3,750
1962	Smooth brown	$775	$1,000

GA-40T Mariner

1962-1967. 1x12" combo, 25 watts, tremolo.

1962-1963	Smooth brown	$850	$1,250
1964	Rough brown	$725	$950
1965-1967	Black	$675	$900

GA-45 RVT Saturn

1965-1967. 2x10", mid power, tremolo, reverb.

1965-1967		$700	$1,125

GA-50/GA-50T

1948-1955. Brown leatherette, 25 watts, 1x12" and 1x8", T had tremolo.

1948-1955	GA-50	$2,500	$3,500
1948-1955	GA-50T	$2,250	$3,250

GA-55 RVT Ranger

1965-1967. Black cover, 4x10", tremolo, reverb.

1965-1967		$750	$1,125

GA-55/GA-55V

1954-1958. 2x12", 20 watts, GA-55V with vibrato.

1954-1958	GA-55	$3,750	$5,000
1954-1958	GA-55 V	$3,750	$5,000

GA-60 Hercules

1962-1963. 25 watts, 1x15, no-frills 1-channel amp, no reverb, no tremolo.

1962-1963		$750	$1,125

MODEL YEAR	FEATURES	LOW	HIGH

GA-60 RV Goldtone
1999-2004. 60 watts, A/B circuit, 2x12", spring reverb, earliest production in England.

| 1999-2004 | | $1,250 | $1,875 |

GA-70 Country and Western
1955-1958. 25 watts, 1x15", 2-tone, longhorn cattle western logo on front, advertised to have extra bright sound.

| 1955-1958 | | $3,750 | $5,000 |

GA-75
1950-1955. Mottled Brown leatherette, 1x15", 25 watts.

| 1950-1955 | | $2,500 | $3,250 |

GA-75 Recording
1964-1967. 2x10" speakers, no reverb or tremolo, 2 channels, dark cover, gray grille.

| 1964-1967 | | $800 | $1,250 |

GA-75L Recording
1964-1967. 1x15" Lansing speaker, no reverb or tremolo, 2 channels, dark cover, gray grille.

| 1964-1967 | | $750 | $1,125 |

GA-77
1954-1959. 1x15" JBL, 25-30 watts, 2x6L6 power tubes, 2-tone covering, near top-of-the-line for the mid-'50s.

| 1954-1958 | 2-tone salt/maroon, leather handle | $2,250 | $3,000 |
| 1958-1959 | 2-tone blue/blond, metal handle | $2,250 | $3,000 |

GA-77 RET Vanguard
1964-1967. Mid-power, 2x10", tremolo, reverb, echo.

| 1964 | Rough brown | $1,250 | $1,750 |
| 1965-1967 | Black | $1,000 | $1,500 |

GA-77 RETL Vanguard
1964-1967. GA-77 RET with 1x15" Lansing speaker option (L).

| 1964-1967 | | $900 | $1,375 |

GA-77 RVTL Vanguard
1962-1967.

| 1962-1967 | | $900 | $1,375 |

GA-77 Vanguard
1960-1961. 1x15" JBL, 25-30 watts, 2 6L6 power tubes, tweed cover, first use of Vanguard model name.

| 1960-1961 | | $1,875 | $2,875 |

GA-78 Bell Stereo
1960. Gibson-branded amp made by Bell, same as GA-79 series, Bell 30 logo on front, 30 watts, 2x10" wedge cab.

| 1960 | | $2,500 | $3,500 |

GA-79 RV
1960-1962. Stereo-reverb, 2x10", 30 watts.

| 1960-1961 | Tweed | $2,750 | $4,000 |
| 1962 | Textured brown | $2,500 | $3,500 |

GA-79 RVT Multi-Stereo
1961-1967. Introduced as GA-79 RVT, Multi-Stereo was added to name in '61. Stereo-reverb and tremolo, 2x10", tweed (black and brown also available), 30 watts.

1961	Tweed	$2,750	$4,000
1961-1962	Gray sparkle	$2,500	$3,500
1963-1965	Textured brown	$2,500	$3,500
1965-1967	Black	$2,500	$3,500

GA-80/GA-80T/Vari-Tone
1959-1961. 25 watts, 1x15", 2 channels, described as "6-in-1 amplifier with improved tremolo," 6 Vari-Tone push buttons which give "six distinctively separate sounds," 7 tubes, tweed cover.

| 1959-1961 | | $2,000 | $3,000 |

GA-83S Stereo-Vibe
1959-1961. Interesting stereo amp with front baffle mounted 1x12" and 4x8" side-mounted speakers (2 on each side), 35 watts, Gibson logo on upper right corner of the grille, tweed cover, brown grille (late '50s Fender-style), 3 pointer knobs and 3 round knobs, 4 inputs.

| 1959-1961 | | $2,750 | $3,750 |

GA-85 Bass Reflex
1957-1958. Removable head, 25 watts, 1x12", very limited production.

| 1957-1958 | | $1,375 | $2,000 |

GA-86 Ensemble
1960. 25-watt head plus 1x12" cab, tweed.

| 1960 | | $1,875 | $2,500 |

GA-88S Stereo Twin
1960. Control panel and 2 separate 1x12" speaker cabs, 35 watts, 8 tubes, tweed.

| 1960 | | $4,250 | $5,500 |

GA-90 High Fidelity
1953-1960. 25 watts, 6x8", 2 channels, advertised for guitar, bass, accordion, or hi-fi.

| 1953-1960 | | $1,750 | $2,500 |

GA-95 RVT Apollo
1965-1967. 90 watts, 2x12", black vinyl, black grille, tremolo, reverb.

| 1965-1967 | | $750 | $975 |

GA-100 Bass
1960-1963. 35 watts, 1x12" cabinet, for '60-'61 tweed and tripod included for separate head, for '62-'63 brown covering and Crestline Tuck-A-Way head.

| 1960-1961 | Tweed | $1,500 | $2,250 |
| 1962-1963 | Smooth brown | $925 | $1,375 |

GA-200 Rhythm King
1957-1961. Introduced as GA-200, renamed Rhythm King in '60, 2-channel version of GA-400. Bass amp, 60 watts, 2x12".

1957-1959	2-tone	$2,500	$3,500
1959-1961	Tweed	$2,500	$3,500
1961	Smooth brown	$2,250	$3,000

GA-300 RVT Super 300
1962-1963. 60 watts, 2x12" combo, reverb, tremolo, smooth brown.

| 1962-1963 | | $2,250 | $3,000 |

GA-400 Super 400
1956-1961. 60 watts, 2x12", 3 channels, same size as GA-200 cab, 1 more tube than GA-200.

1956-1959	2-tone	$2,500	$3,500
1959-1961	Tweed	$2,500	$3,500
1961	Smooth brown	$2,500	$3,500

GA-CB Custom-Built
1949-1953. 25-30 watts, 1x15", the top model in Gibson's '51 line of amps, described as having sound quality found only in the finest public address broadcasting systems, about 47 made, this high-end

1958 Gibson GA-70
Country and Western
RT Jackson

1964 Gibson GA-77
RET Vanguard
Rick Buckendahl

1961 Gibson GA-79 RV

AMPS

Gibson Plus-50
Imaged by Heritage Auctions, HA.com

1963 Gibson Titan III
Imaged by Heritage Auctions, HA.com

Goodsell Super 17 MkIV

MODEL YEAR	FEATURES	LOW	HIGH

amp was replaced by the GA-77 and a completely different GA-90.

| 1949-1953 | | $2,250 | $3,500 |

Gibsonette
1952-1954. Gibsonette logo on front, round hole. See GA-8 Gibsonette for later models.

| 1952-1954 | | $625 | $950 |

GM05
2009-2012. Small 5-watt solidstate amp usually sold with Maestro guitar pack.

| 2009-2012 | | $30 | $40 |

GSS-50
1966-1967. Solidstate, 50 watts, 2x10" combo, reverb and tremolo, black vinyl cover, silver grille, no grille logo.

| 1966-1967 | | $450 | $650 |

GSS-100
1966-1967, 1970. Solidstate, 100 watts, two 24"x12" 2x10" sealed cabs, black vinyl cover, silver grille, 8 black knobs and 3 red knobs, slanted raised Gibson logo. Speakers are prone to distortion. Reissued in '70 in 3 variations.

| 1966-1967 | | $450 | $650 |

Lancer
1968-1969. CMI-Chicago produced, small combo, black upright cab, dark grille, post-McCarty era Gibson logo.

| 1968-1969 | | $95 | $150 |

LP-1/LP-2 Set
1970. Les Paul model, piggyback amp and cab set, LP-1 head and LP-2 4x12" plus 2 horns cab, large vertical speaker cabinet, rather small compact 190-watt solidstate amp head.

| 1970 | | $450 | $600 |

Medalist 2/12
1968-1970. Vertical cabinet, 2x12", reverb and temolo.

| 1968-1970 | | $550 | $750 |

Medalist 4/10
1968-1970. Vertical cabinet, 4x10", reverb and tremolo.

| 1968-1970 | | $550 | $750 |

Mercury I
1963-1965. Piggyback trapezoid-shaped head with 2x12" trapezoid cabinet, tremolo, brown.

| 1963-1965 | | $650 | $950 |

Mercury II
1963-1967. Mercury I with 1x15" and 1x10", initially brown trapezoid cabinets, then changed to black rectangular.

| 1963-1964 | Trapezoid cabs | $750 | $1,125 |
| 1965-1967 | Rectangular cabs | $775 | $1,250 |

Plus-50
1966-1967. 50 watts, powered extension amplifier. Similar to GSS-100 cabinet of the same era, 2x10" cab, black vinyl cover, silver grille, slant Gibson logo.

| 1966-1967 | | $600 | $800 |

Super Thor Bass
1970-1974. Solidstate, part of the new G-Series (not GA-Series), 65 watts, 2x15", black tolex, black grille, upright vertical cab with front control, single channel.

| 1970-1974 | | $500 | $750 |

MODEL YEAR	FEATURES	LOW	HIGH

Thor Bass
1970-1974. Solidstate, smaller 2x10" 50-watt version of Super Thor.

| 1970-1974 | | $450 | $600 |

Titan I
1963-1965. Piggyback trapezoid-shaped head and 2x12" trapezoid-shaped cabinet, tremolo.

| 1963-1965 | | $625 | $900 |

Titan III
1963-1967. Piggyback trapezoid-shaped head and 1x15" + 2x10" trapezoid-shaped cabinet, tremolo.

| 1963-1964 | Brown | $650 | $975 |
| 1965-1967 | Black | $650 | $975 |

Titan Medalist
1964-1967. Combo version of Titan Series with 1x15" and 1x10", tremolo only, no reverb, black.

| 1964-1967 | | $650 | $975 |

Titan V
1963-1967. Piggyback trapezoid-shaped tube head and 2x15" trapezoid-shaped cabinet, tremolo.

| 1963-1964 | Brown | $650 | $975 |
| 1965-1967 | Black | $650 | $975 |

TR-1000 T/TR-1000 RVT Starfire
1962-1967. Solidstate, 1x12" combo, 40 watts, tremolo, RVT with reverb.

| 1962-1967 | | $350 | $500 |

Ginelle

Rick Emery builds his tube combo amps in Ardmore, Pennsylvania starting in 1996.

Giulietti

1962-1965. The Giulietti Accordion Company, New York, offered guitars and amps in the '60s. The amps were made by Magnatone and the models and model numbers are often similar to the Magnatone model.

Pearloid Lap Steel
1962-1965. Small student level, 1x12", 2-channel, tremolo.

| 1962-1965 | | $250 | $400 |

S 1x12" Combo
1962-1965. Tremolo, 2-channel.

| 1962-1965 | | $1,250 | $1,750 |

S-9 (Magnatone 460)
1962-1965. 35 watts, 2x12 plus 2 tweeters, true vibrato combo, black sparkle.

| 1962-1965 | | $1,625 | $2,500 |

Gjika Amplification

1980-present. Premium and presentation grade tube amp heads and cabinets built by Robert Gjika in Escondido, California.

Gnome Amplifiers

Dan Munro builds professional grade, production, guitar amps and cabinets, starting in 2008, in Olympia, Washington. He also builds effects.

Gomez Amplification

2005-2015. Tube combo amps built by Dario G. Gomez in Rancho Santa Margarita, California.

The Vintage Guitar Price Guide shows values for an all-original condition amplifier, and where applicable, with original cover.

MODEL YEAR	FEATURES	LOW	HIGH

Goodsell

2004-present. Tube head and combo amps built by Richard Goodsell in Atlanta, Georgia.

Gorilla

1980s-2009. Small solidstate entry-level amps, distributed by Pignose, Las Vegas, Nevada.

Compact Practice Student

1980s-2009. Solidstate, 10 to 30 watts, compact design.

1980s-2009		$25	$50

Goya

1955-1996. Goya was mainly known for acoustics but offered a few amps in the '60s. The brand was purchased by Avnet/Guild in '66 and by Martin in the late '70s.

Grammatico Amps

2009-present. Production/custom, professional and premium grade, hand-wired, guitar and bass amps built by John Grammatico in Austin, Texas.

Green

1993-present. Amp model line made in England by Matamp (see that brand for listing), bright green covering, large Green logo on the front.

Greer Amplification

1999-present. Tube guitar amps and speaker cabinets built by Nick Greer in Athens, Georgia. He also builds effects.

Gregory

1950s-1960s. Private branded amps sold via music wholesalers, by late '60s solidstate models made by Harmony including the 007, C.I.A., Mark Six, Mark Eight, Saturn 80, most models were combo amps with Gregory logo.

Solidstate

1950s-60s	Various models	$350	$525

Gretsch

1883-present. In '05, Gretsch again started offering amps after previously selling them from the 1950s to '73. Initially private branded for them by Valco (look for the Valco oval or rectangular serialized label on the back). Early-'50s amps were covered in the requisite tweed but evolved into the Gretsch charcoal gray covering. The mid-'50s to early-'60s amps were part of the Electromatic group of amps. The mid-'50s to '62 amps often sported wrap-around and slanted grilles. In '62, the more traditional box style was introduced. In '66, the large amps went piggyback. Baldwin-Gretsch began to phase out amps effective '65, but solidstate amps continued being offered for a period. The '73 Gretsch product line only offered Sonax amps, made in Canada and Sho-Bud amps made in the U.S. In '05, they introduced a line of tube combo amps made in U.S. by Victoria Amp Company.

Artist

1946. Early post-war Gretsch amp made before Valco began to make their amps. Appears to be made by Operadio Mfg. Co., St. Charles, Illinois. Low power small combo amp, Gretsch Artist script logo on grille, round speaker baffle hole.

1946		$300	$450

Broadkaster Mini Lead 50

Late-1960s. Solidstate compact verticle combo amp.

1969		$250	$350

Carousel

Early-1960s. Solidstate,1x10" and 1x3" speakers, tremolo speed and depth knobs, brown cover.

1960s		$550	$775

Electromatic (5222)

1947-1949. Valco-made with era-typical styling, 3 slat speaker baffle openings, leather handle, two-tone leatherette, 3 tubes with small speaker, single volume knob.

1947-1949		$700	$1,125

Electromatic Artist (6155)

1950s. Small amp, 2x6V6 power, 1x10", volume and tone knobs.

1950s		$600	$950

Electromatic Deluxe (6163)

1950s. 1x12", 2x6L6, brown tweed grille. Also offered in Western Finish.

1950s		$975	$1,500

Model 6150 Compact

Late-1950s-1960s. Early amps in tweed, '60s amps in gray covering, no tremolo, single volume knob, no treble or bass knob, 1x8".

1950s	Brown tweed	$525	$750
1960s	Gray	$525	$750

Model 6151 Electromatic Standard/Compact Tremolo

Late-1940s-late-1960s. 1x8", various covers.

1940s-60s		$550	$775

Model 6152 Compact Tremolo Reverb

Ca.1964-late-1960s. Five watts, 11"x6" elliptical speaker early on, 1x12" later.

1964-1969		$800	$1,125

Model 6153T White Princess

1962. Compact combo, 6x9" oval speaker, higher priced than the typical small amp because it is relatively rare and associated with the White Princess guitar - making it valuable in a set, condition is very important, an amp with any issues will be worth much less.

1962		$1,125	$1,500

Model 6154 Super-Bass

Early-1960s-mid-1960s. Gray covering, 2x12", 70 watts, tube.

1960s		$800	$1,125

Model 6156 Playboy

Early-1950s-1966. Tube amp, 17 watts, 1x10" until '61 when converted to 1x12", tweed, then gray, then finally black covered.

1950s-1960	Tweed, 1x10"	$1,000	$1,375
1961-1962	Tweed, 1x12"	$1,000	$1,375
1963-1966	Black or gray, 1x12"	$1,000	$1,375

Green Electric

Greer Mini Chief

1947 Gretsch 5222 Electromatic

AMPS

Gretsch 6161 Electromatic Twin
Imaged by Heritage Auctions, HA.com

1969 Gretsch 6162 Dual Twin
Rivington Guitars

1955 Gretsch Model 6169
Electromatic Twin Western

MODEL YEAR	FEATURES	LOW	HIGH

Model 6156 Playboy (Reissue)
2005-2007. Model G6156, made by Victoria, 15 watts, 1x12" combo amp with retro Gretsch styling.

2005-2007		$1,125	$1,625

Model 6157 Super-Bass (Piggyback)
Mid-late-1960s. 35 watts, 2x15" cabinet, single channel.

1960s		$650	$975

Model 6159 Dual Bass
Mid-late-1960s. 35 watts, tube, 2x12" cabinet, dual channel, black covering. Replaced by 6163 Chet Atkins Piggyback Amp.

1960s		$900	$1,375

Model 6160 Chet Atkins Country Gentleman
Early-late-1960s. Combo tube amp, 35 watts, 2x12" cabinet, 2 channels. Replaced by 6163 Chet Atkins Piggyback amp with tremolo but no reverb.

1960s		$800	$1,250

Model 6161 Dual Twin Tremolo
Ca.1962-late-1960s. 19 watts (later 17 watts), 2x10" with 5" tweeter, tremolo.

1962-1967		$950	$1,500

Model 6161 Electromatic Twin
Ca.1953-ca.1960. Gray Silverflake covering, two 11x6" speakers, 14 watts, tremolo, wraparound grille '55 and after.

1953-1960		$1,500	$2,000

Model 6162 Dual Twin Tremolo/Reverb
Ca.1964-late-1960s. 17 watts, 2x10", reverb, tremolo. Vertical combo amp style introduced in '68.

1964-1967	Horizontal	$1,125	$1,500
1968-1969	Vertical	$975	$1,250

Model 6163 Chet Atkins (Piggyback)
Mid-late-1960s. 70 watts, 1x12" and 1x15", black covering, tremolo, reverb.

1960s		$800	$1,250

Model 6163 Executive
1959. 1x15, gray cover.

1959		$1,625	$2,250

Model 6163 Executive (Reissue)
2005-2007. Model G6163, boutique quality made by Victoria for FMIC Gretsch, 20 watts, 1x15", cabinet Uses to the modern retro early '60s Supro Supreme modified-triangle front grille pattern, maroon baffle with white grille, tremolo and reverb.

2005-2007		$1,250	$1,875

Model 6164 Variety
Early-mid-1960s. 35 watts, tube, 2x12".

1960s		$700	$975

Model 6165 Variety Plus
Early-mid-1960s. Tube amp, 35 watts, 2x12", reverb and tremolo, separate controls for both channels.

1960s		$850	$1,250

Model 6166 Fury (Combo)
Mid-1960s. Tube combo stereo amp, 70 watts, 2x12", separate controls for both channels, large metal handle, reverb.

1960s		$850	$1,250

Model 6169 Electromatic Twin Western
Ca.1953-ca.1960. Western finish, 14 watts, 2-11x6" speakers, tremolo, wraparound grill '55 and after.

1953-1960		$7,500	$10,000

Model 6169 Fury (Piggyback)
Late-1960s. Tube amp, 70 watts, 2x12", separate controls for both channels.

1960s		$950	$1,375

Model 6170 Pro Bass
1966-late-1960s. 25 or 35 watts, depending on model, 1x15", vertical cabinet style (vs. box cabinet).

1966-1969		$675	$950

Model 7154 Nashville
Introduced in 1969. Solidstate combo amp, 4' tall, 75 watts, 2x15", reverb, tremolo, magic echo.

1969-1970s		$525	$775

Model 7155 Tornado PA System
Introduced in 1969. Solidstate piggyback head and cab, 150 watts, 2 column speaker cabs, reverb, tremolo, magic echo.

1969-1970s 2x2x15"		$450	$650
1969-1970s 2x4x15"		$525	$750

Model 7517 Rogue
1970s. Solidstate, 40 watts, 2x12", tall vertical cabinet, front control panel.

1970s		$250	$375

Rex Royal Model M-197-3V
1950s. Small student compact amp, low power, 1x8", Rex Royal logo on grille, Fred Gretsch logo on back panel, single on-off volume knob.

1951		$450	$650

Gries

2004-present. Dave Gries builds his intermediate and professional grade, production/custom, amps and cabinets in Mattapoisett, Massachusetts.

Groove Tubes

1979-2008. Started by Aspen Pittman in his garage in Sylmar, California, Groove Tubes is now located in San Fernando. GT manufactures and distributes a full line of tubes. In '86 they added amp production and in '91 tube microphones. Aspen is also the author of the Tube Amp Book. The Groove Tubes brand was purchased by Fender in June, '08.

Guild

1952-present. Guild offered amps from the '60s into the '80s. Some of the early models were built by Hagstrom.

Double Twin
1953-1955. 35 watts, 2x12" plus 2 tweeters, 2-tone leatherette covered cab.

1953-1955		$1,125	$1,500

G-1000 Stereo
1992-1994. Stereo acoustic combo amp with cushioned seat on top, 4x6 and 1x10 speakers.

1992-1994		$725	$1,125

Master
Ca. 1957- Ca. 1959. Combo 2x6L6 power, tremolo, 2-tone tweed and leatherette.

1957-1959		$600	$875

MODEL YEAR	FEATURES	LOW	HIGH

Maverick

Late-1960s-early-1970s. Dual speaker combo, 6 tubes, verticle cab, tremolo, reverb, red/pink control panel, 2-tone black and silver grille.

1960s-70s		$500	$750

Model One

Mid-1970s-1977. Solidstate 1x12" vertical cab combo, 30 watts, reverb and tremolo.

1970s		$175	$275

Model Two

Mid-1970s-1977. Solidstate 2x10" vertical cab combo, 50 watts, reverb and tremolo.

1977-1978		$250	$375

Model Three

Mid-1970s-1977. Solidstate 1x15" vertical cab bass combo, 60 watts, organ and guitar.

1977-1978		$200	$300

Model Four

Early-1980s. Solidstate, 6 watts.

1980s		$125	$175

Model Five

Early-1980s. Solidstate, 10 watts, 6.25" speaker.

1980s		$175	$275

Model Six

Early-1980s. Same as Model Five but with reverb.

1980s		$200	$300

Model Seven

Early-1980s. Solidstate, 12 watts, small amp for guitar, bass and keyboard.

1980s		$200	$300

Model 50-J

Early-1960s. 14 watts, 1x12", tremolo, blue/gray vinyl.

1962-1963		$675	$975

Model 66

1953-1955. 15 watts, 1x12", tremolo, 2-tone leatherette.

1953-1955		$700	$1,125

Model 66-J

1962-1963. 20 watts, 1x12", tremolo, blue/gray vinyl.

1962-1963		$700	$1,125

Model 98-RT

1962-1963. The only stand-alone reverb amp from Guild in the early '60s, 30 watts, 1x12", blue/gray vinyl.

1962-1963		$875	$1,250

Model 99

1953-1955. 30 watts, 1x12", tremolo, 2-tone leatherette.

1953-1955		$725	$1,125

Model 99-J

Early-1960s. 30 watts, 1x12", tremolo, blue/gray vinyl.

1962-1963		$600	$875

Model 99-U Ultra

Early-1960s. Piggyback 30-watt head with optional 1x12" or 1x15" cab, cab and head lock together, tremolo, blue/gray vinyl.

1962-1963		$725	$1,125

Model 100-J

1958-1959, 1962-1963. Masteramp series, 35 watts, 1x15", blue/gray vinyl.

1958-1959		$2,500	$4,500
1962-1963		$725	$1,125

MODEL YEAR	FEATURES	LOW	HIGH

Model 200-S Stereo Combo

Early-1960s. 25 watts per channel, total 50 watts stereo, 2x12", tremolo, blue/gray vinyl, wheat grille.

1962-1963		$1,000	$1,375

Model RC-30 Reverb Converter

Early-1960s. Similar to Gibson GA-1 converter, attaches with 2 wires clipped to originating amp's speaker, 8 watts, 1x10", blue/gray vinyl.

1962-1963		$750	$1,125

Superbird

1968. Piggyback tube amp with 2x12 cab.

1968		$850	$1,125

SuperStar

Ca.1972-ca.1974. 50 watts, all tubes, 1x15" Jensen speakers, vertical combo, reverb, tremolo, black vinyl cover, 2-tone black/silver grille.

1972-1974		$550	$775

Thunder 1

1965-1972. Combo with single speaker, no reverb, light tan cover, 2-tone tan grille.

1965-1972	1x10"	$450	$650
1965-1972	1x12"	$450	$650

Thunder 1 (Model T1-RVT)/T1

1965-1972. Combo with dual speakers and reverb, light tan cover, 2-tone tan grille.

1965-1972		$675	$1,125

ThunderBass

1965-1972. Piggyback combo, 2x15".

1965-1972	100-watt	$675	$1,125
1965-1972	200-watt	$675	$1,125

ThunderBird

1965-1972. 50 watts, tube, 2x12", reverb, tremolo, with or without TD-1 dolly, black vinyl, black/silver grille.

1965-1972		$675	$1,125

ThunderStar Bass

1965-1972. Piggyback bass tube head or combo, 50 watts.

1965-1972	Full stack, 2x1x15"	$750	$1,250
1965-1972	Half stack, 1x1x15"	$675	$1,125

ThunderStar Guitar

1965-1972. Combo, 50 watts, 1x12".

1965-1972		$675	$975

Guyatone

1933-present. Started offering amps by at least the late '40s with their Guya lap steels. In '51 the Guyatone brand is first used on guitars and most likely amps. Guyatone also made the Marco Polo, Winston, Kingston, Kent, LaFayette and Bradford brands.

Guytron

1995-present. Tube amp heads and speaker cabinets built by Guy Hedrick in Columbiaville, Michigan. In January, '09, GDS Amplification bought the assets of Guytron Amplification.

Hagstrom

1921-1983, 2004-present. The Swedish guitar maker built a variety of tube and solidstate amps from ca. 1961 into the '70s. They also supplied amps to Guild.

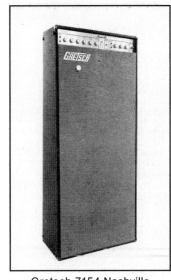

Gretsch 7154 Nashville
Imaged by Heritage Auctions, HA.com

Guild Master
Imaged by Heritage Auctions, HA.com

1970 Guild ThunderBass

AMPS

1963 Harmony H-303A
Rivington Guitars

AMPS

1965 Harmony H400A
Imaged by Heritage Auctions, HA.com

Harry Joyce Classic 30 Watt

Hanburt
1940-ca. 1950. Harvey M. Hansen built electric Hawaiian guitars in Seattle, Washington, some sold as a set with a small amp. The wooden amps have a large HB in the speaker cutout. He also built at least one mandolin.

Harmony
1892-1976, late-1970s-present. Harmony was one of the biggest producers of guitars and offered amps as well. MBT International offered Harmony amps for 2000-'02.

H Series
1940s-1960s. Harmony model numbers begin with H, such as H-304, all H series models shown are tube amps unless otherwise noted as solidstate.

MODEL YEAR	FEATURES	LOW	HIGH
1940s-50s	H-190/H-191	$475	$725
1940s-50s	H-200	$475	$725
1950s	H-204, 18w, 1x12	$475	$725
1960s	H-303A, 8w, 1x8	$250	$375
1960s	H-304, low power	$250	$375
1960s	H-305A, low power	$250	$375
1960s	H-306A, 1x12	$375	$575
1960s	H-306C, 2x12	$450	$675
1960s	H-400, vol	$225	$325
1960s	H-400A, vol/tone	$250	$425
1960s	H-410A, 10w, 1x10	$450	$700
1960s	H-415, 18w, 2x12	$625	$950
1960s	H-420, 20w, 1x15	$475	$725
1960s	H-430, 30w, 2x10	$575	$875
1960s	H-440, 2x12, trem/verb	$650	$975
1960s	H-512, solidstate	$675	$1,000
1960s	H-530, solidstate	$575	$875

Solidstate
1970s. Various models, dark covering, dark grille.

MODEL YEAR	FEATURES	LOW	HIGH
1970s	Large models	$200	$300
1970s	Small models	$30	$40

Harry Joyce
1993-2011, 2015-present. Hand-wired British tube amps, combos, and cabinets from builder/designer Harry Joyce. Joyce was contracted to build Hiwatt amps in England during the '70s. Joyce died in 2002, and the brand was carried on by Charles Bertonazzi and George Scholz until 2011. Brand brought back by Kevin Wood and Scholz through Harry Joyce USA with new versions of the classic models.

Hartke
1984-present. Guitar and bass amps, combos and cabinets made in the U.S. Founded by Larry Hartke, since the mid-'80s, Hartke has been distributed by Samson Technologies. Hartke also offered basses in the past.

Haynes
Haynes guitar amps were built by the Amplifier Corporation of America (ACA) of Westbury, New York. ACA also made an early distortion device pow-

ered by batteries. Unicord purchased the company in around 1964 and used the factory to produce its Univox line of amps, most likely discontinuing the Haynes brand at the same time.

Jazz King II
1960s. Solidstate, stereo console-style, 2x12", Haynes logo upper left side.

MODEL YEAR	FEATURES	LOW	HIGH
1960s		$325	$450

Headstrong
2003-present. Tube combo amps and cabinets built by Wayne Jones in Asheville, North Carolina.

Henriksen JazzAmp
2006-present. Professional grade, production, solidstate amps voiced for jazz guitar built by Peter Henriksen in Golden, Colorado.

Heritage
Founded in 2004 by Malcolm MacDonald and Lane Zastrow who was formerly involved with Holland amps. Located in the former Holland facility in Brentwood, Tennessee, they built tube combo and piggyback amps.

Hilgen
1960s. Mid-level amplifiers from Hilgen Manufacturing, Hillside, New Jersey. Dark tolex covering and swiggle-lined light color grille cloth. Examples have been found with original Jensen speakers.

Basso B-2501
1960s. 25 watts, 1x15" combo, swirl grille, Hilgen crest logo, compact size.

MODEL YEAR	FEATURES	LOW	HIGH
1965		$350	$450

Basso B-2502
1960s. 25 watts, 1x15" combo, swirl grille, Hilgen crest logo, large cab.

| 1965 | | $400 | $525 |

Basso Grande B-2503
1960s. Brown sparkle cover, piggyback, 2x12".

| 1965 | | $500 | $650 |

Basso Profondo B-2502
1965. Combo 1x15".

| 1965 | | $400 | $525 |

Champion R-2523
Mid-1960s. Highest offering in their amp line, piggyback with 2x12" cab, tremolo, reverb, swirl grille cloth.

| 1965 | | $500 | $650 |

Galaxie T-2513
1960s. 25 watts, 2x12" piggyback cab, tremolo.

| 1965 | | $500 | $650 |

Metero T-2511
Mid-1960s. Compact 1x12" combo, tremolo.

| 1965 | | $400 | $550 |

Pacesetter R-2521
Mid-1960s. 1x12" combo, tremolo, reverb, swirl grille cloth.

| 1965 | | $400 | $550 |

Star T-2512
1960s. 25 watts, 1x12" combo, tremolo.

| 1965 | | $400 | $550 |

MODEL YEAR	FEATURES	LOW	HIGH

Troubadour T-1506
Mid-1960s. Small practice amp.

1965		$300	$400

Victor R-2522
Mid-1960s. 1x12" combo, larger cab, reverb, tremolo.

1965		$500	$650

HiWatt
1963-1984, ca.1990-present. Amp builder Dave Reeves started his Hylight Electronics in a garage in England in the early 1960s, doing amp and other electronic repairs. By 1964 he had produced the first amps bearing the Hiwatt brand. By the early '70s, Hiwatt's reputation was growing, and production was moved to a factory in Kingston-upon-Thames, expanding the amp line and adding PA gear. In '81, Reeves suffered a fatal fall, and ownership of Hiwatt was taken over by Biacrown Ltd, a company made up of Hiwatt employees. Biacrown struggled and closed in '84. From ca.1990 to ca.1994, a line of American-made Hiwatts, designed by Frank Levi, were available. By the mid-'90s, amps with the Hiwatt brand were again being built in England and, separately, imported from Asia by Fernandes.

Bass 100 Head

1980s	100 watts, England	$1,750	$2,500

Bulldog SA112
1980s, 1994-2019. 50 watts, combo, 1x12".

1980s		$1,500	$2,000
1994-2019		$1,500	$2,000

Bulldog SA112FL
1980s-1990s. 100 watts, combo, 1x12".

1980s		$1,500	$2,000
1990s		$1,500	$2,000

Custom 100 Head

2007	100 watts	$1,625	$2,500

DR-103 Custom 100 Head
1970-late-1980s, 2005-present. Tube head, 100 watts, custom Hiwatt 100 logo on front.

1970s		$3,750	$6,000
1980s		$2,500	$3,500

DR-201 Hiwatt 200 Head
1970s. 200-watt amp head, Hiwatt 200 logo on front.

1970s		$3,000	$4,000

DR-405 Hiwatt 400 Head
1970s. 400-watt amp head.

1970s		$3,500	$5,000

DR-504 Custom 50 Head
1970-late-1980s, 1995-1999. Tube head, 50 watts.

1970-1980s		$3,000	$4,000

DR-508 50-Watt Head
1966. Tube head, 50 watts, gold script logo.

1966		$7,500	$10,000

Harry Joyce 50-Watt Head
1997. Custom Harry Joyce 50 gold script logo.

1997		$3,500	$4,500

Lead 20 (SG-20) Head
1980s. Tube amp head, 30 watts, black cover, rectangular HiWatt plate logo.

1980s		$775	$1,125

Lead 30 Combo
1980s. Combo tube amp, 30 watts, 1x12".

1980s		$975	$1,250

Lead 50R Combo
1980s. Combo tube amp, 50 watts, 1x12", reverb, dark cover, dark grille, HiWatt rectangular plate logo.

1980s		$1,125	$1,500

OL-103 Lead 100 Head

1982	100 watts, England	$1,750	$2,375

PW-50 Tube
1989-1993. Stereo tube amp, 50 watts per channel.

1989-1993		$1,125	$1,500

S50L Head
1989-1993. Lead guitar head, 50 watts, gain, master volume, EQ.

1989-1993		$950	$1,250

SA 112 Combo

1970s	50 watts, 1x12"	$3,250	$5,000

SA 212 Combo

1970s	50 watts, 2x12"	$3,500	$5,250

SA 412 Combo

1970s	50 watts, 4x12"	$4,250	$6,500

SE 2150 Speaker Cabinet

1970s	2x15" vertical	$2,250	$3,500

SE 4121 Speaker Cabinet

1970s	4x12", half stack	$2,500	$3,750

SE 4122 (Lead) Speaker Cabinet
1971- mid-1980s. 4x12", Fane speakers, 300 watts.

1971-1980s	4x12", half stack	$2,500	$3,500

SE 4123 (Bass) Speaker Cabinet
1970s. Bass version of SE, often used with DR103 head, straight-front cab and stackable, black tolex with gray grille, Hiwatt logo plate in center of grille.

1970s	4x12", half stack	$2,500	$3,500

SE 4129 (Bass) Speaker Cabinet
1970s. SE series for bass, 4x12", often used with DR 201 head.

1970s		$2,500	$3,500

SE 4151 Speaker Cabinet
1970s. SE series with 4x15".

1970s		$2,500	$3,500

Hoagland
Professional grade, production, guitar amps built by Dan Hoagland in Land O Lakes, Florida starting in 2008.

Hoffman
1993-present. Tube amps, combos, reverb units, and cabinets built by Doug Hoffman from 1993 to '99, in Sarasota, Florida. Hoffman no longer builds amps, concentrating on selling tube amp building supplies, and since 2001 has been located in Pisgah Forest, North Carolina.

Hoffmann
1983-present. Tube amp heads for guitar and other musical instruments built by Kim Hoffmann in Hawthorne, California.

Headstrong Lil' King

1977 HiWatt DR-505 Head

Imaged by Heritage Auctions, HA.com

Hoffmann 15

AMPS

Hottie Super Chef

Humphrey

Jet City 800 Hand-wired
Custom 50 Sable

Hohner

1857-present. Matthias Hohner, a clockmaker in Trossingen, Germany, founded Hohner in 1857, making harmonicas. Hohner has been offering guitars and amps at least since the early '70s.

Panther Series
1980s. Smaller combo amps, master volume, gain, EQ.

1980s	Various models	$75	$125

Sound Producer Series
1980s. Master volume, normal and overdrive, reverb, headphone jack.

1980s	Various models	$75	$125

Holland

1992-2004. Tube combo amps from builder Mike Holland, originally in Virginia Beach, Virginia, and since 2000 in Brentwood, Tennessee. In 2000, Holland took Lane Zastrow as a partner, forming L&M Amplifiers to build the Holland line. The company closed in '04.

Holmes

1970-late 1980s. Founded by Harrison Holmes. Holmes amplifiers were manufactured in Mississippi and their product line included guitar and bass amps, PA systems, and mixing boards. In the early '80s, Harrison Holmes sold the company to On-Site Music which called the firm The Holmes Corp. Products manufactured by Harrison have an all-caps HOLMES logo and the serial number plate says The Holmes Company.

Mississippi Blues Master
Solid state, head only.

1980s		$450	$600

Performer PB-115 Bass
60 watts, 1x15", black tolex.

1980s		$125	$195

Pro Compact 210S
60 watts, 2x10", 2 channels, active EQ, black tolex.

1980s		$125	$195

Pro Compact 212S
2x12" version of Pro.

1980s		$150	$225

Rebel RB-112 Bass
35 watts, 1x12", black tolex.

1980s		$125	$225

Hondo

1969-1987, 1991-2005. Hondo has offered imported amps over the years. 1990s models ranged from the H20 Practice Amp to the H160SRC with 160 watts (peak) and 2x10" speakers.

Various Models

1970s-90s	Mid-size	$65	$100
1970s-90s	Small	$35	$50

Hottie

Jean-Claude Escudie and Mike Bernards started in 2005, build budget and intermediate grade, production/custom, solid state "toaster" amps in Portland, Oregon. They also offered guitars in '09.

Hound Dog

1994-1998. Founded by George Alessandro as the Hound Dog Corporation. Name was changed to Alessandro in 1998 (see that brand for more information).

Hughes & Kettner

1985-present. Hughes & Kettner offers a line of solidstate and tube guitar and bass amps, combos, cabinets and effects, all made in Germany.

Humphrey

2010-present. Custom, professional and premium grade, tube amps built in Chanhassen, Minnesota by Gerry Humphrey. He also builds preamps and reverb units.

Hurricane

Tube guitar and harmonica combo amps built by Gary Drouin in Sarasota, Florida. Drouin started the company in 1998 with harp master Rock Bottom, who died in September 2001.

Hy Lo

1960s-1970s. Budget grade, small compact amps made in Japan, Hy Lo logo on grille.

Ibanez

1932-present. Ibanez added solidstate amps to their product line in '98. They also build guitars, basses and effects.

Idol

Late-1960s. Made in Japan. Dark tolex cover, dark grille, Hobby Series with large Idol logo on front.

Hobby Series

1968	Hobby 10	$100	$150
1968	Hobby 100	$200	$300
1968	Hobby 20	$110	$175
1968	Hobby 45	$175	$275

Impact

1963-early 1970s. Based in London, England, tube amps made by Don Mackrill and Laurie Naiff for Pan Musical Instrument Company and their music stores. About a dozen different models of combos, piggyback half-stacks and PAs were offered.

Imperial

Ca.1963-ca.1970. The Imperial Accordion Company of Chicago, Illinois offered one or two imported small amps in the '60s.

Jack Daniel's

2004-2017. Tube guitar amp built by Peavey for the Jack Daniel Distillery, offered until about '10. They offered guitars until '17.

MODEL YEAR	FEATURES	LOW	HIGH

Jackson

1980-present. The Jackson-Charvel Company offered budget to intermediate grade amps and cabinets in the late '80s and the '90s.

Jackson Ampworks

2001-present. Brad Jackson builds his tube amp heads and speaker cabinets in Bedford, Texas.

Jackson-Guldan

1920s-1960s. The Jackson-Guldan Violin Company, of Columbus, Ohio, offered lap steels and small tube amps early on. They also built acoustic guitars.

Jay Turser

1997-present. Smaller, inexpensive imported solidstate guitar and bass amps. They also offer basses and guitars.

JCA Circuits

Premium and presentation grade tube guitar combo amps built by Jason C. Arthur in Pottstown, Pennsylvania, starting in 1995.

Jennings

Late 1960s. Tom Jennings formed another company after resigning from Vox. Large block letter Jennings logo on front panel, Jennings Amplifier logo on back control plate with model number and serial number.

Jet City Amplification

2009-present. Budget to professional grade, production/custom, guitar amps and cabinets designed in Seattle, Washington by Doug White, Dan Gallagher, Michael Soldano and built in Asia.

Jim Kelley

1979-1985. Channel-switching tube amps, compact combos and heads, hardwood cabinets available, made by Jim Kelley at his Active Guitar Electronics in Tustin, California. He produced about 100 amps a year. In 1978 and early '79 he produced a few amps under the Fortune brand name for Fortune Guitars.

JMI (Jennings Musical Industries)

2004-present. Tom Jennings built the Vox amps of the 1960s. They are back with tube amp heads and cabinets based on some of their classic models. Large block letter Jennings logo on front panel, Jennings Amplifier logo on back control plate with model number and serial number. They also offer effects.

Johnson

Mid-1990s-present. Line of solidstate amps imported by Music Link, Brisbane, California. Johnson also offers guitars, basses, mandolins and effects.

Johnson Amplification

Intermediate and professional grade, production, modeling amps and effects designed by John Johnson, starting 1997 in Sandy, Utah. The company is part of Harman International. In 2002, they quit building amps, but continue the effects line.

JoMama

1994-present. Tube amps and combos under the JoMama and Kelemen brands built by Joe Kelemen in Santa Fe, New Mexico.

Jordan

1966-early 1970s. Jordan Electronics, of Alhambra, California, built a range of electronics, including, starting around 1966, solid state guitar amps and effects.

Juke

Tube guitar and harmonica amps built by G.R. Croteau, starting 1989, in Troy, New Hampshire. He also built the Warbler line of amps.

Kafel

Jack Kafel built his tube amp heads in Chicago, Illinois, starting in 2004.

Kalamazoo

1933-1942, 1965-1970. Kalamazoo was a brand Gibson used on one of their budget lines. They used the name on amps from '65 to '67.

Bass

1965-1967. Enclosed back, 2x10", flip-out control panel, not a commonly found model as compared to numerous Model 1 and 2 student amps.

1965-1967		$625	$875

Bass 30

Late 1960s-early 1970s. Tube combo, vertical cabinet, 2x10".

1970		$475	$675

KEA

1948-1952. Small compact amp, round speaker baffle grille, slant Kalamazoo logo on front, oxblood leatherette.

1948-1952		$500	$725

Lap Steel

1940s. Kalamazoo logo on front lower right, low power with 1-6V6, round speaker grille opening, red/brown leatherette.

1940s		$425	$575

Model 1

1965-1967. No tremolo, 1x10", front control panel, black.

1965-1967		$300	$425

Model 2

1965-1967. Same as Model 1 with tremolo, black.

1965-1967	Black panel	$425	$850
1967	Silver panel	$250	$400

Model 3

Late 1960s-early 1970s. Made by CMI Electronics in Chicago, post Gibson Kalamazoo era, student compact

Jordan Entertainer J 110
Rivington Guitars

Juke Warbler Muse
Carter Vintage guitars

Kalamazoo Bass 30
Rivington Guitars

AMPS

Kendrick Double Trouble

1967 Kingston
Rivington Guitars

KJL Companion

MODEL YEAR	FEATURES	LOW	HIGH

solidstate combo, Kalamazoo 3 logo on front panel, Kalamazoo Model 3 logo on label on speaker magnet.

| 1960s-70s | | $115 | $150 |

Model 4

Late 1960s-early 1970s. Made by CMI Electronics in Chicago, post Gibson Kalamazoo era, student compact solidstate combo, 3 control knobs, tone, tremolo, volume, Kalamazoo 4 logo on front panel, Kalamazoo Model 4 logo on label on speaker magnet.

| 1960s-70s | | $115 | $150 |

Reverb 12

1965-1967. Black vinyl cover, 1x12", reverb, tremolo.

| 1965-1967 | | $625 | $925 |

Kay

Ca.1931-present. Kay originally offered amps up to around '68 when the brand changed hands. Currently they offer a couple of small solidstate imported amps. They also make basses, guitars, banjos, mandolins, ukes, and violins.

K506 Vibrato 12

1960s. 12 watts, 1x12", swirl grille, metal handle.

| 1960s | | $550 | $750 |

K507 Twin Ten Special

1960s. 20 watts, 2x10", swirl grille, metal handle.

| 1960s | | $650 | $900 |

K700 Series

Introduced in 1965. Value Leader/Vanguard/Galaxie models, transistorized amps promoted as eliminates tube-changing annoyance and reliable performance, combo amps with tapered cabinets, rear slant control panel, rich brown and tan vinyl cover, brown grille cloth.

| 1965-1966 | Various models | $200 | $500 |

Model 703

1962-1964. Tube student amp, small speaker, 3 tubes, 1 volume, 1 tone, 2-tone white front with brown back cabinet, metal handle, model number noted on back panel, Kay logo and model number badge lower front right.

| 1962-1964 | | $250 | $375 |

Model 803

1962-1964. Student amp, 1x8", 3 tubes, 1 volume, 1 tone, metal handle, 14.75x11.75x6.75" cabinet with dark gray cover.

| 1962-1964 | | $250 | $375 |

Model 805

1965. Solidstate, 35 watts, 1x10", 4 control knobs, 2-tone cabinet.

| 1965 | | $125 | $175 |

Small Tube

1940s	Wood cabinet	$375	$575
1950s	Various models	$375	$575
1960s	Models K503,		
	K504, K505	$450	$725

Kelemen

1994-present. Tube amps and combos under the JoMama and Kelemen brands built by Joe Kelemen in Santa Fe, New Mexico.

Kendrick

1989-present. Founded by Gerald Weber in Austin, Texas and currently located in Kempner, Texas. Mainly known for their intermediate to professional grade, tube amps, Kendrick also offers guitars, speakers, and effects.

Kent

Ca.1962-1969. Imported budget line of guitars and amps.

Guitar and Bass

1960s. Various models.

1960s	1475	$80	$130
1960s	2198	$80	$130
1960s	5999	$115	$150
1960s	6104	$160	$225
1960s	6610	$55	$100

Kiesel

See Guitar section.

King Amplification

Tube combo amps, head and cabinets built by Val King in San Jose, California starting in 2005.

Kingsley

1998-present. Production/custom, professional grade, tube amps and cabinets built by Simon Jarrett in Vancouver, British Columbia.

Kingston

1958-1967. Economy solidstate amps imported by Westheimer Importing, Chicago, Illinois.

Cat Series

Mid-1960s. Solidstate Cat Series amps have dark vinyl and dark grilles.

1960s	P-1 3w	$90	$125
1960s	P-2, 5w	$90	$125
1960s	P-3, 8w	$90	$125
1960s	P-8T, 20w	$90	$125

Cougar BA-21 Bass Piggyback

Mid-1960s. Solidstate, 60 watts, 2x12" cab, dark vinyl, light silver grille.

| 1960s | | $175 | $250 |

Cougar PB-5 Bass Combo

Mid-1960s. Solidstate, 15 watts, 1x8".

| 1960s | | $100 | $150 |

Lion 2000 Piggyback

Mid-1960s. Solidstate, 90 watts, 2x12" cab.

| 1960s | | $225 | $325 |

Lion 3000 Piggyback

Mid-1960s. Solidstate, 250 watts, 4x12" cab.

| 1960s | | $275 | $400 |

Lion AP-281 R Piggyback

Mid-1960s. Solidstate, 30 watts, 2x8" cab, dark vinyl cover, light silver grille.

| 1960s | | $175 | $275 |

Lion AP-281 R10 Piggyback

Mid-1960s. Solidstate, 30 watts, 2x10" cab.

| 1960s | | $200 | $300 |

MODEL				
YEAR	FEATURES	LOW	HIGH	

Kinsman

2012-present. Budget and intermediate grade, production, guitar amps and cabinets built in China and distributed worldwide by John Hornby Skewes & Co. Ltd. in England. They also use the brand on a line of guitar effects.

Kitchen-Marshall

1965-1966. Private branded for Kitchen Music by Marshall, primarily PA units with block logos. Limited production.

JTM 45 MKII 45-Watt Head

1965-1966. Private branded for Kitchen Music, JTM 45 Marshall with Kitchen logo plate, 45 watts.

1965-1966		$7,000	$11,000

Slant 4x12 1960 Cabinet

1965-1966. Slant front 4x12" 1960-style cab with gray bluesbreaker grille, black on green vinyl, very limited production.

1965-1966		$4,000	$6,000

KJL

Founded in 1995 by Kenny Lannes, MSEE, a professor of Electrical Engineering at the University of New Orleans. KJL makes budget to intermediate grade, tube combo amps, heads and an ABY box.

KMD (Kaman)

1986-ca.1990. Distributed by Kaman (Ovation, Hamer, etc.) in the late '80s, KMD offered a variety of amps and effects.

Koch

1988-present. Koch Guitar Electronics produces all-tube combo amps, heads, effects and cabinets built in The Netherlands.

Komet

1999-present. Intermediate to professional grade, tube amp heads built in Baton Rouge, Louisiana, by Holger Notzel and Michael Kennedy with circuits designed by Ken Fischer of Trainwreck fame. They also build a power attenuator.

Kona Guitar Company

2001-present. Budget solidstate amps made in Asia. They also offer guitars, basses, mandolins, ukes and banjos.

Krank

1996-2013, 2015-2020. Founded by Tony Krank and offering tube amp heads, combos and speaker cabinets built in Tempe, Arizona. They also built effects.

Kustom

1965-present. Kustom, a division of Hanser Holdings, offers guitar and bass combo amps and PA equipment. Founded by Bud Ross in Chanute, Kansas, who offered tuck-and-roll amps as early as '58 but began using the Kustom brand name in '65. From '69 to '75 Ross gradually sold interest in the company (in the late '70s, Ross introduced the line of Ross effects stomp boxes). The brand changed hands a few times, and by the mid-'80s it was no longer in use. In '89 Kustom was in bankruptcy court and was purchased by Hanser Holdings Incorporated of Cincinnati, Ohio (Davitt & Hanser) and by '94, they had a new line of amps available.

Prices are for amps with no tears in the tuck-and-roll cover and no grille tears. A tear in the tuck-and-roll will reduce the value, sometimes significantly.

Kustom model identification can be frustrating as they used series numbers, catalog numbers (the numbers in the catalogs and price lists), and model numbers (the number often found next to the serial number on the amp's back panel). Most of the discussion that follows is by series number (100, 200, 300, etc.) and catalog number. Unfortunately, vintage amp dealers use the serial number and model number, so the best way is to cross-check speaker and amplifier attributes. Model numbers were used primarily for repair purposes and were found in the repair manuals. In many, but not all cases, the model number is the last digit of the catalog number; for example, the catalog lists a 100 series Model 1-15J-1, where the last digit 1 signifies a Model 1 amplifier chassis which is a basic amp without reverb or tremolo. A Model 1-15J-2 signifies a Model 2 amp chassis that has reverb and tremolo. In this example, Kustom uses a different model number on the back of the amp head. For the 1-15J-2, the model number on the back panel of the amp head would be K100-2, indicating a series 100 (50 watts) amp with reverb and tremolo (amp chassis Model 2).

Model numbers relate to the amplifier's schematic and electronics, while catalog numbers describe the amp's relative power rating and speaker configuration.

Amp Chassis Model Numbers ('68-'72)
Model 1 Amp (basic)
Model 2 Amp with reverb
Model 3 Amp with Harmonic Clip and Boost
Model 4 Amp with reverb, tremolo, vibrato, Harmonic Clip and Selective Boost
Model 5 PA with reverb
Model 6 Amp (basic) with Selectone
Model 7 Amp with reverb, tremolo, vibrato, boost (different parts)
Model 8 Amp with reverb, tremolo, vibrato, boost (different parts)

Naugahyde Tuck-&-Roll 200 ('65-'67)
The very first Kustoms did not have the model series on the front control panel. The early logo stipulated Kustom by Ross, Inc. The name was then updated to Kustom Electronics, Inc. 1965-'67 amp heads have a high profile/tall "forehead" area (the area on top of the controls) and these have been nicknamed "Frankenstein models." The '65-'67 catalog numbers were often 4 or 5 digits, for example J695. The first digit represents the speaker type (J

Koch Ventura

Komet Songwriter 30

Kustom Hustler

AMPS

1971 Kustom K100
Bob Calla

1971 Kustom K150-8
Tom Pfeifer

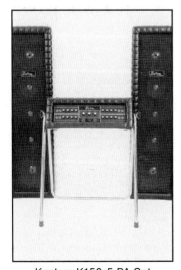

Kustom K150-5 PA Set
Imaged by Heritage Auctions, HA.com

MODEL YEAR	FEATURES	LOW	HIGH

= Jensen, etc.), other examples are L995, L1195, L795RV, etc. Some '67 catalog numbers changed to 2 digits followed by 3 digits, like 4-D 140f, or 3-15C (3 CTS speakers), etc. Others sported 5 characters like 4-15J-1, where 4 = 4 speakers, 15 = 15" speakers, J = Jensen, and 1 = basic amp chassis with no effects. The fifth digit indicated amp chassis model number as described above.

Naugahyde Tuck-&-Roll 100/200/400 ('68-'71)

Starting in '68, the Kustom logo also included the model series. A K100, for example, would have 100 displayed below the Kustom name. The model series generally is twice the relative output wattage, for example, the 100 Series is a 50-watt amp. Keep in mind, solidstate ratings are often higher than tube-amp ratings, so use the ratings as relative measurements. Most '68-'70 Kustom catalog numbers are x-xxx-x, for example 1-15L-1. The first digit represents the number of speakers, the 2nd and 3rd represent the speaker size, the fourth represents the speaker type (A = Altec Lansing, L = J.B.L., J = Jensen, C = C.T.S. Bass), the fifth digit represents the amp chassis number. The power units were interchangeable in production, so amps could have similar front-ends but different power units (more power and different effect options) and vice versa. Some '68 bass amp catalog numbers were 4 digits, for example 2-12C, meaning two 12" CTS speakers. Again, there were several different numbers used. Kustom also introduced the 200 and 400 amp series and the logo included the series number. The catalog numbers were similar to the 100 series, but they had a higher power rating of 100 equivalent watts (200 series), or 200 equivalent watts (400 series). Kustom U.S. Naugahyde (tuck-&-roll) covers came in 7 colors: black (the most common), Cascade (blue/green), silver (white-silver), gold (light gold), red, blue, and Charcoal (gray). The market historically shows color options fetching more. The market has not noticeably distinguished power and features options. Condition and color seem to be the most important. Gold and Cascade may be the rarest seen colors.

Naugahyde Tuck-&-Roll 150/250/300/500/600 (c.'71-c.'75)

The amp heads changed with a slightly slanted control panel and the Kustom logo moved to the right/upper-right portion of the front panel. They continued to be tuck-&-roll offered in the same variety of colors. The sales literature indicated a 150 series had 150 watts, 250 had 250 watts, etc.

Naugahyde Tuck-&-Roll SC (Self Contained) Series

Most SC combo amps were rated at 150 watts, with the 1-12SC listed at 50 watts. They were offered in 7 colors of tuck-and-roll. Again, the model numbers indicate the features as follows: 4-10 SC is a 4 x 10", 2-10 SC is a 2x10", etc.

Super Sound Tuck-and-Roll Combo Series

The last tuck-and-roll combo amps with slightly smaller tucks. The Amp control panel is noticeably smaller and the Kustom logo is in the right side of

MODEL YEAR	FEATURES	LOW	HIGH

the control panel.

Black Vinyl ('75-c.'78)

By '75 ownership changes were complete, and the colorful tuck-and-roll was dropped in favor of more traditional black vinyl. The products had a slant Kustom logo spelled-out and placed in a position on the grille similar to a Fender blackface baffle. Models included the I, II, III, and IV Lead amps. Heads with half- and full stacks were available. Bass amps included the Kustom 1, Bass I, II, III, IV, and IV SRO.

Black Vinyl K logo ('78-'83)

This era is easily recognized by the prominent capital K logo.

Bass V

1990s. Large Kustom Bass V logo upper right side of amp, 35 watts, 1x12", black vinyl.

1990s		$85	$130

Challenger Combo

1973-1975. 1x12" speaker.

1973-1975	Black	$300	$450
1973-1975	Color option	$425	$600

Hustler Combo

1973-1975. Solidstate, 4x10", tremolo, tuck-and-roll.

1973-1975	Black	$325	$500
1973-1975	Color option	$450	$650

K25/K25 C-2 SC

1960s. SC (self-contained) Series, small combo tuck-and-roll, 1x12", solidstate, reverb, black control panel.

1971-1973	Black	$300	$450
1971-1973	Color option	$450	$650

K50-2 SC

1971-1973. Self-contained (SC) small combo tuck-and-roll, 1x12", reverb and tremolo.

1971-1973	Black	$300	$450
1971-1973	Color option	$450	$650

K100-1 1-15C Bass Set

1968-1972. The K100-1 with 1-15C speaker option with matching 1x15" cab, black tuck-and-roll standard, but several sparkle colors offered, C.T.S. bass reflex speaker.

1968-1972	Black	$300	$450
1968-1972	Color option	$450	$650

K100-1 1-15L-1/1-15A-1/1-15J-1 Set

1968-1972. K100-1 with matching 1x15" cab, black tuck-and-roll standard, but several colors offered, speaker options are JBL, Altec Lansing or Jensen.

1968-1972	Black	$300	$450
1968-1972	Color option	$450	$650

K100-1 1-D140F Bass Set

1968-1972. K100-1 with matching 1x15" JBL D-140F cab, black tuck-and-roll standard, but several sparkle colors offered.

1968-1972	Black	$300	$450
1968-1972	Color option	$450	$650

K100-1 2-12C Bass Set

1968-1972. K100-1 with matching 2x12" cab, black tuck-and-roll standard, but several sparkle colors offered, C.T.S. bass reflex speakers.

1968-1972	Black	$350	$500
1968-1972	Color option	$750	$1,125

MODEL YEAR	FEATURES	LOW	HIGH

K100-2 1-15L-2/1-15A-2/1-15J-2 Set
1968-1972. K100-2 head and matching 1x15" cab, black tuck-and-roll standard, but several sparkle colors offered.

1968-1972	Black	$300	$450
1968-1972	Color option	$450	$650

K100-2 2-12A-2/2-12J-2 Set
1968-1972. K100-2 head with matching 2x12" cab, black tuck-and-roll standard, but several sparkle colors offered.

1968-1972	Black	$350	$500
1968-1972	Color option	$750	$1,125

K100-5 PA Head
1968-1972. 50 watts, 2 channels with 8 control knobs per channel, reverb.

1968 1972	Black	$400	$600

K100-6 SC
1970-1972. Basic combo amp with selectone, no reverb.

1970-1972	Black	$250	$350

K100-7 SC
1970-1972. Combo amp with reverb, tremolo, vibrato and boost.

1970-1972	Black	$300	$450
1970-1972	Color option	$450	$650

K100-8 SC
1970-1972. Combo amp with reverb, tremolo, vibrato and boost.

1970-1972	Black	$300	$450
1970-1972	Color option	$450	$650

K100C-6 Combo
1968-1970. Kustom 100 logo middle of the front control panel, 1x15" combo, selectone option.

1968-1970	Black	$300	$450
1968-1970	Color option	$450	$650

K100C-8 Combo
1968-1970. Kustom 100 logo middle of the front control panel, 4x10" combo, reverb, tremolo, vibrato.

1968-1970	Black	$400	$600

K150-1 Set
1972-1975. Piggyback, 150 watts, 2x12", no reverb, logo in upper right corner of amp head, tuck-and-roll, black or color option.

1972-1975	Color option	$450	$650

K150-2 Set
1972-1975. K150 with added reverb and tremolo, piggyback, 2x12", tuck-and-roll, black or color option.

1972-1975	Color option	$450	$650

K150-5 PA Set
1972-1975. PA head plus 2 PA cabs.

1972-1975		$400	$600

K150/150C Combo
1972-1975. Combo, 2x10".

1972-1975	Black	$275	$400

K200-1/K200B Bass Set
1966-1972. K200 head with 2x15" cab.

1966-1972	Black	$425	$650
1966-1972	Color option	$675	$975

K200-2 Reverb/Tremolo Set
1966-1972. K200-2 head with 2x15" or 3x12" cab, available with JBL D-140F speakers, Altec Lansing (A)

speakers, C.T.S. (C), or Jensen (J).

1966-1972	Black	$425	$625
1966-1972	Color option	$675	$975

K250 Set
1971-1975. K250 head with 2x15" cab, tuck-and-roll cover.

1971-1975	Black	$375	$550
1971-1975	Color option	$700	$950

K300 PA Amp and Speaker Set
1971-1975. Includes 302 PA, 303 PA, 304 PA, 305 PA, head and 2 cabs.

1971-1975	Color option	$675	$950

K400-2 Reverb/Tremolo Set
1968-1972. 200 relative watts, reverb, tremolo, with 6x12" or 8x12" cab, available with JBL D-140F speakers, Altec Lansing (A), C.T.S. (C), or Jensen (J). The K400 was offered with no effects (suffix 1), with reverb and tremolo (suffix 2), with Harmonic Clipper & Boost (suffix 3), and Reverb/Trem/Clipper/Boost (suffix 4). The 400 heads came with a separate chrome amp head stand.

1968-1972	Black	$350	$500
1968-1972	Color option	$775	$1,125

KBA-10 Combo
Late-1980s-1990s. Compact solidstate bass amp, 10 watts, 1x8".

1990s		$40	$60

KBA-20 Combo
Late-1980s-early-1990s. KBA series were compact solidstate bass amps with built-in limiter, 20 watts, 1x8".

1989-1990		$40	$60

KBA-30 Combo
Late-1980s-early-1990s. 30 watts, 1x10".

1989-1990		$40	$60

KBA-40 Combo
Late-1980s-early-1990s. 40 watts, 1x12".

1989-1990		$65	$100

KBA-80 Combo
Late-1980s-early-1990s. 80 watts, 1x15".

1989-1990		$100	$150

KBA-160 Combo
Late-1980s-early-1990s. Solidstate bass amp with built-in limiter, 160 watts, 1x15".

1989-1990		$130	$200

KGA-10 VC
1999-2006. 10 watts, 1x6.5" speaker, switchable overdrive.

1999-2006		$40	$60

KLA-15 Combo
Late-1980s-early-1990s. Solidstate, overdrive, 15 watts, 1x8".

1989-1990		$65	$100

KLA-20
Mid-1980s-late-1980s. 1x10", MOS-FET, gain, EQ, reverb, headphone jack.

1986		$65	$100

KLA-25 Combo
Late-1980s-early-1990s. Solidstate, overdrive, reverb, 25 watts, 1x10".

1989-1990		$65	$100

1968 Kustom K200-2
Imaged by Heritage Auctions, HA.com

AMPS

Kustom K250
Tom Pfeifer

Kustom K400-2 Reverb

AMPS

Laboga AD5200 SA
Carter Vintage Guitars

Landry LS30

1980 Legend Rock & Roll 50
Alex Xenos

MODEL YEAR	FEATURES	LOW	HIGH

KLA-50 Combo
Late-1980s-early-1990s. Solidstate, overdrive, reverb, 50 watts, 1x12".

1989-1990		$100	$150

KLA-75
Mid-1980s-late-1980s. 75 watts, reverb, footswitching.

1987		$125	$175

KLA-100 Combo
Late-1980s-early-1990s. Solidstate, reverb, 100-watt dual channel, 1x12".

1989-1990		$125	$175

KLA-185 Combo
Late-1980s-early-1990s. Solidstate, reverb, 185-watt dual channel, 1x12".

1989-1990		$150	$200

KPB-200 Bass Combo
1994-1997. 200 watts, 1x15".

1994-1997		$250	$350

SC 1-12 SC
1971-1973. 50 watts, 1x12" Jensen speaker.

1971-1973	Black	$325	$500
1971-1973	Color option	$450	$650

SC 1-15 SC
1971-1973. 150 watts, 1x15" C.T.S. speaker.

1971-1973	Black	$325	$500
1971-1973	Color option	$450	$650

SC 1-15AB SC
1971-1973. 150 watts, 1x15" Altec Lansing speaker.

1971-1973	Black	$325	$500
1971-1973	Color option	$450	$650

SC 2-12A SC
1971-1973. 150 watts, 2x12" Altec Lansing speakers.

1971-1973	Black	$350	$550
1971-1973	Color option	$450	$650

SC 2-12J SC
1971-1973. 150 watts, 2x12" Jensen speakers.

1971-1973	Black	$350	$550
1971-1973	Color option	$450	$650

SC 4-10 SC
1971-1973. 150 watts, 4x10" Jensen speakers.

1971-1973	Black	$350	$550
1971-1973	Color option	$450	$650

Lab Series

1977-1980s. Five models of Lab Series amps, ranging in price from $600 to $3,700, were introduced at the '77 NAMM show by Norlin (then owner of Gibson). Two more were added later. The '80s models were Lab Series 2 amps and had a Gibson logo on the upper-left front.

B120 Bass Combo
Ca.1984. 120 watts, 2 channels, 1x15".

1984		$375	$550

G120 R-10 Combo
Ca.1984. 120 watts, 3-band EQ, channel switching, reverb, 4x10".

1984		$425	$600

G120 R-12 Combo
Ca.1984. 120 watts, 3-band EQ, channel switching, reverb, 2x12".

1984		$425	$600

MODEL YEAR	FEATURES	LOW	HIGH

L2 Head
1977-ca.1983. 100 watts, black covering.

1977-1983		$325	$425

L3 Combo
1977-ca.1983. 60-watt 1x12".

1977-1983		$375	$550

L4 Head
1977-ca.1983. Solidstate, 200 watts, black cover, dark grille, large L4 logo on front panel.

1977-1983		$300	$450

L5 Combo
1977-ca.1983. Solidstate, 100 watts, 2x12" combo.

1977-1983		$425	$600

L5 Set
1977-ca.1983. Solidstate, 100 watts, 2x12" piggyback.

1977-1983		$425	$600

L7 Set
1977-ca.1983. Solidstate, 100 watts, 4x10" piggyback.

1977-1983		$475	$650

L9 Combo
1977-ca.1983. Solidstate, 100 watts, 1x15".

1977-1983		$375	$550

L11 Set
1977-ca.1983. 200 watts, 8x12" piggyback.

1977-1983		$525	$750

Laboga

1973-present. Adam Laboga builds intermediate and professional grade, production, tube guitar amps and cabinets in Wroclaw, Poland.

Lace Music Products

1979-present. Lace Music Products, founded by pickup innovator Don Lace Sr., offered amplifiers for a while starting in '96. They also offered amps under the Rat Fink and Mooneyes brands.

Lafayette

Ca.1963-1967. Japanese-made guitars and amps sold through the Lafayette Electronics catalogs.

Tube
1960s. Japanese-made tube, gray speckle 1x12" with art deco design or black 2x12".

1960s	Larger, 2 speakers	$275	$375
1960s	Small, 1 speaker	$225	$300

Landry

2008-present. Production, professional grade, amps and cabinets built by Bill Landry in St. Louis, Missouri.

Laney

1968-present. Founded by Lyndon Laney and Bob Thomas in Birmingham, U.K. Laney offered tube amps exclusively into the '80s. Currently they offer intermediate and professional grade, tube and solidstate amp heads and combos and cabinets.

L60 60-Watt Head

1968-1969		$1,500	$2,000

MODEL YEAR	FEATURES	LOW	HIGH

L100 100-Watt Head
1968-1969. Similar to short head Plexi Marshall amp cab, 100 watts, large Laney with underlined "y" logo plate on front upper left corner, black vinyl cover, grayish grille.

1968-1969		$1,500	$2,000

Lectrolab
1950s-1960s. Budget house brand for music stores, made by Sound Projects Company of Cicero, Illinois. Similar to Valco, Oahu, and Danelectro student amps of the '50s, cabinets were generally made from inexpensive material. The Lectrolab logo can generally be found somewhere on the amp.

Tube

1950s-60s	Larger	$425	$650
1950s-60s	Small	$350	$500

Legend
1978-1984. From Legend Musical Instruments of East Syracuse, New York, these amps featured cool wood cabinets. They offered heads, combos with a 1x12" or 2x12" configuration, and cabinets with 1x12", 1x15", 2x12" or 4x12".

A-30
1978-1984. Natural wood cabinet, 30 watts, 1x12".

1978-1984		$475	$650

A-60
1978-1984. Natural wood cabinet, transtube design dual tube preamp with solidstate power section.

1978-1984		$600	$850

Rock & Roll 50
1978-1983. Mesa-Boogie-style wood compact amp, head/half stack or 1x12", 1x15" or 2x12" combo, tube preamp section and solidstate power supply.

1978-1983	1x12" combo	$450	$675
1978-1983	1x15" combo	$450	$675
1978-1983	2x12" combo	$600	$825
1978-1983	Half stack set	$850	$1,250

Super Lead 50
1978-1983. Rock & Roll 50-watt model with added bass boost and reverb, 1x12", hybrid tube and solidstate.

1978-1983		$450	$650

Super Lead 100
1978-1983. 100-watt version, 2x12".

1978-1983		$575	$800

Lenahan
Professional grade, production/custom, vintage-style amps and cabinets built by James T. Lenahan – presently in Fort Smith, Arkansas and prior to '91 in Hollywood, California – starting in 1983. He also built guitar effects.

Leslie
Most often seen with Hammond organs, the cool Leslie rotating speakers have been adopted by many guitarists. Many guitar effects have tried to duplicate their sound. And they are still making them.

16 Rotating Speaker Cabinet
1960s-1970s. 1 cab.

1960s-70s		$775	$2,000

60M Rotating Speaker Cabinets
1960s-1970s. 2 cabs.

1960s-70s		$500	$650

103
1960s. Maximum power 22 watts.

1960s		$500	$650

118
1960s. 1x12".

1960s		$775	$1,250

122A
1960s. Hammond-only model, considered the official Hammond B-3 Leslie. RV indicates reverb.

1960s		$1,250	$2,000

125
Late-1960s. All tube amp with 2-speed rotating 1x12" speaker, bottom rotor only, less features.

1960s		$950	$1,500

142
1960s. Hammond-only model, smaller cabinet than 122 amp.

1960s		$1,250	$2,000

145
1960s. Similar to 147 amp, but smaller and easier to move.

1960s		$1,250	$2,000

147A
1960s. Universal-use model, "7" denotes "universal" usage. RV has added reverb.

1960s		$1,250	$2,000

Lickliter Amplification
In 2009, Michael Lickliter began building professional and premium grade, custom, guitar amps in Punta Gorda, Florida.

Line 6
1996-present. Founded by Marcus Ryle and Michel Doidic and specializing in digital signal processing in both effects and amps. They also produce tube amps. Purchased by Yamaha in 2014.

Little Lanilei
1997-present. Small hand-made, intermediate grade, production/custom, amps made by Mahaffay Amplifiers (formerly Songworks Systems & Products) of Aliso Viejo, California. They also build a reverb unit and a rotary effect.

Little Walter
2008-present. Phil Bradbury builds his professional grade, production, amp heads and cabinets in West End, North Carolina.

London City
Late 1960s-early 1970s. Intermediate to professional grade amps and cabinets made in Netherlands, London City logo.

1967 Leslie 330
Imaged by Heritage Auctions, HA.com

Little Lanilei

Little Walter 30W

AMPS

Louis Electric Deltone

Mad Professor OS 21RT

Magnatone 108 Varsity

AMPS

MODEL YEAR	FEATURES	LOW	HIGH

Louis Electric Amplifier Co.

1993-present. Founded by Louis Rosano in Bergenfield, New Jersey. Louis produces custom-built tweeds and various combo amps from 35 to 80 watts.

Luker

Professional grade, production/custom, guitar and bass amps and cabinets built in Eugene, Oregon by Ken Luker, starting in 2006.

Luna Guitars

2005-present. Located in Tampa, Florida, Yvonne de Villiers imports her budget to professional grade, production, acoustic and electric guitars from Japan, Korea, and China. She also imports guitars, basses and ukes.

Lyric

Late 1950s-ca. 1965. One of several private brands that Magnatone made for others, these were built for Lyric Electronics, located in Lomita, California.

Model 660 Custom

Ca. 1959-ca. 1965. 2x12" combo amp, 35 watts.

1959-1965		$1,750	$2,250

Mack

2005-2019. Made in Toronto, Ontario by builder Don Mackrill, the company offered intermediate and professional grade, production, tube amps.

Mad Professor

2002-present. Bjorn Juhl and Jukka Monkkonen build their premium grade, production/custom, tube amps in Tampere, Finland. They also offer effects pedals.

Maestro

Maestro amps are associated with Gibson and were included in the Gibson catalogs. For example, in the '62-'63 orange cover Gibson catalog, tweed Maestro amps were displayed in their own section. Tweed Maestro amps are very similar to Gibson tweed amps. Maestro amps were often associated with accordions in the early-'60s but the amps featured standard guitar inputs. Gibson also used the Maestro name on effects in the '60s and '70s and in 01, Gibson revived the name for a line of effects, banjos, and mandolins and added guitars and amps in '09.

The prices listed are for amps with fully intact logos. A broken or missing logo may diminish the value of the amp. Amps with a changed handle, power cord, and especially a broken logo, should be taken on a case-by-case basis.

Amp models in '58 include the Super Maestro and Maestro, in '60 the Stereo Maestro Accordion GA-87, Super Maestro Accordion GA-46 T, Standard Accordion GA-45 T, Viscount Accordion GA-16 T, in '62 the Reverb-Echo GA-1 RT, Reverb-Echo GA-2 RT, 30 Stereo Accordion Amp, Stereo Accordion GA-78 RV.

MODEL YEAR	FEATURES	LOW	HIGH

GA-1 RT Reverb-Echo

1961. Tweed, 1x8".

1961		$700	$1,000

GA-2 RT Deluxe Reverb-Echo

1961. Deluxe more powerful version of GA-1 RT, 1x12", tweed.

1961		$1,500	$2,000

GA-15 RV/Bell 15 RV

1961. 15 watts, 1x12", gray sparkle.

1961		$825	$1,125

GA-16T Viscount

1959-1961. 14 watts, 1x10", white cab with brown grille.

1959-1961		$650	$900

GA-45 Maestro

1955-1961. 14-16 watts, 4x8", 2-tone.

1955-1961		$1,500	$2,000

GA-45 RV Standard

1961. 16 watts, 4x8", reverb.

1961		$1,500	$2,000

GA-45T Standard Accordion

1961. 16 watts, 4x8", tremolo.

1961		$1,500	$2,000

GA-46T Super Maestro Accordion and Bass

1957-1961. Based on the Gibson GA-200 and advertised to be designed especially for amplified accordions, 60 watts, 2x12", vibrato, 2-tone cover, large Maestro Super logo on top center of grille.

1957-1961		$2,250	$3,000

GA-78 Maestro Series

1960-1961. Wedge stereo cab, 2x10", reverb and tremolo.

1960-1961	GA-78 RV Maestro 30	$2,500	$3,750
1960-1961	GA-78 RVS	$2,250	$3,500
1960-1961	GA-78 RVT	$2,250	$3,500

Magnatone

Ca.1937-1971, 2013-present. Magnatone made a huge variety of amps sold under their own name and under brands like Dickerson, Oahu, Bronson, and Estey (see separate listings). They also private branded amps for several accordion companies or accordion teaching studios like Ariatone, Audio Guild, Da Vinci, Excelsior, Giulietti, Lyric, Noble, PAC-AMP, PANaramic, Titano, Tonemaster, Twilighter, and Unique (see separate listings). In 2013, Ted Kornblum revived the Magnatone name on a line of tube amps based on the earlier models and built in St. Louis, Missouri.

Model 108 Varsity/Varsity Deluxe

1948-1954. Gray pearloid cover, small student amp or lap steel companion amp.

1948-1954		$450	$650

Model 109 Melodier Deluxe

1950s. 10 watts, 2 speakers.

1950s		$850	$1,250

Model 110 Melodier

1953-1954. 12 watts, 1x10", brown leatherette cover, light grille.

1953-1954		$775	$1,125

MODEL YEAR	FEATURES	LOW	HIGH

Model 111 Student
1955-1959. 1x8", 2-3 watts, brown leatherette, brown grille.

1955-1959		$500	$750

Model 112/113 Troubadour
1955-1959. 18 watts, 1x12", brown leatherette, brown grille, slant back rear control panel.

1955-1959		$1,000	$1,500

Model 118
1960. Compact, tubes, low power, volume and tone knobs, brown tolex era, Model 118 logo on rear-mounted control panel.

1960		$550	$800

Model 120B Cougar Bass
1967-1968. Initial Magnatone entry into the solid-state market, superseded by Brute Series in '68, 120 watts, 2x12" solidstate bass piggyback amp, naugahyde vinyl cover with polyester rosewood side panels.

1967-1968		$450	$650

Model 120R Sting Ray Reverb Bass
1967-1968. Initial Magnatone entry into the solid-state market, superseded by Brute Series in '68, 150 watts, 4x10" solidstate combo amp, naugahyde vinyl cover with polyester rosewood side panels.

1967-1968		$525	$750

Model 130V Custom
1969-1971. Solidstate 1x12" combo amp.

1969-1971		$325	$500

Model 150R Firestar Reverb
1967-1968. Initial Magnatone entry into the solid-state market, superseded by Brute Series in '68, 120 watts, 2x12" solidstate combo amp, naugahyde vinyl cover with polyester rosewood side panels.

1967-1968		$350	$550

Model 180 Triplex
Mid-to-late-1950s. Mid-level power using 2 6L6 power tubes, 1x15" and 1x8" speakers.

1950s		$1,125	$1,625

Model 192-5-S Troubadour
Early-1950s. 18 watts, 1x12" Jensen Concert speaker, brown alligator covering, lower back control panel, 3 chicken-head knobs, Magnatone script logo on front, Troubadour script logo on back control panel.

1950s		$775	$1,125

Model 194 Lyric
1947-mid-1950s. 1x12" speaker, old-style tweed vertical cab typical of '40s.

1940s		$650	$950

Model 195 Melodier
1951-1954. Vertical cab with 1x10" speaker, pearloid with flowing grille slats.

1951-1954		$650	$850

Model 196
1947-mid-1950s. 1x12", 5-10 watts, scroll grille design, snakeskin leatherette cover.

1940s		$650	$950

Model 197 V Varsity
1948-1952. Small compact student amp, 1x8", tubes, Varsity model logo and model number on back panel, old style layout with back bottom-mounted chassis, curved crossbars on front baffle, brown lizard leatherette, leather handle.

1948-1952		$600	$875

Model 198 Varsity
1948-1954. 1x8", tubes.

1948-1954		$650	$950

Model 199 Student
1950s. About 6 to 10 watts, 1x8", snakeskin leatherette cover, metal handle, slant grille design.

1950s		$650	$950

Model 210 Deluxe Student
1958-1960. 5 watts, 1x8", vibrato, brown leatherette, V logo lower right front on grille.

1958-1960		$650	$950

Model 213 Troubadour
1957-1958. 10 watts, 1x12", vibrato, brown leatherette cover, V logo lower right of grille

1957-1958		$1,500	$2,000

Model 240 SV Magna-Chordion
1967-1968. Initial Magnatone entry into the solid-state market, superseded by Brute Series in '68, 240 watts, 2x12" solidstate stereo accordion or organ amp, naugahyde vinyl cover, polyester rosewood side panels, input jacks suitable for guitar, reverb and vibrato, lateral combo cab, rear mounted controls.

1967-1968		$450	$650

Model 250 Professional
1958-1960. 20 watts, 1x12", vibrato, brown leatherette with V logo lower right front of grille.

1958-1960		$1,250	$1,875

Model 260
1957-1958. 35 watts, 2x12", brown leatherette, vibrato, V logo lower right front corner of grille.

1957-1958		$1,750	$2,500

Model 262 Jupiter/Custom Pro
1961-1963. 35 watts, 2x12", vibrato, brown leatherette.

1961-1963		$1,375	$1,750

Model 280/Custom 280
1957-1958. 50 watts, brown leatherette covering, brown-yellow tweed grille, 2x12" plus 2x5" speakers, double V logo.

1957-1958		$1,875	$2,500

Model 280A
1958-1960. 50 watts, brown leatherette covering, brown-yellow tweed grille, 2x12" plus 2x5" speakers, V logo lower right front.

1958-1960		$1,875	$2,500
1958-1960 With matching cab		$2,500	$3,500

Model 410 Diana
1961-1963. Five watts, 1x12", advertised as a 'studio' low power professional amp, brown leatherette cover, vibrato.

1961-1963		$825	$1,250

Model 411 Estey
1960s. Tubes, 15 watts, 1x8".

1960s		$1,500	$2,250

Model 412
1960s. Estey era compact student amp, low power, 1x8", tubes.

1960s		$350	$475

1950s Magnatone Model
192-5 Troubadour
Tom Pfeifer

Magnatone 195 Melodier
Tom Pfeifer

1958 Magnatone Model 210
tednugentlives

AMPS

Magnatone 480 Venus

1961 Magnatone Model 410

1966 Magnatone MP-1

MODEL YEAR	FEATURES	LOW	HIGH
Model 413 Centaur			
1961-1963. 18 watts, 1x12", brown leatherette cover, vibrato.			
1961-1963		$1,250	$1,875
Model 415 Clio Bass			
1961-1963. 25 watts, 4x8", bass or accordion amp, brown leatherette cover.			
1961-1963		$1,250	$1,875
Model 422			
1966-1967. Low power 1x12", 3 inputs, black vinyl, light swirl grille.			
1966-1967		$675	$950
Model 425			
1961. Tube, 55 watts, 4x12".			
1961		$1,625	$2,250
Model 432			
Mid-1960s. Compact student model, wavey-squiggle art deco-style grille, black cover, vibrato and reverb.			
1960s		$775	$1,125
Model 435 Athene Bass			
1961-1963. 55 watts, 4x10", piggyback head and cab, brown leatherette.			
1961-1963		$1,500	$2,250
Model 440 Mercury			
1961-1963. 18 watts, 1x12", vibrato, brown leatherette.			
1961-1963		$1,375	$1,750
Model 450 Juno/Twin Hi-Fi			
1961-1963. 25 watts, 1x12" and 1 oval 5"x7" speakers, reverb, vibrato, brown leatherette.			
1961-1963		$1,500	$2,250
1961-1963	Extension cab only	$775	$1,125
Model 460 Victory			
1961-1963. 35 watts, 2x12" and 2 oval 5"x7" speakers, early-'60s next to the top-of-the-line, reverb and vibrato, brown leatherette.			
1961-1963		$1,625	$2,250
Model 480 Venus			
1961-1963. 50 watts, 2x12" and 2 oval 5"x7" speakers, early-'60s top-of-the-line, reverb and stereo vibrato, brown leatherette.			
1961-1963		$1,500	$2,250
Model M2			
1963-1964. 1x8", 12-15 watts, 1 channel.			
1963-1964		$475	$650
Model M6			
1964 (not seen in '65 catalog). 25 watts, 1x12", black molded plastic suitcase amp.			
1964		$650	$950
Model M7 Bass			
1964-1966. 38 watts, 1x15" bass amp, black molded plastic suitcase amp.			
1964-1966		$675	$975
Model M8			
1964-1966. 27 watts, 1x12", reverb and tremolo, black molded plastic suitcase amp.			
1964-1966		$750	$1,125
Model M9			
1964-1966. 38 watts, 1x15", tremolo, no reverb, black molded plastic suitcase amp.			
1964-1966		$750	$1,125

MODEL YEAR	FEATURES	LOW	HIGH
Model M10/M10A			
1964-1966. 38 watts, 1x15", tone boost, tremolo, transistorized reverb section, black molded plastic suitcase amp.			
1964-1966		$700	$1,125
Model M12 Bass			
1964-1966. 80 watts, 1x15" or 2x12", mid-'60s top-of-the-line bass amp, black molded plastic suitcase amp.			
1964-1966		$750	$1,125
Model M13 Imperial			
Mid-1963-1964. 1x15", 45 watts, 3 channels.			
1963-1964		$750	$1,125
Model M14			
1964-1966. Stereo, 75 watts, 2x12" plus 2 tweeters, stereo vibrato, no reverb, black molded plastic suitcase amp.			
1964-1966		$950	$1,500
Model M15			
1964-1966. Stereo 75 watts, 2x12" plus 2 tweeters, stereo vibrato, transistorized reverb, black molded plastic suitcase amp.			
1964-1966		$975	$1,500
Model M27 Bad Boy Bass			
1968-1971. 150 watts, 2x15" (1 passive), reverb, vibrato, solidstate, vertical profile bass amp, part of Brute Series.			
1968-1971		$400	$550
Model M30 Fang			
1968-1971. 150 watts, 2x15" (1 passive), 1 exponential horn, solidstate, vibrato, reverb, vertical profile amp.			
1968-1971		$400	$550
Model M32 Big Henry Bass			
1968-1971. 300 watts, 2x15" solidstate vertical profile bass amp.			
1968-1971		$400	$550
Model M35 The Killer			
1968-1971. 300 watts, 2x15" and 2 horns, solidstate, vibrato, vertical profile amp.			
1968-1971		$400	$550
Model MP-1 (Magna Power I)			
1966-1967. 30 watts, 1x12", dark vinyl, light grille, Magnatone-Estey logo on upper right of grille.			
1966-1967		$725	$1,125
Model MP-3 (Magna Power 3)			
1966-1967. Mid-power, 2x12", reverb, dark vinyl, light grille, Magnatone-Estey logo on upper right of grille.			
1966-1967		$850	$1,250
Model MP-5 (Magna Power)			
1966-1967. Mid-power, piggyback 2x12", Magnatone-Estey logo on upper right of grille.			
1966-1967		$900	$1,375
Model PS150			
1968-1971. Powered slave speaker cabinets, 150 watts, 2x15" linkable cabinets.			
1968-1971		$250	$350
Model PS300			
1968-1971. Powered slave speaker cabinets, 300 watts, 2x15" (1 passive) linkable cabinets.			
1968-1971		$250	$350

The *Vintage Guitar Price Guide* shows values for an all-original condition amplifier, and where applicable, with original cover.

MODEL YEAR	FEATURES	LOW	HIGH

Small Pearloid
1947-1955. Pearloid (MOTS) covered low- and mid-power amps generally associated with pearloid lap steel sets.

1947-1955	Fancy grille	$475	$750
1947-1955	Plain grille	$325	$500

Starlet Model 107
1951-1952. Student model, 1x8", pearloid cover early, leatherette later, low power, single on-off volume control, Starlet logo on back panel, Magnatone logo plate upper left front of grille.

1951-1954	Pearloid	$450	$600
1955-1959	Leatherette	$400	$550

Starlite Model 401
1964-1966. Magnatone produced the mid-'60s Starlite amplifier line for the budget minded musician. Each Starlite model prominently notes the Magnatone name. The grilles show art deco wavy circles. Magnatone 1960-'63 standard amps offer models starting with 12" speakers. Starlite models offer 10" and below. Model 401 has 15 watts, 1x8" and 3 tubes.

1964-1966		$400	$550

Starlite Model 411
1964-1966. 15 watts, 1x8", 5 tubes, tremolo (not advertised as vibrato), art deco wavy grille.

1964-1966		$450	$600

Starlite Model 441A Bass
1964-1966. Lower power with less than 25 watts, 1x15", tube amp.

1964-1966		$675	$975

Starlite Model Custom 421
1964-1966. Tube amp, 25 watts, 1x10".

1964-1966		$675	$975

Starlite Model Custom 431
1964-1966. Tube amp, 30 watts, 1x10", vibrato and reverb.

1964-1966		$700	$1,125

Mahaffay Amplifiers
2009-present. See Little Lanilei.

Mako
1985-1989. Line of solidstate amps from Kaman (Ovation, Hamer). They also offered guitars and basses.

Marlboro Sound Works
1970-1980s. Economy solidstate amps imported by Musical Instruments Corp., Syosset, New York. Initially, Marlboro targeted the economy compact amp market, but quickly added larger amps and PAs.

Solid State

1970-1980s	Various models	$45	$65

Marshall
1962-present. Drummer Jim Marshall (1923-2012) started building bass speaker and PA cabinets in his garage in 1960. He opened a retail drum shop for his students and others and soon added guitars and amps. When Ken Bran joined the business as service manager in '62, the two decided to build their own amps. By '63 they had expanded the shop to house a small manufacturing space and by late that year they were offering the amps to other retailers. Marshall also made amps under the Park, CMI, Narb, Big M, and Kitchen-Marshall brands.

Mark I, II, III and IVs are generally '60s and '70s and also are generally part of a larger series (for example JTM) or have a model number that is a more specific identifier. Describing an amp only as Mark II can be misleading. The most important identifier is the Model Number, which Marshall often called the Stock Number. To help avoid confusion we have added the Model number as often as possible. In addition, when appropriate, we have included the wattage, number of channels, master or no-master info in the title. This should help the reader more quickly find a specific amp. Check the model's description for such things as two inputs or four inputs, because this will help with identification. Vintage Marshall amps do not always have the Model/Stock number on the front or back panel, so the additional identifiers should help. The JMP logo on the front is common and really does not help with specific identification. For example, a JMP Mark II Super Lead 100-Watt description is less helpful than the actual model/stock number. Unfortunately, many people are not familiar with specific model/stock numbers. VG has tried to include as much information in the title as space will allow.

Marshall amps are sorted as follows:
AVT Series - Advanced Valvestate Technology
Club and Country Series (Rose-Morris)-introduced in '78
JCM 800 Series - basically the '80s
JCM 900 Series - basically the '90s
JCM 2000 Series - basically the '00s
JTM Series
Micro Stack Group
Model Number/Stock Number (no specific series, basically the '60s, '70s) - including Artist and Valvestate models (Valvestate refers to specific Model numbers in 8000 Series)
Silver Jubilee Series

Acoustic Soloist (AS) Series
1994-present. Acoustic guitar amps, models include AS50R and D (50 watts, 2 channels, 2x8"), AS80R (40-watt x2 stereo, 3 channels, 2x8"), AS100D (50-watt x2 stereo, 4 channels, 2x8").

1994-2023	Various models	$225	$300

AVT 20
2001-2011. Solidstate, 20 watts, 12AX7 preamp tube, 1x10", Advanced Valvestate Technology (AVT) models have black covering and grille, and gold panel.

2001-2011	Combo	$150	$200

AVT 50
2001-2011. Solidstate, 50 watts, 4x12".

2001-2011	Combo	$200	$275
2001-2011	Head & cab	$425	$575

AVT 100
2001-2011. Solidstate, 100 watts, tube preamp, 1x12".

2001-2011		$250	$350

1950 Magnatone
Small Pearloid

Magnatone Starlet 107

Imaged by Heritage Auctions, HA.com

Marshall AS100D

Marshall Code 25

1986 Marshall JCM 800 2204
Scott Davis

Marshall JCM 900 Model
4100 Dual Reverb

Imaged by Heritage Auctions, HA.com

MODEL YEAR	FEATURES	LOW	HIGH
AVT 150			
2001-2011. Solidstate, additional features over AVT 100. Combo (100 watts, 1x12"), Half-Stack (150 watts, 4x12") and Head only (150 watts).			
2001-2011	Combo	$250	$350
2001-2011	Half-stack	$325	$450
AVT 275			
2001-2007. Solidstate DFX stereo, 75 watts per side, 2x12".			
2001-2007	Combo	$300	$400
Capri			
1966-1967. Only about 100 made, 5 watts, 1x8, 2x8 or 1x10 combo, red cover.			
1966-1967		$2,000	$3,000
Class 5			
2009-2014. 5 watts, 1x10" tube combo.			
2009-2014	Head	$250	$350
2009-2014	Head & cab	$275	$375
Club and Country Model 4140			
1978-1982. Tubes, 100 watts, 2x12" combo, Rose-Morris era, designed for the country music market, hence the name, brown vinyl cover, straw grille.			
1978-1982		$850	$1,125
Club and Country Model 4145			
1978-1982. Tubes, 100 watts, 4x10" combo, Rose-Morris era, designed for the country music market, hence the name, brown vinyl, straw grille.			
1978-1982		$850	$1,125
Club and Country Model 4150 Bass			
1978-1982. Tubes, 100 watts, 4x10" bass combo, Rose-Morris era, designed for the country music market, hence the name, brown vinyl cover, straw grille.			
1978-1982		$850	$1,125
Code Series			
2016-present. Marshall-Softube (MST) modelling, digital capabilities, series includes CODE25, 50, 100 and 100H. Number indicates watts.			
2016-2023		$120	$165
Haze (MHZ) Series			
2009-2014. All tube, multi-functional amps, MHZ15 (15w, head, 2 cabs), 40C (40w, 1x12 combo) 215 (15w, 2x1x12).			
2009-2014	MHZ15	$600	$800
2009-2014	MHZ40C	$325	$450
JCM 600 Series			
1997-2000. All tube, 60-watt models with modern features, includes the JCM600 head, JCM601 1x12" combo and JCM602 2x12" combo.			
1997-2000	JCM600	$425	$600
1997-2000	JCM601	$450	$650
1997-2000	JCM602	$550	$750
JCM 800 Model 1959 Head			
1981-1991. 100 watts.			
1981-1991		$1,500	$2,000
JCM 800 Model 1987 Head			
1981-1991. 50 watts.			
1981-1991		$1,500	$2,000
JCM 800 Model 1992 Bass Head			
1981-1986. Active tone circuit.			
1981-1986		$1,500	$2,000

MODEL YEAR	FEATURES	LOW	HIGH
JCM 800 Model 2000 Head			
1981-1982. 200 watts.			
1981-1982		$1,500	$2,000
JCM 800 Model 2001 Head			
1981-1982. Bass head, 300 watts.			
1981-1982		$1,500	$2,000
JCM 800 Model 2004 Head			
1981-1990. 50 watts, master.			
1981-1990		$1,500	$2,000
JCM 800 Model 2004S Head			
1986-1987. 50 watts, short head.			
1986-1987		$1,500	$2,000
JCM 800 Model 2005 Full Stack			
1983-1990. Limited Edition, 2005 head with 2 2x12 cabs.			
1983-1990		$2,000	$3,000
JCM 800 Model 2005 Head			
1983-1990. 50 watts, split channel.			
1983-1990		$1,500	$2,000
JCM 800 Model 2203 20th Anniversary Half Stack			
1982. 20th Anniversary plate in lower right corner of matching 1960A cab, matching white tolex cover.			
1982		$2,500	$4,000
JCM 800 Model 2203 Head			
1981-1990, 2002-2020. 100 watts, master volume, reissued '02 in Vintage Series.			
1981-1990		$1,500	$2,000
2002-2020	Reissue	$950	$1,500
JCM 800 Model 2203KK Kerry King Signature			
2008-2012. King Signature logo, 100 watts, 3-band EQ.			
2008-2012		$1,000	$1,500
JCM 800 Model 2203ZW Zack Wylde Signature			
2002. About 600 amp heads and 60 half-stacks made.			
2002	Half-stack	$3,000	$4,500
2002	Head only	$1,750	$2,500
JCM 800 Model 2204 Head			
1981-1990. 50 watts, 1 channel, 2 inputs, master volume, front panel says JCM 800 Lead Series, back panel says Master Model 50w Mk 2.			
1981-1990		$1,500	$2,000
JCM 800 Model 2204S Head			
1986-1987. Short head, 50 watts.			
1986-1987		$1,500	$2,000
JCM 800 Model 2205			
1983-1990. 50 watts, split channel (1 clean and 1 distortion), switchable, both channels with reverb, 4x12" cabinet, front panel reads JCM 800 Lead Series.			
1983-1990	Cab	$550	$850
1983-1990	Head only	$1,500	$2,000
JCM 800 Model 2210 Head			
1983-1990. 100 watts.			
1983-1990		$1,500	$2,000
JCM 800 Model 4010 Combo			
1980-1990. 50 watts, 1x12", non-reverb ('80), reverb begins '81, single channel master volume.			
1980-1990		$1,500	$2,000

MODEL YEAR	FEATURES	LOW	HIGH

JCM 800 Model 4103 Combo
1981-1990. Lead combo amp, 100 watts, 2x12".

1981-1990		$1,500	$2,000

JCM 800 Model 4104 Combo
1980-1990. Tube lead amp, 50 watts, 2x12".

1980-1990	Black	$1,500	$2,000
1980-1990	Head only	$1,250	$1,750
1980-1990	White option	$1,500	$2,000

JCM 800 Model 4210 Combo
1982-1990. 50 watts, 1x12" tube combo, split-channel, single input, master volume.

1982-1990		$1,500	$2,000

JCM 800 Model 4211 Combo
1983-1990. Lead combo amp, 100 watts, 2x12".

1983-1990		$1,500	$2,000

JCM 800 Model 4212 Combo
1983-1990. 50-watt, 2x12" combo.

1983-1990		$1,500	$2,000

JCM 800 Model 5010 Combo
1983-1991. Solidstate, 30 watts, master volume, 1x12".

1983-1991		$350	$500

JCM 800 Model 5150 Combo
1987-1991. Solidstate, 150 watts, 12" Celestion, 2 channels, presence and effects-mix master controls.

1987-1991		$400	$600

JCM 800 Model 5210 Combo
1986-1991. Solidstate, 50 watts, channel switching, 1x12".

1986-1991		$350	$500

JCM 800 Model 5212 Combo
1986-1991. Solidstate, 50 watts, 2x12" split channel reverb combo.

1986-1991		$450	$650

JCM 800 Model 5213 Combo
1986-1991. Solidstate, 2x12", channel-switching, effects loop.

1986-1991		$350	$500

JCM 800 Model 5215 Combo
1986-1991. Solidstate, 1x15", Accutronics reverb, effects loop.

1986-1991		$350	$500

JCM 900 Model 2100 Mark III Head
1990-1993. FX loop, 100/50-watt selectable lead head.

1990-1993		$800	$1,125

JCM 900 Model 2100 SL-X Head
1992-1998. Hi-gain 100-watt head amp, additional 12AX7 preamp tube.

1992-1998		$800	$1,125

JCM 900 Model 2500 SL-X Head
1990-2000. 50-watt version of SL-X.

1992-1998		$800	$1,125

JCM 900 Model 4100 Dual Reverb
1990-2017. Vintage Series, 100/50 switchable head, JCM 900 on front panel, 4x10 or 2x12 matching cab, black with black front.

1990-2017	4x10 or 2x12	$500	$750
1990-2017	Head only	$525	$850

JCM 900 Model 4101 Combo
1990-2000. All tube, 100 watts, 1x12" combo.

1990-2000		$800	$1,125

JCM 900 Model 4102 Combo
1990-2000. Combo amp, 100/50 watts switchable, 2x12".

1990-2000		$800	$1,125

JCM 900 Model 4500 Head
1990-2000. All tube, 2 channels, 50/25 watts, EL34 powered, reverb, effects loop, compensated recording out, master volume, black.

1990-2000		$650	$975

JCM 900 Model 4501 Dual Reverb Combo
1990-2000. 50/25 switchable, 1x12".

1990-2000		$750	$1,125

JCM 900 Model 4502 Combo
1990-2000. 50/25 switchable, 2x12".

1990-2000		$775	$1,125

JCM 2000 DSL Series
1998-2015. DSL is Dual Super Lead, 2 independent channels labelled classic and ultra, JCM 2000 and DSL logos both on front panel.

1998-2015	Half-stacks/combos	$250	$350

JCM 2000 TSL Series
1998-2013. TSL is Triple Super Lead, 3 independent channels labelled clean, crunch and lead, 8 tubes, JCM 2000 and TSL logos both on front panel.

1998-2013	Full-stacks	$1,250	$1,625
1998-2013	Half-stacks/combos	$675	$900

JCM Slash Signature Model 2555SL Set
1996. Based on JCM 800 with higher gain, matching amp and cab set, JCM Slash Signature logo on front panel, single channel, Slash Signature 1960AV 4x12" slant cab, black.

1996	4x12 cab	$750	$1,125
1996	Head only	$1,625	$2,500

JMD Series
2010-2013. JMD is Jim Marshall Digital. Models include JMD50 & 100 heads and JMD 102 (100w, 2x12) & 501 (50w, 1x12) combos.

2010-2013	501	$500	$675

JTM 30 Series
1995-1997. Tube combo, reverb, 30 watts, effects loops, 5881 output sections, foot switchable high-gain modes. Available as 1x15", 1x12", 2x12" or 3x10" combo or as 4x10" half-stack.

1995-1997	Combo 1x12	$425	$575
1995-1997	Combo 2x10	$450	$575
1995-1997	Combo 2x12	$475	$625
1995-1997	Combo 3x10	$475	$625

JTM 45 Head
1962-1964. Amp head, 45 watts. The original Marshall amp. Became the Model 1987 45-watt for '65-'66.

1962	Coffin logo	$18,500	$27,000
1963-1964	Block logo	$9,500	$17,000

JTM 45 Model 1961 MK IV 4x10 Combo
1965-1966. 45 watts, 4x10", tremolo, JTM 45 MK IV on panel, Bluesbreaker association.

1965-1966		$8,000	$12,000

JTM 45 Model 1962 MK IV 2x12 Combo
1965-1966. 45 watts, 2x12", tremolo, JTM 45 MK IV on panel, Bluesbreaker association.

1965-1966		$8,500	$12,000

2003 Marshall JCM 2000 DSL
Imaged by Heritage Auctions, HA.com

1964 Marshall JTM 45
Eddie Daurelle

Marshall JTM 45 1961 MK IV
Pang Leo

AMPS

Marshall JTM 50 Model 1962
Bluesbreaker Reissue

Marshall JVM210C

Marshall MG10

MODEL YEAR	FEATURES	LOW	HIGH

JTM 45 Model 1987 Head Reissue
1988-1999. Black/green tolex.

1988-1999		$1,500	$2,000

JTM 45 Model 1987 Mark II Lead Head
1965-1966. Replaced JTM 45 Amp ('62-'64) but was subsequently replaced by the Model 1987 50-watt Head during '66.

1965-1966		$7,000	$11,000

JTM 45 Offset Limited Edition Set Reissue
Introduced in 2000. Limited run of 300 units, old style cosmetics, 45-watt head and offset 2x12" cab, dark vinyl cover, light gray grille, rectangular logo plate on front of amp and cab, Limited Edition plate on rear of cab, serial number xxx of 300.

2000		$3,000	$4,500

JTM 50 Head
1966-1967. Script logo, JTM 50 panel logo, EL34 power tubes.

1966-1967		$8,000	$12,000

JTM 50 Model 1961 MK IV 4x10 Combo
1965-1972. 50 watts, 4x10", Bluesbreaker association, tremolo, JTM 50 MK IV on front panel to '68, plain front panel without model description '68-'72.

1966-1967		$8,500	$15,000
1968		$7,500	$12,000
1969		$6,500	$10,000
1970		$5,500	$8,500
1971-1972		$5,000	$7,500

JTM 50 Model 1962 Bluesbreaker Reissue
1989-1999. 50 watts, 2x12", Model 1962 reissue Bluesbreaker.

1989-1999		$1,500	$2,000

JTM 50 Model 1962 MK IV 2x12 Combo
1966-1972. 50 watts, 2x12", tremolo, Bluesbreaker association, JTM 50 MK IV on front panel to '68, plain front panel without model description '68-'72.

1966-1967	Used on Bluesbreaker album	$15,000	$22,000
1968		$8,000	$15,000
1969		$7,000	$12,000
1970		$6,500	$10,000
1971-1972		$5,500	$8,500

JTM 50 Model 1963 PA Head
1965-1966. MK II PA head, block logo.

1965-1966		$2,500	$3,500

JTM 60 Series
1995-1997. Tube, 60 watts, 1x12", 1x15", 2x12" or 3x10" combo or as 4x10" half-stack.

1995-1997	1x12 Combo	$500	$650
1995-1997	2x12 Combo	$525	$700
1995-1997	3x10 Combo	$550	$725
1995-1997	4x10 Mini half-stack	$550	$725

JTM 310
1995-1997. JTM 30 with 2x10".

1995-1997		$500	$675

JTM 612 Combo
1995-1997. Tube combo amp, 60 watts, 1x12", EQ, reverb, effects loop.

1995-1997		$500	$650

MODEL YEAR	FEATURES	LOW	HIGH

JVM Series
2007-present. Models (H for Head, C Combo) include 205H/205C (50-watt head/combo 2x12), 210H/210C (100-watt head/combo 2x12), 215C (50-watt 1x12 combo), 410H/410C (100-watt head/combo 2x12, 4-channel).

2007-2017	JVM410C	$1,000	$1,375
2008-2023	JVM205H	$850	$1,125
2008-2023	JVM210C	$1,125	$1,500
2008-2023	JVM210H	$900	$1,250

MA Series
2009-2013. Models include 50C (50 watts, 1x12"), 50H (50-watt head), 100C (100 watts, 2x12"), 100H (100-watt head) and 412 (4x12" slant cabinet).

2009-2013	Half-stacks/combos	$400	$550

MB Series
2006-2012. Bass Combo Series, models include 30C (30watts, 1x10").

2006-2012	MB30C	$125	$175

MG Series
1999-present. Models include 10KK (10 watts, 1x6"), 15CD, 15RCD or CDR (15 watts, 1x8"), 15MS (15 watts, micro stack, 1x8" slant and straight cabs), 15MSII, (in '02, 10" speakers), 15MSZW (15 watts, 2x1x10"), 50DFX (50 watts, 1x12"), 100DFX (100 watts, combo), 100HDFX (100-watt head), 100RCD (Valvestate Series, 100-watt), 102FX (100 watts, 2x12"), 250DFX (250 watts, combo), 412A (4x12" cabinet).

1999-2023	Various models	$50	$450

MGP Series
1980s-1990s. Solidstate rackmount preamps.

1980s-90s	Various models	$175	$225

Micro Stack 3005
1986-1991. Solidstate head, 12 watts, 2 1x10" stackable cabs (one slant, one straight). The standard model is black, but was also offered in white, green, red, or the silver Silver Jubilee version with Jubilee 25/50 logo.

1986-1991	Black	$350	$500
1986-1991	Green or red	$450	$650
1986-1991	White	$450	$650
1987-1989	Silver Jubilee/silver	$550	$1,000

Mini-Stack 3210 MOS-FET Head
1984-1991. Model 3210 MOS-FET head with 2 4x10" cabs, designed as affordable stack.

1984-1991		$400	$600

Model 1710 Bass Cabinet
1990s. 1x15" speaker.

1990s		$325	$450

Model 1912 Cabinet
1989-1998, 2013-2017. 1x12", 150 watts.

2013-2017		$325	$450

Model 1917 PA-20 Head
1967-1973. PA head with 20 watts, but often used for guitar, matching cabinet.

1967-1968	Matching cab	$1,750	$2,500
1967-1968	Plexi head	$3,500	$5,500
1969-1973	Aluminum head	$2,750	$4,000
1969-1973	Matching cab	$1,500	$2,000

Model 1922 Cabinet
1989-present. 2x12" extension cab for JCM 800 Series amps.

1989-2023		$325	$450

MODEL YEAR	FEATURES	LOW	HIGH

Model 1923 85th Anniversary
2008. Based on Jim Marshall's 85th birthday amp, limited edition, 50 watts.

2008		$1,000	$1,500

Model 1930 Popular Combo
1969-1973. 10 watts, 1x12", tremolo.

1969-1972		$3,250	$5,000
1973		$3,500	$5,750

Model 1933 Amp Cabinet
1981-1991. 1x12" extension cab for JCM 800 Series amps.

1981-1991		$325	$450

Model 1935/1935A/1935B Bass Cabinet
1967-1990s. Models 1935, 4x12", black, A slant front, B straight front.

1967-1970	75w	$2,250	$3,000
1971-1972	Black, weave	$1,125	$1,500
1973-1975	Black, checkerboard	$1,125	$1,500
1976-1979	Black	$975	$1,375
1979-1983	260w	$600	$850
1983-1986	280w	$525	$775
1990s		$450	$600

Model 1936 Cabinet
1981-2011. Extension straight-front cab for JCM 800/900 Series amps, 2x12" speakers, black.

1981-2011		$425	$550

Model 1937 Bass Cabinet
1981-1986. 4x12", 140 watts.

1981-1986		$525	$675

Model 1958 18-Watt Lead Combo
1965-1972. 18 watts, 2x10", Bluesbreaker cosmetics, black.

1965-1968		$11,000	$17,000
1968		$6,000	$9,000
1969		$5,500	$8,000
1970		$5,000	$7,500
1971-1972		$4,500	$7,000

Model 1959 Super Lead 100-Watt Head
1966-1981. Two channels, 100 watts, 4 inputs, no master volume. Plexiglas control panels until mid-'69, aluminum after. See Model T1959 for tremolo version. Early custom color versions are rare and more valuable. Becomes JCM 800 1959 in '81.

1966-1969	Black, plexi	$6,500	$12,000
1966-1969	Custom color, plexi	$8,500	$15,000
1969-1970	Black, aluminum	$3,000	$4,500
1969-1970	Custom color, aluminum	$6,000	$9,000
1971-1972	Black, hand-wired, small box	$3,000	$4,500
1971-1972	Custom color, hand-wired	$3,500	$5,500
1973-1975	Black, printed CB, large box	$2,000	$3,000
1973-1975	Custom color, printed CB	$2,750	$4,000
1976-1979	Black	$1,750	$2,750
1976-1979	Custom color	$2,000	$3,000
1980-1981	Black	$1,625	$2,500
1980-1981	Custom color	$1,875	$2,750

Model T1959 Super Lead (Tremolo) Head
1966-1973. 100 watts, plexi until mid-'69, aluminum after. Tremolo version of the Model 1959 Amp.

1966-1969	Black, plexi	$6,500	$12,000
1966-1969	Custom color, plexi	$8,500	$15,000
1969-1970	Black, aluminum	$2,750	$4,000
1969-1970	Custom color, aluminum	$6,000	$9,000
1971-1973	Black, hand-wired, small box	$2,500	$3,500
1971-1973	Custom color, hand-wired	$3,500	$5,000

35th Anniversary Marshall Limited Edition Set
1997. Limited Edition 1997 logo, includes matching Super Lead MKII 100-watt head, PB100 power brake and MKII 1960A slant cab, all in white covering.

1997		$2,500	$3,750

Model 1959 SLP Reissue Head
1992-2017. Vintage Series, Super Lead Plexi (SLP), vinyl covering, black, purple or white.

1992-1999	Black	$1,125	$1,500
1992-1999	Purple or white	$1,375	$2,000
2000-2017	Black	$1,375	$1,750

Model 1959 SLP Reissue Set
1992-2013. Vintage Series, 100-watt Super Lead head and matching 4x12" slant cab.

1992-2013	4x12 Cab	$550	$750

Model 1959HW
2005-present. Hand-wired, 100 watts, 4x12" slant front cab.

2005-2014	Cab	$550	$750
2005-2023	Head only	$1,250	$1,500

Model 1959RR Randy Rhoads Limited Edition
2008-2013. Randy Rhoads Tribute, full stack, 100 watts.

2008-2013		$3,000	$4,500

Model 1960 4x12 Speaker Cabinet
1964-1979. Both straight and slant front. The original Marshall 4x12" cab designed for compact size with 4x12" speakers. First issue in '64/'65 is 60-watt cab, from '65-'70 75 watts, from '70-'79 100 watts. After '79, model numbers contained an alpha suffix: A for slant front, B straight.

1966-1970	Black, weave	$2,250	$3,500
1966-1970	Custom color, weave	$3,250	$5,000
1971-1972	Black, weave	$1,250	$2,000
1971-1972	Custom color, weave	$1,750	$3,000
1973-1975	Black, checkerboard	$1,000	$1,500
1973-1975	Custom color, checkerboard	$1,375	$2,000
1976-1979	Black	$950	$1,375
1976-1979	Custom color	$1,375	$2,000

Model 1960A/1960B 4x12 Speaker Cabinet
1980-1983 (260 watts), '84-'86 (280 watts, JCM 800 era), '86-'90 (300 watts, JCM 800 era), '90-present (300 watts, JCM 900 era, stereo-mono switching). A slant or B straight front.

1980-1983	Black	$550	$1,000
1980-1983	Custom color	$750	$1,500

Marshall Micro Stack 3005
Tim McClutchy

Marshall 1958 18-Watt Lead
Kris Blakely

Marshall Model 1959HW

AMPS

Marshall Model 1962
Bluesbreaker Combo

Marshall 1974X

Marshall 1987X
Ted Wulfers

MODEL YEAR	FEATURES	LOW	HIGH
1984-1986	Black	$450	$650
1984-1986	Custom color	$700	$1,000
1984-1986	Rare color	$950	$1,250
1987-1990	Black	$450	$600
1987-1990	Custom color	$600	$800
1987-1990	Rare color	$850	$1,250
2000-2007	A, Black	$400	$550
2000-2007	B, Black	$450	$600

Model 1960AC/1960BC Classic Speaker Cabinet

2005-2013. 100 watts, 4x12" Celestion G-12M-25 greenback speakers, black, AC slant front, BC straight front.

2005-2013	AC	$700	$900
2005-2013	BC	$650	$850

Model 1960AHW/1960BHW 4x12 Cabinet

2005-present. Half stack cab for HW series, AHW slant or BHW straight front.

2005-2023	A or B	$700	$900

Model 1960AV/1960BV 4x12 Cabinet

1990-present. JCM 900 updated, stereo/mono switching, AV slant, BV straight front.

1990-1999	Red vinyl, tan grille	$550	$725
1990-2012	Black vinyl, black grille	$550	$725
1990-2023	Various colors	$450	$600

Model 1960AX/1960BX 4x12 Cabinet

1990-present. Cab for Model 1987X and 1959X reissue heads, AX slant, BX straight.

1990-2023	AX	$550	$725
1990-2023	BX	$550	$725

Model 1960TV 4x12 Slant Cabinet

1990-2012. Extra tall for JTM 45, mono, 100 watts.

1990-2012	Various colors	$450	$600

Model 1962 Bluesbreaker Combo

1997-2017. Vintage Series, similar to JTM 45 but with 2 reissue 'Greenback' 25-watt 2x12" speakers and addition of footswitchable tremolo effect. Limited Edition 35th Anniversary model was produced in '97 with white tolex, only 250 made.

1997	35th Anniv	$3,500	$4,500
1997-2017		$1,500	$2,000

Model 1964 Lead/Bass 50-Watt Head

1973-1976. Head with 50 watts, designed for lead or bass.

1973-1976		$1,000	$1,500

Model 1965A/1965B Cabinet

1984-1991. 140-watt 4x10" slant front (A) or straight front (B) cab.

1984-1991		$400	$550

Model 1966 Cabinet

1985-1991. 150-watt 2x12" cab.

1985-1991		$400	$550

Model 1967 Major 200-Watt Head

1968-1974. 200 watts, the original Marshall 200 Pig was not popular and revised into the 200 'Major'. The new Major 200 was similar to the other large amps and included 2 channels, 4 inputs, but a larger amp cab.

1968	Plexi	$4,000	$6,000
1969-1970	Aluminum	$3,000	$4,000
1971-1972	Small box	$1,500	$2,250
1973-1974	Large box	$1,500	$2,250

MODEL YEAR	FEATURES	LOW	HIGH

Model 1967 Pig 200-Watt Head

1967-early-1968 only. Head with 200 watts. The control panel was short and stubby and nicknamed the Pig, the 200-watt circuit was dissimilar (and unpopular) to the 50-watt and 100-watt circuits.

1967-1968		$3,500	$5,000

Model 1968 100-Watt Super PA Head

1966-1975. PA head with 100 watts, 2 sets of 4 inputs (identifies PA configuration), often used for guitar, matching cabinet.

1966-1969	Matching cab	$2,000	$3,000
1966-1969	Plexi	$4,000	$5,500
1969-1972	Aluminum	$2,500	$3,500
1969-1975	Matching cab	$1,000	$1,500

Model 1973 Combo

1965-1968. Tube combo, 18 watts, 2x12".

1965		$15,000	$22,000
1966		$12,000	$18,000
1967		$7,000	$12,000
1968		$6,500	$10,000

Model 1973 JMP Lead/Bass 20

1973 only. Front panel: JMP, back panel: Lead & Bass 20, 20 watts, 1x12" straight front checkered grille cab, head and cab black vinyl.

1973		$2,500	$4,000

Model 1974 Combo

1965-1968. Tube combo, 18 watts, 1x12".

1965		$14,000	$20,000
1966		$12,000	$18,000
1967		$7,000	$12,000
1968		$6,500	$10,000

Model 1974X/1974CX

2004-present. Handwired Series, reissue of 18-watt, 1x12" combo, extension cabinet available (CX).

2004-2023	1974CX cab	$600	$800
2004-2023	Combo	$1,375	$1,750

Model 1982/1982A/1982B Cabinet

1967-1987. Bass and lead 4x12", 100-watt 1982/1982B, upped to 120 watts in '70. Becomes higher powered 320 and 400 watts Model 1982A/B in '81 and '82.

1967-1970		$2,500	$3,500
1971-1980		$1,125	$1,500
1981-1982		$550	$850
1983-1987		$550	$850

Model 1986 50-Watt Bass Head

1966-1981. Bass version of 1987, 50-watt, black.

1966-1969	Plexi	$4,000	$6,000
1969-1970	Aluminum	$2,750	$4,000
1971-1972	Hand-wired small box	$2,250	$3,500
1973-1975	Printed CB, large box	$2,000	$3,000
1976-1979		$1,625	$2,750
1980-1981		$1,500	$2,500

Model 1987 50-Watt Head

1966-1981. Head amp, 50 watts, plexiglas panel until mid-'69, aluminum panel after.

1966-1969	Black, plexi	$6,500	$9,500
1966-1969	Custom color, plexi	$9,500	$13,000
1969-1970	Black, aluminum	$3,125	$4,500

MODEL YEAR	FEATURES	LOW	HIGH
1969-1970	Custom color, aluminum	$5,500	$8,500
1971-1972	Black, hand-wired, small box	$2,500	$3,500
1971-1972	Custom color, hand-wired	$3,750	$5,500
1973-1975	Black, printed CB, large box	$2,125	$3,000
1973-1975	Custom color, printed CB	$2,750	$4,000
1976-1979	Black	$1,750	$2,500
1976-1979	Custom color	$2,125	$3,000
1980-1981	Black	$1,750	$2,500
1980-1981	Custom color	$2,000	$3,000

Model 1987X Head
1992-present. Vintage Series amp, all tube, 50 watts, 4 inputs, plexi.

1992-2023		$1,250	$1,625

Model 1992 Super Bass Head
1966-1981. 100 watts, plexi panel until mid-'69 when replaced by aluminum front panel, 2 channels, 4 inputs.

1966-1969	Black, plexi	$6,000	$9,000
1966-1969	Custom color, plexi	$8,500	$13,000
1969-1970	Black, aluminum	$3,500	$5,000
1969-1970	Custom color, aluminum	$6,500	$10,000
1971-1972	Black, hand-wired, small box	$3,500	$5,000
1971-1972	Custom color, hand-wired	$3,750	$5,500
1973-1975	Black, printed CB, large box	$2,500	$3,500
1973-1975	Custom color, printed CB	$3,000	$4,500
1976-1979	Black	$2,000	$2,750
1976-1979	Custom color	$2,500	$3,500
1980-1981	Black	$1,750	$2,500
1980-1981	Custom color	$2,000	$3,000

Model 1992LEM Lemmy Signature Super Bass
2008-2013. Lemmy Kilmister specs, matching 100-watt head with 4x12" and 4x15" stacked cabinets.

2008-2013	Full-stack	$3,500	$5,000

Model 2040 Artist 50-Watt Combo
1971-1978. 50 watts, 2x12" Artist/Artiste combo model with a different (less popular?) circuit.

1971-1978		$1,750	$2,500

Model 2041 Artist Head/Cabinet Set
1971-1978. 50 watts, 2x12" half stack Artist/Artiste cab with a different (less popular?) circuit.

1971-1978		$2,250	$3,000

Model 2046 Specialist 25-Watt Combo
1972-1973. 25 watts, 1x15" speaker, limited production due to design flaw (amp overheats).

1972-1973		$650	$975

Model 2060 Mercury Combo
1972-1973. Combo amp, 5 watts, 1x12", available in red or orange covering.

1972-1973		$750	$975

Model 2061 20-Watt Lead/Bass Head
1968-1973. Lead/bass head, 20 watts, plexi until '69, aluminum after, black. Reissued in '04 as the Model 2061X.

1968-1969	Plexi	$3,750	$5,000
1969-1970	Aluminum	$2,750	$3,500
1971-1972	Aluminum	$2,000	$2,500
1973	Aluminum	$1,875	$2,250

Model 2061X 20-Watt Lead/Bass Head Reissue
2004-2017. Handwired Series, reissue of 2061 amp head, 20 watts.

2004-2014	1x12 cab	$450	$600
2004-2015	2x12 cab	$450	$600
2004-2017	Head only	$1,000	$1,375

Model 2068 Artist (JMP) Set
1971-1978. 100-watt head with matching Artist cab, reverb, small logo.

1971-1978		$1,750	$2,250

Model 2078 Combo
1973-1978. Solidstate, 100 watts, 4x12" combo, gold front panel, dark cover, gray grille.

1973-1978		$850	$1,250

Model 2103 100-Watt 1-Channel Master Combo
1975-1981. One channel, 2 inputs, 100 watts, 2x12", first master volume design, combo version of 2203 head.

1975-1981		$1,250	$1,875

Model 2104 50-Watt 1-Channel Master Combo
1975-1981. One channel, 2 inputs, 50 watts, 2x12", first master volume design, combo version of 2204 head.

1975-1981		$1,250	$1,875

Model 2144 Master Reverb Combo
1978 only. Master volume similar to 2104 but with reverb and boost, 50 watts, 2x12".

1978		$1,500	$2,000

Model 2150 100-Watt 1x12 Combo
1978. Tubes.

1978		$850	$1,250

Model 2159 100-Watt 2-Channel Combo
1977-1981. 100 watts, 2 channels, 4 inputs, 2x12" combo version of Model 1959 Super Lead head.

1977-1981		$1,250	$1,750

Model 2199
1979. Solidstate 2x12" combo.

1979		$600	$750

Model 2200 100-Watt Lead Combo
1977-1981. 100 watts, 2x12" combo, early solidstate, includes boost section, no reverb.

1977-1981		$650	$850

Model 2203 Lead Head
1975-1981. Head amp, 100 watts, 2 inputs, first master volume model design, often seen with Mark II logo.

1975-1981	Black	$1,500	$2,000
1975-1981	Fawn Beige	$1,500	$2,000

Model 2203X JCM800 Head Reissue
2002-2010. 100 watts.

2002-2010		$1,500	$2,000

1968 Marshall Model 1992 Super Bass Head

1972 Marshall 2040 Artist
Mark K

Marshall Model 2203X JCM800 Head Reissue

Marshall 4001 Studio 15
Imaged by Heritage Auctions, HA.com

Marshall 6100 30th
Anniversary
Imaged by Heritage Auctions, HA.com

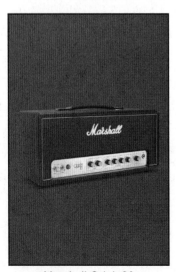

Marshall Origin20

MODEL YEAR	FEATURES	LOW	HIGH

Model 2204 50-Watt Head
1975-1981. Head only, 50 watts with master volume.

1975-1981		$1,500	$2,000

Model 2266 50-Watt Combo
2007-2013. Vintage Modern series, 2x12".

2007-2013		$700	$900

Model 2466 100-Watt Head
2007-2013. Vintage Modern series.

2007-2013		$700	$900

Model 3203 Artist Head
1986-1991. Tube head version of earlier '84 Model 3210 MOS-FET, designed as affordable alternative, 30 watts, standard short cab, 2 inputs separated by 3 control knobs, Artist 3203 logo on front panel, black.

1986-1991		$450	$600

Model 3210 MOS-FET Head
1984-1991. MOS-FET solidstate head, refer Mini-Stack listing for 3210 with 4x10" stacked cabinets. Early-'80s front panel: Lead 100 MOS-FET.

1984-1991		$350	$450

Model 3310 100-Watt Lead
1988-1991. Solidstate, 100 watts, lead head with channel switching and reverb.

1988-1991		$500	$650

Model 4001 Studio 15
1985-1992. 15 watts using 6V6 (only model to do this up to this time), 1x12" Celestion Vintage 30 speakers.

1985-1992		$750	$1,000

Model 4104 50-Watt Combo
1981-1990. Combo version of 2204 head, 50 watts, 2x12", master volume.

1981-1990		$1,250	$1,750

Model 4203 Artist 30-Watt Combo

1986-1991		$400	$500

Model 5002 Combo
1984-1991. Solidstate combo amp, 20 watts, 1x10", master volume.

1984-1991		$200	$300

Model 5005 Lead 12
1983-1991. Solidstate student amp, 12 watts, master volume, 1x10".

1983-1991		$250	$325

Model 5205 Reverb 12
1986. Solidstate, 12 watts, 1x10", Reverb 12 logo on front panel.

1986		$250	$325

Model 5302 Keyboard
1984-1988. Solidstate, 20 watts, 1x10", marketed for keyboard application.

1984-1988		$200	$275

Model 5502 Bass
1984-ca.1992. Solidstate bass combo amp, 20 watts, 1x10" Celestion.

1984-1992		$200	$275

Model 6100 30th Anniversary
1992-1998. Head with 100/50/25 switchable watts and 4x12" cabinet (matching colors), first year and into early '93 was blue tolex, black afterwards.

1992-1998	4x12 cab	$450	$600
1992-1998	Head only	$850	$1,125

Model 6101 30th Anniversary Combo
1992-1998. 1x12" combo version of 6100 amp, first year and into early '93 was blue tolex, black afterwards.

1992-1998		$1,125	$1,500

Model 8008 Valvestate Rackmount
1991-2001. Valvestate solidstate rack mount power amp with dual 40-watt channels.

1991-2001		$175	$225

Model 8010 Valvestate VS15 Combo
1991-1997. Valvestate solidstate, 10 watts, 1x8", compact size, black vinyl, black grille.

1991-1997		$150	$200

Model 8040 Valvestate 40V Combo
1991-1997. Valvestate solidstate with tube preamp, 40 watts, 1x12", compact size, black vinyl, black grille.

1991-1997		$175	$250

Model 8080 Valvestate 80V Combo
1991-1997. Valvestate solidstate with tube 12AX7 preamp, 80 watts, 1x12", compact size, black vinyl, black grille.

1991-1997		$175	$250

Model 8100 100-Watt Valvestate VS100H Head
1991-2001. Valvestate solidstate head, 100 watts.

1991-2001		$200	$275

Model 8200 200-Watt Valvestate Head
1993-1998. Valvestate solidstate reverb head, 2x100-watt channels.

1993-1998		$225	$300

Model 8222 Valvestate Cabinet
1993-1998. 200 watts, 2x12 extention cab, designed for 8200 head.

1993-1998		$175	$250

Model 8240 Valvestate Stereo Chorus
1992-1996. Valvestate, 80 watts (2x40 watts stereo), 2x12" combo, reverb, chorus.

1992-1996		$250	$350

Model 8280 2x80-Watt Valvestate Combo
1993-1996. Valvestate solidstate, 2x80 watts, 2x12".

1993-1996		$275	$375

Model 8412 Valvestate Cabinet
1991-2001. 140 watts, 4x12 extention cab, designed for 8100 head.

1991-2001		$225	$300

MS-2/R/C
1990-present. Microamp series, 1 watt, battery operated, miniature black half-stack amp and cab. Red MS-2R and checkered speaker grille and gold logo MS-2C added in '93.

1990-2023		$40	$55

MS-4
1998-present. Full-stack version of MS-2, black.

1998-2023		$45	$60

Origin (OR) Series
2018-present. Various tube models include ORI-GIN5, 20C, 20H and 50C. Number indicates watts, C is combo, H is head only.

2018-2023		$275	$350

AMPS

MODEL YEAR	FEATURES	LOW	HIGH

Silver Jubilee Model 2550 50/25 (Tall) Head

1987-1989. 50/25 switchable tall box head for full Jubilee stack, silver vinyl and chrome control panel.

1987-1989		$2,500	$3,750

Silver Jubilee Model 2551 4x12 Cabinet

1987-1989. Matching silver 4x12" cabs for Jubilee 2550 head, various models, silver vinyl.

1987-1989	2551A, slant	$1,250	$1,750
1987-1989	2551AV, Vintage 30	$1,250	$1,750
1987-1989	2551B, straight	$1,250	$1,750
1987-1989	2551BV, Vintage 30	$1,250	$1,750

Silver Jubilee Model 2553 50/25 (Short) Head

1987-1988. 50/25 switchable small box head for mini-short stack, silver vinyl and chrome control panel.

1987-1988		$2,250	$3,500

Silver Jubilee Model 2554 1x12 Combo

1987-1989. 50/25 watts, 1x12" combo using 2550 chassis, silver vinyl and chrome control panel.

1987-1989		$2,500	$3,750

Silver Jubilee Model 2555 Head

1987-1989. 100/50 version of 2550 head, silver vinyl and chrome control panel.

1987-1989		$2,250	$3,500

Silver Jubilee Model 2556 2x12 Cabinet

1987-1989. Matching silver 2x12" cabs for Jubilee heads, various models, silver vinyl.

1987-1989	2556A, slant	$1,250	$1,750
1987-1989	2556AV, Vintage 30	$1,250	$1,750
1987-1989	2556B, straight	$1,250	$1,750
1987-1989	2556BV, Vintage 30	$1,250	$1,750

Silver Jubilee Model 2558 2x12 Combo

1987-1989. 50/25 watts, 2x12" combo using 2550 chassis, silver vinyl and chrome control panel.

1987-1989		$2,250	$3,500

Silver Jubilee Model 3560 600 Head

1987. Rackmount 2x300 watts.

1987		$500	$750

SL-5

2013-2015. Tube combo, 5 watts, 1x12", script logo signature on front panel.

2013-2015		$750	$975

Super 100 40th Anniversary JTM45 MK II Full Stack

2005. 100 watts, 2 4x12 cabs, 250 made.

2005		$4,000	$6,000

Martin

Martin has dabbled in amps a few times, under both the Martin and Stinger brand names. The first batch were amps made by others introduced with their electric acoustics in 1959.

Model 110

1959-1961. Tube, 1x10" combo.

1959-1961		$4,000	$5,500

Model 112T

1959-1961. Branded C.F. Martin inside label, made by Rowe-DeArmond, 1x12 combo, limited production, 2x6V6 power tubes, 2x12AX7 preamp tubes, with tube rectifier, 4 inputs, 3 control knobs.

1959-1961		$4,000	$5,500

MODEL YEAR	FEATURES	LOW	HIGH

SS140

1965-1966. Large amp.

1965-1966		$950	$1,250

Stinger FX-1

1988-1990. 10 watts, EQ, switchable solidstate tube-synth circuit, line out and footswitch jacks.

1988-1990		$165	$225

Stinger FX-1R

1988-1990. Mini-stack amp, 2x10", 15 watts, dual-stage circuitry.

1988-1990		$175	$250

Stinger FX-6B

1989-1990. Combo bass amp, 60 watts, 1x15".

1988-1990		$175	$250

Masco

1940s-1950s. The Mark Alan Sampson Company, Long Island, New York, produced a variety of electronic products including tube PA amps and small combo instrument amps. The PA heads are also popular with harp players.

Massie

1940s. Ray Massie worked in Leo Fender's repair shop in the 1940s and built tube amps. He later worked at the Fender company.

Matamp

1966-present. Tube amps, combos and cabinets built in Huddersfield, England, bearing names like Red, Green, White, Black, and Blue. German-born Mat Mathias started building amps in England in '58 and designed his first Matamp in '66. From '69 to '73, Mathias also made Orange amps. In '89, Mathias died at age 66 and his family later sold the factory to Jeff Lewis.

1x15" Cabinet

1970s		$950	$1,250

GT-120 Green Stack

1990s. 120-watt GT head with 4x12" straight front cab.

1993-1999		$1,875	$2,500

GT-120 Head

1971		$2,500	$3,250

Matchless

1989-1999, 2001-present. Founded by Mark Sampson and Rick Perrotta in California. Circuits based on Vox AC-30 with special attention to transformers. A new Matchless company was reorganized in 2001 by Phil Jamison, former head of production for the original company.

Avalon 35 Head

2009-2010. 35 watts head, reverb.

2009-2010		$1,625	$2,500

Brave 40 112

1997-1999. 40 watts class A, 1x12", foot switchable between high and low inputs.

1997-1999		$1,625	$2,250

Brave 40 212

1997-1999. 2x12" version of Brave.

1997-1999		$1,750	$2,500

1987 Marshall Silver Jubilee Model 2555 Head
Imaged by Heritage Auctions, HA.com

AMPS

1950s Masco MU-5
Imaged by Heritage Auctions, HA.com

Matamp GT2 MK II

1995 Matchless Chieftan 212
Imaged by Heritage Auctions, HA.com

Matchless Clubman 35
David Nicholas

Matchless Nighthawk

MODEL YEAR	FEATURES	LOW	HIGH
Chief Head			
1995-1999. 100 watts class A, head.			
1995-1999		$2,750	$4,000
Chief 212			
1995-1999. 100 watts class A, 2x12", reverb.			
1995-1999		$3,000	$4,000
Chief 410			
1995-1999. 100 watts class A, 4x10", reverb.			
1995-1999		$3,000	$4,000
Chieftan Head			
1995-1999. 40 watts class A head, reverb, chicken-head knobs.			
1995-1999		$1,875	$2,500
Chieftan 112			
1995-1999, 2001-present. 40 watts class A, 1x12", reverb.			
1995-1999		$2,500	$3,500
2001-2023	Jamison era	$2,500	$3,500
Chieftan 210			
1995-1999. 40 watts class A, 2x10", reverb.			
1995-1999		$2,500	$3,500
Chieftan 212			
1995-1999, 2001-present. 40 watts class A, 2x12", reverb.			
1995-1999		$2,750	$3,500
2001-2019	Jamison era	$2,750	$3,500
Chieftan 410			
1995-1999. 40 watts class A, 4x10", reverb.			
1995-1999		$2,750	$4,000
Clipper 15 112			
1998-1999. 15 watts, single channel, 1x12".			
1998-1999		$1,250	$1,625
Clipper 15 210			
1998-1999. 15 watts, single channel, 2x10".			
1998-1999		$1,250	$1,750
Clubman 35 Head			
1993-1999. 35 watts class A head.			
1993-1999		$2,000	$3,000
DC-30 Standard Cabinet			
1991-1999. 30 watts, 2x12", with or without reverb.			
1991-1999		$3,000	$4,500
DC-30 Exotic Wood Cabinet (Option)			
1995-1999. 30 watts, 2x12", gold plating, limited production.			
1995-1999		$5,000	$8,000
ES/EB Cabinet			
ES = speaker cabinets and EB = bass speaker cabinets.			
1991-1999	1x12	$475	$650
1993-1999	2x10	$575	$825
1993-1999	2x10+2x12	$725	$1,000
1993-1999	2x12	$600	$850
1993-1999	4x12	$800	$1,125
1997-1999	1x15	$475	$675
1997-1999	4x10	$675	$975
HC-30 Head			
1991-1999, 2003. The first model offered by Matchless, 30 watts class A head.			
1991-1999		$2,250	$3,000
2003	Jamison era	$2,250	$3,000

MODEL YEAR	FEATURES	LOW	HIGH
HC-85 Head			
1992. Only 25 made, similar to HC-30 but more flexible using various tube substitutions.			
1992		$2,500	$3,500
Hurricane Head			
1997. 15 watts class A head.			
1997		$1,375	$2,000
Hurricane 112			
1994-1997. 15 watts class A, 1x12".			
1994-1997		$1,375	$2,000
Hurricane 210			
1996-1997. 15 watts class A, 2x10".			
1996-1997		$1,625	$2,250
Independence 35 Head			
2005-2017. 35 watts, with or without reverb.			
2005-2017		$2,000	$3,000
JJ-30 112 John Jorgensen			
1997-1999. 30 watts, DC-30 chassis with reverb and tremolo, 1x12" Celestion 30, offered in white, blue, gray sparkle tolex or black.			
1997-1999		$4,000	$5,500
Lightning 15 Head			
1994-1997, 2005-present. 15 watts class A head.			
1994-1997		$1,500	$2,000
Lightning 15 112			
1994-1999, 2001-present. 15 watts class A, 1x12".			
1994-1999		$2,000	$3,000
2001-2023	Jamison era	$2,000	$3,000
Lightning 15 210			
1996-1997, 2001-2006. 15 watts class A, 2x10".			
1996-1997		$2,250	$3,000
2001-2006	Jamison era	$2,250	$3,000
Lightning 15 212			
1998, 2001-2022. 15 watts class A, 2x12".			
1998-2022		$2,250	$3,000
Little Monster/The Little Monster			
2007-2009. 9 watts, offered as head, and 1x12" or 2x12" combo.			
2007-2009		$1,500	$2,000
Nighthawk			
2003-present. 15 watts, offered as head, and 1x12", 2x10" or 2x12" combo.			
2003-2014	2x10	$1,375	$2,000
2003-2023	1x12	$1,250	$1,750
2003-2023	2x12	$1,500	$2,250
Phoenix 35 (PH-35) Head			
2003-present. 35-watt head, black or red.			
2003-2023		$2,125	$2,750
SC-30 Standard Cabinet			
1991-1999. 30 watts class A, 1x12".			
1991-1999		$3,000	$4,000
2001-2006	Jamison era	$2,750	$4,000
SC-30 Exotic Wood Cabinet			
1995-1999. 30 watts class A, 1x12", gold plating, limited production.			
1995-1999		$5,000	$8,000
Skyliner Reverb 15 112			
1998-1999. 15 watts, 2 channels, 1x12".			
1998-1999		$1,000	$1,500

The *Vintage Guitar Price Guide* shows values for an all-original condition amplifier, and where applicable, with original cover.

MODEL YEAR	FEATURES	LOW	HIGH

Skyliner Reverb 15 210
1998-1999. 15 watts, 2 channels, 2x10".

1998-1999		$1,125	$1,625

Spitfire 15 Head
1997. 15 watts, head.

1997		$1,375	$2,000

Spitfire 15 112
1994-1997. 15 watts, 1x12".

1994-1997		$1,500	$2,125

Spitfire 15 210
1996-1997. 15 watts, 2x10".

1996-1997		$1,625	$2,250

Starliner 40 212
1999. 40 watts, 2x12".

1999		$1,750	$2,375

Superchief 120 Head
1994-1999. 120 watts, class A head.

1994-1999		$2,750	$3,750

TC-30 Standard Cabinet
1991-1999. 30 watts, 2x10" class A, low production numbers make value approximate with DC-30.

1991-1999		$3,000	$4,250

TC-30 Exotic Wood Cabinet
1991-1999. 30 watts, 2x10" class A, limited production.

1991-1999		$5,000	$8,000

Thunderchief Bass Head
1994-1999. 200 watts, class A bass head.

1994-1999		$2,125	$3,000

Thunderman 100 Bass Combo
1997-1998. 100 watts, 1x15" in portaflex-style flip-top cab.

1997-1998		$3,000	$4,500

Tornado 15 112
1994-1995. Compact, 15 watts, 1x12", 2-tone covering, simple controls - volume, tone, tremolo speed, tremolo depth.

1994-1995		$1,000	$1,375

Maven Peal

Amps, combos and cabinets built by David Zimmerman in Plainfield, Vermont, beginning in 1999. Serial number format is by amp wattage and sequential build; for example, 15-watt amp 15-001.

Mega Amplifiers

Budget and intermediate grade, production, solidstate and tube amps from Guitar Jones, Inc. of Pomona, California.

Merlin

Rack mount bass heads built in Germany by Musician Sound Design. They also offer MSD guitar effects.

Mesa-Boogie

1971-present. Founded by Randall Smith in San Francisco, California. Circuits styled on high-gain Fender-based chassis designs, ushering in the compact high-gain amp market. Mesa was acquired by Gibson in early 2021.

The following serial number information and specs courtesy of Mesa Engineering.

.50 Caliber/.50 Caliber+ Head
Jan. 1987-Dec. 1988, 1992-1993. Serial numbers: SS3100 - SS11,499. Mesa Engineering calls it Caliber .50. Tube head amp, 50 watts, 5-band EQ, effects loop. Called the .50 Caliber Plus in '92 and '93.

1987-1988	Caliber	$1,000	$1,500
1992-1993	Caliber+	$1,000	$1,500

.50 Caliber+ Combo
Dec. 1988-Oct. 1993. Serial numbers FP11,550 - FP29,080. 50 watts, 1x12" combo amp.

1988-1993		$1,125	$1,750

20/20
Jun. 1995-2010. Serial numbers: TT-01. 20-22 watts per channel.

1995-2010		$775	$1,125

50/50 (Fifty/Fifty)
May 1989-2001. Serial numbers: FF001-. 100 watts total power, 50 watts per channel, front panel reads Fifty/Fifty, contains 4 6L6 power tubes.

1989-2001		$775	$1,250

395
Feb. 1991-Apr. 1992. Serial numbers: S2572 - S3237.

1991-1992		$1,125	$1,500

Bass 400/Bass 400+ Head
Aug. 1989-Aug. 1990. Serial numbers: B001-B1200. About 500 watts using 12 5881 power tubes. Replaced by 400+ Aug.1990-present, serial numbers: B1200- . Update change to 7-band EQ at serial number B1677.

1989-1990	Bass 400	$1,250	$1,625
1990-1999	Bass 400+	$1,375	$1,750

Big Block Series
2004-2014. Rackmount bass amps, models 750 (750w head) and Titan V-12 (650/1200w).

2004-2014	750	$1,250	$1,875
2006-2010	Titan V-12	$1,250	$1,875

Blue Angel Series
Jun. 1994-2004. Serial numbers BA01-. Switchable between 15, 33 or 38 watts, offered as head, 1x12" combo or 4x10" combo, blue cover.

1994-2004	Combo 1x12	$950	$1,250
1994-2004	Combo 4x10	$1,000	$1,375

Buster Bass Combo
1999-2001. 200 watts, 2x10", wedge cabinet, black vinyl, metal grille.

1999-2001		$825	$1,500

Buster Bass Head
Dec. 1997-Jan. 2001. Serial numbers: BS-1-999. 200 watts via 6 6L6 power tubes.

1997-2001		$775	$1,500

Coliseum 300
Oct. 1997-2000. Serial numbers: COL-01 - COL-132. 200 watts/channel, 12 6L6 power tubes, rack mount.

1997-2000		$1,375	$1,750

D-180 Head
Jul. 1982-Dec. 1985. Serial numbers: D001-D681. All tube head amp, 200 watts, preamp, switchable.

1982-1985		$1,250	$1,750

Matchless Spitfire 15 112

Maven Peal RG88

Mesa-Boogie Blue Angel

AMPS

Mesa-Boogie Express 5:50

Mesa-Boogie Lone Star 1x12

1970s Mesa-Boogie
Mark I Combo

Tom Allen

MODEL YEAR	FEATURES	LOW	HIGH
DC-3			
Sep. 1994-Jan. 1999. Serial numbers: DC3-001 - DC3-4523. 35 watts, 1x12".			
1994-1999	Combo 1x12	$850	$1,250
1994-1999	Head only	$700	$1,000
DC-5			
Oct. 1993-Jan. 1999. Serial numbers: DC1024 - DC31,941. 50-watt head, 1x12" combo.			
1993-1999	Combo 1x12	$925	$1,250
1993-1999	Head only	$700	$950
DC-10			
May 1996-Jan. 1999. Serial numbers: DCX-001 - DCX-999. Dirty/Clean (DC), 100 watts (6L6s), 2x12".			
1993-1996	Combo 2x12	$1,000	$1,375
1996-1999	Head only	$875	$1,250
Electra Dyne Head			
2009-2013. 45/90 watts, Black Taurus/black grille or British Tan Bronco/tan grille.			
2009-2013		$1,125	$1,500
Express Series			
2007-2017. Compact combo tube amps with power switching.			
2007-2016	5:50, 2x12, 5-50w	$1,125	$1,500
2007-2017	5:25, 1x10, 5-25w	$975	$1,250
2007-2017	5:50, 1x12, 5-50w	$1,125	$1,500
2008	5:25, short head, 25w	$950	$1,250
Extension Cabinet			
1980s-present. Mesa-Boogie offered 'extension cabinets' which could be mixed and matched with amp heads, using different configurations with correct impedance. Other manufacturers often consider an extension cab as an extra cab, but Mesa Engineering considers it to be the main cab (not an extra). The company has generic cabs as well as cabs associated with specific models, but both generic and model-specific fall into similar price ranges. Some other variances include vertical or horizontal, open back or closed, slant or straight front, grille could be metal or cloth, and some cabs are designated for bass guitar. Specialized cabinets may be more than values shown.			
1980-2023	Various sizes	$350	$450
F-30			
2002-Feb. 2007. Combo, 30 watts, 1x12".			
2002-2007		$575	$750
F-50			
2002-Feb. 2007. Combo, 50 watts, 1x12", AB 2 6L6 power.			
2002-2007		$800	$1,125
2002-2007	Head only	$750	$1,000
F-100			
2002-Feb. 2007. Combo, 100 watts, 2x12".			
2002-2007	Combo 2x12	$1,000	$1,375
2002-2007	Head only	$900	$1,250
Fillmore 100 Combo			
2019-present. 100 watts, 1x12" or 2x12", 2 foot-switchable channels.			
2019-2023		$1,500	$2,250
Formula Preamp			
Jul. 1998-2002. Serial numbers: F-01. Used 5 12AX7 tubes, 3 channels.			
1998-2002		$500	$700

MODEL YEAR	FEATURES	LOW	HIGH
Heartbreaker Combo			
Jun. 1996-2001. Serial numbers: HRT-01. 60 to 100 watts switchable, 2x12" combo, designed to switch-out 6L6s, EL34s or the lower powered 6V6s in the power section, switchable solidstate or tube rectifier.			
1996-2001		$1,250	$1,875
Heartbreaker Head			
1996-2001. Head only, 100 watts.			
1996-2001		$1,500	$2,250
Lone Star Series			
2004-2020. Designed by founder Randall Smith and Doug West with focus on boutique-type amp. Class A (EL84) or AB (4 6L6) circuits, long or short head, 1x12" combo, 2x12" combo, and short head 4x10" cab, and long head 4x12" cab.			
2004-2016	Combo 1x12, hardwood	$2,500	$3,750
2004-2016	Combo 4x10, blue	$2,000	$2,625
2004-2020	Combo 1x12	$1,750	$2,500
2004-2020	Combo 2x12	$2,000	$2,750
2004-2020	Head, class A or AB	$1,625	$2,250
Lone Star Special			
2005-2020. Smaller lighter version using EL84 power tubes, 5/15/30 watts, long or short head amp or 1x12", 2x12" or 4x10" combo.			
2005-2020	Combo 1x12	$1,875	$2,500
M-180			
Apr. 1982-Jan. 1986. Serial numbers: M001-M275. Rack mount tube power amp.			
1982-1986		$825	$1,125
M-190			
1980s. Rack mount tube power amp.			
1980s		$600	$850
M-2000/Bass-2000 Head			
Jun. 1995-2003. Serial numbers: B2K-01.			
1995-2003		$850	$1,125
M6 Carbine Bass Head			
2011-2017. 600-watt head, also offered in 2x12 combo.			
2011-2017		$700	$950
Mark I Combo (Model A)			
1971-1978. The original Boogie amp, not called the Mark I until the Mark II was issued, 60 or 100 watts, 1x12", Model A serial numbers: 1-2999, very early serial numbers 1-299 had 1x15".			
1971-1978	1x12 or 1x15	$2,750	$4,500
Mark I Head			
1990. 60/100 watts, tweed cover.			
1990		$2,750	$4,500
Mark I Reissue			
Nov. 1989-Sept. 2007. Serial numbers: H001-. 100 watts, 1x12", reissue features include figured maple cab and wicker grille.			
2000-2007	Hardwood cab	$1,500	$2,250
2000-2007	Standard cab	$1,250	$1,750
Mark II B Combo			
1980-1983. Effective Aug. '80 1x12" models, serial numbers 5575-110000. May '83 1x15" models, serial numbers 560-11000. The 300 series serial numbers K1-K336.			
1981-1983	1x12 or 1x15	$1,750	$2,625
1981-1983	Hardwood cab	$2,375	$3,500

MODEL YEAR	FEATURES	LOW	HIGH

Mark II B Head

1981-1983. Head only.

| 1981-1983 | | $1,250 | $1,875 |

Mark II C/Mark II C+ Combo

May 1983-Mar. 1985. Serial numbers 11001-14999 for 60 watts, 1x15", offered with optional white tolex cover. 300 series serial numbers after C+ are in the series K337-K422.

| 1983-1985 | | $4,500 | $7,000 |
| 1985 | Hardwood cab | $5,500 | $8,000 |

Mark II C+ Head

1983-1985. 60-watt head.

| 1983-1985 | Hardwood cab | $6,000 | $9,000 |
| 1983-1985 | Standard cab | $5,000 | $7,500 |

Mark II Combo

1978-1980. Late-'78 1x12", serial numbers: 3000-5574. Effective Aug.'80 1x15", serial numbers: 300-559 until Mark II B replaced.

| 1978-1980 | 1x12 or 1x15 | $1,500 | $2,125 |

Mark III Combo

Mar. 1985-Feb. 1999. Serial numbers: 15000-28384. 300 series serialization K500-. Graphic equalizer only Mark III since Aug.'90, 100 watts, 1x12" combo. Custom cover or exotic hardwood cab will bring more than standard vinyl cover cab. There is also a Simul-Class Mark III which can run in 25, 60 or 85 watts.

1985-1990	Black	$1,750	$2,750
1985-1990	Custom color	$2,250	$3,500
1985-1999	Custom hardwood	$3,000	$4,500
1990-1999	Graphic EQ, standard cab	$2,125	$3,250

Mark III Head

1985-1999. 100 watts, black vinyl.

1985-1990		$2,750	$4,500
1985-1990	Custom hardwood	$4,250	$6,500
1990-1999	Graphic EQ	$3,250	$4,750

Mark IV (Rack Mount) Head

1990-May 2008. Rack mount version.

| 1990-2008 | | $1,125 | $1,500 |

Mark IV Head

1990-May 2008. Clean rhythm, crunch rhythm and lead modes, 85 watts, EQ, 3-spring reverb, dual effects loops, digital foot switching. Also available in custom hardwood cab with wicker grille.

| 1990-2008 | Custom hardwood | $2,875 | $4,250 |
| 1990-2008 | Short head, tolex | $1,875 | $3,000 |

Mark IV/Mark IV B Combo

May 1990-May 2008. Changed to Model IV B Feb.'95, serial numbers: IV001. Clean rhythm, crunch rhythm and lead modes, 40 watts, EQ, 3-spring reverb, dual effects loops, digital foot switching.

1991-1999		$2,125	$3,250
1991-1999	Custom hardwood	$3,500	$5,250
2000-2008		$2,125	$3,250
2000-2008	Custom hardwood	$3,500	$5,250

Mark V Private Reserve

2011-2016. Special order, 1x12" combo.

| 2011-2016 | | $4,500 | $6,750 |

Mark V Private Reserve 40th Anniversary

2009-2010. Limited production, 1x12 combo, 40th Anniversary logo.

| 2009-2010 | | $4,750 | $7,000 |

Mark V/Mark Five

2010-present. 3 channels, 10/45/90 watts, also in 1x12" combo.

| 2010-2023 | Combo 1x12 | $2,125 | $3,250 |
| 2010-2023 | Head | $2,000 | $2,750 |

Mark V:35/Mark Five:35

2015-present. 35/25/10 watts, also 1x12 combo, black.

| 2015-2023 | Combo 1x12 | $1,750 | $2,500 |
| 2015-2023 | Head | $1,875 | $2,750 |

Maverick Dual Rectifier Combo

1997-Feb. 2005. Dual channels, 4 EL84s, 35 watts, 1x12", 2x12" or 4x10" combo amp, 5AR4 tube rectifier, cream vinyl covering. Serial number: MAV. Also available as head.

1997-2005	1x12	$1,125	$1,500
1997-2005	2x12	$1,250	$1,750
2005	4x10	$1,250	$1,750

Maverick Dual Rectifier Head

1994-Feb. 2005. 35 watts, Dual Rectifier head, white/blond vinyl cover.

| 1994-2005 | | $1,000 | $1,500 |

Mini Rectifier Twenty-Five Head

2012-present. Ultra compact design, 10/25 watts, 2 channels.

| 2012-2023 | | $900 | $1,250 |

M-Pulse 360

Jul. 2001-2005. Serial numbers: MP3-01-. Rack mount, silver panel.

| 2001-2003 | | $900 | $1,250 |

M-Pulse 600

Apr. 2001-2011. Serial numbers: MP6-01- . Rack mount bass with 600 watts, tube preamp.

| 2001-2011 | | $900 | $1,250 |

Nomad 45 Combo

Jul. 1999-Feb. 2005. Serial numbers: NM45-01. 45 watts, 1x12, 2x12" or 4x10" combo, dark vinyl cover, dark grille.

1999-2005	1x12	$650	$950
1999-2005	2x12	$700	$1,000
1999-2005	4x10	$850	$1,250

Nomad 45 Head

1999-Feb. 2005. 45 watts, dark vinyl cover, dark grille.

| 1999-2005 | | $575 | $850 |

Nomad 55 Combo

Jul. 1999-2004. Serial numbers: NM55-01. 55 watts, 1x12", 2x12" or 4x10" combo.

| 1999-2004 | 1x12 | $650 | $1,000 |
| 1999-2004 | 2x12 | $700 | $1,125 |

Nomad 55 Head

1999-2004. 55 watts.

| 1999-2004 | | $575 | $850 |

Nomad 100 Combo

Jul. 1999-Feb. 2005. 100 watts, 1x12" or 2x12" combo, black cover, black grille.

| 1999-2005 | 1x12 | $700 | $1,000 |
| 1999-2005 | 2x12 | $725 | $1,125 |

Nomad 100 Head

Jul. 1999-Feb. 2005. 100 watts, black cover, black grille.

| 1999-2005 | | $650 | $950 |

Mesa-Boogie Mark II C+

1980s Mesa-Boogie
Mark III Combo

Imaged by Heritage Auctions, HA.com

Mesa-Boogie Mark V

AMPS

Mesa-Boogie Rect-O-Verb I
Imaged by Heritage Auctions, HA.com

1984 Mesa-Boogie Son Of Boogie
Tom Pfeifer

Mesa-Boogie Stiletto
Imaged by Heritage Auctions, HA.com

MODEL YEAR	FEATURES	LOW	HIGH

Princeton Boost Fender Conversion
1970. Fender Princeton modified by Randall Smith, Boogie badge logo instead of the Fender blackface logo on upper left corner of the grille. About 300 amps were modified and were one of the early mods that became Mesa-Boogie.
1970 — $2,875 $4,250

Quad Preamp
Sep. 1987-1992. Serial numbers: Q001-Q2857. Optional Quad with FU2-A footswitch Aug.'90-Jan.'92, serial numbers: Q2022-Q2857.
1990-1992 With footswitch $775 $1,250

Recto Recording Preamp
2004-2018. Rack mount preamp.
2004-2018 $1,125 $1,500

Rect-O-Verb Combo
Dec. 1998-2001. Serial numbers R50-. 50 watts, 1x12", black vinyl cover, black grille.
1998-2001 $1,125 $1,500

Rect-O-Verb I Head
Dec. 1998-2001. Serial numbers: R50-. 50 watts, head with 2 6L6 power tubes, upgraded Apr.'01 to II Series.
1998-2001 $1,000 $1,500

Rect-O-Verb II Combo
April 2001-2010. Upgrade R5H-750, 50 watts, AB, 2 6L6, spring reverb.
2001-2010 $1,125 $1,625

Rect-O-Verb II Head
Apr. 2001-2010. Upgrade, serial number R5H-750.
2001-2010 $1,000 $1,500

Road King Dual Rectifier Combo
2002-2015. 2x12" combo version, Series II upgrades start in '06.
2002-2005 Select watts $2,875 $4,000
2006-2015 Series II $2,875 $4,000

Road King Dual Rectifier Head
2002-May 2017. Tube head, various power tube selections based upon a chassis which uses 2 EL34s and 4 6L6, 2 5U4 dual rectifier tubes or silicon diode rectifiers, 50, 100 or 120 watts. Series II upgrades start in '06.
2002-2011 $2,625 $4,000
2006-2017 Series II $2,625 $4,000

Roadster Dual Rectifier
2006-May 2017. 50/100 watts, head only, 1x12" or 2x12" combo.
2006-2014 Combo 1x12 $2,125 $3,250
2006-2017 Combo 2x12 $2,250 $3,500
2006-2017 Head $2,000 $3,000

Rocket 44
2011. 45 watts, 1x12" combo, spring reverb, FX loop.
2011 $600 $800

Rocket 440
Mar. 1999-Aug. 2000. Serial numbers: R440-R44-1159. 45 watts, 4x10".
1999-2000 $775 $1,125

Satellite/Satellite 60
Aug. 1990-1999. Serial numbers: ST001-ST841. Uses either 6L6s for 100 watts or EL34s for 60 watts, dark vinyl, dark grille.
1990-1999 $725 $1,000

Solo 50 Rectifier Series I Head
Nov. 1998-Apr. 2001. Serial numbers: R50. 50-watt head.
1998-2001 $850 $1,125

Solo 50 Rectifier Series II Head
Apr. 2001-2011. Upgrade, serial numbers: S50-S1709. Upgrades preamp section, head with 50 watts.
2001-2011 $850 $1,125

Solo Dual Rectifier Head
1997-2011. Dual Rectifier Solo logo on front panel, 3x5U4, 150 watts.
1997-2011 $2,750 $5,000

Solo Triple Rectifier Head
1997-2011. Triple Rectifier Solo logo on front panel, 3x5U4, 150 watts.
1997-2011 $2,875 $3,750

Son Of Boogie
May 1982-Dec. 1985. Serial numbers: S100-S2390. 60 watts, 1x12", considered the first reissue of the original Mark I.
1982-1985 $725 $1,250

Stereo 290 (Simul 2-Ninety)
Jun. 1992-2021. Serial numbers: R0001-. Dual 90-watt stereo channels, rack mount.
1992-2021 $1,000 $1,375

Stereo 295
Mar. 1987-May 1991. Serial numbers: S001-S2673. Dual 95-watt class A/B stereo channels, rack mount. Selectable 30 watts Class A (EL34 power tubes) power.
1987-1991 $675 $950

Stiletto Ace
2007-2011. 50 watts, 2 channels, head or combo.
2007-2011 Combo 1x12 $1,250 $1,625
2007-2011 Combo 2x12 $1,250 $1,625
2007-2011 Head only $1,250 $1,625

Stiletto Series
2004-2011. Series includes the Deuce (50 or 100 watts, 4 EL-34s) and Trident (50 or 150 watts, 6 EL-34s).
2004-2011 Deuce $1,375 $2,000
2004-2011 Trident $1,500 $2,250

Strategy 400
Mar. 1987-May 1991. Serial numbers: S001-S2627. 400 to 500 watts, power amplifier with 12 6L6 power tubes.
1987-1991 $1,125 $1,500

Strategy 500
Jun. 1991-Apr. 1992. S2,552-. Rack mount, 500 watts, 4 6550 power tubes.
1991-1992 $1,250 $1,750

Studio .22/Studio .22+
Nov. 1985-1988. Serial numbers: SS000-SS11499, black vinyl, black grille, 22 watts, 1x12". Replaced by .22+ Dec. '88-Aug. '93. Serial numbers: FP11,500-FP28,582. 22 watts.
1985-1988 22 $700 $1,000
1988-1993 22+ $700 $1,000

Studio Caliber DC-2
Apr. 1994-Jan. 1999. Serial numbers: DC2-01 - DC2-4247 (formerly called DC-2). 20 watts, 1x12" combo, dark vinyl, dark grille.
1994-1999 $575 $850

The Vintage Guitar Price Guide shows values for an all-original condition amplifier, and where applicable, with original cover.

MODEL YEAR	FEATURES	LOW	HIGH

Studio Preamp
Aug. 1988-Dec. 1993. Serial numbers: SP000-SP7890. Tube preamp, EQ, reverb, effects loop.
1988-1993 $575 $850

Subway Reverb Rocket
Jun. 1998-Aug. 2001. Serial numbers: RR1000-RR2461. 20 watts, 1x10".
1998-2001 $700 $1,000

Subway Rocket (Non-Reverb)
Jan. 1996-Jul. 1998. Serial numbers: SR001-SR2825. No reverb, 20 watts, 1x10".
1996-1998 $700 $1,000

Subway/Subway Blues
Sep. 1994-Aug. 2000. Serial numbers: SB001-SB2515. 20 watts, 1x10".
1994-2000 $700 $1,000

TA-15 Head
2010-2015. TransAtlantic series, lunchbox-sized tube head, 2 channels, 5/15/25 watts.
2010-2015 $700 $1,000

TA-30 Combo
2012-2015. TransAtlantic series, 15/30/40 watts, 1x12" or 2x12" combo, 2 channels.
2012-2015 $1,125 $1,750

Trem-O-Verb Dual Rectifier Combo
Jun.1993-Jan.2001. Serial numbers: R- to about R-21210. 100 watts, 2x12" Celestion Vintage 30.
1993-2001 $1,250 $2,000

Trem-O-Verb Dual Rectifier Head
Jun. 1993-Jan. 2001. 100-watt head version.
1993-2001 $1,250 $2,000
1993-2001 Rackmount version $1,250 $2,000

Triaxis Programmable Preamp
Oct. 1991-2016. Serial numbers: T0001-. 5 12AX7 tube preamp, rack mount.
1991-2016 $1,250 $2,000

Venture Bass (M-Pulse)
2007-2009 $1,125 $1,500

V-Twin Rackmount
May 1995-Jun. 1998. Serial numbers: V2R-001 to V2R-2258.
1995-1998 $600 $850

WalkAbout M-Pulse Bass Head
Sep. 2001-May 2017. Serial numbers: WK-01-. Lightweight 13 pounds, 2 12AX7s + 300 MOS-FET.
2001-2017 $750 $1,125

WalkAbout Scout Convertible Combo
2001-May 2017. Head and 1x12 combo.
2001-2017 $1,125 $1,625

Meteoro
1986-present. Guitar, bass, harp and keyboard combo amps, heads, and cabinets built in Brazil. They also build effects.

Metropoulos Amplification
2004-present. George Metropoulos builds his professional and premium grade amps in Flint, Michigan.

MG
2004-present. Tube combo guitar amps built by Marcelo Giangrande in São Paulo, Brazil. He also builds effects.

Mighty Moe Ampstraps
Peter Bellak built his guitar amp straps in Sacramento, California, starting in 2007. He also offered an amp strap for ukulele.

Milbert Amplifiers
2009-present. Professional and premium grade, production/custom, amps for guitars and cars, built in Gaithersburg, Maryland by Michael Milbert.

Mission Amps
1996-present. Bruce Collins' Mission Amps, located in Arvada, Colorado, produces a line of custom-made combo amps, heads, and cabinets.

Mojave Amp Works
2002-present. Tube amp heads and speaker cabinets by Victor Mason in Apple Valley, California.

Montgomery Ward
Amps for this large retailer were sometimes branded as Montgomery Ward, but usually as Airline (see that listing).
1x12" Combo
1950s. 1x12", about 2 6L6 power tubes, includes Model 8439 and brown covered Maestro C Series with cloverleaf grille.
1950s $500 $750
Model 55 JDR 8437
1950s. 4x8" speakers in 'suitcase' amp cabinet, brown control panel.
1950s $600 $850

Mooneyes
Budget solid state amp line from Lace Music Products. They also offered amps under the Rat Fink and Lace brands. Lace had a Mooneyes guitar model line.

Morley
Late-1960s-present. The effects company offered an amp in the late '70s. See Effects section for more company information.
Bigfoot
1979-ca.1981. Looks like Morley's '70s effects pedals, produced 25 watts and pedal controlled volume. Amp only, speakers were sold separately.
1979-1981 $250 $375

Mosrite
1968-1969. Mosrite jumped into the amp business during the last stages of the company history, the company was founded as a guitar company in 1954 and attained national fame in the '60s but by the time the company entered the amp business, the guitar boom began to fade, forcing the original Mosrite out of business in '69.

1988 Mesa-Boogie Studio .22
Rivington Guitars

Mesa-Boogie Road King II Dual Rectifier Combo

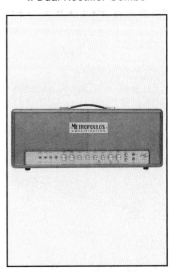
Metropoulos Super-Plex

AMPS

1979 Music Man Seventy Five
Rivington Guitars

1982 Music Man 110 RD Fifty
Richard Potter

1980 Music Man 212 Sixty-Five
Imaged by Heritage Auctions, HA.com

MODEL YEAR	FEATURES	LOW	HIGH

Model 400 Fuzzrite
1968-1969. Solidstate, 1x15 combo, black tolex with silver grille, reverb and tremolo.

1968-1969		$850	$1,250

Model SS-550 The Gospel
1968. Solidstate, 1 speaker combo, 2 channels normal and tremolo, reverb, black tolex.

1968		$750	$1,125

Mountain
Mountain builds a 9-volt amp in a wood cabinet. Originally built in California, then Nevada; currently being made in Vancouver, British Columbia.

Multivox
Ca.1946-ca.1984. Multivox was started as a subsidiary of Premier to manufacture amps, and later, effects. Generally student grade to low intermediate grade amps.

Murph
1965-1967. Amps marketed by Murph Guitars of San Fernado, California. At first they were custom-made tube amps, but most were later solidstate production models made by another manufacturer.

Music Man
1972-present. Music Man made amps from '73 to '83. The number preceding the amp model indicates the speaker configuration. The last number in model name usually refers to the watts. RD indicated Reverb Distortion. RP indicated Reverb Phase. Many models were available in head-only versions and as combos with various speaker combinations.

Sixty Five Head
1973-1981 65-watt		$475	$675

Seventy Five Reverb/75 Reverb
1973-1981. Head, 75 watts, reverb.

1973-1981		$475	$675

110 RD Fifty
1980-1983. 50 watts, 1x10", reverb, distortion.

1980-1983		$550	$775

112 B Bass
1983. 50 watts, 1x12".

1983		$550	$775

112 RD Fifty
1980-1983. 50 watts, 1x12", reverb, distortion.

1980-1983		$550	$775

112 RD Sixty Five
1978-1983. 65 watts, 1x12", reverb, distortion.

1978-1983		$550	$775

112 RD One Hundred
1978-1983. 100 watts, 1x12", reverb, distortion, EVM option for heavy duty 12" Electro-Voice speakers.

1978-1983		$625	$950
1978-1983 EVM option		$625	$950

112 RP Sixty Five
1978-1983. 65 watts, 1x12", reverb, built-in phaser.

1978-1983		$625	$950

MODEL YEAR	FEATURES	LOW	HIGH

112 RP One Hundred
1978-1983. Combo amp, 100 watts, 1x12", reverb, built-in phaser.

1978-1983		$625	$950

112 Sixty Five
1973-1981. Combo amp, 65 watts, 1x12", reverb, tremolo.

1973-1981		$625	$950

115 Sixty Five
1973-1981. Combo amp, 65 watts, 1x15", reverb, tremolo.

1973-1981		$625	$950

210 HD130
1973-1981. 130 watts, 2x10", reverb, tremolo.

1973-1981		$725	$1,125

210 Sixty Five
1973-1981. 65 watts, 2x10", reverb, tremolo.

1973-1981		$725	$1,125

212 HD130
1973-1981. 130 watts, 2x12", reverb, tremolo.

1973-1981		$725	$1,125

212 Sixty Five
1973-1981. 65 watts, 2x12", reverb, tremolo.

1973-1981		$725	$1,125

410 Sixty Five
1973-1981. 65 watts, 4x10", reverb, tremolo.

1973-1981		$725	$1,125

410 Seventy Five
1982-1983. 75 watts, 4x10", reverb, tremolo.

1982-1983		$725	$1,125

HD-130 Head
1973-1981. 130 watts, reverb, tremolo.

1973-1981		$550	$950

HD-150 Head
1973-1981. 75/100 watts.

1973-1981		$500	$775

RD Fifty Head
1980-1983. 50 watts, reverb, distortion.

1980-1983		$500	$775

Nady
1976-present. Wireless sound company Nady Systems started offering tube combo and amp heads in '06.

NARB
1973. Briefly made by Ken Bran and Jim Marshall, about 24 made, all were Marshall 100-watt tremolo half-stack, NARB logo on amp and cabinet.

100 Watt Half-Stack
1973. 100 watts, 4x12".

1973		$4,000	$6,000

National
Ca.1927-present. National/Valco amps date back to the late-'30s. National introduced a modern group of amps about the same time they introduced their new Res-O-Glas space-age guitar models in '62. In '64, the amp line was partially redesigned and renamed. By '68, the Res-O-Glas models were gone and National introduced many large vertical and

MODEL YEAR	FEATURES	LOW	HIGH

horizontal piggyback models which lasted until National's assets were assigned during bankruptcy in '69. The National name went to Chicago importer Strum N' Drum. Initially, Strum N' Drum had one amp, the National GA 950 P Tremolo/Reverb piggyback.

Aztec
1948-1950s. Combo, early '50s version with 3 Rola 7x11" speakers using 3 speaker baffle openings, about 20 watts using 2x6L6 power tubes, 2-tone brown leatherette and tweed cover. By '56, amp has one 15" speaker and does not have segmented grill.

1948-1950s 3 Rola 7x11		$1,000	$1,375
1950s	1x15	$950	$1,250

Bass 70/Bass 75
1962-1967. 35 watts (per channel), 2x12" (often Jensen) speakers, large knobs, Raven Black tolex with silver and white grille, designed for bass. New model name in '64 with nearly identical features but listed as total of 70 watts, in '62 called Bass 70 but renamed Bass 75 in '64.

1962-1963	Bass 70	$775	$1,125
1964-1967	Bass 75 N6475B	$775	$1,125

Chicagoan Model 1220
1940s-1950s. 17 watts, 1x10", tube, says "Valco Chicago 51" on control panel.

1940s-50s		$850	$1,250

Dynamic 20
1962-1963. 17 watts, 2x8" (often Jensen) speakers, 2 large knobs, Raven Black tolex with silver and white grille, compact student-intermediate amp.

1962-1963		$900	$1,250

Glenwood 90
1962-1967. 35 watts, 2x12" (often Jensen) speakers, large knobs, reverb, tremolo, Raven Black tolex with silver and white grille, top of the line, becomes the nearly identical N6490TR in '64.

1962-1963		$1,375	$1,750
1964-1967	Model N6490TR	$1,250	$1,625

Glenwood Vibrato
Two 12" speakers, reverb, tremolo.

1964-1967	Model N6499VR	$1,375	$1,750

Model 75
1940s. Vertical tweed combo cabinet, volume and tone knobs, 3 inputs.

1940s		$600	$775

Model 100
1940s. Tube amp, 40 watts, 1x12".

1940s		$675	$950

Model 1202 Twin
1954. 18 watts, 2x8" Jensen speaker, 2 channels (Instrument and microphone), horizontal flying bird logo on grille.

1954		$900	$1,250

Model 1210 High Fidelity
1954. 20 watts, 1x15" Jensen speaker, 4 input jacks, 2 channels (instrument and microphone), 20x24x10" combo, metal handle.

1954		$900	$1,250

Model 1212
1954. 12 watts, 1x12", 5 tubes, 3 inputs, 15x18x8" combo, diving flying bird logo on grille, plastic handle.

1954		$850	$1,250

Model 1215
1952. 1x12", 2 channels.

1952		$850	$1,250

Model 1275
1953. Combo 1x10", 12 watts, 5 tubes, light tan weave cover, deep brown grille cloth.

1953		$825	$1,250

Model GA 950-P Tremolo/ Reverb Piggyback
1970s. Strum N' Drum/National model, solidstate, 50 watts, 2-channel 2x12" and 1x7" in 32" tall vertical cabinet, black.

1970s		$325	$450

Model N6800 - N6899 Piggyback
1968-1969. National introduced a new line of tube amps in '68 and most of them were piggybacks. The N6895 was sized like a Fender piggyback Tremolux, the N6875 and N6878 bass amps were sized like a '68 Fender large cab piggyback with a 26" tall vertical cab, the N6898 and N6899 were the large piggyback guitar amps. These amps feature the standard Jensen speakers or the upgrade JBL speakers, the largest model was the N6800 for PA or guitar, which sported 3x70-watt channels and 2 column speakers using a bass 2x12" + 1x3" horn cab and a voice-guitar 4x10" + 1x3" horn cab.

1968-1969		$650	$850

Model N6816 (Model 16)
1968-1969. Valco-made tube amp, 6 watts, 1x10" Jensen speaker, 17" vertical cab, tremolo, no reverb, black vinyl cover and Coppertone grille.

1968-1969		$450	$600

Model N6820 Thunderball Bass
1968-1969. Valco-made tube amp, about 35 watts, 1x15" Jensen speaker, 19" vertical cab, black vinyl cover and Coppertone grille.

1968-1969		$550	$725

Model N6822 (Model 22)
1968-1969. Valco-made, 6 watts tube (4 tubes) amp, 1x12" Jensen speaker, 19" vertical cab, tremolo and reverb, black vinyl cover and Coppertone grille.

1968-1969		$500	$650

National Dobro
1930s. Sold by the National Dobro Corp. when the company was still in Los Angeles (they later moved to Chicago). National Dobro plate on rear back panel, suitcase style case that flips open to reveal the speaker and amp, National logo on outside of suitcase.

1930s	Early metal baffle	$700	$950
1930s	Later standard baffle	$525	$700
1930s	Suitcase style	$650	$900

Newport 40
1964-1967. 17 watts, 2x10", tremolo only.

1964-1967	Model N6440T	$850	$1,125

Newport 50
1964-1967. 17 watts, 2x10", tremolo and reverb.

1964-1967	Model N6450TR	$850	$1,125

Newport 97
1964-1967. 35 watts, 1x15", rear mounted chassis, tremolo.

1964-1967	Model N6497T	$850	$1,125

1967 National Bass 75

Tom Pfeifer

1964 National Glenwood Vibrato

Imaged by Heritage Auctions, HA.com

National Model 100

Imaged by Heritage Auctions, HA.com

1950 Oahu
Bill Parsons

Omega

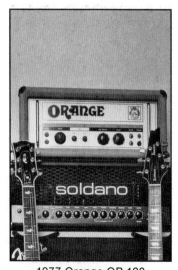

1977 Orange OR-120
Eric Van Gansen

MODEL YEAR	FEATURES	LOW	HIGH

Sportsman
1950s. Tweed combo with brown leatherette speaker surround, 1x10".

1950s		$850	$1,125

Student Practice
1970s. Strum N' Drum era, small solidstate, single control.

1970s		$45	$60

Studio 10
1962-1967. Five watts, 1x8", 3 tubes, 1 channel, 1 volume control, no tone control, no reverb or tremolo.

1962-1963		$550	$750
1964-1967	Model N6410	$550	$750

Tremo-Tone Model 1224
1956-1959. Small combo, tremolo, dual Rola oval 6x11" speakers, tweed, by Valco, flying bird pattern on lower front grille.

1956-1959		$1,125	$1,500

Val-Pro 80
1962-1963. 35 watts, 2x12" (often Jensen) speakers, 8 tubes, large control knobs, tremolo, black cover with white and silver trim, replaced by Glenwood 90 in '64 with added reverb.

1962-1963		$1,250	$1,625

Val-Trem 40
1962-1963. 17 watts, 2x10" (often Jensen) speakers, large knobs, Val-Trem logo on back panel, Clear-Wave tremolo, Raven Black tolex with silver and white grille, open back combo amp, became Newport 40 in '64.

1962-1963		$1,000	$1,375

Val-Verb 60
1962-1963. 17 watts, 2x10" (often Jensen) speakers, large knobs, Val-Verb logo on back panel, reverb, no tremolo, Raven Black tolex with silver and white grille, open back combo amp.

1962-1963		$1,250	$1,625

Westwood 16
1964-1967. Five watts using 1 6V6 power, 2 12AX7 preamp, 1 5Y3GT rectifier, tremolo, 2x8", dark vinyl cover, silver grille.

1964-1967	Model N6416T	$850	$1,125

Westwood 22
1964-1967. 5 watts, 2x8", reverb and tremolo, 1 channel, 6 tubes.

1964-1967	Model N6422TR	$925	$1,250

Naylor Engineering
1994-present. Joe Naylor and Kyle Kurtz founded the company in East Pointe, Michigan, in the early '90s, selling J.F. Naylor speakers. In '94 they started producing amps. In '96, Naylor sold his interest in the business to Kurtz and left to form Reverend Guitars. In '99 David King bought the company and moved it to Los Angeles, California, then to Dallas, Texas. Currently Naylor builds tube amps, combos, speakers, and cabinets.

Nemesis
From the makers of Eden amps, Nemesis is a line of made-in-the-U.S., FET powered bass combos and extension cabinets. The brand is a division of U.S. Music Corp.

MODEL YEAR	FEATURES	LOW	HIGH

Newcomb
1950s. Newcomb Audio Products, Hollywood, California, Newcomb script logo on back panel along with model number, they offered instrument amplifiers that could also be used as small PA.

Model G 12
1953. 1x12" (Rolla) combo amp, 2 controls (volume and tone), large metal handle, oxblood-brown leatherette.

1953		$450	$600

Nobels
1997-present. Effects manufacturer Nobels Electronics of Hamburg, Germany also offers a line of small practice and portable amps.

Noble
Ca. 1950-ca. 1969. From Don Noble and Company, of Chicago, Illinois, owned by Strum N' Drum by mid-'60s. They also offered guitars and amps.

Model 381/Custom 381
1950s. 2x12" and 2x5".

1958-1960		$1,500	$2,000

Norma
1965-1970. Economy line imported and distributed by Strum N' Drum, Wheeling (Chicago), Illinois. As noted in the National section, Strum N' Drum acquired the National brand in the '70s. Some early amps were tube, but the majority were solidstate.

Solid State

1969-1970	Various models	$80	$112

Oahu
The Oahu Publishing Company and Honolulu Conservatory, based in Cleveland, Ohio, started with acoustic Hawaiian and Spanish guitars, selling large quantities in the 1930s. As electric models became popular, Oahu responded with guitar/amp sets. The brand has been revived on a line of U.S.-made tube amps.

Mid-Size Combo

1940s-50s	1x10	$500	$750

Small Combo
1965. Small 1x10" combo, 1 6V6, 4 12AX7. 15Y3GT, white cover, light grille, Oahu script logo upper left grille.

1965		$750	$1,125

Small Guitar/Lap Steel
1940s-1950s. 1x8", various colors.

1940s-50s		$400	$600

Thunderbolt
1965. 1x12", 6 tubes.

1965		$1,750	$2,500

Oliver
Ca.1966-ca. 1978. The Oliver Sound Company, Westbury, New York, was founded by former Ampeg engineer, Jess Oliver, after he left Ampeg in '65. Tube amp designs were based upon Oliver's work at Ampeg. The Oliver Powerflex Amp is the best-known

MODEL YEAR	FEATURES	LOW	HIGH

design, and featured an elevator platform that would lift the amp head out of the speaker cabinet.

Model B-120 Head

1970s. B-120 logo on front panel, 35 watts, all tube head.

1970s		$525	$825

Model G-150R Combo

1970s. Reverb, tremolo, 2 6L6 power tubes, 40 watts, 1x15", black tolex with black grille, silver control panel.

1970s		$625	$925

Model P-500 Combo

1960s. All tube combo with 15" motorized amp chassis that rises out of tall lateral speaker cabinet as amp warms up.

1960s		$875	$1,250

Orbital Power Projector

Late-1960s-early-1970s. Rotating speaker cabinet with horn, Leslie-like voice.

1960s-70s		$1,000	$1,500

Sam Ash Oliver Head

Late-1960s-early-1970s. Private branded for Sam Ash Music, about 30 watts using the extinct 7027A power tubes, Sam Ash script logo on front grille.

1960s-70s		$400	$625

Omega

2009-present. James Price builds his premium grade, production/custom, amps in Moravian Falls, North Carolina.

Orange

1968-1981, 1995-present. Orange amps and PAs were made in the U.K. by Cliff Cooper and Matthew Mathias. The Orange-colored amps were well-built and were used by many notable guitarists. Since '95, Cliff Cooper is once again making Orange amplifiers in the U.K., with the exception of the small Crush Practice Combo amps, which are made in Korea. '68-'70 amps made by Matamp in Huddersfield; classic designs started in '71 at Bexleyheath/London plant.

Model GRO-100 Graphic Overdrive Head

1969-1971. Four EL34 power, only 2 pre-amp tubes, short-style head, model number on back panel.

1969-1971		$4,000	$6,000

Model OR-50 Limited Edition Head

2008. Switches between 30 and 50 watts.

2008		$1,500	$2,000

Model OR-50H Head (Reissue)

2012. Single channel, 50 watts, footswitch master volume.

2012		$1,000	$1,500

Model OR-80

1971-1981. Half-stack head and cab, 80 watts, 4x12" straight-front cab with Orange crest on grille, orange vinyl and light orange grille.

1971-1975		$3,500	$5,500
1976-1981		$3,250	$4,500

Model OR-80 Combo

1971-1981. About 80 watts, 2x12" combo.

1971-1975		$3,250	$4,500
1976-1981		$2,500	$4,000

Model OR-120 Graphic

1972-1981. Half-stack head and cab, 120 watts, 4x12" straight front cab with Orange crest on grille, orange vinyl and light orange grille.

1972-1975		$3,500	$5,500
1976-1981		$3,250	$5,000

Model OR-200 212 Twin

1970s. 120 watts, 2x12" combo, orange vinyl, dark grille, Orange crest on grille, reverb and vibrato, master volume.

1971-1975		$3,500	$5,500
1976-1981		$3,000	$4,500

Orepheus

Early 1960s. Private branded for Coast Wholesale Music Co., Orepheus logo on control panel along with model number.

Student Compact

1960s. Small student compact tube amps, some with 2 knobs, volume and tone.

1960s		$400	$500

Orpheum

Late-1950s-1960s. Student to medium level amps from New York's Maurice Lipsky Music.

Mid-Size/Small

Late-1950s-1960s. U.S.-made, 2 6V6 power tubes, Jensen P12R 12" speaker, light cover with gray swirl grille.

1950s-60s Mid-Size		$650	$975
1950s-60s Small		$450	$700

Osborne Sound Laboratories

Late 1970s. Guitar amps built by Ralph Scaffidi and wife guitarist Mary Osborne in Bakersfield, California. They also offered guitars.

Ovation

1966-present. Kaman made few amps under the Ovation name. They offered a variety of amps under the KMD brand from '85 to around '94.

Little Dude

1969-ca.1971. Solidstate combo, 100 watts, 1x15" and horn, matching slave unit also available.

1970s		$200	$300

The Kat (Model 6012)

1970s. Solidstate, 2x12" combo.

1970s		$200	$300

Overbuilt Amps

1999-2007. Tube amps and combos built by Richard Seccombe in West Hills, California. He nows works at Fender R&D.

PAC-AMP (Magnatone)

Late-1950s-early-1960s. Private branded by Magnatone, often for accordion studios.

Model 213 Troubadour

1957-1958. 10 watts, 1x12".

1957-1958		$1,250	$1,750

Naylor Dual 38

Nobles Streetman 15

Ovation 6012 The Kat

Imaged by Heritage Auctions, HA.com

MODEL YEAR	FEATURES	LOW	HIGH

Model 280-A
1961-1963. About 50 watts, 2x12" + 2x5", brown leatherette, light brown grille, stereo vibrato, PAC-AMP nameplate logo.

| 1961-1963 | | $1,875 | $2,500 |

Palette Amps
Robert Wakeling began building his tube amp heads and combos and speaker cabinets in Stillwater, Oklahoma in 2003.

PANaramic (Magnatone)
1961-1963. Private branded equivalent of '61-'63 Magnatone brown leatherette series, large PANaramic logo. Many Magnatone private brands were associated with accordion companies or accordian teaching studios. PANaramic was a brand name of PANaramic accordion. They also made guitars.

Model 260/262-Style
1961-1963. 35 watts, 2x12", gray vinyl and light grille, vibrato, large PANaramic logo.

| 1961-1963 | | $1,750 | $2,750 |

Model 413-Style
1961-1963. 18 watts, 1x12", black leatherette cover, light silver grille, vibrato, large PANaramic logo.

| 1961-1963 | | $1,125 | $1,750 |

Model 450-Style
1961-1963. 20 watts, 1x12", reverb and vibrato, reverb not generally included in an early-'60s 1x12" Magnatone amp, dark vinyl, dark cross-threaded grille, large PANaramic logo.

| 1961-1963 | | $1,500 | $2,500 |

Model 1210 (250-Style)
1961-1963. 1x12" combo, 20 watts, 2.5 channels, true vibrato.

| 1961-1963 | | $1,250 | $2,000 |

Paris
1960s. Brand name used on a line of solidstate amps distributed by a music wholesaler. Possibly built by Kay.

Master Series
1960s. Compact combo, 1x12", black tolex-style cover, silver grille, rear mounted slanted control panel.

| 1960s | | $95 | $150 |

Park
1965-1982, 1993-1998, 2013-present. Park amps were made by Marshall from '65 to '82. Park logo on front with elongated P. In the '90s, Marshall revived the name for use on small solidstate amps imported from Asia. Brand name acquired by Mitch Colby (Colby Amps) in '13 and used on tube head amps and cabs built in New York City.

G Series
1992-2000. Student compact amps, models include G-10 (10 watts, 1x8"), G-25R (25w, reverb), G-215R (15w, 2x8") and GB-25 (25w, 1x12" bass).

1990s	G-10	$60	$125
1990s	G-15R	$65	$125
1990s	G-215R	$75	$125
1990s	G-25R	$70	$125
1990s	GB-25	$70	$125

Model 50 Head
1967-1969. Plexi, 50 watts.

| 1967-1969 | | $3,500 | $5,500 |

Model 1001L Lead Head

| 1967-1969 | Plexi | $5,000 | $8,000 |
| 1969-1971 | Aluminum | $3,000 | $4,500 |

Model 1008A 4x12 Slant Cabinet
Late-1960s-early-1970s. Similar to Marshall 1960 4x12" cab.

| 1960s-70s | | $2,250 | $3,500 |

Model 1206 50W Master Volume Head
Late-1970s-1982. 50 watts, similar to JCM 800 50-watt made during same era.

| 1970s-1982 | | $2,250 | $3,500 |

Model 1212 50W Reverb Combo
Late-1960s-early-1970s. 50 watts, 2x12", reverb, tube.

| 1960s-70s | | $2,875 | $4,000 |

Model 1213 100W Reverb Combo
Late-1960s-early-1970s. 100 watts, 2x12", reverb, tube.

| 1960s-70s | | $2,875 | $4,000 |

Model 1228 50W Lead Head
Late-1970s-1982. 50 watts, based upon Marshall 50-watt made during same era.

| 1970s-1982 | | $2,250 | $3,500 |

Model 1229 100W Lead Head
Late-1970s-1982. 100 watts, tube.

| 1970s-1982 | | $2,250 | $3,500 |

Model 1231 Vintage 20 LE Combo
Late-1970s-1982. 20 watts, 1x12".

| 1970s-1982 | | $2,500 | $3,750 |

Model 1239 50W Master Volume Reverb Combo
Late-1970s-1982. 50 watts, 1x12".

| 1970s-1982 | | $2,500 | $3,750 |

Paul Reed Smith
1985-present. In the late '80s, PRS offered two amp models. Only 350 amp units shipped. Includes HG-70 Head and HG-212 Combo. HG stands for Harmonic Generator, effectively a non-tube, solidstate amp. In '09, PRS introduced tube combo and head amps and cabinets designed by Doug Sewell.

Paul Ruby Amplifiers
2000-present. Professional grade, custom, tube amps built by Paul Ruby in Folsom, California.

Peavey
1965-present. Hartley Peavey's first products were guitar amps. He added guitars to the mix in '78. Headquartered in Meridan, Mississippi, Peavey continues to offer a huge variety of guitars, amps, and PAs. TransTube redesign of amps occurs in '95.

3120 Head
2009-2016. Tubes, 120 watts, 3 foot-switchable channels.

| 2009-2016 | | $375 | $550 |

1966 PANaramic Model 1210
Rivington Guitars

Park G-25R

PRS Archon

MODEL YEAR	FEATURES	LOW	HIGH

5150 212 Combo

1995-2004. Combo version of 5150 head, 60 watts, 2x12", large 5150 logo on front panel, small Peavey logo on lower right of grille.

1995-2004		$550	$925

5150 EVH Head/Cabinet Set

1995-2008. Half stack 5150 head and 4x12" cab, large 5150 logo on front of amp.

1995-2008	Half-stack	$1,125	$1,500

5150 II

1999-2004. Has 5051 II logo on front, look for 'II' designation.

1999-2004	Half-stack	$1,000	$1,375

6505 Series

2008-present. Promoted for modern "heavy" metal sound.

2008-2019	6505, combo 2x12, 60w	$450	$700
2008-2019	6505+, combo 1x12	$450	$700
2008-2023	6505+ head, 120w	$450	$700

Alphabass

1988-1990. Rack mount all tube, 160 watts, EQ, includes 2x15" Black Widow or 2x12" Scorpion cabinet.

1988-1990		$250	$375

Artist

Introduced in 1975 as 120 watts, 1x12", bright and normal channels, EQ, reverb, master volume.

1970s		$250	$400

Artist 110

1990s. TransTubes, 10 watts.

1990s		$125	$175

Artist 240

1975-1980s. 120-watt combo, 1x12".

1975-1980s		$200	$275

Artist 250

1990s. 100 watts, 1x12", solidstate preamp, 4 6L6 power tubes.

1990s		$200	$275

Artist VT

1990s. Combo amp, 120 watts, 1x12".

1990s		$275	$375

Audition 20

1980s-1990s. 20 watts, single speaker combo.

1980-90s		$55	$75

Audition 30

1980s-1990s. 30 watts, 1x12" combo amp, channel switching.

1980-90s		$55	$75

Audition 110

1990s. 25 watts, 1x10" combo, 2 channels.

1990s		$60	$95

Audition Chorus

1980s. 2x10-watt channels, 2x6", channel switching, post gain and normal gain controls.

1980s		$100	$125

Audition Plus

1980s. Solidstate, 20 watts, 1x10".

1980s		$65	$100

Backstage 30/Plus/50/110

1977-1991. 1x10 combo, Backstage 30 (15 then 18 watts) '77-'83, Backstage Plus (35w) '84-'87, Backstage 50 (50w) '88-'89, Backstage 110 (65w) '89-'91. Name reused in 2000s on small 10-watt amp.

1977-1991		$60	$125

Backstage Chorus 208

1990-1996. 150 watts, 2x8", reverb, channel switching.

1990-1996		$125	$175

Bandit/65/75

1981-1989. 1x12" combo, originally 50 watts, upped to 65 watts in '85 and 75 in '87, renamed Bandit 112 in '90.

1981-1984	Bandit	$125	$200
1985-1986	Bandit 65	$125	$200
1987-1989	Bandit 75	$125	$200

Bandit 112/Bandit II 112

1990-present. 80 watts (II is 100), 1x12", active EQ circuit for lead channel, active controls. TransTube series in '95.

1990-1994		$150	$225
1995-2023	TransTube	$200	$250

Basic 40

1980s. 40 watts, 1x12".

1980s		$90	$130

Basic 60

1988-1995. Solidstate combo amp, 50-60 watts, 1x12", 4-band EQ, gain controls, black.

1988-1995		$125	$175

Basic 112 Bass

1996-2006. 75 watts, 1x12" bass combo, 2000-era red border control panel.

1996-2006		$125	$175

Blazer 158

1995-2005. 15 watts, 1x8", clean and distortion, later called the TransTube Blazer III.

1995-2005		$75	$100

Bluesman

1992. Tweed, 1x12" or 1x15".

1992		$250	$350

Bravo 112

1988-1994. All tube reverb, 25 watts, 1x12", 3-band EQ, 2 independent input channels.

1988-1994		$225	$300

Butcher Head

1985-1987, 2010-2017. All tube head, 120 watts. Current version is all tube, 100 watts with half power switch.

1985-1987		$350	$500

Century 200H Head

2000s. 100 watts.

2000s		$225	$300

Classic 20

1990s. Small tube amp with 2xEL84 power tubes, 1x10" narrow panel combo, tweed cover.

1990s		$325	$450

Classic 30/112

1994-present. Tweed combo, 30 watts, 1x12", EL84 tubes.

1994-2023	Narrow panel	$375	$550
2008-2014	Badge front	$375	$550
2008-2014	Head	$325	$500

Paul Ruby Amplifiers

Peavey 6505

Peavey Classic 30/112

AMPS

AMPS

Peavey Delta Blues
Imaged by Heritage Auctions, HA.com

Ca.1980s Peavey Deuce
Imaged by Heritage Auctions, HA.com

Peavey KB-100
Imaged by Heritage Auctions, HA.com

MODEL YEAR	FEATURES	LOW	HIGH
Classic 50/212			
1990-2023. Combo, 50 watts, 2x12", 4 EL84s, 3 12AX7s, reverb, high-gain section.			
1990-2023		$400	$600
Classic 50/410			
1990-2023. Combo amp, 4x10", EL84 power, reverb, foot switchable high-gain mode.			
1990-2023		$500	$600
Classic 120 Head			
1988-ca.1990. Tube, 120 watts.			
1988-1990		$300	$450
Combo 300			
1982-1993. 1x15" bass combo, 300 watts.			
1982-1993		$150	$250
DECA/750			
1989-ca.1990. Digital, 2 channels, 350 watts per channel, distortion, reverb, exciter, pitch shift, multi-EQ.			
1989-1990		$200	$300
Decade			
1970s. Practice amp, 10 watts, 1x8", runs on 12 volt or AC.			
1970s		$100	$150
Delta Blues			
1995-2014. 30 watts, tube combo, 4 EL84 tubes, 1x15" or 2x10", tremolo, large-panel-style cab, blond tweed.			
1995-2014		$450	$600
Deuce			
1972-1980s. 120 watts, tube amp, 2x12" or 4x10".			
1972-1980s		$225	$325
Deuce Head			
1972-1980s. Tube head, 120 watts.			
1972-1980s		$175	$250
Ecoustic Series			
1996-2022. Acoustic combo amps, 110 (1x10) and 112 (1x12, offered until '10) at 100 watts, digital effects (EFX, later E) added in '03. E20 and E208 added in '11.			
1996-2010	112	$150	$250
2003-2022	E110	$150	$250
Encore 65			
1983. Tube combo, 65 watts.			
1983		$250	$350
Envoy 110			
1988-2020. Solidstate, 40 watts, 1x10", TransTubes.			
1988-2020		$115	$150
Heritage VTX			
1980s. 130 watts, 4 6L6s, solidstate preamp, 2x12" combo.			
1980s		$175	$300
Jazz Classic			
1980s. Solidstate, 210 watts, 1x15", electronic channel switching, 6-spring reverb.			
1980s		$175	$300
JSX (Joe Satriani)			
2004-2010. Joe Satriani signature, 120-watt tube head. Also offered were JSX 50 (50 watts, '09-'10), JSX 212 Combo ('05-'10) and 5-watt JSX Mini Colossal ('07-'10).			
2004-2010	120w head	$575	$875
2004-2010	Combo 2x12	$575	$875

MODEL YEAR	FEATURES	LOW	HIGH
KB Series			
1980s. Keyboard amp, models include KB-60 (60 watts, 1x12", reverb), KB-100 (100w, 1x15"), and KB-300 (300w, 1x15" with horn).			
1980s	KB-100	$150	$200
1980s	KB-300	$200	$250
1980s	KB-60	$125	$150
LTD			
1975-1980s. Solidstate, 200 watts, 1x12" Altec or 1x15" JBL.			
1975-1982		$175	$250
Mace Head			
1976-1980s. Tube, 180 watts.			
1976-1980s		$275	$400
Mark III Bass Head			
1978-1983. 300 watts, 2 channels, graphic EQ.			
1978-1983		$200	$275
MegaBass			
1986-ca. 1992. Rack mount preamp/power amp, 200 watts per 2 channels, solidstate, EQ, effects loop, chorus.			
1986-1992		$180	$250
Microbass			
1988-2005. 20 watts, 1x8" practice amp, made in China.			
1988-2005		$45	$65
Minx 110 Bass			
1987-2005. Solidstate, 35 watts RMS, 1x10" heavy-duty speaker.			
1987-2005		$95	$135
Musician Head			
Introduced in 1965 as 120-watt head, upped to 210 watts in '72.			
1965-1970s		$150	$200
Nashville 112 Steel Guitar			
2008-present. Compact size, 1x12", 80 watts.			
2008-2023		$400	$550
Nashville 400 Steel Guitar			
1982-2000. 210 watts, 1x15" solidstate steel guitar combo amp.			
1982-2000		$400	$550
Nashville 1000 Steel Guitar			
1998-2008. 1x15" speaker, solidstate steel guitar combo amp.			
1998-2008		$400	$550
Pacer			
1974-1985. Master volume, 45 watts, 1x12", 3-band EQ.			
1974-1985		$75	$100
Penta Head/Gary Rossington Signature Penta			
2005-2015. Tubes, 140 watts, 4x12", 5 selectable preamp settings. Becomes the Gary Rossington Signature Penta in 2009.			
2005-2015	Cab	$275	$375
2005-2015	Head	$300	$400
ProBass 1000			
1980s. Rack mount, effects loops, preamp, EQ, crossover, headphone output.			
1980s		$175	$250

The *Vintage Guitar Price Guide* shows values for an all-original condition amplifier, and where applicable, with original cover.

MODEL YEAR	FEATURES	LOW	HIGH

Rage/Rage 158
1988-2008. Compact practice amp, 15 watts, 1x8". 158 starts '95. Replaced by 25-watt Rage 258.

1988-2008		$50	$65

Reno 400
1984-late 1980s. Solidstate, 200 watts, 1x15" with horn, 4-band EQ.

1980s		$150	$200

Renown 112
1989-1994. Crunch and lead SuperSat, 160 watts, 1x12", master volume, digital reverb, EQ.

1989-1994		$150	$200

Renown 212
1989-1994. Crunch and lead SuperSat, 160 watts, 2x12", master volume, digital reverb, EQ.

1989-1994		$150	$250

Renown 400
1981-late 1980s. Combo, 200 watts, 2x12", channel switching, Hammond reverb, pre- and post-gain controls.

1980s		$200	$300

Revolution 112
1992-2002. 100 watts, 1x12" combo, black vinyl, black grille.

1992-2002		$175	$250

Session 400
1974-ca. 1999. 200 watts, 1x15 or early on as 2x12, steel amp, available in the smaller box LTD, offered as a head in '76, available in wedge-shaped enclosure in '88.

1974-1999		$400	$550

Session 500
1979-1980s. 250 watts, 1x15", steel amp.

1979-1985		$400	$550

Special 112
1981-1994. 160 watts, 1x12". In 1988, available in wedge-shaped enclosure.

1981-1994		$150	$250

Special 130
1980s. 1x12", 130 watts.

1980s		$200	$300

Special 212
1995-2005. 160 watts, 2x12", transtube, solidstate series.

1995-2005		$200	$300

Stereo Chorus 212
1990s. 2x12" combo.

1990s		$275	$375

Studio Pro 50
1986-late 1980s. 50 watts, 1x12".

1980s		$110	$150

Studio Pro 112
1980s. Repackaged and revoiced in 1988. Solidstate, 65 watts, 1x12", Peavey SuperSat preamp circuitry, new power sections.

1980s		$125	$200

TKO Series Bass
1978-2011. Solidstate, 1x15, original TKO was 40 watts, followed by TKO 65 (65 watts) for '82-'87, TKO 75 for '88-'90, and TKO 80 for '91-'92. Renamed TKO 115 in '93 with 75, 80 or 100 watts until '09 when jumping to 400 watts.

1982-1987	TKO 65	$110	$150
1988-1990	TKO 75	$150	$200
1991-1992	TKO 80	$185	$250

TNT Series Bass
1974-2009. Solidstate, 1x15, original TNT was 45 watts, upped to 50 for '79-'81, followed by TNT 130 (130 watts) for '82-'87, TNT 150 for '88-'90, and TNT 160 for '91-'92. Renamed TNT 115 in '93 with 150, 160 or 200 watts until '09 when jumping to 600 watts (Tour TNT 115 - see Tour Series).

1982-1987	TNT 130	$250	$350
1988-1990	TNT 150	$250	$350
1991-1992	TNT 160	$250	$350

Tour Series
2004-2019. Imported bass heads and cabinets, various models.

2004-2019	Various models	$275	$400

Transchorus 210
1999-2000. 50 watts, 2x10 combo, stereo chorus, channel switching, reverb.

1999-2000		$250	$350

Triple XXX Series
2001-2009. Made in the USA.

2001-2009	Head, 120 watts	$650	$850
2001-2009	Super 40, 40w, 1x12	$500	$700

Triumph 60 Combo
1980s. Tube head, effects loop, reverb, 60 watts, 1x12", multi-stage gain.

1980s		$175	$250

Triumph 120
1989-1990. Tube, 120 watts, 1x12", 3 gain blocks in preamp, low-level post-effects loop, built-in reverb.

1989-1990		$200	$275

Ultra 60 Head
1991-1994. 60 watts, all tube, 2 6L6 power, black, black grille.

1991-1994		$350	$500

Ultra Series
1998-2002. All tube combos and cabs.

1998-2002	Ulta 112, 60 watts	$275	$350
1998-2002	Ulta 212, 60 watts	$325	$450
1998-2002	Ulta 410, 60 watts	$325	$450
1998-2002	Ulta Plus, 120 watts	$350	$475

ValveKing Series
2005-2018. Tube head, combos and cabs.

2005-2016	VK212, 100w, 2x12	$325	$450
2005-2018	VK100, 100w head	$275	$350
2005-2018	VK112, 50w, 1x12	$300	$400

Vegas 400
1984-late 1980s. 210 watts, 1x15, some prefer as a steel guitar amp.

1980s		$350	$450

VTM Series
1987-1993. Vintage Tube Modified series, tube heads, 60 or 120 watts.

1987-1993	VTM120, 120w	$450	$800
1987-1993	VTM60, 60w	$450	$800

Vypyr Series
2008-2014. Modeling amp heads and combos, 60 and 120-watt tube and 15, 30, 75 and 100-watt solidstate models. Changes to Vypyr VIP in late '14.

2008-2014	15w, combo	$65	$100
2008-2014	30w, combo 1x12	$135	$200
2010	75w, combo	$200	$300

Peavey Nashville 400
Imaged by Heritage Auctions, HA.com

Peavey TKO 80

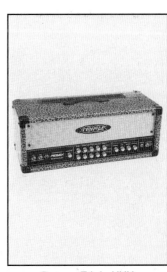
Peavey Triple XXX
Imaged by Heritage Auctions, HA.com

Penn The Pennalizer 35

Plush PRB 1000S

Imaged by Heritage Auctions, HA.com

Polytone Taurus

Imaged by Heritage Auctions, HA.com

MODEL YEAR	FEATURES	LOW	HIGH

Wiggy 212
2001-2008. 100-watt head in mono (2x75-watt in stereo) with matching 2x12" cab, 2 EQ, 5-band sliders, rounded amp head.

2001-2008		$450	$650

Windsor Head
Introduced 2006 summer NAMM. All tube, 100- or 300-watt head.

| 2000s | 100w | $275 | $400 |
| 2000s | 300w | $275 | $400 |

Penn
Tube amps, combos, and cabinets built by Billy Penn, starting in 1994, originally in Colts Neck, then in Long Branch, New Jersey.

Pignose
1972-present. Pignose was started by people associated with the band Chicago, including guitarist Terry Kath, with help from designers Wayne Kimball and Richard Erlund. In 2023, Aria Guitars assumed ownership. They also offer guitars and have offered effects in the past.

7-100 Practice
1972-present. The original Pignose, 7"x5"x3" battery-powered portable amplifier, 1x5".

1972-2023		$55	$100

30/60
1978-ca.1987. Solidstate, 30 watts, 1x10", master volume.

1978-1987		$75	$125

60R Studio Reverb
Solidstate, 30 watts.

1980		$100	$150

G40V
1997-2009. Tubes, 1x10", 40 watts.

1997-2009		$215	$350

G60VR
1998-2009. Tubes, 1x12", 60 watts.

1998-2009		$225	$350

Hog Rechargeable Portable
1995-2023. Small rechargeable solidstate, models include Hog 20 (20W, 6.5" speaker) and Hog 30 (30W, 8").

1995-2023		$120	$175

Plush
Late 1960s-early 1970s. Tuck and roll covered tube amps made by the same company that made Earth Sound Research amps in Farmingdale, New York.

Tube
Early-1970s. All tube heads and combos including the 450 Super 2x12" combo, 1000/P1000S head, and 1060S Royal Bass combo.

1971-1972	Various models	$975	$1,375

Point Blank
2002-2004. Tube amps built by Roy Blankenship in Orlando, Florida before he started his Blankenship brand.

Polytone
Beginning in the 1960s and made in North Hollywood, California, Polytone offers compact combo amps, heads, and cabinets and a pickup system for acoustic bass.

Guitar or Bass

1980-2000s	Various models	$365	$500

Port City
2005-present. Daniel Klein builds his amp heads, combos, and cabinets in Rocky Point, North Carolina.

Premier
Ca.1938-ca.1975, 1990s-2010. Produced by Peter Sorkin Music Company in Manhattan. First radio-sized amplifiers introduced by '38. After World War II, established Multivox subsidiary to manufacture amplifiers ca.'46. By the mid-'50s at least, the amps featured lyre grilles. Dark brown/light tan amp covering by '60. By '64 amps covered in brown woodgrain and light tan. Multivox amps were made until around '84.

B-160 Club Bass
1963-1968. 15 to 20 watts, 1x12" Jensen speaker, '60s 2-tone brown styling, 6V6 tubes.

1963-1968		$800	$1,125

Model 50
1940s-1960s. In '62 this was their entry-level amp, 4 to 5 watts, 1x8" similar to Fender Champ circuit with more of a vertical suitcase-style cab.

1940s-60s		$500	$725

Model 71
1961-1962. Combo with 1x12" (woofer) and 2 small tweeters, 24 watts. '61 styling with circular speaker baffle protected with metal X frame, 2 tweeter ports on upper baffle, 2-tone light tan and brown, 8 tubes, tremolo. The '62 styling changed to baffle with a slight V at the top, and 2-tone cover.

| 1961 | Round baffle | $1,125 | $1,500 |
| 1962 | V-baffle | $1,125 | $1,500 |

Model 76
1950s-1960s. Suitcase latchable cabinet that opens out into 2 wedges, 2-tone brown, lyre grille, 1x12".

1950s-60s		$900	$1,125

Model 88 Multivox
1962. Multi-purpose combo amp, organ-stop control panel, 1x15" woofer with 2 tweeters, vertical suitcase cab, 2-tone cover, classic circular speaker baffle with X brace, 10 tubes, top-of-the-line in '62 catalog.

1962		$1,125	$1,750

Model 88N
1950s-1961. Rectangular suitcase cabinet, 2-tone tan and brown, Premier and lyre logo, 25 watts, 1x12".

1950s-1961		$1,125	$1,750

Model 100R
1960s. Combo amp, 1x12", reverb and tremolo.

1960s		$1,125	$1,750

Model 110
1962. 12-watt 1x10 student combo, lyre grille logo, 2-tone cab.

1962		$700	$975

The Vintage Guitar Price Guide shows values for an all-original condition amplifier, and where applicable, with original cover.

MODEL YEAR	FEATURES	LOW	HIGH

Model 120/120R
1958-1963. 12-watt 1x12" combo, tremolo, reverb ('62), 2-tone brown cab.

| 1958-1963 | | $800 | $1,125 |
| 1962 | With reverb | $900 | $1,250 |

Model 200 Rhythm Bass
1962. 1x15" combo bass amp.

| 1962 | | $850 | $1,250 |

T-8 Twin-8
1950s, 1964-1966. 20 watts, 2x8", tremolo, reverb.

| 1950s | | $1,625 | $2,250 |
| 1964-1966 | | $1,500 | $2,000 |

T-12 Twin-12
1958-1962. Early reverb amp with tremolo, 2x12", rectangular cabinet typical of twin 12 amps (Dano and Fender), brown cover.

| 1958-1959 | | $1,750 | $2,375 |
| 1960-1962 | | $1,625 | $2,000 |

Pritchard Amps
Professional grade, production/custom, single and two-channel amps and cabinets built, beginning in 2004, by Eric Pritchard in Berkeley Springs, West Virginia.

Pyramid Car Audio
Inexpensive student models, imported.

Quantum
1980s. Economy amps distributed by DME, Indianapolis, Indiana.

Q Terminator Economy
1980s. Economy solidstate amps ranging from 12 to 25 watts and 1x6" to 1x12".

| 1980s | Various models | $30 | $50 |

Quidley Guitar Amplifiers
Intermediate and professional grade, production/custom, tube guitar amp heads, combos and cabinets built by Ed Quidley in Wilmington, North Carolina, starting in 2006.

Quilter
2011-present. Patrick Quilter builds his intermediate and professional grade, production, guitar amps in Costa Mesa, California.

Quinn
Professional and premium grade, production/custom, amps and cabinets built by Shadwell J. Damron III, starting 2005, in Vancouver, Washington.

Randall
1960s-present. Randall Instruments was originally out of California and is now a division of U.S. Music Corp. They have offered a range of tube and solidstate combo amps, heads and cabinets over the years.

Rastop Designs
2002-present. Professional grade, custom amps built by Alexander Rastopchin in Long Island City, New York. He also builds effects.

Rat Fink
Early 2000s. Solidstate amp line from Lace Music Products. They also sold guitars and basses under this brand and offered amps under the Mooneyes and Lace brands.

Realistic
Radio Shack offered a couple made-in-the-U.S. combo tube amps in the '60s, including the Entertainer 34 with a flip down record turntable in the back! Their radio and stereo gear were also branded Realistic.

Reason
2007-2016. Professional grade, production/custom, amps and cabinets built by Obeid Khan and Anthony Bonadio in St. Louis, Missouri.

Red Bear
1994-1997. Tube amps designed by Sergei Novikov and built in St. Petersburg, Russia. Red Bear amps were distributed in the U.S. under a joint project between Gibson and Novik, Ltd. Novik stills builds amps under other brands.

MK 60 Lead Tube
1994-1997. Head with 4x12" half stack, Red Bear logo on amp and cab.

| 1994-1997 | | $700 | $950 |

MK 100 Full Stack
1994-1997. 100 watts, 2x4x12".

| 1994-1997 | | $1,125 | $1,500 |

Red Iron Amps
2001-present. Paul Sanchez builds his tube amp heads in Lockhart, Texas.

RedPlate Amps
2006-present. Professional and premium grade, production/custom, guitar amplifiers built in Phoenix, Arizona by Henry Heistand.

Reeves Amplification
2002-present. Started by Bill Jansen, Reeves builds tube amps, combos, and cabinets in Cincinnati, Ohio, based on the classic British designs of Dan Reeves.

Regal
Ca.1895-1966, 1987-present. The original Regal company distributed instruments built by them and others.

Gibson EH
1936. Rare private-branded Gibson EH amp, 1x10", single control, alligator tweed.

| 1936 | | $750 | $1,125 |

1964 Premier B-160 Club Bass
Imaged by Heritage Auctions, HA.com

Quilter OverDrive 202

Reeves Custom 12

AMPS

Retro-King Catalina
Reverb Amp

Rickenbacker Model M-8
Rivington Guitars

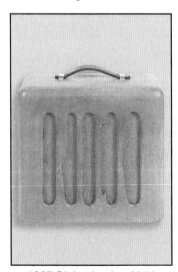

1937 Rickenbacher M-11

MODEL YEAR	FEATURES	LOW	HIGH

Reinhardt

2004-2012. Bob Reinhardt builds his professional grade, production/custom, guitar and bass amps and cabinets in Lynchburg, Virginia. He also builds effects pedals.

Resonant Amplifiers

Owners Wes Kuhnley and Peter Bregman build their professional grade, vacuum tube guitar and hi-fi amps in Minneapolis, Minnesota, starting in 2007. They also build the Field Effects.

Retro-King Amplifier Company

2004-present. Tube combo and head amps built by Chuck Dean in Marcellus, New York.

Revenge Amps

Greg Perrine began building in 1996, intermediate grade, production/custom, guitar amplifiers and attenuators in Conway, Arkansas. He also imports a line of amps.

Reverend

1996-present. Joe Naylor started building amps under the Naylor brand in '94. In '96 he left Naylor to build guitars under the Reverend brand. From '01 to '05, Reverend offered tube amps, combos, and cabinets built in Warren, Michigan, that Naylor co-designed with Dennis Kager.

Rex

1950s-1960s. Tube amps built by the Lamberti Bros. Co. in Melbourne, Australia. They also built guitars. In the 1920s-1940s, Gretsch has an unrelated line of guitars with that brand.

Reynolds Valveart

1997-present. Professional and premium grade, production/custom, amps and cabinets built by Peter Reynolds in Windsor, Australia.

Rickenbacker

1931-present. Rickenbacker made amps from the beginning of the company up to the late '80s. Rickenbacker had many different models, from the small early models that were usually sold as a guitar/amp set, to the large, very cool, Transonic.

E-12

1963. 1x12" combo with tremolo depth and speed, volume, and on-off tone knobs.

1963		$650	$875

Electro-Student

Late-1940s. Typical late-'40s vertical combo cabinet, 1x12" speaker, lower power using 5 tubes, bottom mounted chassis, dark gray leatherette cover.

1948-1949		$625	$850

Hi Fi Model 98

1956. Tube amp, long horizontal cab with 3 speakers, Rickenbacker Hi Fi and Model 98 logo on back panel, blond cover, wheat grille cloth.

1956		$1,375	$1,875

MODEL YEAR	FEATURES	LOW	HIGH

Model B-9E

1960s. 1x12" combo, 4 knobs, gray.

1960s		$825	$1,125

Model M-8

1950s-1960s. Gray, 1x8".

1950s-60s		$550	$775

Model M-9

1960s. Green, 1x12".

1960s		$700	$975

Model M-10

1930s. Silver metal, 1x10".

1935		$575	$925

Model M-11

1950s. 12-15 watts, 1x12", 2x6V6 power. There was a different M-11 offered in the 1930s.

1950s		$875	$1,250

Model M-12

1950s. 12-15 watts, 1x12", M-12 logo on back panel, brown leatherette. There was a different M-12 offered in the 1930s.

1950s		$875	$1,250

Model M-14A

Late 1950s-early 1960s. 1x12 combo, mid-power 2x6V6, dual channel with vibrato, rough-brown tolex cover.

1950s-60s		$875	$1,250

Model M-15

1950s-Early 1960s. 1x15" combo, 35 watts, 2 x 6L6 power tubes, model name on top panel.

1950s-60s		$875	$1,250

Model M-16

1950s-Early 1960s. 1x15", 35 watts, model name on top panel.

1950s-60s		$875	$1,250

Model M-30 EK-O-Sound

1961. Recording echo chamber and amp in 1x12 combo format, 11 tubes, gray grille and cover, very limited production.

1961		$4,500	$6,000

Model M-59

1930s. Small lap steel amp.

1935		$475	$725

Professional Model 200-A

1938. 15 watts, was sold with the Vibrola Spanish guitar.

1938		$625	$825

RB and RG Series

1987-1989. Various bass (RB) and guitar (RG) amp models.

1987-1989		$150	$250

Supersonic Model B-16

1960s. 4x10" speakers, gray cover.

1960s		$950	$1,250

Supersonic Model B-22 Head

1960s. Tube head, gray cover.

1960s		$750	$1,000

TR7

1978-1982. Solidstate, 7 watts, 1x10", tremolo.

1978-1982		$150	$200

TR14

1978-ca.1982. Solidstate, 1x10", reverb, distortion.

1978-1982		$145	$200

MODEL YEAR	FEATURES	LOW	HIGH

TR25
1979-1982. Solidstate, 1x12" combo, reverb, tremolo, distortion.

1979-1982		$225	$325

TR35B Bass
1978-ca.1982. Solidstate, mid-power, 1x15".

1978-1982		$225	$325

TR50
1977-ca. 1982. Solid state with Rick-o-Sound stereo inputs.

1977-1982		$175	$250

TR75G
1978-ca.1982. 75 watts, 2x12", 2 channels.

1978-1982		$225	$350

TR75SG
1978-ca.1983. 1x10" and 1x15" speakers.

1978-1982		$225	$350

TR100G
1978-ca.1982. Solidstate, 100 watts with 4x12", 2 channels.

1978-1982		$225	$350

Transonic TS100/TS200
1967-1973. Trapezoid shaped combo, solidstate, 100-watt (2x12") or 200-watt (2x15"), Rick-O-Select.

1967-1973	100w	$7,500	$10,000
1967-1973	200w	$8,500	$12,000

Risson

1970-1984, 2012-present. Bob Rissi builds his intermediate, professional and premium grade, production/custom, guitar and bass amplifiers in Placentia, California. From 1970-84 they were built in Santa Ana.

Rivera

1985-present. Amp designer and builder Paul Rivera modded and designed amps for other companies before starting his own line in California. He offers heads, combos, and cabinets. He also builds guitar pedals.

Chubster 40
2000-present. 40 watts, 1x12" combo, burgundy tolex, light grille.

2000-2023		$800	$1,125

Clubster 25
2005-2016. 25 watts, 1x10", 6V6.

2005-2016		$650	$950

Clubster 45
2005-2015. 45 watts, 1x12" combo.

2005-2015		$800	$1,125

Fandango 112 Combo
2001-present. 55 watts, 2xEL34, 1x12".

2001-2023		$1,000	$1,500

Fandango 212 Combo
2001-2015. 55 or 100 watts, 2x12" tube amp.

2001-2015		$1,125	$1,500

Jake Studio Combo
1997. 55 watts, 1x12", reverb and effects loop.

1997		$800	$1,125

MODEL YEAR	FEATURES	LOW	HIGH

Knucklehead 55
1994-2002. 55-watt amp head, replaced by reverb model.

1994-2002		$650	$950

Knucklehead 100
1994-2002. 100-watt amp head, replaced by reverb model.

1994-2002		$700	$1,125

Knucklehead Reverb 112
2003-2007. 55 watts, 1x12" amp combo, reverb.

2003-2007		$1,000	$1,500

Los Lobottom/Sub 1
1999-2004. 1x12" cabinet with 300-watt powered 12" subwoofer.

1999-2004		$450	$700

M-60 Head
1990-2009. 60 watts.

1990-2009		$575	$850

M-60 112 Combo
1989-2009. 60 watts, 1x12".

1989-2009		$675	$950

M-100 Head
1990-2009. 100 watts.

1990-2009		$625	$900

M-100 212 Combo
1990-2009. 100 watts, 2x12" combo.

1990-2009		$750	$1,125

Pubster 25
2005-2017. 25 watts, 1x10".

2015-2017		$450	$700

Pubster 45
2005-2014. 45 watts, 1x12".

2005-2014		$475	$750

Quiana Combo
2000-present. Combo, 55 watts.

2000-2014	2x12	$900	$1,250
2000-2014	4x10	$1,000	$1,375
2000-2019	1x12	$800	$1,125

R-30 112 Combo
1993-2007. 30 watts, 1x12", compact cab, black tolex cover, gray-black grille.

1993-2007		$825	$1,250

R-100 212 Combo
1993-2007. 100 watts, 2x12".

1993-2007		$900	$1,250

Sedona 112
2008-2020. 55 watts, 1x12".

2008-2020		$1,125	$1,500

Sedona Lite 55
2005-present. For electric and acoustic guitars, 55 watts, 1x12".

2005-2023		$1,000	$1,500

Suprema R-55 112/115 Combo
2000-present. Tube amp, 55 watts, 1x12" (still available) or 1x15" ('00-'01).

2000-2023	1x12 or 1x15	$950	$1,500

TBR-1
1985-1999. First Rivera production model, rack mount, 60 watts.

1985-1999		$750	$1,125

1980 Rickenbacker TR-100GT
Imaged by Heritage Auctions, HA.com

Rivera Fandango

Rivera Suprema R-55

AMPS

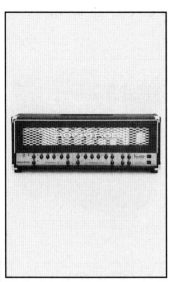

Rocktron Vendetta

1979 Roland Cube 60B
Imaged by Heritage Auctions, HA.com

Roland Micro Cube

MODEL YEAR	FEATURES	LOW	HIGH
Venus Series			
2007-present. Series includes the 7/15-watt 3 combo (1x10 or 1x12), and the 15-watt 5 and 35-watt 6, both as combos (1x12, 2x12) and heads with cabs (1x12, 2x12).			
2007-2023	Venus 6, 1x12	$950	$1,375
2007-2023	Venus 6, 2x12	$1,000	$1,500
2007-2023	Venus 6, head	$925	$1,375
2009-2017	Venus 3, 1x10	$875	$1,250
2009-2023	Venus 5, 1x12	$875	$1,250

Roccaforte Amps

1993-present. Tube amps, combos, and cabinets built by Doug Roccaforte in San Clemente, California.

Rocktron

1980s-present. Tube and solidstate amp heads, combos and cabinets. Rocktron is a division of GHS Strings and also offers stomp boxes and preamps.

Rogue

2001-present. They offered student-level solidstate import (Korea) compact amps up to around '06. They also offer guitars, basses, lap steels, mandolins, banjos, ukuleles and effects.

MODEL YEAR	FEATURES	LOW	HIGH
Small Solidstate			
2001-2006. Various models.			
2001-2006		$45	$100

Roland

Japan's Roland Corporation's products include amplifiers and keyboards and, under the Boss brand, effects.

MODEL YEAR	FEATURES	LOW	HIGH
Acoustic Chorus (AC) Series			
1995-present. Number in model indicates wattage.			
1995-2009	AC-100, 1x12, 2x5	$375	$525
1995-2020	AC-90, 2x8	$375	$525
1995-2023	AC-60, 2x6	$300	$425
Blues Cube			
1996-present.			
1996	BC60, 3x10	$275	$400
1996-2023	BC30, 1x12	$225	$300
1996-2023	BC60, 1x12	$250	$325
Bolt 60			
Early 1980s. Solidstate/tube, 1x12".			
1980s		$200	$300
Cube Series			
1978-present. Number in model indicates wattage..			
1978-1982	Cube 100, 1x12	$200	$275
1978-1982	Cube 20, 1x8	$115	$150
1978-1983	Cube 40, 1x10	$200	$275
1978-1983	Cube 60, 1x12	$200	$275
1978-1983	Cube 60B, 1x12	$200	$275
2000-2009	Cube 30 Bass, 1x10	$130	$175
2000s	Cube 80GX, 1x12	$200	$275
2000s	Cube 80XL, 1x12	$200	$275
2006-2010	Cube 30X, 1x10	$130	$175
2006-2013	Cube 15X, 1x8	$115	$150
2006-2013	Cube 20X, 1x8	$115	$150
2008-2013	Cube 80X, 1x12	$200	$275

MODEL YEAR	FEATURES	LOW	HIGH
Jazz Chorus (JC) Series			
1975-present. Includes the JC-50 (50 watts, 1x12"), JC-55 (50 watts, 2x8"), JC-77 (80 watts, 2x10"), JC-90 (90 watts, 2x10") and JC-120 (120 watts, 2x12" and 4x12").			
1975-2014	JC-120, 2x12	$550	$850
1980s	JC-50, 1x12	$350	$500
1987-1994	JC-55, 2x8	$350	$500
1987-1994	JC-77, 2x10	$400	$550
1990s	JC-120, 4x12	$475	$700
1990s	JC-90, 2x10	$400	$550
Micro Cube			
2000-present. Compact AC power or battery, 2 watts, 1x5".			
2000-2023	Various models	$90	$125
Spirit Series			
1982-1989. Compact, model number indicates wattage.			
1982-1989	Spirit 30, 1x12	$90	$150
1982-1989	Spirit 40A, combo	$90	$150
1982-1989	Spirit 50, combo	$90	$150
Studio Bass			
1979		$250	$325
VGA3 V-Guitar			
2003-2009. GK digital modeling amp, 50 watts, 1x12" combo.			
2003-2009		$225	$300
VGA5 V-Guitar			
2001-2004		$225	$300
VGA7 V-Guitar			
2000-2009		$250	$350

S.S. Maxwell

See info under Danelectro.

Sadowsky

1980-present. From '05 to '07, luthier Roger Sadowsky built a bass tube amp head in Brooklyn, New York. He also builds basses and guitars.

Sam Ash

1960s-1970s. Sam Ash Music was founded by Sam Ash (formerly Ashkynase) in Brooklyn, New York, in 1924, and by '66 there were about four Ash stores. During the '60s they private branded their own amp line, was built by Jess Oliver of Oliver Amps and based upon Oliver's Ampeg designs.

MODEL YEAR	FEATURES	LOW	HIGH
Sam Ash Mark II Pro Combo			
1960s. 2x12" with reverb combo amp.			
1960s		$675	$950

SamAmp

2004-present. Intermediate and professional grade, boutique amps built by Sam Timberlake in Vestavia Hills, Alabama.

Sano

1951-ca. 1980. Combos, heads and cabinets were made in three factories around New Jersey. Founded by Joseph Zonfrilli, Louis Iorio, and Nick Sano, initially offering accordion pickups, amplifiers, and all-electric accordions. Sano patented his accordion

MODEL YEAR	FEATURES	LOW	HIGH

pickup in '44 and also developed a highly acclaimed stereophonic pickup accordion and matching amp. By '66 the Sano augmented their all-tube accordion amps with new solidstate circuitry models. In the mid-'60s they offered a new line of amps specifically designed for the guitar and bass market. Sano amps are generally low-gain, low power amplifiers. They also marketed reverb units and guitars.

Compact Combo

1960s	160R, 15w, 1x12	$525	$750
1960s	Sano-ette	$425	$600

Satellite Amplifiers

2004-present. Professional and premium grade, production/custom, tube amps, preamps and cabinets built by Adam Grimm in San Diego, California. He also builds effects.

Savage

1994-present. Tube combos, amp heads and cabinets built by Jeff Krumm at Savage Audio, in Savage, Minnesota.

Sceptre

1960s. Canadian-made. Sceptre script logo on upper left side of grille ('60s Fender-style and placement).

Signet

1960s. Low power, 1x10", Class-A 6V6 power.

1960s		$350	$475

Schaller

The German guitar accessory company began in 1945, main products in the late '50s were tube amps and they had solid-state amps in the '60s.

Schertler

Made in Switzerland, model logo on front, intermediate to professional grade, modern designs for modern applications.

SDG Vintage

2003-present. Intermediate and professional grade, production/custom, tube amps, combos and heads built by Steven Gupta in Bristow, Virginia.

Selmer

1930s-late 1970s. The Selmer UK distributor offered mid- to high-level amps starting as early as 1935 and by the '50s was one of the strongest European brands of amps.

Bassmaster 50

1960s. Amp and cabinet set.

1960s		$2,375	$3,250

Constellation 14

1962-1965. Single speaker combo, 14 watts, gray snakeskin tolex-type cover.

1962-1965		$2,500	$3,500

Futurama Caravelle

1960s. Mid-size 1x12" combo.

1960s		$1,125	$1,500

MODEL YEAR	FEATURES	LOW	HIGH

Futurama Corvette

1960s. Class A low power 1x8", 4 tubes, volume and tone controls, plus amplitude and speed tremolo controls, large script Futurama logo on front of amp, Futurama Corvette and Selmer logo on top panel.

1960s		$900	$1,250

Goliath Bass Set

1960s. 50 watts, 1x18".

1960s		$1,375	$1,750

Little Giant

1960s. Small combo, red.

1963		$1,250	$1,750

Mark 2 Treble and Bass Head

1960s. About 30 watts (2xEL34s), requires power line transformer for U.S. use, large Selmer logo on grille.

1960s		$1,250	$1,750

Thunderbird Twin 30

1960s. 30 watts, 2x12".

1962-1965		$4,500	$6,000

Thunderbird Twin 50

1960s. 50 watts, 2x12".

1964		$4,500	$6,000
1968		$2,750	$3,875

Truvoice

1960s. Truvoice and Selectortone logo on top-mounted chassis, 30-watt combo, 1x15 or 2x12 Goodmans speaker, 2xEL34 power tubes, tremolo, 6 push button Selectortone Automatic.

1961	1x15 combo	$2,375	$3,250
1965	2x12 combo	$3,000	$4,250

Zodiac Twin 30

1964-1971. Combo amp, gray snakeskin tolex cover.

1964-1971		$3,500	$5,000

Sewell

1998-2008. Doug Sewell built his tube combo and head amps in Texas. He currently is the senior amp designer for Paul Reed Smith.

Seymour Duncan

Pickup maker Seymour Duncan, located in Santa Barbara, California, offered a line of amps from around 1984 to '95.

84-40/84-50

1989-1995. Tube combo, 2 switchable channels, 1x12", includes the 84-40 ('89-'91, 40 watts) and the 84-50 ('91-'95, 50 watts).

1989-1995	84-40 or 84-50	$300	$400

Bass 300 x 2

1986-1987. Solidstate, 2 channels (300 or 600 watts), EQ, contour boost switches, effects loop.

1986-1987		$300	$400

Bass 400

1986-1987. Solidstate, 400 watts, EQ, contour boost, balanced line output, effects loop.

1986-1987		$300	$400

Convertible

1986-1995. 60-watt; dual-channel; effects loop; Accutronics spring reverb; 3-band EQ.

1986-1987	Head only	$425	$500
1988-1995	Combo	$425	$500

1975 Sano Supernova
Tom Pfeifer

Satellite Amplifiers Barracuda

Selmer Zodiac Twin 30
Ron Cascisa

AMPS

Shaw Tonerod MG

Sherlock Fat Head

1972 Sho-Bud Twin Tube

MODEL YEAR	FEATURES	LOW	HIGH

KTG-2075 Stereo
1989-1993. Part of the King Tone Generator Series, 2 channels with 75 watts per channel.

1989-1993		$300	$400

SG Systems

1970s. A Division of the Chicago Musical Instrument Company (CMI), who also owned Gibson Guitars. Gibson outsourced amplifier production from Kalamazoo to CMI in '67 and CMI (Chicago) continued for a year or two with Gibson-branded amplifiers. In the early '70s CMI introduced the SG Systems brand of hybrid amplifiers, which had a tube power section and a solidstate preamp section. CMI was trying to stay modern with SG Systems by introducing futuristic features like the Notch Shift which would quickly switch between popular rock sounds and mellow jazz delivery. SG amps have a large SG logo on the front baffle and were built with metal corners. Amplifiers have similar power specs; for example, the models issued in '73 all were rated with 100-watt RMS with 200-watts peak music power, so models were based on different speaker configurations.

SG Series

1970s	SG115, 1x15	$450	$600
1970s	SG212, 2x12	$450	$650
1970s	SG215 Bass, 2x15	$450	$650
1970s	SG410, 4x10	$450	$650
1970s	SG610, 6x10	$475	$700
1970s	SG812 PA	$300	$400

Shaw

2008-present. Custom/production, intermediate and professional grade, guitar amp heads and cabinets built by Kevin Shaw in Lebanon, Tennessee.

Sherlock Amplifiers

1990-present. Dale Sherlock builds his intermediate to premium grade, production/custom, tube guitar amps and cabinets in Melbourne Victoria, Australia.

Sherwood

Late 1940s-early 1950s. Amps made by Danelectro for Montgomery Ward. There are also Sherwood guitars and lap steels made by Kay.

Sho-Bud

Introduced and manufactured by the Baldwin/Gretsch factory in 1970. Distributed by Kustom/Gretsch in the '80s. Models include D-15 Model 7838, S-15 Model 7836, Twin Tube Model 7834, and Twin Trans Model 7832.

Compactra 100
1960s. Hybrid tube, 45 watts, 1x12", model name logo on lower left control panel.

1960s		$600	$850

D15 Double
Introduced in 1970. Solidstate, 100 watts. 2 channels 1x15" JBL speaker.

1970s		$575	$850

MODEL YEAR	FEATURES	LOW	HIGH

S15 Single
Introduced in 1972. Like D15, but with single channel.

1970s		$400	$550

Sho-Bass
Introduced in 1972. 100 watts, 1x15", solidstate combo, black grille, black vinyl cover.

1970s		$400	$550

Twin Trans
Introduced in 1972. 100 watts, solidstate combo, 2x12", reverb, black vinyl cover, dark grille, Sho-Bud script logo front upper right.

1970s		$550	$850

Twin Tube
Introduced in 1972. 100-watt tube combo, 4 6L6s, 2x12", reverb, black vinyl cover, dark grille.

1970s		$700	$1,125

Siegmund Guitars & Amplifiers

Chris Siegmund builds his tube amp heads, combos and cabinets in Los Angeles, California. He founded the company in Seattle in 1993, moving it to Austin, Texas for '95-'97. He also builds effects pedals and guitars.

Silvertone

1941-ca.1970, present. Brand used by Sears. All Silvertone amps were supplied by American companies up to around '66.

Model 1300
1948. Vertical combo cab, treble-clef logo on grille, 2-tone, 3 inputs, 2 controls.

1948		$500	$700

Model 1304
1949-1951. 18 watts, 1x12, 2x6L6 power tubes, 2-tone leatherette cover, round speaker baffle hole, volume, treble, bass and tremolo control knobs, becomes Model 1344.

1949-1951		$500	$700

Model 1330
1954-1957. Introduced in Sears Fall '54 catalog, 3 tubes (with rectifier), 1x6", wide-panel 13x13.75x7.5" cab in tan artificial leather, 9 lbs., replaced Model 1339 at the same price but with new wide-panel style, small Silvertone logo above the grille, replaced in '58 by Model 1390 Silvertone Meteor.

1954-1957		$250	$400

Model 1331
1954-1957. Made by Danelectro, 14 lbs., 1x8" student combo, 3 tubes (with rectifier), 1 volume, 1 tone, 2 inputs, tan tweed-effect cover with brown alligator trim, large-thread wheat-gold grille, brown metal control panel.

1954-1957		$300	$450

Model 1333
1954-1957. Made by Danelectro, 23 lbs., 1x12" combo, 2x6V6 power, 5 tubes (with rectifier), 2 volumes, 1 tone, 3 inputs, 2-control vibrato, tan tweed-effect cover with brown alligator trim, large-thread wheat-gold grille, brown metal control panel.

1954-1957		$525	$750

MODEL YEAR	FEATURES	LOW	HIGH

Model 1334

1954-1957. Made by Danelectro, 29 lbs., heavy-duty 1x12" combo, 6 tubes (with rectifier), 2 volumes, 2 tones, 3 inputs, 2-control vibrato, tan tweed-effect cover with brown alligator trim, large-thread wheat-gold grille, brown metal control panel.

1954-1957		$550	$800

Model 1335

1954-1957. Made by Danelectro, 99 lbs., heavy-duty 1x15" combo, 6 tubes (with rectifier), 2 volumes, 2 tones, 4 inputs, 2-control vibrato, tan tweed-effect cover with brown alligator trim, large-thread wheat-gold grille, brown metal control panel.

1954-1957		$600	$900

Model 1336 (Twin Twelve)

1954-1957. Made by Danelectro, 26.75x17.5x9.25" cab, 45 lbs., 2x12" combo, 4x6L6 power tubes, 3 volumes, 2 tones, 4 inputs, 2-control vibrato, tan tweed-effect cover with brown alligator trim, large-thread wheat-gold grille, brown metal control panel.

1954-1957		$900	$1,250

Model 1337 "Wide Range Eight Speaker"

1956. Odd-looking suitcase cab that opens into 2 separate speaker baffles each containing 4x8" speakers, 2 preamps, 2 channels with separate controls for volume, bass and treble, 2-control vibrato, 42 lbs.

1956		$900	$1,250

Model 1339

Ca.1952-1954. Sears lowest-priced amp, 3 tubes (with rectifier), 1x6", 1 input, 1 knob, maroon artificial leather cover over 10.5x8x5" vertical cab, script Silvertone logo on low right grille, 7 lbs.

1952-1954		$300	$450

Model 1340

Ca.1952-1954. Sears second lowest-priced amp, 3 tubes (with rectifier), 1x6", 2 inputs, 1 knob, brown and white imitation leather cover over 15x12x8.5" vertical cab, script Silvertone logo on low right grille, 14 lbs.

1952-1954		$300	$450

Model 1342 Streamlined

Ca.1952-1954. Sears third lowest-priced amp, 4 tubes (with rectifier), 1x12", 3 inputs, 2 knobs, green and beige imitation leather cover over 16x19x7.25" slanted-side cab, script Silvertone logo on low right grille, 23 lbs.

1952-1954		$525	$750

Model 1344

1950-1954. Retro-styled vertical 22.5x15.5x9.5" cab with round speaker baffle hole, 1x12" combo, first Silvertone built-in vibrato, 6 tubes (with rectifier), 3 inputs, 3 controls (treble, bass, volume) plus vibrato control, maroon imitation leather cover with sports-stripe around the bottom, 33 lbs., script Silvertone logo low right side of cab.

1952-1954		$525	$750

Model 1346 Twin Twelve

Ca.1952-1954. Danelectro-made, brown control panel, 2x12", 4 6L6s, vibrato, leather handle, tan smooth leatherette cover, 2 speaker baffle openings.

1952-1954		$900	$1,250

Model 1390 Meteor

1958-1959. Renamed from Model 1330, Meteor logo on front panel, 1x6" practice amp, 3 tubes (with rectifier), tan simulated leather cover, in '60 renamed Model 1430 (but no longer a Meteor).

1958-1959		$300	$450

Model 1391

1958-1959. Modern-style cab, 3 tubes (with rectifier), 5 watts, 1x8".

1958-1959		$300	$450

Model 1392

1958-1959. Modern-style cab, 6 tubes (with rectifier), 10 watts, 1x12", vibrato.

1958-1959		$525	$750

Model 1393

1958-1959. Modern-style cab, 7 tubes (with rectifier), 15 watts, heavy-duty 1x12", vibrato.

1958-1959		$525	$750

Model 1396 Two-Twelve

1958-1959. Script Two-Twelve logo on lower left front and Silvertone logo on lower right front, 50 watts, 2x12", 4x6L6 power tubes, 9 tubes (with rectifier), vibrato, 26.75x17.5x9.25" with gray and metallic fleck cover, white grille, 45 lbs.

1958-1959		$900	$1,250

Model 1420

1968. Tube-powered, 5 watts, 1x8" student combo.

1968		$325	$500

Model 1421

1968. Tube-powered, 10 watts, 1x8" combo, covered in dark olive vinyl.

1968		$325	$500

Model 1422

1968. Tube-powered, 40 watts, 1x12" combo, covered in dark olive vinyl.

1968		$525	$750

Model 1423

1968. Solidstate, 125 watts, 2x12" cab, 55 lbs., dark olive.

1968		$425	$600

Model 1425

1968. Solidstate, 200 watts, 6x10" cab, 86 lbs., dark olive.

1968		$1,000	$1,500

Model 1426

1968. Solidstate, 250 watts, 6x15" cab, slide switches instead of control knobs, automatic E-tone for tuning, casters for 149 lb. head and cab.

1968		$1,000	$1,500

Model 1428

1968. Solidstate, 60 watts, 1x15" cab, 36 lbs., dark olive.

1968		$425	$600

Model 1430

1959-1966. Silvertone's lowest-price model, 3 tubes, 1x6", previously called Model 1390 Meteor, and prior to that named Model 1330, retro cab basically unchanged since first introduced in '54.

1959-1966		$300	$450

Silvertone 1331
Tom Pfeifer

Silvertone 1336
Imaged by Heritage Auctions, HA.com

1953 Silverton Model 1346 Twin Twelve
Rivington Guitars

AMPS

1961 Silvertone 1474
Twin Twelve

Imaged by Heritage Auctions, HA.com

AMPS

1966 Silvertone 1482

Larry Niven

Silvertone Model 1483

Imaged by Heritage Auctions, HA.com

MODEL YEAR	FEATURES	LOW	HIGH

Model 1431
1959-1961. 5 watts, 1x8", overhanging-top wraparound grille cab, 3 tubes (with rectifier), light gray cover with white grille.

1959-1961		$300	$450

Model 1431 Bass
1968. Solidstate, 200 watts, 6x12" cab, 91 lbs., dark olive.

1968		$1,000	$1,500

Model 1432
1959-1961. 10 watts, 1x12", vibrato, overhanging-top wrap-around grille cab, 6 tubes (with rectifier), dark gray tweed-effect cover with white grille.

1959-1961		$525	$750

Model 1433
1959-1961. 15 watts, 1x15", vibrato, overhanging-top wrap-around grille cab, 7 tubes (with rectifier), gray with metallic fleck cover with white grille.

1959-1961		$700	$1,000

Model 1434 Twin Twelve
1959-1961. 50 watts using 4x6L6 power, 2x12" combo, vibrato, 2 channels each with volume, bass and treble controls, black cover with gold-colored trim.

1959-1961		$1,000	$1,500

Model 1459
1960s. Student tube amp, 3 watts, 1x8", black vinyl, square cab, 1 tone, 1 volume, 1 channel, 2 inputs.

1967-1968		$325	$500

Model 1463 Bass
1967-1968. Solidstate, 1x15", piggyback, 60 lbs., reverb, tremolo.

1967-1968		$425	$600

Model 1464
1967-1968. Solidstate, 100 watts, 2x12", piggyback, 60 lbs., reverb, tremolo, gray vinyl cover.

1967-1968		$500	$750

Model 1465
1966-1968. Solidstate, piggyback, 150 watts, 6x10", reverb, tremolo, gray vinyl cover, replaces Model 1485.

1966-1968		$900	$1,250

Model 1466 Bass
1966-1968. Solidstate, 150 watts, 6x10", gray vinyl cover.

1966-1968		$725	$1,000

Model 1471
1961-1963. 5 watts, 1x8", 3 tubes, 1 volume, 1 tone, 2 inputs, black leathette cover with white grille.

1961-1963		$325	$500

Model 1472
1960s. 10 watts, 2 6V6s provide mid-level power, 1x12", front controls mounted vertically on front right side, black cover with silver grille, large stationary handle, tremolo.

1961-1963		$525	$800

Model 1473 Bass
1961-1963. Designed for bass or accordion, 25 watts, 1x15" combo, 6 tubes (with rectifier), 2 channels, 4 inputs, 19x29x9" cab, 43 lbs., black leatherette with white grille.

1961-1963		$700	$1,000

Model 1474 Twin Twelve
1961-1963. Silvertone's first reverb amp, 50 watts, 4x6L6 power, 10 tubes (with rectifier), 2x12" combo, 2 control vibrato with dual remote footswitch, 2 channels each with bass, treble, and volume, 4 inputs, ground switch, standby switch, 19x29x9" combo cab, 54 lbs., black leatherette with silver grille.

1961-1963		$900	$1,250

Model 1481
1963-1968. Compact student amp, 5 watts, 1x8", 3 tubes (with rectifier), volume and tone controls, gray leatherette cover with white grille, replaces Model 1471.

1963-1968		$325	$500

Model 1482
1960s. 15 watts, 1x12", 6 tubes, control panel mounted on right side vertically, tremolo, gray leatherette.

1963-1968		$525	$750

Model 1483 Bass
1963-1966. 23 watts, 1x15" piggyback tube amp, gray tolex and gray grille.

1963-1966		$700	$1,000

Model 1484 Twin Twelve
1963-1966. 60 watts, 2x12" piggyback tube amp, tremolo and reverb, gray cover with light grille.

1963-1966		$1,000	$1,500

Model 1485
1963-1965. 120 watts, 6x10" (Jensen C-10Q) piggyback, 10 tubes with 5 silicon rectifiers, 2 channels, reverb, tremolo, charcoal-gray tolex-style cover, white grille, replaced in '66 by solidstate Model 1465.

1963-1965		$1,250	$1,750

Model 4707 Organ
1960s. Interesting '60s family room style cabinet with legs, 45-watt tube amp with vibrato, 1x12", front controls, could be used for organ, stereo, or record player turntable.

1960s		$500	$750

Simms-Watts

Late 1960s-1970s. Tube amp heads, combos, PA heads and cabinets made in London, England. Similar to Marshall and HiWatt offerings of the era.

Skip Simmons

1990-present. Custom and production tube combo amps built by Skip Simmons in Loma Rica, California.

Skrydstrup R&D

1997-present. Production/custom, premium grade, amps and cabinets built by Steen Skrydstrup in Denmark. He also builds effects.

Sligo Amps

2004-present. Intermediate and professional grade, production/custom, amps built by Steven Clark in Leesburg, Virginia.

SMF

Mid-1970s. Amp head and cabinets from Dallas Music Industries, Ltd., of Mahwah, New Jersey.

The *Vintage Guitar Price Guide* shows values for an all-original condition amplifier, and where applicable, with original cover.

MODEL YEAR	FEATURES	LOW	HIGH

Offered the Tour Series which featured a 150-watt head and 4x12" bottoms with metal speaker grilles and metal corners.

Tour MK 2 Head
Mid-1970s. 150-watt head, high- and low-gain inputs, master volume, 8xEL34 power tubes, black.

1970s		$1,250	$1,750

SMF (Sonic Machine Factory)
2002-2009. Tube amps and cabinets designed by Mark Sampson (Matchless, Bad Cat, Star) and Rick Hamel (SIB effects) and built in California.

Smicz Amplification
Tube combos and extension cabinets built by Bob Smicz in Bristol, Connecticut.

Smith Custom Amplifiers
All tube combo amps, heads and speaker cabinets built by Sam Smith in Montgomery, Alabama starting in 2002.

Smokey
1997-present. Mini amps often packaged in cigarette packs made by Bruce Zinky in Flagstaff, Arizona. He also builds Zinky amps and effects and has revived the Supro brand on a guitar and amp.

Snider
Jeff Snider has been building various combo tube amps in San Diego, California, since '95. In 1999 he started branding them with his last name.

Soldano
1987-present. Made in Seattle, Washington by amp builder Mike Soldano, the company offers a range of all-tube combo amps, heads and cabinets. They also offer a reverb unit.

Astroverb 16 Combo
1997-2020. Atomic with added reverb.

1997-2020		$875	$1,500

Atomic 16 Combo
1996-2001. Combo, 20 watts, 1x12".

1996-2001		$725	$1,125

Avenger Head
2004-2020. Single channel, 4 preamp tubes, 100-watt with 4 power tubes, or 50-watt with 2.

2004-2020		$1,375	$1,750

Decatone Combo
1998-2020. 2x12" 100-watt combo, rear mounted controls, still available as a head.

1998-2008 Combo 2x12		$2,000	$2,750
2009-2020 Head only		$1,500	$2,000

HR 50/Hot Rod 50/50+ Head
1992-2012. 50-watt single channel head.

1992-2012		$1,125	$1,500

HR 100/Hot Rod 100/100+ Head
1994-2001. 100-watt single channel head.

1994-2001		$1,125	$1,750

Lucky 13 Combo
2000-2020. 100 watts (50 also available), 2x12" combo.

2000-2020		$1,500	$2,250

Reverb-O-Sonic Combo
1990s-2020. 50 watts, 2 channels, 2x12" combo, reverb.

1990s-2020		$1,250	$1,750

SLO-100 Super Cabinet
1988-2019. 4x12" slant-front or straight-front cabinet, prices shown are for slant, deduct $100 for straight.

1988-1989		$850	$1,250
1990-2019		$750	$1,125

SLO-100 Super Lead Overdrive
1988-2020. First production model, 100-watt amp head, snakeskin cover, 4x12" cabinet. Replaced by SLO-100 Classic in '21.

1988-1989		$3,000	$4,500
1990-2009		$2,750	$4,000
2010-2020		$2,750	$4,000

Sommatone
1998-present. Jim Somma builds his tube combo and head amps and cabinets in Somerville, New Jersey.

Sonax
Introduced in 1972. Budget line of solidstate amps offered by Gretsch/Baldwin, made by Yorkville Sound (Traynor) in Toronto. Introduced with dark grille and dark cover.

530-B Bass
1970s. Solidstate, 30 watts, 1x12".

1970s		$150	$200

550-B Bass
1970s. Solidstate, 50 watts, 1x15".

1970s		$175	$250

720-G
1970s. Solidstate student amp, 20 watts, 2x8", reverb.

1970s		$175	$250

730-G
1970s. Solidstate, 30 watts, 2x10", reverb and tremolo.

1970s		$250	$350

750-G
1970s. Solidstate, 50 watts, 2x12", reverb and tremolo.

1970s		$275	$350

770-G
1970s. Solidstate, 75 watts, 4x10", reverb and tremolo.

1970s		$275	$350

Songworks Systems
See the listing under Little Lanilei.

Sonny Jr.
Harmonica amplifiers built by harmonica player Sonny Jr. in conjunction with Cotton Amps in Tolland, Connecticut. Was started in 1996.

1967 Silvertone Model 1484 Twin Twelve
Tom Pfeifer

AMPS

Smokey

Soldano SLO-100
Imaged by Heritage Auctions, HA.com

MODEL			
YEAR	FEATURES	LOW	HIGH

Sound City 120 and L-412

Imaged by Heritage Auctions, HA.com

Sound Electronics X-101

Tom Novak

Sovtek Mig 100

Sonola

Tube combo amps made for the Sonola Accordian company of Chicago in the 1950s and '60s, possibly built by Guild or Ampeg. There are also Sonola tube amp heads from the '70s made by MHB Amplifiers in Adelaide, South Australia.

Sound City

Made in England from 1966-'67 to the late-'70s, the tube Sound City amps were Marshall-looking heads and separate cabinets. They were imported, for a time, into the U.S. by Gretsch.

50 PA Plus
Late-1960s-late-1970s. Similar to 50 Plus but with 4 channels.

1970s		$850	$1,125

50 Plus/50R Head
Late-1960s-late-1970s. Amp head, labeled 50 Plus or 50 R.

1960s-70s		$1,125	$1,625

120 Energizer Slave Unit
1970s. 120-watt power amp only, no preamp, Energizer Slave Unit logo on front panel.

1970s		$700	$950

120/120R Head
Early-late-1970s. The 120-watt head replaced the late-1960s 100-watt model.

1970s	120, no reverb	$1,125	$1,500
1970s	120R, reverb	$1,250	$1,625

200 Plus Head

1970s		$1,375	$1,750

Concord Combo
80 watts, 2x12" Fane speakers, cream, basketweave grille.

1968		$1,125	$1,500

L-80 Cabinet
1970s. 4x10" speaker cabinet.

1970s		$600	$800

L-412 Cabinet
1970s. 4x12" speaker cabinet.

1970s		$700	$950

X-60 Cabinet
1970s. 2x12" speaker cabinet.

1970s		$650	$850

Sound Electronics

Sound Electronics Corporation introduced a line of amplifiers in 1965 that were manufactured in Long Island. Six models were initially offered, with solidstate rectifiers and tube preamp and power sections. Their catalog did not list power wattages but did list features and speaker configurations. The initial models had dark vinyl-style covers and sparkling silver grille cloth. The amps were combos with the large models having vertical cabinets, silver script Sound logo on upper left of grille. The larger models used JBL D120F and D130F speakers. Standalone extension speakers were also available.

Various Models
Mid-1960s. Made in U.S.A., models include X-101, X-101R, X-202 Bass/Organ, X-404 Bass and Organ, X-

505R amps, hi-fi chassis often using 7868 power tubes.

1960s		$600	$850

Southbay Ampworks/ Scumback Amps

2002-present. Tube combo amps and speaker cabinets built by Jim Seavall in Whittier, California. He also builds Scumback Speakers. In '14, name changed to Scumback Amps.

Sovtek

1992-1996. Sovtek amps were products of Mike Matthews of Electro-Harmonix fame and his New Sensor Corporation. The guitar and bass amps and cabinets were made in Russia.

Mig Cabinet

1992-1996	2x12"	$350	$450

Mig Series Head
1992-1996. Tube amp heads, model number indicates watts, point-to-point wiring, models include Mig 30, 50, 60, 100, 100B (bass).

1992-1996	Various models	$500	$850

Space Tone

See Swart Amplifiers.

Specimen Products

1984-present. Luthier Ian Schneller added tube amps and speaker cabinets in '93. He also builds guitars, basses and ukes in Chicago, Illinois.

Speedster

1995-2000, 2003-2007. Founded by Lynn Ellsworth, offering tube amps and combos designed by Bishop Cochran with looks inspired by dashboards of classic autos. In '03, Joe Valosay and Jevco International purchased the company and revived the brand with help from former owner Cory Wilds. Amps were originally built by Soldono, but later ones were built by Speedster in Gig Harbor, Washington. They also built effects pedals.

Splawn

2004-present. Production, professional grade, tube amps and cabinets built by Scott Splawn in Dallas, North Carolina.

St. George

1960s. There were Japanese guitars bearing this brand, but these amps may have been built in California.

Mid-Size Tube
1965. Low power, 1x10" Jensen, 2 5065 and 2 12AX7 tubes.

1960s		$225	$300

Standel

1952-1974, 1997-present. Bob Crooks started custom building amps part time in '52, going into full time standard model production in '58 in Temple City, California. In '61 Standel started distributing

MODEL YEAR	FEATURES	LOW	HIGH

guitars under their own brand and others. By late '63 or '64, Standel had introduced solidstate amps, two years before Fender and Ampeg introduced their solidstate models. In '67 Standel moved to a new, larger facility in El Monte, California. In '73 Chicago Musical Instruments (CMI), which owned Gibson at the time, bought the company and built amps in El Monte until '74. In '97 the Standel name was revived by Danny McKinney who, with the help of original Standel founder Bob Crooks and Frank Garlock (PR man for first Standel), set about building reissues of some of the early models in Ventura, California.

A-30 B Artist 30 Bass
1964-early-1970s. Artist Series, the original Standel solidstate series, 80 watts, 2x15".

| 1964-1969 | | $450 | $625 |

A-30 G Artist 30 Guitar
1964-early-1970s. Solidstate, 80 watts, 2x15".

| 1964-1974 | | $500 | $650 |

A-48 G Artist 48 Guitar
1964-early-1970s. Solidstate, 80 watts, 4x12".

| 1964-1974 | | $550 | $750 |

A-60 B Artist 60 Bass
1964-early-1970s. Solidstate, 160 watts, 4x15".

| 1964-1974 | | $550 | $750 |

A-60 G Artist 60 Guitar
1964-early-1970s. Solidstate, 160 watts, 4x15".

| 1964-1974 | | $550 | $750 |

A-96 G Artist 96 Guitar
1964-early-1970s Solidstate, 160 watts, 8x12"

| 1964-1974 | | $600 | $850 |

Artist XV
1960s. Piggyback, hybrid solidstate preamp with power tubes.

| 1962 | | $450 | $575 |

C-24 Custom 24
Late-1960s-1970s. Custom Slim Line Series, solidstate, 100 watts, 2x12", dark vinyl, dark grille.

| 1960s-70s | | $550 | $750 |

I-30 B Imperial 30 Bass
1964-early-1970s. Imperial Series, the original Standel solidstate series, 100 watts, 2x15".

| 1964-1974 | | $550 | $750 |

I-30 G Imperial 30 Guitar
1964-early-1970s. Imperial Series, the original Standel solidstate series, 100 watts, 2x15".

| 1964-1974 | | $550 | $750 |

S-10 Studio 10
Late-1960s-1970s. Studio Slim Line Series, solidstate, 30 watts, 1x10", dark vinyl, dark grille.

| 1960s-70s | | $350 | $475 |

S-24 G
1970s. Solidstate, 2x12".

| 1970s | | $425 | $550 |

S-50 Studio 50
Early-late-1960s. Not listed in '69 Standel catalog, 60 watts, gray tolex, gray grille, piggyback.

| 1960s | | $475 | $650 |

SM-60 Power Magnifier
1970s. Tall, verticle combo solidstate amp, 100 watts, 6x10".

| 1970 | | $425 | $550 |

Tube
1953-1958. Early custom-made tube amps made by Bob Crooks in his garage, padded Naugahyde cabinet with varying options and colors. There are a limited number of these amps, and brand knowledge is also limited, therefore there is a wide value range. Legend has it that the early Standel amps made Leo Fender re-think and introduce even more powerful amps.

| 1953-1958 | Various models | $3,500 | $5,000 |

Star
Tube amps, combos and speaker cabinets built by Mark Sampson in the Los Angeles, California area, starting 2004. Sampson has also been involved with Matchless, Bad Cat, and SMF amps.

Starcaster
See listing under Fender.

Starlite
Starlite was a budget brand made and sold by Magnatone. See Magnatone for listings.

Stella Vee
1999-2005. Jason Lockwood built his combo amps, heads, and cabinets in Lexington, Kentucky.

Stephenson
1997-present. Mark Stephenson builds his intermediate to premium grade, production/custom, tube amps and cabinets in Regina, Saskatchewan 1997-'99, in Hope, British Columbia 2000-'06, and since in Parksville, British Columbia. He also offers effects.

Stevenson
1999-present. Luthier Ted Stevenson, of Lachine, Quebec, added amps to his product line in '05. He also builds basses and guitars.

Stimer
Brothers Yves and Jean Guen started building guitar pickups in France in 1946. By the late '40s they had added their Stimer line of amps to sell with the pickups. Early amp models were the M.6, M.10 and M.12 (6, 10 and 12 watts, respectively). An early user of Guen products was Django Reinhardt.

Stinger
1980s-1990s. Stinger was a budget line of guitars and solidstate amps imported by Martin.

Strad-O-Lin/Stradolin
Ca.1920s-ca.1960s. The Strad-O-Lin company primarily made mandolins for wholesalers but around '57 Multivox/Premier bought the company and used the name on guitars and amps.

Compact Solidstate
1960s. Made in U.S.A., logo on control panel and grille, black grille and cover.

| 1960s | | $125 | $175 |

Splawn Supersport

AMPS

Standel 25L15

Stephenson B-100

Suhr Badger
Rob Bernstein

1970 Sunn Sceptre
Imaged by Heritage Auctions, HA.com

1968 Sunn Solarus
Imaged by Heritage Auctions, HA.com

MODEL YEAR	FEATURES	LOW	HIGH

Stramp

1970s. Stramp, of Hamburg, Germany, offered audio mixers, amps and compact powered speaker units, all in aluminum flight cases.

Solidstate

1970s. Solidstate amp head in metal suitcase with separate Stramp logo cabinet.

1970s		$350	$500

Straub Amps

2003-present. Harry Straub builds his professional grade, production/custom, amps in St. Paul, Minnesota.

Suhr

1997-present. John Suhr builds his production/custom amps in Lake Elsinore, California. He also builds guitars and basses.

Sundown

1983-1988. Combo amps, heads and cabinets designed and built by Dennis Kager. By '88, he had sold his interest in the company.

Sunn

1965-2002. Started in Oregon by brothers Conrad and Norm Sundhold (Norm was the bass player for the Kingsman). Sunn introduced powerful amps and extra heavy-duty bottoms and was soon popular with many major rock acts. Norm sold his interest to Conrad in '69. Conrad sold the company to the Hartzell Corporation of Minnesota around '72. Fender Musical Instruments acquired the brand in '85 shortly after parting ways with CBS and used the brand until '89. They resurrected the brand again in '98 but quit offering the name in '02.

100S Amp and Cabinet Set

1965-1970s. 60 watts, 1x15" JBL D130F and 1 LE 100S JBL Driver and Horn, piggyback, 5 tubes (with rectifier).

1965-1969		$1,750	$2,500

190L Amp and Cabinet Set

1970s. Solidstate, 80 watts, 2 speakers.

1970s		$850	$1,375

200S/215B Amp and Cabinet Set

1966-1970s. 60 watts, 2x6550s, large vertical cab with 1x15" or 2x15" speakers.

1966-1969	1x15	$1,500	$2,250
1966-1969	2x15	$1,500	$2,250
1966-1969	Head only	$900	$1,375

601-L Cabinet

1980s. 6x10" plus 2 tweeters cab.

1980s		$400	$600

2000S

1968-1970s. 4x6550 power tubes, 120 watts.

1968-1970s	Head & cab	$1,500	$2,375
1968-1970s	Head only	$1,250	$1,750

Alpha 112

1980s. Solidstate, MOS-FET preamp section, 1x12" combo, reverb, overdrive, black.

1980s		$200	$300

MODEL YEAR	FEATURES	LOW	HIGH

Alpha 115

1980s. Solidstate, MOS-FET preamp section, 1x15", clean and overdrive.

1980s		$200	$300

Alpha 212 R

1980s. Solidstate, MOS-FET preamp section, 2x12", reverb.

1980s		$250	$350

Beta Bass

1978-1980s. Solidstate 100-watt head and combos, large Beta Bass logo on front panel.

1978-1980s 4x12		$725	$1,250
1978-1980s 6x10		$725	$1,250
1978-1980s Combo 1x15		$725	$1,250
1978-1980s Combo 2x12		$725	$1,250
1978-1980s Combo 4x10		$725	$1,250

Coliseum 300 Bass

1970s. Solidstate, Coliseum-300 logo on front.

1970s	Head & cab	$950	$1,250
1970s	Head only	$500	$750

Coliseum Lead

1970s. Solidstate, Coliseum Lead logo on front.

1970s	Head & cab	$950	$1,250
1970s	Head only	$650	$950

Coliseum Lead Full Stack

1970s. Coliseum Lead logo on amp head, two 4x12" cabs.

1970s		$1,500	$2,125

Concert 215S Bass Set

1970s. Solidstate head, 200 watts, Model 215S tall vertical cabinet with 2x12" Sunn label speakers, dark vinyl cover, silver sparkle grille.

1970s		$875	$1,250

Concert Lead 610S Set

1970s. Solidstate, 200 watts, 6x10" piggyback, reverb and built-in distortion.

1970s		$1,125	$1,500

Enforcer

1980s. Tube, 60/100-watt 2x12" or 100 watt head.

1980s	Combo	$850	$1,250
1980s	Head & cab	$900	$1,375

Fuse 200S

1970s. Sunn Fuse logo and model number on front panel, 140 watts.

1970s		$1,375	$2,000

Model T Head

Early-1970s. 100 watts.

1970s	Head only	$3,500	$5,500

Model T (Reissue)

1998-2002. Reissue of '70s Model T, 100-watt head, with 4x12" cab.

1998-2002 Head & cab		$1,250	$1,875

SB-160 Bass

1985. Combo, 60 watts.

1985		$375	$550

SB-200

1985. 200 watts, 1x15", 4-band EQ, master volume, compressor.

1985		$400	$600

Sceptre

1968-1972. 60 watts, 6550 power tubes, tremolo, reverb.

1968-1972 Head only		$1,250	$1,750

AMPS

MODEL YEAR	FEATURES	LOW	HIGH

Sentura
1967-1970s. Rectifier and power tubes, I and II versions.

1967-1969	I, 1x15 set	$1,250	$1,750
1967-1969	II, 2x15 set	$1,375	$2,000

SL 250
1980s. 60 watts, 2x12" combo, SL 250 logo.

1980s		$500	$750

SL 260
1982-ca.1985. 60 watts, 2x12" combo with reverb, SL 260 logo.

1982-1985		$550	$800

Solarus
1967-1970s. Tube amp (EL34s), reverb, tremolo, 2x12" 40-watt combo to '68; 60 watt head with 2x12" cab for '69 on.

1967-1968	Combo	$775	$1,250
1969-1970s	Head and cab	$950	$1,375

Solo II
Early-1970s. Solo II logo on front panel, 120 watts, 2x12" combo, black tolex.

1970s		$700	$975

Sonaro
Early-1970s. Head and 1x15" cab, 60 watts.

1970s	Head and cab	$700	$975

Sonic 1-40
1967-1969. Tube head, 1x15" bass amp, 40 watts.

1967-1969	Head and cab	$1,250	$1,750

Sonic I
1967-1969. 125 watts, 1x15" JBL D130F in short cabinet, 5 tubes (with rectifier), piggyback, dark tolex.

1967-1969	Head and cab	$1,000	$1,500

Sonic II
1967-1969. 250 watts, 2x15" JBL D130F in folding horn large cabinet, 5 tubes (with rectifier), piggyback, dark tolex.

1967-1969	Head and cab	$1,000	$1,500

Sorado
1970s. 50 watts, tubes, 2x15" matching cab.

1970s	Head and cab	$1,000	$1,500

Spectrum I
1967-1969. 125 watts, 1x15" JBL D130F large cabinet, 5 tubes (with rectifier), piggyback, dark tolex cover.

1967-1969	Head and cab	$1,000	$1,500

Spectrum II
1967-1969. 250 watts, 2x12", piggyback, 5 tubes (with rectifier), Spectrum II logo on front panel.

1967-1969	Head and cab	$1,000	$1,500

SPL 7250
Dual channels, 250 watts per channel, forced air cooling, switch-selectable peak compressor with LEDs.

1989	Head and cab	$525	$750

Stagemaster
1980s. 120 watts, 2x12".

1980s	Combo	$425	$600
1980s	Head and cab	$525	$750

T50C
1998-2002. Fender era, combo 1x12", 50 watts.

1998-2002		$600	$950

Supersound
1952-1974. Founded in the U.K. by Alan Wootton, building custom amps and radios, the firm continued to build amps and effects into the early '60s. They also built guitars and basses.

Supertone
1914-1941. Supertone was a brand used by Sears for their musical instruments. In the '40s Sears started using the Silvertone name on those products. Amps were made by other companies.

Various Models

1930s		$325	$500

Supro
1935-1968, 2004-present. Supro was a budget brand of the National Dobro Company, made by Valco in Chicago, Illinois. Amp builder Bruce Zinky revived the Supro name in '04 for a line of guitars and amps. In '13, Absara Audio, LLC acquired the Supro trademark and started releasing amps in July '14.

'64 Reverb/'64 Super
2020-present. 5 watts, 1x8", reverb, Jensen speaker, blue. Renamed Super in '22.

2020-2023	1605RJ	$550	$800

Accordion 1615T
1957-1959. Compact combo, 1x15", 24 watts, 2x6L6 power, 5V4, 3x12AX7, 2 channels, tremolo, 3 control knobs, Accordion (model) logo upper left corner of grille, Supro logo lower right, Rhino-Hide gray with white sides.

1957-1959		$975	$1,375

Bantam
1961-1966. Petite, 4 watts, 3 tubes, 1x 8" Jensen, gold weave Saran Wrap grille, Spanish Ivory fabric cover, red in '64, gray in '66. Also sold as matching set, for example in '64 with student-level red and white lap steel, add 65% to price for matching guitar and amp set.

1961-1963	1611S, Spanish ivory	$500	$650
1964-1965	S6411, red cover	$500	$650
1966	Gray cover	$500	$650

Bass Combo
Early 1960s. 35 watts, 2x12", 2 channels (bass and standard), 7 tubes, tremolo, woven embossed black and white tolex that appears grey. The '61 model 1688T has a narrow panel body style somewhat similar to the Fender narrow panel cab style of the late '50s, in '62 the cab panel was removed, and the 'no panel' style became the 1688TA model, the new cab was less expensive to build and Supro offered a price reduction on applicable models in '62.

1961	1688T, narrow panel	$950	$1,375
1962-1963	1688TA, no panel	$950	$1,375

Big Star Reverb S6451TR
1964. 35 watts, 2x12", reverb and tremolo, 'no panel' cab.

1964		$1,250	$1,875

Black Magick
2017-present. 25 watts, 1x12", head (1695TH), tremolo combo (1695TJ), reverb and tremolo combo (1696RT). Extention cabinets also offered.

2017-2023	1695TH, head	$750	$975

Sunn Solo
Imaged by Heritage Auctions, HA.com

Sunn Stagemaster
Robert Curd

Supro 1688T
Carter Vintage Guitars

AMPS

Supro Corsica
Imaged by Heritage Auctions, HA.com

AMPS

Supro Model 24
Michael Wright

1965 Supro Thunderbolt S6420(B)
Imaged by Heritage Auctions, HA.com

MODEL YEAR	FEATURES	LOW	HIGH
2017-2023	1x12 cab	$325	$450
2017-2023	2x12 cab	$425	$575
2018-2023	1696RT	$975	$1,375
2020-2023	1695TJ	$875	$1,250

Blues King
2019-2020. 5 watts, 1x10".

2019-2020		$275	$400

Blues King 8
2020. 1 watt, 1x8".

2020	1808	$250	$350

Brentwood 1650T
Mid-1950s. Advertised as Supro's "finest amplifier", model 1650T described as the "professional twin speaker luxury amplifier", 2 channels including high-gain, tremolo with speed control.

1956		$1,250	$1,875

Combo
1961-1964. 24 watts, 6 tubes, 1x15" Jensen, Rhino-Hide covering in black and white, light grille, tremolo.

1961	1696T, narrow panel	$900	$1,375
1962-1963	1696TA, no panel	$900	$1,375

Combo Tremolo S6497T
1964. 35 watts, 1x15", standard 'no panel' cab, tremolo.

1964		$1,000	$1,500

Comet 1610B
1957-1959. Gray Rhino-Hide, 1x10".

1957-1959		$875	$1,250

Comet 1610E
Mid-1950s. Supro's only 1x10" amp from the mid-'50s, 3 input jacks, 2 control knobs, woven tweed and leatherette 2-tone covering.

1956		$875	$1,250

Coronado
1960-1963. 24 watts, 2x10", tremolo, 2 channels, 6 tubes, Supro logo upper right above grille, black and white mixed tolex appears gray, described as tremolo twin-speaker pro amp, '61 has 'narrow panel' body style, new body style in '62 becomes 1690TA model with grille only and no panel.

1960-1961	1690T, narrow panel	$1,125	$1,625
1962-1963	1690TA, no panel	$1,125	$1,625

Corsica
Mid-1960s. Redesigned vertical combo amp, reverb, tremolo, blue control panel, black tolex, silver grille.

1965-1967		$750	$1,125

Delta King 8
2020-2021. 1 watt, 1x8", tweed/black (1818TB) or black/cream (1818BC).

2020-2021		$275	$375

Delta King 10
2020-2021. 5 watts, 1x10", reverb, tweed/black (1820RTB) or black/cream (1820RBC).

2020-2021		$350	$450

Delta King 12
2020-2021. 15 watts, 1x12", reverb, tweed/black (1822RTB) or black/cream (1822RBC).

2020-2021		$400	$550

Dual-Tone
1961-1965, 2014-2020. 17 watts, 6 tubes, 1x12" Jensen, organ tone tremolo, restyled in '64, Trinidad

Blue vinyl fabric cover, light color grille. Reintroduced in '14, 24 watts.

1961	1624T, narrow panel	$975	$1,500
1962-1963	1624TA, no panel	$975	$1,500
1964-1965	S6424T, no panel	$975	$1,500
2014-2020	1624T, no panel	$575	$850

Galaxy
2019-2020. 50 watts, 1x12".

2019-2020	1697R	$850	$1,125

Galaxy Tremolo S6488
1965. 35 watts, 2x12" (often Jensen), 7 tubes, tremolo, multi-purpose for guitar, bass and accordion.

1965		$1,000	$1,375

Galaxy Tremolo S6688
1966-1967. 35 watts, 2x12" (often Jensen), turquoise front control panel with Supro logo (not on grille), model name/number also on front control panel.

1966-1967		$1,000	$1,375

Golden Holiday 1665T
Mid-1950s. Supro's model for the 'semi-professional', 2 oval 11x6" speakers, 14 watts, 6 tubes, tremolo, 2 control knobs, black and tweed cover.

1956		$1,125	$1,500

Keeley Custom
2020-2021. Designed with Robert Keeley (Keeley Electronics), 25 watts, 1x10" (Custom 10) or 1x12" (Custom 12).

2020-2021	Custom 10	$600	$800
2020-2021	Custom 12	$725	$950

Model 24
1965. 18 watts, 1x12 combo, 2 channels each with bass and treble inputs, tremolo, Model 24 logo on top panel, Calypso Blue vinyl cover.

1965		$975	$1,500

Reverb 1650R
1963. 17 watts, 1x10", 'no panel' grille front style cab, reverb.

1963		$1,000	$1,500

Royal Reverb 1650TR
1963-1965. 17 watts, 15 tubes, 2x10" Jensens, catalog says "authentic tremolo and magic-reverberation."

1963-1965		$1,375	$1,875

Royal Reverb S6650
1965-1967. Updated cabinet with turquoise-blue front control panel, 2x10" combo, 2 channels (standard and reverb-tremolo).

1965-1967		$800	$1,125

Special 1633E
Mid-1950s. Supro's entry level student amp, 1x8", 3 tubes, large Supro stencil logo on grille, 2-tone red and white fabric cover, leather handle, available with matching Special Lap Steel covered in wine-maroon plastic.

1956		$600	$850

Spectator 1614E
Mid-1950s. 1x8", 3 tubes, 2 control knobs, white front with red and black body.

1956		$675	$1,000

Sportsman S6689
1966. Piggyback, twin speakers.

1966		$950	$1,375

The *Vintage Guitar Price Guide* shows values for an all-original condition amplifier, and where applicable, with original cover.

MODEL YEAR	FEATURES	LOW	HIGH

Statesman S6699
1966-1967, 2017-2020. Piggyback with blue-green control panel, 4x6L6 power, horizontal 2x12" cab, reverb, tremolo, script Statesman logo with model number on upper left front of chassis. Reintroduced in '17, 50 watts, 1x12" combo.

1966-1967	Piggyback	$900	$1,250
2017-2020	Combo	$1,000	$1,375

Studio 1644E
Mid-1950s. Supro's student model for teaching studios, 2 input jacks for student and instructor or guitar and lap steel guitar, 3 tubes, advertised for "true Hawaiian tone reproduction", covered in royal blue leatherette (in '56), available with a matching Studio Lap Steel covered in blue plastic.

1956-1957	Blue leatherette	$650	$900

Super
1961-1963, 2017-2020. 4.5 watts, 3 tubes, 1x8", 1606S has contrasting black and white covering with old narrow panel cab, in '63 new 1606B has 'no panel' style cab with lighter (gray) covering. Reintroduced in '17, 5 watts, 1x8".

1961-1962	1606S	$625	$850
1963	1606B	$625	$850
2017-2020	1606	$500	$650

Super 1606E
Mid-1950s. Supro advertising states, "with features important to women", oval 11x6" Rola speaker, 3 tubes, 1 control knob, 2 inputs, white (front) and grey sides, elliptical baffle soundhole with Supro logo, model number with E suffix common for '50s Supro's.

1956	White and grey	$675	$950

Super Six S6406
1964-1965. Student practice amp, 4.5 watts, 1x8", blue vinyl cover.

1964-1965		$625	$900

Super Six S6606
1966. Updated version of student compact amp.

1966		$675	$950

Supreme
1961-1963. 17 watts, 1x10", designed for use with Model 600 Reverb Accessory Unit, value shown does not include the Model 600 (see Effects Section for reverb unit). The initial 1600R model was designed with a triangle-like shaped sound hole, in '62 the more typical Supro no panel cab was introduced which Supro called the new slope front design.

1961	1600R	$1,250	$1,750
1962-1963	1600S, no panel	$1,250	$1,750

Supreme 17 S6400
1964-1965. 17 watts, 1x10", cab larger than prior models of this type.

1964-1965		$975	$1,500

Supreme Twin Speaker 1600E
Mid-1950s. 2 oval 11x6" speakers, 5 tubes, 3 input jacks, 2 control knobs, grille logo states "Twin Speaker" but unlike most Supro amps of this era the Supro logo does not appear on the front.

1956		$900	$1,375

Thunderbolt S6420(B) Bass
1964-1967. 35 watts, 1x15" Jensen, introduced in the '64 catalog as a no frills - no fancy extra circuits amp.

MODEL YEAR	FEATURES	LOW	HIGH

Sometimes referred to as the "Jimmy Page" based on his use of this amp in his early career.

1964-1967		$1,750	$2,500

Thunderbolt S6920
1967-1968. Redesign circuit replaced S6420B, 35 watts, 1x12".

1967-1968		$875	$1,250

Tremo-Verb S6422TR
1964-1965. Lower power using 4 12AX7s, 1 5Y3GT, and 1 6V6, 1x10", tremolo and reverb, Persian Red vinyl cover.

1964-1965		$1,250	$1,750

Trojan Tremolo
1961-1966. 5 watts, 4 tubes, 1 11"x6" oval (generally Rolla) speaker, '61-'64 black and white fabric cover and Saran Wrap grille, '64-'66 new larger cab with vinyl cover and light grille.

1961	1616T, narrow panel	$600	$850
1962-1963	1616TA, no panel	$600	$850
1964-1966	S6461, blue cover	$600	$850

Vibra-Verb S6498VR
1964-1965. Billed as Supro's finest amplifier, 2x35-watt channels, 1x15" and 1x10" Jensens, vibrato and reverb.

1964-1965		$1,875	$2,500

Surreal Amplification
2007-present. Production/custom, professional grade amp heads, combos and cabinets built in Westminster, California by Jerry Dyer.

Swampdonkey
2006-present. Professional and premium grade, production/custom, guitar amp heads, combos and speaker cabinets built in Rural Rocky View, Alberta by Chris Czech.

Swanpro Amps
Robert Swanson started building tube combo and head amps and cabinets in Denver, Colorado in 2004.

Swart Amplifier Co. (Space Tone)
2003-present. Michael J. Swart builds tube combo and head amps and cabinets under the Swart and Space Tone brand names in Wilmington, North Carolina. He also builds effects.

SWR Sound
1984-2013. Founded by Steve W. Rabe in '84, with an initial product focus on bass amplifiers. Fender Musical Instruments Corp. acquired SWR in June 2003.

Baby Blue Studio Bass System
1990-2003. Combo, all tube preamp, 150 watts solidstate power amp, 2x8", 1x5" cone tweeter, gain, master volume, EQ, effects-blend.

1990-2003		$400	$550

Surreal Cult 45

Swampdonkey Gypsy

Swart AST HHead Mk II

AMPS

SWR California Blonde
Imaged by Heritage Auctions, HA.com

Talos Basic 2011

Tanglewood T3

MODEL YEAR	FEATURES	LOW	HIGH

Basic Black
1992-1999. Solidstate, 100 watts, 1x12", basic black block logo on front, black tolex, black metal grille.

1992-1999		$325	$450

California Blonde
2000s. Vertical upright combo, 100 watts, 1x12" plus high-end tweeters, blond cover, thin black metal grille.

2003		$325	$700

Goliath III Cabinet
1996-2008. Black tolex, black metal grille, includes the Goliath III Jr. (2x10") and the Goliath III (4x10").

1996-2008	2x10"	$275	$400
1996-2008	4x10"	$325	$450

Strawberry Blonde
1998-2011. 80 watts, 1x10" acoustic instrument amp.

1998-2011		$325	$450

Strawberry Blonde II
2007-2011. 90 watts, 1x10" acoustic instrument amp.

2007-2011		$325	$450

Studio 220 Bass Head
1988-1995. 220-watt solidstate head, tube preamp

1988-1995		$200	$275

Workingman's Series
1995-2004. Includes 10 (200w, 2x10), 12 (100w, 1x12), 15 (bass, 1x15), replaced by WorkingPro in '05.

1995-2004	Various models	$225	$350

Symphony

1950s. Probably a brand from a teaching studio, large Symphony script red letter logo on front.

Small Tube
1950s. Two guitar inputs, 1x6" speaker, alligator tweed suitcase.

1950s		$325	$450

Synaptic Amplification

Intermediate to premium grade, production/custom, amps built in Brunswick, Maine by Steven O'Connor, starting in 2007.

Takt

Late-1960s. Made in Japan, tube and solidstate models.

GA Series
1968. GA-9 (2 inputs and 5 controls, 3 tubes), GA-10, GA-11, GA-12, GA-14, GA-15.

1968	GA-14/GA-15	$75	$100
1968	GA-9 thru GA-12	$50	$75

Talos

Doug Weisbrod and Bill Thalmann build their tube amp heads, combo amps, and speaker cabinets in Springfield, Virginia. They started building and testing prototypes in '01.

Tanglewood Guitar Company UK

1991-present. Intermediate and professional grade, production, acoustic amps imported from China by Dirk Kommer and Tony Flatt in the U.K. They also import guitars, basses, mandolins, banjos and ukes.

MODEL YEAR	FEATURES	LOW	HIGH

Tech 21

1989-present. Long known for their SansAmp tube amplifier emulator, Tech 21 added solidstate combo amps, heads and cabinets in '96.

Teisco

1946-1974. Japanese brand first imported into the U.S. around '63. Teisco offered both tube and solidstate amps.

Checkmate CM-10
1960s. Tubes or solidstate, 10 watts.

1960s	Solidstate	$55	$75
1960s	Tubes	$225	$300

Checkmate CM-15
Late-1960s. Tubes, 15 watts.

1960s		$250	$325

Checkmate CM-16
1960s. Tubes or solidstate, 15 watts.

1960s	Solidstate	$75	$100
1960s	Tubes	$250	$325

Checkmate CM-17
1960s. Tubes, 1x10", reverb, tremolo.

1960s		$375	$500

Checkmate CM-20
Late-1960s. Tubes, 20 watts.

1960s		$375	$500

Checkmate CM-25
Late-1960s. Tubes, 25 watts.

1960s		$375	$500

Checkmate CM-50
Late-1950s-early-1960s. Tubes, 2 6L6s, 50 watts, 2x12" open back, reverb, tremolo, piggyback, gray tolex cover, light gray grille.

1960s		$500	$650

Checkmate CM-60
Late-1960s. Tubes, 60 watts, piggyback amp and cab with wheels.

1960s		$300	$400

Checkmate CM-66
Late-1960s. Solidstate, dual speaker combo, Check Mate 66 logo on front panel.

1960s		$80	$100

Checkmate CM-88
1960s. Solidstate, 10 watts, 2x8".

1960s		$80	$100

Checkmate CM-100
Late-1960s. Tubes, 4x6L6 power, 100 watts, piggyback with Vox-style trolley stand.

1960s		$325	$425

King 1800
Late-1960s. Tubes, 180 watts, piggyback with 2 cabinets, large Teisco logo on cabinets, King logo on lower right side of one cabinet.

1960s		$550	$725

Teisco 8
Late-1960s. Solidstate, 5 watts.

1960s		$80	$100

Teisco 10
Late-1960s. Solidstate, 5 watts.

1960s		$80	$100

The *Vintage Guitar Price Guide* shows values for an all-original condition amplifier, and where applicable, with original cover.

MODEL YEAR	FEATURES	LOW	HIGH

Teisco 88
Late-1960s. Solidstate, 8 watts.

1960s		$110	$150

Tempo
1950s-1970s. Tube (early on) and solidstate amps, most likely imported from Japan by Merson Musical Products. They also offered basses and guitars.

Model 39

1950s. Compact amp, vertical cab, tweed, 3 tubes, single control knob for on-off volume.

1953		$300	$400

Teneyck
1960s. Solidstate amp heads and speaker cabinets built by Bob Teneyck, who had previously done design work for Ampeg.

THD
1987-present. Tube amps and cabinets built in Seattle, Washington, founded by Andy Marshall.

The Valve
Guitar luthier Galeazzo Frudua also builds a line of professional grade, production/custom, amps in San Lazzaro di Savena, Italy.

ThroBak Electronics
2004-present. Jonathan Gundry builds his tube combo guitar amps in Grand Rapids, Michigan. He also builds guitar effects and pickups.

Titano (Magnatone)
1961-1963. Private branded by Magnatone, often for an accordion company or accordion studio, uses standard guitar input jacks.

Model 262 R Custom

1961-1963. 35 watts, 2x12" + 2x5", reverb and vibrato make this one of the top-of-the-line models, black vinyl, light silver grille.

1961-1963		$1,375	$2,125

Model 313

1961-1963. Like Magnatone 213 Troubadour, 10 watts, 1x12" combo, vibrato, brown tolex, brownish grille.

1961-1963		$1,250	$2,000

Model 415 Bass

1961-1963. 25 watts, 4x8", bass or accordion amp, black cover, darkish grille.

1961-1963		$1,250	$1,875

TomasZewicZ Amplifiers
2008-present. Intermediate and professional grade, production/custom, tube guitar amp heads and combos built by John Tomaszewicz in Coral Springs, Florida. He also builds effects.

Tombo
This Japanese harmonica manufacturer introduced a solidbody electric ukulele and a Silvertone-esque case with onboard amplifier in the mid-1960s.

Tone Americana
2011-2014. David and Caroline Brass built intermediate and professional grade, production/custom, amp heads, combos and cabinets in Calabasas, California. They also offered an amp combo built in Asia.

Tone King
1993-present. Tube amps, combos, and cabinets built by Mark Bartel in Baltimore, Maryland. The company started in New York and moved to Baltimore in '94.

Tonemaster (Magnatone)
Late-1950s-early-1960s. Magnatone amps private branded for Imperial Accordion Company. Prominent block-style capital TONEMASTER logo on front panel, generally something nearly equal to Magnatone equivalent. This is just one of many private branded Magnatones. Covers range from brown to black leatherette and brown to light silver grilles. They also offered guitars.

Model 214

1959-1960. Ten watts, 1x12", vibrato, brown leatherette, V logo front lower right corner, large TONEMASTER logo.

1959-1960		$1,250	$1,875

Model 260

1961-1963. About 30 watts, 2x12", vibrato, brown leatherette and brown grille, large TONEMASTER logo on front.

1961-1963		$1,875	$2,500

Model 261 Custom

1961-1963. Tonemaster Custom 261 High Fidelity logo on back chassis panel, Tonemaster logo on front panel, 35 watts, 2x12" combo, 2 channels, vibrato.

1961-1963		$1,875	$2,500

Model 380

1961-1963. 50 watts, 2x12" and 2 oval 5"x7" speakers, vibrato, no reverb.

1961-1963		$1,875	$2,500

Model 381 Custom

1961-1963. Tonemaster Custom 381 High Fidelity logo on back chassis panel, Tonemaster logo on front panel, 2x12", 1x5".

1961-1963		$1,875	$2,500

Small Combo

1950s-1960s. 1x8", tremolo, light tan.

1950s-60s		$675	$975

ToneTron Amps
2006-present. Professional grade, custom, guitar and bass tube amps and cabinets built in Minneapolis, Minnesota by Jeffrey Falla.

ToneVille Amps
Matthew Lucci and Phil Jung began in 2013, building professional grade, production, amps and cabinets in Colorado Springs, Colorado.

Tech 21 Trademark 60

Tone King Royalist 15
Carter Vintage Guitars

ToneTron Hall Rocker

AMPS

Tonic Torpedo

Top Hat King Royal

Traynor YGM3 Guitar
Mate Reverb

MODEL YEAR	FEATURES	LOW	HIGH

Tonic Amps

2003-present. Darin Ellingson builds professional and premium grade, production/custom, amps and cabinets in Redwood City, California.

Top Hat Amplification

1994-present. Mostly Class A guitar amps built by Brian Gerhard, previously in La Habra, California, and Apex, North Carolina, and currently in Fuquay-Varina, North Carolina. He also makes effects.

Ambassador 100 TH-A100 Head
Jan.1999-2013. 100 watts, Class AB, 4 6L6s, reverb, dark green vinyl cover, white chicken-head knobs.

1999-2013		$1,125	$1,500

Ambassador T-35C 212
1999-2013. 35 watts, 2x12" combo, reverb, master volume, blond cover, tweed-style fabric grille.

1999-2013		$1,250	$1,625

Club Deluxe
1998-2009. 20 watts, 6V6 power tubes, 1x12".

1998-2009		$1,250	$1,625

Club Royale TC-R1
Jan.1998-2020. Class A using EL84s, 20 watts, 1x12". Replaced by Club Royal 20 in '21.

1998-2020		$775	$1,000

Club Royale TC-R2
Jan.1999-2014. Class A using EL84s, 20 watts, 2x12".

1999-2014		$1,125	$1,500

Emplexador 50 TH-E50 Head
Jan.1997-2020. 50 watts, Class AB vint/high-gain head. Replaced by Emplexador E-50 in '21.

1997-2020		$1,125	$1,500

King Royale/Royal
1996-present. 35 watts, Class A using 4 EL84s, 2x12". Name changed to King Royal in '21.

1996-2023		$1,250	$1,500

Portly Cadet TC-PC
Jan.1999-2004. Five watts, 6V6 power, 1x8", dark gray, light gray grille.

1999-2004		$525	$675

Prince Royale TC-PR
Jan.2000-2002. Five watts using EL84 power, 1x8", deep red, light grille.

2000-2002		$525	$675

Super Deluxe TC-SD2
Jan.2000-2012. 30 watts, Class A, 7591 power tubes, 2x12".

2000-2012		$1,250	$1,500

Torres Engineering

Founded by Dan Torres, the company builds tube amps, combos, cabinets and amp kits originally in San Mateo, California, then San Carlos and since '11 in Milton, Washington. Dan wrote monthly columns for Vintage Guitar magazine for many years and authored the book Inside Tube Amps.

Trace Elliot

1978-present. Founded in Essex, U.K. The U.S. distribution picked up by Kaman (Ovation) in '88

MODEL YEAR	FEATURES	LOW	HIGH

which bought Trace Elliot in '92. In '98 Gibson acquired the brand and in early '02 closed the factory and moved what production was left to the U.S. In '05 Peavey bought the brand name, hiring back many of the old key people, and currently offers professional grade, production, tube and solidstate, acoustic guitar and bass amp heads, combos, and cabinets, with product built in the U.K. and U.S.

Trainwreck

1983-2006. Limited production, custom-made, high-end tube guitar amp heads built by Ken Fischer in Colonia, New Jersey. Models include the Rocket, Liverpool and Express, plus variations. Instead of using serial numbers, he gave each amp a woman's name. Due to illness, Fischer didn't build many amps after the mid '90s, but he continued to design amps for other builders. His total production is estimated at less than 100. Each amp's value should be evaluated on a case-by-case basis. Ken wrote many amp articles for Vintage Guitar. He died in late 2006.

Ken Fisher Custom Built

1983-1998		$35,000	$75,000

Traynor

1963-present. Started by Pete Traynor and Jack Long in the back of Long & McQuade Music in Toronto, Canada where Traynor was a repairman. Currently offering tube and solidstate amp heads, combos and cabinets made by parent company Yorkville Sound, in Pickering, Ontario.

YBA1 Bass Master Head
1963-1979. 45 watts, called Dynabass for 1963-'64, this was Pete Traynor's first amp design.

1963-1979		$650	$1,125

YBA1A Mark II Bass Master Head
1968-1976. Like YBA1, but with 90 watts and cooling fan.

1968-1976		$650	$1,125

YBA3 Custom Special Bass Set
1967-1972. Tube head with 130 watts and 8x10" large vertical matching cab, dark vinyl cover, light grille.

1967-1972		$1,125	$1,500

YBA4 Bass Master
1967-1972. 45-watt 1x15" combo.

1967-1972		$875	$1,375

YCV80 Custom Valve
2003-2009. Tube, 80 watts, 4x10" combo.

2003-2009		$400	$650

YGA1 Head
1966-1967. 45 watts guitar amp, tremolo.

1966-1967		$600	$875

YGL3 Mark III
1971-1979. All tube, 80 watts, 2x12" combo, reverb, tremolo.

1971-1979		$775	$1,125

YGM3 Guitar Mate Reverb
1969-1979. Tubes, 25 watts, 1x12", black tolex, gray grille until '74, black after.

1969-1979		$775	$1,125

MODEL YEAR	FEATURES	LOW	HIGH

YGM3 Guitar Mate Reverb Reissue
2011-2013. 1x12" combo, 'flying wing' Traynor badge.

2011-2013		$450	$600

YRM1 Reverb Master Head
1973-1979. 45-watt tube amp, reverb, tremolo.

1973-1979		$550	$725

YRM1SC Reverb Master
1973-1979. YRM1 as a 4x10" combo.

1973-1979		$800	$1,125

YSR1 Custom Reverb Head
1968-1973. 45-watt tube amp, reverb, tremolo.

1968-1973		$550	$725

YVM Series PA Head
1967-1980. Public address heads, models include tube YVM-1 Voice Master, and solidstate YVM-2 and 3 Voice Mate and YVM-4, all with 4 inputs.

1967-1972	1, tubes	$475	$600
1969-1975	2, solidstate	$195	$275
1970-1980	3, solidstate, reverb	$250	$350
1972-1977	4, solidstate, reverb	$250	$350

Trillium Amplifier Company
2007-present. Brothers Stephen and Scott Campbell build their professional and premium grade, production/custom tube amps in Indianapolis, Indiana.

Trinity Amps
2003-present. Stephen Cohrs builds his production/custom, professional grade, tube amps and cabinets in Toronto, Ontario.

True Tone
1960s. Guitars and amps retailed by Western Auto, manufactured by Chicago guitar makers like Kay.

Hi-Fi 4 (K503 Hot-Line Special)
1960s. Similar to K503, 4 watts from 3 tubes, gray cabinet, gray grille, metal handle.

1960s		$275	$400

Model 5 (K503A)
1960s. 4 tubes, 1x8".

1960s		$275	$400

Vibrato 704
1960s. Solidstate, 10 watts, 1x8", white sides and gray back, gray grille.

1960s		$135	$175

Vibrato 706
1960s. Solidstate, 15 watts, 1x15", white sides and gray back, brown grille.

1960s		$145	$200

Tube Works
1987-2004. Founded by B.K. Butler in Denver, Tube Works became a division of Genz Benz Enclosures of Scottsdale, Arizona in 1997. Tube Works' first products were tube guitar effects and in '91 they added tube/solidstate amps, cabinets, and DI boxes to the product mix. In '04, Genz Benz dropped the brand.

Twilighter (Magnatone)
Late-1950s-early-1960s. Magnatone amps private branded for LoDuca Brothers. Prominent block-style capital TWILIGHTER logo on front panel, generally something nearly equal to Magnatone equivalent. This is just one of many private branded Magnatones. Covers range from brown to black leatherette, and brown to light silver grilles.

Model 213
1961-1963. About 20 watts, 1x12", vibrato, brown leatherette and brown grille.

1961-1963		$1,250	$1,875

Model 260R
1961-1963. About 18 to 25 watts, 1x12", vibrato, brown leatherette cover.

1961-1963		$1,500	$2,250

Model 280A
Late-1950s-early-1960s. About 35 watts, 2x12", vibrato, brown leatherette cover.

1961-1963		$1,500	$2,250

Two-Rock
1999-present. Tube guitar amp heads, combos and cabinets built by Joe Mloganoski and Bill Krinard (K&M Analog Designs) originally in Cotati, California, currently in Rohnert Park. They also build speakers.

Ugly Amps
2003-present. Steve O'Boyle builds his tube head and combo amps and cabinets in Burbank, California and Reading, Pennsylvania.

UltraSound
A division of UJC Electronics, UltraSound builds acoustically transparent amps, designed by Greg Farres for the acoustic guitarist, in Adel, Iowa.

Unique (Magnatone)
1961-1963. Private branded, typically for an accordion company or accordion studio, uses standard guitar input jacks.

Model 260R
1961-1963. Based on Magnatone 260 Series amp, 35 watts, 2x12" but with reverb, black vinyl-style cover with distinctive black diamond-check pattern running through the top and sides.

1961-1963		$1,750	$2,500

Model 460
1961-1963. 35 watts, 2x12" and oval 5"x7" speakers, reverb and vibrato make it one of the top models, black vinyl, black grille.

1961-1963		$1,500	$2,000

Universal (Audio Guild)
See Audio Guild amps.

Univox
1964-ca.1978. From '64 to early-'68, these were American-made tube amps with Jensen speakers. By '68, they were using Japanese components in

1969 Traynor YSR1
Custom Reverb
Scott Anderson

AMPS

Trinity Tweed

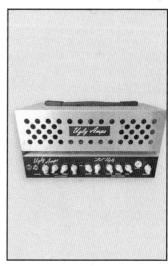
Ugly Lil' Ugly

1971 Univox U1226
Carter Vintage Guitars

Ca. 1951 Valco Chicago 51
Rivington Guitars

Vega Commander
Imaged by Heritage Auctions, HA.com

MODEL YEAR	FEATURES	LOW	HIGH

American cabinets, still with Jensen speakers. Electronics were a combination of tube and transistors during this time; this type lasted until the mid-'70s. Around '71, Univox introduced a line of all solidstate amps, as well.

Lead Model Tube
1960s. Tube amp, 2x10" or 2x12".

1965-1969		$675	$875

Model U45B Bass
1965-1968. 1x12" combo tube bass amp, 10 watts.

1965-1968		$325	$450

Model U60A
1965-1968. 1x12" tube combo.

1965-1968		$375	$500

Model U65R
1965-1968. 20 watts, 1x12" tube combo.

1965-1968		$425	$550

Model U65RD Lead 65
1976-1978. Solidstate, 65 watts, reverb, 1x12" or 2x12" in a vertical cab.

1976-1978		$50	$75

Model U102
1965-1968. 1x12" tube combo.

1965-1968		$425	$550

Model U130B Bass
1976-1978. Solidstate, 130 watts, 1x15".

1976-1978		$135	$175

Model U130L Lead
1976-1978. Solidstate, 130 watts.

1976-1978		$135	$175

Model U155R
1965-1968. 20 watts, 1x12" tube combo.

1965-1968		$550	$750

Model U202R
1965-1968. 1x12" tube combo.

1965-1968		$550	$750

Model U305R
1965-1968. 30 watts, 1x15" tube combo.

1965-1968		$650	$850

Model U1011 Lead Head
1976-1978. Solidstate, 100 watts, reverb, tremolo. Name also used on earlier tube head.

1976-1978		$200	$250

Model U1061 Bass Head
1976-1978. Solidstate.

1976-1978		$200	$250

Model U1220
1968-1971. Tubes or tube-hybrid, piggyback, 2x12".

1968-1971		$325	$450

Model U1226 Head
1971-1972. 60-watt tube amp head.

1971-1972		$550	$750

Model U1246B Bass Head
1976-1978. Solidstate, 60 watts.

1976-1978		$200	$275

Model U1246L Lead Head
1976-1978. Solidstate.

1976-1978		$200	$275

Valco

Valco, from Chicago, Illinois, was a big player in the guitar and amplifier business. Their products were private branded for other companies like National, Supro, Airline, Oahu, El Grande and Gretsch.

Valvetech

Production/custom, professional grade, amps built by Rob Pierce, starting in 1997, in Ossian, Indiana.

Valvetrain Amplification

2005-present. Tube combos, amp heads, and speaker cabinets built by Rick Gessner in Sorrento, Florida. He also builds reverb units.

Vamp

1970s. Tube and solidstate amps and speaker cabinets built at Triumph Electronics in England.

Bass Master Head

1970s	100 watts	$1,250	$1,625

VanAmps

Tim Van Tassel, started in 1999, builds professional, production/custom, amps and cabinets in Golden Valley, Minnesota. He also builds effects.

Vega

The original Boston-based company (1903) was purchased by C.F. Martin in '70. In '80, the Vega trademark was sold to a Korean company.

A-49
1960s. Tubes, 6 watts, 1x8", tan cover.

1960s		$325	$450

Director Combo
1950s. Small to mid-size tube amp, 2-tone cover, 2 volume and 1 tone controls, rear mounted control chassis similar to Fender or Gibson from the '50s.

1950s		$500	$650

Lap Steel
1930s-1940s. Various models.

1930s	1x12, dark cover	$500	$650
1940s	1x10, tweed	$500	$650

Super
Early 1950s. 1 6L6, 1x10", vertical combo amp typical of the era.

1950s		$500	$650

Triumphal
Late-1940s. Vega Triumphal logo on back control pane, 6L6 power, 1x12".

1940s		$500	$650

Versatone (Audio Guild)

See Audio Guild amps.

Vesta Fire

1980s. Japanese imports by Shiino Musical Instruments Corp.; later by Midco International. Mainly known for effects pedals.

MODEL YEAR	FEATURES	LOW	HIGH

VHT

Founded by Steven M. Fryette in 1989, VHT built amps, combos, and cabinets in Burbank, California. At the beginning of '09 AXL guitars acquired the VHT name and manufactures their own product under that brand. Fryette continues to build the VHT amp models under Fryette Amplification.

Vibe Amplification

2008-2013. Intermediate grade, production, tube amps, imported from Asia by Lorenzo Brogi in Bologna, Italy.

Victor

Late-1960s. Made in Japan.

Victoria

1994-present. Tube amps, combos, and reverb units built by Mark Baier in Naperville, Illinois. In '08, they changed the logo from the original script Victoria Amp Co. to the current stylized lightning bolt Victoria logo.

Cherry Bomb
2011-present. Tube tremolo, 40 watts, 1x15", alligator/cream tolex.

		LOW	HIGH
2011-2023		$1,500	$2,000

Double Deluxe
1994-present. 35 watts, 2x12".

1994-2023		$1,500	$2,000

Electro King
2008-present. 1957 GA-40 type circuit, tubes, 15 watts, 1x12".

2008-2023		$1,375	$1,875

Golden Melody
2008-present. Tubes, reverb, 50 watts, 2x12", alligator/brown tolex.

2008-2023		$1,500	$2,000

Ivy League
2010-present. Tweed Harvard specs, 14 watts, 1x10".

2011-2023		$1,125	$1,500

Model 518
1994-present. Tweed, 1x8".

1994-2023		$850	$1,125

Model 5112-T
2001-present. Tweed, 5 watts, 5F1 circuit, 1x12".

2001-2023		$875	$1,125

Model 20112
1994-present. Tweed, 20 watts, 1x12", tweed.

1994-2023		$1,125	$1,500

Model 35115
1994-present. Tweed combo, 28 watts, 1x15".

1994-2023		$1,375	$1,875

Model 35210
1994-present. Tweed, 28 watts, 2x10", tweed.

1994-2023		$1,500	$2,000

Model 35212-T
1990s. Tweed, 35 watts, 2x12".

1990s		$1,500	$2,000

Model 35310-T
1994-present. Tweed, 28 watts, 3x10".

1994-2023		$1,625	$2,125

Model 45115-T
2008-2009. Tweed, 45 watts, 1x15".

2008-2009		$1,375	$1,875

Model 45410-T
1994-present. Tweed, 45 watts, 4x10" combo, tweed.

1994-2023		$1,500	$2,000

Model 50212-T
2002-present. Tweed, 50 watts, 2x12" combo.

2002-2023		$1,500	$2,000

Model 80212
1994-present. Tweed, 80 watts, 2x12", tweed.

1994-2023		$1,625	$2,125

Regal
2004-2006. Class A with 1 x 6L6, 15 watts, 1x15", brown tolex cover, rear mount controls

2004-2006		$1,375	$1,875

Regal II/Regal
2006-present. Class A, 35 watts, 1x15", tweed or vanilla tolex, rear mount controls. The II removed from name about '13.

2006-2023		$1,375	$1,875

Reverberato
1996-2016. Tube reverb unit with vibrato, tweed or color options.

1996-2016		$1,125	$1,500

Silver Sonic
2011-present. Tube reverb, 20 watts, 1x12", 2-tone black/cream cab with Sonic Blue or black tolex.

2011-2023		$1,500	$2,000

Trem d'La Trem
2007-present. Tweed design, 14 watts, 1x15".

2007-2023		$1,375	$1,875

Victoriette
2001-present. 20 watts, 1x12" or 2x10", reverb, tremolo in '01.

2001-2023	2x10	$1,500	$2,000

Victorilux
2001-present. 45 watts, 2x12", 3x10" or 1x15", EL84s, reverb, tremolo.

2001-2023	3x10	$1,625	$2,250

Victoria 35115
Carter Vintage Guitars

Victoria Silver Sonic

Vintage47

2010-present. Founder/builder David Barnes, of California, builds retro-inspired compact amps that reflect old-school Valco values, handwired, intermediate and professional grade.

Vivi-Tone

1933-1938. Founded in Kalamazoo, Michigan, by former Gibson designer Lloyd Loar and others, Vivi-Tone sold small amps built by Webster Electric to accompany their early electric solidbody guitars.

V-M (Voice of Music) Corp.

1944-1977. Started building record changers in Benton Harbor, Michigan. By the early '50s had added amplified phonographs, consoles, and tape recorders as well as OEM products for others. Their portable PA systems can be used for musical instruments. Products sport the VM logo.

Vintage 47 VA-20

AMPS

1961 Vox AC4
Frank Silvestry

Vox AC10C1

1963 Vox AC30 Twin
KC Cormack

MODEL YEAR	FEATURES	LOW	HIGH

Small Portable
1950s. Standard phono input for instrument, phono and microphone controls, wood combo cabinet, 1x10" or 1x12" Jensen.

1950s		$350	$500

Voltmaster
Trapezoid-shaped combo amps and reverb units made in Plano, Texas, in the late 1990s.

Voodoo
1998-present. Tube amp heads and speaker cabinets built in Lansing, New York by Trace Davis, Anthony Cacciotti, and Mike Foster.

Vox
1954-present. Tom Jennings and Dick Denney combined forces in '57 to produce the first Vox amp, the 15-watt AC-15. The period between '57-'68 is considered to be the Vox heyday. Vox produced tube amps in England and also the U.S. from '64 to '65. English-made tube amps were standardized between '60 and '65. U.S.-made Vox amps in '66 were solid-state. In the mid-'60s, similar model names were sometimes used for tube and solidstate amps. In '93 Korg bought the Vox name and current products are built by Marshall. Those amps that originally came with a trolley or stand are priced including the original trolley or stand, and an amp without one will be worth less than the amount shown. Smaller amps were not originally equipped with a trolley or stand (if a speaker cabinet mounts to it and it tilts, it is called a trolley; otherwise referred to as a stand).

4120 Bass
1966-1967. Hybrid solidstate and tube bass amp.

1966-1967		$450	$650

7120 Guitar
1966-1967. Hybrid solidstate and tube amp, 120 watts.

1966-1967		$450	$650

AC4
1961-1965. Made in England, early Vox tube design, 3.5 watts, 1x8", tremolo.

1961-1965		$1,250	$2,000

AC4TV
2009-2019. Tube, 4 watts, in 1x10 (AC4TV8 is 1x8) combo or amp head with 1x12 cab, EL84 power tube, 12AX7 powered preamp. AC4TVmini combo has 6.5-inch speaker.

2009-2013	1x12	$120	$200
2009-2013	1x8	$125	$200
2009-2013	Head only	$140	$200
2009-2019	1x10	$140	$200

AC10
1958-1965. Made in England, 12 watts, 1x10", tremolo, this tube version not made in U.S. ('64-'65).

1958-1965		$3,500	$5,500

AC10 Twin
1962-1965. Made in England, also made in U.S. '64-'65, 12 watts (2xEL84s), 2x10".

1962-1965		$4,000	$6,500

MODEL YEAR	FEATURES	LOW	HIGH

AC10C1
2015-present. Custom series, 10 watts, 1x10", black and maroon 2-tone.

2015-2023		$350	$500

AC15
1958-1965. 15 watts, 1x12", TV front changed to split front in fall '60.

1958	TV front	$4,250	$6,500
1958-1965	Split front	$3,500	$5,000

AC15 Twin
1961-1965. Tube, 2x12", 18 watts.

1961-1965	Standard colors	$4,000	$6,000
1962-1965	Custom colors	$7,500	$11,000

AC15 50th Anniversary
2007. 50th Anniversary 1957-2007 plaque on lower left front of grille, hand wired, white tolex.

2007		$750	$1,125

AC15C1
2010-2020. Custom Series, made in China, 15 watts, 1x12", tube, reverb and tremolo.

2010-2020		$400	$600

AC15CC (Custom Classic)
2006-2012. Made in China, 15 watts, 1x12" tube combo, master volume, reverb, tremolo, 2-button footswitch.

2006-2012		$400	$600

AC15H1TV
2008-2009. Part of Heritage Collection, limited edition, 200 made, hand wired, oiled mahogany cabinet.

2008-2009		$1,000	$1,500

AC15HW1
2015-2021. Hand-wired, 15 watts, 1x12".

2015-2021		$925	$1,250

AC15TB/TBX
1996-2004. 15 watts, top boost, 1x12" Celestion (lower cost Eminence available).

1996-2004	TB	$825	$1,250
1996-2004	TBX	$1,000	$1,500

AC30 Reissue Model
1980s-1990s-2000s. Standard reissue and limited edition models with identification plate on back of amp. Models include the AC30 Reissue and Reissue custom color (1980s-1990s), AC30 25th Anniv. (1985-1986), AC30 30th Anniv. (1991), AC30 Collector Model (1990s, mahogany cabinet), AC30HW Hand Wired (1990s) and HW Limited (2000s).

1980s	Rose Morris era	$1,500	$2,500
1985-1986	25th Anniv	$1,500	$2,500
1990s	Collector model	$2,000	$3,000
1990s	Custom colors	$1,500	$2,000
1990s	Hand wired	$2,250	$3,000
1990s	Reissue	$1,250	$2,000
1991	30th Anniv	$1,750	$2,500
1995	TBT, LE, tan	$1,625	$2,250
2000s	Hand wired LE	$2,250	$3,000
2000s	Reissue	$1,375	$2,000

AC30 Super Twin Set
1960-1965. Piggyback head and 2x12" pressure cabinet with amp trolley.

1960-1965		$4,000	$6,500

The Vintage Guitar Price Guide shows values for an all-original condition amplifier, and where applicable, with original cover.

AMPS

MODEL YEAR	FEATURES	LOW	HIGH

AC30 Twin/AC-30 Twin Top Boost
1960-1973. Made in England, tube, 30-watt head, 36 watts 2x12", Top Boost includes additional treble and bass, custom colors available in '60-'63.

1960-1963	Custom colors	$6,000	$9,000
1960-1965	Black	$4,000	$6,000
1966	Black	$2,500	$4,500
1967-1973	Black	$2,000	$3,500

AC30BM Brian May Limited Edition
2006-2007. Limited run of 500, 30 watts, 2x12" combo.

2006-2007		$1,250	$1,750

AC30C2X Custom
2004-2018. 30 watts, 2x12" Celestion Alnico Blue speakers.

2004-2018		$550	$800

AC30CC (Custom Classic)
2004-2012. 30 watts, 2x12", tubes, 2-button footswitch.

2004-2012		$550	$800

AC30VR Valve Reactor
2010-2019. 2x12" combo, digital reverb, 30 watts.

2010-2019		$350	$500

AC50 Cabinet

1963-1975	Black	$850	$1,250

AC50 Head
1963-1975. Made in England, 50-watt head, U.S. production '64-'65 tube version is Westminster Bass, U.S. post-'66 is solidstate.

1963-1975		$2,750	$3,750

AC100 MK I
1963-1965. All tube 100-watt with 4x12 cab, due to reliability concerns it was transitioned to AC100 Super De Luxe MK II in '65.

1963-1965		$4,250	$6,500

AC100 Super De Luxe/MK II
1965. Solidstate 100-watt head with 4x12 cab on speaker trolley.

1965		$2,500	$4,000

AD Series
2004-2008. Import small to large modeling amps with single 12AXT preamp tube, chrome grills, includes applicable footswitch, some available with amp trolley (i.e. AD60VT).

2004-2006	AD120VT	$400	$550
2004-2006	AD60VT	$250	$350
2004-2008	AD100VTH	$200	$275
2004-2008	AD15VT	$110	$150
2004-2008	AD30VT	$120	$150
2004-2008	AD50VT	$155	$200
2006-2008	AD100VT	$275	$350

Berkeley II V108 (Tube)
1964-1966. U.S.-made tube amp revised '66-'69 to U.S.-made solidstate model V1081, 18 watts, 2x10" piggyback.

1964-1966		$1,125	$1,500

Berkeley II V1081 (Solidstate)
1966-1967. U.S.-made solidstate, 35 watts, 2x10" piggyback, includes trolley stand.

1966-1969		$725	$1,000

Berkeley III (Solidstate)
1968. Berkeley III logo on top panel of amp.

1968-1969		$925	$1,250

Buckingham
1966-1968. Solidstate, 35 watts, 2x12" piggyback, includes trolley stand.

1966-1968		$825	$1,125

Cambridge 15
1999-2001. 15 watts, 1x8", tremolo.

1999-2001		$150	$200

Cambridge 30 Reverb
1999-2002. 30 watts, 1x10", tremolo and reverb.

1999-2002		$175	$250

Cambridge 30 Reverb Twin 210
1999-2002. 30 watts hybrid circuit, 2x10", reverb.

1999-2002		$225	$300

Cambridge Reverb V1031/ V1032 (Solidstate)
1966-1968. Solidstate, 35 watts, 1x10", model V1031 replaced tube version V103.

1966-1968		$775	$1,125

Cambridge Reverb V3/V103 (Tube)
1965-1966. U.S-made tube version, 18 watts, 1x10", a Pacemaker with reverb, superseded by solidstate Model V1031 by '67.

1965-1966		$1,125	$1,625

Churchill PAV119 Head and V1091 Cabinet Set
Late-1960s. PA head with multiple inputs and 2 column speakers.

1960s	PA head only	$475	$650
1960s	Set	$850	$1,125

Climax V125/VO125 Lead Combo
1970-1991. Solidstate, 125 watts, 2x12" combo, 5-band EQ, master volume.

1970-1991	Combo	$700	$1,000
1970-1991	Half-Stack	$925	$1,250

DA Series
2006-2013. Small digital modeling amps, AC/DC power, solidstate.

2006-2013	DA5, 5w, 1x65	$95	$150
2007-2009	DA10, 10w, 2x6	$125	$175
2007-2009	DA20, 20w, 2x8	$125	$175
2010	DA15, 15w, 1x8	$100	$150

Defiant
1966-1970. Made in England, 50 watts, 2x12" + Midax horn cabinet.

1966-1970		$1,500	$2,250

Escort
Late 1960s-1983. 2.5 watt battery-powered portable amp.

1968-1986		$350	$500

Essex V1042 Bass
1966-1968. U.S.-made solidstate, 35 watts, 2x12". Also called Essex Bass Deluxe.

1966-1968		$550	$750

Foundation Bass
1966-1970. Tube in '66, solidstate after, 50 watts, 1x18", made in England only.

1966	Tubes	$1,625	$2,250
1967-1970	Solidstate	$675	$925

2018 Vox AC30C2
Ted Wulfers

1967 Vox Berkeley II V108
Rivington Guitars

Vox Buckingham
Imaged by Heritage Auctions, HA.com

AMPS

AMPS

1967 Vox Royal Guardsman
Imaged by Heritage Auctions, HA.com

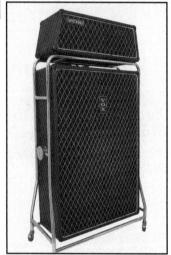

1966 Vox Super Beatle V1141
Imaged by Heritage Auctions, HA.com

Vox VT20+

MODEL YEAR	FEATURES	LOW	HIGH
Kensington V1241 Bass			
	1966-1968. U.S.-made solidstate bass amp, 22 watts, 1x15", G-tuner, called Kensington Bass Deluxe in '67.		
1966-1968		$650	$950
Night Train Series			
	2009-2016. Small tube head and combo, 2 channels, Celestion speaker, models available; NT15C1 (15w, 1x12 combo), NT15H-G2 (15w, 1x12 head/cab), NT50H-G2 (50w, 2x12 head/cab).		
2009-2016	NT, 2x12 cab	$250	$350
2009-2016	NT15H-G2, cab	$200	$300
2009-2016	NT15H-G2, head	$325	$450
2015-2016	NT15C1, combo	$475	$650
Pacemaker V1021 (Solidstate)			
	1966-1968. U.S.-made solidstate amp, 35 watts, 1x10", replaced Pacemaker model V102.		
1966-1968		$450	$650
Pacemaker V2/V102 (Tube)			
	1965-1966. U.S.-made tube amp, 18 watts, 1x10", replaced by solidstate Pacemaker model V1021.		
1965-1966		$925	$1,250
Pathfinder (Import)			
	1998-present. Compact amps with 1960s cosmetics.		
1998-2013	15, 15w, 1x8	$75	$100
2002-2023	10, 10w, 1x65	$60	$85
Pathfinder V1/V101 (Tube)			
	1965-1966. U.S.-made tube amp, 4 watts, 1x8", '66-'69 became U.S.-made solidstate V1011.		
1965-1966		$925	$1,250
Pathfinder V1011 (Solidstate)			
	1966-1968. U.S.-made solidstate, 25 watts peak power, 1x8".		
1966-1968		$425	$650
Royal Guardsman V1131/V1132			
	1966-1968. U.S.-made solidstate, 50 watts piggyback, 2x12" + 1 horn, the model below the Super Beatle V1141/V1142.		
1966-1968		$1,250	$2,000
Scorpion (Solidstate)			
	1968. Solidstate, 120 watts, 4x10" Vox Oxford speaker.		
1968		$550	$750
Super Beatle Reissue Cabinet			
	2011-2012. 2x15" cab only.		
2011-2012		$350	$500
Super Beatle V1141/V1142			
	1965-1966. U.S.-made 120-watt solidstate, 4x12" + 2 horns, with distortion pedal (V1141), or without (V1142).		
1965-1966		$3,000	$4,500
T60			
	1962-1966. Solidstate bass head, around 40 watts, sold with 2x15" or 1x12" and 1x15" cabinet.		
1962-1966		$725	$1,000
VBM1 Brian May Special			
	2010. Compact 10-watt, 1x6" speaker, also called VBM1 Brian May Recording Amp, white cover, includes headphone/recording line out, Brian May logo on lower right grille.		
2010		$125	$200

MODEL YEAR	FEATURES	LOW	HIGH
Viscount V1151/V1152			
	1966-1968. U.S.-made solidstate, 70 watts, 2x12" combo, 1151, 1153, and 1154 with distortion.		
1966-1968		$800	$1,250
VT Valvetronix/Valvetronix + Series			
	2008-present. Line of digital modeling combo amps, ranging from the 15-watt, 1x8" VT15 ('08-'11) to the Valvetronix+ 120-watt, 2x12" VT120+.		
2008-2011	VT15	$100	$150
2012-2023	VT20+	$100	$150
2015-2016	VT80	$165	$250
2015-2023	VT40+	$150	$225
Westminster V118 Bass			
	1966-1969. Solidstate, 120 watts, 1x18".		
1966-1969		$650	$900

V-Series
See Crate.

Wabash
1950s. Private branded amps, made by others, distributed by the David Wexler company. They also offered lap steels and guitars.

Model 1158

1950s. Danelectro-made, 1x15", 2x6L6 power tubes, tweed.

		LOW	HIGH
1950s		$600	$850

Small Tube

		LOW	HIGH
1950s	3 tubes	$225	$350

Wallace Amplification
2000-present. Production/custom, professional grade, amps built by Brian Wallace in Livonia, Michigan. (Not affiliated with a 1970's amp company from the United Kingdom also called Wallace that has since gone out of business.)

Warbler
See listing under Juke amps.

Warwick
1982-present. Combos, amp heads and cabinets from Warwick Basses of Markneukirchen, Germany.

Washburn
1962-present. Imported guitar and bass amps. Washburn also offers guitars, banjos, mandolins, and basses.

Watkins
1957-present. England's Watkins Electric Music (WEM) was founded by Charlie Watkins. Their first commercial product was the Watkins Dominator (wedge Gibson stereo amp shape) in '57, followed by the Copicat Echo in '58. They currently build accordion amps.

Clubman

1960s. Small combo amp with typical Watkins styling, blue cover, white grille.

		LOW	HIGH
1960s		$750	$1,000

MODEL YEAR	FEATURES	LOW	HIGH

Dominator MK Series
1970s. Similar circuit to '50s tube amps except solidstate rectifier, 25 watts, different speaker used for different applications.

1970s	MK I, bass, 1x15	$550	$750
1970s	MK II, organ, 1x12	$550	$750
1970s	MK III, guitar, 1x12	$550	$750

Dominator V-Front
Late-1950s-1960s, 2004. 18 watts, 2x10", wedge cabinet similar to Gibson GA-79 stereo amp, tortoise and light beige cab, light grille, requires 220V step-up transformer. Was again offered in '04.

1959-1962		$2,500	$4,500

Joker
1960-1962. Watkins logo on front, 25-watt 1x12, tubes, 2-tone red and grey covering.

1960-1962		$2,500	$4,500

Scout
1960s. Watkins and Scout logo on top control panel, 17 watts, 1x10 combo, 6 tubes.

1960s		$1,000	$1,500

Westminster Tremolo
1959-1962. 10-watt 1x10" combo, Westminster Tremolo logo on top panel, 3 control knobs, blue and white cover.

1959-1962		$1,000	$1,500

Webcor
1940s-1950s. The Webster-Chicago Company built recording and audio equipment including portable amplifiers suitable for record turntables, PAs, or general utility. Low power with one or two small speakers.

Small

1950s	1 or 2 speakers	$325	$500

West Laboratories
1965-1970s, 2005-2015. Founded by David W. West in Flint, Michigan, moved to Lansing in '68. The '71 catalog included three tube and two solidstate amps, speaker cabinets, as well as Vocal Units and Mini Series combo amps. Amps were available as heads, piggyback half-stacks and full stacks, with the exception of the combo Mini Series. The Fillmore tube amp head was the most popular model. West equipment has a West logo on the front and the cabinets also have a model number logo on the grille. David West reestablished his company in 2005, located in Okemos, Michigan, with models offered on a custom order basis, concentrating on lower power EL84 designs. West died November, '15.

Avalon Head
1965-1970s. 50 watts, 2 6CA7 output tubes.

1965-1970s		$850	$1,250

Fillmore Head
1970s. 200 watts, 4 KT88 output tubes.

1965-1970s		$1,500	$2,500

Grande Head
1970s. 100 watts, 2 KT88 output tubes.

1965-1970s		$1,000	$1,500

MODEL YEAR	FEATURES	LOW	HIGH

Mini IR
1970s. 50 watts, 1x12 tube combo with reverb, black tolex, large West logo and model name Mini IR on front panel.

1965-1970s		$1,000	$1,500

White
1955-1960. The White brand, named after plant manager Forrest White, was established by Fender to provide steel and small amp sets to teaching studios that were not Fender-authorized dealers. The amps were sold with the matching steel guitar. See Steel section for pricing.

White (Matamp)
See Matamp listing.

Winfield Amplification
2001-present. Intermediate and professional grade, production, vacuum tube amps built by Winfield N. Thomas first in Greensboro, Vermont and presently in Cochise, Arizona.

Wizard
1988-present. Professional and premium grade, production/custom, guitar and bass, amps and cabinets built by Rick St Pierre in Cornwall, Ontario.

Woodson
Early 1970s. Obscure builder from Bolivar, Missouri. Woodson logo on front panel and Woodson Model and Serial Number plate on back panel, solidstate circuit, student level pricing.

Working Dog
2001-2014. Lower cost tube amps and combos built by Alessandro High-End Products (Alessandro, Hound Dog) in Huntingdon Valley, Pennsylvania.

Wright Amplification
Aaron C. Wright builds his professional grade, production/custom, amps and cabinets in Lincoln, Nebraska starting in 2004.

Yamaha
1946-present. Yamaha started building amps in the '60s and offered a variety of guitar and bass amps over the years. The current models are solidstate bass amps. They also build guitars, basses, effects, sound gear and other instruments.

Budokan HY-10G II
1987-1992. Portable, 10 watts, distortion control, EQ.

1987-1992		$55	$75

Budokan HY-20G
1988-1992. Portable, 20 watts, distortion, EQ.

1988-1992		$65	$85

G30-112
1983-1992. Solidstate combo, 30 watts, 1x12".

1983-1992		$130	$175

1970s Watkins Dominator MK III
Jeffrey Phelps

AMPS

Wallace Amplification Sophia

West Laboratories Mini I
Mark Harvey

1968 Yamaha TA-60
Tom Pfeifer

Yamaha YTA-95

AMPS

MODEL YEAR	FEATURES	LOW	HIGH
G50-112			
1983-1992. 50 watts, 1x12".			
1983-1992		$175	$250
G100-112			
1983-1992. 100 watts, 1x12" combo, black cover, striped grille.			
1983-1992		$175	$250
G100-212			
1983-1992. 100, 2x12" combo, black cover, striped grille.			
1983-1992		$200	$275
JX30B			
1983-1992. Bass amp, 30 watts.			
1983-1992		$125	$175
T50			
1988-1992. Made by Soldano, 50-watt head, 2 channels.			
1988-1992		$500	$750
T100			
1988-1992. Made by Soldano, 100-watt head, 2 channels.			
1988-1992		$850	$1,250
TA-20			
1968-1972. Upright wedge shape with controls facing upwards, solidstate.			
1968-1972		$100	$150
TA-25			
1968-1972. Upright wedge shape with controls facing upwards, 40 watts, 1x12", solidstate, black or red cover.			
1968-1972		$125	$175
TA-30			
1968-1972. Upright wedge shape, solidstate.			
1968-1972		$150	$200

MODEL YEAR	FEATURES	LOW	HIGH
TA-50			
1971-1972. Solidstate combo, 80 watts, 2x12", includes built-in cart with wheels, black cover.			
1971-1972		$150	$200
TA-60			
1968-1972. Upright wedge shape, solidstate, most expensive of wedge-shape amps.			
1968-1972		$450	$650
VR3000			
1988-1992. Combo 1x12", 2 channels, identical control sections for each channel, settings are completely independent.			
1988-1992		$125	$175
VR4000			
1988-1992. 50-watt stereo, 2 channels, EQ, stereo chorus, reverb and dual effects loops.			
1988-1992		$200	$275
VR6000			
1988-1992. 100-watt stereo, 2 channels which can also be combined, EQ, chorus, reverb and dual effects loops.			
1988-1992		$500	$700
VX-15			
1988-1992. 15 watts.			
1988-1992		$100	$150
VX-65D Bass			
1984-1992. 80 watts, 2 speakers.			
1984-1992		$125	$175
YBA-65 Bass			
1972-1976. Solidstate combo, 60 watts, 1x15".			
1972-1976		$125	$175
YTA-25			
1972-1976. Solidstate combo, 25 watts, 1x12".			
1972-1976		$125	$175

MODEL YEAR	FEATURES	LOW	HIGH

YTA-45
1972-1976. Solidstate combo, 45 watts, 1x12".

| 1972-1976 | | $125 | $175 |

YTA-95
1972-1976. Solidstate combo, 90 watts, 2x12".

| 1972-1976 | | $125 | $175 |

YTA-100
1972-1976. Solidstate piggyback, 100 watts, 2x12".

| 1972-1976 | | $150 | $200 |

YTA-110
1972-1976. Solidstate piggyback, 100 watts, 2x12" in extra-large cab.

| 1972-1976 | | $150 | $200 |

YTA-200
1972-1976. Solidstate piggyback, 200 watts, 4x12".

| 1972-1976 | | $175 | $250 |

YTA-300
1972-1976. Solidstate piggyback, 200 watts, dual cabs with 2x12" and 4x12".

| 1972-1976 | | $275 | $375 |

YTA-400
1972-1976. Solidstate piggyback, 200 watts, dual 4x12".

| 1972-1976 | | $275 | $375 |

Z.Vex Amps

2002-present. Intermediate grade, production amps built by Zachary Vex in Minneapolis, Minnesota with some subassembly work done in Michigan. He also builds effects.

Zapp

Ca.1978-early-1980s. Zapp amps were distributed by Red Tree Music, Inc., of Mamaroneck, New York.

Z-10
1978-1980s. Small student amp, 8 watts.

| 1979-1982 | | $25 | $40 |

Z-50
1978-1980s. Small student amp, 10 watts, reverb, tremelo.

| 1978-1982 | | $30 | $50 |

Zeppelin Design Labs

2014-present. Brach Siemens and Glen van Alkemade build budget and intermediate grade amps and cabinets in Chicago, Illinois. They also offer their products as DIY kits.

Zeta

1982-2010. Solid state amps with MIDI options, made in Oakland, California. They also made upright basses and violins.

Zinky

Tube head and combo amps and cabinets built by Bruce Zinky, starting in 1999, in Flagstaff, Arizona. He also builds the mini Smokey amps (since '97), effects, and has revived the Supro brand on a guitar and amp.

ZT Amplifiers

2009-present. Ken Kantor of Berkeley, California imports intermediate grade, production, solid state compact amps from China. He also offers effects.

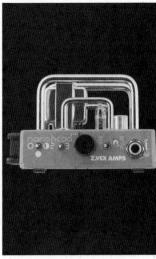

Z.Vex Nano Head

AMPS

ZT Jazz Club

EFFECTS

Ace Tone Fuzz Master FM-2
Antonio Rebolledo Ferrari

ADA MP-1

Akai E2 Headrush

EFFECTS

MODEL YEAR	FEATURES	LOW	HIGH

Vintage pedals and effects are the most volatile segment in the vintage guitar marketplace. Their values can change rapidly. This is because there are many "influencers" on YouTube that demonstrate and compare effects. Some pedals become very popular after being featured.

Two prices are shown for the effects. The first is the median price of an all-original pedal that functions perfectly. The vast majority of these vintage pedals will show signs of wear and tear. The second is the "exceptional condition price." This is for an all-original excellent condition pedal that still functions perfectly. Pedals that come in their original box, have associated "box candy" (instructions, warranty cards, stickers, etc.), and no Velcro or tape marks on bottom are highly desired. Collectors will often pay 10- to 20-percent more for these pedals.

Able Electronics
1990s. Started by John Rogers and based in Pwllheli, Wales.
Bassmaker
1990s. Octave pedal.

1990s		$250	$350

Ace Tone
1968-1972. Effects from Ace Electronic Industry, which was a part of Sakata Shokai Limited of Osaka, Japan, which also made organs, amps, pioneering Rhythm Ace FR-1 and FR-2 drum machines, etc. Their Ace Tone effects line was the predecessor to Roland and Boss.
Echo Chamber EC-10
1968-1972. Solidstate tape echo.

1968-1972		$650	$850

Expander EXP-4
1968-1972. "Expander" effect.

1968-1972		$350	$500

Fuzz Master FM-1
1968-1972. Distortion and overdrive.

1968-1972		$650	$850

Fuzz Master FM-2
1968-1972. Fuzz. Black housing. 2 Control knobs.

1968-1972		$300	$450

Fuzz Master FM-3
1968-1972. Distortion and clean boost.

1968-1972		$475	$700

Stereo Phasor LH-100
1968-1972. Phaser.

1968-1972		$600	$775

Wah Master WM-1
1968-1972. Filter wah.

1968-1972		$130	$175

Acoustyx
1977-1982. Made by the Highland Corporation of North Springfield, Vermont.
Image Synthesizer IS-1
1977-ca.1982. Synthesizer effects.

1977-1982		$75	$100

MODEL YEAR	FEATURES	LOW	HIGH

Phase Five
1977-ca.1982. Used 6 C cell batteries!

1977-1982		$75	$100

ADA
1975-2002. Analog/Digital Associates was located in Berkeley, California, and introduced its Flanger and Final Phase in '77. The company later moved to Oakland and made amplifiers, high-tech signal processors, and a reissue of its original Flanger.
Final Phase
1977-1979. Reissued in '97.

1977-1979		$400	$500

Flanger
1977-1983, 1996-2002. Reissued in '96.

1977-1979	No control pedal	$400	$500
1977-1979	With control pedal	$450	$575
1980-1983		$100	$150
1996-2002		$275	$350

MP-1
1987-1995. Tube preamp with chorus and effects loop, MIDI.

1987-1995	No foot controller	$400	$650
1987-1995	With optional foot controller	$550	$875

MP-2
Ca.1988-1995. Tube preamp with chorus, 9-band EQ and effects loop, MIDI.

1988-1995		$600	$950

Pitchtraq
1987. Programmable pitch transposer including octave shifts.

1987		$250	$350

Stereo Tapped Delay STD-1
Introduced in 1981.

1980s		$250	$450

TFX4 Time Effects
Introduced in 1982, includes flanger, chorus, doubler, echo.

1980s		$250	$350

Aguilar
1995-present. The New York, New York amp builder also offers a line of tube and solidstate pre-amps.

Akai (Akai Electric Company Ltd.)
1984-present. In '99, Akai added guitar effects to their line of electronic samplers and sequencers for musicians.
UniBass UB1
2000s. Bass octave pedal.

2000s		$225	$450

Alamo
1947-1982. Founded by Charles Eilenberg, Milton Fink, and Southern Music, San Antonio, Texas. Distributed by Bruno & Sons. Mainly known for guitars and amps, Alamo did offer a reverb unit.

MODEL YEAR	FEATURES	LOW	HIGH

Reverb Unit
1965-ca.1979. Has a Hammond reverb system, balance and intensity controls. By '73 the unit had 3 controls - mixer, contour, and intensity.

1965-1970		$375	$550

Alesis
1992-present. Alesis has a wide range of products for the music industry, including digital processors and amps for guitars.

Allen Amplification
1998-present. David Allen's company, located in Richwood, Kentucky, mainly produces amps, but they also offer a tube overdrive pedal.

Altair Corp.
1977-1980s. The company was in Ann Arbor, Michigan.

Power Attenuator PW-5
1977-1980. Goes between amp and speaker to dampen volume.

1977-1980		$85	$200

Amdek
Mid-1980s. Amdek offered many electronic products over the years, including drum machines and guitar effects. Most of these were sold in kit form so the quality of construction can vary.

Delay Machine DMK-200
1983. Variable delay times.

1983		$225	$350

Octaver OCK-100
1983. Produces tone 1 or 2 octaves below the note played.

1983		$125	$200

Phaser PHK-100
1983		$85	$135

Phlanger
1983		$85	$135

Ampeg
Ampeg entered the effects market in the late-1960s. Their offerings in the early-'60s were really amplifier-outboard reverb units similar to the ones offered by Gibson (GA-1). Ampeg offered a line of imported effects in '82-'83, known as the A-series (A-1 through A-9), and reintroduced effects to their product line in '05.

Analog Delay A-8
1982-1983. Made in Japan.

1982-1983		$225	$300

Chorus A-6
1982-1983. Made in Japan.

1982-1983		$150	$200

Compressor A-2
1982-1983. Made in Japan.

1982-1983		$150	$200

Distortion A-1
1982-1983. Made in Japan.

1982-1983		$150	$200

Echo Jet Reverb EJ-12
1963-1965. Outboard, alligator clip reverb unit with 12" speaker, 12 watts, technically a reverb unit. When used as a stand-alone amp, the reverb is off. Named EJ-12A in '65.

1963-1965		$600	$800

Echo Satellite ES-1
1961-1963. Outboard reverb unit with amplifier and speaker alligator clip.

1961-1963		$650	$850

Flanger A-5
1982-1983. Made in Japan.

1982-1983		$150	$200

Multi-Octaver A-7
1982-1983. Made in Japan.

1982-1983		$150	$200

Over Drive A-3
1982-1983. Made in Japan.

1982-1983		$150	$200

Parametric Equalizer A-9
1982-1983. Made in Japan.

1982-1983		$150	$200

Phaser A-4
1982-1983. Made in Japan.

1982-1983		$150	$200

Phazzer
1975-1979. Phase shifter, single speed knob.

1975-1979		$250	$350

Scrambler Fuzz
1969-1970. Distortion pedal, black housing. 2 Control knobs. Reissued in '05.

1969-1970		$600	$1,250

Sub Blaster SCP-OCT
2005-2007. Bass octave pedal.

2005-2007		$350	$450

Amplifier Corporation of America
Late '60s company that made amps for Univox and marketed effects under their own name.

Amptweaker
2010-present. James Brown, an amp design engineer previously employed by Peavey, then for Kustom amps, now designs and builds effects in Batavia, Ohio.

amukaT Gadgets
Guitar effects built by Takuma Kanaiwa, starting 2006, in New York, New York.

Analog Man
1994-present. Founded by Mike Piera in '94 with full-time production by 2000. Located in Danbury, Connecticut (until '07 in Bethel), producing chorus, compressor, fuzz, and boost pedals by '03.

Astro Tone
2000s-present. Fuzz.

2000s-2023		$160	$350

Bad Bob
2000s-present. Boost.

2000s-2023		$160	$250

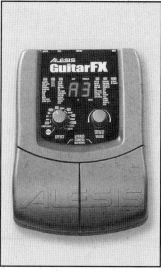
Ampeg Scrambler Fuzz

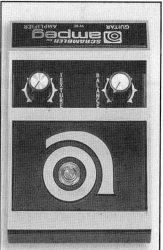
Ampeg Scrambler Fuzz

Amptweaker Big Rock Pro II

Analog.Man King of Tone

Analog.Man Sun Face

1967 Applied Big Bass Boost
Rivington Guitars

MODEL YEAR	FEATURES	LOW	HIGH
Beano Boost			
2000s-present. Boost.			
2000s-2023		$185	$275
Dual Analog Delay			
2000s-present. Delay.			
2000s-2023		$350	$525
Envelope Filter			
2000s-present. Envelope 'auto-wah'.			
2000s-2023		$175	$250
Juicer			
2000s-present. Compressor.			
2000s-2023		$150	$200
King of Tone			
2000s-present. Overdrive pedal, 4 generations, numerous options available.			
2000s-2023		$575	$950
Peppermint Fuzz			
2000s-present. Fuzz.			
2000s-2023		$145	$250
Prince of Tone			
2000s-present. Overdrive.			
2000s-2023		$185	$200
Sun Bender			
2000s-present. Fuzz.			
2000s-2023		$250	$350
Sun Face			
2000s-present. Fuzz.			
2000s-2023		$275	$400
2010s-2015 White Dot NKT 275		$1,500	$2,000

Aphex Systems

1975-present. Founded in Massachusetts by Marvin Caesar and Curt Knoppel, to build their Aural Exciter and other pro sound gear. Currently located in Sun Valley, California, and building a variety of gear for the pro audio broadcast, pro music and home-recording markets.

Apollo

Ca.1967-1972. Imported from Japan by St. Louis Music, includes Fuzz Treble Boost Box, Crier Wa-Wa, Deluxe Fuzz. They also offered basses and guitars.

Crier Wa-Wa			
Ca.1967-1972.			
1967-1972		$150	$250
Fuzz/Deluxe Fuzz			
Ca.1967-1972. Includes the Fuzz Treble Boost Box and the Deluxe Fuzz.			
1967-1972		$150	$250
Surf Tornado Wah Wah			
Ca.1967-1972.			
1967-1972		$275	$350

Applied

1960s. Effects brand of the Goya Music Company. Some models may have been sold under the Nomad brand.

Banshee Fuzz			
1960s. Also sold as the Nomad Banshee Fuzz.			
1960s		$175	$300

Arbiter

Ivor Arbiter and Arbiter Music, London, began making the circular Fuzz Face stompbox in 1966. Other products included the Fuzz Wah and Fuzz Wah Face. In '68 the company went public as Arbiter and Western, later transitioning to Dallas-Arbiter. Refer to Dallas-Arbiter for listings.

Area 51

2003-present. Guitar effects made in Newaygo, Michigan (made in Texas until early '06), by Dan Albrecht. They also build amps.

Aria/Aria Pro II

1956-present. Aria provided a line of effects, made by Maxon, in the mid-'80s.

Analog Delay AD-10			
1983-1985. Dual-stage stereo.			
1983-1985		$100	$150
Chorus ACH-1			
1986-1987. Stereo.			
1986-1987		$75	$100
Chorus CH-10			
1983-1985. Dual-stage stereo.			
1983-1985		$75	$100
Chorus CH-5			
1985-1987		$75	$100
Compressor CO-10			
1983-1985		$75	$100
Digital Delay ADD-100			
1984-1986. Delay, flanging, chorus, doubling, hold.			
1984-1986		$125	$175
Digital Delay DD-X10			
1985-1987		$125	$175
Distortion DT-10			
1983-1985. Dual stage.			
1983-1985		$75	$100
Distortion DT-5			
1985-1987		$75	$100
Flanger AFL-1			
1986. Stereo.			
1986		$75	$100
Flanger FL-10			
1983-1985. Dual-stage stereo.			
1983-1985		$75	$100
Flanger FL-5			
1985-1987		$75	$100
Metal Pedal MP-5			
1985-1987		$75	$100
Noise Gate NG-10			
1983-1985		$50	$75
Over Drive OD-10			
1983-1985. Dual stage.			
1983-1985		$75	$100
Parametric Equalizer EQ-10			
1983-1985		$75	$100
Phase Shifter PS-10			
1983-1984. Dual stage.			
1983-1984		$75	$100

MODEL YEAR	FEATURES	LOW	HIGH

Programmable Effects Pedal APE-1

1984-1986. Compression, distortion, delay, chorus.

| 1984-1986 | | $175 | $250 |

Arion

1984-2014. Arion offers a wide variety of budget imported effects.

Guitar and Bass Effects

| 1984-2014 | | $25 | $100 |

Arteffect

Tom Kochawi and Dan Orr started building analog effects in 2006, in Haifa and Natanya, Israel.

Artesania Sonora Lab

2010s-present. Based in Fortaleza, Brazil.

Fabrica del Fuzz

| 2016-2023 | | $100 | $150 |

Asama

1970s-1980s. This Japanese company offered solidbody guitars with built-in effects as well as stand-alone units. They also offered basses, drum machines and other music products.

Astro Amp

Late 1960s. Universal Amplifier Corporation of New York City made and sold Astro Amps as well as Astro effects. The company also made the Sam Ash Fuzzz Boxx.

Astrotone

| 1966 | | $1,000 | $1,500 |

ATD

Mid-1960s-early 1980s. Made by the All-Test Devices corporation of Long Beach, New York. In the mid-'60s, Richard Minz and an associate started making effects part-time, selling them through Manny's Music in New York. They formed All-Test and started making Maestro effects and transducer pickups for CMI, which owned Gibson at the time. By '75, All-Test was marketing effects under their own brand. All-Test is still making products for other industries, but by the early to mid-'80s they were no longer making products for the guitar.

PB-1 Power Booster

1976-ca.1980.

| 1979-1980 | | $100 | $150 |

Volume Pedal EV-1

1979-ca.1980.

| 1979-1980 | | $100 | $150 |

Wah-Wah/Volume Pedal WV-1

1979-ca.1981.

| 1979-1981 | | $100 | $150 |

Audio Disruption Devices

2010s. Based in Mooresville, Indiana.

Optical Ring V2

2010s. Ring modulator.

| 2010s | | $150 | $200 |

Audio Matrix

1979-1984. Effects built by B.K Butler in Escondido, California. He later designed the Tube Driver and founded Tube Works in 1987. He now operates Butler Audio, making home and auto hybrid tube stereo amps.

Mini Boogee B81

1981. Four-stage, all-tube preamp, overdrive, distortion.

| 1981 | | $250 | $500 |

Audio-Phonic

1970s. Effects built in Argentina.

Mu-Tron III

1970s. Musitronics Mu-Tron III copy.

| 1970s | | $800 | $1,500 |

Audioworks

1980s. The company was located in Niles, Illinois.

F.E.T. Distortion

| 1980s | | $75 | $100 |

Auralux

2000-2011. Founded by Mitchell Omori and David Salzmann, Auralux built effects and tube amps in Highland Park, Illinois.

Austone Electronics

1997-2009. Founded by Jon Bessent and Randy Larkin, Austone offered a range of stomp boxes, all made in Austin, Texas. Bessent passed away in '09.

Overdrive and Fuzz Pedals

1997-2009. Various overdrive and fuzz boxes.

| 1997-2009 | | $200 | $250 |

Automagic

Wah pedals and distortion boxes made in Germany by Musician Sound Design, starting in 1998.

Avalanche

Late 1980s. Effects built by Brian Langer in Toronto, Ontario.

Brianizer

Late-1980s. Leslie effect, dual rotor, adjustable speed and rate.

| 1980s | | $150 | $200 |

Axe

1980s. Early '80s line of Japanese effects, possibly made by Maxon.

B&M

1970s. A private brand made by Sola/Colorsound for Barns and Mullens, a U.K. distributor.

Fuzz Unit

1970s. Long thin orange case, volume, sustain, tone knobs, on-off stomp switch.

| 1970s | | $1,000 | $1,500 |

Area 51 The Alienist

1985 Aria DT-10 Distortion
Rivington Guitars

EFFECTS

Banzai Cold Fusion Overdrive

Bad Cat Double Drive

BBE Sonic Stomp

Beigel Sound Lab Tru-Tron 3X

MODEL YEAR	FEATURES	LOW	HIGH

Backline Engineering

Guitar multi-effects built by Gary Lee, starting 2004 in Camarillo, California. In '07, they added tube amps.

Bad Cat Amplifier Company

2000-present. Amp company Bad Cat, originally of Corona, California, also offers guitar effects. In '09 the company was moved to Anaheim.

Baldwin

1965-1970. The piano maker got into the guitar market when it acquired Burns of London in '65 and sold the guitars in the U.S. under the Baldwin name. They also marketed a couple of effects at the same time.

Banzai

2000-present. Effects built by Olaf Nobis in Berlin, Germany.

Bartolini

The pickup manufacturer offered a few effects from around 1982 to '87.

Tube-It

1982-ca.1987. Marshall tube amplification simulator with bass, treble, sustain controls.

1982-1987	Red case	$300	$400

Basic Systems' Side Effects

1980s. This company was in Tulsa, Oklahoma.

Audio Delay

1986-ca.1987. Variable delay speeds.

1986-1987		$150	$200

Triple Fuzz

1986-ca.1987. Selectable distortion types.

1986-1987		$100	$150

BBE

1985-present. BBE, owner of G&L Guitars and located in California, manufactures rack-mount effects and added a new line of stomp boxes in '05.

Behringer

1989-present. The German professional audio products company added modeling effects in '01 and guitar stomp boxes in '05. They also offer guitars and amps.

Beigel Sound Lab

Music product designer Mike Beigel helped form Musitronics Corp, where he made the Mu-Tron III. In 1978 he started Beigel Sound Lab to provide product design in Warwick, New York, where in '80 he made 50 rackmount Enveloped Controlled Filters under this brand name. In 2013, Mike Beigel's Beigel Sound Lab started making a Mu-FX Tru-Tron 3X and Octave Divider.

Boostron 3

2016-2017. Combines preamp boost, compression, and distortion in one pedal.

2016-2017		$350	$475

MODEL YEAR	FEATURES	LOW	HIGH

Octave Divider

2015. Updated and expanded version of original Musitronics Mu-Tron Octave Divider.

2015		$400	$900

Tru-Tron 3X

2015-2019. Updated and expanded version of original Musitronics Mu-Tron III envelope filter.

2015-2019		$400	$900

Bell Electrolabs

1970s. This English company offered a line of effects in the '70s.

Vibrato

1970s		$150	$200

Bennett Music Labs

Effects built in Chatanooga, Tennessee by Bruce Bennett.

Bigsby

1948-1966. Paul Bigsby made steel guitars, pedal steels, and electric guitars and mandolins, as well as developing the Bigsby vibrato tailpiece and other components.

Foot Volume and Tone Control

1950s-1960s. Beautifully crafted pedal in a cast-aluminum housing featuring a side-to-side tone sweep.

1950s-60s		$500	$650

Binson

Late 1950s-1982. Binson, of Milan, Italy, made several models of the Echorec, using tubes or transistors. They also made units for Guild, Sound City and EKO.

Echorec

Ca.1960-1979. Four knob models with 12 echo selections, 1 head, complex multitap effects, settings for record level, playback and regeneration. Includes B1, B2, Echomaster1, T5 (has 6 knobs), T5E, and Baby. Used a magnetic disk instead of tape. Guild later offered the Guild Echorec by Binson which is a different stripped-down version.

1960s	Tube	$6,000	$8,000
1970s	Solidstate	$1,500	$2,000

Bixonic

1995-2007. The round silver distortion pedals were originally distributed by SoundBarrier Music, later by Godlyke, Inc.

Expandora EXP-2000

1995-2000. Analog distortion, round silver case, internal DIP switches.

1995-2000		$200	$250

Expandora EXP-2000R

2005-2007. Reissue, round silver case with red print.

2005-2007		$250	$350

Black Arts Toneworks

2010s. Founded by Mark Wentz of Chattanooga, Tennessee.

Pharaoh

2010s		$100	$150

MODEL YEAR	FEATURES	LOW	HIGH

Ritual Fuzz
2010s. Inspired by the Colorsound Fuzz Box.

2010s		$100	$150

Black Cat Pedals

1993-2007, 2009-2022. Founded by Fred Bonte and located in Texas until late 2007 when production was discontinued. In '09, using Bonte's same designs, new owner Tom Hughes restarted production in Foxon, Connecticut.

Black Cat OD-1
2010-2022. Overdrive.

2010-2022		$100	$150

Blackbox Music Electronics

2000-2009. Founded by Loren Stafford and located in Minneapolis, Minnesota, Blackbox offered a line of effects for guitar and bass. The Blackbox models are now made under the Ooh La La brand.

Blackout Effectors

Kyle Tompkins began building effects pedals in 2007, in Vancouver, British Columbia and now builds them in Asheville, North Carolina.

Blackstar Amplification

2007-present. Guitar effects pedals built by Joel Richardson in Northampton, U.K. He also builds amps.

Blackstone Appliances

1999-present. Distortion effects crafted by Jon Blackstone in New York City.

Mosfet Overdrive
1999-present. Though the designation doesn't appear on the housing, the original was subsequently called 2Sv1 after later versions were issued.

1999	2Sv1, no controls on top	$250	$325
2000	2Sv2	$200	$275
2006-2023	2Sv3, 2Sv31, 2Sv32, 2Sv33	$200	$275
2012	Billybox Limited Edition	$300	$400

Bon, Mfg

Bon was in Escondido, California.

Tube Driver 204
1979-ca.1981.

1979-1981		$150	$200

Boomerang

1995-present. Effects pedals built in Grapevine, Texas by Boomerang Musical Products, Ltd.

Boss

1976-present. Japan's Roland Corporation first launched effect pedals in '74. A year or two later the subsidiary company, Boss, debuted its own line. They were marketed concurrently at first but gradually Boss became reserved for effects and drum machines while the Roland name was used

on amplifiers and keyboards. Boss still offers a wide line of pedals.

Acoustic Simulator AC-2
1997-2007. Four modes that emulate various acoustic tones.

1997-2007		$60	$85

Acoustic Simulator AC-3
2007-present. Four modes that emulate various acoustic tones.

2007-2023		$60	$125

Auto Wah AW-2
1991-1999. Becomes Dynamic Wah (AW-3) in 2000.

1991-1999		$70	$125

Bass Chorus CE-2B

1987-1995		$85	$135

Bass Equalizer GE-7B
1987-1995. Seven-band, name changed to GEB-7 in '95.

1987-1995		$70	$125

Bass Flanger BF-2B

1987-1994		$90	$150

Bass Limiter LM-2B

1990-1994		$60	$85

Bass Limiter/Enhancer LMB-3

1990s		$60	$125

Bass Overdrive ODB-3
1994-present. Yellow case.

1994-2023		$60	$125

Blues Driver BD-2
1995-present. Blue case.

1995-2023		$75	$90
1995-2023	Keeley modded	$225	$300

Chorus Ensemble CE-1
1976-1978. Vibrato and chorus.

1976-1978		$750	$1,000

Chorus Ensemble CE-2

1979-1982		$250	$350

Chorus Ensemble CE-3

1982-1992		$70	$175

Chorus Ensemble CE-5
1991-present. Pale blue case.

1991-2020		$60	$125

Compressor Sustainer CS-1

1978-1982		$90	$175

Compressor Sustainer CS-2

1981-1986		$130	$185

Compressor Sustainer CS-3
1986-present. Blue case.

1986-2023		$65	$85
1986-2023	JHS modded	$125	$175

Delay DM-2
1979-1985. Analog, hot pink case.

1979-1980	MN3025 Chip	$350	$400
1981-1985	MN3005 Chip	$200	$250

Delay DM-3

1984-1988		$150	$200

Digital Delay DD-2

1983-1986		$150	$250

Black Arts Toneworks
Pharaoh Supreme
Rivington Guitars

Blackstone Mosfet Overdrive

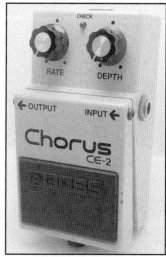

Boss Chorus Ensemble CE-2
Keith Myers

To get the most from this book, be sure to read "Using *The Guide*" in the introduction.

1984 Boss Distortion DS-1
Rivington Guitars

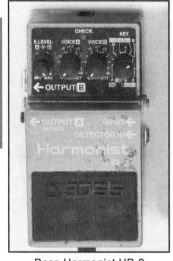

Boss Harmonist HR-2
Imaged by Heritage Auctions, HA.com

Boss Metal Zone MT-2

MODEL YEAR	FEATURES	LOW	HIGH
Digital Delay DD-3			
	1986-present. Up to 800 ms of delay, white case.		
1986-1989		$90	$150
1986-2023	Keeley modded	$150	$250
1990-2023		$75	$125
Digital Delay DD-5			
	1995-2005. Up to 2 seconds of delay.		
1995-2005		$90	$150
Digital Delay DD-6			
	2003-2007. Up to 5 seconds of delay.		
2003-2007		$75	$125
Digital Delay DD-7			
	2008-2022. Up to 6.4 seconds of delay, crème case.		
2008-2022		$90	$135
Digital Dimension C DC-2			
	1985-1989. Two chorus effects and tremolo.		
1985-1989		$250	$350
Digital Metalizer MZ-2			
1987-1992		$150	$250
Digital Reverb RV-2			
1987-1990		$120	$200
Digital Reverb RV-5			
	2003-2019. Dual input and dual output, four control knobs, silver case.		
2003-2019		$90	$125
Digital Reverb/Delay RV-3			
1994-2004		$120	$175
Digital Sampler/Delay DSD-2			
1985-1986		$120	$175
Digital Space-D DC-3/			
Digital Dimension DC-3			
	1988-1993. Originally called the Digital Space-D, later changed to Digital Dimension. Chorus with EQ.		
1988-1993		$175	$275
Digital Stereo Reverb RV-70			
	1994-1995. Rack mount, MIDI control, reverb/ delay, 199 presets.		
1994-1995		$175	$225
Distortion DS-1			
	1978-1989, 1990s-present. Orange case.		
1978-1989		$125	$225
1978-2023	Keeley modded	$175	$250
1990-1999		$60	$80
2000-2023		$30	$40
Dr. Rhythm DR-55			
	1979-1989. Drum machine.		
1979-1989		$200	$400
Dual Over Drive SD-2			
1993-1998		$125	$165
Dynamic Filter FT-2			
	1986-1988. Auto wah.		
1986-1988		$225	$350
Dynamic Wah AW-3			
	2000-present. Auto wah with humanizer, for guitar or bass.		
2000-2023		$85	$125
Enhancer EH-2			
1990-1998		$60	$100
Flanger BF-1			
1977-1980		$225	$400

MODEL YEAR	FEATURES	LOW	HIGH
Flanger BF-2			
1980-1989		$125	$175
1990-2005		$90	$125
Foot Wah FW-3			
1992-1996		$90	$125
Graphic Equalizer GE-6			
	1978-1981. Six bands.		
1978-1981		$120	$175
Graphic Equalizer GE-7			
	1981-present. Seven bands, white case.		
1982-1989		$90	$150
1990-2023		$60	$80
1990-2023	Analogman modded	$250	$300
Graphic Equalizer GE-10			
	1976-1985. 10-band EQ for guitar or bass.		
1976-1985		$150	$300
Harmonist HR-2			
	1994-1999. Pitch shifter.		
1994-1999		$100	$125
Heavy Metal HM-2			
	1983-1991. Distortion.		
1983-1991		$150	$225
Hyper Fuzz FZ-2			
1993-1997		$225	$350
Hyper Metal HM-3			
1993-1998		$90	$150
Limiter LM-2			
1987-1992		$90	$125
Line Selector LS-2			
	1991-2021. Select between 2 effects loops, white case.		
1991-2021	With adapter	$60	$95
Mega Distortion MD-2			
	2003-present. Red case.		
2003-2023		$60	$80
Metal Zone MT-2			
	1991-present. Distortion and 3-band EQ, grey case.		
1991-2023		$125	$200
1991-2023	Keeley modded	$175	$225
Multi Effects ME-5			
	1988-1991. Floor unit.		
1988-1991		$120	$225
Multi Effects ME-6			
1992-1997		$70	$100
Multi Effects ME-8			
1996-1997		$125	$175
Multi Effects ME-20			
1990-2000s		$115	$150
Multi Effects ME-25			
1990-2000s		$120	$150
Multi Effects ME-30			
1998-2002		$90	$125
Multi Effects ME-50			
	2003-2009. Floor unit.		
2003-2009		$150	$195
Multi Effects ME-70			
2000s		$150	$200
Multi Effects ME-80			
	2000s-present.		
2000s-2023		$150	$200
Noise Gate NF-1			
1979-1988		$75	$95

The *Vintage Guitar Price Guide* shows values for an all-original condition guitar effect.

MODEL YEAR	FEATURES	LOW	HIGH
Noise Suppressor NS-2			
1987-present. White case.			
1987-2023		$60	$150
Octaver OC-2/Octave OC-2			
1982-2003. Originally called the Octaver.			
1982		$200	$275
1983-2003		$125	$175
Overdrive OD-1			
1977-1979		$400	$500
1980-1985		$300	$350
Overdrive OD-2			
1990s		$80	$125
Overdrive OD-3			
1997-present. Yellow case.			
1997-2023		$95	$125
Parametric Equalizer PQ-4			
1991-1997		$175	$300
Phase Shifter PH-3			
2000-present. Added effects, light green case.			
2000-2023		$85	$125
Phaser PH-1			
1977-1981. Green box, 2 knobs.			
1977-1981		$225	$300
Phaser PH-1R			
1982-1985. Resonance control added to PH-1.			
1982-1985		$175	$225
Phaser PH-2			
1984-2001. 12 levels of phase shift, 4 knobs.			
1984-2001		$80	$125
Pitch Sifter/Delay PS-2			
1987-1993		$135	$175
Reverb Box RX-100			
1981-mid-1980s.			
1981-1985		$135	$325
Rocker Distortion PD-1			
1980-mid-1980s. Variable pedal using magnetic field.			
1980-1985		$185	$250
Rocker Volume PV-1			
1981-mid-1980s.			
1980-1985		$60	$125
Rocker Wah PW-1			
1980-mid-1980s. Magnetic field variable pedal.			
1980-1985		$65	$125
Slow Gear SG-1			
1979-1982. Violin swell effect, automatically adjusts volume.			
1979-1982		$375	$500
Spectrum SP-1			
1977-1981. Single-band parametric EQ.			
1977-1981		$350	$650
Super Chorus CH-1			
1989-present. Blue case.			
1989-2023		$70	$95
Super Distortion & Feedbacker DF-2			
1984-1994. Also labeled as the Super Feedbacker & Distortion.			
1984-1994		$175	$250
Super Octave OC-3			
2004-2021. Brown case.			
2004-2021		$125	$175

MODEL YEAR	FEATURES	LOW	HIGH
Super Over Drive SD-1			
1981-present. Yellow case.			
1981-1989		$125	$225
1990-2023		$60	$85
Super Phaser PH-2			
1984-1989		$125	$175
1990-2001		$60	$80
Super Shifter PS-5			
1999-2013. Pitch shifter/harmonizer, aqua case.			
1999-2013		$125	$150
Touch Wah TW-1/T Wah TW-1			
1978-1987. Auto wah, early models were labeled as Touch Wah.			
1978-1987		$125	$175
Tremolo TR-2			
1997-present. Aqua case.			
1997-2023		$75	$95
1997-2023	Analogman modded	$200	$250
1997-2023	Keeley modded	$130	$175
Tremolo/Pan PN-2			
1990-1995		$275	$350
Turbo Distortion DS-2			
1987-present. Orange case.			
1987-2023		$75	$95
Turbo Over Drive OD-2			
1985-1994. Called OD-2R after '94, due to added remote on/off jack.			
1985-1994		$90	$125
Vibrato VB-2			
1982-1986. True pitch-changing vibrato, warm analog tone, 'rise time' control allows for slow attach, 4 knobs, aqua-blue case.			
1982-1986		$425	$675
Volume FV-50H			
1987-1997. High impedance, stereo volume pedal with inputs and outputs.			
1987-1997		$60	$85
Volume FV-50L			
1987-1997. Low impedance version of FV-50.			
1987-1997		$55	$75
Volume Pedal FV-100			
Late-1980s-1991. Guitar volume pedal.			
1987-1991		$45	$75

Brimstone Audio

2011-present. Shad Sundberg builds his guitar effects in California.

Browntone Electronics

2006-2012. Guitar effects built in Lincolnton, North Carolina by Tim Brown.

Bruno

Music distributor Bruno and Sons had a line of Japanese-made effects in the early '70s.

Fuzz Machine

1970s. Rebranded version of the Ibanez No. 59 Standard Fuzz.

MODEL YEAR	FEATURES	LOW	HIGH
1970s		$300	$400

Boss Super Over Drive SD-1
Rivington Guitars

1995 Boss Super Phaser PH-2
Rivington Guitars

EFFECTS

Boss Rocker Wah PW-1
Marco Antonio Rebolledo Ferrari

MODEL			
YEAR	FEATURES	LOW	HIGH

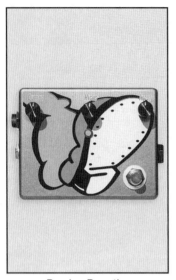

Burriss Boostier

Budda

1995-present. Wahs and distortion pedals originally built by Jeff Bober and Scott Sier in San Francisco, California. In '09, Budda was acquired by Peavey Electronics. They also build amps.

Bud Wah

1997-2018. Wah pedal.

1990s-2018		$135	$275

Phat Bass

2000s		$175	$275

Build Your Own Clone

2005-present. Build it yourself kits based on vintage effects produced by Keith Vonderhulls in Othello, Washington. Assembled kits are offered by their Canadian distributor.

Burriss

2001-present. Guitar effects from Bob Burriss of Lexington, Kentucky. He also builds amps.

Carl Martin

1993-present. Line of effects from Søren Jongberg and East Sound Research of Denmark. In '06 they added their Chinese-made Vintage Series. They also build amps.

Carl Martin Bass drive

Carlsbro

1959-present. English amp company Carlsbro Electronics Limited offered a line of effects from '77 to '81.

Fuzz

1970s. Tone Bender MkIII fuzz built by Sola Sound.

1970s		$800	$1,000

Suzz

1970s. Built by Sola Sound.

1970s		$500	$700

Suzz Wah Wah

1970s. Built by Sola Sound.

1970s		$200	$275

Carrotron

Late-1970s-mid-1980s. Carrotron was out of California and offered a line of effects.

Noise Fader C900B1

1981-ca.1982.

1981-1982		$75	$125

Preamp C821B

1981-ca.1982.

1981-1982		$75	$125

Carvin

1946-present. Carvin introduced its line of Ground Effects in '02 and discontinued them in '03.

Castle Instruments

Early 1980s. Castle was located in Madison, New Jersey, and made rackmount and floor phaser units.

Phaser III

1980-1982. Offered mode switching for various levels of phase.

1980-1982		$350	$500

Catalin Bread Sabbra Cadabra

Rivington Guitars

Catalinbread

2003-present. Nicholas Harris founded Catalinbread Specialized Mechanisms of Music in Seattle, Washington, in '02 to do mods and in '03 added his own line of guitar effects.

Adineko

2000s		$130	$180

Belle Epoch

2000s		$130	$180

Callisto

2000s		$130	$180

Echorec

2000s		$140	$195

Formula No. 5

2000s		$150	$230

Naga Viper

2000s		$100	$150

Perseus

2000s		$130	$160

Rah

2000s		$150	$180

Sabbra Cadabra

2000s		$130	$150

Semaphore

2000s		$130	$150

Super Chili Picoso

2000s		$100	$150

Topanga

2000s		$110	$175

Cat's Eye

Dean Solorzano and Lisa Kroeker began building their analog guitar effects in Oceanside, California in 2001.

Cause & Effect Pedals

Guitar effects pedals built in Ontario by Mark Roberts and Brian Alexson, starting in 2009.

Celmo

The Celmo Sardine Can Compressor is made by Kezako Productions in Montcaret, France, starting in 2008.

Chandler

Located in California, Chandler Musical Instruments offers instruments, pickups, and pickguards, as well as effects.

Digital Echo

1992-2000. Rackmount, 1 second delay, stereo.

1992-2000		$250	$500

Tube Driver

1984-1991. Uses a 12AX7 tube. Not to be confused with the Tube Works Tube Driver.

1984-1987	Made by BK Butler	$600	$800
1988-1991		$250	$300

Chapman

1970-present. From Emmett Chapman, maker of the Stick.

EFFECTS

MODEL YEAR	FEATURES	LOW	HIGH

Patch of Shades
1981, 1989. Wah, with pressure sensitive pad instead of pedal. 2 production runs.

1980s		$500	$650

Chicago Iron
1998-present. Faithful reproductions of classic effects built by Kurt Steir in Chicago, Illinois.

Chunk Systems
1996-present. Guitar and bass effects pedals built by Richard Cartwright in Sydney, Australia.

Clark
1960s. Built in Clark, New Jersey, same unit as the Orpheum Fuzz and the Mannys Music Fuzz.

SS-600 Fuzz
1960s. Chrome-plated, volume and tone knobs, toggle switch.

1960s		$250	$350

Clark Amplification
1995-present. Amplifier builder Mike Clark, of Cayce, South Carolina, offers a reverb unit and started building guitar effects as well, in '98.

ClinchFX
2006-present. Handmade pedals by Peter Clinch in Brisbane, Queensland, Australia.

CMI
1970s. English music company.

Fuzz Unit
1970s. Built by Colorsound based on its Jumbo Tone Bender.

1970s		$600	$800

Coffin
Case manufacturer Coffin Case added U.S.-made guitar effects pedals to their product line in 2006.

Cohrane
2010s. Effects built by Paul Cohrane.

Tim
2010s. Overdrive pedal.

2010s		$600	$700

Timmy
2010s. Upgraded from Tim pedal.

2010s		$250	$175

Timmy V3
2019. Overdrive pedal.

2019		$200	$250

Colorsound
1967-2010. Colorsound effects were produced by England's Sola Sound, beginning with fuzz pedals. In the late-'60s, wah and fuzz-wah pedals were added, and by the end of the '70s, Colorsound offered 18 different effects, an amp, and accessories. Few early Colorsound products were imported into the U.S., so today they're scarce. Except for the Wah-Wah pedal,

Colorsound's production stopped by the early '80s, but in '96 most of their early line was reissued by Dick Denny of Vox fame. Denny died in 2001. Since then, Anthony and Steve Macari have built Colorsound effects in London. Mutronics offered a licensed rack mount combination of 4 classic Colorsound effects for a short time in the early 2000s.

Chuck-a-Wah
1975-1977. Auto wah pedal.

1975-1977		$500	$650

Dipthonizer
1970s. "Talking" pedal with foot control.

1970s		$500	$650

Dopplatone Phase Unit
1970s. Large phase and vibrato effect with Bubble control.

1970s		$500	$650

Electro Echo
1979-1980s. Analog delay pedal.

1979-1980s		$500	$650

Flanger

1970s		$375	$500

FuzzPhaze
Introduced in 1973.

1970s		$500	$650

Jumbo Tone-Bender
1974-early 1980s. Replaced the Tone-Bender fuzz, with wider case and light blue lettering.

1974-1980s		$750	$1,750

Octivider
Introduced in 1973.

1970s		$600	$800

Overdriver
Introduced in 1972. Controls for drive, treble and bass.

1970s		$1,000	$2,000

Phazer
Introduced in 1973. Magenta/purple-pink case, slanted block Phazer logo on front.

1970s		$375	$500

Power Boost

1970s		$750	$975

Ring Modulator
Introduced in 1973. Purple case, Ring Modulator name with atom orbit slanted block logo on case.

1970s		$600	$800

Supa Tone Bender
1977-early 1980s. Sustain and volume knobs, tone control and toggle. Same white case as Jumbo Tone-Bender, but with new circuit.

1970s		$600	$800

Supa Wah-Swell
1970s. Supa Wah-Swell in slanted block letters on the end of the pedal, silver case.

1970s		$500	$650

Supaphase

1970s		$600	$800

Supasustain

1960s		$375	$500

Swell

1970s		$175	$300

Clark Amplification Gainster

ClinchFX EP-PRE

Colorsound Power Boost

EFFECTS

Coopersonic Germaniac

Crazy Tube Circuits Ziggy
Rivington Guitars

Crucial Audio Vacuum Tube
Direct Box Recording Interface

MODEL YEAR	FEATURES	LOW	HIGH
Tremolo			
1970s		$200	$300
Tremolo Reissue			
1996-2009. Purple case.			
1996-2009		$200	$300
Vocalizer			
1979-1980s. "Talking" pedal with foot control.			
1979-1980s		$1,000	$2,500
Wah Fuzz Straight			
Introduced in 1973. Aqua-blue case, Wah-Fuzz-Straight in capital block letters on end of wah pedal.			
1970s		$375	$500
Wah Fuzz Swell			
Introduced in 1973. Yellow case, block letter Wah Fuzz Swell logo on front, three control knobs and toggle.			
1970s		$500	$650
Wah Swell			
1970s. Light purple case, block letter Wah-Swell logo on front.			
1970s		$500	$650
Wah Wah			
1970s. Dark gray case, Wah-Wah in capital block letters on end of wah pedal.			
1975		$750	$975
Wah Wah Reissue			
1996-2005. Red case, large Colorsound letter logo and small Wah Wah lettering on end of pedal.			
1996-2005		$200	$275
Wah Wah Supremo			
1970s. Silver/chrome metal case, Wah-Wah Supremo in block letters on end of wah pedal.			
1975		$2,000	$2,500

Companion

1970s. Private branded by Shin-ei of Japan, which made effects for others as well.

MODEL YEAR	FEATURES	LOW	HIGH
Tape Echo			
1960-1970		$600	$800
Wah Pedal			
1970s		$250	$300

Conn

Ca.1968-ca.1978. Band instrument manufacturer and distributor Conn/Continental Music Company, of Elkhart, Indiana, imported guitars and effects from Japan.

MODEL YEAR	FEATURES	LOW	HIGH
Strobe Tuner			
Brown or later, grey, case.			
1960s	ST-4	$200	$350
1960s	ST-6	$200	$350
1960s	ST-8	$200	$350
1968	ST-2	$200	$350
1970s	Strobotuner ST-11	$200	$350
1970s	Strobotuner ST-12	$200	$350

Coopersonic

2006-present. Martin Cooper builds his guitar effects in Nottingham, UK.

Coron

1970s-1980s. Japanese-made effects, early ones are close copies of MXR pedals.

Cosmosound

Italy's Cosmosound made small amps with Leslie drums and effects pedals in the late '60s and '70s. Cosmosound logo is on top of pedals.

MODEL YEAR	FEATURES	LOW	HIGH
Wah Fuzz CSE-3			
1970s. Volume and distortion knobs, wah and distortion on-off buttons, silver case.			
1970s		$300	$400
Wild Sound			
1970s		$250	$300

Crazy Tube Circuits

2004-present. Guitar effects designed and built by Chris Ntaifotis in Athens, Greece.

Creation Audio Labs

2005-present. Guitar and bass boost pedal and re-amplifying gear built in Nashville, Tennessee.

Crowther Audio

1976-present. Guitar effects built by Paul Crowther, who was the original drummer of the band Split Enz, in Auckland, New Zealand. His first effect was the Hot Cake.

Crucial Audio

2005-present. Effects by Steve Kollander engineered and assembled in Sussex County, Delaware, with chassis manufactured by machine shops within the U.S. They also provide OEM products and design engineering services to companies including Matchless, Requisite Audio & West Coast Pedal Boards.

MODEL YEAR	FEATURES	LOW	HIGH
Apollo-18 Vacuum Tube Leslie Interface			
2015-present. High-voltage vacuum tube interface module for Leslie 122 or 147 type rotary speaker systems; can be used with a tube preamp and/or two channel vacuum tube direct box.			
2015-2023		$1,000	$1,250
Das Götterdämmerung - Germanium Fuzz/Ring Modulator			
2017-2023. Provides full function controls combined with germanium fuzz generated from matched NOS 2N404.			
2017-2023		$325	$400
Echo-Nugget Vacuum Tube Analog Delay			
2008-present. Tube-driven analog delay with selectable boost/tone preamp.			
2008-2023		$500	$600
Time Warp Vacuum Tube Analog Delay			
2008-present. Tube-driven analog delay with selectable modulation/warp function.			
2008-2023		$500	$600
Vacuum Tube Direct Box Recording Interface (DUB-5)			
2016-present. Interface for recording studios or live sound to sweeten the tone of instruments.			
2016-2023		$400	$500

Cruzer

Effects made by Korea's Crafter Guitars. They also build guitars, basses and amps under that brand.

MODEL YEAR	FEATURES	LOW	HIGH

Crybaby

See listing under Vox for early models, and Dunlop for recent versions.

CSL

1970s. Charles Summerfield Ltd., was an English music company with a line of effects made by Sola Sound.

Power Boost

1970s		$1,000	$1,500

Super Fuzz

1970s		$1,000	$1,500

Cusack Music

2003-present. Effects built in Holland, Michigan by Jon Cusack.

Dallas/Dallas Arbiter

Dallas Arbiter, Ltd. was based in London, and it appeared in the late-1960s as a division of a Dallas group of companies headed by Ivor Arbiter. Early products identified with Dallas logo with the company noted as John E. Dallas & Sons Ltd., Dallas Building, Clifton Street, London, E.C.2. They also manufactured Sound City amplifiers and made Vox amps from '72 to '78. The Fuzz Face is still available from Jim Dunlop.

Fuzz Face

1966-1975, 1977-1981, 1986-1987. Late '70s and '80s version was built for Dallas Arbiter by Crest Audio of New Jersey. The current reissue is built by Jim Dunlop USA (see that listing).

1966-1967	Grey, Black or Red, NKT275	$5,500	$7,000
1968-1969	Red, BC108	$2,500	$5,000
1970-1980	Blue	$1,000	$1,500
1981	Grey, reissue	$650	$1,000

Fuzz Wah Face

1970s	Black	$300	$400
1990s	Reissue copy	$85	$150

Rangemaster Fuzzbug

1966. Tone Bender Mk1.5 effect built by Sola Sound.

1966		$2,500	$3,000

Rangemaster Treble Booster

1966. 2000s. Grey housing. 1 Control knob. On-off slider switch. Old-style round-barrel 9-volt battery powered; many converted to later rectangular battery. Various current reissues built by JMI and other firms.

1966		$3,000	$4,000
2000s	JMI reissue	$350	$500

Sustain

1970s		$650	$900

Treble and Bass Face

1960s		$850	$1,250

Trem Face

Ca.1970-ca.1975. Reissued in '80s, round red case, depth and speed control knobs, Dallas-Arbiter England logo plate.

1970-1975		$850	$1,250

Wah Baby

1970s. Gray speckle case, Wah Baby logo caps and small letters on end of pedal.

1970s		$850	$1,250

Damage Control

2004-2009. Guitar effects pedals and digital multi-effects built in Moorpark, California. The company was founded with the release of a line of tube-driven effects pedals. In '09, it began developing products under the Strymon brand name.

Demonizer

2004-2009. Class A distortion preamp pedal powered by dual vacuum tubes.

2004-2009		$200	$275

Liquid Blues

2004-2009. Class A overdrive pedal powered by dual vacuum tubes.

2004-2009		$200	$275

Solid Metal

2004-2009. Class A distortion pedal powered by dual vacuum tubes.

2004-2009		$200	$275

TimeLine

2004-2009. Delay pedal powered by dual vacuum tubes.

2004-2009		$450	$600

Womanizer

2004-2009. Class A overdrive preamp pedal powered by dual vacuum tubes.

2004-2009		$250	$350

Dan Armstrong

1976-1981. In '76, Musitronics, based in Rosemont, New Jersey, introduced 6 inexpensive plug-in effects designed by Dan Armstrong. Perhaps under the influence of John D. MacDonald's Travis McGee novels, each effect name incorporated a color, like Purple Peaker. Shipping box labeled Dan Armstrong by Musitronics. They disappeared a few years later but were reissued by WD Products from '91 to '02 (See WD for those models). From '03 to '06, Vintage Tone Project offered the Dan Armstrong Orange Crusher. Since '06, a licensed line of Dan Armstrong effects that plug directly into the output of a guitar or bass (since '07 some also as stomp boxes) has been offered by Grafton Electronics of Grafton, Vermont. Dan Armstrong died in '04.

Blue Clipper

1976-1981. Fuzz, blue-green case.

1976-1981		$200	$300

Green Ringer

1976-1981. Ring Modulator/Fuzz, green case.

1976-1981		$300	$400

Orange Squeezer

1976-1981. Compressor, orange case.

1976-1981		$400	$500

Purple Peaker

1976-1981. Frequency Booster, light purple case.

1976-1981		$200	$300

Cusack Effects Tap-A-Delay
Rivington Guitars

1969 Dallas Arbiter Fuzz Face
Dean Nissen

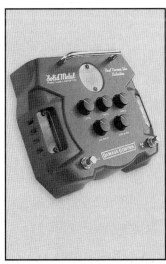

Damage Control Solid Metal

EFFECTS

MODEL YEAR	FEATURES	LOW	HIGH

Danelectro Daddy-O
Jim Schreck

Red Ranger
1976-1981. Bass/Treble Booster, light red case.

1976-1981		$150	$250

Yellow Humper
1976-1981. Yellow case.

1976-1981		$150	$250

Danelectro

1946-1969, 1996-present. The Danelectro brand was revived in '96 with a line of effects pedals. They have also offered the Wasabi line of effects. Prices do not include AC adapter, add $10 for the Zero-Hum adapter.

Chicken Salad Vibrato
2000-2009. Orange case.

2000-2009		$85	$110

Cool Cat Chorus
1996-2018. Blue case.

1996-2018		$75	$110

Corned Beef Reverb
2000-2009. Blue-black case.

2000-2009		$50	$65

Daddy-O Overdrive
1996-2009. White case.

1996-2009		$50	$65

Dan Echo
1998-2009. Lavender case.

1998-2009		$50	$75

Echo Box
1953-ca. 1958. Reverb unit, metal housing with black endplates.

1953-1958		$225	$450

Fab Tone Distortion
1996-2014. Red case.

1996-2014		$85	$110

Reel Echo
2000s. Light green case.

2000s		$125	$250

Reverb Unit Model 9100
1962-ca. 1967. Tube-driven spring reverb, long grey housing.

1962-1967		$600	$750

Daredevil

2012-present. Guitar effects pedals built in Chicago, Illinois by Johnny Wator.

Daredevil Silver Solo

Davoli

1960s-1970. Davoli was an Italian pickup and guitar builder and is often associated with Wandre guitars.

TRD
1970s. Solidstate tremolo, reverb, distortion unit.

1970s		$200	$275

DDyna Music

2008-present. Dan Simon builds his guitar effects pedals in Bothell, Washington.

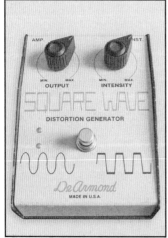

DeArmond Square Wave
Distortion Generator
Jim Schreck

Dean Markley

The string and pickup manufacturer offered a line of effects from 1976 to the early-'90s.

Overlord Classic Overdrive Model III
1990-1991. Battery-powered version of Overlord pedal. Black case with red letters.

1990-1991		$125	$200

Overlord Classic Tube Overdrive
1988-1991. Uses a 12AX7A tube, AC powered.

1988-1991		$125	$200

Voice Box 50 (Watt Model)

1976-1979		$125	$150

Voice Box 100 (Watt Model)
1976-1979, 1982-ca.1985.

1976-1979		$125	$150

Voice Box 200 (Watt Model)

1976-1979		$125	$150

DeArmond

In 1946, DeArmond may have introduced the first actual signal-processing effect pedal, the Tremolo Control. They made a variety of effects into the '70s, but only one caught on - their classic volume pedal. DeArmond is primarily noted for pickups.

Pedal Phaser Model 1900
1974-ca.1979.

1974-1979		$200	$275

Square Wave Distortion Generator
1977-ca.1979.

1977-1979		$300	$400

Thunderbolt B166
1977-ca.1979. Five octave wah.

1977-1979		$250	$300

Tone/Volume Pedal 610
1978-ca.1979.

1978-1979		$200	$250

Tornado Phase Shifter
1977-ca.1979.

1977-1979		$150	$200

Tremolo Control Model 60A/60B
The Model 60 Tremolo Control dates from ca. 1946 to the early-1950s. Model 60A dates from mid- to late-'50s. Model 60B (plastic housing), early-'60s. Also labeled as the Trem-Trol or 601.

1950s	60A	$950	$1,250
1960s	60B	$325	$425
1960s	800 Trem-Trol	$325	$425

Twister 1930
1980. Phase shifter.

1980		$200	$300

Volume Pedal Model 602

1960s		$75	$150

Volume Pedal Model 1602
1978-ca. 1980s.

1970s		$75	$150

Volume Pedal Model 1630
1978-1980s. Optoelectric.

1970s		$75	$150

Weeper Wah Model 1802
1970s. Weeper logo on foot pedal.

1970s		$125	$175

MODEL YEAR	FEATURES	LOW	HIGH

Death By Audio

2001-present. Oliver Ackermann builds production and custom guitar effects in Brooklyn, New York.

Absolute Destruction

2000s-2023		$125	$200

Apocalyse

2000s-2023		$165	$325

Armageddon

2006		$175	$300

Crash Modulator

2005		$175	$300

Deep Animation

2000s-2023		$175	$225

Echo Dream 2

2000s-2023		$175	$250

Echo Master

2000s-2023		$175	$250

Evil Filter

2000s-2023		$125	$225

Fuzz Fuzz Fuzz

2006		$175	$300

Fuzz War

2000s-2023		$125	$300

Interstellar Overdriver

2000s-2023		$110	$150

Interstellar Overdriver 2

2000s-2021		$175	$225

Interstellar Overdriver Deluxe

2000s-2023		$180	$250

Micro Dream

2000s-2023		$125	$165

Micro Harmonic Transformer

2000s-2023		$125	$165

Reverberation Machine

2000s-2023		$180	$300

Robot

2000s-2023		$150	$250

Rooms

"Stereo Reverberator" pedal.

2000s-2023		$180	$350

Soundwave Breakdown

2000s-2023		$100	$150

Space Galaxy

Prototype pedal.

2009		$375	$800

Sunshine Reverberation

Designed in collaboration with Ty Seagall, limited edition of 100 pedals.

2013		$375	$800

Supersonic Fuzz Gun

2000s-2023		$125	$225

Time Shadows

Collaboration with EarthQuaker Devices, limited edition of 1,000 pedals.

2020		$250	$350

Total Sonic Annihilation

2000s-2021		$125	$165

Total Sonic Annihilation 2

2000s-2023		$125	$200

Waveformer Destroyer

2000s-2023		$175	$350

DeltaLab Research

Late 1970s-early 1980s. DeltaLab, which was in Chelmsford, Massachusetts, was an early builder of rackmount gear.

DL-2 Acousticomputer

1980s. Delay.

1980s		$750	$1,250

DL-4 Time Line

1980s. Delay.

1980s		$750	$1,250

DL-5

1980s. Various digital processing effects, blue case, rackmount.

1980s		$750	$1,250

DLB-1 Delay Control Pedal

1980s. Controls other DeltaLab pedals, chrome, Morley-looking pedal.

1980s		$50	$95

Electron I ADM/II ADM

1980s. Blue case, rackmount effects. Models include the Electron I ADM, and the Electron II ADM.

1980s	Electron I ADM	$300	$600
1980s	Electron II ADM	$300	$600

Demeter

1980-present. Amp builder James Demeter and company, located in Van Nuys, California, also build guitar effects.

Denio

Line of Japanese-made Boss lookalikes sold in Asia and Australia.

Devi Ever : Fx

2009-present. Devi Ever builds his guitar effects in Portland, Oregon. Prior to '09 he built the Effector 13 effects.

Diamond Pedals

2004-present. Designed by Michael Knappe and Tim Fifield, these effects are built in Bedford, Nova Scotia.

Diaz

Early-1980s-2002, 2004-2022. Line of effects from the amp doctor Cesar Diaz. Diaz died in '02; in '04, his family granted Diaz's friend Peter McMahon the license to resume production. Helping to differentiate the builder, Diaz and McMahon pedals are often signed inside.

Texas Ranger

1980s-2002, 2004-2022. Treble booster. 2 control knobs. Variety of colorful housings.

1980s-2002	Signed by Diaz	$1,000	$1,250
2004-2022		$800	$1,000

Texas Square Face

1980s-2002, 2004-2022. Fuzz pedal. 2 control knobs. Variety of colorful housings.

1980s-2002	Signed by Diaz	$2,000	$2,500
2004-2022		$1,500	$2,000

Death By Audio
Interstellar Overdriver

Diamond Pedals
Boost-EQ BEQ1

Diaz Texas Ranger

EFFECTS

DLS Reckless Driver

1981 DOD AB Box 270

Rivington Guitars

DOD Studio Bifet Preamp

Keith Myers;

MODEL YEAR	FEATURES	LOW	HIGH
Tremodillo			
1980s-2002, 2004-2022. Tremolo pedal. 2 control knobs. Variety of colorful housings.			
1980s-2002		$800	$1,000
2004-2022		$600	$800

DigiTech

The DigiTech/DOD company is in Utah and the effects are made in the U.S.A. The DigiTech name started as a line under the DOD brand in the early 1980s; later spinning off into its own brand. They also produce vocal products and studio processors and are now part of Harman International Industries.

MODEL YEAR	FEATURES	LOW	HIGH
Digital Delay and Sampler PDS 2000			
1985-1991. 2 second delay.			
1985-1991		$100	$200
Digital Delay PDS 1000			
1985-ca.1989. One second delay.			
1985-1989		$100	$150
Digital Delay PDS 2700 Double Play			
1989-1991. Delay and chorus			
1989-1991		$100	$250
Digital Stereo Chorus/Flanger PDS 1700			
1986-1991		$100	$150
Echo Plus 8 Second Delay PDS 8000			
1985-1991		$200	$400
Guitar Effects Processor RP 1			
1992-1996. Floor unit, 150 presets.			
1992-1996		$100	$150
Guitar Effects Processor RP 3			
1998-2003. Floor unit.			
1998-2003		$100	$150
Guitar Effects Processor RP 5			
1994-1996. Floor unit, 80 presets.			
1994-1996		$100	$150
Guitar Effects Processor RP 6			
1996-1997. Floor unit.			
1996-1997		$100	$150
Guitar Effects Processor RP 7			
1996-1997. Floor unit.			
1996-1997		$100	$150
Guitar Effects Processor RP 10			
1994-1996. Floor unit, 200 presets.			
1994-1996		$150	$200
Guitar Effects Processor RP 14D			
1999. Floor unit with expression pedal, 1x12AX7 tube, 100 presets.			
1999		$150	$200
Guitar Effects Processor RP 100			
2000-2006		$100	$150
Guitar Effects Processor RP 200			
2001-2006. 140 presets, drum machine, Expression pedal.			
2001-2006		$100	$150
Hot Box PDS 2730			
1989-1991. Delay and distortion			
1989-1991		$100	$150
Modulator Pedal XP 200			
1996-2002. Floor unit, 61 presets.			
1996-2002		$100	$150

MODEL YEAR	FEATURES	LOW	HIGH
Multi Play PDS 20/20			
1987-1991. Multi-function digital delay.			
1987-1991		$125	$250
Pedalverb Digital Reverb Pedal PDS 3000			
1987-1991		$125	$250
Programmable Distortion PDS 1550			
1986-1991	Yellow case	$75	$175
Programmable Distortion PDS 1650			
1989-1991	Red case	$75	$175
Rock Box PDS 2715			
1989-1991. Chorus and distortion.			
1989-1991		$75	$175
Two Second Digital Delay PDS 1002			
1987-1991		$100	$200
Whammy Pedal Reissue			
2000-present. Reissue version of classic WP-1 with added dive bomb and MIDI features.			
2000-2020		$125	$140
Whammy Pedal WP I			
1990-1993. Original Whammy Pedal, red case, reissued as WP IV in '00.			
1990-1993		$300	$650
Whammy Pedal WP II			
1994-1997. Can switch between 2 presets, black case.			
1994-1997		$225	$450

DiMarzio

The pickup maker offered a couple of effects in the late-1980s to the mid-'90s.

MODEL YEAR	FEATURES	LOW	HIGH
Metal Pedal			
1987-1989		$250	$425
Very Metal Fuzz			
Ca.1989-1995. Distortion/overdrive pedal.			
1989-1995		$200	$350

Dino's

A social co-op founded by Alessio Casati and Andy Bagnasco, in Albisola, Italy. It builds a line of boutique analog pedals as well as guitars.

Dinosaur

2004-2015. Guitar effects pedals imported by Eleca International. They also offered amps.

Divided By Thirteen

Mid-1990s-present. Fred Taccone builds his stomp box guitar effects in the Los Angeles, California area. He also builds amps.

DLS Effects

1999-present. Guitar effects pedals built by Dave Sestito in Fairport, New York.

DNA Analogic

Line of Japanese-built guitar effects distributed first by Godlyke, then Pedals Plus+ Effects Warehouse.

DOD

DOD Electronics started in Salt Lake City, Utah in 1974. Today, they're a major effects manufacturer

EFFECTS

with dozens of pedals made in the U.S. They also market effects under the name DigiTech and are now part of Harman International Industries.

MODEL YEAR	FEATURES	LOW	HIGH
6 Band Equalizer EQ601			
1977-1982		$65	$80
AB Box 270			
1978-1982		$40	$45
American Metal FX56			
1985-1991		$75	$125
Analog Delay 680			
	1979-ca. 1982.		
1979-1982		$150	$350
Attacker FX54			
	1992-1994. Distortion and compressor.		
1992-1994		$65	$100
Bass Compressor FX82			
	1987-ca.1989.		
1987-1989		$65	$100
Bass EQ FX42B			
1987-1996		$65	$100
Bass Grunge FX92			
1995-1996		$120	$300
Bass Overdrive FX91			
	1998-2012. Yellow case.		
1998-2012		$75	$125
Bass Stereo Chorus Flanger FX72			
1987-1997		$65	$100
Bass Stereo Chorus FX62			
1987-1996		$65	$100
Bi-FET Preamp FX10			
1982-1996		$100	$150
Buzz Box FX33			
	1994-1996. Grunge distortion.		
1994-1996		$200	$400
Chorus 690			
	1980-ca.1982. Dual speed chorus.		
1980-1982		$200	$400
Classic Fuzz FX52			
1990-1997		$65	$100
Classic Tube FX53			
1990-1997		$65	$100
Compressor 280			
	1978-ca.1982.		
1978-1982		$65	$100
Compressor FX80			
1982-1985		$85	$125
Compressor Sustainer FX80B			
1986-1996		$65	$85
Death Metal FX86			
	1994-2009. Distortion.		
1994-2009		$75	$125
Delay FX90			
	1984-ca.1987.		
1984-1987		$85	$150
Digital Delay DFX9			
	1989-ca.1990.		
1989-1990		$75	$100
Digital Delay Sampler DFX94			
1995-1997		$85	$150

MODEL YEAR	FEATURES	LOW	HIGH
Distortion FX55			
	1982-1986. Red case.		
1982-1986		$65	$125
Edge Pedal FX87			
1988-1989		$100	$150
Envelope Filter 440			
1981-1982		$200	$300
Envelope Filter FX25			
	1982-1997. Replaced by FX25B.		
1982-1997		$100	$150
Envelope Filter FX25B			
	1981-2013. Light aqua case.		
1998-2013		$95	$125
Equalizer FX40			
1982-1986		$65	$100
Equalizer FX40B			
	1987-2010. Eight bands for bass.		
1987-2010		$65	$100
Fet Preamp 210			
	1981-ca.1982.		
1981-1982		$100	$225
Flanger 670			
1981-1982		$125	$250
Gate Loop FX30			
1980s		$65	$85
Gonkulator			
1980s		$100	$175
Graphic Equalizer EQ-610			
	1980-ca.1982. Ten bands.		
1980-1982		$65	$85
Graphic Equalizer EQ-660			
	1980-ca.1982. Six bands.		
1980-1982		$65	$75
Grunge FX69			
	1993-2009. Distortion.		
1993-2009		$100	$175
Hard Rock Distortion FX57			
	1987-1994. With built-in delay.		
1987-1994		$100	$165
Harmonic Enhancer FX85			
	1986-ca.1989.		
1986-1989		$65	$85
I. T. FX100			
	1997. Intergrated Tube distortion, produces harmonics.		
1997		$85	$165
IceBox FX64			
	1996-2008. Chorus, high EQ.		
1996-2008		$65	$100
Juice Box FX51			
1996-1997		$125	$250
Master Switch 225			
	1988-ca.1989. A/B switch and loop selector.		
1988-1989		$40	$50
Meat Box FX32			
1994-1996		$150	$300
Metal Maniac FX58			
1990-1996		$100	$150
Metal Triple Play Guitar Effects System TR3M			
1994		$90	$125

DOD Compressor
Sustainer FX80B

DOD Equalizer FX40B

DOD Gonkulator FX 13
Vinny Roth

EFFECTS

EFFECTS

1979 DOD Mini Chorus 460
Rivington Guitars

1981 DOD Phasor 201
Rivington Guitars

Dunlop Cry Baby EVH Wah

MODEL YEAR	FEATURES	LOW	HIGH
Metal X FX70			
1993-1996		$100	$200
Milk Box FX84			
1994-2012. Compressor/expander, white case.			
1994-2012		$100	$175
Mini-Chorus 460			
1981-ca.1982.			
1981-1982		$90	$175
Mixer 240			
1978-ca.1982.			
1978-1982		$25	$35
Momentary Footswitch			
Introduced in 1987. Temporally engages other boxes.			
1980s		$25	$35
Mystic Blues Overdrive FX102			
1998-2012. Medium gain overdrive, purple case.			
1998-2012		$100	$150
Noise Gate 230			
1978-1982		$100	$150
Noise Gate FX30			
1982-ca.1987.			
1982-1987		$65	$75
Octoplus FX35			
1987-1996. Octaves.			
1987-1996		$65	$85
Overdrive Plus FX50B			
1986-1997		$65	$100
Overdrive Preamp 250			
1978-1982, 1995-2020. Reissued in '95, yellow case.			
1978-1981	Gray box	$600	$750
1981-1984	Yellow box	$200	$300
1995-2020		$100	$150
Overdrive Preamp FX50			
1982-1985		$75	$150
Performer Compressor Limiter 525			
1981-1984		$75	$150
Performer Delay 585			
1982-1985		$75	$175
Performer Distortion 555			
1981-1984		$75	$165
Performer Flanger 575			
1981-1985		$75	$165
Performer Phasor 595			
1981-1984		$75	$165
Performer Stereo Chorus 565			
1981-1985. FET switching.			
1981-1985		$75	$150
Performer Wah Filter 545			
1981-1984		$75	$150
Phasor 201			
1981-ca.1982. Reissued in '95.			
1981-1982		$175	$300
Phasor 401			
1978-1981		$100	$250
Phasor 490			
1980-ca.1982.			
1980-1982		$100	$200
Phasor FX20			
1982-1985		$100	$150
Psychoacoustic Processor FX87			
1988-1989		$100	$135

MODEL YEAR	FEATURES	LOW	HIGH
Punkifier FX76			
1997		$200	$300
Resistance Mixer 240			
1978-ca.1982.			
1978-1982		$30	$40
Silencer FX27			
1988-ca.1989. Noise reducer.			
1988-1989		$35	$45
Stereo Chorus FX60			
1982-1986		$100	$150
Stereo Chorus FX65			
1986-1996. Light blue case.			
1986-1996		$100	$150
Stereo Flanger FX70			
1982-ca.1985.			
1982-1985		$65	$125
Stereo Flanger FX75			
1986-1987. Silver case with blue trim.			
1986-1987		$65	$125
Stereo Flanger FX75B			
1987-1997		$100	$150
Stereo Phasor FX20B			
1986-1999		$85	$100
Stereo Turbo Chorus FX67			
1988-1991		$100	$125
Super American Metal FX56B			
1992-1996		$100	$200
Super Stereo Chorus FX68			
1992-1996		$65	$100
Supra Distortion FX55			
1986-2012. Red case.			
1986-2012		$40	$65
Thrash Master FX59			
1990-1996		$100	$175
Vibrothang FX22			
1990s		$100	$135
Votec Vocal Effects Processor and Mic Preamp			
1998-2001		$75	$100
Wah-Volume FX-17 (pedal)			
1987-2000		$75	$100

Dredge-Tone
Located in Berkeley, California, Dredge-Tone offers effects and electronic kits.

DST Engineering
2001-2014. Jeff Swanson and Bob Dettorre built reverb units in Beverly, Massachusetts. They also built amps.

Dunlop
Jim Dunlop, USA offers the Crybaby, MXR (see MXR), Rockman, High Gain, Heil Sound (see Heil), Tremolo, Jimi Hendrix, Rotovibe, Uni-Vibe and Way Huge brand effects.

Cry Baby Bass
1985-present. Bass wah.

	LOW	HIGH
1985-2023	$80	$110

The *Vintage Guitar Price Guide* shows values for an all-original condition guitar effect.

MODEL YEAR	FEATURES	LOW	HIGH

Cry Baby EVH Wah
1990's-present.

1990s-2023		$100	$150

Cry Baby Multi-Wah 535/535Q
1995-present. Multi-range pedal with an external boost control.

1995-2023		$75	$110

Cry Baby Wah-Wah GCB-95
1982-present. Dunlop began manufacturing the Cry Baby in '82.

1982-1989		$55	$85
1990-1999		$50	$80
2000-2023		$45	$75

Fuzz Face Distortion JDF2
1993-present. Reissue of the classic Dallas Arbiter effect (see that listing for earlier versions).

1993-2023	Red, reissue	$100	$150

High Gain Volume + Boost Pedal

1983-1996		$45	$75

High Gain Volume Pedal GCB-80

1983-2010		$45	$75

Jimi Hendrix Fuzz JH-2 (Round)
1987-1993. Round face fuzz, JH-2S is the square box version.

1987-1993		$100	$200

Rotovibe JH-4S Standard
1989-1998. Standard is finished in bright red enamel with chrome top.

1989-1998		$150	$275

Tremolo Volume Plus TVP-1
1995-1998. Pedal.

1995-1998		$115	$300

Uni-Vibe UV-1
1995-2012. Rotating speaker effect.

1995-1999		$350	$500
2000 2012		$250	$325

Durham Electronics

2001-present. Alan Durham builds his line of guitar effects in Austin, Texas.

Dutch Kazoo

2013-present. Guitar effects pedals built in Parker Ford, Pennsylvania by Corinne Mandell.

Dynacord

1950-present. Dynacord is a German company that makes audio and pro sound amps, as well as other electronic equipment and is now owned by TELEX/EVI Audio (an U.S. company), which also owns the Electro-Voice brand. In the '60s they offered tape echo machines and guitars. In '94 a line of multi-effects processors was introduced under the Electro-Voice/Dynacord name, but by the following year they were just listed as Electro-Voice.

EchoCord
Introduced in 1959. Tape echo unit.

1959-1960s		$400	$800

Dyno

See Dytronics.

MODEL YEAR	FEATURES	LOW	HIGH

Dytronics

Mid-1970s-early 1980s. The Japanese Dytronics company made a chorus rackmount unit for electric piano called the Dyno My Piano with flying piano keys or a lightning bolt on the front. Another version was called the Tri-Stereo Chorus and a third, called the Songbird, had a bird's head on the front.

E Bow

See Heet Sound Products.

E.W.S. (Engineering Work Store)

2007-present. Guitar effects pedals built in Tokyo, Japan for Prosound Communications in Van Nuys, California.

EarthQuaker Devices

2005-present. Jamie Stillman started building Fuzz Face and Rangemaster clones for friends and in '07, he built a modified Big Muff for Dan Auerbach of the Black Keys, who he tour-managed at the time. After extensive revisions, this became the Hoof Fuzz and he began retailing his pedals.

Acapulco Gold
2015-present. Power amp distortion. Grandma Cyclops limited-edition version was made '16 in collaboration with visual artist and Devo co-founder Mark Mothersbaugh and the Akron Art Museum.

2015-2023		$85	$115
2016	Grandma Cyclops	$90	$120

Afterneath
2014-present. Ambient reverb.

2014-2023		$110	$150

Amp Hammer II

2009		$65	$110

Arpanoid
2013-2023. Polyphonic arpeggiator.

2013-2023		$165	$220

Arrows
2014-present. Preamp boost.

2014-2023		$55	$90

Avalanche Run
2016-present. Stereo reverb and delay.

2016-2023		$200	$250

Bellows
2016-2019. Fuzz driver.

2016-2019		$85	$120

Bit Commander
2011-present. Guitar synthesizer.

2011-2023		$100	$145

Black Eye

2007		$65	$110

Bows
2016-2019. Germanium preamp.

2016-2019		$90	$120

Chrysalis

2010		$65	$110

Cloven Hoof
2014-2020. Fuzz grinder.

2014-2020		$90	$120

Dunlop Cry Baby
Multi-Wah 535Q

EarthQuaker Devices Bellows

EarthQuaker Devices
Bit Commander

EFFECTS

EarthQuaker Devices
Fuzz Master General

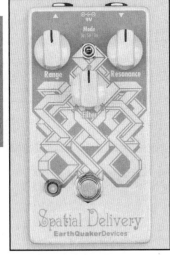

Earthquaker Devices
Spatial Delivery

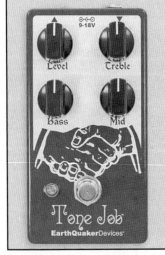

EarthQuaker Devices Tone Job

MODEL YEAR	FEATURES	LOW	HIGH
Cloven Hoof Reaper			
2015-2017. Fuzz.			
2015-2017		$110	$150
Crimson Drive			
2007		$65	$110
Dirt Transmitter			
2008-2019. Fuzz driver.			
2008-2019		$100	$130
Disaster Transport			
2007. Delay pedal.			
2007		$65	$150
Disaster Transport Jr.			
2010		$65	$100
Disaster Transport Sr.			
2013-2021. Advanced modulation delay and reverb.			
2013-2021		$200	$250
Dispatch Master			
2011-present. Hi-fi digital delay and reverb.			
2011-2023		$110	$150
Dream Crusher			
2009		$65	$110
Dunes			
2015-2020. Mini mega overdrive.			
2015-2020		$100	$170
Erupter			
2017-2022. Fuzz.			
2017-2022		$100	$120
Fuzz Master General			
2015-2019. Octave fuzz pedal.			
2015-2019		$100	$140
Ghost Disaster			
2010		$65	$110
Ghost Echo			
2009-present. Vintage-voiced reverb.			
2009-2023		$110	$150
Grand Orbiter			
2009-present. Phaser/vibrato.			
2009-2023		$110	$150
Gray Channel			
2016-2020. Dynamic dirt doubler.			
2016-2020		$110	$150
Hoof			
2007-present. Germanium/silicon hybrid fuzz.			
2007-2023		$110	$140
Hoof Reaper			
2012-present. Dual fuzz octave.			
2012-2023		$175	$250
Hummingbird			
2007-present. Repeat percussion/tremolo.			
2007-2023		$110	$150
Interstellar Orbiter			
2015-2020. Dual resonant filter built in collaboration with turntablist Kid Koala for his "Turntable Orchestra" tour. Features original artwork by Koala.			
2015-2020		$135	$200
Levitation			
2008-2021. Psychedlic reverb.			
2008-2021		$100	$130
Monarch			
2010		$65	$110

MODEL YEAR	FEATURES	LOW	HIGH
Night Wire			
2016-present. Harmonic tremolo.			
2016-2023		$125	$170
Organizer			
2012-present. Polyphonic organ emulator.			
2012-2023		$110	$150
Palisades			
2014-2022. Mega ultimate overdrive.			
2014-2022		$135	$185
Park Fuzz Sound			
2015-present. Reissue of the Park Amplification fuzz pedal built in cooperation with Park.			
2015-2023		$110	$150
Pitch Bay			
2014-2017. Dirty polyphonic harmonizer.			
2014-2017		$110	$180
Pulse Machine Tremolo			
2007		$65	$110
Rainbow Machine			
2011-present. Polyphonic pitch-shifting modulator.			
2011-2023		$135	$200
Royal Drive			
2007		$65	$110
Sea Machine			
2010-present. Chorus.			
2010-2023		$90	$150
Sound Shank			
2009		$65	$110
Space Spiral			
2017-2021. Modulation delay.			
2017-2021		$110	$150
Spatial Delivery			
2016-present. Envelope filter with sample and hold functions.			
2016-2023		$110	$150
Spires			
2016-2019. Nü-Face double fuzz.			
2016-2019		$110	$150
Stealth Fuzz			
2007		$65	$110
Talons			
2012-2017. Hi-gain overdrive.			
2012-2017		$110	$150
Tentacle			
2015-present. Analog octave up. Grandpa Cyclops limited-edition version was made '16 in collaboration with visual artist and Devo co-founder Mark Mothersbaugh and the Akron Art Museum.			
2015-2023		$110	$150
2016	Grandpa Cyclops	$110	$150
Terminal			
2014-2019. Fuzz.			
2014-2019		$110	$150
The Depths			
2013-2017. Optical vibrato.			
2013-2017		$100	$140
The Grim Reefer			
2014-2017. Fuzz pedal.			
2014-2017		$110	$150

The *Vintage Guitar Price Guide* shows values for an all-original condition guitar effect.

MODEL YEAR	FEATURES	LOW	HIGH
The Warden			
2013-present. Optical compression.			
2013-2023		$110	$150
Time Shadows			
2020. Collaboration with EarthQuaker Devices, limited edition of 1,000 pedals.			
2020		$225	$350
Tone Job			
2012-present. EQ and boost.			
2012-2023		$110	$150
Tone Reaper			
2009		$110	$150
Transmisser			
2016-2019. Reverb.			
2016-2019		$140	$200
White Light			
2008		$150	$250
Zap Machine			
2010		$65	$110
Z-Drive			
2015-2017. Overdrive built in collaboration with Dr. Z Amplification.			
2015-2017		$190	$230

EBS

1992-present. Bass and guitar effects built in Stockholm, Sweden by the EBS Sweden AB company. They also build bass amps.

Ecco-Fonic

1959-1968. The Ecco-Fonic was designed by Ray Stolle and sold from his radio and TV repair shop in Los Angeles. Theis first Ecco Ecco-Fonic was distributed by Fender in 1958-'59. Stolle sold the company to E.S. "Eddie" Tubin in late 1959 '60, who sold the company in 1961 to Milton Brucker. Starting in 1963, Fender offered a solidstate Ecco-Fonic designed by new-owner Bob Marks and Russ Allee and labeled as the Fender Echo.

Model 109

1959-1960. Tube-driven tape-echo unit, 2 control knobs, revised to 3 knobs, 1-piece top, gold housing.

1959	Brown case	$1,500	$2,000

Model 109-B

1960-1962. Tube-driven tape echo unit, 4 Control knobs, 2-piece top, gold housing.

1960-1962	Brown or black case	$1,000	$1,500

Model 109-C

1961-1962. Tube-driven tape echo unit, multiple playback heads, black housing.

1961-1962	Black case	$1,500	$2,500

Echoplex

The Echoplex tape echo unit was invented around 1959 in Akron, Ohio, by Don Dixon and Mike Battle, who originally produced it in small numbers. Production was soon moved to Market Electronics in Cleveland, and those units were sold under the Maestro brand (see listings under Maestro). After Maestro dropped the Echoplex, it was marketed under the Market Electronics name from the late-'70s

to the late-'80s (see listing under Market Electronics for '80s models). In '94, Gibson's Oberheim division introduced a rackmount unit called the Echoplex. In '01, it was relabeled as Gibson.

Echoplex

1959. Dixon- and Battle-built pre-Maestro production tube-driven tape echo. Black case.

1959		$1,500	$2,500

EchoSonic

2010s. Ray Butts of EchoSonic amp fame crafted a pioneering fuzz circuit that never went into production. Tim Masters of Florida built a limited run of stompboxes with the circuitry.

Ray-O-Fuzz

2010s. Metal housings in various colors with the logo surrounded by lightning bolts. Attack and Volume controls plus footswitch.

2010s		$275	$500

Eden Analog

Guitar effects pedals built by Chris Sheppard and Robert Hafley in Pelham, Alabama, starting in 2004.

Effector 13

2002-2008. Guitar effects built by Devi Ever in Minneapolis, Minnesota. Located in Austin, Texas until mid-'04. Name changed to Devi Ever : Fx in '09.

Effectrode

1996-present. Effects pedals built in Corvallis, Oregon by Phil Taylor.

EFX

1980s. Brand name of the Los Angeles-based EFX Center; they also offered a direct box and a powered pedal box/board.

Switch Box B287

1984. Dual effects loop selector.

1984		$35	$45

EKO

1959-1985, 2000-present. In the '60s and '70s EKO offered effects made by EME and JEN Elettronica, which also made Vox effects.

Eleca

2004-present. Guitar effects pedals imported by Eleca International. They also offer guitars, mandolins, and amps.

Electra

1970-1984, 2013-present. Guitar importer St. Louis Music offered Electra effects in the late '70s.

Chorus 504CH

Ca.1975-ca.1980.

1975-1980		$100	$150

EarthQuaker Devices
The Warden

EBS ValveDrive DI

Eleca EBB-1

EFFECTS

Electra Phase 501

Christopher Wright

EFFECTS

Electro-Harmonix 16
Second Digital Delay

1974 E-H Big Muff PI

Suzie Williams

MODEL YEAR	FEATURES	LOW	HIGH
Compressor 502C/602C			
Ca.1975-ca.1980.			
1975-1980		$50	$65
Distortion 500D			
Ca.1976-ca.1980.			
1976-1980		$150	$225
Flanger (stereo) 605F			
Ca.1975-ca.1980.			
1975-1980		$90	$150
Fuzz Wah			
Ca.1975-ca.1980.			
1975-1980		$135	$300
Pedal Drive 515AC			
Ca.1976-ca.1980. Overdrive.			
1976-1980		$50	$65
Phaser Model 501P			
Ca.1976-ca.1980.			
1976-1980		$110	$200
Phaser Model 875			
Ca.1975-ca.1980.			
1975-1980		$110	$200
Roto Phase I			
1975-ca.1980. Small pocket phaser.			
1975-1980		$80	$100
Roto Phase II			
1975-ca.1980. Pedal phasor.			
1975-1980		$90	$115

Electro-Harmonix

1968-1984, 1996-present. Founded by Mike Matthews in New York City, the company initially produced small plug-in boosters such as the LPB-1. In '71, they unveiled the awe-inspiring Big Muff Pi fuzz and dozens of innovative pedals followed. After closing in '84, Matthews again began producing reissues of many of his classic effects as well as new designs in '96.

MODEL YEAR	FEATURES	LOW	HIGH
10 Band Graphic Equalizer			
1977-1981. Includes footswitch.			
1977-1981		$90	$115
16-Second Digital Delay			
Early-1980s, 2004-2008. An updated version was reissued in '04.			
1980s	No foot controller	$600	$750
1980s	With foot controller	$850	$1,125
1990s		$400	$550
2004-2008		$350	$500
3 Phase Liner			
1981		$55	$75
5X Junction Mixer			
1977-1981		$30	$75
Attack Equalizer			
1975-1981. Active EQ, a.k.a. "Knock Out."			
1975-1981		$150	$200
Attack/Decay			
1980-1981. Tape reverse simulator.			
1980-1981		$1,250	$1,500
Axis			
1969-1970s. Modified Mosrite Fuzzrite circuit.			
1969-1970s		$775	$1,000

MODEL YEAR	FEATURES	LOW	HIGH
Bad Stone Phase Shifter			
1975-1981.			
1975-1981	Three knobs	$350	$500
1975-1981	Two knobs, color switch	$300	$400
Bass Micro-Synthesizer			
1981-1984, 1999-present. Analog synthesizer sounds.			
1981-1984		$250	$350
1999-2023		$200	$300
Bassballs			
1978-1984, 1998-present. Bass envelope filter/ distortion.			
1978-1984		$150	$200
Big Muff Pi			
1971-1984. Sustain, floor unit, issued in 3 different looks, as described below.			
1970s	V1, Black graphics, knobs in triangle pattern	$1,000	$1,250
1970s	V2, "Rams Head"	$1,250	$1,500
1976	V3, GE transitor, no LED, red/black graphics	$500	$600
1977	V4, Integrated op amp ckt	$400	$500
1978-1980	V5, Tone bypass	$300	$400
1980s	RV6, GE transitor	$250	$350
Big Muff Pi (Reissue)			
1996-present. Originally made in Russia, but currently both Russian- and U.S.-made versions are available.			
1996-2023	Russian-made	$150	$300
Big Muff Sovtek			
2000s. Big Muff Pi, Electro Harmonix, and Sovtek logos on an olive-green case. Sold in a wooden box.			
2000s	With wooden box	$400	$500
Black Finger Compressor Sustainer			
1977, 2003-2019. The original has 3 knobs in triangle pattern.			
1977		$350	$450
2003-2019		$175	$225
Clap Track			
1980-1984. Drum effect.			
1980-1984		$350	$500
Clone Theory			
1977-1981. Chorus effect, The Clone Theory logo.			
1977-1981		$500	$750
Crash Pad			
1980-1984. Percussion synth.			
1980-1984		$100	$300
Crying Tone Pedal			
1976-1978. Wah-wah.			
1976-1978		$200	$250
Deluxe Big Muff Pi			
1978-1981. Sustain, AC version of Big Muff Pi, includes a complete Soul Preacher unit.			
1978-1981	Red graphics	$250	$400
Deluxe Electric Mistress Flanger			
1977-1983, 1996-present. AC.			
1977-1979		$500	$650
1980-1983		$225	$400

The *Vintage Guitar Price Guide* shows values for an all-original condition guitar effect.

MODEL YEAR	FEATURES	LOW	HIGH
Deluxe Memory Man			
1977-1983, 1996-present. Echo and delay, featured 4 knobs '77-'78, from '79-'83 it has 5 knobs and added vibrato and chorus.			
1977-1978	4 knobs	$700	$900
1979-1983	5 knobs	$700	$900
1996-2023	3-prong power cord	$1,000	$1,250
Deluxe Octave Multiplexer			
1977-1981		$350	$400
Digital Delay/Chorus			
1981-1984. With digital chorus.			
1981-1984		$350	$400
Digital Rhythm Matrix DRM-15			
1981-1984		$350	$500
Digital Rhythm Matrix DRM-16			
1979-1983		$150	$400
Digital Rhythm Matrix DRM-32			
1981-1984		$600	$1,250
Doctor Q Envelope Follower			
1976-1983, 2001-2020. For bass or guitar.			
1976-1983		$100	$150
2001-2020		$50	$75
Domino Theory			
1981. Sound sensitive light tube.			
1981		$65	$100
Echo 600			
1981		$200	$250
Echoflanger			
1977-1982. Flange, slapback, chorus, filter.			
1977-1982		$875	$1,250
Electric Mistress Flanger			
1976-1979. $750-$1,500			
1980-1984		$350	$450
Electronic Metronome			
1978-1980		$100	$125
Frequency Analyzer			
1977-1984, 2001-2022. Ring modulator.			
1977-1984		$350	$500
Full Double Tracking Effect			
1978-1981. Doubling, slapback.			
1978-1981		$100	$200
Fuzz Wah			
Introduced around 1974.			
1970s		$250	$300
Golden Throat			
1977-1984		$400	$550
Golden Throat Deluxe			
1977-1979. Deluxe has a built-in monitor amp.			
1977-1979		$500	$650
Golden Throat II			
1978-1981		$150	$300
Guitar Synthesizer			
1981. Sold for $1,495 in May '81.			
1981		$200	$250
Hog's Foot Bass Booster			
1977-1980		$100	$150
Holy Grail			
2002-present. Digital reverb.			
2002-2023		$75	$150

MODEL YEAR	FEATURES	LOW	HIGH
Hot Foot			
1977-1978. Rocker pedal turns knob of other E-H effects, gold case, red graphics.			
1977-1978		$150	$250
Hot Tubes			
1978-1984, 2001-2007. Tube distortion.			
1978-1984		$250	$400
Linear Power Booster LPB-1			
1968-1983.			
1976-1979		$125	$200
1980-1983		$50	$75
Linear Power Booster LPB-2			
Ca.1968-1983.			
1968-1983		$125	$200
Little Big Muff Pi			
1976-1980, 2006-present. Sustain, 1-knob floor unit.			
1976-1980		$150	$300
2006-2023		$50	$75
Little Muff Pi			
1971-1975. Sustain, 1-knob floor unit, issued in 2 styles: blue or red graphics.			
1971-1975		$250	$350
Memory Man/Stereo Memory Man			
1976-1984, 1999-present. Analog delay, newer version in stereo.			
1976-1979		$500	$800
1980-1984		$250	$350
Micro Synthesizer			
1978-1984, 1998-present. Mini keyboard phaser.			
1978-1984		$400	$500
1998-2023		$150	$200
Mini Q-Tron/Micro Q-Tron			
2002-present. Battery-operated smaller version of Q-Tron envelope follower, changed to identical effect in smaller box Micro in '06			
2002-2023		$65	$100
Mini-Mixer			
1978-1981. Mini mic mixer, reissued in '01.			
1978-1981		$100	$150
MiniSynthesizer			
1981-1983. Mini keyboard with phaser.			
1981-1983		$350	$450
MiniSynthesizer With Echo			
1981		$450	$600
Mole Bass Booster			
1968-1978.			
1968-1969		$95	$125
1970-1978		$50	$75
Muff Fuzz			
1976-1983. Fuzz and line boost, silver case with orange lettering.			
1976-1983		$125	$250
Muff Fuzz Crying Tone			
1977-1978. Fuzz, wah.			
1977-1978		$175	$300
Octave Multiplexer Floor Unit			
1976-1980		$175	$300
Octave Multiplexer Pedal			
1976-1977, 2001-2022.			
1976-1977		$500	$650
2001-2022		$50	$65

E-H Deluxe Memory Man

E-H Digital Rhythm Matrix DRM-15

Jim Schreck

1978 E-H Linear Power Booster LPB-2

Rivington Guitars

EFFECTS

E-H Small Clone

E-H Soul Food

E-H Soul Preacher

Jim Schreck

MODEL YEAR	FEATURES	LOW	HIGH
Panic Button			
1981. Siren sounds for drums.			
1981		$100	$200
Poly Chorus/Stereo Polychorus			
1981, 1999-2021. Same as Echoflanger.			
1981		$550	$800
1999-2021		$150	$200
Polyphase			
1979-1981. With envelope.			
1979-1981		$300	$550
Pulsar/Stereo Pulsar			
2004-present. Variable wave form tremolo.			
2004-2023		$50	$65
Pulse Modulator			
Ca.1968 -ca.1972. Triple tremolo.			
1968-1969		$300	$400
1970-1972		$250	$300
Q-Tron			
1997-2017. Envelope controlled filter.			
1997-2017		$200	$250
Q-Tron +			
1999-present. With added effects loop and Attack Response switch.			
1999-2023		$115	$150
Queen Triggered Wah			
1976-1978. Wah/Envelope Filter.			
1976-1978		$500	$750
Random Tone Generator RTG			
1981		$60	$75
Rhythm 12 (Rhythm Machine)			
1978		$150	$200
Rolling Thunder			
1980-1981. Percussion synth.			
1980-1981		$50	$65
Screaming Bird Treble Booster			
Ca.1968-1980. In-line unit.			
1968-1980		$150	$200
Screaming Tree Treble Booster			
1977-1981. Floor unit.			
1977-1981		$150	$200
Sequencer Drum			
1981. Drum effect.			
1981		$450	$800
Slapback Echo			
1977-1978. Stereo.			
1977-1978		$150	$200
Small Clone			
1983-1984, 1999-present. Analog chorus, depth and rate controls, purple face plate, white logo.			
1983-1984		$500	$700
1999-2023		$60	$100
Small Stone Phase Shifter			
1975-1984, 1996-present. Both Russian and U.S. reissues were made.			
1975-1979		$300	$400
1980-1984		$150	$200
Solid State Reverb			
1980s. Input, output, blend, and feedback controls.			
1980s		$250	$500

MODEL YEAR	FEATURES	LOW	HIGH
Soul Food			
2000s		$50	$65
2000s	JHS modded	$125	$175
Soul Preacher			
1977-1983, 2007-present. Compressor sustainer. Nano version for present.			
1977-1983		$125	$250
Space Drum/Super Space Drum			
1980-1981. Percussion synthesizer.			
1980-1981		$150	$200
Switch Blade			
1977-1983. A-B Box.			
1977-1983		$50	$75
Talking Pedal			
1977-1978. Creates vowel sounds.			
1977-1978		$350	$550
The Silencer			
1976-1981. Noise elimination.			
1976-1981		$75	$150
Tube Zipper			
2001-2018. Tube (2x12AX7) envelope follower.			
2001-2018		$125	$150
Vocoder			
1978-1981. Modulates voice with instrument.			
1978-1981	Rackmount	$450	$550
Volume Pedal			
1978-1981.			
1978-1981		$50	$65
Wiggler			
2002-2019. All-tube modulator including pitch vibrato and volume tremolo.			
2002-2019		$150	$300
Worm/The Worm			
2002-present. Wah/Phaser.			
2002-2023		$60	$75
Y-Triggered Filter			
1976-1977		$150	$200
Zipper Envelope Follower			
1976-1978. The Tube Zipper was introduced in '01.			
1976-1978		$200	$300

Electrosonic Amplifiers

2002-2010. Amp builder Josh Corn also offers a preamp pedal, built in Boonville, Indiana.

Elektronika

1980s-1990s. Russian effects pedals by the Soviet Ministry of Electronic Industry.

MODEL YEAR	FEATURES	LOW	HIGH
Compressor-Sustainer			
1980s		$150	$225
Equalizer E-02			
1980s		$150	$225
Fazer-2			
1980s		$150	$225
Flanger FL-01			
1980s		$150	$300
Flanger PE-05			
1980s		$150	$225
Jet-Phaser			
1980s		$150	$225
Synchro-Wah			
1980s		$150	$225

MODEL YEAR	FEATURES	LOW	HIGH

Volna
1980s. Auto wah.

1980s		$150	$225

Elk Gakki
Late-1960s. Japanese company Elk Gakki Co., Ltd. mainly made guitars and amps, but did offer effects as well.

Big Muff Sustainer
1970s. Electro-Harmonix Big Muff Pi copy.

1970s		$300	$850

Elka
In the late '60s or early '70s, Italian organ and synthesizer company Elka-Orla (later just Elka) offered a few effects, likely made by JEN Elettronica (Vox, others).

EMMA Electronic
Line of guitar effects built in Denmark and distributed by Godlyke.

ReezaFRATzitz RF-1/ReezaFRATzitz II
2004-present. Overdrive and distortion, red case.

2004-2023		$85	$125

Empress Effects
2005-present. Guitar effects pedals built by Steve Bragg and Jason Fee in Ottawa, Ontario.

EMS
1969-1979. Peter Zinnovieff's English synth company (Electronic Music Studios) also offered a guitar synthesizer. The company has reopened to work on original EMS gear.

Eowave
2002-present. Effects built first in Paris and now in Burgundy, France by Marc Sirguy.

Epiphone
Over the years, Epiphone offered a variety of different effect lines. Epiphone pedals which are labeled G.A.S Guitar Audio System were offered from around 1988 to '91.

Pedals
Various models with years available.

1988-1989	Chorus EP-CH-70	$45	$60
1988-1989	Delay EP-DE-80	$55	$75
1988-1991	Compressor EP-CO-20	$45	$60
1988-1991	Distortion EP-DI-10	$45	$60
1988-1991	Flanger EP-FL-60	$55	$75
1988-1991	Overdrive EP-OD-30	$45	$60

Rocco Tonexpressor
1937. Designed by steel-guitar ace Anthony Rocco, this pedal allows steel guitarists to adjust volume and tone with their foot.

1937		$300	$500

Ernie Ball
1972-present. The Ernie Ball company also builds Music Man instruments.

Volume Pedals
1977-present. Aluminum housing.

1977-2023		$35	$75

Euthymia Electronics
Line of guitar effects built by Erik Miller in Alameda, California.

Eventide
1971-present. This New Jersey electronics manufacturer has offered studio and rackmount effects since the late '70s. In '08 they added guitar effects pedals.

EXR
The EXR Corporation was in Brighton, Michigan.

Projector
1983-ca.1984. Psychoacoustic enhancer pedal.

1983-1984		$70	$100

Projector SP III
1983-ca.1984. Psychoacoustic enhancer pedal, volume pedal/sound boost.

1983-1984		$70	$100

Farfisa
The organ company offered effects pedals in the 1960s. Their products were manufactured in Italy by the Italian Accordion Company and distributed by Chicago Musical Instruments.

Model VIP 345 Organ
Mid-1960s. Portable organ with Syntheslalom used in the rock and roll venue.

1960s		$550	$650

Repeater

1969		$165	$300

Sferasound
1960s. Vibrato pedal for a Farfisa Organ but it works well with the guitar, gray case.

1960s		$300	$400

Wah/Volume

1969		$110	$150

Fargen
1999-present. Guitar effects built in Sacramento, California by Benjamin Fargen. He also builds amps.

Fender
1946-present. Although Fender has flirted with effects since the 1950s (the volume/volume-tone pedal and the Ecco-Fonic), the company concentrated mainly on guitars and amps. Fender effects ranged from the sublime to the ridiculous, from the tube Reverb to the Dimension IV. In 2013 Fender added a line of pedals.

'63 Tube Reverb
1994-2017. Reissue spring/tube Reverb Units with various era cosmetics as listed below. Currently offered in brown or, since '09, in lacquered tweed.

1994	White (limited run)	$800	$1,125
1994-1997	Black	$800	$1,125
1994-1997	Blond	$800	$1,125

E-H Switch Blade
Jim Schreck

1977 E-H Zipper
Rivington Guitars

EFFECTS

Fender '63 Tube Reverb

Fender Electronic
Echo Chamber

1971 Fender Fuzz Wah
Rivington Guitars

1962 Fender Reverb Unit
Michael Alonz

MODEL YEAR	FEATURES	LOW	HIGH
1994-1997	Tweed	$800	$1,125
1994-2008	Brown	$800	$1,125
2009-2017	Lacquered Tweed	$1,000	$1,250

Blender
1968-1977, 2005-2010. Battery-operated unit with fuzz, sustain, and octave controls.

1968-1969		$475	$650
1970-1977		$375	$600
2005-2010	Reissue	$200	$300

Contempo Organ
1967-1968. Portable organ, all solidstate, 61 keys including a 17-key bass section, catalog shows with red cover material.

1967-1968		$650	$1,250

Dimension IV
1968-1970. Multi-effects unit using an oil-filled drum.

1968-1970		$325	$425

Echo and Electronic Echo Chamber
1963-1968. Solidstate tape echo built by Ecco-Fonic, up to 400 ms of delay, rectangle box with 2 controls '63-'67, slanted front '67-'68.

1963-1967		$450	$800
1967-1968		$325	$600

Echo-Reverb
1966-1970. Solidstate, echo-reverb effect produced by rotating metal disk, black tolex, silver grille.

1966-1970		$500	$650

Fuzz-Wah
1968-1984, 2007-2011. Has Fuzz and Wah switches on sides of pedal '68-'73, has 3 switches above the pedal '74-'84. The newer version ('07-'11) has switches on sides.

1968-1973	Switches on side	$250	$325
1974-1984	Switches above	$175	$225
2007-2011	Switches on side	$110	$150

Phaser
1975-1977, 2007-2011. AC powered, reissued in '07.

1975-1977		$225	$300
2007-2011		$65	$130

Reverb Unit
1961-1966, 1975-1978. Fender used a wide variety of tolex coverings in the early-'60s as the coverings matched those on the amps. Initially, Fender used rough blond tolex, then rough brown tolex, followed by smooth white or black tolex.

1961	Blond tolex, Oxblood grille	$2,500	$3,750
1961	Brown tolex	$1,750	$3,500
1962	Blond tolex, Oxblood grille	$1,750	$3,500
1962	Brown tolex, Wheat grille	$1,500	$2,500
1963	Brown tolex	$1,500	$2,500
1963	Rough blond tolex	$1,500	$2,500
1963	Smooth white tolex	$1,500	$2,500
1964	Black tolex	$1,250	$2,000
1964	Brown tolex, gold grille	$1,250	$2,000
1964	Smooth white tolex	$1,250	$2,000
1965-1966	Black tolex	$1,250	$2,000
1966	Solidstate, flat cabinet	$350	$450
1975-1978	Tube reverb reinstated	$975	$1,500

MODEL YEAR	FEATURES	LOW	HIGH

Vibratone
1967-1972. Fender's parent company at the time, CBS, bought Leslie in 1965, and Fender began offering a Leslie-type rotating-speaker-emulator as the Vibratone in 1967. Based on the Leslie Model 16 cabinet and made specifically for the guitar, it featured a single fixed 4-ohm 10-inch speaker fronted by a rotating drum. Designed to be powered by an external amp. 2-speed motor. Black tolex.

1967-1968	Fender cast logo in upper left corner	$850	$2,000
1968-1972	Fender logo plate through center	$700	$1,500

Volume-Tone Pedal
1954-1984, 2007-2018. Swivel foot controller.

1954-1984		$400	$525
2007-2018		$45	$60

Fernandes
1970s. Japanese guitar and effects maker.
Funky-Filter FR-3F
1970s. Built by Univox for Fernandes.

1970s		$225	$300

Field Effects by Resonant Electronic Design
Guitar effects pedals, starting in 2010, built in Minneapolis, Minnesota by Wes Kuhnley and Peter Bregman. They also build the Resonant brand amps.

Fishman
2003-present. Larry Fishman of Andover, Massachusetts offers a line of acoustic guitar effects pedals. He also builds amps.

FJA Mods
Jerry Pinnelli began building guitar effects in 2002, in Central Square, New York. He added professional grade, production, guitar amps in '07, then relocates to Charlotte, North Carolina in '18 and takes a hiatus from building.

FlexiSound
FlexiSound products were made in Lancaster, Pennsylvania.
F. S. Clipper
1975-ca.1976. Distortion, plugged directly into guitar jack.

1975-1976		$60	$75

The Beefer
1975. Power booster, plugged directly into guitar jack.

1975		$45	$60

Flip
Line of tube effects by Guyatone and distributed in the U.S. by Godlyke Distributing.
Tube Echo (TD-X)
2004-2017. Hybrid tube power delay pedal.

2004-2017		$110	$150

The *Vintage Guitar Price Guide* shows values for an all-original condition guitar effect.

MODEL			
YEAR	FEATURES	LOW	HIGH

FM Acoustics

FM Acoustics pedals were made in Switzerland.

E-1 Pedal
1975. Volume, distortion, filter pedal.

1975		$75	$100

Foxx

Foxx pedals are readily identifiable by their fur-like covering. They slunk onto the scene in 1971 and were extinct by '78. Made by Hollywood's Ridinger Associates, their most notable product was the Tone Machine fuzz. Foxx-made pedals also have appeared under various brands such as G & G, Guild, Yamaha, and Sears Roebuck, generally without fur. Since 2005, reissues of some of the classic Foxx pedals are being built in Provo, Utah.

Clean Machine
1974-1978		$250	$350

Down Machine
1971-1977. Bass wah.

1971-1977	Blue case	$250	$350

Foot Phaser
1975-1977, 2006.

1975-1977		$650	$850

Fuzz and Wa and Volume
1974-1978, 2006. Currently called the Fuzz Wah Volume.

1974-1978		$500	$650

Guitar Synthesizer I
1975		$625	$1,750

Loud Machine
1970s. Volume pedal.

1970s		$65	$150

O.D. Machine
1972-ca.1975.

1972-1975		$250	$325

Phase III
1975-1978		$200	$250

Tone Machine
1971-1978, 2005. Fuzz with Octave, blue or black housing.

1971-1978		$500	$650

Wa and Volume
1971-1978		$375	$500

Wa Machine
1971-ca.1978.

1971-1978		$250	$325

Framptone

Founded by Peter Frampton in the year 2000, Framptone offers hand-made guitar effects.

3 Banger
2000-2021. Three-way amp switch box, white housing.

2000-2021		$250	$500

Amp Switcher
2000-2021. A-B switch box, white housing.

2000-2021		$200	$250

Talk Box
2000-2021. Talk box, white housing, no control knobs, on-off footswitch.

2000-2021		$250	$500

Frantone

1994-present. Effects and accessories hand built in New York City.

Fulltone

1991-present. Effects based on some of the classics of the past and built in Los Angeles, California, by Michael Fuller.

Choralflange
2000s. Dark green and silver case.

2000s		$250	$400

DejàVibe
1991-2004. Uni-Vibe-type pedal, later models have a Vintage/Modern switch. A stereo version also available.

1991-1993	Mono, gold housing	$350	$550
1993-2004	Mono, black housing	$275	$350

DejàVibe 2
1997-2018. Like DejàVibe but with built-in speed control. A stereo version also available.

1997-2018	Mono	$350	$550

Distortion Pro
2002-2008. Red case, volume, and distortion knobs with four voicing controls.

2002-2008		$125	$175

Fat Boost
2001-2007. Clean boost, silver-sparkle case, volume, and drive knobs.

2001-2007		$150	$200

Full-Drive 2
1995-present. Blue case, four control knobs.

1995-2023		$150	$400

Mini-DejàVibe
2004-2018. Uni-Vibe-type pedal, white housing, 3 Control knobs, stereo version also available.

2004-2018	Mono	$200	$400

OCD
1990-present. Obsessive compulsive drive.

1990-2012	V11 to V13	$250	$300
2013-2023	V14 to V17	$100	$150

Octafuzz
1996-2019. Copy of the Tycobrahe Octavia.

1996-2019		$150	$400

Soul Bender
1994-present. Volume, tone, and dirt knobs.

1994-2023		$200	$550

Supa-Trem
1996-2019. Black case, white Supa-Trem logo, rate, and mix controls.

1996-2019		$150	$200

Supa-Trem2
2000s. Yellow housing, 3 control knobs.

2000s		$200	$450

Tube Tape Echo
2000s. Echo-Plex-style echo unit, white case.

2000s		$775	$1,750

Tube Tape Echo TTE
2004-2022. Echoplex-style tube-powered tape unit, different colored housings.

2004-2022		$775	$1,750

Fishman Fission Bass Powerchord

2006 Fulltone Octafuzz
Rivington Guitars

Fulltone Tube Tape Echo TTE

EFFECTS

George Dennis Elite Wah

Gizmoaudio Sawmill

Goran Fat Boy

Furman Sound

1993-present. Located in Petaluma, California, Furman makes audio and video signal processors and AC power conditioning products for music and other markets.

LC-2 Limiter Compressor
1990s. Rackmount unit with a black suitcase and red knobs.

1990s		$65	$85

PQ3 Parametric EQ
1990s. Rackmount preamp and equalizer.

1998-1999		$225	$400

PQ6 Parametric Stereo

1990s		$225	$400

RV1 Reverb Rackmount

1990s		$225	$400

Fxdoctor

2003-present. Joshua Zalegowski originally built his effects in Amherst, Massachusetts, and in 2005 moved to Boston.

Fxengineering

2002-present. Production and custom guitar effects built by Montez Aldridge in Raleigh, North Carolina.

G.M. Electronics

1960s. Based in Detroit, Michigan.

Dual Range Fuzz Up FD3-A
1960s. Fuzz pedal combining 2 Gibson Maestro FZ-1 Fuzz Tone circuits.

1960s		$125	$300

Fuzz Up FM3-B
1960s. Clone of the Gibson Maestro FZ-1 Fuzz Tone.

1960s		$125	$300

G.S. Wyllie

2000s. Glenn Wyllie built effects in North Carolina.

Moonrock
2000s. Octave fuzz.

2000s		$450	$1,000

NewMoon
2000s. Updated version of Moonrock octave fuzz.

2000s		$450	$1,000

Ozo
2000s. Ring modulator.

2000s		$450	$1,000

X-Fuzz
2000s. High-gain fuzz.

2000s		$450	$1,000

G2D

1999-present. David Manning and Grant Wills build their guitar effects pedals in Auckland, New Zealand.

Garcia

Guitar effects built by Matthew Garcia in Myrtle Beach, South Carolina, starting in 2004. He also built amps.

Geek MacDaddy

See listing under The Original Geek.

George Dennis

1991-present. Founded by George Burgerstein, the original products were a line of effects pedals. In '96 they added a line of tube amps. The company is in Prague, Czech Republic.

Gibson

Gibson did offer a few effects bearing their own name, but most were sold under the Maestro name (see that listing).

Echoplex Digital Pro Plus
1994-2010. Rackmount unit with digital recording, sampling, and digital delay. Labeled as just Echoplex until '01 when Gibson name added.

1994-2010		$425	$550

GA-3RV Reverb Unit
1964-1967. Small, compact, spring reverb unit, black tolex, gray grille.

1964-1967		$400	$550

GA-4RE Reverb-Echo Unit
1964-1967. Small, compact, lightweight accessory reverb-echo unit that produces complete reverberation and authentic echo, utilizes Gibson's "electronic memory" system for both reverb and echo, black tolex, gray grille.

1964-1967		$400	$550

Gig-FX

2004-present. Founder Jeff Purchon of Waltham, Massachusetts, imports guitar effects pedals built at his company-owned factory in Shenzhen, China.

Gizmo, Inc.

Ca.1980. Short-lived company that grew out of the ashes of Musitronics' attempt to make the Gizomotron. See Mu-Tron.

Gizmoaudio

2009-present. Guitar effects built by Charles Luke in Cumming, Georgia.

Gnome Amplifiers

Guitar effects pedals built by Dan Munro in Olympia, Washington. He started in 2008 and builds amps.

Godbout

Godbout sold a variety of effects do-it-yourself kits in the 1970s, which are difficult to value because quality depends on skills of builder.

Effects Kits

1970s		$25	$35

Godley Crème

1978-1980. Kevin Godley and Lol Crème, members of the band 10cc, developed the Gizmotron, which mounted on the face of a bass or guitar and continuously strummed the strings to give a bowed-string effect. The

MODEL YEAR	FEATURES	LOW	HIGH

device was built by Musitronics of New Jersey, which built the MuTron III and other effects.

Gizmotron

1978-1980. A "ultimate sustain" mechanical add-on to guitar or bass bridges with rotating plectrums.

1978-1980		$350	$500

Goodrich Sound

1970s-present. Originally located in Michigan, and currently in Dublin, Georgia, Goodrich currently offers volume pedals and a line boost.

Match Box Line Boost

Early-1980s-2011. Small rectangular line buffer/driver.

1980s-2011		$125	$175

Volume Pedal 6122

Late-1970s-1980s. Uses a potentiometer.

1970s		$125	$175

Volume Pedal 6400ST

Late-1970s-1980s. Stereo pedal, using photocells.

1970s		$125	$175

Volume Pedal 6402

Late-1970s-1980s. Uses photocell.

1970s		$125	$175

Goran Custom Guitars

1998-present. Luthier Goran Djuric from Belgrade, Serbia also offers guitar pedals.

Goya

1960s. Goya Music sold effects under the brands Goya, Applied, Nomad, Conrad and maybe more.

Fury Box

1960s		$100	$150

Greer Amplification

1999-present. Guitar stomp box effects built by Nick Greer in Athens, Georgia. He also builds amps.

Gretsch

Gretsch has offered a limited line of effects from time to time.

Controfuzz

Mid-1970s. Distortion.

1970s		$250	$350

Deluxe Reverb Unit Model 6149

1963-1969. Similar to Gibson's GA-1 introduced around the same time.

1963-1969		$650	$850

Expandafuzz

Mid-1970s. Distortion.

1970s		$300	$400

Reverb Unit Model 6144 Preamp Reverb

1963-1967. Approximately 17 watts, preamp functionality, no speaker.

1963-1967		$650	$1,000

Tremofect

Mid-1970s. Tremolo effect, 3-band EQ, speed, effect, bass, total, and treble knobs.

1970s		$400	$550

Guild

Guild marketed effects made by Binson, Electro-Harmonix, Foxx, WEM and Applied in the 1960s and '70s.

Copicat

1960s-1979. Echo.

1970s		$750	$1,500

DE-20 Auto-Rhythm Unit

1971-1974. 50-watt rhythm accompaniment unit. Included 20 rhythms and a separate instrument channel with its own volume control. 1x12" plus tweeter.

1971-1974		$300	$400

Echorec (by Binson)

Ca.1960-1979. Stripped-down version of the Binson Echorec.

1960s		$5,500	$7,500

Foxey Lady Fuzz

1968-1977. Distortion, sustain.

1968-1975	2 knobs, made by E-H	$750	$1,000
1976-1977	3 knobs in row, same as Big Muff	$850	$1,250

Fuzz Wah FW-3

1975-ca.1979. Distortion, volume, wah, made by Foxx.

1970s		$150	$300

HH Echo Unit

1976-ca.1979.

1970s		$350	$550

VW-1

1975-ca.1979. Volume, wah, made by Foxx.

1970s		$200	$250

Guyatone (Tokyo Sound Company)

1930s-present. Founded by Mitsuo Matsuki, maker of guitars, amps, and effects. Imported stomp boxes, tape echo units and outboard reverb units distributed by Godlyke Distributing. In 2013 they merged with DeMont Guitars of Oswego, Illinois and effects are made in the US and Japan.

Bazz Box FS-1

1960s. Vox V828 Tone Bender copy.

1960s		$200	$300

Bazz Box FS-2

1960s. Univox Super-Fuzz copy.

1960s		$200	$300

Crazy-Face

1970s. Dallas-Arbiter Fuzz Face copy.

1970s		$300	$600

Sustainer FS-6

1970s. Circular Fuzz Face-like housing.

1970s		$500	$800

Wah-Fuzz FS-5

1970s		$200	$450

HAO

Line of guitar effects built in Japan by J.E.S. International, distributed in the U.S. by Godlyke.

Harden Engineering

2006-present. Distortion/boost guitar effects pedals built by William Harden in Chicago, Illinois. He also builds guitars.

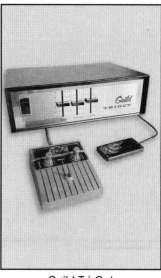

Guild Tri-Oct
Mary-Anne Hammer

1970s Guyatone PS-104
Crossover Auto Wah
Rivington Guitars

HAO Rust Driver

EFFECTS

MODEL			
YEAR	**FEATURES**	**LOW**	**HIGH**

Henretta Engineering
The Valley Reverb

Hughes & Kettner Rotosphere
Imaged by Heritage Auctions, HA.com

Ibanez Analog Delay AD9
Rivington Guitars

Heathkit

1960s. These were sold as do-it-yourself kits and are difficult to value because quality depends on the skills of builder.

TA-28 Distortion Booster

1960s. Fuzz assembly kit, heavy '60s super fuzz, case-by-case quality depending on the builder.

1960s		$250	$350

Heavy Metal Products

Mid-1970s. From Alto Loma, California, products for the heavy metal guitarist.

Raunchbox Fuzz

1975-1976		$150	$200

Switchbox

1975-1976. A/B box.

1975-1976		$30	$40

Heet Sound Products

1974-present. The E Bow concept goes back to '67, but a hand-held model wasn't available until '74. Made in Los Angeles, California.

E Bow

1974-1979, 1985-1987, 1994-present. The Energy Bow, hand-held electro-magnetic string driver.

1974-1979		$70	$90

E Bow for Pedal Steels

1979. Hand-held electro-magnetic string driver.

1979		$50	$70

Heil Sound

1960-present. Founded by Bob Heil, Marissa, Illinois. Created the talk box technology as popularized by Joe Walsh and Peter Frampton. In the '60s and '70s Heil was dedicated to innovative products for the music industry. In the late-'70s, innovative creations were more in the amateur radio market, and by the '90s Heil's focus was on the home theater market. The Heil Sound Talkbox was reissued by Jim Dunlop USA in '89.

Talk Box

1976-ca.1980, 1989-present. Reissued by Dunlop.

1976-1980		$150	$200
1989-1999		$85	$110
2000-2023		$80	$110

Henretta Engineering

2009-present. Analog guitar effects built by Kevin Henretta first in Chicago, Illinois and presently Saint Paul, Minnesota.

Hermida Audio

2003-2013. Alfonso Hermida built his guitar effects in Miramar, Florida. Hermida was acquired by Lovepedal in '13.

High Gain

See the listing under Dunlop.

Hohner

Hohner offered effects in the late-1970s.

Dirty Booster

1977-ca.1978. Distortion.

1977-1978		$550	$775

Dirty Wah Wah'er

1977-ca.1978. Adds distortion.

1977-1978		$225	$300

Fuzz Wah

1970s. Morley-like volume pedal with volume knob and fuzz knob, switch for soft or hard fuzz, gray box with black foot pedal.

1970s		$225	$350

Multi-Exciter

1977-ca.1978. Volume, wah, surf, tornado, siren.

1977-1978		$250	$350

Tape Echo/Echo Plus

1970s. Black alligator suitcase.

1970s		$300	$550

Tri-Booster

1977-ca.1978. Distortion, sustain.

1977-1978		$550	$775

Vari-Phaser

1977-ca.1978.

1977-1978		$300	$400

Vol-Kicker Volume Pedal

1977-ca.1978.

1977-1978		$225	$350

Wah-Wah'er

1977-ca.1978. Wah, volume.

1977-1978		$225	$350

HomeBrew Electronics

2001-present. Stomp box effects hand made by Joel and Andrea Weaver in Glendale, Arizona.

Honey

1967-1969. Honey Company Ltd. Was formed by ex-Teisco workers after that firm was acquired by Kawai. Honey launched several effects designed by engineer Fumio Mieda, before going bankrupt in March, '69. The company was reborn as Shin-ei and many of its designs continued production in various forms; see Shin-ei for more.

Baby Crying

1960s. Univox Super-Fuzz copy.

1960s		$450	$550

Psychedelic Machine

1967-1969. Amp head-sized effect with numerous controls.

1967-1969		$3,000	$5,000

Special Fuzz

1967-1970s		$550	$850

Vibra Chorus

1967-1969. Original version of the Uni-Vibe, which Shin-ei would produce after Honey went bankrupt.

1967-1969		$2,000	$3,000

Hughes & Kettner

1985-present. Hughes & Kettner builds a line of tube-driven guitar effects made in Germany. They also build amps and cabinets.

MODEL YEAR	FEATURES	LOW	HIGH

Ibanez

1932-present. Ibanez effects were introduced ca. 1974 and were manufactured by Japan's Maxon Electronics. Although results were mixed at first, a more uniform and modern product line, including the now legendary Tube Screamer, built Ibanez's reputation for quality. They continue to produce a wide range of effects.

60s Fuzz FZ5 (SoundTank)
1991-1992, 1996-1998. Fuzz with level, tone and distortion controls, black plastic case, green label.

1990s		$55	$75

7th Heaven SH7 (Tone-Lok)
2000-2004. Lo, high, drive and level controls, gray-silver case, blue-green label.

2000-2004		$50	$75

Acoustic Effects PT4
1993-1998. Acoustic guitar multi-effect with compressor/limiter, tone shaper, stereo chorus, digital reverb, with power supply.

1993-1998		$200	$500

Analog Delay 202 (Rack Mount)
1981-1983. Rack mount with delay, doubling, flanger, stereo chorus, dual inputs with tone and level.

1981-1983		$300	$400

Analog Delay AD9
1982-1984, 2000s. 3 control analog delay, Hot Pink metal case, reissued in the 2000s.

1982-1984		$150	$350
2000s	Reissue	$85	$150

Analog Delay AD80
1980-1981. Pink case.

1980-1981		$200	$300

Analog Delay AD99
1996-1998. Reissue, 3 control knobs and on/off switch, winged-hand logo, black case.

1996-1998		$100	$150

Analog Delay AD100 (Table Unit)
1981-1983. Stand-alone table/studio unit (not rack mount) with power cord.

1981-1983		$200	$250

Analog Delay ADL

1985-1986		$100	$130

Auto Filter AF9
1982-1984. Replaces AF201 model.

1982-1984		$200	$300

Auto Filter AF201
1981. Two min-max sliders, 3 mode toggle switches, orange metal case.

1981		$200	$350

Auto Wah AW5 (SoundTank)
1994-1999. Plastic case SoundTank series.

1994-1999		$50	$90

Auto Wah AW7 (Tone-Lok)
2000-2010. Silver case.

2000-2010		$50	$100

Bass Compressor BP10

1986-1991		$80	$125

Bass Stack BS10

1987-1988		$450	$600

Bi-Mode Chorus BC9
1984. Dual channel for 2 independent speed and width settings.

1984		$150	$225

Chorus CS-505
1980-1981. Speed and depth controls, gray-blue case, stereo or mono input, battery or external power option.

1980-1981		$200	$250

Chorus Flanger CF7 (Tone-Lok)
1999-2010. Speed, depth, delay, regeneration controls, mode, and crazy switches.

1999-2010		$75	$125

Chorus Flanger DCF-10

1986-1989		$175	$225

Classic Flange FL99
1997-1999. Analog reissue, silver metal case, winged-hand artwork, 4 controls, 2 footswitch buttons.

1997-1999		$275	$350

Classic Phase PH99
1995-1999. Analog reissue, silver metal case, winged-hand artwork, speed, depth, feedback, effect level controls, intense and bypass footswitches.

1995-1999		$125	$150

Compressor CP5 (SoundTank)

1991-1998		$30	$45

Compressor CP10

1986-1992		$85	$125

Compressor CP830

1975-1979		$100	$150

Compressor II CP835

1980-1981		$125	$150

Compressor Limiter CP9

1982-1984		$75	$100

DCP Distortion PDS1

1980s		$75	$100

DCP Parametric EQ PPE1

1980s		$110	$200

Delay Champ CD10
1986-1989. Red case, 3 knobs.

1986-1989		$120	$160

Delay Echo DE7 (Tone-Lok)
1999-2010. Stereo delay/echo.

1999-2010		$100	$125

Delay Harmonizer DM1000
1983-1984. Rack mount, with chorus, 9 control knobs.

1983-1984		$175	$225

Delay II DDL10

1986-1988		$125	$175

Delay III DDL20 Digital Delay
1988-1989. Filtering, doubling, slap back, echo S, echo M, echo L, Seafoam Green coloring on pedal.

1988-1989		$130	$150

Delay PDD1 (DPC Series)
1988-1989. Programmable Digital Delay (PDD) with display screen.

1988-1989		$125	$150

Digital Chorus DSC10
1990-1992. 3 control knobs and slider selection toggle.

1990-1992		$100	$125

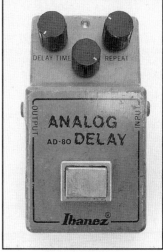

1980 Ibanez Analog Delay AD80
Bernunzio Uptown Music

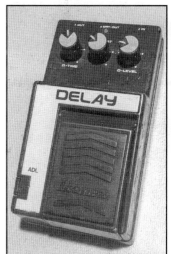

Ibanez Analog Delay ADL
Keith Myers

1983 Ibanez Compressor Limiter CP9
Mark Mondahl

EFFECTS

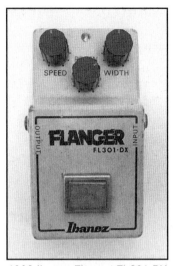

1982 Ibanez Flanger FL301-DX
Bernunzio Uptown Music

1975 Ibanez Overdrive OD850
Rivington Guitars

1977 Ibanez Phase
Tone II PT707
Keith Myers,

MODEL YEAR	FEATURES	LOW	HIGH
Digital Delay DL5 (SoundTank)			
1991-1998		$40	$80
Digital Delay DL10			
1989-1992. Digital Delay made in Japan, blue case, 3 green control knobs, stompbox.			
1989-1992		$100	$130
Distortion Charger DS10			
1986-1989		$110	$150
Distortion DS7 (Tone-Lok)			
2000-2010. Drive, tone, and level controls.			
2000-2010		$45	$65
Dual Chorus CCL			
1990s		$100	$150
Echo Machine EM5 (SoundTank)			
1996-1998. Simulates tape echo.			
1996-1998		$200	$300
Fat Cat Distortion FC10			
1987-1989. 3-knob pedal with distortion, tone, and level controls.			
1987-1989		$150	$300
Flanger FFL5 (Master Series)			
1984-1985. Speed, regeneration, width, D-time controls, battery or adapter option.			
1984-1985		$75	$100
Flanger FL5 (SoundTank)			
1991-1998		$40	$60
Flanger FL9			
1982-1984. Yellow case.			
1982-1984		$100	$200
Flanger FL301			
1979-1982. Mini flanger, 3 knobs, called the FL-301 DX in late '81-'82.			
1979-1982		$120	$150
Flanger FL305			
1976-1979. Five knobs.			
1976-1979		$300	$400
Flying Pan FP777			
1976-1979. Auto pan/phase shifter, 4 control knobs, phase on/off button, pan on/off button, silver metal case with blue trim and Flying Pan winged-hand logo.			
1976-1979		$350	$450
Flying Pan FP777 Reissue			
2007	777 made	$250	$350
Fuzz FZ7 (Tone-Lok)			
2000-2010. Drive, tone and level controls, gray-silver case, blue green FZ7 label.			
2000-2010		$60	$80
Graphic Bass EQ BE10			
1986-1992. Later labeled as the BEQ10.			
1986-1992		$70	$100
Graphic EQ GE9			
1982-1984. Six EQ sliders, 1 overall volume slider, turquoise blue case.			
1982-1984		$100	$200
Graphic EQ GE10			
1986-1992. Eight sliders.			
1986-1992		$75	$130
Graphic Equalizer GE601 (808 Series)			
1980-1981. 7-slider EQ, aqua blue metal case.			
1980-1981		$75	$100

MODEL YEAR	FEATURES	LOW	HIGH
Guitar Multi-Processor PT5			
1993-1997. Floor unit, programmable with 25 presets and 25 user presets, effects include distortion, chorus, flanger, etc, green case.			
1993-1997		$100	$150
Jetlyzer JL70			
1975-1977. Phase shifter and jet plane effect, orange and black case.			
1975-1977		$350	$550
LA Metal LM7			
1988-1989. Silver case.			
1988-1989		$100	$135
LoFi LF7 (Tone-Lok)			
2000-2010. Filter, 4 knobs.			
2000-2010		$100	$175
Metal Charger MS10			
1986-1992. Distortion, level, attack, punch and edge control knobs, green case.			
1986-1992		$100	$125
Metal Screamer MSL			
1985. 3 control knobs.			
1985		$150	$200
Modern Fusion MF5 (SoundTank)			
1990-1991. Level, tone and distortion controls.			
1990-1991		$80	$160
Modulation Delay DM500			
1983-1984. Rack mount.			
1983-1984		$100	$200
Modulation Delay DM1000			
1983-1984. Rack mount with delay, reverb, modulation.			
1983-1984		$100	$200
Modulation Delay PDM1			
1988-1989. Programmable Digital Modulation pedal.			
1988-1989		$100	$200
Mostortion MT10			
1990-1992. Mos-FET circuit distortion pedal, 5 control knobs, green case.			
1990-1992		$450	$650
Multi-Effect PUE5/PUE5 Tube (Floor Unit)			
1990-1993. Yellow version has tube, blue one does not. Also available in PUE5B bass version.			
1990-1993 Tube		$300	$400
Multi-Effect UE300 (Floor Unit)			
1983-1984. Floor unit, 4 footswitches for super metal, digital delay, digital stereo chorus, and master power, 3 delay modes.			
1983-1984		$250	$350
Multi-Effect UE300B (Floor Unit)			
1983-1984. Floor unit for bass.			
1983-1984		$250	$350
Multi-Effect UE305 (Floor Unit)			
1983-1984		$200	$300
Multi-Effect UE400 (Rackmount)			
1980-1984. Rack mount with foot switch.			
1980-1984		$300	$375
Multi-Effect UE405 (Rackmount)			
1981-1984. Rack mount with analog delay, parametric EQ, compressor/limiter, stereo chorus and loop.			
1981-1984		$300	$375

The *Vintage Guitar Price Guide* shows values for an all-original condition guitar effect.

MODEL YEAR	FEATURES	LOW	HIGH
Noise Buster NB10			
1988-1989. Eliminates 60-cycle hum and other outside signals, metal case.			
1988-1989		$70	$100
Overdrive OD850			
1975-1979		$300	$400
Overdrive II OD855			
1977-1979. Distortion, tone, and level controls, yellow/green case, large Overdrive II logo.			
1977-1979		$300	$400
Pan Delay DPL10			
1990-1992. Royal Blue case, 3 green control knobs.			
1990-1992		$100	$125
Parametric EQ PQ9			
1982-1984		$125	$200
Parametric EQ PQ401			
1981. 3 sliders, dial-in knob, light aqua blue case.			
1981		$200	$275
Phase Tone II PT707			
1976-1979. Blue box, script logo for first 2 years.			
1976-1979		$100	$130
Phase Tone PT909			
1979-1982. Blue box, 3 knobs, early models with flat case (logo at bottom or later in the middle) or later wedge case.			
1979-1982		$140	$200
Phase Tone PT999			
1975-1979. Script logo, 1 knob, round footswitch, becomes PT-909.			
1975-1979		$125	$150
Phase Tone PT1000			
1974-1975. Morley-style pedal phase, light blue case, early model of Phase Tone.			
1974-1975		$200	$300
Phaser PH5 (SoundTank)			
1991-1998		$40	$70
Phaser PH7 (Tone-Lok)			
1999-2010. Speed, depth, feedback, and level controls.			
1999-2010		$60	$75
Phaser PT9			
1982-1984. Three control knobs, red case.			
1982-1984		$125	$220
Powerlead PL5 (SoundTank)			
1991-1998. Metal case '91, plastic case '91-'98.			
1991	Metal	$25	$35
1991-1998	Plastic	$30	$50
Renometer			
1976-1979. 5-band equalizer with preamp.			
1976-1979		$150	$200
Rotary Chorus RC99			
1996-1999. Black or silver cases available, requires a power pack and does not use a battery.			
1996-1999	Black case	$125	$175
Session Man SS10			
1988-1989. Distortion, chorus.			
1988-1989		$300	$450
Session Man II SS20			
1988-1989. 4 controls plus toggle, light pink-purple case.			
1988-1989		$200	$300

MODEL YEAR	FEATURES	LOW	HIGH
Slam Punk SP5 (SoundTank)			
1996-1999		$50	$70
Smash Box SM7 (Tone-Lok)			
2000-2010		$70	$85
Sonic Distortion SD9			
1982-1984		$150	$200
Standard Fuzz (No. 59)			
1974-1979. Two buttons (fuzz on/off and tone change).			
1974-1979		$400	$600
Stereo Bass Chorus BC10			
1986-1993. Purple case.			
1986-1993		$100	$125
Stereo Box ST800			
1975-1979. One input, 2 outputs for panning, small yellow case.			
1975-1979		$125	$250
Stereo Chorus CS9			
1982-1984		$125	$250
Stereo Chorus CSL (Master Series)			
1985-1986		$100	$125
Super Chorus CS5 (SoundTank)			
1991-1998		$25	$40
Super Metal SM9			
1984. Distortion.			
1984		$150	$220
Super Stereo Chorus SC10			
1986-1992		$100	$150
Super Tube Screamer ST9			
1984-1985. 4 knobs, light green metal case.			
1984-1985		$450	$600
Super Tube STL			
1985		$150	$275
Swell Flanger SF10			
1986-1992. Speed, regeneration, width and time controls, yellow case.			
1986-1992		$130	$250
Time Machine AD190 Delay			
1978-1980. Analog delay and flanger.			
1978-1980		$400	$500
Trashmetal TM5 (SoundTank)			
1990-1998. Tone and distortion pedal, 3 editions (1st edition, 2nd edition metal case, 2nd edition plastic case).			
1990-1998		$50	$70
Tremolo Pedal TL5 (SoundTank)			
1995-1998		$40	$70
Tube King TK999			
1994-1995. Has a 12AX7 tube and 3-band equalizer.			
1994-1995	Includes power pack	$150	$200
Tube King TK999US			
1996-1998. Has a 12AX7 tube and 3-band equalizer, does not have the noise switch of the original TK999. Made in the U.S.			
1996-1998	Includes power pack	$150	$200
Tube Screamer TS5 (SoundTank)			
1991-1998		$25	$100
Tube Screamer TS7 (Tone-Lok)			
1999-2010. 3 control knobs.			
1999-2010		$60	$100

1984 Ibanez Phaser PT9
Rivington Guitars

1984 Ibanez Super Metal SM9
Mark Mondahl

Ibanez Tube Screamer TS5

EFFECTS

Ibanez Tube Screamer TS9

JAM Pedals Delay Llama

JAM Pedals LucyDreamer
Supreme

MODEL YEAR	FEATURES	LOW	HIGH
Tube Screamer TS9			
1982-1984, 1993-present. Reissued in '93.			
1982-1984		$350	$450
1993-2023		$125	$175
1993-2023	AnalogMan modded	$175	$225
1993-2023	Keeley modded	$225	$300
Tube Screamer Classic TS10			
1986-1993		$350	$500
Tube Screamer TS808			
1980-1982, 2004-present. Reissued in '04.			
1980-1982	Original	$1,000	$1,250
2004-2023	Reissue	$100	$130
Turbo Tube Screamer TS9DX			
1998-present. Tube Screamer circuit with added 3 settings for low-end.			
1998-2023		$100	$150
Twin Cam Chorus TC10			
1986-1989. Four control knobs, light blue case.			
1986-1989		$75	$180
Virtual Amp VA3 (floor unit)			
1995-1998. Digital effects processor.			
1995-1998		$75	$125
Visual Super Product SK-10			
1986. Very rare, limited run for small shop in Japan.			
1986		$3,000	$3,500
VL10			
1987-1997. Stereo volume pedal.			
1987-1997		$50	$75
Wah Fuzz Standard (Model 58)			
1974-1981. Fuzz tone change toggle, fuzz on toggle, fuzz depth control, balance control, wah volume pedal with circular friction pads on footpedal.			
1974-1981		$125	$275
Wah WH10			
1987-1996		$100	$300
Wau Wau Fuzz			
1970s. Volume plus fuzz control.			
1970s		$150	$250

Ilitch Electronics
2003-present. Ilitch Chiliachki builds his effects in Camarillo, California.

Indy Guitarist
See listing under Wampler Pedals.

InterFax Electronics
Mid-1970s-1980s. Started by Ed Giese, located in Milwaukee, Wisconsin.
HP-1 Harmonic Percolator
Mid-1970s. Distortion/fuzz unit, harmonics and balance sliders.

1970s		$175	$300

Intersound
1970s-1980s. Intersound, Inc. was in Boulder, Colorado and was a division of Electro-Voice.
Reverb-Equalizer R100F
1977-1979. Reverb and 4-band EQ, fader.

1977-1979		$75	$100

J. Everman
Analog guitar effects built by Justin J. Everman in Richardson, Texas, starting in 2000.

Jack Deville Electronics
2008-present. Production/custom, guitar effects built in Portland, Oregon by Jack Deville.

Jacques
One-of-a-kind handmade stomp boxes and production models made in France.

JAM Pedals
2007-present. Pedals built by Jannis Anastasakis Marinos of Athens, Greece.

MODEL YEAR	LOW	HIGH
Black Muck		
2017-2018. Fuzz distortion.		
2017-2018	$200	$250
Boomster		
2007-present. Silicon clean boost.		
2007-2023	$80	$100
Boomster Mini		
2017-2022. Silicon clean boost.		
2017-2022	$55	$100
DanComp		
2007-2015. Compressor based on the Dan Armstrong Orange Squeezer compressor circuit.		
2007-2015	$200	$250
Delay Llama		
2007-present. Analog delay.		
2007-2023	$150	$200
Delay Llama Supreme		
2014-2019. Analog delay with tap tempo modulation.		
2014-2019	$300	$350
Delay Llama+		
2009-2019. Analog delay with hold function.		
2009-2019	$175	$225
Dyna-ssoR		
2007-present. Compression/sustainer.		
2007-2023	$150	$200
Fuzz Phase		
2007-2018. Germanium fuzz.		
2007-2018	$200	$250
LucyDreamer Supreme		
2017-present. Overdrive/boost.		
2017-2023	$200	$250
Rattler		
2008-present. Distortion.		
2008-2023	$150	$200
Rattler+		
2008-2018. Distortion with low-gain stage.		
2008-2018	$200	$250
Red Muck		
2008-2018. Fuzz distortion.		
2008-2018	$150	$200
Retro Vibe		
2007-present. Vibe/vibrato.		
2007-2023	$250	$300
Ripple		
2007-present. Two-stage phaser.		
2007-2023	$125	$175

MODEL YEAR FEATURES	LOW	HIGH

Ripply Fall
2017-present. Chorus/vibrato/phaser.

2017-2023	$225	$300

Rooster
2007-2018. Frequency booster.

2007-2018	$175	$225

The Big Chill
2011-2023. Super tremolo with 2 speeds and chop effect.

2011-2023	$200	$250

The Chill
2007-present. Sine-wave tremolo.

2007-2023	$125	$175

Tube Dreamer 58/Tubedreamer
2007-present. Overdrive with selectable high-gain stage.

2007-2023	$125	$175

Tube Dreamer 72
2007-2018. Overdrive.

2007-2018	$150	$200

Tube Dreamer 88
2007-2018. Double overdrive.

2007-2018	$175	$225

Tube Dreamer+
2007-2017. Overdrive with footswitchable high-gain stage.

2007-2017	$150	$200

Wahcko/Wahcko+
2007-present. Wah-wah.

2007-2023	$200	$250

WaterFall
2007-present. Chorus/vibrato.

2007-2023	$175	$225

JangleBox

2004-present. Stephen Lasko and Elizabeth Lasko build their guitar effects in Springfield, Virginia and Dracut, Massachusetts.

Jan-Mar Industries

Jan-Mar was in Hillsdale, New Jersey.

The Talker
1976. 30 watts.

1976	$75	$150

The Talker Pro
1976. 75 watts.

1976	$100	$150

Jax

1960s-1970. Japanese imports made by Shin-ei.

Fuzz Master

1960s	$400	$500

Fuzz Wah

1960s	$200	$350

Vibrachorus
1969. Rotating-speaker simulator, with control pedal. Variant of Uni-Vibe.

1969	$800	$1,500

Wah-Wah

1960s	$500	$600

MODEL YEAR FEATURES	LOW	HIGH

Jen

Italy's Jen Elettronica company made a variety of guitar effects pedals in the 1960s and '70s for other brands such as Vox and Gretsch name. They also offered many of them, including the Cry Baby, under their own name.

Jennings

1960s. Dick Denny, of Vox fame, designed a short-lived line of effects for Jennings Electronic Developments of England.

Growler
1960s. Fuzz and wah effect with a rotary foot control.

1960s	$875	$1,500

Jersey Girl

1991-present. Line of guitar effects pedals made in Japan. They also build guitars.

Jet Sounds LTD

1977. Jet was located in Jackson, Mississippi.

Hoze Talk Box
1977. Large wood box, 30 watts.

1977	$100	$150

Jetter Gear

2005-present. Brad Jeter builds his effects pedals in Marietta, Georgia.

JHD Audio

1974-1990. Hunt Dabney founded JHD in Costa Mesa, California, to provide effects that the user installed in their amp. Dabney is still involved in electronics and builds the BiasProbe tool for tubes.

SuperCube/SuperCube II
1974-late 1980s. Plug-in sustain mod for Fender amps with reverb, second version for amps after '78.

1974-1980s	$50	$75

JHS Pedals

2007-present. Located in Mississippi 2007-08, Josh Scott presently builds his guitar and bass effects in Kansas City, Missouri.

Bonsai

2007-2023	$150	$200

Colour Box V2

2007-2023	$275	$350

Emperor

2007-2022	$110	$175

Feedback Looper

2007-2022	$100	$130

Haunting Mids

2007-2023	$80	$125

HoneyComb

2007-2022	$110	$200

Lime AID

2007-2022	$130	$250

Morning Glory

2007-2023	$130	$250

Prestige

2007-2023	$60	$100

JAM Pedals Ripply Fall

Jetter Monster

JHS Pedals Bonsai

EFFECTS

JHS Pedals Pulp 'N' Peel

JHS Superbolt
Rivington Guitars

Jordan Boss Tone Fuzz

MODEL YEAR	FEATURES	LOW	HIGH
Pulp 'N' Peel			
2007-2023		$130	$200
Spring Tank Reverb			
2007-2023		$90	$130
SuperBolt			
2007-2023		$100	$150

Jimi Hendrix
See the listing under Dunlop.

John Hornby Skewes & Co.
Mid-1960s-present. Large English distributor of musical products, which has also self-branded products from others, over the years. The early Zonk Machines, Shatterbox and pre-amp boosts were designed and built by engineer Charlie Ramskirr of Wilsic Electronics, until his death in '68. Later effects were brought in from manufacturers in Italy and East Asia.

MODEL YEAR	FEATURES	LOW	HIGH
Bass Boost BB1			
1966-1968. Pre-amp.			
1966-1968		$1,000	$1,375
Fuzz FZIII			
1970s. Fuzz pedal, 2 control knobs, 1 footswitch.			
1970s		$225	$400
Phaser PZ111			
1970s. Phaser pedal made in Italy, 2 control knobs, 1 footswitch.			
1970s		$225	$400
Selectatone TB2			
1966-1968. Pre-amp combining treble and bass boost.			
1966-1968		$1,000	$1,375
Treble Boost TB1			
1966-1968. Pre-amp.			
1966-1968		$1,000	$1,375
Zonk Machine I			
1965-1968. Fuzz pedal, gray-blue housing, 2 control knobs, 1 footswitch, 3 germanium transistors.			
1965-1968		$3,000	$4,000
Zonk Machine II			
1966-1968. Fuzz pedal, gray-blue housing, 2 control knobs, 1 footswitch, 3 silicon transistors.			
1966-1968		$2,500	$3,500
Zonk Machine Reissue			
2000s. Reissued by JMI starting in 2013, reissues also made by the British Pedal Company, 2 control knobs, 1 footswitch.			
2000s		$150	$200
Zonk Shatterbox			
1966-1968. Combined the Zonk Machine II fuzz circuit with the Treble Boost, 2 control knobs, gold housing, 2 foot switches.			
1966-1968		$3,000	$4,000
Zonk Shatterbox Reissue			
2000s. Reissues made by the British Pedal Company, gold housing, 2 foot switches.			
2000s		$150	$200
Zoom Spring Reverb Unit			
1967-1968		$550	$750

Johnson
Mid-1990s-present. Budget line of effects imported by Music Link, Brisbane, California. Johnson also offers guitars, amps, mandolins and basses.

Johnson Amplification
Modeling amps and effects designed by John Johnson, of Sandy, Utah, starting in 1997. The company is part of Harman International. In '02, they quit building amps, but continued the effects line.

Jordan
1966-early 1970s. Jordan Electronics - originally of Alhambra, California, later in Pasadena - built a range of electronics, including, starting around 1966, solid state guitar amps and effects. Sho-Bud of Nashville, Tennessee, licensed the Boss Tone and sold it as the Sho-Sound Boss Tone. Mahoney later reissued the Boss Tone as the Buzz Tone.

MODEL YEAR	FEATURES	LOW	HIGH
Boss Tone Fuzz			
1967-1970s. Tiny effect plugged into guitar's output jack, 2 control knobs, black plastic housing, extremely delicate wiring.			
1967-70s		$200	$350
Compressor J-700			
1967-1970s. Sustain and Level control knobs.			
1967-70s		$150	$300
Creator Volume Sustainer Model 600			
1967-1970s. Volume pedal and sustainer, side controls for Sustain and Tone.			
1967-70s		$500	$600
Gig Wa-Wa Volume Pedal			
1967-1970s.			
1967-70s		$150	$300
Phaser			
1967-1970s. Black case, yellow knobs.			
1967-70s	Black case	$150	$300
Vibrasonic			
1967-70s		$150	$300

Kay
1931-present. Kay was once one of the largest instrument producers in the world, offering just about everything for the guitarist, including effects.

MODEL YEAR	FEATURES	LOW	HIGH
Effects Pedals			
1970s. Various models, includes the Graphic Equalizer GE-5000 and Rhythme.			
1970s		$55	$75
Fuzz Tone F-1			
1970s		$300	$700
Tremolo T-1			
1970s		$200	$300
Wah			
1970s		$100	$200

Kazan
1970s-1980s. Effects made in Kazan, Tatarstan Republic.

MODEL YEAR	FEATURES	LOW	HIGH
Booster			
1970s. Fuzz pedal with foot control.			
1970s		$150	$250

MODEL YEAR	FEATURES	LOW	HIGH

Kvaker
1970s. Wah pedal.

1970s		$150	$250

Keeley
2001-present. Line of guitar effects designed and built by Robert Keeley in Edmond, Oklahoma. Keeley Electronics also offers a range of custom modifications for other effects.

Java Boost

2001-2022		$135	$250

Katana

2001-2023		$125	$200

Keio
1970s. Keio Electronic Laboratories of Japan would later become Korg in the '80s.

Synthesizer Traveler F-1
1970s. Multi-effects unit with foot pedal.

1970s		$500	$800

Kendrick
1989-present. Texas' Kendrick offers guitars, amps, and effects.

ABC Amp Switcher

1990s		$130	$170

Buffalo Pfuz

1990s		$200	$250

Model 1000 Reverb
1991-2003. Vintage style, 3 knobs: dwell, tone, and mix, brown cover, wheat grille with art deco shape.

1991-2003		$800	$1,000

Powerglide Attenuator
1998-present. Allows you to cut the output before it hits the amp's speakers, rack mount, metal cab.

1998-2023		$200	$250

Kent
1961-1969. This import guitar brand also offered a few effects.

Kern Engineering
Located in Kenosha, Wisconsin, Kern offers pre-amps and wah pedals.

Kinsman
2012-present. Guitar effects pedals built in China and distributed by John Hornby Skewes & Co. Ltd.

Klon
Originally located in Brookline, then in Cambridge, Massachusetts, Klon was started by Bill Finnegan, in 1994, after working with two circuit design partners on the Centaur Professional Overdrive.

Centaur
2010. Smaller overdrive unit with burnished silver case.

2010		$850	$1,500

Centaur Professional Overdrive
1994-2009. Standard size with gold case. A smaller unit was introduced in '10.

1994-2009	Gold, horse logo	$6,000	$7,000
1994-2009	Silver, no horse logo	$3,000	$4,000

KTR
2010. Smaller overdrive unit with red case.

2010		$500	$700

KMD (Kaman)
1986-ca. 1990. Distributed by Kaman (Ovation, Hamer, etc.) in the late '80s.

Effects Pedals

1986-1990	Analog Delay	$120	$150
1986-1990	Overdrive	$80	$125
1987-1990	Distortion	$100	$135
1987-1990	Flanger	$80	$120
1987-1990	Phaser	$80	$120
1987-1990	Stereo Chorus	$80	$120

Knight
1967-1972. Effects kits sold via mail-order by Chicago's Allied Radio Company.

Fuzz Box KG-389

1967-1972		$200	$400

Korg
Formed from Keio Electronic Laboratories of Japan. Most Korg effects listed below are modular effects. The PME-40X Professional Modular Effects System holds four of them and allows the user to select several variations of effects. The modular effects cannot be used alone. This system was sold for a few years starting in 1983. Korg currently offers the Toneworks line of effects.

PEQ-1 Parametric EQ
1980s. Dial-in equalizer with gain knob, band-width knob, and frequency knob, black case.

1980s		$60	$160

PME-40X Modular Effects

1983-1986	KAD-301 Delay	$90	$100
19831-1986	KCH-301 Chorus	$40	$50
1983-1986	KCO-101 Compressor	$70	$80
1983-1986	KDI-101 Distortion	$70	$80
1983-1986	KDL-301 Echo	$135	$150
1983-1986	KFL-401 Flanger	$60	$70
1983-1986	KGE-201 Graphic EQ	$40	$50
1983-1986	KNG-101 Noise Gate	$40	$50
1983-1986	KOD-101 Over Drive	$70	$80
1983-1986	KPH-401 Phaser	$70	$80
1983-1986	OCT-1 Octaver	$100	$125

PME-40X Professional Modular Effects System
1983-ca.1986. Board holds up to 4 of the modular effects listed below.

1983-1986		$150	$200

SSD 3000 Digital Delay
1980s. Rack mount, SDD-3000 logo on top of unit.

1980s		$500	$650

Keeley Hooke Reverb

1997 Klon Centaur Overdrive
Folkway Music

1989 Korg PEQ-1 Parametric EQ
Rivington Guitars

EFFECTS

KR Musical Mega Vibe
Keith Myers

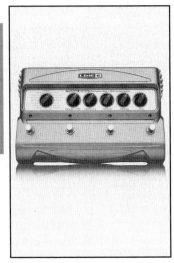

Line 6 DL-4 Delay Modeler

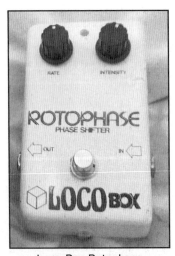

**Loco Box Rotophase
Phase Shifter**
Jeff Jordan

MODEL YEAR	FEATURES	LOW	HIGH

KR Musical Products

2003-2022. Kevin Randall presently builds his vintage style, guitar effects in White Marsh, Virginia.

Krank

1996-2013, 2015-2020. Tempe, Arizona, amp builder Tony Krank also built effects pedals.

Kustom

1965-present. Founded in '64 by Charles "Bud" Ross in his Chanute, Kansas, garage to build amps for his band. While Fender, Rickenbacker, and others tried and failed with solid-state amps, Ross' Kustom creations were a big hit. Kustom likely only ever made one foray into effects, producing The Bag, designed by Doug Forbes.

The Bag

1969-1971. Pioneering "talk box" effect housed in a "bota" wineskin-type bag worn over the player's shoulder. Covered in multiple styles of mod fabrics.1,500

1969-1971		$1,500	$2,500

Lafayette Radio Electronics

1960s-1970s. Effects that claimed to be made in the U.S. but were most likely built by Shin-ei of Japan.

Deluxe AC Super Fuzz

1969-1970s. Made by Shin-ei, AC power.

1969-70s		$400	$500

Echo Verb/Echo Verb II

1970s. Solid-state echo/reverb. Likely made by Shin-ei.

1970s	2 instrument inputs	$200	$350
1970s	Instrument & mic inputs	$100	$300

Fuzz Sound

1970s. Likely made by Shin-ei.

1970s		$200	$350

Roto-Vibe

1969-1970s. Rotating-speaker simulator, with control pedal. Variant of Uni-Vibe made by Shin-ei.

1969-70s		$600	$850

Super Fuzz

1969-1970s. Made by Shin-ei.

1969-70s		$400	$500
1969-70s	Battery power	$400	$500

Laney

1968-present. Founded by Lyndon Laney and Bob Thomas in Birmingham, U.K., this amp builder also offered a reverb unit.

Reverberation Unit

1968-1969. Sleek reverb unit, plexi-style front panel, black vinyl cover.

1968-1969		$300	$400

Larry Alan Guitars

2003-present. Luthier Larry Alan Daft offers effects pedals built in Lansing, Michigan. He also builds guitars and basses.

MODEL YEAR	FEATURES	LOW	HIGH

Lectronx

1990s. Founded by Edwin C. Clothier in North Hollywood, California.

Shark

1990s. Stereo filter pedal designed to use with 2 amps.

1990s		$200	$350

Lehle

2001-present. Loop switches from Burkhard Georg Lehle of Lehle Gitarrentechnik in Voerde, Germany.

D.Loop Signal Router

2004		$150	$180

Lenahan

Amp builder James Lenahan also offered a line of guitar pedals, built in Fort Smith, Arkansas.

Leslie

1966-1970s. In 1941, Donald Leslie began building speakers for Hammond organs to emulate pipe-organ sounds. Using a rotating baffle in front of a stationary speaker, he replicated the tremolo sound. He sold his company to CBS in 1965, and Fender launched its Vibratone based on Leslie technology in 1967. Leslie also offered its Model 16 and 18 speakers for guitarists. The Leslie 16/18 were also sold by Selmer as the Selmer-Leslie.

Model 16

1966-1970s. Rotating-speaker emulator, single fixed 4-ohm 10-inch speaker fronted by a rotating drum. Designed to be powered by an external amp. Black covering, cast Leslie badge in upper left corner.

1966-70s		$1,000	$1,500

Model 18

1966-1970s. Rotating-speaker emulator, single fixed 4-ohm 12-inch speaker fronted by a rotating drum. Designed to be powered by an external amp. Black covering, cast Leslie badge in upper left corner.

1966-70s		$850	$1,000

Line 6

1996-present. Founded by Marcus Ryle and Michel Doidic. Purchased by Yamaha in 2014. They also produce amps and guitars. All prices include Line 6 power pack if applicable.

AM-4 Amp Modeler

1996-2002. Red case.

1996-2002		$70	$120

DL-4 Delay Modeler

1999-present. Green case.

1999-2023		$95	$175

DM-4 Distortion Modeler

1999-2018. Yellow case.

1999-2018		$90	$165

FM-4 Filter Modeler

2001-2018. Purple case.

2001-2018		$170	$270

MM-4 Modulation Modeler

1999-2018. Aqua blue case.

1999-2018		$100	$200

The *Vintage Guitar Price Guide* shows values for an all-original condition guitar effect.

MODEL YEAR	FEATURES	LOW	HIGH

POD 2.0
2001-2014. Updated version of the original Amp Modeler.

2001-2014		$60	$120

Little Lanilei
1997-present. Effects made by Mahaffay Amplifiers (formerly Songworks Systems & Products) of Aliso Viejo, California. They also build amps.

Lizard Leg Effects
2007-2016. Steve Miller built a line of effects pedals in Gonzales, Louisiana.

Lock & Rock
Line of floor pedal guitar and microphone effects produced by Brannon Electronics, Inc. of Houston, Texas starting in 2003.

Loco Box
1982-1983. Loco Box was a brand of effects distributed by Aria Pro II for a short period starting in '82. It appears that Aria switched the effects to their own brand in '83.
Effects

1982-1983	Various models	$150	$300

Lotus Pedal Designs
2009-ca. 2018. Guitar effects pedals built in Duluth, Minnesota by Sean Erspamer.

Loud Button Electronics
Founded in 2009 by Shawn Schoenberger in Minneapolis, Minnesota.
Morphine Dream
2010s. Analog phase shifter and distortion, based on Roland AP-7 Jet Phaser.

2010s		$350	$450

Lovepedal
2000-present. Sean Michael builds his preamps and guitar stomp boxes in Detroit, Michigan.

Lovetone
Hand-made analog effects from Oxfordshire, U.K. starting in 1995.

Ludwig
For some reason, drum builder Ludwig offered a guitar synth in the 1970s.
Phase II Guitar Synth
1970-1971. Oversized synth, mushroom-shaped footswitches, vertical silver case.

1970-1971		$2,000	$2,500

M.B. Electronics
Made in San Francisco, California.
Ultra-Metal UM-10
1985. Distortion.

1985		$40	$50

Mad Professor
2002-present. Guitar effects pedals built by Bjorn Juhl and Jukka Monkkonen in Tampere, Finland. They also build amps.

Maestro
1950s-1970s, 2001-2012, 2022-present. Maestro was a Gibson subsidiary; the name appeared on 1950s accordion amplifiers. The first Maestro effects were the Echoplex tape echo and the FZ-1 Fuzz-Tone, introduced in the early-'60s. Maestro products were manufactured by various entities such as Market Electronics, All-Test Devices, Lowrey and Moog Electronics. In the late-'60s and early-'70s, they unleashed a plethora of pedals; some were beautiful, others had great personality. The last Maestro effects were the Silver and Black MFZ series of the late-'70s. In 2001, Gibson revived the name for a line of effects, banjos and mandolins, adding guitars and amps in '09. By '12 the brand was no longer listed but was reintroduced on a line of Gibson effects in '22.

Bass Brassmaster BB-1
1971-ca.1974. Added brass to your bass.

1971-1974		$2,000	$2,500

Boomerang
Ca.1969-ca.1972. Wah pedal made by All-Test Devices.

1969-1972		$200	$400

Boomerang BG-2
1972-ca.1976. Wah pedal made by All-Test Devices.

1972-1976		$250	$350

Echoplex EM-1 Groupmaster
Ca.1970-ca.1977. Two input Echoplex, solidstate.

1970-1977	Without stand	$1,750	$3,000

Echoplex EP-1
1959-mid-1960s. Original model, smaller green box, tube-driven tape echo, separate controls for echo volume and instrument volume, made by Market Electronics. Though not labeled as such, it is often referred to as the EP-1 by collectors.

1959-60s	Earlier small box	$1,500	$2,500

Echoplex EP-2
Mid-1960s-ca.1970. Larger gray or green box than original, tube-driven tape echo, single echo/instrument volume control, made by Market Electronics. Around '70, the EP-2 added a Sound-On-Sound feature. Limited-edition EP6T reissue made by Market in 1980s (see Market Electronics listing).

1960s	Larger box	$1,250	$2,000

Echoplex EP-3
Ca.1970-1977. Solidstate, made by Market Electronics, black box.

1970-1977		$950	$1,500

Echoplex EP-4 (IV)
1977-1978. Solidstate, the last version introduced by Maestro. See Market Electronics and Echoplex brands for later models.

1977-1978		$1,000	$1,500

Lovepedal Amp Eleven

1972 Maestro Bass
Brassmaster BB-1
John Krylow

1973 Maestro Echoplex EP-3
Rivington Guitars

EFFECTS

Maestro Fuzz-Tone FZ-1B
Mike Lakis

1968 Maestro Octave Box
Rivington Guitars

Maestro Rover RO-1
Kyle Stevens.

MODEL YEAR	FEATURES	LOW	HIGH
Echoplex Groupmaster EM-1			
1970s. Large, multi-channel echo unit.			
1970s		$1,500	$2,500
Echoplex Sireko ES-1			
Ca.1971-mid-1970s. A budget solidstate version of the Echoplex, made by Market.			
1971-1975		$350	$500
Envelope Modifier ME-1			
1971-ca.1976. Tape reverse/string simulator, made by All-Test.			
1971-1976		$200	$350
Filter Sample and Hold FSH-1			
1975-ca.1976.			
1975-1976		$775	$1,500
Full Range Boost FRB-1			
1971-ca.1975. Frequency boost with fuzz, made by All-Test.			
1971-1975		$250	$450
Fuzz MFZ-1			
1976-1979. Made by Moog.			
1976-1979		$350	$600
Fuzz Phazzer FP-1			
1971-1974		$300	$600
Fuzztain MFZT-1			
1976-1978. Fuzz, sustain, made by Moog.			
1976-1978		$300	$600
Fuzz-Tone FZ-1			
1962-1963. Brown housing, uses 2 AA batteries.			
1962-1963		$500	$700
Fuzz-Tone FZ-1A			
1965-1967, 2001-2009. Brown housing, uses 1 AA battery. Early model "Kalamazoo, Michigan" on front, later "Nashville, Tennessee".			
1965-1967	Kalamazoo	$400	$600
2001-2009	Nashville	$250	$350
Fuzz-Tone FZ-1B			
Late-1960s- early-1970s. Black housing, uses 9-volt battery.			
1970s		$400	$600
Mini-Phase Shifter MPS-2			
1976. Volume, speed, slow and fast controls.			
1976		$350	$500
Octave Box OB-1			
1971-ca.1975. Made by All-Test Devices.			
1971-1975		$300	$500
Parametric Filter MPF-1			
1976-1978. Made by Moog.			
1976-1978		$700	$1,000
Phase Shifter PS-1			
1971-1975. With or without 3-button footswitch, made by Oberheim.			
1971-1975	With footswitch	$350	$800
1971-1975	Without footswitch	$300	$700
Phase Shifter PS-1A			
1976		$350	$800
Phase Shifter PS-1B			
1970s		$350	$800
Phaser MP-1			
1976-1978. Made by Moog.			
1976-1978		$300	$500

MODEL YEAR	FEATURES	LOW	HIGH
Repeat Pedal RP-1			
1970s		$300	$500
Rhythm King MRK-2			
1971-ca.1974. Early drum machine.			
1971-1974		$800	$1,000
Rhythm 'n Sound G-2			
Ca.1969-1970s. Multi-effect unit.			
1969-1975		$1,875	$2,500
Rhythm Queen MRQ-1			
Early 1970s. Early rhythm machine.			
1970s		$300	$500
Ring Modulator RM-1			
1971-1975	No control pedal	$650	$1,500
1971-1975	With MP-1 pedal	$750	$1,875
Rover Rotating Speaker			
1971-ca.1973. Rotating Leslie effect that mounted on a large tripod.			
1971-1973	RO-1 model	$1,500	$2,000
Sound System for Woodwinds W-1			
1960s-1970s. Designed for clarinet or saxophone input, gives a variety of synthesizer-type sounds with voices for various woodwinds, uses Barrel Joint and integrated microphone.			
1960-1970s		$750	$900
Stage Phaser MPP-1			
1976-1978. Has slow, fast and variable settings, made by Moog.			
1976-1978		$300	$500
Super Fuzz-Tone FZ-1S			
1971-1975		$400	$750
Sustainer SS-2			
1971-ca.1975. Made by All-Test Devices.			
1971-1975		$300	$500
Theramin TH-1			
1971-mid-1970s. Device with 2 antennae, made horror film sound effects. A reissue Theremin is available from Theremaniacs in Milwaukee, Wisconsin.			
1971-1975		$1,500	$2,500
Wah-Wah/Volume WW-1			
1970s. Wah-Wah Volume logo on end of pedal, green foot pad.			
1971-1975		$300	$500

Magnatone

Ca.1937-1971, 2013-present. Magnatone built very competitive amps from '57 to '66. In the early-'60s, they offered the RVB-1 Reverb Unit. The majority of Magnatone amps pre-'66 did not have on-board reverb.

Model RVB-1 Reverb Unit

1961-1966. Typical brown leatherette cover, square box-type cabinet. From '64-'66, battery operated, solidstate version of RVB-1, low flat cabinet.

1961-1963		$275	$400
1964-1966	Battery & solidstate	$200	$300

Mahoney

2000s. Reissues of the Jordan Boss Tone.

Buzz Tone

2000s. Similar black-plastic housing to the original Boss Tone. 2 Control knobs.

2000s		$75	$100

The *Vintage Guitar Price Guide* shows values for an all-original condition guitar effect.

MODEL YEAR	FEATURES	LOW	HIGH

Manny's

Effects issued by New York-based retailer Manny's Music.

Fuzz

1960s. Same unit as the Orpheum Fuzz and Clark Fuzz.

1960s		$950	$1,250

Market Electronics

Market, from Ohio, made the famous Echoplex line. See Echoplex and Maestro sections for earlier models.

Echoplex EP-6T

1980-ca.1988. Limited-edition all-tube reissue of the Echoplex EP-2.

1980-1988		$550	$650

Marshall

1962-present. The fuzz and wah boom of the '60s led many established manufacturers, like Marshall, to introduce variations on the theme. They got back into stomp boxes in '89 with the Gov'nor distortion, and currently produce several distortion/overdrive units.

Blues Breaker

1992-1999, 2024-present. Replaced by Blues Breaker II in 2000-'23. Back to Blues Breaker in '24.

1992-1999		$450	$550

Blues Breaker II BB-2

2000-2023. Overdrive pedal, 4 knobs.

2000-2023		$50	$100

Drive Master

1992-1999, 2024-present. Overdrive pedal, 5 knobs. Reissued '24.

1992-1999		$150	$300

Guv'nor

1989-1991, 2024-present. Distortion, Guv'nor Plus introduced in '99. Reissued '24.

1989-1991		$200	$300

Jackhammer JH-1

1999-2023. Distortion pedal.

1999-2023		$50	$100

Power Brake PB-100

1993-1995. Speaker attenuator for tube amps.

1993-1995		$350	$450

Shred Master

1992-1999, 2024-present. High-gain pedal, 5 knobs. Reissued '24.

1992-1999		$200	$350

Supa Fuzz

Late-1960s. Made by Sola Sound (Colorsound).

1967		$850	$2,500

Supa Wah

Late-1960s. Made by Sola Sound (Colorsound).

1969		$400	$800

Vibratrem VT-1

1999-2023. Vibrato and tremolo.

1999-2023		$50	$100

Matchless

1989-1999, 2001-present. Matchless amplifiers offered effects in the '90s.

MODEL YEAR	FEATURES	LOW	HIGH

AB Box

1990s. Split box for C-30 series amps (DC 30, SC 30, etc.).

1990s		$400	$600

Coolbox

1997-1999. Tube preamp pedal.

1997-1999		$400	$600

Dirtbox

1997-1999. Tube-driven overdrive pedal.

1997-1999		$950	$1,200

Echo Box

1997-1999. Limited production because of malfunctioning design which included cassette tape. Black case, 8 white chicken head control knobs.

1990s	Original unreliable	$500	$800
1990s	Updated reliable	$800	$1,000

Hotbox/Hotbox II

1995-1999. Higher-end tube-driven preamp pedal.

1995-1999		$400	$600

Mix Box

1997-1999. 4-input tube mixer pedal.

1997-1999		$400	$600

Reverb RV-1

1993-1999. 5 controls, tube-driven spring-reverb tank, various colors.

1993-1999		$1,750	$2,250

Reverb RV-2

2000s. 5 controls, tube-driven spring-reverb tank, various colors.

2000s		$1,250	$1,500

Split Box

1990s. Tube AB box.

1997	Standard AB	$400	$600

Tremolo/Vibrato TV-1

1993-1995. Tube unit.

1993-1995		$400	$600

Maxon

1970s-present. Maxon was the original manufacturer of the Ibanez line of effects. Currently offering retro '70s era stomp boxes distributed in the U.S. by Godlyke.

AD-9/AD-9 Pro Analog Delay

2001-2021. Purple case.

2001-2021		$150	$250

CS-550 Stereo Chorus

2001-2017. Light blue case.

2001-2017		$115	$175

DS-830 Distortion Master

2001-2021. Light blue-green case.

2001-2021		$115	$175

OD-820 Over Drive Pro

2001-2021. Green case.

2001-2021		$150	$200

PH-350 Rotary Phaser

2001-2021. Orange case.

2001-2021		$400	$750

McQuackin FX Co.

Rich McCracken II began building his analog guitar effects in 1997, first in Nashville, Tennessee, then Augusta, Georgia.

1968 Maestro Sound System for Woodwinds W-1
Rivington Guitars

Maestro Wha-Wha/ Volume WW-1
Robbie Keene

Marshall Blues Breaker II BB-2

EFFECTS

Meteoro Doctor Metal

Mica Wau Wau Fuzz
Marco Antonio Rebolledo Ferrari.

Mooer Baby Water

MODEL YEAR	FEATURES	LOW	HIGH

Mesa-Boogie

1971-present. Mesa added pre-amps in the mid '90s, then pedals in 2013. Mesa was acquired by Gibson in early 2021.

V-Twin Bottle Rocket

| 2000-2004 | | $100 | $180 |

V-Twin Preamp Pedal

Dec. 1993-2004. Serial number series: V011-. 100 watts, all tube preamp, floor unit, silver case.

| 1993-1999 | | $250 | $425 |
| 2000-2004 | Updated tone adj | $250 | $425 |

Metal Pedals

2006-present. Brothers Dave and Mike Pantaleone build their guitar effects in New Jersey.

Meteoro

1986-present. Guitar effects built in Brazil. They also build guitar and bass amps.

MG

2004-present. Guitar effects built by Marcelo Giangrande in São Paulo, Brazil. He also builds amps.

Mica

Early 1970s. These Japanese-made effects were also sold under the Bruno and Marlboro brand names.

Tone Fuzz

1970s. Silver case, black knobs.

| 1970s | | $200 | $350 |

Tone Surf Wah Siren

1970s. Wah pedal.

| 1970s | | $200 | $350 |

Wailer Fuzz

| 1970 | | $200 | $350 |

Wau Wau Fuzz

1970s. Wau Wau Fuzz logo on end of pedal, black.

| 1970s | | $200 | $350 |

Mooer

2012-present. A line of guitar pedals built by Mooer Audio in China.

Moog/Moogerfooger

1964-present. Robert Moog, of synth fame, introduced his line of Moogerfooger analog effects in 1998. They also offer guitars.

Misc. Effects

2004-present.

| 2004-2010 | MF-105 MuRF | $700 | $1,500 |
| 2004-2010 | Theremin | $400 | $700 |

Moonrock

Fuzz/distortion unit built by Glenn Wyllie and distributed by Tonefrenzy starting in 2002.

Morley

Late-1960s-present. Founded by brothers Raymond and Marvin Lubow, Morley has produced a wide variety of pedals and effects over the years, changing with the trends. In '89, the brothers sold the company to Accutronics (later changed to Sound Enhancements, Inc.) of Cary, Illinois.

MODEL YEAR	FEATURES	LOW	HIGH

ABY Switch Box

1981-ca.1985. Box no pedal.

| 1981-1985 | | $40 | $80 |

Auto Wah PWA

1976-ca.1985.

| 1976-1985 | | $40 | $80 |

Bad Horsie Steve Vai Signature Wah

1997-present.

| 1997-2023 | | $70 | $85 |

Black Gold Stereo Volume BSV

| 1985-1991 | | $40 | $80 |

Black Gold Stereo Volume Pan BSP

| 1985-1989 | | $40 | $80 |

Black Gold Volume BVO

| 1985-1991 | | $40 | $80 |

Black Gold Wah BWA

| 1985-1991 | | $40 | $80 |

Black Gold Wah Volume BWV

| 1985-1989 | | $40 | $80 |

Chrystal Chorus CCB

1996-1999. Stereo output.

| 1996-1999 | | $40 | $80 |

Deluxe Distortion DDB

1981-1991. Box, no pedal.

| 1981-1991 | | $40 | $80 |

Deluxe Flanger FLB

1981-1991. Box, no pedal.

| 1981-1991 | | $40 | $80 |

Deluxe Phaser DFB

1981-1991. Box, no pedal.

| 1981-1991 | | $40 | $80 |

Distortion One DIB

1981-1991. Box, no pedal.

| 1981-1991 | | $40 | $80 |

Echo Chorus Vibrato ECV

1982-ca.1985.

| 1982-1985 | | $200 | $400 |

Echo/Volume EVO-1

1974-ca.1982.

| 1974-1982 | | $200 | $400 |

Electro-Pik-a-Wah PKW

1979-ca.1982.

| 1979-1982 | | $40 | $80 |

Emerald Echo EEB

1996-1999. 300 ms delay.

| 1996-1999 | Green case | $40 | $80 |

Jerry Donahue JD-10

1995-1997. Multi-effect, distortion, overdrive.

| 1995-1997 | | $100 | $150 |

Power Wah PWA/PWA II

1992-2006. Wah with boost. Changed to II in '98.

| 1992-2006 | | $40 | $80 |

Power Wah PWO

Ca.1969-1984, 2006-present. Reissued in '06 as 20/20 Power Wah.

| 1969-1984 | | $60 | $150 |

EFFECTS

MODEL YEAR	FEATURES	LOW	HIGH
Power Wah/Boost PWB			
Introduced in 1973, doubles as a volume pedal.			
1970s		$100	$150
Power Wah/Fuzz PWF			
Ca.1969-ca.1984.			
1969-1984		$300	$450
Pro Compressor PCB			
1978-1984. Stomp box without pedal, compress-sustain knob and output knob.			
1978-1984		$40	$80
Pro Flanger PFL			
1978-1984		$200	$300
Pro Phaser PFA			
1975-1984		$200	$300
Rotating Sound Power Wah Model RWV			
1971-1982		$200	$300
Select-Effect Pedal SEL			
1980s. Controls up to 5 other pedals.			
1980s		$100	$150
Slimline Echo Volume 600			
1983-1985. 20 to 600 ms delay.			
1983-1985		$100	$150
Slimline Echo Volume SLEV			
1983-1985. 20 to 300 ms delay.			
1983-1985		$100	$150
Slimline Variable Taper Stereo Volume SLSV			
1982-1986		$100	$150
Slimline Variable Taper Volume SLVO			
1982-1986		$100	$150
Slimline Wah SLWA			
1982-1986. Battery operated electro-optical.			
1982-1986		$100	$150
Slimline Wah Volume SLWV			
1982-ca.1986. Battery operated electro-optical.			
1982-1986		$100	$150
Stereo Chorus Flanger CFL			
1980-ca. 1986. Box, no pedal.			
1980-1986		$100	$150
Stereo Chorus Vibrato SCV			
1980-1991. Box, no pedal.			
1980-1991		$100	$150
Stereo Volume CSV			
1980-ca. 1986. Box, no pedal.			
1980-1986		$100	$150
Volume Compressor VCO			
1979-1984		$100	$150
Volume Phaser PFV			
1977-1984. With volume pedal.			
1977-1984		$150	$200
Volume VOL			
1975-ca.1984.			
1975-1979		$100	$150
1980-1984		$100	$150
Volume XVO			
1985-1988		$40	$80
Volume/Boost VBO			
1974-1984		$100	$150
Wah Volume CWV			
1987-1991. Box, no pedal.			
1987-1991		$100	$150

MODEL YEAR	FEATURES	LOW	HIGH
Wah Volume XWV			
1985-ca.1989.			
1985-1989		$100	$150
Wah/Volume WVO			
1977-ca.1984.			
1977-1984		$100	$150

Morpheus

Guitar effects pedals manufactured in Salt Lake City, Utah by the same builders of the Bolt brand amps.

Mosferatu

Line of guitar effects pedals built by Hermida Audio Technology

Mosrite

Semie Moseley's Mosrite company dipped into effects in the 1960s.

Fuzzrite

1960s-1970s, 1999. Silver housing as well as some painted housings, 2 front-mounted control knobs. Sanner reissued in '99.

1960s-70s	Mosrite logo	$500	$1,000
1999	Reissue, Sanner logo	$125	$225

Mu-FX

See Beigel Sound Lab.

Multivox

New York-based Multivox offered a variety of effects in the 1970s and '80s.

Big Jam Effects

Multivox offered the Big Jam line of effects from 1980 to ca. '83.

1980-1983	Analog Echo/Reverb	$250	$350
1980-1983	Bi-Phase 2, Flanger, Jazz Flanger	$150	$200
1980-1983	Chorus	$115	$150
1980-1983	Compressor, Phaser, 6-Band EQ, Spit-Wah	$100	$130
1980-1983	Distortion	$175	$225
1980-1983	Octave Box	$100	$130
1981-1983	Noise Gate, Parametric EQ	$85	$110
1981-1983	Space Driver, Delay	$150	$200
1982-1983	Volume Pedal	$75	$100

Full Rotor MX-2

1978-ca.1982. Leslie effect.

1978-1982		$450	$550

Little David LD-2

1970s. Rotary sound effector in mini Leslie-type case.

1970s	With pedal	$500	$650
1970s	Without pedal	$500	$650

Multi Echo MX-201

1970s. Tape echo unit, reverb.

1970s		$500	$650

Morley Bad Horsie Steve Vai

Morley Rotating Wah RWV

Nate Westgor

Morley Stereo Chorus
Flanger CFL

1970s Multivox Full Rotor MX-2
Keith Myers

Mu-Tron Flanger
Marco Antonio Rebolledo Ferrari

Mu-Tron III Envelope Filter

MODEL YEAR	FEATURES	LOW	HIGH

Multi Echo MX-312
1970s. Tape echo unit, reverb.

MODEL YEAR	FEATURES	LOW	HIGH
1970s		$500	$650

Rhythm Ace FR6M
1970s. 27 basic rhythms.

| 1970s | | $300 | $400 |

Mu-Tron

1972-ca.1980. Made by Musitronics, founded by Mike Beigel and Aaron Newman in Rosemont, New Jersey, these rugged and unique-sounding effects were a high point of the '70s. The Mu-Tron III appeared in '72, and more products followed, about 10 in all. Musitronics also made the U.S. models of the Dan Armstrong effects. In '78 ARP synthesizers bought Musitronics and sold Mutron products to around '80. In '78, Musitronics also joined with Lol Creme and Kevin Godley of 10cc to attempt production of the Gizmotron, which quickly failed (see listing under Godley Crème). A reissue of the Mu-Tron III was made available in '95 by NYC Music Products and distributed by Matthews and Ryan Musical Products. As of 2013, Mike Beigel's Beigel Sound Lab has started making a hot-rodded Tru-Tron III.

Bi-Phase
1975-ca.1980. Add $50-$75 for Opti-Pot pedal.

| 1971-1980 | Optical pedal option | $2,000 | $3,000 |
| 1975-1980 | 2-button footswitch | $2,000 | $3,000 |

C-100 OptiPot Control Pedal

| 1975-1980 | Blue case | $600 | $900 |

C-200 Volume-Wah

| 1970s | | $500 | $650 |

Flanger
1977-ca.1980.

| 1977-1980 | | $2,000 | $2,500 |

III Envelope Filter
1972-ca.1980. Envelope Filter.

| 1972-1980 | | $1,250 | $1,500 |

Micro V
Ca.1975-ca.1977. Envelope Filter.

| 1970s | | $350 | $750 |

Octave Divider
1977-ca.1980.

| 1977-1980 | | $500 | $800 |

Phasor
Ca.1974-ca.1976. Two knobs.

| 1974-1976 | | $350 | $400 |

Phasor II
1976-ca.1980. Three knobs.

| 1976-1980 | | $400 | $450 |

Muza

Digital guitar effects made in China, starting in 2006, by Hong Kong's Medeli Electronics Co., Ltd. They also build digital drums.

MWFX

2008-present. Effects pedals built by Matt Warren in Somerset, England.

Glitch

| 2000s | Wooden case | $250 | $400 |

MXR

1972-present. MXR Innovations launched its line of pedals in '72. Around '77, the Rochester, New York, company changed lettering on the effects from script to block and added new models. MXR survived into the mid-'80s. In '87, production was picked up by Jim Dunlop. Reissues of block logo boxes can be differentiated from originals as they have an LED above the switch and the finish is slightly rough; the originals are smooth.

Six Band EQ
1975-1982. Equalizer.

| 1975-1979 | | $150 | $200 |
| 1980-1982 | | $150 | $200 |

Six Band EQ M109 (Reissue)
1987-present. Reissued by Jim Dunlop.

| 1987-2023 | | $40 | $50 |

Ten Band EQ M108
1975-1981, 2004-present. Graphic equalizer, with AC power cord.

| 1975-1981 | | $100 | $150 |

Analog Delay
1975-1981. Green case, power cord.

| 1975-1979 | Earlier 2-jack model | $350 | $450 |
| 1980-1981 | Later 3-jack model | $200 | $300 |

Blue Box
1972-ca.1978. Octave pedal, M-103.

| 1970s | Earlier script logo | $250 | $350 |
| 1970s | Later block logo | $225 | $325 |

Blue Box M103 (Reissue)
1995-present. Reissued by Jim Dunlop, blue case. Produces 1 octave above or 2 octaves below.

| 1995-2023 | | $50 | $100 |

Carbon Copy M169
1987-present. Analog delay. 3 Control knobs. I Toggle switch. Green housing.

| 1987-2023 | | $75 | $250 |

Commande Effects
1981-1983. The Commande series featured plastic housings and electronic switching.

1981-1983	Overdrive	$60	$90
1981-1983	Phaser	$160	$250
1981-1983	Preamp	$60	$90
1981-1983	Stereo Chorus	$100	$150
1981-1983	Sustain	$100	$150
1981-1983	Time Delay	$120	$200
1982-1983	Stereo Flanger	$120	$200

Distortion +
1972-1982.

1970s	Earlier script logo	$250	$300
1970s	Later block logo	$150	$350
1980s	Block logo	$85	$125

Distortion + (Series 2000)

| 1983-1985 | | $130 | $175 |

Distortion + M104 (Reissue)
1987-present. Reissued by Jim Dunlop, yellow case.

| 1987-1990 | | $65 | $85 |
| 1991-2023 | | $55 | $75 |

Distortion II

| 1981-1983 | With AC power cord | $175 | $350 |

MODEL YEAR	FEATURES	LOW	HIGH
Distortion III M115			
1987-present. 3 Control knobs. Red housing.			
1987-2023		$50	$65
Double Shot Distortion M151			
2003-2005. 2 channels.			
2003-2005		$55	$90
Dyna Comp			
1972-1982. Compressor.			
1970s	Block logo, battery	$125	$250
1970s	Script logo, battery	$250	$300
1980s	Block logo, battery	$85	$125
Dyna Comp (Series 2000)			
1982-1985		$110	$130
Dyna Comp M102 (Reissue)			
1987-present. Reissued by Jim Dunlop, red case.			
1987-2023		$55	$70
Envelope Filter			
1976-1983		$250	$300
Flanger			
1976-1983, 1997-present. Analog, reissued by Dunlop in '97.			
1976-1979	AC power cord, 2 inputs	$250	$350
1980-1983	AC power cord	$200	$375
1997-2023	M-117R reissue	$65	$85
Flanger/Doubler			
1979	Rack mount	$500	$650
Fullbore Metal M116			
1987-present. 6 Control knobs. Bare metal housing.			
1987-2023		$55	$100
Limiter			
1980-1982. AC, 4 knobs.			
1980-1982	AC power cord	$225	$300
Loop Selector			
1980-1982. A/B switch for 2 effects loops.			
1980-1982		$85	$115
Micro Amp			
1978-1983, 1995-present. Variable booster, creme case, reissued in '95.			
1978-1983		$150	$200
1995-2023	M-133 reissue	$50	$65
Micro Chorus			
1980-1983. Yellow case.			
1980-1983		$150	$300
Micro Flanger			
1981-1982		$175	$300
Noise Gate Line Driver			
1974-1983.			
1970s	Script logo	$85	$165
1980s	Block logo	$85	$125
Omni			
1980s. Rack unit with floor controller, compressor, 3-band EQ, distortion, delay, chorus/flanger.			
1980s		$350	$500
Phase 45			
Ca.1976-1982. Battery, earlier script logo, later block.			
1970s	Script logo	$250	$350
1980s	Block logo	$175	$225
Phase 90			
1972-1982.			

MODEL YEAR	FEATURES	LOW	HIGH
1970s	Earlier script logo	$350	$450
1970s	Later block logo	$250	$350
1980s	Block logo	$150	$200
Phase 90 M101 (Reissue)			
1987-present. Reissued by Jim Dunlop, orange case.			
1987-1989	Block logo	$100	$150
1990-2023	Block or script logo	$65	$85
Phase 100			
1974-1982.			
1970s	Earlier script logo	$300	$400
1970s	Later block logo, battery	$200	$300
Phaser (Series 2000)			
1982-1985. Series 2000 introduced cost cutting die-cast cases.			
1982-1985		$65	$85
Pitch Transposer			
1980s		$600	$900
Power Converter			
1980s		$55	$75
Smart Gate M135			
2002-present. Noise-gate, single control, battery powered, gray case.			
2002-2023		$65	$85
Stereo Chorus			
1978-1985. With AC power cord.			
1978-1979		$200	$350
1980-1985		$200	$250
Stereo Chorus (Series 2000)			
1983-1985.			
1983-1985		$65	$85
Stereo Flanger (Series 2000)			
1983-1985.			
1983-1985		$65	$85
Super Comp M132			
2002-present. 3 knobs, black case.			
2002-2023		$45	$60
Wylde Overdrive ZW44			
2000s. Zakk Wylde signature pedal.			
2000s		$75	$100

Nobels

Early 1990s-present. Effects pedals from Nobels Electronics of Hamburg, Germany. They also make amps.

ODR-1 Natural Overdrive

1990s-present. Classic overdrive, green case.

1990s	Early original version	$500	$800
1997-2023		$60	$100

TR-X Vintage Tremolo

1997-2017. Tremolo effect using modern technology, purple case.

1997-2017		$60	$100

Nomad

1960s. Effects that claimed to be made in the U.S., but most likely built by Shin-ei of Japan. Models include the Verberola and the Fuzz wah, both of which were sold under other brands such as Applied, Jax USA, and Companion.

MXR Carbon Copy M169

MXR Fullbore Metal M116
Keith Myers

MXR Phase 100
Marco Antonio Rebolledo Ferrari

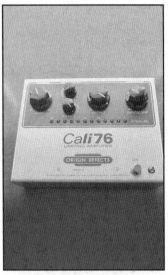

Origin Effects Cali 76

Pearl Flanger FG-01

Peavey Companded
Chorus CMC-1

MODEL YEAR	FEATURES	LOW	HIGH

Fuzz Wah
1960s. Fuzz wah pedal similar to Morley pedals of the era with depth and volume controls and fuzz switch, silver and black.

1960s		$100	$175

Oberheim Electronics Inc.
1970s. Electronics company based in Santa Monica, California, which offered effects under its own name as well as building effects for Gibson/ Maestro.

Voltage Controlled Filter VCF-200
1970s. Voltage-controlled filter, envelope follower and sample-and-hold circuit.

1970s		$700	$900

Oddfellow Effects
Jon Meleika, began in 2013, builds guitar effects pedals in Riverside, California.

Olson
Olson Electronics was based in Akron, Ohio.

Reverberation Amplifier RA-844
1967. Solidstate, battery-operated, reverb unit, depth and volume controls, made in Japan.

1967		$100	$150

Ooh La La Manufacturing
2007-2014. Hand-made guitar effects built in St. Louis Park, Minnesota, including the models formerly offered under the Blackbox brand.

Option 5
2002-present. Jay Woods builds his guitar effects pedals in Mishwaka, Indiana.

Origin Effects
2012-present. Custom-built and production guitar effects made in Oxfordshire, U.K. by Simon Keats.

Ovation
Ovation ventured into the solidstate amp and effects market in the early '70s.

K-6001 Guitar Preamp
1970s. Preamp with reverb, boost, tremolo, fuzz, and a tuner, looks something like a Maestro effect from the '70s, reliability may be an issue.

1970s		$200	$300

PAIA
1967-present. Founded by John Paia Simonton in Edmond, Oklahoma, specializing in synthesizer and effects kits. PAIA did make a few complete products but they are better known for the various electronic kit projects they sold. Values on kit projects are difficult as it depends on the skills of the person who built it.

Roctave Divider 5760
1970s. Kit to build analog octave divider.

1970s		$100	$200

MODEL YEAR	FEATURES	LOW	HIGH

Pan*Damn*ic
2007-2012. Guitar effects pedals made by PLH Professional Audio in West Chester, Pennsylvania.

Park
1965-1982, 1992-2000. Sola/Colorsound made a couple of effects for Marshall and their sister brand, Park. In the '90s, Marshall revived the name for use on small solidstate amps.

Pax
1970s. Imported Maestro copies.

Fuzz Tone Copy

1970s		$200	$300

Octave Box Copy
1970s. Dual pushbuttons (normal and octave), 2 knobs (octave volume and sensitivity), green and black case.

1970s		$200	$300

Pearl
Pearl, located in Nashville, Tennessee, and better known for drums, offered a line of guitar effects in the 1980s.

Analog Delay AD-08
1983-1985. Four knobs.

1983-1985		$100	$175

Analog Delay AD-33
1982-1984. Six knobs.

1982-1984		$175	$250

Chorus CH-02
1981-1984. Four knobs.

1981-1984		$100	$200

Chorus Ensemble CE-22
1982-1984. Stereo chorus with toggling between chorus and vibrato, 6 knobs.

1982-1984		$100	$200

Compressor CO-04

1981-1984		$100	$200

Distortion DS-06

1982-1986		$80	$180

Flanger FG-01
1981-1986. Clock pulse generator, ultra-low frequency oscillator.

1981-1986		$100	$200

Graphic EQ GE-09

1983-1985		$80	$180

Octaver OC-07

1982-1986		$150	$300

Overdrive OD-05

1981-1986		$100	$200

Parametric EQ PE-10

1983-1984		$80	$180

Phaser PH-03
1981-1984. Four knobs.

1981-1984		$100	$200

Phaser PH-44
1982-1984. Six knobs.

1982-1984		$200	$300

Stereo Chorus CH-22
1982-1984. Blue case.

1982-1984		$100	$200

EFFECTS

MODEL YEAR	FEATURES	LOW	HIGH

Thriller TH-20

1984-1986. Exciter, 4 knobs, black case.

| 1984-1986 | | $100 | $200 |

Peavey

1965-present. Peavey made stomp boxes from '87 to around '90. They offered rack mount gear after that.

Effects

| 1980s | Various models | $75 | $100 |

PedalDoctor FX

1996-present. Tim Creek builds his production and custom guitar effects in Nashville, Tennessee.

Pedalworx

Bob McBroom and George Blekas began building guitar effects in 2001, in Manorville, New York and Huntsville, Alabama. They also make modifications to wahs.

Pharaoh Amplifiers

1998-2010. Builder Matt Farrow builds his effects in Raleigh, North Carolina.

Pignose

1972-present. Guitar stomp boxes offered by the amp builder in Las Vegas, Nevada. They also offer guitars.

Pigtronix

2003-present. Dave Koltai builds his custom guitar effects originally in Brooklyn, and currently in Yonkers, New York and offers models built in China.

Plum Crazy FX

Guitar effects built by Kaare Festovog in Apple Valley, Minnesota starting in 2005.

Premier

Ca.1938-ca.1975, 1990-2010. Premier offered a reverb unit in the '60s.

Reverb Unit

1961-late-1960s. Tube, footswitch, 2-tone brown.

| 1960s | | $400 | $550 |

Prescription Electronics

Located in Portland, Oregon, Jack Brossart began offering a variety of hand-made effects in 1994.

Dual-Tone

1998-2009. Overdrive and distortion.

| 1998-2009 | | $165 | $175 |

Throb

1996-2014. Tremolo.

| 1996-2014 | | $165 | $175 |

Yardbox

1994-2014. Patterned after the original Sola Sound Tonebender.

| 1994-2014 | | $90 | $125 |

Pro Tone Pedals

2004-present. Guitar effects pedals built by Dennis Mollan in Dallas, Texas until early-2011, and presently in Summerville, South Carolina.

ProCo

1974-present. Located in Kalamazoo, Michigan and founded by Charlie Wicks, ProCo produces effects, cables and audio products.

Rat

1979-1987. Fuzztone, large box until '84. The second version was 1/3 smaller than the original box. The small box version became the Rat 2. The current Vintage Rat is a reissue of the original large box.

| 1979-1984 | Large box | $500 | $1,500 |
| 1984-1987 | Compact box | $300 | $500 |

Rat 2

1987-present. Classic distortion.

| 1987-1999 | | $150 | $300 |
| 2000-2023 | | $55 | $75 |

Turbo Rat

1989-present. Fuzztone with higher output gain, slope-front case.

| 1989-2023 | | $100 | $150 |

Vintage Rat

1992-2005. Reissue of early-'80s Rat.

| 1992-2005 | | $150 | $250 |

Pro-Sound

The effects listed here date from 1987, and were, most likely, around for a short time.

Chorus CR-1

| 1980s | | $40 | $55 |

Delay DL-1

1980s. Analog.

| 1980s | | $55 | $75 |

Distortion DS-1

| 1980s | | $35 | $45 |

Octaver OT-1

| 1980s | | $40 | $55 |

Power and Master Switch PMS-1

| 1980s | | $25 | $35 |

Super Overdrive SD-1

| 1980s | | $35 | $45 |

Providence

1996-present. Guitar effects pedals built in Japan for Pacifix Ltd. and distributed in the U.S. by Godlyke Distributing, Inc.

Radial Engineering

1994-present. Radial makes a variety of products in Port Coquitlam, British Columbia, including direct boxes, snakes, cables, splitters, and, since '99, the Tonebone line of guitar effects.

Rands

1960s. Japanese music company.

Resly Machine RM-29

1960s. Copy of Maestro PS-1 Phase Shifter built by Shin-ei.

| 1960s | | $300 | $400 |

Prescription Electronics
Yardbox

Rivington Guitars

ProCo Rat 2

Radial Tonebone Texas
Dual Overdrive

EFFECTS

Red Witch Synthotron
Rodger Reed

Rocktron Banshee Talk Box
Rivington Guitars

Rocktron Hush The Pedal

MODEL YEAR	FEATURES	LOW	HIGH

Rapco

The Jackson, Missouri based cable company offers a line of switch, connection, and D.I. Boxes.

The Connection AB-100

1988-2017. A/B box.

1988-2017		$35	$45

Rastop Designs

2002-present. Alexander Rastopchin builds his effects in Long Island City, New York. He also builds amps.

Ray Butts Music Co.

1950s. Ray Butts ran a music store in Cairo, Illinois, where he built his famous EchoSonic amp. He experimented with building a pioneering fuzz box that never went into production and offered his NovaMatch buffer in limited production.

NovaMatch

Late-1950s. Buffer with 1Db of gain in a lipstick-tube-like unit that plugged into guitar jacks.

1950s		$250	$350

Real McCoy Custom

1993-present. Wahs and effects by Geoffrey Teese. His first wah was advertised as the Real McCoy, by Teese. He now offers his custom wah pedals under the Real McCoy Custom brand. He also used the Teese brand on a line of stomp boxes, starting in '96. The Teese stomp boxes are no longer being made. In '08 he moved to Coos Bay, Oregon.

Recycled Sound

2009-present. Greg Perrine designs attenuators in Conway, Arkansas, which are then built in China.

Red Panda

2010s-present. Based in Pittsburgh, Pennsylvania.

Bitmap

2016		$110	$200

Raster

2015		$150	$250

Red Witch

2003-present. Analog guitar effects, designed by Ben Fulton, and made in Paekakariki, New Zealand.

Reinhardt

2004-2012. Amp builder Bob Reinhardt of Lynchburg, Virginia also offers a line of effects pedals.

Retro FX Pedals

2006-ca. 2010. Guitar effects pedals built by John Jones in St. Louis, Missouri.

Retroman

2002-present. Joe Wolf builds his retro effects pedals in Janesville, Wisconsin.

Retro-Sonic

2002-present. Tim Larwill builds effects in Ottawa, Ontario.

Reverend

1996-present. Reverend offered its Drivetrain effects from '00 to '04. They also build guitars.

RGW Electronics

Guitar effects built by Robbie Wallace, starting in 2003, in Lubbock, Texas.

Rivera

1985-present. Amp builder Paul Rivera also offers a line of guitar pedals built in California.

Rocco

Introduced in 1937, the Rocco Tonexpressor was a volume pedal designed by New York City steel-guitarist Anthony Rocco and built and distributed by Epiphone. Generally credited with being the first guitar effect pedal.

Rockman

See listings under Scholz Research and Dunlop.

Rocktek

1986-2009. Imports formerly distributed by Matthews and Ryan of Brooklyn, New York; and later by D'Andrea USA.

Effects

1986-2009	Various models	$50	$60

Rocktron

1980s-present. Rocktron is a division of GHS Strings and offers a line of amps, controllers, stomp boxes, and preamps.

Austin Gold Overdrive

1997-2011. Light overdrive.

1997-2011		$30	$70

Banshee Talk Box

1997-present. Includes power supply.

1997-2023		$65	$125

Hush Rack Mount

1980s-present.

2000-2023		$70	$120

Hush The Pedal

1996-present. Pedal version of rackmount Hush.

1996-2023		$40	$80

Rampage Distortion

1996-2013. Sustain, high-gain and distortion.

1996-2013		$60	$80

Surf Tremolo

1997-2000		$60	$80

Tsunami Chorus

1996-2009. Battery or optional AC adapter.

1996-2009	Battery power	$60	$80
1996-2009	With power supply	$65	$85

EFFECTS

MODEL YEAR	FEATURES	LOW	HIGH
Vertigo Vibe			
2003-2006. Rotating Leslie speaker effect.			
2003-2006	Battery power	$60	$80
2003-2006	With power supply	$60	$80
XDC			
1980s. Rack mount stereo preamp, distortion.			
1980s		$100	$150

Roger Linn Design

2001-present. Effects built in Berkeley, California by Roger Linn.

Roger Mayer Electronics

1964-present. Roger Mayer started making guitar effects in the U.K. in '64 for guitarists like Jimmy Page and Jeff Beck. He moved to the U.S. in '69 to start a company making studio gear and effects. Until about 1980, the effects were built one at a time in small numbers and not available to the public. In the '80s he started producing larger quantities of pedals, introducing his rocket-shaped enclosure. He returned to the U.K. in '89.

MODEL YEAR	FEATURES	LOW	HIGH
Axis Fuzz			
1987-present.			
1987-2023		$350	$450
Classic Fuzz			
1987-present. The Fuzz Face.			
1987-2020		$350	$450
Metal Fuzz			
Early 1980s-1994.			
1987-1994		$350	$450
Mongoose Fuzz			
1987-2017.			
1987-2017		$350	$450
Octavia			
1981-present. Famous rocket-shaped box.			
1981-2023		$400	$550
Voodoo-1			
Ca.1990-present.			
1990-2023		$350	$450

Rogue

2001-present. Budget imported guitar effects. They also offer guitars, basses, lap steels, mandolins, banjos, ukuleles, and amps.

Roland

Japan's Roland Corporation first launched effect pedals in 1974; a year or two later the subsidiary company, Boss, debuted its own line. They were marketed concurrently at first, but gradually Boss became reserved for compact effects while the Roland name was used on amplifiers, keyboards, synths, and larger processors.

MODEL YEAR	FEATURES	LOW	HIGH
Analog Synth SPV			
1970s. Multi-effect synth, rack mount.			
1970s		$750	$1,500
Bee Baa AF-100			
1975-ca.1980. Fuzz and treble boost.			
1975-1980		$325	$550

MODEL YEAR	FEATURES	LOW	HIGH
Bee Gee AF-60			
1975-ca.1980. Sustain, distortion.			
1975-1980		$300	$500
Double Beat AD-50			
1975-ca.1980. Fuzz wah.			
1975-1980		$250	$450
Expression Pedal EV-5			
1970s		$55	$75
Expression Pedal EV-5 Reissue			
2000. Black pedal, blue foot pad.			
2000		$30	$40
Guitar Synth Pedal GR-33 and Pickup GK-2A			
2000-2005. Requires optional GK-2A pickup, blue case.			
2000-2005		$300	$500
Human Rhythm Composer R-8			
1980s. Drum machine, keypad entry.			
1980s		$250	$450
Human Rhythm Composer R-8 MK II			
2000s. Black case.			
2000s		$450	$1,000
Jet Phaser AP-7			
1975-ca.1978. Phase and distortion.			
1975-1978		$300	$650
Phase Five AP-5			
1975-ca.1978.			
1975-1978		$350	$550
Phase II AP-2			
1975-ca.1980. Brown case.			
1975-1980		$150	$350
Space Echo Unit			
1974-ca. 1980. Tape echo and reverb, various models.			
1970s	RE-101	$750	$1,000
1970s	RE-150	$750	$1,000
1970s	RE-200	$1,000	$1,500
1970s	RE-201	$1,500	$2,000
1970s	RE-301	$1,500	$2,000
1970s	RE-501	$1,500	$2,000
1970s	SRE-555 Chorus Echo	$1,500	$2,000
Vocoder SVC-350			
Late-1970s-1980s. Vocal synthesis (vocoder) for voice or guitar, rack mount version of VP-330.			
1980		$1,000	$2,500
Vocoder VP-330 Plus			
Late-1970s-1980s. Analog vocal synthesis (vocoder) for voice or guitar, includes 2 1/2 octaves keyboard.			
1978-1982		$2,000	$2,500
Wah Beat AW-10			
1975-ca.1980.			
1975-1980		$150	$250

Rosac Electronics

1969-1970s. Founded by Ralph Scaffidi and former Mosrite engineer Ed Sanner with backing from Morris Rosenberg and Ben Sacco in Bakersfield, California. Made the Nu-Fuzz which was a clone of Mosrite's Fuzzrite and the Nu-Wah. Closed in mid- to late-'70s and Scaffidi went on to co-found Osborne Sound Laboratories.

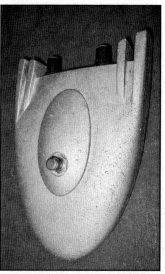
Roger Mayer Classic Fuzz

Roger Mayer Voodoo Axe

Roland Space Echo

EFFECTS

MODEL			
YEAR	**FEATURES**	**LOW**	**HIGH**

1978 Ross Compressor

1978 Ross Distortion

Rivington Guitars

Sam Ash Fuzzz Boxx

Ross

Founded by Bud Ross, who also established Kustom, in Chanute, Kansas, in the 1970s. Ross produced primarily amplifiers. In about '78, they introduced a line of U.S.-made effects. Later production switched to Asia.

10 Band Graphic Equalizer

1970s		$50	$120

Compressor
1970s. Gray or black case.

1970s		$700	$800

Distortion
1978-ca.1980. Brown.

1979-1980		$150	$250

Flanger
1977-ca.1980. Red.

1977-1980		$150	$300

Phase Distortion R1
1979. Purple.

1979		$150	$200

Phaser
1978-ca.1980. Orange.

1978-1980		$150	$200

Stereo Delay
1978-ca.1980.

1978-1980		$200	$300

Rotosound

1960s. English musical company.

Fuzz Box
1967-1968. Fuzz built by Sola Sound.

1967-1968		$500	$650

Rotovibe

See the listing under Dunlop.

Royal

1960s. Japanese effects company with product built by other makers, including the Thunder Electronic Co. Ltd. Of Tokyo.

Double Effect Machine RFC-1
1960s. Built by Shin-ei.

1960s		$300	$600

Fuzz Box RF-1
1960s. Expanded version of Univox Super-Fuzz with tone effects foot switch.

1960s		$300	$600

S. Hawk Ltd.

1970s. Various effect pedals, no model names on case, only company name and logo.

Hawk I Fuzz
1970s. Linear pre-amp, fuzz, headphone amp, 1 slider.

1970s		$600	$700

SAM

1970s-1980s. Effects made by the SAM Electro-mechanical Plant in Moscow, Russia.

Effekt-1 Fuzz-Wah-Vibrato
1970s. Fuzz pedal with foot control.

1970s		$150	$250

Sam Ash

1960s-1970s, 2013-present. Sam Ash (nee Askynase) founded Sam Ash Music, in '24, in Brooklyn, and by '66, there were about four Ash stores. During this time, Ash Music private branded their own amps and effects. In 2013, Sam Ash reissued the Fuzz Boxx.

Fuzzola
1960s. Rebranded version of the Shin-ei Uni-Fuzz. There is also a Fuzzola II.

1960s		$300	$400

Fuzzz Boxx
1966-1967, 2013-2019. Red, made by Astro/Universal Amplifier Company, same as Astro Amp Astrotone fuzz. Reissued in '13.

1966-1967		$450	$850
2013-2019	Reissue	$150	$175

Volume Wah
1970s. Italian-made.

1970s		$250	$325

Sangil

1960s. Ed Sanner – designer of the Mosrite Fuzzrite – also built and sold effects through his own company, Sangil.

Iron Butterfly
1960s. Fuzz wah pedal.

1960s		$300	$400

Sanner

1999. Reissue from Ed Sanner, who was the engineer behind the 1960s Mosrite Fuzzrite, using identical circuitry as the original. Issued as a limited edition.

Sano

1944-ca. 1970. Sano was a New Jersey-based accordion company that built their own amps and a reverb unit. They also imported guitars for a few years, starting in '66.

Satellite Amplifiers

2004-present. Analog effects pedals made in San Diego, California by amp builder Adam Grimm.

Schaffer-Vega

1975-1982. After Mick Jagger's wireless system for the 1975 Rolling Stones Tour of the Americas began broadcasting police calls and lottery numbers, New York recording engineer Ken Schaffer invented his Schaffer-Vega Diversity System (SVDS) as a better wireless system – although it also could be used to affect guitar tones, offering overdrive as used by AC/DC's Angus Young. SoloDallas began offering Schaffer replicas in 2015.

Diversity System
1975-1982. Wireless mic and guitar transmitter and receiver.

1975-1982		$1,500	$2,500

MODEL			
YEAR	FEATURES	LOW	HIGH

Schaller

The German guitar accessories company, which began in 1945, offered guitar effects off and on since the '60s and currently has reissue versions of its volume pedal and tremolo.

Scholz Research

1982-1995. Started by Tom Scholz of the band Boston. In '95, Jim Dunlop picked up the Rockman line (see Dunlop).

Equalizer
| 1980s | | $250 | $325 |

Power Soak
| 1980s | | $175 | $275 |

Rockadapter
| 1980s | | $80 | $100 |

Rockman
| 1980s | | $350 | $400 |

Rockman X100
1980s. Professional studio processor.
| 1980s | | $650 | $700 |

Soloist
1980s. Personal guitar processor.
| 1980s | | $250 | $350 |

Stereo Chorus
| 1980s | | $250 | $500 |

Stereo Chorus Delay
| 1980s | | $400 | $500 |

Stereo Echo
| 1980s | | $1,000 | $1,250 |

Sustainer 200
| 1980s | | $700 | $900 |

Wah Volume
| 1980s | | $100 | $150 |

Seamoon

1973-1977, 1997-2002. Seamoon made effects until '77, when Dave Tarnowski bought up the remaining inventory and started Analog Digital Associates (ADA). He reissued the brand in '97.

Fresh Fuzz
1975-1977. Recently reissued by ADA.
| 1975-1977 | | $500 | $750 |

Funk Machine
1974-1977. Envelope filter. Recently reissued by ADA.
| 1974-1977 | | $300 | $400 |

Studio Phase
1975-1977. Phase shifter.
| 1975-1977 | | $500 | $650 |

Sears, Roebuck & Co.

1970s. Department-store and mail-order giant Sears sold inexpensive effects likely made in Japan by Guyatone.

Fuzz & Wa & Volume Control Pedal
| 1970s | | $125 | $200 |

Fuzz-Tone Control
1970s. Dallas-Arbiter Fuzz Face/Guyatone Crazy-Face copy.
| 1970s | | $250 | $350 |

MODEL			
YEAR	FEATURES	LOW	HIGH

Sekova

Mid-1960s-mid-1970s. Entry level instruments imported by the U.S. Musical Merchandise Corporation of New York.

Big Muff SE-2015
1972-1973. "Triangle" Big Muff Pi copy built by Shin-ei.
| 1972-1973 | | $300 | $450 |

Fuzz
| 1960s | | $150 | $250 |

Selmer

1960s. English music company based in London.

Buzz-Tone
| 1960s | | $350 | $500 |

Seymour Duncan

In late 2003, pickup maker Seymour Duncan, located in Santa Barbara, California, added a line of stomp box guitar effects.

Shin-ei

1969-1970s. When the Honey company went bankrupt in March, '69, it was reborn as Shin-ei and many Honey designs continued in production in various forms. Their chief engineer was Fumio Mieda who later did design work for Korg. Shin-ei also made effects for Univox (including the Uni-Fuzz, Super-Fuzz and Uni-Vibe), Companion, Applied, Apollo, Jax, Nomad, Shaftsbury, Pax, Crown, Royal, Mica, Kent, Marlboro, Memphis, Bruno, Boomer, Alex, Ace Tone, Aria, Goya, Kimbara, Lord, National, Northland, Tele Star, Tempo, and probably others.

Fuzz Wah
| 1970s | | $200 | $300 |

FY-2 Fuzz Box
1969-1970s. 2 transistors.
| 1969-1970s | | $200 | $300 |

FY-6 Super Fuzz
1969-1970s. Built from fuzz circuitry of Psychedelic Machine, 6 transistors.
| 1969-1970s | | $500 | $600 |

Mica Tone Fuzz Wah
| 1970s | | $200 | $300 |

Octave Box OB-28
1970s. Version of the Gibson Maestro OB-1 Octave Box.
| 1970s | | $200 | $300 |

Phase Tone PT-18
1970s. Tremolo, vibrato and phase effects.
| 1970s | | $500 | $1,000 |

Psychedelic Machine
1969. Amp head-sized effect with numerous controls.
| 1969 | | $2,000 | $3,000 |

Resly (Repeat Time) Machine
1970s. Black case, 3 speeds.
| 1970s | | $2,000 | $2,500 |

Sho-Bud

1956-1980. This pedal steel company offered volume pedals as well.

Seamoon Funk Machine

Seymour Duncan Dirty Deed

Seymour Duncan Fooz

EFFECTS

Siegmund DoubleDrive

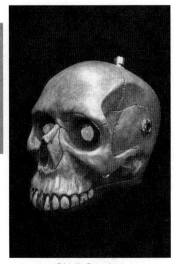

Skull Crusher

Snarling Dogs Mold Spore
Psycho-Scumatic

Garrett Tung

MODEL YEAR	FEATURES	LOW	HIGH

Sho-Sound Boss Tone
1970s-1980. Licensed version of the Jordan Boss Tone, 2 control knobs, similar black plastic housing.

1970s-80		$100	$200

Volume Pedal
1965		$100	$200

SIB
Effects pedals from Rick Hamel, who helped design SMF amps.

Siegmund Guitars & Amplifiers
Los Angeles, California amp and guitar builder Chris Siegmund added effects to his product line in '99.

Sitori Sonics
Emanual Ellinas began building his guitar effects in Birmingham, Alabama, in 2006.

Skrydstrup R&D
1997-present. Effects pedals built by Steen Skrydstrup in Denmark. He also builds amps.

Skull Crusher
2009-2015. Partners John Kasha and Shawn Crosby of Tone Box Effects built their guitar effects in Simi Valley, California.

Snarling Dogs
Started by Charlie Stringer of Stringer Industries, Warren, New Jersey in 1997. Stringer died in May '99. The brand is now carried by D'Andrea USA.

Sobbat
1995-present. Line of effects from Kinko Music Company of Kyoto, Japan.

Solasound/Colorsound
1962-2010. Sola was founded by London's Macari's Musical Exchange in '62, which was launched by former Vox associate Larry Macari and his brother Joe. The first product was the Tone-Bender fuzz box, designed by Gary Stewart Hurst and modeled in part on the Maestro Fuzz-Tone FZ-1. The first readily available fuzz in Britain was an instant success. Sola soon began making effects for Vox, Marshall, Park, and B & M and later under their own Colorsound brand. Refer to Colorsound for further listings and more company info.

Tone Bender Mk1.5
1966-1969		$2,000	$2,500

Tone Bender MkI
1965-1966		$2,500	$4,000

Tone Bender MkIII
1968-1970s		$2,500	$4,000

Tone Bender Professional MkII
1960s		$1,250	$1,800

MODEL YEAR	FEATURES	LOW	HIGH

Soldano
1987-present. Seattle, Washington amp builder Soldano also built a reverb unit.

Sho-Space Box
1987-2018. Tube-driven spring reverb.

1987-2018		$1,000	$1,500

SoloDallas
2015-present. Started by Filippo "SoloDallas" Olivieri to build replicas of the Schaffer-Vega Diversity System. Based in San Diego, California.

Schaffer Boost Solo-X
2015-2022		$80	$125

Schaffer Replica Classic
2015-2023. Stompbox replicating the SVDS guitar effect.

2015-2023		$150	$200

Schaffer Replica Storm
2015-present. Stompbox replicating the SVDS guitar effect.

2015-2023		$95	$150

Schaffer Replica Tower
2015-present. Replica of the original SVDS made by SoloDallas.

2015-2023		$1,000	$1,375

Songbird
See listing for Dytronics.

Sonic Edge
Guitar and bass effects pedals built by Ben Fargen in Sacramento, California starting in 2010. He also builds the Fargen amps.

Sonuus
2009-present. Guitar effects built in China and imported by owners James Clark and John McAuliffe in the U.K.

Sovtek (New Sensor Corporation)
1990s. Started by Mike Matthews, of Electro-Harmonix fame, to build EHX effects in Russia. See also Electro-Harmonix.

Bass Balls
1990s		$350	$450

Big Muff
1990s		$450	$550

Electric Mistress
1990s		$350	$450

Red Army Overdrive
1990s		$1,500	$2,500

Small Stone
1990s		$350	$450

Speedster
1995-2000, 2003-2007. Amp builder Speedster added guitar effects pedals to their product line in '04, built in Gig Harbor, Washington.

The *Vintage Guitar Price Guide* shows values for an all-original condition guitar effect.

Spektr

1970s-1980s. Effects made in Novosibirsk, Russia.

Spektr-1
1970s. Analog multi-effects pedal with foot control.

1970s		$150	$200

Spektr-2
1970s. Fuzz wah.

1970s		$150	$200

Spektr-3
1970s. Volume pedal with boost, fuzz, wah and auto-wah.

1970s		$250	$350

Spektr-4

1970s		$300	$400

StarTouch

Tony Chostner began in 2001, builds production/custom, effects pedals in Salem, Oregon.

Stephenson

1997-present. Amp builder Mark Stephenson in Parksville, British Columbia also offers a line of guitar pedals.

Stinger

Stinger effects were distributed by the Martin Guitar Company from 1989 to '90.

Effects

		LOW	HIGH
1989-1990	CH-70 Stereo Chorus	$50	$65
1989-1990	CO-20 Compressor	$60	$75
1989-1990	DD-90 Digital Delay	$80	$100
1989-1990	DE-80 Analog Delay	$95	$125
1989-1990	DI-10 Distortion	$75	$95
1989-1990	FL-60 Flanger	$75	$95
1989-1990	OD-30 Overdrive	$75	$95
1989-1990	TS-5 Tube Stack	$80	$100

Strymon

2009-present. Founded in 2004 as Damage Control, the company began offering effects pedals under the Strymon name in 2009. Owners Gregg Stock, Pete Celi, and Dave Fruehling build their line of guitar pedals in Chatsworth, California.

Big Sky
2013-present. Reverberator pedal.

2013-2023		$375	$475

BlueSky
2010-present. Digital reverb pedal.

2010-2023		$225	$300

Brigadier
2010-present. dBucket delay.

2010-2023		$225	$300

Deco
2014-present. Tape saturation and doubletracker pedal.

2014-2023		$250	$325

DIG
2015-present. Dual digital delay.

2015-2023		$225	$300

El Capistan
2010-present. Tape echo.

2010-2023		$225	$300

Flint
2012-present. Tremolo and reverb.

2012-2023		$225	$300

Lex
2011-present. Rotary effects pedal.

2011-2023		$225	$300

Mobius
2012-present. Modulation pedal.

2012-2023		$375	$475

OB.1
2009-2020. Optical compressor and clean boost.

2009-2020		$125	$175

Ojai
2016-present. High current DC power supply.

2016-2023		$125	$175

Ola
2010-present. dBucket chorus and vibrato.

2010-2023		$225	$300

Orbit
2010-present. dBucket flanger.

2010-2023		$225	$300

Riverside
2016-present. Multistage drive.

2016-2023		$225	$300

Sunset
2017-present. Dual overdrive pedal.

2017-2023		$225	$300

TimeLine
2011-present. Delay pedal.

2011-2023		$325	$425

Zuma
2016-present. High current DC power supply.

2016-2023		$225	$300

Studio Electronics

1989-present. Synth and midi developer Greg St. Regis' Studio Electronics added guitar pedal effects to their line in '03.

Subdecay Studios

2003-present. Brian Marshall builds his guitar effects in Woodinville, Washington.

Supersound

1952-1974. Founded by England's Alan Wootton, Supersound built echo units in the 1960s. They also built amps, guitars, and basses.

Supro

1935-1968, 2004-present. Supro offered a few reverb units in the '60s. The brand name was revived in '04.

500 R Standard Reverb Unit
1962-1963. Outboard reverb unit.

1962-1963		$300	$500

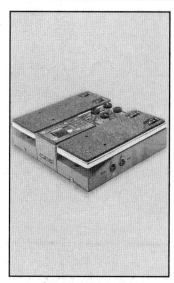

Spektr-3 Fuzz Wah
Ilya Shlepako

StarTouch AB Stereo

Strymon TimeLine

Swart FuzzyBoost

TC Electronic HOF Mini
Keith Myers

1999 Tech 21 XXL Distortion

MODEL YEAR	FEATURES	LOW	HIGH

600 Reverb Power Unit
1961. Independent reverb unit amp combination to be used with Supro Model 1600R amp or other amps, 3 tubes, 1x8" speaker.

1961		$400	$700

Swart Amplifier
2003-present. Effects pedals built by Michael J. Swart in Wilmington, North Carolina. He also builds amps.

Sweet Sound
Line of effects from Bob Sweet beginning in 1994, originally made in Trenton, Michigan, and then in Coral Springs, Florida. Bob died in 2008. Currently built by his brother Gerald.

Swell Pedal Company
1997-2012. Mike Olienechak builds his line of tube pedals for guitar and bass in Nashville, Tennessee.

SynapticGroove
Benjamin Harrison and Chrystal Gilles build their guitar effects in Edmond, Oklahoma, starting in 2013.

Systech (Systems & Technology in Music, Inc)
1975-1979. Started by Greg Hockman, Systech was in Kalamazoo, Michigan.

Envelope & Repeater

1975-1979		$250	$350

Envelope Follower
1975-1979. Decay and drive controls.

1975-1979		$300	$400

Flanger
1975-1979. Sweep rate, depth, and gain controls.

1975-1979		$300	$400

Harmonic Energizer
1975-1979. Filter/distortion with bandwidth, center frequency and gain controls. Silver body early, black body later.

1975-1979		$1,000	$1,500

Overdrive
1975-1979. EQ, distortion, and gain controls. Silver body early, black body later.

1975-1979		$350	$750

Phase Shifter
1975-1979. Dual sweep rate controls plus emphasis control.

1975-1979		$350	$500

T.C. Jauernig Electronics
Tim Jauernig, of Rothschild, Wisconsin, built effects for several years before launching his T.C. Jauernig brand in 2004.

TC Electronic
1976-present. Brothers Kim and John Rishøj founded TC Electronic in Risskov, Denmark, and

made guitar effects pedals for several years before moving into rack-mounted gear. Currently they offer a wide range of pro audio gear and rack and floor guitar effects.

Booster + Distortion

1980s		$300	$400

Dual Parametric Equalizer

1980s		$200	$375

Stereo Chorus/Flanger SCF
Introduced in 1982 and reissued in '91.

1980s		$250	$350

Sustain + Equalizer

1980s		$200	$350

Tech 21
1989-present. Tech 21 builds their SansAmp and other effects in New York City. They also build amps.

Sansamp
1989-present. Offers a variety of tube amp tones.

1989	1st year	$350	$500
1990-2023		$150	$200

XXL Pedal
1995-2000, 2005-2012. Distortion, fuzz.

1995-2012		$75	$100

Teese
Geoffrey Teese's first wah was advertised as the Real McCoy, by Teese. He now offers his custom wah pedals under the Real McCoy Custom brand. The Teese brand was used on his line of stomp boxes, starting in '96. The Teese stomp boxes are no longer being made.

Ten
2013-present. Guitar effects built in Spokane, Washington by Ryan Dunn and Doug Harrison. From 2001-'13 they used the ToadWorks brand.

The Original Geek
Jeff Rubin began building guitar effects pedals in Los Angeles, California under the Geek MacDaddy brand in 2004. After a breakup with his business partner in '09 he began using The Original Geek brand.

Theremaniacs
2010s-present. Started by Chuck Collins, builder of Theremins, based in Big Bend, Wisconsin.

Harmonic Percolator
2010s-present. Replica of '70s InterFax Harmonic Percolator.

2010s-2023		$350	$450

Thomas Organ
The Thomas Organ Company was heavily involved with Vox from 1964 to '72, importing their instruments into the U.S. and designing and assembling products, including the wah-wah pedal. Both Thomas Organ and JMI, Vox's European distributor, wanted to offer the new effect. The problem was solved by labeling the Thomas Organ wah the

MODEL YEAR	FEATURES	LOW	HIGH

Crybaby. Dunlop now offers the Crybaby. Refer to Vox listing for Crybaby Stereo Fuzz Wah, Crybaby Wah, and Wah Wah.

ThroBak Electronics
2004-present. Jonathan Gundry builds his guitar effects in Grand Rapids, Michigan. He also builds guitar amps and pickups.

ToadWorks
See listing for Ten.

TomasZewicZ or TZZ
2008-present. Guitar effects pedals built by John Tomaszewicz in Coral Springs, Florida, which he labels TZZ. He also builds amps.

Tone Box Effects
See listing for Skull Crusher.

Tonebone
See Radial Engineering listing.

ToneCandy
2007-present. Mike Marino builds his guitar effects pedals in Santa Rosa, California.

Top Gear
1960s-1970s. Top Gear was a London music store. Their effects were made by other manufacturers.
Rotator
1970s Leslie effect

1970s		$350	$750

Top Hat Amplification
1994-present. Brian Gerhard builds his amps and effects in Fuquay-Varina, North Carolina. He previously built them in La Habra, California and Apex, North Carolina.

Traynor
1963-present. Amp and PA builder Traynor also built two spring reverb units, one tube and one solidstate, in Canada from 1966-'72 and a 7-band EQ from '73-'78.

Tremolo
See the listing under Dunlop.

T-Rex
2003-present. Made in Denmark and imported by European Musical Imports.

TSVG
Mike Klein started building his guitar effects in his shop located in Philadelphia, Pennsylvania in 2011.

Tube Works
1987-2004. Founded by B.K. Butler (see Audio Matrix) in Denver, Colorado, Tube Works became

MODEL YEAR	FEATURES	LOW	HIGH

a division of Genz Benz Enclosures of Scottsdale, Arizona in 1997 which dropped the brand in 2004. They also offered tube/solidstate amps, cabinets, and DI boxes.

Blue Tube
1989-2004. Overdrive bass driver with 12AX7A tube.

1989-2004		$150	$200

Real Tube
Ca.1987-2004. Overdrive with 12AX7A tube.

1987-1999		$150	$200

Tube Driver
1987-2004. With tube.

1987-2004		$150	$250

TWA (Totally Wycked Audio)
2009-present. Boutique analog effect pedals made in the U.S. and offered by Godlyke, Inc.

Tycobrahe
The Tycobrahe story was over almost before it began. Doing business in 1976-1977, they produced only three pedals and a direct box, one the fabled Octavia. The company, located in Hermosa Beach, California, made high-quality, original devices, but they didn't catch on. Now, they are very collectible. Reissues were made by Chicago Iron.

Octavia
1976-1977, 2000s. Octave doubler.

1976-1977		$3,500	$5,000
2000s	Octavia & Octavian reissue	$350	$500

Parapedal
1976-1977, 2000s. Wah.

1976-1977		$800	$1,250
2000s	Reissue, light blue	$350	$500

Pedalflanger
1976-1977. Blue pedal-controlled flanger.

1976-1977		$1,000	$1,500

UMI (United Musical Industries)
1960s. UMI was based in Farmingdale, New York.

Tone Booster
1960s. Primitive EQ unit with treble and bass boost controls.

1960s		$250	$350

Uni-Vibe
See listings under Univox and Dunlop.

Univox
Univox was a brand owned by Merson (later Unicord), of Westbury, New York. It marketed guitars and amps and added effects in the late-'60s. Most Univox effects were made by Shin-ei, of Japan. They vanished in about '81.

Drum Machine SR-55

1970s		$300	$400

Ten Bananas At Large Stereo Buffer

ThroBak Electronics Strange Master

TWA Little Dipper LD-01

1975 Univox EC-100 Echo
Rivington Guitars

1969 Univox Uni-Vibe
Imaged by Heritage Auctions, HA.com

**Visual Sound Visual VLM
10th Anniversary**

MODEL YEAR	FEATURES	LOW	HIGH
EC-80 A Echo	*Early-1970s-ca.1977. Tape echo, sometimes shown as The Brat Echo Chamber.*		
1970s		$450	$600
EC-100 Echo	*1970s. Tape, sound-on-sound.*		
1970s		$350	$500
Echo-Tech EM-200	*1970s. Disc recording echo unit.*		
1970s		$500	$750
Fuzz FY-2			
1970s		$500	$650
Micro 41 FCM41 4 channel mixer			
1970s		$50	$75
Micro Fazer	*1970s. Phase shifter.*		
1970s		$125	$200
Noise-Clamp EX110			
1970s		$100	$200
Phaser PHZ1	*1970s. AC powered.*		
1970s		$200	$350
Pro-Verb UR-3	*1970s. Reverb (spring) unit, black tolex, slider controls for 2 inputs, 1 output plus remote output.*		
1970s		$150	$250
Square Wave SQ150	*Introduced in 1976. Distortion, orange case.*		
1970s		$300	$500
Super-Fuzz	*1968-1973. Made by Shin-ei and similar to the FY-6 Super Fuzz, built from fuzz circuitry of Honey/Shin-ei Psychedelic Machine, 6 transistors, battery powered.*		
1968-1973	Gray box, normal bypass switch	$700	$900
1968-1973	Orange and blue	$800	$1,000
Surf Siren	*1970s. Wah pedal.*		
1970s		$200	$300
Uni-Comp	*1970s. Compression limiter.*		
1970s		$150	$250
Uni-Drive			
1970s		$1,000	$1,250
Uni-Fuzz	*1969-1973. Fuzz tone in blue case, 2 black knobs and slider switch. Made by Shin-ei, AC-powered version of Super-Fuzz, built from fuzz circuitry of Honey/Shin-ei Psychedelic Machine.*		
1969-1973		$600	$1,000
Uni-Tron 5	*1975. A.k.a. Funky Filter, envelope filter.*		
1975		$500	$700
Uni-Vibe	*1968-1973. Rotating-speaker simulator, with control pedal. Made by Shin-ei, built from circuitry of Honey/Shin-ei Psychedelic Machine.*		
1968-1973		$3,500	$5,000
Uni-Wah Wah/Volume			
1970s		$175	$250

MODEL YEAR	FEATURES	LOW	HIGH
VanAmps			

Amp builder Tim Van Tassel of Golden Valley, Minnesota, also offers a line of reverb effects pedals.

Vesta Fire
Ca.1981-ca.1988. Brand of Japan's Shiino Musical Instrument Corp.

MODEL YEAR	FEATURES	LOW	HIGH
Chorus/Flange FLCH			
1981-1988		$100	$150
Distortion DST			
1981-1988		$100	$150
Flanger			
1981-1988		$100	$150
Noise Gate			
1981-1988		$50	$65
Stereo Chorus SCH			
1981-1988		$100	$150

Vintage Tone Project
Line of guitar effects made by Robert Rush and company in Delmar, New York, starting in 2003. They also built reissues of Dan Armstrong's '70s effects from '03 to '06.

VintageFX
2003-present. Effects based on vintage pedals from the '60s and '70s built by Dave Archer in Grand Island, New York.

Visual Sound
1995-2015. Effects pedals designed by Bob Weil and R.G. Keen in Spring Hill, Tennessee and built in China. They changed name to Truetone in '15.

VooDoo Lab
1994-present. Line of effects made by Digital Music Corp. in California.

MODEL YEAR	FEATURES	LOW	HIGH
Analog Chorus	*1997-2012. Based on '76 CE-1.*		
1997-2012		$125	$175
Bosstone	*1994-1999. Based on '60s Jordan Electronics Fuzz.*		
1994-1999		$100	$175
Micro Vibe	*1996-2022. Uni-Vibe rotating-speaker simulator.*		
1996-2022		$100	$175
Overdrive	*1994-2002. Based on '70s overdrive.*		
1994-2002		$100	$150
Proctavia	*1990s. Based on '70s classic fuzz/octave.*		
1990s		$100	$150
Superfuzz	*1999-present. Vintage fuzz.*		
1999-2023		$100	$150
Tremolo	*1995-2022. Vintage tube amp trem tone.*		
1995-2022		$75	$125

MODEL YEAR	FEATURES	LOW	HIGH

Vox

1954-present. The first Vox product was a volume pedal. Ca. '66, they released the Tone Bender, one of the classic fuzzboxes of all time. A year or so later, they delivered their greatest contribution to the effects world, the first wah-wah pedal. The American arm of Vox (then under Thomas Organ) succumbed in '72. In the U.K., the company was on-again/off-again.

Clyde McCoy Wah-Wah Pedal

Introduced in 1967, reissued in 2001-2008. Clyde's picture on bottom cover.

1967	Clyde's picture	$2,000	$3,000
1968	No picture	$1,250	$1,750
2001-2008	Model V-848	$200	$300

Crybaby Wah

Introduced in 1968. The Thomas Organ Company was heavily involved with Vox from '64 to '72, importing their instruments into the U.S. and designing and assembling products. One product developed in conjunction with Vox was the wah-wah pedal. Both Thomas Organ and JMI, Vox's European distributor, wanted to offer the new effect. The problem was solved by labeling the Thomas Organ wah the Crybaby. The original wahs were built by Jen in Italy, but Thomas later made them in their Chicago, Illinois and Sepulveda, California plants. Thomas Organ retained the marketing rights to Vox until '79 but was not very active with the brand after '72. Dunlop now offers the Crybaby brand.

1960s	Jen-made	$300	$400
1970	Sepulveda-made	$200	$300

Double Sound

1970s. Jen-made, Double Sound model name on bottom of pedal, double sound derived from fuzz and wah ability.

1970s		$300	$400

Flanger

1970s		$300	$400

King Wah

1970s. Chrome top, Italian-made.

1970s		$200	$300

Repeat Percussion

Late-1960s. Plug-in module with on-off switch and rate adjustment.

1968		$200	$250

Stereo Fuzz Wah

1970s		$200	$250

Tone Bender V-828

1966-1970s. Fuzz box, reissued as the V-829 in '93.

1966-1968	Mark I, gray case	$1,250	$1,875
1969	Mark II, black case	$1,000	$1,500
1970s	Mark III	$1,000	$1,500

ToneLab Valvetronix

2003-2019. Multi-effect modeling processor (ToneLab EX or ToneLab ST), 12AX7 tube preamp.

2003-2019		$150	$250

V-807 Echo-Reverb Unit

1967. Solidstate, disc echo.

1967		$300	$400

V-837 Echo Deluxe Tape Echo

1967. Solidstate, multiple heads.

1967		$400	$500

V-846 Wah

1969-1970s. Chrome top, Italian-made.

1969	Made in Italy	$800	$1,250
1970s	Sepulveda-made	$300	$400

V-847 Wah-Wah

1992-present. Reissue of the original V-846 Wah.

1992-2023		$75	$100

Volume Pedal

1954-late 1960s. Reissued as the V850.

1960s		$50	$75

Wampler Pedals

2004-present. Brian Wampler began building effects under the brand Indy Guitarist in 2004 and changed the name to Wampler Pedals in 2007. They are built in Greenwood, Indiana.

Warmenfat

2004-present. Pre-amps and guitar effects built in Sacramento, California, by Rainbow Electronics.

Wasabi

2003-2008. Line of guitar effect pedals from Danelectro.

Washburn

Washburn offered a line of effects from around 1983 to ca. '89.

Effects

1980s	Analog Delay AX:9	$50	$65
1980s	Flanger FX:4	$55	$75
1980s	Phaser PX:8	$65	$85
1980s	Stack in a Box SX:3	$50	$65

Watkins/WEM

1957-present. Charlie Watkins founded Watkins Electric Music (WEM). Their first commercial product was the Watkins Dominator amp in '57, followed by the Copicat Echo in '58.

Copicat Tape Echo

1958-1970s, 1985-present. The Copicat went through several detail changes, subsequently known as the Marks I, II, III, and IV versions. It has been reissued in various forms by Watkins.

1958-1970s	Solidstate	$750	$1,500
1958-1970s	Tube	$1,250	$1,750

Way Huge Electronics

1995-1998, 2008-present Way Huge offered a variety of stomp boxes, made in Sherman Oaks, California. Jim Dunlop revived the brand in '08.

Foot Pig Fuzz

1990s		$800	$1,000

Green Rhino Overdrive II

1990s		$400	$1,000

Piercing Moose Octafuzz

1990s		$650	$850

Swollen Pickle Jumbo Fuzz

1990s		$400	$650

1967 Vox Tone Bender
Dean Nissen

Wampler Clarksdale

Watkins Copicat Tape Echo
Rivington Guitars

Whirlwind OC-Bass
Optical Compressor

Xotic SL Drive

Xotic Effects Soul Driven

MODEL YEAR	FEATURES	LOW	HIGH

WD Music

Since 1978, WD Music has offered a wide line of aftermarket products for guitar players. From '91 to '02, they offered a line of effects that were copies of the original Dan Armstrong color series (refer to Dan Armstrong listing).

Blue Clipper
1991-2002. Fuzz.

1991-2002		$60	$80

Orange Squeezer
1991-2002. Signal compressor.

| 1991-2002 | Light Orange case | $60 | $80 |

Purple Peaker
1991-2002. Mini EQ.

| 1991-2002 | | $60 | $80 |

Westbury

1978-ca.1983. Brand imported by Unicord.

Tube Overdrive
1978-1983. 12AX7.

| 1978-1983 | | $200 | $300 |

Whirlwind

1976-present. Effects from Michael Laiacona, who helped found MXR, originally made in Rochester, New York. Currently the company offers guitar effects, DI boxes and other music devices built in Greece, New York.

Commander
1980s. Boost and effects loop selector.

| 1980s | | $75 | $100 |

Wilsic

1970s. Enginer Charlie Ramskirr designed effects for Hornby Skewes, but also offered DIY mail-order kits under the brand Wilsic.

Sound Vibration

| 1970s | | $75 | $100 |

Wilson Effects

2007-present. Guitar effects built by Kevin Wilson in Guilford, Indiana.

WMD (William Mathewson Devices)

2008-present. William Mathewson builds his instrument effects in Denver, Colorado.

Wurlitzer

Wurlitzer offered the Fuzzer Buzzer in the 1960s, which was the same as the Clark Fuzz.

Xotic Effects

2001-present. The roots of Xotic go back to a small garage in the San Fernando Valley of Southern California in 1996, producing and designing bass guitars and bass preamps, soon expanding to build boutique pedals.

MODEL YEAR	FEATURES	LOW	HIGH

AC Booster
2002-2020. Light overdrive with 20db+ of boost and 2-band EQ.

| 2002-2020 | | $100 | $130 |

AC Plus
2007-2018. Stackable 2-channel light overdrive with 3-band EQ and compression.

| 2007-2018 | | $130 | $175 |

AC-COMP
2010-2018. Custom Shop light overdrive with 3 compression modes. Internal DIP switches control level of compression, tonal character, and treble/presence levels.

| 2010-2018 | | $160 | $200 |

Bass BB Preamp
2006-present. Bass overdrive with 2 overlapping EQs and ±15dB boost/cut.

| 2006-2023 | | $175 | $225 |

Bass RC Booster
2006-present. Bass boost with 2-band active EQ and ±15dB boost/cut.

| 2006-2023 | | $65 | $85 |

BB Plus
2008-2020. Stackable 2-channel overdrive with 3-band EQ and compression.

| 2008-2020 | | $150 | $200 |

BB Preamp
2005-2020. Overdrive with 30dB+ boost and 2-band EQ.

| 2005-2020 | | $100 | $130 |

BBP-COMP
2011-2018. Custom Shop overdrive with 3 compression modes and 2-band EQ.

| 2011-2018 | | $175 | $225 |

BBP-MB
2009-2018. Custom Shop overdrive with 12dB+ mid-treble boost and 2-band EQ.

| 2009-2018 | | $150 | $200 |

EP Booster
2009-present. Mini boost pedal with 20db+ of boost. Internal DIP switches control boost frequencies and EQ.

| 2009-2023 | | $100 | $130 |

RC Booster
2002-2017. Clean boost with 20dB+ of transparent boost and 2-band EQ.

| 2002-2017 | | $65 | $85 |

RC Booster V2
2016-present. Clean boost with 20dB+ transparent boost and 2-band EQ. Added gain channel with gain 2 control knob.

| 2016-2023 | | $100 | $130 |

Robotalk
1998-2009. Envelope filter, random arpeggiator and low-pass filter. Ultra-boutique pedal, made from scratch, in limited quantities.

| 1998-2009 | | $250 | $325 |

Robotalk 2
2009-2022. Envelope filter with 2 separate envelope filter channels that can be combined or used individually. Internal input pad controls passive/active signals. Internal DIP switches control frequency settings.

| 2009-2022 | | $150 | $200 |

EFFECTS

MODEL YEAR	FEATURES	LOW	HIGH

Robotalk-RI
2011-2018. Custom Shop envelope filter with an enhanced arpeggiator for more wonderfully strange and mesmerizing sounds.

2011-2018		$175	$225

SL Drive
2013-present. Mini overdrive pedal produces tones from legendary amplifiers, the Super Lead and Super Bass. Internal DIP switches control boost frequencies and EQ settings.

2013-2023		$85	$110

Soul Driven
2017-present. Boost/overdrive with mid-boost and tone knobs. Internal bass boost DIP switches control up to 6dB+ of boost.

2017-2023		$175	$225

SP Compressor
2012-present. Mini compressor featuring a wide variety of compressor tones from vintage to subtle to modern, and more. Internal DIP switches control attack.

2012-2023		$110	$150

Stereo X-Blender
2011-2017. Custom Shop effects looper with 3 parallel effects loops equipped with a transparent buffer amplifier allowing feeding and mixing of effects without signal deterioration.

2011-2017		$175	$225

X-Blender
2006-present. Series and parallel effects looper with boost switch for 6dB+ volume boost, treble and bass EQ and phase inverter switch. Dry/Wet knob in parallel mode.

2006-2023		$110	$150

Xotic Wah
2014-present. Wah pedal that features a 20% smaller size, bias, wah-Q, treble, and bass controls, plus internal DIP switches for even more tonal possibilities.

2014-2023		$225	$300

Yack
1960s. Japanese effects company.

Fuzz Box YF-2

1960s		$150	$400

Yamaha
1946-present. Yamaha has offered effects since at least the early '80s. They also build guitars, basses, amps, and other musical instruments.

Analog Delay E1005
1980s. Free-standing, double-space rack mount-sized, short to long range delays, gray case.

1980s		$175	$325

Yubro
Yubro, of Bellaire, Texas, offered a line of nine effects in the mid- to late-'80s.

Analog Delay AD-800

1980s	300 ms	$75	$125

Stereo Chorus CH-600

1980s		$55	$75

MODEL YEAR	FEATURES	LOW	HIGH

Zinky
Amp builder Bruce Zinky added guitar effects in late 2003, in Flagstaff, Arizona. He also builds amps and has revived the Supro brand on a guitar and amp.

Zoom
Effects line from Samson Technologies Corp. of Syosset, New York.

503 Amp Simulator

1998-2000		$40	$55

504 Acoustic Pedal
1997-2000. Compact multi-effects pedal, 24 effects, tuner, replaced by II version.

1997-2000		$40	$55

505 Guitar Pedal
1996-2000. Compact multi-effects pedal, 24 effects, tuner, replaced by II version.

1996-2000		$45	$60

506 Bass Pedal
1997-2000. Compact multi-effects bass pedal, 24 effects, tuner, black box, orange panel. Replaced by II version.

1997-2000		$55	$75

507 Reverb

1997-2000		$40	$55

1010 Player
1996-1999. Compact multi-effects pedal board, 16 distortions, 25 effects.

1996-1999		$60	$75

ZT Amplifiers
2009-present. Effects pedals built in China and offered by Ken Kantor in Berkeley, California. He also imports amps.

ZVex Effects
1995-present. Zachary Vex builds his effects in Minneapolis, Minnesota, with some subassembly work done in Michigan. Painters on staff create stock and custom versions of many pedals, which often bring higher prices. Vexter pedals are silk-screened pedals made in Taiwan. U.S. Vexters are manufactured in Taiwan but engraved in Minnesota. California Mini models are manufactured in California. In 2000-'02, Vex built the solidbody Drip Guitar with an onboard Wah. In '02, Vex also began building amps.

Basstortion
2011-present. Bass distortion, bright/dark switch.

2011-2023		$95	$130

Box of Metal
2007-present. High-gain distortion, switchable noise gate.

2007-2023		$120	$150

Box of Rock
2005-present. 2-in-1 pedal. Tube amp-type distortion pedal and clean post-gain boost.

2005-2023		$100	$150

Channel 2
2014-2023. Mini boost pedal, master volume.

2014-2023		$70	$90

Xotic Effects X-Blender

ZT Amplifiers Extortion

ZVex Effects Basstortion

EFFECTS

ZVex Effects Double Rock

ZVex Instant Lo-Fi Junky

ZVex Super Seek Trem

EFFECTS

Distortion
2009-2020. Tube amp-style distortion, sub contour and gain switches.
2009-2020 — $60 / $75

Double Rock
2012-present. Dual switchable distortion/boost pedal.
2012-2023 — $175 / $200

Fat Fuzz Factory
2011-present. Fuzz Factory with additional 3-position mini toggle to select frequency range.
2011-2023 — $175 / $200

Fuzz Factory
1995-present. Powerful, tweaky, and unique germanium fuzz pedal, with idiosyncratic hand-painted housings. Also available as Vexter and US Vexter models.
1995-2014 — $120 / $145
1995-2023 Hand-painted — $140 / $200

Fuzz Factory 7
2013-present. Limited edition Fuzz Factory with footswitchable EQ and 9-position rotary frequency selector.
2013-2023 — $300 / $375

Fuzz Probe
2000-present. Theremin-controlled Fuzz Factory.
2000-2023 — $100 / $175

Fuzzolo
2014-present. Mini footprint 2-knob silicon fuzz for guitar and bass.
2014-2023 — $80 / $100

Instant Lo-Fi Junky
2011-present. Filter, compression, and wave shapeable vibrato and blend for chorus effect.
2011-2023 — $150 / $175

Inventobox
2010-2021. Dual pedal chassis for DIY builders or for use with Z.Vex modules.
2010-2021 — $150 / $200

Jonny Octave
2005-present. Octave pedal.
2005-2023 — $140 / $185

Lo-Fi Loop Junky
2002-present. Sampler, single 20-second sample with vibrato.
2002-2023 — $150 / $200

Loop Gate
2012-present. Audio looping mixer with foot switchable noise gate.
2012-2023 — $100 / $130

Machine
1996-present. Crossover distortion generator.
1996-2023 — $150 / $200

Mastrotron
2009-present. Silicon fuzz with mini toggle sub contour.
2009-2023 — $70 / $95

Octane I, II, and III
1995-2023. Ring modulator fuzz.
1995-2023 — $85 / $125

Ooh Wah I and II
2003-2013. 8-step sequencer using wah filters with random sequencing.
2003-2013 — $90 / $115

Ringtone and Ringtone TT
2006-2013. 8-step sequencer using ring modulator.
2006-2013 — $175 / $190

Seek Trem I and II
2006-2013. 8-step sequencer using volume.
1999-2013 — $135 / $175

Seek Wah I and II
2006-2013. 8-step sequencer using wah filters.
2006-2013 — $140 / $180

Sonar Tremolo and Stutter
2012-present. Tremolo with wave shaping, distortion circuit, tap tempo, and auto tempo ramping.
2012-2023 — $175 / $190

Super Duper 2-in-1
2001-present. Dual boost with master volume on 2nd channel.
2001-2023 — $120 / $170

Super Hard On
1996-present. Sparkly clean boost.
1996-2023 — $110 / $170

Super Ringtone
2013-present. 16-step sequencer using ring modulator with MIDI sync, tap tempo, tap tempo sync, and glissando.
2013-2023 — $150 / $225

Super Seek Trem
2013-present. 16-step sequencer using volume with MIDI sync, tap tempo, tap tempo sync, and glissando.
2013-2023 — $150 / $195

Super Seek Wah
2013-present. 16-step sequencer using wah filters with MIDI sync, tap tempo, tap tempo sync, and glissando.
2013-2023 — $150 / $195

Tremolo Probe
2000-2023. Theremin-controlled volume.
2000-2023 — $100 / $175

Tremorama
2004-2013. 8-step sequencer using volume with random sequencing.
2004-2013 — $195 / $230

Volume Probe
2000-2002. Theremin-controlled volume using coiled cable for antenna.
2000-2002 — $100 / $175

Wah Probe
2000-2023. Theremin-controlled wah.
2000-2023 — $100 / $175

Woolly Mammoth
1999-present. Silicon fuzz for guitar and bass.
1999-2023 — $200 / $290

MANDOLINS

MODEL		EXC. COND.	
YEAR	FEATURES	LOW	HIGH

1900s American
Conservatory Bowlback

Imaged by Heritage Auctions, HA.com

Apitius Grand Classic

Airline

Ca. 1958-1968. Brand for Montgomery Ward. Instruments were built by Kay, Harmony and Valco.
Acoustic
1960s. Acoustic, plain features.

1960s		$250	$350

Electric (Kay K390)
Early-1960s. In '62 the K390 was advertised as the Kay Professional Electric Mandolin. Venetian shape with sunburst spruce top, curly maple back and sides, tube-style pickup, white 'guard, rope-style celluloid binding.

1962		$450	$575

Alvarez

1965-present. An import brand for St. Louis Music, Alvarez currently offers intermediate grade, production, mandolins. They also offer guitars, lap steels and banjos.
Model A
1970s-2000s. Classic A-style mandolin features, round soundhole or f-holes.

1970s		$500	$650

Model F
1970s-2000s. Classic F-style mandolin features, round soundhole or f-holes.

1970s		$550	$725

American Conservatory (Lyon & Healy)

Late-1800s-early-1900s. Mainly catalog sales of guitars and mandolins from the Chicago maker. Marketed as a less expensive alternative to the Lyon & Healy Washburn product line.
Arched Back
1910s. Flat back with a mild arch, standard appointments, nothing fancy.

1910s		$225	$450

Bowl Back
1917. Bowl back style, 14 ribs, Brazilian.

1917		$125	$400

Bowl Back Style G2603
Early-1900s. Bowl back-style, 28 rosewood ribs (generally more ribs and use of rosewood ribs versus mahogany indicates higher quality), color corded soundhole and edge inlay, inlaid tortoise shell celluloid guard plate underneath strings and below the soundhole, bent top, butterfly headstock inlay.

1917		$225	$600

Bowl Back Style G2604
Early-1900s. Bowl back-style, 42 rosewood ribs (generally more ribs indicated higher quality), extra fancy color corded soundhole and edge inlay around, extra fancy inlaid tortoise shell celluloid guard plate underneath strings and below the soundhole, bent top, butterfly headstock inlay.

1917		$400	$725

Anderson

1976-2019. Gerald Anderson began working with luthier Wayne Henderson in 1976, until opening his own shop in 2005. He died suddenly in '19.

F-5

1994		$5,500	$7,500

Apitius

1976-present. Luthier Oliver Apitius builds his premium and presentation grade, production/custom, mandolins in Shelburne, Ontario.

Applause

Applause offered intermediate grade, production, Ovation-styled, imported mandolins, starting in 1994. They also offer ukes.
Various Models

1990s		$125	$225

Aria/Aria Pro II

1956-present. Intermediate grade, production, acoustic and electric mandolins from Aria/Aria Pro II, which added Japanese and Korean mandolins to their line in '76.
AM200/BS Style A
1994-2012. Pear-shaped A body, plywood.

1994-2012		$225	$300

AM400/BS Style F
1994-2012. F-style, plywood.

1994-2012		$350	$450

AM600 Style F
1994-2008. F-style, solid wood.

1994-2008		$400	$500

PM750 Style F
1976-ca. 1982. F-style Loar copy, maple plywood body, sunburst.

1976-1982		$600	$750

Bacon & Day

Established in 1921 by David Day and Paul Bacon, primarily known for fine quality tenor and plectrum banjos in the '20s and '30s.
Orchestra Mando Banjo
1920s. Mandolin neck and banjo body with open back, headstock with Bacon logo.

1920s		$350	$450

Professional Mando Banjo
1920s. Figured birch back and sides, spruce top, oval sound hole, 2-point flat back, The Bacon tailpiece.

1920s		$1,375	$1,875

Senorita Mando Banjo
1930s. Mandolin neck and banjo body, 19-fret tenor.

1930s		$750	$975

Silverbell #1 Mando Banjo
1920s. Fancy appointments, closed-back resonator.

1920s		$850	$1,125

Bauer (George)

1894-1911. Luthier George Bauer built guitars and mandolins in Philadelphia, Pennsylvania. He also built instruments with Samuel S. Stewart (S.S. Stewart).

MANDOLINS

MODEL YEAR	FEATURES	EXC. COND. LOW	HIGH

Acme Professional Bowl Back
1894-1911. Brazilian, 29 ribs.

1894-1911	Fancy	$550	$725
1894-1911	Mid-level	$400	$525
1894-1911	Plain	$275	$350

Beltone
1920s-1930s. Acoustic and resonator mandolins and banjo-mandolins made by others for New York City distributor Perlberg & Halpin. Martin did make a small number of instruments for Beltone, but most were student-grade models most likely made by one of the big Chicago builders. They also made guitars.

Resonator
1930s. F-hole top, banjo-style resonator back.

1930s		$475	$625

Bohmann
1878-ca.1926. Established by Czechoslavakian-born Joseph Bohmann in Chicago, Illinois.

Bowl Back
1890-1900. Spruce top, marquetry trimmed, inlay, pearl.

1890-1900	Fancy	$725	$1,250
1890-1900	Mid-level	$550	$725
1890-1900	Plain	$375	$500

Brandt
Early 1900s. John Brandt started making mandolin-family instruments in Chicago, Illinois around 1898.

Mandola
1900s. Spruce top, rosewood body, scroll headstock, pearl and abalone fretboard binding.

1900s		$750	$1,250

Presentation
1900s. Spruce top, tortoise shell-bound.

1900s		$500	$1,125

Breedlove
1990-present. Breedlove started building professional and premium grade, mandolins in Bend, Oregon in 1997. In '15, they ceased U.S. mando production, but continued with their import line. They also produce guitars, basses, laps and ukes.

Alpine
2000s-2013. Master Class series, O-style body, spruce/maple.

2000s-2013		$2,000	$2,500

K-5
1990s. Asymmetric carved top, maple body.

1990s		$1,750	$2,250

Olympic
1990s. Solid spruce top, teardrop-shaped, oval soundhole, highly flamed maple back, sunburst.

1990s		$1,375	$1,750

Quartz OF/OO
2000s. Basic A-style body with f-holes.

2000s		$950	$1,250

MODEL YEAR	FEATURES	EXC. COND. LOW	HIGH

Bruno and Sons
Established in 1834 by Charles Bruno, primarily as a distributor, Bruno and Sons marketed a variety of brands, including their own. In the '60s or '70s, a Japanese-made solidbody electric mandolin was sold under the Bruno name.

Banjo Mando
1920s. Open back, 10" model.

1920s		$125	$350

Bowl Back
1890s-1920s. Brazilian rosewood, spruce, rosewood ribs.

1920s	Fancy	$550	$725
1920s	Less fancy	$350	$450

Calace
1825-present. Nicola Calace started The Calace Liuteria lute-making workshop in 1825 on the island of Procida, which is near Naples. The business is now in Naples and still in the family.

Lyre/Harp-Style
Late-1800s-early-1900s. Lyre/harp-style, 8 strings, round soundhole, slightly bent top. Condition is important for these older instruments and the price noted is for a fully functional, original or pro-restored example.

1900		$1,125	$1,500

Carvin
1946-present. Carvin offered solidbody electric mandolins from around '56 to the late '60s, when they switched to a traditional pear-shaped electric/acoustic. They also offer guitars, basses and amps.

MB Models
1956-1968. Solidbody, 1 pickup, single-cut Les Paul shape until '64, double-cut Jazzmaster/Strat shape after. Models include the #1-MB and the #2-MB, with different pickups.

1950s	#1-MB	$1,500	$2,000

Cole
1890-1919. After leaving Fairbanks & Cole in 1890, W.A. Cole started his own line. He also made guitars and banjos.

Imperial G Bowl Back
1905-1910. 27 ribs.

1905-1910		$950	$1,250

Collings
1986-present. Professional and premium grade, production/custom, mandolins built in Austin, Texas. Collings added mandolins to their line in '99. They also build guitars and ukuleles.

MF
1999-present. F-style, carved top and back.

1999-2023		$3,375	$4,375

MF-5 Deluxe
2005-2006. Limited production, varnish finish, hand engraved nickel tailpiece unique to each instrument.

2005-2006		$8,000	$10,000

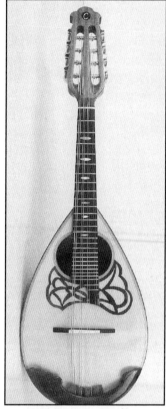

Calace Mandolino Ripa

Collings MF

MANDOLINS

Collings MT

MODEL YEAR	FEATURES	EXC. COND. LOW	HIGH

MF-5V
2007. Carved Adirondack spruce top, highly flamed maple body.

2007		$6,750	$8,750

MT
1999-present. A-style, 2 f-holes, carved top and back, matte finish, tortoise-bound top.

1999-2023		$2,250	$3,000

MT-2
2009-present. A-style, red spruce top, premium maple back and sides.

1999-2023		$3,250	$4,500

MT-2V
2009-present. Like MT-2, but with oil-based varnish finish and ivoroid-bound ebony 'guard.

2009-2023		$3,625	$4,750

Crestwood
1970s. Copy models imported by La Playa Distributing Company of Detroit.

Various Models
1970s. Includes models 3039 (electric A-style), 3041 (bowl back-style, flower 'guard), 3043 (bowl back-style, plain 'guard), 71820 (A-style), and 71821 (F-style).

1970s		$185	$250

Cromwell
1935-1939. Private branded instruments made by Gibson at their Parsons Street factory in Kalamazoo, Michigan. Distributed by a variety of mail order companies such as Continental, Grossman, and Richter & Phillips.

GM-2
1935-1939. Spruce top, mahogony back and sides, similar to KM-11.

1935-1939		$500	$650

GM-4
1935-1939. Style A, f-holes, solid wood arched top, mahogany back and sides, block capital letter Cromwell headstock logo, dot markers, elevated 'guard, sunburst.

1935-1939		$600	$750

Dayton
1910-late 1930s. Mandolins built by luthier Charles B. Rauch in Dayton, Ohio. He also built banjos, violins, guitars and banjo-ukuleles.

Style B

1910-1930s		$1,625	$2,125

DeLucia, Vincenzo
1910s-1920s. Luthier Vincenzo DeLucia built mandolins in Philadelphia, Pennsylvania.

Various Models
Early-1900s. High quality material, rosewood body, fine ornamentation.

1910s		$1,125	$1,500

Ditson
Mandolins made for the Oliver Ditson Company of Boston, an instrument dealer and music publisher. Turn of the century and early-1900s models were bowl back-style with the Ditson label. The '20s Ditson Style A flat back mandolins were made by Martin. Models were also made by Lyon & Healy of Boston, often with a Ditson Empire label.

Mandola
1920. Bowl back.

1920		$1,125	$1,500

Style A
1920s. Style A flat back made by Martin, mahogany sides and back, plain ornamentation.

1920s		$1,125	$1,500

Style B
Style B flat back made by Martin, Adirondack top, Brazilian rosewood sides and back, herringbone soundhole trim.

1918		$2,000	$2,500

Victory
1890s. Brazilian rib bowl back with fancy inlays.

1890s		$725	$950

Dobro
1929-1942, 1954-2019. Dobro offered mandolins throughout their early era and from the '60s to the mid-'90s.

Resonator
1930s-1960s. Resonator on wood body.

1930s-60s		$1,000	$1,375

Dudenbostel
1989-present. Luthier Lynn Dudenbostel builds his limited production, premium and presentation grade, custom, mandolins in Knoxville, Tennessee. He started with guitars and added mandolins in '96.

F-5
1996-2012. Loar-style, about 30 made.

1996-2012		$20,000	$25,000

Duff Mandolins
1982-present. Premium and presentation grade, custom/production, mandolin family instruments built by luthier Paul Duff in Palmyra, Western Australia.

F-5
1990-present. Loar-style, various woods.

1990-2023 Adirondack		$5,750	$7,500

H-5 Mandola
2000-present. Various woods.

2000-2023 Adirondack		$6,500	$8,500

EKO
1961-1985, 2000-present. The Italian-made EKOs were imported by LoDuca Brothers of Milwaukee. The brand was revived around 2000, but does not currently include mandolins.

Baritone
1960s. Baritone mandolin with ornate inlays.

1960s		$450	$575

Octave
1960s. Octave mandolin with ornate inlays.

1960s		$450	$575

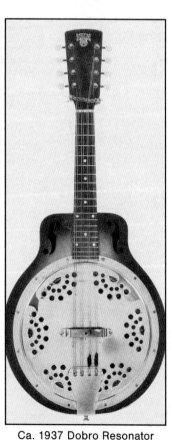

Ca. 1937 Dobro Resonator
Imaged by Heritage Auctions, HA.com

MANDOLINS

MODEL YEAR	FEATURES	EXC. COND. LOW	HIGH

Epiphone

1928-present. Intermediate grade, production, acoustic mandolins. Epiphone has offered several mandolin-family models over the years. Those from the '30s to the '60s were U.S.-made, the later models imported.

Adelphi

1932-1948. A-style body, maple back and sides, f-holes, single-bound top and back.

1932-1948		$1,000	$1,375

Mandobird VIII

2004-2012. Reverse Firebird-style body with mandolin neck, electric, various colors.

2004-2012		$200	$250

MM Series

1979-present. Imported A and F styles.

1979-1985	MM70, F-style	$500	$650
1979-2013	MM50, F-style	$400	$500
1980-2023	MM30, A-style	$150	$200
1998-2013	MM20, A-style	$125	$175

Strand

1932-1958. Walnut back and sides, f-holes, multi-bound, sunburst.

1944-1947		$1,000	$1,375

Venetian Electric

1961-1970. Gibson-made, pear-shaped body, 4 pole P-90 'dog-ear' mounted pickup, volume and tone knobs, dot markers, sunburst finish.

1961-1970		$1,500	$2,000

Windsor Special

1936-1949. Scroll body, f-holes, slot-block inlays.

1940s	Rare, high-end	$10,000	$15,000

Zephyr

1939-1958. A-style, electric, f-holes, maple body, 1 pickup, slotted block inlay.

1950s		$725	$950

Esquire

1930s. Student level instruments with painted Esquire logo and painted wood grain.

A-Style

1930s. Laminate A-style wood body, sunburst.

1930s		$300	$400

Fairbanks

1875-1922. Primarily known for banjos, Fairbanks also offered banjo mandolins when owned by Vega.

Little Wonder Banjo Mando

1920s. Banjo body, mando neck, dot inlays.

1921		$500	$650

Style K Banjo Mando

1920s. Banjo body, mando neck, dot inlays.

1920		$450	$600

Fender

1946-present. Intermediate grade, production, acoustic and acoustic/electric mandolins. Fender also offered an electric mandolin for 20 years.

Electric Solidbody

1956-1976. Often referred to as the Mandocaster by collectors.

1956-1957	Blond	$3,500	$5,000
1958-1959	Sunburst	$3,500	$5,000
1960-1965	Sunburst	$3,000	$4,000
1966-1976	Sunburst	$2,500	$3,500

FM Series

2001-2017. Made in Korea, acoustic and acoustic-electric, models include 52E (acou-elec, A-style), 53S (acoustic, A-style), 60E (5 string, 2 pu) and 61SE (8-string, 1 pu), 62SE (acou-elec, double-cut, extended 'board), 62SCE (acou-elec, double-cut, block-end 'board), 63S (acoustic, F-style), 63SE (acou-elec, F-style), 100 (acoustic, A-style).

2001-2002	FM-60E/61SE	$400	$500
2001-2007	FM-62SE/62SCE	$400	$500
2001-2014	FM-52E	$150	$200
2001-2017	FM-53S	$175	$250
2001-2017	FM-63S	$325	$425
2011-2017	FM-63SE/63SCE	$400	$525
2013-2017	FM-100	$95	$125

Leo Deluxe

Chrome-plated, fancy inlays.

Flatiron

1977-2003, 2006-2009. Gibson purchased Flatiron in 1987. Production was in Bozeman, Montana until the end of '96, when Gibson closed the Flatiron mandolin workshop and moved mandolin assembly to Nashville, Tennessee. General production tapered off after the move and Flatirons were available on a special order basis for a time. The brand was revived in '06 on an import model sold through Epiphone.

A-Style

Includes A-style Performer series (1990-'95, maple back & sides, mahogany neck, ebony board, top binding, sunburst) and Festival series (1988-'95, same, in cherry finish and with no binding).

1988-1995	Festival	$1,375	$1,750
1990-1995	Performer	$1,500	$2,000

A-2

1977-1987	Early, no truss rod	$3,000	$4,000

A-5

Teardrop shape, f-holes, figured maple body and neck, carved spruce top, X-bracing, unbound ebony 'board, nickel hardware, fleur-de-lis headstock inlay.

1987-1994	Gibson Montana	$1,750	$2,250
1996-2003		$1,750	$2,250

A-5 1

Carved top and back, bound body, dot inlays, The Flatiron headstock inlay.

1983-1985	Pre-Gibson	$3,500	$4,500

A-5 2

Carved top and back, bound body, neck, headstock and pickguard, dot inlays, modified fern headstock inlay.

1983-1985	Pre-Gibson	$3,500	$4,500

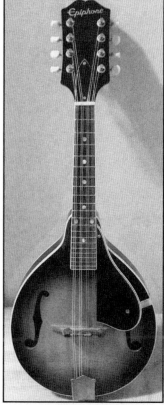

1966 Epiphone Venetian
Kerry Brown

1993 Flatiron A-5
Steven Squire

MANDOLINS

1924 Gibson A
David Stone

1914 Gibson A-1

MODEL YEAR	FEATURES	EXC. COND. LOW	HIGH
A-5 Artist			
A-5 with highly figured maple body and neck, bound ebony headstock, gold hardware, fern headstock inlay.			
1987-1990	Gibson Montana	$3,000	$4,000
1996-2003		$2,500	$3,250
A-5 Junior			
As A-5 but with tone bar bracing, mahogany neck, The Flatiron headstock inlay.			
1987-1990	Gibson Montana	$1,250	$1,625
1996-2003		$1,250	$1,625
Cadet			
Flat-top, teardrop body, spruce top, maple body, rosewood 'board, nickel hardware.			
1990-1996		$650	$850
F-Style			
Includes F-style Performer series (1990-'95, maple back & sides and neck, ebony board, fern/banner headstock inlay, top and back of body and headstock bound, sunburst top) and Festival series (1988-'95, same, but without headstock or back binding).			
1988-1995	Festival	$3,250	$4,250
1990-1995	Performer	$3,250	$4,250
2001	Festival, Gibson Montana	$3,250	$4,250
F-2			
1977-1987	Early, no truss rod	$6,750	$8,750
F-5			
F-style body, f-holes, flamed maple body and neck, carved spruce top, tone bar bracing, bound ebony 'board and headstock, nickel hardware, flower pot headstock inlay, cherry finish.			
1987-1990	Gibson Montana	$4,250	$5,500
F-5 Artist			
F-5 but with X-braces, bound ebony 'board, gold hardware, fern headstock inlay, and sunburst.			
1984-1985	Pre-Gibson	$5,000	$6,500
1987-1995	Gibson Montana	$4,750	$6,250
1996-2003	Modified fern	$4,750	$6,250
Model 1			
Oval shape, spruce top, maple body, rosewood 'board, walnut headstock veneer.			
1977-1987	Pre-Gibson	$1,000	$1,375
1988-1995	Gibson Montana	$825	$1,125
Model 1 Mandola			
Model 1 features.			
1977-1987	Pre-Gibson	$1,000	$1,375
1983-1995	Gibson Montana	$825	$1,125
Model 2			
Like Model 1, but with curly maple (MC) or birdseye maple (MB) back and sides, ebony 'board, rosewood headstock veneer.			
1977-1987	Pre-Gibson	$950	$1,250
1977-1995	Flamed koa back/sides	$1,000	$1,500
1988-1995	Gibson Montana	$900	$1,125
Model 2 Mandola			
Model 2 features, birdseye maple (MB) or curly maple (MC) body.			
1977-1987	Pre-Gibson	$1,125	$1,500
1988-1995	Gibson Montana	$1,000	$1,375

MODEL YEAR	FEATURES	EXC. COND. LOW	HIGH
Model 3 Octave			
Model 2 features, birdseye maple (MB) or curly maple (MC) body.			
1977-1987	Pre-Gibson	$1,125	$1,500
1988-1995	Gibson Montana	$1,000	$1,375

Framus
1946-1977, 1996-present. Founded in Erlangen, Germany by Fred Wilfer. In the '60s, Framus instruments were imported into the U.S. by Philadelphia Music Company. They offered acoustic and electric mandolins. The brand was revived in '96.

MODEL YEAR	FEATURES	EXC. COND. LOW	HIGH
12-String			
1960s		$475	$625

Freshwater
1992-2011. Luthier Dave Freshwater and family built mandolin family instruments in Beauly, Inverness, Scotland. They also built bouzoukis, dulcimers and harps.

Galiano/A. Galiano
New Yorkers Antonio Cerrito and Raphael Ciani offered instruments built by them and others under the Galiano brand during the early 1900s.

MODEL YEAR	FEATURES	EXC. COND. LOW	HIGH
Bowl Back			
Some fancy appointments.			
1920s		$375	$500

Gaylord
1940s. Private brand made by Harmony, painted Gaylord logo on headstock.

MODEL YEAR	FEATURES	EXC. COND. LOW	HIGH
Artistic A			
1940s	Painted logo	$200	$275

Gibson
1890s (1902)-present. Orville Gibson created the violin-based mandolin body-style that replaced the bowl back-type. Currently Gibson offers professional, premium and presentation grade, production/custom, mandolins.

Special Designations:
Snakehead headstock: 1922-1927 with production possible for a few months plus or minus.
Lloyd Loar era: Mid-1922-late 1924 with production possible for a few months plus or minus.

MODEL YEAR	FEATURES	EXC. COND. LOW	HIGH
A-Style (Orville Gibson)			
1890s-1902. Mandolin models built during Orville Gibson era, before he sold out to others in 1902, covering a range of features and levels of appointments.			
1890s-1902	Fancy, rare	$21,000	$31,000
1890s-1902	Plain	$2,750	$7,000
A			
1902-1933. Oval soundhole, snakehead headstock '22-27, Loar era mid-'22-late-'24.			
1902-1918	Orange	$1,500	$2,000
1918-1921	Brown	$1,500	$2,000
1922-1924	Loar era	$2,500	$3,000
1925-1933		$2,250	$2,750

MANDOLINS

MODEL YEAR	FEATURES	EXC. COND. LOW	HIGH

A-0

1927-1933. Replaces A Jr., oval soundhole, dot inlay, brown finish.

1927-1933		$1,500	$2,000

A-00

1933-1943. F-hole, dot inlay, carved bound top.

1933-1943	Sunburst	$1,500	$2,000

A-1

1902-1918, 1922-1927, 1933-1943. Snakehead headstock '23-'27.

1902-1918	Orange	$1,500	$2,000
1922-1924	Loar era	$3,000	$4,000
1925-1927	Black	$2,125	$2,750
1927	Not snaked	$2,250	$3,000
1927	Snaked	$2,250	$3,000
1929		$2,250	$3,000
1932	Re-intro, oval	$2,250	$3,000
1933-1943	Sunburst, f-holes	$1,375	$1,875

A-2/A-2Z

1902-1908, 1918-1928. A-2Z '22-'27. Renamed A-2 '27-'28. Snakehead headstock '23-'27. Lloyd Loar era mid-'22-late-'24.

1902-1908	Orange	$1,750	$2,250
1918-1921	Brown	$1,750	$2,250
1922-1924	Loar era	$5,000	$6,500
1923-1924	Loar era, extra binding	$5,000	$6,500
1925-1928		$2,250	$3,000

A-3

1902-1922. Oval soundhole, single-bound body, dot inlay.

1902-1917	Orange	$2,250	$3,000
1918-1922	Ivory	$2,250	$3,000

A-4

1902-1935. Oval soundhole, single-bound body, dot inlay, snakehead '23-'27.

1902-1917	Various colors	$3,000	$4,000
1918-1921	Dark mahogany	$3,000	$4,000
1922-1924	Loar era	$6,000	$7,500
1925-1935	Various colors	$3,000	$4,000

A-5

1957-1979. Oval soundhole, maple back and sides, dot inlay, scroll headstock, sunburst. Name now used on extended neck version.

1957-1964		$1,375	$1,750
1965-1969		$1,250	$1,625
1970-1979		$1,250	$1,625

A-5G

1988-1996. Less ornate version of the A-5 L, abalone fleur-de-lis headstock inlay.

1988-1996		$1,250	$1,625

A-5L/A-5

1988-2013. Extended neck, raised 'board, flowerpot headstock inlay, curly maple and spruce, sunburst, based on custom-made 1923 Loar A-5. L has been dropped from name.

1988-2013		$2,500	$3,250

A-9

2002-2013. Spruce top, maple back and sides, black bound top, satin brown finish.

2002-2013		$1,250	$1,625

A-12

1970-1979. F-holes, long neck, dot inlay, fleur-de-lis inlay, sunburst.

1970-1979		$1,125	$1,500

A-40

1948-1970. F-holes, bound top, dot inlay, natural or sunburst.

1948-1949		$1,500	$2,000
1950-1959		$1,375	$1,875
1960-1964		$1,250	$1,625
1965-1970		$1,125	$1,500

A-50

1933-1971. A-style oval bound body, f-holes, sunburst.

1933	Oval soundhole	$1,626	$2,250
1934-1941	Larger 11.25" body	$1,625	$2,250
1942-1949	Smaller 10" body	$1,375	$1,875
1950-1959		$1,250	$1,875
1960-1964		$1,125	$1,500
1965-1971		$1,125	$1,500

A-75

1934-1936. F-holes, raised fingerboard, bound top and back.

1934-1936		$2,250	$3,000

A-C Century

1933-1934, 1936-1937. A body, built to commemorate the 1933-1934 Century of Progress Exhibition in Chicago, pearloid 'board.

1933-1937		$3,500	$5,000

A-Junior

1920-1927. The Junior was the entry level mandolin for Gibson, but like most entry level Gibsons (re: Les Paul Junior), they were an excellent product. Oval soundhole, dot markers, plain tuner buttons. Becomes A-0 in '27.

1920-1927	Sheraton Brown	$1,500	$2,000

AN-Custom (Army-Navy)

Mid-1990s. Made in Bozeman, Montana, round teardrop shape, flat spruce top, flat maple back, maple rims, Gibson script logo on headstock.

1995		$1,250	$1,625

Army and Navy Special Style DY/Army-Navy

1918-1922. Lower-end, flat top and back, round soundhole, no logo, round label with model name, brown stain. Reintroduced as Army-Navy (AN Custom) '88-'96.

1918-1922		$775	$1,000

C-1

1932. Flat top, mahogany back and sides, oval soundhole, natural, painted on 'guard, a '32 version of the Army and Navy Special. This model was private branded for Kel Kroydon in the early-'30s.

1932		$775	$1,000

CB-3 Mando-Cello (Cello Banjo)

1930s. TB-3 Mastertone rim, 4 strings.

1930s		$4,000	$5,000

D "The Alrite"

1917. Round body style, round soundhole, The Alrite on inside label, colored wood on top binding and around center hole.

1917		$900	$1,250

1920 Gibson A-4
Craig Brody

1950 Gibson A-50
Imaged by Heritage Auctions, HA.com

MANDOLINS

1954 Gibson EM-150
Tom Smiley

1924 Gibson F-4
Bob Moreland

MODEL YEAR	FEATURES	EXC. COND. LOW	HIGH
EM-100/EM-125			

1938-1943. Initially called EM-100, renamed EM-125 in '41-'43. Style A (pear-shape) archtop body, 1 blade pickup, 2 knobs on either side of bridge, dot markers, tortoise 'guard, sunburst.

MODEL YEAR	FEATURES	EXC. COND. LOW	HIGH
1938-1940	EM-100	$1,375	$1,875
1941-1943	EM-125	$1,375	$1,875
EM-150			

1936-1971. Electric, A-00 body, 1 Charlie Christian pickup early on, 1 P-90 later, bound body, sunburst.

1936-1940	Charlie Christian	$2,750	$3,750
1941-1949	Rectangular pu	$1,500	$2,000
1949-1964	P-90 pickup	$1,500	$2,000
1965-1971	P-90 pickup	$1,250	$1,625
EM-200/Florentine			

1954-1971. Electric solidbody, 1 pickup, gold-plated hardware, 2 control knobs, dot markers, sunburst. Called the EM-200 in '60 and '61.

1954-1960	Florentine	$2,250	$3,000
1960-1961	Renamed EM-200	$2,250	$3,000
1962-1971	Renamed Florentine	$2,250	$3,000
F			

1900-1903. 1900 model has O.H. Gibson Kalamazoo label, 3-point unbound body, early Gibson F-style, historically important design, inlaid star and crescent headstock. 1903 model is 3-point F-style, bound top rope-style, fancy inlay below-the-string guard, inlaid star and crescent headstock, large dot markers, black finish. Early F-style mandolin ornamentation can vary and values will vary accordingly.

1900	Signed by Orville	$6,250	$27,000
1900	Unsigned	$4,250	$22,000
1901-1902		$3,250	$14,000
1903		$2,750	$13,000
Bill Monroe Signature Model F			

1991-1995. Limited run of 200, sunburst.

1991-1995	Lacquer	$8,500	$15,000
1991-1995	Varnish	$8,500	$15,000
Doyle Lawson Signature Model F			

2003-2018. Artist Series, F-5 style, carved spruce top, figured maple sides and back, sunburst finish.

2003-2018		$6,000	$8,000
F-2			

1902-1934. Oval soundhole, pearl inlay, star and crescent inlay on peghead.

1902-1909	3-point	$3,750	$5,000
1910-1917	2-point	$3,750	$5,000
1918-1921	2-point	$3,500	$4,500
1922-1924	Loar era	$5,000	$6,500
1925-1934		$4,250	$5,750
F-3			

1902-1908. Three-point body, oval soundhole, scroll peghead, pearl inlayed 'guard, limited production model, black top with red back and sides.

1902-1908		$4,250	$5,500
F-4			

1902-1943. Oval soundhole, rope pattern binding, various colors.

1902-1909	3-point	$5,500	$7,500
1910-1921	2-point	$5,500	$7,500
1922-1924	Loar era	$6,500	$8,500
1925-1943		$4,000	$5,500

MODEL YEAR	FEATURES	EXC. COND. LOW	HIGH
F-5			

1922-1943; 1949-1980. F-holes, triple-bound body and 'guard. The '20s Lloyd Loar era F-5s are extremely valuable. Reintroduced in '49 with single-bound body, redesigned in '70. The Loar era F-5 market is very specialized to the point that individual instrument valuations can vary based upon the actual sound of the particular instrument. Valuations should be considered on a case-by-case basis.

1922	Loar no virzi	$75,000	$130,000
1923	Loar Apr. 12, 1923	$80,000	$130,000
1923	Loar Feb. 8, 1923	$80,000	$130,000
1923	Loar Jul. 9, 1923, side bound, Monroe date	$85,000	$130,000
1923	Loar non-side bound	$80,000	$130,000
1924	Late-1924, unsigned	$55,000	$75,000
1924	Loar Feb. 18, 1924	$85,000	$130,000
1924	Loar Mar. 31, 1924	$85,000	$130,000
1924	Loar no virzi	$80,000	$130,000
1924	Loar with virzi	$75,000	$130,000
1925-1929	Fern, Master Model	$50,000	$65,000
1928-1929	Fern, not Master Model	$35,000	$50,000
1930-1931	Fern peghead inlay	$35,000	$45,000
1932-1935	Fern peghead inlay	$30,000	$40,000
1936-1937	Fern peghead inlay	$20,000	$25,000
1938-1940		$20,000	$25,000
1940-1943	Fleur-de-lis peghead inlay	$16,000	$22,000
1949	Flower pot, mahogany neck	$8,500	$12,000
1950-1953	Flower pot maple neck	$6,500	$8,500
1954	Flower pot peghead inlay	$6,500	$8,500
1955-1956	Flower pot peghead inlay	$6,000	$8,000
1957-1959	Flower pot peghead inlay	$5,500	$7,500
1960-1965		$5,500	$7,500
1966-1969	Sunburst	$5,500	$7,500
1970-1980	Sunburst	$5,000	$7,000
F-5 CMS			

2016. Flamed maple back and sides, aged hand-carved spruce top.

2016		$6,000	$7,500
F-5 Distressed Master Model			

2004-2009. Aged finish and hardware.

2004-2009		$12,000	$15,000
F-5 Fern			

2003-2010. Custom Shop model.

2003-2010		$7,000	$9,500
F-5 Goldrush			

2007-2018. Custom Shop, sitka spruce top, flamed maple back and sides, abalone fern inlay.

2007-2018		$6,500	$7,500

MANDOLINS

MODEL YEAR	FEATURES	EXC. COND. LOW	HIGH

F-5 Master Model
2002-2018. F-holes, triple-bound body and guard, red spruce top, maple back and sides, flowerpot inlay.

2002-2018		$12,000	$15,000

F-5G/F-5G Deluxe
1997-2018. Two-point style F, Deluxe has a slightly wider neck profile.

1997-1999		$3,500	$4,500
2000-2018		$3,750	$5,000

F-5L/F-5L "The Fern"
1978-2018. Reissue of Loar F-5, gold hardware, fern headstock inlay (flowerpot inlay with silver hardware also offered for '88-'91), sunburst.

1978-1984	Kalamazoo-made	$5,250	$7,000
1984-1999		$5,250	$7,000
2000-2018		$4,250	$5,500

F-5V
1990s-2000s. Based on Lloyd Loar's original F-5s of 1922-24, varnish Cremona Brown Sunburst finish.

1990-2000s		$6,750	$9,000

F-5X
1996. F-5 Fern model, X-braced.

1996		$4,750	$6,500

Adam Steffey Signature F-5
2002-2003. Only 50 offered, signature logo on truss rod cover.

2002-2003		$5,250	$7,500

Bella Voce Signature F-5
1989. Custom Shop master-built model, high-end materials and construction, engraved tailpiece with Bella Voce F-5, sunburst.

1989		$7,500	$10,000

Bruce Weber Signature F-5
1995-1996. Label signed by Weber.

1995-1996		$5,500	$7,500

Ricky Skaggs Distressed F-5 Master Model
2007-2008. Distressed Master Model (DMM), limited to 30, hand-carved red spruce top, hand-carved Eastern flamed maple back, sides and neck.

2007-2008		$15,000	$20,000

Sam Bush Signature F-5
2000-2018. Artist Series model, carved spruce top, gold hardware, built at Opry Mill plant in Nashville.

2000-2018		$6,000	$9,500

Wayne Benson Signature F-5
2003-2006. Limited edition of 50, solid spruce top, figured maple back, sides and neck, gold hardware, vintage red satin.

2003-2006		$5,250	$7,000

F-7
1934-1940. F-holes, single-bound body, neck and 'guard, short neck, fleur-de-lis peghead inlay, sunburst.

1934-1937		$8,500	$11,000

F-9
2002-2018. F-5 style, carved spruce top, no inlays, black bound body.

2002-2018		$2,250	$3,000

F-10
1934-1936. Slight upgrade of the '34 F-7 with extended 'board and upgraded inlay, black finish.

1934-1936		$13,000	$17,500

F-12
1934-1937, 1948-1980. F-holes, bound body and neck, scroll inlay, raised 'board until '37, 'board flush with top '48-on, sunburst.

1934-1937		$9,500	$12,000
1948-1959		$3,750	$5,000
1960-1964		$3,500	$4,750
1965-1969		$3,000	$4,000
1970-1980		$3,000	$4,000

H-1 Mandola
1902-1936. Has same features as A-1 mandolin, but without snakehead headstock.

1902-1908	Orange	$2,000	$2,500
1918-1921	Brown	$2,500	$3,500
1922-1924	Loar era	$3,500	$4,500
1925-1928		$3,250	$4,250

H-1E Mandola
Late-1930s. Limited number built, electric with built-in adjustable bar pickup, sunburst.

1938		$4,000	$5,500

H-2 Mandola
1902-1922. Has same features as A-4 mandolin.

1902-1917	Various colors	$3,250	$4,500
1918-1922	Dark mahogany	$4,000	$5,500

H-4 Mandola
1910-1940. Same features as F-4 mandolin.

1910-1921		$8,000	$11,000
1922-1924	Loar era	$9,250	$12,000
1925-1940		$7,750	$11,000

H-5 Mandola
1923-1929 (available by special order 1929-1936), 1990-1991. Same features as the high-end F-5 Mandolin. This is a very specialized market and instruments should be evaluated on a case-by-case basis.

1923-1929	Loar era	$60,000	$85,000
1990-1991	Limited production	$5,000	$6,500

J Mando Bass
1912-1931. Large 24" wide A-style body, 4 strings, extension endpin for upright bass-style playing, optional colors available.

1912-1917	Sunburst	$5,000	$6,500
1918-1922	Brown	$5,000	$6,500
1923-1931	Black	$5,000	$6,500

K-1 Mandocello
1902-1943. Same features as H-1 mandola, off & on production, special order available.

1902-1908	Orange	$3,250	$4,500
1918-1921	Brown	$3,250	$4,500
1922-1924	Loar era	$3,750	$5,000
1925-1943		$3,750	$5,000

K-2 Mandocello
1902-1922. Same features as A-4, black or red mahogany.

1902-1917		$3,750	$5,000
1918-1922		$3,750	$5,000

K-4 Mandocello
1912-1929 (offered as special order post-1929). Same features as F-4 mandolin, sunburst.

1912-1921		$7,750	$10,000
1922-1924	Loar era	$14,000	$18,000
1925-1929		$8,000	$11,000

1954 Gibson F-12
Frank Manno

1920s Gibson K-2
Bernunzio Uptown Music

MANDOLINS

1926 Gibson MB-3
Bernunzio Uptown Music

1970s Harmony Model H8025
Bernunzio Uptown Music

MANDOLINS

MODEL YEAR	FEATURES	EXC. COND. LOW	HIGH
M-6 (Octave Guitar)			
2002-2006. A-style mandolin body, short-scale 6-string guitar neck.			
2002-2006		$1,250	$1,625
MB-00 Mando Banjo			
1932-1942. Banjo body, 6-string mandolin neck.			
1932-1942		$800	$1,000
MB-1 Mando Banjo			
1922-1923, 1925-1937. Banjo body, 8-string mandolin neck.			
1922-1923	Trap door	$425	$600
1925-1937		$625	$850
MB-2 Mando Banjo			
1920-1923, 1926-1937. Banjo body, 8-string.			
1920-1923	Trap-door	$575	$775
1926-1937		$800	$1,125
MB-3 Mando Banjo			
1923-1939. Banjo body, 8-string.			
1923-1924	Trap-door	$800	$1,125
1925-1939		$1,750	$2,375
MB-4 Mando Banjo			
1923-1932. Fleur-de-lis inlay.			
1923-1924	Trap-door	$850	$1,125
1925-1932		$2,000	$2,500
MB-11 Mando Banjo			
1931-1942. Pearloid headstock with fancy inlay.			
1931-1942		$2,875	$4,000
MB-Jr. Mando Banjo			
1924-1925. Junior, open back, budget level.			
1924-1925		$425	$600
SPF-5			
1938. F-style, single bar pickup with volume and tone controls, very limited production, natural.			
1938		$22,000	$30,000

Gilchrist

1977-present. Premium and presentation grade, custom, mandolins made by luthier Steve Gilchrist of Camperdown, Australia. Custom ordered but were also initially distributed through Gruhn Guitars, Nashville, Tennessee and then exclusively by Carmel Music Company. Designs are based upon Gibson mandolins built between 1910 and '25.

MODEL YEAR	FEATURES	EXC. COND. LOW	HIGH
Mandola			
1999. Classical styling.			
1999		$20,000	$27,000
Model 1			
2000s-present. A-style, maple back and sides, black binding.			
2000-2023		$7,500	$10,000
Model 3			
2011-present. A-style, sugar maple back and sides, ivoroid binding, black/white purfling.			
2011-2023		$15,000	$20,000
Model 4			
1978-present. F-style, sugar maple back and sides, ivoroid binding.			
1978-2023		$15,000	$20,000

MODEL YEAR	FEATURES	EXC. COND. LOW	HIGH
Model 4 Junior			
2012-present. F-style, sugar maple back and sides, ivoroid binding.			
2012-2023		$12,000	$15,000
Model 5			
1978-present. Based on the Gibson '22-'24 Loar-era F-5 mandolin, Gilchrist slant logo, spruce top, flamed maple back, sides, and neck, ebony 'board, multiple binding, sunburst.			
1978-2023		$20,000	$25,000
1980	G5 Model, 2 made	$28,000	$36,000
Model 5C Classical			
Part of "Classical" quartet commissioned by the Nashville Mandolin Ensemble.			
1993	Blond	$20,000	$27,000

Givens

1962-1992. Luthier R. L. (Bob) Givens hand-crafted about 800 mandolins and another 700 in a production shop.

MODEL YEAR	FEATURES	EXC. COND. LOW	HIGH
A			
1962-1975. Early production A-style.			
1962-1975		$3,500	$4,500
A-3			
1975-1988. Distinguished by use of decal (the only model with Givens decal).			
1975-1988		$3,500	$4,500
A-4			
1988-1993. No 'board binding, simple block-like multiple-line RL Givens inlay, nicer maple.			
1988-1993		$3,500	$4,500
A-5			
1988-1993. Bound 'board, pearl headstock inlay.			
1988-1993		$3,500	$4,500
A-6 (Torch)			
1988-1992. Narrow neck, torch inlay (the only A model with this), gold hardware, snowflake markers.			
1988-1992		$3,750	$5,000
A-6 Custom			
1991-1992. Elaborate customized A-6 model.			
1991-1992		$4,250	$5,500
A-6 Legacy			
2007. Givens brand made by long time associate Steven Weill, Engelmann spruce top, Mother-of-Pearl and abalone R.L. Givens flowerpot inlay, 3-tone sunburst.			
2007		$2,000	$2,750
F-5 (Fern)			
1973-1985. Givens' own version with fern ornamentation.			
1973-1985		$8,000	$11,000
F-5 (Loar)			
1962-1972. Givens' own version based upon the Loar model F-5.			
1962-1972		$8,000	$11,000
F-5 (Torch)			
1988-1992. Givens F-5 with torch inlay (the only F model with this).			
1988-1992		$9,000	$12,000
F-5 (Wheat Straw)			
1986-1988. Givens F-5-style with wheat straw ornamentation.			
1986-1988		$8,500	$11,000

The *Vintage Guitar Price Guide* shows values for all-original, excellent condition instruments and, where applicable, with original case.

MODEL YEAR	FEATURES	EXC. COND. LOW	HIGH

Godin

1987-present. Intermediate grade, production, acoustic/electric mandolins from luthier Robert Godin. They also build basses and guitars.

A-8

2000-2020. Single-cut chambered body, acoustic/electric.

2000-2020		$450	$575

Goya

1955-1996. Originally made in Sweden, by the late '70s from Japan, then from Korea.

Japan/Korea-Made

1960s		$300	$375

Sweden-Made

1960s-70s		$550	$750

Gretsch

1883-present. Gretsch started offering mandolins by the early 1900s, then stopped after the late '50s. In 2012 they again offered mandolins.

New Yorker

Late 1940s-late 1950s. Teardrop shape, f-holes, arched top and back, spruce top, maple back, sides, and neck, rosewood 'board.

1940s-50s		$550	$750

G Series

2012-2017. Part of the Roots Collection, spruce top, mahogany body, rosewood 'board, includes New Yorker G9300 Standard, G9310 Supreme (antique mahogany) and G9320 Deluxe.

2012-2017	G9300 Standard	$95	$125
2012-2017	G9320 Deluxe	$115	$150

GTR

1974-1978. GTR (for George Gruhn, Tut Taylor, Randy Wood) was the original name for Gruhn Guitars in Nashville, Tennessee (it was changed in '76). GTR imported mandolins and banjos from Japan. An A-style (similar to a current Gibson A-5 L) and an F-style (similar to mid- to late-'20s F-5 with fern pattern) were offered. The instruments were made at the Moridaira factory in Matsumoto, Japan by factory foreman Sadamasa Tokaida. Quality was relatively high but quantities were limited.

A-Style

1974-1978. A5-L copy with GTR logo on headstock.

1974-1978		$1,250	$1,625

F-Style

1974-1978. F-5 Fern copy with slant GTR logo on headstock, sunburst, handmade in Japan.

1974-1978		$2,125	$2,750

Harmony

1892-1976, late 1970s-present. Founded by Wilhelm Schultz in 1892, and purchased by Sears in 1916. The company evolved into one of the largest producers of stringed instruments in the U.S. in the '30s.

Baroque H35/H835 Electric

Late 1960s-1970s. Electric version of Baroque H425 with single pickup and two controls.

1969-1970	H35	$425	$575
1971-1976	H835	$425	$575

Baroque H425/H8025

Late 1960s-1970s. F-style arched body, extreme bass bout pointy horn, close grained spruce top, sunburst.

1969-1970	H425	$425	$650
1971-1976	H8025	$425	$650

Lute H331/H8031

1960s-1970s. A-style, flat top and back, student level.

1960s	H331	$425	$650
1970s	H8031	$425	$650

M-100

1980s. A-style, sunburst.

1980s		$200	$300

Monterey H410/H417/H8017 Mandolin

1950s-1970s. A-style arched body with f-holes, sunburst.

1950s-70s	All models	$225	$300

Heritage

1985-present. Heritage offered mandolins for a number of years.

H-5

1986-1990s. F-style scroll body, f-holes.

1986-1990s		$2,750	$3,500

Höfner

1887-present. Höfner has offered a wide variety of instruments, including mandolins, over the years. They currently again offer mandolins.

Model 545/E545

1960s. Pear-shaped A-style with catseye f-holes, 545 (acoustic), E545 (acoustic-electric), block-style markers, engraved headstock, Genuine Höfner Original and Made in Germany on back of headstock, transparent brown.

1968-1969	545	$450	$600
1968-1969	E545	$550	$750

Hondo

1969-1987, 1991-2005. Budget grade, production, imported mandolins. They also offered banjos, basses and guitars. Hondo also offered mandolins from around '74 to '87.

Acoustic

1974-1987. Hondo offered A-style, F-style, and bowl back mandolin models.

1974-1987		$120	$165

Acoustic-Electric

1974-1987		$200	$275

F-Style (Loar)

1974-1987		$275	$350

Howe-Orme

1897-ca. 1910. Elias Howe patented a guitar-shaped mandolin on November 14, 1893 and later partnered with George Orme to build a variety of mandolin family instruments and guitars in Boston.

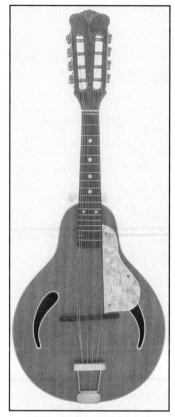

1960s Höfner Model 545
Imaged by Heritage Auctions, HA.com

1985 Hondo F-Style
Imaged by Heritage Auctions, HA.com

MANDOLINS

1900s Howe-Orme Mandolin Style 6
Lowell Levinger

1930s Kalamazoo KM-21
Imaged by Heritage Auctions, HA.com

| MODEL | | EXC. COND. | |
YEAR	FEATURES	LOW	HIGH

Mandola
1897-early-1900s. Guitar body-style with narrow waist, not the common mandolin F- or S-style body, pressed (not carved) spruce top, mahogany back and sides, flat-top guitar-type trapeze bridge, decalomania near bridge.

| 1890s | | $1,500 | $2,000 |

Style 3
Brazilian rosewood, plain style.

| 1900 | | $1,500 | $2,000 |

Style 4
Guitar-shaped, Brazilian rosewood, fancy style.

| 1900 | | $1,750 | $2,250 |

Style 6
Brazilian rosewood, top-of-the-line.

| 1900 | | $3,750 | $5,000 |

Ianuario Mandolins
1990-2009. Professional and premium grade, custom, mandolins built by luthier R. Anthony Ianuario in Jefferson, Georgia. He also built banjos and violins. Tony and his wife Ann died in an auto accident in '09.

Ibanez
1932-present. Ibanez offered mandolins from '65 to '83. In '04 they again added mandolins to the product line.

Model 511
1974-1980. A-style, f-holes, dot markers, sunburst.

| 1974-1980 | | $275 | $350 |

Model 513
1974-1979. A-5 copy with double cutaways, oval sound hole, dot markers, sunburst.

| 1974-1979 | | $275 | $375 |

Model 514
1974-1979. Arched back, spruce, rosewood, dot inlays, sunburst.

| 1974-1979 | | $275 | $375 |

Model 522
1974-1978. Symmetrical double point.

| 1974-1978 | | $375 | $550 |

Model 524 Artist
1974-1978. F-5 Loar copy, solid wood carved top and solid wood carved top and solid wood back, sunburst.

| 1974-1978 | | $800 | $1,125 |

Model 526 (Electric)
1974-1978. A-style body, single pickup, two control knobs, sunburst.

| 1974-1978 | | $450 | $600 |

Model 529 Artist
1982-1983. F-5 Loar era copy, solid wood carved top and solid wood spruce top and solid maple sides and back, sunburst.

| 1982-1983 | | $950 | $1,250 |

Model M500 Series
2004-present. F-Style and A-Style bodies, acoustic and acoustic-electric option, various finishes.

| 2004-2023 | Various models | $150 | $200 |

Imperial
1890-1922. Imperial mandolins were made by the William A. Cole Company of Boston, Massachusetts.

Bowl Back

| 1890s | | $275 | $375 |

J.L. Smith
2008-present. Custom, intermediate and professional grade, mandolins built by luthier John L. Smith first in Myrtle Beach, South Carolina, and presently in Sebastian, Florida.

Johnson
Mid-1990s-present. Budget and intermediate grade, production, mandolins imported by Music Link, Brisbane, California. Johnson also offers guitars, amps, basses and effects.

MA Series A-Style
Mid-1990s-2013. Import, A-style copy. Several levels offered; range shown is for all value levels.

| 1990s-2013 | | $150 | $200 |

MF Series F-Style
Mid-1990s-2006. Import, F-style copy. Several levels offered; range shown is for all value levels.

| 1990s-2006 | | $225 | $300 |

Kalamazoo
1933-1942, 1946-1947, 1965-1970. Budget brand produced by Gibson in Kalamazoo, Michigan. They offered mandolins until '42.

Kalamazoo/Oriole A-Style
1930s. Kalamazoo and Oriole on the headstock, KM/A-style.

| 1930s | | $750 | $1,125 |

KK-31 Mandocello
1935-1938. Archtop, f-hole body, sunburst.

| 1935 | | $3,000 | $4,000 |

KM-11
1935-1941. Gibson-made, A-style, flat top and back, round soundhole, dot inlay, sunburst.

| 1935-1941 | | $550 | $750 |

KM-12N
1935-1941. A-style with f-holes, spruce top, flamed maple sides and back, bound top and bottom, natural finish.

| 1935-1941 | | $650 | $875 |

KM-21
1936-1940. Gibson-made, A-style, f-holes, arched bound spruce top and mahogany back, sunburst.

| 1936-1940 | | $800 | $1,125 |

KM-22
1939-1942. Same as KM-21 with bound top and back.

| 1939-1942 | | $900 | $1,250 |

KMB Banjo-Mando
1930s. Banjo-mandolin with resonator.

| 1930s | | $400 | $550 |

The *Vintage Guitar Price Guide* shows values for all-original, excellent condition instruments and, where applicable, with original case.

MODEL		EXC. COND.	
YEAR	FEATURES	LOW	HIGH

Kay

1931-present. Located in Chicago, Illinois, the Kay company made an incredible amount of instruments under a variety of brands, including the Kay name. From the beginning, Kay offered several types of electric and acoustic mandolins. In '69, the factory closed, marking the end of American-made Kays. The brand survives today on imported instruments.

K68/K465 Concert

1952-1968. Pear-shape, spruce top, mahogany back and sides, natural. Renamed the K465 in '66. Kay also offered a Venetian-style mandolin called the K68 in '37-'42.

1952-1968		$375	$500

K70

1939-1966. Venetian-style, bound top and back, f-holes.

1939-1959		$675	$900

K73

1939-1952. Solid spruce top, maple back and sides, A-style body, f-holes, cherry sunburst.

1939-1952		$375	$500

K390/K395 Professional Electric

1960-1968. Modified Venetian-style archtop, 1 pickup, f-hole, spruce top, curly maple back and sides, sunburst finish. Renamed K395 in '66.

1960-1968		$475	$650

K494/K495 Electric

1960-1968. A-style archtop, single metal-covered (no poles) pickup, volume and tone control knobs, sunburst. The K494 was originally about 60% of the price of the K390 model (see above) in '65. Renamed K495 in '66.

1960-1968		$375	$500

Kay Kraft

1931-1937. First brand name of the newly formed Kay Company. Brand replaced by Kay in '37.

Mandocello

1928-1935. Venetian octave mandolin.

1935		$1,125	$1,500

Mandola

1937		$675	$900

Style C Octave

1928-1935. Deluxe Venetian, rosewood back and sides.

1935		$1,500	$2,000

Venetian/Teardrop

1931-1937. Kay Kraft offered Venetian- and teardrop-shaped mandolins.

1931-1937		$400	$550

Kel Kroydon (by Gibson)

1930-1933. Private branded budget level instruments made by Gibson. They also had guitars and banjos.

KK-20 (Style C-1)

1930-1933. Flat top, near oval-shaped body, oval soundhole, natural finish, dark finish mahogany back and sides.

1930-1933		$1,125	$1,500

Kent

1961-1969. Japanese-made instruments. Kent offered teardrop, A style, and bowlback acoustic mandolins up to '68.

Acoustic

1961-1968. Kent offered teardrop, A-style, and bowl back acoustic mandolins up to '68.

1961-1968		$200	$275

Electric

1964-1969. Available '64-'66 as a solidbody electric and '67-'69 as hollowbody Venetian-style.

1964-1969		$250	$325

Kentucky (Saga M.I.)

1977-present. Brand name of Saga Musical Instruments currently offering budget, intermediate, and professional grade, production, A- and F-style mandolins. Early models made in Japan, then Korea (roughly the '90s), currently made in China.

KM Series

1980s-present. Originally made in Japan, then Korea and now China.

1980s	KM-1000 F-style	$1,000	$1,375
1980s	KM-180 A-style	$275	$375
1980s	KM-650 F-style	$525	$700
1980s	KM-700 F-style	$525	$700
1980s	KM-800 F-style	$725	$975
1988-2009	KM-850 F-style	$1,125	$1,500
1990-2000s	KM-250S A-style	$300	$400
1990s	KM-200S A-style	$300	$400
1990s	KM-500S A-style	$550	$750
1990s	KM-620 F-style	$550	$750
1990s	KM-675 F-style	$500	$650
1990s-2023	KM-505 A-style	$425	$575
2000-2017	KM-675 F-style	$550	$750
2000-2017	KM-700 F-style	$350	$475
2000-2023	KM-1000 F-style	$1,000	$1,375
2000-2023	KM-140 A-style	$115	$150
2000-2023	KM-150 A-style	$175	$250
2000-2023	KM-160 A-style	$175	$250
2000-2023	KM-750 F-style	$750	$1,125
2000s	KM-380S A-style	$250	$350
2000s	KM-620 F-style	$325	$450
2000s	KM-630 F-style	$375	$500
2000s	KM-800 F-style	$350	$450
2010-2023	KM-1500 Master F-5	$1,750	$2,375
2010-2023	KM-606 F-style	$575	$775
2010s	KM-615 F-style	$400	$550
2011	KM-171 A-style	$225	$300
2011-2017	KM-900 A-style	$700	$950
2020-2023	KM-670 F-style	$800	$1,125
2020-2023	KM-855 F-style	$950	$1,250
2022-2023	KM-256 A-style	$375	$500

Kimble

2000-present. Luthier Will Kimble builds his premium grade, custom/production, mandolins, mandocellos, and mandolas in Cincinnati, Ohio.

1960s Kay K95

Kentucky KM-1000
Master F-Style

MANDOLINS

Lyon & Healy Style C
Imaged by Heritage Auctions, HA.com

1953 Martin Style 2-15
Greg Perrine

MODEL YEAR	FEATURES	EXC. COND. LOW	HIGH

Kingston

Ca. 1958-1967. Mandolins imported from Japan by Jack Westheimer and Westheimer Importing Corporation of Chicago, Illinois. They also offered guitars, basses and banjos.

Acoustic

| 1960s | Various models | $175 | $250 |

EM1 Electric

1964-1967. Double-cut solidbody electric, 15.75" scale, 1 pickup.

| 1960s | | $225 | $300 |

Knutsen

1890s-1920s. Luthier Chris J. Knutsen of Tacoma and Seattle, Washington. He moved to Los Angeles, California around 1916. He also made guitars, steels, and ukes.

Harp Mando

1910s. Harp mandolin with tunable upper bass bout with 4 drone strings, and standard mandolin neck. The mandolin version of a harp guitar.

| 1910s-20s | | $2,000 | $2,500 |

Lakeside (Lyon & Healy)

1890-early-1900s. Mainly catalog sales of guitars and mandolins from the Chicago maker. Marketed as a less expensive alternative to the Lyon & Healy Washburn product line.

Style G2016 12-String

1890-early-1900s. 12-string, 18 mahogany ribs with white inlay between, celluloid guard plate.

| 1890-1900s | | $375 | $500 |

Lyle

Ca. 1969-1980. Instruments imported by distributor L.D. Heater of Portland, Oregon. Generally Japanese-made copies of American designs. They also had basses and guitars.

TM-200

| 1970s | A-style | $175 | $250 |

Lyon & Healy

1864-present. Lyon & Healy was an early large musical instrument builder and marketer, and produced instruments under many different brands.

Style A Mandocello

1910s-1920s. Scroll peghead, symmetrical 2-point body, natural.

| 1910s-20s | | $6,500 | $8,500 |

Style A Professional

1918-1920s. Violin scroll peghead, natural.

| 1918-1920s | Basic options | $6,500 | $8,500 |
| 1918-1920s | Fancy options | $8,250 | $11,000 |

Style B

1920s. Maple back and sides, 2-point body, natural.

| 1920s | | $2,375 | $3,250 |

Style C

1920s. Like Style A teardrop Gibson body style, oval soundhole, carved spruce top, carved maple back, natural.

| 1920s | | $2,500 | $3,375 |

MODEL YEAR	FEATURES	EXC. COND. LOW	HIGH

Lyra

1920s-1930s. Private brand made by Regal, Lyra name plate on headstock.

Style A (Scroll)

1920s-1930s. Scroll on upper bass bout.

| 1925-1935 | | $475 | $650 |

Mann Mandolins

2002-present. Luthier Jonathan Mann builds his professional grade, production/custom, acoustic and electric mandolins in Joelton, Tennessee.

Martin

1833-present. Martin got into the mandolin market in 1895 starting with the typical bowl back designs. By 1914, Gibson's hot selling, innovative, violin-based mandolin pushed Martin into a flat back, bent top hybrid design. By '29, Martin offered a carved top and carved back mandolin. Most models were discontinued in '41, partially because of World War II. Production resumed and standard models are offered up to 1993. From '94 to '02 mandolins are available on a custom order basis only. Martin offered a Backpacker mandolin up to '06.

Backpacker

1998-present. Travel guitar, bell-shaped body.

| 1998-2023 | | $130 | $175 |

Style 0

1905-1925. Bowl back-style, 18 rosewood ribs, solid peghead.

| 1905-1925 | | $750 | $975 |

Style 00

1908-1925. Bowl back-style, 9 rosewood ribs (14 ribs by '24), solid peghead.

| 1908-1925 | | $750 | $925 |

Style 000

1914 only. Bowl back, solid peghead, dot inlay, 9 mahogany ribs.

| 1914 | | $750 | $925 |

Style 1

1898-1924. Bowl back, German silver tuners, 18 ribs.

| 1898-1924 | | $950 | $1,250 |

Style 2

1898-1924. Bowl back, 26 rosewood ribs, higher appointments than Style 1.

| 1898-1924 | | $1,250 | $1,625 |

Style 2-15

1936-1964. Carved spruce top, maple back and sides, f-hole, single-bound back, solid headstock.

| 1936-1964 | | $1,250 | $1,625 |

Style 2-20

1936-1942. Carved spruce triple-bound top and bound maple back and sides, f-hole, dot inlay.

| 1936-1942 | | $1,875 | $2,500 |

Style 2-30

1937-1941. Carved spruce top and maple back and sides, multi-bound, f-holes, diamond and square inlays.

| 1937-1941 | | $2,125 | $2,750 |

Style 3

1898-1922. Bowl back, 26 rosewood ribs, abalone and ivory-bound soundhole.

| 1898-1922 | | $1,500 | $2,000 |

MANDOLINS

MODEL YEAR	FEATURES	EXC. COND. LOW	HIGH

Style 4
1898-1921. Bowl back, 30 rosewood ribs.

1898-1921		$1,500	$2,000

Style 5
1898-1920. Bowl back, vine inlay, abalone top trim.

1898-1920		$1,625	$2,125

Style 6
1898-1921. Bowl back, top bound with ivory and abalone, vine or snowflake inlay.

1898-1921		$1,750	$2,250

Style 20
1929-1942. Symmetrical 2-point body, carved top and back with oval soundhole, dot markers.

1929-1942		$2,000	$2,500

Style A
1914-1995. Flat back, oval soundhole, dot inlay, solid headstock.

1914-1949		$850	$1,500
1950-1995		$750	$1,250

Style AA Mandola
1915-1931, 1935, 1941. Mandola version of Style A mandolin.

1915-1941		$1,750	$2,250

Style AK
1920-1937. Koa wood version of Style A, flat back.

1920-1937		$1,500	$2,000

Style A Bitting Special
1917. Private branded, small number produced, Martin and model impressed on back of headstock.

1917		$950	$1,250

Style B
1914-1946, 1981-1987. Flat back with bent top, spruce top and rosewood back and sides, herringbone back stripe, multi-bound.

1914-1939		$1,500	$2,000
1940-1946		$1,250	$1,750
1981-1987		$950	$1,250

Style BB Mandola
1917-1921, 1932-1939. Brazilian rosewood, herringbone trim, features like Style B mandolin. This is the only Mandola offered.

1917-1939		$2,250	$3,000

Style C
1914-1934. Flat back.

1914-1916		$1,875	$2,500
1917-1934		$2,250	$3,000

Style D
1914-1916. Flat back.

1914-1916		$2,875	$3,750

Style E
1915-1937. Flat back, rosewood back and sides, bent spruce top, Style 45 snowflake fretboard inlay and other high-end appointments. Highest model cataloged.

1915-1919		$5,000	$6,500
1920-1937		$6,000	$7,750

May Flower

Ca. 1901-1910. H. J. Flower's Chicago-based May Flower Music Company offered bowl back mandolins that he may or may not have built. There were also May Flower harp guitars built by others.

MODEL YEAR	FEATURES	EXC. COND. LOW	HIGH

Bowl Back
1901-1910. Mid-level bowl back-style with 19 rosewood ribs and mid-level appointments.

1901-1910	Fancy	$850	$1,125
1901-1910	Plain	$700	$975

Menzenhauer & Schmidt

1894-1904. Founded by Frederick Menzenhauer and Oscar Schmidt International. Menzenhauer created the guitar-zither in the U.S. He had several patents including one issued in September 1899 for a mandolin-guitar-zither. Control of operations quickly went to Oscar Schmidt.

12-String
1890s. Bowl back mandolin with 3 strings per course that were tuned in octaves, designed during an experimental era for mandolin-related instruments, 13 rosewood ribs, spruce top, inlays.

1890s		$275	$350

Mid-Missouri/The Big Muddy Mandolin Company

1995-present. Intermediate grade, production, acoustic and electric mandolins and mandolas built by luthier Michael Dulak in Columbia, Missouri. In late '06, they changed their name to The Big Muddy Mandolin Company.

M Series
1995-present. Teardrop A-style body, solid spruce top, solid maple, mahogany or rosewood back and sides.

1995-1999	M-0	$350	$450
1995-1999	M-1	$350	$450
1995-2016	M-3	$400	$525
1995-2023	M-15 Mandola	$525	$675
1995-2023	M-2	$375	$500
1995-2023	M-4	$475	$625

Mix

Carbon fiber mandolins built by Peter Mix, Will Kimball, and Matt Durham of New Millennium Acoustic Design (NewMAD) in Waterville, Vermont. They started in 2007.

Monteleone

1971-present. Primarily a guitar maker, luthier John Monteleone also builds presentation grade, custom, mandolins in West Islip, New York.

Morales

Ca.1967-1968. Japanese-made, not heavily imported into the U.S.

Electric

1967-1968		$400	$525

Mozzani

Late-1800s-early-1900s. Founder Luigi Mozzani was an Italian (Bologna) master luthier and renowned composer and musician. There are original Mozzani-built mandolins and also factory-built instruments made later at various workshops.

1907 Martin Style 4
Imaged by Heritage Auctions, HA.com

1916 Martin Style B
Larry Briggs

MANDOLINS

MANDOLINS

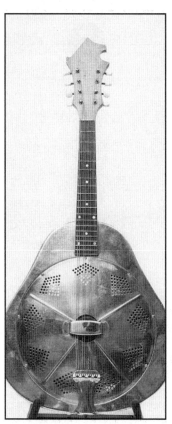

1935 National Style 1
Bernunzio Uptown Music

Ratliff R-5

MODEL YEAR	FEATURES	EXC. COND. LOW	HIGH

Original Bowl Back
Late-1800s-early-1900s. Handcrafted by Luigi Mozzani, about 24 ribs, soundhole ornamentation, snowflake-like markers.

| 1800-1900s | | $1,125 | $1,500 |

Factory Bowl Back
1920s. Factory-built bowl back model.

| 1920s | | $400 | $550 |

National
Ca.1927-present. The National brand has gone through many ownership changes and offered resonator mandolins from around 1927 to '41.

Style 0
1931-early-1940s. Metal body with Hawaiian scenes, single cone resonator.

| 1931-1940s | | $2,500 | $3,250 |

Style 1
1928-1936 Plain metal body, single or tricone resonator.

| 1928-1936 | Single cone | $2,250 | $3,000 |
| 1928-1936 | Tricone version | $3,000 | $4,000 |

Style 2
1928-1936. Metal body with rose engraving, single or tricone resonator.

| 1928-1936 | Single cone | $3,500 | $4,500 |
| 1928-1936 | Tricone version | $7,500 | $9,500 |

Style 3
1928-1936. High-quality decorative engraving, single or tricone resonator.

| 1928-1936 | Single cone | $4,500 | $6,000 |
| 1928-1936 | Tricone version | $8,500 | $12,000 |

Style 97
1936-1940. Metal body, tricone resonator.

| 1936-1940 | | $5,500 | $7,000 |

Triolian
1928-1940. Metal body with palm trees, single cone resonator.

| 1928-1940 | | $2,750 | $3,500 |

Nouveau (Gibson)
1986-1989. Mandolin bodies and necks made in Japan, assembled and finished in U.S. Became Nouveau (by Epiphone) in '88 and the brand was discontinued in '89. They also made guitars.

C7
1986-1987. F-style, white wood body and neck.

| 1986-1987 | | $1,625 | $2,125 |

Nugget
1970s-present. Luthier Mike Kemnitzer builds his premium grade mandolins in Central Lake, Michigan.

O'Dell, Doug
See listing under Old Town.

Old Hickory
2005-2010. Budget grade, production, imported F- and A-style acoustic mandolins from Musician's Wholesale America, Nashville, Tennessee. They also offer banjos.

MODEL YEAR	FEATURES	EXC. COND. LOW	HIGH

Style A
2005-2010	AC-100 mid-level	$125	$175
2005-2010	FC-100 high-level	$155	$200
2005-2010	M-1 low-level	$75	$100

Style F
| 2005-2010 | Various models | $185 | $250 |

Old Kraftsman
1930s-1960s. Brand name used by the Siegel Company on instruments made by Kay and others (even Gibson). Quality was mixed, but some better-grade instruments were offered.

Various Models
| 1950s | | $325 | $425 |

Old Town
1974-2007. Luthier Doug O'Dell built his professional and premium grade, production/custom acoustic and electric mandolins in Ohio.

EM Series Electric
| 1980s-2007 | Various models | $2,000 | $2,500 |

Old Wave
1990-present. Luthier Bill Bussmann builds his professional and premium grade, production/custom, mandolins and mandolas in Caballo, New Mexico. He has also built guitars and basses.

Orpheum
1897-1942, 1944-early 1970s, 2001-2006. Intermediate grade, production, mandolins. They also offered guitars. An old brand often associated with banjos, 1930s branded guitars sold by Bruno and Sons. 1950s branded guitars and mandolins sold by Maurice Lipsky Music, New York, New York. The brand was revived for '01 to '06 by Tacoma Guitars.

Mando-Banjo
1910-1930. Mandolin neck on small banjo body, fancy headstock and fretboard inlay, carved heel.

1910-1930	Model No. 1	$400	$550
1910-1930	Model No. 2	$500	$650
1910-1930	Model No 3	$550	$725

Model 730 E Electric
1950s. Private branded for Maurice Lipsky as a student model, A-style body, 1 bar pickup, 2 side-mounted knobs, maple back and sides, dots, sunburst.

| 1950s | | $575 | $750 |

Style A
| 1950s | | $375 | $500 |

Oscar Schmidt
1879-ca. 1939, 1979-present. Currently offering budget and intermediate grade, production, mandolins. They also offer guitars, basses, banjos, ukuleles and the famous Oscar Schmidt autoharp. The original Schmidt company offered innovative mandolin designs during the 1900-'30 mandolin boom.

Mando-Harp Style B
1890s. More zither-autoharp than mandolin, flat autoharp body with soundhole.

| 1890s | | $200 | $275 |

MODEL YEAR	FEATURES	EXC. COND. LOW	HIGH

Sovereign
1920s. Bowl back, bent top, rope-style binding, mahogany ribs, dot inlay, plain headstock, natural.

1920s	Basic	$325	$425
1920s	Fancy	$825	$1,125

Ovation
1966-present. Ovation added mandolins in '94 and currently offers intermediate and professional grade, production, mandolins. They also offer guitars and basses.

MCS148 (Celebrity)
1994-2017. Single-cut, small Ovation body, Ovation headstock, red sunburst.

1994-2017		$425	$550

Paris Swing
2005-2008. Intermediate grade, production, imported acoustic mandolins from The Music Link, which also offers instruments under Johnson and other brands.

Phoenix
Premium grade, production/custom, mandolins built by luthier Rolfe Gerhardt (formerly builder of Unicorn Mandolins in the '70s) in South Thomaston, Maine. Gerhardt's Phoenix company, which started in 1990, specializes in a 2-point Style A (double-cut) body style.

Ramsey
1990s. Built by luthier John Ramsey of Colorado Springs, Colorado.

Ratliff
1982-present. Professional and premium grade, production/custom, mandolin family instruments built by luthier Audey Ratliff in Church Hill, Tennessee.

R Series
1990s-present. R-5 is an F-style mando, R-4 is round-hole version of 5.

1995-2016	R-4	$1,625	$2,125
1995-2023	R-5	$2,500	$3,250

Silver Eagle
1998	A-style	$1,500	$2,000

Recording King
1929-1943. Montgomery Ward house brand. Suppliers include Gibson, Kay, Regal, and Gretsch. Brand name revived by The Music Link in '05.

Style A
1929-1943. Gibson-made, plain appointments, sunburst.

1929-1943		$475	$625

Red Diamond
Early 1980s-present. Luthier Don MacRostie builds his premium grade, production/custom, mandolins in Athens, Ohio.

MODEL YEAR	FEATURES	EXC. COND. LOW	HIGH

Regal
Ca. 1895-1966, 1987-present. Large Chicago-based manufacturer which made their own brand name and others for distributors and mass merchandisers. Absorbed by the Harmony Company in 1954.

A-Style
1920s		$375	$500

Bicentennial 76
1976. A-style body, flat back, oval soundhole, '76 logo on 'guard, white body, red peghead, blue stars on front and back.

1976		$450	$575

Octofone
1920s-1930s. It had 8 strings, but Regal's marketing department named this the Octo because it was "eight instruments in one" as it could be tuned as a mandolin, tenor banjo, tenor guitar and other instruments.

1920s-30s		$450	$600

Resonator
1937	Model 250	$1,125	$1,500
1950s	.	$675	$875

Standard
1930s		$475	$625

Ultra Grand Deluxe
1930s		$675	$875

Rickenbacker
1931-present. Rickenbacker had the Electro Mandolin in the late '30s and introduced 4-, 5- and 8-string electric models in 1958 and currently offers one model.

Model 5002V58
1958-present. 8 strings, maple front, walnut back, rosewood 'board.

1958-2023		$1,500	$2,000

Rigel
1990-2006. Professional and premium grade, production/custom mandolins and mandolas built by luthier Pete Langdell in Hyde Park, Vermont.

Roberts
1980s. Built by luthier Jay Roberts of California.

Tiny Moore Jazz 5
1980s. Based on Bigsby design of the early-1950s as used by Tiny Moore, five-string electric, sunburst.

1985		$1,625	$2,125

Ryder
1992-present. Luthier Steve Ryder builds his professional and premium grade, production/custom solid and semi-hollowbody electric mandolins, mandola and octave mandolins in South Portland, Maine.

S. S. Stewart
1878-1904. S.S. Stewart of Philadelphia was primarily known for banjos. Legend has it that Stewart was one of the first to demonstrate the mass production assembly of stringed instruments.

2010 Ovation MCS148 Celebrity
Imaged by Heritage Auctions, HA.com

MANDOLINS

1930s Regal Flat Back Teardrop
Bernunzio Uptown Music

Stiver F-5

1930s Strad-O-Lin Style A
Bernunzio Uptown Music

MODEL YEAR	FEATURES	EXC. COND. LOW	HIGH

Mando-Banjo
Early-1900s. Mandolin neck and a very small open back banjo body, star inlay in headstock.
| 1900s | | $275 | $350 |

Sekova
Mid-1960s-mid-1970s. Entry level, imported by the U.S. Musical Merchandise.
Electric
1960s-1970s. Kay-Kraft-style hollowbody with f-holes, 1 pickup and Sekova logo on the headstock.
| 1960s-70s | | $400 | $525 |

Sigma
1970-2007. Budget and intermediate grade, production, import mandolins distributed by C.F. Martin Company. They also offered guitars, basses and banjos.
SM6
1970-2007. Made in Korea.
| 1970-2007 | | $275 | $375 |

Silvertone
1941-ca.1970, present. Brand name used by Sears on their musical instruments.
Arched
1941-ca.1970. Arched top and back, sunburst.
| 1940s-50s | | $325 | $425 |

Sovereign
Ca. 1899-ca. 1938. Sovereign was originally a brand of the Oscar Schmidt company of New Jersey. In the late '30s, Harmony purchased several trade names from the Schmidt Company, including Sovereign. Sovereign then ceased as a brand, but Harmony continued using it on a model line of Harmony guitars.
Bent-Top
1920s-1930s. Old-style bent top.
| 1920s-30s | | $325 | $425 |

Stanley Mandolins
Luthier Chris Stanley builds his premium grade, production/custom, A-style and F-style mandolins in Rhinelander, Wisconsin. He started in 2003.

Stathopoulo
1903-1916. Original design instruments, some patented, by Epiphone company founder A. Stathopoulo.
A-Style
1903-1916. A-style with higher-end appointments, bent-style spruce top, figured maple back and sides.
| 1903-1916 | | $800 | $1,125 |

Stella
Ca. 1899-1974, 2000s. Stella was a brand of the Oscar Schmidt Company which was an early contributor to innovative mandolin designs and participated in the 1900-'30 mandolin boom. Pre-World War II Stella instruments were low-mid to mid-level instruments. In '39, Harmony purchased the Stella name and '50s and '60s Stella instruments were student grade, low-end instruments. The Stella brand was reintroduced in the 2000s by MBT International.
Banjo-Mando
1920s. One of several innovative designs that attempted to create a new market, 8-string mandolin neck with a banjo body, Stella logo normally impressed on the banjo rim or the side of the neck.
| 1920s | | $165 | $250 |
Bowl Back
1920s. Typical bowl back, bent top-style mandolin with models decalomania, about 10 (wide) maple ribs, dot markers.
| 1920s | | $165 | $250 |
Pear-Shape
1940s-1960s. Harmony-made lower-end mandolins, pear-shaped (Style A) flat back, oval soundhole.
| 1940s-60s | | $225 | $300 |

Stelling
1974-present. Mainly known for banjos, Stelling also builds premium grade, production/custom mandolins in Afton, Virginia.

Sterling
Early-1900s. Distributed by wholesalers The Davitt & Hanser Music Co.

Stiver
1971-present. Premium grade, custom/production, mandolins built by luthier Louis Stiver in Polk, Pennsylvania.
A Model
| 1982-2023 | | $2,750 | $3,500 |
F-5
| 1982-2023 | | $3,500 | $4,500 |

Strad-O-Lin/Stradolin
Ca.1920s-ca.1960s. The Strad-O-Lin company was operated by the Hominic brothers in New York, primarily making mandolins for wholesalers. In the late '50s, Multivox/Premier bought the company and used the name on mandolins, guitars and amps.
Baldwin Electric
1950s-1960s. A-Style, single pickup, tone and volume knobs, spruce top, maple back and sides, Baldwin logo on headstock, natural.
| 1950s-60s | Various models | $325 | $450 |
Junior A
1950s-1960s. A-Style, Stradolin Jr. logo on headstock, dot markers, sunburst.
| 1950s-60s | | $195 | $250 |
Style A
1920s-1950s. A-style body with f-holes, dot markers.
| 1940s-50s | | $475 | $625 |
Various Models
| 1920s-30s | | $475 | $625 |

MANDOLINS

MODEL YEAR	FEATURES	EXC. COND. LOW	HIGH

Summit

1990-present. Professional and premium grade, production/custom mandolins built by luthier Paul Schneider in Hartsville, Tennessee. He was originally located in Mulvane, Kansas.

Supertone

1914-1941. Brand used by Sears before they switched to Silvertone. Instruments made by other companies.

Various Models

Spruce top, mahogany back and sides, some with decalomania vine pattern on top.

1920s-30s	Basic	$300	$400
1920s-30s	Fancy	$475	$600

Supro

1935-1968, 2004-present. Budget line from the National Dobro Company. Brand name was revived in '04.

T30 Electric

1950s		$725	$950

Tacoma

1995-2009. Tacoma offered intermediate, professional and premium grade, production, electric and acoustic mandolins up to '06. They also built guitars and basses.

M Series

1999-2006. Solid spruce top, typical Tacoma body-style with upper bass bout soundhole, E (i.e. M-1E) indicates acoustic/electric.

1999-2004	M2/M2E, rosewood	$475	$625
1999-2006	M1/M1E, mahogany	$400	$525
1999-2006	M3/M3E, maple	$500	$650

Unicorn

1970s-late 1980s. Luthier Rolfe Gerhardt (currently luthier for Phoenix Mandolins) founded Unicorn in the mid-'70s. Gerhardt built 149 mandolins before selling Unicorn to Dave Sinko in '80. Sinko closed Unicorn in the late-'80s.

Vega

The original Boston-based company started in 1889 and was purchased by C.F. Martin in '70. The Deering Banjo Company acquired the brand in '89 and uses it on a line of banjos.

Lansing Special Bowl

1890s. Spruce top, abalone, vine inlay.

1890s	$400	$550

Little Wonder Mando-Banjo

1920s. Maple neck, resonator.

1920s	$400	$550

Mando Bass

1910s-1920s. Large upright bass-sized instrument with bass tuners, body-style similar to dual-point A-style, scroll headstock.

1910s-20s	$3,500	$4,500

Mando Cittern

1910s. Vague A-style with oval soundhole and cylinder back,10-string (five double strings tuned in 5ths), natural.

1910s	$2,000	$2,500

Mandola Lute

1915. Few made, 15" scale, 10-string.

1915	$2,125	$2,750

Style 202 Mando-Lute

Early-1900s. Basic A-style with small horns, natural spruce top, mahogany sides and cylinder back, dot markers.

1915	$2,000	$2,500

Style 205 Cylinder Back

1910s-1920s. Rounded tube cylinder shape runs the length of the back.

1910s	$1,375	$1,750
1920s	$1,250	$1,625

Style A

1910s	$525	$700

Style D 100 Electric Hollowbody

1940	$575	$750

Style F

1910s. Scroll upper bass bout, oval soundhole, Vega and torch inlay in headstock.

1910s	$825	$1,125

Style K Mando-Banjo

1910s-30s	$275	$375

Style L Mando-Banjo/Whyte Laydie

1910s-1920s. Open back banjo body and mandolin 8-string neck.

1910s-20s	$725	$950

Style S Mando-Banjo

1915	$625	$850

Super Deluxe

1910s	Sunburst	$825	$1,125

Tubaphone Style X Mando-Banjo

1922-1923	$825	$1,125

Vinaccia

Italian-made by Pasquale Vinaccia, luthier.

Bowl Back

1900-1920s. High-end appointments and 'guard, 30 rosewood ribs.

1900-1920s	$1,750	$2,250

Vivi-Tone

1933-ca. 1936. Lloyd Loar's pioneering guitar company also built early electric mandolins and mandocellos in Kalamazoo, Michigan.

Acoustic

1933-1935. Spruce top, back and sides.

1933-1935	$4,750	$6,000

Electric

1933-1935. Vivi-Tone silkscreen logo on headstock.

1933-1935	$4,750	$6,000

Electric Mandocello

1933-1935. Traditonal guitar-arch body, Vivi-Tone silkscreen logo on headstock.

1933-1935	$5,500	$7,500

Electric Mandola

1933-1935. Traditonal European teardrop/pear-shaped top, Vivi-Tone silkscreen logo on headstock.

1933-1935	$5,000	$6,500

1920s Supertone

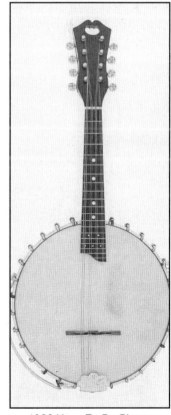

1922 Vega Tu-Ba-Phone

Imaged by Heritage Auctions, HA.com

MANDOLINS

Ca. 1898 Washburn Model 118
Izzy Miller

Weber Bitterroot A14-O
Bernunzio Uptown Music

MODEL YEAR	FEATURES	EXC. COND. LOW	HIGH

Waldo
1891-early 1900s. Mandolin family instruments built in Saginaw, Michigan.
Bowl Back
1890s. Alternating rosewood and maple ribs, some with script Waldo logo on pickguard.

1890s	Various models	$200	$275

Washburn
1962-present. Currently offering imported intermediate and professional grade, production, mandolins.
Various Models
1974-present. Various imported models plywood to fancy carved.

1974-2023		$85	$350

Washburn (Lyon & Healy)
1880s-ca.1949. Washburn was founded in Chicago as one of the lines for Lyon & Healy to promote high quality stringed instruments, ca. 1880s. The rights to Washburn were sold to Regal which built Washburns by the mid-'30s until ca. '49. In '74 the brand resurfaced.
Bowl Back
1890s-1900s. Lyon and Healy sold a wide variety of bowl back mandolins, some Brazilian ribs with fancy inlays and bindings.

1890-1900s	Fancy	$900	$1,125
1890-1900s	Plain	$275	$350
1900s	Standard appointments	$375	$500

Style A
1920s. Professional quality.

1920s		$2,750	$3,500

Style E
1915-1923. Brazilian rosewood.

1915-1923		$600	$775

Weber
1996-present. Intermediate, professional, and premium grade, production/custom, mandolins, mandolas, and mandocellos. Many former Flatiron employees, including Bruce Weber, formed Sound To Earth, Ltd., to build Weber instruments when Gibson moved Flatiron from Montana, to Nashville. Originally in Belgrade, Montana, and after '04, in Logan, Montana. They also build guitars. In '12, Two Old Hippies (Breedlove, Bedell) acquired the brand, moving production in '13 to Oregon where Bruce Weber oversees development.
Absaroka
2000s. A style body, white binding, diamond inlays.

2002		$2,000	$2,625

Alder #1 Mandola
Celtic A style body, black binding, diamond inlays.

1997		$1,250	$1,625

Alder #2 Mandola
2000-2012. Teardrop body, X-braced, spruce top, maple back and sides.

2000-2012		$1,250	$1,625

Aspen #1
1997-2011. Teardrop A-style, solid spruce top, maple sides and back, mahogany neck.

1997-2011		$950	$1,250

Aspen #2
1997-2011. Like #1, but with maple neck.

1997-2011		$950	$1,250

Beartooth
1997-2009. Teardrop A-style, solid spruce top, curly maple sides, back, and neck.

1997-2009		$2,000	$2,625

Big Sky

1999	F-style	$3,250	$4,250

MODEL YEAR	FEATURES	EXC. COND. LOW	HIGH

Bighorn
2006-2008. A-style, oval, double Venetian.

2006-2008		$2,750	$3,500

Bitterroot
2002-present. Style A or F.

2002-2023	A-style	$2,250	$3,000
2002-2023	F-style	$2,500	$3,250

Bridger
2000-2015. A-Celtic style, long neck.

2000-2015		$2,000	$2,625

Custom Vintage
2007-present. Heritage Series.

2007-2023	A-style	$3,000	$4,000
2007-2023	F-style	$4,000	$5,250

Fern
1997-present. Heritage Series, top of the product line.

1997-2023	A-style	$3,500	$4,500
1997-2023	F-style	$4,250	$5,500

Gallatin
1999-present. Spruce top, Amber Burst finish.

1999-2023	A-style	$1,125	$1,500
1999-2023	F-style	$1,750	$2,250

Octar
2008. Octave mando, 15" archtop body.

2008		$2,000	$2,625

Sage #1 Octave
2003-2006. Octave mando, diamond inlays.

2003-2006		$1,000	$1,375

Sweet Pea
2009-2012. Travel mando.

2009-2012		$350	$550

Y2K
2000-2002. Celtic-style teardrop body, satin natural finish.

2000-2002		$650	$850

Yellowstone
1997-present. A-style and F-style available, solid spruce top, curly maple sides, back, and neck, sunburst.

1997-2023	A-style	$2,500	$3,250
1997-2023	F-style	$3,250	$4,250
2003-2023	Mandola	$3,250	$4,250
2010-2023	Octave	$2,500	$3,250

Weymann

1864-1940s. H.A. Weymann & Sons was a musical instrument distributor located in Philadelphia. They also built their own instruments.

Keystone State Banjo-Mando
1910s. Maple rim and back, ebony fretboard.

1910s		$350	$450

Mando-Banjo
1920s. Mandolin neck on an open banjo body.

1920s	Various models	$325	$425

Mando-Lute
1920s. Lute-style body, spruce top, flamed maple sides and back, rope binding, deluxe rosette, natural.

1920s	Various models	$625	$825

Wurlitzer

The old Wurlitzer company would have been considered a mega-store by today's standards. They sold a wide variety of instruments, gave music lessons, and operated manufacturing facilities.

Banjolin
1920s. Mandolin neck on banjo body.

1920s		$475	$625

Mando-Banjo
1900-1910. Mandolin neck on open back banjo body, plain-style.

1900-1910		$225	$300

Various Models
1920s. Various woods and appointments.

1920s		$475	$650

Weber Yellowstone A Style

Wurlitzer
Imaged by Heritage Auctions, HA.com

MANDOLINS

BANJOS

Bacon Blue Ribbon
Intermountain Guitar and Banjo

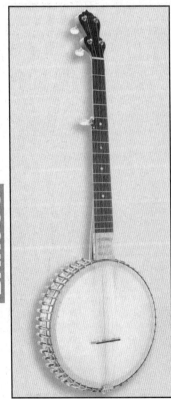

Ca. 1890 Benary and Sons Celebrated Benary
Elderly Instruments

Banjo collectors, hobbyists, and dealers often think nothing of changing the neck on a banjo; a banjo may have a true vintage neck or a new replacement neck. So, our all original parts concept that applies to the rest of this Price Guide doesn't always apply to vintage banjos.

The banjo market operates somewhat differently than many of the other markets that are covered in the Guide. The prices shown are guidance prices only and each instrument should be evaluated on a case-by-case basis.

Acme

1893-early 1900s. Banjos made for Sears by S.S. Stewart, and later George Bauer, both of Philadelphia.

The Pearl
Open back, 5-string, pearl fretboard.

MODEL YEAR	FEATURES	LOW	HIGH
1908		$825	$1,125

The Professor
Tree-of-Life board, 5-string.

1900		$825	$1,125

Aria/Aria Pro II

1956-present. Aria offered banjos from time to time under both the Aria and Aria Pro II brand names. They also make guitars, basses, and mandolins.

Resonator 5-String
1976-1978. 5-string resonator back, Aria Pro II brand, models PB450, PB550 and PB650.

1975		$450	$600

August Pollmann

1880s-1890s. These are thought to have been made for August Pollman's New York based company, by luthier Pehr Anderberg who had a shop in Boston, Massachusetts.

Royal Professional

1890s	5-String	$350	$500

Bacon

1906-1967. Frederick Bacon was a well-known banjo player when he started selling banjos under his own name. The earliest Bacon banjos were built by other companies. By 1920, they were building their own models including the B&D (Bacon & Day) models. In 1940 Gretsch purchased the company and took over production.

FF Professional No. 3

1906-1907	5-string	$10,500	$14,000

Special

1914	5-string	$2,000	$2,500

Style C/Super Tenor

1920-1926	Tenor	$450	$600

Bacon & Day

1921-1967. B&D was not a separate company, but a line of banjos from the Bacon Banjo Company. David Day left Vega to join up with Fred Bacon in '21. Gretsch purchased Bacon in '40, and offered Bacon and B&D banjos until '67.

MODEL YEAR	FEATURES	LOW	HIGH
Blue Bell			
1922-1939	Tenor	$650	$850
Blue Ribbon 17			
1933-1939	Tenor	$525	$675
Blue Ribbon Deluxe			
1933-1939	Tenor	$1,500	$2,000
Blue Ribbon Orchestra			
1933-1939	Tenor	$1,500	$2,000
FF Professional No. 1			
1921	5-string	$1,250	$1,750
FF Professional No. 2			
1921	5-string	$1,250	$1,750
FF Professional No. 3			
1920-1922	Tenor	$575	$750
Ne Plus Ultra			
1920s	#5, Plectrum	$5,500	$7,000
1920s	#5, Tenor	$5,500	$7,000
1920s	#6, Plectrum	$6,500	$8,500
1920s	#6, Tenor	$6,000	$7,500
1920s	#7, Plectrum	$9,500	$12,500
1920s	#7, Tenor	$9,000	$11,500
1920s	#8, Plectrum	$15,000	$20,000
1920s	#8, Tenor	$15,000	$20,000
1920s	#9, Plectrum	$15,000	$20,000
1920s	#9, Tenor	$15,000	$20,000
1930s	Tenor	$6,000	$8,000
1948	Plectrum	$2,250	$3,000
1950s-60s	Tenor	$1,500	$2,000
Ne Plus Ultra Style 6			
1920s	Plectrum or Tenor	$7,500	$10,000
Roy Smeck			
1930s. Silver Bell #1, tenor.			
1930s		$1,500	$2,000
Senorita			
1930s	Plectrum	$550	$725
1950s	4-String	$400	$525
Silver Bell #1 Series			
1920-1933	#1 Plectrum	$1,500	$2,000
1920-1933	#1 Tenor	$1,500	$2,000
1920-1939	#1 5-String	$2,750	$3,500
1933-1939	#1 Montana, Plectrum	$1,500	$2,000
1933-1939	#1 Montana, Tenor	$1,500	$2,000
1933-1939	#1 Serenader, Tenor	$1,500	$2,000
1933-1939	#1 Symphonie, Tenor	$1,625	$2,125
Silver Bell #2 Series			
1920-1933	#2 Tenor	$1,500	$2,000
Silver Bell #3 Series			
1920-1933	#3 Montana, Tenor	$1,875	$2,500
1920-1933	#3 Tenor	$1,750	$2,250
1931	#3 Sultana, Tenor	$2,000	$2,500
1933-1939	#3 Montana, Plectrum	$2,125	$2,750
Silver Bell #4 Series			
1928	#4 Montana, Tenor	$2,750	$3,500
1928	#4 Tenor	$2,750	$3,500
Silver Bell #5 Series			
1920s	#5 5-String	$3,750	$5,000
Silver Bell #6 Series			
1927	#6 Montana, Tenor	$4,000	$5,250

The *Vintage Guitar Price Guide* shows values for all-original, excellent condition instruments and, where applicable, with original case.

BANJOS

MODEL YEAR	FEATURES	EXC. COND. LOW	HIGH
Super			
1920-1925	Tenor, non-carved neck	$650	$850
1926-1927	5-String, carved neck	$2,000	$2,500
1926-1927	5-String, non-carved neck	$1,875	$2,375
1926-1927	Plectrum	$925	$1,250
1926-1927	Tenor, non-carved neck	$825	$1,125

Symphonie Silver Bell

1960. By Gretsch, script Symphonie logo on headstock, fancy ornamentation, gold-plated hardware.

1960	5-String	$1,750	$2,250

Baldwin

1966-1976. Baldwin was one of the largest piano retailers in the Midwest and in 1965, they got into the guitar market. In '66 they bought the ODE Banjo company. From '66 to '71 the banjos were labeled as Baldwin; after that ODE was added below the Baldwin banner. In '76 Gretsch took over ODE production.

Ode 2R

1968	Plectrum, 4-String	$775	$1,000

Ode Style C

1968	Bluegrass, 5-String	$1,000	$1,500

Style D

1968-1969	5-String	$2,250	$3,000

Barratt

1890s. Made by George Barratt in Brooklyn, New York.

Style D 5-String

1890s	Victorian era	$300	$400

Benary and Sons

1890-1899. Manufactured by the James H. Buckbee Co. for music instrument wholesaler Robert Benary.

Celebrated Benary

1890-1899. 5-string, open back, plain appointments.

1890-1899		$400	$550

Bishline

1985-present. Professional and premium grade, production/custom, banjos built by luthier Robert Bishline in Tulsa, Oklahoma.

Boucher

1830s-1850s. William Boucher's operation in Baltimore is considered to be one of the very first banjo-shops. Boucher and the Civil War era banjos are rare. The price range listed is informational guidance pricing only. The wide range reflects conservative opinions. 150 year old banjos should be evaluated per their own merits.

Double Tack

1840s		$8,000	$10,000

Single Tack

1840s		$7,000	$9,000

Bruno and Sons

Established in 1834 by Charles Bruno, primarily as a distributor, Bruno and Sons marketed a variety of brands, including their own.

Royal Artist Tenor

1920s	Figured resonator	$500	$650

Buckbee

1863-1897. James H. Buckbee Co. of New York was the city's largest builder. The company did considerable private branding for companies such as Benery, Dobson, and Farland.

5-String

1890-1897. 5-string, open back, plain appointments.

1890-1897	High-level	$1,250	$1,625
1890-1897	Low-level	$450	$600
1890-1897	Mid-level	$650	$850

Christy

1960s. Banjos built by luthier Art Christianson in Colorado.

5-String Long Neck Folk

1965	Rare	$500	$650
1965	Standard	$350	$450

Cole

1890-1919. W.A. Cole, after leaving Fairbanks & Cole, started his own line in 1890. He died in 1909 but the company continued until 1919. He also made guitars and mandolins.

Eclipse

1890-1919	Dot diamond inlays	$1,500	$2,000
1890-1919	Flower inlays	$1,750	$2,250
1890-1919	Man-in-the-moon inlays	$2,000	$2,500

Model 4000

Fancy pearl, carved heel.

1890		$3,500	$4,500

Deering

1975-present. Greg and Janet Deering build their banjos in Spring Valley, California. In 1978 they introduced their basic and intermediate banjos. They also offer banjos under the Goodtime and Vega brands.

40th Anniversary

2015	5-String	$2,250	$3,000

B-6

1986-2002. Mahogany neck and resonator, ebony 'board, 6 strings, satin finish.

1986-2002		$850	$1,125

Basic

Resonator back, 5 strings.

1979-1982		$800	$1,125

Black Diamond

1998-2020. Black head, mahogany neck, 5 strings, ebony 'board, diamond inlays, resonator back.

2001		$1,125	$1,500

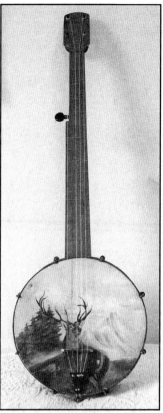

Ca.1890s Buckbee
Kenneth Parr

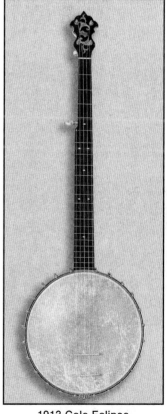

1913 Cole Eclipse

BANJOS

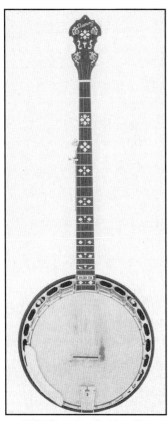

1993 Deering Golden Era
Imaged by Heritage Auctions, HA.com

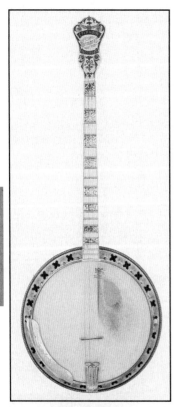

**1930s Epiphone
Recording Concert**
Imaged by Heritage Auctions, HA.com

MODEL YEAR	FEATURES	EXC. COND. LOW	HIGH

Boston

1982-present. Mahogany resonator and neck, 5 or 6 strings, ebony 'board, seed and vine inlays.

| 1982 | 5-String | $775 | $1,000 |
| 2012 | 6-String | $1,125 | $1,500 |

Calico

1998-present. Curly maple resonator and neck, 5 strings, ebony 'board, plectrum and tenor available.

| 2007-2010 | | $2,750 | $3,500 |

Calico Custom

1997-2007.

| 2007 | 5-String | $3,250 | $4,500 |

Crossfire

1998-2016. Alder body, maple neck, 5 strings, ebony 'board, diamond inlays. Available in tenor.

| 2005-2016 | | $2,000 | $2,500 |

D-6 Banjo-Guitar

| 1995 | Resonator, 6-String | $1,625 | $2,250 |

Deluxe

1995-2020. Mahogany resonator, mahogany or maple neck, ebony 'board, white and gold inlays on 6-string. Available 5-, 6- or 12-string, plectrum 4-string, 17- or 19-fret tenor 4-string.

| 1995-2003 | 5- or 6-String | $1,750 | $2,250 |
| 1995-2003 | Plectrum 4-String | $1,375 | $1,750 |

Eagle II

2010-present. Resonator back, available as 5-string, 6-string, open back 5-string and 19-fret tenor.

| 2010-2016 | 5-String | $1,500 | $2,000 |

G.D.L. Greg Deering Limited Edition

2001-2010. Figured walnut neck, burl walnut resonator, abalone and mother-of-pearl inlays, ebony 'board, 5 strings.

| 2001 | | $3,500 | $4,500 |

Golden Era

1995-present. Deeper resonator sound chamber, curly maple, 5 strings, ebony 'board, Cremona Sunburst stain finish.

| 1995-2016 | | $2,500 | $3,500 |

Golden Wreath

2006-present. Deep resonator, 5 strings, mahogany neck, ebony 'board, mother of pearl wreath inlay.

| 2006 | | $2,500 | $3,500 |

Goodtime 5-String

| 2010-2013 | | $450 | $600 |

Goodtime Special

2001-present. Maple neck, rim and resonator, black inlays and binding. Available 4-string plectrum and 19-fret tenor, or 5-string open back.

| 2010-2013 | 5-string | $700 | $950 |

Grand Ole Opry

2005. Limited Edition for Opry's 80th anniversary, hand signed by Greg and Janet Deering, only 80 produced.

| 2005 | 5-string | $4,000 | $5,000 |

Ivanhoe

High-end appointments, 5-string.

| 1986 | | $8,000 | $11,000 |

John Hartford

Resonator back, curly maple, 5-string, offered in 22 or 24 frets.

| 2007-2015 | | $2,500 | $3,250 |

MODEL YEAR	FEATURES	EXC. COND. LOW	HIGH

Maple Blossom

1983-present. Dark walnut stained maple neck, 4, 5, or 6 strings, fancy inlays, high gloss finish. Originally called the Advanced ('78-'82).

| 1983-2016 | 5-string | $2,000 | $2,500 |
| 1983-2016 | Tenor | $1,500 | $2,000 |

Saratoga Star

| 2004 | 5-string | $3,750 | $4,875 |

Sierra

1998-present. Mahogany or maple neck and resonator, maple rim, ebony 'board, 4- or 5-string, electric/acoustic or openback.

| 1996-2014 | | $1,250 | $1,625 |

Standard

| 1992 | 5-string | $1,250 | $1,625 |

Tenbrooks Saratoga Star

Curly maple neck and deep resonator, 5-string, ebony 'board.

| 2010 | | $3,500 | $4,500 |

Texas Calico

1986. Limited run of 150, Texas and 1836-1986 logo on fretboard, engraved gold-plated metal hardware, 5 strings.

| 1986 | | $8,500 | $11,000 |

Ditson

1916-1930. The Oliver Ditson Company of Boston offered a variety of musical instruments.

Tenor

Resonator with typical appointments, 4 strings.

| 1920 | | $500 | $650 |

Dobro

1929-1942, ca. 1954-2019. Guitars and mandolins were also made under the Dobro name. In '93 Gibson purchased the brand and built Dobros in Nashville, Tennessee. For more info refer to the guitar section.

Dojo

Resonator guitar body with 5-string banjo neck.

| 1988-1994 | | $1,500 | $2,000 |

Dobson, C. Edgar

1880s. The Dobson brothers – Henry Clay, Charles Edgar, George Clifton, Frank Prescott, and Edward Clarendon – were banjo teachers and performers who marketed banjos in various ways over the years.

Great Echo

| 1888 | 5-String | $950 | $1,250 |

Dobson, George

1870-1890. Marketed by renown banjo instructor George C. Dobson of Boston, Massachusetts.

Matchless

| 1880s | 5-String | $850 | $1,125 |

Dobson, H.C.

1860s-early 1900s. The oldest of the Dobson brothers, Henry C. was a successful musical instrument distributor out of New York. They were designed by Henry, but most, if not all, were made by others.

MODEL YEAR	FEATURES	EXC. COND. LOW	HIGH
Silver Chime			
1870-1890	Fancy, 5-String	$1,250	$1,750
1870-1890	Plain, 5-String	$725	$1,125

Epiphone

1873-present. Epiphone introduced banjos in the early 1920s, if not sooner, offering them up to WW II. After Gibson bought the company in '57, they re-introduced banjos to the line, which they still offer.

Black Beauty Tenor

1920		$450	$600

EB-44 Campus

1962 1970. Long neck, open back, folk-era 5-string.

1962-1970		$950	$1,250

EB-88 Minstrel

1961-1969. Flat head, standard neck, 5 strings.

1961-1969		$1,500	$2,000

EB-99

1970s. Import, higher-end, 5-string.

1970s		$650	$850

EB-188 Plantation

1962-1968. Long neck, open back, 5 strings.

1962-1968		$1,375	$1,750

Electar (Electric)

1930s	Tenor	$900	$1,125

MB-200

1998-2015. Mahogany neck and body, rosewood 'board, 5 strings.

2009		$275	$350

MB-250

1998-2013. Mahogany resonator body and neck, rosewood 'board, 5 strings.

2012		$450	$600

Peerless Plectrum

1920-1925. Has Epiphone and Peerless logo on fancy headstock.

1920-1925		$475	$625

Recording A

Ca. 1925-ca. 1935. Epiphone Recording logo on headstock, flamed maple neck and resonator, fancy pearl inlay markers.

1920s	Tenor	$2,000	$2,500

Recording B

Ca. 1925-ca. 1935.

1930s	Tenor	$2,250	$3,000

Recording Concert C Special

1930s. Tenor, maple body, fancy appointments, resonator.

1932		$3,000	$4,000

TB-100

Mid-1960s. Tenor, 11" rim.

1960s		$750	$975

White Beauty Tenor

1920. Closed-back resonator, large dot markers, White Beauty headstock logo.

1920		$500	$650

Excelsior

Ca.1885-ca. 1990. Brand name of guitars and banjos marketed by Boston's John C. Haynes & Company. Instruments were more basic without tone rings. Brand most likely faded out in very early 1890s when Haynes started their more refined line of Bay State instruments.

Model 218

1889	Open back, 5-string	$1,250	$1,625

Fairbanks/Vega Fairbanks/ A.C. Fairbanks

1875-1922. From 1875 to 1880, A. C. Fairbanks built his own designs in Boston. In 1880, W. A. Cole joined the company, starting Fairbanks & Cole, but left in 1890 to start his own line. The company went by Fairbanks Co. until it was purchased by Vega in 1904. The banjos were then branded Vega Fairbanks (see Vega listings) until 1922.

Acme (F & C)

1880-1890. 5-string, open back, fancy markers.

1880-1890		$750	$950

Electric 5-String Series

1890s	Electric	$3,500	$4,500
1890s	Imperial	$2,000	$2,750
1890s	No. 3	$3,500	$4,500
1890s	No. 5	$5,000	$6,500
1890s	No. 6	$5,500	$7,000
1901	Special	$2,375	$3,000

Electric Banjeaurine

1890s	5-string	$2,000	$2,500

Imperial Open Back

1888	5-string	$2,000	$2,500

Regent

1900-1904	5-string	$2,000	$2,500

Senator No. 1

1900-1909	5-string	$950	$1,250

Special #0

1890-1904		$650	$850

Special #2

1890-1904	5-string	$800	$1,000

Special #4

1900-1904	5-string	$1,000	$1,375

Tubaphone #3

1908	5-string	$2,500	$3,500

Whyte Laydie #2

1901-1904	5-string	$3,500	$4,500

Whyte Laydie #7

1901	1st year	$7,500	$8,000
1902-1908		$7,000	$8,500

Farland

Ca. 1890-1920s. Buckbee and others made instruments for New York banjo teacher and performer A. A. Farland.

Concert Grand

1900-1920	5-string	$950	$1,250

Grand Artist No. 2

1890s-1910. Ornate floral markers, open back, 5-string.

1890s-1910		$1,625	$2,125

Fender

1946-present. Fender added banjos to their product mix in the late 1960s, and continues to offer them.

Fairbanks Electric
Intermountain Guitar and Banjo

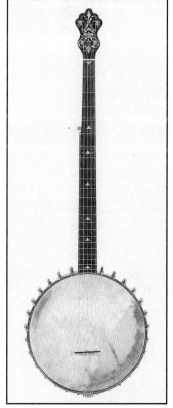

Farland

BANJOS

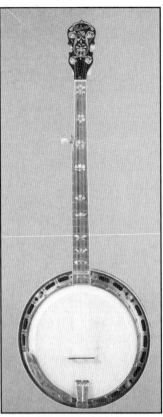

1927 Gibson Bella Voce
William Ritter/Gruhn Guitars

1924 Gibson GB-5
Intermountain Guitar and Banjo

MODEL YEAR	FEATURES	EXC. COND. LOW	HIGH
Allegro			
Late 1960s-1970s. Tenor or 5-string.			
1960s		$850	$1,125
Artist			
1960s-70s	5-string	$1,500	$2,000
FB Series			
1998-2017. Various imported 5-string models.			
2007-2012	FB-54	$250	$350
2007-2012	FB-55	$400	$550
2007-2012	FB-58	$500	$650
2007-2012	FB-59	$650	$850
Leo Deluxe			
1970s-1988. Japanese-made, fancy inlay.			
1970s		$850	$1,125

Framus

1946-1977, 1996-present. The new Framus company, located in Markneukirchen, Germany, continues to offer banjos.

MODEL YEAR	FEATURES	EXC. COND. LOW	HIGH
Various Models			
1960s		$300	$400
1970s		$200	$275

Gibson

1890s (1902)-present. Gibson started making banjos in 1918. Vega and Gibson were the only major manufacturing companies that offered banjos in their product catalog in the '50s.

RB prefix = regular banjo (5-string)
TB prefix = tenor banjo (4-string, tenor tuning)
PB prefix = plectrum banjo (4-string, plectrum tuning)
The prices shown are guidance prices only and each instrument should be evaluated on a case-by-case basis.

All American
1930-1937, 1970-1986. Tenor banjo, fancy appointments, historic art, gold hardware. Reissue offered in RB, TB, or PB.

MODEL YEAR	FEATURES	EXC. COND. LOW	HIGH
1930-1937	Arch top, 2-pc. Flange	$10,000	$13,000
1930-1937	Flat head, 1-pc. flange, rare	$40,000	$50,000
1975-1980	5-string	$6,500	$8,500

Bella Voce
1927-1931. Tenor or plectrum, fancy appointments, flower-pattern art, gold hardware.

1927-1931	Plectrum	$10,000	$13,000
1927-1931	Tenor	$10,000	$13,000

Christmas Limited Edition
2008-2009. Christmas theme, 5-string, flame maple, gold parts, 12 offered.

2008-2009		$7,000	$9,000

Earl Scruggs '49 Classic
1992-2008. Figured maple resonator and neck, rosewood 'board, multiple bindings.

2001-2002		$3,500	$4,500

Earl Scruggs Flint Hill Special
2005. Commemorative Limited Edition, 20 made with first 5 signed by Earl, Flint Hill Special on headstock, figured maple resonator and neck, classic

MODEL YEAR	FEATURES	EXC. COND. LOW	HIGH
Amber Brown finish.			
2005		$4,500	$6,000
Earl Scruggs Golden Deluxe			
1991-2010. Satin gold hardware, hearts and flowers inlay.			
1997		$4,500	$6,000
Earl Scruggs Standard			
1984-2010. 5-string, high-end appointments, Standard added to model name in '92.			
1984-2010		$3,500	$4,500
ETB Electric Tenor			
1938-1941. Electric Tenor Banjo, Charlie Christian pickup.			
1934-1941		$3,000	$4,000
Flint Hill Special			
2005-2006. Earl Scruggs style, 5-string.			
2005-2006		$4,000	$5,500
Florentine Plectrum			
1927-1937. High-end appointments, gold hardware.			
1925-1930	2-piece flange	$10,000	$13,000
Florentine Tenor			
1927-1937. High-end appointments, gold hardware.			
1927-1935	40-hole	$10,000	$13,000

GB-1
1922-1940. Guitar-banjo, style 1 appointments, 6-string neck, walnut. Trap door '22-'24, resonator diamond-flange '25-'30, 1-piece flange '31-'40.

1922-1924		$1,500	$2,000
1925-1930		$2,000	$2,500
1931-1940		$2,500	$3,500

GB-3
1918-1937. Guitar-banjo, style 3 appointments, mahogany. Trap door '18-'24. Mastertone, 2-piece flange, ball-bearing arch-top tone ring for '25-'26 and cast arch-top tone ring for '26-'29. Mastertone, 40-hole tone ring '28-'37. Flat head option '31-'37.

1918-1924		$1,250	$1,625
1925-1926		$3,000	$4,000
1926-1929		$3,000	$4,000
1928-1937		$3,000	$4,000

GB-4
1918-1931. Guitar-banjo, style 4 appointments, maple. Very early models were called GB without -4 suffix. Trap door '18-'24. Mastertone, 2-piece flange, ball-bearing arch-top tone ring for '25-'26 and cast arch-top tone ring for '26-'29. Mastertone, 40-hole tone ring '28-'31. Flat head option

1918-1924	GB/GB-4	$2,500	$3,375
1925-1926		$3,750	$5,000
1926-1929		$3,750	$5,000
1928-1931		$3,750	$5,000

GB-5
1924. Rare, gold plated, trap door.

1924		$6,500	$8,500

GB-6/GB-6 Custom
1922-1934. Guitar-banjo, style 6 appointments, special order availability. Trap door '22-'24. Mastertone, 2-piece flange, ball-bearing arch-top tone ring for '25-'26 and cast arch-top tone ring for '26-'29. Mastertone, 40-hole tone ring '28-'34. Flat head option '31-'34.

1922-1924		$3,500	$4,500

BANJOS

MODEL YEAR	FEATURES	EXC. COND. LOW	HIGH
1925-1926		$5,500	$7,000
1926-1929		$5,500	$7,000
1928-1934		$5,250	$6,500

Granada PB
1929-1939. Plectrum, flat head tone ring.

1929-1939		$90,000	$120,000

Granada RB
1925-1939. 5-string banjo with either a 2-piece flange ('25-'30), or a 1-piece flange ('33-'39).

1925-1926	Ball bearing	$15,000	$20,000
1927-1930	40-hole arched	$25,000	$30,000
1929-1939	Flat head	$175,000	$250,000

Granada RB (Reissue)
1986-2010. Resonator back, hearts & flowers or flying eagle inlay, 5-string.

1986-2006	Flying eagle	$4,000	$5,000
1986-2010	Hearts & flowers	$4,000	$5,000

Granada RB Pot and Reneck
1933-1939. Original pot and replacement neck, flat head tone ring.

1933-1939		$45,000	$60,000

Granada TB
1925-1930. Tenor banjo with a 2-piece flange.

1925-1926	Ball bearing	$5,500	$7,000
1927-1930	40-hole arched	$7,000	$9,500

PB-1
1926-1930s. Plectrum Banjo (PB), bracket-shoe.

1920s		$1,000	$1,375

PB-2
1920s-1930s. Plectrum, bracket-shoe for '20s and 1-piece flange for '30s.

1920s	Bracket-shoe	$1,000	$1,375
1930s	1-piece flange	$3,500	$4,500

PB-3
1925-1927, 1929-1939. Laminated maple resonator Mastertone model, plectrum neck and tuning. Tube and plate, 2-piece flange for '25-'27. Flat head tone ring '29-'39.

1925-1927	Tube & plate	$2,250	$3,000
1929-1939	Flat head	$65,000	$85,000

PB-4
1925-1940. Plectrum with either a 2-piece flange ('25-'32), or 1-piece ('33-'40).

1925-1927	Ball bearing	$2,750	$3,500
1928-1932	Archtop	$3,500	$4,500
1933-1940	Archtop	$9,000	$12,000
1933-1940	Flat head	$50,000	$65,000

PB-7
1937-1943. Plectrum, 40-hole flat tone ring.

1940		$50,000	$65,000

PB-11
1931-1942. Plectrum, 1-piece flange, pearloid 'board, headstock and resonator cover.

1931-1942		$3,500	$4,500

PB-100
1948-1979. Plectrum with either a 1-piece flange ('48-'68), or 2-piece ('69-'79).

1969-1979		$1,000	$1,375

RB Jr.
1924-1925. Budget line, 5-string, open back.

1924-1925		$1,250	$1,625

RB-00
1932-1942. Maple resonator, 1-piece flange.

1933-1939		$4,000	$5,000

RB-1
1922-1940. Resonator Banjo (RB), 1-piece or diamond flange.

1922-1930	Early specs	$4,000	$5,500
1930-1932	1-piece flange	$4,000	$5,500
1933-1940	Diamond flange	$4,000	$5,500

RB-1 Reissue
1990-1993. Fleur-de-lis, brass tone ring.

1990-1993		$2,000	$2,500

RB-2

1933-1939		$7,000	$9,000

RB-3
1923-1937. Resonator, dot inlay, 5 strings, trap door or non-trap '22-'24. Mastertone, ball bearing '25-'26. Mastertone, archtop, 40-hole or no hole for '27-'29.

1922-1924		$2,500	$3,250
1925-1926		$7,500	$9,500
1927-1929		$12,000	$16,000

RB-3 Reissue
1988-2010. Called the RB-3 Wreath at end of production.

1988-2010		$3,250	$4,250

RB-4
1922-1937. Resonator 5-string, trap or non-trap door on earlier models ('22-'24), either a 2-piece flange ('25-'31), or 1-piece ('33-'37).

1922-1924		$3,000	$4,000
1925-1931	Archtop	$14,000	$18,000
1929-1937	Flat head tone ring	$80,000	$100,000
1933-1937	Archtop	$28,000	$38,000

RB-4/R-4/Retro 4
1991-2006. Resonator, flying eagle inlay, multibound.

1998-2006		$4,000	$5,500

RB-5
1995-2008. Resonator.

1995-2008		$6,000	$8,000

RB-6 New Century
1995-2008. Style 6, 5-string, figured-maple, gold sparkle binding.

2005		$6,000	$8,000

RB-7 Top Tension
1994-2008. Maple, bow-tie inlay.

2003		$4,000	$5,500

RB-11
1931-1942. Pearloid covered 'board, headstock and resonator.

1933-1939		$5,000	$7,000

RB-12
1995-2008. Carved walnut resonator, rosewood 'board, art deco inlay.

1996-2003		$4,000	$5,500

RB-75 J.D. Crowe Blackjack
1997-2006. Resonator 5-string, mahogany neck finished in vintage brown/red with aged white binding, rosewood 'board.

1997-2006		$3,500	$4,500

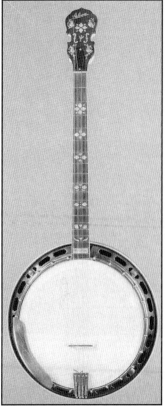

1927 Gibson Granada TB
William Ritter/Gruhn Guitars

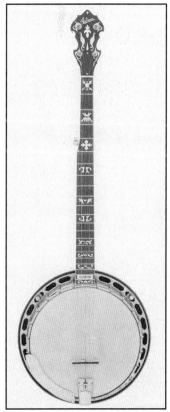

2000 Gibson RB-4 Mastertone
Imaged by Heritage Auctions, HA.com

BANJOS

To get the most from this book, be sure to read "Using *The Guide*" in the introduction.

1959 Gibson RB-250
Jay Hunt

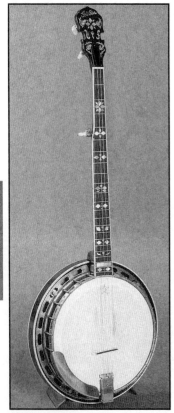

Gold Star G-11HF
Elderly Instruments

MODEL YEAR	FEATURES	EXC. COND. LOW	HIGH
RB-100			
1948-1979. Maple resonator.			
1948-1965		$2,000	$2,500
1966-1979		$1,500	$2,000
RB-150			
1948-1959. Laminated mahogany resonator, bow tie inlay.			
1948-1959		$2,250	$3,000
RB-170			
1960-1973. No resonator, 5-string, dot markers, decal logo, multi-ply maple rim.			
1960-1973		$1,125	$1,500
RB-175			
1962-1973. 2000s. Open back, long neck typical of banjos of the '60s. Models include the RB-175, RB-175 Long Neck, RB-175 Folk.			
1962	RB-175	$1,250	$1,625
1962-1964	Long Neck	$1,250	$1,625
1965-1969	Folk	$1,250	$1,625
1970-1973	RB-175	$1,250	$1,625
RB-180			
1961-1967. Longneck.			
1961-1967		$2,000	$2,500
RB-250			
1954-1999, 2002-2010. Mahogany, 2-piece flange until '88, 1 after.			
1954-1959		$3,000	$4,000
1960-1965		$3,000	$4,000
1966-1969	Flat head	$2,000	$2,500
1970-1989	Mastertone	$2,000	$2,500
1990-1999		$2,000	$2,500
2002-2004	Reissue	$2,000	$2,500
RB-500			
1964-1969. Maple, 1-piece flange, gold hardware.			
1967		$3,500	$4,500
RB-800			
1964-1971, 1979-1986. Maple resonator, 1-piece flange until '69, 2 after.			
1964-1986		$3,500	$4,500
TB			
1918-1923. Renamed TB-4.			
1919		$1,125	$1,500
TB-00			
1939-1944. Maple resonator, 1-piece flange.			
1939-1944		$1,750	$2,375
TB-1			
1922-1939. Tenor banjo with a 1-piece flange.			
1922-1925		$675	$875
1926		$725	$950
1933-1939		$3,000	$4,000
TB-2			
1922-1928 Wavy flange		$850	$1,125
1933-1937	Pearloid board	$3,000	$4,000
TB-3			
1925-1937. Tenor banjo with either a 2-piece flange, or a 1-piece flange.			
1925-1926		$1,750	$2,375
1927-1929		$3,000	$4,000
1930-1937		$6,000	$8,000

MODEL YEAR	FEATURES	EXC. COND. LOW	HIGH
TB-4			
1922-1937. Dot inlay.			
1922-1924	Trap door	$1,000	$1,500
1925-1926	Ball bearing	$3,000	$4,000
1927-1931	40 or no hole ring	$3,000	$4,000
1933-1937	40 or no hole ring	$5,000	$6,500
TB-5			
1922-1924	Trap door	$1,125	$1,500
1925-1926	Ball bearing	$7,000	$9,500
1927-1931	40 or no hole ring	$9,000	$12,000
TB-6			
1927-1939	Tube plate flange	$11,500	$15,000
TB-11			
1931-1942. Pearloid covered 'board, headstock and resonator.			
1931-1942		$2,250	$3,000
TB-12			
1937-1939. Produced in limited quantities, 1-piece flange, flat head tone ring, double bound walnut resonator, price levels include both original and conversion instruments, conversions with original flat head tone rings are somewhat common in the vintage banjo market.			
1937		$48,000	$65,000
TB-18			
1937. Rare model, flat head top tension.			
1937		$68,000	$90,000
TB-100			
1949-1959		$1,125	$1,500
1960-1969		$1,125	$1,500
TB-150			
1949-1959		$1,500	$2,000
TB-250			
1954-1959		$1,750	$2,500
1960-1969	Mastertone	$1,500	$2,000
1970-1996	Mastertone	$1,375	$1,875
TB-800			
1964	2 made	$3,500	$4,500
1975	Flying eagle markers	$3,000	$4,000
Trujo Plectrum			
1928-1934		$2,500	$3,500

Gold Star

1970s-present. A brand name of Saga Musical Instruments offering professional and premium grade, production banjos.

5-String

1970s-present. Various 5-string models.

1970s	G-11HF	$1,375	$1,750
1980s-2017	GF-85	$1,375	$1,750
1984	JD Crowe	$4,250	$5,500
2000-2017	GF-200	$1,375	$1,750
2006-2022	GF-100FE	$1,375	$1,750
2020	GF-100JD	$1,125	$1,500

Gold Tone

1993-present. Professional and premium grade, production/custom banjos and banjitars built by Wayne and Robyn Rogers in Titusville, Florida. They also offer guitars, basses, lap steels, mandolins and ukuleles.

BANJOS

MODEL YEAR	FEATURES	EXC. COND. LOW	HIGH
5-String			
Various 5-string models.			
2009	Banjola Deluxe	$650	$850
2011	BG-250F BG Special	$550	$725
2011	CC-100 Cripple Creek	$500	$650
2011	OB-250AT	$975	$1,250
2011	OT-800	$875	$1,125
2014	TB-250 Travel	$875	$1,125
2014	WL-250 Open Back	$875	$1,125
Tenor			
Various tenor models.			
2011	IT250R Irish (China)	$475	$625

Goya

1952-1996. Martin offered Goya banjos while they owned the brand name in the '70s.

Student 5-String

1976-1996. Goya-Martin era.

1976-1996		$275	$350

Gretsch

1883-present. Gretsch offered banjos in the '20s and again in the '50s and '60s. In 2012 they again started building them.

5-String

1977		$400	$550

Broadkaster

1920s-1939. Tenor or 5-string banjo with pearloid head and board.

1920s	Tenor	$500	$650
1932-1939	5-string	$950	$1,250
1932-1939	Tenor	$350	$450

Model 6536 Folk

1960s. Open-back, 5-string, long-neck style.

1964		$550	$725

New Yorker

1930s-1960s. New Yorker logo on headstock, 5-string or tenor.

1930s-60s		$275	$350

Orchestella

1925-1929. Tenor or 5-string banjo with gold engravings.

1925-1929	5-string	$1,500	$2,000
1925-1929	Tenor	$600	$775

Tenor Short-Scale

1925-1929	Plain styling	$300	$400
1950s	Plain styling	$300	$400

GTR

1974-1978. GTR (for George Gruhn, Tut Taylor, Randy Wood) was the original name for Gruhn Guitars in Nashville, and they imported mandolins and banjos from Japan.

5-String Copy

1974-1978		$750	$1,000

Harmony

1892-1976, late 1970s-present. Huge, Chicago-based manufacturer of fretted instruments, mainly budget models under the Harmony name or for many other American brands and mass marketers.

MODEL YEAR	FEATURES	EXC. COND. LOW	HIGH
Bicentennial			
1976. Red, white and blue, '76 logo, 5-string.			
1976		$650	$850
Electro			
1950s. Electric banjo, 5-string, wood body, 1 pickup.			
1950s		$650	$850
Holiday Folk			
1960s. Long neck, 5-string.			
1960s		$250	$325
Reso-Tone Tenor			
1960s		$225	$300
Roy Smeck Student Tenor			
1963		$225	$300
Sovereign Tenor			
1960s		$225	$300

Howard

Howard is a brand name of Cincinnati's Wurlitzer Co. used in the 1920s on banjos built by The Fred Gretsch Manufacturing Co. The brand name was also appeared on guitars in the mid-'30s by Epiphone.

Tenor

1930s	Open back	$175	$225
1930s	Resonator	$375	$500

Huber

1999-present. Premium grade, production, 5-string banjos built by luthier Steve Huber in Hendersonville, Tennessee.

Ibanez

1932-present. Ibanez introduced their Artist line of banjos in 1978 in a deal with Earl Scruggs, but they were dropped by '84.

Model 591

1978-1984. Flat head, 5-string.

1978-1984		$1,000	$1,250

Model 593

1977. Vine inlay, 5-string.

1977		$1,250	$1,625

John Wesley

Introduced in 1895 by Kansas City, Missouri instrument wholesalers J.W. Jenkins & Sons, founded by cello builder John Wesley Jenkins. May have been built by Jenkins until circa 1905, but work was later contracted out to others.

Kalamazoo

1933-1942, 1965-1970. Budget brand built by Gibson. Made flat-tops, solidbodies, mandolins, lap steels, banjos and amps.

KPB Plectrum

1935-1940		$450	$550

KRB 5-String

1935-1941		$750	$975

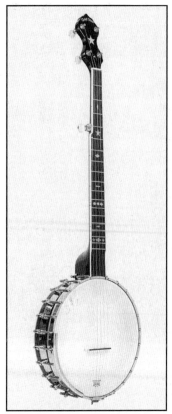

Gold Tone OT-800

Kalamazoo KPB Plectrum

BANJOS

1964 Kay
Rivington Guitars

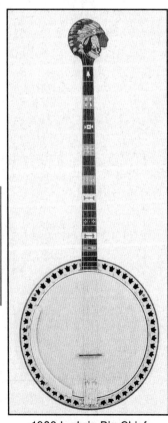

1930 Ludwig Big Chief
Imaged by Heritage Auctions, HA.com

MODEL YEAR	FEATURES	EXC. COND. LOW	HIGH

Kay

Ca. 1931 (1890)-present. Kay was a huge manufacturer and built instruments under their name and for a large number of other retailers, jobbers, and brand names.

Silva

1950s. Top of the line 5-string, Silva verticle logo along with Kay logo on headstock, block markers.

1950s		$500	$650

Student Tenor

1950s		$200	$250

Kel Kroydon

1930-1933. Private branded budget level instruments made by Gibson. They also had guitars and banjos. The name has been revived on a line of banjos by Tom Mirisola and made in Nashville.

KK-11 Tenor

1933-1937		$2,500	$3,250

Kingston

Ca. 1958-1967. Imported from Japan by Westheimer Importing Corp. of Chicago. They also offered guitars, basses and mandolins.

Student Tenor

1965		$65	$85

Lange

1920s-1942, Late 1940s. The William L. Lange Company began selling Paramount banjos, guitar banjos and mandolin banjos in the early 1920s. Gretsch picked up the Paramount name and used it on acoustics and electrics for a time in the late '40s. See Paramount for more listings.

Tourraine Deluxe

1920s	Tenor	$600	$750

Leedy

1889-1930. Founded in Indianapolis by U. G. Leedy, the company started making banjos in 1924. Leedy was bought out by C. G. Conn in '30.

Arcadian

1925	Plectrum	$450	$600

Olympian

1930	Tenor	$450	$600

Solotone

1924-1930	A Tenor	$850	$1,125
1924-1930	B Tenor	$1,125	$1,500
1924-1930	C Tenor	$1,125	$1,500
1924-1930	D Tenor	$1,250	$1,750

Libby Bros.

1890s. Made in Gorham, Maine, rarity suggests limited production.

Open Back

1890-1895. Fancy position markers, 5-string.

1890-1895		$1,000	$1,375

Ludwig

The Ludwig Drum Company was founded in 1909. They saw a good business opportunity and

MODEL YEAR	FEATURES	EXC. COND. LOW	HIGH

entered the banjo market in '21. When demand for banjos tanked in the '30s, Ludwig dropped the line and concentrated on its core business.

Ambassador

1920s-1932	Tenor	$850	$1,125

Bellevue

1920s. Tenor, closed-back banjo with fancy appointments.

1920s		$650	$850

Big Chief

1930. Carved and engraved plectrum banjo.

1930		$5,500	$7,000

Capitol

1920s		$550	$725

Columbia

1920s	Tenor, student-level	$350	$450

Commodore

1930s. Tenor or plectrum, with gold hardware and fancy appointments.

1930s	Tenor	$1,125	$1,500
1932	Plectrum	$1,250	$1,625

Deluxe

1930s. Tenor, engraved, gold hardware.

1930s		$1,625	$2,125

Dixie

1930s	Tenor	$300	$400

Kenmore

1920s. Plectrum with open back or tenor resonator.

1920s	Plectrum	$500	$650

Kingston

1924-1930	Tenor	$500	$650

Standard Art Tenor

1924-1930. Tenor banjo with fancy appointments.

1924-1930		$2,500	$3,250

The Ace

1920s. Tenor banjo, resonator and nickel appointments.

1920s		$950	$1,250

Luscomb

1888-1898. John F. Luscomb was a well-known banjo player who designed a line of instruments for Thompson & Odell of Boston.

Open Back 5-String

1890s		$600	$775

Lyric (by Gretsch)

1930s. There are also Lyric-branded banjos made by William Schmick in the 1910s as well as current Asian-made ones.

Tenor

1930	Resonator back	$500	$650

Matao

1967-1983. Japanese copies of American brands, offered guitars, basses, banjos and ukes.

Bluegrass

1970s	5-string	$275	$350

MODEL		EXC. COND.	
YEAR	FEATURES	LOW	HIGH

Mitchell (P.J.)
1850s. Early gut 5-string banjo maker from New York City.
Gut 5-String
1850s		$2,500	$3,250

Morrison
Ca. 1870-ca. 1915. Marketed by New Yorker James Morrison, made by Morrison or possibly others like Buckbee. After 1875, his instruments sported the patented Morrison tone ring.
5-String
1885-1890		$550	$725

ODE/Muse
1961-1980. Founded by Charles Ogsbury in Boulder, Colorado, purchased by Baldwin in '66 and moved to Nashville. Until '71 the banjos were branded as Baldwin; afterwards as Baldwin ODE. Gretsch took over production in '76. Muse was a retail store brand of banjos produced by ODE from '61 to '66. In '71, Ogsbury started the OME Banjo Company in Colorado.
Model C
1976-1980. Resonator, 5-string, fancy markers.
1976-1980		$1,500	$2,000

Model D
1976-1980. Resonator, 5-string, gold engravings.
1976-1980	.	$2,125	$2,750

OME
1971-present. Charles Ogsbury started OME outside Boulder, Colorado after he sold his first banjo company, ODE, to Baldwin.
Bright Angel
2012-2019	5-string	$2,500	$3,250

Columbine
2012-2015	Tenor	$3,000	$4,000

Grubstake
1972-1980	5-string	$950	$1,250

Juggernaut
1973-1979	5-string	$2,000	$3,500

Juggernaut II
1974	5-string	$2,500	$3,500

Juniper Megatone
2016	5-string	$2,500	$3,500

Magician
1997	5-string, gold	$3,000	$4,000

Mogul
1973	5-string, silver	$2,500	$3,500
1973	Plectrum, black	$2,500	$3,500
1973	Plectrum, silver	$2,500	$3,500
1974	5-string, gold	$3,250	$4,500

Monarch
1985-1990	5-string	$2,500	$3,500
1986	Plectrum	$2,000	$2,500

Primrose
2013-2019	5-string	$2,500	$3,500

X 5-String
1971		$1,000	$1,375

XX 5-String
1971		$1,125	$1,500
1972	Extra long neck	$1,000	$1,375
1975		$1,000	$1,375

XX Tenor
1973		$1,000	$1,375

XXX 5-String
1971		$1,500	$2,000

Orpheum
1897-1922. Lange and Rettberg purchased the J.H. Buckbee banjo factory in 1897 and started making banjos under the Orpheum label. William Lange took control in 1922 and changed the name to Paramount.
Model #1
1910s-20s	Tenor	$575	$750
1914-1916	5-string	$2,000	$2,500
1920-1922	Plectrum	$650	$850

Model #2
1920-1922	5-string	$1,500	$2,000
1920-1922	Tenor	$725	$950

Model #3
1900-1910s	5-string	$3,000	$4,000
1910s	Plectrum, fancy	$1,625	$2,125
1910s	Tenor, fancy	$900	$1,125

Paramount
1921-1935. William Lange and his Paramount company are generally accredited with commercializing the first modern flange and resonator in 1921.
Aristocrat
1921-1935	Plectrum	$1,375	$1,875
1921-1935	Tenor	$1,125	$1,500

Aristocrat Special
1921-1935. Plectrum or tenor with fancy appointments.
1921-1935	Plectrum	$2,000	$2,750
1921-1935	Tenor	$1,625	$2,125

Artists Supreme
1930s. High-end appointments, 19-fret tenor, engraved gold-plated hardware.
1930s	Tenor	$3,500	$4,750

Banjo-Harp
Wood resonator, all wood including spruce top, fancy.
1924	5-string	$1,250	$1,625
1924	Tenor, 4-string	$900	$1,250

Junior
1921-1935	Plectrum	$650	$875
1921-1935	Tenor	$450	$600

Leader
1921-1935	Plectrum	$800	$1,000
1921-1935	Tenor	$700	$950

Style 1
1921-1935	Plectrum	$700	$950
1921-1935	Tenor	$525	$700

Style 2
1921-1935. Tenor, resonator and plain appointments.
1921-1935		$550	$750

2003 OME Mockingbird Grand Artist SB Plectrum
William Ritter/Gruhn Guitars

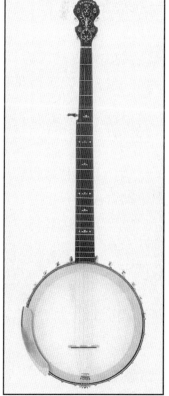

1920s Orpheum Model #1
Imaged by Heritage Auctions, HA.com

BANJOS

1930s Paramount Style A Tenor
Imaged by Heritage Auctions, HA.com

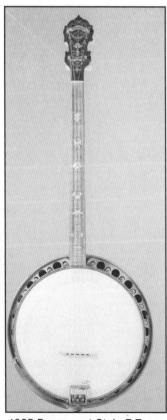

1925 Paramount Style E Tenor
William Ritter/Gruhn Guitars

MODEL YEAR	FEATURES	EXC. COND. LOW	HIGH
Style A			
1921-1935. Models include the Style A Tenor, Plectrum, and the 5-string (with resonator and fancy appointments).			
1921-1935	5-string	$1,500	$2,000
1921-1935	Plectrum	$1,000	$1,375
1921-1935	Tenor	$825	$1,125
Style B			
1921-1935. Models include the Style B Tenor, and the Plectrum (with resonator and fancy appointments).			
1921-1935	Plectrum	$1,500	$2,000
1921-1935	Tenor	$1,250	$1,625
Style C			
1921-1935. Models include the Style C Tenor, Plectrum, and the 5-string (with resonator and fancy appointments).			
1921-1935	5-string	$3,000	$4,000
1921-1935	Plectrum	$1,000	$1,375
1921-1935	Tenor	$1,000	$1,375
Style D			
1921-1935	Plectrum	$1,500	$2,000
1921-1935	Tenor	$1,375	$1,875
Style E			
1921-1935	Plectrum	$2,000	$2,750
1921-1935	Tenor	$1,750	$2,375
Style F			
1921-1935	Plectrum	$2,750	$3,750
1921-1935	Tenor	$2,500	$3,375
Super/Super Paramount			
1929-1935	Plectrum	$3,000	$4,000
1929-1935	Tenor	$2,750	$3,750
Trooper			
1921-1935	Plectrum	$550	$750
1921-1935	Tenor	$450	$600

Penco

Ca. 1974-1978. Japanese-made banjos imported into Philadelphia. They also offered guitars, basses and mandolins.

Deluxe Tenor			
1970s	Japan	$225	$300

Recording King

1929-1932, 1936-1941. Brand name used by Montgomery Ward for instruments made by various American manufacturers, including Kay, Gibson and Gretsch.

M-6 Tenor			
1938		$1,500	$2,000
Studio King Tenor			
1929-1932. Gibson-made, 40 hole archtop.			
1929-1932		$3,000	$4,000

Regal

Ca. 1895-1966, 1987-present. Mass manufacturer Regal made brands for others as well as marketing its own brand. In '87 the Regal name was revived by Saga.

Bicentennial '76			
1976. Part of a series of Regal instruments with Bicentennial themed appointments.			
1976	5-string	$400	$500

S.S. Stewart

1878-1904. S.S. Stewart of Philadelphia is considered to be one of the most important and prolific banjo manufacturers of the late 19th century. It's estimated that approximately 25,000 banjos were made by this company. The brand name was used on guitars into the 1960s.

20th Century			
1890s		$900	$1,250
American Princess			
1890s. 5-string, 10" rim.			
1890s	.	$850	$1,125
Banjeaurine			
1890s. Open back, 10" head, 5-string.			
1890s	Plain appointments	$900	$1,250
1890s	Style 3, fancy	$1,750	$2,250
Champion			
1895. Open back, 5-string.			
1895	Plain appointments	$900	$1,125
Concert No. 1 Pony			
Open back, 5-string, short scale.			
1891		$900	$1,125
Orchestra			
1890s. 5-string, various styles.			
1893-1894	#1, with frets	$1,125	$1,500
1893-1894	#2, fretless	$2,375	$3,250
1893-1894	#2, with frets	$1,875	$2,500
Piccolo			
1880s-1890s. 5-string, 7" rim, plain appointments.			
1880s-90s		$1,000	$1,375
Special Thoroughbred			
1890s-1900s. Open back, 5-string, carved heel, plain appointments.			
1890-1900s		$900	$1,125
Universal Favorite			
1892. 11" head, plain appointments.			
1892		$800	$1,125

Sekova

1960s-1970s. Imported from Japan, budget grade.

5-String			
1970s		$250	$350

Silvertone

1941-ca. 1970, present. Brand of Sears instruments which replaced their Supertone brand in '41. Currently, Samick offers a line of amps under the Silvertone name.

4-String			
1960s		$125	$175
5-String			
1960s		$275	$350

Slingerland

Ca. 1914-2019. The parent company was Slingerland Banjo and Drums, Chicago, Illinois. The company offered other stringed instruments into the '40s. In 2019, Slingerland Drums was acquired (from Gibson) by Drum Workshop (DW).

Deluxe			
1920s	Tenor, high-end	$1,250	$1,625

BANJOS

MODEL YEAR	FEATURES	EXC. COND. LOW	HIGH
May Bell			
1920s-30s	Various styles	$250	$1,000
Student/Economy			
1930s	Tenor	$175	$300

Stathopoulo

1917-1928. House of Stathopoulo evolved from the A. Stathopoulo brand in 1917 and in 1929 became the Epiphone Banjo Corporation, which later became Epiphone, the well known guitar brand.

Super Wonder XX Tenor

1920s		$750	$1,125

Stelling

1974-present. Founded by Geoff Stelling, building premium and presentation grade, production/custom banjos in Afton, Virginia. They also build mandolins.

5-String

1974-present. Various 5-string models.

1976-1984	Staghorn	$4,000	$5,000
1977-1978	Bell Flower	$2,500	$3,500
1978-1981	Whitestar	$2,000	$2,750
1980-1985	Golden Cross	$3,000	$4,000
1983	Hartford	$2,500	$3,250
1985-1995	Master Flower	$3,000	$4,000
1985-2003	Sunflower	$3,000	$4,000
1990	Masterpiece	$4,500	$6,000
2001	Red Fox	$2,500	$3,250
2004	Crusader Deluxe	$4,250	$5,500
2006	Crusader	$3,000	$4,000
2012	Swallowtail	$3,000	$4,000

Stetson, J.F.

1880s-1900s. J. F. Stetson branded banjos were distributed by W.J. Dyer & Bros. of St. Paul, Minnesota and others.

Presentation

1890s. By Fairbanks, few made, highest-end style, open back, 5-string.

1890s		$10,000	$12,000

Studio King

1930s. Banjos made by Gibson, most likely for a mail-order house or a jobber.

TB-3 Tenor

1933-1934	2-piece flange	$3,750	$5,000
1935-1937	1-piece flange	$6,000	$8,000

Superb

1920s. Private brand made by House of Stathopoulo, Inc., the company name of Epiphone from 1917 to 1928. The brand was also used on banjo ukuleles.

Tenor

1920s		$400	$550

Supertone

1914-1941. Brand used by Sears, Roebuck and Company for instruments made by various American manufacturers, including its own Harmony subsidiary Harmony. In '40, Sears began making a transition to the Silvertone brand.

Various Models

1915-1930s		$300	$500

Thompson & Odell

1875-1898. Boston instrument importers Thompson & Odell started building banjos in the 1880s. They sold the company to Vega in 1898.

Artist

1880s	Various models	$650	$850

Tilton

1850s-late 1800s. Built by William B. Tilton, of New York City. He was quite an innovator and held several instrument-related patents. He also built guitars.

Toneking

1927. Private brand of the NY Band Instruments Company, Toneking logo on headstock.

Tenor

1927		$300	$400

Univox

1964-1978. Instruments imported from Japan by the Merson Musical Supply Company, later Unicord, Westbury, New York.

Tenor

1970s	Import	$300	$400

Van Eps

1920s. Designed by virtuoso banjo artist Fred Van Eps and sold through Lyon & Healy.

Recording

1920s	5-string	$1,000	$1,375
1920s	Tenor	$1,000	$1,375

Vega

1889-1980s, 1989-present. Vega of Boston got into the banjo business in 1904 when it purchased Fairbanks. Vega and Gibson were the only major manufacturing companies that offered banjos in their product catalog in the 1950s. The Deering Banjo Company acquired the brand in '89 and uses it on a line of banjos.

Artist

1927-1929	Tenor	$1,125	$1,500
1929	Plectrum, open back	$1,125	$1,500
Artist Deluxe			
1931	Tenor	$1,500	$2,000
Artist Professional #9			
1923-1929	Tenor	$2,000	$2,500
Earl Scruggs STII			
1967-1969	5-string, resonator	$1,750	$2,250
Folk Ranger FR-5			
1960s	5-string, open back	$600	$800
Folk Wonder			
1960s	5-string	$700	$900

Stelling Master Flower
Elderly Instruments

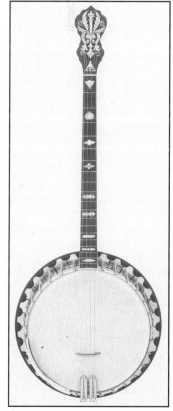

1927 Vega Artist
Imaged by Heritage Auctions, HA.com

BANJOS

1924 Vega Style X No. 9 Tenor
Intermountain Guitar and Banjo

MODEL YEAR	FEATURES	EXC. COND. LOW	HIGH
Folklore SS-5			
1966. Open back, long neck folk banjo.			
1963-1966	5-string	$1,000	$1,375
FP-5 Folk Professional			
1961	5-string, rare	$1,500	$2,000
Imperial Electric			
1918-1921	5-string	$2,000	$2,750
Little Wonder			
1910s-20s	Guitar-banjo	$1,000	$1,375
1920s	Plectrum	$600	$850
1920s-30s	Tenor	$600	$850
1950s	5-string	$950	$1,250
Moderne Tenor			
1931		$1,500	$2,000
Pete Seeger			
1958-1971. 5-string, long neck banjo.			
1958-1961	Dowel-stick	$3,000	$4,000
1962-1965	PS-5	$3,000	$4,000
1966-1971	PS-5	$2,750	$3,500
Professional			
1960. 5-string banjo with a Tubaphone tone ring.			
1960	Pro II, slits	$1,375	$1,875
1960	Professional, holes	$1,500	$2,000
Ranger			
1960s. Standard appointments, 5-string, dot markers.			
1966		$550	$750
Regent			
1920s. Open back, 5-string, dot markers.			
1920s		$1,500	$2,000
Soloist			
1920s-1930s. Oettinger tailpiece.			
1927	5-string	$2,000	$3,000
1930	Tenor	$1,000	$1,375
Style M			
1920-1929. Tenor, with Tubaphone TR.			
1920-1929		$900	$1,250
Style N			
1910s-20s	Tenor	$450	$600
Style X No. 1			
1922-1930	Tenor	$1,500	$2,000
Style X No. 9			
1922-1930. Tenor with fancy appointments.			
1922-1930	Tenor	$1,750	$2,375
Tubaphone #3			
1908-1930	5-string	$1,750	$2,375
Tubaphone #9			
1921-1929	5-string	$5,750	$8,000

MODEL YEAR	FEATURES	EXC. COND. LOW	HIGH
Tubaphone Deluxe			
1920s. Higher-end appointments, carved heel, Deluxe logo on tailpiece.			
1923	5-string	$8,000	$11,000
V.I.P.			
1970s. Open back, 4-string, fancy engraved pearl markers, on-board electronics.			
1970	Tenor	$1,250	$1,625
1973-1974	5-string	$1,375	$1,875
V-45			
1970. Plectrum banjo, flat head tone ring, fancy appointments.			
1970s		$2,750	$3,750
Vega Lady's			
1913		$950	$1,250
Vegaphone De-Luxe			
1929	Plectrum	$3,000	$4,000
Vegaphone Professional			
1920s	Plectrum	$1,250	$1,625
1920s-30s	Tenor	$1,125	$1,500
1960s	5-string	$950	$1,250
Vegavox I 5-String			
1964		$1,500	$2,000
Vegavox I Plectrum			
1956-1959		$1,500	$2,000
Vegavox I Tenor			
1930s-1969. Vox-style deep resonator, alternating block/dot markers.			
1930s		$2,000	$2,750
1956-1959		$1,500	$2,000
1960-1969		$1,500	$2,000
Vegavox IV			
1956-1975. IV logo on truss rod cover, high-end appointments, 4-string plectrum neck.			
1956-1975	Plectrum or Tenor	$2,750	$3,750
Vegavox IV Deluxe			
1970-1973	Tenor	$3,500	$4,750
Whyte Laydie			
1975	5-string	$1,750	$2,375
Whyte Laydie #2			
1919	Vega Fairbanks	$3,000	$4,000
1923-1928	5-string	$3,000	$4,000
1923-1928	Plectrum	$1,125	$1,500
Whyte Laydie #7			
1905	5-string	$6,500	$8,000
1909	5-string	$6,000	$7,500
1920s	5-string	$5,500	$7,500
1920s	Tenor	$2,250	$3,000

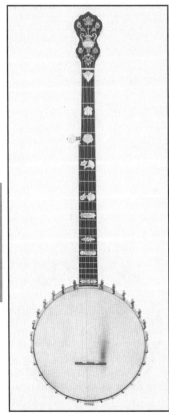

1923 Vega Whyte Laydie #7
Imaged by Heritage Auctions, HA.com

BANJOS

The *Vintage Guitar Price Guide* shows values for all-original, excellent condition instruments and, where applicable, with original case.

MODEL YEAR	FEATURES	EXC. COND. LOW	HIGH
Whyte Laydie Style L			
1922		$1,000	$1,375
Whyte Laydie Style R			
1920s-1930s. Tenor banjo with closed back.			
1920s-30s		$1,000	$1,375
Wonder			
Made by C.F. Martin (brand owner in the '70s), closed back resonator style, tenor or plectrum.			
1967	Plectrum	$750	$1,000
1973	Tenor	$750	$1,000

Vega/Deering

1989-present. Deering purchased the Vega brand in '89. They also make banjos under the Deering brand.

Kingston Trio

1990s-present. Folk-style banjo similar to '50s and '60s Vega Long Neck, 5-string.

1990-2000s		$2,625	$3,500

Little Wonder

Maple neck, ebony 'board, 5-string.

1999		$500	$650

Long Neck

2006	5-string	$2,625	$3,500

Old Tyme Wonder

2012-2018. Maple neck, ebony 'board, 5 strings, brown stained satin finish.

2012-2018		$1,000	$1,375

Senator

2009-present. Open back, 5-string.

2009-2011		$1,125	$1,500

Tubaphone #2

2005-2011. Open back, 5-string.

2005-2011		$2,375	$3,250

Washburn (Lyon & Healy)

1880s-ca.1949. Washburn was the brand name of Lyon & Healy of Chicago. They made banjos from 1880-1929.

5-String

1896	Old 1890s style	$850	$1,125

Irene

1920s	5-string	$750	$1,125

Model 1535

1917	5-string, open back	$1,500	$2,000

MODEL YEAR	FEATURES	EXC. COND. LOW	HIGH
Weymann			

1864-1940s. The Weymann company was founded in 1864 and got seriously into the banjo manufacturing business in 1917. They manufactured banjos until around 1930.

Keystone State Style 2

1920s		$850	$1,125

Plectrum

1924-1928	Style A	$750	$1,125
1927	Style #1	$1,250	$1,625
1927	Style #2	$1,375	$1,750

Tenor

1922	Banjo-Harp, wood top	$1,500	$2,000
1924-1928	Style #1	$1,125	$1,500
1924-1928	Style #2	$1,250	$1,625
1924-1928	Style #4	$2,250	$3,000
1924-1928	Style #50	$500	$650
1924-1928	Style #6	$3,750	$5,000
1924-1928	Style A, low pro	$750	$1,125

Wildwood Banjos

1973-2018. Traditional and bluegrass banjos made originally in Arcata, California, and after '07, in Bend, Oregon.

Minstrel

1990s-2018. Maple neck, ebony 'board, tubaphone-style tone ring, 5 strings.

2013		$1,125	$1,500

Paragon

1990s-2018. Curly maple or Claro black walnut neck, ebony 'board, mother-of-pearl inlay, 5 strings.

1990s		$1,500	$2,000

Troubador

1973-2018. Curly maple neck, ebony 'board, tubaphone-style tone ring, 5 strings.

1973-2018		$1,250	$1,625

Wilson Brothers

1915-1928. Brand name, possibly made by Lyon & Healy, for the Wilson Brothers Manufacturing Company, of Chicago, which was better known as a builder of drums.

Tenor

1920s-30s	Resonator	$375	$500

Yosco

1900-1930s. Lawrence L. Yosco was a New York City luthier building guitars, round back mandolins and banjos under his own brand and for others.

Style 3

1920s	Tenor	$1,000	$1,375

Vega Senator

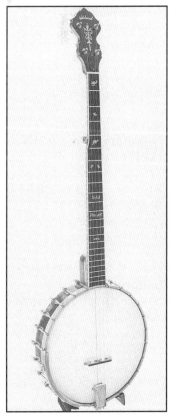

Wildwood Troubador
Elderly Instruments

BANJOS

DEALER DIRECTORY
A GEOGRAPHICAL GUIDE

Canada
Folkway Music
22 Dupont Street East
Waterloo, Ontario N2J-2G9
(855) 772-0424 (toll free)
info@folkwaymusic.com
www.folkwaymusic.com

Twelfth Fret
Chris Bennett
2132 Danforth Avenue
Toronto, Ontario M4C 1J9
416-423-2132
416-423-1554 (Repairs)
sales@12fret.com
www.12fret.com

England
Ampaholics
Paul Goodhand-Tait
PO Box 542
Surrey, GU1-12F
001-44-1483-825102
ampaholics@aol.com
www.ampaholics.org.uk

Japan
H I Guitars
No.1 Furukawa Building
3-8-6-B1 Kanda Kajicho
Chiyoda-Ku, Tokyo 101-0045 Japan
001-81-3257-7117
higuitars@aol.com
www.hi-guitars.com

United States of America
California
California World Guitar Shows
Larry Briggs
918-288-2222
www.CalShows.TV

Drew Berlin's Vintage Guitars
Drew Berlin
213-400-4244
Drew@DrewBerlin.com
www.DrewBerlin.com

Guitars West
Gary Hernandez
41110 Sandalwood Cir STE 113
Murrieta, CA 92562
619-988-9777
www.guitarswest.net

Gryphon Strings
Richard Johnston
211 Lambert Ave
Palo Alto, CA 94306
650-493-2131
info@gryphonstrings.com
www.gryphonstrings.com

Neal's Music
Neal Shelton
Huntington Beach, CA
714-330-9428
nealmuzic@aol.com
www.nealsmusic.com

Players Vintage Instruments
Lowell Levinger
Inverness, CA
415-669-1107
info@vintageinstruments.com
www.vintageinstruments.com

Schoenberg Guitars
Eric Schoenberg
106 Main Street
Tiburon, CA 94920
415-789-0846
eric@om28.com
www.om28.com

Union Grove Music
Richard Gellis
PO Box 2635 Aptos CA 95001
831-427-0670
www.uniongrovemusic.com/

Florida
Guitar Broker
Craig & Dustin Brody
816 NW 6th Ave
Ft. Lauderdale, FL 33311

954-646-8819
vintage@guitarbroker.com
www.guitarbroker.com

Kummer's Vintage
Timm Kummer
954-752-6063
prewar99@gmail.com
www.kummersvintage.com

Replay Guitar Exchange
Jim Brady
3944 Britton Plaza
Tampa, FL 33611
813-254-8800
info@replayguitar.com
www.replayguitar.com

Georgia
Atlanta Vintage Guitars
Greg Henderson
3778 Canton Road, Ste. 400
Marietta, GA 30066
770-433-1891
atlantavintageguitars@gmail.com
www.atlantavintageguitars.com

Illinois
Chicago Guitar Show
Ruth Brinkmann
817-312-7659
ruthmbrinkmann@gmail.com
www.amigoguitarshows.com

Chicago Music Exchange
Daniel Escaruiza
3316 N Lincoln Ave
Chicago, IL 60657
773-525-7773
info@chicagomusicexchange.com
www.CME6.com

SS Vintage
George Coutretsis
4422 N Clark St
Chicago,IL 60640
773-472-3333

george@ssvintage.com
www.ssvintage.com

Maryland
Garrett Park Guitars
Rick Hogue
7 Old Solomans Island Rd
Annapolis, MD 21401
410-571-9660
info@gpguitars.com
www.gpguitars.com

Nationwide Guitars, Inc.
Bruce or Brad Rickard
P.O. Box 2334
Columbia, MD 21045
410-489-4074
nationwideguitar@gmail.com
www.nationwideguitars.com

Southworth Guitars
Gil Southworth
southworthguitar@aol.com
www.southworthguitars.com

Massachusetts
Bay State Vintage Guitars
A.J. Jones
481 Washington St
Norwood, MA 02062
617-267-6077
info@baystatevintageguitars.com
www.baystatevintageguitars.com

Mill River Music and Guitars
Jon Aronstein
135 King St
Northampton, MA 01060
413-505-0129
Info@millrivermusic.com
www.millrivermusic.com

Michigan
Elderly Instruments
Stan Werbin
100 North Washington
Lansing,MI 48906
800-473-5810
elderly@elderly.com
www.elderly.com

Minnesota
Vintage Guitars & Parts Guitarville by Eddie Vegas
Ed Matthews
Cloquet, MN 55720
218-879-3796

Ed@eddievegas.com
www.eddievegas.com

Willie's American Guitars
1382 Eustis St
St. Paul, MN 55108
651-699-1913
info@williesguitars.com
williesguitars.com

Missouri
Fly by Night Music
Dave Crocker
204 N College
Neosho, MO 64850-1816
417-850-4751
crocker@joplin.com
www.amigoguitarshows.com

Killer Vintage
Dave Hinson
PO Box 190561
St. Louis, MO 63119
314-647-7795
info@killervintage.com
www.killervintage.com

Nevada
A.J.'s Music
Peter Trauth
1203 Santa Ynez
Henderson, NV 89002
702-436-9300
ajsmusic@earthlink.net
www.ajsmusic.com

New Hampshire
Retromusic
Jeff Firestone
38 Washington Street
Keene, NH 03431
603-357-9732
retromusicnh@gmail.com
www.retroguitar.com

New Jersey
Kebo's Bassworkd
Kevin 'Kebo' Borden and Dr. Ben
Sopranzetti
info@kebosbassworks.com
www.kebosbassworks.com

Lark Street Music
Buzz Levine
479 Cedar Ln
Teaneck, NJ 07666
201-287-1959

larkstreet@gmail.com
www.larkstreetmusic.com

New Mexico
GuitarVista
Stanley Burg
3117 Silver Ave SE
Albuquerque, NM 87106
505-268-1133
gitmaven@yahoo.com
www.guitarvistanm.com

New York
Bernunzio Uptown Music
122 East Ave
Rochester, NY 14604
585-473-6140
info@bernunzio.com
www.bernunzio.com

Imperial Guitars
Bill Imperial
2A Cherry Hill Rd
New Paltz, NY 12561
845-255-2555
IGS55@aol.com
www.imperialguitar.com

Laurence Wexer, LTD
Larry Wexer
By appointment only
NY, NY 10016
917-848-2399
lwexer@gmail.com
www.wexerguitars.com

Rivington Guitars
Howie Statland
73 E 4th St
NY, NY 10003
212-505-5313
rivingtoninfo@gmail.com
www.rivingtonguitars.com

We Buy Guitars
Richie Friedman
PO Box 60736
Staten Island, NY 10306
516-221-0563
Webuyguitars@aol.com

Well Strung Guitars
David Davidson / Paige Davidson
330 Conklin St Unit 4
Farmigndale, NY 11735
516-221-0563

info@wellstrungguitars.com
www.wellstrungguitars.com

North Carolina
Coleman Music
Chip Coleman
1021 S Main St
China Grove, NC 28023-2335
704-857-5705
OR120@aol.com
www.colemanmusic.com

Midwood Guitar Studio
Douglas Armstrong
1517 Central Ave
Charlotte, NC 28205-5013
980-265-1976
sales@midwoodguitarstudio.com
www.midwoodguitarstudio.com

Ohio
Gary's Classic Guitars
Gary Dick
Cincinnati, OH
513-891-9444
garyclssc@aol.com
www.garysguitars.com

Mike's Music
Mike Reeder
2615 Vine St
Cincinnati, OH 45219
513-281-4900
www.mikesmusicohio.com

The Loft at Lay's
Dan Shinn
974 Kenmore Blvd
Akron, OH 44314
330-848-1392
info@laysguitar.com
www.theloftatlays.com

Oklahoma
Strings West
Larry Briggs
PO Box 999 - 109 N Cincinnati Ave
Sperry, OK 74073
918-288-2222
larryb@stringswest.com
www.stringswest.com

Oregon
McKenzie River Music
Artie Leider
455 West 11th
Eugene, OR 97401

541-343-9482
artie@mrmgtr.com
www.mckenzierivermusic.com

Pennsylvania
Heritage Insurance
Ed Pokrywka
826 Bustleton Pike Ste 203
Feasterville, PA 19053
800-289-8837
edp@his-pa.com
www.musicins.com

Jim's Guitars
Jim Singleton
651 Lombard Rd #119
Red Lion, PA 17356
717-417-5655
sunburst549@aol.com
www.jimsguitars.com

Vintage Blues Guitars
Bruce Roth / Tom Wentzel
717-393-5393 / 717-917-3738
info@vintagebluesguitars.com
www.vintagebluesguitars.com

Vintage Instruments
Fred Oster
507 South Broad Street
Philadelphia, PA 19147
215-545-1000
vintagephiladelphia@gmail.com
www.vintage-instruments.com

Tennessee
Carter's Vintage Guitars
Kim Sherman
625 8th Ave S
Nashville, TN 37203
615-915-1851
kim@thenorthamericanguitar.com
www.cartervintage.com

Gruhn Guitars
George Gruhn
2120 8th Ave S
Nashville, TN 37204
615-256-2033
gruhn@gruhn.com
www.gruhn.com

Rumble Seat Music
Eliot Michael
1805 8th Ave S
Nashville, TN 37203
615-915-2510

sales@rumbleseatmusic.com
www.rumbleseatmusic.com

Tone Central Station
Jamie Jackson and Todd (Toddzilla)
Austin
615-812-8890 (Jamie)
1056 E Trinity Lane #102
Nashville, TN 37216
tonecentralstation@gmail.com
www.tonecentralstation.com

Texas
Boingosaurus Music LLC
Garrett Tung
Austin, TX
boingosaurusmusic@gmail.com
www.boingosaurus.com

Dallas International Guitar Festival
Jimmy Wallace
PO Box 4997186
Garland, TX 75049
972-240-2206
info@guitarshow.com
www.guitarshow.com

Heritage Auctions
Aaron Piscopo
2801 W Airport Fwy
Dallas, TX 75261
214-409-1183
AaronP@HA.com
www.HA.com

Killer Vintage Specialty Guitars of Texas
Dave Hinson
3738 Haggar Way Ste 108
Dallas, TX 75209
972-707-0409
killervintagedallas@gmail.com
www.killervintagespecialtyguitars.com

Texas Amigos Guitar Shows
Ruth Brinkmann
800-473-6059
www.amigoguitarshows.com

Van Hoose Vintage Instruments
Thomas VanHoose
2722 Raintree Drive
Carrollton, TX 75006
972-998-8176
tv0109@yahoo.com
www.vanhoosevintage.com

Utah
Intermountain Guitar and Banjo
By appointment only
Bountiful, UT
801-322-4682/801-450-7608
guitarandbanjo@earthlink.net
www.guitarandbanjo.com

Virginia
Action Music
Matt Baker
111 Park Ave.
Falls Church, VA 22046
703-534-4801
action.music@comcast.net
www.actionguitar.com

Vintage Sound
Bill Holter
PO Box 11711
Alexandria, VA
22312 703-300-2529
bhvsound@vintagesound.com
www.vintagesound.com

Wisconsin
Brian Goff's Bizarre Guitars
Brian Goff
Madison, WI
608-235-3561
Bdgoff@sbcglobal.net
www.bizarreguitars.net

Cream City Music
John Majdalani
12505 W Bluemound Rd
Brookfield, WI 53005-8026
262-860-1800
johnm@creamcitymusic.com
www.creamcitymusic.com

Dave's Guitar Shop
Dave Rogers
1227 South 3rd St
LaCrosse, WI 54601
608-785-7704
info@davesguitar.com
www.davesguitar.com

Dave's Guitar Shop
Dave Rogers
914 S 5th St
Milwaukee, WI 53204
608-790-9816
info@davesguitar.com
www.davesguitar.com

Dave's Guitar Shop
Dave Rogers
110 Market St.
Sun Prairie, WI 53590
608-405-8770
info@davesguitar.com
www.davesguitar.com

Dave's Guitar Shop
Dave Rogers
200 South Central Ave
Marshfield, WI 54449
715-207-0525
info@davesguitar.com
www.davesguitar.com

MANUFACTURER
DIRECTORY

Alabama
Alleva Coppolo
Jimmy Coppolo
Gadsden, AL 35901
909-981-9019
jimmy@allevacoppolo.com
www.allevacoppolo.com

California
Chatsworth Guitars
www.chatsworthguitars.com

Dumble Amps
Drew Berlin - Tone Chaperone
213-400-4244
Drew@DrewBerlin.com
www.Dumble.com

Oklahoma
Keeley Effects
Robert Keeley
www.RKFX.com

Other
Bill Tuli
Ramtuli.com

Lindy Fralin Pickups
www.fralinpickups.com

Tunerette Guitar Tuner
www.tunerette.net

TECH/REPAIR

California
Dumble Amps
Drew Berlin - Tone Chaperone
213-400-4244

Drew@DrewBerlin.com
www.Dumble.com

National Guitar Repair
Marc Schoenberger

805-481-8532, 805-471-5905
Luthier17@aol.com
www.nationalguitarrepair.com

Skip Simmons Amp Repair
Skip Simmons
4824 Bevan Rd
Loma Rica, CA 95901
530-771-7345

Delaware
Dana Sound Research
Danta Sutcliffe, Master Luthier
Wilmington, DE 19810
danasoundresearch@gmail.com
www.danamusic.com

Massachusetts
Mill River Music and Guitars
Jon Aronstein
135 King St.
Northampton, MA 01060
413-505-0129
Info@millrivermusic.com
www.millrivermusic.com

Ohio
Lays Guitar Restoration
Dan Shinn
974 Kenmore Blvd.
Akron, OH 44314
330-848-1392
info@laysguitar.com
www.laysguitar.com

Wyoming
Anton's Musical Instrument Repair
Anton
1841 Lane 12
Powell, WY 82435
307-754-5341
luthier82435@yahoo.com
www.antonsinstrumentrepair.com

Notes

Notes

Notes

Notes

Notes

Notes